AN INTRODUCTION TO
POSITIVE ECONOMICS

SEVENTH EDITION

RICHARD G. LIPSEY

Canadian Institute for Advanced Research
and Professor of Economics, Simon Fraser University,
Vancouver, B.C.

Weidenfeld and Nicolson London

© 1989 by Richard G. Lipsey

First published 1963

Second edition 1966
Reprinted 1967, 1968, 1969, 1970 (twice)

Third edition 1971
Reprinted 1972

Paperback edition first published 1972
Reprinted 1973, 1974

Fourth edition 1975
Reprinted 1976

Fifth edition 1979
Reprinted 1980 (twice), 1982

Sixth edition 1983
Reprinted 1985 (twice), 1987, 1988

Seventh edition 1989

Part of this seventh edition appeared in the United States in
Economics by Richard G. Lipsey, Peter O. Steiner and
Douglas D. Purvis, © 1987, published by Harper and Row.

George Weidenfeld and Nicolson Ltd
91 Clapham High St, London SW4 7TA

ISBN 0 297 79554 6 cased
ISBN 0 297 79555 4 paperback

Phototype set by Keyspools Ltd
Golborne, Lancs

Printed in Great Britain by
Butler & Tanner Ltd
Frome and London

To Diana

Contents

Fact and theory
in economics

'... Einstein started from facts – the Morley Michelson measurements of light, the movements of the planet Mercury, the unexplained aberrancies of the moon from its predicted place. Einstein went back to facts or told others where they should go, to confirm or to reject his theory – by observation of stellar positions during a total eclipse.

'... It is not necessary, of course, for the verification of a new theory to be done personally by its propounder. Theoretical reasoning from facts is as essential a part of economic science as of other sciences, and in a wise division of labour there is room, in economics, as elsewhere, for the theoreticians pure and simple, for one who leaves the technical business of verification to those who have acquired a special technique of observation. No one demanded of Einstein that he should visit the South Seas in person, and look through a telescope; but he told others what he expected them to see, if they looked, and he was prepared to stand or fall by the result. It is the duty of the propounder of every new theory, if he has not himself the equipment for observation, to indicate where verification of his theory is to be sought in facts – what may be expected to happen or to have happened if his theory is true, what will not happen if it is false.

'[Now consider by way of contrast the behaviour of the participants in a current controversy in economics.] ... None of them takes the point that the truth or falsehood of ... [a] ... theory cannot be established except by an appeal to the facts; none of them tests it by facts himself. The distinguishing mark of economic science as illustrated by this debate is that it is a science in which verification of generalizations by reference to facts is neglected as irrelevant. ... I do not see how ... [members of the public who survey the controversy] ... can avoid the conclusion that economics is not a science concerned with phenomena, but a survival of medieval logic, and that economists are persons who earn their livings by taking in one another's definitions for mangling.

'... I know that in speaking thus I make enemies. I challenge a tradition of a hundred years of political economy, in which facts have been treated not as controls of theory, but as illustrations. I shall be told that in the Social Sciences verification can never be clean enough to be decisive. I may be told that, in these sciences, observation has been tried and has failed, has led to shapeless accumulations of facts which themselves lead nowhere. I do not believe for a moment that this charge of barrenness of past enquiries can be sustained; to make it is to ignore many achievements of the past and to decry solid work that is being done at this School and elsewhere. But if the charge of barrenness of realistic economics in the past were justified completely, that would not be a reason for giving up observations and verification. It would only be a reason for making our observations more exact and more numerous. If, in the Social Sciences, we cannot yet run or fly, we ought to be content to walk, or to creep on all fours as infants. ... For economic and political theorizing not based on facts and not controlled by facts assuredly does lead nowhere.

'There can be no science of society till the facts about society are available. Till 130 years ago we had no census, no knowledge even of the numbers and growth of the people; till fifteen years ago we had no comprehensive records about unemployment even in this country, and other countries are still where we were a generation or more ago; social statistics of every kind – about trade, wages, consumption – are everywhere in their infancy.

'... From Copernicus to Newton is 150 years. Today, 150 years from the *Wealth of Nations*, we have not found, and should not expect to find, the Newton of economics. If we have travelled as far as Tycho Brahe we may be content. Tycho was both a theorist and an observer. As a theorist, he believed to his last day in the year 1601 that the planets went round the sun and that the sun and the stars went round the earth as the fixed centre of the universe. As an observer, he made with infinite patience and integrity thousands of records of the stars and planets; upon these records Kepler, in due course, based his laws and brought the truth to light. If we will take Tycho Brahe for our example, we may find encouragement also. It matters little how wrong we are with our existing theories, if we are honest and careful with our observations.'

Extracts from Lord Beveridge's farewell address as Director of the London School of Economics, 24 June 1937. Published in *Politica*, September 1937.

Foreword

TO EVERYONE: THEMES OF THIS BOOK

This is an introductory textbook, starting at an elementary stage and progressing, in some places, to an intermediate level. Although it is designed to be read as a first book in economics, I hope it will not be without interest for someone who has already studied one of the many existing textbooks written at a pre-university standard such as Lipsey and Harbury's *First Principles of Economics* (London: Weidenfeld and Nicolson, 1988).

The book had its beginnings when I was asked, many years ago, to give the basic economic theory lectures for the B.Sc.(Econ.) degree at the London School of Economics. This, its seventh edition, has had the most thorough rewriting of any edition. I hope that the result will continue to prove valuable as an introduction to economics for beginners who are serious about their subject, and that students will continue to find it useful as an overview throughout their undergraduate studies.

The five main themes, discussed below, have been stressed from the first to the present edition.

Full explanations: There is a tradition in many textbooks of trying to sneak quite complex bits of analysis past students without telling them what is happening. This may be the best thing to do if the object is to get through an examination a large mass of people who have neither interest nor ability in economics, and who are hostile to the basic idea of a Social Science. I am not interested in reaching such a public. I have assumed that my readers are intelligent students who are interested in the subject and who wish to know, at every stage, what is going on and why.

I have always given first priority to making the theoretical analysis readable and fully understandable. Nowhere is a theoretical concept introduced merely to be bowed to. Instead, everything that is introduced is fully explained. This requires a great deal of space, which is obtained at the cost of leaving out much illustrative empirical data – data which students will find in whatever applied and descriptive book they are reading alongside this text.

Criticism and assessment: One of the troubles with the traditional approach of sneaking analysis past the student is that, when the intelligent student feels that there is something wrong with what has been taught, he or she does not know how to go about being critical of it in an effective way. I have made a point of telling readers what is going on, to say 'now we are doing comparative-static equilibrium analysis' or whatever it might be, and I have devoted considerable space to an analysis of both sensible and silly criticisms of the theories described – much more space than can be found in any other textbook written at a comparable level.

I do not accept the view that the possibility of criticizing what has been learned should go unmentioned because, if it is raised, students will only make hasty and confused criticisms. Good students will always attempt criticisms and evaluations. It seems to me that their criticisms are more likely to be informed and relevant if they are given instruction in how to set about effectively challenging what they have been taught, than if they meet a conspiracy of silence on this topic.

Theory and observation: All too often, economic theory is taught merely as logical analysis, and is, at best, only vaguely related to the world, while applied economics becomes description unenlightened by any theoretical framework. Economic theory is meant to be about the real world. We seek, by the use of theory, to explain, understand and predict real-world phenomena, and our theory must therefore be related to, and tested by, empirical observations. The student of economic theory needs to ask at every stage what are the relevant empirical magnitudes and quanties. This is the theme set by the quotation from Beveridge that opens this book.[1] It is also a theme that I have stressed by ending many of the Parts with a chapter devoted to issues of measuring and testing the theories and relationships studied in that Part.

---

[1] I take it that in the last sentence quoted, Beveridge is saying that it does not matter how wrong present theories may be as long as we make careful observations of the facts on which these theories stand or fall and then discard or amend theories when they are found to be inconsistent with the facts. A more modern statement of the relation between theory and observation, made by a famous theoretical physicist, the late Richard Feynmen, can be found in Box 2.1 on page 18.

Theory and policy: The distinction between positive and normative statements is well known to professional economists, but all too often we fail to communicate its significance to our students. Economic theory cannot, of course, ever show us what we ought to do, but only what will happen if we do certain things. The uses and limitations of economic theory in dealing with matters of public policy is a theme which recurs throughout the book. Policy issues are raised for purposes of illustration in many chapters; a whole Part – Chapters 23–25 – is devoted to microeconomic policy, while three chapters – 37, 38 and 40 – deal with macroeconomic policy issues.

Emphasis on economic theory: This is a book about economic theory. Although I have tried to relate the theory to the real world and although I have described British institutions where the theory is inextricably bound up with institutions – as with the theory of monetary policy – I have not had space to provide either extensive illustrative empirical data, or details of the institutions and structure of any one economy. Instead I have joined forces with Professor Colin Harbury of City University, London, to write a descriptive companion to *Positive Economics*. This book, *An Introduction to the UK Economy* (London: Pitman, 3rd edn 1989), is designed to give the institutional and factual background needed for an application of economic theory to the UK economy. Of course there are many other valuable books on the UK economy, although some are in our view too detailed while others are not detailed enough. *I assume that all my UK readers are simultaneously studying at least one such book.*

The use of algebra in macroeconomics: There is one further theme that was not introduced until the sixth edition. There, for the first time, I used elementary algebra in the development of the macroeconomic theory that occupies the second half of the book.

All of the mathematics used is well within the capabilities of anyone who has passed O-Level mathematics. The use of algebra in the text does, however, pose problems for two different types of student. To those who have difficulty with O-Level mathematics, some of the algebra may seem formidable. It is not. It is in fact intellectually simpler than some of the issues in the micro part of the book that are expressed through words and graphs. With some practice to breed familiarity, no one who is capable of understanding the ideas expressed throughout this book is incapable of handling the very elementary algebra that I use.

There is a different problem for students who know mathematics, say at an A-Level standard. The algebra used will be so simple for them that there is a danger they will conclude that the economics comprehended by the algebra is trivial. This is not so. Indeed some very subtle economic ideas can be expressed by some very simple mathematics. The subtlety is in the economic behaviour that lies behind, and gives rise to, the results that are derived using simple mathematics.

Because of these problems, I have not relied exclusively, or even mainly, on the algebra. On all points I have used words and geometry as well. Indeed I have spent much more time than in the sixth edition explaining what is going on when algebra is being used and explaining in words the transition from one step in the algebraic treatment to the next. This should help readers to learn how to relate verbal and geometrical discussions to their algebraic counterparts. For any student of economics wishing to overcome a fear of symbolic expression and simple mathematical reasoning, the macro half of this book is an excellent beginning. Once one does get used to it, the algebra provides a simplicity and a finality to theoretical arguments that often seem both complex and uncertain when expressed in verbal and geometric terms alone.

TO THE STUDENT: THE USE OF THIS BOOK

The study of economics can be both interesting and rewarding. If you are not intending to specialize in economics, it can give you some understanding of the functioning of the economy, and some appreciation of the issues involved in current controversies concerning economic policy. It may also give you some idea of the methods which have been applied with some modest success in one Social Science.

If you are a would-be economics specialist, the study of an introductory book, such as this one, can be the beginning of a real adventure. The scope of your chosen science opens up before you. At first you encounter theories which add to your understanding of the world, but soon you begin to encounter problems: observations for which there are no satisfactory explanations, and theories which are generally agreed to be unsatisfactory, but which have not been adequately tested. Both of these constitute a challenge, in the first case for the development of new theories and in the second for the making of a careful set of observations to test an existing theory.

You need to study a book on economics in a different way than you would study a book on, say, history or English literature. Economic theory has a logical structure that builds on itself from stage to stage. Thus if you only imperfectly understand some concept or theory, you will run into increasing difficulty when, in subsequent chapters, this concept or theory is taken for granted and built upon. Because of its logical structure, quite long chains of reasoning are encountered; if A than B, if B then C, if C then D, and if D then E. Each step in the argument may seem simple enough, but the cumulative effect of several steps, one on top of the other, may be bewildering on first encounter. Thus when, having followed the argument step by step, you encounter the statement 'it is now obvious that if A then E', it may not seem at all obvious to you. This is a problem which everyone encounters with chains of reasoning. The only way to deal with it is to follow the argument through several times. Eventually, as the reasoning becomes familiar, it will become obvious that, *if A then E.*

Economics has its own technical language or jargon. At first you may feel that you are merely being asked to put complicated names to common-sense ideas. To some extent this is true. It is a necessary step, however, because loose thinking about vaguely formed ideas is a quick route to error in economics. Furthermore, when you begin to put several ideas together to see what follows from them, jargon – the single clearly defined term to refer to these ideas – becomes a necessary part of your equipment. To help you recognize them as such, technical terms are printed in **bold type** the first time they are used. As a further aid, their definitions are gathered together into a Glossary printed at the end of the book.

A book on economics is to be worked at, and understood step by step. It is usually good to read a chapter quickly in order to see the general run of the argument, and at this stage you might omit the captions to the Figures. You must then reread the chapter carefully, making sure that the argument is understood step by step. On this reading, you *must* study the captions to all the Figures carefully. They contain the reasoning on which the intuitive discussion of the text is based. If you do not understand the captions, you have not understood economics. You should not be discouraged if, occasionally at this stage, you find yourself spending an hour on only two or three pages.

A pencil and paper are necessary pieces of equipment in your reading. Difficult arguments should be followed by building up one's own diagram while the argument unfolds, rather than relying on the printed diagram which is, perforce, complete from the beginning. Numerical examples should be invented to illustrate general propositions.

The Summaries and Topics for Review are there to help you. After your reading of each chapter, and when revising for exams, you should read them and check that you understand the meaning of the Topics and the reasoning behind the Summary points. Difficulties in doing so provide a signal that you need to reread some or all of the chapter.

After the book has been read in this detailed manner, it should be reread fairly quickly from cover to cover; it is often difficult to understand why certain things are done until one knows the end-product, and, on a second reading, much that seems strange and incomprehensible will be seen to have an obvious place in the analysis.

In short, the technical vocabulary aside, one must seek to understand economics, not to memorize it. Theories, principles and concepts are always turning up in slightly unfamiliar guises. If you have understood your economics, this poses no problem; if you have merely memorized it, this spells disaster.

A further aid that is available to you is the *Workbook* prepared by David Forrest, Wendy Olsen and myself. It is very easy to think you understand a verbal presentation, only to dis-

cover that you do not when you come to use what you have tried to learn. The *Workbook* is designed to test your comprehension at every stage and to send you back to the relevant part of the text when your comprehension is faulty. Without using the *Workbook,* or doing its equivalent in class exercises, most readers will get much less than they could out of this book.

Economics is a subject in which one never stops learning. I am grateful to many users – students and teachers – who have taken the trouble to write to me pointing out errors, making comments and offering suggestions. I hope that readers will continue to teach me with as many further comments and criticisms as they have in the past. I try to acknowledge every such letter. If you write and do not hear from me, write again – the post (or my filing system) has let us down! Unfortunately, however, the world being a very large place, it is beyond my financial means to oblige the many people who write asking me to send them free copies of my book.

TO THE INSTRUCTOR: NOTES ON THE SEVENTH EDITION

This edition has been extensively revised in both form and substance.

Form

In this edition, I have introduced a number of important changes in the form of presentation, many of which have been found in introductory American textbooks for some time, and some of which Professor Steiner and I pioneered in the 1970s in our US textbook, *Economics.*

Figures, tags and captions: By far the most important change in format lies in transferring the analysis related to each Figure from the body of the text to a caption attached to the Figure. This is an advantage in keeping the reasoning physically attached to its associated Figure and in allowing that reasoning to be studied at the point that seems best to the reader. The text is made self-sufficient by providing an intuitive explanation of the formal reasoning given in each Figure caption. This means that the text can be read on its own, without the Figure captions – say, on first reading or for revision. The basic analytical reasoning that is the core of economics is, however, given in the captions *all of which must be carefully studied by all students.*

Captioning also permits both a fast reading of the text for the general intuitive drift of the argument without captions, and an easy revision of specific points by reading some captions on their own.

Each Figure caption begins with a tag line in bold type that states its main message.

Summaries: Every chapter now ends with a set of summary points. They provide a useful review as well as a warning that some of the chapter needs to be reread when the reasoning behind one or more of the summary points cannot be reconstructed.

Topics for review: Every chapter also ends with a series of topics for review. These can be treated in the same way as the summaries: as checks on what has just been learned, and as signals during revision.

Boxes: Frequent use is now made of Boxes which are set off from the body of the chapter by a different type and a background colour screen. These Boxes contain material that can be omitted without loss of continuity. They include empirical illustrations, more detailed elaborations of various points made in the text, points of historical interest and occasional formal proofs, all of which may be of interest to some, but not all, readers.

Glossary: The first time a technical term is used extensively in the text it is printed in **bold** type so that it can be easily recognized as such. The definitions of all such terms are gathered together in a Glossary printed at the end of the book.

Substance

The need to transfer the discussion of Figures from text to caption, and to write new intuitive presentations in the text, has required a rewriting of much of the book's teaching material. In the course of this, I have tried to provide a clear and complete presentation of all the points covered. I have not hesitated to use all the length required to

achieve that goal. I hope the result is an example of *longer and fuller* being easier than *shorter and terser.*

The four introductory chapters have been reordered from the sixth edition. The chapter on economic issues now comes first, on the grounds that it is better to describe the subject-matter of economics before raising issues related to social sciences in general. Chapter 4 prepares the ground for the theory of Part 2 by introducing a number of key concepts such as the household, the firm and the economy.

Chapter 5, on Demand, Supply and Price, has been simplified by going straight to the demand curve and then introducing the influence of other variables by showing how they shift that curve.

Chapter 6 now has a new section introducing the important concept of consumers' surplus. It is common to derive consumers' surplus from marginal utility theory, but this is not necessary. The text treats it as a direct consequence of the negative slope of demand curves. Having the tool of consumers' surplus available early on, permits evaluations to be made of certain situations before it is possible to introduce all the formal criteria of optimality.

Chapter 7, on Applications of Price Theory, has been streamlined to place more emphasis on practice in tool-using, rather than on the detailed content of the specific illustrations of rent control and agricultural-support policies. The chapter ends with some general lessons about the price system which are what one hopes students will remember long after they have forgotten some of the more obtruse points of economic theory.

The main burden of demand theory is now carried by the Indifference-Preference Theory of Chapter 8. The appendix on Marginal Utility Theory presents that theory for those who wish to cover it. The significant insights of marginal utility theory that used to be included, when it was covered in a chapter, are now given in Chapter 6 in the section on consumers' surplus.

Chapter 9 contains a revised version of the original edition's treatment on Measurement and Testing of Demand Relations, but it also has an entirely new first section on risk – a topic that plays such an important part in many modern economic theories.

Chapter 14, on Imperfect Competition, has been heavily revised. It now includes a discussion of the non-cooperative, Cournot equilibrium which forms the basis of much of the modern theorizing in what is called the New Industrial Organization Theory (the new I.O.). It continues to include the discussion, introduced in the sixth edition, of why manufacturing firms tend to fix prices and allow quantities to adjust in the short run. This behaviour lies at the heart of modern micro underpinnings of macroeconomics.

Chapter 18, on Labour, has been thoroughly revised. The discussion of the causes of wage differentials now includes modern material on the return to human capital from both formal and on-the-job education, discrimination and alternative market structures.

Chapter 21 contains a fuller discussion of economies of scale, learning-by-long and dynamic comparative advantage as additional sources of the gains from trade.

Chapter 22 has been updated to include material on non-tariff barriers to trade, and other matters that are subject to negotiations in the current Uruguay round of GATT negotiations and the run up to Europe-1992.

Part 7, on Microeconomic Policy, has been expanded to become three instead of two chapters. Chapter 23 gives the economist's case for the free market, first, in the intuitive terms used by classical economists and many of their successors and, second, in the formal terms developed by modern welfare economists. Chapter 24 gives the case against the completely free market, based on such concepts as public goods and externalities. This is followed by the case for government intervention which includes an assessment of the costs, as well as the potential benefits, of intervention. Public choice theory is given attention under the topic of costs.

Chapter 25, on the Aims and Objectives of Government Policy, has been expanded from earlier editions to include a fuller discussion of the goals of efficiency, equity and growth as well as the issues of nationalization, privatization and deregulation.

Chapter 26 introduces the concepts and issues of macroeconomics. From that point on, all of the details of the presentation of the macroeconomics have been reworked. Although the treatment continues to use O-Level algebra, each step is taken more slowly, and is more fully explained, than in the sixth edition. Words and graphs are

relied on more heavily and no student – once a fear of working with equations is overcome – should have problems with the treatment. After all, it is intellectually less demanding than many of the more subtle ideas in microeconomics that are handled in words and graphs.[1]

As in the previous edition, the theory of the determination of national income is developed in three steps, (i) the interest rate and the price level are exogenous, (ii) the interest rate is endogenous, and (iii) the interest rate and the price level are endogenous. The third step, taken in Chapter 33 on Aggregate Demand and Aggregate Supply, now occurs at a much earlier stage than in the sixth edition, while the Philips curve is brought in where it most naturally belongs – as a part of the discussion of inflation in Chapter 34.

Chapter 28, on the Consumption Function, elaborates on key concepts that used to be covered briefly in an appendix. Life-cycle and permanent-income explanations of consumption behaviour are now too important to be relegated to an appendix.

The introductory chapter on money, Chapter 30, has been expanded to include a more detailed explanation of the classical distinction between the real and the monetary sectors of the economy and now has a full coverage of the Classical

---

[1] Some readers of the manuscript have asked 'why mathematics in the macro part but not in the micro part?' The answer is that microeconomics, being based on behavioural relations that are essentially non-linear, is involved with calculus almost from the onset and, being based on maximizing models, soon requires the techniques of constrained maximization. Not only are these techniques beyond the O-Level syllabus, some of them are beyond A-Level. In contrast, elementary macro models, not being maximizing models, do not need constrained maximizing techniques. Even more important, there is nothing fundamentally non-linear about the relations. We can, therefore, linearize all behavioural relations at the onset, as I do, and use very elementary algebra. It is, of course, possible to use general functional forms for all behavioural relations. The models are then solved by substituting definitional and behavioural equations into the equilibrium conditions, totally differentiating these, setting the results up in matrix form and solving using Cramers' rule. Although dropping the assumption of linearity in basic macro models is good practice for more advanced theorizing, it produces no new insights at this level since all of the results are essentially the same – the only difference being that partial derivatives replace the parameters of the linearized version.

Quantity Theory of money that was formerly covered only briefly, and later in the book. The material on the creation of deposit money has also been transferred to this chapter.

Chapter 31 has a much expanded treatment of the monetary transmission mechanism. The new flow charts should help to fix the causal mechanism in readers' minds. Frequent back-references are given in subsequent chapters whenever this mechanism is relied upon.

Chapters 37 and 38, on Fiscal and Monetary Policy, have had a major update as has the material on the open economy in Chapters 39–40.

ACKNOWLEDGEMENTS

Finally I should like to say a word of thanks to all those people who have made this book possible. In so far as the ideas and viewpoints expressed in the first edition were novel, they were the common property of all my colleagues who in the late 1950s and early 1960s were members of the L.S.E. *Staff Seminar on Methodology, Measurement and Testing in Economics*. All I did in the first edition was to give a slightly personal expression to this general viewpoint. At one time or another, I have been given valuable comments or suggestions by K. Klappholz, R. Cassen, G. C. Archibald, John Black, Claire Rubin, Diana Lipsey, Joanna Lipsey, Douglas Purvis, Bryan Hurl, Somnath Sen, David Tash and Robert York. David Tash has also helpfully provided material that has formed the basis of several illustrative boxes used in this edition. The largest single debt of all I owe to Professor P.O. Steiner, who co-authored with me the American textbook *Economics*. To Professor Steiner, who was everywhere my severe critic and often my teacher, I and the substance of the present book, owe a great debt.

The executor of Lord Beveridge's estate has kindly granted permission to quote extracts from Beveridge's farewell address at the London School of Economics. Thanks are also due to Macmillan and McGraw-Hill for permission to quote from Lord Robbins' *Essay on the Nature and Significance of Economic Science* and *The British Economy* respectively. Harper and Row have been generous in giving their permission to use material first prepared for the 8th edition of the American textbook *Economics*, written by Professors P. O. Steiner, D. D. Purvis and myself.

Through the various editions, valuable research assistance has been provided by M. J. Blanden, June Wickins, P. Geary, J. Stilwell, A. Popoff, D. Gilchrist, T. Whitehead and K. MacMillan. Sarah Craig, Evelyn Dean, Tina Brown, Joanne Marlieb, Marlene Rego, Laura Elston, Cynthia Price, and Elaine Fitzpatrick have shown unlimited patience in dealing with manuscripts. Thing 1, George, Chekov, Pushkin, and Tiger Lilly have sat on my manuscript, chewed my pen and otherwise offered invaluable feline assistance through successive editions. The usual disclaimer of course holds here: for all shortcomings and mistakes I am solely to blame.

R.G. Lipsey
Simon Fraser University
Vancouver B.C.
March 1989

PART 1

Scope and Method

1

Economic
Issues

Why has the history of most industrial nations been one of several years of boom and plenty, followed by several years of recession and unemployment with consequent poverty for many citizens? Why, during the 1930s in most countries, was up to one person in four unemployed while factories lay idle and raw materials went unused; why, in short, was everything available to produce urgently needed goods and yet nothing happened? Why, in the 1980s, did unemployment in most countries reach the highest levels ever attained since the Great Depression of the 1930s? Is it really true that while the Great Depression of the 1930s overwhelmed unwitting and powerless governments, the great slump of the 1980s was deliberately engineered by governments who knew full well what they were doing?

What determines the level of wages and what influences do unions have on the share of national income received by labour? What functions do unions fulfil in today's world? Is it possible that having fully achieved the purpose of putting labour on an equal footing with management, they have outlived their usefulness?

Must all modern economies make use of money? Could money be eliminated in a truly socialist state? How is it that new money can be created by ordinary commercial banks within broad limits, and by governments without limits? If money is valuable, why do economists insist that countries with large supplies of it are no richer than countries with small supplies?

Why did inflation accelerate so dramatically in most countries in the mid-1970s? Was the massive unemployment of the 1980s the necessary cost of bringing inflation under control, as many governments argued, or could inflation have been cured at much less cost?

Is government intervention needed to keep markets working effectively, or would we be better off with a policy of *laissez-faire* that minimized government intervention? What are the effects of a government's taxing and spending policies?

These are a few of the questions with which economists concern themselves, and on which the theories of economics are designed to shed some light. Such a list may give you a better idea of the scope of economics than could be obtained at this stage from an enumeration of the common textbook definitions.

THE SOURCE OF ECONOMIC PROBLEMS

All of the above issues, as well as many others that we will meet in our study, have common features – features that make them economic rather than something else, such as political or biological. Our first task in this chapter is to look for some of the similarities that suggest an underlying unity to these apparently diverse issues.

Most of the problems of economics arise out of a basic fact of life:

> **the production that can be obtained by fully utilizing all of a nation's resources is insufficient to satisfy all the wants of the nation's inhabitants; because resources are scarce, it is necessary to choose among the alternative uses to which they could be put.**

Resources and Scarcity

Kinds of resources: The resources of a society consist not only of the free gifts of nature, such as land, forests and minerals, but also of human capacity, both mental and physical, and of all sorts of man-made aids to further production, such as tools, machinery and buildings. It is sometimes useful to divide these resources into three main groups: (1) all those free gifts of nature, such as land, forests, minerals, etc., commonly called *natural resources* and known to economists as **land**; (2) all human resources, mental and physical, both inherited and acquired, which economists call **labour**; and (3) all those man-made aids to further production, such as tools, machinery and factories, which are used up in the process of making other goods and services rather than being consumed for their own sake, and which economists call **capital**. Often a fourth resource is distinguished. This is **entrepreneurship** from the French word *entrepreneur*, meaning the one who undertakes tasks.

Entrepreneurs take risks by introducing both new products and new ways of making old products. They organize the other factors of production and direct them along new lines. (When it is not distinguished as a fourth factor, entrepreneurship is included under labour.)

Collectively these resources are called **factors of production** because they are used in the process of production.

Kinds of production: The things that are produced by the factors of production are called **commodities**. Commodities are divided into goods and services: **goods** are tangible, as are cars or shoes; **services** are intangible, as are haircuts and education. This distinction, however, should not be exaggerated: goods are valued because of the services they yield. A car, for example, is valued because of the transportation that it provides, and possibly also for the flow of satisfaction the owner gets from displaying it as a status symbol. The total output of all commodities in one country over some period, usually taken as a year, is called its *national product*.

The act of making goods and services is called **production**, and the act of using these goods and services to satisfy wants is called **consumption**. Anyone who helps to make goods or services is called a **producer**, and anyone who consumes them to satisfy his or her wants is called a **consumer**.

Judging definitions: The division of resources into land, labour, capital and entrepreneurship, and the division of consumption commodities into goods and services, are matters of definition. Definitions are to be judged not as matters of fact but on the grounds of usefulness and convenience. The question 'Is this division likely to be a useful one?' can be discussed fruitfully. The question 'Is this fourfold division the correct one?' is unlikely to give rise to fruitful discussion and it certainly has no definite answer.

Useless arguments about which of many definitions is the correct one are so common that they have been given a name: *essentialist arguments*. An essentialist argument takes place whenever we agree about the facts of the case, but we argue about what name to use to indicate the agreed facts. We may agree, for example, about what happened in the USSR between 1921 and 1925, but argue about whether that can be called true communism.

Scarcity: In most societies goods and services are not regarded as desirable in themselves; few people are interested in piling them up endlessly in warehouses, never to be consumed. Usually the purpose of producing goods and services is to satisfy the wants of the individuals who consume them. Goods and services are thus regarded as *means to an end*, the satisfaction of wants.

In relation to the known desires of individuals for such commodities as better food, clothing, housing, schooling, holidays, hospital care and entertainment, the existing supplies of resources is woefully inadequate.[1] They are sufficient to produce only a small fraction of the goods and services that people desire. This gives rise to the basic economic problem of *scarcity*.

Choice and Opportunity Cost

Choices are necessary because resources are scarce. Because a country cannot produce every-thing its citizens would like to consume, there must exist some mechanism to decide what will be done and what left undone; what goods will be produced and what left unproduced; what quant-ity of each will be produced; and whose wants will be satisfied and whose left unsatisfied. In most societies these choices are influenced by many different people and organizations, such as individual consumers, business organizations, labour unions and government officials. One of the differences among economies such as those of the United States, the United Kingdom, India and the Soviet Union is the amount of influence that various groups have on these choices.

If you choose to have more of one thing, then, where there is an effective choice, you must have less of something else. Think of a man with a certain income who considers buying bread. We could say that the cost of this extra bread is so many pence per loaf. A more revealing way of looking at the cost, however, is in terms of what other consumption he must forgo in order to obtain his bread. Say that he decides to give up some cinema attendances. If the price of a loaf is one-fifth of the price of a cinema seat, then the cost of five more loaves of bread is one cinema attendance forgone or, put the other way around, the cost of one more cinema attendance is five loaves of bread forgone.

---

[1] We do not need to decide if it would ever be possible to produce enough goods and services to satisfy all human wants. We only need to observe that it would take a vast increase in production to raise all the citizens of any country to the standard at present enjoyed by its richer citizens. It is doubtful that, even if this could be done, all citizens would find their wants fully satisfied.

Now consider the same problem at the level of a whole society. If the government elects to build more roads, and finds the required money by cutting down on its school construction pro-gramme, then the cost of the new roads can be expressed as so many schools per mile of road. If the government decides that because more re-sources must be devoted to arms production, less will be available to produce civilian goods then a choice has been made between 'guns and butter'. The cost of one can be expressed in terms of the amount of the other forgone. The economist's term for costs expressed in terms of forgone alternatives is **opportunity cost**.

The concept of opportunity cost emphas-izes the problem of choice by measuring the cost of obtaining a quantity of one commodity in terms of the quantity of other commodities that could have been obtained instead.

Our discussion may now be summarized briefly. Most of the issues studied in economics are related to the use of scarce resources to satisfy human wants. Resources are employed to pro-duce goods and services, which are used by consumers to satisfy their wants. Choices are necessary because resources are scarce in relation to the virtually unlimited wants that they could be used to satisfy.

Basic Economic Problems

Most of the specific questions posed at the beginning of this chapter (and many other ques-tions as well) may be regarded as aspects of seven more general questions that arise in all economies, whether they be capitalist, socialist or communist.

(1) *What commodities are being produced and in what quantities?* The answer to this question determines the allocation of the economy's scarce resources among alternative uses, called its **re-source allocation**. Choosing to produce a parti-cular combination of goods means choosing a particular allocation of resources among the industries producing these goods. For example, producing a large output of one good requires that a large amount of resources be allocated to its production. In free-market economies, most de-cisions concerning resource allocation are made through the price system, and the study of how

this system works is a major topic in economics.

(2) *By what methods are these commodities produced?* This question arises because there is almost always more than one technically possible way in which output can be produced. Agricultural goods, for example, can be produced by farming a small quantity of land very intensively, using large quantities of fertilizer, labour and machinery, or by farming a large quantity of land extensively, using only small quantities of fertilizer, labour and machinery. Both methods can be used to produce the same quantity of some good; one method is frugal with land but uses larger quantities of other resources, whereas the other method uses large quantities of land but is frugal in its use of other resources. The same is true of manufactured goods. Any particular output can usually be produced by several different techniques, ranging from ones using a large quantity of labour and only a few simple machines, to ones using a large quantity of automated machines and only a few workers. Questions about why one method of production is used rather than another, and the consequences of these choices about production methods, are important topics in the *theory of production.*

(3) *How is society's output of goods and services divided among its members?* Why do some individuals and groups consume a large share of the national output, while other individuals and groups consume only a small share? The superficial answer is because the former earn large incomes while the latter earn small incomes. But this only pushes the question one stage back. Why do some individuals and groups earn large incomes while others earn only small incomes? The basic question concerns the division of the national product among individuals and groups. Economists wish to know why any particular division occurs in a free-market society and what forces, including government intervention, can cause it to change.

When they speak of the division of the national product among any set of groups in the society, economists speak of the **distribution of income**. The question of what determines the distribution of income is dealt with in the *theory of distribution.*

(4) *How efficient is the society's production and distribution?* These questions quite naturally arise out of questions 1, 2 and 3. Having asked what quantities of goods are produced, how they are produced and to whom they are distributed, it is natural to go on to ask whether the production and distribution decisions are efficient.

The concept of efficiency is quite distinct from the concept of justice. The latter is what we will learn in Chapter 2 to call a normative concept. A just distribution of the national product would be one that our value judgements told us was a *good* or a *desirable* distribution. Efficiency and inefficiency are what we will learn in Chapter 2 to call positive concepts. Production is said to be inefficient if it would be possible to produce more of at least one commodity – without simultaneously producing less of any other – by merely reallocating resources. The economy's output is said to be inefficiently distributed if it could be redistributed among the individuals in the society so as to make at least one person better off without simultaneously making anyone worse off. Questions about the efficiency of production and allocation belong to the branch of economic theory called **welfare economics**.

Questions 1 to 4 are related to the allocation of resources and the distribution of income and are intimately connected, in a market economy, to the way in which the price system works. They are grouped under the general heading of **microeconomics**.

(5) *Are the country's resources being fully utilized, or are some of them lying idle?* We have already noted that the existing resources of any country are not sufficient to satisfy even the most pressing needs of all its citizens. Surely, then, if resources are so scarce that there are not enough of them to produce all of those commodities which are urgently required, there can be no question of leaving idle any of the resources that are available. Yet one of the most disturbing characteristics of free-market economies is that such waste sometimes occurs. When this happens the resources are said to be involuntarily unemployed (or, more simply, unemployed). Unemployed workers would like to have jobs, the factories in which they could work are available, the managers and owners wish to operate their factories profitably, raw materials are available in abundance, and the goods that could be produced by these resources are urgently required by individuals in the community. Yet, for some

reason, nothing happens: the workers stay unemployed, the factories lie idle and the raw materials remain unused. The cost of such unemployment is felt both in terms of the goods and services that could have been produced by the idle resources, and in terms of the effects on people who are unable to find work for prolonged periods.

Why do market societies experience such periods of involuntary unemployment *which are unwanted by virtually everyone in the society*, and can such unemployment be prevented by government action?

(6) *Is the purchasing power of money constant,*

FIGURE 1.1 A Production-Possibility Boundary

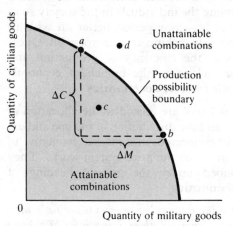

The downward-sloping boundary shows the combinations that are just attainable when all of the society's resources are efficiently employed. The quantity of military goods produced is measured along the horizontal axis, the quantity of civilian goods along the vertical axis. Thus any point on the diagram indicates some amount of each kind of good produced. The production-possibility boundary separates the attainable combinations of goods such as *a, b* and *c* from unattainable combinations such as *d*. It slopes downward because resources are scarce: in a fully employed economy more of one good can be produced only if resources are freed by producing less of other goods. For example, moving from point *a* to point *b* implies producing Δ*M* more military goods at an opportunity cost of Δ*C* fewer civilian goods. Points *a* and *b* represent efficient uses of all of society's resources. Point *c* represents either inefficient use of resources or failure to use all the available resources. By moving upwards and to the right from point *c* the economy can produce more of everything.

---

or is it being eroded because of inflation? The world's economies have often experienced periods of prolonged and rapid changes in price levels. Over the long swing of history, price levels have sometimes risen and sometimes fallen. In recent decades, however, the course of prices has almost always been upward. The 1970s saw a period of accelerating inflation in Europe, in the United States and in most of the world; in the 1980s inflation subsided.

Inflation is closely related to the amount of money in the economy. Money is the invention of human beings, not of nature, and the amount in existence can be controlled by them. Economists ask many questions about the causes and consequences of changes in the quantity of money and the effects of such changes on the price level. They also ask about other causes of inflation. Questions 5 and 6 are both studied in a branch of economics called **macroeconomics**.

(7) *Is the economy's capacity to produce goods and services growing from year to year or is it remaining static?* The misery and poverty described in the England of a century and a half ago by Charles Dickens are no longer with us as a mass phenomenon. This is largely due to the fact that the capacity to produce goods and services has grown about 2 per cent per year faster than population since Dickens' time. Why the capacity to produce grows rapidly in some economies, slowly in others, and not at all in yet others is a critical problem which has exercised the minds of some of the best economists since the time of Adam Smith. Although a certain amount is now known in this field, a great deal remains to be discovered. Problems of this type are topics in the *theory of economic growth*.

There are, of course, other questions that arise, but these seven are the major ones common to all types of market economies. Most of the rest of this book is devoted to their detailed study. We shall study how decisions on these questions are made in free-market societies, the (often unexpected) consequences of settling these questions through the price system, and why governments sometimes intervene in an attempt to alter the decisions.

The Production Possibility Boundary

Four of the above questions that are most easily

confused can be distinguished by introducing a simple diagram. Consider one choice that faces all economies today: how many resources to devote to producing 'guns for defence' and how many to devote to producing goods for all other purposes. This is a problem in the allocation of resources, which is illustrated in Figure 1.1. The horizontal axis measures the quantity of military goods produced while the vertical axis measures the quantity of all other goods, which we call *civilian goods*. Next we plot all those combinations of military and civilian goods that can be produced if all resources are fully employed. We join up these points and call the resulting line a **production-possibility boundary**. Points inside the boundary show the combinations of military and civilian goods that can be obtained given the society's present supplies of resources. Points outside the boundary show combinations that cannot be obtained because there are not enough resources to produce them. Points on the boundary are just obtainable; they are the combinations that can just be produced using all the available supplies of resources.

A production-possibility boundary illustrates three concepts: scarcity, choice and opportunity cost. Scarcity is implied by the unattainable combinations beyond the boundary; choice, by the need to choose among the attainable points on the boundary; opportunity cost, by the downward slope of the boundary.

Question 1. The question of where to produce on the production-possibility boundary is a question about the allocation of resources. In this example it is the allocation of resources between the production of military and civilian goods.

Questions 4 and 5. An economy can always be located inside its boundary. This is wasteful because production of both types of commodity is then less than it could be if points on the boundary were attained. An economy can be producing inside its production-possibility boundary either because some of its resources are lying idle (question 5), or because its resources are being used inefficiently in production (question 4).

Question 7. If the economy's capacity to produce goods is increasing through time, the production-possibility boundary will be moving

FIGURE 1.2 The Effect of Economic Growth on the Production-Possibility Boundary

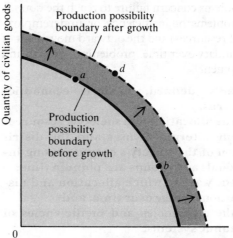

Economic growth shifts the boundary outward and makes it possible to produce more of all commodities. Before growth in productive capacity, points *a* and *b* were on the production-possibility boundary and point *d* was an unattainable combination. After growth, point *d* and many other previously unattainable combinations are attainable, as shown by the dark-shaded band.

outwards over time, as illustrated in Figure 1.2. If the economy remains on its outward-shifting boundary, more of all goods can be produced.

Notice that if an economy is at some point on an unchanging production-possibility boundary, having more of one thing necessarily implies having less of something else. It is, however, possible to have more of everything if: (i) resources previously unemployed are now employed; (ii) resources previously used inefficiently are now used efficiently; or (iii) economic growth shifts the production-possibility boundary outwards.

Economics: A Working Definition

Listing the problem areas of economics outlines its scope more fully than can be done with short definitions. Economics today is regarded much more broadly than it was even half a century ago. Earlier definitions stressed only the alternative and competing uses of resources, and focused on choices among alternative points on a stationary production-possibility boundary. Other important problems concern failure to reach the boundary (problems of inefficiency or underemployment of resources) and the outward movement of the boundary over time (problems of growth and development).

Broadly defined, modern economics concerns:
(1) the allocation of a society's resources among alternative uses and the distribution of the society's output among individuals and groups at a point in time;
(2) the ways in which allocation and distribution change over time; and
(3) the efficiencies and inefficiencies of economic systems.

THE EVOLUTION OF MARKET ECONOMIES

The great seventeenth-century philosopher Thomas Hobbes described life in a state of nature as 'nasty, brutish and short'. Modern study of the several surviving food-gathering societies suggests that Hobbes' ideas were wide of the mark. In fact, societies in the pre-agricultural stage are characterized by a

'relative simplicity of the material culture (only 94 items exist among Kung bushmen); the lack of accumulation of individual wealth [and mobility] ... Subsistence requirements are satisfied by only a modest effort – perhaps two or three days' work a week by each adult; they do not have to struggle over food resources; the attitudes towards ownership are flexible and their living groups open.'[1]

Such features set hunters and gatherers apart from more technologically developed societies whose very survival depends upon their ability to maintain order and to control property.

Many of the characteristic problems of modern economies do not arise in these primitive societies. Indeed the economic problem as we

know it today has been with us only ten thousand or so years – little more than an instant compared to the tens of millions of years that hominid creatures have been on earth. It began with the original agricultural revolution, dated somewhere this side of 10,000 BC, when people first found it possible to stay in one place and survive. Gradually abandoning the old nomadic life of food gathering, people began to settle down, tending crops that they themselves had learned to plant and animals that they had learned to domesticate. Since that time societies have faced the all-pervading problem of choice under conditions of scarcity.

Specialization, Surplus and Trade

Along with permanent settlement, the agricultural revolution brought surplus production: farmers could produce substantially more than they needed to survive. The agricultural surplus led to the appearance of new occupations such as artisans, soldiers, priests and government officials. Freed from having to grow their own food, these people turned to producing specialized services and goods other than food. They too produced more than they themselves needed, so they traded the excess to obtain whatever else they required.

Economists call this allocation of different jobs to different people **specialization of labour**. Specialization has proved extraordinarily efficient compared to universal self-sufficiency, for at least two reasons. First, individual abilities differ, and specialization allows each person to do what he or she can do relatively best. Second, a person who concentrates on one activity becomes better at it than could a jack-of-all-trades.

Probably the exchange of goods and services in early societies took place by simple, mutual agreement among neighbours. In the course of time, however, trading became centred in particular gathering places called markets. Today we use the term **market economy** to refer to a society in which people specialize in productive activities and meet most of their material wants through exchanges voluntarily agreed upon by the contracting parties.

Specialization must be accompanied by trade. People who produce only one thing

---

[1] *The Times Atlas of World History*, ed. G.Barraclough (London: Times Books, 1978), p. 35.

BOX 1.1 BARTER IN THE MODERN WORLD

Although barter is the dominant form of exchange only in very primitive societies, barter transactions are not unknown in modern societies. When you agree to do a job for your neighbour in return for a job your neighbour does for you, the two of you are bartering.

More sophisticated barter transactions also occur. In the 1970s, for example, many chemical plants were built in the Soviet Union by contractors based in Western countries. The contracting firms were paid not in money, but by a promise of some proportion of the output of those plants for a number of years after they first became productive. This had two advantages for the Soviets: it gave the contractors an incentive to ensure that the plant would produce the desired chemicals to the full design capacity; it also conserved the Soviets' scarce supplies of Western currencies.

Since 1983 the Saudi Arabian government has been buying American jumbo jets, British Rolls-Royce engines and French military aircraft, each

time paying in oil. For another example, the British car manufacturer Talbot agreed in early 1985 to supply kits for the construction of its cars to Iran, with payment to be made in oil.

In the same year the South American country of Guyana had agreements to use rice to pay for spare parts from East Germany and oil from Trinidad. It also paid for Japanese lorries with bauxite (the ore from which aluminium is made). Guyana had other barter arrangements with the governments of Yugoslavia, China and Brazil.

Until February 1986, barbers in Warsaw, Poland, obtained modern equipment from firms in West Germany, in return for hair cuttings which were made into West German wigs.

What all of these examples have in common is that they involve *international* trade, so that *two* currencies would be involved if the transaction used money, and the government of at least one of the countries does not (perhaps cannot) allow its currency to be freely traded for the other currency involved.

must trade most of it to obtain all of the other things they require.

Early trading was by means of **barter**, the trading of goods directly for other goods. But barter is costly in terms of time spent searching out satisfactory exchanges. If a farmer has wheat but wants a hammer, he must find someone who has a hammer and wants wheat. A successful barter transaction thus requires what is called a *double coincidence of wants*.

Money eliminates the cumbrous system of barter by separating the transactions involved in the exchange of commodities. If a farmer has wheat and wants a hammer, he does not have to find someone who has a hammer and wants wheat. He merely has to find someone who wants wheat. The farmer takes money in exchange, then finds a person who wishes to trade a hammer, and gives up the money for the hammer.

By eliminating the cumbrousness of barter, money greatly facilitates trade and specialization.

Most transactions in the modern world make use of money. As Box 1.1 shows, however, barter is sometimes resorted to even today.

Factor Services and the Division of Labour

Market transactions in early economies involved mostly goods and services for consumption. Producers specialized in making some commodity and then traded it for the other products they needed. The labour services required to make the product would usually be provided by the makers themselves, by apprentices who were learning to become craftsmen, or by slaves. Over the last several hundred years many technical advances in methods of production have made it efficient to organize agriculture and industry on a very large scale. These technical developments have made use of what is called the **division of labour**. This term refers to specialization within the production process of a particular commodity. The labour involved is divided into repetitive tasks, and each individual does one task that may be a minute fraction of those necessary to produce the commodity. Indeed, it is possible today for an individual to spend years doing a production-line job without knowing what commodity emerges at the end of the line! Adam Smith, the great British economist, was one of the first to perceive the enormous importance of the division of labour, and a fragment of his

BOX 1.2 ADAM SMITH ON THE DIVISION OF LABOUR

Adam Smith began *The Wealth of Nations* with a long study of the division of labour. Among other things, he had this to say.

'The greatest improvements in the productive powers of labour ... have been the effects of the division of labour.

To take an example ... the trade of the pinmaker; a workman not educated to this business (which the division of labour has rendered a distinct trade), nor acquainted with the use of the machinery employed in it could scarce, perhaps, with his utmost industry, make one pin in a day, and certainly could not make twenty. But in the way in which this business is now carried on ... it is divided into a number of branches. ... One man draws out the wire, another straightens it, a third cuts it, a fourth points it, a fifth grinds it at the top for receiving the head; to make the head requires two or three distinct operations; to put it on, is a peculiar business, to whiten the pins is another; it is even a trade by itself to put them into the paper; and the important business of making a pin is, in this manner, divided into about eighteen distinct operations, which, in some manufactories, are all performed by distinct hands, though in others the same man will sometimes perform two or three of them.'

Smith observes that even in small factories, where the division of labour is exploited only in part, output is as high as 4,800 pins per person per day!

Later Smith discusses the general importance of the division of labour and the forces that limit its application.

'Each animal is still obliged to support and defend itself, separately and independently, and derives no sort of advantage from that variety of talents with which nature has distinguished its fellows. Among men, on the contrary, the most dissimilar geniuses are of use to one another; the different products of their respective talents, by the general disposition to truck, barter, and exchange, being brought, as it were, into a common stock, where every man may purchase whatever part of the produce of other men's talents he has occasion for.

As it is the power of exchanging that gives occasion to the division of labour, so the extent of this division must always be limited by the extent of that power, or, in other words, by the extent of the market. When the market is very small, no person can have any encouragement to dedicate himself entirely to one employment for want [i.e. lack] of the power to exchange all that surplus part of the produce of his own labour, which is over and above his own consumption, for such parts of the produce of other men's labour as he has occasion for.'

Smith notes that there is no point in specializing to produce a large quantity of pins, or anything else, unless there are enough persons making other commodities to provide a market for all the pins that are produced. Thus, the larger the market, the greater the scope for the division of labour and the higher the resulting opportunities for efficient production.

writings on this matter is given in Box 1.2.

To take advantage of the division of labour, production had to be organized in large and expensive factories. With this development, workers lost their status as craftsmen (or peasants) and became members of the proletariat, wholly dependent on their ability to sell their labour to factory (or farm) owners and without any plot of land to fall back on for subsistence in times of need.

Today's typical workers do not earn their incomes by selling commodities they themselves have produced; rather they sell their labour services to firms and receive money wages in return.

Interestingly enough, individual artisans have

recently reappeared in some lines of production. They are responding to a revival in the demand for individually crafted, rather than mass-produced, commodities. People who earn their living by selling commodities produced primarily by their own labour continue, however, to account for a very small part of the nation's total productive effort.

HOW MARKET ECONOMIES WORK

In a market economy, millions of consumers decide what commodities to buy and in what quantities; a vast number of firms produce those commodities and buy the factor services that are needed to make them; and millions of owners of factors of production decide to whom and on what terms they will sell these services. These individual decisions collectively determine the economy's allocation of resources among competing uses.

In a market economy, the allocation of resources is the outcome of millions of independent decisions made by consumers and producers, all acting through the medium of markets.

Early economists observed the market with wonder. They saw that although most commodities were made by a large number of independent producers, they were made in approximately the quantities that people wanted to purchase. Natural disasters aside, there were neither vast surpluses nor severe shortages in relation to the demand for these commodities. These economists also saw that most labourers were able to sell their services to employers most of the time, in spite of the fact that the kinds of products made, the techniques used to make them and the places in which they were made changed over time.

How does the market produce this order without conscious direction by some central co-ordinating body? It is one thing to have the same commodities produced year in and year out when people's wants and incomes do not change; it is quite another to have production adjusting continually to changing wants, incomes and techniques of production. Yet this *relatively* smooth adjustment is accomplished by the market – albeit with occasional, and sometimes serious, interruptions. Because of the importance of prices in market economies, we say that they employ a **price system**. This term refers to the role that prices play in determining the allocation of resources and the distribution of national product. The great insight is that:

markets function without conscious control because individuals take their private decisions in response to publicly known signals such as prices, while these signals in turn respond to the collective actions entailed by the sum of all individual decisions; in short, the price system is an automatically functioning social-control mechanism.

A social-control mechanism is a technical term for anything that influences social behaviour. Prices, which provide an incentive for people to adopt certain patterns of behaviour voluntarily, are one example; laws, which force behaviour into certain patterns, are another example.

In 1776, Adam Smith published *The Wealth of Nations*. This great book was the culmination of the early attempts to understand the workings of market economies. Smith spoke of the price system as 'the invisible hand' because it co-ordinated decision-taking that was decentralized among millions of individual producers and consumers.

A word of warning: Be careful not to be one of those who confuse the word automatic, which we have used to describe the working of a free market, with the phrase perfectly functioning, which we have not used. It is beyond dispute that the free market works as a social-control mechanism to allocate scarce resources among competing uses without conscious central control. How well the market does this job in comparison with other systems that might be used is an important, and much debated, issue. Before we even raise that question, however, we need to understand how free markets do the job.

We may now study two illustrations designed to give some intuitive understanding of how the price system works in market economies.

A Change in Demand

First consider how the market reacts to a change in the tastes of individual consumers. Let us say, for example, that consumers experience a greatly increased desire for Brussels sprouts and a diminished desire for carrots. The cause is unimportant; all that matters is that consumers desire more sprouts and fewer carrots.

What will be the effects of this change? First, consumers will buy more Brussels sprouts and fewer carrots. With production unchanged, a shortage of Brussels sprouts and a glut of carrots will develop. In order to unload their surplus stocks of carrots, merchants will reduce carrot prices on the principle that it is better to sell them at a reduced price than not to sell them at all. On the other hand, merchants will find that they cannot keep Brussels sprouts on their shelves.

Sprouts will become a scarce commodity and the merchants will raise their price. As the price rises, fewer sprouts will be bought. Thus the consumers' demand will be limited to the available supply by the means of making the commodity more expensive.

Farmers will now observe that the price of sprouts is rising while the price of carrots is falling. Brussels sprout production will be more profitable than in the past, for while the costs of producing them are unchanged, their market price has risen. Carrot production will be less profitable than it was because costs are unchanged but prices have fallen. Thus the change in consumers' tastes, working through the price system, causes the allocation of resources to change in such a way that less resources are devoted to carrot production and more to sprout production. Economists use the term **reallocation of resources** to refer to a change in the use of the economy's resources.

As the production of carrots declines, the glut on the market will diminish, and carrot prices will begin to rise. On the other hand, the expansion in Brussels sprout production will reduce the shortage and prices will fall. These price movements will continue until it no longer pays farmers to reduce carrot production and to increase the production of sprouts.

Let us review this last point. When the price of carrots was very low and the price of sprouts very high, carrot production was unprofitable and sprout production was very profitable. Therefore more sprouts and fewer carrots were produced. These changes in production caused sprout prices to fall, and carrot prices to rise. Once the prices of these goods became such that it no longer paid farmers to transfer out of carrots into sprouts, production settled down and price movement ceased.

We can now see how the reallocation of resources takes place. Carrot producers will be reducing their production, and they will therefore be laying off workers and generally demanding fewer factors of production. On the other hand, Brussels sprout producers will be expanding production by hiring workers and generally increasing their demands for factors of production. Labour can probably switch from carrot to sprout production without much difficulty. If, however, there are certain resources, in this case

say certain areas of land, which are much better suited for sprout-growing than for carrot-growing, and other resources, say other areas of land, which are much better suited for carrot-growing than sprout-growing, then their prices will be affected. Since farmers are trying to increase sprout production, they will be increasing their demand for factors which are especially suited for this activity. This will create a shortage and cause the prices of these factors to rise. On the other hand, carrot production will be falling, and hence the demand for resources especially suited for carrot-growing will be reduced. There will thus be a surplus of these resources and their prices will be forced down.

The changes in factor prices in turn influence the distribution of income. Factors particularly suited to sprout production will be earning more than previously, and they will obtain a higher share of total national income than before. Factors particularly suited for carrot production, on the other hand, will be earning less than before and so will obtain a smaller share of the total national product than before.

Thus the change in consumers' tastes sets off market changes which cause a reallocation of resources in the required direction and, in the process, causes changes in the distribution of total national income among factors of production. We shall study changes of this kind more fully later. For now, the important thing to notice is how a change initiated in consumers' tastes causes a reallocation of resources in the direction required to cater to the new set of tastes.

A Change in Supply

For a second example, consider a change originating with producers. Begin as before by imagining a situation in which farmers find it equally profitable to produce sprouts and carrots, and consumers are willing to buy, at prevailing market prices, the quantities of these two commodities that are being produced. Now imagine that, with no change in the prices of sprouts and carrots, farmers become more willing to produce sprouts than in the past and less willing to produce carrots. This change might be caused, for example, by a rise in carrot costs and a fall in sprout costs raising the profitability of sprout production relative to carrot production.

What will happen now? For a short time, nothing at all. The existing supplies of sprouts and carrots are the results of decisions taken by farmers some time in the past. But farmers will now plant fewer carrots and more sprouts, and soon the quantities seen on the market will change. The amounts available for sale will rise in the case of sprouts and fall in the case of carrots. A shortage of carrots and a glut of sprouts will result. The price of carrots will rise and the price of sprouts will fall. As carrots become more expensive and sprouts become cheaper, fewer carrots and more sprouts will be bought by consumers. On the other hand, the rise in carrot prices and the fall in sprout prices will act as an incentive for farmers to move back into carrot production and out of sprout production. We started from a position in which there was a shortage of carrots, which caused carrot prices to rise. The rise in carrot prices removed the shortage in two ways: first by reducing the demand for the increasingly expensive carrots, and second by increasing the output of carrots which became increasingly profitable. We also started from a position in which there was a surplus of Brussels sprouts, which caused their price to fall. The fall in price removed the surplus in two ways: first by encouraging consumers to buy more of this commodity as it became less and less expensive, and second by discouraging the production of this commodity as it became less and less profitable.

Who Controls the Free Market?

These examples illustrate several features of the price system. First, the market responds to the collective actions of consumers and producers, even though the actions of *any one of them* would go unnoticed. There are millions of purchasers of carrots and Brussels sprouts, and a change in the tastes of a single one has a negligible effect on market prices and resource allocation. But if many consumers change their tastes, the effect will be significant. The situation is similar for producers. There are thousands of farmers, and the effect on market prices of the change in the behaviour of a single one of them is negligible. But if many farmers alter their behaviour, the effect on prices will be significant and there will be changes in the allocation of resources.

The second point that is illustrated is the market's systematic adaptation to changes in demand and supply, which take place without being consciously co-ordinated by anyone. When shortages develop, prices rise and profit-seeking farmers are led to produce more of the goods in short supply. When surpluses occur, prices fall and production is voluntarily contracted. The price system provides a series of automatic signals so that a large number of independent decision-taking units react in a co-ordinated way.

We have seen that although no single individual may be able to exert any significant control over a free market, the decisions of two groups, producers and consumers, do determine what is produced and sold. Thus the decisions of both groups influence the allocation of resources. A change in either consumers' demand or producers' supply will affect the allocation of resources and thus also the pattern of production and consumption.

It is often remarked that in a free-market society the consumer is king. Such a maxim reveals only half the truth. Prices are determined by supply as well as demand. A free-market society gives sovereignty to two groups, producers and consumers, and the decisions of both groups affect the allocation of resources.

Under certain conditions, known as *perfect competition*, the producer loses his sovereignty and becomes a mere automaton responding to the will of consumers. These very special conditions are described in Chapter 12. Aside from this case, however, producers do exercise considerable power over the allocation of resources.

Empirical evidence shows that, for many agricultural commodities and industrial raw materials, the price system works very much as described above. In any retail or wholesale produce market, prices can be observed to react to the state of demand and supply, rising when there is a shortage and falling when there is a surplus. Even the most casual observation of agriculture will show farmers varying their production of different crops as market prices vary. Is it valid, however, to extend this view of the price system to cover all commodities? This more difficult question must be postponed until the theory of price has been developed more fully.

SUMMARY

1. Scarcity is a fundamental problem faced by all economies because not enough resources – land, labour, capital and entrepreneurship – are available to produce all the goods and services that people would like to consume. Scarcity makes it necessary to choose. All societies must have a mechanism for choosing what commodities will be produced and in what quantities.

2. The concept of opportunity cost emphasizes scarcity and choice by measuring the cost of obtaining a unit or one commodity in terms of the number of units of other commodities that could have been obtained instead.

3. Some basic questions that concern all economies are: What commodities are being produced and in what quantities? How are they being produced? How is income distributed? How efficient is production and distribution? What commodities are being consumed and by whom? What are the unemployment and inflation rates, and are they related? Is productive capacity changing?

4. A production-possibility boundary shows all of the combinations of goods that can be produced by an economy whose resources are fully employed. Movement from one point to another on the boundary shows a shift in the bundle of goods being produced. This requires a reallocation of resources.

5. Modern economies are based on the specialization and division of labour, which necessitates the exchange of goods and services. Exchange takes place in markets and is facilitated by the use of money. Much of economics is devoted to a study of how markets work to co-ordinate millions of individual, decentralized decisions.

6. A free-market economy is one in which the allocation of resources is determined by the production, sales, and purchase decisions made by firms and households acting in response to such market signals as prices and profits.

TOPICS FOR REVIEW

- Factors of production
- Commodities, goods and services
- Scarcity, choice and opportunity cost
- Production-possibility boundary
- Resource allocation
- Growth in productive capacity
- Specialization and the division of labour
- Price system as a social control mechanism

2
Economics as a Social Science

Poetry is an art; nuclear physics is a science. By classifying economics as a social science, economists place their subject in the category of science rather than art. In so doing they advance the claim that there can be scientific studies of social as well as physical phenomena.

Both controversy and confusion centre around this claim. You should understand that calling economics a science implies a claim that the truth and applicability of economic theories can be supported or challenged by the test that all sciences accept: the degree to which theories correspond to observations of the real world. Calling economics a science does *not*, however, imply a claim for the universal truth of its current theories.

The claim that economics is scientific stands or falls, therefore, on the claim that economists can improve their ability to understand and predict events in the real world by stating theories, subjecting the theories to the test of real-world observations and by improving the theories in the light of what is learned thereby.

In this chapter we look at economics as a social science. We start by distinguishing between positive and normative statements – a distinction that is basic to all scientific enquiry. We then go on to consider whether or not it is actually possible to conduct a scientific study of *any* aspect of human behaviour. The questions dealt with in this chapter, namely 'What can we hope to learn?' and 'How can we go about it?', are fundamental to the whole subject. Indeed, these are also questions which inspire disagreement among professionals and misunderstanding, even superstition, among the general public.

POSITIVE AND NORMATIVE STATEMENTS

A key contributor to the success of modern science is the ability to separate views on *what actually happens* from views on *what one would like to happen*. For example, until the nineteenth century virtually all Christians, Jews and Muslims believed that the earth was only a few thousand years old. About two hundred years ago, evidence began to accumulate that some existing rocks were millions of years old, possibly even thousands of millions. Most people found this hard to accept; it would force them to rethink their religious beliefs and abandon those that were based on a literal reading of the Old Testament. Many wanted the evidence to be wrong; they wanted rocks to be only a few thousand years old. By the mid-nineteenth century, however, the age of the earth came to be dated in thousands of millions of years. This advance in our knowledge came because the question 'How old are rocks?' could be separated from the feelings of scientists (many of them devoutly religious) about the age they would have liked the rocks to be.

Definitions and Illustrations

Distinguishing what is from what we would like, or what we feel ought to be,[1] depends partly on knowing the difference between **positive** and **normative** statements.

> **Positive statements concern what is, was or will be; they assert alleged facts about the universe in which we live. Normative statements concern what ought to be; they depend on our *value judgements*, which are our judgements about what is good and what is bad. And as such, they are inextricably bound up with our philosophical, cultural and religious positions.**

To illustrate the distinction, consider some assertions, questions and hypotheses which can be classified as positive or normative. The statement 'It is impossible to break up atoms' is a positive one that can quite definitely be (and of course has been) refuted by empirical experimentation; while the statement 'Scientists ought not to break up atoms' is a normative statement that involves ethical judgements, and cannot be proved right or wrong by any evidence. In economics the questions 'What policies will reduce unemployment?' and 'What policies will

prevent inflation?' are positive ones, while the question 'Ought we to be more concerned about unemployment than about inflation?' is a normative one. The statement 'An increase in government spending will reduce unemployment and increase inflation' is a positive hypothesis. The statement 'Unemployment is a more serious social problem than inflation' is normative.

As an example of the importance of this distinction in the social sciences, consider the question 'Has the payment of generous unemployment benefits increased the amount of unemployment?' This positive question can be turned into a testable hypothesis by asserting, for example, 'The higher are the benefits paid to the unemployed, the higher will be the total amount of unemployment.' If we are not careful our value judgements may get in the way of our study of this hypothesis. Some people are opposed to the welfare state and believe in an individualist, self-help ethic. They may hope that the hypothesis will be found correct because its truth could then be used as an argument against welfare measures in general. Others feel that the welfare state is a good thing, reducing misery and contributing to human dignity. They may hope that the hypothesis is wrong because they do not want welfare measures to produce results of which people disapprove. In spite of different value judgements and social attitudes, evidence is accumulating on this particular hypothesis. As a result, we have much more knowledge than we had ten years ago of the effect that unemployment benefits have on unemployment. This evidence could never have been accumulated, or accepted, if investigators had not been able to distinguish their feelings on this controversial subject from their ability to observe how people actually behave.

Positive statements, such as the one just considered, assert things about the world. If it is possible for a statement to be proved wrong by empirical evidence, we call it a *testable statement*. Many positive statements are testable, and disagreements over them are appropriately handled by an appeal to the facts.

In contrast to positive statements, which are often testable, normative statements are never testable. Disagreements over such normative statements as 'It is wrong to steal' or 'It is immoral for someone to have sexual relations

---

[1] The word 'ought' has two distinct meanings: the 'logical ought' and the 'ethical ought'. The logical ought refers to the consequences of certain things: e.g. 'you ought to leave now if you wish to arrive on time'. The ethical ought refers to the desirability of certain things: e.g. 'arriving late is impolite and you ought to be polite'. The text refers to the ethical ought.

with another person of the same sex' cannot be settled by an appeal to empirical observations. Normative questions can be discussed rationally, but doing so requires techniques that differ from those required for a rational decision on positive questions. For this reason, it is convenient to separate normative from positive enquiries. This is done not because the former are less important than the latter, but merely because they must be investigated by different methods.

Some Points of Possible Confusion

Having made the basic distinction between positive and normative, a number of related points require attention. Although we deal with them only briefly, any one of them could be the subject of extended discussion.

The classification is not exhaustive: A classificatory system is exhaustive if every item can be placed in one or another of the defined classes. All statements cannot, however, be classed as either 'positive' or 'normative'. For example, there is an important class, called *analytic statements*, whose truth or falsehood depends only on the rules of logic. Such statements are thus neither positive nor normative. Consider the single sentence: 'If every X has the characteristic Y, and if this item Z is in fact an X, then it has the characteristic Y.' This sentence is true by the rules of logic, and its truth is independent of what particular items we substitute for X, Y and Z. Thus the sentence '*If* all men are immortal *and if* you are a man, *then* you are immortal' is a true analytic statement. It tells us that *if* two things are true *then* a third thing must be true. The truth of the whole statement is not dependent on whether or not its individual parts are factually correct. Indeed the sentence 'All men are immortal' is a positive statement which has been refuted by countless deaths. Yet no amount of empirical evidence on the mortality of men can upset the truth of the sentence '*If* all men are immortal, *and if* you are a man, *then* you are immortal.'

Not all positive statements are testable: A positive statement may be empirically true or false in the sense that what it asserts may or may not be true of reality. Many positive statements

are refutable: if they are wrong this can be ascertained (within a margin for error of observation) by checking them against data. For example, the positive statement that the earth is less than five thousand years old was tested and refuted by a mass of evidence which was accumulated in the eighteenth and nineteenth centuries. The statement 'Angels exist and occasionally visit the earth in visible form' is, however, also a positive statement. But we can never refute it with evidence because, no matter how hard we search, believers can argue that we have not looked in the right places or in the right way, or that angels won't reveal themselves to non-believers, or any one of a host of other alibis. Thus, statements that could conceivably be refuted by evidence if they are wrong are a subclass of positive statements; other positive statements are irrefutable.

The distinction is not unerringly applied: Because the positive–normative distinction helps the advancement of knowledge, it does not follow that all scientists automatically and unerringly apply it. Scientists are human beings! Many have strongly held views and they sometimes let their value judgements get in the way of their assessment of evidence. For example, many scientists are not even prepared to consider evidence that there may be differences in intelligence among races because as good liberals they feel that all races ought to be equal. Nonetheless, the desire to separate *what is* from *what we would like to be* is the guiding light of science. The ability to do so, even if imperfectly, is attested to by the final acceptance of many ideas that were initially extremely unpalatable – ideas such as the extreme age of the earth and the evolution of man from other animal species. Another case in point is described in Box 2.1.

Ideals can be important even though they are not universally applied. Consider an analogy. (1) Many people try to be good (according to their own lights). (2) Most people do not live up to their own standards of goodness all of the time. (3) Ideas of goodness are an important force in motivating human behaviour. All three of these statements are probably true: the truth of (1) does not preclude the truth of (2) and the truth of (2) does not preclude the truth of (3). In an analogous way, all three of the following statements are

BOX 2.1 POSITIVE AND NORMATIVE IDEAS IN PHYSICS

Distinguishing how the world is from how we would like it to be, is at the basis of a scientific approach to the study of any issue. Nowhere was the issue more starkly presented than with the development of the quantum theory of light, earlier in this century. The 4,000-year-old dream of science, that the world was like a machine in which given causes always had given effects, was upset within a generation and replaced by a probabilistic or statistical view of the universe. In the probabilistic world, given causes are followed by results that occur with given levels of probability, and it is never possible to know everything with certainty.

Albert Einstein could not bring himself to accept quantum theory, although his early work had pioneered its development. His intuition told him that, as he put it in his famous saying, 'God does not play dice with the universe.' As always, however, it was observation of what is, rather than feelings about what ought to be, that settled the issue – in this case against Einstein and in favour of the 'ridiculous' quantum theory.

Here is how a famous physicist, Richard Feynman, described the issue in his lectures on quantum electrodynamics.*

'I'm going to describe to you how Nature is – and if you don't like it, that's going to get in the way of your understanding it. It's a problem that physicists have learned to deal with: They've learned to realize that whether they like a theory or they don't like a theory is *not* the essential question. Rather, it is whether or not the theory gives predictions that agree with experiment. It is not a question of whether or not the theory is philosophically delightful, or easy to understand, or perfectly reasonable from the point of view of common sense. The theory of quantum electrodynamics described Nature as absurd from the point of view of common sense. And it agrees fully with experiment. So I hope you can accept Nature as She is – absurd.

I'm going to have fun telling you about this absurdity, because I find it delightful. Please don't turn yourself off because you can't believe Nature is so strange. Just hear me all out, and I hope you'll be as delighted as I am when we're through.'

* Richard P. Feynman, *QED: The Strange Theory of Light and Matter* (Princeton: Princeton University Press, 1985), p. 10.

probably true. (1) Positive and normative statements can be distinguished. (2) Not all scientists do, or even could, maintain the distinction all of the time. (3) The distinction has been a potent force in the advancement of knowledge and in the separation of knowledge from prejudice. Statement (1) does not preclude (2), and (2) does not preclude (3).[1]

Economists do not need to confine their discussions to positive statements: Some critics have mistakenly assumed that economists must try to deal only in statements that are positive and testable. In fact, positive economists must frequently consider the correctness of analytic statements: 'Is a certain prediction actually implied by a certain set of assumptions?' Fur-

thermore, theories from which positive, testable statements are deduced often contain some untestable assumptions. Nor need economists shrink from discussing value judgements, as long as they know what they are doing.

This last point is important. Just because positive economics does not include normative questions (because its tools are inappropriate to them), it does *not* follow that economists must stop their enquiry as soon as someone says the word 'ought'. The pursuit of what appears to be a normative statement will often turn up positive hypotheses on which our *ought* conclusion depends. For example, although many people have strong emotional feelings about government control of industry, few probably believe that such control is good or bad in itself. Their advocacy or opposition will be based on certain beliefs about relations which can be stated as positive rather than normative hypotheses. For example: 'Government control reduces (or increases) efficiency, changes (or does not change) the distribution of income, leads (or does not lead) to an increase in state control in other spheres.' A careful study of

[1] Many critics of the idea of positive science have argued otherwise. They feel that because no person can be perfectly objective about other people, the idea of an objective, fact-guided science of human behaviour is a contradiction. Fortunately, science based on the testing of positive hypotheses is possible even though no one individual can always be relied on to separate completely his judgement of facts from his desires on what he would like the facts to be.

this emotive subject will reveal an agenda for positive economic enquiry that could keep a research team of economists occupied for a decade.

THE NATURE OF POSITIVE ECONOMICS

We begin this section by summarizing the above discussion. Positive economics is concerned with the development of knowledge about the behaviour of people and things. This means that its practitioners are concerned with developing propositions that fall into the positive, testable class. This does not mean, however, that every single statement and hypothesis to be found in positive economics will actually be positive and testable. Some time ago a philosophy of knowledge called *logical positivism* was popular. It held that every single statement in the theory had to be positive and testable. This proved to be a harmful and unnecessary strait-jacket.

All that positive economists ask is that something that is positive and testable should emerge from their theories somewhere – for if it does not, their theories will be unrelated to the real world.

The Use of Evidence

Scientists seek to answer positive questions by relating them to evidence. This approach is one of the characteristics that distinguish scientific enquiries from other types of enquiry.[1] Experimental sciences, such as chemistry and some branches of psychology, have an advantage because they can produce relevant evidence through controlled laboratory experiments. Other sciences, such as astronomy and economics, must wait for evidence to be produced in the natural course of events.

The ease with which one can collect evidence does not determine whether a subject is scientific,

although many people have thought otherwise.[1] The techniques of scientific enquiry do, however, differ radically between fields in which laboratory experiment is possible and those in which it is not. Here we consider general problems more or less common to all sciences. Later in the chapter we deal with problems peculiar to the non-experimental sciences.

It is often said that we live in a scientific age. In recent centuries, the citizens of most Western countries have enjoyed the fruits of innumerable scientific discoveries; but the scientific advances that have so profoundly affected them have been made by a small minority. Most people have accepted these advances without the slightest idea either of the technical nature of the discoveries involved or of the attitude of mind that made them possible. If we take as a measure of the influence of science the degree to which the fruits of science are enjoyed by the public, then we live in a profoundly scientific age; but if we take as our measure the degree to which the public appreciates the scientific approach, then we are in a largely pre-scientific era. Indeed, the scientific discipline of answering questions by appealing to a carefully collected and co-ordinated body of facts is a method often ignored by the public.

Consider, for example, the argument about capital punishment that continues today even in many of the countries that have abolished the death penalty. It is possible to advocate capital punishment as an act of pure vengeance, or because we believe that morally a person who kills *ought* himself to be killed. If we argue on these grounds, we are dealing with normative issues that depend on value judgements. The majority of arguments for capital punishment, however, are not of this type. Instead, they depend on predictions about observable behaviour, and thus belong to the field of science. These are usually variants of the general argu-

---

[1] Other approaches might be to appeal to authority, for example, to Aristotle or the Scriptures, to appeal by introspection to some inner experience (to start off 'all reasonable men will surely agree'), or to proceed by way of definitions to the 'true' nature of the problem or concepts under consideration.

[1] It is often thought that scientific procedure consists of grinding out answers by following blind rules of calculation, and that only in the arts is the exercise of real imagination required. This view is misguided. What the scientific method gives is an impersonal set of criteria for answering some questions. What questions to ask, exactly how to ask them and how to obtain the evidence, are difficult problems for which there are no rules. They often require great imagination and ingenuity.

ment that capital punishment is a deterrent to murder.

People often take a stand on the issue of deterrance without considering the available evidence. For example, many people involved in these debates know nothing of the mass of evidence on murder rates before and after the abolition of capital punishment in the large number of jurisdictions where it has been abolished and in those few where it has been reimposed. Indeed, popular arguments for and against capital punishment often involve empirical questions which are answered without appeal to empirical evidence.

We may conclude that many hotly debated issues of public policy involve positive, not normative, questions, but that the scientific approach to them is often avoided.

Stability in Human Behaviour?

The preceding discussion raises the question of whether or not it is possible to have a scientific study in the field of human behaviour. A necessary condition for such a science is that human beings should show stable response patterns to various stimuli. Is it reasonable to expect such stability in human behaviour?

It is often argued that natural sciences deal with inanimate matter that is subject to natural 'laws', while the social sciences deal with people, who have free will and cannot, therefore, be made the subject of such (inexorable) laws. Such an argument, however, concentrates on the physical sciences; it omits biology and the other life sciences which deal successfully with animate matter. When this point is granted, it may then be argued that the life sciences deal with simple living material, while only the social sciences deal with human beings, who are the ultimate in complexity and who alone possess free will. Today, when we are increasingly aware of our common heritage with primates in general, and apes in particular, an argument that human behaviour is totally different from the behaviour of other animals finds few adherents among informed students of animal behaviour.

Nonetheless, many social observers while accepting the success of the natural and the life sciences, hold that there cannot be a successful social science. Stated carefully, this view implies that inanimate and non-human animate matter will show stable responses to certain stimuli, while humans will not. For example, if you put a match to a dry piece of paper, the paper will burn; while if you try to extract vital information from unwilling human beings by torture, some will yield, while others will not, and, more confusingly, the same individual will react differently at different times. Whether or not human behaviour shows sufficiently stable responses to be predictable within an acceptable margin of error is a positive question. It can only be settled by an appeal to evidence, and not by *a priori* speculation.[1]

If group human behaviour were in fact random and capricious, existence would be impossible. Neither law nor justice nor airline timetables would be more reliable than a roulette wheel; a kind remark could as easily provoke fury as sympathy; one's landlady might put one out tomorrow or forgive one the rent. One cannot really imagine a society of human beings that could possibly work like this. Indeed a major part of brainwashing techniques is to mix up rewards and punishments until the victim genuinely does not know 'where he is': unpredictable pressures drive human beings mad. In fact, we live in a world which is a mixture of the predictable, or average, or 'most of the people most of the time', and of the haphazard, contrary or random.

When we try to analyse our world, and apply our orderly models to it, we need help from specialists in probability – statisticians – but we have not yet found that we need the advice of experts in the study of systems whose underlying behaviour is purely random.

The 'Law' of Large Numbers

We may now ask how it is that group behaviour can show stable responses even though we can never be quite sure what each single individual will do. As a first step, we must distinguish between *deterministic* and *statistical* hypotheses. Deterministic hypotheses permit no exceptions. An example would be the statement: 'If you torture any man over this period of time with these methods, he will *always* break down.'

---

[1] *A priori* is a phrase commonly used by economists. It may be defined as that which is prior to actual experience, i.e. innate rather than acquired by experience.

Statistical hypotheses, however, permit exceptions and purport to predict the probability of certain occurrences. An example would be: 'If you torture a man over this period of time with these methods, he will *very probably* break down; in fact if you torture a large number of men under the stated circumstances about 95 per cent of them will break down.' Such a hypothesis does not predict what an individual will certainly do, but only what she will probably do. This does allow us, however, to predict within a determinable margin of error what a large group of individuals will do.

Successful predictions about the behaviour of large groups are made possible by the statistical 'law' of large numbers. Very roughly, this 'law' asserts that random movements of a large number of items tend to offset one another. The law is based on one of the most beautiful constants of behaviour in the whole of science, and yet the law can be derived from the fact that human beings make errors! This constant is the *normal curve of error* which you will encounter in elementary statistics.

Let us consider what is implied by the law of large numbers. Ask one person to measure the length of a room and it will be almost impossible to predict in advance what sort of error of measurement he or she will make. Furthermore, one individual may make one error today and quite a different error tomorrow. But ask one thousand people to measure the length of the same room and we can predict with a high degree of accuracy how this *group* will make its errors! We can assert with confidence that more people will make small errors than will make large errors, that approximately the same number of people will overestimate as will underestimate the distance, and that the average error of all the individuals will be close to zero.[1] Here then is a truly remarkable constant pattern of human behaviour, a constant on which much of the theory of statistical inference is based.

If a common stimulus should act on all members of the group, we can successfully predict their average behaviour, even though any one member of the group may act in a surprising fashion. If, for example, we give all our thousand individuals a tape-measure which understates 'actual' distances, we can predict that, on the average, the group will now understate the length

of the room. It is, of course, quite possible that one member who had in the past been consistently undermeasuring distance because she was depressed will now overestimate the distance because her health has changed; but something else may happen to some other individual that will turn him from an overmeasurer into an undermeasurer. Individuals may do peculiar things which, as far as we can see, are inexplicable, but the group's behaviour, when the inaccurate tape-measure is substituted for the accurate one, will nonetheless be predictable, *precisely because the odd things that one individual does will tend to cancel out the odd things some other individual does.*

THE NATURE OF SCIENTIFIC THEORIES

We have seen that human behaviour does show stable response patterns, but how do we construct theories about such behaviour? Theories develop in answer to the question 'Why?' Some sequence of events, some regularity between two or more behavioural patterns is observed, and someone asks why this should be so. A theory attempts to explain why. One of the main practical consequences of a theory is that it enables us to predict as yet unobserved events. For example, the theory of market behaviour predicts that, if there is a partial failure of the potato crop, the total income earned by potato farmers will increase!

Theories are used in explaining observed phenomena. A successful theory enables us to predict behaviour.

Any explanation whatsoever of how given

---

[1] For purposes of measuring the error, we define the 'true' distance to be that measured by the most precise instruments of scientific measurement (whose range of error will be very small relative to the range of error of our one thousand laymen all wielding tape-measures). Those familiar with statistical theory will realize that the predictions in the text assume that all the necessary conditions, such as the existence of a large number of independent factors causing individuals to make errors, are fulfilled. The purpose of the discussion in the text is not to give readers a full appreciation of the subtleties of statistical theory, but to persuade them that free will, and the absence of deterministic certainty about human behaviour, do not make its scientific study impossible.

observations are linked together is a theoretical construction. Theories are used to impose order on our observations. Without theories there would be only a shapeless mass of meaningless observations.

The choice is not between theory and observation but between better or worse theories to explain observations.

Misunderstandings about the role of theories in scientific explanation give rise to many misconceptions. Consider, for example, the common saying that something is 'True in theory, but not in practice.' The next time you hear someone say this (or, indeed, the next time you say it yourself) you should immediately reply, 'All right then, tell me what does happen in practice.' Usually you will not be offered mere facts, but rather you will be given an alternative theory – a different explanation of the facts. The speaker should have said, 'The theory in question provides a poor explanation of the facts (that is, it is contradicted by some factual observations). I have a different theory that does a much better job.'

The Components of a Theory

A theory consists of (1) a set of definitions that clearly describe the *variables* to be used, (2) a set of *assumptions* that outline the conditions under which the theory is to apply, (3) one or more *hypotheses* about the behaviour of these variables, (4) *predictions* that are deduced from the assumptions of the theory, and that (5) can be tested against actual data. We consider these five constituents in the following five sections.

Variables

A **variable** is a magnitude that can take on different possible values. Variables are the basic elements of theories, and each one needs to be carefully defined.

Price is an example of an important economic variable. The price of a commodity is the amount of money that must be given up to purchase one unit of that commodity. To define a price we must first define the commodity to which it attaches. Such a commodity might be one dozen grade-A large eggs. The price of such eggs sold in, say, supermarkets in Newmarket defines a variable. The particular values taken on by that

variable might be £0.90 on 1 July 1988, £1.00 on 8 July 1989, and £0.95 on 15 July 1990.

There are many distinctions between kinds of variables; two of the most important are discussed below.

Endogenous and exogenous variables: An **endogenous variable** is a variable that is explained within a theory. An **exogenous variable** influences endogenous variables but is itself determined by factors outside the theory.

To illustrate, consider this theory: the price of apples in Glasgow on a particular day depends on several things, one of which is the weather in southern England during the previous apple-growing season. We can safely assume that the state of the weather is not determined by economic conditions. In this theory, the price of apples is an endogenous variable – something determined within the framework of the theory. The state of the weather in southern England is an exogenous variable: the weather influences apple prices (by affecting the output of apples), but the state of the weather is not influenced by apple prices.

Other words are sometimes used to make the same distinction. One frequently used pair is *induced* for endogenous and *autonomous* for exogenous.

Stock and flow variables: A flow variable has a time dimension; it is so much per unit of time. The quantity of grade-A large eggs purchased in Glasgow is a flow variable. No useful information is conveyed if we are told that the number purchased was 2,000 dozen eggs unless we are also told the period of time over which these purchases occurred. Two thousand dozen per hour would indicate an active market in eggs, while 2,000 dozen per month would indicate a sluggish market.

A stock variable has no time dimension; it is just so much. Thus, the number of eggs in an egg producer's warehouse – for example, 20,000 dozen eggs – is a stock variable. All those eggs are there at one time, and they remain there until something happens to change the stock held by the producer. The stock variable is just a number, not a rate of flow of so much per day or per month.

Economic theories use both flow variables and stock variables, and it takes a little practice to keep them straight. The amount of income earned is a flow – there is so much per year or per month or per hour. The amount of a household's expenditure is also a flow – so much spent per week or per month. The amount of money in a bank account or a miser's hoard (earned, perhaps, in the past, but unspent) is a stock – just so many thousands of pounds sterling. The key test is always whether a time dimension is required to give the variable meaning.

Assumptions

Assumptions are essential to theorizing. Students are often greatly concerned about the justification of assumptions, particularly if they seem unrealistic.

An example will illustrate some of the issues involved in this question of realism. Much of the theory that we are going to study in this book uses the assumption that the sole motive of all those who run firms is to make as much money as they possibly can, or, as economists put it, firms are assumed to be run so as to *maximize their owners' profits*. The assumption of profit maximization allows economists to make predictions about the behaviour of firms. They study the effects that alternative choices would have on profits, and then predict that the alternative selected will be the one that produces the most profits.

But profit maximization may seem a rather crude assumption. Surely the managers of firms sometimes have philanthropic or political motives. Does this not discredit the assumption of profit maximization by showing it to be unrealistic?

To make successful predictions, however, the theory does not require that managers are solely and always motivated by the desire to maximize profits. All that is required is that profits are a sufficiently important consideration that a theory based on the assumption of profit maximization will produce predictions that are substantially correct.

This illustration shows that it is not always appropriate to criticize a theory because its assumptions seem unrealistic. *All theory is an abstraction from reality*. If it were not, it would merely duplicate the world and would add nothing to our understanding of it. A good theory abstracts in a useful way; a poor theory does not. If a theory has ignored really important factors, then some of its predictions will be contradicted by the evidence.

Hypotheses

Relations among variables: The critical step in theorizing is formulating hypotheses. A hypothesis is a statement about how two or more variables are related to each other. For example, it is a basic hypothesis of economics that the quantity produced of any commodity depends upon its own price in such a way that the higher the price the larger the quantity produced. To illustrate, the higher the price of eggs the larger the quantity of eggs that farmers will produce. Stated in more formal terms, the hypothesis is that the two variables, price of eggs and quantity of eggs, are positively related to each other. Notice that when two variables are related in such a way that an increase in one is associated with an increase in the other, we say they are **positively related**; when two variables are related in such a way that an increase in one is associated with a decrease in the other, we say they are **negatively related**.

Predictions

A theory's predictions are the propositions that can be deduced from that theory. An example of a prediction would be the deduction: *if* firms maximize their profits, and *if* certain other assumptions and hypotheses of the theory hold true, *then* a rise in the rate of business income tax will cause a reduction in the amount of investment that firms make in new plant and equipment. The prediction is that the rise in the tax rate will be accompanied by a fall in investment. The reasons that lie behind the prediction are contained in the assumptions and hypotheses that constitute the theory in question.

It should be apparent from this discussion that a scientific prediction is not the same thing as a prophecy.

A scientific prediction is a conditional statement that takes the form: *If* **you do this,** *then* **such and such will follow.**

For example, *if* the government cuts taxes, *then* the rate of unemployment will decrease. It is most important to realize that this prediction is very different from the statement: 'I prophesy that in two years' time there will be a large reduction in unemployment because I believe the government will decide to cut tax rates.' The government's decision to cut tax rates in two years' time will be the outcome of many influences, both economic and political. If the economist's prophecy about unemployment turns out to be wrong because in two years' time the government does not cut tax rates, then all that has been learned is that the economist is not good at guessing the behaviour of the government. However, *if* the government does cut tax rates (in two years' time or at any other time) and *then* the rate of unemployment does not decrease, a conditional scientific prediction in economic theory has been contradicted.

In general discussions of theories, definitions, assumptions and hypotheses are often lumped together and called the theory's assumptions. This general use is implicit, for example, when people speak of a theory's predictions being deduced from its assumptions.

Tests

A theory is tested by confronting its predictions with evidence. It is necessary to see if certain events are followed by the consequences predicted by the theory. For example, is an increase in the rate of tax on business income followed by a decline in business investment?

Generally, theories tend to be abandoned when they are no longer useful. Theories cease to be useful when they cannot predict better than an alternative. When a theory consistently fails to predict better than an available alternative, it is either modified or replaced.[1]

Refutation or confirmation: The scientific approach to any phenomenon consists in setting up a theory that will explain it and then seeing if that theory can be refuted by evidence.

The alternative to this approach is to set up a theory and then look for confirming evidence. Such an approach is hazardous because the world is sufficiently complex for *some* confirming evidence to be found for almost any theory, no matter how unlikely the theory may be.

An example of the unfruitful approach of seeking confirmation is frequently seen when a leader – be it the British Prime Minister or a foreign dictator – is surrounded by yes-men who filter out evidence that conflicts with the leader's existing views. This approach is usually a road to disaster because the leader's decisions become more and more out of touch with reality. A wise leader adopts a scientific approach instinctively; constantly checking the validity of his or her views by encouraging subordinates to criticize them. This tests how far the leader's existing views correspond to all available evidence and encourages amendment in the light of conflicting evidence.

Theory and evidence, which came first? The old question of the chicken and the egg is often raised when discussing economic theories. In the first instance, it was observation that preceded economic theories. People were not born with economic theories embedded in their minds. Instead, economic theories first arose when people observed certain market behaviour and asked themselves why such behaviour occurred. But, once economics had begun, theories and evidence interacted with each other and it has become impossible to say that one now precedes the other. In some cases, tests of theories may suggest inadequacies that require the development of better theories. In other cases, an inspired guess may lead to a theory that has little current empirical support but is subsequently found to explain many observations.[1]

The State of Economics

Any developing science will be continually hav-

---

[1] The development of a new theory to account for existing observations is often the result of creative genius of an almost inspired nature. This step in scientific development is the exact opposite of the popular conception of the scientist as an automatic rule-follower. One could argue for a long time whether there was more original creative genius embodied in a first-class symphony or a new theory of astronomy. Fascinating studies of the creative process may be found in A. Koestler, *The Sleep Walkers* (London: Hutchinson, 1959), especially the section on Kepler, and J. D. Watson, *The Double Helix* (London: Weidenfeld & Nicolson, 1968).

---

[1] This type of procedure is quite common these days in physics where theories that are put forward to explain known facts gain wide acceptance mainly because of their elegance and aesthetic appeal. Experimentalists often spend years looking for some new particle or other phenomenon predicted by the theory. In the end, however, the theory stands or falls on the balance of evidence between it and competing theories.

FIGURE 2.1 The Interaction of Deduction and Measurement in Theorizing

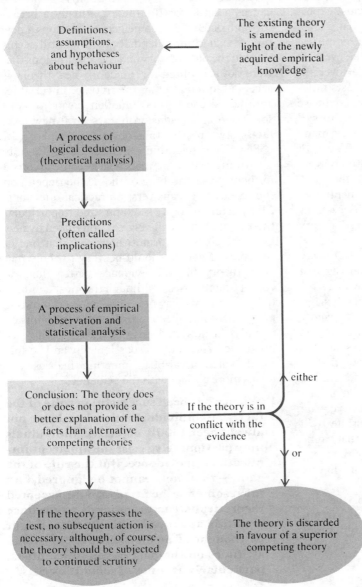

Theory and observation are in continuous interaction. Start at the top left because description must start somewhere. Using the theory's assumptions, the definitions of relevant terms, and hypothesis about behaviour, the theorist deduces everything that is implied by the assumptions. These implications are the predictions of the theory. The theory is then tested by confronting its predictions with evidence, using factual observations and the techniques of statistical analysis. If the theory is in conflict with the evidence, it will usually be amended to make it consistent with those facts (thereby making it a better theory); in extreme cases it will be discarded, to be replaced by a superior alternative. The process then begins again: the new or amended theory is subjected first to logical analysis and then to empirical testing.

ing some of its theories rejected; it will also be cataloguing observations that cannot be explained by any existing theory. These observations indicate the direction required for the development of new theories or for the extension of existing ones. On the other hand there will be many implications of existing theories that have not yet been tested, either because no one has yet figured out how to test them, or merely because no one has got around to doing the job. These untested hypotheses provide an agenda for new empirical studies.

Economics provides no exception. On the one hand, there are many observations for which no fully satisfactory theoretical explanation exists. On the other hand, there are many predictions which no one has yet satisfactorily tested. Thus serious students of economics must not expect to find a set of answers to all possible questions as they progress in their study. They must expect very often to encounter nothing more than a set of problems for further theoretical or empirical research. Even when they do find answers to problems, they should accept these answers as tentative and ask, even of the most time-honoured theory: 'What observations might we make that would be in conflict with this theory?' Economics is still a very young science with many issues remaining almost untouched. Those of you who venture further in this book may well, only a few years from now, publish a theory to account for some of the problems mentioned herein, or else you may make a set of observations which will upset some time-honoured theory described within these pages.

Having counselled disrespect for the authority of accepted theory, it is necessary to warn against adopting an approach that is too cavalier. No respect attaches to the person who merely says: 'This theory is for the birds; it is *obviously* wrong.' This is too cheap. To criticize a theory on logical grounds (economists sometimes say 'on theoretical grounds') one must show that it contains some internal contradictions,[1] or that alleged predictions do not follow from its assumptions. To criticize a theory effectively on empirical grounds, one must demonstrate by a carefully made set of observations that some aspect of the theory is contradicted by the facts. These tasks are seldom easily or lightly accomplished.

Figure 2.1 provides a summary of the discussion of theories. It shows a closed circuit, because theory and observation are in continuous interaction with each other.

Scientific Crises

Sciences often appear to evolve through a series of stages. At first, an existing theory seems to be working well and the main scientific tasks are to extend it in various directions. Then, gradually, observations begin to accumulate that conflict with the theory. For a long time these exceptions are explained away on an ad hoc basis, but eventually the weight of conflicting evidence causes a crisis for the theory. Finally a breakthrough occurs, and some genius develops a new theory that comprehends both what still seems right in the older theory *and* the observations that were not accounted for. Once the new theory is accepted, often after an interlude of uncertainty and heated controversy, another period of consolidation and extension occurs until new conflicts between theory and observation emerge.

Periods of scientific crisis can be profoundly disturbing to the scientists who become involved in them, to say nothing of those who depend on the scientists for answers to practical questions. Many economists are so committed to particular theories that they will never be convinced by new evidence. It is important, however, that one of the rules of debate should be 'Try to show that your theory fits the evidence better than do competing theories.' Although the most committed protagonists may never change their minds, a new generation of economists, not so committed to old and outdated positions, may be able to judge the issues more dispassionately and be able to tell which of various competing theories conforms more closely with the evidence.

Science has been successful in spite of the fact that individual scientists have not always been totally objective. Individuals may passionately resist the apparent implications of evidence. But the rule of the game – that facts cannot be ignored, and must somehow be fitted into the accepted theoretical structure – tends to produce scientific advance in spite of what might be thought of as unscientific, emotional attitudes on the part of many scientists, particularly at times of scientific crisis.

But if existing protagonists ever succeed in changing the rules of the game by encouraging economists to ignore inconvenient facts or define them out of existence, this would be a major blow to scientific enquiry in economics.[1]

---

[1] This is what Einstein did in his famous thought experiment in which he imagined what would happen, according to Newtonian physics, if a particle were to be accelerated to the speed of light.

[1] One of the best introductions to methodology for economists is Mark Blaug, *The Methodology of Positive Economics: Or How Economists Explain* (Cambridge: Cambridge University Press, 1980), which is, however, probably better read after one has studied a certain amount of economics.

SUMMARY

1. A key to the success of scientific inquiry lies in separating positive questions about the way the world works from normative questions about how one would like the world to work, formulating positive questions precisely enough so that they can be settled by an appeal to evidence, and then finding means of gathering the necessary evidence.

2. Some people argue that although natural phenomena can be subject to scientific inquiry and 'laws' of behaviour, human phenomena cannot. The evidence, however, is otherwise. Social scientists have observed many stable human behavioural patterns. These form the basis for successful predictions of how people will behave under specified conditions.

3. The fact that people sometimes act strangely, even capriciously, does not destroy the possibility of scientific study of group behaviour. The odd and inexplicable things that one person does will tend to cancel out the odd and inexplicable things that another person does. As a result, systematic patterns can often be seen in the behaviour of large groups of individuals.

4. Theories are designed to give meaning and coherence to observed sequences of events. A theory consists of a set of definitions of the variables to be employed, a set of assumptions concerning conditions under which the theory is meant to apply, and a set of hypotheses about how things behave. These are often collectively referred to as the theory's assumptions. Any theory has certain logical implications that must be true if its assumptions are true. These are the theory's predictions.

5. A theory provides conditional predictions of the type '*if* one event occurs, *then* another event will also occur'. An important method of testing theories is to confront their predictions with evidence. The progress of any science lies in finding better explanations of events than are now available. Thus, in any developing science, one must expect periodically to discard present theories, replacing them with demonstrably superior alternatives.

TOPICS FOR REVIEW

- Positive and normative statements
- Testable statements
- The law of large numbers and the predictability of human behaviour
- Endogenous and exogenous variables
- Stock and flow variables
- Negative and positive relations between variables
- Variables, assumptions, hypotheses and predictions

3

The Tools of Economics

In this chapter we discuss two of the major tools of economic analysis, looking first at the tools of theoretical analysis and then at those of statistical analysis. The Appendix covers some elementary concepts in school mathematics and geometry that are used throughout any economics textbook. Readers who had difficulty with school maths, or who find the material in this chapter tough going, might be well advised to read the Appendix first.

THE TOOLS OF THEORETICAL ANALYSIS

The left-hand side of Figure 2.1 on page 25 contains darkly coloured rectangles. The first stands for the movement from the assumptions to the implications, or predictions, of theories. To make this move, economists use the tools of logical deduction or, as they are often called, the tools of theoretical analysis.

Expressing Hypotheses

We have already noted that an economic theory contains definitions, assumptions and hypotheses about behaviour, often collectively called assumptions.

> **The assumptions of economic theory may be described in words, formulated mathematically or illustrated graphically. Once they are expressed in a precise way, their implications may also be derived by verbal, mathematical or geometrical analysis.[1]**

To a great extent all of these methods are interchangeable; any piece of logical reasoning that can be done verbally or geometrically can also be done mathematically. Some things that are done in mathematics, however, cannot be done rigorously verbally or geometrically.

Correspondences and Functions

Science is based on studying how variables are related to each other. When two variables are

---

[1] Geometry is, of course, a branch of mathematics, but it is convenient to distinguish between 'geometrical' and 'mathematical' methods – meaning by the latter term mathematical other than the geometrical.

related in some way, we say that there is a *correspondence* between them. When the relationship is such that to any value of the variable X there corresponds one and only one value of the variable Y, then Y is said to be a *function* of X. For example, in the relation

$$Y = a + bX + cX^2 \qquad (1)$$

Y is a function of X because each value of X gives rise to one and only one value of Y.[1] In what follows we confine ourselves to the subclass of correspondences that are functions. To illustrate our points, we consider a functional relation that we shall encounter later in this book. It states that the amount a household spends on purchasing goods and services is related to that household's after-tax income. Two steps are needed in order to express this functional relation in symbols. First, each variable needs to be given a symbol. We let C stand for the household's expenditure on goods and services, and Y stand for its after-tax income. Second, we designate a symbol to express the relation of one variable to the other. If we agree to use the letter f, we can now write:

$$C = f(Y) \ . \qquad (2)$$

This is read 'consumption is a function of income'. The variable on the left-hand side is called the dependent variable, since its value depends on the value of the variable on the right-hand side. The variable on the right-hand side is called the independent variable, since it can take on any value whatsoever. The letter f tells us that a functional relation is involved. This means that a knowledge of the value of the variable (or variables) within the parentheses on the right-hand side allows us to determine the value of the variable on the left-hand side. Although, in this case, we have used f (a memory-aid for function), any convenient symbol can be used to denote the existence of a functional relation.

Functional notation can seem intimidating. But it *is* helpful. Since the functional concept is basic to all science, the notation is worth mastering.

The expression $C = f(Y)$ states that C is

related to Y; it says nothing about the *form* that this relation takes. The term *functional form* refers to the specific nature of the relation between the variables in the function. The following is one possible form of the general relation between consumption and income:

$$C = 0.75Y \ . \qquad (3)$$

Equation (2) expresses the general hypothesis that a household's consumption depends upon its after-tax income. Equation (3) expresses the more specific hypothesis that expenditure on consumption will be three-quarters of the household's income. There is no reason why either of these hypotheses *must* be true; indeed, neither may be consistent with the facts. But those are matters for testing. What we do have in each equation is a concise statement of a particular hypothesis.

Thus the existence of some relation between two variables, Y and X, is denoted by $Y = f(X)$, whereas any precise relation may be expressed by a particular form such as $Y = 2X$, $Y = 4X^2$, or $Y = X + 2X^2 + 0.5X^3$.

Recall that if Y increases as X increases (e.g., $Y = 10 + 2X$), Y and X are said to be positively related to each other. If Y decreases as X increases (e.g., $Y = 10 - 2X$), Y and X are said to be negatively related to each other.[1]

The Error Term

The functional relation considered above was *deterministic*, in the sense that, given the value of Y, we knew the value of C exactly. Relations in economics are seldom of this sort, except where definitions are being expressed. When an economist says that the world behaves so that $Y = f(X)$, he does not expect that knowing X will tell him *exactly* what Y will be, but only that it

---

[1] It is worth noting that Y being a function of X does not imply that X is a function of Y. For example, in equation (1), X cannot be expressed as a function of Y because for many values of Y there correspond two values of X.

[1] The terms 'directly' and 'inversely related' are sometimes used instead of 'positively' and 'negatively related'. These alternative terms can, however, be ambiguous. Direct might be taken to mean the opposite of indirect, and inverse might be taken to refer to the specific inverse relation $Y = 1/X$. To avoid these possible ambiguities, we usually use the terms 'positively' and 'negatively related' in the text.

Because economists often think of graphs as flowing from left to right, they sometimes speak of negatively and positively sloped curves as 'sloping downwards' and 'sloping upwards' respectively. We usually avoid this terminology, which can be a source of confusion to persons trained in other disciplines.

will tell him what Y will be *within some margin of error*.

The error in predicting Y from a knowledge of X arises for two quite distinct reasons. First, there may be other variables that also affect Y. Although we may say that the quantity of butter demanded is a function of the price of butter, $q_b = f(p_b)$, we know that other factors will also influence this demand. A change in the price of margarine will certainly affect the demand for butter, even though the price of butter does not change. Thus we do not expect to find a perfect relation between q_b and p_b that will allow us to predict q_b exactly, from a knowledge of p_b. Second, we can never measure our variables exactly, so that, even if X is the only cause of Y, our measurements will give various Ys corresponding to the same X. In the case of the demand for butter, our errors of measurement might not be so large. In other cases, errors can be substantial. In the case of a relation between total spending on consumption goods and total income earned in the nation ($C = f(Y)$), our measurements of both C and Y may be subject to quite wide margins of error. We may thus observe various values of C associated with the same measured value of Y, not because C is varying independently of Y, but because our error of measurement is itself varying from period to period.

If all the factors other than X that affect the measured value of Y are summarized into an *error term*, ε, we write

$$Y = f(X, \varepsilon) .$$

This says that the observed value of Y is related to the observed value of X as well as to a lot of other things, both observational errors and other causal factors, all of which will be lumped together and called ε (the Greek letter epsilon). In economic theory this error term is almost always suppressed, and we proceed as if our functional relations were deterministic. (When we come to test our theories, however, some very serious problems arise because functional relations do not hold exactly.)

It is important to remember, both when interpreting a theory in terms of the real world and when testing a theory against facts, that the deterministic formulation

is a simplification. The error term is really present in all the functional relations dealt with in economics.

Alternative Methods of Representing Functional Relations

A functional relation can be expressed in words, in graphs or in mathematical equations. (It can also be illustrated by displaying specific values in a *table* or, as it is sometimes called, a *schedule*.) As a simple example let us consider a specific form of the general relation given in (2) above. This new example is different from the one given in (3) and can be expressed in any of the following three ways.

(1) **Verbal statement.** When income is zero, the household will spend £800 a year (either by borrowing the money or by consuming past savings), and for every pound of income that the household obtains net of taxes (called its 'disposable income'), the household will increase its expenditure by £0.80.

(2) **Mathematical (algebraic) statement.** $C = 800 + 0.8Y$ is the equation of the relation just described in words. As a check you can substitute any two values of Y that differ by £1, multiply each by 0.80 and add 800, and then satisfy yourselves that the corresponding two values of consumption differ by £0.80.

FIGURE 3.1 A Relation Between a Household's Expenditure and its Income

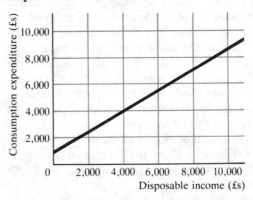

The graph shows consumption expenditure as an increasing function of income. Plotting income on one axis and consumption expenditure on the other produces a visual representation of the assumed relation between the two variables.

---

(3) **Geometrical (graphical) statement.** Figure 3.1 shows the same relation on a graph. Comparison of the values on the graph with the values derived from the equation just stated shows that these are two alternative expressions of the same relation between C and Y. Box 3.1 gives some further dicussion of the ways in which such functions can be graphed.

Deriving Implications from Functional Relationships

After laying out the functional relations, the next step is to discover what they imply. In the process of making logical deductions from theories, economists may again employ verbal, geometrical or mathematical forms of reasoning. The main concerns are to ensure that the reasoning processes are both correct, so that deductions are actually implied by the theory, and efficient, so that everything that is implied by the theory is discovered. The worries that many people have about the use of mathematical analysis in economics are further discussed in Box 3.2 on page 34.

Examples of Theoretical Reasoning

In later chapters you will encounter many interesting examples of the process of logical deduction in economics. In the meantime we can illustrate the procedure with some very simple manipulation of the household's consumption function $C = 800 + 0.8Y$. What can we discover about the behaviour of a household which has such a consumption function? First, it is clear that when its income is zero, the household is using up past savings or going into debt at the rate of £800 per year. Second, it is clear that an increase in income of £1 leads to an increase in consumption of 80p. Third, there will be a level of income at which the household is neither running into debt nor saving any of its income. This is called the *break-even level of income*, and it is easily discovered by finding the level of Y such that C and Y are equal.

To discover the break-even level algebraically, we need to solve the two simultaneous equations $C = 800 + 0.8Y$ and $C = Y$. The first tells us

how the household's consumption expenditure varies with its income, and the second imposes the condition that consumption expenditure should equal disposable income. If you solve these two equations, you will discover that the break-even level of income for this household is £4,000. A little further experimentation will show that at any level of income less than £4,000, expenditure exceeds income, while at any income level over £4,000, expenditure is less than income. The graphical determination of the break-even level of income is shown in Figure 3.2.

As a final example of elementary theoretical reasoning, let us ask by how much the break-even level of income will increase if the household's behaviour changes so that, at each level of income, consumption expenditure is £800 higher than before. The changed behaviour is described by the new equation: $C = 1,600 + 0.8Y$. To find the new break-even level of income, we solve this simultaneously with $C = Y$ and find the solution to be £8,000. Thus, when consumption is in-

FIGURE 3.2 The Determination of the Break-even Level of Income

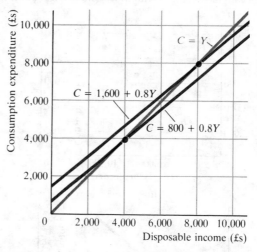

The graph shows pictorially the solution of two simultaneous equations. The lines graphing the consumption function $C = 800 + 0.8Y$ and the condition that C should equal Y intersect at income £4,000. This is the solution to the two equations.

The lines graphing the consumption function $C = 1,600 + 0.8Y$ and the condition $C = Y$ intersect at income £8,000. This tells us that when this consumption function shifts upwards by £800, the break-even level of income rises by £4,000.

BOX 3.1   GRAPHING ECONOMIC RELATIONS

The consumption function given in the text is $C = 800 + 0.8Y$. Let us start by taking five different levels of income, £0, £2,500, £5,000, £7,000 and £10,000, and calculating the level of consumption expenditure that would be associated with each. The Table shows these values and, for further reference, assigns a letter to each pair of values.

Part (i) of the Figure plots these data on a co-ordinate grid.

Part (ii) plots not only these five points, but a line relating C to every value of Y in the range covered by the graph. You should take the equation $C = 800 + 0.8Y$, and calculate and plot as many points as are needed to satisfy yourself that all points generated by the equation lie on this straight line.

Once we have plotted this line, we have no further need for the co-ordinate grid, and the Figure will be less cluttered if we suppress it, as in part (iii).

For some purposes we do not really care about the specific numerical values of the function; we are content merely to represent it as a positively sloped, straight line. This is done in part (iv). We have now replaced the specific numerical values of the variables C and Y with the letters C_1, C_2, Y_1 and

Y_2, each of which indicates some specific value. For example, part (iv) tells us that if we increase the quantity of disposable income from OY_1 to OY_2, consumption expenditure will increase from OC_1 to OC_2.

In speaking of the quantity of Y as OY_1 or OY_2 we are following good geometric practice and recognizing that a *value* of Y is a *distance* on the Y axis. For brevity, we will usually use a shorter notation and speak of the quantity of Y as Y_1 or Y_2 to stand for a specific value of the variable. It is the value that would occur on the axis at that point. This is less cumbrous, but it is important to remember that *any point on the axis represents the distance from the origin to that point*. For example, Y_1 stands

Selected Values of the Function

Y(£s)	C(£s)	Reference letter
0	800	A
2,500	2,800	B
5,000	4,800	C
7,500	6,800	D
10,000	8,800	E

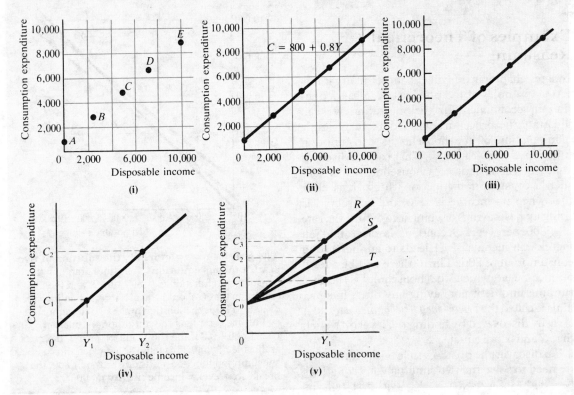

geometrically for the distance from O to Y_1.

The beginning student may feel that we have lost ground by omitting so much in moving from part (ii) to part (iv). It is in the form of (iv), however, that most diagrams appear in economics texts. The great advantage of illustrating functional relations graphically is that we can easily compare different relations without specifying them in precise numerical form.

Suppose, for example, that we wish to compare and contrast three households, R, S and T, whose consumption functions are shown in part (v) of the Figure. All three consumption functions have the same intercept, C_0, indicating that they all have the same level of consumption when their incomes are zero. The function for R is steeper than that for S, which is in turn steeper than that for T. This shows that R's consumption responds more to a change in income than does S's, which in turn responds more than does T's. Thus, for example, when the incomes of all three households rise from zero to Y_1, their respective levels of consumption rise from C_0 to C_1 for T, C_2 for S and C_3 for R. Note that all these comparisons have been made without specifying the precise numerical values of any of the three households' consumption functions.

creased by £800 at each level of income, the break-even level of income rises by £4,000. This result, which is illustrated in Figure 3.2, is perhaps a little less obvious than the previous ones.

Is this an accident depending upon the numbers chosen, or is there some more general relation being illustrated by this particular example? A bit of experimentation with the algebra or geometry of this case should allow you to prove that, with the consumption function $C = a + bY$, any change in the constant a by an amount Δa will change the break-even level of income by $\Delta a/(1-b)$. This is a general result that holds for all straight-line consumption functions.[1]

Notice how far we have come. We began with a very simple economic hypothesis relating two variables, consumption expenditure and disposable income. We took a numerical example and expressed it algebraically and geometrically. We then made certain simple logical deductions about what was implied by the hypothesis. At first these deductions were obvious, but the last one – that if £800 more is spent at each level of income, the break-even level of Y rises by £4,000 – was not quite so obvious. We then wondered if this not-quite-so-obvious result was an accident

depending on the particular numbers we chose. Experimentation showed that there was a single general result for all linear consumption functions: break-even Y rises by $1/(1-b)$ times the rise in the constant a.

All of this illustrates how the tools of logical analysis do allow us to discover what is implied by our assumptions. It also shows how theorizing tends to become cumulative: we obtain one result, possibly quite an obvious one, and this suggests another possible result to us; we check this and find that it is true and this suggests something else. Then we wonder if what we have discovered applies to cases other than the one we are analysing. Before we know it, we are led off on a long chase that ends only when we think we have found all of the interesting implications of the theory. Of course, when we say the chase ends, we mean it ends for the particular investigator, for he is usually wrong when he thinks he has found all the implications of a complex theory. Some new and ingenious investigator is likely to discover new implications or generalizations, and so, for her, the chase begins again.

THE TOOLS OF STATISTICAL ANALYSIS

Look once again at Figure 2.1 on page 25 and notice the second of the two darkly coloured rectangles. It refers to statistical analysis which is used for two related purposes: first, to test the predictions of theories against evidence, and, second, to estimate the magnitude of relations among variables. For example, statistical analysis has not only been used to test the prediction that

---

[1] This last result can be taken on trust for the moment since we will study it in some detail later in the book. You can, however, prove with simple algebra, using the Δ notation for changes explained in more detail in the Appendix to this chapter on page 44. We have two equations; the first expresses the consumption function, and the second expresses the condition for the break-even level, that consumption should equal income: $C = a + bY$; and $C = Y$. Solving these simultaneously for Y yields: $Y = a/(1-b)$. First differencing for Y and a yields $\Delta Y = \Delta a/(1-b)$.

BOX 3.2 THE USE OF MATHEMATICS IN THEORETICAL REASONING

Many people – not just beginning students – are disturbed by the use of mathematics in economic reasoning. 'Surely', they argue, 'human behaviour is too subtle and complex to be reduced to mathematical formulae.' At least four issues can be distinguished here.

First, we might wonder if we can ever understand enough about human behaviour to be able to build useful theories about it. This has to do with our ability to understand, not with the language we should use to express what we do understand.

Second, we might wonder if it is possible to express assumptions about human behaviour in mathematical terms. If such assumptions can be stated at all, they can be stated mathematically, since mathematics is just another language like English or Polish – albeit more precise than any of the languages of common speech. Any hypothesis about how two or more things are related can be expressed mathematically.

Third, we might wonder if the subtlety and complexity of human behaviour make mathematics less appropriate than a verbal language such as English for expressing our assumptions. Verbal expression may sometimes be so vague as to hide our ignorance, but verbal expression can never overcome our ignorance. Mathematical expression is more precise than verbal expression. Not only can a relation between two or more things be stated mathematically, but any qualifications to that relation can also be stated mathematically, if it is clearly understood. It is an advantage, not a disability, of mathematical formulation that it exposes what is being said and what is left unsaid, and that it makes it hard to employ imprecise qualifications.

Fourth, we might worry about the application of long chains of mechanical, mathematical deductions to our theories. Once the assumptions of a theory have been fully stated, the theorist must discover their implications. This stage simply requires logical deduction. It is not a criticism to say that a technique is mechanical if by mechanical we mean that it allows us to discover efficiently and accurately what is, and is not, implied by our assumptions. It is never an advantage to use a technique that leaves us in doubt on this. If we accept the view that, somehow, verbal analysis (or 'judgement') can solve problems, even though we are unable to state clearly how we have reached the solutions, then we are involved not in a science but in a medieval mystery, in which the main problem is to be able to distinguish between the true and the false prophet.

Mathematics is neither the maker nor the destroyer of good economic theory. It is merely a precise and compact means of expression and an efficient tool for deriving implications from assumptions. Irrelevant or factually incorrect assumptions will yield irrelevant or factually incorrect implications, whatever logical tools are used to derive them.

people spend more when their after-tax incomes rise, but to measure by how much expenditure rises for each rise in income.

An understanding of the intricacies of statistical analysis when used for either of these purposes can be gained only from a detailed study of statistical theory. In this chapter we take a brief look at how statistical analysis is used in economics. Because this is a book about economic theory, we concentrate on the use of statistics in testing theories. Later, however, we shall often refer to statistical estimates of the magnitude of specific relations.

Kinds of Sciences

In order to determine whether or not predictions are correct within some acceptable margin of error, they are tested against evidence. This is not a task that is easily accomplished (or briefly described), particularly in non-laboratory sciences.

Laboratory sciences: In some sciences, it is possible to obtain all necessary observations from controlled experiments made under laboratory conditions. In such experiments, all the factors that are thought to affect the outcome of the process being studied can be controlled. They are varied one by one, while all other factors are held constant so that the influence of each factor can be studied one at a time.

Non-laboratory sciences: In other sciences, such as astronomy and economics, controlled laboratory experiments are, as a general rule, impossible. (In recent years, however, some economists have conducted controlled experiments to observe people's behaviour with respect to many of the choices that are studied in economic theory.)

Although economics is mainly a non-laboratory science, a mass of data is being generated continually by the economy. Every day, for example, consumers are comparing prices and deciding what to buy; firms are comparing prices and deciding what to produce and offer for sale; and governments are intervening with taxes, subsidies and direct controls. All of these acts can be observed and recorded to provide empirical observations against which theories can be tested. Given the complexity of data generated under non-experimental conditions, casual observation is insufficient for testing economic hypotheses.[1] Modern statistical analysis was developed to test hypotheses rigorously in situations in which many things were varying at once.

An Example of Statistical Testing

To illustrate how data may be used to test theories even while other things are not held constant, we take the very simple, and intuitively plausible, hypothesis that the personal income taxes paid by UK households increase as their incomes increase.

A Sample

To begin with, observations must be made of household income and tax payments. It is not practical to do so for all households, so a small number (called a sample) is studied on the assumption that those included in the sample will be typical of the entire group.

---

[1] Often in ordinary conversation a person advances a possible relation (e.g. between education and some facet of character), while someone else will 'refute' this theory by citing a single counter-example (e.g. 'My friend went to that school and did not turn out like that'). It is a commonplace in everyday conversation to dismiss a hypothesis with some such remark as 'Oh, that's just a generalization.' All interesting hypotheses are generalizations and it will always be possible to notice some real or apparent exceptions. What we need to know is whether or not the mass of evidence supports the hypothesis as a statement of a general tendency for two or more things to be related to each other. This issue can never be settled one way or the other by the casual quoting of a few bits of evidence that just happened to be readily available.

It is important that the sample is what is called a random sample. A *random sample* is chosen according to a rigidly defined set of conditions guaranteeing, among other things, that every member of the group from which we are selecting the sample has an equal chance of being selected. Choosing the sample in a random fashion has two important consequences.

First, it reduces the chance that the sample will be unrepresentative of the entire group from which it is selected. Second, and more important, it allows us to calculate just how likely it is that the sample will be unrepresentative by any specified amount. For example, if the average amount of income tax paid by the households in a sample is £1,000, then it is most likely that the average tax paid by all households in the country is close to £1,000. But that is not necessarily so. The sample might be so unrepresentative that the actual figure for average tax paid by all households is £2,000. We can never be certain that we will avoid such misleading results. However, if the sample is random, we are able to calculate the probability that the actual data for the whole population differ from the data in our sample by any stated amount.

The reason for the predictability of random samples is that such samples are chosen by chance, and chance events are predictable.

That chance events are predictable may sound surprising, but consider these questions. If you pick a card from a deck of ordinary playing cards, how likely is it that you will pick a heart? An ace? An ace of hearts? You play a game in which you pick a card and win if it is a heart and lose if it is anything else; a friend offers you £3 if you win against £1 if you lose. Who will make money if the game is played a large number of times? The same game is played again, but now you get £5 if you win and pay £1 if you lose. Who will make money over a large number of draws? That these questions can be answered tells us that chance events are in some sense predictable.

Analysis of the Data

To test the hypothesis about taxes, a random sample of 227 households was chosen and its income and the taxes it paid were recorded for each family. There are several ways in which the

BOX 3.3 GRAPHING ECONOMIC DATA

Economists study economic data for many reasons, including testing their theories and applying these theories to specific situations. Data may be collected, and presented, in many ways. This box mentions a few of the key distinctions.

Types of Data
Economic data come in two basic forms. The first is called *cross-sectional data,* which means a number of different observations all taken at the same point in time. For example, we might study how much meat was bought by dozens of different households during some given month. If we were interested in how a household's income affected its meat purchases, we would also obtain data for each household's income. The result would be cross-sectional data showing each household's income, and its purchases of meat, where all observations referred to the same point in time.

The second type of data is called *time-series data.* It refers to observations taken on the same variable, or variables, at successive points in time. For example, we might obtain data for the meat purchases of one specific household each month over ten years. The result would be a time series of 120 observations showing the variations in one household's meat purchases over time.

Graphing Data
Two main forms in which data may be graphed are the time series graph and the scatter diagram. A *time-series graph* plots data for a single series at successive points of time. If we measure months on the horizontal axis and meat on the vertical axis, we can draw a time-series chart showing how the meat purchases of a single household varied over time. Each point on a time-series chart gives the value of the variable at the time indicated. Examples of time-series charts are shown on pages 447 and 454, and it would be a good idea to glance at these now.

A second main way in which data can be presented is in a *scatter diagram.* This type of diagram is designed to show the relation between two different variables, such as meat purchases and household income. To plot a scatter diagram, values of one variable are measured on the horizontal axis and values of the second variable are measured on the vertical axis. Any point on the diagram relates a specific value of one variable to a specific value of the other. For example, if a household that had an income of £10,000 bought 10 lbs of meat in the period under consideration, this would be shown by a point whose co-ordinates were 10 lbs on the meat axis and £10,000 on the income axis. An example of a scatter diagram is given in the text where taxes paid by households are related to household income.

Note that a scatter diagram can be drawn whenever we have a series of observations on any two variables. These observations themselves may be cross-sectional or time-series data. All that matters is that they give a set of observations on the two variables in which we are interested.

For example, if we wished to study how purchases of meat varied with household income, we could obtain cross-sectional data showing the incomes and the meat purchases of a number of households at one point in time. These data could then be plotted on a scatter diagram where each point referred to the income and meat purchases of one household.

We could also obtain time-series data for one household, observing its income and its meat purchases during several time periods, say each month for several years. These data could also be plotted on a scatter diagram in which each point refers to the household's income and its meat purchases during one particular month.

data may be used to evaluate the hypothesis. Box 3.3 discussed graphical presentations in more general terms; the text that follows uses the technique relevant to the problem at hand.

Scatter diagram: Figure 3.3 is a *scatter diagram* that relates family income to income-tax payments. The pattern of the dots suggests that there is a strong tendency for tax payments to be higher when family income is higher. It thus supports the hypothesis.

There is some scattering of the dots because the relationship is not 'perfect'; in other words, there is some variation in tax payments that cannot be associated with variations in family income. These variations in tax payments occur mainly for two reasons. First, factors other than income influence tax payments, and some of these other factors will undoubtedly have varied among the households in the sample. Second, there will inevitably be some errors in measurement. For example, a family might have incorrectly reported its tax payments to the person who collected the data.

FIGURE 3.3 A Scatter Diagram Relating Taxes Paid to Household Income

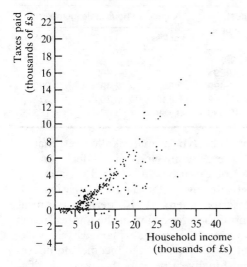

The scatter pattern shows a clear tendency for taxes paid to rise with household income.
Household income is measured along the horizontal axis, and income taxes paid along the vertical axis. Each dot represents a single household in the sample and is located on the graph according to the family's income and taxes paid. The dots fall mainly within a narrow, rising band, suggesting the existence of a systematic relationship between income and taxes paid. But they do not fall along a single line, which suggests that things other than household income affect taxes paid. (Negative amounts of tax liability arise because of such things as capital losses that may be carried forward.)

Cross-classification table: A cross-classification table provides another way to examine the hypothesis that tax payments vary directly with income. Table 3.1 cross-classifies households by their income and their average tax payments. In the Table the data on 227 households are grouped into the income classes shown in the first column. The average tax payment for households in each income group is calculated and listed in the second column. This second column shows a steady rise in tax payments. This cross-classification reduces 227 individual observations to 6. More (or less) detail could have been preserved by varying the size of the income classes used in the first column. At the cost of losing considerable detail, the table makes clear the general tendency for tax payments to rise as income rises.

Regression analysis: While both the scatter diagram and the cross-classification table reflect the general relationship between income-tax payments and family income, neither characterizes what the precise relationship is. Regression analysis does this by calculating a regression equation that is the best estimate of the average relationship between the variables. The equation can be used in the present example to describe the tendency for higher family income to be associated with higher tax payments.

How closely are tax payments related to household income? This question is answered by a measure called the *coefficient of determination* (r^2), which tells us the percentage of the variance in the dependent variable (tax payments in this case) that can be accounted for by variations in the independent variable (household income in this case). For our sample, $r^2 = 0.73$. This number tells us that 73 per cent of the variance in tax payments can be 'explained' by associating it with variations in family incomes.

A significance test can be applied to determine the odds that the relation discovered in the sample does not exist for the whole population but has arisen by chance because the households selected happen not to be representative of the entire set of households in the country. It turns out that in this example there is less than one chance in a million that the rising pattern of dots shown in Figure 3.3 would have been observed if there were no positive association between income and tax payments for all households. We therefore conclude, with less than one chance in a million of being wrong, that the hypothesis that tax payments and family income are positively related is correct. Statistically the relationship is said to be significant.

TABLE 3.1 Tax Payments Cross-classified by Household Income

Annual household income (£s)	Average tax payment (£s)	Number of households
Less than 5,000	148	38
5,000–9,999	907	76
10,000–14,999	2,381	42
15,000–19,999	3,904	28
20,000–24,999	6,642	28
25,000–49,999	14,869	15

Extending the Analysis to Three Variables

The scatter diagram and the regression equation show that all the variation in income-tax payments cannot be accounted for by observed variations in household income. If it could, all the dots would lie on a line. Since they do not, some other factors must influence tax payments.

Why might one household with an income of £10,000 pay 20 per cent more in income taxes than another household with the same income? One reason is that tax laws provide exemptions based on the number of dependants in each household. (There will be other reasons too, such as differences in deductions for allowable expenses or charitable donations.) Fortunately, the survey also collected data on household size. This gives us three observations for each of the 227 households: annual income, income-tax payments and number of persons in the household.

How should these data be handled? The scatter diagram technique is not available because the relation between three sets of data cannot conveniently be shown on a two-dimensional graph. The data may, however, be classified into groups once again. This time we are testing two variables that are thought to influence tax payments, and the data have to be cross-classified in a more complicated manner, as shown in Table 3.2. Each observation in the body of the Table shows the average tax payments made by households with incomes indicated by its row and the number of persons indicated by its column.

The Table can be used to hold one variable roughly constant while allowing another to vary. Reading along each row, we see that income is held constant within a specified range and household size is varied; reading down each column, we see that size of household is held constant within a specified range and income is varied. The declining numbers across each row show that, for each income group, tax payments tend to decline as household size increases. Each column in the Table shows the effect of income on tax payments for a given family size. The increase in taxes paid as we move down each column shows that tax payments increase with household income.

A technique called *multiple regression analysis* can be used to estimate the numerical relation among household income, family size and tax

TABLE 3.2 Tax Payments Cross-classified by Household Income and Household Size

Annual family income (£s)	Number of household members:		
	3 or less	4 or 5	6 or more
0–4,999	175	142	26
5,000–9,999	1,028	995	507
10,000–14,999	2,950	2,491	935
15,000–19,999	5,349	3,802	2,372
20,000–49,999	9,459	8,624	4,193

payments. This type of analysis allows estimation of both the separate and joint effects on tax payments of variations in size and variations in income by fitting to the data an equation that 'best' describes them. It also permits the measurement of the proportion of the total variation in tax payments that can be explained by associating it with variations both in income and household size. Finally, it permits the use of significance tests to determine how likely it is that the relations found in the sample are the result of chance and thus do not reflect a similar relationship for all households. Chance plays a role because by bad luck an unrepresentative sample of households might have been chosen.

Testing and Measurement

Statistical techniques help us to judge the probability that any particular theory is false. This is an extremely valuable thing to be able to do. What statistical techniques cannot do is prove with certainty that an hypothesis is either true or false.

Can we Prove that a Hypothesis is True?

Most hypotheses in economics are universal. They state that, whenever certain conditions are fulfilled, cause *X* always produces effect *Y*.

Universal hypotheses cannot be proved to be correct because we can never rule out the possibility that we shall in the future make observations that conflict with the theory.

Indeed science progresses by upsetting currently accepted universal hypotheses, and replacing them with new hypotheses that include what was correct in the earlier hypotheses, while explaining new evidence.

Can we Prove that a Hypothesis is False?

Hypotheses can be divided into those that are deterministic and those that are statistical. A *deterministic hypothesis* admits no exceptions. For example, an increase in a household's income will always lead to increased spending. A *statistical hypothesis* describes a general tendency and so admits exception. For example, an increase in a household's income will 'normally' (or 'typically' or 'usually') be observed to lead to an increase in expenditure.

We cannot hope categorically to refute statistical hypotheses. Consider, for example, the hypothesis 'Most crows are black.' We observe fifty crows; forty-nine are grey and only one is black. Have we disproved the hypothesis? The answer is no, for it is possible that this was just bad luck and if we could observe all the crows in the world it would indeed prove to be the case that most are black.

What, then, is required if we are to be able to refute any hypothesis? First, the hypothesis must be deterministic, admitting of no exceptions; it must say, for example, 'All crows are black'. Second, we must be certain that any apparently refuting observations are not mistaken. The observation of forty-nine black crows and one grey refutes the hypothesis that all crows are black only if we are sure that we genuinely saw a grey crow. But are we sure that the odd bird really was a crow? Are we sure that what looked like a grey crow was not a dusty black crow?[1] Errors in observation may always be present. Thus:

a hypothesis cannot be refuted on the basis of a single conflicting observation, and indeed it can never be categorically refuted, no matter how many conflicting observations we make.

If we observe forty-nine grey crows and only one black one, our faith in the hypothesis that all

crows are black may well be shaken and as a practical measure we may choose to abandon the hypothesis (see below). We can never be certain, however, that all forty-nine cases were not due to errors of observation and had we persisted we might have ended up observing 999,951 black crows and 49 grey ones. (This would make the hypothesis look pretty good, since a measurement error on 0.005 per cent of our cases might not seem at all improbable.)

Rules for Decision-taking

Although we can neither prove nor refute a hypothesis conclusively, no matter how many observations we make,[1] we do have to make decisions. We act as if some hypotheses were refuted by rejecting them and we act as if some hypotheses were proved by accepting them. Such decisions are always subject to error and hence are tentative ones. Fortunately statistical analysis allows us to calculate and control the chance of making errors even if we cannot eliminate them.

Consider an example. When studying taxes our hypothesis might have been that the tax paid by households *falls* as their income rises. We would then ask what the chances were of making the observations shown in Figure 3.3 if the hypothesis were correct. There is always some chance that our sample was untypical of all households in the country or that the relationship appears as it is because of measurement errors. Assume we calculate (using the tools taught in courses on statistics) that there is less than one chance in 100 of making the observations in Figure 3.3 *if* the hypothesized relation that tax payments fall as income rises actually holds for all households. We would then abandon the hypothesis and for practical purposes regard it as refuted.

It is important, however, to understand, first, that we can never be certain that we are right in

---

[1] Even if we satisfy ourselves that we saw a grey crow, future generations may not accept our evidence unless they go on observing the occasional grey crow. After all we no longer accept the mass of well-documented evidence accumulated several centuries ago on the existence and power of witches, even though it fully satisfied most contemporary observers. Clearly the existence of observational errors on a vast scale has been shown to be possible even though it may not be frequent.

[1] This is because I take all hypotheses about observable events to be statistical ones due to unavoidable errors of observation. We do, of course, make arbitrary decisions to reject statistical hypotheses but so also do we make arbitrary decisions to accept them. These rules of thumb for taking decisions have nothing to do with the methodological questions of whether any hypothesis can be conclusively refuted and whether any hypothesis can be conclusively proved. My answer to both questions is no. Those who are not convinced by my arguments may proceed with the text as long as they are prepared to accept that most hypotheses in economics are statistical hypotheses.

rejecting a statistical hypothesis and, second, that there is nothing magical about our arbitrary cut-off points. The cut-off point (less than one chance in 100 of being wrong in this case) is used because some decision has to be made. Notice also that decisions can always be reversed should new evidence come to light.

Judging Among Hypotheses

Older methodologies tended to emphasize the testing of theories one at a time. As it has become clearer that theories in economics could be neither confirmed nor refuted with finality, newer methodologies have tended to emphasize the use of statistical analysis to choose among two or more competing theories.

Although we can never be absolutely sure of two theories that one is right and the other is wrong, we can hope to show that the data favour one over the other.

To make such tests we must first find out where theories A and B make predictions that conflict with each other. Theory A might, for example, predict a close relation between variables X and Y because, according to it, X causes Y; theory B might predict no strong relation between the two variables because, according to it, X has no effect on Y one way or the other. The empirical relation between X and Y can then be studied and conclusions reached about the probability that what we saw could have happened if theory A were correct or if theory B were correct.

Quantitative Measurement of Economic Relations

Economic theories are seldom of much use until we are able to give quantitative magnitudes to our relations. For estimating such magnitudes, our common sense and intuitions do not get us very far. Common sense might well have suggested that the taxes paid by households would rise rather than fall as income rose, but only careful observation is going to show by how much it typically rises. One of the major uses of statistical analysis is to quantify the general relations suggested by theory. In practice, we can use actual observations both to test the hypothesis that two things are related and to estimate the numerical values of the relations that do exist.

Although theories can never be accepted

or rejected with finality, statistical analysis can be used, first, to establish the probability that observations are consistent with some specific theory; second, to establish the balance of probabilities between two competing theories; and, third, to measure the quantitative relations among those variables that some theory suggests are related.

Words of Warning

Chapters 2 and 3 have made a case that economics can be a scientific enquiry. Some words of caution are now in order.

The statistical techniques mentioned in this chapter are often difficult to apply, and the pitfalls ready to trap the unwary user of inappropriate statistical procedures are too numerous to mention. The techniques were first developed to analyse data from controlled experiments in the natural sciences. They were used with some success in economics and they have given rise to a whole new subject called econometrics that has been developed to handle the special problems that arise when the available data does not come from controlled experiments.

To test our theories against facts, we need reliable facts. Because this is not a textbook in economic statistics, we do not stress the problems involved in collecting reliable observations. Such problems can, however, be formidable, and there is always the danger of rejecting a theory on the basis of mistaken observations. Unreliable observations are all too frequently encountered. Note, however, that if we think all our observations are totally unreliable, we have nothing to explain and, hence, no need for any economic theory. If, on the other hand, we believe that we do have observations reliable enough to require explanation, then we must also believe that we have observations reliable enough to provide tests for the predictive powers of our theories.

Because there are major differences among the sciences, methods that work well in one may not be suitable in another. In particular, what works in physics, the queen of sciences, may not work well in a social science such as economics. What unites all sciences is the explanation and prediction of observed phenomena. The successes and failures of all sciences are judged by their abilities to further these objectives.

SUMMARY

1. Economic theory is based on relations among various magnitudes. Because all such relations can be expressed mathematically, mathematics is important in economics. Once hypotheses have been written down as algebraic expressions, mathematical manipulation can be used to discover their implications.
2. A functional relation can be expressed in words, in a graph or in a mathematical equation. Deducing the consequences of assumptions is a logical process that can often be done verbally, geometrically or mathematically.
3. In non-laboratory sciences where controlled experiments are impossible, statistical techniques are used to examine the influence of each independent variable *ceteris paribus*.
4. Empirical observations can neither prove nor refute hypotheses with absolute finality. Hypotheses can never be proven to be true because the possibility of making conflicting observations in the future can never be entirely ruled out. Hypotheses can never be shown to be certainly false since the possibility of errors of observation – sometimes on a massive scale – cannot be totally ruled out.
5. Nonetheless, practical decisions to accept some hypotheses and to reject others are made all the time. Statistical analysis allows the possibility of errors in making such decisions to be controlled even though it cannot be eliminated.

TOPICS FOR REVIEW

- Correspondences and functions
- Ways of expressing a relation between two variables
- Laboratory and non-laboratory sciences
- A sample
- Scatter diagrams
- Cross-classification tables
- Proof and refutation of hypotheses
- Statistical rules for rejecting or accepting hypotheses

APPENDIX to Chapter 3

Some Common Techniques

Certain graphical and mathematical concepts are frequently encountered in economic analysis. In this appendix we deal briefly with the ones most frequently used in this book.

Every student needs to master the elementary techniques described in this appendix before completing his or her study of introductory economics. Those who find they can manage it at this stage should study the appendix carefully now. Those who had difficulty with simple mathematics at school should skim through the appendix now, making a list of the concepts discussed. When these concepts are encountered later in the text they should be reviewed again carefully here.

(1) The Function as a Rule

Using functional notation, we write $Y = f(X)$, and we read it, 'Y is a function of X'. The letter 'f' stands for a rule which we use to go from a value of X to a value of Y. The rule tells us how to operate on X to get Y. Consider, for example, the specific function

$$Y = 5X - 3 .$$

The rule here is 'take X, multiply it by 5 and subtract 3'; this then yields the value of Y. In another case we may have

$$Y = X^2/2 + 6 .$$

This rule says 'take X, square it, divide the result by 2, then add 6'; again, the result is the value of Y. If, for example, X has a value of 2, then the first rule yields $Y = 7$, while the second rule yields $Y = 8$.

The equations displayed above describe two different rules. We may confuse these if we denote both by the same letter. To keep them separate we can write

$$Y = f(X)$$

for the first and

$$Y = g(X)$$

for the second.

Since the choice of symbols to designate different rules *is* arbitrary, we can use any symbols that are convenient. In the above examples we had $Y = 5X - 3$ and $Y = X^2/2 + 6$ and we chose to indicate these rules by 'f' and 'g'. If we wanted to indicate that these were rules for yielding Y we could use that letter, and then use subscripts to indicate that there were two different rules. Thus we would write

$$Y = Y_1(X)$$

and

$$Y = Y_2(X) ,$$

where Y_1 and Y_2 stand for two different rules for deriving Y from any given value of X.

Suppose now that we have two different variables Y and Z both related to X. A specific example would be

$$Y = 3 + 10X$$

and

$$Z = 28 - 2X .$$

Again we have two different rules for operating on X; the first rule yields Y and the second rule yields Z. We could denote these rules $f(X)$ and g(X) but, since the choice of a letter to denote each rule is arbitrary, we could also write

and
$$Y = Y(X)$$
$$Z = Z(X) .$$

In this case the choice of letters is a memory device which reminds us that the first rule, $3 + 10X$, yields Y, while the second rule, $28 - 2X$, yields Z.

(2) Some Conventions in Functional Notation

Assume we are talking about some sequence of numbers, say, 1, 2, 3, 4, 5, ... If we wished to talk about one particular term in this series without indicating which one, we could talk about the ith term, which might be the 5th or the 50th. If we now want to indicate terms adjacent to the ith term, whatever it might be, we talk about the $(i-1)$th and the $(i+1)$th terms.

By the same token we can talk about a series of time periods, say, the years 1900, 1901 and 1902. If we wish to refer to three adjacent years in any series without indicating which three years, we can talk about the years $(t-1)$, t and $(t+1)$.

Consider a functional relation, between the quantity produced by a factory and the number of workers employed. In general, we can write $Q = Q(W)$, where Q is the amount of production and W is the number of workers. If we wished to refer to the quantity of output where ten workers were employed, we could write $Q_{10} = Q(W_{10})$, whereas, if we wished to refer to output when some particular, but unspecified, number were employed, we would write $Q_i = Q(W_i)$. Finally, if we wished to refer to output when the number of workers was increased by one above the previous level, we could write $Q_{i+1} = Q(W_{i+1})$. This use of subscripts to refer to particular values of the variables is a useful notion, and one that we shall use at various points in this book.

We may use time subscripts to date variables. If, for example, the value of X depends on the value of Y three months ago, we write this as $X_t = f(Y_{t-3})$. Another convention is the use of ... to save space in functions of many variables. For example, $f(X_1, ..., X_n)$ indicates a function containing n (some unspecified number of) variables.

(3) Graphing Functions

A co-ordinate graph divides space into four quadrants, as shown in Figure 3A.1. The upper right-hand quadrant, which is the one in which both X and Y are positive, is usually called the *positive quadrant*. Very often in economics we are concerned only with the positive values of our variables, and in such cases we confine our graph to the positive quadrant. Whenever we want one or both of our variables to be allowed to take on negative values we must include some or all of the other quadrants. For example, one of the functions in Figure 3A.2(ii) is extended into the quadrant in which X is positive and Y is negative, while the remaining two functions are not extended beyond the positive quadrant.

(4) Straight Lines and Slopes

Consider the following functional relations:

$$Y = 0.5X ,$$
$$Y = X ,$$
$$Y = 2X .$$

These are graphed in Figure 3A.2(i). You will see that they all pass through the origin. This is also obvious from the fact that if we let $X = 0$ in each of the above relations, Y also becomes 0. In the first equation, Y goes up half a unit every time X goes up by one unit; in the second equation, Y goes up one unit every time X goes up one unit; and in the third equation, Y goes up two units every time X goes up one unit.

FIGURE 3A.1 A Co-ordinate Graph Divides Space into Quadrants

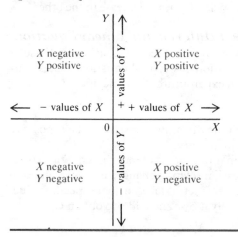

FIGURE 3A.2 Some Linear Functions

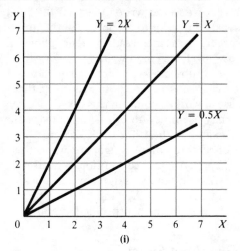

(i)

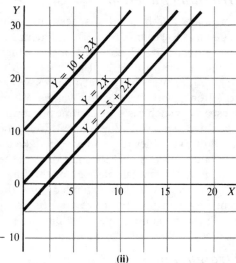

(ii)

We now introduce the symbol Δ to indicate a change in a variable. Thus ΔX means the value of the change in X and ΔY means the value of the change in Y. In the first equation if $X = 10$ then Y is 5 and if X goes up to 16, Y goes up to 8. Thus, in this exercise, $\Delta X = 6$ and $\Delta Y = 3$.

Next consider the ratio $\Delta Y/\Delta X$. In the above example it is equal to 0.5. In general, it will be noted that, for any change we make in X in the first equation, $\Delta Y/\Delta X$ is always 0.5. In the second $\Delta Y/\Delta X$ is unity and in the third the ratio is always 2. In general, if we write $Y = bX$, then, as is proved below, the ratio $\Delta Y/\Delta X$ is always equal to b.

We now define the slope, or gradient, of a straight line to be the ratio of the distance moved up the Y axis to the distance moved along the X axis. Start at the point (X_1, Y_1) and move to the point (X_2, Y_2). The change in X is $X_2 - X_1$ or ΔX. The change in Y is $Y_2 - Y_1$ or ΔY. The ratio $\Delta Y/\Delta X$ is the slope of the straight line. It tells us the ratio of a change in Y to a change in X.

In trigonometry the tangent of an angle is defined as $\Delta Y/\Delta X$; thus the slope of the line is equal to the tangent of the angle between the line and any line parallel to the X axis. Given the scale on any diagram, the larger the ratio $\Delta Y/\Delta X$, the steeper the graph of the relation. Figure 3A.2(i) shows three lines corresponding to $\Delta Y/\Delta X = 0.5$, 1 and 2. Clearly, the steeper the line the larger the change in Y for any given change in X.

Now consider the following equations,

$$Y = 2X$$
$$Y = 10 + 2X$$
$$Y = -5 + 2X \;,$$

which are graphed in Figure 3A.2(ii). All three lines are parallel. In other words, they have the same slope. In all three $\Delta Y/\Delta X$ is equal to 2. Clearly, the addition of a (positive or negative) constant does not affect the slope of the line. This slope is influenced only by the number attached to X. When that number is positive, X and Y are positively related: an increase in one variable is associated with an increase in the other, and a decrease in one with a decrease in the other. When the number is negative, the two variables are negatively related: an increase in either variable is associated with a decrease in the other.

(5) First Differencing Linear Equations

In national-income theory we make much use of linear equations. A typical equation relates consumption expenditure, C, to income Y:

$$C = a + cY \;,$$

where a is any positive constant and c is positive but less than unity.

We can now first difference this equation to get an expression relating changes in C to changes in Y. To do this let Y take on some specific value, Y_1, multiply it by c and add a to obtain C_1:

$$C_1 = a + cY_1 \;.$$

Now do the same thing for a second value of Y called Y_2:

$$C_2 = a + cY_2 .$$

Next, subtract the second equation from the first to obtain

$$C_1 - C_2 = a - a + cY_1 - cY_2$$
$$= c(Y_1 - Y_2) .$$

Now use the delta notation for changes to write

$$\Delta C = c\Delta Y .$$

The constant a disappears and we see that the change in C is c times the change in Y, and also that the ratio of the changes is c, i.e.

$$\Delta C / \Delta Y = c .$$

Thus whenever we see a linear relation of the form $Y = a + bX$, we know immediately that

$$\Delta Y / \Delta X = b .$$

(6) Non-linear Functions

All of the examples used so far in this appendix and most of the examples in the text of Chapter 3 concern *linear relations* between two variables. A linear relation is described graphically by a straight line, and algebraically by the equation $Y = a + bX$. It is characteristic of a linear relation that the effect on Y of a given change in X is the same everywhere on the relation.

Many of the relations encountered in economics are *non-linear*. In these cases the relation will be expressed graphically by a curved line and algebraically by some expression more complex than the one for a straight line. Two common examples are:

$$Y = a + bX + cX^2$$

and

$$Y = a/X^b$$

The first example is a *parabola*. It takes up various positions and shapes depending on the signs and magnitudes of a, b and c. Two examples of parabolas are given in Figures 3A.3 and 3A.4. The second example becomes a rectangular hyperbola if we let $b = 1$, and then the position is determined by the value of a. Three examples where $a = 0.5, 2.5$ and 5 are shown in Figure 3A.5.

There are, of course, many other examples of nonlinear relations between variables. In general,

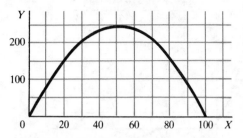

FIGURE 3A.3 A Parabola with a Maximum Value of Y ($Y = 10X - 0.1X^2$)

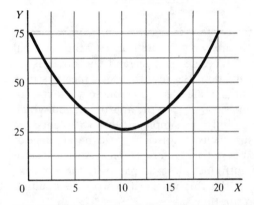

FIGURE 3A.4 A Parabola with Minimum Value of Y ($Y = 75 - 10X + 0.5X^2$)

whatever the relation between X and Y, as long as it can be expressed on a graph it can also be expressed by means of an algebraic equation.

(7) Marginal Values and Incremental Ratios

Economic theory makes much use of what are called 'marginal' concepts. Marginal cost, marginal revenue, marginal rate of substitution and marginal propensity to consume are a few examples. Marginal means on the margin or border and the concept refers to what would happen if there were a small change from the present position.

Marginals refer to functional relations: the independent variable x is determining the dependent variable y and we wish to know what would be the change in Y if X changed by a small amount from its present value. The answer is referred to as the marginal value of Y and is given various names depending on what economic variables X and Y stand for.

FIGURE 3A.5 Three Rectangular Hyperbolae

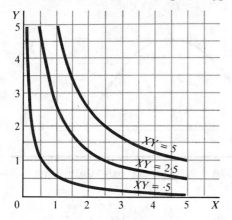

There are two ways of measuring the marginal value of Y. One is exact and the other is an approximation. Because the exact measure uses differential calculus, introductory texts in economics usually use the approximation which depends only on simple algebra. Students are often justifiably confused because the language of economic theory refers to the exact measure while introductory examples use the approximation. For this reason it is worth explaining each at this time.

Consider the example shown in Figure 3A.6 in which a firm's output, Q, is measured on the X axis and the total revenue earned by selling this output, R, is measured on the Y axis. Thus we have the function $R = R(Q)$. (We shall see later that the graph corresponds to the shape of a monopolist's revenue function, but right now we may take its shape as given.)

The marginal concept that corresponds to this function is *marginal revenue*. It refers to the change in the firm's revenue when sales are altered slightly from their present level. But what do we mean by 'altered slightly'? The answer depends on which marginal concept we use.

The approximation to marginal revenue is called the **incremental ratio**. Let sales in Figure 3A.6(i) be 6, with a corresponding revenue of £70. Now increase sales to 8, so that revenue rises to £100. The increase in sales is 2 and the increase in revenue is £30. Using the Δ notation for changes, we can write this as

$$\Delta R/\Delta Q = £30/2 = £15 \ .$$

Thus incremental revenue is £15 per unit when sales change from 6 to 8. This means that sales are increasing at an average rate of £15 *per unit of commodity sold* over the range from 6 to 8 units. We may call this the marginal revenue at 6 units of output but, as we shall see, it is only an approximation to the true marginal revenue at that output.

Graphically, incremental revenue is the slope of the line joining the two points in question. In this case they are the two points on the revenue function corresponding to outputs of 6 and 8. This is shown in Figure 3A.6(ii), which is an enlargement of the relevant section of the function graphed in 3A.6(i). Look at the small triangle

FIGURE 3A.6(i) The Revenue Function of a Firm

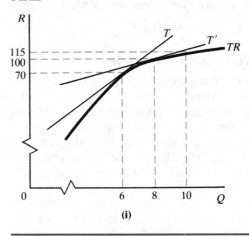

FIGURE 3A.6(ii) An Enlargement of a Section of the Firm's Revenue Function

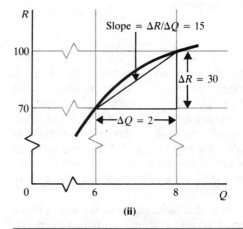

created by these points. Its base is 2 units long and its vertical side is 30 units in height. The slope of the hypotenuse of the triangle is $30/2 = 15$, which is the incremental revenue. Visually it is clear that this slope tells us the average gradient or steepness of the revenue function over the range from $Q = 6$ to $Q = 8$. It thus tells us how fast revenue is changing as output changes over that range of Q.

Incremental revenue will be different at different points on the function. For example, when output goes from 8 to 10, revenue goes from 100 to 115 and this gives us an incremental revenue of

$$\Delta R/\Delta Q = \text{\textsterling}15/2 = \text{\textsterling}7.50 \ .$$

This calculation confirms what visual inspection of the Figure suggests: the larger is output (at least over the ranges graphed in the Figure), the less is the response of revenue to further increases in output.

The incremental ratio is an approximation to the true marginal concept which is based on the derivative of differential calculus. The derivative is symbolized in general by dY/dX, and in the case of the function $R = R(Q)$, by dR/dQ. It measures the tendency for R to change as Q changes *at a precise point on the curve*. (Whereas the incremental ratio measures the average tendency *over a range of the curve*.) The value of the derivative is given by the slope of the tangent at the point on the function in which we are interested. Thus 'true' marginal revenue at 6 units of output is given by the slope of the tangent, T, to the curve at that point.[1] This slope measures the tendency for R to change *per unit change in Q* at the precise value at which it is evaluated (i.e. the point on the function at which the tangent is drawn).[2]

We saw in the example of Figure 3A.6 that, on the particular function being considered, the incremental ratio declines as we measure it at larger and larger values of Q. It should be visually obvious that this is also true for marginal revenue: the slope of the tangent to the function is smaller the larger is the value of Q at which the tangent is taken. Two examples are shown in Figure 3A.6(i); one, T, for $Q = 6$ and the other, T', for $Q = 8$.

Now try measuring the incremental ratio starting at 6 units of output but for smaller and smaller changes in output. Instead of going from 6 to 8, go, for example, from 6 to 7. This brings the two points in question closer together and, in the present case, it steepens the slope of the line joining them. It is visually clear in the present example that as ΔQ is made smaller and smaller, the slope of the line corresponding to the incremental ratio starting from $Q = 6$ gets closer and closer to the slope of the tangent corresponding to the true marginal value evaluated at $Q = 6$.

Let us now state our conclusions in general for the function $Y = Y(X)$.

(1) The marginal value of Y at some initial value of X is the rate of change of Y per unit change in X as X changes from its initial value.

(2) The marginal value is given by the slope of the tangent to the curve graphing the function at the point corresponding to the initial value of X.

(3) The incremental ratio $\Delta Y/\Delta X$ measures the average change in Y per unit change in X over a range of the function starting from the initial value of X.

(4) As the range of measurement of the incremental ratio is reduced (i.e. as ΔX gets smaller and smaller), the value of the incremental ratio eventually approaches the true marginal value of Y. Thus the incremental ratio may be regarded as an approximation to the true marginal value, the degree of approximation improving as ΔX gets very small.[1]

(8) Marginal and Total Values

We saw in a previous section that marginal revenue refers to the change in the total revenue

---

[1] Because of the thickness of the lines, the tangents in the Figures seem to coincide with the curve over a range. It is of course impossible for a curve and a straight line to do this. The true tangents T and T' touch the curve TR at $Q = 6$ and $Q = 8$ respectively, and *lie* a *above the curve for all other values of Q*.
[2] The text discussion refers to functions of a single variable. Where Y is a function of more than one variable, $X_1, \ldots, X_n$, then the marginal concept refers to a *partial* derivative: $\partial Y/\partial X_1$, etc. There is then a marginal value of Y with respect to variations in *each* of the independent variables, $X_1, \ldots, X_n$.

---

[1] This footnote need only concern those who already know some calculus. We must be careful how we state conclusion (4) since, on a wavy function, the degree of approximation may alternately improve and worsen as ΔX gets smaller, but, providing the conditions for a derivative to exist are met, there *must* be a small neighbourhood around the point in question within which the degree of approximation improves as ΔX gets smaller, with the 'error' going to zero as ΔX goes to zero.

as output changes. Figure 3A.7(i) draws a new total revenue curve. Figure 3A.7(ii) gives the corresponding marginal revenue curve. (The equation of the plotted curve is $R = 100q - 0.50q^2$.)

From totals to marginals: Let us now assume that we have only the curve in part (i) of Figure 3A.7, and that we wish to obtain the curve in part (ii). (Note that the two parts are not plotted on the same scales.)

Graphically, the marginal curve is derived by measuring the slope of the tangent to the TR curve at each level of output and plotting the value of that slope against the same level of output in part (ii) of the Figure. One example is shown in the Figure. When output is 60 in part (i), the slope of the tangent to the curve is 40. This value of 40 is then plotted against output 60 in part (ii) of the Figure. Looked at either as the slope of the tangent to the TR curve in part (i), or as the height of the MR curve in part (ii), this value tells us that revenue increases at a rate of *£40 per unit increase in output* when output is 60 units.

Mathematically, the procedure is to differentiate the function showing the dependence of total revenue on output. So, on the function $R = R(q)$, we calculate the derivative dR/dq. If you know the calculus, you can make this simple operation; if not, you know from the previous section what concepts are involved. (In the case plotted the equation of the marginal revenue curve is $MR = dR/dq = 100 - q$.)

From marginals to totals: Now let us assume that we have only the curve in part (ii) of the Figure, and that we wish to derive the curve in part (i). In other words, we know marginal revenue associated with any specific output and we wish to deduce the corresponding total revenue.

If we had a schedule of incremental ratios all we would have to do is to add up the necessary marginal values. This is illustrated in Table 3A.1. For example, the total revenue when output is three units is calculated in the table as the sum of the contributions to total revenue of the first, the second and the third units. This illustrates that, if we know what each unit adds to total revenue, we can calculate the total revenue associated with any amount of output, say q_0, by

FIGURE 3A.7 A Firm's Total and Marginal Revenue Functions

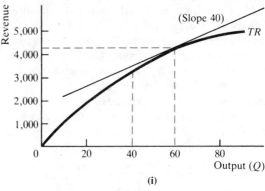

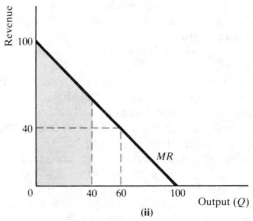

summing the separate contributions to revenue of each of the q_0 units.

Graphically, the same operation is done on a continuous curve by calculating the area under the marginal curve from zero to any given level of output. For example, at output 40 in part (ii) of the Figure, total revenue is given by the shaded area under the MC curve, which is 3,600. The value of this area is the height of the TR curve in part (i) at output 40.

TABLE 3A.1 Total and Marginal Revenues Associated with Various Levels of Output

Output	Marginal revenue	Total revenue
1	99.5	99.5
2	98.5	198.0
3	97.5	295.5
4	96.5	392.0

The common sense of this relation is that the height of the *MR* curve at any given output tells us how much is being added to revenue by a change in output when output has the value in question. Adding all these heights, from zero to the output in question, means summing all the contributions to revenue from each unit of output from zero to the amount in question. On a continuous curve, this summation yields the area under the curve between zero and that output.

Mathematically, going from the marginal to the total revenue curve is merely a matter of integrating the marginal revenue function. Since differentiation derives the marginal function from the total function, and since integration reverses the process of differentiation, integrating the marginal function gets back to the total function.[1]

(9) Maximum and Minimum Values

Consider the function

$$Y = 10X - 0.1X^2 ,$$

which is plotted in Figure 3A.3. *Y* at first increases as *X* increases, but after a while *Y* begins to fall as *X* goes on rising. We say that *Y* rises to a *maximum*, which is reached in this case when $X = 50$. Until $X = 50$, *Y* is rising as *X* rises, but after $X = 50$, *Y* is falling as *X* rises. Thus *Y* reaches a maximum value of 250 when *X* is 50.

A great deal of economic theory is based on the idea of finding a maximum (or a minimum) value. Since *Y* is a function of *X*, we speak of *maximizing the value of the function*, and by this we mean that we wish to find the value of *X* (50 in this case) for which the value of *Y* is at a maximum (250 in this case).

Now consider the function

$$Y = 75 - 10X + 0.5X^2 ,$$

which is graphed in Figure 3A.4. In this case, the value of *Y* falls at first while *X* increases, reaches

a *minimum*, and then rises as *X* goes on increasing. In this case, *Y* reaches a minimum value of 25 when *X* is 10. Here we speak of *minimizing the value of the function*, by which we mean finding the value of *X* for which the value of *Y* is at a minimum.

(10) Functions of More Than One Variable

In most of the examples used so far *Y* has been a function of only one variable, *X*. In many cases, however, the dependent variable is a function of more than one independent variable. The demand for a good might depend, for example, on the price of that good, on the prices of a number of competing products, on the prices of products used in conjunction with the product with which we are concerned, and on consumers' incomes.

When we wish to denote the dependence of *Y* on several variables, say, *V*, *W* and *X*, we write $Y = Y(V, W, X)$, which is read *Y* is a function of *V*, *W* and *X*.

In mathematics and in economics we often wish to discover what happens to *Y* as *X* varies, assuming meanwhile that the other factors that influence *Y* are held constant at some stated level. The result is often phrased '*Y* varies in such and such a way with *X* *other things being equal*' or '*Y* varies with *X* in such and such a way *ceteris paribus*'.

Students who do not know mathematics are often disturbed by the frequent use in economics of arguments that depend on the qualification 'other things being equal' (for which we often use the Latin phrase *ceteris paribus*). Such arguments are not peculiar to economics. They are used successfully in all branches of science and there is an elaborate set of mathematical techniques available to handle them.

When mathematicians wish to know how *Y* is changing as *X* changes when other factors that influence *Y* are held constant, they calculate what is called the *partial derivative of Y with respect to X*. This is written symbolically as $\partial Y/\partial X$. We cannot enter here into a discussion of how this expression is calculated. We only wish to note that finding $\partial Y/\partial X$ is a well recognized and very common mathematical operation, and the answer tells us approximately how *Y* is affected by small variations in *X* *when all other relevant factors are held constant*.

---

[1] If we differentiate a function with a specific constant term and then integrate the resulting function, we get back to the original function but with the specific constant replaced by the undetermined constant of integration. In the case of the total revenue function, we know that the constant on the original function is zero since, when output is zero, nothing is earned from selling output. In other cases, however, adding up the area under the marginal curve gets the total curve except for an undetermined constant of integration.

4

Basic Economic Concepts

Chapter 1 gave a general intuitive discussion of how markets work to determine the allocation of resources. In that chapter we could be satisfied with rather rough and ready notions. To build a formal theory, however, we now need more precise concepts.

DECISION-TAKERS

Economics is about the behaviour of people. Much that we observe in the world, and that we assume in our theories, can be traced back to decisions taken by individuals. There are millions of individuals in most economies. To make our systematic study of their behaviour more manageable, we consolidate them into three important groups: households, firms and central authorities. These are the *dramatis personae* of economic theory, and the stage on which their play is enacted is the market.

Households

We have used the term consumer to mean anyone who consumes commodities to satisfy his or her wants. Much economic theory replaces the concept of the consumer with that of the household. A **household** is defined as all the people who live under one roof and who take, or are subject to others taking for them, joint financial decisions. In our theory we give households a number of attributes.

First, we assume that each household takes consistent decisions as if it were composed of a single individual. Thus we ignore many interesting problems of how the household reaches its decisions. It may be by paternal dictatorship or democratic voting – that does not matter to us. Intra-family conflicts and the moral and legal problems concerning parental control over minors are dealt with by other social sciences.[1] These problems are avoided in economics by the

[1] In academic work, as well as elsewhere, a division of labour is useful. It is important to remember, however, that when economists speak of *the* consumer or *the* individual they are in fact referring to the group of individuals composing the household. Thus, for example, the commonly-heard phrase *consumer sovereignty* really means *household sovereignty*. These two concepts are quite distinct: it is one thing, for example, to say that individuals should be free to decide their own fate, and quite another thing to say that the head of the household should be free to decide the fate of all its members.

assumption that the household is the basic decision-taking atom of consumption behaviour.

Second, we assume that each household seeks to maximize what is variously called its *satisfactions*, or its *well-being* or its *utility*. This it tries to do within the limitations of the resources available to it. The concept of satisfaction or utility maximization can be tricky, and it is considered in some detail in Chapter 8.

Third, we assume that households are the principal owners of factors of production. They sell the services of these factors to producers and receive their incomes in return. It is obvious that labour is 'owned' by those individuals who sell their labour and receive wages and salaries in return. Most capital equipment is owned by firms; but firms are in turn owned by households. Joint stock companies, for example, are owned by the households that hold those companies' stocks. These households provide the firms with the money needed to purchase capital goods and they receive the firms' profits as their income. Land is owned by households and firms, and firms are in turn owned by households. A household may use its land itself or it may make it available to some other user in return for rent which becomes the household's income.[1] In making all these decisions on how much to sell and to whom to sell it, we again assume that households seek to maximize their utility.

Firms

Economists use the terms *producer*, *supplier* and *firm* interchangeably. A **firm** is defined as the unit that employs factors of production to produce commodities that it sells to other firms, to households or to the central authorities (defined below). Firms have a number of attributes.

First, we assume that each firm takes consistent decisions as if it were composed of a single individual. This means that we ignore the internal problems of who reaches particular decisions, and how they are reached. Instead we assume that each firm's decisions are not influenced by its internal organization. This allows us to treat the firm as our atom of behaviour on the production or supply side of commodity markets, just as the

household is treated as the atom of behaviour on the consumption or demand side.

Second, we assume that each firm takes its decisions with respect to a single goal: to make as much *profit* as it possibly can. This goal of profit maximization is analogous to the household's goal of utility maximization.

Third, we assume that firms are the principal users of the services of factors of production. In markets where factor services are bought and sold, the roles of firms and households are thus reversed from what they are in commodity markets: in factor markets, firms do the buying and households do the selling.

Central Authorities

The comprehensive term **central authorities** includes all public agencies, government bodies and other organizations belonging to or owing their existence to both central and local governments. This includes such institutions as the central bank, the civil service, commissions and regulatory agencies, the cabinet, the police force, the judiciary and all other authorities that can exercise control over the behaviour of firms and households. It is not important to draw up a comprehensive list of all central authorities; just keep in mind the general idea of a group of organizations that exist at the centre of legal and political power and exert some control over the rest of us. Economists often use the simpler, though less accurate, terms the *government* or the *state* to refer to the central authorities.

It is *not* a basic assumption of economics that the central authorities always act in a consistent fashion as if they were a single individual. Indeed, conflict among different central-authority agencies is often an important component in theories that analyse government intervention in the economy.

THE CONCEPT OF MARKETS

Markets are basic concepts in economics and we must consider them in some detail.

An Individual Market

Originally the word *market* designated a physical place where commodities were bought and sold.

---

[1] The only organization which owns capital and land without itself being a household, or being owned by a household, is the government. Thus, in the final analysis, all factors of production are owned either by households or by governments.

Once developed, however, theories of market behaviour were easily extended to cover commodities such as wheat, which can be purchased anywhere in the world at a price which tends to be uniform the world over. Thus the concept of 'the wheat market' extends our viewpoint well beyond the idea of a single place to which the householder goes to buy something.

For present purposes a **market** may be defined as an area over which buyers and sellers negotiate the exchange of a well-defined commodity. It must be possible, therefore, for buyers and sellers to communicate with each other and to make meaningful deals over the whole market.

The Separation of Individual Markets

Markets are separated from each other by the commodity sold, by natural economic barriers and by barriers created by the central authorities. To illustrate, consider one example of each type of separation. First, the market for men's shirts is different from the market for refrigerators because different commodities are sold in each. Second, the market for cement in the UK is distinct from the market for cement in the western United States, since transport costs are so high that UK purchasers would not buy American cement even if its price in the western US were very much lower than the price of cement in the UK. Third, the market for textiles is separated among many countries since national tariffs and restrictive quotas make it difficult or impossible for firms in one country to sell to households in another.

The Interlinking of Individual Markets

Although all markets are to some extent separated, most are also interrelated.

Consider again the three causes of market separation: different commodities, spatial separation and government intervention. First, the markets for different kinds of commodities are interrelated because all commodities compete for consumers' income. Thus if more is spent in one market, less will be available to spend in other markets. Second, the geographical separation of markets for similar commodities depends on transport costs. Commodities whose transport costs are high relative to their production costs

tend to be produced and sold in geographically distinct markets. Commodities whose transport costs are low relative to their production costs tend to be sold in what amounts to one world market. But whatever the transport costs, there will be some price differential at which it will pay someone to buy in the low-priced market and ship to the high-priced one. Thus there is always some potential link between geographically distinct markets, even when shipping costs are high. Third, markets are often separated by policy-induced barriers, such as tariffs (which are taxes paid when goods come into a country from abroad). Although high tariffs tend to separate markets, they do not do so completely because, if price differences become large enough, it will pay buyers in the high-cost market to import from the low-cost market and producers in the low-cost one to export to the high-cost one, even though they have to pay the tariff as a result.

Differences Among Markets

Individual markets differ from each other in many ways. Here we distinguish the type of commodity sold and the amount of competition among sellers.

Goods and factor markets: Every distinct good and service has its own market. For many purposes, however, it is useful to divide markets into two types. **Goods markets** are those where goods and services are bought and sold.[1] The sellers in such markets are usually firms; the buyers may be households, other firms or the central authorities. **Factor markets** are those where factor services are bought and sold. The sellers in such markets are the owners of factors of production (usually households, but sometimes firms); the buyers are usually firms and the central authorities.

Competitiveness: Individual markets may differ from each other according to the degree of competition among the various buyers and sellers in each market. In the next few chapters we shall

---

[1] Since these markets include both goods and services, it might seem better to refer to them as *commodity markets*. Unfortunately, this term is in common use in the business world to refer to markets where basic commodities, such as rubber, tin and jute, are sold. To avoid confusion, economists often speak of *goods markets* where, in their own terminology, commodity markets would be better.

confine ourselves to markets in which the number of buyers and sellers is sufficiently large that no one of them has any appreciable influence on price. This is a very rough definition of what economists call *competitive markets*. Later we shall consider the behaviour of markets that do not meet this competitive requirement.

THE CONCEPT OF AN ECONOMY

An **economy** is a rather loosely defined term for any specified collection of interrelated marketed and non-marketed productive activity. It may refer to productive activity in a region of one country, such as *the economy of eastern Canada*; it may refer to one country, such as *the UK economy*, or it may refer to a group of countries, such as *the economy of Western Europe*.

The economies of all countries contain market and non-market sectors. A **free-market economy** is one in which most production is in the market sector, and these markets are relatively free from control by the central authorities. In such an economy the allocation of resources is determined by production, sales and purchase decisions taken mainly by firms and households.

At the opposite extreme from a free-market economy is a **centrally controlled economy** or, as it is sometimes called, a **command economy**. Here all the decisions about the allocation of resources are taken by the central authorities, so that firms and households produce and consume only as they are ordered. In such an economy most production will be in the non-market sector.

Neither the completely free-market economy nor the completely controlled economy has ever existed in modern history.

In practice, all economies are **mixed economies** in the sense that some decisions are taken by firms and households, and some by the central authorities. The emphasis varies, however. In some economies, the influence of the central authorities is substantially less than in others. Not only may the average amount of central control vary among economies, it may also vary among markets within one economy. Thus, in the UK, the day-to-day behaviour of the stock market is relatively free from central control, while the market for rented housing has been heavily controlled by the central authorities for most of this century.

The theory that we will develop applies specifically to the behaviour of free markets, but it can also deal with many types of central control commonly found in Western economies. We shall use the phrase 'free-market economy' to indicate economies in which the decisions of individual households and firms exert a substantial influence over the allocation of resources. The dividing line is an arbitrary one. We must always remember that every possible mixture of centralized and decentralized control exists, and that the economies of Poland and the Soviet Union differ from those of France and the UK only in the *degree* to which the central authorities exert an influence over the markets of each economy.

Free-market economies are sometimes called capitalist economies. Capitalist used as an adjective in this context means that the factor of production, capital, is owned by private individuals rather than by the state. The legal distinction of ownership is, however, less important than the economic distinction of control, so we shall not often use the term capitalist.

Sectors of an Economy

The economy is often conceptually divided into various subdivisions called sectors. Two of the most common separations involve marketed and non-marketed sectors and the public and private sectors.

Market and non-market sectors: There are two basic ways in which commodities may pass from those who make them to those who use them. First, commodities may be sold by producers and bought by consumers. When this happens, the producers must cover their costs by the revenues they obtain from the sale of the product. Such production is called *marketed production* and this part of the country's activity belongs to the **market sector**. Second, the product may be given away. In this case the costs of production must be covered by some means other than sales revenues. This production is called *non-marketed production* and belongs to the **non-market sector**. In the case of private charities, the money required to pay for factor services may be raised from the public by voluntary subscriptions. In the case of production by the government – which accounts for the great bulk of non-marketed production – the money is provided from government revenue, which in turn comes mainly from taxes levied on firms and households.

Whenever a government enterprise *sells* its output, this output is in the market sector. Much government output is, however, in the non-market sector. Some is in the non-market sector because of the nature of the product. One could not imagine, for example, the criminal paying the judge for providing him with the service of criminal justice. Some products are in the non-market sector because the government has decided to remove them from the market sector. In some countries, for example, firms producing medical and hospital services are in the market sector and their products are sold to consumers for a price that must cover their costs. In other countries such as the UK, however, the production of these services is in the non-market sector; they are provided at little or no cost to users, and costs are covered by the state.

Assigning production to one sector or the other is simple when either all or none of its costs are covered by selling the products to users. In other cases, however, production falls partly into one sector and partly into the other. If 10 per cent of costs are covered by small charges made to users and 90 per cent by the government, then the production is 10 per cent in the market sector and 90 per cent in the non-market sector. If private firms get a subsidy from the government to cover 10 per cent of their costs, but meet the rest out of sales revenue, then their production is 10 per cent in the non-market sector and 90 per cent in the market sector.

All the country's national product is produced in either the market or the non-market sector of the economy.

The public and private sectors: The productive activity of a country is often subdivided in a different way to obtain the private and the public sectors. The **private sector** refers to all production that is in private hands; the **public sector** refers to all production that is in public hands. The distinction between the two sectors depends on the legal distinction of ownership. In the private sector, the organization that does the producing is owned by households or other firms; in the public sector, it is owned by the state. The public sector includes all production of goods and services by central authorities, plus all production by nationalized industries that is sold to consumers through ordinary markets.

MICROECONOMICS AND MACROECONOMICS

There are two different but complementary ways of viewing the economy. The first, *microeconomics*, studies the detailed workings of individual markets and interrelations among markets. The second, *macroeconomics*, suppresses much of the detail and concentrates on the behaviour of broad aggregates.

Microeconomics and Macroeconomics Compared

Microeconomics and macroeconomics differ in the question asked and in the level of aggregation used.

> **Microeconomics deals with the determination of prices and quantities in individual markets and with the relations among these markets.**

Thus it looks at the details of the market economy. It asks, for example, how much labour is employed in the restaurant industry and why the amount is increasing. It asks what determines the output of such commodities as Brussels sprouts, pocket calculators, automobiles and beer. It asks, too, about the prices of these things – why some prices go up and others down. Economists interested in microeconomics analyse how prices and outputs respond to exogenous shocks caused by events in other markets or by government policy. They ask, for example, how a technical innovation, a government subsidy or a drought will affect the price and output of sugar and the employment of farm workers.

In contrast:

> **macroeconomics focuses on much broader aggregates. It looks at such things as the total number of people employed and unemployed, the average**

level of prices, total national output and aggregate consumption.

Macroeconomics asks what determines these aggregates and how they vary in response to changing conditions. Whereas microeconomics looks at demand and supply with regard to particular commodities, macroeconomics looks at aggregate demand and aggregate supply.

An Overview of Macroeconomics

The discussion in Chapter 1 on how the market reacts to changes in demand and supply for carrots provided an overview of the microeconomic theory of the behaviour of individual markets.

Macroeconomics, however, is based on an aggregation that suppresses what is happening in individual markets. In macroeconomics we consider *all* the buyers of the nation's output and call their total desired purchases **aggregate demand**. We can also consider *all* the producers of the nation's output and call their total desired sales **aggregate supply**. Some of the most important problems in macroeconomics lie in determining the magnitude of aggregate demand and aggregate supply and in explaining why they change.

Major changes in aggregate demand are called *demand shocks*, and major changes in aggregate supply are called *supply shocks*. Such shocks will cause important changes in the broad averages and aggregates that are the concern of macroeconomics, including total output, total employment, and average levels of prices and wages. Government actions are sometimes the cause of demand or supply shocks, while at other times they are reactions to such shocks and are used in an attempt to cushion or change the effect of such shocks.

The Circular Flow of Income

One way to gain insight into aggregate demand and aggregate supply is to view the economy as a giant set of flows. A major part of aggregate demand arises from the purchases of consumption commodities by the nation's households. These purchases generate income for the firms that produce and sell commodities for consumption. A major part of aggregate supply arises from the production and sale of consumption goods by the nation's firms. This production generates income for all the factors that are employed in making these goods.

The dark grey arrows in Figure 4.1 show the interaction between firms and households in two sets of markets – factor markets and product markets – through which their decisions are co-ordinated. Consider households first. The members of households want commodities to keep themselves fed, clothed, housed, entertained, healthy and secure. They also want commodities to educate, edify, beautify, stupefy and otherwise amuse themselves. Households have resources with which to attempt to satisfy these wants. But not all their wants can be satisfied with the resources available. Households are forced, therefore, to make choices as to which goods and services to buy in product markets that offer them myriad ways to spend their incomes.

Now consider firms. They must choose among the products they might produce and sell, the ways of producing them and the various quantities (and qualities) they can supply. Firms must also buy factors of production. Payments by firms to factor owners provide the factor owners with incomes. The recipients of these incomes are households whose members want commodities to keep themselves fed, clothed, housed and entertained.

We have now come full circle! These interchanges involve firms and households interacting with one another. Payments flow from households to firms through product markets and back to households again through factor markets.

If the economy consisted only of households and firms, if households spent all the income they received on buying goods and services produced by firms, and if firms distributed all their receipts to households either by purchasing factor services or by distributing profits to owners, then the circular flow would be simple indeed. Everything received by households would be passed on to firms, and everything received by firms would be passed back to households. The circular flow would then be a completely closed system: aggregate demand and aggregate supply would consist only of consumption goods, and macroeconomics would involve little more than measuring the

FIGURE 4.1 The Circular Flow of Expenditures and Income

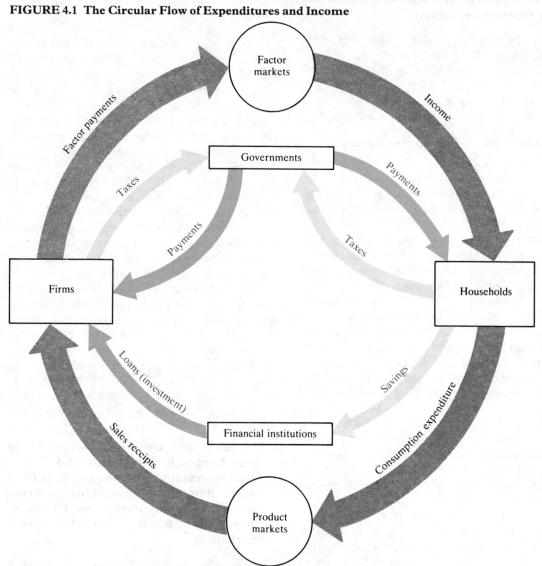

**The interaction of firms and households in product and factor markets
generates a flow of expenditure and income. These flows are also influenced
by other institutions such as governments and the financial system.** Factor
services are sold by households through factor markets. This leads to a flow of income
from firms to households. Commodities are sold by firms through product markets.
This leads to a flow of payments from households to firms. If these primary flows,
shown by the grey arrows, were the only flows, the circular flow would be a closed
system. But other institutions, such as governments and financial institutions, play
roles. For example, governments may inject funds in the form of government
payments to households and firms, and banks may inject funds in the form of loans to
firms for investment expenditures. Such additions or injections are illustrated by the
dark-coloured arrows. Similarly, governments may withdraw funds in the form of
taxes, and financial institutions may do so by accepting funds that households wish to
save. Such leakages or withdrawals are illustrated by the light-coloured arrows.

flows of production of, and expenditure on, consumption goods.

The circular flow is not, however, a completely closed system. First, households do not spend all their income. Some of their income is saved, and some goes to governments as taxes. As a result, total household demand for consumption goods and services falls short of total household income. These two *leakages* from the circular flow are shown by the light-coloured arrows flowing out of the households in Figure 4.1. As shown in the Figure, a third leakage occurs because firms also pay taxes. (Of course, firms may also save, but this leakage is omitted from the Figure for simplicity.)

A second reason why the circular flow is not a closed system is that there are elements of aggregate demand that do not arise from household spending. The two main additional elements are investment and government expenditure. A major component of aggregate demand comes from governments – central and local. They add to total expenditure on the nation's output by spending on a whole range of goods and services from national defence through the provision of justice to the building of roads and schools. These two major additions to the cir-

cular flow of income are shown by the dark-coloured arrows flowing into the firms in Figure 4.1. As shown in the Figure, a third addition arises because households also receive payments from government. (Of course, households may also borrow from financial institutions to finance current consumption expenditure, but for simplicity this fourth addition is omitted from the Figure.)

When any of the elements of aggregate demand change, changes will also occur in aggregate output and in the total income earned by households. Thus, if we are to understand the causes of changes both in the nation's total output and in the employment generated by the production of that output, we need to understand the determinants of total consumption, investment and government spending.

The Next Step

Soon you will be going on to study micro- or macroeconomics. Whichever branch of the subject you study first, it is important to remember that microeconomics and macroeconomics are complementary, not competing, views of the economy. Both are needed for a full understanding of the functioning of a modern economy.

SUMMARY

1. The decision-taking units in economic theory are households for demand, firms for supply, and central authorities for supply of some goods and for regulation and control of the private sector. Given the resources at their command, each household is assumed to act consistently to maximize its satisfaction, and each firm is assumed to act consistently to maximize its profit.

2. Individual markets are partially separated from each other because different commodities are sold in each, and because of barriers to the movement of commodities among markets such as transport costs (a natural barrier) and tariffs (a policy-induced barrier). In spite of a substantial degree of separation, most individual markets are more or less interlinked.

3. An economy refers to an interrelated set of marketed and non-marketed productive activities. The behaviour of free-market economies is primarily determined by individual firms and households; the behaviour of command economies is primarily determined by the central authorities.

4. The distinction between the marketed and non-marketed sectors is an economic one: it depends on whether or not the costs of producing commodities are recovered by selling them to their users. The distinction between the private and the public sectors is a legal one: it depends on whether the firms are owned by private individuals (or groups) or by governments.

5. Microeconomics deals with the action and interaction of individual markets in determining the allocation of resources. Macroeconomics concerns the behaviour of such broad aggregates as total output, total employment, and the average level of all prices. The basic concept of microeconomics is the individual market; the basic concept in macroeconomics is the circular flow of income.

TOPICS FOR REVIEW

- Households, firms and central authorities (the government)
- Individual markets, their separation and interlinking
- Goods and factor markets
- Free-market and command (centrally controlled) economies
- The market and non-market, and the public and private sectors of an economy
- Microeconomics and macroeconomics
- The circular flow of income

PART 2

The Elementary Theory of Demand and Supply

5

Demand, Supply and Price

The preliminaries of Part I are now completed, and we are ready to study one of the most famous aspects of the whole of economics, the laws of supply and demand. The theory is a formalization of Chapter 1's intuitive discussion of the carrot and Brussels sprout markets. In this key chapter we look at the determinants of demand, then of supply, and finally of market price.

DEMAND

The Nature of Demand

The amount of a commodity that households wish to purchase is called the **quantity demanded**. Notice two important things about this concept. First, quantity demanded is a *desired* quantity. It is how much households *wish* to purchase, not necessarily how much they actually succeed in purchasing. We use phrases such as **quantity actually purchased**, or **quantity actually bought and sold**, to distinguish actual purchases from quantity demanded. Second, note that quantity demanded is a *flow*. (See page 22 for the distinction between stocks and flows.) We are concerned not with a single isolated purchase, but with a continuous flow of purchases, and we must, therefore, express demand as so much per period of time – e.g. one million oranges *per day*, or seven million oranges *per week*, or 365 million oranges *per year*.

The concept of demand as a flow appears to raise difficulties when we deal with the purchases of durable consumer goods (often called consumer durables). It makes obvious sense to talk about a household consuming oranges at the rate of thirty per month, but what can we say of a household that buys a new television set every five years? This apparent difficulty disappears if we measure the demand for the *services* provided by the consumer durable. Thus, at the rate of a new set every five years, the television purchaser is using the service (viewing TV programmes) at the rate of 1/60 of a set per month.

The Determinants of Quantity Demanded: The Demand Function

Five main variables influence the quantity of each

commodity that is demanded by each individual household:

(1) the price of the commodity,
(2) the prices of other commodities,
(3) the household's income and wealth,
(4) various 'sociological' factors, and
(5) the household's tastes.

Making use of the functional notation that was introduced in Chapter 3, the above list is conveniently summarized in what is called a **demand function**:

$$q_n{}^d = D(p_n, p_1, \ldots, p_{n-1}, Y, S) \,,$$

where $q_n{}^d$ is the quantity that the household demands of some commodity, which we call commodity n; where p_n is the price of this commodity, where $p_1, \ldots, p_{n-1}$ is a shorthand notation for the prices of all other commodities, where Y is the household's income, where S stands for a host of sociological factors such as number of children and place of residence (e.g. big city, small town, country), and the form of the function, D, is determined by the tastes of the members of the household. The demand function is just a shorthand way of saying that quantity demanded depends on the variables listed on the right-hand side, while the form of the function determines the sign and the magnitude of that dependence.

We will not be able to understand the separate influences of each of the above variables if we ask what happens when everything changes at once. Instead, we consider the influence of the variables one at a time. To do this, we use a device that is frequently employed in economic theory. We assume that all except one of the variables in the right-hand side of the above expression are held constant; we then allow this one variable, say p_n, to change, and we consider how the quantity demanded $(q_n{}^d)$ changes. This means we study the effect of changes in one influence on quantity demanded *assuming that all other influences remain unchanged*, or, as economists are fond of putting it, *ceteris paribus* (which means *other things being equal*).

We can do the same for each of the other variables in turn, and in this way we can come to understand the importance of each variable. Once this is done, we can aggregate the separate influences of each variable to discover what would happen when several variables change at the same time – as they usually do in practice.

Demand and Price

We are interested in developing a theory of how commodities get priced. To do this, we need to study the relation between the quantity demanded of each commodity and that commodity's own price. This requires that we hold all other influences constant and ask: how will the quantity of a commodity demanded vary as its own price varies?

A basic economic hypothesis is that the lower the price of a commodity, the larger the quantity that will be demanded, other things being equal.

Why might this be so? A major reason is that there is usually more than one commodity that will satisfy any given desire or need. Hunger may be satisfied by meat or vegetables; a desire for green vegetables may be satisfied by broccoli or spinach. The need to keep warm at night may be satisfied by several woollen blankets, or one electric blanket, or a sheet and a lot of oil burned in the boiler. The desire for a vacation may be satisfied by a trip to the Scottish Highlands or to the Swiss Alps, the need to get there by airlines, a bus, a car or a train, and so on. Name any general desire or need, and there will usually be several commodities that will satisfy it.

Now consider what happens if we hold income, tastes, population and the prices of all other commodities constant and vary the price of only one commodity.

First, let the price of the commodity rise. The commodity then becomes a more expensive way of satisfying a want. Some households will stop buying it altogether; others will buy smaller amounts; still others may continue to buy the same amount, but no rational household will buy more of it. Because many households will switch wholly, or partially, to other commodities to satisfy the same want, less will be bought of the commodity whose price has risen. As meat becomes more expensive, for example, households may switch to some extent to meat substitutes; they may also forgo meat at some meals and eat less meat at others.

Second, let the price of a commodity fall. This makes the commodity a cheaper method of satisfying any given want. Households will thus buy more of it. Consequently, they will buy less of similar commodities whose prices have not fallen and which, as a result, have become expensive *relative to* the commodity in question. When a bumper tomato harvest drives prices down, shoppers buy more tomatoes and fewer of other vegetables that now look relatively more expensive.

The Demand Schedule and the Demand Curve

A household's demand: A **demand schedule** is one way of showing the relationship between quantity demanded and price. It is a numerical tabulation showing the quantity that is demanded at selected prices.

Table 5.1 is a household's hypothetical demand schedule for carrots. It shows the quantity of carrots that a household would demand at six selected prices. For example, at a price of £40 per ton, the quantity demanded is 10.25 lbs per month. Each of the price-quantity combinations in the Table is given a letter for easy reference. We can now plot the data from Table 5.1 in Figure 5.1, with price on the vertical and quantity on the horizontal axis.[1]

Next, we draw a smooth curve through these points. This curve, also shown in Figure 5.1, is called the **demand curve** for carrots. It shows

---

[1] Readers trained in other disciplines often wonder why economists plot demand curves with price on the vertical axis. The normal convention is to put the independent variable (the variable that does the explaining) on the X (i.e. horizontal) axis and the dependent variable (the variable that is explained) on the Y axis. This convention calls for price to be plotted on the horizontal axis and quantity on the vertical axis.

The axis reversal – now enshrined by nearly a century of usage – arose as follows. The analysis of the competitive market that we use today stems from Leon Walras, in whose theory quantity was the dependent variable. Graphical analysis in economics, however, was popularized by Alfred Marshall, in whose theory price was the dependent variable. Economists continue to use Walras' theory and Marshall's graphical representation and thus draw the diagram with the independent and dependent variables reversed – to the everlasting confusion of readers trained in other disciplines. In virtually every other graph in economics the axes are labelled conventionally, with the dependent variable on the vertical axis.

TABLE 5.1 A Household's Demand Schedule for Carrots

Reference letter	Price (£s per tonne)	Quantity demanded (lbs per month)
a	20	14.0
b	40	10.25
c	60	7.5
d	80	5.25
e	100	3.5
f	120	2.5

The Table shows the quantity of carrots that one household would demand at each selected price, *ceteris paribus.* For example, at a price of £20 the household demands 14 lbs per month while at a price of £120 it only demands 2.5 lbs.

---

the quantity of carrots that the household would like to buy at every possible price; its negative slope indicates that the quantity demanded increases as the price falls.

A single point on the demand curve indicates a single price-quantity relation. *The whole demand curve shows the complete relation between quantity demanded and price.* Economists often speak of

FIGURE 5.1 A Household's Demand Curve

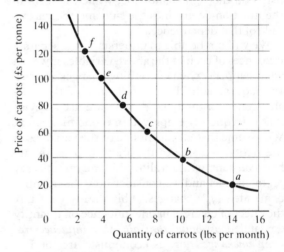

A household's demand curve relates the price of a commodity to the amount that the household wishes to purchase. The curve is drawn from the data in Table 5.1, each point on the Figure relating to a row on the Table. For example, when price is £120, 2.5 lbs are bought per month (point *f*) while when the price is £20, 14 lbs are bought each month (point *a*).

FIGURE 5.2   The Relation Between Household and Market Demand Curves

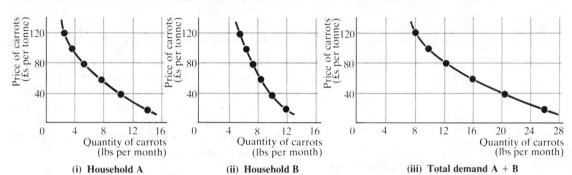

(i) Household A   **(ii) Household B**   **(iii) Total demand A + B**

The market demand curve is the horizontal sum of the individual demand curves of all households in the market. The Figure illustrates aggregation over two households. For example, at a price of £60 per tonne, household A purchases 7.5 units and household B purchases 8.5 units. Thus together they purchase 16 units. No matter how many households are involved, the process is the same.

the conditions of demand in a particular market as given or as known. When they do so they are not referring just to the particular quantity that is being demanded at the moment (i.e. not just to a particular point on the demand curve). They are referring rather to the whole demand curve, to the complete functional relation whereby desired purchases are related to all possible alternative prices of the commodity.

The market demand curve: So far we have discussed how the quantity of a commodity demanded by one household depends on its price, other things being equal. To explain market behaviour, however, we need to know the total demand of all households. To obtain a market demand schedule, we first sum the quantities demanded by all households at a particular price to obtain the total quantity demanded at that price. We then repeat the process for each price to obtain a schedule of a total, or market, demand at all possible prices. A graph of this schedule is called the *market demand curve*. Figure 5.2 shows the summation geometrically. It illustrates the proposition that the market demand curve is the horizontal sum of the demand curves of all the households in the market.[1]

We have illustrated the market demand curve by summing the demands for only two households. An actual market demand curve will represent the demands of all the households who buy in that market. In practice, our knowledge of market curves is usually derived by observing total quantities directly. The derivation of market demand curves by summing individual curves is a theoretical operation. We do it to understand the relation between curves for individual households and market curves.

In Table 5.2 we assume we have data for the market demand for carrots. The schedule tells us the total quantity that will be demanded by all buyers in that market at each market price. The data are plotted in Figure 5.3, and the curve drawn through these points is the market demand curve.

---

[1] When summing curves, students sometimes become confused between vertical and horizontal summation. Such a confusion can only result from the application of memory rather than common sense to one's economics. *Consider what*

would be meant by vertical summation: measure off equal quantities, say 10 lbs in parts (i) and (ii) of Figure 5.2. Now add the price on each household's demand curve to which this quantity corresponds. This is £42 + £40 = £82. If we now plot the point corresponding to £82 and 10 lbs, we have related a given quantity of the commodity to the sum of the prices which the households are separately prepared to pay for this commodity. Clearly, this information is of no interest to us in the present context. *Every graphical operation can be translated into words*. The advantage of graphs is that they make proofs easier; the disadvantage is that they make it possible to make silly errors. To avoid error, you should always translate into words any graphical operation you have performed and ask yourself: 'Does this make sense and is this what I meant to do?'

TABLE 5.2 A Market Demand Schedule for Carrots

Reference letter	Price (£s per tonne)	Quantity demanded (thousand tonnes per month)
U	20	110.0
V	40	90.0
W	60	77.5
X	80	67.5
Y	100	62.5
Z	120	60.0

The Table shows the quantity of carrots that would be demanded by all purchasers at various prices, *ceteris paribus*. For example, row *W* indicates that if the price of carrots were £60 per tonne consumers would desire to purchase 77,500 tonnes of carrots per month, given the values of the other variables that affect quantity demanded, including average household income.

Determinants of Demand Once Again

When we go from the individual household's demand curve to the market demand curve, we must reconsider item (3) in our list of the determinants of demand. 'Household income' now refers to *the total income of all households*. If, for example, the population increases due to immigration and each new immigrant has an income, the demands for most commodities will rise even though existing households have unchanged incomes and face unchanged prices.

When we take total income of all households as our income variable, we must add another factor to the major determinants of demand.

A sixth determinant, income distribution among households: Consider two societies with the same total income. In one society there are some rich households, many poor households, but only a few in the middle-income range. In the second society, most of the households have incomes that do not differ much from the average income for all households. Even if all other variables that influence demand are the same, the two societies will have quite different patterns of demand. In the first there will be a large demand for Mercedes-Benz and Rolls-Royce cars and also for coarse bread and potatoes. In the second, there will be a smaller demand for these products, but a large demand for television sets, medium-sized cars and other

middle-income consumption goods. Clearly, the distribution of income is a major determinant of market demand.

Market Demand: A Recapitulation

The total quantity demanded in any market depends on the price of the commodity being sold, on the prices of all other commodities, on the total income of all the households buying in that market, on the distribution of that income among the households, and on tastes.

To obtain the market demand curve, we hold constant all the factors that influence demand, including total income and its distribution among households.

The market demand curve relates the total quantity demanded of a commodity to its own price on the assumption that all other prices, total household income, its distribution among households, and tastes are held constant.

FIGURE 5.3 A Market Demand Curve for Carrots

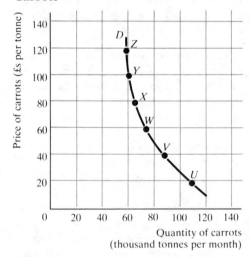

This demand curve relates quantity of carrots demanded to their price; its downward slope indicates that quantity demanded increases as price falls. The six points correspond to the price-quantity combinations shown in Table 5.2. Each row in the Table defines a point on the demand curve. The smooth curve drawn through all of the points and labelled *D* is the demand curve.

FIGURE 5.4 Two Demand Curves for Carrots

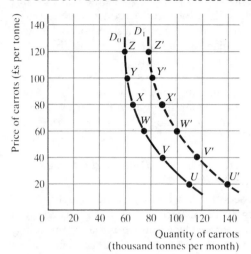

Quantity of carrots
(thousand tonnes per month)

The rightward shift in the demand curve from D_0 to D_1 indicates an increase in the quantity demanded at each price. The lettered points correspond to those in Table 5.3. A rightward shift in the demand curve indicates an increase in demand in the sense that more is demanded at each price and that a higher price would be paid for each quantity. For example at price £60, quantity demanded rises from 77.5 (point W) to 100.8 (point W'); while the quantity of 90, which was formerly bought at a price of £40 (point V), will be bought at a price of £80 after the shift (point X').

Shifts in the Demand Curve

The demand schedule and the demand curve are constructed on the assumption of *ceteris paribus*. But what if other things change, as surely they must? What, for example, if households find themselves with more income? If they spend their extra income, they will buy additional quantities of many commodities *even though market prices are unchanged*. But if households increase their purchases of any commodity whose price has not changed, the new purchases cannot be represented by the original demand curve. Thus the rise in household income *shifts* the demand curve to the right as shown in Figure 5.4.[1] This shift illustrates the operation of an important general rule.

---

[1] The convention used throughout this book for shifts in curves is as follows. The initial position of the curve is indicated by the subscript 0, the position after the first shift by 1, after the second shift by 2, and so on. The equilibrium price

A demand curve is drawn on the assumption that everything except the commodity's own price is held constant. A change in any of the variables previously held constant will shift the demand curve to a new position.

Any change will shift the demand curve to the right if it increases the amount households wish to buy at each price, and to the left if it decreases the amount households wish to buy at each price.

Changes in household income: If households receive more income, they can be expected to purchase more of most commodities even though commodity prices remain the same. Such a shift is illustrated in Table 5.3 and Figure 5.4. A commodity whose demand increases when income increases is called a **normal good**.

A rise in average household income shifts the demand curve for normal commodities to the right, indicating that more will be demanded at each possible price.

For a few commodities, called **inferior goods**, a rise in their income leads households to reduce their purchases (because they can now afford to switch to a more expensive, but superior, substitute).

A rise in income will shift the demand for inferior goods to the left, indicating that less will be demanded at each price.

Changes in other prices: We saw that demand curves have a negative slope because the lower a commodity's price, the cheaper it becomes relative to other commodities that can satisfy the same needs. Those other commodities are called **substitutes**. A commodity becomes cheaper relative to its substitutes if its own price *falls*. This also happens if the substitute's price

---

and quantity associated with the initial curve are indicated by p_0 and q_0, those associated with the curve after one shift by p_1 and q_1, and so on. When there is no curve shift, and hence no room for ambiguity, the subscripts are often dropped. Thus, for example, there are no subscripts on Figure 5.1, but in Figure 5.4 the initial curve is labelled D_0 and the shifted curve D_1.

Where we wish to indicate two alternative curves rather than a shift of a curve, we use prime (') marks. Thus, for example, D_0 and D_1 refer to the curve that starts at D_0 and shifts to D_1 while D, D' and D'' refer to three alternative curves, any one of which might actually exist at any one time.

rises. For example, carrots can become cheap relative to cabbage, either because the price of carrots falls, or because the price of cabbage rises. Either change will increase the amount of carrots households are prepared to buy.

A rise in the price of a commodity's substitute shifts the demand curve for the commodity to the right. More will be purchased at each price.

For example, a rise in the price of cabbage could shift the demand curve for carrots from D_0 to D_1 in Figure 5.4.

Commodities that tend to be used jointly with each other are called **complements**. Cars and petrol are complements; so are golf clubs and golf balls, electric cookers and electricity, an aeroplane trip to Austria and lift tickets on the mountain. Since complements tend to be consumed together, a fall in the price of either will increase the demand for both. For example, a fall in the price of cars that causes more people to become car owners will, *ceteris paribus*, increase the demand for petrol.

A fall in the price of one commodity that is complementary to a second commodity will shift the second commodity's demand curve to the right. More will be purchased at each price.

Changes in tastes: If there is a change in

tastes in favour of a commodity, more will be demanded at each price, causing the demand curve to shift to the right. In contrast, if there is a change in tastes away from a commodity less will be demanded at each price, causing the entire demand curve to shift left.

Figure 5.5 summarizes our discussion of the causes of shifts in the demand curve. Notice that since we are generalizing beyond our example of carrots, we have relabelled our axes 'price' and 'quantity', dropping the qualification 'of carrots'.

Movements Along Demand Curves Versus Shifts

Suppose you read in today's newspaper that a soaring price of carrots has been caused by a greatly increased demand for that commodity. Then tomorrow you read that the rising price of carrots is greatly reducing the typical household's demand for carrots as shoppers switch to potatoes, yams and peas. The two statements appear to contradict each other. The first associates a rising price with a rising demand; the second associates a rising price with a declining demand. Can both statements be true? The answer is that they can be because they refer to different things. The first refers to a shift in the demand curve: the second refers to a movement along a demand curve in response to a change in price.

Consider first the statement that the increase in

TABLE 5.3 Two Alternative Market Demand Schedules for Carrots

(1)	Price of carrots (£s per tonne) (2)	Quantity of carrots demanded at original level of household income (thousand tonnes per month) (3)	Quantity of carrots demanded when household income rises to new level (thousand tonnes per month) (4)	(5)
U	20	110.0	140.0	U'
V	40	90.0	116.0	V'
W	60	77.5	100.8	W'
X	80	67.5	90.0	X'
Y	100	62.5	81.3	Y'
Z	120	60.0	78.0	Z'

An increase in average household income increases the quantity demanded at each price. When average income rises, quantity demanded at a price of £60 per tonne rises from 77,500 tonnes per month to 100,800 tonnes per month. A similar rise occurs at every other price. Thus the demand schedule relating columns 2 and 3 is replaced by the one relating columns 2 and 4. The graphical representations of these two schedules are labelled D_0 and D_1 in Figure 5.4.

FIGURE 5.5 Shifts in the Demand Curve

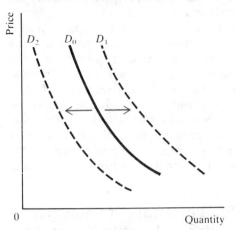

A shift in the demand curve from D_0 to D_1
indicates an increase in demand; a shift from
D_0 to D_2 indicates a decrease in demand. An
increase in demand means that more is demanded at
each price. Such a rightward shift can be caused by a
rise in income, a rise in the price of a substitute, a fall
in the price of a complement, a change in tastes that
favours the commodity, an increase in population, or
a redistribution of income toward groups who favour
the commodity.

A decrease in demand means that less is demanded
at each price. Such a leftward shift can be caused by a
fall in income, a fall in the price of a substitute, a rise
in the price of a complement, a change in tastes that
disfavours the commodity, a decrease in population,
or a redistribution of income away from groups who
favour the commodity.

the price of carrots has been caused by an
increased demand for carrots. This statement
refers to a shift in the demand curve for carrots.
In this case, the demand curve must have shifted
to the right, indicating more carrots demanded at
each price. This shift will, as we shall see later in
this chapter, increase the price of carrots.

Now consider the statement that fewer carrots
are being bought because carrots have become
more expensive. This refers to a movement along
a given demand curve and reflects a change
between two specific quantities being bought,
one before the price rose and one afterwards.

So what lay behind the two stories might have
been something like the following.

(1) A rise in the population shifts the demand
curve for carrots to the right as more and more are
demanded at each price. This in turn is raising
the price of carrots (for reasons we will soon
study in detail). This was the first newspaper
story.

(2) The rising price of carrots is causing each
individual household to cut back on its purchase
of carrots. This causes a movement upward to the
left along any particular demand curve for carrots. This was the second newspaper story.

To prevent the type of confusion caused by our
two newspaper stories, economists have developed a specialized vocabulary to distinguish
shifts of curves from movements along curves.
Demand refers to one *whole* demand curve.
Change in demand refers to a *shift* in the whole
curve, that is, a change in the amount that will be
bought at *every* price.

**An increase in demand means that the
whole demand curve has shifted to the
right; a decrease in demand means that
the whole demand curve has shifted to
the left.**

Any one point on a demand curve represents a
specific amount being bought at a specified price.
It represents, therefore, a particular quantity
demanded. A movement along a demand curve
is referred to as a **change in the quantity
demanded.**[1]

**A movement down a demand curve is
called an increase (or a rise) in the quantity demanded; a movement up the demand curve is called a decrease (or a fall)
in the quantity demanded.**

To illustrate this terminology, look again at
Table 5.3. First, at the original level of household
income, a decrease in price from £80 to £60
increases *the quantity demanded* from 67.5 to 77.5
thousand tonnes a month. Second, the increase in
average household income *increases demand* from
what is shown by column 3 to what is shown by
column 4. The same contrast is shown in Figure
5.4, where a fall in price from £80 to £60
increases the quantity demanded from the quan-

---

[1] Sometimes a movement along a demand curve is referred to
as an *expansion* or a *contraction* of demand: an expansion
referring to what we have called an increase in the quantity
demanded and a contraction to a decrease in the quantity
demanded.

FIGURE 5.6 Shifts of and Movements Along the Demand Curve

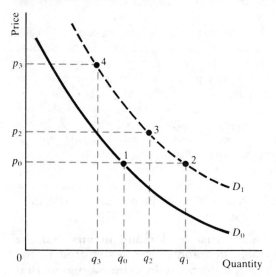

A rise in demand means that more will be bought at each price, but it does not mean that more will be bought under all circumstances. The demand curve is originally D_0 and price is p_0 at which q_0 is bought (point 1). Demand then increases to D_1. At the old price of p_0, the quantity demanded is now q_1 (point 2). Next assume that the price rises above p_0. This causes quantity demanded to be reduced below q_1. The net effect of these two shifts can be either an increase or a decrease in the quantity demanded. If price rises to p_2, the quantity demanded of q_2 still exceeds the original quantity q_0 (point 3); while a rise in price to p_3 leaves the final quantity of q_3 (point 4) below the original quantity of q_0.

tity shown by point x to the quantity shown by point w. An increase in household income increases demand from curve D_0 to curve D_1.

Figure 5.6 illustrates the combined effect of (i) a rise in demand, and (ii) a fall in the quantity demanded. The first of these is shown by a rightward shift in the whole demand curve. The second is shown by a movement upward, along a given demand curve.

SUPPLY

The Nature of Supply

The amount of a commodity that firms are able and willing to offer for sale is called the **quantity**

supplied. Supply is a desired flow: how much firms are willing to sell per period of time, not how much they actually sell.

We make a brief study of supply in this chapter, establishing only what is necessary for a theory of price. In later chapters we study the determinants of supply in some detail. In those chapters we first study the behaviour of individual firms, and then aggregate individual behaviour to obtain the behaviour of market supply. For present purposes, however, it is sufficient to go directly to market supply, the collective behaviour of all the firms in a particular market.

The Determinants of Quantity Supplied: The Supply Function

Four major determinants of the quantity supplied in a particular market are:

(1) the price of the commodity,
(2) the prices of factors of production,
(3) the goals of producing firms, and
(4) the state of technology.

This list of factors can be summarized in a **supply function**:

$$q_n^s = S(p_n, F_1, \ldots, F_m) \ ,$$

where q_n^s is the quantity supplied of commodity n, p_n is the price of that commodity, $F_1, \ldots, F_m$ is shorthand for the prices of all factors of production, and where the goals of producers and the state of technology determine the form of the function S. (Recall, once again, that the form of the function refers to the precise quantitative relation between the variable on the left-hand side and the variables on the right-hand side.)

Supply and Price

For a simple theory of price we need to know how quantity supplied varies with a commodity's own price, all other things being held constant. We are only concerned, therefore, with the *ceteris paribus* relation, $q_n^s = S(p_n)$. We will have much to say in later chapters about the relation between quantity supplied and price. For the moment it is sufficient to state the hypothesis that, *ceteris paribus, the quantity of any commodity that firms will produce and offer for sale is positively related to*

TABLE 5.4 A Market Supply Schedule for Carrots

Reference letter	Price of carrots (£s per tonne)	Quantity supplied (thousand tonnes per month)
u	20	5.0
v	40	46.0
w	60	77.5
x	80	100.0
y	100	115.0
z	120	122.5

The Table shows the quantities that producers wish to sell at various prices, *ceteris paribus.* For example, row *y* indicates that if the price were £100 per tonne producers would wish to sell 115,000 tonnes of carrots per month.

the commodity's own price, rising when price rises and falling when price falls. The reason is that, *ceteris paribus*, the higher the price of the commodity, the greater the profits that can be earned, and thus the greater the incentive to produce the commodity and offer it for sale.

FIGURE 5.7 A Supply Curve for Carrots

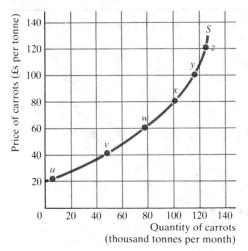

This supply curve relates quantity of carrots supplied to the price of carrots; its positive slope indicates that quantity supplied increases as price increases. The six points correspond to the price-quantity combinations shown in Table 5.4. Each row in the Table defines a point on the supply curve. The smooth curve drawn through all of the points, and labelled *S*, is the supply curve.

We now extend the numerical example of the carrot market to include the quantity of carrots supplied. The **supply schedule** given in Table 5.4 is analogous to the demand schedule in Table 5.2, but it records the quantities all producers wish to produce and sell at a number of alternative prices, rather than the quantities consumers wish to buy.

Next, the six points corresponding to each price-quantity combination shown in the Table are plotted in Figure 5.7. When we draw a smooth curve through the six points, we obtain a **supply curve** for carrots. The curve shows the quantity produced and offered for sale at each price. Since we are not considering individual firms in this chapter, all supply curves are market curves showing the behaviour of all firms in the market. Where that is obvious from the context, the adjective 'market' is usually omitted.

Shifts in the Supply Curve

A shift in the supply curve means that, at each price, a different quantity will be supplied. An increase in the quantity supplied at each price is illustrated in Table 5.5 and plotted in Figure 5.8. This change appears as a rightward shift in the supply curve. A decrease in the quantity supplied at each price would appear as a leftward shift.

For supply-curve shifts, there is an important general rule similar to the one stated earlier for demand curves:

> **a change in any of the variables (other than the commodity's own price) that affect the amount of a commodity that firms are willing to produce and sell will shift the whole supply curve for that commodity.**

The major possible causes of such shifts are summarized in the caption of Figure 5.9 and are considered briefly below.

Prices of inputs: All things that a firm uses to produce its outputs – such as materials, labour and machines – are called the firm's *inputs*. Other things being equal, the higher the price of any input used to make a commodity, the less will be the profit from making that commodity. Thus the higher the price of any input used by a firm, the lower will be the amount that the firm will produce and offer for sale at any given price of the commodity.

TABLE 5.5 Two Alternative Market Supply Schedules for Carrots

(1)	Price of carrots (£s per tonne) (2)	Original quantity supplied (thousand tonnes per month) (3)	New quantity supplied (thousand tonnes per month) (4)	(5)
u	20	5	28	u'
v	40	46	76	v'
w	60	77.5	102	w'
x	80	100	120	x'
y	100	115	132	y'
z	120	122.5	140	z'

A cost-saving innovation increases the quantity supplied at each price. As a result of a cost-saving innovation, the quantity that is supplied at £100 per tonne rises from 115,000 to 132,000 tonnes per month. A similar rise occurs at every price. Thus, the supply schedule relating columns 2 and 3 is replaced by one relating columns 2 and 4.

A rise in the costs of inputs shifts the supply curve to the left, indicating that less will be supplied at any given price; a fall in the cost of inputs shifts the supply curve to the right.

Goals of the firm: In economic theory, firms are usually assumed to have a single goal: profit maximization. Firms could, however, have other goals either in addition to, or as substitutes for, profit maximization. If firms worry about risk, they will pursue safer lines of activity even though these lines promise lower probable profits. If firms value size, they may produce and sell more than the profit-maximizing quantities. If they worry about their image in society, they may forsake highly profitable activities (such as the production of dioxin) when there is major public disapproval.

As long as firms prefers higher to lower profits, they will respond to changes in the profitabilities of alternative lines of action, and supply curves will slope upward. But if the importance that firms give to other goals changes, the supply curve will shift, indicating a changed willingness to supply the quantity at each given price.

Technology: At any time what is produced and how it is produced depends on what is known. Over time, knowledge changes; so do the quantities of individual commodities supplied. The enormous increase in production per worker that has been going on in industrial societies for about 200 years is largely due to improved methods of production. Discoveries in chemistry have led to lower costs of production of well-

established products, such as paints, and to a large variety of new products such as those made of plastics and synthetic fibres. The invention of transistors and silicon chips has radically changed products such as computers, audio-visual equipment and guidance-control systems, and the development of small computers is revolutionizing the production of countless other products.

FIGURE 5.8 Two Supply Curves for Carrots

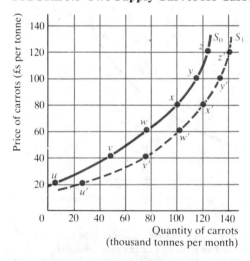

The rightward shift in the supply curve from S_0 to S_1 indicates an increase in the quantity supplied at each price. The lettered points correspond to those in Table 5.5. A rightward shift in the supply curve indicates an increase in supply in the sense that more carrots are supplied at each price.

FIGURE 5.9 Shifts in the Supply Curve

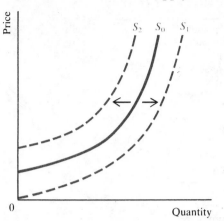

A shift in the supply curve from S_0 to S_1
indicates an increase in supply; a shift from S_0
to S_2 indicates a decrease in supply. An increase
in supply means that more is supplied at each price.
Such a rightward shift can be caused by certain
changes in producers' goals, improvements in
technology, or decreases in the costs of inputs that
are important in producing the commodity.

A technological change that decreases costs
will increase the profits earned at any given price
of the commodity. Since increased profitability
leads to increased production, this change shifts
the supply curve to the right, indicating an
increased willingness to produce the commodity
and offer it for sale at each possible price.

Movements Along Supply Curves Versus Shifts

As with demand, it is essential to distinguish
between a movement along the supply curve
(caused by a change in the commodity's own
price) and a shift of the whole curve (caused by a
change in something other than the commodity's
own price). We adopt the same terminology as
with demand: **supply** refers to the whole relation
between price and quantity supplied, and **quantity supplied** refers to a particular quantity
actually supplied at a particular price of the
commodity. Thus, when we speak of an *increase
or a decrease in supply*, we are referring to shifts in
the supply curve such as the ones illustrated in
Figures 5.8 and 5.9. When we speak of a *change in*

the quantity supplied, we mean a movement from
one point on the supply curve to another point on
the same curve.[1]

THE DETERMINATION OF PRICE

So far, demand and supply have been considered
separately. We now come to a key question: how
do the two forces of demand and supply interact
to determine price in a competitive market?
Table 5.6 brings together the demand and supply
schedules from Tables 5.2 and 5.4. Figure 5.10
shows both the demand and the supply curves on
a single graph; the six points on the demand curve
are labelled with upper-case letters, while the six
points on the supply curve are labelled with
lower-case letters, each letter referring to a
common price on both curves.

Quantity Supplied and Quantity Demanded at Various Prices

Consider first the point at which the two curves in
Figure 5.10 intersect: the market price is £60; the
quantity demanded is 77.5 thousand tonnes and
the quantity supplied is the same. Thus at that
price consumers wish to buy exactly the same
amount as producers wish to sell. Provided that
the demand curve is negatively sloped and the
supply curve positively sloped throughout their
entire ranges, there will be no other price at
which the quantity demanded equals the quantity supplied.

Now, consider prices below £60. At these
prices, consumers' desired purchases exceed producers' desired sales. It is easily seen, and you
should again check one or two examples, that at
all prices below £60, the quantity demanded
exceeds the quantity supplied. Furthermore, the
lower the price, the larger the excess of the one
over the other. The amount by which the quantity demanded exceeds the quantity supplied is
called the **excess demand**, which is defined as
quantity demanded *minus* quantity supplied
$(q^d - q^s)$.

---

[1] As with demand, an alternative terminology refers to an
increase in the quantity supplied as an *expansion of supply* and
a reduction in the quantity supplied as a *contraction of supply*.

TABLE 5.6 Demand and Supply Schedules for Carrots and Equilibrium Price

Price per tonne (£s)	Quantity demanded (thousand tonnes per month)	Quantity supplied (thousand tonnes (per month)	Excess demand (quantity demanded minus quantity supplied) (thousand tonnes per month)
20	110.0	5.0	105.0
40	90.0	46.0	44.0
60	**77.5**	**77.5**	**0.0**
80	67.5	100.0	−32.5
100	62.5	115.0	−52.5
120	60.0	122.5	−62.5

Equilibrium occurs where quantity demanded equals quantity supplied – where there is neither excess demand nor excess supply. These schedules are repeated from Tables 5.2 and 5.4. The equilibrium price is £60. For lower prices, there is excess demand; for higher prices, there is excess supply.

Finally, consider prices higher than £60. At these prices consumers wish to buy less than producers wish to sell. Thus quantity supplied exceeds quantity demanded. It is easily seen, and you should check a few examples, that for any price above £60, quantity supplied exceeds quantity demanded. Furthermore, the higher the price, the larger the excess of the one over the other. In this case there is negative excess demand ($q^d - q^s < 0$). Negative excess demand is usually, however, referred to as **excess supply**, which measures the amount by which supply exceeds demand ($q^s - q^d$).

Changes in Price When Quantity Demanded Does Not Equal Quantity Supplied

Where there is excess demand, households will be unable to buy all they wish to buy; when there is excess supply, firms will be unable to sell all they wish to sell. In both cases some people will not be able to do what they would like to do, and we might expect some action to be taken as a result.

To develop a theory about how the market does behave in the face of excess demand or excess supply, we now make two further assumptions. First we assume that *when there is excess supply, the market price will fall*. Producers,

unable to sell some of their goods, may begin to offer to sell at lower prices; purchasers, observing the glut of unsold output, may begin to offer lower prices. For either or both of these reasons, the price will fall.

Second, we assume that *when there is excess demand, market price will rise*. Individual households, unable to buy as much as they would like to buy, may offer higher prices in an effort to get more of the available goods for themselves; suppliers, who could sell more than their total production, may begin to ask higher prices for the quantities that they have produced. For either or both of these reasons, prices will rise.

The Equilibrium Price

For any price above £60, according to our theory, the price tends to fall; for any price below £60, the price tends to rise. At a price of £60, there is neither excess demand creating a shortage, nor excess supply creating a glut; quantity supplied is equal to quantity demanded and there is no tendency for the price to change. The price of £60, where the supply and demand curves intersect, is the price towards which the actual market price will tend. It is called the **equilibrium price**: the price at which quantity demanded equals quantity supplied. The amount that is bought and sold at the equilibrium price is called the **equilibrium quantity**. The term *equilib-*

FIGURE 5.10 Determination of the Equilibrium Price of Carrots

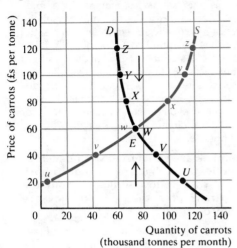

The equilibrium price corresponds to the intersection of the demand and supply curves. Point *E* indicates the equilibrium. At a price of £60 quantity demanded equals quantity supplied. At prices above equilibrium there is excess supply and downward pressure on price. At prices below equilibrium there is excess demand and upward pressure on price. The pressures on price are represented by the vertical arrows.

rium means a state of balance; it occurs when desired purchases equal desired sales.

When quantity demanded equals quantity supplied, we say that the market is in **equilibrium**. When quantity demanded does not equal quantity supplied we say that the market is in **disequilibrium**. We may now summarize our *theory*.

Hypotheses concerning a competitive market:

(1) **all demand curves have a negative slope throughout their entire range,**

(2) **all supply curves have a positive slope throughout their entire range,**

(3) **price changes if, and only if, there is excess demand; rising if excess demand is positive and falling if it is negative.**

Implications:

(1) **there is no more than one price at which quantity demanded equals**

quantity supplied: equilibrium is unique,

(2) **only at the equilibrium price will market price be constant,**

(3) **if either the demand or the supply curve shifts, the equilibrium price and quantity will change.**

Shifts in Demand and Supply

Earlier in this chapter, we studied shifts in demand and supply curves. Recall that a rightward shift in the relevant curve means that more is demanded or supplied *at each market price*, while a leftward shift means that less is demanded or supplied *at each market price*. How does a shift in either curve affect price and quantity?

The answers to this question are called the 'laws' of supply and demand. Each of the laws summarizes what happens when an initial position of equilibrium is upset by some shift in either the demand or the supply curve, and a new equilibrium position is then established. The sense in which it is correct to call these propositions 'laws' is discussed in Box 5.1.

To discover the effects of each of the curve shifts that we wish to study, we use the method known as **comparative statics.**[1] We start from a position of equilibrium and then introduce the change to be studied. The new equilibrium position is determined and compared with the original one. The differences between the two positions of equilibrium must result from the change that was introduced, for everything else has been held constant.

The four laws of demand and supply are derived in Figure 5.11, which generalizes our specific discussion about carrots. Previously, we had given the axes specific labels, but from here on we will simplify. Because it is intended to apply to any commodity, the horizontal axis is simply labelled *Quantity*. This should be understood to mean quantity per period in whatever units output is measured. *Price*, the vertical axis, should be understood to mean the price measured as £s per unit of quantity for the same

---

[1] The term *static* is used because we are not concerned about the actual path by which the market goes from the first equilibrium position to the second. Analysis of that path would be described as *dynamic analysis*.

BOX 5.1 THE 'LAWS' OF SUPPLY AND DEMAND

As with all theories, the implications of the theory of demand and supply may be looked at in two quite distinct ways. First, they are logical deductions from a set of assumptions about behaviour. When we consider the truth of the implications, we are concerned with whether or not they are logically correct deductions. If we discovered that we made mistakes in our reasoning process, then we would conclude that the alleged implications are false in the sense that they do not follow from the assumptions of the theory. Second, the implications are predictions about real-world events. When we consider the truth of the implications, we are concerned with whether or not they are empirically correct. If one or more of the assumptions are empirically incorrect, the predictions of the theory are likely to be found to be at variance with the facts. In this case, we would conclude that the predictions are false in the sense that they are contradicted by real-world observations.

Consider an example. The sentence '*If* the demand curve for motorcars slopes downwards and *if* the supply curve slopes upwards, *then* an increase in demand for cars will raise their equilibrium price' is logically correct in the sense that the 'then' statement follows logically from the two 'if' statements. The single statement 'A rise in the demand for motorcars will increase the price of

motorcars' is one that may or may not be empirically true. If any one of the assumptions of the theory is not empirically correct for motorcars, the statement may be found to be empirically false, even though it is a correct logical deduction from the theory's assumptions. If, for example, the market for cars does not respond to excess demand with a rise in price, the statement may be empirically false: even though a rise in demand for motorcars does create excess demand, market price will not rise.

Economists are concerned with developing implications that are correct in both senses – they follow logically from the assumptions of a theory, and they are factually correct.

The use of the term 'laws' in the popular phrase 'the laws of supply and demand' implies that the four implications have been shown to be true in the empirical sense. We must remember, however, that these 'laws' are nothing more than predictions that are always open to testing. There is considerable evidence that the predictions are consistent with the facts in many markets. In other markets, especially those for durable consumer goods such as cars and TV sets, it is not so clear that they are fully consistent with empirical observations.

commodity. The laws of supply and demand are:

(1) **A rise in the demand for a commodity (a rightward shift of the demand curve) causes an increase in both the equilibrium price and the equilibrium quantity bought and sold.**

(2) **A fall in the demand for a commodity (a leftward shift of the demand curve) causes a decrease in both the equilibrium price and the equilibrium quantity bought and sold.**

(3) **A rise in the supply of a commodity (a rightward shift of the supply curve) causes a decrease in the equilibrium price and an increase in the equilibrium quantity bought and sold.**

(4) **A fall in the supply of a commodity (a leftward shift of the supply curve) causes an increase in the equilibrium price and a decrease in the equilibrium quantity bought and sold.**

In Figures 5.5 and 5.9 we summarized the many events that cause demand and supply curves to shift. Using the four 'laws' just worked out, we can understand the link between these events and changes in market prices and quantities. To take one example, a rise in the price of butter will lead to an increase in both the price of margarine and the quantity bought (because a rise in the price of one commodity causes a rightward shift in the demand curves for its substitutes, and 'law' (1) tells us that such a shift causes price and quantity to increase).

The theory of the determination of price by demand and supply is beautiful in its simplicity and yet powerful in its range of applications

Prices in Inflation

Up to now we have developed the theory of the prices of individual commodities under the assumption that all other prices remained constant. Does this mean that the theory is inapplicable during an inflationary period when almost

FIGURE 5.11 The 'Laws' of Demand and Supply

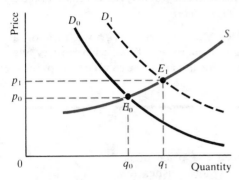

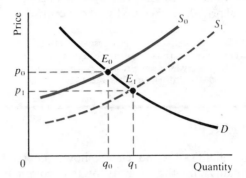

(i) The effect of shifts in the demand curve   **(ii) The effect of shifts in the supply curve**

The effects on equilibrium price and quantity of shifts in either demand or supply are called the laws of demand and supply. *An increase in demand.* In (i) assume that the original demand and supply curves are D_0 and S, which intersect to produce equilibrium at E_0, with a price of p_0 and a quantity of q_0. An increase in demand shifts the demand curve to D_1, taking the new equilibrium to E_1. Price rises to p_1 and quantity rises to q_1.

A decrease in demand. In (i) assume that the original demand and supply curves are D_1 and S, which intersect to produce equilibrium at E_1, with a price of p_1 and a quantity of q_1. A decrease in demand shifts the demand curve to D_0, taking the new equilibrium to E_0. Price falls to p_0 and quantity falls to q_0.

An increase in supply. In (ii) assume that the original demand and supply curves are D and S_0, which intersect to produce an equilibrium at E_0, with a price of p_0 and a quantity of q_0. An increase in supply shifts the supply curve to S_1, taking the new equilibrium to E_1. Price falls to p_1 and quantity rises to q_1.

A decrease in supply. In (ii) assume that the original demand and supply curves are D and S_1, which intersect to produce an equilibrium at E_1, with a price of p_1 and a quantity of q_1. A decrease in supply shifts the supply curve to S_0, taking the new equilibrium to E_0. Price rises to p_0, and quantity falls to q_0.

all prices are rising? Fortunately the answer is no.

We have mentioned several times that what matters for demand and supply is the price of the commodity in question relative to the prices of other commodities. This is called a **relative price**.

In an inflationary world, a commodity's relative price can be measured by changes in the commodity's own price relative to changes in the average price of all other commodities. If, during a period when the general price level rose by 40 per cent, the price of oranges rose by 60 per cent, then the price of oranges rose relative to the price level as a whole. Oranges became *relatively* expensive. However, if the price of oranges had risen by only 30 per cent when the general price level rose by 40 per cent, then the relative price of oranges would have fallen. Although the money price of oranges rose substantially, oranges became *relatively* cheap.

In Lewis Carroll's famous story *Through the Looking Glass*, Alice finds a country where everyone has to run in order to stay still. So it is with inflation. A commodity's price must rise as fast as the general level of prices just to keep its relative price constant.

It has been convenient in this chapter to analyse a change in a particular price in the context of a constant price level. The analysis is easily extended, however, to an inflationary period by remembering that any force that raises the price of one commodity when other prices remain constant will, given general inflation, raise the price of that commodity faster than the price level is rising. For example, a change in tastes in favour of carrots that would raise their price by 20 per cent when other prices were constant, would raise their price by 32 per cent if the general price level goes up by 10 per cent.[1] In

each case the price of carrots rises 20 per cent *relative to the average of all prices*. This average is called *the price level*.

In price theory, whenever we talk of a change in the price of one commodity, we mean a change relative to all other prices.

---

[1] Let the price level be 100 in the first case and 110 in the second. Let the price of carrots be 120 in the first case and x in the second. To preserve the same relative price, we need x such that $120/100 = x/110$, which makes $x = 132$.

SUMMARY

1. A household's demand curve shows the relation between the price of a commodity and the quantity of that commodity the household wishes to purchase per period of time. It is drawn on the assumption that income, tastes and all other prices remain constant. Its negative slope indicates that the lower the price of the commodity, the more the household wishes to purchase.

2. The market demand curve is the horizontal sum of the demand curves of all the individual households. The demand curve for a normal good shifts right when average income rises, or the price of a substitute rises, or the price of a complement falls or tastes change in favour of the commodity. It shifts left with the opposite changes.

3. A movement along a demand curve indicates a change in quantity demanded in response to a change in the commodity's own price; a shift in a demand curve indicates a change in the quantity demanded at each price in response to a change in one of the conditions held constant along a demand curve.

4. The supply curve for a commodity shows the relationship between its price and the quantity producers wish to produce and offer for sale per period of time. It is drawn on the assumption that all other forces that influence quantity supplied remain constant, and its positive slope indicates that the higher the price, the more producers wish to sell.

5. A supply curve shifts in response to changes in the prices of the inputs used by producers, and to changes in technology. The shift represents a change in the amount supplied at each price. A movement along a supply curve indicates that a different quantity is actually being supplied in response to a change in the commodity's own price.

6. At the *equilibrium price* the quantity demanded equals the quantity supplied. At any price below equilibrium there will be excess demand; at any price above equilibrium there will be excess supply. Graphically, equilibrium occurs where the demand and the supply curves intersect.

7. A rise in demand raises both equilibrium price and quantity; a fall in demand lowers both. A rise in supply raises equilibrium quantity but lowers equilibrium price; a fall in supply lowers equilibrium quantity but raises equilibrium price. These are the so-called laws of supply and demand.

8. Price theory is most simply developed in the context of a constant price level. Price changes discussed in the theory are changes relative to the average level of all prices. In an inflationary period a rise in the *relative price* of one commodity means that its price rises by more than the rise in the general price level; a fall in its relative price means that its price rises by less than the rise in the general price level.

TOPICS FOR REVIEW

- Quantity demanded and the demand function
- The demand schedule and the demand curve for an individual and for the market
- Shifts in the demand curve and movements along the curve
- Substitutes and complements
- Quantity supplied and the supply function
- The supply schedule and the supply curve
- Shifts in the supply curve and movements along the curve
- Excess demand and excess supply
- Equilibrium and disequilibrium prices
- The 'laws' of demand and supply
- Money prices and relative prices

6

Elasticity and Consumers' Surplus

PRICE ELASTICITY OF DEMAND

Often it is not enough just to know whether quantity rises or falls in response to a change in price; it may be important to know by how much. To measure this we use the concept of elasticity.

Suppose there is a rise in the supply of a farm crop. According to our 'laws', this will lead to a fall in price and a rise in quantity sold. But will these changes be large or small? Figure 6.1 shows that the answers depend, at least partly, on the slope of the demand curve. *Ceteris paribus*, the price change tends to be larger when the demand curve is steep and smaller when it is flat.

The difference between the two cases analysed in Figure 6.1 may be significant for policy. Consider what will happen, for example, if the government pays a subsidy for each tonne of carrots grown. This will shift the supply curve of carrots to the right because more will be produced at each price. If the demand for carrots is as shown in part (i) of the Figure, the effect of the government's policy will be to reduce carrot prices slightly, while greatly increasing the quantity grown and consumed. If, however, the demand is as shown in part (ii), the effect of the policy will be to reduce carrot prices greatly but to increase carrot production and consumption by only a small amount. If the purpose of the policy is to increase the quantity that is produced and consumed, then the policy will be a great success when the demand curve is similar to the one shown in part (i), but a failure when the demand curve is similar to that shown in part (ii). If, however, the main purpose of the policy is to achieve a large reduction in the price of carrots, the policy will be a failure when demand is as shown in part (i) but a great success when demand is as shown in part (ii).

Measuring the Responsiveness of Demand to Price

The degree to which quantity demanded responds to changes in the commodity's own price is called the *responsiveness of demand*. Sometimes we wish to know how the responsiveness of one product changes over time, or we may wish to compare the responsiveness of several products or several alternative demand curves for one

FIGURE 6.1 The Effect of the Shape of the Demand Curve

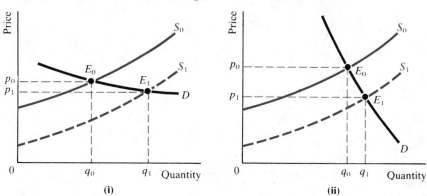

(i)   (ii)

The flatter the demand curve, *ceteris paribus*, the less the change in price and the greater the change in quantity. Both parts of the Figure are drawn on the same scale. Both show the same rightward shift in the supply curve. In each part, the initial equilibrium is at price p_0 and quantity q_0, while the new equilibrium is at p_1 and q_1. In part (i), the effect of the shift in supply from S_0 to S_1 is a slight fall in the price and a large increase in quantity. In part (ii), the effect of the identical shift in the supply curve from S_0 to S_1 is a large fall in the price and a relatively small increase in quantity.

product. In Figure 6.1 we were able to compare the responsiveness of quantity demanded along the two demand curves because they were drawn on the same scale. But you should not try to compare two curves without making sure that the scales are the same. Also, you must not leap to conclusions about responsiveness of quantity demanded on the basis of the apparent steepness of a single curve. The hazards of so doing are illustrated in Figure 6.2. Both parts of the Figure plot the same demand curve, but the choice of scale on the quantity axis serves to make one curve look steep and the other flat.

Rather than look at geometrical shape, as we just did, we might concentrate on actual quant-

ities. Assume that we have the information shown in Table 6.1. Does this tell us enough to make meaningful comparisons?

There are two problems. First, a reduction of, say, 10 pence will be a large price cut for a low-priced commodity, but an insignificant price cut for a high-priced commodity. It is more revealing for purposes of comparison to know the percentage change in the prices of the various commodities. Second, by a similar argument, the amount by which quantity demanded changes is not very revealing, unless we know the original quantity. An increase of 10,000 tonnes is a very significant change if the quantity formerly bought was, say, 15,000 tonnes, while it is but a drop in a very large

TABLE 6.1 Changes in Prices and Quantities

Commodity	Reduction in price	Increase in quantity demanded
Sausages	£0.10 per pound	7,500 lbs
Men's ties	£0.15 per tie	4,500 ties
Radios	£0.05 per radio	20 radios

Data for absolute changes in prices and quantities do not allow us to judge the degree of responsiveness. The Table shows hypothetical data for a change in price and the resulting change in quantity demanded for these commodities.

FIGURE 6.2 One Demand Curve Drawn on Two Scales

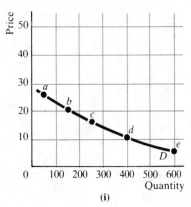
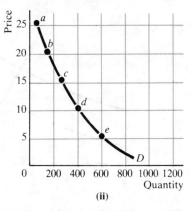

Suitable choice of scale can make any demand curve appear steep or flat.
The curves in parts (i) and (ii) are the same demand curve, as can easily be checked by
noting that each lettered point in part (ii) measures the same price-quantity relation as
in part (i). Because the same distance on the quantity axes stands for twice as much in
part (ii) as in part (i), the curve is steeper when plotted in graph (ii) than when plotted
in graph (i).

bucket if the original quantity was 10,000,000
tonnes.

Table 6.2 records the original levels of price
and quantity, as well as the changes. From it we
can derive more relevant information on how
large is the decrease in price, expressed as a
percentage of the original price, and how large is
the increase in quantity, expressed as a percentage of the quantity originally being sold? This
information is recorded in the last two columns of
the Table.

They show that quite a large percentage
change in the price of sausages brought about a
much smaller percentage change in quantity
purchased. On the other hand, although the

increase in the number of radios purchased was
only twenty, this is quite a large percentage
change in the quantity *in comparison to the
percentage change in price that brought it about.*

A Formal Definition

The above example leads us to the concept of the
price elasticity of demand, which is defined as
the percentage change in quantity demanded
divided by the percentage change in price that
brought it about. This elasticity is usually symbolized by the Greek letter eta, η:

$$\eta = \frac{\text{percentage change in quantity demanded}}{\text{percentage change in price}}.$$

TABLE 6.2 Original and New Prices and Quantities

Commodity	Original price	Change in price	Original quantity	Change in quantity	% change in price	% change in quantity
Sausages (lb)	£0.80	−£0.10	108.750	7,500	−12.50	6.90
Men's ties	£4.98	−£0.15	144,750	4,500	− 3.01	3.11
Radios	£50.00	−£0.05	9,980	20	− 0.10	0.20

**The importance of changes in prices and quantities can be judged when
original prices and quantities are known.** The data shows the original price-
quantity combinations from which the changes shown in Table 6.1 occurred. By
calculating percentages of original prices and quantities, the significance of the price
and quantity changes can be assessed.

Many different elasticities are used in economics. To distinguish η from the others, the full term *price elasticity of demand* can be used. Since η is by far the most commonly used elasticity, economists often drop the adjective *price* and refer to it merely as *elasticity of demand*, or sometimes just as *elasticity*. When more than one kind of elasticity could be involved, however, η should be given its full title.

When the above formula is used to calculate elasticity, two problems arise. First, when we deal with a percentage change, we must define the change as a percentage of something. Should it be the original amount? This is simple but has the disadvantage of making the percentage change, and hence the elasticity, depend on the direction of the movement. Thus if we define the percentage change in price as the change from the original price, a movement from £1.00 to £1.20 is a 20 per cent change (price increased by 1/5), while a movement from £1.20 to £1.00 is only a $16\frac{2}{3}$ per cent change (price decreased by 1/6). If, however, we take the percentage change to be the change in price divided by the average price (£1.10), both the change from £1.00 to £1.20 and the change from £1.20 to £1.00 are a percentage change of 18.18 per cent. It is desirable that the elasticity measured between two points on a demand curve should have a unique value, whether the movement is from the first point to the second or the second point to the first. To ensure that this is the case, we calculate the percentage change in price as the change in price divided by the *average* of the original and the new price. Similarly, the percentage change in quantity is the change in quantity divided by the *average* of the original and the new quantities.

The second problem arises from the sign of the elasticity measure. Because of the negative slope of the demand curve, the price and quantity will always change in opposite directions from each other. One change will be positive and the other negative, making the measured elasticity of demand negative. This would pose no problem except for two unfortunate habits of economists. First, sometimes either by carelessness or by design, the minus sign is dropped and elasticity

reported as a positive number. Second, it is almost universal practice when comparing two elasticities to compare their absolute, not their algebraic, values. For example, if commodity X has an elasticity of -2 while commodity Y has an elasticity of -10, economists will say that Y has a greater elasticity than X (in spite of the fact that -10 is *less than* -2). As long as it is understood that absolute and not algebraic values are being compared, this usage is acceptable.[1] After all, the demand curve with the larger absolute elasticity *is* the one where quantity demanded is more responsive to price changes. For example, an elasticity of -10 indicates greater response of quantity to price than does an elasticity of -2.

The issues just discussed need not cause us trouble as long as we remember the basics:

demand elasticity is measured by the ratio of the percentage change in quantity demanded divided by the percentage change in price that brought it about; for normal, negatively sloped demand curves elasticity is negative, but two elasticities are compared by comparing their absolute values.

We may now calculate the elasticities implied by the data in Table 6.2. This is done in Table 6.3. According to the calculated elasticities, the demand for radios is more responsive to a price change than the demand for sausages and men's ties. The percentage change in the quantity of radios demanded is twice as large as the percentage change in price that brought it about ($\eta = 2$); the percentage change in the quantity of men's ties demanded is the same as the price change that brought it about ($\eta = 1$); but the percentage change in the quantity of sausages demanded is only half as large as the price change that brought it about ($\eta = 0.5$).

Interpreting Demand Elasticity

The value of elasticity of demand ranges from zero to minus infinity. In this section, however, we concentrate on absolute values, and so ask by how much the value *exceeds zero*. It is zero if there is no change in quantity demanded when price changes, i.e. when quantity demanded does not respond to a price change. A demand curve of zero elasticity is shown in Figure 6.3(i). It is said to be *perfectly* or *completely* inelastic.

---

[1] The absolute value is the magnitude without the sign. Thus, for example, -2 and $+2$ have the same absolute value of 2.

TABLE 6.3 Calculation of Price Elasticities

	Old amount	New amount	Change in amount	Average amount	Percentage change	Elasticity
Sausages						
Price (£s)	0.80	0.70	−0.10	0.750	$\dfrac{-0.10}{0.750}100 = -13.33$	$\left.\rule{0pt}{40pt}\right\}\ \eta = \dfrac{+6.67}{-13.33} = -0.5$
Quantity (lbs)	108,750	116,250	7,500	112,500	$\dfrac{7{,}500}{112{,}500}100 = +6.67$	
Men's ties						
Price (£s)	4.98	4.83	−0.15	4.905	$\dfrac{-0.15}{4.905}100 = -3.06$	$\left.\rule{0pt}{40pt}\right\}\ \eta = \dfrac{+3.06}{-3.06} = -1.0$
Quantity	144,750	149,250	4,500	147,000	$\dfrac{4{,}500}{147{,}000}100 = +3.06$	
Radios						
Price (£s)	50.00	49.95	−0.05	49.975	$\dfrac{-0.05}{49.975}100 = -0.10$	$\left.\rule{0pt}{40pt}\right\}\ \eta = \dfrac{+0.20}{-0.10} = -2.0$
Quantity	9,980	10,000	20	9,990	$\dfrac{20}{9{,}990}100 = +0.20$	

Elasticity is the ratio of the appropriately calculated percentage changes in price and quantity. The first steps in the Table calculate the average of the original and the new prices and quantities. The changes are then expressed as percentages of these averages. Finally elasticity is calculated as the ratio of the percentage change in quantity to the percentage change in price.

As long as there is some positive response of quantity demanded to a change in price, the absolute value of elasticity will exceed zero. The more the response, the larger the elasticity. As long as this value is less than one, however, the percentage change in quantity is less than the percentage change in price.

When elasticity is equal to one, the two percentage changes are then equal to each other. This is the important boundary case of *unit elasticity*. A demand curve having this elasticity over its whole range is shown in Figure 6.3(ii).[1]

When the percentage change in quantity demanded exceeds the percentage change in price, the elasticity of demand is greater than one. When elasticity is infinitely large, there exists some small price reduction that will raise demand from zero to infinity. Above the critical price, consumers will buy nothing. At the critical price, they will buy all that they can obtain (an infinite amount, if it were available). The graph of a demand curve having infinite price elasticity is shown in Figure 6.3(iii). Such a demand curve is said to be *perfectly* or *completely elastic*. (This

---

[1] The curve is called a rectangular hyperbola. Any rectangular hyperbola has the formula *x* times *y* equals a constant. In this case, the two variables are price, *p*, and quantity, *q*, so the formula of the unit-elastic demand curve is $pq = C$. Beginners are often confused by the fact that any demand curve having a constant elasticity other than zero or infinity is a curve and *not* a straight line. In Figure 6.3(ii), as we move down on the price axis, equal *absolute* changes in price (say, continuous price cuts of 10p) represent larger and larger *percentage* changes. But as we move outwards on the quantity axis, equal *absolute changes* represent smaller and smaller *percentage changes* in quantity, because the quantity from which we start is becoming larger and larger. If the ratio *percentage change in quantity/percentage change in price* is to be kept constant, equal absolute price cuts must be met with larger and larger absolute increases in quantity. Thus, geometrically, the curve must get flatter as price becomes lower and lower. This increasing flatness of the demand curve indicates an increasing responsiveness of the absolute quantity demanded to any given absolute price change.

FIGURE 6.3 Four Demand Curves

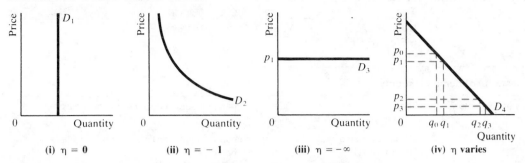

(i) $\eta = 0$ (ii) $\eta = -1$ (iii) $\eta = -\infty$ (iv) η **varies**

**Elasticity is constant along the first three curves but variable along the
fourth.** D_1 has *zero elasticity*: the quantity demanded does not change at all when
price changes. D_2 has *unit elasticity*: a given percentage increase in price brings an
equal percentage decrease in quantity at all points on the curve. D_3 has *infinite
elasticity*: at price p_1, an infinitely large quantity is demanded, but any price increase,
no matter how small, reduces demand to zero. D_4 has a *variable elasticity*. The change
in price from p_0 to p_1 is a small percentage of the average price ($[p_0 + p_1]/2$) while the
change in quantity from q_0 to q_1 is a large percentage of the average quantity
($[q_0 + q_1]/2$). Thus elasticity is high. However, the change in price from p_2 to p_3 is a
large percentage of the average price, while the change in quantity from q_2 to q_3 is a
small percentage of the average quantity. Thus elasticity is low.

unlikely looking case will turn out to be important later when we study the demand for the
output of a single firm with many competitors.)

When the percentage change in quantity is less
than the percentage change in price (elasticity
less than one), the demand is said to be **inelastic**.
When the percentage change in quantity is
greater than the percentage change in price
(elasticity greater than one), the demand is said to
be **elastic**. Box 6.1 on page 84 summarizes the
discussion. The terminology in the Table is
important, and you should become familiar with
it.

A demand curve need not have the same
elasticity over its entire range. A downward-
sloping straight line, such as the one shown in
part (iv) of Figure 6.3, has an elasticity that varies
from infinity at the price axis to zero at the
quantity axis. The intuitive reason is that, along
this demand curve, equal absolute changes in
price cause equal absolute changes in quantity,
but near the price intercept these equal changes
result in large *percentage* changes in quantity and
small percentage changes in price, while near the
quantity intercept they result in large percentage
changes in price and small percentage changes in
quantity.

Price Elasticity and Changes
in Total Expenditure

The total revenue received by the sellers is the
total amount spent by purchasers (minus any part
of the selling value that represents government
taxes, which for simplicity we here assume to be
zero). How does this revenue react when the price
of a product is changed? The simplest example
will show that it may rise or fall in response to a
decrease in price. Suppose 100 units of a commodity are being sold at a unit price of £1. The
price is then cut to £0.90. If the quantity sold
rises to 110, the total revenue of the sellers falls
from £100 to £99; but if quantity sold rises to
120, total revenue rises from £100 to £108.

The change in total revenue when price
changes is related to the elasticity of demand. If
elasticity is less than unity, the percentage change
in price will exceed the percentage change in
quantity. The price change will then be the more
important of the two changes, so that total
revenue will change in the same direction as the
price changes. If, however, elasticity exceeds
unity, the percentage change in quantity will
exceed the percentage change in price. The
quantity change will then be the more important

BOX 6.1 THE TERMINOLOGY OF ELASTICITY

TERMINOLOGY	NUMERICAL MEASURE OF ELASTICITY	VERBAL DESCRIPTION
Price elasticity of demand (supply)		
Perfectly or completely, inelastic	Zero	Quantity demanded (supplied) does not change as price changes
Inelastic	Greater than zero, but less than one	Quantity demanded (supplied) changes by a smaller percentage than does price
Unit elasticity	One	Quantity demanded (supplied) changes by exactly the same percentage as does price
Elastic	Greater than one, but less than infinity	Quantity demanded (supplied) changes by a larger percentage than does price
Perfectly, or completely or infinitely, elastic	Infinity	Purchasers (sellers) are prepared to buy (sell) all they can at some price and none at all at an even slightly higher (lower) price
Income elasticity of demand		
Inferior good	Negative	Quantity demanded decreases as income increases
Normal good	Positive	Quantity demanded increases as income increases:
Income inelastic	Greater than zero, but less than one	less than in proportion to income increase
Income elastic	Greater than one	more than in proportion to income increase
Cross-elasticity of demand		
Substitute	Positive	Price increase of a substitute leads to an increase in quantity demanded of this good (and also less of substitute)
Complement	Negative	Price increase of a complement leads to a decrease in quantity demanded of this good (and also less of the complement)

change, so that total revenue will change in the same direction as quantity changes (that is, in the opposite direction to the change in price).

(1) If elasticity of demand exceeds unity (demand elastic), a fall in price increases total consumer expenditure and a rise in price reduces it.

(2) If elasticity is less than unity (demand inelastic), a fall in price reduces total expenditure and a rise in price increases it.

(3) If elasticity of demand is unity, a rise or a fall in price leaves total expenditure unaffected.[1]

You should now take the earlier example of radios, ties and sausages and calculate what happened to total revenue when price fell in each case. When you have done this, you will see that

---

[1] Algebraically, total revenue is price *times* quantity. If, for example, the equilibrium price and quantity are p_1 and q_1, then total revenue is $p_1 q_1$. On a demand-curve diagram, price is given by a vertical distance and quantity by a horizontal distance. It follows that on such a diagram total revenue is given by the *area* of a rectangle, the length of whose sides represent price and quantity.

in the case of sausages, where the demand was inelastic, a cut in price lowered the revenue of sellers; in the case of radios, where the demand was elastic, a cut in price raised the revenue earned by sellers. The borderline case is provided by men's ties – here the demand elasticity was unity, and the cut in price left total revenue unchanged.

What Determines Elasticity of Demand?

The main determinant of elasticity is the availability of substitutes. Some commodities, such as margarine, cabbage, lamb and Renault 5s, have quite close substitutes – butter, other green vegetables, beef and similar makes of cars. A change in the price of any one of these commodities, *the prices of the substitutes remaining constant,* will lead consumers to substitute one commodity for another. A fall in price leads consumers to buy more of the commodity and less of its substitutes; and a rise in price leads consumers to buy less of the commodity and more of its substitutes. More broadly defined commodities, such as all foods, all clothing, cigarettes and petrol, have few if any satisfactory substitutes. A rise in their price can be expected to cause a smaller fall in quantity demanded than would be the case if close substitutes were available.

> **A commodity with close substitutes tends to have an elastic demand, one with no close substitutes an inelastic demand.**

Closeness of substitutes – and thus measured elasticity – depends both on how the commodity is defined and on the time-period under consideration. This is explored in the following sections.

Definition of the commodity: Food is a necessity of life; there is no substitute for food. Thus, for food taken as a whole, demand is inelastic over a large price range. It does not follow, however, that any one food, such as white bread or beef, is a necessity in the same sense; each of these has close substitutes, such as brown bread and pork. Individual foods can have quite elastic demands, and they frequently do.

Durable goods provide a similar example. Durables as a whole have less elastic demands than do individual kinds of durable goods. For

example, when the price of television sets rises, many households may replace their lawnmower or their vacuum cleaner instead of buying that extra television set. Thus, while their purchases of television sets fall, their total purchases of durables may not.

Because most specific manufactured goods have close substitutes, they tend to have price-elastic demands. Millinery, for example, has been estimated to have an elasticity of -3.0. In contrast, clothing in general tends to be inelastic.

> **Any one of a group of related products will tend to have an elastic demand, even though the demand for the group as a whole may be inelastic.**

Long-run and short-run elasticity of demand: Because it takes time to develop satisfactory substitutes, a demand that is inelastic in the short run may prove elastic when enough time has passed. For example, when cheap electric power was first brought to rural areas of the United States in the 1930s, few households were wired for electricity. The initial measurements showed demand for electricity to be very inelastic. Some commentators even argued that it was foolish to have invested so much money in rural electrification because farmers did not buy electricity even at low prices. But gradually households became electrified and purchased electric appliances, while new industries moved into the area to take advantage of the cheap electric power. Thus, when measured over several years, the response of quantity demanded to the fall in price was quite large, even though, when measured over a short period, the response was quite small.

Petrol provides a similar, more recent example. Before the first OPEC price shocks of the mid-1970s, the demand for petrol was thought to be highly inelastic because of the absence of satisfactory substitutes. But the large price increases over the 1970s led to the development of smaller, more fuel-efficient cars and to less driving. The most recent estimates of elasticity of demand for petrol have risen from around 0.6 to around unity. Given another decade in which to develop substitutes, petrol demand might have proved elastic had the price not fallen back towards its earlier relative level. Each of these measures relates the change in price at one point in time to the change in quantity over time. What is found is that the larger the time-period over which the change in quantity is measured, the larger the elasticity tends to be.

The response of quantity demanded to a given price change, and thus the measured price elasticity of demand, will tend to be greater the longer the time-span considered.

The different quantity responses can be shown by different demand curves. Every demand curve shows the response of consumer demand to a change in price. For such commodities as corn-flakes and pillowcases, the full response occurs quickly and there is little reason to worry about longer-term effects. For these commodities a single demand curve will suffice. Other commodities are typically used in connection with highly durable appliances or machines. A change in price of, say, electricity or petrol may not have its major effect until the stock of appliances and machines using these commodities has been adjusted. This adjustment may take a long time. It is useful to identify two kinds of demand curve for such commodities. A *short-run demand curve* shows the response of quantity demanded to a change in price, *given* the existing quantities of the durable goods that use the commodity, and *given* existing supplies of substitute commodities. A different short-run demand curve will exist for each such structure of durable goods and substitute commodities.

The *long-run demand curve* shows the response of quantity demanded to a change in price after enough time has passed to allow all adjustments to be made. The relation between long-run and short-run demand curves is shown in Figure 6.4. Assume for example that there is a large rise in the price of electricity. The initial response will be along the short-run demand curve. There will be some fall in quantity demanded, but the percentage drop is likely to be less than the percentage rise in price, making short-run demand inelastic. Over time, however, many people will replace their existing electric cookers with gas cookers as they wear out. New homes will also be more often equipped with gas rather than electric appliances. Over time, factories will switch to relatively cheaper sources of power. When all these types of long-run adaptations

FIGURE 6.4 Short-run and Long-run Demand Curves

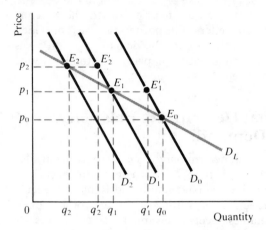

The long-run demand curve is more elastic than the short-run curves. D_L is a long-run demand curve. Suppose consumers are fully adjusted to price p_0. Equilibrium is then at E_0, with quantity demanded q_0. Now suppose price rises to p_1. In the short run, consumers will react along the short-run demand curve D_0 and reduce consumption to q'_1. Once enough time has passed to permit the full range of adjustments to the new price, p_1, a new equilibrium at E_1 will be reached with quantity at q_1.

Now that all adjustments have been made, there will be a new short-run demand curve, D_1, passing through the point E_1. A further rise in price to p_2 would lead first to a short-run equilibrium at E'_2 with quantity q'_2, but eventually to a new long-run equilibrium at E_2 with quantity q_2. The grey long-run demand curve is more elastic than the short-run curves.

have been made, the demand for electricity will have fallen a great deal. Indeed, over this longer period of time, the percentage reduction in quantity demanded may exceed the percentage increase in price. If so, the long-run demand for electricity will be elastic.

The principal conclusion in the discussion of elasticity is:

the long-run demand curve for a commodity that is used in conjunction with durable commodities will tend to be substantially more elastic than any of the short-run demand curves.

This distinction will prove valuable in several of the chapters that follow.

BOX 6.2 ELASTICITY AND INCOME

It is often argued that the demand for a commodity will be more inelastic the smaller the proportion of income spent on it. The argument runs as follows. When only a small proportion of income is spent on some commodity, consumers will hardly notice a price rise. Hence they will not react strongly to price changes one way or the other. The most commonly quoted example of this alleged phenomenon is salt.

Salt is, however, a poor example for the argument being advanced. Not only does it take up a very small part of consumers' total expenditure, it also has few close substitutes. Consider another commodity, say one type of mints. These mints no doubt account for only a small portion of the total expenditure of mint-suckers, but there are many close substitutes – other types of mints and other sucking sweets. The makers of Polo mints know, for example, that if they raise Polo prices greatly, mint-suckers will switch to other brands of mints and to other types of sucking sweets. They thus face an elastic demand for their product.

Similar considerations apply to any one brand of matches. If the makers of Swan Vesta matches raise their prices significantly, people will switch to other brands of matches rather than pay much more than is necessary.

What this discussion shows is that:

goods with close substitutes will tend to have elastic demands whether they account for a large or a small part of consumers' incomes.

There is, however, another aspect of the influence of income. To see this, consider any good that has an inelastic demand. A rise in its price causes more to be spent on it. If consumers spend more on that commodity, they must spend less on all others taken as a group. But the higher is the proportion of income spent on the commodity the less likely is this to occur. After all, if a household spends all of its income on potatoes, its demand must have a unit elasticity. As price rises, its purchases must fall in proportion since it has only a given income to spend. Thus:

for a good to have a highly inelastic demand it must have few good substitutes, *and* it must not take up too large a proportion of consumers' total expenditure.

One common misconception about demand elasticity is discussed in Box 6.2.

OTHER DEMAND ELASTICITIES

So far we have discussed *price elasticity of demand*, the response of the quantity demanded to a change in the commodity's own price. The concept of demand elasticity can, however, be broadened to measure the response to changes in *any* of the factors that influence demand. How much, for example, do changes in income and the prices of other commodities affect quantity demanded?

Income Elasticity

The reaction of demand to changes in income is an important economic variable. In many economies, economic growth has been doubling real national income every twenty or thirty years.

This rise in income is shared by most households. As they find their incomes increasing, households increase their demands for many commodities. In the richer countries the demand for food and basic clothing does not increase with income nearly so much as does the demand for many other commodities. In most of these richer countries, the demands that are increasing most rapidly as incomes rise are the demands for durable goods. In a few of the very richest of the Western countries; however, the demand for services is rising more rapidly than the demand for durables as income rises.

The responsiveness of demand for a commodity to changes in income is termed **income elasticity of demand**, and is defined as

$$\eta_y = \frac{\text{percentage change in quantity demanded}}{\text{percentage change in income}}.$$

For most commodities, increases in income lead to increases in quantity demanded, and income elasticity is therefore positive. For such commodities, we have the same subdivisions of income elasticity as for price elasticity. If the

FIGURE 6.5 The Relation Between Quantity Demanded and Income

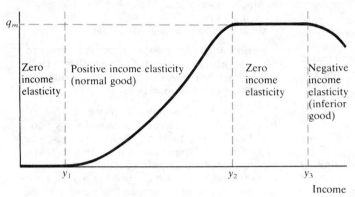

Zero income elasticity

Positive income elasticity (normal good)

Zero income elasticity

Negative income elasticity (inferior good)

y_1 y_2 y_3

Income

Normal goods have positive income elasticities. Inferior goods have negative elasticities. The graph relates the quantity of some good demanded to income. Nothing is demanded at incomes less than y_1, so for incomes between 0 and y_1 income elasticity is zero. Between incomes of y_1 and y_2, quantity demanded rises as income rises, making income elasticity positive. Between incomes of y_2 and y_3, quantity demanded stays constant at q_m, making income elasticity once again zero. At incomes above y_3, increases in income cause reductions in quantity demanded, making income elasticity negative.

resulting percentage change in quantity demanded is larger than the percentage increase in income, η_y will exceed unity. The commodity's demand is then said to be **income elastic**. If the percentage change in quantity demanded is smaller than the percentage change in income, η_y will be less than unity. The commodity's demand is then said to be **income inelastic**. In the boundary case, the percentage changes in income and quantity demanded are equal, making η_y unity. The commodity is said to have a *unit income elasticity of demand*.

Virtually all commodities have negative price elasticities. Both positive and negative income elasticities, are, however, commonly found.

Goods with positive income elasticities are called normal goods. Goods with negative income elasticities are called inferior goods; for them, a rise in income is accompanied by a fall in quantity demanded. Normal goods are much more common than inferior goods. The boundary case between normal and inferior goods occurs when a rise in income leaves quantity demanded unchanged, so that income elasticity is zero.

The important terminology of income elasticity is summarized in Figure 6.5 on this page and Box 6.1 on page 84. You should spend time studying the terminology and committing it to memory. Figure 6.5 shows a commodity with all types of income elasticity, positive, zero and

negative. This is to illustrate all of the possible reactions. Specific goods do not need to show all of these. For example a good may have a positive income elasticity at all levels of income. (You should be able to explain, however, why no good can have a negative income elasticity at *all* levels of income.)

Cross-Elasticity

The responsiveness of quantity demanded of one commodity to changes in the prices of other commodities is often of considerable interest. Producers of, say, beans and other meat substitutes find the demands for their products rising when cattle shortages force the price of beef up. Producers of large cars found their sales rising when the price of petrol fell dramatically.

The responsiveness of demand for one commodity to changes in the price of another commodity is called **cross-elasticity of demand**. It is defined as

$$\eta_{xy} = \frac{\text{percentage change in quantity demanded of commodity } X}{\text{percentage change in price of commodity } Y}$$

Cross-elasticity can vary from minus infinity to plus infinity. Complementary goods have negative cross-elasticities and substitute goods have positive cross-elasticities.

Bread and butter, for example, are complements: a fall in the price of butter causes an increase in the consumption of both commodities. Thus changes in the price of butter and in the quantity of bread demanded will have opposite signs. In contrast, butter and margarine are substitutes: a fall in the price of butter increases the quantity of butter demanded, but reduces the quantity of margarine demanded. Changes in the price of butter and in the quantity of margarine demanded will, therefore, have the same sign. The terminology of cross-elasticity is also summarized in Box 6.1.

ELASTICITY OF SUPPLY

We have seen that elasticity of demand measures the response of quantity demanded to changes in any of the factors that influence it. Similarly elasticity of supply measures the response of quantity supplied to changes in any of the factors that influence it. Because we wish to focus on the commodity's own price as a factor influencing its supply, we shall be concerned with *price elasticity of supply*. We shall follow the usual practice of dropping the adjective 'price', and will refer simply to 'elasticity of supply' whenever there is no ambiguity in this usage.

Supply elasticities are important in economics. The brevity of our treatment here reflects two main facts: first, much of the technique of demand elasticity carries over to the case of supply and does not need repeating; second, we

will have more to say about the determinants of supply elasticity later in this book.

A Formal Definition

The **price elasticity of supply** is defined as the percentage change in quantity supplied divided by the percentage change in price that brought it about. Letting the Greek letter epsilon, ε, stand for this measure, its formula is

$$\varepsilon = \frac{\text{percentage change in quantity supplied}}{\text{percentage change in price}}.$$

> **Supply elasticity is a measure of the degree of responsiveness of quantity supplied to changes in the commodity's own price.**

Since supply curves normally have positive slopes, supply elasticity is normally positive. As with demand elasticity, it is best to calculate percentage changes on the average of the new and old prices and the new and the old quantities, when applying the above formula.

Interpreting Supply Elasticity

Figure 6.6 illustrates three cases of supply elasticity. The case of zero elasticity is one in which the quantity supplied does not change as price changes. This would be the case, for example, if suppliers persisted in producing a given quantity and dumping it on the market for whatever it would bring. Infinite elasticity occurs at some price if nothing at all is supplied at lower prices, but an indefinitely large amount is supplied at

FIGURE 6.6 Four Supply Curves

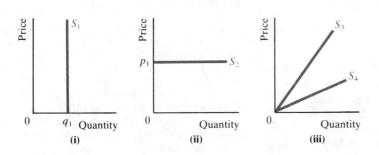

(i)   (ii)   (iii)

All four curves have constant elasticity. Curve S_1 has a *zero elasticity* since the same quantity, q_1, is supplied whatever the price. Curve S_2 has an infinite elasticity at the price p_1. Nothing at all will be supplied at any price below p_1 while a indefinitely large quantity will be supplied at the price of p_1. The curves S_3 and S_4, as well as all other straight lines through the origin, have a unit elasticity, indicating that the percentage change in quantity equals the percentage change in price between any two points on the curve. (See the Appendix to this chapter for a proof.)

that price. Any straight-line supply curve drawn through the origin has an elasticity of unity. For a proof of this, see proposition (4) on page 98 of the Appendix to this chapter.

The case of unit supply elasticity illustrates that the warning given earlier for demand applies equally to supply: do not confuse geometric steepness of supply curves with elasticity. Since *any* straight-line supply curve that passes through the origin has an elasticity of unity, it follows that there is no simple correspondence between geometrical steepness and supply elasticity. The reason is that varying steepness (when the scales on both axes are unchanged) reflects varying *absolute* changes, while elasticity depends on *percentage* changes. The terminology of supply elasticity is also summarized in Box 6.1.

What Determines Elasticity of Supply?

What determines the response of producers to a change in the price of the commodity that they supply? The size of the response depends in part on how easily producers can shift from the production of other commodities to the one whose price has risen. If agricultural land and labour can be readily shifted from one crop to another, the supply of any one crop will be more elastic than if labour cannot easily be shifted. Here also, as with demand, length of time for response is critical. It may be difficult to change quantities supplied in response to a price increase in a matter of weeks or months, but easy to do so over a period of years. An obvious example concerns the planting cycle of crops. Also, new oilfields can be discovered, wells drilled and pipelines built over a period of years, but not in a few months. Thus the elasticity of supply of oil is much greater over five years than over one year.

The treatment of supply elasticity is brief here because elasticity is strongly influenced by how costs respond to output changes, an issue that will be treated at length in later chapters.

CONSUMERS' SURPLUS

The negative slope of the demand curve gives rise to a phenomenon called consumers' surplus, a concept that has often been influential in guiding economic policy. We will define the term later; first let us see how the surplus arises.

The Meaning of the Concept

Consumers' surplus is a direct consequence of downward-sloping demand curves. To illustrate this, suppose that we have interviewed a consumer to learn about his purchase of some commodity – milk, for example. The results are shown in Table 6.4. Our first question is: if you were getting no milk at all, how much would you be willing to pay for one glass per week? With no hesitation the consumer replies £3.00. We then ask: if you had already consumed that one glass, how much would you pay for a second glass per week? After a bit of thought he replies £1.50. Adding one glass per week with each question, we discover that he would be willing to pay £1.00 to get a third glass per week and £0.80, £0.60, £0.50, £0.40, £0.30, £0.25 and £0.20 for successive glasses of milk from the fourth to the tenth per week. The sum of the values that he places on each unit gives the *total consumption value* that he places on all units. In the present

TABLE 6.4 Consumers' Surplus

Glasses of milk consumed per week	Amount the consumer would pay to get this glass	Consumers' surplus on each glass if milk costs £0.30 per glass
First	£3.00	£2.70
Second	1.50	1.20
Third	1.00	0.70
Fourth	0.80	0.50
Fifth	0.60	0.30
Sixth	0.50	0.20
Seventh	0.40	0.10
Eighth	0.30	0.00
Ninth	0.25	—
Tenth	0.20	—

Consumers' surplus on each unit consumed is the difference between the market price and the maximum price the consumer would pay to obtain that unit. The Table shows the value that one consumer puts on successive glasses of milk consumed each week. His negatively sloped demand curve shows that he would be willing to pay progressively smaller amounts for each additional glass of milk consumed. As long as he would be willing to pay more than the market price for any glass, he obtains a consumers' surplus on it when he buys it. The marginal glass of milk is the eighth, the one valued just at the market price and on which no consumers' surplus is earned.

example, the consumer values ten units at £8.55. This is the amount he would be willing to pay if faced with the either-or choice of ten glasses of milk or none at all. This is also the amount we could get him to pay if we offered him the glasses of milk one at a time, charging him the maximum he was willing to pay for each.

But the consumer does not have to pay a different price for each glass of milk that he consumes each week; he can buy all he wants at the prevailing market price. Suppose the price is £0.30. He will consume eight glasses per week (one for each weekday and two for Sunday) because he values the eighth glass just at the market price, while valuing all earlier glasses at higher amounts. Because he values the first glass at £3.00 but gets it for £0.30, he makes a 'profit' of £2.70 on that glass. Between his £1.50 valuation of the second glass and what he has to pay for it, he clears a 'profit' of £1.20. He clears £0.70 on the third glass, and so on. These 'profits', which are called his consumer's surpluses on each unit, are shown in column 3 of the Table. The total surplus is £5.70 per week. In the Table, we arrive at the consumers' surplus by summing the surpluses on each glass. We arrive at the same total, however, by first summing what the consumer would pay for all the glasses bought (which is £8.10 in this case) and then subtracting the £2.40 which he does pay.

The value placed by each household on its total consumption of some commodity can be estimated in at least two ways: the valuation that the household places on each successive unit may be summed, or the household may be asked how much it would pay to consume the amount in question if the alternative were to have none.[1]

While other households would put different numerical values into Table 6.4, the negative

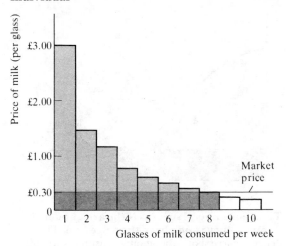

FIGURE 6.7 Consumers' Surplus for an Individual

Consumers' surplus is the sum of the extra valuations placed on each unit above the market price paid for each. This Figure is based on the data in Table 6.4. The consumer will pay the dark-shaded area for the eight glasses of milk he will consume per week when the market price is £0.30 a glass. The total value he places on these eight glasses of milk is the entire shaded area. Hence his consumers' surplus is the light-shaded area.

slope of the demand curve implies that the figures in column 2 would be declining for each household. Since a household will go on buying further units until the value placed on the last unit equals the market price, it follows that there will be a consumers' surplus on every unit consumed except the last one.

In general, **consumers' surplus** is the difference between the total value households place on all the units consumed of some commodity – i.e. the total consumption value of the commodity and the total payment they must make to purchase that amount of the commodity – i.e. the total sale value of the commodity.

The data in columns 1 and 2 of Table 6.4 give the consumer's demand curve for milk. It is his demand curve because he will go on buying glasses of milk as long as he values each glass at least as much as the market price he must pay for it. When the market price is £3.00 per glass he will buy only one glass; when it is £1.50 he will buy two glasses, and so on. The total consump-

---

[1] This is only an approximation, but it is good enough for our purposes. More advanced theory shows that the calculations presented here overestimate consumers' surplus because they ignore the income effect. Although it is sometimes necessary to correct for this bias, none of the corrections that are called for would upset our basic conclusion: *when consumers can buy all units they require at a single market price, they pay much less than they would be willing to pay if faced with the choice between having the quantity they consume and having none.*

FIGURE 6.8 Consumers' Surplus for the Market

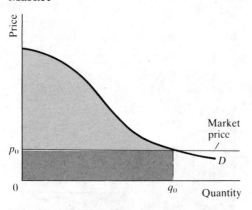

Total consumers' surplus is the area under the demand curve and above the price line. The demand curve shows the amount consumers would pay for each unit of the commodity if they had to buy their units one at a time. The area under the demand curve shows the total valuation consumers place on all units consumed. For example, the total value that consumers place on q_0 units is the entire shaded area under the demand curve up to q_0. At a market price of p_0 the amount paid for q_0 units is the dark-shaded area. Hence consumers' surplus is the light-shaded area.

tion value is the area below his demand curve, and consumers' surplus is that part of the area that lies above the price line. This is shown in Figure 6.7.

Figure 6.8 shows that the same relation holds for the smooth market demand curve that indicates the total amount all consumers would buy at each price.[1]

Some Applications of Consumers' Surplus

In subsequent chapters we will find many uses for the concept of consumers' surplus. In this chapter we show how it can be used to resolve some very old problems.

---

[1] Figure 6.7 is a bar chart because we only allowed the consumer to vary his consumption in discrete units one at a time. Had we allowed him to vary his consumption continuously, we could have traced out a continuous curve for the consumer similar to the one shown in Figure 6.8.

The Paradox of Value

Early economists, struggling with the problem of what determines the relative prices of commodities, encountered what they called the *paradox of value*: necessary commodities, such as water, have prices that are low compared with the prices of luxury commodities, such as diamonds. Water is necessary to our existence, while high-quality diamonds are mostly used for frivolous purposes and could disappear from the face of the earth tomorrow without causing any real hardship. Does it not seem odd, these economists asked, that water, which has such a high consumption value, has such a low market value while diamonds, which must have a lower consumption value, have a much higher market value? It took a long time to resolve this apparent paradox, so it is not surprising that, even today, similar confusions persist and cloud many policy discussions.

The key to resolving the 'paradox' lies in the important distinction between what one would pay to avoid having one's consumption of a commodity reduced to zero and what one would pay to gain the use of one more unit of the commodity. We have already seen in the previous section that the area under the demand curve measures the *total value* that consumers place on *all* of the units consumed. In Figure 6.8 the total consumption value of q_0 units is the entire shaded area (light and dark) under the demand curve.

What about the value that the household places on having *one more*, or *one less*, than the q_0 units it is currently consuming? Faced with a market price of p_0, the household buys all units that it values at p_0 or greater, but it does not purchase any units that it values at less than p_0. It follows that the value households place on the last unit consumed of any commodity is measured by the commodity's price.

Now look at the total amount spent to purchase the commodity – the price paid for it multiplied by the quantity bought and sold – which we can call its *total market value* or *sale value*. In Figure 6.8 it is shown by the dark-shaded rectangle with sides p_0 and q_0.

We have seen that the total consumption value consumers place on a given amount of a commodity exceeds its total market value. The two values do not, however, have to bear any constant relation to each other. Figure 6.9 shows two goods, one where total market value is a very small fraction of its total consumption value and another where total market value is a much higher fraction of total consumption value.

The resolution of the paradox of value is that a good that is very plentiful, such as water, will have a low price and will thus be consumed to the point where all households place a low value on the last unit consumed, whether or not they place a high value on their total consumption of the commodity. On the other hand, a commodity that is relatively scarce will have a high market price and consumption will, therefore, stop at a point at which consumers place a high value on the last unit consumed whatever value they place on their total consumption of the good.

We have now reached an important conclusion:

the market price of a commodity depends on demand *and supply.* Hence no paradox is involved when a commodity on which consumers place a high total consumption value sells for a low price, and hence has only a low total market value (i.e. a low amount spent on it).

Necessities, Luxuries and Elasticity

In ordinary discussion, people often distinguish between necessities and luxuries – necessities being commodities it is difficult to do without and luxuries being commodities that could be fairly

FIGURE 6.9   Total Value Versus Market Value

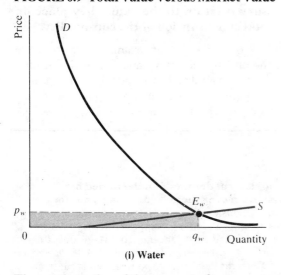

(i) Water

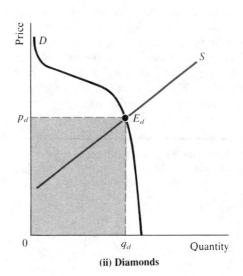

(ii) Diamonds

The market value of the amount of some commodity bears no necessary relation to the total value consumers place on that amount. The two parts of the diagram present hypothetical demand curves for water and diamonds that are meant to be stylized versions of the real curves. The total value that households place on water, as shown by the area under the demand curve, is great – indeed we cannot possibly show the curve for very small quantities because people would pay all they had, rather than be deprived completely of water. The total valuation that households place on diamonds is shown by the area under the demand curve for diamonds. This is less than the total value placed on water.

The supply curve of diamonds makes diamonds scarce and keeps diamonds high in price. Thus, when equilibrium is at E_d the total market value of diamonds sold, indicated by the shaded area of $p_d q_d$, is high.

The supply curve of water makes water plentiful and makes water low in price. Thus when equilibrium is at E_w, the total market value of water consumed, indicated by the shaded area of $p_w q_w$, is low.

easily dispensed with. The distinction is some-what arbitrary. For example, are eggs a necessity or a luxury? Nonetheless, some sense can be made of the distinction by taking it to compare the total values that households place on their consumptions of different commodities. In the previous section we learned to measure these total values by the areas under demand curves. Using this terminology, we would say that a necessity has a very large consumption value as measured by the area under its demand curve; a luxury has a smaller consumption value.

A frequent error occurs when people try to use knowledge of total values to predict demand elasticities. It is sometimes argued that, since luxuries can be given up, they have highly elastic demands; when their prices rise, households can stop purchasing them. Conversely, it is argued that necessities have highly inelastic demands because, when prices rise, households have no choice but to continue to buy them.

But elasticity of demand depends on how consumers value commodities at the margin, not on how much they value the total consumption of the commodity. The relevant question for predicting the response to a price change is 'how much do households value a bit more of the commodity?', not 'how much do they value *all* that they are consuming?'

When the price of a commodity rises, each household will reduce its purchase of that commodity until it values the last unit consumed at the price that it must pay for that unit. Will the reduction in quantity required to raise the valuation be a little or a lot? This depends on the shape of the demand curve in the relevant range. If the demand curve is flat, a large change in quantity is required and demand will be elastic. If the curve is steep, a small change will suffice and demand will be inelastic. This point is illustrated in Figure 6.10, which shows two quite different responses to the same change in price. It leads to this important conclusion:

elasticity depends on the value households place on having a bit more or a bit less of the commodity; it bears no necessary relation to the value they place on total consumption of the commodity.

Box 6.3 provides an example from outside economics of the importance of distinguishing between the total value that people get from some activity and the value they would place on doing a bit more or a bit less of it.

FIGURE 6.10 The Relation of Elasticity of Demand to Total Value

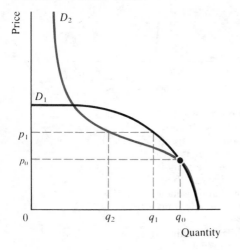

Elasticity of demand is determined by valuation over the relevant range, not total value. Consider two alternative demand curves for a commodity, D_1 and D_2. Suppose price is p_0. Given either demand curve, the household consumes the quantity q_0, where the last unit consumed is valued at p_0. When the price rises to p_1, households cut their consumption.

If the black line D_1 is the demand curve, consumption only falls to q_1 and the demand for the product is quite inelastic. If, however, the coloured line D_2 is the demand curve, consumption falls to q_2 and the demand for the product is more elastic.

Although the shape of the demand curve in the relevant range is important, its shape outside this range is irrelevant for determining elasticity. But total value depends upon the whole area under the curve. Depending on the shape of the curve between 0 and q_0, either curve can show more or less total value than the other. Thus total value has no influence on market behaviour in response to a change in price from p_0 to p_1.

BOX 6.3 WHAT DO ATTITUDE SURVEYS MEASURE?

Consider a type of survey that is popular in the daily newspapers and in sociology and political science. These surveys take the form of asking such questions as:

(1) Do you favour the Conservatives or Labour?
(2) In deciding to live in area A rather than area B, what factors influenced your choice? List the following in order of importance: neighbours, schools, closeness to swimming area, price and quality of housing available, play areas for children, general amenities.
(3) In choosing a university, what factors were important to you? List in order of importance: environment, academic excellence, residential facilities, parents' opinion, school opinion, athletics facilities, tuition.

You should be able to add other examples to this list. All of the above survey questions, and most of those you might add, *attempt to measure the total valuation households place on some activity rather than the valuation they would place on a little more or a little less consumption.*

The total value being asked about includes the consumers' surplus. There is, of course, nothing illegal or immoral about this. People are free to measure anything that interests them, and in some cases knowledge of total valuation may be useful. But in most cases actual behaviour is determined by valuations of a little more or a little less, and anyone who attempts to predict such behaviour from a knowledge of total valuations, even a correct knowledge, will be hopelessly in error.

Where the behaviour being predicted involves an either-or decision, such as a vote for the Conservative or for Labour in a two-party contest, total value attached to each choice will indeed be what matters because the voters are choosing one or the other. But where the decision is between a little more and a little less, total value is not what will determine behaviour.

A recent newspaper poll in a large US city showed that two-thirds of the city's voters rated its excellent school system as an important asset. Yet in a subsequent election the voters refused to accept further borrowing to build new schools. Is this irrational behaviour, as the newspaper editorials charged? Does it show a biased sample in the poll? It demonstrates neither. The poll measured the people's assessment of the total value derived from the school system (high), while the vote on new borrowing depended on the people's assessment of the value of a little more money spent on the school system (low). There is nothing contradictory in anyone's feeling that the total value of the city's fine school system is high, but that the city (or the taxpayer) has other needs that have a higher value at the margin than further money spent on school construction.

A recent survey showed – paradoxically, it claimed – that many parents are getting more pleasure from their families just at the time they are electing to have smaller families. There is nothing paradoxical about a shift in tastes that increases the value of the first one or two children and reduces the value of each further child. Nor is there any paradox in a parent's getting a high total value from the total time spent with the children, but assigning a low value to the prospect of spending additional time with them each evening.

SUMMARY

1. *Elasticity of demand* (also called *price elasticity of demand*) is the percentage change in quantity divided by the percentage change in price that brought it about.
2. When the percentage change in quantity is less than the percentage change in price that brought it about, demand is said to be *inelastic* and a fall in price lowers the total amount spent on the commodity. When the percentage change in quantity is greater than the percentage change in price that brought it about, demand is said to be *elastic* and a fall in price raises total revenue.
3. The main determinant of the price elasticity of demand is the availability of substitutes for the commodity. Any one of a group of close substitutes will tend to have an elastic demand even though the group as a whole may have an inelastic demand.

4. Elasticity of demand tends to be greater the longer the time over which adjustment occurs. Items that have a few substitutes in the short run may develop ample substitutes when consumers and producers have time to adapt.

5. *Income elasticity* is the percentage change in quantity demanded divided by the percentage change in income that brought it about. The income elasticity of demand for a commodity will usually change as income varies.

6. *Cross-elasticity* is the percentage change in quantity demanded divided by the percentage change in the price of some other commodity that brought it about. It is used to define commodities that are substitutes for one another (positive cross-elasticity) and commodities that complement one another (negative cross-elasticity).

7. *Elasticity of supply* is an important concept in economics. It measures the ratio of the percentage change in the quantity supplied of a commodity to the percentage change in its price.

8. The negative slope of the demand curve means that a purchaser would be willing to pay more than the prevailing market price for all but the last unit consumed. Consumers' surplus measures the difference between the total value a household places on all the units consumed of some commodity and the amount actually paid.

9. There is nothing paradoxical in a household putting a high total value on *all* of its consumption of some commodity and only a low value on the *last unit* consumed.

10. Elasticity depends not on total value placed on all units consumed but on the values placed on the marginal units that will be added to, or substracted from, consumption as a result of a small change in price.

TOPICS FOR REVIEW

- Price, income and cross-elasticity of demand
- Zero, inelastic, unitary, elastic and infinitely elastic demand
- The relation between price elasticity and changes in total expenditure
- Determinants of demand elasticity
- Income elasticities for normal and inferior goods
- Cross-elasticities between substitutes and complements
- Long- and short-run elasticity of demand
- Elasticity of supply and its determinants
- Consumers' surplus
- The paradox of value
- Necessities, luxuries and demand elasticities

APPENDIX to Chapter 6

A Formal Analysis of Elasticity

In the text we defined elasticity of demand as the ratio of the percentage change in the quantity demanded to the percentage change in price. This definition uses discrete changes in price and quantity. It is called **arc elasticity** to distinguish it from the definition that uses the concept of a derivative taken from the calculus. This latter concept of elasticity is called **point elasticity**. Arc elasticity, described in Chapter 6, may be regarded as an approximation to point elasticity.

We shall consider arc and then point elasticity, but first we must define some symbols:

$q \equiv$ the original quantity;
$\Delta q \equiv$ the change in quantity;
$p \equiv$ the original price;
$\Delta p \equiv$ the change in price.

We can now express the definition of arc elasticity of demand in symbols:[1]

$$\eta \equiv \frac{\Delta q/q}{\Delta p/p} \ .$$

By inverting the denominator and multiplying, we get

$$\eta \equiv \frac{\Delta q}{q} \cdot \frac{p}{\Delta p} \ .$$

Since it does not matter in which order we do our multiplication (i.e. $q.\Delta p \equiv \Delta p.q$), we may reverse the order of the two terms in the denominator and write

$$\eta = \frac{\Delta q}{\Delta p} \cdot \frac{p}{q} \ . \tag{1}$$

We have now split elasticity into two parts: $\Delta q/\Delta p$, the ratio of the change in quantity to the change in price, which is related to the slope of the demand curve, and p/q, which is related to the place on the curve at which we made our measurement.

Figure 6A.1 shows a straight-line demand curve by way of illustration. If we wish to measure the elasticity at point 1, we take our p and q at the point and consider a price change, taking us, say, to point 2, and measure our Δp and Δq as indicated. The slope of the straight line joining points 1 and 2 is $\Delta p/\Delta q$ (if you have

FIGURE 6A.1 A Straight-line Demand Curve

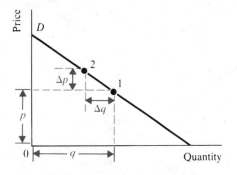

---

[1] In Chapter 6 we also took price and quantity to be the average of the prices and quantities before and after the change being considered; for the more formal treatment in this Appendix it is more satisfactory to take price and quantity to be the ones ruling before the change being considered. The difference between taking p and q as original or as average amounts diminishes as the magnitude of the change being considered diminishes.

forgotten this, refer to the appendix to Chapter 3, pages 43–44), and the term in equation (1) is $\Delta q/\Delta p$, which is the reciprocal of $\Delta p/\Delta q$. We conclude, therefore, that the first term in our elasticity formula is the reciprocal of the slope of the straight line joining the two price–quantity positions under consideration.

We may now develop a number of theorems relating to the elasticity of demand and supply.

(1) *The elasticity of a downward-sloping straight-line demand curve varies from infinity (∞) at the price axis to zero at the quantity axis.* We first notice that a straight line has a constant slope so that the ratio $\Delta p/\Delta q$ is the same anywhere on the line. Therefore, its reciprocal, $\Delta q/\Delta p$, must also be constant. We can now infer the changes in η by inspecting the ratio p/q. At the price axis $q = 0$ and p/q is undefined, but as we let q *approach* zero, without ever quite reaching it, the ratio p/q increases without limit. Thus $\eta \to \infty$ as $q \to 0$. As we move down the line, p falls and q rises steadily; thus p/q is falling steadily so that η is also falling. At the q axis the price is zero, so the ratio p/q is zero. Thus $\eta = 0$.

(2) *Comparing two straight-line demand curves of the same slope, the one farther from the origin is less elastic at each price than the one closer to the origin.* Figure 6A.2 shows two parallel straight-line demand functions. Pick any price, say p, and compare the elasticities of the two curves at that price. Since the curves are parallel, the ratio $\Delta q/\Delta p$ is the same on both curves. Since we are comparing elasticities at the same price on both curves, p is the same, and the only factor left to vary is q. On the curve farther from the origin,

FIGURE 6A.2 Two Parallel Straight-line Demand Curves have Unequal Price Elasticities at *p*

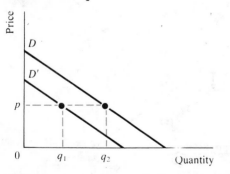

FIGURE 6A.3 Two Intersecting Straight-line Demand Curves have Different Elasticities at the Point Where They Cross

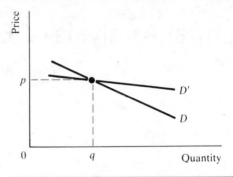

quantity is larger (i.e. $q_2 > q_1$), and hence p/q is smaller; thus η is smaller.

It follows from Theorem 2 that a parallel shift of a straight-line demand curve lowers elasticity (at each price) if the line shifts outward, and raises elasticity if the line shifts inward.

(3) *The elasticities of two intersecting straight-line demand curves can be compared at the point of intersection merely by comparing slopes, the steeper curve being the less elastic.* In Figure 6A.3 we have two intersecting curves. At the point of intersection p and q are common to both curves, and hence the ratio p/q is the same. Therefore η varies only with $\Delta q/\Delta p$. On the steeper curve the absolute value of $\Delta p/\Delta q$ is larger than on the flatter curve; thus the absolute value of the ratio $\Delta q/\Delta p$ is smaller on the steeper curve than on the flatter curve, so that elasticity is lower.

(4) *Any straight-line supply curve through the origin has an elasticity of minus one.* Such a supply curve is shown in Figure 6A.4. Consider the two triangles with the sides p, q, and the S curve, and Δp, Δq, and the S curve. Clearly these are similar triangles. Therefore the ratios of their sides are equal, i.e.

$$\frac{p}{q} = \frac{\Delta p}{\Delta q} \ . \tag{2}$$

Elasticity of supply is defined as

$$\varepsilon = \frac{\Delta q}{\Delta p} \cdot \frac{p}{q} \ , \tag{3}$$

which, by substitution from (2), gives

$$\varepsilon = \frac{q}{p} \cdot \frac{p}{q} \equiv 1 \ . \tag{4}$$

FIGURE 6A.4 A Straight-line Supply Curve Through the Origin has an Elasticity of One

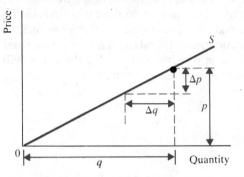

(5) *With a straight-line demand curve, the elasticity measured from any point (p, q), according to equation (1) above, is independent of the direction and magnitude of the change in price and quantity.* This follows immediately from the fact that the slope of a straight line is a constant. If we start from some point (p, q) and then change price, the ratio $\Delta q/\Delta p$ will be the same whatever the direction or the size of the change in p.

(6) *The elasticity measured from any point (p, q), according to equation (1) above, is in general dependent on the direction and magnitude of the change in price and quantity.* Except for a straight-line demand curve (for which the slope does not change) the ratio $\Delta q/\Delta p$ will not be the same at

FIGURE 6A.5 Arc Elasticity Measured from a Particular Point (1) on a Demand Curve that is not a Straight Line

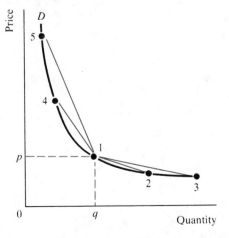

different points on a demand curve. Figure 6A.5 shows a demand curve that is not a straight line. We desire to measure the elasticity from point 1. The figure makes it apparent that the ratio $\Delta q/\Delta p$, and hence the elasticity, will vary according to the size and the direction of the price change. This result is very inconvenient. It happens because we are averaging the reaction of Δq to Δp over a section of the demand curve, and, depending on the range that we take, the *average reaction* will be different.

If we wish to measure the elasticity at a point, we need to know the reaction of quantity to a change in price at that point, not over a whole range. We call the reaction of quantity to price change at a point dq/dp, and we define this to be the reciprocal of the slope of the straight line (i.e. $\Delta q/\Delta p$) tangent to the demand curve at the point in question. In Figure 6A.6 the point elasticity of demand at a is the ratio p/q (as it has been in all previous measures) now multiplied by the ratio of $\Delta q/\Delta p$ measured along the straight-line tangent to the curve at a. This definition may now be written as

$$\eta = \frac{dq}{dp} \cdot \frac{p}{q} \ . \tag{5}$$

The ratio dq/dp, as we have defined it, is in fact the differential-calculus concept of the derivative of quantity with respect to price.

This elasticity is the one normally used in economic theory. Equation (1) may be regarded as an approximation to this expression. It is

FIGURE 6A.6 Point Elasticity of Demand Measured from a Particular Point (a) on the Demand Curve

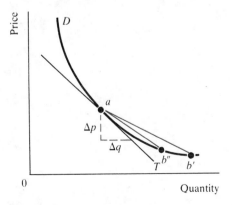

obvious by inspecting Figure 6A.6 that the elasticity measured from (1) will come closer and closer to that measured from (5) the smaller the price change used to calculate the value of (1). From (1), change the price so that we move from a to some point b'; the ratio $\Delta q/\Delta p$ is the reciprocal of the slope of the straight line joining a and b'. The smaller the price change that we make, the closer the point comes to point a and the closer the slope of the line joining the points comes to the slope of the line tangential to the curve at a. If the slopes of those two lines get closer together, so also do the reciprocals of the slopes and, thus, so do the elasticities as measured by equations (1) and (5). Thus, if we consider (1) as an approximation to (5), the error will diminish as the size of Δp diminishes.

7

Applications of Price Theory

Although theory of the determination of price is a powerful tool, there is no point in merely memorizing the laws of supply and demand. The theory should become one's servant, not one's master. Students must aim to understand it well enough to be able to analyse problems on their own. With that objective in view, the present chapter applies the theory to a number of actual cases, which are chosen both to illustrate the use of price theory and to give practice using it.

In order to use our theory to develop predictions which are open to empirical testing we need two further hypotheses: (1) the assumptions of our theory of price determination adequately describe relations that exist in the real world; and (2) if there is a change in the equilibrium price and quantity, the actual price and quantity will move fairly quickly to their new equilibrium values. *If* these hypotheses are correct, *then* the propositions of our theory will provide useful predictions about how prices and quantities actually behave; if not, the predictions of our theory will be frequently contradicted by the evidence.

PRICE CONTROLS

If the government wishes to influence the price at which some product is bought and sold, it has two main alternatives. First, it may change the equilibrium price by altering the commodity's demand or supply. Second, it may alter the price by enacting legislation that regulates the price. **Price controls** refer to the latter alternative: influencing price by laws, rather than by market forces.

Quantity Exchanged at Non-Equilibrium Prices

Controls can be used to hold a commodity's price at a disequilibrium level. What then determines the quantity actually traded on the market? Any voluntary market transaction requires both a willing buyer and a willing seller. Thus, if quantity demanded is less than quantity supplied, demand will determine the amount actually exchanged, and the excess supply will remain in the hands of the unsuccessful sellers. If quantity supplied is less than quantity demanded, however, supply will determine the amount

FIGURE 7.1 The Determination of Quantity Exchanged in Disequilibrium

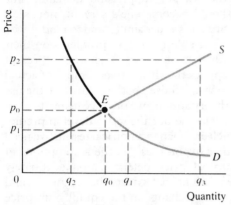

In disequilibrium, quantity exchanged is determined by the lesser of quantity demanded or quantity supplied. When the market is in equilibrium at point E, price is p_0, while quantity demanded equals quantity supplied at q_0. For prices below p_0, the quantity exchanged will be determined by the supply curve. For example, the quantity q_1 will be exchanged at the disequilibrium price p_1 in spite of the excess demand of $q_1 - q_2$. For prices above p_0, the quantity exchanged will be determined by the demand curve. For example, the quantity q_2 will be exchanged at the disequilibrium price p_2, in spite of the excess supply of $q_3 - q_2$. Thus the darker portions of the S and D curves show the actual quantities exchanged at different prices.

actually traded and the excess demand will take the form of desired purchases by unsuccessful buyers. This is shown graphically in Figure 7.1.

At any disequilibrium price, quantity exchanged is determined by the lesser of quantity demanded or quantity supplied.

This result is often expressed by the maxim: *in disequilibrium the short side of the market dominates* (i.e. determines what is bought and sold).

Maximum-price Legislation

Since the dawn of history, governments have passed laws regulating the prices at which certain commodities could be sold. In this section we concentrate on laws setting *maximum* permissible prices, which are often called 'price ceilings'. Such laws have had many purposes. Governments of medieval cities sometimes sought to

protect their citizens from the consequences of crop failures by fixing a maximum price at which bread could be sold. In modern times, many governments have employed rent controls in an attempt to make housing available at a price that could be afforded by lower-income groups.

The effects on price and quantity: Although frequently referred to as *fixed* or *frozen prices*, most price ceilings actually specify the highest permissible price that producers may legally charge. If the ceiling is set above the equilibrium price, it has no effect, since the equilibrium remains attainable. If, however, the ceiling is set below the equilibrium price, it determines the price – in which case it is said to be *binding*. The key consequences of price ceilings are shown in Figure 7.2.

The setting of a maximum price either will have no effect (maximum price set at or above the equilibrium) or will cause a shortage of the commodity (maximum price set below the equilibrium), thereby reducing the quantity actually bought and sold below its equilibrium value.

Allocation of available supply: In the case of a binding price ceiling, production is insufficient to satisfy everyone who wishes to buy the commodity. Since price is not allowed to rise so as to allocate the available supply among the would-be purchasers, some other method of allocation must be found. Theory does not predict what this other method will be, but experience has shown several possibilities.

If shops sell to the first customers who arrive, people are likely to rush to those stores that are rumoured to have any stocks of the scarce commodity. Long queues will develop, and allocation will be on the basis of luck, or to those knowing enough to gain from the principle of 'first come, first served'. This is a system commonly found in the command economies of Eastern Europe, where queuing often becomes a way of life.

Sometimes shopkeepers themselves decide who will get the scarce commodities, and who will not. They may keep commodities under the counter and sell only to regular customers, or only to people of a certain colour or religion. Such a system is called allocation by **sellers' preferences**.

If the central authorities dislike the allocation system that results from price ceilings, they can ration the goods, giving out ration coupons sufficient to purchase the available supply. The authorities then determine, as a conscious act of policy, how the available supply is to be allocated. The coupons might be distributed equally, or on such criteria as age, sex, marital status or number of dependants.

Rationing substitutes the government's preferences for the sellers' preferences, in allocating a commodity that is in excess demand because of a binding price ceiling.

Black markets: Under certain circumstances, price control, with or without rationing, is likely to give rise to a **black market**. This is a market in which goods are sold illegally at prices that violate the legal restrictions. Many products have only a few manufacturers but many retailers.

FIGURE 7.2 A Price Ceiling and Black-market Pricing

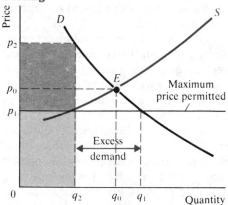

A price ceiling set below the equilibrium price causes excess demand and invites a black market. Equilibrium price is at p_0. If a price ceiling is set at p_1, the quantity demanded will rise to q_1 and the quantity supplied will fall to q_2. Quantity actually exchanged will be q_2. Although excess demand is $q_1 - q_2$, price may not legally rise to restore equilibrium.

Black marketeers would buy q_2 at the controlled price of p_1, paying the amount shown by the light-shaded area $p_1 q_2$. They would sell at the price p_2, earning profits shown by the dark-shaded area between p_1 and p_2.

Although it is easy to police the producers, it is difficult even to locate all those who are, or could be, retailing the product, much less control them.

Figure 7.2 shows the case where the central authorities can fix the price that producers get, but are unable to control the price at which retailers sell to the public. Output is restricted by the low price received by producers, while consumers must pay the high price that equates demand to the available supply. The difference between what consumers pay and what producers get goes as profits to the black marketeers.

The theory predicts that the potential for a profitable black market will exist whenever effective price ceilings are imposed. The actual growth of such a market depends on there being a few people willing to risk heavy penalties by running a black-market supply organization, and a reasonably large number of persons prepared to purchase goods illegally on such a market.

It is unlikely that all of the output will be sold on the black market – both because there are some honest people in every society and because the central authorities usually have some power to enforce their price laws. Thus the normal case is not the extreme result mentioned above. Instead, some of the limited supplies will be sold at the controlled price and some at the black-market price.

Economists can evaluate a black-market situation only when the central authorities' objectives are known. If the authorities are mainly concerned with an equitable distribution of a scarce product, effective price control on manufacturers, plus a largely uncontrollable black market at the retail level, may produce the worst possible result. If, however, they are mainly interested in restricting production in order to release resources for other more urgent needs, such as war production, the policy works effectively, if somewhat unfairly. Where the purpose is to keep prices down, the policy is a failure to the extent that black marketeers succeed in raising prices, and a success to the extent that sales actually occur at the controlled prices.

Empirical evidence: There is much evidence confirming these predictions. In the First and Second World Wars, governments set binding ceilings on many prices. The legislation of maximum prices was always followed by shortages, then by either the introduction of rationing or the growth of some private method of allocation (such as sellers' preferences), and then by the rise of some sort of black market. The ceilings were more effective in limiting consumption than in controlling prices, although they did restrain price increases to some extent. Many socialist countries have followed a policy of controlling food prices at levels that are below the equilibrium prices. Chronic shortages, queues, allocation by sellers' preferences and black markets are the normal result of such policies.

The Theory of Maximum Prices Applied to Rent Controls[1]

Although there is debate on the desirability of rent-control legislation, there is little doubt about its major consequences. They can all be observed in the UK, where rent control was first introduced in 1914 and gradually extended to cover the entire rental market. Over a period of sixty years the market for privately owned unfurnished rental accommodation was largely eliminated. From 45 per cent of households in privately owned rental accommodation in 1945, the figure has fallen steadily, until in the late 1980s it was only 8 per cent. Finally in 1989 the British government announced measures to bring an end to rent controls.

In other countries, rent control has caused severe housing shortages. In the US, rent control is in the hands of individual cities. The existence of controlled markets in some cities and uncontrolled markets in others facilitates testing predictions about rent controls. For example, rent control in the Queens borough of New York was accompanied by severe housing shortages; whole blocks of buildings were abandoned, although they could have lasted for decades. Uncontrolled markets in the south-western United States have seen supplies increase rapidly to meet the growing demands for housing as population moved there. Rent control over lower-rent properties was introduced in the Canadian province of Ontario in 1975, and extended to all rental accommodations in 1985. Since that time the construction of rental accommodation has

halted, except where it is subsidized; conversions to owner-occupancy soared and were then made illegal, entrance fees and subletting have become common and would-be renters have resorted to increasingly desperate measures, ranging from bribes to searching out the families of newly deceased tenants.

Economic theory explains why these consequences always follow, sooner or later, from the imposition of effective rent controls.

Rent controls are just a special case of price ceilings. They are usually imposed to freeze rents at their current levels at times when equilibrium rents are rising either because demand is shifting rightward (due to forces such as rising population and income) or because supply is shifting leftward (due to forces such as rising costs). The result is that the controlled rents are soon well below the free-market equilibrium level and excess demand appears. The following predictions about rent controls are simply applications to the housing market of the results concerning price controls in any competitive market.

(1) There will be a shortage of rental accommodation; quantity demanded will exceed quantity supplied.

(2) The quantity of accommodation occupied will be less than if free-market rents had been charged.

(3) Black markets will appear. Landlords may require large lump-sum entrance fees from new tenants, and may evict existing tenants so as to collect this new entrance fee. Existing tenants may sublet their accommodation, charging the market price while themselves paying only the controlled price. In general, the larger the housing shortage, the bigger the entrance fee that landlords charge, and the bigger the profit that tenants who sublet can earn.

(4) To protect tenants, governments pass security-of-tenure laws, which protect the tenant from eviction and thus give existing tenants priority over potential new tenants. By making it harder to evict undesirable tenants, these laws reduce the expected return from any given rental price. This shifts the supply curve to the left and further aggravates the shortage.

(5) By suppressing price signals, rent controls

---

[1] For a discussion of rent controls in Britain, see C. Harbury and R. G. Lipsey, *An Introduction to the UK Economy* (London: Pitman, 1989), Chapter 6.

lead to large shortages in expanding parts of the country, but may cause no shortages in contracting parts where demand is shrinking as fast as the quantity supplied. Under free-market conditions, rent would rise in expanding areas, such as the southeast of England, and fall in contracting areas, such as the north of England and parts of Scotland. This would provide a signal to private investors to build rental accommodation in the expanding areas, but not in the contracting ones.

To go beyond what we have established so far, we need to say a little about the special aspects of the market for rental accommodation. The supply of accommodation depends on the *stock* of rental housing available, and in any year it is composed mainly of buildings built in earlier years. The stock is added to by conversions of owner-occupied housing, and construction of new buildings. It is diminished by conversions to other uses, and demolition or abandonment of existing buildings whose economic life is over. The stock usually changes slowly.

These considerations mean we can draw more than one supply curve for rental accommodation depending on how much time is allowed for reactions to occur to any given level of rents. We shall distinguish just two such curves. The *long-run supply curve* relates rents to the quantity of rental accommodation that will be supplied after sufficient time has passed for all adjustments to be made. The *short-run supply curve* relates rents to quantity supplied when only a short time – say, a few months – is allowed for immediate adjustments to be made in response to a change in rents. In the short run, very few new conversions and very little new construction can occur.

The long-run supply curve: There is a large potential source of supply of rental accommodation, for it is relatively easy to build a new block of flats or to convert an existing house and offer its units for rent. If the expected return from investing in new rental units rises significantly above the return on comparable other investments, there will be a flow of investment funds into the building of new flats.

Because of the ease of entry, there is a long-run tendency for the rate of profit on rental accommodation to be pushed to the rate that can be earned on similar investments elsewhere in the economy.

If the return from rental accommodation falls significantly below that obtainable on comparable investments, investment will go elsewhere. The construction of new accommodation will fall off and possibly stop altogether. Old flats will not be replaced as they wear out, so the quantity available will fall drastically. Existing flats may be removed from the rental market. Their freehold, or leasehold, will be sold. Conversion takes some time, and depletion of the housing stock, as old flats wear out and are not replaced, can take many decades. So the full long-run adjustment to prices below equilibrium can take a long time.

The long-run supply of rental accommodation is highly responsive to changes in market conditions, making the long-run supply curve quite elastic; long periods of time may be required for full adjustment, particularly where a reduction in the housing stock is called for.

The short-run supply curve: Now consider the supply response over a few months. What happens when rents rise? Even though investment in new blocks of flats immediately becomes profitable, years will pass while land is obtained, plans drawn up and construction completed. Of course, some existing housing can be quickly converted to rental uses, but even this often takes more than a few months.

What if rents fall? New construction will fall off, and this will surely decrease the supply at some time in the future. The owners of existing accommodation with few alternative uses will be willing to rent them for whatever they will earn, providing that the rentals at least cover current out-of-pocket costs such as cleaning and heating. Some rental housing can be abandoned or converted to other uses, but, again, this will not usually happen very quickly.

Thus the short-run supply curve that relates rentals to the quantity supplied tends to be quite *inelastic* at the level of the quantity currently supplied.

The demand for rental accommodation: There are many reasons to expect the demand for rental accommodation to be responsive to variations in rents. As rents rise in a particular area, each of the following will occur:

(1) some people will stop renting and will buy instead;

(2) some will move to where rental accommodation is cheaper;

(3) some will economize on the amount of housing they use by renting smaller, cheaper accommodation (or renting out a room or two in their present accommodation);

(4) some will double up, and others will not 'undouble' (for example, young adults will not move out of parental homes as quickly as they might otherwise have done).

Such behaviour contributes to a substantial elasticity of the demand for rental housing.

Rent Controls Again

These special features of the housing market allow us to be more specific about the effects of controls that keep the price of rental accommodation below its equilibrium value.

As shown in Figure 7.3, most of the initial effects of rent controls are on the demand side. A shortage is caused mainly because quantity demanded exceeds the equilibrium quantity supplied, with only a small shortfall of quantity supplied below its equilibrium value as a secondary cause of the shortage. Over the long term, however, supply falls greatly, and the main cause of the shortage of rental accommodation comes from the supply side. Under free-market conditions, rents would rise and quantity demanded would shrink as people economized on housing.

Rent controls prevent such increases in rents from occurring. Thus, even while the quantity of rental accommodation is contracting for the reasons discussed above, the signal to economize on rental accommodation is *not* given through rising rents. The housing shortage grows as the stock of rental accommodation shrinks while nothing decreases the demand for it.

The long lag helps to explain why rent controls are so often tolerated in spite of the harm that they do in the long run. The first generation of tenants gains from controlled rents while future generations suffer from a drastically reduced supply of rental accommodation.

The growing housing shortage puts pressure

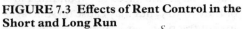

FIGURE 7.3 Effects of Rent Control in the Short and Long Run

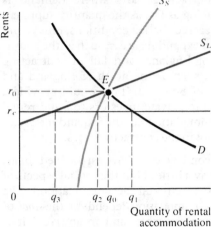

Rent control causes housing shortages that worsen as time passes. The controlled rent of r_c forces rents below their free-market equilibrium value of r_0. The short-run supply of housing is shown by the rather inelastic curve S_S. The controls reduce quantity supplied to q_2 in the short run, and the housing shortage becomes $q_1 - q_2$. Over time, supply falls, as shown by the long-run supply curve S_L. In long-run equilibrium, there are only q_3 units of rental accommodation, far fewer than when controls were instituted. Since the long-run supply is quite elastic, the shortage of rental accommodation of $q_1 - q_3$ that occurs after supply has fully adjusted, ends up being much larger than the initial shortage of $q_1 - q_2$.

on the state to build the accommodation that private investors will not supply at controlled rents. Local authorities have done so for decades in the UK, supplying large quantities of council housing. In response to financial stringency in the 1980s, however, the construction of new council housing was curtailed. As a result, the supply of rental accommodation has fallen from its already low levels.

The shortage of rental accommodation makes existing occupiers reluctant to move from areas of high unemployment to areas where unemployment is low but rent-controlled accommodation hard to find. People are also reluctant to move out of accommodation that is no longer suitable because families have grown up and moved away.

Effective rent control leads to housing shortages, black-market prices, security-

of-tenure laws, pressure for public housing and reluctance of sitting tenants to
move from their present accommodations, even when these are no longer
suitable.

Evaluations

Whatever else it does, rent control does
not, over the long run, provide ordinary
people with a secure supply of rental
accommodation at below market prices.

Although rent control does lower the cost of
accommodation over the short run, which may
last decades, it eventually leads to a severe
reduction in the supply of rental accommodation.

Rent control is not an effective method of
redistributing income from higher- to lower-
income persons. Although some tenants are poor,
many are well off; although some landlords are
wealthy, some are of quite modest means. As a
result, rent control, which redistributes income
from landlords to tenants, causes a haphazard
redistribution of income among income classes.

Rent control does not in the long run help
lower-income persons. The growing shortage of
rental accommodation forces more and more
people to buy freeholds or long leases. It is easier
for higher-income people to save, or borrow, the
purchase price than it is for lower-income people.
Thus the very people that rent controls were
meant to help most are hurt most by its long-run
effects. They are the ones least able to cope with
finding lump-sum purchase prices rather than
weekly, monthly or quarterly rent payments.

Minimum-price Legislation

Governments sometimes pass laws stating that
certain goods and services cannot be sold below
some stated minimum price. In many Western
countries today there are minimum-wage laws
specifying 'floors' for the wages to be paid to
different kinds of labour. Resale price maintenance, which exists in many countries, gives the
manufacturer power to prevent the retailer from
selling below the prices that are set by the
manufacturer.

The effects on price and quantity: The case
of a commodity subject to minimum-price legis-

FIGURE 7.4 A Minimum Price

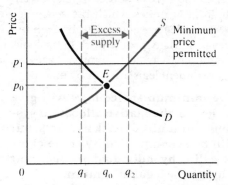

**If a price floor is above the equilibrium price,
quantity supplied will exceed quantity
demanded.** The free-market equilibrium is at E,
with price p_0 and quantity q_0. If the minimum
permitted price is p_1, quantity supplied will exceed
quantity demanded by $q_2 - q_1$. If the government does
nothing, this excess supply will be in private hands,
and either will be wasted or will accumulate as stocks.
If the government buys the excess supply, producers
will be able to sell their output of q_2, but the
government must store or dispose of the quantity
$q_2 - q_1$ each period.

lation is illustrated in Figure 7.4. An effective
minimum raises actual price above the free-
market equilibrium. This causes quantity supplied to rise, while quantity demanded falls. The
result is surplus production.

The setting of minimum prices will have
no effect (minimum prices set at or below
the equilibrium) or will cause a surplus of
the commodity (minimum price set
above the equilibrium), reducing the
quantity actually bought and sold below
its equilibrium value.

**No alternative allocation systems and no
black markets:** At the legally enforced minimum price, there is no scarcity of the controlled
commodity. Therefore, alternative allocative systems will not grow up. Nor will a black market,
where people buy legally at the controlled
price and sell illegally at the free-market price.

There will, however, be a shortage of purchasers, and potential suppliers may compete in
various ways for the available customers. Suppliers will look for ways of cutting prices; some
will find loopholes in the law; others will flout it.

For example, travel clubs and other organizations arose in the 1970s in order to take advantage of cheap group rates which the scheduled airlines were not legally allowed to offer individual passengers. Many people work in the black economy in order to avoid minimum wages set either by government legislation or by unions.

Effective minimum-price laws will give rise neither to alternative allocation systems nor to organized black markets, but they will be accompanied by some clandestine selling by individual producers at prices below the legal minimum.

Empirical evidence: Next, we shall see that the setting of minimum prices in the agricultural sector of the economy has led, just as the theory predicts, to excess supply. Governments responsible for these minimum prices have found embarrassing surpluses of unsold agricultural goods piling up in their warehouses, surpluses that cannot be sold at the legislated minimum prices.

In Chapter 18 we extend the analysis to cover minimum-wage legislation. There we find that the predicted surpluses take the form of unemployment, particularly among young people who cannot find employment at the minimum wage.

Sometimes governments or producers' associations set prices above the competitive level, but avoid surpluses by assigning each producer a quota. Quantity supplied is thus held equal to the quantity demanded at the controlled price. OPEC functions in this way, and IATA – the body that regulates international air fares – is not too dissimilar.

It is remarkable how many predictions the simple theory of market price yields about the effects of minimum and maximum price controls. It is also remarkable how often these predictions have been confirmed by empirical evidence. Nonetheless, many governments continue to pass price-control legislation in apparent ignorance of its likely consequences.

THE PROBLEMS OF AGRICULTURE[1]

To the casual observer, the agricultural sector of almost any advanced Western economy presents a series of paradoxes. Food is a basic necessity of life. Yet, over the last century, agricultural sectors have been declining in relative importance, and many of those persons who have remained on the land have been receiving incomes well below national averages.

Governments have felt it necessary to intervene, and have resorted to a bewildering array of controls and subsidies. These have often led to the accumulation of vast surpluses which have sometimes rotted in storage and sometimes been sold abroad at prices below production costs. All of this has gone on against a backdrop of endemic malnutrition and occasional outbursts of famine in the Third World. We may now use the theory of market price to gain some insight into modern agricultural problems.

Short-term Fluctuations in Prices and Incomes: Supply-side Influences

Agricultural production is subject to large variations due to factors beyond human control: bad weather reduces output below that planned by farmers, while exceptionally good weather pushes production above planned levels. What are the effects of these unplanned fluctuations?

A supply curve shows desired output and sales at each market price. If there are unplanned variations in output, then actual output will diverge from its planned level. By now you should not be surprised to hear that such unplanned fluctuations in output cause fluctuations in prices. Not only does price theory predict this consequence, it also predicts other, less obvious ones that help us to understand some aspects of the agricultural problem.

The basic predictions are derived in Figure 7.5. Variations in farm output cause prices to fluctuate in the opposite direction to crop sizes. A bumper crop sends prices down; a poor crop sends them up. The price changes will be larger the less elastic the demand curve.

Because farm products often have inelastic demands, price fluctuations tend to be large in response to unplanned changes in production.

---

[1] For a discussion of British agricultural policy, see Harbury and Lipsey, op. cit., Chapters 1 and 6.

FIGURE 7.5 The Effect on Price of Unplanned Variations in Output Depends on Elasticity of Demand

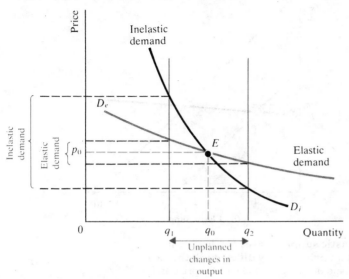

Unplanned fluctuations in output lead to much sharper fluctuations in price if the demand curve is inelastic than if it is elastic. Suppose that the expected price is p_0 and the planned output is q_0. The two curves D_i and D_e are alternative demand curves. If actual production always equalled planned production, the equilibrium price and quantity would be p_0 and q_0 with either demand curve. Unplanned variations in output, however, cause quantity to fluctuate year by year between q_1 (a bad harvest) and q_2 (a good harvest). When demand is inelastic (shown by the black curve), prices will show large fluctuations. When demand is elastic (shown by the grey curve), prices will show much smaller fluctuations. (In both cases, elasticity is measured around the point E.)

Now consider the effects on the revenues received by farmers from the sale of their crops.[1] Here the relations are a bit more complex, but they all follow immediately from the results established on page 84. If the product in question has an elastic demand, farmers' revenues are raised by good harvests and lowered by bad harvests. If the product has an inelastic demand, however, good harvests lower farmers' revenues, while bad harvests raise them.[2] If the demand elasticity happens to be unity, then farmers' revenues will not vary as output and prices vary, because every change in output will be met by an exactly offsetting change in price.

Unplanned variations in output will cause producers' revenues:

(1) to vary in the same direction as output varies whenever demand for the product is elastic;

(2) to vary in the opposite direction as output varies whenever demand for the product is inelastic;

(3) to fluctuate more, the further the elasticity of demand diverges from unity in either direction.

Since many agricultural commodities have inelastic demands, farmers often see their incomes dwindling when nature is unexpectedly kind in producing a bumper crop, while their incomes rise when crops are poor.

Cyclical Fluctuations in Prices and Incomes: Demand-side Influence

Agricultural markets are subject not only to short-run instabilities due to uncontrollable changes in output, but also to cyclical instability due to shifts in demand. In periods of prosperity, employment and wages are high, which implies a strong demand for most commodities. In periods of depressed business activity, employment and wages are diminished, which implies a weak demand for most commodities. Thus the demand curves for most commodities rise and fall as business activity ebbs and flows.

The effects on commodity prices are analysed in Figure 7.6. Industrial products typically have

---

[1] While we can only make predictions in this section about their revenues, such receipts are closely related to farmers' incomes. We can, therefore, without risk of serious error, extend these predictions to incomes.

[2] It does not follow that every individual farmer's income must rise (after all, some farmers may have nothing to harvest); it follows only that the aggregate revenue earned by *all* farmers must rise.

FIGURE 7.6 The Effect on Receipts of a Shift in Demand

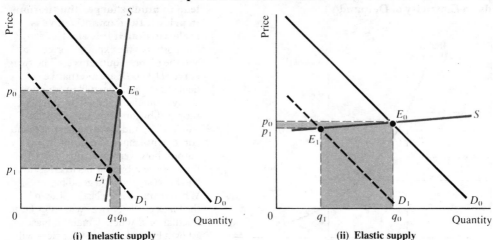

(i) **Inelastic supply**   (ii) **Elastic supply**

**When demand falls both inelastic and elastic supply curves can lead to a
sharp decrease in receipts, but the effect on price is very different in the two
cases.** In each part of the diagram, when demand decreases from D_0 to D_1, price and
quantity decrease from p_0 and q_0 to p_1 and q_1. Total receipts decline by the shaded area.
In (i), which is typical of many agricultural markets, the result is mainly a sharp
decrease in price. Output and employment remain high, but the drastic fall in price
will reduce or eliminate profits and put downward pressure on wages. In (ii), which is
typical of the markets for manufactured goods, the result is primarily a sharp decrease
in quantity. Employment and total profits earned fall drastically, though wage rates
and profit margins on what is produced may remain close to their former levels.

The effects of an increase in demand are merely the reverse of those just studied.
They can be seen by letting the initial demand curve be D_1, while the shift takes it to
D_0.

rather elastic supply curves, so that demand
shifts tend to cause large changes in outputs but
small changes in prices. Agricultural commodities tend to have rather inelastic supplies. Thus,
when demand falls due to a decline in general
business activity, prices tend to fall drastically in
agriculture but to remain fairly stable in manufacturing. In both cases, revenues fluctuate
cyclically.

**When demand falls and the supply is very
inelastic, revenue falls because *price* falls
a great deal; when demand falls and
the supply is very elastic, revenue falls
because *quantity* falls a great deal.**

Agricultural Stabilization Programmes

In free-market economies, agricultural incomes
often tend to *fluctuate* around a low *average* level.

As a result, agricultural stabilization programmes often have two goals: to reduce the
fluctuations and to raise the average level of farm
incomes. We shall see that the two goals, stable
incomes and reasonably high incomes, often
conflict with each other.

Stabilization schemes can be illustrated by
considering those designed to lessen the effect of
unplanned fluctuations in supply. A similar analysis could be carried out for schemes designed
to lessen the effects of fluctuations in demand.

**Market stabilization by a producers'
association:** One method of preventing
fluctuations in prices and incomes is for the
individual farmers to form a producers' association which stabilizes the quantity coming on to
the market, in spite of variations in production.
Under the conditions shown in Figure 7.7, a
producers' association can stabilize price and
income in spite of year-to-year fluctuations in

FIGURE 7.7 Alternative Schemes for Price Stabilization

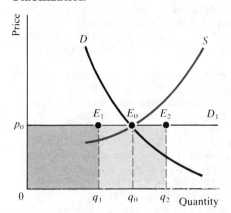

Stabilizing quantity sold stabilizes income: though merely stabilizing price does not. The curve S shows planned supply at each price; p_0 and q_0 are the equilibrium price and quantity, respectively. Actual production is assumed to vary in an unplanned manner between q_1 and q_2.

(i) *A producers' association.* When production is q_2 the producers' association sells q_0 and stores $q_2 - q_0$. When production is q_1 it still sells q_0, supplementing the current production by selling $q_0 - q_1$ from its stocks. Producers' revenue is stabilized at $p_0 \times q_0$.

(ii) *Government purchases and sales at a stabilized price.* The quantity sold to the public is always q_0, and this stabilizes price at p_0. Producers sell their whole crop every year. When production is q_2 the government buys $q_2 - q_0$ and stores it. When production is q_1 the government sells $q_0 - q_1$ from storage. The government policy converts the demand curve facing farmers from D to D_1. If q_0 is average production, there is no trend towards the accumulation of stocks. Farmers' revenue varies from $p_0 \times q_1$ (the darker-shaded area) when production is q_1, to $p_0 \times q_2$ (the entire light- and dark-shaded areas) when production is q_2.

output. It does this by selling the same quantity every year, adding to its stocks when output exceeds that quantity and selling from its stocks when output falls short. Provided that the level of sales to be maintained is equal to the average level of production over good and bad years, the policy can be carried on indefinitely. If, however, the producers attempt to keep the price too high, sales will be less than average production. Then, taken over a number of years, additions to stocks will exceed sales from stocks, and the association's stockpile will grow.

Market stabilization by government sales and purchases: What will happen if a producers' association is not formed but the government itself attempts to stabilize the incomes of farmers? To do this, the government buys and adds to its own stockpile when there is a surplus, and sells when there is a shortage. The government is assumed not to consume any of the commodity but only to hold stocks. If it wishes to stabilize farmers' incomes, should it aim, like the producers' association, at keeping price constant at all times?

This policy will not stabilize farmers' incomes. Farmers are now faced with an infinitely elastic demand at a stabilized price. They are able to sell any amount at that price: whatever the public will not buy, the government will purchase. The second part of the caption to Figure 7.7 shows that, if prices are held constant and farmers sell their whole production each year, farmers' incomes will fluctuate in proportion to fluctuations in production. This government policy, therefore, will not eliminate income fluctuations but will simply reverse their direction. Now, good crops will be associated with high incomes, while poor crops will be associated with low incomes.

What, then, must a government's policy be if it wishes to stabilize farmers' revenues through its own purchases and sales in the open market? Too much price stability causes revenues to vary directly with production, as in the case just considered, while too little price stability causes them to vary inversely with production, as in the free-market case shown in Figure 7.5. It appears that the government should aim at some intermediate degree of price stability. In fact, if it allows prices to vary in inverse proportion to variations in production, revenues will be stabilized. A 10 per cent rise in production should be met by a 10 per cent fall in price, and a 10 per cent fall in production by a 10 per cent rise in price.

Figure 7.8 analyses this policy. Farmers sell their whole crop each year. When production unexpectedly exceeds normal output, the government buys in the market. It allows price to fall, but only by the same proportion that production has increased. When production unexpectedly falls short of normal output, the government enters the market and sells some of its stocks. It allows price to rise, but only by the

**FIGURE 7.8 Government Income Stabilization
with Variable Price**

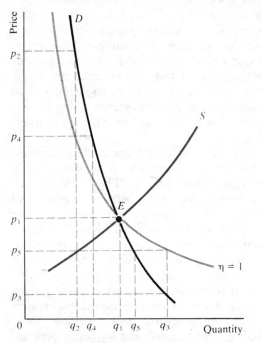

Income stabilization is obtained by allowing
prices to fluctuate in inverse proportion to
output. D is demand, S is planned supply and
equilibrium is at E. However, actual production
fluctuates between q_2 and q_3, and these fluctuations
cause the free-market price to fluctuate between p_2
and p_3.

A curve of unit elasticity through its whole range is
drawn through E and labelled $\eta = 1$. When
production is q_3, market price must be held at p_5, if
income is to be unchanged. But, at market price p_5,
the public only wishes to purchase q_5 and it is
therefore necessary for the government to buy up the
remaining production, $q_3 - q_5$, and add it to its stocks.
Farmers' total sales are q_3 at price p_5, and since the
grey curve is a rectangular hyperbola, it follows that
income $p_5 \times q_3$ is equal to income $p_1 \times q_1$.

When production is equal to q_2, price must be
allowed to rise to p_4 (by construction the area $p_4 \times q_2$ is
equal to the area $p_1 \times q_1$). But at price p_4 the public will
wish to buy q_4, so that the government must sell
$q_4 - q_2$ out of its stocks.

To stabilize income, any given output must be sold
at a price determined by the curve labelled $\eta = 1$. To
achieve that price, the government buys or sells from
its stocks an amount equal to the horizontal distance
between the $\eta = 1$ curve and the demand curve.

same proportion that production has fallen below
normal. Thus, as farmers encounter unplanned
fluctuations in their output, they encounter
exactly offsetting fluctuations in prices so that
their revenues are stabilized.

This policy has the following results. First,
price fluctuations are smaller than they would be
on a completely free market. Second, total
revenues of the producers are stabilized in the
face of fluctuations in production. Finally, the
government scheme is self-financing. In fact, if
we ignore costs of storage, the scheme will show a
profit, for the government will be buying at low
prices – the lower the price, the more it buys –
and selling at high prices – the higher the price,
the more it sells.

Problems with Stabilization Policies

The above analysis illustrates some of the many
types of stabilization schemes and shows how the
theory of price can be used to predict their
consequences. If such schemes have all the
advantages outlined above, why is there so much
trouble with most actual stabilization programmes?

Choosing the proper price: One of the major
problems arises from uncertainty, combined
with political pressure applied by farmers. Demand and supply curves are never known
exactly, so the central authorities do not know
average production over a number of years at
each possible price. They do not know, therefore,
exactly what level of income they can try to
achieve while also keeping average sales from
stocks equal to average purchases for stocks.
Since farmers have votes, there is strong pressure
on any government to be over-generous. If the
price, and hence the level of income, is fixed too
high, then the government will have to buy
unsold crops in most years. Thus stocks will
build up more or less continuously and, sooner or
later, they will have to be destroyed, given away
or dumped on the market for what they will
bring, thus forcing the market price down, de-
feating the purpose for which the crops were
originally purchased.

The government's plan will now show a deficit,
which will have to be covered by taxation. This
means that people in cities will be paying farmers
for producing goods which cannot be sold at a

price covering their costs of production. The next step is often to try to limit the production of each farmer. Quotas may be assigned to individual farmers, and penalties imposed for exceeding them, or bonuses may be paid for leaving land idle. Such measures attempt to avoid the consequence of there being too many resources allocated to the agricultural sector by preventing these resources from producing all that they could.

Government policies that stabilize prices at too high a level will cause excess supply, a rising level of unsold stocks, and pressure for further government intervention to restrict output.

The long-term problem of resource allocation: Even if the temptation to set too high a price is avoided, there is still a formidable problem facing the managers of agricultural-stabilization programmes. Output and real incomes have been rising at an average rate of about 2 per cent per year over the last 100 years in the countries that now form the European Community. As real incomes have risen, however, consumers have chosen to spend more of their extra incomes on durable consumers' goods and less on food and other basic commodities. If the allocation of resources had remained unchanged, production of each commodity would have risen in proportion to the rise of productivity in the

industry producing that commodity. This would cause shortages and surpluses.

Assume for simplicity that productivity expands more or less uniformly in all industries. The demand for commodities with low income elasticities will be expanding more slowly than output; excess supplies will develop, prices and profits will be depressed, and it will be necessary for resources to move out of these industries. Exactly the reverse will happen for commodities with high income elasticities: demand will expand faster than supply, prices and profits will tend to rise, and resources will move into those industries. Table 7.1 provides an illustrative numerical example.

With continuous productivity increases, there will be a *continuous tendency* toward excess supply of commodities with low income elasticities and excess demand for commodities with high elasticities. This will mean a continuous movement of resources out of industries producing the former type of commodities into industries producing the latter.

In a free-market economy, this reallocation will take place under the incentives of low prices, wages and incomes in the declining sector, and high prices, wages and incomes in the expanding sector. Look at Table 7.1 again. Because there is excess supply in the agricultural sector, prices will fall, taking producers' incomes down with

TABLE 7.1 The Long-run Allocation Problem

	Agriculture	Manufacturing
Production originally was	50.0	50.0
Production after productivity change, if there were no reallocation of resources, would be	100.0	100.0
Income elasticity of demand is	0.5	1.5
Therefore quantity demanded after rise in income is	75.0	125.0
Therefore surplus or shortage is	25.0 (surplus)	25.0 (shortage)

As economic growth proceeds, resources must move from industries with low income elasticities to industries with high income elasticities. This simple, illustrative economy is divided into an agricultural and a manufacturing sector. Originally, resources are divided equally between the two. Productivity then doubles in both sectors. The incomes of all consumers double, but the income elasticity of demand for manufactured goods is higher than the income elasticity of demand for agricultural goods. The rise in productivity causes a surplus equal to one-quarter of the agricultural production, and a shortage equal to one-quarter of the manufactured-goods production.

them. There will be a decline in the demand for farm labour and the other factors of production used in agriculture, and the earnings of these factors will also decline. At the same time, the opposite tendencies will be observed in manufacturing. Here demand is expanding faster than supply; prices will rise; incomes and profits of producers will be rising. There will be a large demand for the factors of production used in manufacturing industries, so that the price of these factors, and consequently the incomes that they earn, will be bid upwards. In short, manufacturing will be a buoyant, expanding industry and agriculture will be a depressed, contracting industry.[1]

In a free-market economy, the mechanism for a continued reallocation of resources out of low-income-elasticity industries and into high-income-elasticity ones is a continued tendency for prices and incomes to be depressed in contracting industries, and a continued tendency for prices and incomes to be buoyant in expanding industries.

Stabilization schemes that guarantee a 'reasonable' income to farmers remove the incentive for resources to transfer out of the agricultural sector. Unless some other means is found to persuade resources to transfer, a larger and larger proportion of the resources currently devoted to agriculture will become redundant. Productivity growth will be raising quantity supplied faster than income growth is raising quantity demanded. If, however, the government does not intervene at all, leaving the price mechanism to accomplish the resource allocation, a more or less permanently depressed agricultural sector must be accepted.

Economists cannot prove that governments ought, or ought not, to interfere with the price mechanism. By providing some insight into the workings of the price mechanism, economics can, however, predict some of the gains and losses. It can also point out problems that must be solved if intervention is to be successful.

---

[1] Notice that for purposes of illustration we have divided the economy into only two parts. Thus 'manufacturing' stands for everything but agriculture. Similar problems of reallocation could arise within this 'manufacturing sector'.

If the problem of reallocating resources out of the rural sector is not solved, intervention to secure high and stable levels of farm incomes will be unsuccessful over any long period of time. It will give rise to a characteristic, and predictable, set of problems that will eventually defeat the original purposes of the schemes.

The EC's Agricultural Policy

The Common Agricultural Policy of the European Community, nicknamed the CAP, amply illustrates the validity of the theories just outlined. The policy holds agricultural prices well above their market equilibrium values within the EC. To prevent the flood of imports that would be attracted by these high prices, all imported agricultural goods are subject to a tariff. The high European prices cause production to exceed consumption. Surpluses pile up, only to be destroyed or sold abroad at a fraction of their production costs. EC farmers gain, while taxpayers and efficient foreign producers are the losers. The payments to farmers have risen so much over the years that they threaten the EC with financial crisis, since its spending now consistently exceeds its revenues.

Box 7.1 presents a brief report on EC farm policy taken from *The Economist*. Readers should study it and see what pieces of analysis given earlier in this chapter explain the economic forces lying behind the various issues raised in the article.

SOME GENERAL LESSONS ABOUT THE PRICE SYSTEM

In this chapter we have illustrated the usefulness of the theory of price determination in individual competitive markets. We conclude with some important general observations about the price system.

The Interrelationship of Markets

Our first observation concerns the interrelationship of markets. Markets do not function in isolation from each other. Instead, the economy

BOX 7.1 THE CRISIS IN THE EC's COMMON AGRICULTURAL POLICY*

Farming in most rich countries is in a classic mess. As food prices have tumbled on world markets, subsidies to farmers (paid through taxes or propped-up food prices) have spiralled to more than $100 billion a year. Such protectionism only sharpens the appetite for more; it never achieves its proclaimed goals. Farmers' incomes and land prices are falling, bankruptcies are rising. Now the Americans have urged the EEC to agree to abolish all subsidies and barriers to agricultural trade within ten years. The Americans have good reasons for wanting a change: their own spending on farm support has trebled in the past three years.

The main way in which the EEC's common agricultural policy supports farmers is by Eurocrats setting guaranteed prices for dairy products, beef, cereals, sugar. If market prices fall below the floor, intervention agencies buy the surpluses. This rigged system is buttressed by import levies and export subsidies, and its benefits go mainly to the wrong people. Three-quarters of EEC farm support reaches the biggest and richest 25% of farmers, concentrated in the wealthier northern countries. They get nearly $10,000 a year each from Europe's taxpayers. The other quarter goes to the poorer, southern 75% of farmers. They get about $1,000 a year each. Most distortingly, because German and French politicians want their farmers to have average German and French incomes, the EEC

pays Karl and Jacques to produce butter at five times the price at which New Zealanders can do it; some of this butter is dumped on world markets at under one-fifth of its true cost, making economic New Zealand butter unsellable.

Europe's farm ministers recognise some of these absurdities, but prefer to tackle the symptoms (eg, through curbing surpluses of milk and sugar by imposing production quotas) rather than the cause (which is the gap between Community prices and world prices). Quotas have sometimes made the gap worse, because farmers have received higher prices to compensate them for not being allowed to produce so much of what is not wanted. Quotas also freeze market shares. Trading in quotas mitigates this, but creates nonsenses of its own. In parts of Britain a farmer's milk quotas are now worth more than his land. Curbs on milk output can just mean more beef or cereals. When everything is in surplus, quotas are a nightmare of red tape, with each farmer having to account for his production down to the last bunch of radishes.

Every statesman knows that a better solution would be sharp cuts in support prices, but these are called politically impossible.

* Excerpted from *The Economist*, 3 October 1987, pp. 18–19.

is composed of an interlocking system in which anything happening in one market has profound effects on many other markets and could, potentially, influence all others.

Consider, for example, the effects of a large rise in the demand for some product. Fairly soon it will be met by a rise in production. If the rise in demand is judged to be permanent, firms in the industry will begin to increase their productive capacity. Employment will rise, and producers may try to attract labour from other industries by offering higher wages. Thus one of the first impacts on other markets will be a loss of labour, and possibly a need to raise wages in order to compete for labour with the expanding industry. This will cause profits to fall in these other industries.

The increased employment in the expanding industry may cause some geographical movement of labour. This in turn will cause a rise in the demand for housing in expanding centres and a corresponding fall elsewhere. New housing

construction will lead to a rise in the demand for construction workers and materials. Quarries and brickworks may have to take on additional labour and expand output.

Further, there will be a rise in the demand for materials used in the expanding industry. Firms making component parts elsewhere in the country, and raw-material producers on the other side of the world, may be affected. If new investment in factories and machinery takes place, there will be a rise in the demand for many capital goods; shortages and bottlenecks may develop, and other industries which use these capital goods may find that their costs go up, and they may have trouble meeting delivery dates. There will also be a change in consumers' expenditure because some people's earnings will be increased and other people's reduced. Imports and exports will change and, as a result, the exchange rate may be affected. If sterling rises in value on the foreign-exchange market, this will encourage imports of other commodities and discourage exports. If sterling falls in value, this will have the opposite effects. Thus the influence of a change in one market will spread through the economy rather like the ripples which spread out over the smooth surface of a pond after a pebble has been dropped into it.

The Price System is a Control Mechanism

When shortages develop in a market economy, prices rise and profit-seeking entrepreneurs want to produce more of the commodities in short supply. When surpluses occur, prices fall and producers voluntarily contract supply. It was the great discovery of eighteenth-century economists that a competitive price system produces a co-ordination of effort in which – by seeking their own private gains and responding to such public signals as prices, costs and profit rates – individuals react in a co-ordinated fashion to changes in demand and supply.

> **No one consciously created the price system. No central administrator needs to foresee and consciously co-ordinate the necessary changes; adjustments occur automatically as a result of the separate decisions taken by a large number of individuals, all seeking their own best interests, and all responding to market signals that are there for all to see.**

The reader who believes that behaviour in a free-market economy is unplanned, and unco-ordinated, must abandon this notion. The existence of a co-ordinating mechanism – the price system – is beyond dispute. A case can be made that no practical alternative works as well as the unaided price system. This case is not accepted, however, by advocates of a mixed system in which substantial government intervention is designed to improve the workings of markets.[1] This question of how well the free-market system works in comparison with practical, alternative co-ordinating systems has been debated for two

hundred years, and is still a great unsettled social question. We consider this issue in more detail in later chapters.

Shifts in consumers' demand or producers' costs cause changes in market prices. Rising prices tend to produce rising profits. Rising profits attract further resources into production. Short-term, windfall profits (i.e. profits that bear no relation to current costs) repeatedly occur in market economies; they induce resources to move into the profitable industries until the profits are forced back to levels that can be earned elsewhere in the economy.

Falling prices, and falling profits, provide the opposite motivations. Purchasers are inclined to buy more; sellers are inclined to produce less, and resources move out of the industry and into more profitable alternative uses.

Free-market Prices and Profits Encourage Economical Use of Resources

Prices and profits in a market economy provide signals to both demanders and suppliers. On the demand side, a high and rising price (relative to other prices) provides an incentive to purchasers to economize on the commodity. Consumers may choose to buy substitutes whose prices have not risen, or to shift expenditure to quite different types of commodities. There is substantial scope for such economizing reactions, even for commodities as 'necessary' as housing: *some* housing is necessary, but a particular quantity and quality are not.

On the supply side, changing prices provide the incentive for many types of adaptation. If a particular input such as oil or steel becomes scarce, its price will rise. Firms will have an incentive to economize on its use and to replace it where possible with cheaper substitutes. Thus without ever knowing national scarcities, firms are led to react to them by responding to market prices. They will make lavish uses of resources that are plentiful and less use of resources that are scarce as a natural consequence of trying to maximize their own profits in the face of market prices that reflect national demands and supplies.

> **Free-market prices and profits are signals to producers and consumers.**

---

[1] The experience of contemporary command economies has convinced most observers that a complete command economy is vastly inferior to a mixed-market economy. So most debate is over the optimum degree of government intervention in an economy in which market forces are given substantial play.

Changes in relative prices and profits signal a need for adaptation and change. By responding to these signals, consumers and producers cause the required changes.

Government Controls Require Alternative Allocative Mechanisms

When controls are used to prevent prices from rising in response to an increase in demand, the signal is not given to consumers to economize on a commodity that is in short supply. On the supply side, when prices and profits are prevented from rising (on the grounds, for example, that no more than a 'fair' return should be earned at all times), the profit signals that would attract new resources into the industry are never given. The shortage continues, and the changes in demand and supply that would remove it are not set in motion.

In the opposite case, where there is excess supply, an appropriate response would be an increase in quantity purchased and a decrease in production, accompanied by a shift of resources to production of other, more valued commodities. Falling prices and profits would motivate such shifts. When prices are prevented from falling in the face of temporary surpluses (on the grounds, for example, that producers of an essential product must have a 'fair' return guaranteed to them), the signals that would increase purchases, or move resources out of an industry, are not given.

If the price system is not used to allocate resources, alternative methods will necessarily appear. If prices are held constant, temporary fluctuations in demand and supply give rise to shortages and surpluses. During times of shortage, allocation will be by sellers' preferences, unless the state imposes rationing. During periods of surplus, unsold supplies will accumulate, or prices will be cut illegally, unless the state buys and stores the surpluses. Long-run changes in demand and costs will not induce reallocations through private decisions. As a result, the state will be put under strong, long-run pressure to step in. It will have to force, or order, resources out of industries where prices are held above

their free-market level into industries where prices are held below their free-market level.

Any specific alternative scheme of allocation that is imposed is costly in a number of additional ways. First, the allocation itself usually requires the use of resources for administering and enforcing the rules. Second, centralized bureaucratic systems tend to be less flexible and adaptive than decentralized decision-taking systems. (For example, rules and laws are harder to change than market prices.) Third, the freedom of some individuals to act in what they consider their own best interest is reduced.

Sometimes the benefits of the policies will be judged to justify the costs, sometimes they will not. Justified or not, the costs are always present and need to be taken into account when balancing the pros and cons of any particular policy.

Government intervention that prevents prices and profits from responding to the conditions of demand and supply tends to inhibit the free-market allocation mechanism and requires alternative methods for allocating scarce supplies of output and scarce factors of production among their competing uses.

Costs May Be Shifted, But They Cannot Be Avoided

For society as a whole, there is no such thing as free housing. The average standard of living depends on the amounts of resources available to the economy and the efficiency with which these resources are used. Since resources are scarce, the production of any commodity has an opportunity cost. If, for example, 5 per cent of the nation's resources is required to provide housing to some stated standard, then those resources will not be available to produce other commodities.

It follows that costs of producing goods and services are incurred no matter who provides these to consumers.

Rent controls, housing subsidies or public provision of housing can change the share of the costs of housing paid by particular individuals for others. But such policies cannot make the costs go away. As it is with housing, so it is with all other commodities.

SUMMARY

1. Effective price ceilings lead to excess demand, black markets and non-price methods of allocating the scarce supplies among would-be purchasers.
2. Rent controls are a form of price ceiling. Their major consequence is a shortage of rental accommodation that gets worse due to a slow but inexorable decline in the quantity of rental accommodation.
3. Rent control does not assure a secure supply of cheap housing for lower income households; it redistributes incomes from landlord to tenant, but not necessarily from richer to poorer households.
4. Effective price floors lead to excess supply and cut-price cheating by would-be sellers who cannot find buyers at the floor price.
5. Many free-market agricultural prices are subject to wide fluctuations due to weather-induced, year-to-year fluctuations in supply operating on inelastic demand curves, and cyclical fluctuations in demand operating on inelastic supply curves.
6. Appropriate government policies can stabilize agricultural incomes by reducing price fluctuations through purchases in times of surplus and sales in times of glut.
7. The long-term problems of agriculture arise from a high rate of productivity growth on the supply side and low income elasticity on the demand side. This means that unless many resources are being transferred out of agriculture fairly rapidly, quantity supplied tends to increase faster than quantity demanded year after year.
8. Stabilization schemes that hold prices above their free-market levels on average, over short-term and cyclical swings, frustrate the long-term adjustment process and lead to ever-growing surpluses – as has the EC's Common Agricultural Policy (the CAP).
9. Major lessons about the price system are: (i) that markets are interrelated, so that what happens in one market has repercussions in many others; (ii) that the price system acts as a social control mechanism for co-ordinating decentralized decision-taking; (iii) that the system encourages an economical use of resources without anyone having to be aware of the overall national situation of resource scarcities and surpluses; (iv) that government controls over markets upset the allocative mechanism and require alternative mechanisms, which if not imposed by policy, will grow up on their own; and (v) that although government policy may shift the real cost of production from one group to another, this cost cannot be avoided – someone *must* bear it.

TOPICS FOR REVIEW

- Maximum, or ceiling, prices
- Alternative allocation systems under excess demand
- Short- and long-run effects of rent controls
- Minimum, or floor, prices
- Causes of fluctuations in agriculture prices and incomes
- Schemes for price and income stabilization, and their short- and long-term problems
- Interrelation of markets
- The price system as a social control mechanism
- Price incentives for economical use of resources
- How government controls influence the allocative mechanism
- Why costs can be shifted but not eliminated

The Elementary Dynamic Theory of Price

Statics and Dynamics

The predictions derived in previous chapters are all derived by comparing the new equilibrium position with the original equilibrium position, a technique called comparative statics. Although useful in many situations, it cannot predict the path followed from one equilibrium to another, and it cannot predict whether or not a given equilibrium will be attained. Often we are interested in how the market behaves out of equilibrium. We then require **dynamic analysis**, which is the study of the behaviour of systems in states of disequilibrium.

Agricultural Price Fluctuations

In Chapter 7, we applied comparative statics to agricultural price fluctuations. Planned production was constant and price fluctuations were caused by unplanned changes in supply. After each change, price settled at its new equilibrium level, before supply was subject to another unplanned change. The price fluctuations could thus be viewed as a series of movements between successive equilibrium positions, each one equating the current supply with demand.

Many agricultural markets exhibit systematic oscillations in price which cannot be accounted for by unplanned shifts in supply. Instead, the oscillations result from *planned* fluctuations in farmers' output. This phenomenon is explained by what are called supply lags.

Supply lags

The supply curve relates the price of the commodity to the quantity producers wish to sell. If price changes, they will want to sell a different quantity. But only after sufficient time has elapsed to give effect to decisions to change supply will there be a change in actual quantity supplied. The delay between the decision to do something and its actually being done is called a **time lag**. The delay between the decision to change quantity supplied and its actually being changed is called a **supply lag**.

Output currently coming on to the market is the result of production decisions taken in the past, while current production decisions will not have their effect on quantity supplied until some time in the future.

Every commodity has its own characteristic supply lag. For example, an increase in the demand for raw milk can be met to some extent almost immediately by diverting milk from other uses; to a greater extent within 27 months by not slaughtering calves at birth but allowing them to reach maturity; and to an ever-increasing extent over the long term by allowing the larger population of adult cows to give birth to a larger number of calves. These reactions give rise to a complex lag.

In agriculture the time interval between successive crops often determines the supply lag. A simple lag occurs when farmers look to the existing market price when deciding what crops to plant so that *next year's* supply depends on *this year's* price, while this year's supply depends on last year's price. This gives a time-lag of one year in the adjustment of quantity supplied to a change in price.[1]

When supply lags are unimportant, comparative statics will successfully predict market behaviour. When supply lags exert an important influence, many aspects of market behaviour will require dynamics for their analysis.

Agricultural markets tend to have rather long supply lags. Comparative statics is nonetheless useful in analysing the long-term behaviour of such markets. For example, the secular upward trend in the amount of beef production and in the amount of land devoted to growing grain for cattlefeed can be understood in comparative static terms. Each decade income is higher than in the previous decade. Given the high income elasticity of demand of beef, the demand curves for beef and for feed-grain can be seen as shifting rightwards over time, causing the quantities of beef and grain and their prices (relative to other prices) to rise over time.

Large cyclical ups and downs in cattle prices and production have, however, been superimposed on this upward secular trend. These cyclical movements, particularly when they take prices temporarily to unusually high levels, loom large in newspaper reports and popular discussion. To understand them, we need to take account of supply lags and use at least some elementary dynamic theory.

The Cobweb Theory

We shall now introduce an elementary dynamic theory. We assume that producers' output plans are fulfilled, but with a time-lag, and then show how *planned* changes in supply can give rise to oscillations. We shall consider only the simplest possible time-lag: this year's price has no effect whatsoever on this year's supply, the full adjust-

ment to this year's price being made all at once next year. We have already seen that such lags are typical of many agricultural products that give one crop annually, such as wheat, oats and barley.

Markets subject to simple one-year time-lags are illustrated in Figures 7A.1 and 7A.2. Look first at Figure 7A.1. The demand curve shows the relation between the price ruling in any year and the quantity that will be demanded in the same year; the supply curve shows the relation between the price ruling in any year and the quantity that will be supplied to the market in the following year. The price that equates demand and supply is p_1. At this price q_1 units will be produced and sold.

What will happen if this equilibrium is disturbed by, for example, a temporary fluctuation in either of the curves? If in one year, year t, the price is p_2, farmers will plan to produce q_2 in the following year. In that year, 'year $t+1$', q_2 will come on the market, and, in order that q_2 may be sold, the price will have to fall to p_3. The price of p_3 will induce farmers to produce the quantity q_3. When this quantity comes on the market in the following year, 'year $t+2$', the price will rise to p_4. This price will call forth a supply of q_4 the next year 'year $t+3$', and this will depress the price below p_4. It is clear from this that, in the market described in Figure 7A.1, the price and quantity will oscillate around their equilibrium values in a series of diminishing fluctuations, so that, if nothing further disturbs the market, price and quantity will eventually approach their equilibrium values, p_1 and q_1.

Now consider the case illustrated in Figure 7A.2. Exactly the same argument as in the previous paragraph applies here, and the text of that paragraph should be re-read to describe the process in this market. Notice that here, however, the last sentence of the previous paragraph does *not* apply: this time the oscillations get larger so that the equilibrium is never restored.

The market in Figure 7A.1 has an adjustment mechanism which is *stable*, while Figure 7A.2 has one which is *unstable*. A *stable adjustment mechanism* is one which will take the market to its equilibrium; the actual price and quantity will tend towards their equilibrium values. An *unstable adjustment mechanism* is one which will not take the market to its equilibrium; the actual price and quantity will tend away from equilib-

---

[1] In the terminology of the Appendix to Chapter 3 (page 43) we may write $S_t = S(p_{t-1})$, which reads: supply at time-period t depends on (i.e. is a function of) the price ruling in the previous time-period, $t-1$, where time-periods are measured in years.

FIGURE 7A.1 A Stable Cobweb

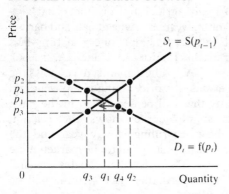

FIGURE 7A.2 An Unstable Cobweb

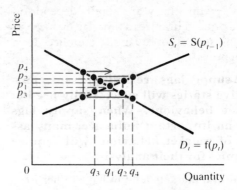

rium values. What makes one of these markets stable and the other unstable?

Given the simple supply lag that we are considering, the difference between the stable and unstable markets is in the relative slopes of the demand and supply curves. In Figure 7A.1 the demand curve is flatter than the supply curve. As price changes, the absolute quantity demanded changes more than the absolute quantity supplied. Excess demand or supply can be eliminated with only a small price change, and the price change in turn causes only a very small change in supply in the following year. Hence the supply change has only a small effect on next year's price. In Figure 7A.2 the supply curve is flatter than the demand curve; the quantity supplied responds more to price changes than the quantity demanded. When there is excess supply, a large price fall is necessary to call forth the required demand. This price fall causes a large reduction in the next year's supply (because supply is very responsive to price). Next year there is a large shortage, and a very big price increase is necessary to reduce quantity demanded to the level of the available supply. This price rise causes a very large increase in quantity supplied the following year, and so it goes, in a series of alternating periods of ever-increasing surplus and shortage.

In the unstable case the oscillations increase continually. In practice, however, the oscillations will tend to reach limits. A full theory of

such a market would require an analysis of the limits, but this is beyond the scope of this book. We have, however, established the following:

Although the price system does allocate resources, it does not always cause adjustments to occur in a smooth fashion. Where supply lags are long, and delayed reactions are large, fluctuations around equilibrium are possible with alternatively too much and too little being produced.

The cobweb model is a very simple theory, and more complicated lags on demand and supply are easy to imagine. Most such complications cannot, however, be handled without the help of mathematical analysis.[1] The study of the simplest cobweb model does, however, serve to introduce dynamic theory, and to illustrate its value by providing a reasonably satisfactory explanation of an interesting real-world phenomenon: the tendency towards oscillation in many agricultural markets with periods of shortages and high prices alternating with periods of surpluses and low prices for reasons that cannot be blamed on such uncontrollable factors as the weather. It also shows in a fairly dramatic way that even very simple competitive markets can show oscillatory behaviour.

---

[1] See, e.g., R. D. G. Allen, *Mathematical Economics* (London: Macmillan, 1966), Chapter 1.

PART 3

The Intermediate Theory of Demand

8

Indifference-Preference Theory

In Chapter 4 we said just enough about the determinants of market demand and market supply curves to enable us to develop the theory of the determination of prices in competitive markets. Now we need to study the household behaviour that lies behind demand curves and the firm behaviour that lies behind supply curves.

The theory of demand will occupy us for only two chapters because we do not need to depart from our assumption that each household is a price-taker, unable to influence by any action of its own the market prices of the commodities it purchases.

The theory of supply requires more space. This is because a large proportion of production is carried on by firms that are able to exert a significant influence on the market prices of the commodities they sell. Therefore, although we do not need to alter any of the hypotheses about demand introduced in Chapter 5, we must amend the hypothesis that there *always* exists a simple relation between market price and firms' supply. But, before we come to these supply complications, we must turn our attention to the theory of demand.

HOW THE HOUSEHOLD REACHES EQUILIBRIUM

To study the household's choice problem, we introduce two concepts. The budget line tells us what choices the household can make; indifference curves tell us what choices the household would like to make.

The Choices Available to the Household

We start by considering a single household that is allocating the whole of its money income between two goods, which we shall call food and clothing.[1]

---

[1] These assumptions are not as restrictive as they at first seem. Two goods are used so that the analysis can be handled geometrically; the argument can easily be generalized to any number of goods with the use of mathematics. Savings are ignored because we are interested in the allocation of expenditure between commodities for current consumption. The possibilities of saving or borrowing (or using up past savings) can be allowed for, but they affect none of the results in which we are interested here.

The Budget Line

The **budget line** shows all those combinations of the goods that are just obtainable, given the household's income and the prices of the commodities that it buys.[1]

Assume, for example, that the household's income is £120 per week, that the price of clothing is £4 per unit, and the price of food is £2 per unit. We denote food by F and clothing by C so that, for example, 20 units of food and 10 units of clothing is written as $20F$ and $10C$. An amount of both goods consumed by a household is called a **bundle** or a **combination** of these goods. Table 8.1 lists a few of the bundles of food and clothing available to this household, while the line ab in Figure 8.1 shows all the possible bundles. Point b, for example, indicates all the household's income spent buying $60F$ and no clothing, while point a indicates all income spent on buying $30C$ and no food. Points on the line between the two end points a and b indicate that the household is buying positive amounts of both commodities.

---

[1] A budget line is analogous to the production-possibility boundary shown in Figure 1.1 on page 6. The budget line shows the combinations of commodities available to one household given its income and prices, while the production-possibility curve shows the combination of commodities available to the whole society given its supplies of resources and techniques of production.

TABLE 8.1   Data for a Budget Line

Quantity of food	Value of food	Quantity of clothing	Value of clothing	Total expenditure
60	£120	0	£0	£120
50	100	5	20	120
40	80	10	40	120
30	60	15	60	120
20	40	20	80	120
10	20	25	100	120
0	0	30	120	120

The Table shows combinations of food and clothing available to a household with an income of £120 and facing prices of £4 for clothing and £2 for food. Any row in this Table indicates a bundle of given amounts of food and clothing. The quantities in each row exactly exhaust the household's income of £120 when the prices are £2 for a unit of food and £4 for a unit of clothing.

FIGURE 8.1   A Budget Line

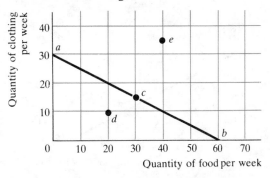

The budget line shows the quantities of goods available to a household given its money income and the price of the goods it buys. Any point indicates a bundle of so much food and so much clothing. Point e, for example, indicates 35 units of clothing and 40 units of food per week. With an income of £120 a week and prices of £2 per unit for food and £4 per unit of clothing, the household's budget line is ab. This line shows all the combinations of F and C available to a household spending that income at those prices.

Bundle d ($10C$ and $20F$) does not use all of the household's income. Bundle e ($35C$ and $40F$) is not available because it would require more than the household's present income.

The Slope of the Budget Line

Figure 8.2 repeats the budget line from Figure 8.1 and highlights two points from Table 8.1. It is clear from the Figure that the absolute value of the slope of the budget line measures the ratio of the change in C to the change in F as we move along the line. This ratio $\Delta C/\Delta F$ is 0.5 in our present example (10/20).

How does the slope of the budget line relate to the prices of the two goods? This question is easily answered if we remember that all points on the budget line represent bundles of goods that just exhaust the household's whole income. It follows that when the household moves from one point on the budget line to another, the change in expenditure on C must be of equal value, but opposite sign, to the change in expenditure on F. Letting ΔC and ΔF stand for the changes in the quantities of clothing and food respectively, and p_c and p_f stand for the prices of clothing and food respectively, we can write this relation as follows:

$$\Delta C p_c = -\Delta F p_f \ .$$

FIGURE 8.2 The Slope of the Budget Line

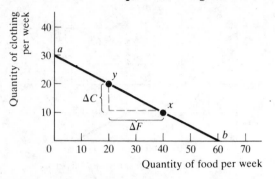

The slope of this budget line measures the opportunity cost of food in terms of clothing.
Points *x* and *y* are both on the budget line and indicate bundles consisting of 40*F* and 10*C* (point *x*) and 20*F* and 20*C* (point *y*). If the household moves from point *y* to point *x* it consumes 20 more *F* and 10 less *C*, the amounts indicated by Δ*F* and Δ*C* in the Figure. Thus the opportunity cost of each unit of *F* added to consumption is 10/20 = 0.5 units of clothing forgone. In the Figure this is Δ*C*/Δ*F*, which is the slope of the budget line *ab*.

There is nothing at all difficult in this. All it says is that if any amount more is spent on one commodity, the same amount less must be spent on the other. A given income imposes this discipline on the household.

If we divide the above equation through, first by Δ*F*, and then by p_c, we get the following:

$$\Delta C/\Delta F = -p_f/p_c \ .$$

So the slope of the budget line is the negative of the ratio of the two prices (with the price of the good that is plotted on the horizontal axis appearing in the numerator).

This gives us the important information that the slope of the budget line depends only on the relation between the two prices, not on their absolute values. To check this, consider an example. If clothing costs £4 and food costs £2, then 0.5 units of clothing must be forgone in order to be able to purchase one more unit of food; if clothing costs £8 and food costs £4 it is still necessary to forgo 0.5 units of clothing to be able to purchase one more unit of food. In fact, as long as the price of clothing is twice the price of food, it will be necessary to forgo half a unit of clothing in order to be able to purchase one more unit of food.

More generally, the amount of clothing that must be given up to obtain another unit of food depends only on *the relation between the price of clothing and the price of food*. If we take the money price of food and divide it by the money price of clothing, we have the opportunity cost of food in terms of clothing (the quantity of clothing that must be forgone in order to be able to purchase one more unit of food). This may be written:

$$\frac{p_f}{p_c} = \begin{array}{l}\text{opportunity cost of food} \\ \text{in terms of clothing}\end{array}$$

where p_f and p_c are the money prices of food and clothing. It is apparent that changing income and/or changing both prices in the same proportion leaves the ratio p_f/p_c unchanged.[1]

As we observed in Chapter 5, any price expressed as a ratio of another price is called a *relative price*. The relative price must be distinguished from the **money price** of a single commodity, which is also called its **absolute price**. These concepts can prove tricky and the reader is urged to experiment with some examples.[2]

The Household's Preferences

The budget line shows the choices available to the household. The choice that the household will make depends on its tastes. These tastes are shown by indifference curves.

A Single Indifference Curve

We start by developing a single indifference curve. To do this we give our imaginary household some quantities of each of two commodities, say 18*C* and 10*F*. This bundle is plotted as point *b* in Figure 8.3. We first consider points in the two shaded areas defined by vertical and

[1] Those who prefer an algebraic derivation may refer now to the proof of this proposition on pages 145–146 of the second Appendix to this chapter.
[2] For example, if the prices of food and clothing are £2 and £6 respectively, what are the values of: (i) the relative price of food, (ii) the relative price of clothing, (iii) the opportunity cost of food measured in units of clothing, (iv) the opportunity cost of clothing measured in units of food, (v) the slope of the budget line drawn with food on the horizontal and clothing on the vertical axis, and (vi) the slope of the budget line drawn with the two commodities on the opposite axes?

horizontal lines drawn through *b*. To do so we introduce our first assumption about tastes:

assumption 1: *ceteris paribus*, the household always prefers more of any commodity to less of that commodity.

This is sometimes referred to as the *non-satiation axiom*. The reason for using this term is that if the household is to prefer more to less of any commodity, it must not be satiated with that commodity.

As the Figure shows, assumption 1 implies that the household will prefer bundle *b* to any point in the dark-shaded area, which has less of both commodities, and will prefer all points in the light-shaded area to *b*, because they have more of

TABLE 8.2 Alternative Bundles Conferring Equal Satisfaction

Bundle	Clothing	Food
a	30	5
b	18	10
c	13	15
d	10	20
e	8	25
f	7	30

Since each of these bundles give the household equal satisfaction, the household is indifferent among them. These hypothetical data illustrate an indifference relation. The household is assumed to be indifferent among all of these bundles of the two goods. None of the bundles contains more F *and* more C than any of the other bundles. The household's indifference among these bundles is not, therefore, in conflict with the assumption that the household prefers more to less of each commodity.

both commodities. But what about points in the two unshaded areas? Compared with bundle *b* the points within these areas have more of one good and less of the other. Further assumptions about the household's tastes are needed if points in these areas are to be ranked against point *b*.

To develop a view of the household's preferences in these two areas, we imagine offering the household an alternative bundle, say 13 units of clothing and 15 units of food. This alternative has 5 units fewer of clothing and 5 units more of food than bundle *b*. Whether the household prefers this bundle depends on the relative value that it places on 5 units more of food and 5 units less of clothing. If it values the extra food more than the forgone clothing, it will prefer the new bundle to the original one. If it values the food less than the clothing, it will prefer the original bundle. There is a third alternative: if the household values the extra food the same as it values the forgone clothing, it would gain equal satisfaction from the two alternative bundles. In this case the household is said to be *indifferent* between the two bundles.

Assume that we have identified a number of bundles shown in Table 8.2, each of which gives equal satisfaction. There will, of course, be other bundles that yield the same level of satisfaction. All of these that lie within the confines of Figure 8.4 are shown by the smooth curve passing

FIGURE 8.3 A Comparison of Consumption Bundles Containing More or Less of Everything

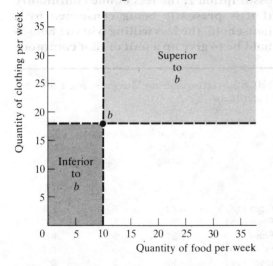

According to assumption 1, bundle *b* is superior to all bundles that have less of both goods and inferior to all bundles that have more of both goods. A vertical and a horizontal line drawn through *b* divides the graph into four areas. The household will regard all points within the dark-shaded area as inferior to bundle *b* because they have less of both commodities (except on the boundaries, where they have less of one and the same amount of the other). The household will regard all points within the light-shaded area as superior to bundle *b* because they have more of both commodities (except the boundaries, where they have the same amount of one and more of the other). Points within the two unshaded areas have more of one commodity and less of the other than bundle *b*.

FIGURE 8.4 An Indifference Curve

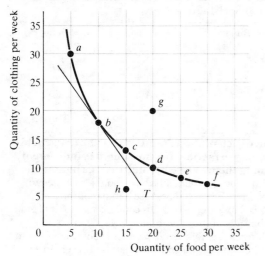

This indifference curve shows combinations of food and clothing that yield equal satisfaction and among which the household is indifferent. Points *a* to *f* are plotted from Table 8.2. The smooth curve through them is an indifference curve; each combination on it gives equal satisfaction to the household. Point *g* above the line is a preferred combination to any point on the line; point *h* below the line is an inferior combination to any point on the line.

The slope of the line *T* gives the marginal rate of substitution at point *b*. Moving down the curve from *b* to *f*, the slope flattens, showing that the more food and the less clothing the household has, the less willing it will be to sacrifice further clothing to get more food.

through the points plotted from the Table. This curve is an indifference curve.

In general, an **indifference curve** shows combinations of commodities that yield the same satisfaction to the household. A household is *indifferent* between the combinations indicated by any two points on one indifference curve.

Now we can rate bundles in the two unshaded portions of Figure 8.3. Any points above and to the right of the curve in Figure 8.4 show combinations of food and clothing that the household would prefer to combinations indicated by points on the curve. Consider, for example, the combination of 20 food and 20 clothing, which is represented by point *g* in the Figure. Although it might not be obvious that this bundle is preferred to bundle *a* (which has more clothing but less

food), assumption 1 tells us that *g* is preferred to bundle *c*, because *g* has more clothing *and* more food than *c*. Inspection of the graph shows that *any* point above the curve will be obviously superior to *some* points on the curve in the sense that it will contain both more food and more clothing than those points on the curve. But since all points on the curve are equal in the household's eyes, the point above the curve must therefore be superior to *all* points on the curve. By a similar argument, points such as *h*, which are below and to the left of the curve, represent bundles of goods that are inferior to all bundles represented by points on the curve.

Diminishing Marginal Rate of Substitution

We now make a second assumption:

> **assumption 2: the less of one commodity that is presently being consumed by a household, the less willing will the household be to give up a unit of that commod-**

TABLE 8.3 Diminishing Marginal Rate of Substitution

Movement	(1) Change in clothing	(2) Change in food	(3) Marginal rate of substitution $[(1) \div (2)] \times [-1]$
From *a* to *b*	−12	5	2.4
From *b* to *c*	−5	5	1.0
From *c* to *d*	−3	5	0.6
From *d* to *e*	−2	5	0.4
From *e* to *f*	−1	5	0.2

The marginal rate of substitution measures the amount of one commodity the consumer must be given to compensate for giving up one unit of the other. This Table is based on the data in Table 8.2. When the household moves from *a* to *b*, it gives up 12 units of clothing and gains 5 units of food; it remains at the same level of overall satisfaction. The household at point *a* was prepared to sacrifice 12 clothing for 5 food (i.e. 12/5 = 2.4 units of clothing per unit of food obtained). When the household moves from *b* to *c*, it sacrifices 5 clothing and gains 5 food (a rate of substitution of 1 unit of clothing for each unit of food). Note that the marginal rate of substitution is the absolute value of the ratio $\Delta C/\Delta F$; hence it is obtained by multiplying this ratio by −1.

ity to obtain an additional unit of a second commodity.

This assumption is usually referred to as **diminishing marginal rate of substitution**. It is illustrated in Table 8.3, which is based on the example of food and clothing shown in Table 8.2. As we move down the Table through points a to f, the household is consuming bundles with less and less clothing and more and more food. In accordance with the hypothesis of diminishing marginal rate of substitution, the rate at which the household is willing to give up further clothing to get more food diminishes. When the household moves from c to d, for example, the Table tells us that the household is prepared to give up 6/10 of a unit of clothing to get a further unit of food, while when it moves from e to f, it will give up only 2/10 of a unit.

The geometrical expression of this hypothesis is found in the shape of the indifference curve. Look closely, for example, at the slope of the curve in Figure 8.4. Its downward slope indicates that, if the household is to have less of one commodity, it must have more of the other to compensate. Diminishing marginal rate of substitution is shown by the fact that the curve is convex viewed from the origin: moving down the curve to the right, its slope gets flatter and flatter. The absolute value of the slope of the curve is the marginal rate of substitution, the rate at which one commodity must be substituted for the other in order to keep total utility constant.

Geometrically the slope of the indifference curve at any point is indicated by the slope of the tangent to the curve at that point. The slope of tangent T drawn to the curve at point b shows the marginal rate of substitution at that point. It is visually obvious that, moving down the curve to the right, the slope of the tangent, and hence the marginal rate of substitution at that point, gets flatter and flatter.[1]

---

[1] Table 8.3 calculates the rate of substitution between distinct points on the indifference curve. Strictly speaking these are the incremental rates of substitution between the two points. Geometrically this incremental rate is given by the slope of the chord joining the two points. The marginal rate refers to the slope of the curve at a single point and is given by the slope of the tangent to the curve at the point. The discussion of the relation between marginal and incremental rates given in section 7 of the Appendix to Chapter 3 should be read, or reread, at this point.

The Indifference Map

So far we have constructed only a single indifference curve. There must, however, be a similar curve through other points in Figure 8.4. Starting at any point, such as g, there will be other combinations that will yield equal satisfaction to the household and, if the points indicating all of *these* combinations are connected, they will form another indifference curve. This exercise can be repeated as many times as we wish, generating a new indifference curve each time.

It follows from the comparisons given in Figure 8.5 that the farther away any indifference curve is from the origin, the higher is the level of satisfaction given by the consumption bundles that it indicates. We refer to a curve that confers a higher level of satisfaction as a *higher curve*.

A set of indifference curves is called an **indifference map**. An example is shown in Figure 8.6. It specifies the household's tastes by showing its rate of substitution between the two commod-

---

FIGURE 8.5 One Consumption Bundle Compared to all Others

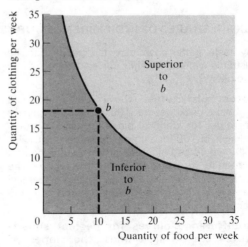

The indifference curve allows any bundle such as *b* to be compared with all other bundles. The household regards all bundles in the dark-shaded area as inferior to b. It regards all bundles in the light-shaded area as superior to b. The indifference curve is the boundary between these two areas. The household regards all points on it as conferring equal satisfaction and is, therefore, indifferent among all such points.

FIGURE 8.6 An Indifference Map

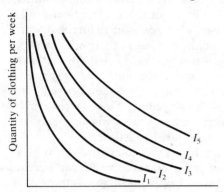

Quantity of food per week

An indifference map consists of a set of indifference curves. All points on a particular curve indicate alternative combinations of food and clothing that give the household equal satisfaction. The further the curve from the origin, the higher the level of satisfaction it represents. For example, I_5 is a higher indifference curve than I_4, which means that all points on I_5 yield a higher level of satisfaction than do the points on I_4.

ities for every level of consumption of these commodities. When economists say that a household's tastes are *given*, they do not mean merely that the household's current consumption pattern is given; rather, they mean that the household's entire indifference map is given.

Box 8.1 shows some specific shapes of indifference curves that correspond to some specific taste patterns.

The Equilibrium of the Household

The budget line tells us what the household *can do*: it can select any consumption bundle on, or below, the line, but not above it. To see what the household *wants to do*, we introduce our third assumption:

assumption 3: the household seeks to maximize its satisfactions, which means reaching the highest possible indifference curve.

BOX 8.1 SHAPES OF INDIFFERENCE CURVES

Any taste pattern we care to specify can be illustrated with indifference curves. Here are a few examples.

Perfect substitutes: Drawing pins that came in yellow packages of 100 would be perfect substitutes for identical pins that came in green packages of 100 for a colour-blind consumer. He or she would be willing to substitute one type of package for the other at a rate of one for one. The indifference curves would thus be a set of parallel lines with a slope of −1. Two such curves, I_1 and I_2, are shown in part (i) of the Figure.

Indifference curves for perfect substitutes are straight lines, the slopes of which indicate the rate at which one good can be substituted for the other.

Perfect complements: Left- and right-hand gloves are perfect complements, since one of them is of no use without the other. This gives rise to the indifference curves shown in part (ii) of the Figure. There is no rate at which the household will substitute one kind of glove for the other when it starts with equal numbers of each. Of course, it

prefers more pairs to less, so the curve I_4 represents a higher level of satisfaction than does curve I_3.

Indifference curves for perfect complements are 'L-shaped'.

A commodity that gives zero utility: When a good gives no satisfaction at all, a person would be unwilling to sacrifice even the smallest amount of other goods to obtain any quantity of the good in question. Such would be the case for meat for a vegetarian household, whose indifference curves are horizontal straight lines indicating a marginal rate of substitution of zero for meat (part iii). Since the household likes vegetables, the curve I_6 indicates a higher level of satisfaction than does I_5 but in both cases its satisfaction is not affected by the amount of meat it has (since, no matter how much it is given, none will be eaten).

Indifference curves for a commodity yielding zero satisfaction are parallel to that commodity's axis.

An absolute necessity: In part (iv) of the Figure, there is some minimum quantity of water,

w_0, that is necessary to sustain life. No amount of other goods will persuade any household to cut its water consumption below that amount. As consumption of water falls towards w_0, increasingly vast amounts of other goods are necessary to persuade the household to cut down on its water consumption even a little bit more. Thus the indifference curve becomes steeper and steeper as it approaches w_0, and the marginal rate of substitution increases. In the limit, it becomes infinite as the indifference curve becomes vertical at w_0.

The marginal rate of substitution for an absolute necessity reaches infinity as consumption falls towards the amount that is absolutely necessary.

A good that confers a negative utility after some level of consumption: Beyond some point, further consumption of many foods, beverages, movies, plays or cricket matches would reduce satisfaction. Beyond that point, the indifference curves begin to slope upwards, because the household would be willing to sacrifice some amount of other goods to be allowed to reduce its consumption of the offending commodity.

Part (v) of the Figure shows a household that is *forced* to eat more and more food. At the amount f_0, it has all the food it could possibly want. Beyond f_0, its indifference curves slope upwards, indicating that it gets *negative* value from consuming the extra food, and so it would be willing to sacrifice some amount of other commodities to avoid consuming it.

When, beyond some level of consumption, the household's utility is reduced by further consumption, the indifference curves slope upwards.

This case does not arise if the household can dispose of the extra unwanted units at no cost. The indifference curves then become horizontal.

A good that is not consumed: Typically a household will consume only one or two of all of the available types of cars, TV sets, dishwashers, tennis rackets. If a household is in equilibrium consuming a zero amount of say, green peas, it will be in what is called a *corner solution*, where (as shown in part (vi) of the Figure) its indifference curve cuts the green pea axis with a slope flatter than its budget line.

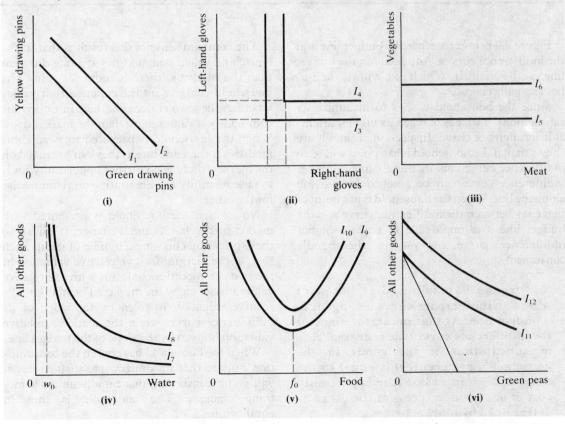

FIGURE 8.7 The Equilibrium of a Household

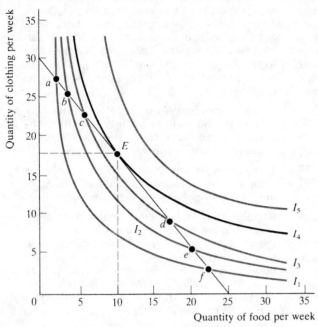

Equilibrium occurs at *E*, where an indifference curve is tangent to the budget line. The household has an income of £150 a week and faces prices of £5 a unit for clothing and £6 a unit for food. A bundle of clothing and food indicated by point *a* is attainable, but by moving along the budget line, higher indifference curves can be reached. The same is true at *b* and *c*. At *E*, however, where the indifference curve I_4 is tangent to the budget line, it is impossible to reach a higher curve by moving along the budget line. If the household did alter its consumption bundle by moving from *E* to *d*, for example, it would move to the lower indifference curve I_3 and thus to a lower level of satisfaction.

Figure 8.7 brings together the budget line and the indifference curves. Any point on the budget line can be attained. Which one will the household actually choose?

Since the household wishes to maximize its satisfactions, it wishes to reach its highest attainable indifference curve. Inspection of the Figure shows that, if the household is at a point where an indifference curve cuts its budget line, a higher indifference curve can be reached by moving along the line. When the household is at a point of tangency between the indifference curve and the budget line it is impossible to reach a higher indifference curve by varying the bundle consumed.

Satisfaction is maximized at the point where an indifference curve is tangent to a budget line. At that point, the slope of the indifference curve (the marginal rate of substitution of the goods in the household's preferences) is equal to the slope of the budget line (the opportunity cost of one good in terms of the other as determined by market prices).

The common sense of this result is that, if the household values commodities at a rate different than the market's, there is room for gain. The household can give up the commodity it values less than the market does and take in return the commodity it values more than the market does. When the household is prepared to swap commodities at the same rate as they can be traded on the market, there is no further opportunity for it to raise its utility by substituting one commodity for the other.

Notice that the household is presented with market prices that it cannot change. It adjusts to these prices by choosing a bundle of goods such that, at the margin, its own relative valuation of the two commodities conforms with the relative valuations given by the market. The household's relative valuation is given by the slope of its indifference curve, while the market's relative valuation is given by the slope of the budget line.

When the household has chosen the consumption bundle that maximizes its satisfactions, it will go on consuming that bundle unless something changes. The household is thus in equilibrium.

HOW THE HOUSEHOLD RESPONDS TO CHANGES

We are now ready to consider how a household responds to various changes in its income and the prices that it faces.

Parallel Shifts in the Budget Line

A change in money income: A change in the household's money income will, *ceteris paribus*, shift its budget line. For example, if the household's income is doubled, it will be able to buy twice as much of both goods compared with any combination on its previous budget line. The budget line will therefore shift out parallel to itself to indicate this expansion in the household's consumption possibilities. (The fact that it will be a parallel shift is established by our demonstration on page 126 that the slope of the budget line depends only on the relation between the prices of the two commodities.) This illustrates the result that is proven (as proposition 1) in the second appendix to this chapter:

> **a change in the household's income shifts the budget line parallel to itself, outwards when income rises and inwards when income falls.**

The effect of income changes is shown in Figure 8.8. For each level of income there will, of course, be an equilibrium position at which an indifference curve is tangent to the relevant budget line. Each such equilibrium position means that the household is doing as well as it possibly can for that level of income. As the household's income is twice increased, the budget line moves outwards from a tangency with indifference curve I_1 to I_2 to I_3. If we join up all the points of equilibrium, we trace out what is called an **income-consumption line**. This line shows how consumption bundles change as income changes, with prices held constant.[1]

---

[1] This income-consumption line can be used to derive the curve relating quantity demanded to income that was introduced on page 88. This is done by plotting the quantity of one of the goods consumed at the equilibrium position against the level of money income that determined the position of the budget line. Repeating this for each level of income produces the required curve.

FIGURE 8.8 An Income-Consumption Line

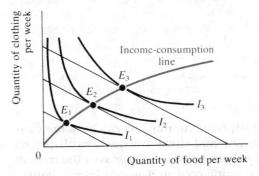

The income-consumption line shows how the household's purchases react to changes in income with relative prices held constant.

The income-consumption line shows how the household's purchases react to changes in income with relative prices held constant.
Increases in income shift the budget line out parallel to itself, moving the equilibrium from E_1 to E_2 to E_3. By joining up all the points of equilibrium, an income-consumption line is traced out.

A proportionate change in all prices: Now let us consider what happens when all prices change in the same proportion. For example, a halving of all prices allows the household to buy twice as much of both commodities as was bought at any point on its previous budget line. This is exactly the same shift in the budget line as when the household's income doubled with prices held constant. On the other hand, a doubling of all prices will cause the budget line to shift inwards in exactly the same way as if its money income had halved with prices held constant.

This illustrates the following general result (which is also proven as proposition 2 in the second appendix to this chapter):

> **an equal proportionate change in all money prices, with money income held constant, shifts the budget line parallel to itself, towards the origin when prices rise and away from the origin when prices fall.**

From this point on, the analysis is the same as in the previous section, since changing money prices proportionately has the identical effect as changing money income.

Offsetting changes in money prices and money incomes: The results in the last two sections suggest that we can have offsetting changes in money prices and money incomes. Consider a doubling of money income that shifts the budget line outwards. Let this be accompanied by a doubling of all money prices that shifts the budget line inwards. The net effect is to leave the budget line where it was before income and prices changed. This illustrates the general result (which is proven as proposition 3 in the second appendix to this chapter):

> **multiplying money income by some constant, λ, and simultaneously multiplying all money prices by $1/\lambda$ leaves the budget line unaffected and hence leaves household purchases unaffected.**

Changes in the Slope of the Budget Line

A change in relative prices: We already know that a change in the relative price of the two goods changes the slope of the budget line. At a given price of clothing, the household has an equilibrium consumption position for each possible price of food. Connecting these positions traces out a **price-consumption line**, as is

FIGURE 8.9 The Price-Consumption Line

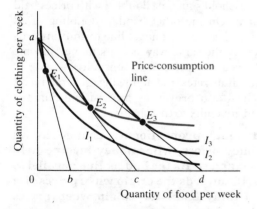

The price-consumption line shows how the household's purchases react to a change in one price with money income and other prices held constant. Decreases in the price of food (with money income and the price of clothing constant) pivot the budget line from *ab* to *ac* to *ad*. The equilibrium position moves from E_1 to E_2 to E_3. By joining up all the points of equilibrium, a price-consumption line is traced out.

shown in Figure 8.9. Notice that, as the relative price of food and clothing changes, the relative quantities of food and clothing purchased also change. In particular, as the price of food falls, the household buys more food.

Real and Money Income[1]

The preceding analysis suggests an important distinction between two concepts of income. **Money income** measures a household's income in terms of some monetary unit; for example, so many pounds sterling or so many dollars. **Real income** measures the purchasing power of the household's money income. A rise in money income of x per cent combined with an x per cent rise in all money prices leaves a household's purchasing power, and hence its real income, unchanged. When we speak of the real value of a certain amount of money, we are referring to the goods and services that can be bought with the money, that is, to the purchasing power of the money.

Allocation of Resources: The Importance of Relative Prices

Price theory predicts that the allocation of resources depends on the structure of relative prices. If the money value of all prices, incomes, debts and credits were doubled, there would, according to our theory, be little noticeable effect. The economy would function as before. The same set of relative prices and real incomes would exist, and there would be no incentive for any reallocation of resources.

This prediction is an implication of the theories of the behaviour of households and firms. We have already seen that doubling all money prices, and money income, leaves the household's budget line unchanged and so, according to the theory of household behaviour, gives the household no incentive to vary the quantity of each commodity that it purchases. As far as producers are concerned, if the prices of all outputs and inputs double, the relative profitabilities of alternative lines of production will be unchanged. Thus producers will have no incen-

---

[1] Now that we have developed the appropriate theoretical tools, this discussion can go further and deeper than the discussion of the same issue at the end of Chapter 5.

tive to alter production rates so as to produce more of some things and less of others.

If *relative* prices change, however, then our theory predicts that resources will be reallocated. Households will buy more of the cheaper commodities and less of the expensive ones, and producers will increase production of those commodities whose prices have risen relatively, and reduce production of those whose prices have fallen relatively (since the latter will be relatively less profitable lines of production).

The theory of price and resource allocation is a theory of relative, not absolute, prices.

Inflation and Deflation: The Importance of Absolute Prices

The average level of all money prices is called the **price level**. If all money prices double, we say that the price level has doubled. An increase in the price level is called an **inflation**, a decrease is called a **deflation**. If a rise in all money prices and incomes has little or no effect on the allocation of resources, it may seem surprising that so much concern is expressed over inflation. Clearly, people who spend all their incomes, and whose money incomes go up at the same rate as money prices, lose nothing from inflation. Their real income is unaffected.

Inflation, while having no effect on households whose incomes rise at the same rate as prices, does nonetheless have serious consequences. These are studied in detail later in this book and for present purposes *we shall assume that the price level is constant.*

Under these circumstances a change in one money price necessarily changes that price *relative* to the average of all other prices. The theory can easily be extended to situations in which the price level is changing. Then every time shifts in demand or supply required a change in a commodity's relative price, its price would change *faster* (its relative price rising) or *slower* (its relative price falling) than the general price level. Explaining this each time can be cumbersome. It is, therefore, simpler to deal with relative prices in a theoretical setting in which the price level is constant. It is important to realize, however, that even though we develop the theory in this way, it is not limited to such situations.

The propositions we develop can be applied to changing price levels merely by making explicit what is always implicit: in the theory of relative prices, 'rise' or 'fall' *always* means rise or fall *relative to the average of all other prices.*

THE HOUSEHOLD'S DEMAND CURVE

To derive the household's demand curve for any commodity, we need to depart from our world of two commodities. We are now interested in what happens to the household's demand for some commodity, say petrol, as the price of that commodity changes, *all other prices being held constant.*

Derivation of the Demand Curve

In part (i) of Figure 8.10 a new type of indifference map is plotted in which the horizontal axis measures litres of petrol and the vertical axis measures the value of all other goods consumed. We have in effect used *everything but petrol* as the second commodity. The indifference curves now give the rate at which the household is prepared to substitute petrol for money (which allows it to buy all other goods).

The derivation of a demand curve is illustrated in Figure 8.10. For a given income, each price of petrol gives rise to a particular budget line, and a particular equilibrium position. Plotting the quantity of petrol consumed against the price that determined the position of the budget line yields one point on the demand curve. Each such price yields a different point, and taken together gives the whole demand curve.

The Slope of the Demand Curve

The price-consumption line in part (i) of Figure 8.10 indicates that, as price decreases, the quantity of petrol demanded increases. But one can draw the indifference curves in such a way that the response to a given decrease in price is for less to be consumed rather than more. This possibility gives rise to the positively sloped demand curve, referred to as a **Giffen good**. Let us see how the conditions leading to this case are analysed using indifference curves.

FIGURE 8.10 Derivation of a Household's Demand Curve

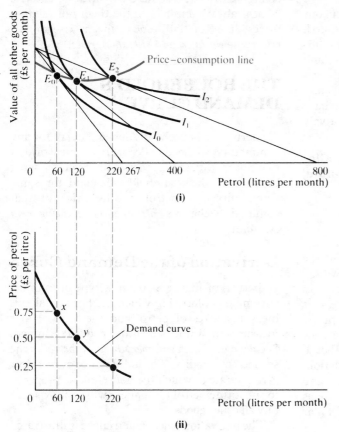

(i)

(ii)

Every point on the price-consumption line corresponds to both a price of the commodity and a quantity demanded; this is the information required for a demand curve. In part (i) the household has an income of £200 per month, and alternatively faces prices of £0.75, £0.50 and £0.25 per litre of petrol, choosing positions E_0, E_1 and E_2. The information for litres demanded at each price is then plotted in part (ii) to yield the household's demand curve. The three points x, y and z in (ii) correspond to the three equilibrium positions E_0, E_1 and E_2 in (i).

Income and substitution effects: The key is to distinguish between what is called the income effect and the substitution effect of a change in price. The separation of the two effects according to indifference theory is shown in Figure 8.11. We can think of the separation occurring in the following way: after the price of the good has fallen, we reduce money income *until the original indifference curve can just be obtained*. The household is now on its original indifference curve but facing the new set of relative prices. Its response is defined as the **substitution effect**. Then, to measure the income effect, we restore money income. The household's response is defined as the **income effect**. The distinction between income and substitution effect is one of the most tricky bits of basic economic theory. The reader is advised, therefore, to study Figure 8.11 with great care.

In Figure 8.11, the income and substitution effects work in the same direction, both tending to increase quantity demanded when price falls. Is this necessarily the case? The answer is no. It follows from the convex shape of indifference curves that the substitution effect is always in the same direction: more is consumed of a commodity whose price has fallen. The income effect, however, can be in either direction: it can lead to more or less being consumed of a commodity whose price has fallen. The direction of the income effect depends on the distinction we drew earlier between normal and inferior goods.

The slope of the demand curve for a Normal Good: For a normal good, an increase in household's real income, due to a decrease in price of the commodity, leads to increased consumption, reinforcing the substitution effect.

FIGURE 8.11 The Income Effect and the Substitution Effect

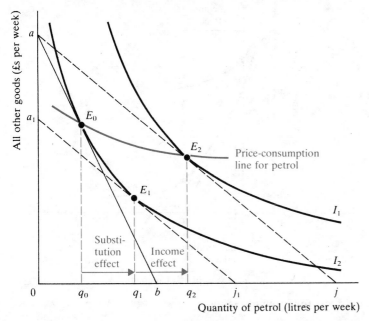

The substitution effect is defined by sliding the budget line around a fixed indifference curve; the income effect is defined by a parallel shift of the budget line. The original budget line is at ab and a fall in the price of petrol takes it to aj. The original equilibrium is at E_0 with q_0 of petrol consumed, and the final equilibrium is at E_2 with q_2 of petrol consumed. To remove the income effect, imagine reducing the household's income until it is just able to attain its original indifference curve at new prices. We do this by shifting the line aj to a parallel line nearer the origin until it just touches the indifference curve that passes through E_0. The intermediate point E_1 divides the quantity change into a substitution effect $q_1 - q_0$ and an income effect $q_2 - q_1$. It can also be obtained by sliding the original budget line ab around the indifference curve until its slope reflects the new relative prices.

Because quantity demanded increases, the demand curve has a negative slope. This is the case illustrated in the Figure 8.11.

The slope of the demand curve for an Inferior Good: Figure 8.12 shows indifference curves for inferior goods. The income effect is negative in each part of the diagram. This follows from the nature of an inferior good: as income rises, less of the good is consumed. In each case the substitution effect serves to increase the quantity demanded as price decreases and is offset to some degree by the negative income effect. The final result depends on the relative strengths of the two effects. In part (i), the negative income effect only partially offsets the substitution effect, and thus quantity demanded

increases as a result of the price decrease, though not as much as for a normal good. This is the typical pattern for inferior goods, and it too leads to negatively sloped demand curves, often relatively inelastic ones.

In part (ii), the negative income effect actually outweighs the substitution effect and thus leads to a positively sloped demand curve. This is the Giffen case. For this to happen the good must be inferior. But that is not enough; the change in price must have a negative income effect *strong enough* to offset the substitution effect. These circumstances are unusual ones; a positively sloped market demand curve is a rare exception to the general rule that demand curves slope downwards.

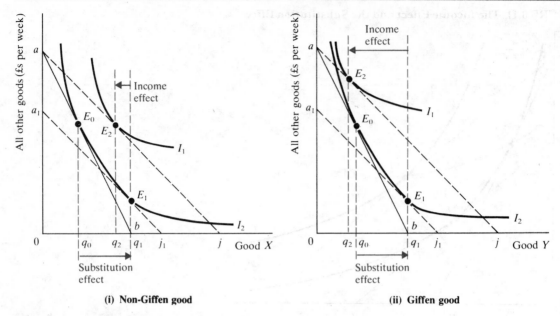

(i) Non-Giffen good   **(ii) Giffen good**

FIGURE 8.12 Income and Substitution Effects for Inferior Goods

Inferior goods have negative income effects. A large enough negative income effect can outweigh the substitution effect and lead to a decrease in consumption in response to a fall in price. In each part of the diagram, the household is in equilibrium at E_0, consuming a quantity q_0 of the good in question. The price then decreases and the budget line shifts to aj, with a new equilibrium at E_2 and quantity consumed q_2. In each case the substitution effect is to increase consumption from q_0 to q_1. In (i) there is a negative income effect of $q_1 - q_2$. Because this is less than the substitution effect, the latter dominates, so good X has a normal, negatively sloped demand curve. In (ii) the negative income effect $q_1 - q_2$ is larger than the substitution effect, and quantity consumed actually decreases. Good Y is thus a Giffen good.

SUMMARY

1. While the budget line describes what the household *can* purchase, indifference curves describe the household's tastes and, therefore, refer to what it *would like* to purchase. A single indifference curve shows combinations of commodities that give the household equal satisfaction, and among which it is therefore indifferent. An indifference map is a set of indifference curves.

2. The basic hypothesis about tastes is that of a diminishing marginal rate of substitution. This hypothesis states that the less of one good and the more of another the household has, the less willing it will be to give up some of the first good to get a further unit of the second. This means indifference curves are downward sloping and convex to the origin.

3. Given its budget line the household achieves an equilibrium that maximizes its satisfactions at the point at which an indifference curve is tangent to its budget line.

4. The income-consumption line shows how quantity consumed changes as income changes with relative prices constant.

5. The price-consumption line shows how quantity consumed changes as relative prices change. The household will normally consume more of the commodity whose relative price falls.

6. The price-consumption line relating the purchases of one particular commodity to all other commodities contains the same information as an ordinary demand curve. The horizontal axis measures quantity, and the slope of budget line measures price. Transferring this price-quantity information to a diagram whose axes represent price and quantity leads to a conventional demand curve.

7. The effect of a change in price of one commodity, all other prices and money income constant, is to change both relative price and real income. The effect of each of these changes on consumption is measured by the substitution effect and the income effect.

8. Demand curves for normal goods slope downward because both income and substitution effects work in the same direction, a decrease in price leading to increased consumption.

9. For an inferior good a decrease in price leads to more consumption via the substitution effect and less consumption via the income effect. In the extreme case of a Giffen good the negative income effect more than offsets the substitution effect, and the consumption of the commodity decreases as a result of a price decrease. This is a theoretical possibility that has seldom if ever been observed in fact.

TOPICS FOR REVIEW

- **Budget line**
- **Absolute and relative prices, and the slope of the budget line**
- **An indifference curve and an indifference map**
- **Slope of an indifference curve and the marginal rate of substitution**
- **Diminishing marginal rate of substitution**
- **Equilibrium of the household**
- **Response of a household to changes in income and prices**
- **Derivation of the demand curve from indifference curves**
- **Income and substitution effects**
- **Normal goods, inferior goods and Giffen goods**

Marginal Utility Theory

The history of demand theory has seen two major breakthroughs. The first was the marginal utility theory, which assumed that the utility people got from consuming commodities could be measured objectively. By distinguishing total and marginal values, this theory explained why what seemed like a paradox – necessary goods that cannot be dispensed with often have low market values, while luxury goods that could easily be dispensed with often have high market values – was not a paradox at all.

The second breakthrough came with indifference theory, which showed that demand theory could dispense with the dubious assumption of measurable utility on which marginal utility theory was based. All that was needed in this new theory was to assume that households could say which of two consumption bundles they preferred without having to say by how much.

The text of this chapter deals with indifference theory. This Appendix deals with marginal utility theory.

Marginal and Total Utility

We confine our attention for the moment to the consumption of a single commodity. The satisfaction a household receives from consuming that commodity is called its **utility**. **Total utility** refers to the total satisfaction from the amount of that commodity consumed. **Marginal utility** refers to the change in satisfaction resulting from consuming a little more or a little less of that commodity. For example, the total utility of consuming 14 eggs a week is the total satisfaction that those 14 eggs provide. The marginal utility of the fourteenth egg consumed is the additional satisfaction provided by the consumption of that unit. Thus marginal utility is the difference in total utility gained by consuming 13 eggs and by consuming 14.

The Hypothesis of Diminishing Marginal Utility

The basic hypothesis of utility theory, sometimes called the *law of diminishing marginal utility*, is as follows:

> **The utility any household derives from successive units of a particular commodity diminishes as total consumption of the commodity increases while the consumption of all other commodities remains constant.**

Consider water. Some minimum quantity is essential to sustain life, and a person would, if necessary, give up all his or her income to obtain that quantity of water. Thus the marginal utility of that much water is extremely high. More than this bare minimum will be drunk, but the marginal utility of successive glasses of water drunk over a period will decline steadily.

You can convince yourself that it is at least reasonable by asking a few questions. How much money would induce you to cut your consumption of water by one glass per week? The answer is very little. How much would induce you to cut it by a second glass? By a third glass? To only one glass consumed per week? The answer to the last question is quite a bit. The fewer glasses you are consuming already, the higher the marginal utility of one more or one less glass of water.

But water has many uses other than for drinking. A fairly high marginal utility will be attached to some minimum quantity for bathing, but much more than this minimum will be used only for more frequent baths or for having a water level in the tub higher than is absolutely necessary. The last weekly gallon used for bathing is likely to have a low marginal utility. Again, some small quantity of water is necessary for tooth brushing, but many people leave the water running while they brush. The water going down the drain between wetting and rinsing the brush surely has a low utility. When all the extravagant uses of water by the modern consumer are considered, it is certain that the marginal utility of the last, say, 30 per cent of all units consumed is very low, even though the total utility of *all* the units consumed is extremely high.

Utility Schedules and Graphs

The schedule in Table 8A.1 is hypothetical. It is constructed to illustrate the assumptions that have been made about utility, using cinema attendance as an example. The Table shows that total utility rises as the number of films attended each month rises. Everything else being equal, the more films the household attends each month, the more satisfaction it gets – at least over the range shown in the Table. But the marginal utility of each additional film per month is less than that of the previous one even though each film adds something to the household's satisfaction. The schedule shows that marginal utility declines as quantity consumed rises. The same data are shown graphically in the two parts of Figure 8A.1.

Maximizing Utility

A basic assumption of the economic theory of household behaviour is that households try to make themselves as well off as they possibly can in the circumstances in which they find themselves. In other words, the members of a household seek to maximize their total utility.

The Equilibrium of a Household

How can a household adjust its expenditure so as

TABLE 8A.1 Total and Marginal Utility Schedules

Number of films attended per month	Total utility	Marginal utility
0	0	
		30
1	30	
		20
2	50	
		15
3	65	
		10
4	75	
		8
5	83	
		6
6	89	
		4
7	93	
		3
8	96	
		2
9	98	
		1
10	99	

Total utility rises, but marginal utility declines as this household's consumption increases. The marginal utility of 20, shown as the second entry in the last column, arises because total utility increases from 30 to 50 – a difference of 20 – with attendance at the second film. To indicate that the marginal utility is associated with the change from one rate of film attendances to another, the figures in the third column are recorded between the rows of the figures in the second column. When plotting marginal utility on a graph, it is plotted at the midpoint of the interval over which it is computed.

to maximize its total utility? Should it go to the point at which the marginal utility of each commodity is the same, that is, the point at which it would value equally the last unit of each commodity consumed? This would make sense only if each commodity had the same price per unit. But if a household must spend £3 to buy an additional unit of one commodity and only £1 for a unit of another, the first commodity would represent a poor use of its money if the marginal utility of each were equal. The household would be spending £3 to get satifaction it could have acquired for only £1.

The household maximizing its utility will allocate its expenditure among commodities so that the utility of the last dollar spent on each is equal.

Imagine that the household is in a position in which the utility of the last £ spent on carrots yields three times the utility of the last £ spent on Brussels sprouts. In this case total utility can be

FIGURE 8A.1 Total and Marginal Utility Curves

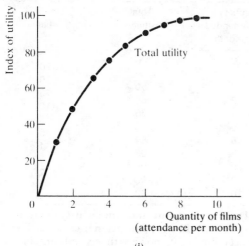

(i)

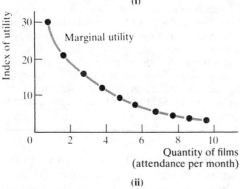

(ii)

The total utility curve rises, but the marginal utility curve falls as the quantity consumed rises. The dots correspond to the points listed in Table 8A.1; smooth curves have been drawn through them.

increased by switching £1 of expenditure from sprouts to carrots and gaining the difference between the utilities of £1 spent on each.

The utility-maximizing household will continue to switch its expenditure from sprouts to carrots as long as £1 spent on carrots yields more utility than £1 spent on sprouts. But this switching reduces the quantity of sprouts consumed and, given the law of diminishing marginal utility, raises the marginal utility of sprouts; at the same time the switching increases the quantity of carrots consumed and thereby lowers the marginal utility of carrots.

Eventually the marginal utilities will have changed enough so that the utility of £1 spent on carrots is just equal to the utility of £1 spent on sprouts. At this point there is nothing to be gained by a further switch of expenditure from sprouts to carrots. If the household persists in reallocating its expenditure, it will further reduce the marginal utility of carrots (by consuming more of them) and raise the marginal utility of sprouts (by consuming less of them). Total utility will no longer be at its maximum because the utility of £1 spent on sprouts will exceed the utility of £1 spent on carrots.

Let us now consider the conditions for maximizing utility in a more general way. Denote the marginal utility of the last unit of commodity X by MU_x and its price by p_x. Let MU_y and p_y refer, respectively, to the marginal utility of a second commodity Y and its price. The marginal utility per pound spent on X will be MU_x/p_x. For example, if the last unit adds 30 units to utility and costs £2, its marginal utility per pound is $30/2 = 15$.

The condition required for a household to maximize its utility is, for any pair of commodities,

$$\frac{MU_x}{p_x} = \frac{MU_y}{p_y}. \qquad (1)$$

This says that the household will allocate its expenditure so that the utility gained from the last pound spent on each commodity is equal.

This is the fundamental equation of the utility theory of demand. Each household demands each good (for example, film attendance) up to the point at which the marginal utility per pound spent on it is the same as the marginal utility of a pound spent on another good (for example, water). When this condition is met, the household cannot shift a pound of expenditure from one commodity to another and increase its utility.

An Alternative Interpretation of Household Equilibrium

If we rearrange the terms in equation (1) we can gain additional insight into household behaviour.

$$\frac{MU_x}{MU_y} = \frac{p_x}{p_y}. \qquad (2)$$

The right side of this equation states the *relative* price of the two goods. It is determined by the market and is outside the control of the individual household; the household reacts to these market prices but is powerless to change them. The left side states the relative ability of the goods to add to the household's satisfaction and is within the control of the household. In determining the quantities of different goods it buys, the household determines also their marginal utilities. (If you have difficulty seeing why, look again at Figure 8A.1(ii).)

If the two sides of equation (2) are not equal, the household can increase its total satisfaction by rearranging its purchases. Assume, for example, that the price of a unit of X is twice the price of a unit of Y $(p_x/p_y = 2)$, while the marginal utility of a unit of X is three times that of a unit of Y $(MU_x/MU_y = 3)$. Under these conditions it pays the household to buy more X and less Y. For example, reducing its purchases of Y by two units frees enough purchasing power to buy a unit of X. Since one extra unit of X bought yields 1.5 times the satisfaction of two units of Y forgone, the switch is worth making. What about a further switch of X for Y? As the household buys more X and less Y, the marginal utility of X falls and the marginal utility of Y rises. The household will go on rearranging its purchases – reducing Y consumption and increasing X consumption – until, in this example, the marginal utility of X is only twice that of Y. At this point total satisfaction cannot be further increased by rearranging purchases between the two commodities.

Now consider what the household is doing. It is faced with a set of prices that it cannot change. The household responds to these prices and maximizes its satisfaction by adjusting the things it can change – the quantities of the various goods it purchases – until equation (2) is satisfied for all pairs of commodities.

The sort of equation – one side representing the choices the outside world gives decision-makers and the other side representing the effect of those choices on their welfare – recurs in economics. It reflects the equilibrium position reached when decision-makers have made the best adjustment they can to the external forces that limit their choices.

When it enters the market, every household faces the same set of market prices. When all households are fully adjusted to these prices, each will have identical ratios of its marginal utilities for each pair of goods. Of course, a rich household may consume more of each commodity than a poor household. However, the rich and the poor households (and every other household) will adjust their *relative* purchases of each commodity so that the relative marginal utilities are the same for all. Thus, if the price of X is twice the price of Y, each household will purchase X and Y to the point at which the household's marginal utility of X is twice its marginal utility of Y. Households with different tastes will, however, have different marginal utility schedules and so may consume differing relative quantities of commodities, even though the ratios of their marginal utilities are the same for all households.

Derivation of the Household's Demand Curve

To derive the household's demand curve for a commodity, it is only necessary to ask what happens when there is a change in the price of that commodity. To do this for sugar take equation (2) and let X stand for sugar and Y for all other commodities. What will happen if, with all other prices constant, the price of sugar rises? The household that started from a position of equilibrium will now find itself in a position in which

$$\frac{MU \text{ of sugar}}{MU \text{ of } Y} < \frac{\text{price of sugar}}{\text{price of } Y} . \quad (3)$$

To restore equilibrium, it must buy less sugar, thereby raising its marginal utility until once again equation (2) (where X is sugar) is satisfied.[1] The common sense of this is that the marginal utility of sugar *per £* falls when its price rises. The household began with the utility of the last £ spent on sugar equal to the utility of the last £ spent on all other goods, but the rise in sugar

---

[1] For most consumers sugar absorbs only a small proportion of total expenditure. If, in response to a change in its price, expenditure on sugar changes by £2 per month, this represents a large change in sugar consumption but only a negligible change in the consumption of other commodities. Hence in the text we proceed by assuming that the marginal utilities of other commodities do not change when the price and consumption of sugar change.

prices changes this. The household buys less sugar (and more of other goods) until the marginal utility of sugar rises enough to make the utility of a £ spent on sugar the same as it was originally.

This analysis leads to the basic prediction of demand theory.

A rise in the price of a commodity (with income and the prices of all other commodities held constant) will lead to a decrease in the quantity of the commodity demanded by each household.

If this is what each household does, it is also what all households taken together do. Thus the theory predicts a downward-sloping market demand curve.

SUMMARY

1. Marginal utility theory distinguishes between the total utility gained from the consumption of all units of some commodity and the marginal utility resulting from the consumption of one more unit of the commodity.
2. The basic assumption made in utility theory is that the utility the household derives from the consumption of successive units of a commodity per period of time diminishes as the consumption of that commodity increases.
3. Households are assumed to maximize utility and thus reach equilibrium when the utility derived from the last £ spent on each commodity is equal Another way of putting this is that the marginal utilities derived from the last unit of each commodity consumed, will be proportional to their prices.
4. When the price of one commodity, X, falls, each household restores equilibrium by increasing its purchases of X. This restores the ratio of X's marginal utility to its new price (MU_x/p_x) to the same level as the household has achieved for all other commodities. Hence demand curves slope downward.

A Formal Analysis of the Budget Line

In this Appendix we use simple algebra to prove the propositions asserted in the chapter.

Let the household's money income be M. Let p_x and p_y be the prices of food and clothing, and let X and Y be the quantities of food and clothing purchased by the household. Total expenditure is thus $p_xX + p_yY$. If we assume, as we did in the text, that the household spends all its income on these two goods, we have the following equation:

$$p_xX + p_yY = M . \qquad (1)$$

Rearrangement of terms yields the equation of the budget line as it is plotted in Figures 8.1 and 8.2. To do this, we subtract p_xX from both sides, and then divide through by p_y to obtain:

$$Y = \frac{M}{p_y} - \frac{p_x}{p_y}X . \qquad (2)$$

Equation (1) is a linear equation of the form

$$Y = a - bX , \qquad (3)$$

where $a = M/p_y$ and $b = p_x/p_y$. The intercept a is the number of units of Y that can be purchased by spending all of M on Y, i.e. money income divided by the price of Y. The slope b depends on the relation between p_x and p_y.

We first prove that the opportunity cost, the slope of the budget line and the relative price are identical. If we take first differences representing changes in quantities, with prices constant, we get from (1):

$$p_x\Delta X + p_y\Delta Y = \Delta M .$$

This says that the sum of any changes in the value of purchases of X and the value of purchases of Y must be equal to the change in income (since income determines the total value of purchases).

Along a budget line expenditure is constant, so we can write

$$p_x\Delta X + p_y\Delta Y = 0 ,$$

which says that if income does not change, the change in the total value of purchases must be zero. Simple manipulation of the above equation yields:

$$p_x/p_y = -\Delta Y/\Delta X . \qquad (4)$$

Now $-\Delta Y/\Delta X$ is the change in Y per unit change in X. It is thus the opportunity cost of X measured in units of Y: the amount of Y sacrificed (gained) per unit of X gained (sacrificed). From (4) this is equal to the relative price of X, which, from (2), is the slope of the budget line.

We may now prove the five propositions used in the text.

Proposition (1): A change in money income, with money prices (and thus, necessarily, relative prices) constant, shifts the budget line parallel to itself, inwards towards the origin when income falls, and outwards away from the origin when income rises.

PROOF: If we change the value of M in (2), we change the value of a in (3) in the same direction: $\Delta a = \Delta M/p_y$, but b is unaffected since M does not appear in that term; thus changing M shifts the budget line inwards ($\Delta M < 0$) or outwards ($\Delta M > 0$) but leaves the slope unaffected.

Proposition (2): An equal percentage change in all absolute prices leaves relative prices unchanged. If money income remains unchanged, it will shift the budget line parallel to itself, inwards towards the origin when prices rise, and outwards away from the origin when prices fall.

PROOF: Multiplying both prices in equation (2) by the same constant λ gives

$$Y = \frac{M}{\lambda p_y} - \frac{\lambda p_x}{\lambda p_y} X .$$

Since the λs cancel out of the slope term, b is unaffected; the a term however is changed. If $\lambda > 1$, then a is diminished, while if $\lambda < 1$ then a is increased.

Proposition (3): Multiplying all money prices by the same constant, λ, while holding money income constant, has exactly the same effect on the budget line as multiplying money income by $1/\lambda$ while holding money prices constant.

PROOF: Multiply both money prices in (2) by λ:

$$Y = \frac{M}{\lambda p_y} - \frac{\lambda p_x}{\lambda p_y} X .$$

Cancelling the λs from the slope term gives:

$$Y = \frac{M}{\lambda p_y} - \frac{p_x}{p_y} X .$$

Finally bringing the λ from the denominator to the numerator of the constant term gives:

$$Y = \frac{(1/\lambda)M}{p_y} - \frac{p_x}{p_y} X .$$

Proposition (4): A change in relative prices causes the budget line to change its slope.

PROOF: The relative price p_x/p_y in (2) is the slope term, b, in (3). Thus changing the relative price is

necessary and sufficient for changing the slope of the budget line.

Note that to pivot the budget line, keeping its Y intercept (and money income) constant as in Figure 8.2, it is necessary to change the relative price by changing p_x only. This can be seen algebraically by inspection of (2), since p_x does not appear in the constant term. If the relative price change is accomplished solely, or partly, by changing p_y, then both the slope and the Y intercept change. This is because in (2) p_y appears in both the a and the b term. The common sense of these results is that the Y intercept measures the quantity of Y that can be consumed by buying only Y and this obviously depends on money income and the price of Y.

We conclude that any change in the relative price necessarily changes the slope of the budget line; while with money income constant, a change in p_y changes the Y intercept and (by analogous reasoning) a change in p_x changes the X intercept of the budget line.

Proposition (5): Equal percentage changes in all absolute prices and in money income leave the budget line unaffected.

PROOF: Multiply M and both prices in equation (2) by λ:

$$Y = \frac{\lambda M}{\lambda p_y} - \frac{\lambda p_x}{\lambda p_y} X .$$

Cancel out the λs from the intercept and the slope terms to obtain:

$$Y = \frac{M}{p_y} - \frac{p_x}{p_y} X$$

which is equation (2) once again.

9

Uncertainty, Risk and Other Issues

This chapter is divided into three sections. The first deals with issues involving uncertainty and risk, the second with measurements of demand curves and elasticities, and the third with some criticisms of the theory of demand.

THE BEHAVIOUR OF THE HOUSEHOLD UNDER UNCERTAINTY

So far, we have studied the behaviour of households when they are presented with choices that involve outcomes that are certain. We asked, for example, if the household would prefer bundle A, containing ten units of food and five units of clothing, to bundle B, containing six units of food and twelve units of clothing. In so doing, we assumed implicitly that when one choice was made, the bundle would be obtained for certain. What happens, however, if the household is faced with only a *probability* of obtaining each bundle?

For example, the household might be told that it must choose between two alternatives. Course A gives it five chances out of six of getting bundle A and one chance out of six of getting nothing. Course B gives it four chances out of six of getting bundle B and two chances out of six of getting nothing.[1]

This is not the type of choice that normally faces a household when one of its members visits a shop. In that case, the shopper knows that if he pays his money, he will get what he has paid for with certainty. Sometimes, however, there is uncertainty about the quality of the products among which selection is made. The buyer may think that the more expensive brand X will last longer and require less maintenance expenditure than the cheaper brand Y. She may not, however, be sure of how much longer it will last, and how much less maintenance is involved.

Other types of choices involve more serious types of uncertainty. Buying a flat in area A rather than area B may reduce the chance of being broken into by robbers, as may installing a

---

[1] The outcomes could be determined by rolling one die. If A is chosen, the favourable result occurs if the numbers one through five turn up, and the unfavourable result if a six turns up. If B is chosen, the favourable result requires one through four to turn up, and the unfavourable result a five or a six.

burglar alarm or bars on the ground-floor windows. But by how much? While households sometimes make choices under conditions of uncertainty, firms do so constantly. Production takes time, and so involves spending money now to produce goods to be sold in the uncertain future.

This chapter is about households, so we concentrate on household behaviour under uncertainty, but we note at the outset that all of the economy's decision-takers operate under conditions of significant uncertainty much of the time.

Many of the principles discussed in this chapter were first developed by analysing such games of chance as roulette or penny tossing. The same principles arise in consumption and production decisions involving uncertainty, but it is often easier to appreciate them in the kind of games that the early theorists studied. The reader is warned at the outset that many of the ideas are quite subtle. To handle them rigorously requires careful definitions and some complex analysis. This section gives only an intuitive overview of what is involved.

The Characterization of Risk

Much of what is involved in risky choices can be captured in two measures: the most likely outcome if the choice is repeated over and over again, which is called the **expected value** of the choice, and the dispersion of possible outcomes, which is called the **degree of risk** attached to making that choice.

Expected value: Say you play a game in which a fair coin is tossed once every minute. You win £1 if the result is a head and lose £1 if the result is a tail. If you play the game for 10 minutes, you may have a lucky run and win £10 for an expenditure of 10 minutes of your time. There is an equal chance that you will have an unlucky run and lose £10. It is much more likely, however, that you will get some heads and some tails and end up winning or losing a sum much smaller than £10. The single most likely outcome is that you will exactly break even. This is because there are more sequences of 10 tosses that will end up with five heads and five tails than any other single combination of heads and tails. For the same

reason, the two next most likely results are that you will win £2 (six heads and four tails) or that you will lose £2 (six tails and four heads). Outcomes with larger gains and larger losses become less and less likely, until one gets to the two least likely results of winning £10 and losing £10.

Now consider playing the game repeatedly day after day. It is still quite possible that you will end up winning £10 or losing £10. After all, if you have broken even after many days of play, the chance that you will now encounter ten heads in a row is the same as it was on your first ten tosses of the coin. But as you go on playing, the average return *per minute spent playing the game* gets smaller and smaller. This return can be expressed as $(H - T)/n$, where H is the number of heads, T is the number of tails, and n is the number of minutes you have spent playing the game. Every time the game is played, n increases by one; the only way the numerator can increase by the same amount is if *every* toss is an H, or every toss is a T. So if your sequence of losses contains a mixture of heads and tails, the average gain or loss per play will tend to decline. Indeed, it can be shown that as you go on playing for longer and longer periods of time, so that n increases without limit, the value of $(H - T)/n$ tends to zero. This is the expected value of the game. It tells you the most likely outcome for a small number of tosses, and what you can expect to earn as an average per toss if you play the game for a long time – in this case it is zero.

Another way of calculating the expected value of the outcome of any game is to add up the various outcomes, each multiplied by its probability of occurrence. The game we are considering has two outcomes on each toss: either you win £1 with probability 0.5 or you lose £1 with probability 0.5. The expected value of the outcome is £1(0.5) – £1(0.5) = £0.5 – £0.5 = 0.

Risk: In the above game you stood to win £1 per toss or lose £1 per toss. If you contract to play for 10 minutes, your maximum possible loss is £10. Now suppose you play the same game but you win £100 on a head and lose £100 on a tail. This is still a fair game, with an expected value of zero for the outcome. But you risk more if you play it for any given amount of time. There is the same chance that you will encounter an unlucky run of 10 tails, but now you stand to lose £1,000 in this event. Clearly there is more risk attached to the second game than to the first. Risk refers to the dispersion of the possible results. In the first game the possible results from 10 minutes play are dispersed over a range running from + £10 to − £10; in the second game the possible results are dispersed over a range running from + £1,000 to − £1,000.

The risk attached to any choice, refers to the variation in the possible outcomes resulting from making that choice.[1]

Fair and Unfair Games

The penny toss games that we have considered so far are fair games in the sense that, if you play them, you have just as much chance of winning as of losing. A lottery, in which all of the ticket money is paid out, is also a fair game. Say, for example, that 100 lottery tickets are sold for £1 each, and a draw then determines which one of the ticket-holders wins £100. This is a fair game because each ticket-holder has one chance in one hundred of winning £99 (the person's own £1 back and £99 of winnings) and ninety-nine chances out of a hundred of losing £1. The expected value of this gamble is £99(1/100) − £1(99/100) = £0.99 − £0.99 = 0.

A mathematically fair game is one for which the expected value of the outcome is zero.

If you play a fair game repeatedly, you may end up winning or losing, depending on the 'luck of the toss', but the *average gain or loss per play* calculated over all plays will tend to approach zero as time passes.

Now consider playing the coin-tossing game under the rules that heads you win £2 and tails you lose £1. The expected value of the outcome of this game is £2(0.5) − £1(0.5) = £1 − £0.50 = £0.50. If you play the game only once, you will either win £2 or lose £1. If you play it repeatedly, however, your average gain will tend towards £0.50 per toss. This is not a fair game.

[1] For many purposes, the variation can be satisfactorily measured by a what is called the *variance* of the possible results, which is the sum of the squares of the deviation of each result from the average, or most likely, result.

Instead it is biased in your favour (and hence biased *against* whoever you are playing with).

Finally, consider the kind of lottery that actually exists. The organizers – be they a firm or, as is the case in many countries, the government – take a proportion of the ticket revenue as their profit and distribute the rest as prize money. All such lotteries are not fair games. They are biased against the participants in the sense that the expected value of participating in the game is negative.

To illustrate, take our previous lottery where 100 tickets are sold at £1 each. Now, however, assume that the organizers take £50 as their profit and pay out the other £50 to the winning ticket. The expected value of a lottery ticket is now £49(1/100) − £1(99/100) = £0.49 − £0.99 = − £0.50. The negative value shows that this is not a fair game; instead it is biased against anyone who plays it.

Another way of seeing this is to ask yourself what would happen if you bought all the tickets. You would spend £100 and win back £50, thus making a loss of £50. This is a loss of £0.50 per ticket which, we have already seen, is the expected value of each ticket. (What do you now think about someone who buys two tickets instead of one and tells you he does this in order 'to increase my chances of coming out a winner'?)

Consumers' Tastes for Risk

Economists distinguish three kinds of decision-takers when risk is involved. Those who are **risk neutral** will be indifferent about playing a fair game, will willingly play one that is biased in their favour, but will not play one that is biased against them. Those who are **risk averse** will only play games that are sufficiently biased in their favour to overcome their aversion to risk, but will be unwilling to play fair games, let alone ones that are biased against them. Finally, people who are **risk lovers** are willing to play games even when they are biased against them, the extent of the love of risk being measured by the degree of bias that a person is willing to accept. (No one would knowingly buy a ticket on a lottery in which the prize was zero, but some extreme risk-lovers might enter a lottery in which only ten per cent of the ticket money was paid out as prize money.)

Let us start by assuming that people are risk-neutral.

Consumer's Valuation of Income

We can get quite some way in explaining household behaviour with respect to risk if we use a second assumption.

> **According to the *hypothesis of diminishing marginal utility of income*, households get less and less satisfaction from successive, equal increases in their income or wealth.**

The argument is that if you only have £1,000 per year, you will spend it satisfying your most urgent wants. The next £1,000 will also go for quite important needs, but ones that are a little less urgent than those satisfied by the first £1,000. If your income is increased progressively by £1,000 increments, less and less urgent needs will be satisfied by each additional £1,000 of income. The general idea, therefore, is that people can arrange their wants in order and will satisfy the ones that give them most utility first, and then, as their incomes increase, they will satisfy wants that give them progressively less and less utility. It follows from this assumption that the utility each household will attach to successive equal increments of income will decrease steadily as income increases.[1] Or, put the other way around, the utility attached to successive equal reductions of income will increase steadily as income is decreased.

Let us accept the hypothesis of diminishing marginal utility of income, and the assumption that all households are risk-neutral, and study two cases, insurance and gambling. Each of these cases is typical of other similar ones. They differ from each other in that, with insurance, one pays a smaller sum for certain to avoid a small chance of a larger loss, while, with gambling, one pays a smaller sum to obtain the chance of a larger gain.

---

[1] This proposition may seem obvious to you. Indeed, it is possible to define terms in such a way that it is true by definition. If we want the hypothesis to be useful in a theory designed to predict behaviour, it must not be made true by definition. It is worth noting that, when stated in the form of a testable hypothesis, there is no general agreement among economists that it is overwhelmingly supported by evidence.

The Demand for Insurance

Say that you feel there is one chance in 100 of some unfavourable outcome in which you will lose some asset (possibly your house) that you value at £100,000 and 99 chances in 100 that nothing will happen at all with respect to this asset. The most likely outcome is that nothing will happen at all, but there is a small chance of a really big loss. Say that someone now offers you a mathematically fair insurance policy which avoids this big loss. The policy costs you £1,000 paid now. If nothing else happens, you have lost the £1,000. However, if the disaster occurs and you suffer the loss of £100,000, you will be fully compensated.

So you have two possible choices. Choice A: you buy the policy, giving up £1,000 for certain, but you avoid the one chance in 100 of losing £100,000. The 'expected value' of A is $-£1,000 = (£1,000(100/100) - £100,000(0))$. Choice B: you reject the policy, and the expected value of your choice is one chance in one hundred of losing £100,000 and 99 chances out of 100 of losing nothing, i.e. $-£100,000(1/100) + 0(99/100) = -£1,000$. The insurance policy represents a fair bargain because the expected values of both courses of action are the same, a loss of £1,000.

Not buying the insurance is, however, a much riskier course than buying it. If you are lucky, you save the £1,000 insurance premium. If you are unlucky, you lose £100,000. Clearly, someone who is risk-averse would buy the policy. But what about someone who is risk-neutral? Both courses have the same expected value so, if there were no other considerations, the risk-neutral person would be indifferent between buying this insurance policy and not buying it.

This is where the hypothesis of diminishing marginal utility of income comes into play. If we think of reducing the household's income by successive units of £1,000, the loss attached to each unit will grow as income is reduced. Thus the utility forgone if £100,000 is lost will be more than one hundred times the utility forgone if £1,000 is lost. It is now rational for a risk-neutral person to prefer the insurance policy. The key is that the utility attached to each £1 lost is not the same. Larger losses of money result in utility forgone that is more than in proportion to the utility forgone as a result of smaller losses. As a result, the expected utility is greater with the policy than without it, even though the expected monetary loss is the same in either case.

There is one further complication that needs to be mentioned. Since insurance companies must themselves make money, they do not offer their policy-holders mathematically fair policies such as the one just described. In the above case, where the risk was one chance in 100 of losing £100,000, an insurance company would charge a premium of more than £1,000. Say it was £1,200. The insurance company expects to pay out an average of £1,000 per policy, so the £200 goes to cover its costs and earn it a profit.

For the purchaser the expected value of buying the policy is now − £1,200. But the expected value of not buying remains at £1,000. If nothing else intervened, a risk-neutral person would not buy the policy, which requires spending £1,200 to avoid a situation (no insurance) whose expected value is − £1,000.

If risk-neutral people buy insurance, diminishing marginal utility of income must be strong enough to make an unfair gamble appear attractive to them.

The Demand to Gamble

Now let us consider any situation where one can either do nothing or pay money to purchase the chance of a gain. This could be a lottery ticket, a ticket on the football pools, a firm investing money in future output, or a person purchasing a share in a firm.

Consider first a mathematically fair possibility. You are offered a ticket on a lottery consisting of 100 tickets sold for £1 each, with a single prize of £100 going to the winning ticket. Now you have 99 chances out of 100 of losing £1 and one chance in 100 of winning £100. If you are risk-neutral, and have diminishing marginal utility of income, you would not buy a ticket. This is a fair monetary bet, since the expected value of a ticket is zero. But given diminishing marginal utility of income, the utility a person will get from winning £100 will be less than 100 times the utility sacrificed by the loss of £1. Thus, because the expected value of the ticket measured in money is zero, the expected value of the ticket measured in utility is negative.

So far we have considered a fair gamble. Most gambling games, however, are not mathematically fair. Instead they are biased against the player. The proprietor of the game takes out some of the money wagered to cover costs and provide a profit (the government may also take some as a betting tax); what is left is distributed as prize money. This is true of lotteries, pools, dog and horse races, casino gambling and every commercial gambling function. (When individuals play games of pure chance with each other, the games are usually fair in the sense that the value of what is won is equal to the value of what is lost, so that the expected value of playing the game is zero.)

Gambling on any event in which the organizers take a profit, and/or on which the government levies a tax, has a negative expected value and is thus inconsistent with risk-neutral participants who are subject to diminishing marginal utility of income.

Yet we observe such behaviour every day. How can we explain it? No less than four possibilities suggest themselves.

One possibility is that people have increasing marginal utilities of income. This could explain why they gamble on games that have negative expected values. It would, however, be inconsistent with their buying insurance policies with negative expected values. So this explanation would only work if there were one class of people who gambled (those with increasing marginal utility of income) and another class who insured (those with decreasing marginal utility of income). The common observation that there are many people who do both, rules out this possibility as a general explanation.

A second possibility is that people are risk-lovers. This would explain why they took part in mathematically unfair gambling games whenever the extra utility from the gambling overcame the diminishing marginal utility attached to the income to be won. This would also be consistent with buying insurance as long as the marginal utility of the income to be lost was a stronger force than the utility attached to taking a risk.

A third possibility is that, although people are not risk-lovers in general, they get utility out of the dreams attached to even a remote possibility of winning a vast sum on the pools or some similar bet. In this case, the gamblers know that the average player will lose money over his or her lifetime, but that does not matter. The gamblers are sustained by the mere thought that, against all the odds, they might win a sum large enough to transform an otherwise dull, or even hopeless life, in the same way that Cinderella's fairy godmother transformed her life. This may go a long way towards explaining why people take part in gambling games where a few very large prizes are to be won. It seems less satisfactory as an explanation of why people bet on horses or dogs where winnings, although more frequent, are not enough to change one's whole lifestyle. Here the answer needs to be a more conventional enjoyment of small risks.

A further poosibility is of course that people are just badly informed. They may not know the expected value of the gamble that they take. It is probably true that many people do not realize the magnitude of the negative expected value of many gambles. (The smaller the *payout ratio* – the ratio of money paid out to money taken in – the larger the magnitude of the negative expected value of the game.)

The Supply of Gambling

This chapter is mainly about households and demand. It is, however, convenient at this point to complete the story of gambling and insurance by explaining why firms are willing to supply these services to households who demand them. We first consider the easy case of gambling, and then go on to the more difficult, but also more interesting case of insurance.

There is no difficulty in understanding why firms are willing to provide such gambling opportunities as the pools or betting on horse or dog races. If firms make their own odds after they know the amounts bet, they are on the right side of a mathematically unfair game from which they must win. Assume, for example, that you run a lottery and are free to take for yourself what you wish from the funds raised and then distribute the rest as prizes. You cannot lose.

Firms providing this type of gambling service sometimes have a government monopoly and sometimes are subject to competition from other firms. If there is competition, then there will be pressure to keep the payout ratio high, providing that ticket purchasers are aware of the prizes given out by competing lotteries. If the lottery has a monopoly, there will be an optimum payout ratio that will maximize the profits of the firm running the game. As the payout ratio goes to one, profits go to zero, since all money taken in is paid out. As the payout ratio goes to zero, profits will also go to zero since fewer and fewer people will be willing to wager money as the size of the winnings and/or the number of winners get smaller.

> **Somewhere in between a ratio of zero and one, will be the optimum payout ratio that maximizes the profits of a monopoly firm runnning a lottery or other betting game.**

The Supply of Insurance

In the gambling case, the firm could decide how much to pay out after it knew how much it had taken in. Insurance is a different matter. The insurance firm takes your money and agrees to pay out a certain sum if the unlucky event strikes you. Conceivably the insurance firm could have an unlucky run of luck in which, in the limit, all of the people it insures suffer loss at the same time. The basis for profitable insurance firms is not, therefore, being on the right side of an unfair game. Instead it lies in the mathematics of what are called *pooled risks*.

Risk Pooling

To see what is involved in the pooling of risks, consider two individuals who get an income which varies according to the toss of a coin. (Once again the coin toss stands for any source of uncertainty.) Each individual tosses a coin each month. If a head comes up, John gets £500; if a tail, he gets nothing. The same applies to June: she gets £500 if she tosses a head and nothing if a tail comes up. The expected value of each person's income is £500(0.50) = £250 per month. Over a long period of time, each person's monthly income will indeed average close to £250. But neither of them may like the possibility of going from £500 to nothing on the toss of a coin each month. Suppose they decide to pool their incomes each month and each take half of

TABLE 9.1   Incomes of Two Persons When Risks Are and Are Not Pooled

	Risks are not pooled		Risks are pooled
	John	June	Both get
T − T	0	0	0
T − H	0	500	250
H − T	500	0	250
H − H	500	500	500

Pooling of independent risks reduces risk. Each person gets an income of £500 if he or she tosses a head and nothing if a tail. There are four possible results, in two of which one head and one tail occurs. In the other two, there are either two tails or two heads. When each accepts his or her own risks, each expects an income of £500 half the time and zero the other half. When the incomes are pooled then split, only one combination in four gives them zero income while half of the time they will get £250. The deviations of their monthly incomes from the expected value of £250 is decreased by pooling.

the resulting amount. The expected value of each person's income is still £250 per month.[1]

Now the variation from month to month will be diminished. The result is shown in Table 9.1. When they were operating on their own, each person's income deviated from its expected value by £250 each month, in good months it was £250 over, and in bad months it was £250 below. When the two incomes are pooled, the expected value is reached whenever one is lucky and the other unlucky, which will tend to be about half the time. Only in one quarter of the outcomes will income be £250 above, and in one quarter will it be £250 below. These results require that both be lucky at the same time or both be unlucky.

If three people pool their incomes, the extreme cases of £500 each and zero each occur only when all three are lucky or unlucky at the same time. These cases each occur with a probability of 1

---

[1] This can be seen in a number of ways. First we merely sum the expected value of each person's income, £250 + £250 = £500 and divide it between the two to get £250. Second, we can evaluate the four possible outcomes: there is a 0.25 chance of the pool being £500; there is a 0.25 chance that John will get £500 and June zero and the same chance that June will get £500 and John zero, i.e. a 0.5 chance of it being £250; and a 0.25 chance of it being £0. This sums to £500(0.25) + £250(0.5) + 0(0.25) = £125 + £125 = £250.

chance in four. (There is one chance in two that any one person will get a head, and $(1/2)(1/2)(1/2) = 1/8$ that all three will get heads at once and 1/8 for tails.) If four people pool incomes, the extreme cases of £500 or £0 income per person will occur only with probability 2/64. If ten people are involved, the two extreme cases will occur only twice in two raised to the 10th power, which is a very small fraction indeed.

The larger the number of independent events that are pooled, the less and less likely is it that extreme results will occur.

The key to this proposition is that the events must be independent; the result of John's coin toss must be independent of the result of June's. In the unpooled case, the extreme result occurs to one of them when one of them is unlucky. The probability of the extreme result is less likely when they pool their incomes because it requires that both be unlucky at the same time.

The same reasoning applies to all kinds of events that may be regarded as chance occurrences, as long as they are independent of each other. There is some probability that any given house in the country will burn down in any given year. Let us say it is one in a thousand. An insurance company takes a premium from house-owners and offers them full compensation if their house burns down. If the company is so small that it only insures ten houses, it may be unlucky in having ten owners who just happen to be careless at the same time and burn their houses down accidentally. This is unlikely, but not impossible. A bad bit of luck over all ten houses insured will ruin the company, which could not meet all of its insured risks at the same time. But let the company be large enough to insure 100,000 houses. Now it is pooling risk over a large number and the chances are that very close to one house in every thousand insured houses will burn down. With 100,000 houses insured, the most likely outcome is that 100 houses will burn down. The company might be unlucky and have 110 burn down, or lucky and have only 90 do so. But to have even 200 burn down is very unlikely indeed, as long as a fire in one house is independent of a fire in another.

This requirement of independence explains why insurance policies normally exclude wars and other situations where some common cause acts on all the insured units. A war may lead to a vast number of houses being destroyed. Since the cause of the loss of one house is not independent of the cause of the loss of another, the insurance company has a high probability, should a war break out, of suffering ruinous losses.

The basic feature of insurance is the pooling of independent events, which is what makes extreme outcomes unlikely. A common cause that affects all insured items in the same way, defeats the principle on which insurance is based.

The typical insurance company, therefore, deals with repeated events such as fires or death in which the probability of each insured item becoming a claimant, is independent of the probability of any other item becoming a claimant.

Risk Sharing

A further practice of insurance companies allows them to extend their coverage to events that are not repeated and where the loss might be large enough to ruin any one company.

Say that a famous pianist wants to insure her hands against any event that would stop her from playing the piano. The amount insured would be colossal, amounting to all the income she will earn over her life if her hands stay unharmed. The company can calculate the chances that any randomly chosen person in the population will suffer such a loss. But it is not insuring the whole population. Only one person is involved. If there is no catastrophe, the company will gain its premium. If there is a catastrophe, the company will suffer a large loss.

The trick in being able to insure the pianist, or any single unique person or thing where the loss would be large, lies in what is called *risk sharing*. One company writes a policy for the pianist and then breaks the policy up into a large number of sub-policies. Each sub-policy carries a fraction of the payout and earns a fraction of the premium. The company then sells each sub-policy to many different firms.

Assume, for illustration, that one hundred firms each write one such primary policy – one on a pianist's hands, one on a footballer's legs, one on a rare treasure being flown to Japan for exhibit, etc., etc. Each then breaks its primary policy up into one hundred sub-parts and sells each part to the other ninety-nine firms. Each firm ends up holding risks that are independent of each other, no one of which is large enough to threaten the firm should it give rise to a claim. This is what Lloyd's of London does. It is a syndication of a large number of insurance underwriters. Each one is prepared to insure almost anything as long as a claim would not break all of the firms when the risk is spread over a large number of them.[1]

This completes our introductory study of the importance of risk. We shall have occasion to return to these problems, and build on the present discussion at several points later in this book.

MEASUREMENT OF DEMAND

Much of what economists do to earn a living involves the use of demand measurements. Will a fare increase help to ease the deficit of London Transport or the Panama Canal? The answer requires a knowledge of price elasticity of demand. The United Nations Food and Agricultural Organization (FAO), and producers' co-ops, use income elasticities of demand to predict future changes in demand for food. Over the past decade many industries have estimated their products' cross-elasticities of demand with petroleum in order to predict the effects of sharply changing petroleum prices. The methods for obtaining this demand information are dealt with in econometrics courses. Solutions to two of the most troubling problems concerning demand measurement are discussed in the next part of this chapter.

The solution of the statistical problems associated with demand measurement has led to a large accumulation of data on demand elasticities. The value of these data to the applied economist shows the usefulness of demand theory.

---

[1] This is also what bookmakers do when they cannot control the odds themselves. When they take bets at odds set by others, one large bet could ruin them by requiring a payout greater than their current assets. To avoid such risks they lay off part of the bet with other bookmakers. In this way no one ends up holding bets that are big enough to threaten their solvency if they suffer an unlucky run of payouts.

TABLE 9.2 Estimated Price Elasticities of Demand for Selected Foods in the UK 1981–86

Beef and Veal	−1.46
Mutton and Lamb	−1.67
Pork	−2.01
Frozen peas	−0.88
Bread	−0.26
Tea	−0.19
Potatoes	−0.13

Source: Annual report of the National Food Survey Committee, Ministry of Agriculture, Fisheries and Food, *Household Food Consumption and Expenditure 1986* (HMSO, 1987).

The demands for meat products are elastic in the UK, while the demands for many other food products are inelastic. Bread, potatoes and tea have very low elasticities. Frozen peas, which are a bit more of a luxury, have an elasticity that is higher although still less than unity. The major meat products have elasticities in excess of unity.

Price Elasticities

Much of the early work on demand measurement concentrated on the agricultural sector. Large fluctuations in agricultural prices provided both the incentive to study this sector and the data on which to base estimates of price elasticities of demand. Nobel laureate Richard Stone, in the UK, and Professor Henry Schultz, in the US, did much of the pioneering work. Many agricultural research centres extended their work, and even today make new estimates of the price elasticities of foodstuffs. The resulting data mostly confirm the existence of low price elasticities for food products as a whole, as well as for many individual products. The policy pay-off of this knowledge in terms of understanding agricultural problems has been enormous; it represents an early triumph of empirical work in economics. (See the discussion in Chapter 7.)

Although agricultural commodities often have inelastic demands, the demand for some commodities, such as beef in the United States and domestically produced lamb and mutton in the United Kingdom, are elastic. The reason for this is that these products have close substitutes. For example, British households can choose between locally produced lamb and mutton and imported varieties (which typically have a somewhat lower quality and price). Similarly, American households can choose among beef, pork and chicken on the basis of price. These data support the generalization that the broader the category of related products, the lower the observed price elasticity of demand.

Table 9.2 shows that even broadly defined meat categories tend to have mildly elastic demands in the UK. As the Table also illustrates, however, many other food products have highly inelastic demands.

Although the importance of the agricultural problem led early investigators to concentrate on the demand for foodstuffs, modern studies have expanded to include virtually the whole range of commodities on which the household spends its income. The demands for consumers' durables such as cars, radios, refrigerators, television sets and houses are of particular interest because they constitute a large fraction of total demand, and because they can vary markedly from one year to the next. A durable commodity can usually be made to last for another year; thus purchases can be postponed with greater ease than can purchases of non-durables such as food and services. If enough households decide simultaneously to postpone purchases of durables for even six months, the effect on the economy can be enormous.

Durables as a whole have an inelastic demand, while many individual durables have elastic demands. This is another example of the general proposition that the broader the category, the lower the elasticity because the fewer the close substitutes. Indeed, whether durable or non-durable, most specific manufactured goods have close substitutes, and studies show that they tend to have price-elastic demands. The accumulated data on price elasticity confirm this generalization:

any one of a group of close substitutes will tend to have an elastic demand, even though the demand for the group as a whole may be inelastic.

Income Elasticities

Income elasticities have been measured frequently. Because changes in income exert a major effect on quantities demanded, the FAO has found it useful to estimate income elasticities for dozens of agricultural products, country by

TABLE 9.3 Estimated Income Elasticities of Demand for Selected Foods in the UK 1960–85

	1960	1975	1985
Beef and Veal	0.16	0.25	0.26
Mutton and Lamb	0.38	0.21	0.19
Pork	0.46	0.39	0.14
Frozen peas	1.53	0.43	0.33
Bread	−0.09	0.01	−0.06
Tea	0.03	−0.10	−0.32
Potatoes	0.07	0.01	−0.23

Source: Annual Reports of the National Food Survey Committee, Ministry of Agriculture, Fisheries and Food *Household Food Consumption and Expenditure* (HMSO, various years).

UK income elasticities tend to be less than unity for almost all food products. At the levels of income achieved in the UK in 1985, most foods were regarded as necessities having very low income elasticities. Back in 1960, frozen peas were still a luxury with an income elasticity of 1.53 but by 1985 that had fallen to 0.33. By 1985, tea and potatoes were definitely inferior goods (the measured values for bread do not differ significantly from zero). In spite of being inferior goods, they had normal price elasticities as shown in Table 9.2, illustrating that it is more common for a good to be an inferior good than to be a Giffen good.

country. The data tend to show that the more basic, or staple, a commodity, the lower its income elasticity.

Table 9.3 illustrates this result for the UK. Note the low income elasticities for all of the food products consumed by households that are listed in the Table. Note also the interesting contrast with the data in Table 9.2. The meat products that have elastic price elasticities nonetheless have inelastic income elasticities. This tells us that changes in relative prices will cause substantial substitution among different types of meat – hence the greater-than-unity price elasticities – but that increases in incomes cause relatively small increases in overall meat consumption – hence the low income elasticities. Some of the non-meat products shown in the Table have negative income elasticities, indicating that they are inferior goods at current levels of household incomes. Thus, although reductions in relative prices lead to increased purchases – normal price elasticities – the goods are inferior with respect to increases in income.

Empirical studies tend to confirm that, as income rises, household expenditures follow broadly similar paths in different countries. Summarizing recent studies, Robert Ferber wrote that they yield low elasticities for food and housing, elasticities close to unity for clothing and education, and higher elasticities for various types of household services, recreation, personal care and other services. Of course there are exceptions to cross-country uniformity. If a commodity plays a very different role in the consumption patterns of different groups, it may be expected to have different demand characteristics, even at comparable levels of income. Wine is a basic part of the French consumption bundle, and its consumption in France is little affected by changes in level of income. A higher income elasticity for wine in Canada and the United States shows that it is regarded as a luxury rather than a necessity, particularly at lower levels of income. Measured differences in income elasticity of demand for poultry between the United Kingdom and Sri Lanka result from differences both in the level of average income and in tastes.

The accumulated data on income elasticity confirm this generalization:

The more basic an item is in the consumption pattern of households, the lower its income elasticity will be.

Cross-elasticities of Demand

In many countries monopoly is illegal. Measurement of cross-elasticities have helped courts to decide on the allegation that a monopoly exists. To illustrate, assume that the government of a particular country brings suit against a company for buying up all the firms making aluminium cable, claiming the company has created a monopoly of the product. The company replies that it needs to own all the firms in order to compete efficiently against the several firms producing copper cable. It argues that these two products are such close substitutes that the firms producing each are in intense competition, so that the only producer of aluminium cable cannot be said to have an effective monopoly over the market for cable. Measurement of cross-elasticity can be decisive in such a case. A cross-elasticity of 10, for example, would support the company by showing that the two products were such close substitutes that a monopoly of either would not be an effective monopoly of the cable market. A cross-elasticity of 0.5, on the other hand, would support the government's contention that the monopoly of aluminium cable was a monopoly over a complete market.

Other Variables

Modern studies show that demand is often influenced by a wide variety of socio-economic factors – family size, age, geographical location, type of employment, wealth, and income expectations – not included in the traditional theory of demand. Although significant, the total contribution of all these factors to changes in demand tends to be small. Typically, less than 30 per cent of the variations in demand are accounted for by these 'novel' factors and a much higher proportion is explained by the traditional variables of current prices and incomes.

Problems of Demand Measurement

The explosion of knowledge of elasticities in recent decades came about when econometricians overcame major problems in measuring demand relationships. A full discussion must be left to a course in econometrics, but some aspects of such measurements are sufficiently troubling to most students to make them worth mentioning here.

Everything is Changing at Once

When market demand changes over time, it is usually because *all* of the influences that affect demand have been changing at the same time. How, then, can the separate influence of each variable be determined?

What, for example, is to be made of the observation that the quantity of butter consumed per capita rose by 10 per cent over a period in which average household income rose by 5 per cent, the price of butter fell by 3 per cent and the price of margarine rose by 4 per cent? How much of the change is due to income elasticity of demand, how much to price elasticity and how much to the cross-elasticity between butter and margarine? If this is all we know, the question cannot be answered. If, however, there are many observations showing, say, quantity demanded,

income, price of butter and price of margarine every month for four or five years, it is possible to discover the separate influence of each of the variables. The standard technique for doing so is called multiple regression analysis, and it was briefly alluded to in Chapter 3.

Separating the Influences of Demand and Supply

A second set of problems concerns the separate estimation of demand and supply curves. We do not observe directly what people wish to buy and what producers wish to sell. Rather, we see what they do buy and what they do sell. The problem of how to estimate both demand and supply curves from observed market data on prices and quantities actually traded is called the **identification problem**.

To illustrate the problem, we assume in Figure 9.1 that all situations observed in the real world are equilibrium ones, in the sense that they are produced by the intersection of demand and supply curves. The first two parts of the Figure show cases where only one curve shifts. Observations made on prices and quantities then trace out the curve that has not shifted. The third part of the Figure, however, shows that when both curves are shifting, observations of prices and quantities are not sufficient to identify the slope of either curve.

The identification problem is surmountable. The key to identifying the demand and supply curves separately is to bring in variables other than price, and then to relate demand to one set and supply to *some other* set. For example, supply of the commodity might be related not only to the price of the commodity but also to its cost of production, and demand might be related not only to the price of the commodity but also to consumers' incomes. Provided that these other variables change sufficiently, it is possible to determine the relation between quantity supplied and price as well as the relation between quantity demanded and price. The details of how this is done will be found in a course on econometrics.

In serious applied work, concern is usually given to the identification problem. Sometimes, however, the problem is ignored. Whenever you see an argument such as, 'We know that the foreign elasticity of demand must be very low because the price of whisky rose by 10 per cent

FIGURE 9.1 The Identification Problem

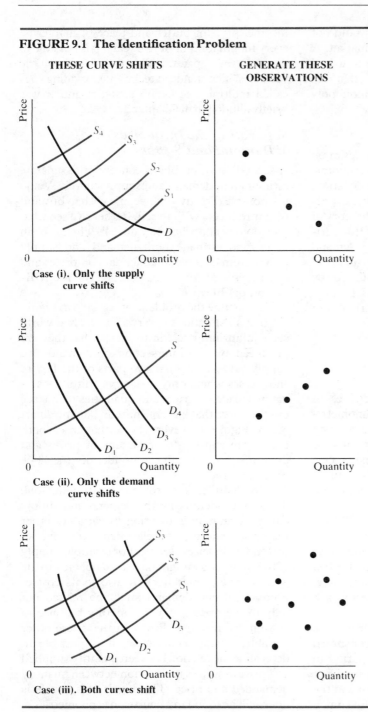

THESE CURVE SHIFTS

GENERATE THESE OBSERVATIONS

Case (i). Only the supply curve shifts

Case (ii). Only the demand curve shifts

Case (iii). Both curves shift

Observations on prices and quantities are sufficient to identify the slope of one of the curves when it is stationary while the other shifts. In each case, the curves in the left-hand panel shift randomly from one numbered position to another. All that one sees, however, are the observations indicated by each of the points in the right-hand panels. The problem is to identify the slope of one of the curves in the corresponding left-hand panel. In case (i) the observations trace out the shape of the demand curve. In case (ii) they trace out the supply curve. In case (iii) neither curve can be identified from the observed prices and quantities.

last year while whisky exports hardly fell at all', you should ask if the author has really identified the demand curve. If the rise in price was due to a rise in foreign demand for whisky, we may actually have discovered that the short-run *supply curve* of whisky is very inelastic (since whisky takes several years to manufacture). The general proposition to keep in mind is:

unless we know that one curve has shifted while the other has not, price and quantity data alone are insufficient to reveal

anything about the shape of either the demand or the supply curve.

Why the Measurement of Demand is Important

The empirical measurements of demand elasticity help to provide the theory of price with empirical content. If we knew *nothing* about demand elasticities, then all of the exercises we have gone through in previous chapters would have very little application to the real world. A different view of the importance of empirical measures of demand, made many years ago by the late Lord Robbins, is discussed in Box 9.1.[1]

Since the time when Lord Robbins made his criticism, modern research has gone a long way in establishing quantitative demand relations. As time goes by, further evidence accumulates, and economists are far beyond merely wondering if demand curves have negative slopes. Not only do we now know the approximate shape of many demand curves, we also have information about how demand curves shift. Our knowledge of demand relations increases significantly every year.

CRITICISMS OF DEMAND THEORY

Students often find demand theory excessively abstract and feel that it is unrealistic. Some very senior critics have often felt more or less the same way. Here we shall take up the question of whether demand theory is obviously unrealistic.

Is Demand Theory in Conflict with Everyday Experience?

It is easy to prove that people do not *always*

---

[1] L. Robbins, *An Essay on the Nature and Significance of Economic Science* (London: Macmillan, 1932), p. 98–101, italics added. This provocative work contains classic statements of many views still held by economists. It also states a view on the nature of economic theory and its relation to empirical observations that is contradictory to the one presented in this book. Many other economists of Lord Robbins' time shared this view. For a similar statement, see L. von Mises, *Human Action* (Hodge, 1949), Chapter 2. For a view much closer to the one presented in this book, however, see L. Robbins, 'The Present Position of Economics', *Rivista Di Economica*, September 1959.

behave in the manner assumed by demand theory. Does that make the theory inapplicable? The answer depends on what we want demand theory to accomplish. Three uses may be distinguished. First, we may be interested in the aggregate behaviour of all households, as shown by the market demand curve for a product. Second, we may want to make probabilistic statements about the actions of individual households. Third, we may want to make statements about what *all* households *always* do.

The aggregate use of the theory of demand is the most common one in economics. All of the predictions developed in Chapter 7 depend on having some knowledge of the shape of the relevant market demand curves, yet they do not require that we be able to predict the behaviour of each individual household. The second use, though much less common than the first, is important; we do sometimes want to be able to say what a single household will probably do. The third use of demand theory is by far the least important of the three. Rarely do we wish to make categorical statements about what all households will always do.

Fortunately, the observation that households occasionally behave in ways not predicted by demand theory would, if carefully documented, refute only the assertion that the theory's predictions *always* applied to *all* households.

Neither the existence of a relatively stable downward-sloping market demand curve nor our ability to predict what a single household will probably do requires that all households invariably behave in the manner assumed by the theory. Such fully consistent behaviour on the part of everyone at all times is sufficient but not necessary for a stable market demand curve. Consider two other possibilities. First, some households may always behave in a manner contrary to the theory. Households whose members are handicapped or are emotionally disturbed are obvious possibilities. The erratic behaviour of such households will not cause market demand curves for normal goods to depart from their downward slope, provided that the households account for a small part of purchases of any product. Their behaviour will be swamped by the normal behaviour of the majority of the households. Second, an occasional irrationality on the part of every household

BOX 9.1 ARE ELASTICITY MEASUREMENTS PART OF ECONOMIC SCIENCE?

Many years ago the late Lord Robbins had this to say about empirical measures of demand:[1]

'Our deductions do not provide any justification for saying that caviare is an economic good and carrion a disutility. Still less do they inform us concerning the intensity of the demand for caviare or the demand to be rid of carrion ... But is it not desirable to transcend such limitations? Ought we not to wish to be in a position to give numerical values to the scales of valuation, to establish quantitative laws of demand and supply? ... No doubt such knowledge would be useful. But a moment's reflection should make it plain that we are here entering upon a field of investigation *where there is no reason to suppose that uniformities are to be discovered* ...

A simple illustration should make this quite clear ... Suppose we are confronted with an order fixing the price of herrings at a point below the price hitherto ruling in the market. Suppose we are in a position to say, 'According to the researches of Blank (1907–1908) the elasticity of demand for common herring (*Clupea harengus*) is 1.3; the present price-fixing order therefore may be expected to leave an excess of demand over supply of two million barrels.'

But can we hope to attain such an enviable position? Let us assume that in 1907–1908 Blank had succeeded in ascertaining that, with a given price change in that year, the elasticity of demand was 1.3 ... But what reason is there to suppose that he was unearthing a constant law? ... Is it possible reasonably to suppose that coefficients derived from the observation of a particular herring market at a particular time and place have any *permanent* significance – save as Economic History?'

Several criticisms can be made of Robbins' argument. First, although *a priori* arguments may strongly suggest that certain relationships will not be stable, they can never establish this. Even if the *a priori* arguments turn out to be correct most of the time, they may be wrong in a few cases. Only observation can reveal the cases in which the *a priori* argument is wrong.

The second major criticism is that the variability of any given relationship is an important matter. If, for example, tastes were so variable that demand curves shift violently from day to day, then all of the comparative-static equilibrium analysis of the previous chapters would be useless. Only by accident would any market be near its equilibrium, and this would occur only momentarily. If, instead, tastes change extremely slowly, then we might do very well to regard the relation between demand and price as being stable over long time-periods. Even if we could show, on *a priori* grounds, that every relation between two or more variables used in economic theory was necessarily not perfectly stable, it would be critical for purposes of theory to know the quantitative amount of the lack of stability. Only observation can show this, and such observations are thus important for economic theory as well as for economic history.

The third criticism is that even if we find substantial variations in our relations, we want to know if these variations appear capricious or if they display a systematic pattern that might lead us to suspect that herring demand is related to other factors. We might, for example, find a strong but sometimes interrupted tendency for the elasticity of demand for herrings to fall over time. We might then find that this systematic variation in price elasticity could be accounted for by income variations (as the population gets richer its demand for herrings is less and less affected by price variations and so the demand becomes more and more inelastic). We might now find that a high proportion of the changes in herring demand could be accounted for by assuming a *stable relation* between demand on the one hand, and price *and* income on the other. In general, what looked like an unstable relation between two variables might turn out to be only part of a more stable relation among three or more variables. All of this leads us to the following conclusion.

Empirical measurements are critical to economics. Without some quantitative evidence of the magnitude and the stability of particular relations we cannot use economic theory to make useful predictions about the real world.

will not upset the downward slope of the market demand curve for a normal good. As long as these are unrelated across households, occurring now in one and now in another, their effect will be swamped by the normal behaviour of most households most of the time.

The negative slope of the demand curve requires only that at any moment of time most households are behaving as is predicted by the theory. This is quite compatible with behaviour contrary to the theory by some households all of the time

and by all households some of the time. Thus we cannot test the theory of market demand by observing the behaviour of an isolated household.

Is Demand Theory Just an Elaborate Way of Saying that Anything can Happen?

Many critics of demand theory argue that the theory has little substantive content. They argue that, with respect to the commodity's own price, the theory says nothing more than that most demand curves slope downwards most of the time. They also argue that, with respect to such other variables as income and the prices of other commodities, the theory says nothing more than that, when any of these change, quantity demanded may go up, go down or stay the same. If all we can say is that anything can happen, we hardly need to base this agnostic position on an elaborate theory. According to these critics, demand theory is a lot of sound and fury signifying (almost) nothing. To weigh their claims, we must consider the relation between quantity demanded and the various factors that influence it.

Demand and tastes: The proposition that demand and tastes are related is not really testable unless we have some way of measuring a change in tastes. Since we do not have an independent measure of taste changes, what we

usually do is infer them from the data for demand. We make such statements as: ' In spite of the rise in price, quantity purchased increased, so there must have been a change in tastes in favour of this commodity.' More generally, we are likely to use prices and incomes to account for all the changes in demand that we can, and then assert that the rest must be due to changes in tastes (and to errors of measurement). This does not concern us unduly because we are not particularly interested in establishing precise relations between tastes and demand.

The fact that we cannot identify those changes in demand that are due to changes in tastes does, however, cause trouble when we come to consider the relation between demand and other factors. Anything that does not seem to agree with our theory can be explained away by saying that tastes must have changed. Say, for example, *incomes and other prices were known to be constant*, while the price of some commodity X rose and, at the same time, more X was observed to be bought. This gives us observations such as the two illustrated in Figure 9.2(i). The demand curve for X might be positively sloped in this case, but another explanation is that the rise in price coincided with a change in tastes, so that the demand curve shifted just as price changed. These possibilities are analysed in Figure 9.2. With only two observations, we are unable to distinguish between these possibilities, since we

FIGURE 9.2 Is the Demand Curve Positively Sloped?

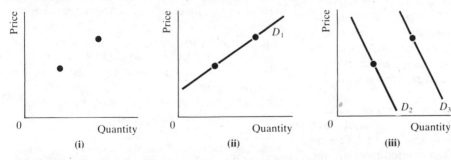

A change in tastes may explain isolated apparent contradictions of the demand curve's negative slope. Part (i) shows two price-quantity observations that are assumed to be made when income and the prices of all other commodities are unchanged. Part (ii) shows the possibility that the observations were generated by a positively sloped demand curve D_1. Part (iii) shows the possibility that the observations were generated by a negatively sloped demand curve, D_2, that shifted to D_3 due to a change in tastes.

FIGURE 9.3 The Demand Curve Appears to be Positively Sloped

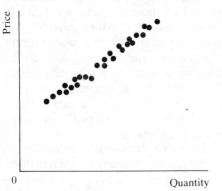

Repeated changes in tastes are unlikely to be a satisfactory explanation of repeated contradictions of the demand curve's negative slope. Each of the 26 dots shows a price-quantity combination. All observations are assumed to be taken over a 26-week period when incomes and other prices did not change. The explanation that the demand curve is positively sloped is more likely to be correct than the explanation that a negatively sloped demand curve had shifted each week so as to generate the data showing a positive association between price and quantity.

have no independent way of telling whether or not tastes changed. If, however, we have many observations, we can get some idea of where the balance of probabilities lies between the two explanations. If *after using appropriate statistical procedures to remove the effects due to changes in income and other prices*, we have the twenty-six observations illustrated in Figure 9.3 (say the commodity's own price changed each week over a period of six months), we will be hard-pressed to avoid the conclusion that the evidence conflicts with the hypothesis of a negatively sloping demand curve.

Of course, we can always explain away these observations by saying that tastes must have changed in favour of this commodity each time its price rose and against the commodity each time its price fell. This 'alibi' can certainly be used with effect to explain away a single conflicting observation, but we would be uncomfortable using the same alibi twenty-six times in six months. Indeed, we should begin to suspect a fault in the hypothesis that demand and price vary inversely with each other.

We now have a problem in statistical testing of the sort described in Chapter 3. We are not prepared to throw away a theory after only one or two conflicting observations, but we are prepared to abandon it once we accumulate a mass of conflicting observations that were very unlikely to have occurred if the theory was correct.[1] Thus, statistically, the theory is testable. Fortunately, there is, as we have seen, a great deal of evidence that most demand curves do have negative slopes. The predictions of the theory have, with a few possible exceptions, been found to be in agreement with the facts.

Demand and the prices of other commodities: In chapter 5, we made a distinction between commodities that are complements to one another and those that are substitutes. Consider the quantity demanded of commodity X. This will be negatively related to the price of a complement (when the price of a complement falls, quantity of X demanded will rise), and positively related to the price of a substitute (when the price of a substitute falls, quantity of X demanded will fall). There may also be a group of commodities for which price variations leave demand for X unchanged. These commodities lie on the boundary dividing substitutes for X from complements to X.

These three reactions – quantity demanded rises, falls or remains unchanged when the price of some other good varies – cover all conceivable possibilities. So far we merely have a set of labels to attach to all possibilities. We do not have a useful theory unless we have a way of *deciding in advance* which goods are substitutable for and which are complementary to X. Fortunately, we can sometimes decide this from technical knowledge alone. To do so is particularly easy when we are considering the demands for inputs in production. Lifts and lift operators, buckets and spades, trains and rails, roads and fences, any

---

[1] If changes in tastes are not related to changes in price, we can easily calculate the odds that the observations in Figure 9.3 are consistent with a negatively sloped, but continually shifting, demand curve. If tastes changed randomly each week, there is a 50–50 chance that tastes changed in the direction needed to offset the first week's price change. In the second week there is also a 50–50 chance. The chances that they changed the 'right' way in both weeks are $(1/2)$ $(1/2) = 1/4$ and the chance that they changed the right way for 25 successive weeks is $(1/2)^{25} = 1/33,544,432$!

piece of equipment and its human operator are all examples of pairs of commodities that are complements to each other. Thus we can predict that a fall in the price of any one will lead to an increase in the demand for the other member of the pair. A similar list can be drawn up for inputs that are substitutes. It would include such things as wood, bricks and concrete in construction; manure and artificial fertilizers; and a building full of statistical clerks with desk calculators and a computer.

There are also many consumer goods for which we can predict complementary or substitutability. Complementarity exists, for example, between electric razors and pre-shave lotion; ordinary razors, razor blades and shaving cream; golf clubs and golf balls; grass seed and lawnmowers; electric stoves and electricity; and marriages and services of divorce-court judges. The list of substitute goods includes such obvious examples as various green vegetables, beef and pork, private automobiles and public transport, open fireplaces and central heating, gas and electric cookers, holidays in Spain and on the Italian Riviera, skiing in Switzerland and Austria – such a list could be extended to cover many pages.

Whenever the technical data tell us which goods are substitutes and which are complements, we can predict in advance the effect of a change in the price of one good on the demand for another.

Demand and income: A change in income can have any conceivable effect on demand: a rise in income may cause the demand for a product to rise, to fall or to remain unchanged. Given this ambiguity, two facts help to give content to the theory. First, *we observe that income elasticities are fairly stable over time.* If, over the last twenty years, the income elasticity of demand for some agricultural product has been observed to fall from 0.70 to 0.40, we are reasonably safe in predicting that a rise in income next year will be met by a less than proportionate rise in the demand for that product. If, on the other hand, the income elasticity of demand for cars and electricity are both observed to have been above unity for several years, it is fairly safe to predict that rises in income in the next few years will be met by more than proportionate rises in the demand for cars and electricity. Because these

elasticities are observed not to change rapidly or capriciously we can predict into the near future from a knowledge of the level and direction of change of existing income elasticities.

The second observation that helps give empirical content to the theory is that *households throughout the world behave in many broadly similar ways.* At low levels of income, food tends to have a fairly high income elasticity of demand. But as the level of income rises, the income elasticity of demand for food tends to fall well below unity. This constant of behaviour that has been observed in many countries allows us to predict (1) that as long as productivity growth continues in agriculture, the long-term drift from the land will continue in Western countries (unless they have a large export market for their agricultural goods), and (2) that when other countries of the world achieve sustained positive rates of growth, they will soon encounter the problem of a declining agricultural sector.

Demand for the commodity and the commodity's own price: The prediction that demand curves have negative slopes has long been known as *the law of demand*. Great interest was attached to a refutation of the law of demand, supposedly made by the Victorian economist Sir Robert Giffen. Giffen was reputed to have observed that an increase in the price of wheat led to an increase in the consumption of bread by nineteenth-century English peasants. If this observation is correct, it does refute the hypothesis that all demand curves always slope downwards. Does it refute the modern theory of demand? The answer is No, because that is just the type of rare exception to the normal case that is envisaged by the modern indifference-preference theory.[1]

Thus the modern theory of demand makes an unequivocal prediction only when we have extraneous information about income elasticities of

---

[1] The reason why a demand curve can slope upwards according to indifference-preference theory is to be found on pages 135–138. the possible explanation is in terms of a negative income effect swamping a normal substitution effect. Wheat accounted for a very large fraction of the total expenditure of the households affected by the price change. If wheat is an inferior good, so that the income effect is negative, it is possible that the large negative income effect overcame the normal substitution effect when the price of wheat rose.

demand. Since incomes change continuously as a result of economic growth, we do have such information about many commodities. When we know that the income effect is positive (income elasticity of demand exceeds zero), as it is for most commodities, we can predict in advance that the quantity demanded will be negatively related to its price. When we know the income effect is negative (i.e. the good is inferior), we cannot be sure of the result. The only thing we can then say is that, the smaller is the proportion of total expenditure accounted for by this commodity, the less important the income effect will be, and, hence, the more likely we are to get the normal result of price and quantity varying negatively with each other. Finally, if we have no knowledge about the income effect, we can still hazard a probabilistic statement. The great weight of existing evidence suggests that if we had to guess with no prior knowledge whether the demand curve for some commodity X was downward or upward sloping, the former choice would be the odds-on favourite.

Alternative Theories of the Source of Household Satisfaction

The only exception to the law of demand admitted within indifference-preference theory is the Giffen good. Further exceptions all arise from making assumptions that contradict those of indifference theory.

Assume, for example, that a household's satisfaction depends not only on the quantities of the various commodities that it consumes but also on the prices it has to pay for them. The household may, for example, buy diamonds not because its members particularly like diamonds *per se*, but because they wish to show off their wealth in an ostentatious but socially acceptable way. The household values diamonds precisely because they are expensive; thus a fall in price might lead the household to stop buying diamonds and switch to a more satifactory object of ostentatious display. Such households will have positively sloping demand curves for diamonds: the lower the price, the fewer they will buy. If enough households act similarly, the market demand curve for diamonds could slope upwards as well.

But a positively-sloping market demand curve for diamonds and other similar products has never been observed. Why? A moment's thought

about the industrial uses of diamonds, and the masses of lower-income consumers who would buy diamonds only if they were sufficiently inexpensive, suggests that positively sloping demand curves for some individual households are much more likely than a positively sloping market demand curve for the same commodity. Recall the discussion on pages 159–161 about the ability of the theory of the negatively sloping demand curve to accommodate odd behaviour on the part of a small group of households (this time the 'odd' group is the rich, rather than the handicapped or the emotionally disturbed).

Conclusion

Today we not only believe that most demand curves have negative slopes, we also have a good idea of the elasticity in many cases. Reasonably precise knowledge about demand curves is needed if we are to make real-world applications of price theory. If we knew nothing at all empirically about these curves, the theory would be devoid of real-world applications. Since we do have this knowledge, we can predict in advance the effects of changes in many factors such as taxes, costs, the amount of competition in a particular market, and so forth. The more accurate our knowledge of the shape of demand curves, the smaller will be the margin of error in such predictions. Fortunately, as we have seen in this chapter, economists have accumulated a great store of the requisite empirical knowledge.[1]

[1] For an interesting discussion of the issues discussed in this chapter, see T.W.Hutchison, *Knowledge and Ignorance in Economics* (Oxford: Basil Blackwell, 1977), especially Chapter 2. Hutchison distinguishes between universal predictions and extrapolations of existing regularities and says that I am concerned only with the latter in this chapter. In the first edition of this book I looked only for universal predictions and criticized demand theory for being almost empty of these. Later, when I contemplated how much economists did that was useful, I came to look beyond universal predictions. I noted many applications – including the triumph of the understanding of the agricultural problem which before econometric measurement had seemed a mystery – that rested on the ability to understand economic events by using theory plus empirical elasticities based on a knowledge of the past. Such studies have been wonderfully successful, compared especially with the lack of equivalent success in other social sciences. I am not sure how to interpret these successes in terms of abstract scientific methodology. I suspect, however, that we need further methodological insights before we can understand these and place them outside Hutchison's dichotomy of generalized predictions and simple extrapolations.

SUMMARY

1. Many economic decisions taken by firms and households involve risky choices which can often be characterized by the expected value of the outcome and the degree of risk as measured by the dispersion of the possible outcomes.
2. Because those providing the insurance, or gambling games, must make profits, those gambling or taking out insurance do not take mathematically fair gambles. Diminishing marginal utility explains why risk-neutral people would buy such insurance policies but predicts that such people would not gamble. Gambling where there is a small chance of a very large gain may be explained by the value placed on the hope (however small) of transforming one's life. Gambling where small gains and losses are involved may be explained by risk loving, while taking out insurance may be explained by increasing marginal utility of units of forgone income.
3. From the firm's point of view, providing gambling games where the odds can be set endogenously is a no-lose situation. Providing insurance is risky, but the risk is minimized by the pooling of independent risks.
4. Over the years, economists have measured many price, income and cross elasticities of demand. Being able to do so requires the use of statistical techniques to measure the separate influence of each of several variables when all are changing at once. It also requires a solution of the identification problem, which refers to measuring the separate shapes of the demand and the supply curves. This cannot be done from price and quantity data alone.
5. Observed demand curves are negatively sloped in spite of odd behaviour on the part of some people some of the time. Such behaviour tends to cancel out as long as individuals behave independently of each other.
6. Because households tend to behave the same the world over, income elasticities measured in one country can be used to predict behaviour in other countries when they reach the first country's level of income. Because price elasticities do not change capriciously, knowledge of price elasticities from the recent past is useful in predicting behaviour in the near future.

TOPICS FOR REVIEW

- Uncertainty, expected value and risk
- Fair and unfair games
- Attitudes to risk
- Risk sharing and risk pooling
- Why people insure against risks and why they gamble
- Measurements of price, income and cross-elasticities of demand
- The identification problem

PART 4

The Intermediate Theory of Supply

10

The Firm, Production and Cost

In Chapter 4 we assumed the existence of a supply curve relating the price of a commodity to the quantity firms would be willing to produce and offer for sale. We now go behind the supply curve to explain how its shape results from the decision of individual firms. Thus Chapters 10 to 12 do for the supply curve what Chapter 8 did for the demand curve. These chapters are also a first step towards dealing with a host of interesting policy questions, such as: What is the effect of various forms of competition or monopoly on the production of an industry? Why do firms combine? What are the causes and consequences of takeover bids? Will taxing the domestic consumption of a good encourage its export?

THE FIRM IN PRACTICE

We start by taking a brief look at the basic unit of production, the firm. After studying firms as we see them in the real world, we go on to see how firms are treated in economic theory.

Forms of Business Organization[1]

There are four main ways of organizing the production of goods and services that are sold on markets: a *single proprietorship*, also known as a sole trader, a *partnership*, a *joint-stock company*, also known as a company (corporation in North America), and a *public corporation*. With a **single proprietorship** there is one owner who is personally responsible for everything that is done. The firm may or may not have employees, but it has just one owner-manager. In the **partnership** there are two or more joint owners, each of whom is personally responsible for all of the partnership debts. A **joint-stock company** is a firm regarded in law as having an identity of its own; its owners are not personally responsible for anything that is done in the name of the firm. A **public corporation** is set up to run a nationalized industry. It is owned by the state but is usually under the direction of a more or less independent, state-appointed board. Although its ownership differs, the organization and legal

[1] For a detailed discussion of the types of business organization, their finance and other related issues, see Harbury and Lipsey, *op. cit.*, Chapter 2.

status of such a public corporation is similar to that of a joint-stock company.[1]

A fifth method of organizing production differs from all the others in that the output is not sold. Instead it is provided to consumers free (or at a nominal price), while costs of production are paid from the tax revenue in the case of government production, and charitable donations in the case of private production. Important examples found in all countries are government agencies providing defence, roads and education, as well as private charities. In the UK we must also add the National Health Service to this list. (In countries without nationalized medical services, hospitals and doctors behave just as other firms do: they purchase factors of production on the open market and gain revenue by selling their services to people who wish to, and can afford to, purchase them.)

The first four types of organizations comprise what in Chapter 4 we called the market sector of the economy. The fifth type comprises the non-market sector.

The Financing of Firms

The money a firm raises for carrying on its business is sometimes called its **financial capital** (or its *money capital*), as distinct from its **real capital** (or *physical capital*), the physical assets that constitute factories, machinery and stocks of material and finished goods.

The use of the term *capital* to refer to both an amount of money and a quantity of goods can be confusing, but which is being referred to is usually made clear by the context. The two uses are not independent, for much of the financial capital raised by a firm will be used to purchase the capital goods the firm requires for production.

There are two basic types of financial capital used by firms: owners' capital, funds provided by the owners, and debt, funds borrowed from outside the firm.

Owners' Capital

The first main source of funds is the firm's owners. In individual proprietorships and partnerships, one or more owners will put up much of the required funds. A joint-stock company acquires funds from its owners by selling **stocks**, **shares** or **equities** (as they are variously called) to them. These are basically ownership certificates. The money goes to the company and the purchasers become owners of the firm, risking the loss of their money, and gaining the right to share in the firm's profits. Profits that are paid out to shareholders are called **dividends**.

One easy way for an established firm to raise money is to retain current profits rather than paying them out to shareholders. Financing investment from *undistributed profits* has become an important source of funds in modern times. Reinvested profit adds to the value of the firm, and hence raises the market value of existing shares; it is in fact capital provided by owners.

Debt

Holders of debentures are the firm's creditors, not its owners. They have loaned money in return for what is called a **debenture**. This is a promise both to pay a stated sum each year and to repay the loan at some stated time in the future. The amount that is paid each year is called the **interest**, while the amount of the loan that will be repaid at the stated date in the future is called the **principal**. The time at which the principal is repaid is called the **redemption date** of the debenture. The amount of time between the debenture's issue and its redemption date is called its **term**. The firm has a legal obligation to make periodic interest payments and to repay the principal on the redemption date.

Many small businesses which are not well established cannot sell stocks to the public and must borrow from banks and other financial institutions to finance their activities in the short term. Such borrowing tends to be expensive for firms, so they usually prefer other methods of raising funds for long-term purposes. Some companies, however, are forced to seek funds from non-bank, financial institutions, at yet higher rates of interest.

---

[1] The recent development of limited partnerships provides a hybrid between the ordinary partnership and the joint-stock company. This hybrid provides for two types of partners. *General partners* take part in the running of the business and have unlimited liability. *Limited partners* take no part in the running of the business and their liability is limited to the amount they actually invest in the enterprise.

In economic theory the term **bond** is used to refer to any piece of paper that provides evidence of a debt carrying a legal obligation to pay interest and repay the principal at some stated future time. Hereafter we refer to debentures, as well as other similar debt instruments, as *bonds*.

THE FIRM IN ECONOMIC THEORY

In Chapter 4 we defined the firm as the unit that takes decisions with respect to the production and sale of commodities. This concept of the firm covers a variety of business organizations, from the single proprietorship to the joint-stock company, and a variety of business sizes, from the single inventor operating in his garage and financed by whatever he can extract from a reluctant bank manager, to vast undertakings with many thousands of shareholders and creditors.

Profit Maximization

We know that the decisions taken by large firms are actually taken by many different individuals. Nonetheless, the firm can be regarded as a single, consistent, decision-taking unit because of the assumption that all its decisions are taken in order to maximize its profits. This assumption is critical to the whole traditional theory of the firm, and we may state it formally as follows:

> **The desire to maximize profits is assumed to motivate all decisions taken within a firm, and such decisions are uninfluenced by who takes them. Thus the theory abstracts from the peculiarities of the persons taking the decisions and from the organizational structure in which they work.**

A firm's profits are the difference between the revenues it received from selling its output and its costs of producing that output. This simple-sounding concept turns out to be a tricky one because, as we shall see later in this chapter, costs of production involve some rather subtle notions.

The assumption of profit maximization allows economists to predict firm behaviour. Economists do this by studying the effect that each of the choices available to the firm would have on its profits. They then predict that the firm will select the alternative that produces the largest profits. Box 10.1 deals with some common worries about the assumptions of profit maximization.

PRODUCTION, COSTS AND PROFITS

Firms seek profits by producing and selling commodities. The materials and factor services used in the production process are called **inputs**, and the products that emerge are called **outputs**. One way of looking at the process is to regard the inputs as being combined to produce the output. One might also regard the inputs as being used up, or sacrificed, to gain the output.

Hundreds of inputs enter into the output of a specific good. Among the inputs entering into car production are, to name only a few, sheet steel, rubber, spark plugs, electricity, the site of the factory, the carpark for its employees, machinists, cost accountants, spray-painting machines, forklift trucks, managers and painters. These inputs can be grouped into four broad classes: (1) those that are inputs to the car firm, but outputs to some other firm, such as spark plugs, electricity and sheet steel; (2) those that are provided directly by nature, such as land; (3) those that are provided directly by households, such as the services of workers and managers; and (4) those that are provided by the factories and machines used for manufacturing cars.

The first class of inputs is made up of goods produced by other firms. They are called *intermediate products*. For example, one firm may mine iron ore and then sell this ore to be used as an input by a second firm which produces steel. Iron ore is thus an intermediate product which is an output of the first firm and an input of the second. Intermediate products thus appear as inputs only because the stages of production are divided among different firms. At any one stage of production, a firm is using as inputs goods produced by other firms at an earlier stage. If these intermediate products are traced back to their sources, all production can be accounted for by the services of the three kinds of inputs which we first discussed in Chapter 1, and which are called *factors of production*. These are the gifts of nature, such as soil and raw materials, called *land*;

BOX 10.1 WORRIES ABOUT THE ASSUMPTION OF PROFIT MAXIMIZATION

Two criticisms are commonly made of the traditional theory of the firm: first, profit maximization is too crude an assumption about motivation and, second, the firm's organizational structure must affect its decisions.

The motivation of the firm: Many critics have argued that it is unrealistic to build an elaborate theory on such a crude assumption as profit maximization. It is well known that some businessmen are not inspired by the desire to make as much money as possible. Some pursue political influence, while others may be influenced by philanthropic urges. Should we not, therefore, say that the assumption that firms seek to maximize profits is refuted by empirical evidence?

The real world is complex. A theory selects certain factors which are assumed to be the most important ones, while those that are ignored are assumed to be relatively unimportant. If it is true that the key factors have been included, then the theory's predictions will be supported by the facts. It follows that it is not an important criticism to point out that a theory ignores some factors known to be present in the world; this tells us nothing more than that we are dealing with a theory rather than a photographic reproduction of reality. If the theory has ignored some really important factors, its predictions will be contradicted by the evidence.

How do these considerations relate to theories based on the assumption of profit maximization? First, such a theory does not require that profit is the only factor that ever influences firms. What it requires is that profits are an important consideration, important enough that assuming profit maximization to be the firm's sole motive will produce predictions that are substantially correct. Thus, pointing out that businessmen are sometimes motivated by considerations other than profits does not constitute a relevant criticism. It may well be that the theory is substantially wrong, but if so, the way to demonstrate this is to show that its predictions are in conflict with the facts. We cannot, of course, even consider such a possibility until we know what the theory does and does not

predict. Accordingly, we shall press on to develop the theory. When we have completed this task, we shall study relevant criticisms.

Organizational structure: In the theory of the firm, it does not matter whether a decision is taken by a small independent proprietor, a plant manager or the board of directors. As far as the theory is concerned, the decision-taker *is* the firm. This is an assumption of heroic proportions. It amounts to saying that we can treat the farm, the corner greengrocer, the large department store and the giant chemical company, all under the umbrella of a single theory of the behaviour of the firm. Even if this is only partially correct, it represents an enormously valuable simplification. It also illustrates the power of theory in revealing unity of behaviour where to the casual observer there is only a bewildering diversity.

Do not be surprised, therefore, if the theory seems rather abstract and out of touch with reality at first encounter. Because it does generalize over such a wide variety of behaviour, it must ignore those features with which we are most familiar, and which, in our eyes, distinguish the grocer from Royal Dutch Shell. Any theory that generalizes over a wide variety of apparently diverse behaviour necessarily has this characteristic, because it ignores those factors that are most obvious to us and which create in our minds the appearance of diversity.

The final test of whether or not organizational factors can be legitimately ignored is an empirical one: if the theory that we develop by ignoring these factors is successful in predicting the outcome of the kind of events in which we are interested, then we can conclude that we were correct in assuming that these factors could be safely ignored.

Criticisms of the theory for ignoring the importance of the firm's institutional structure are discussed in Chapter 16, at which point competing hypotheses about business behaviour are also discussed.

physical and mental efforts provided by people, called *labour*; and factories, machines and other man-made aids to production, called *capital*.

The Definition of Costs

We have said that profit is the difference between revenue and cost. Any rate of output will have a set of inputs associated with it. To arrive at the cost of producing this output, a value must be put on each of the separate inputs used. The assignment of monetary values to physical quantities of inputs is easy in some cases and difficult in others.

Economists study the production behaviour of firms for a variety of reasons:

(1) to predict how the behaviour of firms will respond to specified changes in the conditions they face;

(2) to help firms make the best decisions they can in achieving their goals; and

(3) to evaluate, from society's point of view, how well firms use scarce resources.

The same measure of cost need not be correct for all of these purposes. For example, if the firm happens to be misinformed about the value of a resource, it will behave according to that misinformation. In predicting the firm's behaviour, economists should use the same information as the firm, even if they know it to be incorrect. But in helping firms to achieve their goals, economists should substitute the correct information.

Economists know exactly how to define costs for purposes (2) and (3) above. If we assume that businessmen use the same concept, the economists' definition will also be appropriate for purpose (1). For the moment we assume that this is so. The consequences of this assumption being wrong are discussed in Chapter 16.

The Measurement of Opportunity Cost

All economic costing is governed by a common principle that is sometimes called user cost but is more commonly called opportunity cost:

the cost of using something in a particular venture is the benefit forgone by (or opportunity cost of) not using it in its best alternative use.

In principle, measuring opportunity cost is easy. The firm must assign to each factor of production it uses a monetary value equal to what it sacrifices in order to have the use of that factor.

Purchased and Hired Inputs

Assigning costs is straightforward when the firm buys a factor on a competitive market and uses up the entire quantity purchased during the period of production. Materials purchased by the firm fall into this category. If the firm pays £80 per tonne for coal delivered to its factory, it has sacrificed its claims to whatever else £80 can buy, and thus the purchase price is a reasonable measure of the opportunity cost of using one tonne of coal.

The situation is the same for hired factors of production. Most labour services are hired, but typically the cost is more than the wages paid because employers have to contribute to such things as national insurance and pension funds. The cost of these must be added to the direct wage in determining the opportunity cost of labour.

Imputed Costs

A cost must also be assigned to factors of production that the firm neither purchases nor hires because it already owns them. The costs of using such factors are called **imputed costs**. They are reckoned at values reflecting what the firm could earn if it shifted these factors to their next best use. Important imputed costs arise from the use of owners' money, the use of the firm's own capital equipment, the need to compensate risk-taking, and the need to value any special advantages (such as franchises or patents) that the firm may possess. Correct cost imputation is needed if the firm is to discover the most profitable lines of production.

What is the opportunity cost to a firm of the financial capital it has tied up in its operations – say it is £100,000? The answer can best be broken into two parts. First ask what the firm could earn by lending its £100,000 on a riskless loan to someone else – say by purchasing a government bond which has no significant risk of not being repaid. Say this is 8 per cent per annum. This amount is called the **pure return on capital**. It is clearly a cost to the firm since it could close down operations, lend out its money and earn an 8 per cent return. Next ask what the firm could earn in addition to this amount by lending its money to another firm where the risk of default was equal to the risk of loss in the firm itself. Say this is an additional 6 per cent. This is called the **risk premium** and it is clearly also a cost. If the firm does not expect to earn this much in its own operations, it will pay it to close down and lend its money out to some other equal-risk use earning 14 per cent (8 per cent pure return + 6 per cent risk premium).

Special advantages: Suppose a firm owns a valuable patent or a highly desirable location, or produces a product with a popular brand name such as Tizer, Triumph or Player's. Each of these involves an opportunity cost to the firm in production (even if it was acquired free) because if the firm did not choose to use the special advantage itself, *it could sell or lease it to others.*

The use of the firm's own capital equipment: The cost of using capital equipment the firm owns, such as buildings and machinery, consists of the loss in the value of the asset, called **depreciation**, caused by its use in production. Accountants use various conventional methods of calculating depreciation based on the price originally paid for the asset. While such historical costs are often useful approximations, they may, in some cases, seriously differ from the depreciation required by the opportunity-cost principle. Two examples of possible errors are given in the paragraphs that follow.

Example 1. The owner of a firm buys a £6,000 car that she intends to use for six years for business purposes and then discard. She may think this will cost her £1,000 per year. But if after one year the value of her car on the used-car market is £4,500, it has cost her £1,500 to use the car during the first year. Why should she charge herself £1,500 depreciation during the first year? After all, she does not intend to sell the car for six years. The answer is that one of her alternatives is to buy a one-year-old car and operate it for five years. Indeed, that is the very position she is in after the first year. Whether she likes it or not, she has paid £1,500 for the use of the car during the first year of its life. If the market had valued her car at £5,800 after one year (instead of £4,500), the correct depreciation charge would have been only £200.

Example 2. A firm has just purchased a set of machines for £100,000. The machines have an expected lifetime of ten years and the firm's accountant calculates the 'depreciation cost' of these machines at £10,000 per year. The machines can be used to make only one product, and since they are installed in the firm's factory, they can be leased to no one else. They have a negligible secondhand or scrap value. Assume that if the machines are used to produce the firm's product, the cost of all other factors utilized will amount to £25,000 per year. Immediately after purchasing the machines the firm finds that the price of the product in question has unexpectedly fallen, so that the output can now only be sold for £29,000 per year instead of the £35,000 that had originally been expected. What should the firm do?

If in calculating its costs the firm adds in the historically determined 'depreciation costs' of £10,000 a year, the total cost of operation comes to £35,000; with the revenue at £29,000 this makes a loss of £6,000 per year. It appears that the commodity should not be made. but this is not correct. Since the machines have no alternative use, their opportunity cost to the firm (which is determined by what else the firm could do with them) is zero. The total cost of producing the output is thus only £25,000 per year, and the whole current operation shows a return over cost of £4,000 per year rather than a loss of £6,000. (If the firm did not produce the goods, in order to avoid expected losses, it would earn £4,000 per year less than if it carried on with production.)

Of course, the firm would not have bought the machines had it known that the price of the product was going to fall, but once it has bought them, the cost of using them is zero, and it is profitable to use them as long as they yield any net revenue whatsoever over all other costs.

The principle illustrated by both of these examples may be stated in terms of an important maxim:

bygones are bygones and should have no influence in deciding what is currently the most profitable thing to do.[1]

---

[1] This is an important principle that extends well beyond economics. In many poker games, for example, the cards are dealt a round at a time and betting occurs each time the players have been given an additional card. Players who bet heavily on early rounds because their hands looked promising often stay in through later rounds on indifferent hands because they 'already have such a stake in the pot'. The professional players know that, after each round of cards has been dealt, their bet should be made on the probability that the hand currently held will turn into a winner when all the cards have been dealt. If the probabilities look poor after the fourth card has been dealt (five usually constitutes a complete hand), the player should abandon the hand whether he or she has put 5p or £5 into the pot already. Amateurs who base their current decisions on what they have put into the pot in earlier rounds of betting, will be long-term losers if they play in rational company. In poker, war and economics, bygones *are* bygones, and to take account of them in current decisions is to court disaster!

TABLE 10.1 Profit and Loss Account for *XYZ* Company for the Year Ending 31 December 1990

EXPENDITURE		INCOME	
Variable costs			
Wages	£200,000	Revenue from sales	£1,000,000
Materials	300,000		
Other	100,000		
Total VC	600,000		
Fixed costs			
Rent	50,000		
Managerial salaries	60,000		
Interest on loans	90,000		
Depreciation allowance	50,000		
Total FC	250,000		
Total expenditure	850,000		
Profit			150,000

The profit and loss account shows profits as defined by the firm. The Table gives a simplified version of a real profit and loss statement. The total revenue earned by the firm, minus what it regards as costs, yields profits. Since firms do not count the opportunity cost of capital, this is included in profits as calculated by the firm. (Note that costs are divided into those that vary with output, called variable costs, and those that do not, called fixed costs. This distinction is discussed in detail in Chapter 11.)

The Definition of Profits

We have earlier defined profits as the difference between the revenue the firm gains from selling its output minus the costs of producing that output. Different definitions of profits are in use because of different definitions of costs.

The firm's definition: Firms regard profits as the excess of revenues over the costs calculated by their accountants. The calculation by a firm of its profits is done in a profit and loss statement, a simplified version of which is shown in Table 10.1. Notice that we have divided the firm's costs between those that vary with output, called variable costs, and those that do not, called fixed costs.

What the firm calls its profits includes a return to cover the opportunity cost of its own capital.[1] To get at the economists' concept of profits the imputed opportunity cost must be deducted, as shown in Table 10.2.

[1] Owner-managed firms must be careful to include an imputed cost for the owner's time.

The economist's definition: Pure profit is any excess of revenue over all opportunity costs including those of capital. To discover whether pure profit exists, take the revenue of the firm and deduct the costs of all factors of production other than capital. Then deduct the pure return on capital and any risk premium necessary to compensate the owners of capital for the risks associated with its use in this firm and industry.

TABLE 10.2 Calculation of Pure Profits

Profit as reported by the firm	£150,000
Opportunity cost of capital:	
(i) Pure return on the firm's capital	−100,000
(ii) Risk premium	−40,000
Pure profit	10,000

The economist's definition of profit excludes the opportunity cost of capital. To arrive at the economist's definition of profits, the opportunity cost of capital – the pure return on a riskless investment plus any risk premium – must be deducted from the firm's definition of profits.

Anything that remains is pure profit. It belongs to the owners of the firm and therefore may be regarded as an additional return on their capital. Profit in the sense just defined is variously called *pure profit, economic profit* or, where there is no room for ambiguity, just *profit*.

Alternative terminology in economics:
The opportunity cost of capital is defined by economists as part of total cost. Profits are thus defined in economics as what is left after deducting this cost from what the businessman calls profits. An alternative terminology, still used in some elementary treatments, but seldom in advanced theory, calls the opportunity cost of capital *normal profits*. Any excess of revenue over normal profits is then called supernormal profits. Since you may encounter this alternative terminology, the equivalents are laid out in Table 10.3.

TABLE 10.3 Alternative Terminology of Profits

STANDARD USAGE	ALTERNATIVE USAGE
Opportunity cost of capital =	Normal profits
Pure profits =	Supernormal profits

Alternative terminologies depend on whether or not the opportunity cost of capital is counted as a cost.

PROFITS AND RESOURCE ALLOCATION

When resources are valued by the opportunity-cost principle, their costs show how much these resources would earn if used in their best alternative uses. If there is an industry in which all firms' revenues exceed opportunity costs, all the firms in the industry will be earning profits. Thus the owners of factors of production will want to move resources into this industry because the earnings potentially available to them are greater there than in alternative uses of the resources. If in some other industry firms are incurring losses, some or all of this industry's resources are more highly valued in other uses, and owners of the resources will want to move them to those other uses.

Profits and losses play a crucial signalling role in the workings of a free-market system.

Profits in an industry are the signal that resources can profitably be moved into the industry. Losses are the signal that the resources can profitably be moved elsewhere. Only if there are zero economic profits is there no incentive for resources to move into or out of an industry.

A Preview

We have seen that firms are assumed to maximize their profits (π), which are the difference between the revenues derived from the sale of their output (R) and the cost of producing that output (C):

$$\pi = R - C .$$

Thus what happens to profits depends on what happens to revenues and costs.

We already explained the special meaning that economists give to the concept of costs. In Chapter 11 we develop a theory of how costs vary with output. This theory is common to all firms. We then consider how revenues vary with output and find that it is necessary to deal separately with firms in markets that are competitive (Chapter 12) and monopolistic (Chapters 13 and 14). Costs and revenues are then combined to determine the profit-maximizing behaviour for firms in various market situations. This theory can then be used to predict the outcome of changes in such things as demand, costs, taxes and subsidies.

SUMMARY

1. Firms in the real world are organized as either single proprietorships, with one owner-manager, partnerships, with several fully liable owners, or joint-stock companies, with limited liability for their many owners who are not the firms' managers.

2. Firms compromise the production side of the market sector. The non-market sector consists of organizations that do not seek to cover their costs of production by revenue gained from selling that production.

3. Modern firms finance themselves by obtaining money from their owners by selling them shares or by reinvesting their profits, and by borrowing from both the public and various financial institutions.

4. Economic theory treats all types of firms under one umbrella by assuming that all firms make consistent decisions designed to maximize their profits. The theory thus assumes that the organizational structure of firms, and objectives other than profits, do not exert significant influences on situations whose outcomes are predicted by economic theory.

5. Costs in economic theory refer to opportunity costs. These are correctly measured by the price paid for hired factors. They must be imputed for the costs of using factors owned by the firm. The cost of firms' own capital includes the pure return – what could be earned on a riskless investment – and a risk premium – what could be earned over the pure return elsewhere in the economy on a equally risky investment. Profits are the difference between revenues and costs.

6. Firms do not deduct the cost of their own capital when calculating what they call profits, which thus include the pure return on capital as well as the risk premium. When these two amounts are also deducted from revenues the result is the economist's concept of profit which is sometimes called pure, or economic, profit to distinguish it from what firms call profits.

7. Pure profits play a key role in resource allocation. Positive profits attract resources into an industry, negative profits induce resources to move elsewhere.

TOPICS FOR REVIEW

- Forms of business organization
- Methods of financing modern firms
- Profit maximization
- The definition of costs
- The measurement of opportunity costs for hired and for owned factors
- Imputed costs
- The principle of bygones are bygones
- Alternative definitions of profits

11

Cost and Output

We now know how to calculate the cost, revenue, and profit. To discover which rate of output is the most profitable, firms need to know the cost and revenue associated with each rate of output. This tells them how profit relates to output. Selecting the profit-maximizing output is then a simple matter. In this chapter we shall confine our attention to costs; in subsequent chapters we shall study revenues.

To discover how costs are related to output, we first study how output is related to inputs. We then place a value on these inputs – using the principles established in Chapter 10 – and discover how costs are related to output.

THE PRODUCTION FUNCTION

The **production function** describes the purely technological relation between what is fed into the productive apparatus by way of inputs of factor services and what is turned out by way of product. When using this function, remember that production is a flow: it is so many units *per period of time*. If we speak of raising the level of monthly production from, say, 100 to 101 units, we do not mean producing 100 units this month and one unit next month, but going from a rate of production of 100 units *each month* to a rate of 101 units *each month*.

Using functional notation, the production function is written as:

$$q = q(f_1, \ldots, f_m) \ , \qquad (1)$$

where q is the quantity of output and $f_1, \ldots, f_m$ are the quantities of m different inputs used in production, everything being expressed as rates per period of time.[1]

For the rest of this chapter we shall consider a very simple example relating to the production of some industrial product. We ignore land (since it is relatively unimportant) and deal with the other two factors of production, labour, to which we give the symbol L, and capital, to which we give the symbol K. This gives us the simplified production function:

$$q = q(L, K) \ , \qquad (2)$$

---

[1] If you have any trouble with this form of expression, you should review the first part of the Appendix to Chapter 3 at this time.

where q is tonnes of output per day, L is labour days employed, K is units of capital services used per day (e.g. machine days), and q stands for the relation that links q to K and L. Confining attention to two inputs simplifies without obscuring the essence of the problem.

Suppose that a firm wishes to increase its rate of output. To do so, it must increase the inputs of one or both factors of production. But the firm cannot vary all of its factors with the same degree of ease. It can vary labour on short notice, but time is needed to install more capital.

To capture the fact that different inputs can be varied with different speeds, we abstract from the more complicated nature of real decisions and think of each firm as making three distinct types of decisions: (1) how best to employ its existing plant and equipment; (2) what new plant, equipment and production processes to select, within the framework of existing technology; and (3) what to do about encouraging the development of new technology. The first set of decisions is said to be made over the short run; the second, over the long run; the third, over the very long run.

The short run: The **short run** is defined as the period of time over which the inputs of some factors, called **fixed factors**, cannot be varied. The factor that is fixed in the short run is usually an element of capital (such as plant and equipment), but it might be land, or the services of management, or even the supply of skilled, salaried labour. What matters is that at least one significant factor is fixed.

In the short run, production can be changed only by using more or less of those inputs that can be varied. These inputs are called **variable factors**. In our example, the variable factor is labour services. Thus, in the short run, q is varied by varying L, with K held fixed. (See equation 2.)

The short run is not of the same duration in all industries. In the electric-power industry, for example, where it takes three or more years to build new power stations, an unforeseen increase in demand must be served as well as possible with the existing capital equipment for several years. At the other end of the scale, a machine shop can acquire new equipment in a few weeks, and thus the short run is correspondingly short. The length of the short run is influenced by technological considerations such as how quickly

equipment can be manufactured and installed. These things may also be influenced to some extent by the price the firm is willing to pay.

The long run: The **long run** is defined as the period long enough for the inputs of all factors of production to be varied, but not so long that the basic technology of production changes. Again, the long run is not a specific period of time, but varies among industries.

The special importance of the long run in production theory is that it corresponds to the situation facing the firm when it is *planning* to go into business, or to expand or contract the scale of its operations. The planning decisions of the firm are characteristically made with fixed technical possibilities but with freedom to choose whatever factor inputs seem most desirable. Once these planning decisions are carried out – once a plant is built, equipment purchased and installed, and so on – the firm has fixed factors and makes operating decisions in the short run.

The very long run: Unlike the short and the long run, the **very long run** is concerned with situations in which the technological possibilities open to the firm are subject to change, leading to new and improved products and new methods of production. In the very long run the production function itself changes so that, in the production function of equation (2), *given* inputs of K and L will be associated with *different* amounts of output. The firm may bring about some changes itself, through its research and development; other changes may come from outside.

Next we study the firm's production possibilities, and its costs, under each of these 'runs'.

THE SHORT RUN

In the short run, we are concerned with what happens to output and costs as more, or less, of the variable factor is applied to a given quantity of the fixed factor. To illustrate, we use the simplified production function of (2) above, and assume that capital is fixed and labour is variable.

Short-run Variations in Output

Our firm starts with a fixed amount of capital (say 10 units) and contemplates applying various

TABLE 11.1 Total, Average and Marginal Products in the Short Run

(1) Quantity of labour L	(2) Total product TP	(3) Average product AP	(4) Marginal product MP
1	43	43	43
2	160	80	117
3	351	117	191
4	600	150	249
5	875	175	275
6	1,152	192	277
7	1,372	196	220
8	1,536	192	164
9	1,656	184	120
10	1,750	175	94
11	1,815	165	65
12	1,860	155	45

The relation of output to changes in the quantity of the variable factor can be looked at in three different ways. Capital is assumed to be fixed at ten units. As the quantity of labour increases, the rate of output (the total product) increases, as shown in column (2). The average product in column (3) is found by dividing the total product figure in column (2) by the amount of labour required to produce that product – as shown by the figure in the corresponding row of column (1).

The marginal product is shown between the rows because it refers to the *change* in output from one level of labour input to another. When graphing the schedule, *MP*s of this kind should be plotted at the midpoint of the interval. Thus, graphically, for example, the marginal product of 249 would be plotted to correspond to quantity of labour of 3.5. This is because it refers to the increase in output when labour inputs rise from 3 to 4 units.

amounts of labour to it. Table 11.1 shows three different ways of looking at how output varies with the quantity of the variable factor. As a preliminary step, some terms must be defined.

(1) **Total product (TP)** means just what it says: the total amount produced during some period of time by all the factors of production employed. If the inputs of all but one factor are held constant, the total product will change as more or less of the variable factor is used. This variation is shown in column (2) of Table 11.1, which gives a total product schedule. Figure 11.1(i) shows such a schedule graphically. (The shape of the curve will be discussed shortly.)

(2) **Average product (AP)** is merely the total product per unit of the variable factor, which is labour in the present illustration:

$$AP = \frac{TP}{L} \ .$$

Average product is shown in column (3) of Table 11.1. Notice that as more of the variable factor is used, average product first rises and then falls. The point where average product reaches a maximum is called the *point of diminishing average productivity*. In the Table, average product reaches a maximum when 7 units of labour are employed.

(3) **Marginal product (MP)** is the change in total product resulting from the use of one more (or one less) unit of the variable factor:[1]

$$MP = \frac{\Delta TP}{\Delta L} \ ,$$

where ΔTP stands for the change in the total product and ΔL stands for the change in labour input that caused TP to change. In everything that follows in this chapter, we assume that output is varied in the short run by combining different amounts of the variable factor with a *given* quantity of the fixed factor.[2]

Computed values of the marginal product appear in column (4) of Table 11.1. *MP* in the example reaches a maximum between $L = 5$ and $L = 6$ and thereafter declines. The level of output where marginal product reaches a maximum is called the *point of diminishing marginal returns*.

[1] Strictly speaking, the text defines what is called 'incremental product', that is the rate of change of output associated with a discrete change in an input. Marginal product refers to the rate at which output is tending to vary as input varies at a particular output. Students familiar with elementary calculus will recognize the marginal product as the partial derivative of the total product with respect to the variable factor. In symbols: $MP = \partial Q/\partial L$. In the text we refer only to finite changes, ΔL and ΔTP, but the phrase 'a change of one unit' should read 'a very small change'. At this time it would be helpful to read, or re-read, the discussion of the marginal concept given on pp.145–147 of the Appendix to Chapter 3.
[2] This is not the only thing that can happen in the short run. Instead, *some of the fixed factor can be left unemployed*. Dropping the assumption that all of the fixed factor is always employed in the short run has, as we shall see in Chapter 14, significant effects on the shape of the short-run cost curve. Until then, however, we stay with the assumption that the fixed factor is always fully employed as output varies over the short run.

FIGURE 11.1 Total, Average and Marginal Product Curves

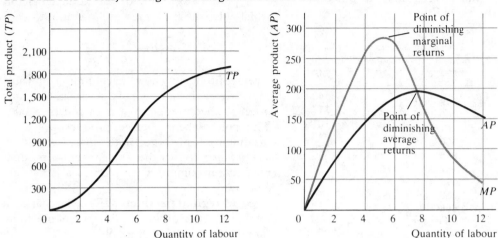

(i) **Total product**

(ii) **Average and marginal product**

Total product (*TP*), average product (*AP*) and marginal product (*MP*)
curves often have the shapes shown here. The curves are plotted from the data in
Table 11.1. In (i) the total product curve shows the total product steadily rising, first at
an increasing rate, then at a decreasing rate. This causes both the average and the
marginal product curves in (ii) to rise at first and then decline. Note that at the point of
maximum average returns (also called the point of diminishing average returns) $MP = AP$.

Figure 11.1(ii) shows the average and marginal
product curves plotted from the data in Table
11.1. Notice (1) that MP reaches its maximum at
a lower level of L than does AP, and (2) that
$MP = AP$ when AP is a maximum. These relations are discussed below.

Finally, bear in mind that the schedules of
Table 11.1 and the curves of Figure 11.1 all
assume a specified quantity of the fixed factor. If
the quantity of capital had been, say, 14 instead of
the 10 units that were assumed, there would be a
different set of total, average and marginal product curves. The reason is that if any specified
amount of labour has more capital to work with,
it can produce more output: its total, average and
marginal products will be greater.

The Law of Diminishing Returns

We now consider the variations in output that
result from applying different amounts of a
variable factor to a given quantity of a fixed
factor. These variations are the subject of a
famous hypothesis called the **law of diminishing returns**.

**The law of diminishing returns states
that if increasing quantities of a variable
factor are applied to a given quantity of a
fixed factor, the marginal product, and
the average product, of the variable factor will eventually decrease.**

As illustrated in Figure 11.2, the law of diminishing returns is consistent with marginal and
average product curves that decline over the
whole range of output (part (i) of the Figure), or
that increase for a while and only later diminish
(part (ii) of the Figure). The latter case arises
when it is impossible to use the fixed factor
efficiently with only a small quantity of the
variable factor (if, say, one man were trying to
farm 1,000 acres). In this case, increasing the
quantity of the variable factor makes possible
more efficient division of labour, so that the
addition of another unit of the variable factor
would make all units more productive than they
were previously. According to the hypothesis
of diminishing returns, the scope for such
economies must eventually disappear, and

FIGURE 11.2 Alternative Average and Marginal Product Curves

PERMISSIBLE SHAPES

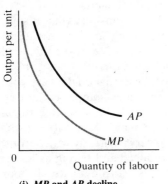

(i) MP and AP decline over all ranges of output

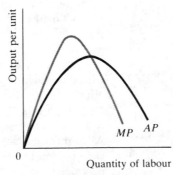

(ii) MP and AP first rise, then decline

NOT PERMISSIBLE SHAPES

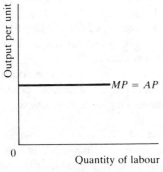

(iii) MP and AP are constant over all ranges of output

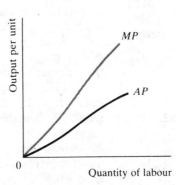

(iv) MP and AP rise over all ranges of output

According to the law of diminishing returns, average and marginal product must decline sooner or later as output increases. The law of diminishing returns permits the average and marginal product curves to decline at all positive levels of output, as shown in part (i). The law also allows the average and marginal products to rise over an initial range of output and only then decline, as shown in part (ii). This is the case where the fixed factor cannot be efficiently used when combined with very small amounts of the variable factor.

The law does not permit average and marginal products that are constant (part (iii)) or rise over the entire range of output (part (iv)).

sooner or later the marginal and average product of additional workers must decline.

Notice that when various amounts of labour are applied to a fixed quantity of capital, the proportions in which the two factors are used is being varied. For this reason,

the law of diminishing returns is also called *the law of variable proportions* because it predicts the consequences of varying the proportions in which factors of production are used.

The common sense of diminishing marginal product is that the fixed factor limits the amount of additional output that can be realized by adding more of the variable factor. Were it not for the law of diminishing returns, there would be no need to fear that the world's population explosion will cause a food crisis. If the marginal product of additional workers applied to a fixed quantity of land were constant, then world food production could be expanded in proportion to the increase in population merely by keeping the same proportion of the population on farms. As it is, diminishing returns means an inexorable decline in the marginal product of each additional labourer as an expanding population is applied, with static techniques, to a fixed world supply of agricultural land. Thus, unless there is a continual and rapidly accelerating improvement in the techniques of production, the population explosion must bring with it declining living standards over much of the world.

The relation between marginal and average product curves: Notice that in Figure 11.2(ii) the *MP* curve cuts the *AP* curve at the latter's maximum point. It is important to understand why. The key is that the average product curve slopes upward as long as the marginal product curve is above it; it makes no difference whether the marginal curve is itself sloping upwards or downwards. The common sense of this relation is that, if an additional worker is to raise the average product of all workers, the worker's output must be greater than the average output of all existing workers. It is immaterial whether his contribution to output is greater or less than the contribution of the worker hired immediately before him; all that matters is that his contribution to output exceeds the average output of *all* the workers hired before him.[1] Since *AP* slopes upwards or downwards depending on whether *MP* is above or below *AP*, it follows that *MP* must equal *AP* at the highest point on the *AP* curve.[2]

Short-run Variations in Cost

We have now learned how, according to economic theory, output varies with factor inputs in the short run, and we know from Chapter 10 how to value the firm's inputs. By combining these two pieces of knowledge, we can discover how a firm's output is related to its cost of production. For the time being, we consider firms that are not

in a position to influence the prices of the factors of production that they employ.

The following brief definitions of several cost concepts are closely related to the product concepts defined earlier in this chapter.

(1) **Total cost (*TC*)** means just what it says: the total cost of producing any given rate of output. Total cost is divided into two parts, total fixed costs (*TFC*) and total variable costs (*TVC*). **Fixed costs** are those costs that do not vary with output; they will be the same if output is 1 unit or 1 million units. These costs are also often referred to as 'overhead costs' or 'unavoidable costs'. All of those costs that vary positively with output, rising as more is produced and falling as less is produced, are called **variable costs**. In our present example, since labour is the variable factor of production, the wage bill would be a variable cost. Variable costs are often referred to as 'direct costs' or 'avoidable costs'. The latter term is used because the costs can be avoided by not hiring the variable factor.

(2) **Average total cost (*ATC*)** is the total cost of producing any given output divided by the number of units produced, or the cost per unit. *ATC* may be divided into **average fixed costs (*AFC*)** and **average variable costs (*AVC*)** in just the same way as total costs were divided.

(3) **Marginal cost (*MC*)** is the increase in total cost resulting from raising the rate of production by one unit. The marginal cost of the 10th unit, for example, is the change in total cost when the rate of production is increased from nine to ten units per period.

These three measures of cost are merely different ways of looking at a single phenomenon, and they are mathematically interrelated.[1] Sometimes it is convenient to use one, and sometimes another.

Short-run Cost Curves

The relations just outlined are most easily understood if we show them as cost curves. To illustrate how this is done, we take the production relationships in Table 11.1 and assume that the price of labour is £20 per unit and the price of

---

[1] To check your understanding, try an example in which five workers produce 50 units of output. In the first case a sixth worker adds 16 and a seventh worker adds 14 to total output. In the second case, the sixth worker adds 14 and the seventh worker adds 16. When you do the calculations you will find that *AP* is rising in both cases, although *MP* is declining in the first case and rising in the second.

[2] This is easily proved for those who know elementary calculus. Our definitions are: $TP = q(n)$, $AP = q(n)/n$, and $MP = q'(n)$, where the single prime mark indicates the first derivative and n is the quantity of the variable factor employed. A necessary condition for the maximum of the *AP* curve is that its first derivative, $[nq'(n) - q(n)]/n^2$, be equal to zero. Setting the above expression equal to zero, adding $q(n)/n^2$ to both sides and multiplying through by n yields: $q'(n) = q(n)/n$, which is to say $MP = AP$.

---

[1] Mathematically, average total cost is *total cost* divided by output while marginal cost is the first derivative of *total cost* with respect to output.

TABLE 11.2 Variation of Costs with Capital Fixed and Labour Variable

INPUTS		OUTPUT	TOTAL COST			AVERAGE COST			MARGINAL COST
(1) Capital	(2) Labour (L)	(3) Output (q)	(4) Fixed (TFC)	(5) Variable (TVC)	(6) Total (TC)	(7) Fixed (AFC)[1]	(8) Variable (AVC)[2]	(9) Total (ATC)[3]	(10) (MC)[4]
10	1	43	£100	£ 20	£120	£2.326	£0.465	£2.791	£0.465
10	2	160	100	40	140	0.625	0.250	0.875	0.171
10	3	351	100	60	160	0.285	0.171	0.456	0.105
10	4	600	100	80	180	0.167	0.133	0.300	0.080
10	5	875	100	100	200	0.114	0.114	0.228	0.073
10	6	1,152	100	120	220	0.087	0.104	0.191	0.072
10	7	1,372	100	140	240	0.073	0.102	0.175	0.091
10	8	1,536	100	160	260	0.065	0.104	0.169	0.122
10	9	1,656	100	180	280	0.060	0.109	0.169	0.167
10	10	1,750	100	200	300	0.057	0.114	0.171	0.213
10	11	1,815	100	220	320	0.055	0.121	0.176	0.308
10	12	1,860	100	240	340	0.054	0.129	0.183	0.444

The relation of cost to the rate of output can be looked at in several different ways. These cost schedules are computed from the product curves of Table 11.1, given the price of capital of £10 per unit and the price of labour of £20 per unit. Marginal cost (in column 10) is shown between the lines of total cost because it refers to the *change* in cost divided by the *change* in output that brought it about. Marginal cost is calculated by dividing the increase in costs by the increase in output when one additional unit of labour is used. This gives the increase in cost per unit of output over that range of output. For example, the *MC* of £0.08 is the increase in total cost of £20 (from £160 to £180) divided by the 249-unit increase in output (from 351 to 600). This tells us that when output goes from 351 to 600 (because labour inputs go from 3 to 4) the increase in costs is £0.08 per unit of output. In constructing a graph, marginal costs should be plotted midway in the interval over which they are computed. The *MC* of £0.08 would thus be plotted at output 475.5.

[1] Col. (4) ÷ col. (3).   [3] Col. (6) ÷ col. (3) = col. (7) + col. (8).
[2] Col. (5) ÷ col. (3)   [4] Change in col. (6) from one row to the next ÷ corresponding change in col. (3).

capital is £10 per unit. In Table 11.2, we present the cost schedules computed for these values. (It is important that you see where the numbers come from;[1] if you do not, review Table 11.1 and the definitions of cost just given.) Figure 11.3(i) shows the total cost curves; Figure 11.3(ii) plots the marginal and average cost curves.

[1] There is one problem associated with our numerical example that has not so far been discussed. We have derived the data in Tables 11.1 and 11.2 by letting inputs of labour vary one unit at a time. This gives rise to variation in output of more than one per unit of time. Marginal cost is defined as the change in cost when output varies one unit at a time. To calculate marginal cost, we divide the *increase in costs when labour inputs rise by one unit* by the *increase in output*. This gives us the increase in costs *per unit of output* over that range of output. This, and similar, problems do not arise when all marginal concepts are defined as derivatives.

How Cost Varies With Output

Since total fixed costs (*TFC*) do not, by definition, vary with output, average fixed cost (*TFC/q*) is negatively related to output while marginal fixed cost is zero. Variable cost is positively related to output, since to produce more requires more of the variable factor which in turn entails spending more to buy the factor. Average variable cost may, however, be negatively or positively related to output. If output rises faster than variable costs, average variable costs will be falling as output rises; if output rises less fast than costs rise, average variable cost will be rising. Marginal variable cost is always positive, indicating that it costs something to increase output, but, as we shall soon see, marginal cost may rise or fall as output rises.

FIGURE 11.3 Total Cost, Average Cost and Marginal Cost Curves

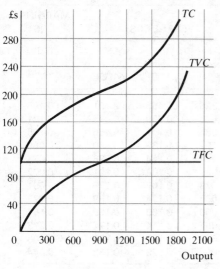

(i) **Total cost curves**

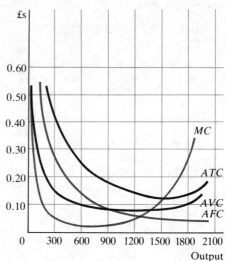

(ii) **Marginal and average cost curves**

Total cost (*TC*), average cost (*AC*) and marginal cost (*MC*) curves often have the shapes shown here. These curves are plotted from Table 11.2. Total fixed cost does not vary with output. Total variable cost and the total of all costs ($TC = TVC + TFC$) rise with output, first at a decreasing rate, then at an increasing rate. The total cost curves in (i) give rise to the average and marginal curves in (ii). Average fixed cost (*AFC*) declines as output increases. Average variable cost (*AVC*) and average total cost (*ATC*) fall and then rise as output increases. Marginal cost (*MC*) does the same, intersecting the *ATC* and *AVC* curves at their minimum points. Capacity output is at the minimum point of the *ATC* curve, which is an output of 1,500 in this example.

Notice that the marginal cost curve cuts the *ATC* and *AVC* curves at their lowest points. This is another example of the relation (discussed above) between a marginal and an average curve. The *ATC* curve, for example, slopes downwards as long as the marginal cost curve is below it; it makes no difference whether the marginal cost curve is itself sloping upwards or downwards.

In Figure 11.3 the average variable cost curve reaches a minimum and then rises. With fixed factor prices, when average product per worker is at a maximum, average variable cost is at a minimum. The common sense is that each new worker adds the same amount to cost but a different amount to output, and when output per worker is rising the cost per unit of output must be falling, and vice versa.

The law of diminishing returns implies eventually increasing marginal and average variable cost.

Short-run *AVC* curves are often drawn U-shaped. This reflects the assumptions that (i) average productivity is increasing when output is low, but that (ii) eventually average productivity begins to fall fast enough to cause average total cost to increase.[1]

The definition of capacity: The output that

---

[1] This point is easily seen if a little algebra is used. (The only new symbol used here is w, which stands for the price of a unit of labour.) By definition $AVC = TVC/q$. But $TVC = L.w$, and $q = AP.L$ (since $AP = q/L$). Therefore

$$AVC = (L.w)/(AP.L)$$
$$= w/AP .$$

In other words, average variable cost equals the price of the variable factor divided by the average product of the variable factor. Since w is constant, it follows that AVC and AP vary inversely with each other, and when AP is at its maximum value AVC must be at its minimum value.

corresponds to the minimum short-run average total cost is very often called **capacity**. Capacity in this sense is not an upper limit on what can be produced, as you can see by looking again at Table 11.2. In the example, capacity output is between 1,536 and 1,656 units, but higher outputs can be achieved. A firm producing *below capacity* is producing at a rate of output less than the one for which average total cost is a minimum. A firm producing *above capacity* is producing more than this amount. It is thus incurring costs per unit of output that are higher than the minimum achievable.

A family of short-run cost curves: A short-run cost curve shows how costs vary with output for a given quantity of the fixed factor – say a given size of plant.

> **There is a different short-run cost curve for each quantity of the fixed factor.**

A small plant for manufacturing nuts and bolts will have its own short-run cost curve. A medium-size and a very large-size plant will each have its own short-run cost curve. If a firm expands by replacing its small plant with a medium-size plant, it will move from one short-run cost curve to another. This change from one size of plant to another is a long-run change. We now study how short-run cost curves of different size plants are related to each other.

THE LONG RUN

In the short run, with only one factor variable, there is only one way to produce a given output: by adjusting the input of that factor until the desired rate of output is achieved. Thus, in the short run, the firm must make a decision about its output, but once it has decided on a rate of output, there is only one technically possible way of achieving that output. In the long run, all factors are variable. If a firm decides on some rate of output, it has an additional decision to make: by which of the many technically possible methods will the output be produced? Should the firm adopt a technique that uses much capital and little labour, or should it adopt one that uses less capital but more labour?

Since there are usually many ways of producing any given total output, the firm must choose one of them. The hypothesis of profit maximization provides a simple rule for making this choice. The rule is called *cost minimization*: any firm that is trying to maximize its profits will select the method of producing a given output that incurs the lowest possible cost. This rule is an implication of profit maximization, since a firm that is not minimizing its costs is not maximizing its profits.

Although profit maximization is sufficient to produce cost-minimizing behaviour, it is not necessary. As long as the firm's goal is to maximize anything that uses economic resources, the firm will wish to minimize the costs it incurs to produce any given level of output. The lower its costs, the more resources it has available to pursue its goals, whatever they may be.

> **For any specific output, the firm chooses the least costly method of production from the alternatives open to it.**

If there is a known, stable, required rate of output, and if the costs of factors are given, this is all there is to it.

Long-run planning decisions are important because today's variable factors are tomorrow's fixed ones. A firm deciding on a new, fully equipped plant will have many alternatives from which to choose, but once installed the capital is fixed for a long time. If the firm errs now, its very survival may be threatened; if it estimates shrewdly and its rivals do not, its owners, and its far-sighted managers, may be rewarded with large profits and bonuses.[1]

Conditions for Cost Minimization

Whenever the firm can substitute one factor for another in such a way as to keep its output constant while reducing its total cost, it has not yet succeeded in minimizing costs.

---

[1] Long-run decisions are among the most difficult and most important the firm makes. They are difficult because the firm must anticipate what methods of production will be efficient, not only today but in the years ahead when costs of labour and raw materials may have changed. They are difficult because the firm must estimate its desired future output. Is the industry growing or declining? Is the firm's share of the market going to increase or decrease? Will new products emerge to render its own products less useful than an extrapolation of past sales might suggest?

To understand this condition, suppose that the last £1 spent on capital added 10 units to output, while the last £1 spent on labour added only 4 units. In such a case, the firm by using £2.50 less of labour would reduce output by 10 units. But it could regain that lost output by spending £1 more on capital. Making such a substitution of capital for labour would leave output unchanged and reduce cost by £1.50. Thus the original set of factor inputs could *not* have been the ones that minimized costs. If, however, the last £1 spent on labour produced the same output, say 5 units, as the last £1 spent on capital, no cost saving could be effected by reducing one factor and increasing the other, keeping output constant.

The general rule illustrated by this example is that the firm will have succeeded in minimizing its cost of producing any given output only when *the last £1 spent on one factor produces the same total output as the last £1 spent on every other factor.*

The next step in the argument is to ask how to find the output that is produced by the last pound spent on each factor. To do this, we divide the factor's marginal product by its price. Thus, for example, if the marginal product of labour is 12 units of output, and labour costs £3 per unit, the output *per additional £1 spent on labour* is 12/3, which is four units. So we can now reword our rule as follows: the firm will have succeeded in minimizing the costs of producing any given output when *the ratio of the marginal product of each factor to its price is the same for all factors.*

In terms of the example that uses two factors, labour and capital, the rule can be written as follows (using p_K and p_L to represent the prices of capital and labour respectively):

$$\frac{MP_K}{p_K} = \frac{MP_L}{p_L} . \tag{3}$$

Whenever the two sides of (3) are not equal, there are factor substitutions that will reduce the cost of producing any given output.

To make sure that you understand this rule, ask yourself what substitution the firm should make if capital costs £10 a unit and has a marginal product of 40 units of output, while labour costs £2 a unit and has a marginal product of 4 units of output. In this case, £1 more spent on capital produces 4 units of output (40/10), while £1 more spent on labour produces only 2 units of output (4/2). If the firm spends £1 less on labour, it loses 2 units of output. If it spends £0.50 more on capital, it gains 2 units of output. Thus it can substitute capital for labour in such a way as to hold output constant while reducing its costs.[1]

Now consider what happens as the firm goes on making the substitutions just discussed. The firm is using more capital, so capital's marginal product must be falling. The firm is using less labour, so labour's marginal product must be rising. The substitution of one factor for the other will continue until equation (3) is fulfilled. Say, for example, that in the above numerical example, where the prices of capital and labour were £10 and £2 respectively, the marginal product of capital falls to 30 units, while the marginal product of labour rises to 6 units. Now £1 more spent on capital yields 3 units of output (30/10), while £1 more spent on labour also yields 3 units of output (6/2). In this case, the firm can obtain no further cost savings by substituting one factor for the other.

Next let us rearrange the terms in (3) in the following way:

$$\frac{MP_K}{MP_L} = \frac{p_K}{p_L} . \tag{4}$$

The ratio of the marginal products on the left-hand side of (4) compares the contribution to output of the last unit of capital employed with the last unit of labour employed. If, for example, the ratio is 4, this means 1 unit more of capital will add 4 times as much to output as 1 unit more of labour. The right-hand side shows how the cost of 1 unit more of capital compares to the cost of 1 unit more of labour. If it is also 4, the firm can gain nothing by substituting capital for labour or vice versa. But suppose the right-hand side is 2. Capital, although twice as expensive, is 4 times as productive, and it will pay the firm to switch to a method of production that uses more capital and less labour. If, however, the right-hand side is 6 (or *any* number more than 4), it will pay to substitute labour for capital.

This formulation shows how the firm can adjust the things over which it has control (the

---

[1] All of the above numerical illustrations assume that marginal products remain constant when small substitutions are made. This will be approximately true as long as the substitutions being made are small.

quantities of factors used, and thus the marginal products of the factors) to the things that are typically given to it by the market (the prices of the factors). An analogous adjustment process is involved when households adjust their consumption of goods to given market prices.

The principle of substitution: Suppose that a firm is producing where the cost-minimizing conditions shown in (3) or (4) are met, but that the cost of labour increases while the cost of capital remains unchanged. As we have just seen, the least-cost method of producing any given output will now use less labour and more capital than was required before the factor prices changed. This prediction, called the **principle of substitution**, follows from the cost-minimizing behaviour of firms.

Methods of production will change if the relative prices of factors change; rela- **tively more of the cheaper factor and relatively less of the more expensive one will be used.**

This proposition is central to the theory of the allocation of resources because it predicts how firms respond to changes in relative factor prices. Such changes are caused by the changing relative scarcities of factors in the whole economy. Individual firms thus use less of factors that have become scarcer in overall supply. The significance of the principle of substitution to the economy as a whole is discussed in Box 11.1.

Cost Curves in the Long Run

There is a best (least-cost) method of producing each rate of output when all factors are free to be varied. If factor prices are given, a minimum cost can be found for each possible level of output and, if this minimum achievable cost is expressed

---

BOX 11.1   THE ECONOMY-WIDE SIGNIFICANCE OF THE PRINCIPLE OF SUBSTITUTION

The relative prices of factors of production in an economy will tend to reflect their relative scarcities. In a country with a great deal of land and a small population, for example, the price of land will be low while, because labour is in short supply, the wage rate will be high. In such circumstances firms producing agricultural goods will tend to make lavish use of (cheap) land and to economize on (expensive) labour; a production process will be adopted that is labour-extensive and land-intensive. On the other hand, in a small country with a large population, the demand for land will be high relative to its supply. Thus land will be very expensive and firms producing agricultural goods will tend to economize on it by using a great deal of labour per unit of land. In this case production will tend to be labour-intensive and land-extensive.

In free markets relative factor prices reflect the relative scarcities (in relation to demand) of different factors of production: abundant factors have prices that are low relative to the prices of factors that are scarce. Firms seeking their own private profit will be led to use much of the factors with which the whole country is plentifully endowed, and to economize on the factors that are in scarce supply.

This discussion provides an example of the price system as an automatic control system. No single firm need be aware of national factor surpluses and scarcities. Since they are reflected in market prices, individual firms that never look beyond their own private profits are led to economize on factors that are scarce in the nation as a whole. We should not be surprised, therefore, to discover that methods of producing the same commodity differ in different countries. In Europe, where labour is highly skilled and very expensive, a steel company may use very elaborate equipment to economize on labour. In China, where labour is abundant and capital scarce, a much less mechanized method of production may be appropriate. The Western engineer who feels that the Chinese are behind because they are using methods abandoned in the West as inefficient long ago, may be missing the significance of economic efficiency.

In spite of the price system's ability to induce profit-maximizing firms to take account of the nation's relative factor scarcities when choosing among possible methods of production, one must avoid jumping to the conclusion that whatever productive processes are adopted are the best possible ones and should never be interfered with. There is, however, a strong common-sense appeal in the idea that:

Any society interested in getting the most out of its resources needs to take account of their relative scarcities in deciding what productive processes to adopt, which is what the price system leads individual firms to do.

as an amount per unit of output, we obtain the long-run average cost of producing each level of output. When this information is plotted on a graph, the result is the **long-run average cost (LRAC) curve**, shown in Figure 11.4. (Notice that since all costs are variable in the long run, we do not need to distinguish between AVC, AFC and ATC as we did in the short run; in the long run there is only one $LRAC$.)

The $LRAC$ curve is determined by the technology of the industry (which is assumed to be fixed) and by the prices of the factors of production. Points below the curve are unattainable; points on the curve are attainable if sufficient time elapses for all factors to be adjusted; points above the curve are also attainable. Indeed, some points above the $LRAC$ curve represent the lowest costs achievable in the short run whenever the current supply of the *fixed* factor is not cost-minimizing for the given output.

> **The $LRAC$ curve divides the cost levels that are attainable with known technology and given factor prices from those that are unattainable.**

The Shape of the Long-run Average Cost Curve

The long-run average cost curve in Figure 11.4 is shown as falling at first and then rising. This curve is often described as being U-shaped. The output, q_m, at which the $LRAC$ curve reaches a

minimum is called the **minimum efficient scale (MES)**.[1]

Decreasing costs: Over the range of output from zero to q_m, the firm has falling long-run average total costs. An expansion of output results in a reduction of costs per unit of output, once enough time has elapsed to allow adjustments in capital as well as labour. Since the prices of factors are assumed to be constant, the reason for the decline in costs per unit must be that output increases faster than inputs as the scale of the firm's production expands. Over this range the firm encounters long-run **increasing returns**, also called **economies of scale**.[2] Increasing returns may arise from increased opportunities for specialization of tasks made possible by the division of labour even with no substitution of one factor of production for another. Or they may arise because of factor substitution. Even the most casual observation of the differences in

---

[1] In Figure 11.4, there is only one output for which $LRAC$ is a minimum. In other cases the curve may be horizontal over some range beyond q_m. In that case, MES is the lowest output at which $LRAC$ is minimized.

[2] Economists often shift back and forth between speaking in physical output terms and cost terms. Thus a firm with increasing (physical) returns to scale (output rises more than in proportion to input in the long run) is also correctly spoken of as a firm with decreasing long-run costs (total costs rise less than in proportion to output as output is increased in the long run).

FIGURE 11.4 A Long-run Average Cost Curve

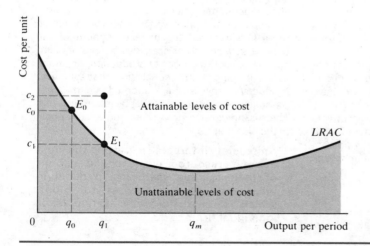

The **long-run average cost (LRAC) curve provides a boundary between attainable and unattainable levels of cost.** If the firm wishes to produce output q_0, the lowest attainable cost level is c_0 per unit. Thus point E_0 is on the $LRAC$ curve. E_1 represents the least-cost method of producing q_1. Suppose a firm is producing at E_0 and desires to increase output to q_1. In the short run it will not be able to vary all factors, and thus costs above c_1, say c_2, must be accepted. In the long run, a plant that is the optimal size for producing output q_1 can be built and costs of c_1 can be attained. At output q_m the firm attains its lowest possible per unit cost of production for the given technology and factor prices.

production technique used in large-size and small-size plants shows that factor proportions do differ in reality. These differences arise because the use of large, specialized machinery is profitable only when the firm's volume of output is large enough to employ that equipment more or less full time.

For example, the use of assembly-line techniques in car production is economically efficient only if individual operations are to be repeated thousands of times. The use of elaborate harvesting equipment (which combines many individual tasks that could be done by hand and by tractor) provides the least-cost method of production on a big farm but not on a few acres. Typically, capital is substituted for labour and complex machines for simpler ones. Automation and robotization

are contemporary examples of this kind of substitution. Electronic devices can handle a very large volume of operations very quickly, but unless the level of production requires very large numbers of operations, it does not make sense to use these techniques. Another example of scale economies is discussed in Box 11.2.

Increasing costs: Over the range of outputs greater than q_m in Figure 11.4, the firm encounters rising costs. An expansion in production, even after sufficient time has elapsed for all adjustments to be made, is accompanied by a rise in average costs per unit of output. If the prices of factors of production are constant, this rise in costs must be the result of an expansion in output which is proportionately less than the expansion

---

BOX 11.2 ECONOMIES OF SCALE IN THE ELECTRICITY INDUSTRY

In the 1940s, 50s and 60s, major economies of scale in electricity generation came from the use of larger and larger generators: from 30MW (= 300,000 kilowatts) generating sets in 1948 to 100MW sets in 1956, 200MW sets in 1959 and 500MW sets in 1966.

Since the 1960s, there has been little increase in the size of generators, with the largest now being installed at 660MW, but the industry has found a new way of reaping scale economies. It has been reducing the *number* of power stations, each station having several generators. The result has been that the average capacity of each power station has continued to rise significantly, bringing a different type of economy of scale. From 233 power stations with an average capacity of 147MW in March 1965, the Central Electricity Generating Board (which is responsible for the generation of all the electricity supplied by area electricity boards in England and Wales) reduced the number of stations to 174 with an average capacity of 324MW by March 1974 and 78 stations with an average capacity of 671MW by March 1987. It is interesting to note that the 'energy crisis' starting in 1973–74 brought a stop to the rapid growth in demand for electricity in Britain, so the overall generating capacity is now *smaller* than it was 15 years ago. Nevertheless, the adoption of larger generating units and their concentration in larger and larger power stations has brought significant scale economies.

The CEGB has also benefitted from economies of scale in bulk transmission of electricity. As long ago as the mid-1960s, the Board began construction of a 'Supergrid' of 400KV (= 400,000 volts) transmission lines based on the knowledge that such a line could replace 3 lines operating at 275KV or 18 lines operating at 132KV, without a corresponding increase in costs.

Economies of scale have allowed the industry to cope with rising *real* prices of its main inputs – coal and labour – without raising the real price of electricity. During the 1960s, when the real price of the major alternative fuel – oil – was falling (this fall itself being the result of the increasing exploitation of economies of scale in oil tankers delivering crude oil from the Middle East), the UK electricity industry was actually able to reduce the real price of electricity, which is one of the reasons for electricity being adopted more and more widely in preference to other fuels.

Strictly speaking, scale economies refer to the effects of increasing output *along* a negatively sloped *LRAS* curve as a result of rising output within the confines of known technology, while changes in technological knowledge *shift* the *LRAS* curve. As this example shows, the two forces usually become mixed in most real-world applications. The rise in demand for electricity in the three decades starting with the 1950s, required an increase in output. The rise in output made the use of higher-capacity equipment possible and thus provided an incentive for the development of such equipment. No fundamental new knowledge was required but the details of the technology of larger generators has to be developed through research rather than being taken from already existing blueprints.

in inputs. Such a firm is said to encounter long-run **decreasing returns** or **diseconomies of scale**.[1] As the firm's scale of operations increases, diseconomies – say of management – are encountered. These increase the quantity of factors that must be used per unit of output produced.

Minimum costs: At the output q_m in Figure 11.4 the firm has reached its lowest possible long-run costs per unit of output. If the firm produces at that output, it is producing efficiently in the sense that the costs per unit of output are as low as they possibly can be (for given technology and factor prices). We shall see in Chapter 12 that under certain conditions (called those of perfect competition) each firm will, in equilibrium, produce at the minimum point on its *LRAC* curve.

Constant costs: The firm's long-run average costs are shown in Figure 11.4 as falling to output q_m and rising thereafter. Another possibility should be noted: the firm's *LRAC* curve might be flat over some range of output around q_m. When such a flat portion exists, the firm is said to encounter constant costs over the relevant range of output. This would mean that the firm's long-run average cost per unit of output was not changing as its output changed. If factor prices are assumed to be fixed, this must mean that the firm's output is increasing exactly as fast as its inputs are increasing. Such a firm would be said to be encountering **constant returns**.

The Relation Between Long-run and Short-run Costs

The various short-run cost curves studied earlier in this chapter, and the long-run cost curve just studied, are all derived from the same production function, and each assumes given prices for all factor inputs. In the long run, all factors can be varied; in the short run, some must remain fixed. The long-run average total cost (*LRAC*) curve shows the lowest cost of producing any output

---

[1] Long-run decreasing returns differ from the short-run diminishing returns that we discussed earlier. In the short run, at least one factor is fixed and the law of diminishing returns ensures that returns to the variable factor must eventually diminish. In the long run, all factors are variable, and physically diminishing returns may never be encountered – at least as long as it is genuinely possible to increase inputs of all factors.

FIGURE 11.5 Long-run Average Cost and Short-run Average Cost Curves

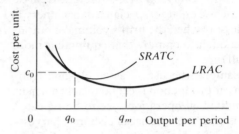

The short-run average total cost (*SRATC*) curve is tangent to the long-run average cost (*LRAC*) curve at the output for which the quantity of the fixed factors is optimal. Assume that output is varied with plant and equipment fixed at the level that is optimal for producing q_0. Costs will then follow the short-run cost curve shown in the Figure. The curves *SRATC* and *LRAC* coincide at output q_0, where the fixed plant is optimal for that level of output. For all other outputs there is too little or too much plant and equipment, and *SRATC* lies above *LRAC*. If some output other than q_0 is to be sustained, costs can be reduced to the level of the long-run curve when sufficient time has elapsed to adjust the size of the firm's plant and equipment.

The output q_m is the lowest point on the firm's long-run average cost curve. It is called the firm's *minimum efficient scale (MES)*. It is the output at which long-run costs are minimized.

---

when all factors are variable. The short-run average total cost (*SRATC*) curve shows the lowest cost of producing any output when one or more factors is not free to vary.

The relation between the short-run cost curves and the long-run curve is illustrated in Figure 11.5. Note that each short-run cost curve is tangent to (touches) the long-run curve at the level of output for which the quantity of the fixed factor is optimal, and lies above the long-run cost curve for all other levels of output. Here is why. One given *SRATC* curve refers to some given amount of capital. It will coincide with the *LRAC* curve at the output for which the given amount of capital is optimal. For all other outputs produced along that *SRATC* curve, there is either too little, or too much, fixed capital and that *SRATC* curve must, therefore, lie above the *LRAC* curve.

We saw earlier in this chapter that a *SRATC* curve, such as the one shown in Figure 11.5, is but one of many such short-run curves. Each one

FIGURE 11.6 The Envelope Long-run Average Cost Curve

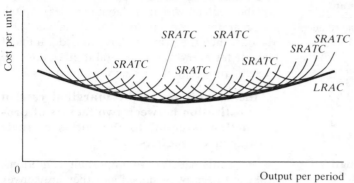

To every point on the long-run average cost (**LRAC**) curve there is an associated short-run average cost (**SRAC**) curve tangent at that point. Each short-run curve shows how costs vary if output varies, with the fixed factor held constant at the level that is optimal for the output at the point of tangency. As a result, each *SRATC* curve touches the *LRAC* curve at one point and lies above it at all other points. This makes the *LRAC* curve the envelope of the *SRATC* curves.

shows how costs vary as output is varied from a base output, holding some factors fixed at the quantities most appropriate to the base output. This is illustrated in Figure 11.6. There is an associated short-run cost curve tangent to every point on the long-run cost curve. Each short-run curve shows how costs vary if output varies, with the fixed factor held constant at the level that is optimal for the output at the point of tangency. The long-run curve is sometimes called an **envelope curve**, which means that it just *encloses* the whole family of short-run curves.[1]

Shifts in Cost Curves

The cost curves we have derived so far show how cost varies with output, given constant factor prices and fixed technology. Changes in either technological knowledge or factor prices will cause the whole family of short- and long-run cost curves to shift. Loss of existing technological knowledge is a rare thing, so technological change normally works in one direction only, to shift cost curves downwards. Factor prices can, however, exert an influence in either direction. If a firm has to pay more for any factor that it uses, the cost of producing each level of output will rise; if the firm has to pay less, costs fall.

A rise in factor prices shifts the whole family of short- and long-run cost curves upwards. A fall in factor prices or a technological advance shifts the whole family of cost curves downwards.

Isoquants: An Alternative Analysis of the Firm's Long-run Input Decisions[1]

The long-run choices of factor proportions that we have just studied can be shown graphically by using a new concept. This concept, which is called an *isoquant*, is defined below.

A Single Isoquant

Table 11.3 gives a hypothetical illustration of those combinations of two inputs (labour and capital) that will produce a given quantity of output. The data from Table 11.3 are plotted in Figure 11.7. A smooth curve is drawn through the points to indicate that there are additional ways, not listed in the Table, of producing 6 units. The curve is called an **isoquant**. It shows the set of technologically efficient possibilities for producing a given level of output – it is 6 units. The isoquant in this example is analogous to an indifference curve that shows all combinations of commodities that yield a given utility.

As we move from one point on an isoquant to another we are *substituting one factor for another* while holding output constant. The **marginal**

---

[1] Each short-run curve touches the long-run curve at one point and lies above it everywhere else. This leads to a subtle consequence. Two curves that are tangent at a point have the same slope at that point. If *LRAC* is decreasing where it is tangent to *SRATC*, then *SRATC* must also be decreasing. What this tell us is that the best way to produce any output q_o where economies of scale are not exhausted is to build a plant whose minimum *SRATC* exceeds q_o and then underutilize it.

---

[1] The material in this section can be omitted without a loss of continuity.

TABLE 11.3 Alternative Methods of Producing Six Units of Output: Points on an Isoquant

Method	K	L	ΔK	ΔL	Rate of substitution $\Delta K / \Delta L$
a	18	2			
b	12	3	−6	1	−6.0
c	9	4	−3	1	−3.0
d	6	6	−3	2	−1.5
e	4	9	−2	3	−0.67
f	3	12	−1	3	−0.33
g	2	18	−1	6	−0.17

An isoquant describes the firm's alternative methods for producing a given output. The Table lists some of the methods indicated by a production function as being available to produce six units of output. The first combination uses a great deal of capital (K) and very little labour (L). As we move down the Table, labour is substituted for capital in such a way as to keep output constant. Finally, at the bottom, most of the capital has been replaced by labour. The rate of substitution between the two factors is calculated in the last three columns of the Table. Note that as we move down the Table, the absolute value of the rate of substitution declines.

rate of substitution (**MRS**) measures the rate at which one factor is substituted for another with output held constant. Graphically this is measured by the absolute value of the slope of the isoquant at a particular point. Table 11.3 shows the calculation of some rates of substitution between various points of the isoquant.[1]

Let us now see how the marginal rate of substitution is related to the marginal products of the factors of production. An example will illustrate this relation. Assume that at the present level of inputs of labour and capital, the marginal product of a unit of labour is 2 units of output while the marginal product of capital is 1 unit of output. If the firm reduces its use of capital and increases its use of labour so as to keep output

constant, it needs to add only 1/2 unit of labour for 1 unit of capital given up. If, at another point on the isoquant with more labour and less capital, the marginal products are 2 for capital and 1 for labour, then the firm will have to add 2 units of labour for every unit of capital it gives up. The general proposition this example illustrates is:

> **the magnitude of the marginal rate of substitution between two factors of production is equal to the ratios of their marginal products.**

Isoquants satisfy two important conditions: they are negatively sloped and they are convex viewed from the origin. What is the meaning of each of these conditions?

The negative slope indicates that each factor of production has a positive marginal product. If the input of one factor is reduced and that of the other is held constant, output must fall. Thus, if one input is reduced, production can only be held

FIGURE 11.7 An Isoquant for Output of Six Units

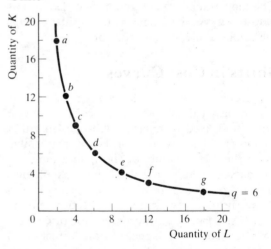

Isoquants are downward-sloping and convex. The lettered points are plotted from the data in Table 11.3. The convex shape of the isoquant reflects a diminishing marginal rate of substitution; moving along the isoquant to the right, its slope becomes flatter. Starting from point *a*, which uses relatively little labour and much capital, and moving to point *b*, 1 additional unit of labour can substitute for 6 units of capital (while holding production constant). But from *b* to *c*, 1 unit of labour substitutes for only 3 units of capital, and so on.

---

[1] The Table calculates the incremental rate of substitution between distinct points on an isoquant. The marginal rate of substitution refers to substitutability at a particular point on the isoquant. Graphically the incremental rate of substitution is related to the slope of the chord joining the two points in question, while the marginal rate of substitution is given by the slope of the tangent to the curve at one particular point. Again the discussion of section (7) of the Appendix to Chapter 3 is relevant.

constant if the other input is increased. This gives the marginal rate of substitution a negative value: decreases in one factor must be balanced by increases in the other factor if output is to be held constant.

Now consider what happens as the firm moves along the isoquant of Figure 11.7 downwards and to the right. This movement means that labour is being added and capital reduced so as to keep output constant. If labour is added in successive increments of exactly one unit, how much capital may be dispensed with each time? The key to the answer is that both factors are assumed to be subject to the law of diminishing returns. Thus the gain in output associated with each additional unit of labour added is *diminishing*, while the loss of output associated with each additional unit of capital forgone is *increasing*. It therefore takes ever larger increases in labour to offset equal reductions in capital in order to hold production constant. This implies that the isoquant is convex viewed from the origin.

An Isoquant Map

The isoquant drawn in Figure 11.7 referred to 6 units of output. There is another isoquant for 7 units, and for every other output. Each isoquant refers to a specific output; it connects alternative

---

FIGURE 11.8 An Isoquant Map

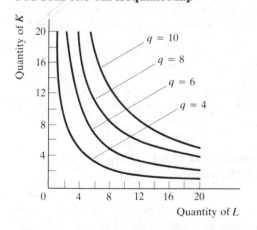

An isoquant map shows a set of isoquants, one for each level of output. The Figure shows four isoquants drawn from the production function and corresponding to 4, 6, 8 and 10 units of production. The higher the level of output, the further is the isoquant from the origin.

FIGURE 11.9 Isocost Lines

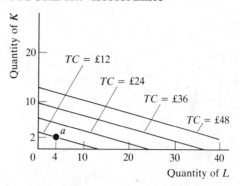

An isocost line shows alternative factor combinations that can be purchased for a given outlay. The graph shows the four isocost lines that result when labour costs £1 a unit and capital £4 a unit, and expenditure is held constant at £12, £24, £36 and £48 respectively. The line labelled $TC = £12$ represents all combinations of the two factors that the firm could buy for £12. Point *a* represents 2 units of K and 4 units of L.

---

combinations of factors that are technologically efficient methods of achieving that output. If we plot a representative set of these isoquants on a single graph, we obtain an **isoquant map**. Such a map is shown in Figure 11.8. The higher the level of output along a particular isoquant, the further away from the origin it will be.

Isoquants and the Conditions for Cost Minimization

Finding the efficient way of producing any output requires finding the least-cost factor combination. To do this when both factors are variable, factor prices need to be known. Suppose, to continue the example, that capital is priced at £4 per unit and labour at £1. We can now draw what are called **iso cost lines**, each one of which shows all of the combinations of the two factors that can be purchased for a given outlay. Four such lines are shown in Figure 11.9. For given factor prices, the parallel isocost lines reflect alternative levels of expenditure on factors. The higher the expenditure, the farther from the origin is the isocost line. Note that the isocost line is similar to the budget line introduced in Chapter 8 which shows all the combinations of two goods that can be bought with a given income.

In Figure 11.10 the isoquant and isocost maps

FIGURE 11.10 The Determination of the Least-cost Method of Output

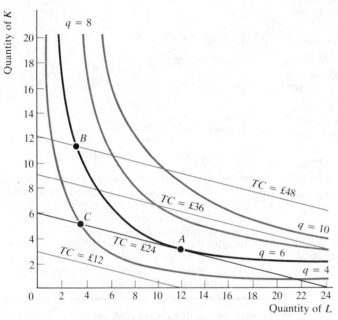

Least-cost methods are represented by points of tangency, such as *A*, between isoquant and isocost lines. The isoquant map of Figure 11.8 and the isocost map of Figure 11.9 are brought together in Figure 11.10. Consider point *A*. It is on the 6-unit isoquant and the £24 isocost line. Thus it is possible to achieve an output of 6 units for a total cost of £24. There are, however, other ways to achieve this output. For example, at point *B*, 6 units are also produced, but at a total cost of £48.

Now consider moving along the isocost line, say from point *A* to point *C*. Although costs are held constant, output falls from 6 to 4 units.

Point *A* thus shows both the least-cost method of producing 6 units of output *and* the maximum output that can be produced for an outlay of £24. Moving along the isoquant from point *A* in either direction clearly increases cost.

are brought together. A careful study of that Figure reveals the following important results. If the isoquant cuts the isocost line, it is possible to move along the isoquant and reach a lower level of cost. Where the isoquant is tangent to the isocost line, however, a movement in either direction along the isoquant is a movement to a higher level of cost. Thus

> **the least-cost method of producing any given output is shown graphically by the point of tangency between the relevant isoquant and an isocost line.**

Notice that point *A* in Figure 11.10 indicates not only the lowest level of cost for 6 units of output but also the highest output for £24 of cost.[1]

The absolute value of the slope of the isocost line is given by the ratio of the prices of the two factors of production.[2] The slope of the isoquant

is given by the ratio of their marginal products. (Both statements refer to absolute values.) When the firm reaches its least-cost position, it has equated the price ratio (which is given to it by the market prices) with the ratio of marginal products (which it can adjust by varying the proportions in which it hires the factors). In symbols,

$$\frac{MP_K}{MP_L} = \frac{p_K}{p_L} .$$

This is equation (4) on page 186. We have now derived this result by use of the isoquant analysis of the firm's decisions.

Isoquants and the Principle of Substitution

Suppose that with technology unchanged – that is, with the isoquant map fixed – the price of one factor changes. Figure 11.11 shows why the change in price changes the least-cost method of producing a given output. An increase in the price of one factor pivots the isocost line inwards and thus increases the cost of producing any output. It also changes the slope of the isocost line and thus changes the least-cost method of

---

[1] Thus we find the same solution if we set out *either* to minimize the cost of producing 6 units of output *or* to maximize the output that can be obtained for £24. One problem is said to be the *dual* of the other.

[2] The isocost line's equation is $Lp_L + Kp_K = t$, where t is total cost. Taking first differences yields $\Delta Lp_L + Kp_K = \Delta t = 0$, since t is held constant. Thus $\Delta K/\Delta L = -p_K/p_L$

FIGURE 11.11 The Effects of a Change in Factor Prices on Costs and Factor Proportions

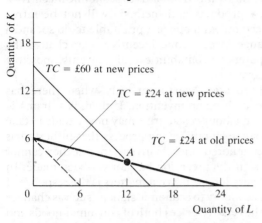
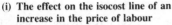

(i) The effect on the isocost line of an increase in the price of labour

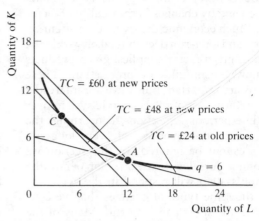

(ii) Substitution of capital for labour resulting from an increase in the price of labour

An increase in the price of labour pivots the isocost line inwards and thus increases the cost of producing any given output. It also changes the slope of the isocost line and thus changes the least-cost method of producing any given output. In (i) the rise in price of L from £1 to £4 a unit (with price of K constant at £4) pivots the $TC = £24$ line inwards. Any output previously produced for £24 will cost more at the new prices if it used any amount of labour. The new cost of producing at A rises from £24 to £60. In (ii) the steeper isocost line is tangent to the 6-unit isoquant at C, not A. Costs at C are £48, which is higher than they were before the price increase but not as high as they would be if the factor substitution had not occurred.

production. Costs at the new least-cost point C are higher than they were before the price increase, but not as high as if the factor substitution had not occurred. The slope of the isocost line has changed, making it efficient to substitute the now relatively cheaper capital for the relatively more expensive labour.

This result illustrates the principle of substitution.

Changes in relative factor prices will cause a partial replacement of factors that have become relatively more expensive by factors that have become relatively cheaper.

Of course, substitution of capital for labour cannot fully offset the effects of a rise in the cost of labour, as Figure 11.11(i) shows. This means that if production is to be held constant, higher costs must be accepted – but because of substitution it is not necessary to accept costs as high as would accompany an unchanged factor proportion.

This leads to the prediction that:

a rise in the price of one factor with all other factor prices constant will (1) shift upwards the cost curves of commodities that use that factor, and (2) lead to a substitution of factors that are now relatively cheaper for the factor whose price has risen.

Both of these predictions were stated in the first part of this chapter; they have now been derived formally using the isoquant technique.

THE VERY LONG RUN

In the long run, when technology – and hence the production function – is given, a certain quantity of inputs produces a certain output. In the very long run, technology may change: the same quantities of inputs may then produce a different quantity of output than before.

Changes in supply over the very long run are strongly influenced by changes in the techniques of production, by changes in the goods being produced and by changes in the quality of factor inputs. Much economic theory focuses attention on short- and long-run decisions taken within the context of given factor supplies, given products and known techniques of production. These decisions are important but, if we are interested in the performance of the economic system over long time-periods, questions concerning the causes and consequences of very-long-run changes cannot be ignored. In this section we shall confine ourselves to the question of how the economic system will respond in the very long run to the same types of changes that we considered in the short and long run. Many of the wider aspects of very-long-run changes must be postponed until Chapter 36, which deals with the whole problem of long-term economic growth.

Productivity

Over the last two centuries the material standard of living of the typical family has increased enormously in all of the world's industrialized countries. Much of this increase has been due to the invention of new, improved ways of making products. This causes an increase in **productivity**, which is output per unit of input employed.

> **The apparently modest rate of increase of output per man-hour of labour of 2.0 per cent per year leads to a doubling of output per man-hour every 36 years.**

Productivity in the United Kingdom has increased at approximately this rate over the last 100 years.

Productivity changes affect the supplies of commodities. Productivity changes are partly an endogenous response to economic signals and incentives and partly an exogenous consequence of spontaneous creative activity. Much of the economy's long-run ability to adjust to various disturbances that impinge on it depends on very-long-run changes being at least partly endogenous.

Inventions and Innovations

An **invention** is defined as the discovery of something new, such as a new production technique or a new product. An **innovation** is defined as the introduction of an invention into use. Innovation responds to economic incentives. New products and methods will not be introduced unless it appears profitable to do so, and a change in economic incentives can change the apparent profitabilities of various possible innovations.

Innovation can occur only when there has already been an invention. If there is a dramatic rise in labour costs, firms may now decide to take up some labour-saving process that hitherto has been ignored since its invention, but they cannot do so if the invention has not yet been made. In the very long run, what matters is the response of the economy to economic signals, such as changes in the relative prices both of consumer goods and of inputs. The extent to which invention responds to such incentives helps to determine the economy's responses.

An example will illustrate why the extent to which invention is endogenous matters.

Hypothesis 1: This is the age of electronics and automation, and scientists just go on inventing methods that replace unskilled labour with capital, thereby creating unemployment among the unskilled. The normal corrective of the price system is for the relative price of unskilled labour to fall, thus inducing a substitution in favour of unskilled labour until the unemployment is eliminated. But, according to this hypothesis, scientists are uninfluenced by the incentives of relative factor prices. Now assume that each new technique invented is *absolutely* more efficient than its predecessors in the sense that it uses less of *all* factors than its predecessors – but it also uses less unskilled labour *relative to* other inputs. Firms will now be motivated to adopt the absolutely more efficient new techniques, but in so doing they will adopt a factor combination that increases the unemployment among the unskilled.

Hypothesis 2: If unemployment amongst the unskilled drives down their relative wage, firms will be led to select from amongst existing techniques those that are more intensive in the use of unskilled labour. If there is still unemployment among the unskilled, their factor services will remain cheap and the profit incentive will cause the development of new techniques that substitute cheap unskilled labour for the more expensive factors.

Thus, in hypothesis 1, the long-term effects of invention and innovation are to increase the problem of 'structural unemployment' of the unskilled, while in hypothesis 2 the effect of the same inventive activity is to reduce this unemployment. Under hypothesis 1, allowing the relative wage of the unskilled to fall will only worsen their plight, while under hypothesis 2 it will cause a burst of inventive and innovative activity that will reduce their unemployment.

Clearly it matters whether, in the long-run, invention proceeds more or less autonomously or under the influence of such economic incentives as relative factor prices. That invention does respond endogenously to economic incentives is well documented. For example, when oil became very expensive from 1972–85 there was a burst of inventive activity directed at the development of alternative energy sources. When the price of oil fell after 1985, this activity slackened substantially. What is less certain are the critical matters of *how much* it responds and *how fast*.

SUMMARY

1. The production function shows how inputs of factor services are related to outputs.

2. In the short run, at least one important input is fixed. In the long run, all inputs can be varied. In the very long run the production function itself changes so that given amounts of inputs produce varying (usually increasing) amounts of output.

3. Short-run variations in a variable input with another input fixed are subject to the law of diminishing returns: equal increments of the variable input sooner or later produce smaller and smaller additions to total output and eventually a reduction in average output per unit of variable input.

4. The marginal product curve intersects the average product curve at the latter's maximum point.

5. Short-run average and marginal cost curves are U-shaped, the rising portion reflecting diminishing average and marginal returns.

6. The marginal cost curve intersects the average cost curve at the latter's minimum point, which is called the firm's capacity output.

7. There is a family of short-run average and marginal cost curves, one for each level of the fixed factor.

8. In the long run the firm will adjust all factor inputs to minimize the cost of producing any given level of output. This requires that the ratio of a factor's marginal product to its price be the same for all factors.

9. The principle of substitution states that, when relative factor prices change, firms will substitute relatively cheaper factors for relatively more expensive ones.

10. Long-run cost curves are often assumed to be U-shaped, indicating decreasing average costs (increasing returns to scale) followed by increasing average costs (decreasing returns to scale). The long-run cost curve may be thought of as the envelope of the family of short-run cost curves, all of which shift when factor prices shift.

11. Long-run decisions can be analysed using isoquants each one of which shows all the combinations of inputs that will produce a given output. Cost minimization occurs where an isocost line is tangent to an isoquant.

12. In the very long run, new methods of production alter the production function. The inventions that cause this are partly exogenous and partly endogenous in that they respond to price and profit incentives.

TOPICS FOR REVIEW

- The production function
- The short, long and very long run
- The law of diminishing returns or variable proportions
- Short-run average, marginal, fixed and total cost
- Capacity and minimum efficient scale (MES)
- Conditions for cost minimization
- The principle of substitution
- The long-run envelope cost curve
- Constant, increasing and decreasing long-run costs
- Isoquants and cost minimization
- Inventions and innovations in the very long run

12

Perfect Competition

In Chapter 10 we hypothesized that firms maximize profit, which is the difference between the total revenue derived from selling their product and the total cost of making it. In Chapter 11 we studied how firms' costs varied with their output. Next we need to know how their revenues vary with their output. When we have done this, we can put the costs and revenues together and study how firms must behave if they wish to maximize their profits.

Various Revenue Concepts

As a first step, we define a number of revenue concepts that apply to all firms. These are the revenue equivalents of the total, average and marginal costs that we defined in Chapter 11. We can look at the firm's revenues as totals, averages or marginal quantities, exactly as we looked at costs in the previous chapter.

(1) **Total revenue (TR)** refers to the total amount of money that the firm receives from the sale of its output. This will vary with a firm's sales, so we may write, using functional notation:

$$TR = R(q) ,$$

where TR is total revenue and, as in the last chapter, q is total output over some period of time. (Note that, since we are not concerned with the holding of stocks, we can equate the firm's output with its sales.) Total revenue is equal to the quantity sold multiplied by the selling price of the commodity, i.e.

$$TR = pq ,$$

where p is the price per unit. The unqualified term *revenue* is often used to refer to total revenue, and whenever we speak of revenue or use the symbol R, we shall mean total revenue.

(2) **Average revenue (AR)** is total revenue divided by the number of units sold (pq/q). Quite obviously, average revenue is the price of the commodity:

$$AR = p .$$

(3) **Marginal revenue (MR)** is the change in total revenue resulting from an increase of 1 unit in the rate of sales per period of time (say per month). The marginal revenue resulting from the sale of the nth unit of a commodity is thus the change in total revenue when sales rise from the

rate of $n - 1$ units per period to the rate of n units. Expressing this in symbols:[1]

$$MR_n = TR_n - TR_{n-1} \; .$$

Do not think that $n - 1$ units are sold at some time and an extra unit at some later time. Marginal revenue refers to alternative sales policies *over the same period of time*. Thus to find the marginal revenue of the 100th unit, we compare the total revenue resulting when 100 units are sold over some period of time, TR_n, with the total revenue that would have resulted if 99 units had been sold over the same period of time, TR_{n-1}.

We now need to discover how total, average and marginal revenues are related to each firm's output. We cannot, however, develop a single theory that applies to all firms because these key relations vary with the different market situations in which the firm operates. To see why this is so, we need to distinguish between two different concepts called competitive behaviour and competitive market structure.

COMPETITIVE BEHAVIOUR AND MARKET STRUCTURE

Is Saxone in competition with Dolcis? Does Selfridge's compete with Marks & Spencer's? Is a Yorkshire wheat farmer in competition with a Somerset wheat farmer? In the everyday meaning of competition, the answers to the first two of these questions are plainly yes, and the answer to the third question is probably no. Saxone and Dolcis both advertise extensively to persuade the same group of buyers to buy *their* own products. Many shoppers check the respective prices and qualities offered by two nearby department stores such as Selfridge's and Marks & Spencer's. There is, however, nothing that the Yorkshire farmer can do to affect the sales or the profits of the Somerset farmer.

To decide who is competing with whom and in

---

[1] Once again the definition uses finite changes and, therefore, refers to incremental revenue. Students familiar with the calculus will realize that marginal revenue refers to the derivative of the total revenue function with respect to quantity: $MR = dTR/dq$. In the text we do not distinguish the two concepts. The distinction is further discussed in the Appendix to Chapter 3, pages 45–47.

what sense they compete, it is necessary to distinguish between the *behaviour* of individual firms and the *type of market* in which the firms operate. Economists use the term *market structure* to refer to the latter concept. In everyday use the term 'competition' usually refers only to competitive behaviour. Economists, however, are interested both in the competitive behaviour of individual firms and in the competitiveness of market structures.

Competitive market structure: The competitiveness of the market structure refers to the extent to which individual firms have power over that market – power to influence the price or other terms on which their product is sold. The less power an individual firm has to influence the market in which it sells its product, the more competitive is that market structure said to be. The extreme of a competitive structure occurs when each firm has zero market power. In such a case, there are so many firms that each must accept the price set by the forces of market demand and supply. This extreme is called the *perfectly competitive market structure*.

Perhaps surprisingly, firms that operate in perfectly competitive markets do not need to compete actively with each other since none has any power over the market. One firm's ability to sell its product does not depend on the behaviour of any other firm.

For example, the Yorkshire and Somerset wheat farmers do not engage in active *competitive behaviour* with each other. They are firms operating in a perfectly competitive market over which they have no power. Neither has significant power to change the market price for its wheat by altering its own behaviour.

Competitive behaviour: In everyday language the term *competitive behaviour* refers to the degree to which individual firms actively compete with one another. For example, Saxone and Dolcis certainly engage in competitive behaviour.

It is also true, however, that Saxone and Dolcis have some power over their markets. Either firm could raise its prices and continue to sell some of its products. Each has the power to decide, within limits set by buyers' tastes and the prices of competing firms, what price consumers will pay for its own products. Thus, although they compete actively with each other, they do so in a market that is not perfectly competitive.

Behaviour versus structure: The distinction made above explains why it is that firms in perfectly competitive markets (e.g. the Yorkshire and Somerset wheat farmers) do not actively compete with each other, while firms that do compete actively with each other (e.g. Saxone and Dolcis) do not operate in perfectly competitive markets.

The Significance of Market Structure

Our next step is to define two important concepts, the market and the industry.

From the point of view of a buyer, the **market** consists of those firms from which a well-defined product can be purchased; from the point of view of a firm, the market consists of those buyers to whom a well-defined product can be sold. A group of firms that sells a well-defined product or closely related set of products is said to constitute an **industry**. The market demand curve is the demand curve for an industry's product.[1]

Consider a firm that produces a specific product for sale in a particular market and competes for customers with other firms in the same industry. If the firm knows the demand curve it faces, it knows the price it could charge for each rate of sales and thus knows its potential revenues. If it also knows its costs, the firm can calculate the profits that would be associated with each rate of output and can choose the rate that maximizes its profits.

But what if the firm knows only its costs and the *market* demand curve for its industry's product? Because it does not know its *own* demand curve, it does not know what its own sales would be at any price that it might charge. To know how its own sales would change as its own price changes, the firm needs to know how other firms will respond to its change in price. If it reduces its price by 10 per cent, will other sellers leave their prices unchanged, or will they also reduce them? If so, by how much? Obviously, these responses will affect the firm's sales and thus its revenues and profits.

---

[1] An industry typically produces many differentiated products and sells them in many different markets. For our elementary treatment, we focus attention on the single-product industry that sells its output in a single market.

We have said that market structure refers to the type of market in which the firm operates. **Market structure** means those characteristics of markets that influence the behaviour and performance of firms that sell in that market. These characteristics are many of the ones that determine the relation between the market demand curve for the industry's product and the firm's own demand curve.

The number of sellers and the nature of the product are important characteristics of market structure. Others are the ease of entering the industry, the nature and number of the purchasers of the firm's products, and the firm's ability to influence demand by advertising. To reduce these characteristics to manageable proportions, economists have focused on a few theoretical market structures that they believe represent a high proportion of the cases actually encountered in market economies. In this and the following chapters, we shall look at four market structures: perfect competition, which is studied in this chapter, monopoly, studied in Chapter 13, and monopolistic competition and oligopoly, studied in Chapter 14.

PERFECT COMPETITION

The theory of the market structure called **perfect competition** is built on two critical assumptions, one about the behaviour of the individual firm and one about the nature of the industry in which it operates.

The Assumptions of Perfect Competition

The *firm* is assumed to be a **price-taker**. This means that it can alter its rate of production and sales within any feasible range without having any significant effect on the price of the product it sells. Thus the firm must passively accept whatever price happens to be ruling on the market.

The *industry* is characterized by **freedom of entry and exit**. This means that any new firm is free to set up production if it so wishes, and that any existing firm is free to leave the industry if it so wishes. Existing firms cannot bar the entry of new firms and there are no legal prohibitions on entry or exit.

The ultimate test of the theory based on these assumptions is the usefulness of its predictions, but because students are often bothered by the first assumption, we examine it more closely. To see what is involved in the assumption of price-taking, contrast the demand for the products of a car manufacturer and a wheat farmer.

A Car Manufacturer

The Ford Motor Company is aware of the fact that it has some market power. If it substantially increases the price of one of its cars, sales will fall off; if it lowers the price substantially, it will be able to sell more. If Ford contemplates a large increase in production of one type of car that is not a response to some known or anticipated rise in demand, it knows that it will have to reduce prices in order to sell the extra output. The car-manufacturing firm is *not* a price-taker who passively accepts whatever price is set by the market. The quantity that it is able to sell will depend on the prices that it sets. In other words, the firm is faced with a downward-sloping demand curve, and it may select any price-quantity combination that is consistent with that demand curve.

A Wheat Farmer

There are many contrasts between a car manufacturer and a wheat farmer. Three will be sufficient to explain the fundamentals of price-taking behaviour.

A homogeneous product: Every type of car Ford produces is distinct from every other type of Ford car and from every car produced by Ford's competitors. We say that car firms sell a **differentiated product**. Each car has characteristics that appeal to particular customers, so Ford can raise the price of one of its cars without instantly losing all of its sales as customers switch *en masse* to other cars. In contrast, one farmer's No. 1 winter wheat is indistinguishable from any other farmer's No. 1 winter wheat. We say that wheat farmers sell a **homogeneous product**. Thus there is no reason why well-informed buyers would buy from anyone but the lowest-price supplier of No. 1 winter wheat. Since anyone who charges more than this minimum can expect to sell nothing, every supplier must sell at the same price.

Price-taking behaviour requires that firms sell a homogeneous product.

Well-informed buyers: The argument just given assumes that buyers know when one firm is asking a higher price than other firms. A necessary condition for price-taking is that buyers are sufficiently well informed that if a firm raises the price of its homogeneous product above the prices of other firms, it will lose its customers.

For price-taking behaviour, buyers must be sufficiently well informed that significant numbers of them do not unknowingly pay more than is necessary for their purchases.

Many sellers: A key distinction between the car and the wheat industries is in the number of sellers. Any one wheat farmer's contribution to the total production of wheat is a very small drop in an extremely large bucket. Ordinarily a farmer will assume that he has no effect on price. Of course, he can have *some* effect on price, but as the calculations in Box 12.1 show, the effect is so minute that he can justifiably neglect it.

It is thus only a slight simplification of reality to say that the firm is unable to influence the world price of wheat, and that it is able to sell all that it can produce at the going world price. In other words, the firm is faced with a perfectly elastic demand curve for its product – it is a price-taker.

The difference between firms producing wheat and firms producing cars is one of degree of market power. The wheat firm, as an insignificant part of the whole market, has no power to influence the world price of wheat. But the car firm does have power to influence the price of cars because its own production represents a significant part of the total supply of cars.

For a firm to be a price-taker, it must be one of a large number of similar firms.

Demand and Revenue Curves for the Perfectly Competitive Firm

In perfect competition, each individual firm faces a perfectly elastic demand curve for its product. Since the market price is unaffected by variations

BOX 12.1 DEMAND UNDER PERFECT COMPETITION: FIRM AND INDUSTRY

Since all products have negatively sloped market demand curves, *any* increase in the industry's output will cause *some* fall in the market price. As the calculations in the following Table show, however, any conceivable increase that one wheat farm could make in its output has such a negligible effect on the industry's price that the farmer correctly ignores it.

The Table calculates the elasticity of demand facing one wheat farmer in two steps. Step 1 shows that a 200 per cent variation in the farm's output leads to only a tiny percentage variation in the world's price. Thus, as step 2 shows, the farm's elasticity of demand is very high: 71,428!

Although the arithmetic used in reaching these measures is unimportant, understanding why the wheat farmer is a price-taker in these circumstances is vital.

Here is the argument which the Table summarizes. The market elasticity of demand for wheat is approximately 0.25. This means that if the quantity of wheat supplied in the world increased by 1 per cent, the price would have to fall by 4 per cent to induce the world's wheat buyers to purchase the entire increase in the crop.

Even huge farms produce a very small fraction of the total crop. In a recent year, one large farm produced 1,750 tonnes of wheat. This was only 0.0035 per cent of the world production of 500 million tonnes. Suppose that the farm decided in one year to produce nothing and in another year managed to produce twice its normal output of 1,750 tonnes. This is an extremely large variation in output. Indeed it is an impossibly large variation for a farm that can normally produce 1,750 tons.

The increase in output from zero to 3,500 tonnes is a 200 per cent variation measured around the farm's average output of 1,750. Yet the percentage increase in world output is only $(3,500/500m)100 = 0.0007$ per cent. The Table shows that this increase would lead to a decrease in the world price of 0.0028 per cent (2.8 in 1,000) and give the farm's own demand curve an elasticity of over 71,000! This is an an enormous elasticity of demand; the farm would have to increase its output by over 71,000 per cent to bring about a 1 per cent decrease in the price of wheat! Because the farm's output cannot be varied this much, the farmer correctly regards the price of wheat as unaffected by any change in output that this one farm could conceivably make. For all intents and purposes, the wheat-producing farm is faced with a perfectly elastic demand curve for its product – *it is a price-taker*.

TABLE The Calculation of the Firm's Elasticity of Demand (η_F) from Market Elasticity of Demand (η_M)

Given $\eta_M = 0.25$
World output = 500 million tonnes.
A large farm with an average output of 1,750 tonnes varies its output between 0 and 3,500.
The variation of 3,500 tonnes on an average output of 1,750 = 200 per cent.
This causes world output to vary by (3,500/500 million) 100 = 0.0007 per cent.

Step 1. Find the percentage change in world price.

$$\eta_M = -\frac{\text{percentage change in world output}}{\text{percentage change in world price}}$$

$$\text{percentage change in world price} = -\frac{\text{percentage change in world output}}{\eta_M}$$

$$= -\frac{0.0007}{0.25}$$

$$= -0.0028$$

Step 2. Compute the farm's elasticity of demand.

$$\eta_F = -\frac{\text{percentage variation in farm's output}}{\text{percentage change in world price}}$$

$$= -\frac{+200}{-0.0028} = +71,428$$

TABLE 12.1   Revenue Concepts for a Price-taking Firm

Quantity sold (units) q	Price p	$TR = p \cdot q$	$AR = TR/q$	$MR = \Delta TR/\Delta q$
10	£3·00	£30·00	£3·00	
11	3·00	33·00	3·00	£3·00
12	3·00	36·00	3·00	3·00
13	3·00	39·00	3·00	3·00

When price is fixed, average revenue, marginal revenue and price are all equal to each other. The Table shows the calculation of total (TR), average (AR) and marginal revenue (MR) when market price is £3.00 and the firm varies its quantity over the range from 10 to 13 units. Marginal revenue is shown between the lines because it represents the change in total revenue in response to a change in quantity. For example, when sales rise from 11 to 12 units, revenue rises from £33 to £36 making marginal revenue $(36–33)/(12–11) = £3$ per unit.

in any one firm's output, it follows that each firm's marginal revenue, resulting from an increase in the volume of sales by one unit, is constant and is equal to the price of the product. For example, at a market price of £3, each additional unit sold will bring in £3. Thus marginal revenue is £3, while the average revenue (equals total revenue/number of units sold) is also £3.

> **In perfectly competitive markets the demand curve facing the firm is identical with both the average and the marginal revenue curves; all three coincide in the same straight line, showing that price = *AR* = *MR*.**

Total revenue does, of course, vary with output; since price is constant, it follows that total revenue varies in direct proportion to output. Calculations of these revenue concepts for a price-taking firm are illustrated in Table 12.1.

SHORT-RUN EQUILIBRIUM

Equilibrium of the Firm

In the short run, all firms have fixed factors and vary their outputs by varying their inputs of variable factors. Thus their short-run costs curves are relevant to their short-run output decisions.

Each firm's profit-maximizing level of output will depend on its costs, and on the demand curve that it faces. We start by stating a set of rules that determine the outputs of profit-maximizing firms operating in all market structures. We then apply these rules to each of the four market structures as we study them.

Rules for Profit Maximization in all Market Structures

Three important rules define the output that maximizes each firm's profits. Economists do not assume that firms consciously follow these rules, but as long as they succeed somehow in maximizing their profits, the rules allow economists to predict how firms behave.

A rule to decide whether or not to produce in the short run: A firm always has the option of producing nothing, in which case it will have an operating loss equal to its fixed costs. If production adds less to revenue than to costs, production will increase the loss suffered by the firm. If production adds more to revenue than to costs, production will reduce the firm's losses (or increase its profits). From this follows our first rule:

> *Rule 1.* **In the short run, a firm should produce if and only if total revenue is not less than total variable cost.**

Another way of stating this rule is that the firm should produce output only if average revenue (price) is not less than average variable cost. In the short run, it pays a firm to stay in production even if it cannot cover its full fixed costs since its fixed costs must be met whether production occurs or not.[1] This rule, which is sometimes called the shutdown rule, is simple to state, but often difficult to apply in practice. Box 12.2 on page 212 uses it to explain some behaviour that often seems odd to the casual observer.

---

[1] In the long run, all costs are variable since the firm need not replace its fixed factors as they wear out. In the long run, therefore, a firm must cover all its costs if it is to stay in production.

A rule that is necessary for profits to be at a maximum:[1] Consider a firm that finds it profitable to produce some output according to Rule 1. How much should it produce? If, on the one hand, the firm finds that, at its present level of production, the cost of making another unit (marginal cost) is less than the revenue that would be gained by selling that unit (marginal revenue), total profit could clearly be increased by producing another unit of output. Thus whenever a firm finds that, at the current level of output, marginal revenue exceeds marginal cost, it can increase its profit by producing more. If, on the other hand, the firm finds that at the present level of production the cost of making the last unit exceeds the revenue gained by selling it, total profit could clearly be increased by not producing the last unit. Thus whenever the firm finds that marginal cost exceeds marginal revenue it can increase its total profit by reducing its output.

Now we have the result that the firm should change its output whenever marginal cost does not equal marginal revenue, raising output if *MR* exceeds *MC* and lowering output if *MC* exceeds *MR*. Thus at the profit-maximizing output the last unit produced should add just as much to revenue as it adds to cost.

> **Rule 2. A necessary condition for the firm to be producing its profit-maximizing output is that marginal revenue should equal marginal cost.**

A rule to ensure that profits are maximized rather than minimized: Figure 12.1 shows that it is possible to fulfil Rule 2 and have profits at a minimum rather than a maximum.

In the Figure there are two outputs where marginal cost equals marginal revenue. Rule 3 is needed to distinguish minimum-profit positions from maximum-profit positions.

> **Rule 3. For an output where marginal cost equals marginal revenue to be profit-maximizing rather than profit-minimizing, it is sufficient that marginal cost be less than marginal revenue at slightly lower outputs and that marginal**

FIGURE 12.1 Two Outputs Where Marginal Cost Equals Marginal Revenue

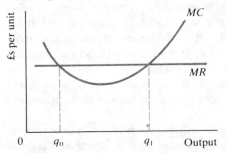

The equality of marginal cost and marginal revenue is necessary, but not sufficient, for profit maximization. The firm is assumed to be able to sell any output at the going market price, so that the market price is the firm's marginal revenue. (If all units can be sold at the prevailing market price then each unit adds that price to the firm's total revenue.) $MC = MR$ at outputs q_0 and q_1. Output q_0 is a minimum-profit position because a change of output in either direction would increase profit: for outputs below q_0, marginal cost exceeds marginal revenue and profits can be increased by *reducing* output; while for outputs above q_0, marginal revenue exceeds marginal cost and profits can be increased by *increasing* output. Output q_1 is a maximum-profit position since at outputs just below it, marginal revenue exceeds marginal cost and profit can be increased by *increasing* output towards q_1; while at outputs just above it, marginal cost exceeds marginal revenue and profit can be increased by *reducing* output towards q_1.

cost exceed marginal revenue at slightly higher outputs.

The geometric statement of this condition is that, at the profit-maximizing output, the marginal cost curve should intersect the marginal revenue curve from below. This ensures that *MC* is less than *MR* to the left of the profit-maximizing output and greater than *MR* to the right of the profit-maximizing output.[1]

The optimum output: The above three rules determine the output that will be chosen by any firm that maximizes its profits in the short run. This output is called the firm's profit-

---

[1] Students familiar with differential calculus will realize that the possibility of a stationary point of inflexion in the profit function is ignored in this treatment.

[1] Those students who are familiar with elementary calculus can follow the formal derivations of these three rules given in the Appendix to this chapter.

maximizing output, and sometimes its optimum output:

- the firm's optimum output is zero if total revenue is less than total variable cost at all levels of output; the optimum output is positive if there is any output for which total revenue exceeds total variable cost;
- when the firm's optimum output is positive, it is where marginal cost equals marginal revenue;
- if output is reduced slightly from the optimum level, marginal cost must be less than marginal revenue; if output is increased slightly from the optimum level, marginal cost must exceed marginal revenue.

When the firm has chosen its optimum output, it is in equilibrium because it has no incentive to alter its behaviour in the short run. Output will thus remain constant in the short run until there is some change in either the revenues, or the cost functions. (Long-run behaviour is considered later in this chapter.)

The Rules for Profit Maximization Applied to Perfect Competition

To apply Rule 2 to a firm operating in perfect competition, we recall that, as shown in Figure 12.2, the firm faces a perfectly elastic demand curve which defines its average and its marginal revenue. So when the profit-maximizing firm equates marginal cost to marginal revenue it is also, if it operates in a perfectly competitive market, equating marginal cost to market price.

As long as market price exceeds its average variable cost (Rule 1), a firm operating in a perfectly competitive market will produce the output at which its marginal cost of production equals the market price (Rule 2).

Unless costs or price change, the firm will continue producing this output because it is doing as well as it can do, given the situation it faces. The firm is then said to be in **short-run equilibrium**, which is illustrated in Figure 12.3.

The market price to which the perfectly competitive firm responds is set by the forces of demand and supply. The individual firm, by adjusting its production to whatever price is ruling on the market, helps to determine market supply. The link between the behaviour of the firm and the behaviour of the competitive market is provided by the market supply curve.

The supply curve of the firm: The supply curve shows the relation between quantity supplied and market price. For each given price we need to ask what quantity will be supplied. This question may be answered by supposing that a price is specified and then determining how much each firm will choose to supply. Next a different price is specified and quantity supplied is again determined – and so on, until all possible prices have been considered. For prices below AVC, the firm will supply zero units (Rule 1). For prices above AVC, the firm will equate price and marginal cost (Rule 2).

FIGURE 12.2 Revenue Curves for a Firm in Perfect Competition

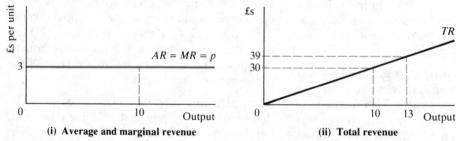

The demand curve for a perfectly competitive firm is a horizontal straight line. The lines graph the data from Table 12.1. Because price does not change, neither marginal nor average revenue varies with output – both are equal to price. When price is constant, total revenue is a rising straight line from the origin whose slope is given by the price.

FIGURE 12.3 The Short-run Equilibrium of a Firm in Perfect Competition

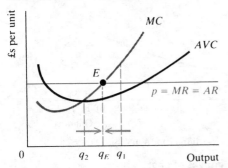

The firm chooses the output for which $p = MC$ above the level of AVC. When price equals marginal cost, as at output q_E, the firm loses profits if it either increases or decreases its output. At any point left of q_E, say q_2, price is greater than the marginal cost, and it pays to increase output (as indicated by the left-hand arrow). At any point to the right of q_E, say q_1, price is less than the marginal cost, and it pays to reduce output (as indicated by the right-hand arrow).

From this it follows that:

in perfect competition the segment of the firm's marginal cost curve that is above the AVC curve is the same as the firm's supply curve.

This result is shown in more detail in Figure 12.4.

Equilibrium of the Industry

The supply curve of the industry: Figure 12.5 illustrates the derivation of an industry supply curve for an example of only two firms. The important general result shown in that Figure is that:

the supply curve for a competitive industry is the horizontal sum of the marginal cost curves of all the individual firms in the industry.

This supply curve, based as it is on the short-run marginal cost curves of the firms in the industry, is the industry's **short-run supply curve**. In Chapter 5, we merely assumed the existence of upward-sloping, short-run, industry supply curves. We have now derived these curves for a competitive industry, and we have seen how they are related to the behaviour of individual, profit-maximizing firms.

Short-run price and output: The short-run equilibrium price and quantity for the industry is determined by the interaction of the industry supply curve that we have just derived, with the industry's demand curve. In such a perfectly competitive market no single buyer, or single

FIGURE 12.4 The Supply Curve for a Price-taking Firm

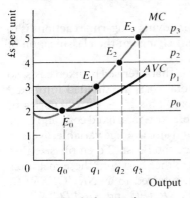

(i) Marginal cost and average variable cost curves

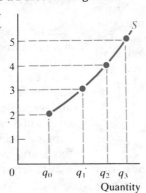

(ii) The supply curve

For a price-taking firm, the supply curve has the same shape as its MC curve above the level of AVC. The point E_0, where price p_0 equals AVC, is the shutdown point. For prices below £2, optimum output is zero, because the firm is better off if it produces nothing. As prices rise from £2 to £3 to £4 to £5, the firm increases its production from q_0 to q_1 to q_2 to q_3. If, e.g., price were £3, the firm would produce output q_1 rather than zero because it would be earning the contribution to fixed costs shown by the shaded rectangle.

The firm's supply curve is shown in (ii). It relates market price to the quantity the firm will produce and offer for sale. It has the same shape as the firm's MC curve for all prices above AVC.

FIGURE 12.5 The Supply Curve for a Group of Firms

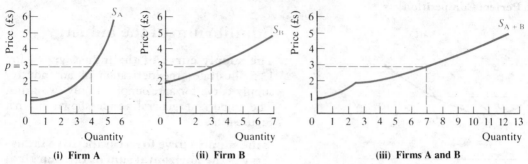

| (i) Firm A | (ii) Firm B | (iii) Firms A and B |

The industry supply curve is the horizontal sum of the supply curves of each of the firms in the industry. At a price of £3, firm A would supply 4 units and firm B would supply 3 units. Together, as shown in (iii), they would supply 7 units. In this example, because firm B does not enter the market at prices below £2, the supply curve S_{A+B} is identical to S_A up to price £2 and is the sum of $S_A + S_B$ above £2.

If there are hundreds of firms, the process is the same: each firm's supply curve (which is derived in the manner shown in Figure 12.4) shows what that firm will produce at each given price. The industry supply curve shows the sum of the quantities produced by all firms at each given price.

seller, can influence the market price significantly. Nonetheless, price is determined by the collective actions of all firms in the industry, as shown by the industry supply curve, and the collective actions of households, as shown by the industry's demand curve.

> **At the equilibrium market price, each firm is producing and selling a quantity for which its marginal cost equals the market price and no firm is motivated to change its output in the short run. Since total quantity demanded equals total quantity supplied, there is no reason for market price to change in the short run; the market, and all the firms in the industry, are in short-run equilibrium.**

Short-run Profitability of the Firm

We know that when the industry is in short-run equilibrium each competitive firm is maximizing its profits. We do not, however, know *how large* these profits are. It is one thing to know that a firm is doing as well as it can in particular circumstances; it is another thing to know how well it is doing.

Figure 12.6 shows three possible positions for a firm in short-run equilibrium. In all three cases, the firm is maximizing its profits; it is doing as well as it can, given the market price and its short-run costs. In part (i) the firm is suffering losses; in part (ii) it is just covering all costs; in part (iii) it is earning pure profits. All three of these are possible equilibrium positions in the short run – but *not* in the long run.

LONG-RUN EQUILIBRIUM

The first step in studying long-run reactions is to note an important change in the classification of costs.

The short run is characterised by fixed costs, so that the firm's total costs are divided into fixed and variable costs. This gives six categories of costs: total variable cost, total fixed cost, and their sum, total cost, and also average variable, average fixed, and average total cost. To emphasize that we are referring to the short run, these measures of cost are often referred to as *SRVC*, *SRFC*, *SRTC*, *SRAVC*, *SRAFC* and *SRATC*. Where there is no room for ambiguity, however, the short-run (*SR*) designation may be omitted.

The long run is characterized by the absence of fixed costs. All costs are variable, so there is no need to separate total costs into the fixed and variable categories. Thus, in the long run, there is only total cost and average total cost, which we refer to as *LRTC* and *LRAC*.

The concept of marginal cost applies both to the short run and to the long run. Both short-run marginal cost (*SRMC*) and long-run marginal cost (*LRMC*) refer to the change in total cost when output is varied one unit from its present level. In the short run, only some inputs, and hence only some input costs, can be varied. In the long run, all inputs, and hence all input costs, can be varied. Long-run marginal cost thus refers to the change in total cost resulting from a one unit change in output, after all factor inputs have been adjusted so as to produce the new output at the lowest possible cost.

The Long Run in Outline

The key to long-run equilibrium under perfect competition is entry and exit. We have seen that when firms are in *short-run* equilibrium they may

be making profits or losses or they may be just breaking even. Since costs include the opportunity cost of capital, firms that are just breaking even are doing as well as they could if they invested their capital elsewhere. Thus there will be no incentive for existing firms to leave the industry; neither will there be an incentive for new firms to enter the industry, because capital can earn the same return elsewhere in the economy. If, however, existing firms are earning profits over all costs, including the opportunity cost of capital, new capital will enter the industry to share in these profits. If existing firms are making losses, capital will leave the industry because a better return can be obtained elsewhere in the economy.

Let us consider the process in more detail. If all firms are in the position of the firm in Figure 12.6(iii), new firms will enter the industry, attracted by existing profits. Suppose that in response to high profits for 100 existing firms, 20 new firms enter. The market supply curve that formerly

FIGURE 12.6 Alternative Short-run Equilibrium Positions for a Firm in Perfect Competition

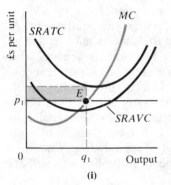 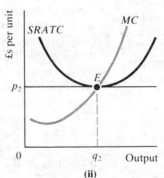 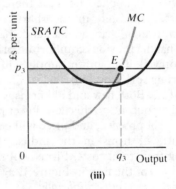

(i)	(ii)	(iii)

When it is in short-run equilibrium, a competitive firm may be suffering losses, breaking even or making profits. The diagrams show a firm with given costs faced with three alternative prices p_1, p_2 and p_3. In each part of the diagram, E is the point at which $MC = MR =$ price. Since in all three cases price exceeds *AVC*, the firm is in short-run equilibrium.

In part (i), price is p_1. Because price is below average total cost, the firm is suffering losses shown by the coloured area. Because price exceeds average variable cost, the firm continues to produce in the short run. Because price is less than *ATC*, the firm will not replace its capital as it wears out.

In part (ii), price is p_2 and the firm is just covering its total costs. It will replace its capital as it wears out since its revenue is covering the full opportunity cost of its capital.

In part (iii), price is p_3 and the firm is earning pure profits in excess of all its costs as shown by the shaded area. As in part (ii), the firm will replace its capital as it wears out.

FIGURE 12.7 The Effect of New Entrants on the Supply Curve

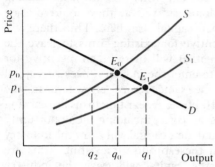

New entrants shift the supply curve to the right and lower the equilibrium price. Initial equilibrium is at E_0 with price p_0 and output q_0. The entry of new firms shifts the supply curve to S_1, the equilibrium price falls to p_1 while output rises to q_1. At this price, before entry, only q_2 would have been produced. The extra output is supplied by the new firms.

added up the outputs of 100 firms now must add up the outputs of 120 firms. Thus, at any price, more will be supplied because there are more suppliers. This shift in the short-run supply curve, with an unchanged market demand curve, means that the previous equilibrium price will no longer prevail. The shift in supply will cause the equilibrium price to fall, as is illustrated in Figure 12.7. Both new and old firms will have to adjust their outputs to this new, lower price.

Entry will proceed, and price will continue to fall, until all firms in the industry are just covering their total costs. Firms will then be in the position of the firm in Figure 12.6(ii), which is called a *zero-profit equilibrium.*

> **Profits in a competitive industry are a signal for the entry of new capital; the industry will expand, forcing price down until the profits earned by firms, old and new, fall to zero.**

If the firms in the industry are in the position of the firm in Figure 12.6(i), they are suffering losses. They are earning more than their variable costs, but the return that they are earning on their capital is less than the opportunity cost of this capital: the firms are not, therefore, covering their total costs. This is a signal for exit of capital.

As plant and equipment wears out, it will not be replaced. As a result, the industry's short-run supply curve shifts left and market price rises. Capital continues to exit and price continues to rise until the remaining firms can cover their total costs – that is, until they are all in the zero-profit equilibrium illustrated in Figure 12.6(ii). Exit then ceases.

> **Losses in a competitive industry are a signal for the exit of capital; the industry will contract, driving price up until the remaining firms are covering their total costs.**

In all of this we see profits fulfilling their function of allocating resources among the industries of the economy.

Marginal and intramarginal firms: When considering possible exit from an industry, it is sometimes useful to distinguish marginal from intramarginal firms. The marginal firm is just covering its full costs and would exit if price fell by even a small amount. The intramarginal firm is earning profits and would require a larger fall in price to persuade it to exit. In the pure abstract model of perfect competition, however, all firms are marginal firms in long-run equilibrium. All firms have access to the same technology and all, therefore, will have identical cost curves when enough time has passed for full adjustment of all capital to be made.[1] In long-run industry equilibrium, all firms are thus in position (ii) in Figure 12.6. If price falls below p_2 in that Figure all firms wish to withdraw. Exit must then be by some contrived process, such as random lot, since there is nothing in the theory to explain who will exit first.

In real-world situations, firms are not identical, since technology changes continually and different firms have different histories. A firm that has recently replaced its capital is likely to have more efficient, lower-cost plant and hence lower cost curves than a firm whose capital is

---

[1] If one firm has some special advantage, such as a patented production process or an unusually good manager, the principle of imputed opportunity cost requires that the extra revenues attributable to such advantages be included as a cost – since the patent or manager could be leased to other firms. This emphasizes once again that all firms have the same costs in long-run perfectly competitive equilibrium.

ageing. The details of each practical case will then determine the identity of the marginal firm that will exit first when price falls. For one example, assume that all firms have identical costs and differ only in the date at which they entered the industry. In this case, the firm whose capital comes up for replacement first will be the marginal firm. It will exit first because it will be the first to confront the long-run decision about replacing its capital in a situation where no firms are covering long-run opportunity costs.

The Response of a Perfectly Competitive Industry to a Change in Technology

As an illustration of the use of long-run analysis, consider the effects of technological progress on a competitive industry. Initially the industry is in long-run equilibrium where each firm is earning zero profits. Now assume that some technological development lowers the cost curves of newly built plants. The technology cannot be used by old plants because it must be *embodied* in new plants and equipment. Since price is just equal to the average total cost for the old plants, new plants will now be able to earn profits and they will be built immediately. But this expansion in

capacity shifts the short-run supply curve to the right and drives price down. The expansion in capacity and the fall in price will continue until price is equal to the *ATC* of the *new* plants. At this price, old plants will not be covering their long-run costs. As long as price exceeds their average variable cost, however, such plants will continue in production. As the outmoded plants wear out they will gradually disappear. Eventually a new long-run equilibrium will be established in which all plants use the new technology.

What happens in a competitive industry in which this type of technological change occurs not as a single isolated event but more or less continuously? Plants built in any one year will tend to have lower costs than plants built in any previous year. Figure 12.8 illustrates such an industry. It will exhibit a number of interesting characteristics.

One is that plants of different ages and different levels of efficiency will exist side by side. This is dramatically illustrated by the variety of vintages of steam turbine generators found in any long-established electricity industry. Critics who observe the continued use of older, less efficient plants and urge that the industry be modernized miss the point of economic efficiency. If the plant

FIGURE 12.8 Plants of Different Ages in an Industry with Continual Technical Progress

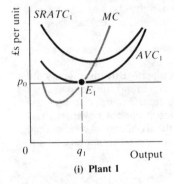 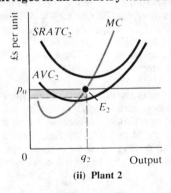 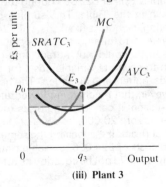

Entry of progressively lower-cost firms forces price down, but older plants with higher costs remain in the industry as long as price covers average variable cost. Plant 3 is the newest plant with the lowest costs. Long-run equilibrium price will be determined by the average total costs of plants of this type, since entry will continue as long as the owners of the newest plants expect to earn profits from them. Plant 1 is the oldest plant in operation; it is just covering its *AVC*, and if the price falls any further it will be closed down. Plant 2 is a plant of intermediate age. It is covering its variable costs and earning some contribution toward its fixed costs. In (ii) and (iii), the coloured areas shows the excess of revenues over variable costs.

is already there, it can be operated profitably as long as it can cover its variable costs. As long as a plant can produce goods that are valued by consumers at an amount above the value of the resources currently used up by its operation (variable costs), the value of society's total output is increased by producing these goods.

A second characteristic of such an industry is that price will be governed by the minimum *ATC* of the most efficient plants. Entry will continue until plants of the latest vintage are just expected to earn normal profits over their lifetimes. The benefits of the new technology are passed on to consumers because all units of the commodity, whether produced by new or old plants, are sold at a price that is related solely to the *ATC*s of the new plants. Owners of older plants find their returns over variable costs falling steadily as increasingly efficient plants drive the price down.

A third characteristic is that old plants will be discarded when the price falls below their *AVC*. This may occur well before the plants are physically worn out. In industries with continuous technical progress, capital is usually discarded because it is economically obsolete, not because it has physically worn out. This illustrates the

BOX 12.2 A PARABLE OF THE ESPLANADE HOTEL

Why do some resort hotels stay open in the off-season, even though to do so they must offer bargain rates that do not even cover their 'full costs'? Why do the managements of other hotels allow them to fall into disrepair even though they are able to attract enough customers to stay in business? Are the former being overly generous, and the latter overly parsimonious? No! both sets of owners may be responding rationally to the circumstances that they face.

To illustrate what is involved, consider the Esplanade Hotel at Quicksand-on-Sea. Its revenues and costs of operating during the in-season and off-season periods are shown in the Table. When charging the profit-maximizing price for its rooms, the hotel earns a return over its total variable costs of £22,000 during the in-season, as shown in the Table. This surplus goes towards meeting the hotel's fixed costs of £24,000.

Were it to charge the same rates in the off-season, it could not attract enough customers even to cover its variable costs for such items as maids, porters and managers. The hotel discovers, however, that by charging lower rates during the off-season, it can let some of its rooms and earn revenues of £20,000. Its costs of staying open are £18,000, and if it allocated the same portion of its fixed costs of £24,000 to each month that it stays open, it would not be covering its total costs (fixed plus variable costs) in the off-season. But it will be earning a surplus of £2,000 over variable costs. This surplus, though relatively small, can go towards covering some part of the fixed costs. Therefore, the hotel stays open the whole year round, offering bargain rates to grateful guests. (Indeed, if it were to close in the winter, it would not be able to cover its total fixed and variable costs solely through its in-season operations.)

Now assume that the off-season revenue falls to £19,000 (everything else the same). The short-run condition for staying open, *TR > TVC*, is met for the in- and the off-seasons. But the long-run condition is not, since the *TR* over the whole year of £77,000 is less than the total cost of £78,000, all of which are variable in the long run. The hotel will remain open as long as it can do so with its present capital – it will produce in the short run. But it will not pay the owners to replace the capital as it wears out.

The hotel will become one of those run-down hotels where guests ask 'why don't they do something about this place?' But the owners are behaving optimally in operating the hotel as long as it covers its variable costs, but not putting more investment into it since it cannot cover its fixed costs. Sooner or later the fixed capital will become too old to be run, or at least to attract customers, and the hotel will be closed.

THE ESPLANADE HOTEL. Total Costs and Revenues (£s)

Season	Total revenue (*TR*)	Total variable costs (*TVC*)	Net revenue (*TR–TVC*)
In-season	58,000	36,000	22,000
Off-season	20,000	18,000	2,000
Total	78,000	54,000	24,000

Note. Fixed costs are £24,000 per annum.

economic meaning of obsolete:

> **old capital is obsolete when its average variable cost exceeds the average total cost of new capital.**

Box 12.2 gives an example that illustrates both the short and the long-run conditions for a firm to remain in an industry.

A More Detailed Analysis of the Long Run

For some purposes it is important to understand some complications omitted from the foregoing broad treatment. The rest of this chapter will be devoted to a more detailed examination of the long-run behaviour of a perfectly competitive industry. It can, however, be omitted without loss of continuity.

Consider the position of the firms and the industry when both are in long-run equilibrium. There is no change that any firm could make, over the short or the long run, that would increase its profits. This requirement can be stated as three distinct conditions.

(1) *No firm will want to vary the output of its existing plants*: short-run marginal cost ($SRMC$) must equal price.

(2) *Profits earned by existing plants must be zero.* This implies that short-run ATC must equal price – that is, firms must be in the position of the firm in Figure 12.6(ii).

(3) *No firm can earn profits by building a plant of a different size.* This implies that each existing firm must be producing at the lowest point on its long-run average cost curve.

We have already seen why the first two conditions must hold. The reasoning behind the third condition is shown in Figure 12.9. Although the firm shown in that Figure is in short-run equilibrium, it is not in long-run equilibrium because its $LRAC$ curve lies below the market price at some higher levels of output. The firm can, therefore, increase its profits by building a plant of larger size, thereby lowering its average total costs. Since the firm is a price-taker, this change will increase its profits.

A price-taking firm is in long-run equilibrium only when it is producing at the minimum points on its $LRAC$ curve.

FIGURE 12.9 Short-run versus Long-run Equilibrium of a Competitive Firm

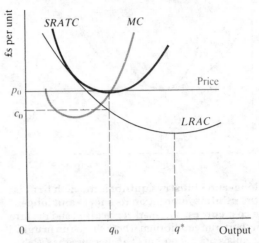

A competitive firm that is not at the minimum point on its $LRAC$ curve cannot be in long-run equilibrium. A competitive firm with short-run cost curves $SRATC$ and MC faces a market price of p_0. The firm produces q_0 where MC equals price and total costs are just being covered. However, the firm's long-run cost curve lies below its short-run curve at output q_0. The firm could produce output q_0 at cost c_0 by building a larger plant so as to take advantage of economies of scale. Profits would rise because average total costs of c_0 would then be less than price p_0. The firm cannot be in long-run equilibrium at any output below q^* because, with any such output, average total costs can be reduced by building a larger plant. The output q^* is the *minimum efficient scale* of the firm.

All three of the conditions listed above are fulfilled when each firm in the industry is in the position shown in Figure 12.10.[1]

The Long-run Response of a Perfectly Competitive Industry to a Change in Demand

Now suppose that the demand for the product increases. Price will rise to equate demand with the industry's short-run supply. Each firm will expand output until its short-run marginal cost

---

[1] The text discussion implies that all existing firms and all new entrants face identical $LRAC$ curves. This merely means that all firms face the same set of factor prices and have the same technology available to them. Do not forget that we are in the long run *where technological knowledge is given and constant*, and all firms have had a chance to adjust their capital to the best that is available.

FIGURE 12.10 Equilibrium of a Firm When the Industry is in Equilibrium

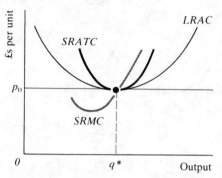

In long-run industry equilibrium, each firm is at the minimum point on its short- and long-run cost curves. The market price is p_0 and the firm is in short-run equilibrium where short-run marginal cost equals price at output of q^*. Because the *LRAC* lies above p_0 everywhere except at q^*, the firm has no incentive to move to another point on its *LRAC* curve by altering the size of its plant.

once again equals price. Each firm will earn profits as a result of the rise in price, and the profits will induce new firms to enter the industry. This will shift the short-run supply curve to the right and force down the price. Entry will continue until all firms are once again just covering average total costs.

Now consider a fall in demand. The industry starts with firms in long-run equilibrium as shown in Figure 12.10 and the market demand curve shifts left and price falls. There are two possible consequences.

First, the decline in demand forces price below *ATC* but leaves it above *AVC*. Firms are then in the position shown in Figure 12.6(i). They can cover their variable costs and earn some return on their capital, so they remain in production for as long as their existing plant and equipment lasts. Exit will occur, however, as old capital wears out and is not replaced. As firms exit, the short-run supply curve shifts left and market price rises. This continues until the remaining firms in the industry can cover their total costs. At this point, it will pay to replace capital as it wears out, and the industry will stop declining. This adjustment may take a long time, for the industry shrinks in size only as existing plant and equipment wears out.

The second possibility is that the decline in demand is large enough to push price below the level of *AVC*. Now firms cannot even cover their variable costs and some will shut down immediately. Reduction in capital devoted to production in the industry occurs rapidly because some existing capacity is scrapped or shifted to other uses. The decline in the number of firms reduces supply and raises the equilibrium price. Once the price rises enough to allow the remaining firms to cover their variable costs, the rapid withdrawal of capital ceases. Further exit occurs more slowly, as described in the previous paragraph.

Entry of new capital into a profitable industry can take place only as fast as new plants can be built and new equipment installed. Exit of existing capital from an unprofitable industry with losses will occur very quickly when price is less than average variable cost, but only at the rate at which old plant and equipment wears out when price exceeds average variable cost.

This adjustment process is examined in greater detail in the following section.

The Long-run Industry Supply Curve

Possible adjustments of the industry to the kinds of changes in demand just discussed are shown by the **long-run industry supply (*LRS*) curve**. This curve shows the relation between equilibrium price and the output firms will be willing to supply after all desired entry or exit has occurred.

The long-run supply curve connects positions of long-run equilibrium after all demand-induced changes have occurred.

When induced changes in factor prices are considered, it is possible for the *LRS* curve to be horizontal or positively or negatively sloped. The various cases are illustrated in Figure 12.11.

In Figure 12.11(i) the long-run supply curve is horizontal. This indicates that given time, the industry will adjust its size to provide whatever quantity is demanded at a constant price equal to the lowest possible average total costs. An industry with a horizontal long-run supply curve is said to be a *constant-cost industry*.

While conditions of constant *LRS* may exist, such conditions are not necessary. This case occurs when the expansion of the industry leaves the long-run cost curves of existing firms unchanged, which requires that the industry's input prices do not change as the whole industry's output expands or contracts. Since new firms have access to the same technology and face the same factor prices, their cost curves will not be higher than those of existing firms. Under these circumstances, the long-run equilibrium with price equal to minimum long-run average total cost can only be re-established when price returns to its original level.

Changing factor prices and rising long-run supply curves: When an industry expands its output, it needs more inputs. The increase in demand for these inputs may bid up their prices.[1]

If costs rise with increasing levels of industry output, so too must the price at which the producers are able to cover their costs. As the industry expands, the short-run supply curve shifts outwards but the firms' $SRATC$ curves shift upwards because of rising factor prices. The expansion of the industry comes to a halt when price is equal to minimum $LRAC$ for existing firms. This must occur at a higher price than ruled before the expansion began, as illustrated in part (ii) of Figure 12.11. A competitive industry with rising long-run supply prices is often called a *rising-cost industry*.

Can the long-run supply curve decline?: So far we have suggested that the long-run supply curve may be horizontal or positively

---

[1] In a fully employed economy the expansion of one industry implies the contraction of some other industry. What happens to factor prices depends on the proportions in which the expanding and the contracting industries use the factors. The relative price of the factor used intensively by the expanding industry will rise, causing the costs of the expanding industry to rise relative to those of the contracting industry. In a two-sector, two-factor model, a rising long-run industry supply curve is normal because of the effect that changes in industry outputs have on relative factor prices.

FIGURE 12.11 Long-run Industry Supply Curves

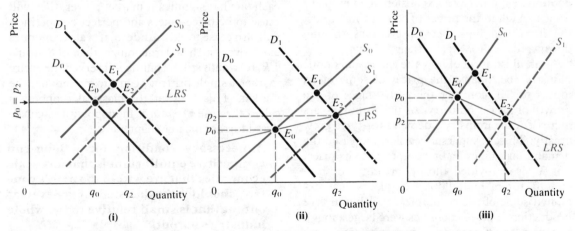

The long-run industry supply curve may be horizontal, or positively or negatively sloped. In all three parts the initial curves are at D_0 and S_0, yielding equilibrium at E_0 with price p_0 and quantity q_0. A rise in demand shifts the demand curve to D_1, taking the short-run equilibrium to E_1. New firms now enter the industry, shifting the supply curve outwards, pushing down price until pure profits are no longer being earned. At this point the supply curve is S_1 and the new equilibrium is E_2 with price at p_2 and quantity q_2.

In part (i), price returns to its original level, making the long-run supply curve horizontal. In part (ii), profits are eliminated before price falls to its original level, giving the LRS curve a positive slope. In part (iii), the price falls below its original level before profits return to normal, giving the LRS curve a negative slope.

sloped. Could it ever decline, thereby indicating that higher outputs were associated with lower prices in long-run equilibrium?

It is tempting to answer yes, because of the opportunities of more efficient scales of operation using greater mechanization and more effective specialization of labour. But this answer would not be correct for perfectly competitive industries, because each firm in long-run equilibrium must already be at the lowest point on its *LRAC* curve. If a firm could lower its costs by building a larger, more mechanized plant, it would be profitable to do so without waiting for an increase in demand. Since any single firm can sell all it wishes at the going market price, it will be profitable to expand the scale of its operations as long as its *LRAC* is falling.

The scale economies that we have just considered are within the control of the firm; they are said to be **internal economies**. A perfectly competitive industry might, however, have falling long-run costs if industries that supply its inputs have increasing returns to scale. Such effects are outside the control of the perfectly competitive firm and are called **external economies**. Whenever expansion of an industry leads to a fall in the prices of some of its inputs, the firms will find their cost curves shifting downwards as they expand their outputs.

As an illustration of how the expansion of one industry could cause the prices of some of its inputs to fall, consider the early stages of the growth of the car industry. As the output of cars increased, the industry's demand for tyres grew greatly. This, as suggested earlier, increased the demand for rubber and tended to raise its price, but it also provided the opportunity for tyre manufacturers to build larger plants that exploited some of the economies available in tyre production. These economies were large enough to offset any factor-price increases, and tyre prices charged to car manufacturers fell. Thus car costs fell, because of lower prices of an important input. This case is illustrated in part (iii) of Figure 12.11. An industry that has a negatively sloped long-run supply curve is often called a *falling-cost industry*.

Notice that, although the economies were external to the car industry, they were internal to the tyre industry. This in turn requires that the supplying industry not be perfectly competitive.

If it were, all its scale economies would already have been exploited. So this case refers to a perfectly competitive industry that uses an input produced by a non-competitive industry, whose own scale economies have not yet been fully exploited because demand is insufficient. An example is provided by perfectly competitive agricultural industries buying their farm machinery from an industry dominated by a few large firms.

Does a Long-run Competitive Equilibrium Exist?[1]

A competitive firm will never be in equilibrium on the falling part of its *LRAC* – if price is given and costs can be reduced by increasing the scale of output, profits can also be increased by doing so. Thus firms will grow in size until all scale economies are exhausted. Provided that the output that yields the minimum *LRAC* for each firm is small relative to the industry's total output, the industry will contain a large number of firms and will remain competitive. If, however, reaching the minimum *LRAC* makes firms so large that each one has significant market power, they will cease to be price-takers and perfect competition will also cease to exist. Indeed, if scale economies exist over such a large range that one firm's *LRAC* would still be falling if it served the entire market, a single firm may come to monopolize the market. This is what the classical economists called the case of *natural* monopoly; it is considered further in later chapters.

A necessary condition for a long-run competitive equilibrium is that any scale economies that are within the firm's control should be exhausted at a level of output that is small relative to the whole industry's output.

Only if the firm's *LRAC* curve is U-shaped will there be a determinate size of the firm in a competitive industry. To see why, assume instead that *LRAC* falls to a minimum at some level of output and then remains constant for all larger outputs. All firms will have to be at least the

----

[1] This section deals with a difficult point that is often postponed until intermediate or even advanced courses. It may be omitted without loss of continuity.

minimum size, but they can be just that size or much larger, since price will equal *LRAC* for any output above the minimum efficient size. In other words, there will then be no unique size for the firm.

There are very good reasons why the *LRAC* curve for a single plant may be U-shaped. Modern technology often results in lower average costs for large, automated factories compared with smaller factories in which a few workers use relatively unsophisticated capital equipment. As a single plant becomes too large, however, costs rise because of the sheer difficulty of planning for, and controlling the behaviour of, a vast integrated operation. Thus we have no problem accounting for a U-shaped cost curve for the *plant*.

What of the U-shaped cost curve for the *firm*? A declining portion will occur for the same reason that the *LRAC* for one plant declines when the firm is so small that it operates only one plant. Now, however, let the firm be operating one plant at the output where its *LRAC* is a minimum. (Call that output q^*.) What if the firm decides to double its output to $2q^*$? If it tries to build a vast plant with twice the output of the optimal-size plant, the firm's average total cost of production may rise (because the vast plant has higher costs than a plant of the optimal size). But the firm has the option of *replicating* its first plant in a physically separate location. If the firm obtains a second parcel of land, builds an identical second plant, staffs it identically, and allows its production to be managed independently, there seems no reason why the second plant's minimum *LRAC* should be different from that of the first plant. *Because the firm can replicate plants and have them managed independently, there seems no reason why any firm, faced with constant factor prices, should have a rising LRAC, at least for integer multiples[1] of the output produced by the optimal-sized plant.*

In the modern theory of perfect competition, a U-shaped cost curve for a *firm* is merely assumed. Without it – although a competitive equilibrium may exist for an arbitrary number of firms – there is nothing to determine the equilibrium size of the firm and hence the number of firms in the industry. If all firms have constant *LRAC*s, then equilibrium requires that price equals *LRAC*, but the equilibrium output can just as well be produced by a large number of firms each producing a small output or a small number of firms each producing a large output.

---

[1] This means multiplying the output of the optimal-sized plant by any whole number, i.e. building and fully utilizing that number of complete new plants. It rules out multiplying it by some fractional number such as 7/2 which would mean only partially utilizing one plant.

SUMMARY

1. A firm maximizes profits by producing the output where the marginal cost curve cuts the marginal revenue from below or by producing nothing if average variable cost exceeds price at all outputs.
2. Competitive *behaviour* refers to the extent that individual firms compete with each other to sell their products. Competitive *market structure* refers to the power that individual firms have over the market – perfect competition occurring where firms have no market power and hence no need to react to each other.
3. Perfect competition requires price-taking behaviour and freedom of entry and exit.
4. A perfectly competitive firm is a quantity adjustor, facing a perfectly elastic demand curve at the given market price and maximizing profits by equating its marginal cost to that price.
5. The supply curve of a firm in perfect competition is its marginal cost curve, and the supply curve of a perfectly competitive industry is the sum of the marginal

cost curves of all its firms. The intersection of this curve with the market demand curve for the industry's product determines market price.

6. Long-run industry equilibrium requires that each individual firm be producing at the minimum point of its *LRAC* curve and be making zero profits.

7. The long-run industry supply curve may be (i) positively sloped, if input prices are driven up by the industry's expansion, (ii) horizontal, if plants can be replicated and factor prices remain constant, or (iii) negatively sloped, if some other industry that is not perfectly competitive produces an input under conditions of falling long-run costs.

TOPICS FOR REVIEW

- Competitive behaviour and competitive market structure
- Behavioural rules for the profit-maximizing firm
- Price-taking and a horizontal demand curve
- Average revenue, marginal revenue, and price under perfect competition
- Relation of the industry supply curve to its firms' marginal cost curves
- The role of entry and exit in achieving equilibrium
- Short-run and long-run equilibrium of firms and industries

A Mathematical Derivation of the Rules of Profit Maximization

In this brief Appendix we provide formal derivations of the three rules for profit maximization. The first derivation uses only algebra and can be read by anyone. The second and third use elementary calculus and should not be attempted by those who are unfamiliar with simple derivatives.

Condition 1: Profits, π, are defined as follows:

$$\pi = R - (F + V) \ ,$$

where R is total revenue, F is total fixed cost and V is total variable cost. Now let subscript n stand for a state where there is no production and p for one where there is production. It pays the firm to produce if there is at least one level of production for which

$$\pi_p \geqslant \pi_n \ .$$

When the firm does not produce, R and V are zero, so the above condition becomes

$$R - F - V \geqslant -F$$

or

$$R \geqslant V.$$

Dividing both sides by output, Q, we get: price $\geqslant$ AVC.

Condition 2:

$$\pi = R - C \ ,$$

where C is total cost $(F + V)$. Both revenues and costs vary with output, i.e. $R = R(Q)$ and $C = C(Q)$. Thus we may write

$$\pi = R(Q) - C(Q) \ .$$

A necessary condition for the maximization of profits is[1]

$$\frac{d\pi}{dQ} = R'(Q) - C'(Q) = 0$$

or

$$R'(Q) = C'(Q) \ .$$

But these derivatives define marginal revenue and marginal cost, so we have

$$MR = MC \ .$$

Condition 3: To ensure that we have a maximum and not a minimum for profits, we require

$$\frac{d^2\pi}{dQ^2} = R''(Q) - C''(Q) = \frac{dMR}{dQ} - \frac{dMC}{dQ} < 0$$

or

$$\frac{dMR}{dQ} < \frac{dMC}{dQ} \ ,$$

which means that the algebraic value of the slope of the marginal cost curve must exceed, at the point of intersection, the algebraic value of the slope of the marginal revenue curve. This translates into the geometric statement that the marginal cost curve should cut the marginal revenue curve from below.

---

[1] Note the convenient use of a prime for a derivative. Thus for the function $F(X)$, the two notations d/dX and $F'(X)$ mean the same thing and d^2/dX^2 and $F''(X)$ mean the same thing.

13

Monopoly

The market structure of **monopoly** is at the opposite extreme from perfect competition. It exists when an industry is in the hands of a single producer. In the case of perfect competition, there are so many individual producers that no one of them has any power whatsoever over the market; any one firm can vary its production without affecting the market price significantly. A monopoly, on the other hand, has power to influence the market price.

A SINGLE-PRICE MONOPOLY

In the first half of this chapter we study monopolies that must charge a single price for the goods that they sell; in the second half we study monopolies that can sell their goods at different prices either to different classes of customers or in different geographical markets.

In contrast to a firm selling in a perfectly competitive market, a monopoly firm is a price-setter, not a price-taker. Since it is the only producer of its product, the demand curve that it faces *is* the market demand curve for that product, and it can pick any price-quantity combination on that curve. The monopolist is sometimes said to be able to *administer* its price. This means that, unlike the perfect competitor, it can, and usually does, select its own price.

Revenue curves for a monopoly: A monopoly firm that charges the same price to all its customers faces an average revenue curve which is the same as the market demand curve. Since this curve has a negative slope, sale of an extra unit forces down the price at which *all* units can be sold. Thus the sale of an extra unit results in a net addition to revenue of an amount less than its own selling price. This important relation is illustrated arithmetically in Table 13.1 and geometrically in Figure 13.1.

> **Whenever the demand curve slopes downward, the marginal revenue associated with an increase in the rate of sales by one unit per period will be less than the price at which that unit is sold.**

Figure 13.2 shows how the total, average and marginal revenue curves, and demand elasticity, are related along a straight-line demand curve.

TABLE 13.1 Total, Average and Marginal Revenue Illustrated

Price $p = AR$	Quantity q	$TR = p \times q$	$MR = \Delta TR/\Delta q$
£9.10	9	£81.90	
£9.00	10	£90.00	£8.10
£8.90	11	£97.90	£7.90

Marginal revenue is less than price because price must be lowered to sell an extra unit. Consider, for example, the marginal revenue of the 11th unit. This is total revenue when 11 units are sold minus total revenue when 10 units are sold. The result is £7.90, which is less than the price of £8.90 at which all 11 units are sold. To see why, notice that to increase sales from 10 to 11 units, the price on all units sold must be reduced from £9.00 to £8.90. The net addition to revenue is the £8.90 gained from selling the extra unit minus £0.10 lost on each of the 10 units already being sold: £8.90 − (£0.10 × 10) = £7.90.

Marginal revenue is shown displaced by half a line to emphasize that it represents the effect on revenue of the *change* in sales.

FIGURE 13.1 The Effect on Revenue of an Increase in Quantity Sold

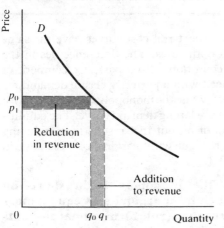

Because the demand curve has a negative slope, marginal revenue is less than price. A reduction of price from p_0 to p_1 increases sales by one unit from q_0 to q_1 units. The revenue from the extra unit sold is shown as the lighter shaded area. But to sell this unit, it is necessary to reduce the price on each of the q_0 units previously sold. The loss in revenue is shown as the darker shaded area. Marginal revenue of the extra unit is equal to the *difference* between the two areas.

FIGURE 13.2 Total, Average and Marginal Revenue Curves and Elasticity of Demand

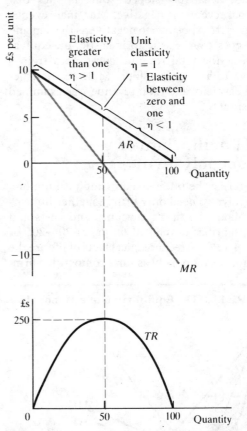

When *TR* is rising, *MR* is positive and demand is elastic. When *TR* is falling, *MR* is negative, and demand is inelastic. In this example, for outputs from 0 to 50, marginal revenue is positive, elasticity is greater than unity and total revenue is rising. For outputs from 50 to 100, marginal revenue is negative, elasticity is less than unity and total revenue is falling.

Consider first that part of the demand curve where elasticity is greater than one. This means that total revenue rises as quantity increases, and hence the total revenue curve is positively sloped. Because total revenue is increasing as quantity is increasing, marginal revenue is positive. Next consider the point at which elasticity of demand is exactly unity. Here total revenue remains constant as quantity sold increases. This implies that marginal revenue is zero. Consider finally the part of the demand curve where elasticity is less than one. This means that total revenue falls as quantity increases, and hence the total revenue curve is negatively sloped. This implies that marginal revenue is negative. Marginal revenue thus goes from positive to negative as the demand curve goes from elastic to inelastic, or, equivalently, as the total revenue curve goes from a positive to a negative slope. (The relation between elasticity and total revenue was examined in Chapter 6.)

The Equilibrium of a Monopoly Firm

To describe the profit-maximizing position of a monopoly, we need only bring together information about the firm's revenues and costs and apply the rules developed on pages 204–205 of Chapter 12. The technological facts of life are the same for the monopoly as for a competitive firm,

FIGURE 13.3   The Equilibrium of a Monopoly

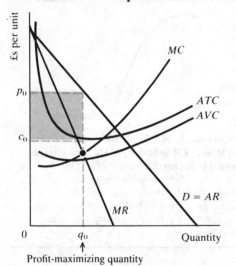

The monopoly maximizes its profits by producing where marginal cost equals marginal revenue. The monopoly produces the output q_0 for which marginal revenue equals marginal cost (Rule 2). At this output, price of p_0 – which is determined by the demand curve – exceeds average variable cost (Rule 1). Profits per unit are the difference between the average revenue of p_0 and the average total cost of c_0. Total profits are the profits per unit of $p_0 - c_0$ multiplied by the output of q_0, which is the shaded area.

FIGURE 13.4   Alternative Profit Possibilities for a Monopolist

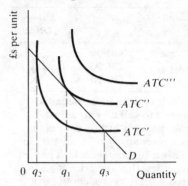

Profit maximization means that the monopoly is doing as well as it can do, given the cost and demand curves that it faces; it does not mean that profits are being earned. The monopolist faces a demand curve of D. Three alternative cost curves are considered. With the curve ATC''', there is no positive output at which the monopolist can avoid making losses. With the curve ATC'', the monopolist covers all costs at output q_1, where the ATC curve is tangent to the D curve. With the curve ATC', profits can be made by producing at any output between q_2 and q_3. (The profit-maximizing output will be some point between q_2 and q_3, where $MR = MC$, which is not shown on the diagram.)

so that the short-run cost curves have the same shapes in both cases. The difference lies in the demand conditions. Each perfectly competitive firm is faced with a perfectly elastic demand for its product, while the monopoly firm is faced with a downward-sloping demand curve. The equilibrium level of output that results from equating marginal revenue with marginal cost is shown in Figure 13.3.

> When the monopoly is in short-run equilibrium, marginal cost equals marginal revenue (rule 2); marginal cost cuts marginal revenue from below (rule 3); and price is greater than average variable cost (rule 1).

Two common misconceptions about monopoly profits need to be cleared up at this point. First, nothing guarantees that a monopoly will make profits in the short run. Figure 13.4 illustrates this by showing three alternative average total cost curves: one where the monopolist can earn pure profits, one where it can just cover its full costs, and one where it makes losses at any level of output.

The second common misconception about monopoly profits is that a monopoly that is not maximizing its profits must be making losses. Figure 13.4 refutes this misconception by showing a demand and cost curve for which the monopolist can make profits over a range of outputs, only one of which maximizes these profits.

Firm and Industry, Short Run and Long Run

Since a monopoly firm is the only producer in an industry, there is no need to have a separate theory of the firm and the industry. The monopoly firm *is* the industry.

Absence of a short-run supply curve under monopoly: Now consider the relation between the price of the product and the quantity supplied under monopoly. In perfect competition there is a unique relation between price and quantity supplied, which depends only on each firm's marginal cost curve. It is the supply curve

for each firm, and aggregation produces the supply curve for the industry. As with all profit-maximizing firms, the monopolist equates marginal cost to marginal revenue; but marginal revenue does not equal price. Hence the monopoly does *not* equate marginal cost to price. In order to know the amount produced at any given price, we need to know the demand curve as well as the marginal cost curve. Under these circumstances it is possible for different demand conditions to cause a given output to be sold at different prices. It is also possible for a given price to be associated with different outputs. The two parts of Figure 13.5 illustrate these two possibilities.

> **In monopoly, there is no unique relation between market price and quantity supplied.**

Box 13.1 deals with an interesting variation of monopoly theory, the pricing of limited editions.

Absence of long-run entry: In a monopolized industry, as in a perfectly competitive one, profits provide an incentive for new firms to enter. If a profitable monopoly is to persist in the long run, other firms must not enter the industry.

FIGURE 13.5 The Absence of a Supply Curve under Monopoly

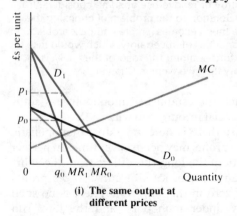
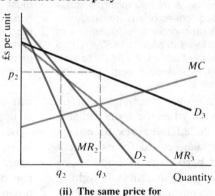

(i) The same output at different prices

(ii) The same price for different outputs

When a firm faces a negatively sloped demand curve, there is no unique relation between the price that it charges and the quantity that it sells. In part (i), the demand curves D_0 and D_1 both have marginal revenue curves that intersect the marginal cost curve at output q_0. But because the demand curves are different, q_0 is sold at p_0 when the demand curve is D_0, and at p_1 when the demand curve is D_1.

In part (ii), the marginal revenue curves MR_2 and MR_3 intersect the marginal cost curve at different outputs, q_2 and q_3. Because the two demand curves have different slopes, both of these outputs are sold at the same price, p_2.

BOX 13.1 DEMAND FOR ONCE-OFF PRODUCTION

An interesting case of monopoly pricing occurs with 'limited editions'. These are art works – sometimes lithographs, etchings and woodcuts by famous artists and sometimes products with less artistic merit, as in the following examples.

One has only to pick up a London telephone directory to see the words 'Limited Edition Print Offer: See inside back cover' in the bottom right-hand corner of a signed coloured sketch (portraying Buckingham Palace, the Tower of London, St Paul's Cathedral or the Houses of Parliament) which decorates the front cover of each of the four volumes. Information on the inside cover reveals that the four watercolours were 'specially commissioned' and would be reproduced 'in a limited edition of 500 prints' to be sold at £25 each or £85 for the set of four. 'Only 500 prints will be made of each image following which the plates will be destroyed.' This suggests that British Telecom feels that limiting the quantity supplied to 500 is necessary to make £25 a reasonable price, in the sense that the quantity demanded at £25 would be around 500, and that making the prints more plentiful would require a significantly lower price in order to 'clear the market'. Of course the estimates of market demand are slightly complicated by the possibility of buying individual prints *or* a set of four prints, but the same principle applies.

Similar examples can be seen in the booklets sent to credit-card users with their monthly statements. A Wedgwood 'collector's plate produced on fine bone china' and depicting 'Meadows of Wheatfields' was offered in March 1987 (with a statement 'Offer closes 15th May 1987') to holders of Midland Bank's *Access* card, with the promise that production would be 'limited to 150 firing days' and that a numbered certificate would accompany the plate. In fact, the sellers must have overestimated the quantity that would be demanded at their price of £16.65 (including postage and packing) as the offer was repeated in October 1987 ('Offer closes 7th December 1987'). Analysing this case helps to illustrate the flexibility of theory when used imaginatively. The normal demand curve is for a repeated flow of purchases, period after period. In this case, the demand is for a stock to be produced and purchased once only. Presumably, however, the smaller the total number of items produced the more people will value each item and the higher the price that can be charged. This gives rise to a negatively sloped demand curve.

If producers know the curve exactly and know their marginal cost of production, choosing the profit-maximizing price/quantity combination is simple. They equate marginal cost with marginal revenue. But since production and sales are not repeated period after period, producers have no chance to learn the shape of the demand curve. They must guess on the basis of the sales of earlier, more or less similar limited editions. What if they guess wrong? If they set the price too low, they will sell all their output but not at its profit-maximizing price. If they set the price too high, they will be left with unsold output which they must destroy or readvertise at some considerable expense. Solution to the problem of choosing the best price then becomes a more complex problem in the economics of uncertainty which would take us much further along the road of the analysis of uncertainty than we went in Chapter 9.

Circumstances that protect the monopolist, by discouraging entry even when the monopolist is earning profits, are called **barriers to entry**. These barriers may take several forms. Patent laws may create and perpetuate monopolies by conferring on the patent-holder the sole right to produce a particular commodity. The government may grant a firm a charter or a franchise that prohibits competition by law. Monopolies may also arise because of economies of scale. The established firm may retain a monopoly through a cost advantage because it can produce at a lower cost than could any new, smaller competitor. A monopoly may also be perpetuated by force: potential competitors can be intimidated by threats ranging from sabotage to a price-cutting war which the established monopoly has sufficient financial resources to win.

Because there is no entry into a monopolistic industry, profits may persist over time. In perfect competition, the long run differs from the short run because the process of entry forces profits down to zero in the long run. There is no such tendency under monopoly, and the long run differs from the short run only in terms of the cost curve on which the monopolist is operating. Consider a monopoly fully adjusted to a given demand curve: the appropriate sized plant has been constructed and *long-run marginal cost* has been equated to marginal revenue. Now assume that there is a permanent rise in demand. The best the firm can do in the short run is to work its existing plant more intensively, expanding output until the short-run marginal cost curve associated with the fixed plant intersects the marginal revenue curve. In the long run, however, a larger plant could be built so that the monopoly is again in a position at which long-run marginal cost equals marginal revenue.

A PRICE-DISCRIMINATING MONOPOLY

So far in this chapter we have assumed that the monopoly charges the same price for every unit of its product no matter to whom, or where, the product is sold. Other situations are also possible. Milk is often sold at one price if it is for drinking, but at a lower price if it is to be used to make ice-cream or cheese. Doctors in private practice, solicitors and business consultants sometimes vary their fees according to the incomes of their clients. Cinemas and airlines sometimes charge lower prices for children and those over 65. Firms often sell their products more cheaply abroad than at home. Electrical companies in many countries sell electricity more cheaply for industrial use than for home use. **Price discrimination** occurs when firms sell different units of their output at different prices *for reasons not associated with differences in costs*.

Why Price Discrimination Pays

A formal analysis of price discrimination is given in the Appendix to this chapter. The key point is that price discrimination allows sellers to capture some of the *consumers' surplus* that would otherwise go to buyers. This can be captured by two types of discrimination, one among units sold to individual buyers, the other among buyers. (You should now review the discussion of consumers' surplus on pages 90–95.)

Discrimination among units sold to one buyer: Look back to Table 6.4 on page 90. If the firm could sell each unit separately, it could extract all the consumers' surplus. In the example it would sell the first unit for £3.00, the second for £1.50, the third for £1.00 and so on until the eighth was sold for £0.30. This would yield a total revenue of £8.10, rather than a mere

£2.40 when all eight units are sold at a common price of £0.30.

Now assume that the firm cannot charge a separate price for each unit that it sells to the consumer, but it can charge two prices. If it sells the first four units at £0.80 and the second four at £0.30, it earns £4.40. This is less than it gets when it charges a separate price on each unit, but substantially more than the revenue of £2.40 that it gets by selling all eight units at a single price.

Discrimination among buyers: Consider a simple example where four buyers each wish to buy one unit per period but are prepared to pay different prices. The first buyer is prepared to pay a maximum price of £4, the second buyer £3, the third £2, and the fourth £1. If the firm wishes to serve all four buyers and must charge a single price, it will charge £1. This yields a total revenue of £4. The first buyer gets a consumers' surplus of £3 (the £4 he is prepared to pay minus the £1 he does pay). The second and third buyers get surpluses of £2 and £1 respectively. Total consumers' surplus is thus £6. If the monopoly firm could sell to each individual separately, it could charge the first £4, the second £3, the third £2 and the fourth £1. Total revenue would then be £10 and the firm would have appropriated the whole of the consumers' surplus for itself. If, however, the firm could charge only two prices, it might charge buyers one and two £3 and buyers three and four £1. This makes the firm's total revenue £8 and leaves £2 of consumers' surplus in the hands of the buyers (£1 for the first and £1 for the third buyer).

Figure 13.6 goes beyond this simple numerical example. It shows that, if the monopolist can discriminate among units sold, it can always earn more than when a single price is charged.

> **For any given level of output there always exists some system of discriminatory prices that will provide a higher total revenue than will any given single price.**

Thus whenever it is possible, price discrimination will always pay because it can be used to increase the revenue associated with any level of output.

Discrimination and total output: Not only does price discrimination increase a monopoly's total revenue for any given output, it will also

FIGURE 13.6 Price Discrimination

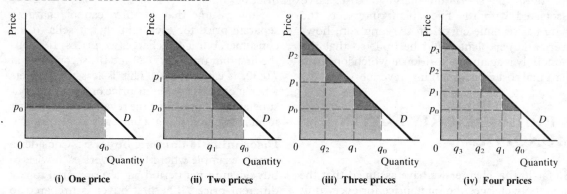

| (i) One price | (ii) Two prices | (iii) Three prices | (iv) Four prices |

Price discrimination turns consumers' surplus into producers' revenue. In each of the four parts a monopolist faces the same demand curve, D, and the total quantity sold is assumed to be q_0. Each firm does a different amount of price discrimination and in each case the firm's revenue is shown by the light-shaded area while consumers' surplus is shown by the dark-shaded area.

In part (i), a single price p_0 is charged.

In part (ii), the first q_1 units are sold at p_1 and the next $q_0 - q_1$ are sold at p_0.

In part (iii), the first q_2 are sold at p_2; the next $q_1 - q_2$ are sold at p_1, and the last $q_0 - q_1$ at p_0.

In part (iv), the first q_3 units are sold at p_3; the next $q_2 - q_3$ at p_2, the next $q_1 - q_2$ at p_1 and the last $q_0 - q_1$ at p_0.

As the amount of price discrimination increases, consumers' surplus diminishes and producers' revenue increases.

encourage the firm to raise its output. The intuitive sense of this proposition concerns marginal revenue under single and discriminatory pricing systems. The monopoly that must charge a single price produces less than the perfectly competitive industry, because it is aware that by selling more it drives down the price against itself. Price discrimination allows the firm to avoid this disincentive. To the extent that it can sell its output in separate blocks, it can sell another block without spoiling the market for the block already being sold.

In the case of *perfect* price discrimination, where every unit of output is sold at a different price, the monopoly output would be the same as the output of a perfectly competitive industry. This is easily seen as follows. If each unit can be sold at a separate price, the seller does nothing to spoil the market for previous units by selling an additional unit. The marginal revenue of selling an additional unit is the price of that unit. Thus the demand curve becomes the marginal revenue curve, and the monopolist reaches equilibrium at a point where the price (in this case, marginal

revenue) equals marginal cost. This is also the point of competitive equilibrium.

When is Price Discrimination Possible?

We have seen that price discrimination is profitable, whenever it is possible. But when is it possible?

Discrimination among units of output sold to the same buyer requires that the seller be able to keep track of the units a buyer consumes each period.

Thus the tenth unit purchased by a given buyer in a given month can be sold at a different price from the fifth unit *only* if the seller can keep track of who buys what. This can be done by sellers of electricity or gas through meter readings, or by magazine publishers who can distinguish between renewals and new subscriptions. This may also be done by service establishments such as car washes or film developers, by giving a certificate for a reduced-price second sale within a stated time from the first sale. It is also done by sellers of goods when they attach coupons to a good bought at full price allowing a reduced-price purchase of the same good within a given period. A similar result is obtained when firms advertise sales: 'Buy one for full price and get a second for only half price.'

The key to being able to discriminate among buyers is that:

discrimination among buyers requires that the goods cannot be resold by the buyer who faces the low price to the buyer who faces the high price.

Often such resale cannot be prevented. However much the local butcher would like to charge the banker twice as much for a lamb chop as he charges the street sweeper, he cannot succeed in doing so. The banker can always go into a supermarket where her occupation is not known. Even if the butcher and the supermarket agreed to charge her twice as much, she could hire the street sweeper to do her shopping for her. On the other hand, the surgeon in private practice may succeed in discriminating because it will not do the banker much good to hire the street sweeper

to have her operations for her. The ability to prevent resale tends to be associated with the character of the product, or the ability to classify buyers into readily identifiable groups. Services are less easily resold than goods, and those goods requiring installation by the manufacturer (such as heavy equipment) are less easily resold than are movable commodities (such as household appliances). Transportation costs, tariff barriers or import quotas serve to separate classes of buyers geographically and may make discrimination possible.

An interesting case of discrimination among buyers is discussed in Box 13.2. The twist in this case is that the motivation may be to maximize the number of units sold, rather than to maximize profits.

The Normative Aspects of Price Discrimination

Price discrimination often has a bad reputation. The very word *discrimination* has undesirable connotations. Whether an individual judges price discrimination to be good or bad is likely to depend upon the details of the case, as well as upon personal value judgements. Certainly there

---

BOX 13.2 PRICE DISCRIMINATION BY THE NATIONAL ECONOMIC DEVELOPMENT OFFICE

A very simple case of genuine price discrimination is the pricing of a publication that many Economics students in the UK may come across. The National Economic Development Office (the administrative branch of the system of the National Economic Development Council and the 30-odd Economic Development Committees) publishes *British Industrial Performance*, of which there have been four editions between 1980 and 1987. This booklet shows the changes experienced by UK industry over the previous decade and makes comparisons between the UK and other major industrial countries. It is useful to many government departments and other public-sector agencies, large firms and organizations with responsibilities towards industry (such as the Confederation of British Industry, which itself plays a major role within the NEDC), and – last but not least – students of economics. One major difference between the last category of users on the one hand, and the administrative/industrial users on

the other, is the students' relative lack of funds, and the corresponding shortage within educational establishments which leads many schools and colleges to buy one copy of useful publications and then – illegally – photocopy it so as to provide a copy for all students. NEDO accordingly sets a relatively high price (£12.50) for the general buyers but charges significantly less (£8.50) to educational establishments, making a further reduction (£7.50) to those schools and colleges buying 6 or more copies – copies that they are likely to be tempted to obtain by the illegal photocopying option. (Discounts for bulk purchase *often* reflect economies of scale, but it is doubtful whether this is relevant here.) As long as no sales occur below the (very low) marginal cost of producing further copies, such price discrimination can add to the profits of the NEDO – as well as increasing the number of people who read its publication. (All prices quoted here were for sales in 1988.)

is nothing in economic theory to suggest that price discrimination is always in some sense worse than non-discrimination. The following examples should serve to illustrate the varying aspects of price discrimination.

Example 1: Some years ago British Rail was not allowed to discriminate among passengers in different regions. To prevent discrimination, a fixed fare per passenger mile was laid down and had to be charged on all lines whatever the density of their passenger traffic and whatever the elasticity of demand for their services. In the interests of economy, branch lines which could not cover costs were often closed down. This meant that some lines closed even though the users preferred rail transport to any of the available alternatives and the strength of their preference was such that they would voluntarily have paid a price sufficient for the line to have covered its costs. The lines were nonetheless closed because it was thought inequitable to charge the passengers on their line more than the passengers on other lines. Subsequently, British Rail was allowed to charge prices that took some account of market conditions, and the effect was an increase in revenues.

Example 2: A very large oil-refining firm agrees to ship its product to a market on a given railway, but only if the railway gives the company a secret rebate on the transportation cost and does not give a similar concession to rival refiners. The railway agrees, and is thus charging discriminatory prices. This rebate gives the oil company a cost advantage that it uses to drive its rivals out of business or to force them into a merger on dictated terms. (John D. Rockefeller is alleged to have used such tactics in forming the original Standard Oil Trust in the US in the late nineteenth century.)

Example 3: Doctors in countries without national health systems usually charge discriminatory prices for their services. When they are accused of behaving unfairly, they point out that if they had to charge a uniform fee for all patients, it would have to be so high – if the doctor were to obtain a reasonable income – as to price their services out of reach of the lower-income groups. The discriminatory price system, they argue, is what allows them to make their services available to all income groups while still securing a high enough income to ensure a continued supply of doctors.

Example 4: A product that a number of people want has cost and demand curves such that there is no single price at which costs can be covered (i.e. the average cost curve lies everywhere above the demand curve). However, if a monopoly is allowed to charge discriminatory prices, it will make a profit.

Each of these examples, as well as those at the beginning of this section, involves price discrimination. Few readers would regard them all as equally good or bad situations. There are two points to be stressed. First, the consequences of price discrimination can differ from case to case; second, no matter what their values, most people will not pass the same verdict of desirable or undesirable on all cases.

SUMMARY

1. A monopoly is an industry containing a single firm. The monopoly firm maximizes its profits by equating marginal cost to marginal revenue which is less than price.
2. The monopoly can earn positive profits in the long run if there are barriers to entry. These may be man-made, such as patents or exclusive franchises, or natural, such as sufficiently large-scale economies.
3. If a monopolist can discriminate either among different units or different customers, it will always sell more and earn greater profits than if it must charge a single price.
4. For price discrimination to be possible, the seller must be able to distinguish

individual units bought by a single buyer or to separate buyers into classes among whom resale is impossible.

5. No simple judgement that price discrimination is either always beneficial or always harmful to the interests of consumers seems justified. Each case needs to be evaluated on its own merits.

TOPICS FOR REVIEW

- Relationship between price and marginal revenue for a monopolist
- Relationships among marginal revenue, total revenue, and elasticity for a monopolist
- Short- and long-run monopoly equilibrium
- Natural and created entry barriers
- Price discrimination among different units and different buyers

APPENDIX to Chapter 13

A Formal Analysis of Price Discrimination Among Buyers

Consider a monopoly firm that sells a single product in two distinct markets, A and B, whose demand and marginal curves are shown in Figure 13A.1. Resale among customers is impossible and a single price must be charged in each market.

What is the best price for the firm to charge in each market? The simplest way to discover this is to imagine the firm deciding how best to allocate any given total output Q^*, between two markets. Since output is fixed arbitrarily at Q^*, there is nothing the monopolist can do about costs. The best thing it can do, therefore, is to maximize the revenue that it gets by selling Q^* in the two

markets. *To do this it will allocate its sales between the markets until the marginal revenues are the same in each market.* Consider what would happen if the marginal revenue in market A exceeded the marginal revenue in market B. The firm could keep its overall output constant at Q^* but reallocate a unit of sales from B to A, gaining a net addition in revenue equal to the difference between the marginal revenues in the two markets. Thus it will always pay a monopoly firm to reallocate a given total quantity between its markets as long as marginal revenues are not equal in the two markets.

If we assume that marginal cost is constant, we

FIGURE 13A.1 Equilibrium of a Price-discriminating Monopolist with Constant Marginal Costs

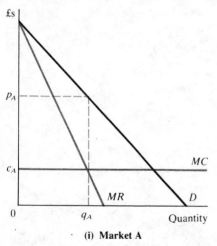

(i) Market A

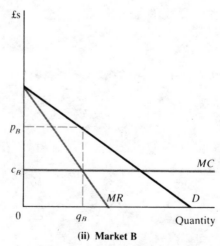

(ii) Market B

FIGURE 13A.2 Equilibrium of a Price-discriminating Monopolist with Variable Marginal Costs

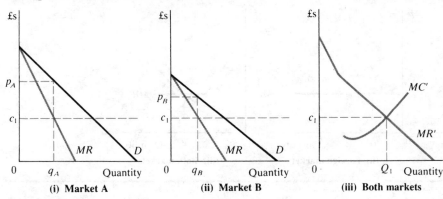

(i) **Market A**   (ii) **Market B**   (iii) **Both markets**

can determine the profit-maximizing course of action from Figure 13A.1. The MC curve in both figures shows the constant marginal cost. The firm's total profits are maximized by equating MR in each market to its constant MC, thus selling q_A at p_A in market A and q_B at p_B in market B. Marginal revenue is the same in each market $(c_A = c_B)$ so that the firm has its total output correctly allocated between the two markets and marginal costs equals marginal revenue, showing that the firm would lose profits if it produced more or less total output.

Next assume that marginal cost varies with output, being given by MC' in Figure 13A.2(iii). Now we cannot just put the MC curve on to the diagram for each market, since the marginal cost of producing another unit for sale in market A will depend on how much is being produced for sale in market B and vice versa. To determine what overall production should be, we need to know overall marginal revenue. To find this we merely sum the separate quantities in each market that correspond to each particular marginal revenue. If, for example, the 10th unit sold in market A and the 15th unit sold in market B each have a marginal revenue of £1 in their separate markets, then the marginal revenue of £1 corresponds to overall sales of 25 units (divided 10 units in A and 15 in B). This example illustrates the general principle: the overall marginal revenue curve to a discriminating monopolist is the horizontal sum of the marginal revenue curves in each of its markets. This overall curve shows the marginal revenue associated with an increment to

production on the assumption that sales are divided between the two markets so as to keep the two marginal revenues equal.

This overall MR curve is shown in Figure 13A.2(iii) and is labelled MR'. The firm's total profit-maximizing output is at Q_1 where MR' and MC' intersect (at a value of c_1). By construction, marginal revenue is c_1 in each market although price is different. To find the equilibrium price and quantity in each market, find the quantities, q_A and q_B, that correspond to this marginal revenue; then find the prices in each market that correspond to q_A and q_B. All of this is illustrated in parts (i) and (ii) of the figure.

An Application

In some industries firms sell competitively on international markets while enjoying a home market that is protected from foreign competition by tariffs or import quotas. To illustrate the issues involved consider the following extreme case. A firm is the only producer of product X in country A. There are thousands of producers of X in other countries so that X is sold abroad under conditions of perfect competition. The government of country A grants the firm a monopoly in the home market by prohibiting imports of X. The firm is now faced with a downward-sloping demand curve at home and a perfectly elastic demand curve abroad at the prevailing world price of X.

What will it do? To maximize profits the firm will divide its sales between the foreign and the home markets so as to equate marginal revenues

FIGURE 13A.3 Equilibrium of a Firm with a Monopoly in the Home Market but Selling under Perfectly Competitive Conditions Abroad

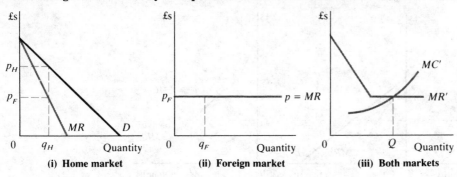

   (i) **Home market**   (ii) **Foreign market**   (iii) **Both markets**

in the two. On the world market its average and marginal revenues are equal to the world price. Thus the firm will equate marginal revenue in the home market with the world price, and since price exceeds marginal revenue at home (because the demand curve slopes downwards), price at home must exceed price abroad.

The argument is illustrated in Figure 13A.3. The home market is shown in (i), the foreign market in (ii) and the sum of the two marginal revenue curves in (iii). Provided that the mar-

ginal cost curve cuts the marginal revenue curve to the right of the kink (i.e. MC does not exceed the world price when only the home market is served), both markets will be served at prices of p_H at home and p_F abroad. The total quantity sold will be Q, of which q_H is allocated to the home market and the rest ($q_F = Q - q_H$) is sold abroad.[1]

---

[1] It is an interesting exercise to consider the effect on the firm's exports of a tax on the sale of X in the home market.

14

Imperfect Competition

The two extreme market structures of perfect competition and monopoly do not cover all of the economic activity that we see today. Most firms involved in the production, distribution and retailing of consumer goods and services, as well as capital goods, come under intermediate market structures. They are not monopolies because their industries contain several firms which often compete actively against each other. They do not do so, however, in perfectly competitive markets. Usually, the number of competing firms is small, but, even when the number is large, *the firms are not price-takers*.

Firms manufacturing cars, refrigerators, TV sets, breakfast cereals, and just about any other consumers' good, operate in industries containing several close rivals (often foreign as well as domestic). Even in small towns, residents find more than one chemist, garage, hairdresser and greengrocer competing for their patronage.

PRICING UNDER ALTERNATIVE MARKET STRUCTURES

In perfect competition, firms sell a homogeneous product, face a market price that they are quite unable to influence, and adjust their quantities to that price. When market conditions change, the signal that the firm sees is a change in market prices.

> In perfect competition, firms are price-takers and quantity-adjusters. Changes in market conditions are signalled to firms by changes in their market prices.

In most manufacturing industries, firms sell *differentiated products*. These are products which are similar enough to constitute a single group, but which are sufficiently different for purchasers to distinguish one from another. Although the products produced by various firms in an industry may be close substitutes for each other, they are not exact substitutes as in perfect competition. Firms thus have some control over their prices; they must decide on a price to quote for each of their product lines. If they are unsatisfied with their price-output position, they can change their price – but they must quote some price. In such circumstances we say that firms 'administer' their prices. The term **administered prices** refers to prices that are set by the decisions of individual firms rather than by impersonal market forces.

When a firm sets its price, the amount that it sells is determined by its demand curve. Changes in market conditions will be signalled to the firm by changes in the amount that it sells at its administered price. The changed conditions may or may not lead the firm to change its price.

> **With market structures other than perfect competition, firms set their prices and let demand determine their sales. Changes in market conditions are signalled to firms by changes in their sales.[1]**

IMPERFECT COMPETITION AMONG THE MANY

The Development of Monopolistic Competition

Dissatisfaction with the two polar market structures of perfect competition and monopoly led the American economist Edward Chamberlin to develop the theory of a market structure called **monopolistic competition**. The dissatisfaction that motivated his theorizing lay in conflicts between theories and evidence.

Observations showed that many manufacturing firms were producing on the falling portion of their long-run average cost curves. The theory of perfect competition predicted, however, that no unexploited scale economies could exist in long-run equilibrium. Further conflicts between theory and evidence concerned advertising, and many other forms of inter-firm rivalry, which cannot be accounted for by either polar theory. A perfectly competitive firm can sell all it wants at the going price, and hence has no need to advertise, or to engage in any form of competitive behaviour directed at other firms. A monopoly

might advertise in an effort to shift the market demand curve, but it has no other firms against whom it needs to compete.

Assumptions of monopolistic competition: In an attempt to get closer to reality, the theory of monopolistic competition dealt with a market that was competitive in the sense that it contained a large number of firms that could freely enter into, and exit from, the industry and that were in active competition with each other. The market was monopolistic, however, in the sense that each firm sold a product that was differentiated from the product sold by each other firm in the industry. For example, each firm's toothpaste would be different in colour, taste and packaging from each other firm's toothpaste. This market structure was similar to perfect competition, except for the single key assumption that each firm sold a differentiated product.

The theory was an important step in the development of models of intermediate market structures.[1] Its main predictions are outlined below, and a more detailed discussion is given in the Appendix to this chapter.

Monopolistically Competitive Equilibrium

Short-run equilibrium: Because each firm has a monopoly over its own product, each firm faces a negatively sloped demand curve. But the curve is rather elastic because similar products sold by other firms provide many close substitutes. The negative slope of the demand curve provides the potential for monopoly profits in the short run, as illustrated in Figure 14.1(i).

Long-run equilibrium: Freedom of entry and exit forces profits to zero in the long run. If profits are being earned by existing firms in the industry, new firms will enter. Their entry will mean that the demand for the product must be shared among more and more brands. Thus the

---

[1] Of course, given a demand curve, a manufacturing firm could set its price, which implies a quantity of sales, or set quantity of sales, which implies a price. In practice, however, there is no impersonal auction market to set price, so each firm *must* quote a price at which it is prepared to sell each of its differentiated products. If it has a quantity target, it must vary its price until it meets that target.

[1] Another attempt to reconcile theory with the same observations was made by the British economist Joan Robinson. She assumed that each industry was monopolized. Although her work led to important clarifications of the theory of monopoly, it proved a dead end in explaining the behaviour of manufacturing industries. Instead it was Chamberlin's work which set the direction that more modern explanations have successfully followed.

demand curve for each existing firm's brand shifts to the left.[1] Entry continues until profits fall to zero.

Excess capacity: The absence of positive profits requires that each firm's demand curve be nowhere above its long-run average cost curve. The absence of losses, which would cause exit, requires that each firm be able to cover its costs. Thus average revenue must equal average cost at some output. Together these requirements imply that when a monopolistically competitive industry is in long-run equilibrium, each firm will be producing where its demand curve is tangent to

---

[1] How the demand curve shifts is determined by Chamberlin's critical *symmetry assumption*: a new entrant takes sales equally from all existing firms.

(i.e. just touching at one point) its average total cost curve.

Two curves that are tangent at a point have the same slope at that point. If a negatively sloped demand curve is to be tangent to the *LRAC* curve, the latter must also be negatively-sloped at the point of tangency. This situation is shown in Figure 14.1(ii): the typical firm is producing an output less than the one for which its *LRAC* reaches its minimum point.

This is the famous **excess-capacity theorem** of monopolistic competition. Each firm is producing its output at an average cost that is higher than it could achieve by producing its capacity output. In other words, each firm has *unused* or *excess* capacity. So:

the theory of monopolistic competition

FIGURE 14.1 Equilibrium of a Typical Firm in Monopolistic Competition

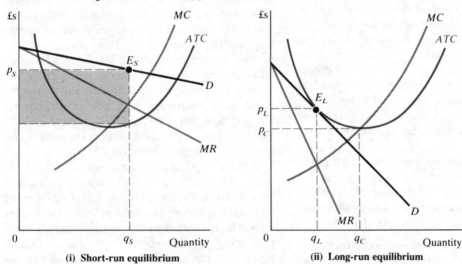

(i) Short-run equilibrium   **(ii) Long-run equilibrium**

In the short run, a typical firm may make pure profits, but in the long run it will only cover its costs. In part (i), a typical monopolistically competitive firm is shown in short-run equilibrium at point E_S. Output is q_S, where $MC = MR$; price is p_S and profits are the shaded area.

In part (ii), the firm is in long-run equilibrium at point E_L. Entry of new firms has pushed the existing firms' demand curve to the left until the curve is tangent to the *ATC* curve at output q_L. Price is p_L, and total costs are just being covered. Excess capacity is $q_C - q_L$. If the firm did produce at capacity, its costs would fall from p_L per unit of output to p_C.

Note that to make the points q_L and q_C visually distinct, the demand curve in part (ii) has been drawn more steeply sloped than in part (i). The flatter demand curve of part (i) is what is expected in monopolistic competition. If it were drawn on part (i), q_L would more realistically be closer to q_C, but the differences being illustrated by the Figure would be harder to see.

shows that an industry can be competitive, in the sense of containing numerous competing firms, and yet contain unexploited scale economies, in the sense that each firm is producing on the negatively sloped portion of its average cost curve.

The explanation, however, seemed to imply waste and inefficiency. Production was at higher cost than was necessary, and firms typically invested in capacity that was not fully utilized.

Is excess capacity wasteful?: The excess-capacity theorem aroused passionate debate for decades. Was it really true that the free-market system caused waste and inefficiency whenever an industry produced differentiated products?

The debate was finally resolved with a negative answer in the 1960s by considering the question: What is the optimal number of differentiated products that should be produced?

People clearly have different tastes. For example, each brand of breakfast food, hi-fi set, car and watch has its sincere devotees. Increasing the number of differentiated products has two effects. First, it increases the amount of excess capacity in the production of each product because the total demand must be divided among more products. Second, the increased diversity of available products will better satisfy diverse tastes.

Now consider how to maximize consumers' satisfactions in these circumstances. The correct policy is *not* to reduce the number of differentiated products until each remaining product can be produced at its least-cost output. Instead:

> **to maximize consumers' satisfactions, the number of differentiated products should be increased until the gain in consumers' satisfaction from increasing diversity equals the loss from having to produce each existing product at a higher cost.**

For this reason, among others, the charge that large-group monopolistic competition would lead to a waste of resources is no longer accepted as necessarily, or even probably, true.[1]

---

[1] Important demonstrations of this result were given by several economists, including Kelvin Lancaster, formerly of the London School of Economics and now at Columbia University in New York.

The Empirical Relevance of Large-group Monopolistic Competition

A long controversy raged over several decades as to the empirical relevance of monopolistic competition. Of course, product differentiation is an almost universal phenomenon in many industries, including those producing virtually all consumers' goods. Nonetheless, many economists maintained that the monopolistically competitive market structure was almost never found in practice.

To see why, we need to distinguish between products and firms. In many manufacturing industries numerous differentiated products are produced by only a few firms. The vast variety of breakfast foods, for example, is produced by a mere three firms. Similar circumstances exist in soap, chemicals, cigarettes and numerous other industries where many competing products are produced by a few very large firms. These industries are clearly not perfectly competitive and neither are they monopolies. Are they monopolistically competitive? The answer is no, because they contain only a few firms who often take account of each other's reactions when determining their own behaviour. Furthermore, these firms often earn large profits without attracting new entry. In fact, they operate under a market structure called oligopoly, which we consider in the next section.

While accepting that many differentiated products are produced by industries that are not monopolistically competitive, some economists feel that the theory is useful in analysing industries which contain many relatively small firms producing a differentiated product.[1] Others agree with the late Nicholas Kaldor who maintained in his long debate with Chamberlin that because every variety of a differentiated product

---

[1] At first sight, retailing may appear to be closer to the conditions of large-group monopolistic competition than is manufacturing. Every city has many retailers selling any one commodity, and differentiated from each other mainly by their geographical location. Each firm, however, tends to have only a few close neighbours and many more distant ones. Thus a model of interlocking oligopolies, with every firm in strong competition with only a few close neighbours, seems to be a better model for retailing than the model of large-group monopolistic competition, in which every firm competes directly, and equally, with all other firms in the industry. These, and other related matters, are further discussed in the Appendix to the chapter.

was not an equally good substitute for every other variety, even these many-firm industries were better studied in a model of overlapping oligopolies. (The debate is discussed further in the Appendix to this chapter.)

The last decade has seen a great outburst of theorizing concerning all aspects of product differentiation. Interestingly, the theory that deals with market structures where a small number of firms compete to sell a large number of differentiated products has taken the name *monopolistic competition*. The term now refers to any industry containing more than one firm, all of whom sell differentiated products. The qualifiers *large-group* and *small-group* are then often used to distinguish Chamberlin's theory of monopolistic competition from the more empirically relevant theory of monopolistic competition among a few oligopolistic firms.

The modern theory of small-group monopolistic competition is the direct descendant of the earlier large-group theories. The focus remains on product differentiation, and on industrial structures thought to describe the nature of the modern economy. The newer theories are consistent with Chamberlin's famous propositions that it pays firms to differentiate their products, to advertise heavily and to engage in many other forms of competitive behaviour. These are characteristics to be found in the world, but not in perfect competition. Most modern industries that sell differentiated products, however, contain only a few firms. This is the market structure of oligopoly that is discussed in the next sections.

IMPERFECT COMPETITION AMONG THE FEW

An **oligopoly** is an industry that contains only a few competing firms. Each firm has enough market power to prevent its being a price-taker, but each firm is subject to enough inter-firm rivalry to prevent its considering the market demand curve as its own. In most modern economies this is the dominant market structure for the production of consumer's and capital goods as well as many basic industrial materials such as steel and aluminium. Services, however, are often produced under more competitive conditions.

Why Bigness?

Why are so many industries dominated by a few large firms? In many cases the answer is to be found in falling costs due to the economies of large-scale production. This was the basis of the assembly line which revolutionized the mass production of many goods earlier in this century, and it still underlies economies of large-scale production in many industries such as steel and cars.

The production of differentiated products by many of today's industries is subject to a different sort of scale economy. Developing a new product is costly, and it may be replaced by some superior version of the same basic commodity within a relatively short time. The fixed costs of developing a new product must be recovered from the sales revenue, and the larger are the firm's sales, the less is the cost that has to be recovered from each unit sold. Consider a product that costs £10 million to develop and market. If one million units are to be sold, then £1 of the selling price of each must go to recovering development costs. If, however, the firm expects to sell 10 million units, then each unit need only contribute £0.10 to these costs and the market price can be lowered accordingly. With the enormous development costs of some of today's 'high tech' products, firms that can sell large volumes have a distinct pricing advantage over firms that sell much smaller volumes.

Other economies are related to financing and marketing. It is costly to set up a presence in a market, establish a selling organization and make consumers aware of one's product. Funds to cover these expenditures, as well as development costs, have to be raised, which often requires that large amounts be borrowed. The smaller the volume of the firm's sales, the higher must be the price per unit sold, if the firm is to cover all of these costs.

These, and other similar reasons, mean that there are major advantages of large size for firms in many industries. Where this is the case, there may be room for only a few firms producing at their MES, even when the total market is quite large. This cost advantage of size will dictate that the industry be an oligopoly unless some form of government regulation prevents the firms from growing to their efficient size.

In other cases, as we shall see later in this chapter, the existing firms in the industry may create barriers to entry where natural ones do not exist. The industry will then be dominated by a few large firms only because they are successful in preventing the entry of new firms.

Short-run Price Stickiness

One of the most striking contrasts between perfectly competitive markets, on the one hand, and all markets where prices are administered, on the other hand – including oligopoly and mono-poly markets – concerns the behaviour of prices. In perfect competition, prices change continually in response to changes in demand and supply. Administered prices change less frequently. Manufacturers prices for radios, cars, television sets and men's suits do not change with anything like the frequency that prices change in markets for basic materials or foreign exchange or bonds.

This phenomenon is often referred to as the *stickiness* of administered prices. Before con-sidering possible explanations of why prices may be sticky, it is important to recognize that these prices do also change.

Changing prices: Administered prices usu-ally change when there are major changes in costs of production. Increases in raw materials prices, or wage rates, are passed on fairly quickly through increases in input prices. This is because cost increases threaten to eliminate profits unless they are at least partly passed on in terms of higher prices. Also, major reductions in costs, as when a new product such as the personal com-puter is being developed, are usually followed by reductions in prices. This is because of the rivalry among oligopolistic firms. If one firm fails to cut price when costs fall, another firm will do so, seeking thereby to increase its market share.

Oligopoly prices also often change in response to large unexpected shifts in demand. If an industry finds itself faced with an apparently permanent downward shift in demand, firms will often cut prices in an attempt to retain their markets until longer-term adjustments can be made.

Sticky prices: The rigidity of administered prices occurs mainly in the face of cyclical and seasonal fluctuations in demand. The existence of

trade cycles – i.e. alternating periods of high and low demand for output – is well known to firms, even if the precise course of each cycle cannot be predicted in advance. Oligopolistic firms tend to hold their administered prices fairly constant through cyclical fluctuations in demand while allowing output to vary.

Price stickiness is short-term behaviour that need not affect our longer-term view of how the economy functions. Nonetheless, the stickiness is an interesting problem in its own right, and it has important implications for macroeconomics.[1]

Three of the explanations of this price sticki-ness that have been offered concern fear of competitors' reactions, full-cost pricing policies, and the cost of changing prices. Each may have validity in certain circumstances.

The Kinked Demand Curve

One explanation looks to each firm's anticipation of its competitors' reactions. According to this theory, each oligopolist conjectures that its rivals will match any price decreases it makes, but will not follow it in any price increases. If one firm raises its price and its competitors do not follow, it will lose market share and its sales will fall off drastically. Thus its demand curve for a rise in price will be rather flat. On the other hand, if the firm lowers price and its competitors all follow, it will not gain market share. Its sales will expand only in proportion to the expansion in the industry's sales. The firm's demand curve for price reductions will thus be steeper than its demand curve for price increases. The resulting *kinked oligopoly demand curve* is shown in Figure 14.2.

Whenever oligopolists make these assump-tions about their competitors' reactions, they will be reluctant to change prices in response to shifts in costs. Their profit-maximizing strategy will be to hold prices constant in the face of significant shifts in marginal costs even though the profit-maximizing behaviour for the group as a whole would be to raise price.

If the market demand curves for the whole set

---

[1] A major problem of macroeconomics is why in the short run it is mainly output, rather than prices, that responds to changes in the total demand for goods and services across the whole economy. The behaviour studied in this section provides an important part of the explanation of this phenomenon.

FIGURE 14.2 The Kinked Oligopoly Demand Curve

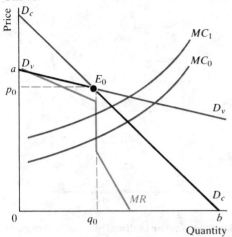

Price stickiness in the face of varying costs can result if the firm assumes that its competitors will match its price reductions but not its price increases. The firm is in equilibrium at E_0, charging a price of p_0 and selling q_0. Its demand curve, drawn on the assumption that all other firms follow any price changes it makes, is the curve D_c. The firm's market share is constant along this curve. (So this curve is labelled D_c for *constant* market share.) The firm's demand curve, drawn on the assumption that all other firms hold their prices constant, is D_v. Along this curve the firm's market share varies negatively with the price it charges – the higher its price, the lower its market share. (So this curve is labelled D_v for *variable* market share.)

Since the firm assumes its competitors will match its price cuts but not its price increases, its demand curve is given by D_c below E_0 and D_v above E_0. Thus the whole demand curve is the solid black line running from a to E_0 to b, with a kink at E_0 where there is a change in the curve that is relevant. The marginal revenue curve for this kinked demand curve takes a jump at quantity q_0. For lower quantities, where the curve D_v is relevant, its *MR* curve is high up and relatively flat. For larger quantities, where the curve D_c is relevant, its *MR* curve is lower down and steeper.

The marginal cost curves of MC_0 and MC_1 both give equilibrium output at q_0 with price p_0 because both pass through the point where the marginal cost curve 'jumps'.

of differentiated products produced by the industry shifts to the left, or to the right, each firm will be led to change its price – unless, by coincidence, the kink on the new demand curve occurs at the

same price as the kink on the original curve. Such a coincidence is not impossible but it is unlikely to be the reason behind the *general tendency* for oligopolistic prices to be sticky in the face of shifts in demand.

This theory may well explain oligopolistic price stickiness in the face of cost changes – at least when oligopolists make these specific assumptions about their competitors' reactions. As we shall soon see, however, oligopolists' assumptions about their competitors' reactions tend to vary with the market circumstances in which they find themselves. They are thus unlikely to be the same at all times, so that a theory based on the assumption of particular reactions is unlikely to explain all cases.

Also the theory does not explain the observed cyclical price stickiness on the part of monopolists, who have no competitors to worry about, or of oligopolists who are colluding with each other to charge the monopoly price, or of oligopolists who do indulge in price competition with each other, or of monopolistic competitors who are, by definition, unconcerned about the reaction of the numerous firms in their industry.

Full-cost Pricing

An early interpretation stems from the pioneering work of two Oxford economists, Robert Hall and Charles Hitch. Their view was that businessmen were conventional creatures of habit who were not profit-maximizers. Businessmen calculated their full costs at normal capacity and then added a conventional mark-up to determine price. They then sold whatever they could at that price, so that demand fluctuations caused quantity rather than price fluctuations. This view of the conventional mark-up was successful in explaining the observed oligopolistic price stickiness, but provided no explanation of the variations in mark-ups that did occur from time to time.

The Cost of Changing Prices

The third explanation of sticky prices concerns the cost of making price changes. Modern firms selling differentiated products typically have hundreds, sometimes even thousands, of distinct products in their price lists. The cost of changing such a long list of administered prices includes the costs of printing new list prices, the costs of notifying all customers, the accounting and billing difficulty of keeping track of frequently changing prices, and the loss of customer and retailer loyalty and goodwill due to the uncertainty caused by frequent changes in prices. These costs are seldom insignificant to the firm.

> **The daily or even hourly changes in prices that occur in markets where prices are set by the impersonal forces of demand and supply would be extremely costly to make in markets where prices are administered by multiproduct manufacturing firms.**

In spite of the costs of changing prices, maintaining sticky prices in the face of fluctuating demand and output would not be profitable if costs varied greatly with output. A firm whose costs varied drastically with output would make losses if it varied output widely while holding prices constant. A firm with a flat cost curve, however, can do so. Part of the explanation of sticky prices in the presence of price-adjustment costs is found, therefore, in the fact that many manufacturing firms – monopolistic competitors, oligopolists and monopolists – have rather flat cost curves.

FIGURE 14.3 A Saucer-shaped, Average Variable Cost Curve

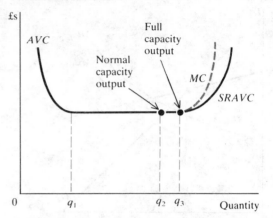

When the fixed factor is divisible, the average variable cost curve will be flat over a range of output. At outputs between q_1 and q_3, the AVC curve is flat because output is varied by using more or less labour and capital in constant proportions. Normal-capacity output is q_2 and full-capacity output is q_3. When output reaches q_3, the fixed stock of capital is fully employed, and further increases in output can only be achieved at rising cost as more labour is applied to a fixed quantity of capital.

FIGURE 14.4 Sticky Oligopoly Prices

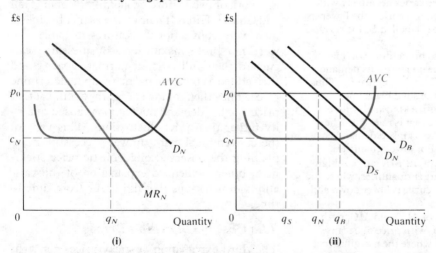

This firm fixes price at its profit-maximizing level and builds a plant whose normal capacity is the profit-maximizing output. Variations in demand are then met by variations in output. In part (i), D_N is the normal demand curve, and p_0 and q_N the profit-maximizing price and output. The plant is built so that q_N is normal-capacity output. In (ii), demand fluctuates between slump and boom, from a low of D_S to a high of D_B. Price is held constant at p_0 while output varies from q_S to q_B.

These curves, which are steep at either extreme and flat over a long middle portion, are often referred to as being *saucer-shaped*. One such curve is shown in Figure 14.3, and Box 14.2 on page 242 discusses the reason for their shape.

Although the saucer-shaped cost curves typically found in manufacturing, do not *force* firms to adopt sticky pricing policies, they do make it possible.

The explanation of sticky prices based on flat cost curves and the cost of changing prices is illustrated in Figure 14.4. Firms estimate their *normal* demand curve, that is, the average of what they can expect to sell at each price over booms and slumps. Having built a plant consistent with this normal demand, and with the expected fluctuations in output, they adopt the profit-maximizing price derived from their normal demand curve as their 'normal price'. Short-run fluctuations in demand are met by holding price constant and varying output. This avoids all the costs involved in repeated changes of prices.

The behaviour just described is consistent with profit maximization if the costs of changing prices are high enough and production cost curves are flat enough. The best thing a firm can then do is to set the price that maximizes profits for average demand and then adjust output rather than price, as demand varies over the cycle. The theory applies equally well to firms in oligopoly, monopolistic competition, and monopoly. Manufacturing firms in all of these market structures find it costly to change prices and usually have saucer-shaped cost curves. Furthermore, the theory predicts stickiness in the face of short-term shifts in demand, which clearly does occur, while allowing price changes in the face of shifts in costs, which also seems to conform with available evidence.

An interesting case of what appears to be oligopolistic price stickiness in the market for a primary product is discussed in Box 14.1.

COMPETITION AMONG OLIGOPOLISTIC FIRMS

The Basic Dilemma of Oligopoly

So far we have explained the short-run pricing behaviour of individual firms. The essence of much of the oligopoly problem, however, is the interrelation among firms.

If Dolcis watches Saxone, so does Saxone watch Dolcis. More importantly, each firm *knows* it is being carefully watched by the other. So when Dolcis makes some marketing decision, it may take into account how it thinks Saxone will react, and Saxone is likely to do the same with

---

BOX 14.1 OLIGOPOLISTIC PRICE STICKINESS IN THE MARKET FOR A PRIMARY PRODUCT

Price stickiness is common in manufactured goods most of which are produced under conditions of oligopoly. Primary products are usually produced and sold under conditions that come closer to those of perfect competition. An interesting exception occurs in the case of germanium, a rare metal which is used to make semi-conductors. One source said that there were 13 producers in 1977/78, with the top 5 accounting for nearly 80 per cent of world output. A reference book published in 1985 listed 5 suppliers of germanium dioxide, one in each of five countries, and 9 suppliers of the metal itself (in a total of six countries). This material can thus be regarded as the product of an oligopolistic industry.

The first source mentioned above shows absolute stability for the price of germanium from 1970 until 1976. More recently, the periodical *Metal Bulletin*, which publishes current prices in each issue, showed the price as 13,075 Belgian francs from March 1979 until January 1980, price rises in January, March and July and then a price of 22,275 Belgian francs from July 1980 until April 1981. The new price, of 31,200 Belgian francs, lasted for five months, and a price of 38,900 Belgian francs for a further 5½ months. The price set in February 1982 – 42,100 Belgian francs – lasted until April 1986, and the prices of two grades of germanium oxide were similarly unchanged: completely stable prices for about four years (at the end of which the prices fell by a mere 1 per cent). This is quite unlike the behaviour of most mineral prices, which fluctuate continuously in response to changes in both demand and supply.

BOX 14.2 SAUCER-SHAPED FIRM COST CURVES

Ever since economists began measuring the cost curves of manufacturing firms more than 50 years ago, they have reported flat, short-run variable cost curves. The evidence shows that in most manufacturing industries, and in some others, cost curves are shaped like the curve shown in Figure 14.3. For such a saucer-shaped curve, there is a large range of output over which average variable costs are constant. Over that range, marginal costs are equal to average variable costs, and thus they, too, are constant per unit of output.

Does the flat portion of the cost curve violate the law of diminishing returns? That law predicts that short-run returns, and hence short-run costs, must vary whenever a varying amount of one factor is applied to a fixed amount of another factor? According to that law, manufacturing firms will have U-shaped short-run cost curves whenever a variable amount of labour is applied to a fixed amount of capital. Starting from zero output, and zero use of the variable factor, as more of that factor is used, a more nearly optimal combination with the fixed factor is achieved. Once the optimal combination is arrived at, the use of further units of the variable factor leads to too much of that factor being used in combination with the fixed factor, and thus to rising average variable costs. Only one quantity of labour leads to the least-cost factor proportions.

These changing combinations of fixed and variable factors must occur in the short run whenever all of the fixed factor must be used all of the time; in other words, when the fixed factor is *indivisible*.

The constraint that lies behind the U-shaped cost curve is that the amount of the fixed factor actually used in the short run must always equal the fixed amount that is available.

Even though the firm's plant and equipment may be fixed in the short run, so that no more than what exists is available, it is usually possible to utilize *less* than all the fixed capital. For that reason, the flat cost curve is not inconsistent with the law of diminishing returns. The *divisibility* of the 'fixed factor' means that diminishing returns do not apply for outputs up to full capacity because variations below full capacity are accomplished by reducing the input of both labour and capital.

The constraint that gives rise to the saucer-shaped cost curve is that the
amount of the fixed factor actually used in the short run cannot exceed (but can be less than) the amount that is actually available.[1]

Consider as a simple example a factory that consists of 10 sewing machines in a shed, each with a productive capacity of 20 units per day when operated by 1 operator for 1 shift. If 200 units per day are required, then all 10 machines are operated by 10 workers on a normal shift. If demand falls to 180, then 1 operator can be laid off. But there is no need to have the 9 remaining operators dashing about trying to work 10 machines. Clearly, 1 machine can be 'laid off' as well, and the ratio of *employed* labour to *employed* machines held constant. Production can go from 20 to 40 to 60 all the way to 200 without any change in factor proportions for the factors in use. In this case we would expect the factory to have constant marginal and average variable costs from 20 to 200 units and only then to encounter rising costs, as production must be extended by overtime and other means of combining more labour with the maximum available supply of 10 machines.

In such a case, the fixed factor is *divisible*. Since some of it can be left unemployed, there is no need to depart from the most efficient ratio of *labour used* to *capital used* as production is decreased. Thus, average variable costs can be constant over a large range, up to the point at which all of the fixed factor is used.

A similar situation occurs when a plant is put on short time. An unchanged number of workers is tending the machines, but both workers and machines are employed fewer hours per week. The same result arises when the firm has many plants. For example, a plywood manufacturer with 10 plants may choose to reduce its output by temporarily closing one or more plants while operating the rest at normal-capacity output. The *firm's* short-run variable costs tend to be constant over a large range of output because there is no need to depart from the optimal combination of labour and capital in those plants that are kept in operation.

---

[1] In formal language, the two curves differ by an equality and an inequality constraint. Let $\bar{K}$ be the fixed quantity of capital available in the short run and let K_e be the amount actually employed. The U-shaped curve occurs when the short-run constraint is $K_e = \bar{K}$ and the saucer-shaped curve occurs when $K_e \leqslant \bar{K}$.

respect to Dolcis. So what Dolcis does may depend on what it *thinks* Saxone will do, and the outcome of Dolcis' actions will depend on what Saxone *actually* does do. In the face of this interdependence there is no obvious way to derive the firm's own demand curve. What then can be done?

Firms in oligopolistic industries that recognize their interdependence, face a basic dilemma: to compete against each other or to co-operate with each other:

> **the firms in an oligopolistic industry will make more profits as a group if they co-operate; any one firm, however, may make more profits for itself if it competes.**

The co-operative equilibrium: If they co-operate, either overtly or tacitly, to produce among themselves the monopoly output, oligopolistic firms can maximize their joint profits. If they do this, they reach what is called the **co-operative equilibrium**, which is the equilibrium that a single monopoly firm would reach if it owned all the firms in the industry.

The non-cooperative equilibrium: If all firms are at the co-operative equilibrium, it will usually pay any one of them to cut its price or raise its output – as long as the others do not do so. However, if everyone does the same, they will be worse off as a group and may all be worse off individually. An equilibrium reached by firms when they procede by calculating only their own gains, without worrying about the reactions of others, is called a **non-cooperative equilibrium**.

Other considerations: The above two paragraphs refer to a static world which shows the conflict between competition and co-operation in its starkest form. In the real world, other considerations will sometimes operate to push firms away from the co-operative equilibrium. If one firm can conceal its cheating for some time, using tactics such as secret rebates to favoured customers, or if its competitors are slow to react, the firm that departs from the co-operative equilibrium may make large profits before the non-cooperative equilibrium is achieved. Also, in a world in which technology and product characteristics are constantly being changed, a firm that

choses to behave rivalrously may be able to maintain a larger market share and larger profits than it would under co-operation, even though all firms' joint profits are lower.

Having outlined the basic dilemma, we can now look in a little more detail first at co-operative, and then at non-cooperative, behaviour.

Types of Co-operative Behaviour

When firms agree to co-operate in order to restrict output and raise profits, their behaviour is called **collusion**. Collusive behaviour may occur with, or without, an actual agreement to collude. Where explicit agreement occurs, economists speak of *overt* or *covert collusion*, depending on whether the agreement is open or secret. Where no agreement actually occurs, economists speak of **tacit collusion**. In this case, all firms behave co-operatively without an explicit agreement to do so. They merely understand that it is in their mutual interest to restrict output and raise prices.

While collusive behaviour is frowned on by governments, a small group of firms that recognize the influence that each has on the other, may act in a common manner without any explicit agreement to do so. In such tacit agreements, the oligopolist's dilemma is still evident. The firms have a common interest in co-operating to maximize their joint profits at the co-operative equilibrium. Each firm is, however, interested in its own profits and any one of them can usually increase it profits by behaving in a rivalrous fashion.

The most obvious way to do this is for one firm to produce more than its share of the joint-profit-maximizing output. But there are other ways as well.

Even if joint profits are maximized, there is the problem of market shares. How is the profit-maximizing level of sales to be divided among the competing firms? Competition for market shares may upset the tacit agreement to hold to joint-maximizing behaviour. In an industry with many differentiated products and where sales are often by contract between buyers and sellers, cheating may be covert rather than overt. Secret discounts and rebates can allow a firm to increase its sales at the expense of its competitors while appearing to hold to the tactily agreed monopoly price.

Another reason why the monopoly level of profits may not be achieved, even if the monopoly price is maintained, is that firms often compete for market shares by various forms of non-price competition such as advertising. Since such competition is costly, it will reduce industry profits.

Types of Non-cooperative Behaviour

To study the consequences of non-cooperative behaviour among oligopolists in its purest form, we will start with the pathbreaking attack on the oligopoly problem that was made by the French economist A. A. Cournot. The non-cooperative equilibrium that he demonstrated in 1838 has become one of the basic tools in the recent development of modern oligopoly theory known as 'the new industrial organization' (or the 'new IO' for short).

Cournot confined his attention to the special case of an industry containing only two firms, called a **duopoly**. He then assumed that the two firms sold an identical product which was produced at zero marginal cost.[1] Each chose its profit-maximizing output *on the assumption that the other firm would hold its output constant.*

Cournot Equilibrium

Figure 14.5 shows the situation as it looks to either firm when Cournot's assumptions are made. Let us call the firm we are looking at Firm One, and its rival Firm Two. For any given quantity produced by Firm Two, call it q_2, Firm One only needs to subtract that quantity from the market demand curve to obtain its own demand curve. Firm One can then calculate its profit-maximizing output by equating its marginal cost to its marginal revenue in the usual way.[2] Call this output q_1. Repeating this process for each given q_2, yields a set of corresponding q_1's. We

[1] The simplifying assumption of zero marginal costs does not restrict the usefulness of the conclusions, none of which are affected in any important way, if marginal costs are assumed positive.
[2] Since we have simplified by assuming marginal cost to be zero, the firm will produce at the point where its MR curve cuts the quantity axis, i.e. the output for which marginal revenue is zero.

now have what is called Firm One's **reaction curve**. It shows Firm One's profit-maximizing output for each given quantity sold by Firm Two. Such a curve is shown in Figure 14.6.

The whole procedure can now be repeated for Firm Two. For each given output for Firm One, q_1, that output can be subtracted from the market demand curve to obtain Firm Two's own demand curve. Firm Two's profit-maximizing output, q_2, can then be calculated. Repeating the procedure for each possible output of Firm One yields a set of corresponding profit-maximizing outputs for Firm Two. This gives us Firm Two's

FIGURE 14.5 Calculation of a Firm's Own Demand Curve in Cournot's Model

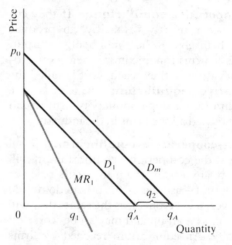

If one firm's output is given, the other firm's demand curve is easily calculated. The market demand curve is D_m. On that curve, quantity demanded is q_A when price is zero, and it falls to zero when price reaches p_0. Firm One assumes that Firm Two will hold its output constant at q_2. Subtracting this fixed quantity from the market demand curve yields Firm One's demand curve which tells Firm One what it can sell at each price. This curve, labelled D_1 in the diagram, is the market demand curve shifted to the left by the amount q_2, which is the distance $q_A - q'_A$ in the Figure. Firm One's marginal revenue curve, MR_1, is derived from its own demand curve. Equating MR to zero (since marginal cost is zero in this example) yields Firm One's profit-maximizing output, q_1, *given Firm Two's output of q_2.*

Firm One has its own demand curve, its own marginal cost curve and its own desired output for each given quantity that it assumes Firm Two will produce.

FIGURE 14.6 Cournot Equilibrium

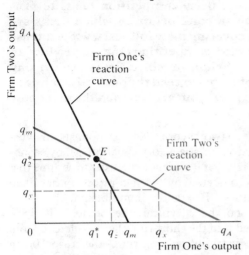

Cournot equilibrium occurs when, given each firm's present output, the other firm's profit-maximizing output is its present output. The Figure shows each firm's reaction curve. Firm One's curve shows its profit-maximizing output for each *given* output of Firm Two. Firm Two's reaction curve shows its profit-maximizing output for *given* outputs of Firm One. The quantity q_m is the monopoly output measured on both axes because it shows what each firm would like to produce if the other's production were zero. The quantity q_A, measured on both axes, is equal to the intercept on the market demand curve in Figure 14.4 because, when its competitor sells that quantity, the firm in question can sell nothing.

The outputs where the two reaction curves interesect (at E) are the equilibrium outputs. At that point, given q_2^*, Firm One's desired output is q_1^*; and given q_1^*, Firm Two's desired output is q_2^*.

No other combination of outputs is an equilibrium. For example, if Firm One produces output q_x, Firm Two will want to produce q_y; but if Firm Two produces q_y, Firm One will want to change its output to q_z.

reaction curve, showing its profit-maximizing output for each given output by Firm One. This curve is also given in Figure 14.6.

Inspection of Figure 14.6 shows the Cournot equilibrium. There is the pair of outputs, call them q_1^* and q_2^*, such that *if Firm One produces q_1^*, then Firm Two will wish to produce q_2^*; and if Firm Two produces q_2^*, then Firm One will wish to produce q_1^*.* This is an equilibrium in the sense that, if these outputs are established, neither firm

will wish to depart from them, given the assumptions made about their behaviour.

In the Cournot equilibrium, the two firms are making profits that exceed those earned under perfect competition but are less than those that would be earned by a monopoly. They earn less than a monopoly would earn because their joint outputs exceed the monopoly output. They earn more than perfectly competitive firms would make since each is aware that it drives the price down when it increases its own output. Thus, even if each takes its competitor's output as given, the demand curve that they assume they are facing is negatively sloped; so each stops short of the output for which marginal cost equals price.

Bertrand Equilibrium

Some fifty years after Cournot's book was published (and largely ignored) it was reviewed by the French mathematician Bertrand. He argued that Cournot's analysis was unrealistic because each firm determined its own best quantity *on the assumption that the other would hold its quantity constant*. Instead, Bertrand had each firm assume that the other would hold its *price* constant, and then ask itself what is the best *price* to charge.

The result was destructive competition which drove price to the level of short-run marginal cost, so that firms would not be covering their fixed costs. To see why, assume that firms start in the Cournot equilibrium as shown in Figure 14.6. Firm One then follows Bertrand's reasoning and asks: 'If Firm Two holds its price constant, what is my best price?' The answer is to undercut Firm Two's price by a marginal amount. Firm One then gains the whole market in return for a small price cut. For example, if each firm was selling 1,000 units at a price of £1, and Firm One cuts its price to £0.99, it will sell 2,000 units and increase its total revenue from £1,000 (1,000 units at £1) to £1,980 (2,000 units at £0.99). But Firm Two will now reason in the same way. At a price of £1, its sales are now zero, but at a price of £0.98 it could capture the entire market and earn £1,960 (2,000 units at £0.98)[1].

The incentive for price-cutting is always pre-

---

[1] The figures in this paragraph imply a completely inelastic market demand, since 2,000 units are sold whatever the price. If the demand curve has the normal negative slope, the

sent as long as each firm can increase its profits by capturing the whole market. The only stable position is when price has been driven to short-run marginal cost (which is zero in the present case). At this price, neither firm has any incentive to cut price. Although it would gain the entire market, selling at a price below the marginal cost of production is never profitable.

Do the Theories Employ Unrealistic Assumptions?

For many years it was popular to criticize both Cournot's and Bertrand's theories on the grounds that they employed unrealistic assumptions. Surely, it was argued, each firm would learn that its competitors did not sit idly by, holding their prices, or their outputs, constant, while the firm adopted its own best strategy. Indeed, if these theories were meant to explain how equilibrium was reached, the theories would be naive. As the process of price or quantity undercutting continued, each firm would learn that it was wrong to assume that the other firm would not react. But the theories are not meant to be about the process by which equilibrium is reached, although many critics have thought otherwise. Instead, they are about the existence of an equilibrium which, if reached by any means, will be self-perpetuating.

The great significance of both Cournot's and Bertrand's equilibria is that they are self-policing.

If firms compete actively with each other by varying the quantities that they sell, and if they reach Cournot's equilibrium by any path whatsoever, they will tend to stay there. Any other combination of outputs is not self-policing in the sense that each firm will be tempted to vary its *output*. The same is true of Bertrand's equilibrium. If firms compete with each other by varying prices, and if price is at marginal cost, there is no incentive for any one firm to depart from this *price*. Raising price will reduce sales to zero, while cutting price will capture the entire market but at a price below variable costs.

incentive to undercut the competitor becomes even stronger. The undercutting strategy then increases the firm's sales by the amount that it takes from the other firm, plus the amount that market quantity demanded increases as a result of a fall in the market price.

Consequences

Intense price competition tends to produce an equilibrium in which firms are not covering their full costs, while intense quantity competition tends to produce an equilibrium in which firms are earning profits that exceed the perfectly competitive result, but are less than the monopoly result.

These two theories left economists in what seemed an unsatisfactory situation. Many economists felt that it was more realistic to assume that firms competed by setting prices rather than quantities. Bertrand's equilibrium, however, could not be a typical one because, if firms reached it in the short run, they would exit from the industry in the long run – the reason being that if short-run marginal costs are constant and equal to price, firms cannot be covering their fixed costs.[1]

Examples of Bertrand-style price competition do seem to occur from time to time. In unusually bad recessions, price competition sometimes drives price well below average total costs. Similar behaviour is sometimes found in the aircraft industry even in good times. When the major aircraft companies are competing to sell a new generation of aircraft, most of the development costs have already been incurred. Although direct production costs are not zero, they are a small part of average total costs because the costs of developing a new line of aircraft are enormous. Under these circumstances, the few major aircraft companies compete to sell their similar planes to the world's major airlines. If an order is lost, nothing is earned. If an order is gained at any price above variable costs it contributes something to fixed costs. The resulting competition to obtain large orders can lead to something close to Bertrand's equilibrium. Rather than lose an order, price is cut well below average total cost

[1] Under perfect competition in the long run, price is equal to short-run marginal cost and to long-run average total cost because the firms' cost curves are U-shaped. (See Figure 12.10 on page 214.) If short-run marginal costs are constant, and equal to short-run average variable costs as in Figure 14.3, marginal cost will be less than average total cost. For example, if *every* unit produced costs £5 in direct production costs, and is sold for £5, there is no revenue available to cover fixed costs.

and little more than marginal production cost is covered. Such competition is costly to firms, but once the fixed costs have been incurred, it is hard to prevent price-cutting when large orders can be won or lost.

Price or Quantity Competition?

Until recently, economists were left to choose between Cournot's quantity competition and Bertrand's price competition by arguing on intuitive grounds which theory made the more reasonable assumptions – a most unsatisfactory way of choosing between two competing theories. More recently, however, economists, developing what is called *the new theories of industrial organization (the new IO)*, have investigated circumstances under which each type of competition is more likely to occur. For example, in the aircraft case, where fixed costs are all paid before sales take place, and the firms have capacity to fill many more orders than they may get, price competition is likely. In other cases, where the production process takes a long time, firms may commit themselves to some level of output, and then sell it for what they can get. In this case, competition is in quantities.

The most important result of these studies, however, concerns capacity.

> **One firm's temptation to undercut its rival's price, and capture all the market which underlies Bertrand's model, is only present when that firm has the capacity to serve the whole market.**

To see this, assume that two firms are in a Cournot equilibrium such as is shown in Figure 14.6. Now also assume that both firms' plants are operating at full capacity; they cannot produce any larger output. Under these circumstances, there is no reason to cut price, since output cannot be increased beyond its present levels in either firm.

An important result using this insight has recently been established by two American economists, Kreps and Scheinkman[1]. They study a case in which firms first decide how much capacity to install. (How large a plant should I build?) Having built their plants, firms then compete with each other to sell their outputs. When firms decide on their own best capacity, they know whether the subsequent competition will be in prices (Bertrand) or quantities (Cournot). Under these circumstances, profit-maximizing firms build plants just big enough to supply the output that would occur in Cournot equilibrium. Then, whether they subsequently compete by deciding on quantities, as in Cournot's theory, or on prices, as in Bertrand's theory, they end up in Cournot's equilibrium. They cover their total costs and make profits that are less than a monopoly but more than a perfectly competitive industry. When they do reach the Cournot equilibrium, they are not tempted to cut prices because they are already producing at full capacity.[1]

The intuitive reason for this result is:

> **Firms often recognize the self-destructive nature of the price competition that was analysed by Bertrand. Having recognized it, they take steps to avoid it. They do this by limiting their capacity to produce.**

This very suggestive theory leads us to expect Cournot's results when demand is such that firms can just use their capacity, and Bertrand's results when firms unexpectedly find themselves with large quantities of unused capacity. Thus, for example, when demand persists at unexpectedly low levels, firms will have excess capacity and will be tempted to engage in price competition that may drive price below average total costs. But when demand is at its expected level, firms will not find themselves with the excess capacity that tempts them to undercut their competitors, and so driving price below Cournot's equilibrium level. This is no accident; firms will have planned it that way.

---

[1] D.M.Kreps and J.A.Scheinkman, 'Quantity Precommitment and Bertrand Competition yield the same results', *Bell Journal*, 11:326–37.

[1] The firms are engaged in what is called a two-stage game that uses the equilibrium concept of sub-game perfection. The two stages are the decision on plant size and the competition between the firms once their plants are built. Sub-game perfection means that, in making its first decision on capacity, each firm understands the kind of competitive game it will be playing in the second stage when it competes to sell its output. Recent research has focused on the conditions for Cournot's equilibrium to be the outcome of this two-stage game. The important result, however, is that Bertrand's equilibrium is never the outcome if demand is correctly foreseen.

Qualified Maximization

We have seen that co-operation leads to the monopoly result, that competition in quantities leads to smaller profits while competition in prices can lead to losses. Which outcome will be reached?

One set of answers is provided by the *hypothesis of qualified joint profit maximization*. It states that the relative strengths of the incentives to co-operate and to cheat vary from industry to industry in a systematic way that is associated with observable characteristics of firms, markets and products. Here are some of the characteristics that the hypothesis states will affect the strength of the two incentives.

(1) *The tendency toward joint maximization is greater for small numbers of sellers than for larger numbers.* This involves both motivation and ability. When there are few firms, they will know that one of them cannot gain sales without inducing retaliation by its rivals. Also, a few firms can tacitly co-ordinate their policies with less difficulty than can many firms.

(2) *The tendency towards joint maximization is greater for producers of similar products than for producers of sharply differentiated products.* The more nearly identical are the products of sellers, the closer will be the direct rivalry for customers, and the less the ability of one firm to gain a lasting advantage over its rivals. Such sellers will tend to prefer joint efforts to achieve a larger pie, to individual attempts to increase their own shares.

(3) *The tendency toward joint maximization is greater in a growing than in a contracting market.* When demand is growing, firms can produce at full capacity without any need to 'steal' their rivals' customers. When firms have excess capacity, they are tempted to give price concessions to attract customers; but when their rivals retaliate, price cuts become general.

(4) *The tendency toward joint maximization is greater when the industry contains a dominant firm rather than a set of more or less equal competitors.* A dominant firm may become a *price leader*, that is, a firm that sets the industry's price while all other firms fall into line. Even if a dominant firm is not automatically a price leader, other firms may look to it for judgement about market conditions, and its decisions may become a tentative focus for tacit agreement.

(5) *The tendency toward joint profit maximization is greater when non-price rivalry is absent or limited.* When firms seek to suppress their basic rivalry by avoiding price competition, rivalry will tend to break out in other forms unless it is expressly curtailed. Firms may seek to increase their market shares through extra advertising, quality changes, the establishment of new products, giveaways, and a host of similar schemes that leave their prices unchanged but increase their costs and so reduce their joint profits.

(6) *The tendency toward joint profit maximization is greater when the barriers to entry of new firms are greater.* The high profits of existing firms attract new entrants, who will drive down price and reduce profits. The greater the barriers to entry, the less this will occur. Thus the greater the entry barriers, the closer the profits of existing firms can be to their joint-maximizing level without being reduced by new entry.

LONG-RUN CONSIDERATIONS: THE IMPORTANCE OF ENTRY BARRIERS

Oligopolists not only have to worry about competing with their existing rivals, they also need to worry about potential competition from firms that might be tempted to enter their industry. Entry barriers are critical to the behaviour of firms in oligopolistic markets.

Suppose such firms succeed in raising prices above long-run average total costs and earn substantial profits that are not eliminated by non-price competition. Why do these profits not cause new firms to enter the industry, increasing output and forcing prices down to the zero-profit level? The answer lies in barriers to entry.

Natural entry barriers were discussed in Chapter 13 (pages 223–224.) In this chapter, we discuss firm-created barriers.

If there are no natural barriers to entry, oligopolistic firms will earn profits in the long run only if they can create barriers that prevent entry. To the extent to which this can be done, existing firms can move in the direction of joint profit maximization without fear of new entrants attracted by the high profits. We discuss below ways in which such barriers can be created.

Brand Proliferation

Differentiated products usually have several characteristics which can be varied over a wide range. Thus, there is room for a large number of similar products, each with a somewhat different mix of characteristics. Consider, for example, the many different kinds of breakfast cereals or cars. Although the multiplicity of brands is no doubt partly a response to consumers' tastes, it may also be partly the result of a deliberate attempt to discourage the entry of new firms. Such brand proliferation can be an entry barrier because, when the existing firms sell a wide array of differentiated products, entry on a small scale by a new firm is made difficult.

To illustrate why brand proliferation may be a formidable barrier to a small potential entrant, assume that the product is of the type where there is a substantial amount of brand switching by consumers. In this case, the larger the number of brands sold by existing firms, the smaller the expected sales of a new entrant. Assume that an industry contains three large firms, each selling one brand of cigarettes, and further assume that 30 per cent of all smokers change brands in a random fashion each year. If a new firm enters the industry, it can expect to pick up 25 per cent of these smokers (it has one brand out of a total of four available brands). This would give it 7.5 per cent (25 per cent of 30 per cent) of the total market in its first year of operation, merely by picking up its share of the random switchers. It would then go on increasing its share year by year thereafter. (As long as it is smaller than its rivals, it will lose fewer customers to them by random switching than it will gain from them.) If, however, the existing three firms have five brands each, fifteen brands are already available, and a new small firm selling one new brand could expect to pick up only one-sixteenth of the brand switchers, giving it less than 2 per cent of the total market the first year. Its gains in subsequent years are also correspondingly less.

This is an extreme case but it illustrates a general result:

the larger the number of differentiated products sold by existing oligopolists, the smaller the market available to a new firm entering with a single new product.

An interesting illustration of brand proliferation in the industry producing beer and spirits is given in Box 14.3.

BOX 14.3 BRAND PROLIFERATION IN ALCOHOLIC DRINKS

Allied-Lyons PLC is one of Britain's largest companies. This is partly because of the diversity of its activities – manufacturing and selling beers and other alcoholic drinks, producing a wide variety of food products and operating restaurants – but even within a limited field like alcoholic drinks, the range of apparently competing brands for which the company is responsible is staggering.

In addition to the beers produced by the original Ind Coope group and Benskins in the south of England, Allied is responsible for Tetley Bitter, Ansells Bitter, John Bull Bitter and Draught Burton Ale, all of which originated in the north of England or the Midlands but are increasingly being found in the south. Even if the Scottish brewers in the group – Drybrough Brewery and Alloa Brewery Company – do not compete much with those further south, there is a wealth of lager brands from which to choose: Lowenbrau, Castlemaine XXXX, Skol and Oranjeboom. If you want to encourage competition in the cider field, it's no good switching from Gaymer's Olde English to Whiteways: they're both made by Allied. Of course, you could ponder the situation while sipping a whisky: Allied won't mind whether you choose Ballantine's or Teacher's as they own both, while having a 50 per cent share in Grant's Steadfast and Glenfiddich whiskies. Try a Lamb's Navy Rum for a change, and you're still buying from Allied. You may prefer fortified wines like Harvey's sherries or Cockburn's ports; your sophisticated friends go for Tico mixer sherry; your less sophisticated acquaintances for British wines like VP or Rougemont Castle: you're all drinking the products of Allied-Lyons PLC.

The production of such a wide range of differentiated products helps to satisfy consumers' clear demand for diversity. It also has the effect of making it more difficult for a new firm to enter the industry. If the new firm wishes to compete over the whole range of differentiated products it must enter on a massive scale. If it wishes to enter on only a small scale it faces a formidable task of establishing brand images and customer recognition with only a few products over which to spread these expenses of entry.

Set-up Costs

Existing firms can create entry barriers by imposing on new entrants significant fixed costs of setting up operations in that market. This is important if there are no economies of large-scale production to provide natural barriers to entry.

Advertising is one means by which existing firms can impose heavy set-up costs on new entrants. Advertising, of course, has effects other than creating barriers to entry. It may perform the useful function of informing buyers about their alternatives, thereby making markets work more smoothly. Indeed, a new firm may find that advertising is essential, even when existing firms do not advertise at all, simply to call attention to its entry into an industry. Nonetheless, advertising can also operate as a potent entry barrier by increasing the set-up costs of new entrants. Effective brand-image advertising means that a new firm will have to advertise in order to catch the public's attention. If the firm's sales are small, advertising costs *per unit sold* will be large. Unit costs will only be reduced sufficiently to make a new entrant profitable when sales are large, so that the fixed advertising costs needed to break into the market can be spread over a large number of units.

Figure 14.7 illustrates how heavy advertising can shift the cost curves of a firm with a low *MES* to make it one with a high *MES*.

A new entrant with small sales, but large set-up costs, finds itself at a substantial cost disadvantage relative to its established rivals.

Although we have discussed advertising, the same argument applies to any once-and-for-all cost of entering a market. For example, there is often a high cost of developing a new product that is similar to existing products. Even if there are few economies of scale in production, large development costs can lead to a falling long-run average total cost curve over a wide range of output and create a natural entry barrier.

An Application

We have seen that brand proliferation and advertising can act as entry barriers. The combined use of the two help to explain why one firm often sells multiple brands of the same product, which compete actively against one another as well as against the products of other firms.

The soap and cigarette industries provide examples. Since all available scale economies can be realized by quite small plants, both industries have few natural barriers to entry. Both contain a few large firms, each of which produces an array of heavily advertised products. The array of products makes it harder for a new entrant to obtain a large market niche with one new product. Each firm's heavy advertising designed to compete against all other products in the industry – many of which are also produced by that firm – creates an entry barrier. It increases the set-up costs of a new product that seeks to gain the attention of consumers and establish its brand image.

Together many differentiated products and heavy advertising provide a formidable entry barrier to any new firm.

FIGURE 14.7 Advertising as a Barrier to Entry

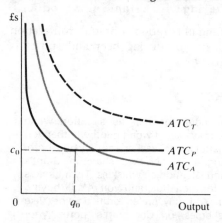

Large advertising costs can increase the minimum efficient scale (MES) of production and thereby increase entry barriers. The curve ATC_P refers to production costs and has an *MES* at a low level of output, q_0, where unit costs are c_0. The curve ATC_A declines over its whole range. It shows the effect of a fixed level of advertising costs being spread over more and more units of output, so that advertising costs per unit of output fall as output rises. The summation of production and advertising costs per unit gives the curve labelled ATC_T, which is average total cost. Costs fall significantly over a much larger range of output along ATC_T than along ATC_P. Advertising gives a scale advantage to large sellers, and thus creates a barrier to entry.

OLIGOPOLY AND THE FUNCTIONING OF THE ECONOMY

Oligopoly is the most commonly encountered market structure in modern economies. Does the recognition of the impossibility of achieving perfect competition, and of the necessity for oligopoly over a large part of the economy, significantly change our views of the working of the price system?

Oligopolies do not fulfil the technical conditions of allocative efficiency that we study later in this book. In many industries, however, scale economies make perfect competition impossible. There is just not room for a large number of firms all operating at, or near, their minimum efficient scales. Important issues for public policy thus concern how to evaluate the performance of oligopolistic industries. In doing this, two questions are key. First, in their price and output behaviour, where do oligopoly firms typically settle between the extremes of the monopoly, and the perfectly competitive, outcomes? Second, how much do oligopolists contribute to economic growth by engaging in innovative activity in the very long run?

Resource Allocation

We have seen that, under perfect competition, prices are set by impersonal market forces and that firms respond to market conditions by adjusting quantities to market prices.

Firms in oligopolistic markets administer their prices. The market-signalling system works slightly differently when prices are administered rather than determined by the market. Changes in the market conditions for both inputs and outputs are signalled to perfectly competitive firms by changes in the prices of their inputs and outputs. Changes in the market conditions for inputs are also signalled to oligopolistic firms by changes in the prices of its inputs. Changes in the market conditions for the outputs of oligopoly firms are, however, typically signalled by changes in their sales at their administered prices.

Rises in costs of inputs will shift cost curves upwards, and oligopolistic firms will be led to raise price and lower output. Rises in demand will cause the sales of oligopolistic firms to rise.

Firms will then respond by increasing output, thereby increasing the quantities of society's resources that are allocated to producing that commodity.

The market system reallocates resources in response to changes in demand and costs in roughly the same way under oligopoly as it does under perfect competition.

Some oligopolies succeed in coming close to joint profit maximization. Others compete so intensely among themselves that they come close to competitive prices and outputs. The consequences for the behaviour of the economic system vary accordingly. Box 14.4 discusses one recent theory that outlines some of the conditions under which oligopoly can be pushed closer to the competitive equilibrium by potential, rather than actual, entry.

Innovation

An important issue is how much oligopolies contribute to economic growth by engaging in innovative activity in the very long run. Some economists have theorized that intermediate market structures, such as oligopoly, would lead to more innovation than would occur under either perfect competition or monopoly. They argue that the oligopolist is faced with strong competition from existing rivals and cannot afford the more relaxed life of the monopolist. At the same time, however, the oligopolistic firm expects to keep a good share of the profits that it earns because of the barriers to entry and its ability to avoid excessive price competition with existing rivals. The empirical evidence seems broadly consistent with this hypothesis. Professor Jesse Markham of Harvard University concluded a survey of empirical findings by saying:

'If technological change and innovational activity are, as we generally assume, in some important way a product of organized R & D activities financed and executed by business companies, it is clear that the welfare payoffs that flow from them can to some measurable extent be traced to the doorsteps of large firms operating in oligopolistic markets.'

Everyday observation provides some confirmation of this finding. Leading firms that operate

BOX 14.4 CONTESTIBLE MARKETS

The American professors William Baumol, Robert Willig and John Panzer have recently developed a theory of what they call *contestible markets*. This theory argues that markets do not have to contain many firms, or to show actual entry, for profits to be held near the competitive level. Potential entry can do the job just as well as actual entry, as long as (i) entry could be easily accomplished, and (ii) existing firms take potential entry into account.

Entry is usually costly to the entering firm. It may have to build a plant, it may have to develop new versions of the industry's differentiated product, and it may have to advertise in order to call attention to its product. These and many other costs of entry are often what are called *sunk costs*. A sunk cost is a cost that cannot subsequently be recovered. So sunk costs of entry are those that must be incurred to enter the market and cannot be recovered if the firm subsequently exits. For example, if an entering firm builds a product-specific factory that has no resale value, this is a sunk cost of entry. However, the cost of a factory that is not product-specific, and can be resold for something close to its original cost, is not a sunk cost of entry.

A market in which new firms can enter and leave without incurring any sunk costs is called a *perfectly contestible market*. A market can be perfectly contestible even if the firm must pay some costs of entry, as long as these can be recovered when the firm exits. Since there are no markets that do not require some sunk costs, contestibility must be understood as a variable. The lower the sunk costs of entry, the more contestible the market.

In a contestible market, the existence of profits even if they are due to transitory causes, will attract entry. Firms will enter, attracted by these profits, and will exit when the transitory situation has changed.

Consider, for example, the market for air travel between two cities. It will be quite contestible as long as space at the airline terminals is available to new entrants. An airline not currently serving the cities in question can shift one of its existing planes to the market with little sunk costs. Some training of personnel to become familiar with that route, and that airport, may be needed. This is a sunk cost that cannot be recovered if the cities in question are no longer to be served. But most of the airline's costs are not sunk. If it subsequently decides to leave that city, the rental of terminal space will stop while the airplane and the ground equipment can be shifted to another location.

Sunk costs of entry constitute a barrier to entry, and the larger these are, the larger can the profits of existing firms be without attracting entry. The flip side of this coin is that markets without large sunk costs of entry will not earn large profits because, if they do, firms can enter costlessly to capture the profits while they last and then exit costlessly.

Contestibility, where it is possible, is a force limiting the profits of existing oligopolists. Even if entry does not occur, the ease with which it can be accomplished will keep oligopolists away from the co-operative equilibrium.

This is another example, in a somewhat refined form, of the key point that entry is the major force preventing the exploitation of market power to restrict output and raise prices. It also emphasizes the importance of the natural barriers to entry into many markets where large sunk costs such as product development, advertising and the setting up of distribution networks must be incurred.

in highly concentrated industries have been highly innovative over many years.

While this hypothesis has substantial credibility, it is not universally valid. Some oligopolistic industries appear to have lagged far behind their foreign competitors, particularly when protected by tariffs. Evidently, a sustained absence of competition can lead them to become complacent and relatively inefficient.

A Final Word

Oligopoly is an important market structure in today's economy because there are many indus-

tries where the MES is simply too large to allow many competing firms to co-exist. Rivalrous oligopoly, however, may produce more satisfactory results than monopoly. Oligopoly may also be effective in producing very-long-run adaptations that develop both new products and cost-reducing methods of producing old ones.

The defence of oligopoly as a market structure is that it may be the best of the available alternatives when MES is large. The challenge to public policy is to keep oligopolists competing and directing their competitive energies towards improving products and lowering costs, rather than merely towards erecting entry barriers.

SUMMARY

1. Firms in market structures other than perfect competition face negatively sloped demand curves and must administer their prices.
2. In the theory of large-group monopolistic competition, many firms compete to sell differentiated products. Each may make pure profits in the short run but in the long run freedom of entry shifts its demand curve until it is tangent to the *ATC* curve, leading to excess capacity and production at average costs above the minimum possible level. Examples of such industries are rare in the real world.
3. The prices of manufactured goods, whether produced under conditions of oligopoly or monopoly, tend to be sticky in the face of cyclical fluctuations in demand. With flat cost curves and costs associated with continual changes in price, it can pay firms to set price at the profit-maximizing output for normal capacity and adjust output as demand fluctuates seasonally and cyclically.
4. Competition among oligopolists may lead to a non-cooperative equilibrium which is self-policing in the sense that no one has an incentive to depart from it unilaterally. Competition in quantities produces Cournot's equilibrium with profits above the competitive but below the monopoly level. Competition in prices, where each firm has the capacity to serve the whole market, produces the Bertrand, short-run equilibrium with price driven to marginal cost and negative profits. If firms can choose their capacity knowing the dangers of destructive price competition, they will restrict their capacity in such a way that they will not be tempted into Bertrand-type price competition except in the face of unexpected reductions in demand.
5. Oligopolistic profits can persist only if there are entry barriers. Natural barriers include economies of large-scale production and large fixed costs of entering the market. Artificial barriers include brand proliferation and high levels of advertising.
6. In qualititive terms the workings of the allocative system under oligopoly is similar (but not identical) to what it is under perfect competition. Whether oligopoly or perfect competition is more conducive to long-run growth of productivity is an open question.

TOPICS FOR REVIEW

- The assumptions of monopolistic competition
- Excess capacity under monopolistic competition
- Reasons for price stickiness under oligopoly
- Cooperative and non-cooperative equilibria
- Bertrand and Cournot equilibrium for duopoly
- Conjectural variations
- Entry barriers
- Resource allocation under oligopoly

APPENDIX to Chapter 14

The Rise and Fall of the Theory of Large-group Monopolistic Competition

The theory of monopolistic competition recognized that manufacturing firms typically sell differentiated products. Indeed, an impressive array of differentiated products, no one precisely the same as another, greets the buyer on any shelf of any supermarket or in any part of a large department store. Product differentiation is a fact of life. It means that every firm has some control over the price of each of its products and that it cannot sell an unlimited amount of each at its current price: the firm faces downward-sloping demand curves, not a perfectly elastic one. This is the 'monopolistic' part of the theory.

Chamberlin chose to analyse a market that had freedom of entry and that contained a large group of sellers rather than a small group. This is the 'competition' part of monopolistic competition. Indeed, he maintained all the assumptions of perfect competition except the one that all firms sell a homogeneous product. In other words, he let otherwise perfectly competitive firms sell a slightly differentiated product. This little change had enormous consequences; it produced what came to be called the monopolistic competition revolution.[1]

---

[1] Chamberlin devoted some space to product differentiation in markets with a few firms and to both free and blockaded entry. Yet the main thrust of the monopolistic competition revolution was in the direction of the large-group case. In the words of the historian of economic thought, Mark Blaug, 'the 12 pages in *The Theory of Monopolistic Competition* on "mutual interdependence recognized" constituted a then original contribution to the theory of oligopoly, but this was not the core of Chamberlin's book.' (*Economic Theory in Retrospect*, 3rd edn, Cambridge: Cambridge University Press, 1978, p. 415.)

The Theory

The short-run equilibrium of the firm in monopolistic competition, shown in Figure 14.1(i) on page 235, is the same as that of monopoly. Short-run profits will attract entry. As more firms enter, the total demand for the product must be shared among the larger number of firms, so each can expect to have a smaller share of the market. At any given price, each firm can expect to sell less than it could before the influx of new firms. At this point Chamberlin makes the critical *assumption of symmetry*: *that the entry of one new firm will shift the demand curve for each of the firms already in the industry by the same (small) amount to the left.*

This movement will continue as long as there are profits. At equilibrium, the monopolistically competitive firm is in the zero-profit tangency solution with excess capacity of $q_C - q_L$ shown in Figure 14.1(ii).

Modern Developments

A major theoretical criticism of the large-group case began with Nicholas Kaldor in the 1930s but was fully articulated only with the work by Kelvin Lancaster on the 'New Theory of Demand' in the 1970s.

Differentiated products have several characteristics, and each product can be thought of as being located in its 'characteristics space'. This can be represented by a graph in which amounts of each characteristic are measured on each axis. A new product must occupy some point in characteristic space – that is, the product must have quantities of each characteristic. Thus a new product will have some closely competing products (those whose characteristics are very similar), more less close competitors, and even more further distant competitors. Consequently the new entrant will not affect the demand curves for all the industry's products to the same degree. Closely similar products will have their demands shifted a lot, less similar products less so, and so on. *Chamberlin's symmetry assumption does not apply to products differentiated in characteristics space.*

A similar argument applies to geographic differentiation. A large city may have hundreds of chemists' shops that are only slightly differentiated from each other in all non-geographic characteristics. But each has a specific location and thus a different level of convenience to each buyer. When a new shop enters the industry at one specific location, its arrival will have a major impact on the demand curves facing chemists in nearby locations, a smaller effect on chemists further away and virtually no effect on chemists located at the other end of the city. Consequently a new shop entering such a market will not shift the demand curves of existing shops to the same degree. Nearby shops will be affected a lot, more distant shops less so, and so on. *Chamberlin's symmetry assumption does not apply to firms differentiated in geographic space.*

The above shows why Chamberlin's large-group case, where, because of the symmetry assumption, each product or shop is *equally* in competition with every other product or shop, has few real applications. A model in which the many firms in an industry are in intense competition with only a relatively few close neighbours seems a better fit to the world of experience.[1]

The above arguments would hold even if each shop or product were owned by a separate firm. Empirically, a further shortcoming of the large-group case (as observed in the text of Chapter 14) is that a large number of differentiated *products* is

much more common than is a large number of differentiated *firms*. In soap or cigarettes for example there is a large number of products but each firm produces many products, so there is only a small number of firms. Also chains such as Trusthouse Forte or Boots are common in spatially differentiated industries so that although many shops is the typical case, few firms is also often typical. Thus when we look at firms, which are the decision units, rather than products, we find once again that small-group is much more common than large-group monopolistic competition in the real world. As Mark Blaug puts it (*op. cit.*, p. 415):

> The most damaging criticism that can be made against the theory of monopolistic competition is not that some of its assumptions are unrealistic but that most of the product markets that appear at first glance to conform to the requirements of the Chamberlinian tangency solution turn out on closer examination to involve the 'conjectural interdependence' characteristic of oligopoly: product differentiation takes place typically in a market environment of 'competition among the few'.

Consequently, the main thrust of the development of the modern theory of product differentiation has been in the small-group case: a small number of firms compete, each selling its own range of differentiated products. Indeed in modern terminology, monopolistic competition has come to mean product differentiation (the monopolistic aspect) rather than large numbers (the competitive aspect), so most modern work on what is called monopolistic competition is work on the case of differentiated oligopoly (a small group of firms selling a number of differentiated products).

The modern theory has suggested its own form of the excess-capacity theorem: that firms may sometimes create more capital than they need for their own current production, the excess being a barrier to the entry of new firms. There is a difference, however. In the older theory, firms were forced into excess capacity by the impersonal market forces of entry; in the new theory, existing firms may consciously create excess capacity as a barrier to entry. This proposition, still a subject of controversy, takes us to the very frontier of current research.

---

[1] We have discussed these matters in more detail elsewhere in a paper that is accessible only to more advanced students. See B.C.Eaton and R.G.Lipsey, 'Product Differentiation', in R.Schmallensee and R.Willig (eds), *A Handbook of Industrial Organization* (Amsterdam: North Holland Press, 1989). See also G.C.Archibald, B.C.Eaton and R.G.Lipsey, 'Address Models of Value Theory', in J.Stiglitz and R.Mathewson (eds), *New Developments in the Theory of Monopolist's Competition* (Boston: MIT Press, 1987).

Conclusion

Looking back, we see that the original theory of monopolistic competition contributed at least two important things to the development of economics. At the time that it was first developed, perfect competition was under attack for the lack of realism of its assumptions. The theory of monopolistic competition allowed for the facts of product differentiation, of the ability of firms to influence prices and of advertising. The incor-poration of these into a new theory encouraged economists to consider the question of their effects on the operation of the price system.

A second major contribution of the theory is that many economists have been profoundly influenced by it. It rekindled economists' interest in such important things as how and when firms took each other's reactions into account, what made for easy or restricted entry, and the signifi-cance to competition of different products that were roughly similar to one another.

15

Applications

In this chapter we use the theories that we have just examined to predict how industries will react to some of the forces that affect them. The predictions can be viewed in two different ways. First, they are logical implications of the theory's assumptions. From this point of view, the truth of a certain proposition is a matter of logic: the proposition either is, or is not, implied by the theory. Second, the predictions may be regarded as empirical hypotheses. Their consistency with the facts is then a matter for testing.

Whether or not a given proposition is implied by some theory is a question that can be settled definitely without reference to facts; whether or not a given proposition (which follows from a theory) is consistent with the facts, can be settled only by observation.

THE DRIVE TO MONOPOLIZE PERFECTLY COMPETITIVE INDUSTRIES

Cocoa producers in West Africa, farmers in the EC, coffee growers in Brazil, oil producers in the OPEC countries, taxi drivers in many cities and labour unions throughout the world have all sought to obtain, through collective action, some of the benefits of departing from perfect competition.

The motivation behind this drive for monopoly power is analysed in Figure 15.1. As the Figure shows, the equilibrium of a perfectly competitive industry is *invariably* one in which a restriction of output, and a consequent increase in price, would raise the joint profits of all the firms in the industry. This is because at any competitive equilibrium, each firm is producing where marginal cost equals price. But as long as the demand curve slopes downwards, marginal revenue for the industry is less than price, and thus also less than marginal cost. It follows that in competitive equilibrium the last unit sold necessarily contributes less to the industry's revenue than to its costs.

It always pays the producers in a perfectly competitive industry to enter into an output-restricting agreement.

FIGURE 15.1 The Cartelization of a Perfectly Competitive Industry

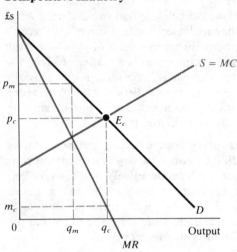

Cartelization of a perfectly competitive industry can always increase that industry's profits. Equilibrium for a perfectly competitive industry occurs at E_c, where the supply and demand curves intersect. Equilibrium price and output are at p_c and q_c. Because the industry demand curve has a negative slope, marginal revenue is less than price. In the diagram, marginal revenue is m_c at the competitive equilibrium output of q_c.

If the industry is cartelized, profits can be increased by reducing output. All units between q_c and q_m add less to revenue than to cost – the marginal revenue curve lies below the marginal cost curve. (Recall from Figures 12.4 and 12.5 that the industry's supply curve is the sum of the marginal cost curves of the firms in the industry.) If the units between q_c and q_m are not produced, output is reduced to q_m and price rises to p_m. This price-output combination maximizes the industry's profits because it is where marginal revenue equals marginal cost.

FIGURE 15.2 Conflicting Forces Affecting Cartels

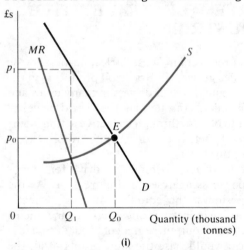 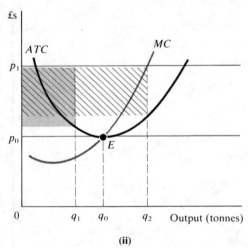

(i)   (ii)

Co-operation leads to the monopoly price, but individual self-interest leads to production in excess of the monopoly output. Market conditions are shown in (i), and the situation of a typical firm in (ii). (Note the different scales in the two figures.) Initially, the market is in competitive equilibrium with price p_0, and quantity Q_0. The individual firm is producing output q_0, and is just covering its total costs.

The cartel now enforces quotas on individual firms sufficient to reduce the industry's output to Q_1, which maximizes the joint profits of the cartel members. Price rises to p_1 as a result. The typical firm has a quota of q_1 and its profits rise from zero to the amount shown by the grey-shaded area. At price p_1, however, the individual firm's profit-maximizing output is q_2, where marginal cost is equal to the new price. The firm's profits would then be the amount shown by the diagonally striped area. But if all firms increase their outputs above their quotas, industry output will increase beyond Q_1. Price will be driven down and the profits earned by all firms will fall.

A producers' association formed for such a purpose is often called a **cartel**.

Figure 15.2 shows the disruptive forces that operate whenever an output-restricting agreement is in existence. Price is raised when all firms agree to restrict output. Any single firm can increase its profits, however, by violating the output restrictions. Selling more will not significantly affect price, but will increase its revenue. Thus, unless the cartel has the power to enforce its output restrictions, there will be a tendency for individual firms to violate the restrictions once prices have been raised. Furthermore, the cartel must have power over all producers, not merely over its members; otherwise a firm could avoid the output restrictions merely by leaving the cartel.

If one member succumbs to the temptation, it is better off and no one else loses since one firm's output is too small to affect price significantly. But if all members succumb to the temptation, output will rise significantly, price will be driven back to the competitive level, and all firms will lose.

> **Each individual cartel member can increase its profits by violating the output restrictions, provided that the other members do not violate theirs.**

These two predictions highlight the dilemma of any cartel, whether it be OPEC or a local producers' association. Each firm is better off if the cartel is effective in restricting output and so raising price. But each is even better off if everyone else co-operates while it cheats. Yet if all cheat, all will be worse off.

The Organization of Petroleum Exporting Countries as an Illustration of Oligopoly

The Organization of Petroleum Exporting Countries (OPEC) provides an example of the cartelization of a formerly competitive industry, and it illustrates both the problems of oligopolistic industries and the functioning of the price system.

The OPEC Cartel

Prior to 1973 the oil industry was not perfectly competitive. There were so many oil-producing countries, however, that no one country could significantly influence the price of oil by withholding its own output from the market. Thus, at least in the price-taking aspect, the various oil-producing countries sold their oil in a perfectly competitive market. There was large productive capacity in the OPEC countries, making the short-run world supply highly elastic at a world price which was close to OPEC's production costs.

OPEC did not become a cartel, nor attract world attention, until 1973. In that year, however, members of OPEC voluntarily restricted their outputs by negotiating quotas. At the time, OPEC countries accounted for about 70 per cent of the world's supply of crude oil and 87 per cent of world oil exports. So, although it was not quite a complete monopoly, the cartel had substantial monopoly power. As a result of the output restrictions, the world price of oil nearly quadrupled within a year. What happened is analysed in more detail in Figure 15.3.

The Success of OPEC

OPEC's policy succeeded for several reasons. First, the member countries provided a large part of the total world supply of oil; second, other producing countries could not quickly increase their outputs in response to price increases; and third, the world demand for oil proved to be highly inelastic in the short run.

OPEC's exports were about 31 million barrels per day in 1973. In order to raise prices within a year from an average of $3.37 per barrel to an average of $11.25 a barrel, exports had only to be restricted to 28.5 million barrels per day. A reduction in OPEC's exports of less than 10 per cent was sufficient to more than triple the world price! (Note that oil prices are usually expressed in terms of US dollars.)

The higher prices were maintained for the remainder of the decade. As a result, OPEC countries found themselves suddenly enjoying vast wealth, while oil-importing countries found their real incomes substantially diminished.

No early temptation to cheat: So great was the increase in the wealth of the member countries that the temptation to cheat, in order to gain even more, was small during the rest of the 1970s. Indeed, the development programmes of many

FIGURE 15.3 OPEC as a Successful Cartel

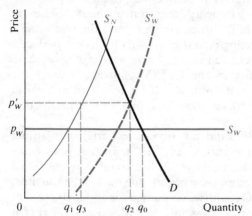

Given a rising, non-OPEC supply curve of oil, OPEC could determine equilibrium price by choosing its contribution to total supply. The curve S_N represents the non-OPEC supply curve of oil. When the OPEC countries were prepared to supply all that was demanded at the world price of p_W, the world supply curve was S_W. At that price, production was q_1 in non-OPEC countries, and $q_0 - q_1$ in OPEC countries.

By fixing its production, OPEC shifted the world supply curve to S'_W, where the horizontal distance between S_N and S'_W is OPEC's production. The world price rose to p'_W. Production became q_3 in non-OPEC countries, and $q_2 - q_3$ in the OPEC countries.

OPEC increased its oil revenues because, although sales fell, the price rose more than in proportion. Non-OPEC countries gained doubly because they were free to produce more, and to sell it at the new, higher world price.

OPEC countries were constrained, not by funds, but by physical limits to their growth. For example, ships carrying supplies needed to build roads, warehouses and other basic facilities often lay in harbour for months because of insufficient port facilities. Even when they were unloaded, supplies often sat at the harbour side for further months because of inadequate internal transport facilities. Because further funds were not urgently needed by OPEC members, the temptation to cheat was weak, making the enforcement of OPEC's output quotas an easy matter.

Longer-term market forces, however, were working against OPEC.

Pressure on the Cartel

Monopolistic producers always face a dilemma.

The closer are their prices to the profit-maximizing level, the greater their short-term profits, but also the greater the incentive for market reactions that will reduce their profits in the longer term. In OPEC's case, the market reactions came from both the demand and the supply sides of the market.

Increasing world supply: The high prices and high profits achieved by the OPEC cartel spurred major additions to the world's oil supply by non-OPEC producers. This was, in effect, new entry. In 1973, OPEC produced more than 70 per cent of the world's oil, by 1979 its share was less than 60 per cent, and by 1985 only 30 per cent. North Sea oil, Mexican oil, Soviet oil and increased American and Canadian production gradually replaced output that had been withdrawn from the market by OPEC. Higher prices encouraged new exploration and induced the oil companies to produce more from already proven reserves. The increased supply of non-OPEC oil tended to drive the world price down. To maintain the price, OPEC had to reduce its own output so as to hold world output constant. The OPEC countries lost revenue if they held their output constant because their prices fell; if they took steps to maintain prices, output had to be reduced.

Declining world demand: The market demand curve for oil shows how the puchases of oil will vary as price varies, *other things being equal*. But, other things being equal, there was little that users could do to reduce their consumption of petroleum products in response to the price rise. Car drivers could take fewer Sunday trips, and some took a train or bus to work when petrol prices soared. Householders and office managers turned their heating down a bit. Factories tried to economize on their fuel consumption. But, overall, the response of world demand to the initial price increase was modest. The market demand curve was thus highly inelastic.

Over a longer period of time, however, major economies proved possible – as they almost always do for any product whose relative price rises greatly. When it came time to replace the family car, many households responded to the high price of petrol by buying smaller, more fuel-efficient cars. Householders and office managers found that they could greatly reduce their fuel bills by properly insulating their buildings or by turning to such alternative sources of heating as natural gas. New factories were able to use newly designed power plants that used alternative fuels or were much more economical in their use of oil. A host of longer-term adaptations economized on petroleum products within known technology. The long-run demand curve proved to be much more elastic than the short-run demand curve. (See Figure 6.4 on page 86, for an elaboration of the distinction between short- and long-run demand curves.)

Very-long-run forces were also unleashed. The high price of petroleum led to a burst of scientific research to develop more petroleum-efficient technologies, and alternatives to petroleum. Solar-heating technology was advanced, as was technology concerning many longer-term alternatives such as tidal power and heat from the interior of the earth. Had the price of petroleum remained at its 1980 peak, this research would have continued at an intense pace, and would have borne increasing fruits in the decades that followed.

As a result of the long- and very-long-run reactions, other things did not remain equal over the period of a decade. Instead, the market demand curve for oil began to shift to the left.[1]

The combined effect of decreasing demand and increasing supply is illustrated in Figure 15.4. The shrinking market for OPEC oil at the high OPEC price necessitated ever stiffer production limitations if the cartel was to maintain its prices. By 1981 OPEC exports were only 18 million barrels per day, two-thirds of the 1973 level, and by 1985 maintaining prices required that production be cut to only 15 million barrels per day.

The pressure to cheat: We have seen that, as world output of oil grew, OPEC output had to be reduced substantially to hold prices high. As a result, incomes in OPEC countries declined

---

FIGURE 15.4 OPEC in Trouble

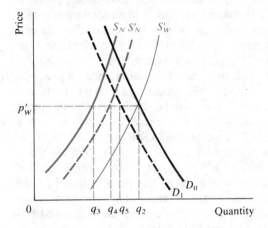

As demand declined and non-OPEC oil supply increased, declining OPEC production was required to maintain the world price. The Figure repeats the post-OPEC equilibrium from Figure 15.3. The world demand curve is D_0, and the non-OPEC supply curve is S_N. OPEC's production is $q_2 - q_3$, making the world supply curve S'_W, and the world price p'_W.

Over time, the discovery and development of new oil sources shifted the supply curve of the non-OPEC countries to S'_N. At the same time, long-term economization, and adoption of other energy sources, shifted the market demand curve for oil to D_1. At the world price, p'_W, non-OPEC production rises to q_4. To maintain that price, OPEC production must be contracted to $q_5 - q_4$.

---

sharply. Many oil-producing countries had become used to their new wealth, and thus the instabilities inherent in any cartel began to be felt seriously from within OPEC. In 1981 the cartel price reached its peak of US $35 per barrel. In real terms, this was about five times as high as the 1972 price, but production quotas were less than half of OPEC's capacity. Anxious to increase their oil revenues, many individual OPEC members gave in to the pressures that were analysed in Figure 15.2 – they began to exceed their production quotas.

OPEC members met every few months to debate quotas, deplore cheating and argue about strategy. Saudi Arabia, the giant of OPEC with 40 per cent of all OPEC oil reserves, maintained a semblance of order after 1981 by a combination of threats to flood the market with oil if cheating

---

[1] One reason why these demand reactions took so long to develop was government policies in many countries designed to hold domestic prices far below world prices in order to cushion the blow on domestic consumers. This delayed many of the reactions on both the demand and the supply sides. Governments exhorted people to economize on petrol and fuel oil, but the response was slight until the incentive of higher domestic prices was allowed to operate.

continued, and willingness to take a lion's share of the additional cuts required to keep prices high. Between 1981 and 1983 Saudi Arabia cut its production from 9.8 to 5.1 million barrels per day, accounting for virtually all of the reduction in total OPEC production during those years.

By late 1985, Saudi Arabia indicated it would not tolerate further cheating by its partners, and demanded that others share equally in quota reductions. But agreement proved impossible and in December 1985 OPEC decided to eliminate production quotas. Early in 1986 the price fell below $10 a barrel which, corrected for inflation, was equal to the price ruling in 1970 before the supply restrictions were first introduced. The price since then has fluctuated between $10 and $20 a barrel.

Hurt dramatically by the collapse of their cartel arrangements, OPEC countries, this time with some tacit assistance of non-OPEC producers, slowly achieved some fragile co-operation. As a result, the price of oil settled around $18 a barrel by mid 1987. The agreement continued to be fragile; some serious violations of quotas led to further fluctuations in the range $12–$18 over the next two years. Maintaining an $18 price will depend on the ability to sustain the co-operative behaviour of the oil-producing countries, each one of which has a self-interest in producing to the point where its own marginal cost of production equals the world price.

The Relevance of the OPEC Experience to Oligopoly

OPEC's experience illustrates some basic problems of monopolies and of cartels.

Restriction of output below the competitive level can lead to immense profits in the short term.

This is particularly so if the market demand curve turns out to be highly inelastic. There is thus substantial incentive for an industry to be monopolized, or for a group of producers to co-operate in exercising their collective market power.

Maintaining market power becomes increasingly difficult as time passes.

Supply is likely to increase as new producers find ways of overcoming entry barriers in order to share in the large profits. Demand is likely to decrease as new substitutes are invented and put into production. These long-term adjustments limit the market power of monopolies and cartels, but only with a significant time-lag.

Producers with market power face a basic trade-off between profits in the short term and profits in the longer term.

The closer does the single producer, or a cartel, get price to the monopoly level, the higher are the short-run profits, but the greater is the incentive for longer-term, profit-reducing reactions from both the supply side and the demand side of the market.

Output restriction by voluntary agreement among several firms is difficult to maintain in the long run.

When there are many producers the perfectly competitive equilibrium is the self-policing, non-cooperative equilibrium. The monopoly solution is a co-operative equilibrium and, because it is not self-policing, it tends to be hard to maintain. This is particularly so if declining demand and increasing competition from new sources, or new products, leads to a steadily shrinking share of the market and falling profits.

CHANGES IN DEMAND AND COSTS

How do markets respond to changing demands and costs? The analysis of this question is important because it sets the stage for a study of the effects of taxes, subsidies, innovations and a host of other things, all of which affect either the revenues or the costs of firms. As in any study using comparative statics, we must start in the appropriate equilibrium position – in this case it is one of long-run equilibrium. (Appropriate corrections must be made if one wishes to apply the results to cases in which the initial position is one of disequilibrium.)

Changes in Demand

Competition: The effects of shifts in demand in perfect competition have been analysed on pp. 213–216 of Chapter 12. For completeness, we summarize these results here.

In the short run, a rise in demand in a competitive industry will cause:
(1) **price to rise;**
(2) **an increase in the quantity supplied by each firm and hence by the industry;**
(3) **each firm to earn profits.**

The long-run effects follow from the third prediction. Profits will attract new investment. New entry will cause an increase in supply that will force the price below the previously established, short-run equilibrium. This will continue until profits have returned to zero.

In the long run, a rise in demand in a competitive industry will cause:
(1) **the scale of industry to expand;**
(2) **profits to return to zero; and**
(3) **the new equilibrium price to be above, below or equal to the original price; but (i) constant factor prices and (ii) identical, and unchanged, cost curves for new and old firms ensure that price returns to its original level.**

Now consider the effects of a fall in demand.

In the short run, a fall in demand in a competitive industry will cause:
(1) **price to fall;**
(2) **a decrease in the quantity supplied by each firm and hence by the industry;**
(3) **each firm to make losses; and**
(4) **firms to cease production immediately if they are unable to cover their variable costs of production.**

The long-run effects follow from the third prediction. Losses make the industry an unattractive place in which to invest. No new capital will enter; as old plant and equipment wear out, it will not be replaced. As the supply diminishes, the price of the product will rise until the remaining firms can cover their total costs.

In the long run, a fall in demand in a competitive industry will cause:
(1) **the scale of the industry to contract;**
(2) **losses to be eliminated eventually; and**
(3) **price to be above, below or equal to its**
original level; but (i) constant factor prices and (ii) identical, and unchanged, cost curves for all firms ensure that price returns to its original level.

Oligopoly: When we consider market structures other than perfect competition, we must distinguish short-run cyclical fluctuations in demand from changes that are perceived to be longer lasting. We saw in Chapter 14 that oligopolies tend to adjust quantity rather than price when demand fluctuates in the short term (see pages 238–242). Thus cyclical fluctuations in demand cause output to change at a (more or less) constant price in oligopolistic industries.

Long-term changes in demand lead to more familiar adjustments. Permanent decreases in demand cause capital to leave the industry. Price then rises or falls depending on what happens to the costs of the remaining firms, and to their degree of competition. Permanent increases in demand cause capital to enter the industry. Price rises or falls depending on what happens to firms' costs and to the degree of competition. Even if the number of firms does not change, existing firms will alter their outputs. They will then wish to move to a different point on their *LRAC* curves by altering their plant size. (Recall that perfect competition is the only market structure in which firms must be on the lowest point of their *LRAC* curve in equilibrium.)

Monopoly: Short-term cyclical fluctuations have the same effect as in oligopoly and for the same reasons: it does not always pay the monopolist to vary price in response to shifts in demand that are expected to be transitory.

Now consider a shift in demand that is assumed to be long-lasting. In the section on the absence of a supply curve under monopoly (see Figure 13.5), we saw that a rise in demand need not always cause an increase in a monopolist's price and output, even in the short run. It is possible, provided that the elasticity of demand changes sufficiently, for a rise in demand to cause a fall either in price or in output.

At this level of generality, we are left with the implication that a rise in demand for a monopoly can cause both its price and its output to rise, but that either price or output might fall. This may seem a disappointingly vague conclusion, but it is

FIGURE 15.5 Shifts in a Monopolist's Demand Curve

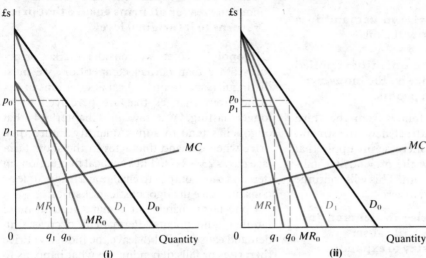

When a monopolist's demand curve either shifts parallel to itself or pivots
through the price intercept, both price and quantity change in the same
direction. In both parts of the Figure, the original demand curve is D_0. The marginal
revenue curve MR_0 and the marginal cost curve intersect at output q_0, which is sold at
price p_0. The demand curve then shifts to D_1. The new marginal revenue curve, MR_1,
intersects the unchanged MC curve to produce a new equilibrium price and quantity
of p_1 and q_1. Both price and quantity fall. (Both rise if the shift is a rise in demand from
D_1 to D_0.) The difference between the two parts is in the nature of the demand shift.

In part (i), the demand curve shifts parallel to itself, indicating the same *absolute
change* in quantity demanded at each price, and the same *absolute change* in price at
which each quantity will be bought.

In part (ii), the demand curve pivots through the price intercept, indicating the
same *percentage change* in quantity demanded at each price.

---

all that the theory implies. In order to get a more
specific prediction we need to know more about
the precise shape of the demand curve.

There are some cases in which predictions are
possible. Two are of particular interest: (i) every
point on the demand curve shifts by the same
amount, and (ii) the demand curve pivots
through its point of intersection on the price axis.
Figure 15.5 shows that, in both of these cases,
both price and quantity rise when demand rises,
and fall when demand falls. The first case applies
in the effects of a per-unit tax or subsidy on the
monopolist's output. A specific tax can be shown
as a shift of the firm's demand curve vertically
downwards by the amount of the tax. Case (ii)
applies when the market expands because of the
addition of new customers with the same tastes as
those initially in the market. In this case, if the

number of customers increased by x per cent, the
quantity demanded also increases by x per cent at
each price.

Changes in Costs

Competition: Figure 15.6 analyses the effects
of a reduction in costs of production in a competitive industry. The short-run supply curve shifts
downwards by the amount of the downward shift
in the firms' marginal cost curves. This leads to a
higher output and a lower price. The price will
fall, however, by less than the fall in costs, while
profits will now be earned because of the lower
costs of production.

**In the short run under perfect compe-
tition, a fall in variable cost causes price
to fall but by less than the reduction in**

marginal cost. The benefit of the reduction in cost is thus shared between consumers, in terms of lower prices, and producers, in terms of higher profits.

In the long run, however, profits cannot persist in an industry having freedom of entry. New firms will enter the industry, increasing output and reducing price until all profits are eliminated.

In the long run under perfect competition, all of the benefits of lower costs are passed on to consumers in terms of higher output and lower prices.

The case of a rise in costs is just the reverse. In the short run, the effects will be shared between consumers, in terms of higher prices, and producers, in terms of losses. In the long run, however, firms will leave the industry until those remaining can cover all their costs. Therefore,

the effects of higher costs are fully borne by consumers in terms of lower output and higher prices.

Oligopoly: In oligopoly, a fall in costs yields a fall in the profit-maximizing price at normal-capacity output. Therefore, price will fall and output will rise. Also profits will rise so that, once again, pressure will occur for new entry. A battle may then ensue between new firms desiring entry and existing firms pursuing entry-barring strategies.

Monopoly: A fall in marginal costs will cause a reduction in price and an increase in output. (You should draw your own Figure to demonstrate this.) Thus the direction of the change in price and output, in response to a change in costs, is the same in monopoly as in perfect competition. But the magnitude of the change will be less in

FIGURE 15.6 A Fall in Costs in a Competitive Industry (Short-run Effects)

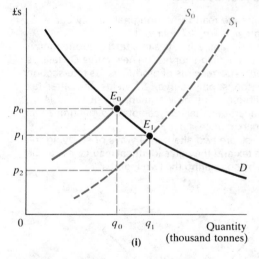
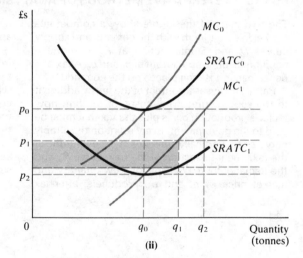

A fall in costs in a competitive industry leads to a fall in price, an increase in output and the emergence of profits. In part (i), the original demand and supply curves of D and S_0 intersect at E_0 to yield a price and quantity of p_0 and q_0. When each firm's production costs fall, the supply curve – which is the sum of the marginal cost curves of all firms in the industry – shifts downward by the amount of the fall in costs, to S_1. If price fell by the full amount that costs had fallen, price would become p_2. Instead, price falls to p_1 while quantity rises to q_1, at the new equilibrium E_1.

In part (ii), the typical firm in the industry is shown in equilibrium at price p_0 with cost curves $SRATC_0$ and MC_0. The cost curves then shift to $SRATC_1$ and MC_1. The firm would be willing to produce output q_0 at price p_2. Instead price only falls to p_1, and the firm increases its output to q_1. At this price-quantity combination, it earns profits shown by the shaded area.

monopoly than in competition. Since a monopoly firm necessarily has barriers to entry (or it would not be a monopoly), the higher profit that it earns as a result of a fall in its costs does *not* attract new entrants. Thus there is no long-run force to drive profits back to their original level.

In monopoly, in both the short run and the long run, the effects of rising or falling costs are shared between the consumers, in terms of price and output variations, and the firm, in terms of profit variations.

We now have a powerful tool at our command: once we can relate anything in which we are interested to change in either costs or revenues, we have a series of predictions already worked out. We shall see examples of how this can be done in the next section of this chapter, and later in this book.

THE EFFECT OF TAXES ON PRICE AND OUTPUT

There are many kinds of taxes which affect the costs of firms. We shall consider three of them here: a tax that is a fixed amount per unit produced; a tax that is a fixed amount; and a tax that is a fixed percentage of profits. The first is called a per-unit tax, the second a lump-sum tax, and the third a profits tax.

Per-unit Tax

Box 15.1 shows two methods of analysing the effects of a per-unit tax. The method that we use in what follows is to observe that with a per-unit tax the firm must pay the tax to the government on each unit that it produces. Thus the tax may be thought of as increasing the costs associated with producing each unit. The marginal cost curve of every firm shifts vertically upwards by

---

BOX 15.1 ALTERNATIVE METHODS OF ANALYSING A SALES TAX

The two parts of the Figure show a competitive market in equilibrium with the demand and supply curves D and S intersecting at E_0 to produce equilibrium price and output of p_0 and q_0. A tax of T pence per unit is then placed on the commodity.

Part (i) analyses the effect of the tax by adding it to the supply curve. The 'costs' of the firm now include production costs plus the tax that must be paid to the government. Every point on the supply curve shifts vertically upwards by the amount of the tax. The intersection of the new curve S_T and the demand curve D yields the new quantity and market price of q_1 and p_1. Producers' after-tax

receipts are read for the original supply curve, S, and are p_2 $(= p_1 - T)$ per unit.

Part (ii) analyses the same tax by subtracting it from the demand curve. The new curve D_T tells us the after-tax receipts of producers. Its intersection with the supply curve, S, yields the after-tax equilibrium. The new equilibrium quantity is q_1, producers get after-tax receipts of p_2 per unit while the market price is p_1.

These are two alternative ways of studying the same tax and they give identical results, as can be seen by comparing the two Figures.

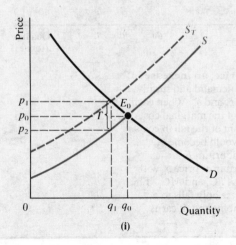

(i)

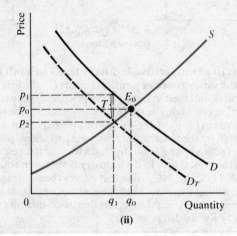

(ii)

BOX 15.2 THE PRICE OF HAIRCUTS AND THE PROFITS OF BARBERS

Suppose that there are many barber shops and freedom of entry into barbering: anyone can set up as a barber. Assume that the going price for haircuts is £5 and that at this price all barbers believe their incomes are too low.

The barbers hold a meeting and decide to form a trade association. The purpose of the association is to persuade the government to impose a price of £7 for haircuts. What is the result?

We need to distinguish between the short-run and the long-run effects of an increase in the price of haircuts. In the short run the number of barbers is fixed. Thus, in the short run the answer depends only on the elasticity of the demand for haircuts. If demand elasticity is less than 1, total expenditure on haircuts will rise and so will the incomes of barbers; if demand elasticity exceeds 1, the barbers' revenues will fall. Thus to answer the question we need some knowledge about the size of the elasticity of demand for haircuts.

Suppose we estimate the elasticity of demand over the relevant price range to be 0.45. We then predict that barbers will be successful in raising incomes in the short run. A 40 per cent rise in price will be met by an 18 per cent fall in quantity of haircuts, so the total revenue of the typical barber will rise by about 15 per cent.*

Now what about the long run? If barbers were just covering costs before the price change, they will now be earning profits. Barbering will become an attractive trade relative to others requiring equal skill and training, and there will be a flow of barbers into the industry. As the number of barbers rises, the same amount of business must be shared among more and more barbers, so the typical barber will find business – and thus earnings – decreasing.

Profits may also be squeezed from another direction. With fewer customers coming their way, barbers may compete against one another for the limited number of customers. The government (or their agreement) does not allow them to compete through price cuts, but they can compete in service. They may spruce up their shops, offer their customers expensive magazines to read, and so forth. This kind of non-price competition will raise operating costs.

These changes will continue until barbers are just covering their opportunity costs, at which time the attraction for new entrants will vanish. The industry will settle down in a new long-run equilibrium in which individual barbers make incomes only as large as they did before the price rise. There will be more barbers than there were in the original situation, but each barber will be working for a smaller fraction of the day and will be idle for a larger fraction (the industry will have excess capacity). Customers will have shorter waits even at peak periods, and they will get to read a wide choice of magazines, but they will be paying £7 for haircuts.

If the government agreed to the plan in order to raise the average income of barbers, it will have failed. It has created more jobs for barbers, but not a higher income for each.

The general lesson is clear: one cannot raise income by raising price above the competitive level unless one can prevent new entry or otherwise reduce the quantity of the product or service provided.

---

*Let p and q be the price and quantity before the price increase. Total revenue after the increase is $TR = (1.4p)(0.82q) = 1.148pq$.

the amount of the tax, where marginal cost now refers to the total outlay – factor payments and taxes – associated with each additional unit of production.

Perfect competition: In perfect competition, the upward shift in marginal cost curves means that the industry supply curve shifts upward by the amount of the tax. Now we can refer to the results of our previous study of cost changes in order to obtain the required predictions.

The effects of a per-unit tax on the output of a competitive industry are:

(1) in the short run, the price will rise but by less than the amount of the tax, so that the burden will be shared by consumers and producers;

(2) in the long run, the industry will contract, profits will return to normal and the whole burden will fall on consumers;

(3) if cost curves of firms remaining in the industry are unaffected by the contraction in the size of the industry, price will rise in the long run by the full amount of the tax.

The second of the above predictions is an example of a most important general proposition:

in an industry with freedom of entry or exit and where there is room for a large number of firms, profits will always be pushed to zero in the long run. Thus any temporary advantage or disadvantage given to the industry by government policy, by private conniving or by anything else must be dissipated in the long run – free entry and exit always ensures that surviving firms earn zero profits.

Government intervention in an industry with freedom of entry and exit can influence the size of the industry, the total volume of its sales and the price at which its goods are sold; but intervention cannot influence the long-run profitability of the firms that remain in the industry.

Many a government policy has started out to raise the profitability of a particular industry, and ended up only increasing the number of firms operating at an unchanged level of profits. A further illustration of this important point is given in Box 15.2.

Monopoly: Although the monopoly firm has no supply curve, the tax does shift its marginal cost curve. The analysis of the previous section on cost shifts allows us to state that:

In the short run and in the long run, the burden of a per-unit tax on a monopoly will be shared between consumers, in terms of lower output and higher prices, and the producer, in terms of lower profits.

Lump-sum Tax

Lump-sum taxes increase the fixed costs of the firm but do not increase marginal costs. As long as a firm is able to cover its variable costs, it will remain in production. Since both marginal costs and marginal revenues are unaffected by the taxes, the profit-maximizing level of output must be unchanged.

A lump-sum tax leaves the short-run equilibrium price and output unchanged in all market structures, unless the tax is so high that it causes firms simply to abandon production at once.

This result is shown in Figure 15.7(i). The long-run effects of a lump-sum tax differ between monopolistic and competitive industries.

Perfect competition: If a perfectly competitive industry was in equilibrium with zero profits before the tax was instituted, then the tax will cause losses. Although nothing will happen in the short run to price and output, equipment will not be replaced as it wears out. Thus, in the long run, the industry will contract, and price will rise until the *whole tax* has been passed on to consumers and the firms remaining in the industry are again covering total costs.

A lump-sum tax will have no effect on a competitive industry in the short run, but in the long run it will cause the exit of firms; output will fall and price will rise until the whole of the tax is borne by consumers.

Monopoly: Assuming that the firm was previously making profits, the tax merely reduces the level of these profits. But, since the tax reduces the profit associated with every output by the same amount, it does not change the profit-maximizing output. Therefore, the tax leaves the monopoly's price and output unchanged.

In the long run, the lump-sum tax that does not drive a monopolist out of business has no effect on its price and output; hence the whole tax is paid by the monopolist.

Of course, if the tax is so large that, even at the profit-maximizing output, profits become negative, the monopolist will cease production in the long run.

Profits Tax

A famous prediction is that a tax levied as a percentage on what economists call profits will have no effect on price and output under any market structure. Let us first see how the prediction is derived, and then consider its application to real-world situations.

Perfect competition: In perfect competition, there are no profits in long-run equilibrium. Thus the firms in a perfectly competitive industry will pay no profit tax in the long run (x per cent of zero is zero). It follows that the tax does not affect the firm's long-run behaviour.

FIGURE 15.7 A Tax on Pure Profits

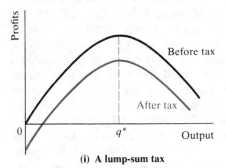

(i) A lump-sum tax

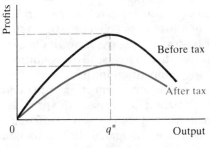

(ii) A percentage tax

A tax on pure profits leaves equilibrium price and output unchanged.

In both parts of the diagram, the upper curve shows how profits vary with output in the absence of a tax. The profit-maximizing output is q^*. The lower curve shows how profits vary with output after a tax is imposed on profits.

In part (i), the tax is a lump sum. Every point on the upper curve shifts down by the same amount. The profit-maximizing output remains at q^*.

In part (ii), the tax is 20 per cent of profits. Every point on the lower curve is 20 per cent less than the corresponding point on the upper curve. The profit-maximizing output remains at q^*.

Monopoly: A monopoly firm usually earns profits in the long run and, therefore, would pay a profits tax. The tax would reduce its profits but would not cause the firm to alter its quantity produced nor (hence) its price. Since the firm's previous output yields higher profits than any other output, taxing away a percentage of the firm's profits cannot make any other output yield more profits than the previous profit-maximizing output. This result is illustrated in Figure 15.7(ii).

A tax on profit, as defined in economics, affects neither price nor output in perfect

competition and in monopoly. Hence it has no effect on the allocation of resources.

A qualification: Does this prediction apply to real-world 'profit taxes'? The answer is no because profits, as they are defined in tax law, are different from profits as defined in economics. In particular, the tax-law definition includes the opportunity cost of capital and the reward for risk-taking. To economists, this is a cost; for tax purposes, it is profit.

Consider some of the consequences of a tax on the return to capital. First, perfectly competitive firms will pay such taxes even in long-run equilibrium, since they use capital and must earn enough money to pay a return on it. Second, the tax will affect costs differently in different industries. To see this, compare two industries. One is very labour-intensive, so that 90 per cent of its costs of production go to wages and only 10 per cent to capital and other factors. The other is very capital-intensive, so that fully 50 per cent of its costs (in the economists' sense) are a return to capital. The tax on the return to capital will take a small part of the total earnings of the first industry and a large part of those of the second industry. If the industries were equally profitable (in the economists' sense) before the tax, they would not be afterwards, and producers would be attracted into the first industry and out of the second one. This would cause prices to change until both industries became equally profitable, after which no further movement would occur.

A tax on profits as they are defined in tax law has an effect on the allocation of resources.

Other ways in which 'profit taxes' influence the allocation of resources could be mentioned. Enough has been said, however, to show the importance of distinguishing between taxes levied on what economists mean by profits, and taxes levied on what the government defines as profits.

THE PREDICTIONS OF THE THEORY OF SUPPLY

In this chapter we have developed a number of quite general predictions of the theory of the firm and industry, and we have also illustrated the use of the theory in yielding predictions after certain specific information has been added to its general assumptions. The theory is an outstanding intellectual achievement.

The theory of perfect competition shows in a quite general way how a large number of separate profit-maximizing firms can, with no conscious co-ordination, produce an equilibrium which depends only on the 'technical data' of demand and costs. Individual attitudes of producers, and a host of other factors, are successfully ignored, and an equilibrium is shown to follow solely from the conditions of costs and demand.

The analysis extends, with necessary corrections, to the cases of monopolistic competition and monopoly. It does not extend so easily, however, to oligopoly. It is here that the traditional theory has had the least success. A great burst of recent theorizing on small-group monopolistic competition (i.e. oligopolies with differentiated products) is, however, beginning to yield some real advances in this area. Non-cooperative equilibria are relatively easy to analyse and have important applications. In dynamic adjustments, however, strategies matter and the number of possible cases proliferates.

The consumer goods with which the ordinary citizen is most familiar – motorcars, radios, TV sets, washing machines, cookers, etc. – are mostly produced by oligopolistic industries. This has led many superficial observers to conclude that the perfectly competitive model is inapplicable to the modern economy. This is emphatically not so.

Markets where buyers and sellers adjust quantities to a given price that they cannot change by their own individual efforts abound in the economy. Foreign-exchange markets, markets for raw materials, markets for many agricultural commodities, real estate, most futures markets, the markets for gold and other precious metals and securities markets are but a few whose behaviour is comprehensible with, but makes no sense without, the basic model of perfect competition (usually augmented by one or two specific additional assumptions to catch the key institutional details of each case).

Manufactured consumer goods are, as already mentioned, dominated by oligopolistic industries. Retail trades and many service industries were once thought to come close to the conditions of monopolistic competition in that there is free entry, a large number of competing firms and product differentiation (the person who provides the service matters, and each person is different). Because of the nature of spatial differentiation, however, a model of overlapping oligopolies seems closer to the mark than does that of large-group monopolistic competition. (This matter is discussed in more detail in the Appendix to Chapter 14.)

An array of market structures is relevant to our economy. Happily, as illustrated in this chapter, existing theories do make many useful predictions about how our economy behaves. Unhappily, however, there are situations for which current theory does not provide clear predictions, particularly in oligopolistic markets.

SUMMARY

1. An industry's profits can always be increased by co-operating to depart from a perfectly competitive equilibrium and reducing output until marginal cost equals the industry's marginal revenue. At this co-operative equilibrium, each firm can increase its profits by increasing its output. If all try to do this, price will be driven back to its perfectly competitive level.

2. The OPEC experience shows the value to producers of restricting output below the perfectly competitive level, as well as the difficulties of maintaining the co-operative solution for a long time. It also shows the powerful response to price signals: high relative prices and profits call forth increased supplies and long-term reductions in demand.

3. In perfectly competitive industries, demand and cost shifts cause changes in

the prices paid by consumers and the profits earned by producers in the short run. In the long run, however, free entry and exit ensure that profits will not be affected, so that all gains and losses will be passed on to consumers.

4. In monopoly the gains and losses arising from shifts in demand and costs will be shared between the firm and its customers.

5. Taxes and subsidies will affect the profits of perfectly competitive firms in the short run. In the long run, they will affect price and output, but will have no effect on the profits of producers.

6. Lump-sum taxes and taxes on economic profits do affect profits, but affect neither price nor output in monopoly industries (provided they are not so high as to drive the monopoly firm out of business). Taxes on output and on the return to capital (called profit taxes) will affect price, output and profits in a monopoly industry.

TOPICS FOR REVIEW

- The gains from monopolizing a perfectly competitive industry
- OPEC
- The incentives to cheat on a cartel
- The effect of changes in demand and in costs under competition, oligopoly and monopoly
- The effect of taxes on output and profits under competition, oligopoly and monopoly

16

Criticisms and Tests

In previous chapters we have derived testable implications from the theory of supply. The theory is tested every time one of these implications is confronted with facts in such a way that a conflict between theory and observation is possible. In many cases, if a particular implication is found to be in conflict with the facts, only a minor change in the basic theory is needed. In other cases, however, alleged empirical observations strike at the more important parts of the theory. If these conflicting observations were substantiated, it would be necessary to make very drastic amendments to the existing theory or to replace it by a competing alternative.

In this chapter we first discuss some general approaches to testing the theory, and then consider a number of criticisms. The final section discusses the ideas of Professor J. K. Galbraith. In a number of famous books, running from *The Affluent Society* to *The New Industrial State*, Professor Galbraith has attacked some of the most fundamental aspects of the theory.

APPROACHES TO TESTING THE THEORY

Although the theory of the behaviour of firms and industries does not cover all issues in which we might be interested, it does provide predictions about many interesting situations. But is the theory right? Are we not being misled by its predictions? How can we assess such worries? Four of the several approaches to answering these questions are considered below.

Formulate an Alternative Theory

Given two alternative theories, we can derive their conflicting predictions, and choose to accept the one that comes closer to predicting what is observed. One competing theory hypothesizes, for example, that firms choose to maximize their sales rather than their profits. A valid way of testing between profit- and sales-maximizing theory is to identify those predictions of each theory that conflict with each other, and confront them with the evidence. This way of choosing between two theories is satisfactory – although it is seldom easy to carry out.

Ask Decision-takers How They Behave

Another approach to testing the theory of profit maximizing is to ask businessmen: 'Do you seek to maximize profits?' This approach has from time to time been tried and it will not surprise you to learn that, when asked if their sole motive was to make as much money as possible, businessmen replied that it was not; that they sought instead to charge a 'fair price', to make only a reasonable profit and generally to conduct their affairs in a manner conducive to the social good. Asking people what they do, and why they do it, can suggest hypotheses about behaviour for further testing. For example, if you have always taken it for granted that people do a certain thing and inquiry shows that everyone denies it, then this may make you suspicious and lead you to check your theories further. But consider what the denials might mean: (i) the people were lying; (ii) the people told what they thought was the truth, but they were not aware of their own motives and actions; (iii) the denials were true.

One needs only a nodding acquaintance with elementary psychology to realize that we are not likely to discover very much about human motivation by asking people what motivates them. Usually they will have either no idea at all, or else only a pleasantly acceptable rationalization. Direct questioning at best (assuming the subject tries to be scrupulously honest) tells us what people who are questioned think they are doing. Such information can never refute an hypothesis about what people are actually doing. To challenge such an hypothesis, we must observe what they do, not ask them what they think they do.

Observe Decision-takers Within the Firm

Carefully conducted case studies can reveal much about behaviour. For example, the management of a firm may be observed consistently to reject alternatives that would increase profits. Such studies can only cover a small sample of firms and worries naturally arise about the representativeness of the firms that are studied and about comparability between studies made by different researchers.

In spite of such doubts, case studies are fruitful in suggesting new theories. If studies show, for example, that firms habitually follow certain procedures that lead them away from profit maximization, we can formulate a new theory in which these procedures play a prominent role. We would then have two conflicting theories, and we could proceed to test between them in the manner discussed in the earlier section.

Observe Decision-takers Under Laboratory Conditions

Economists have only recently begun to use the methods of behavioural psychologists. Several centres of experimental economics now exist, and increasing numbers of researchers are studying economic decisions taken under controlled conditions. It is too early to evaluate the success of this work, although some very suggestive results have been obtained. It will be a long time, however, before economists will be willing to discard theories solely as a result of tests taken under what many would regard as artificial conditions. What is more likely is that some of the results that persist under laboratory conditions will be used to formulate new theories of behaviour – theories that will then be subjected to conventional testing.

ALTERNATIVE MAXIMIZING THEORIES

We shall now consider two major types of criticism of the theory of short-run profit maximization. The first holds that the firm seeks to maximize something other than short-run profits, while the second denies that the firm can be understood as a maximizing agent.

Long-run Profit Maximization

In order to take account of various observations that seem to conflict with short-run profit maximization, some economists modify the firm's objective to be that of long-run profit maximization. For example, the sales-maximization hypothesis considered below might be interpreted as long-run profit maximization because sales are the key to growth and growth is the key to future profits. This may eliminate the apparent conflict between sales and profit maximization. In much the same way, the 'long-run' approach can be used to account for other facts that appear to contradict predictions based on short-run profit maximization. For one example, consumer goodwill gained by not raising prices to take advantage of temporary shortages may be worthwhile in terms of long-run profits, particularly in oligopolistic markets. For another example, a firm may be right to avoid risky ventures, even if large short-run profits might be earned, because the surest way to earn long-run profits is to survive in the short run. Long-run profitability requires survival, and survival may require caution.

Rational profit-maximizing must occur over a realistic time-horizon. The rational maximizing firm seeks to maximize the 'present value' of its entire stream of expected future profits. In this sense, rational maximizing theory is concerned with long-run maximization. However, given a fairly large rate of discount – due partly to increasing uncertainty about profits further and further into the future – profits in the near future tend to exert the main influence on the firm's behaviour.[1]

One must beware, however, of using this theory to provide *ad hoc* explanations for all evidence that a firm is not maximizing its profits. Conflicting evidence can always by explained away by asserting that the firm was maximizing over *some time-period other than* the one to which the evidence applies. Such misuse of the theory makes it consistent with any conceivable business behaviour and, as a result, makes it uninteresting.

Maximization of Managers' Rather than Shareholders' Interests

The owners of the firm are its shareholders, and their interest clearly lies in profit maximization, or (what is the same thing) maximizing the value of the firm's shares. The shareholders do not, however, take the firm's decisions. Instead shareholders elect directors who appoint managers. Directors are supposed to represent shareholders' interests and to determine broad

policies that the managers merely carry out. In order to conduct the complicated business of running a large firm, a full-time professional management group *must* be given broad powers of decision. Although managerial decisions can be reviewed from time to time, they cannot be supervised in detail. In fact, the links are typically so weak that top management often does control the destiny of the company over long periods of time. As long as directors have confidence in the managerial group, they accept and ratify their proposals, and shareholders characteristically elect and re-elect directors who are proposed to them. If the managers behave badly, they may be replaced, but this drastic and disruptive action is infrequently employed. Within very wide limits, then, effective control of the company's activities does reside with the managers, who need not even be shareholders.

For the separation of ownership and control to be important, it is necessary not only that the managers should be able to exert effective control over business decisions, but also that they act differently from the way the shareholders and directors wish them to act. If managers maximize the firm's profits – either because it is in their own interests to do so or because they voluntarily choose to reflect the shareholders' interests – it does not matter that they have effective control over decisions. If managers pursue other goals, firm behaviour will vary according to whether the managers or the owners are in control.

Sales Maximization

The hypothesis of *sales maximization* offers an example of a different goal. In the giant corporation, the managers need to make some minimum level of profits to keep the shareholders satisfied; after that, according to this hypothesis, they seek growth unhampered by profit considerations. Salary, power and prestige of management are all more closely related to the size of a firm than to its profits; the manager of a large, normally profitable corporation may well earn a salary considerably higher than that earned by the manager of a small but highly profitable corporation.

The sales-maximization hypothesis says that managers of firms seek to maximize their sales revenue, subject to a profit constraint.

---

[1] Chapter 19 shows how the firm's rate of discount is used to put a present value on its expected stream of future profits.

FIGURE 16.1 Alternative Objectives of Firms

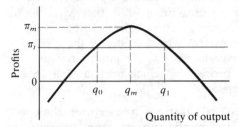

Quantity of output

Sales maximization leads to a higher output than profit maximization. A profit-maximizing firm produces output q_m and earns profits π_m. A sales-maximizing firm, with a minimum profit constraint of π_t, produces the output q_1. Thus sales maximization predicts a higher output than does profit maximization.

The satisficing firm that is happy with the profits of π_t, and is not following a maximizing strategy, will be content with any output between q_0 and q_1.

Figure 16.1 demonstrates that sales maximization, subject to a profit constraint, causes firms to sacrifice some profits by setting price below, and output above, the profit-maximizing levels.

Sales-maximizing behaviour is, however, constrained by outside forces. If the management departs too far from profit-maximizing behaviour, the firm is vulnerable to a takeover bid by a new owner who does intend to maximize profits. This is discussed later in this chapter.

Principal-agent Problems

Sales maximization on the part of managers of firms whose shareholders desire profit maximization is – in so far as these are genuinely different goals – an example of a principal-agent issue. The principal is someone who wants a job done, the agent is someone who is hired to do it.

> **A principal-agent problem arises whenever the self-interest of the agent is opposed to the self-interest of the principal.**

A solution is to provide incentives for the agent to carry out the principal's wishes. In small organizations this can be done by supervision. If the agent does not do what the principal wishes, the agent is dismissed and someone who will do the job is hired. Here the incentive system is of the stick variety: 'if you don't serve my interests, you will lose your job,' says the principal to the agent.

In large companies the required degree of supervision is impossible. Directors, let alone shareholders, can have very little idea of the impact of day-to-day decisions made by managers.

So alternative solutions seek to use carrot-type rather than stick-type incentives. The key here is to change the incentives facing managers so that their interest lies in maximizing profits. Simple examples are to make a significant part of the manager's income depend on the firm's profits. Two such methods are profit-linked bonus schemes and schemes that make managers into shareholders.

Firms, and professional economists, have studied principal-agent issues in recent years. Some ingenious solutions have been proposed and some have been instituted. They all have the same characteristic:

> a principal-agent problem is solved whenever the incentive system can be changed to give the agents (in this case managers) interests in common with the principals (in this case shareholders).

Self-interest can then be relied on to motivate managers in the desired direction. Supervision can be directed at weeding out the incompetent rather than at enforcing behaviour that is not in the managers' own interests.

Institutions matter: The traditional theory of the firm ignores the institutional structures of firms by assuming that all firms seek to maximize their profits. This amounts to assuming that there is no principal-agent problem, that all managers do seek the self-interest of shareholders. In so far as there is a principal-agent problem in large companies we would expect behaviour to vary with the institutions of the firm. Those firms whose institutions did not provide the correct managerial incentives would be following the self-interest of managers. Those whose institutions had solved the principal-agent problem would be following profit-maximizing behaviour.

NON-MAXIMIZING THEORIES

Many students of large and complex organizations have been critical of economic theory for regarding modern corporations as 'simple profit-maximizing computers'. They believe that firms are *profit-oriented* in the sense that, *ceteris paribus*, they prefer more profits to less. They do not believe, however, that firms are *profit maximizers*.

Maximization has two aspects. A firm is a *local maximizer* if it maximizes profits that can be earned with its present range of commodities and its present markets. A firm is a *global maximizer* if it surveys all possible courses of action and then chooses the most profitable one. Possible courses of action will include new products, new markets, and new sales and production techniques. It is fairly easy to gather evidence showing that most firms are not global maximizers; it is more difficult to do the same for local maximization.

Non-maximization Due to Ignorance

One group of critics say that profit-maximizing theory is inadequate because firms, however hard they may try, cannot reach decisions in the way the theory predicts. This criticism has several aspects, some crude and some quite sophisticated.

Businessmen do not understand marginal concepts: One of the crudest criticisms is based on the observation that businessmen do not calculate in the manner assumed by the theory. Sometimes businessmen are interviewed and it is discovered (apparently to the surprise of the interviewer) that many have never heard of the concepts of marginal cost and marginal revenue. It is then argued that maximizing theory is refuted because businessmen cannot be employing concepts of which they are unaware.

This observation, assuming it to be correct, does refute the theory that firms take decisions by calculating marginal values and consciously equating them. But it does not refute the theory that firms maximize profits. The mathematical concepts of marginal cost and marginal revenue are used by economic theorists to discover what will happen as long as, by one means or another – be it guess, hunch, clairvoyance, luck or good judgement – the firms do approximately succeed in maximizing their profits. The constructs of the theory are not meant to be descriptions of *how*

firms reach their decisions. If firms are maximizing their profits, then the tools of economic theory allow us to predict how they will react to certain changes, such as the introduction of a new tax. The methods used to derive these predictions have no necessary connection with the thought process by which firms actually reach their decisions.

Business calculations are cruder than assumed by profit-maximizing theory: A similar argument stems from the observation that firms do not calculate down to a single unit with such a nice degree of accuracy as is assumed in profit-maximizing theory. In the verbal presentation of the theory of the firm, it is usually stated that firms will increase production until the cost of producing the very last unit is just equal to the revenue gained from its sale. This is merely a verbal statement of the mathematical conditions for the maximization of the profit function. The observation that firms do not calculate down to single units is not of itself relevant as a test of the theory. Marginal analysis allows us to predict how firms will respond to certain changes that affect them. If they are maximizing their profits, they will respond in the predicted manner even though they calculate in a much cruder fashion than mathematicians do.

Firms have inadequate information: More sophisticated critics argue that the information available to decision-takers is simply not adequate to permit them to reach the decisions that economists predict they will reach. This argument generally takes one of three forms: that firms base their decisions on accounting concepts, which differ from economic ones; that the natural lag between accumulating and processing data is such that important decisions must be made on fragmentary and partially out-of-date information; or that firms cannot afford to acquire as much information as economists assume them to have. All of this suggests that although firms may be profit seekers, they may not be profit maximizers.

Non-maximizing by Choice

The following theories all have in common the view that firms *choose* not to be profit maximizers.

Full-cost Pricing

Most manufacturing firms are price-setters: they must quote a price for their products rather than accept a price set on some impersonal competitive market. Simple profit-maximizing theory predicts that these firms will change their prices in response to every change in demand and cost that they experience. In the short run, prices of manufactured goods do not vary in response to every shift in the firm's demand. Instead they appear to change rather sluggishly.

This short-run behaviour is consistent with the hypothesis of **full-cost pricing**, which we have already discussed on page 239 in Chapter 14. It was first advanced following a series of detailed case studies of actual pricing decisions made in Oxford. Case studies in the intervening decades have continued to reveal the widespread use of full-cost pricing procedures.

The full-cost pricer, instead of equating marginal revenue with marginal cost, sets price equal to average cost at normal-capacity output, plus a conventional mark-up.

The firm changes its prices when its average costs change substantially (as a result of such events as a new union contract or a sharp change in the prices of key raw materials), and it may occasionally change its mark-up. However, its short-run pricing behaviour appears conventional rather than profit maximizing.

Modern critics of profit-maximizing theory accept the evidence that full-cost prices are sometimes changed in the profit-maximizing direction. They hold, however, that the prevalence of conventional full-cost practices shows that prices are typically not at their profit-maximizing level. They also hold that the prevalence of full-cost pricing shows that firms are creatures of custom that at most make profit-oriented changes at infrequent intervals.

We have seen in Chapter 14 that the short-term stickiness of oligopolistic prices can be accounted for under profit-maximizing theory by the fact that it is costly for a multi-product firm to change its list prices. If so, the possible conflict between full-cost and profit-maximizing theory concerns only the setting of the mark-up that relates prices to costs. If mark-ups are conventional, and only rarely revised, then there is a conflict. If, however, the mark-up is the profit-maximizing one for normal-capacity output, full-cost pricing is consistent with profit maximization when it is costly to change prices.

Organization Theory

According to **organization theory**, decisions are taken by large companies after much discussion by groups and committees, and the structure of the process affects the substance of the decisions.

The central prediction of organization theory is that different decisions will result from different kinds of organizations, even when all else is unchanged.

One proposition that follows from this theory is that large and diffuse organizations find it necessary to develop standard operating procedures to help them in making decisions. These decision rules arise as compromises among competing points of view and, once adopted, are changed only reluctantly. An important prediction following from this hypothesis is that the compromises will persist for long periods of time despite changes in conditions affecting the firm. Even if a particular compromise were the profit-maximizing strategy in the first place, it would not remain so when conditions changed. Thus profits will not usually be maximized.

Another prediction is that decision by compromise will lead firms to adopt conservative policies that avoid large risks. Smaller firms, not faced with the necessity of compromising competing views of their own employees, will take bigger risks than larger firms.

An alternative to profit maximization, called **satisficing**, was first suggested by Professor Herbert Simon of Carnegie-Mellon University, who in 1978 was awarded the Nobel Prize in economics for his work on the behaviour of firms. According to the satisficing hypothesis, firms will strive to achieve certain target levels of profits, but having achieved them, they will not strive to improve their profit position further. This means, as shown in Figure 16.1, that the firm could produce any one of a range of outputs that yield at least the target level of profits. Thus:

Satisficing theory predicts a range of

possible outputs, rather than a unique output. The range includes the profit-maximizing output, and has the sales-maximizing output as its upper bound.

Evolutionary Theories

The modern evolutionary theories advanced by such economists as Richard Nelson and Sidney Winter of Yale University[1] build on the earlier theories of full-cost pricing and satisficing. Evolutionary theorists have gathered much evidence to show that tradition often dominates firms' planning. The basic effort at the early stages of planning is directed, they argue, toward the problem of performing reasonably well in established markets and maintaining established market shares. They quote evidence to show that suggestions, made in preliminary planning documents, to do radically new things, are usually weeded out in the reviewing process. They believe that most firms spend very little effort on *planning* to enter entirely new markets, and still less on direct efforts to leave, or even reduce, their share in long-established markets. These attitudes were illustrated by one firm which, although faced with obviously changing circumstances, reported that 'We have been producing on the basis of these raw materials for more than 50 years with success, and we have made it a policy to continue to do so.'

The evolutionary theory of the firm draws many analogies with the biological theory of evolution. Here are two of the most important.

The genes: In biological theory, behavioural patterns are transmitted over time by genes. Rules of behaviour fulfil the same function in the evolutionary theory of the firm. In Nelson and Sidney Winter's words: 'That a great deal of firm decision behaviour is routinized ... is a "stylized fact" about the realities of firm decision process. Routinized ... decision procedures .. cover decision situations from pricing practices in retail stores to such "strategic" decisions as advertising or R and D effort, or the question of whether or not to invest abroad.' Winter talks of firms 'remembering by doing' according to repetitive routines. He adds that government policymakers tend to have unrealistic expectations about firms'

flexibility and responsiveness to changes in market incentives. These expectations arise from the maximizing model, whose fatal flaw, Winter alleges, is to underestimate the importance, and difficulty, 'of the task of merely continuing the routine performance, i.e. of preventing undesired deviations'.

The mutations: In the theory of biological evolution, mutations are one vehicle of change. In the evolutionary theory of the firm this role is played by innovations. The most familiar innovation concerns the introduction of new products and new production techniques. However, a further important class of innovations in evolutionary theory is the introduction of new rules of behaviour. Sometimes innovations are thrust on the firm; at other times the firm consciously plans for, and creates, this type of innovation.

According to maximizing theory, innovations are the result of incentives – the 'carrot' of new profit opportunities. In evolutionary theory, the firm is much more of a satisficer. It usually innovates only under the incentive of the 'stick', either of unacceptably low profits or of some form of external prodding. Firms change routines when they get into trouble, not when they see a chance to improve an already satisfactory performance. For example, in the growing markets of the 1960s and 1970s, many firms adopted wasteful practices that they shed fairly easily when their profits were threatened in the more difficult economic climate of the 1980s.

The Significance of Non-maximizing Theories

An impressive array of evidence can be gathered in apparent support of various non-maximizing theories. What would be the implications if they were accepted as being better theories of the behaviour of the economy than profit maximization?

If non-maximizing theories are correct, the economic system does not perform with the delicate precision that follows from profit maximization. But the system described by many of these alternative theories *does* function. Firms sell more when demand goes up and less when it goes down. They also alter their prices and their input mixes when hit with the 'stick' of sufficiently large changes in input prices.

---

[1] R. Nelson and S. Winter, *The Evolutionary Theory of the Firm* (New Haven: Yale University Press, 1984).

Profit-oriented, non-maximizing theories do not upset the broad case for the price system: that it is an effective coordinator of decentralized decisions.

But profit-oriented, non-maximizing firms will also exhibit a great deal of inertia. They will not respond quickly and precisely to small changes in market signals from either the private sector or government policy. Nor will they always make radical changes in their behaviour even when the profit incentives to do so are large. This casts doubt on the efficacy of those government policies that make relatively small changes in incentives, expecting that firms will respond to these as profit maximizers.

Non-maximizing models imply sensitivity of the price system to large, but not to small, changes in signals caused by changes in demand, costs or public policy.

CAN FIRMS CONTROL THEIR OWN MARKETS?: THE GALBRAITH THESIS

A very different hypothesis from the ones considered so far has been advocated by John Kenneth Galbraith of Harvard University. Galbraith observes that modern firms must make enormous investments whose profitability is threatened by the unpredictability of future events. In response, according to Galbraith, firms render the future less unpredictable by actively manipulating market demand, and by co-opting government agencies that are supposed to control their activities.

The most important unpredictable events that may jeopardize corporate investments are unexpected shifts in market demand curves. To guard against unexpected declines in demand, corporations spend vast sums on advertising to allow them to sell what they want to produce rather than what consumers want to buy. At the same time, corporations decide not to produce some products that consumers would like to buy. This reduces the risks inherent in investing in new and untried products and avoids the possibility that successful new products might spoil the market for existing products.

According to this hypothesis, consumers are the victims of the corporations; they are pushed around at the corporate whim, persuaded to buy things they do not really want and denied products they would like to have.

In spite of all the efforts that firms undoubtedly do make to control the demands for their products, shifts in demand do occur, some rapidly, some gradually. Are these explained by manipulation of consumers' tastes through advertising as Galbraith would have us believe, or by more basic changes? Advertising has two major aspects: it seeks to inform consumers of the characteristics of the available products and it seeks to influence consumers by altering their tastes and, hence, their demands. The first aspect, **informative advertising**, plays an important part in the efficient operation of any free-market system; the second aspect, **competitive advertising**, is one through which firms seek to control the market instead of being controlled by it. This does not mean that competitive advertising is to be condemned out of hand. It also plays a key role in inter-firm competition.

Clearly, however, advertising does influence consumers' demand. If Volkswagen stopped advertising, it would surely lose sales to Ford and Fiat, but it is hard to believe that the automotive society was conjured up by the advertising industry. Advertising may persuade a London-bound Italian family to fly BA rather than Alitalia, but could it persuade them to use a canal barge, a bicycle or even a bus? Careful promotion can influence the success of one rock group over another, but could it sell the waltz to today's youth? Advertising is to some extent taste-making. It unquestionably plays a role in shaping demand, but so too do more basic human attitudes, psychological needs, technological opportunities, and many fads and fashions stemming from sources other than advertising.

Certainly, advertising shifts demands among very similar products. It is hard to believe, however, that the economy, or the average citizen's system of values, would be fundamentally changed if one more or one less make of car or TV set or brand of shoes were made available. A look at those products that have brought basic changes to the economy – and perhaps to value systems – suggests that these products succeeded *because consumers wanted them*, not because the advertising industry brainwashed people into buying them. Consider a few of the major examples.

The washing machine, the dishwasher, the vacuum cleaner, detergents and a host of other household aids liberated married women from dawn-to-dusk hard labour and contributed to women's liberation in ways hard to appreciate by those who grew up accepting these conveniences. Few women needed to be brainwashed by advertisers to accept the freedom offered by these products. Could advertising persuade them to give them up and return to a life of household drudgery? The motorcar transformed society and is now in demand everywhere in the world, even in Communist countries where only informative advertising exists. Films, particularly those made in Hollywood, had an enormous influence in shaping society and in changing values; they are eagerly attended everywhere in the world, whether or not they are accompanied by a ballyhoo of advertising. The aeroplane – and the jet in particular – has shrunk the size of the world: it has made the international conference a commonplace among professionals; it has made foreign holidays a reality for the many rather than a luxury for the very few. For better or worse, the revolution in behaviour caused by generally available, cheap and effective methods of birth control is still being worked out. TV has changed the activities of children (and adults) in fundamental ways and has brought to viewers a sense of immediacy about distant events that newspapers could never achieve. The pocket calculator replaced the sliderule within five years. The personal computer and word-processor dominates many offices and is used in many homes.

Many factors, including advertising and salesmanship, affect consumers' purchasing patterns. However, the new products that have really influenced the allocation of resources and the pattern of society – such as those mentioned in the previous paragraph – have succeeded because consumers wanted them; most of those that failed did so because they were not wanted – at least not at prices that would cover their costs of production.

The evidence suggests that the allocation of resources among major product groups – but possibly not among different brands of one basic product – owes more to the tastes and values of consumers than it does to advertising and related activities.

SOME FINAL WORDS

The Importance of Profits

Economics is a continually developing subject; its theories are under constant scrutiny and attack. Some of the major debates concerning the profit-maximizing theory of the firm have been reviewed in this chapter. On the one hand, the Galbraithian view that firms create their own market conditions seems difficult to maintain in the face of the evidence; on the other hand, simple profit-maximizing theory seems unlikely to be able to capture all aspects of firm behaviour. Thus this theory may sooner or later be expanded to include elements of such theories as satisficing, sales maximization and evolutionary behaviour.

Profits, however, are unmistakably a potent force in the life – and death – of firms. The resilience of profit-maximizing theory, and its ability to predict much economic behaviour, suggests that firms are motivated by the pursuit of profits. Other things being equal, firms seem to prefer more profits to less profits.

If *profit-maximizing* theory should eventually give way to some more organizationally dominated theory, the new theory will still be *profit-oriented*. The search for profits, and the avoidance of losses, is a powerful force that drives the economy even when firms do not turn out to be precise maximizers.

How Far can Firms Depart from Profit-maximizing Behaviour?

Many of the criticisms that we have just considered assume that firms seek to do things other than maximize their profits. If the present management elects not to maximize its profits, this implies that some other management could make more money by operating the firm. One major restraint on existing managements is the threat of a takeover bid. As we shall see in some detail in Chapter 19, the maximum amount one can profitably pay for any asset depends on how much it is expected to earn. If one firm can make an asset produce more than another, that firm can rationally outbid the other for it.

A management that fails to come close to achieving the profit potential of the assets it controls becomes a natural target for acquisition. Indeed, some firms specialize in taking over inefficiently run firms. The management of the acquiring firm makes a *tender offer* (or a *takeover bid* as it is often called) to the shareholders of the target firm, offering them what amounts to a premium for their shares, a premium it can pay because it expects to increase the firm's profits. Managers who wish to avoid takeover bids cannot let the profits of their firm slip far from the profit-maximizing level – because their unrealized profits provide the incentives for takeovers. Some, though by no means all, of the so-called conglomerate firms have specialized in this kind of merger.

The threat of takeovers clearly limits the discretion of corporate management to pursue goals other than profit maximization.

The General Demand and Supply Theory of a Market Economy

We have noted that some markets, such as those for agricultural goods and other primary products, do function as assumed in the theory of competitive price determination. We have now studied alternative market structures sufficiently to realize that we cannot in fact apply the simple demand-and-supply theory to a whole economy. It is a theory of *competitive* markets, markets with many buyers and many sellers. Most manufactured goods, however, are produced by oligopolistic industries containing only a few firms. These firms may or may not compete actively with each other; in cases in which they do compete, they are likely to change their prices only occasionally and to compete from day to day by adjusting such things as service, delivery dates, quality and special features.

Does it matter that manufacturing is primarily oligopolistic? Does this fact undermine our ability to use economic theory as a successful predictive device? At least two things seem fairly clear.

First, we do have difficulty predicting the detailed effects on the manufacturing industries of changes in such things as tax rates, the number of firms in an industry, demands, costs and government regulations. In administered-price situations there is considerable non-price competition. Since we do not have a well-tested theory of non-price competition, it is often, although by no means always, unclear what will be the effects of changes such as those just listed.

Second, if we wish to predict general long-term responses to such major events as changes in the price of oil, our theory is more helpful. Evidence supports each of the following statements. The prices of most primary products are set on competitive markets and these prices fluctuate in response to shifts in demands and supplies. Large changes in the relative prices of inputs do cause firms to change the proportions in which they use factors, since most objectives are better served by minimizing costs, rather than by wasting money unnecessarily. Continual changes in the prices of inputs sooner or later lead firms to change the prices of their outputs. (Even a non-profit-maximizing monopoly cannot afford to let its profits become significantly negative.) This means that, over the long term, relative prices of manufactured commodities do reflect major changes in the relative costs of producing these commodities. When relative prices of commodities change, consumers react. Many long-term changes in consumption patterns that are often casually ascribed to changes in tastes, fashions and habits, are actually responses to changes in relative prices. Observers who predict the economy's broad reactions to major shocks, such as changes in energy prices, make disastrous errors when they ignore this general long-term adaptability. Because it is so adaptable, the economy behaves – at least in broad outline – as would a perfectly competitive economy.

This assessment probably commands widespread acceptance among economists. But just *how* bad is our ability to predict in detail (especially in the oligopolistic part of the economy), and just *how* good is our ability to predict long-term trend reactions to major events? (Do not forget that we are not trying to foretell the future, but to make conditional predictions about the reactions of the economy to given events.) Because it is hard to assemble the mass of available evidence so as to focus on this issue, economists are left to their personal assessments of the balance between success and failure, and the debate goes on among those who assess it differently. It does, however, seem safe to say two things: when judged by its ability to predict the outcome of events in which we are interested, the theory of the allocation of resources reveals many substantial successes, and some major failures; no alternative theory that can do even half as well has yet been proposed.

SUMMARY

1. Properly understood, profit-maximizing means maximizing the present value of the discounted flow of all expected future profits. There is a danger, however, of using long-run maximization as an *ad hoc* way of explaining away all observations that appear to conflict with profit maximization.
2. A class of alternative theories assumes that managers (agents) have different objectives than shareholders (principals) and that they are able to pursue these objectives. One example is maximizing sales rather than profits.
3. Another class of theories claim that firms are not *maximizers* of anything. This may be because they lack sufficient knowledge, or because they choose not to do so.
4. Full-cost pricing with conventional mark-ups makes firms creatures of convention. The same theory with mark-ups determined at the profit-maximizing level for normal-capacity output (plus the assumption that changing prices is costly) is consistent with profit maximization.
5. Organization theory assumes that the firm satisfices – which means that it is satisfied with any level of output and prices that meets its minimum-profit constraint.
6. Evolutionary theories see firms as profit oriented but not profit maximizing. Firms follow rules of behaviour that have been shown to work and change these only when forced to by major changes in market conditions.
7. Galbraith argued that modern firms could create their own demand through advertising so that the concept of consumer sovereignty was outdated. Although advertising clearly influences consumers' choices among different brands of similar commodities, there is little evidence that consumers' desires to consume major classes of goods – such as cars, washing machines, TV sets and rock concerts – are primarily determined by advertising.
8. Although detailed prediction of the economy's reactions to every change, large and small, that impinges on it is not possible, broad-brush predictions of overall reactions to major changes are.

TOPICS FOR REVIEW

- Approaches to testing the theory of supply
- Sales maximization
- Principal-agent problems
- Reasons for non-maximization of profits
- Organization theory and satisficing
- Evolutionary theories
- The Galbraith hypothesis
- Takeovers as a constraint on non-maximizing behaviour

PART 5

The Theory of Distribution

17

Factor Incomes in Competitive Markets[1]

Are the poor getting poorer and the rich richer, as Karl Marx thought they would? Are the rich getting relatively poorer and the poor relatively richer, as Alfred Marshall hoped they would? Is the inequality of income a social constant, determined by forces that are possibly beyond man's understanding and probably beyond his control, as Vilfredo Pareto thought they were? These questions concern what is called the **size distribution of income**, which is a classification of income according to the amount of income received by each individual irrespective of the sources of that income.

The great classical economists, Adam Smith, David Ricardo and Karl Marx, were mainly concerned with how income was shared among the three great social classes of their day – workers, landowners and capitalists. They defined three basic factors of production: labour, land and capital, according to the functions that they fulfilled in production. Their incomes split the national product into three parts: wages, rent and the return on capital (interest and profit). This investigation concerns what is called the **functional distribution of income**. This way of looking at distribution classifies income according to its source, i.e. according to the amounts of income received by the various factors of production rather than the amounts received by various individuals or households.

Much of the attention of modern economists and policy-makers is devoted to the size distribution of income, and most distributional policies are designed to alter the size distribution of income rather than the functional distribution. After all, some capitalists (such as the owners of small retail stores) are in the lower part of the income scale, while some wage-earners (such as skilled athletes) are at the upper end of the income scale. Moreover, if a family is poor, this poverty is the same whether they are capitalists or workers.

Inequality in the size distribution of income is shown graphically in Figure 17.1. This curve of income distribution, called the *Lorenz curve*, shows how much of total income is accounted for by given proportions of the nation's families.

---

[1] For the factual background concerning various aspects of the distribution of income, see Harbury and Lipsey, *op. cit*, Chapter 4.

FIGURE 17.1 A Lorenz Curve of Family Income in the UK

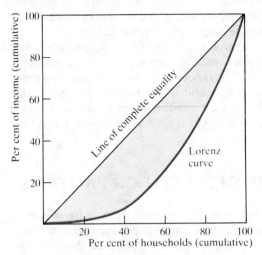

The size of the shaded area between the Lorenz curve and the diagonal is a measure of the inequality of income distribution. If there were complete income equality, the bottom 20 per cent of income earners would receive 20 per cent of the income, the bottom 40 per cent would receive 40 per cent of the income, and so forth. The Lorenz curve would then coincide with the diagonal line. Because of income inequality (e.g. the lower 20 per cent receive only 2 per cent of the income), the Lorenz curve lies below the diagonal. The extent to which it bends away from the straight line indicates the amount of inequality in the distribution of income.

(The further the curve bends away from the diagonal, the more unequal is the distribution of income.) In 1986, the bottom 20 per cent of all UK households received just over 2 per cent of all income earned, while the top 1 per cent received over 6 per cent of the income. This represents a much greater degree of inequality of income than is found, for example, in the United States. (See the US Lorenz curve on page 742).

THE NEO-CLASSICAL THEORY OF DISTRIBUTION IN OUTLINE

Why does the market system reward some people with high incomes, while others earn very little? It is tempting to give superficial answers such as:

'People are paid what they are worth.' But we may wonder: Worth what, and to whom? What gives them value? Sometimes it is said that people earn according to their ability. But note that incomes are distributed in a very much more unequal fashion than any measured index of ability such as IQ or physical strength. In what sense is Cleo Laine twenty times as able as a promising new pop singer? She earns twenty times as much. In what sense is a lorrydriver more able than a schoolteacher? If answers couched in terms of worth and ability seem superficial, so are answers such as 'It's all a matter of luck', or 'It's just the system'.

According to the traditional or *neo-Classical* theory, the distribution of income is simply a special case of price theory.

How this works can be summarized in the following three points.

- The income of any factor of production (and hence the amount of the national product that it is able to command) depends on the price that is paid for the factor and the amount that is used.
- Factor prices and quantities are determined by demands and supplies in factor markets in exactly the same way that the prices and quantities of commodities are determined in commodity markets.
- To explain distribution, through price theory, all that is needed, therefore, is to identify the main determinants of the demand for, and supply of, factors of production and allow for any intervention into free markets caused by governments, unions, or other similar institutions.

Figure 17.2 illustrates the neo-Classical theory by showing how competitive market forces determine one factor's income. In order to ensure that we are speaking of relative and not just absolute amounts we assume that, when the changes studied in the Figure occur, *the price of all other factors of production, the prices of all goods, and the level of national income are given and constant*[1] Under these circumstances, fluctuations in a factor's equilibrium price and quantity cause fluctuations (i) in the money earnings of that factor, (ii) in its earnings relative to other factors,

FIGURE 17.2 Factor Income Determined in Competitive Markets

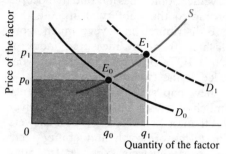

The interaction of demand and supply in competitive factor markets determines a factor's equilibrium price and quantity, and hence its income. The original demand and supply curves are D_0 and S. Equilibrium is at E_0, with price p_0 and quantity employed q_0. The factor's income is its price times its quantity, which is shown by the dark-shaded area in the Figure. When the demand curve shifts to D_1, equilibrium shifts to E_1, with price p_1 and quantity q_1. The factor's income rises by the amount of the light-shaded area.

and (iii) in the share of national income going to the factor. Assume, for example, that the money price of one factor changes from some value p_0 to a higher value p_1, while the quantity employed changes the amount from q_0 to q_1. This means that (i) the factor's *relative price* rises from p_0/F to p_1/F, where F is the constant, average price of *all* other factors; and (ii) because the factor's total earnings change from p_0q_0 to p_1q_1, the share of income going to this factor changes from p_0q_0/Y to p_1q_1/Y, where Y is the constant total national income.

In the next part of this chapter we enquire into the determinants of factor demands and supply. Then we study how they interact in factor markets to determine equilibrium prices and quantities, and hence factor incomes.

As we observed in Chapter 10 (see page 170), the *intermediate inputs* used by firms are the outputs of other firms. These can be netted out to

---

[1] We make these assumptions because we are concerned with a factor's relative share of total national income. As we observed on pages 74–76, these assumptions are only a simplifying device for our analysis; they do not prevent it from being applied to inflationary situations.

show that, for the economy as a whole, there are three basic factor inputs, land (defined in its broad sense to include all natural resources), labour, and capital. When we are concerned with either the size or the functional distributions of income over the economy as a whole, we are concerned with incomes going to these basic factors. The theory of factor pricing is, however, quite flexible and it can be used to discuss the market price, and the income earned, by *any* input into *any* firm's, or *any* industry's, productive process.

THE DEMAND FOR FACTORS

Firms require land, labour, raw materials, machines and other inputs to produce their outputs. The demand for any input depends, therefore, on the demand for the goods that it helps to make. We say that the demand is a **derived demand**.

Examples abound. The demand for computer programers is growing as industry turns increasingly to electronic computers. The demand for university teachers varies directly with the number of students going to university. The demand for coalminers and coalmining equipment declines as the demand for coal declines. Typically, of course, one factor will be used in making many different goods. Steel is used, for example, in dozens of industries, as are the services of carpenters. The total demand for a factor will be the sum of the derived demands in all of its uses.

> **Derived demand provides a link between the pricing of factors and the pricing of products. It connects the theory of the firm to the theory of distribution.**

The Quantity of a Factor Demanded in Equilibrium

We first derive a famous relation that holds in equilibrium for every factor employed by a wide class of firms. In Chapter 12, we established the rules for the maximization of a firm's profits in the short run. When one factor is fixed and another is variable, the profit-maximizing firm increases its output until the last unit produced adds just as much to cost as to revenue, i.e. until marginal cost equals marginal revenue. Another way of stating exactly the same thing is to say that *the profit-maximizing firm will increase production up to the point at which the last unit of the variable factor employed adds just as much to revenue as it does to cost.*

The marginal cost of a variable factor is the addition to the total cost resulting from the employment of one more unit of that factor. The amount that a unit of a variable factor adds to revenue is the marginal revenue produced by the last unit of that factor. Since we have already used the term *marginal revenue* to refer to the change in revenue resulting from the sale of an additional unit of product, we shall use another term, **marginal revenue product (MRP)**, to mean *the addition to a firm's revenue resulting from the sale of the output produced by an additional unit of the variable factor.*

Using our new terminology, we can restate the condition for maximizing profits as follows:

marginal cost   marginal revenue
of each variable = product of   (1)
factor (*MC*)   that factor (*MRP*).

To check your understanding of (1), consider an example. Assume that the variable factor is available to the firm at a cost of £10 a unit. If another unit taken on would add £15 to revenue, then hiring that unit brings in £5 more than it costs. *The firm will take on more of the factor whenever MRP exceeds MC.* Now assume, however, that another unit of the variable factor would add only £7 to revenue. The firm would lose if it hired that unit at a cost of £10. Further assume that by laying off one unit of the variable factor, revenue would be reduced by £8. Clearly, the firm can increase profits by cutting back on its use of the factor, since laying off one unit reduces revenues by £8 while reducing costs by £10. *The firm will lay off units of the variable factor whenever MRP is less than MC.* Finally assume that another unit of the factor taken on, or laid off, changes revenue by £10. Now the firm cannot increase its profits by altering its employment of the variable factor in either direction. *The firm cannot increase its profits by altering employment of the variable factor whenever MRP equals MC.*

Now consider each of the two sides of equation (1) separately. First we look at the marginal cost and then at the marginal revenue product of the variable factor.

The Marginal Cost of the Variable Factor

In this chapter we confine our attention to firms that are price-takers in the markets for their inputs, which means that they cannot influence the prices of the factors that they purchase. For them, the marginal cost of a factor is merely its market price. The cost, for example, of obtaining an extra machinist is the market wage for that type of machinist. For firms that are price-takers in factor markets, condition (1) can be restated as:

price of   marginal revenue product
the factor = of that factor.   (2)

Marginal Revenue Product of a Variable Factor

We have seen that the *MRP* is defined as the addition to total revenue resulting from the use of an additional unit of a variable factor. This may be broken up into a physical and a value component, and we now consider how each of these varies as the quantity of the factor varies.

The physical component: As the quantity of the variable factor varies, output will vary. The hypothesis of diminishing returns, first discussed in Chapter 11, predicts what will happen: as the firm adds further units of the variable factor to a given quantity of the fixed factor, the additions to output will eventually get smaller and smaller. The extra output produced by an additional unit of the variable factor is called its **marginal physical product (MPP)**. It is illustrated in Figure 17.3, using hypothetical data which has the same general characteristics as the data in Table 11.1 on p. 179. Note that the MPP curve is negatively sloped. Because of the law of diminishing returns, each unit of labour adds less to total output than the previous unit.

The value component: To convert the marginal physical product curve of Figure 17.3(i) into a marginal revenue product curve, we need to know the value of the extra physical product. The marginal physical product depends solely on the technical conditions of production, but the value to the firm of this extra product depends on the price of the product. There are two cases to consider. In the first case the firm sells its product in a perfectly competitive market. The firm is a price-taker in its product markets, and the price of its product measures the value to the firm of an additional unit of output. In this case:

$$MRP = \text{multiplied by the price of the} \quad (3)$$
marginal physical product
product

(for any firm that is a price-taker in its output market)

This is the case illustrated in Figure 17.3.

In the second case, the firm is not a price-taker in the market for its product. Instead, it faces a downward-sloping demand curve. The value to the firm of an extra unit of output will now be less than its price because, to sell the extra unit, the firm will have to reduce the price on all units sold. In this case, the marginal revenue due to an extra unit of output is less than its price. Thus, where any firm faces a downward-sloping demand

curve for its product, the marginal revenue product is given by:

$$MRP = \begin{array}{l}\text{marginal physical product} \\ \text{multiplied by the} \\ \text{marginal revenue from} \quad (4) \\ \text{the sale of an extra unit}\end{array}$$

(for a firm that is not a price-taker in its output market)

In both cases the firm is interested in the gain in revenue resulting from taking on another unit of the variable factor. In both cases an extra unit of the variable factor adds the same physical amount to output. The difference between the two cases lies in what this addition to output does to revenue. In one case, the addition to revenue is just the market price of the addition to output (3 above). In the other case, the addition to revenue is less than the market price of the additional

FIGURE 17.3 From Marginal Physical Product to Demand Curve

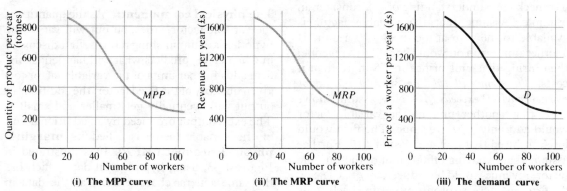

(i) The MPP curve   (ii) The MRP curve   (iii) The demand curve

Each additional unit of the factor employed adds a certain amount to total product (part i) and hence a certain amount to total revenue (part ii), and this determines the amount of the factor firms will demand at each price (part iii). Part (i) assumes data that is consistent with marginal productivity theory; it shows the addition to the firm's *output* produced by additional units of labour hired. The curve is downward-sloping because of the law of diminishing returns.

Part (ii) shows the addition to the firm's *revenue* caused by the employment of each additional unit of labour. It is the marginal physical product from part (i) multiplied by the price at which that product is sold. In this case the price is assumed to be £2. (The multiplication is by market price because the firm is assumed to be a price-taker in the market for its output. If it were not, MPP would be multiplied by marginal revenue to obtain MRP.)

Since the firm will hire the factor until the marginal value product is equal to the factor's price, the firm's demand curve in part (iii) is the same as the marginal revenue product curve in part (ii).

output – because selling the extra output drives down the price at which all units of output must be sold (case 4).[1]

The Firm's Demand Curve for a Variable Factor

Conditions (1) and (2) describe relations that hold in equilibrium. We now wish to derive the firm's demand curve for factors of production when the firm is a price-taker in factor markets. For the moment we shall also assume that there is only a single variable factor of production. This allows us to use condition (2) to derive the firm's demand for the factor from the factor's marginal revenue product curve. This curve comes from either (3) or (4) depending on whether or not the firm is a price-taker in the market for its output.

Part (ii) of Figure 17.3 shows a marginal revenue product curve for labour on the assumption that the firm sells its product in a competitive market at a price of £2 a unit. This curve shows how much would be added to revenue by employing one more unit of the factor for each level of total employment of the factor. Condition (2) states that the profit-maximizing firm will employ additional units of the factor up to the point at which the marginal revenue product equals the price of the factor. If, for example, the price were £1,200 per year, then it would be most profitable to employ fifty workers. (There is no point in employing a fifty-first, since that would add just less than £1,200 to revenue, but a full £1,200 to costs.)

The curve in part (iii) of Figure 17.3 shows the quantity of labour employed at each price of labour. Such a curve can be derived from part (ii) of the Figure by picking various prices of the variable factor, and reading off the amount used from the marginal revenue product curve in just the way described above for the price of £1,200.

Note that the curve in part (iii) has an identical shape to the marginal revenue product curve in part (ii). The curve in part (iii) relates the price of the variable factor to the quantity employed. Hence, it is the variable factor's demand curve.

---

[1] We have avoided unnecessary terminology by referring to both (3) and (4) as *marginal revenue product*. Sometimes, however, when it is desirable to distinguish between the two, (3) is called *the value of the marginal product*, while the terms *marginal revenue product*, or *marginal value product*, are reserved for (4).

Recapitulation

All of the above analysis no doubt sounds very forbidding at first reading. It is an example of a chain of reasoning, referred to in the Foreword, where each step is simple enough, but the cumulative effect of several steps can seem complex. And there are more steps to come! Perhaps it would be a good idea, before going on, to summarize the argument so far.

- **Any profit-maximizing firm will hire a variable factor up to the point at which the last unit adds as much to revenue as to costs.**
- **The addition to costs is the price of the factor (if the firm buys factors in a competitive input market).**
- **The addition to revenue is either the marginal physical product multiplied by the price of the product, if the firm sells in a competitive output market, or the marginal physical product multiplied by marginal revenue, if the firm faces a negatively sloped demand curve.**
- **In both cases, the curve showing the addition to revenue resulting from the employment of each additional unit of the factor is identical in shape to the firm's demand curve for the factor.**

The Industry's Demand for a Factor

We now wish to derive the demand curve for a factor on the part of all firms in a perfectly competitive industry. When we derived the market demand curve for a commodity, we merely summed the demands of individual households. We cannot, however, rely on such a simple procedure in the case of a factor of production. The individual firm's demand curve shows how the quantity of the factor demanded varies with the factor's price, *assuming that the price of the firm's product remains constant*. If the price of the variable factor changes, however, *all* firms will vary their production, and this will cause the market price of output to change. If, for example, the price of the factor falls, then all firms will hire more of the variable factor, and the resulting increase in output will cause a fall in the market

BOX 17.1 THE DERIVATION OF A COMPETITIVE INDUSTRY'S DEMAND CURVE FOR A FACTOR

We wish to derive an industry's demand curve for a variable factor when all firms in the industry respond to a factor price change by varying their outputs. We are given the marginal physical product curves for all firms in the industry, and the demand curve for the industry's product. We proceed in the following manner.

(1) Assume some particular price of the factor and find the equilibrium price for the product. This is done in the manner described in Chapter 12: once the factor price is known, the marginal physical product curves can be translated into marginal cost curves for each firm; these cost curves are then summed, giving an industry supply curve which, together with the market demand curve, determines the equilibrium price of the product.

(2) Next, take the marginal physical product curve of the firm in which we are interested, and multiply each quantity by the market price determined in (1) above. This gives a marginal revenue product curve on the assumption that market price remains constant as output is varied. This is the curve MRP_0 shown in the Figure. *This curve, MRP_0, is the firm's demand curve for the variable factor, on the assumption that the price of the commodity is fixed; its slope depends solely on the technical conditions of production, i.e. on the slope of the marginal physical product curve.* Locate on it the point A, corresponding to the existing price of the factor and the quantity actually being employed.

(3) Now consider a lower price of the factor, say p_1, instead of p_0. In an effort to maximize profits, our firm will hire more labour and increase its output. But so will all other firms and, as a result, the price of the product will fall. This causes

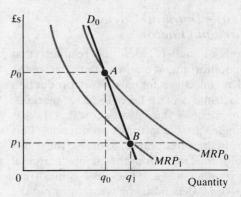

the curve showing marginal physical product (MPP) multiplied by existing market-price to *shift inwards towards the origin* – to MRP_1 in the Figure. Thus the firm moves towards equilibrium in two ways: by hiring more labour and by having its curve showing marginal physical product *times* current market price shift inwards. A possible equilibrium is illustrated by point B. The lower price of the product gives rise to a new curve showing MPP *times* market price and the new quantity of labour hired is q_1 instead of q_0. Repeat the procedure for each possible price of labour and generate a set of points such as A and B. Now join up these points to obtain a demand curve for labour allowing for the price changes in the final product. This curve, which is shown by the line labelled D_0 in the Figure, is steeper than any of the fixed-price demand curves. How much steeper depends upon how much the price of the product falls as all firms expand output, i.e. on the elasticity of the market demand for the product. To derive the industry's demand curve for the factor, we aggregate the demand curves we have developed.

price of that output. This fall in price will cause each firm to hire less of the factor than it would have hired if the price of its output had remained constant.

As a result, the industry's demand curve for a factor is steeper (indicating a smaller increase in employment when the factor's price falls) than it would have been if the price of the industry's output had remained constant as production increased. So if each firm has a negatively sloped demand curve for a factor, the industry's demand curve for that factor must also be negatively sloped. This negative slope is all that matters for the analysis that follows. Those who wish to see

the industry's curve derived formally, however, should study Box 17.1.

Elasticity of Factor Demand

We have seen that the demand curve for a factor is negatively sloped, indicating that the lower the factor's price, the greater the quantity that will be demanded. But what determines the elasticity of such a demand curve? Some of the forces that influence elasticity depend on the technical conditions of production; others depend on the demand for the industry's product.

Technical determinants: One determinant

FIGURE 17.4 A Factor's Price and a Firm's Output

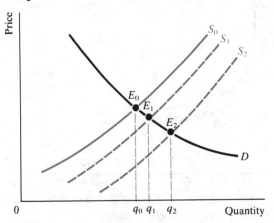

A fall in a factor's price shifts the industry's supply curve, the amount of the shift depending on the importance of the factor in the firm's total cost. The demand curve for the industry's product is D and, given the factor's original price, the industry supply curve is S_0. Equilibrium is at E_0 with output at q_0. The factor's price then falls.

If the factor accounts for a small part of the industry's total costs, each firm's marginal cost curve shifts downwards by only a small amount. So also does the industry supply curve, as illustrated by the supply curve S_1. Output only expands a small amount to q_1 which implies only a small increase in the quantity of the variable factor demanded.

If the factor accounts for a large part of the industry's total costs, each firm's marginal cost curve shifts downwards a great deal. So also does the industry supply curve, as illustrated by the curve S_2. Output expands greatly to q_2, which implies a large increase in the quantity of the variable factor demanded.

of short-run demand elasticity is the rate at which diminishing returns set in, as shown by the slope of the *MRP* curve in Figure 17.3 (i).

First, assume that diminishing returns set in slowly, so that each unit of the factor adds only a little less to the total product than did the previous unit. The *MPP* curve will thus be quite flat. This will make the *MRP* curve, and hence the demand curve, flat as well. The common sense of this flat curve is that, if each additional unit adds almost as much to output as did the previous unit, the firm will need only small reductions in the price of its input to induce it to take on many more units.

Next, assume that returns diminish rapidly so that each unit adds much less to output than the previous unit. The curves in Figure 17.3 will then be quite steep. The common sense of the steep demand curve is that, if each additional unit adds much less than previous units, the firm will need large reductions in the price of its input to induce it to take on many extra units.

(1) In the short run, the demand curve for a factor is more elastic the less rapidly do returns diminish as more units of the factor are employed.[1]

A second technical determinant is the importance of the factor in the firm's total costs. This influence is analysed in Figure 17.4. To illustrate what is involved, compare a labour-intensive industry, B, with a capital-intensive industry, A. Assume for purposes of this illustration that expenditure on labour accounts for 2 per cent of the total costs of production in industry A and for 50 per cent of total costs in industry B. Now consider a 1 per cent change in the price of labour. This change will shift the marginal cost curves by more in industry B than in industry A. Clearly, the smaller the shift in the marginal cost curve, the smaller the shift in the industry's supply curve and, hence, the smaller the change in equilibrium output. The smaller the change in output, the smaller the change in the quantity of the variable factor required as an input. This chain of reasoning leads to the conclusion[2] that:

(2) The smaller the proportion of total cost accounted for by a factor, the more inelastic is the demand for it.

---

[1] The argument in the text goes from slopes to elasticities. In doing so, it relies on point 3 in the appendix to Chapter 6 (see page 98). The full statement is '*at any given price-quantity point* the demand for a factor will be more elastic the less rapidly do returns diminish'.

[2] Like most propositions in economics this is based on *ceteris paribus* assumptions. When there is more than one variable factor, the elasticity of demand depends both on the proportion of costs accounted for by the factor and on the ease with which other factors can be substituted for it. Thus we would not expect there to be an inelastic demand on British building sites for Irish labourers from the city of Cork because, although they usually account for a low proportion of total costs, other labourers are perfect substitutes for them. On the other hand, we would expect there to be an inelastic demand for door handles because, not only are they a small proportion of the total cost of building a house, it is very hard to build a satisfactory house without them.

FIGURE 17.5 Factor Prices and Factor Substitutability

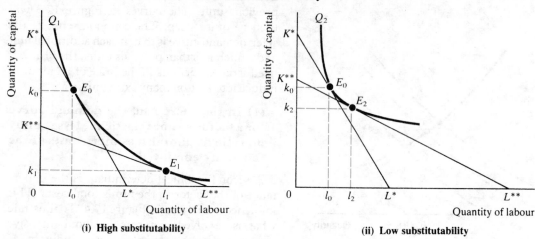

(i) **High substitutability**   (ii) **Low substitutability**

The higher the degree of substitutability, the greater the increase in demand for a factor when its price falls. In each part of the Figure, the quantity of labour used by some firm is plotted on the horizontal axis and the quantity of capital is plotted on the vertical axis. Each isoquant shows the alternative quantities of labour and capital that can be used to produce a given output per period. The initial factor-price ratio is given by the slope of the isocost line running from K^* to L^* – a given expenditure will buy K^* of capital and no labour, L^* of labour and no capital, or any combination of the two factors that lies on the line joining these points. The firm produces its output by using l_0 of labour and k_0 of capital. The price of labour then falls, so that the relative price is now shown by the slope of the line running from K^{**} to L^{**}.

In part (i), the isoquant Q_1 bends only slowly, indicating that the technical conditions of production are such that capital can be substituted for labour over a wide range, at nearly a constant rate. When the price of labour falls, the firm produces its given output by increasing its use of labour a great deal, to l_1, and reducing its use of capital a great deal, to k_1.

In part (ii), the isoquant Q_2 bends sharply, indicating that it is technically difficult to substitute labour for capital: even when a great deal of additional labour is used, the amount of capital employed can only be reduced slightly. When the price of labour falls, the firm produces its given output by increasing its use of labour by only a small amount, to l_2, and reducing its use of capital by only a small amount, to k_2.

In the long run, the major technical condition that influences elasticity is the ease with which one factor can be substituted for another. If it is very easy to substitute capital for labour, then a small increase in the price of labour will lead to a large replacement of labour by capital. If such substitutions are not easy, then only a small replacement will occur in response to a rise in the price of labour. This is demonstrated in Figure 17.5, using the isoquants first introduced in Figure 11.7.

(3) In the long run, the higher the degree of substitutability between factors, the greater the elasticity of demand for the factor.

It is very easy to underestimate the degree of substitutability. It is fairly obvious that a bushel of wheat can be produced by combining land, either with a lot of labour and a little capital, or with a little labour and a lot of capital. It is common, however, to think in terms of using inputs in fixed proportions in manufacturing. Factor proportions are, however, highly variable over time in manufacturing. Although one would never guess it by considering their physical qualities, even glass and steel can be good substi-

**FIGURE 17.6 The Demand for the Product and
the Demand for the Factor**

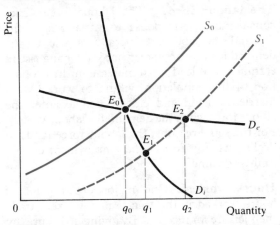

**The more elastic the demand for the industry's
product, the more elastic the demand for a
factor used by the industry.** The original demand
and supply curves intersect at E_0 to produce an
industry output of q_0. A fall in the price of a factor
causes the industry's supply curve to shift downwards
to S_1.

When the demand curve is relatively inelastic, as
shown by the curve D_i, the industry's output only
increases by a small amount, to q_1. The quantity of the
variable factor demanded will only increase by a
correspondingly small amount.

When the demand curve is relatively elastic, as
shown by the curve D_e, the industry's output
increases by a large amount to q_2. The quantity of the
variable factor demanded will then increase by a
correspondingly large amount.

tutes for each other. In the car industry, for
example, one of these can be substituted for the
other merely by varying the dimensions of the
windows. An interesting example of substitution
among inputs in the electricity industry is given
in Box 17.2.

Demand determinants: All of the influences
studied so far have been on the supply or cost
side. Now let us consider the influence of the
demand for the commodity made by the factor. A

change in a factor's price shifts the supply curve
for the industry's output. The more elastic the
demand for the product made by the industry,
the greater will be the change in quantity sold as a
result of a given shift in supply. The more the
change in quantity sold, the more the change in
the quantity of inputs demanded.

**(4) The more elastic the demand for the
industry's product, the more elastic the
demand for each factor that it uses.**

BOX 17.2 ELECTRICITY GENERATION: SUBSTITUTION IN PRACTICE

One field in which the principle of substitution has
been important, but has not always worked in the
same direction, is the choice of fuels used to
generate electricity.

During the 1950s and 1960s, economies of
scale in shipping crude oil from the Middle East to
Western Europe made oil-based fuels more and
more competitive. The relative price of fuels for
industrial use fell by even more than the production cost of petrol as it was the demand for petrol
which was mainly responsible for the derived
demand for crude oil. Other outputs of the oil-
refining process were by-products. The Central
Electricity Generating Board responded to the
falling relative price of 'bunker' oil by building
more and more oil-fired power stations and gradually closing down (or converting) the older coal-
fired stations. From 85–87 per cent of electricity
generated from coal and 11–14 per cent from oil in
1962–65, the CEGB steadily changed the 'mix', so
that by 1971–74 it was generating 63–66 per cent

from coal and 24–26 per cent from oil.

Then came the 'oil shocks' of 1973/74 and
1979/80, when the OPEC countries dramatically
raised the price of crude oil, leading to correspondingly dramatic increases in the prices of all
oil products. Even though people in coal-mining
saw an opportunity to raise coal prices substantially, the *relative* price of oil was significantly
higher in the 1980s than it had been in the 1960s
and early 1970s. The CEGB accordingly switched
back to increasing reliance on coal-firing, generating 77–81 per cent of its electricity from coal and
only 5–7 per cent from oil in 1982–84.

Nevertheless, the CEGB clearly retained the
ability to switch back to oil rapidly if required: in
1984/85, the coal miners' strike which lasted
almost the whole year led to an amazing 41 per
cent of electricity being generated from oil (with
total output slightly higher than the previous year)
and only 42 per cent from coal. After the strike the
figures quickly returned to their 1982–84 levels.

This proposition is derived in Figure 17.6. Note once again the long string of reasoning which occurs because we are dealing with derived demand. We start with a change in the factor price, this changes the industry's costs and so shifts its supply curve, this changes its output *by an amount that depends on the market demand curve for the industry's product*, and this in turn changes the quantities of all variable factors that are demanded.

THE SUPPLY OF FACTORS

There is an important distinction between the total supply of a factor to the whole economy and the supply of that factor to one industry or to one firm. We deal first with the total supply of a factor to the economy.

The Total Supply of Factors

At first glance it may seem plausible to assume that the total supply of most factors is fixed. After all, there is only so much land in the world, or in England, or in London. There is an upper limit to the number of workers. There is only so much coal, oil, copper and iron ore in the earth. These considerations do indeed set a maximum to the supply of each factor. That upper limit, however, is seldom reached, so we do need to consider what determines changes in the total amount of factors that are actually supplied to the market.

Labour

The number of people willing to work is called the *labour force*; the total number of hours they are willing to work is called the **supply of effort** or, more simply, the **supply of labour**.

> **The supply of effort depends on three influences: the size of the population, the proportion of the population willing to work, and the number of hours worked by each individual.**

Population: Populations vary in size, and these variations are influenced to some extent by economic forces. There is some evidence, for example, that the birth rate and the net immigration rate (immigration minus emigration) is higher in good times than in bad. Much of the variation in population is, however, explained by factors outside economics.

The labour force: The labour force varies considerably in response to variations in the demand for labour. Generally, a rise in the demand for labour, and an accompanying rise in earnings, will lead to an increase in the proportion of the population willing to work. More married women and elderly people enter the labour force when the demand for labour is high. For the same reasons, the labour force tends to decline when earnings and employment opportunities decline.

Hours worked: One major determinant of hours worked is the wage rate. Workers trade their leisure for incomes. By giving up leisure (by working), they obtain income with which to buy goods. They can, therefore, be thought of as trading leisure for goods.

A rise in the wage rate implies a change in the relative price of goods and leisure. Goods become cheaper relative to leisure, since each hour worked buys more goods than before. The other side of the same change is that leisure becomes more expensive, since each hour of leisure consumed is at the cost of more goods forgone.

This change in relative prices has both the income and the substitition effects that we studied on pages 136–137. The substitution effect leads the individual to consume more of the relatively cheaper goods, and less of the relatively more expensive leisure – i.e. to trade more leisure for goods. The income effect, however, leads the individual to consume more goods *and* more leisure. The rise in the wage rate makes it possible for the individual to have more goods and more leisure. For example, if the wage rate rises by 10 per cent, and the individual works 5 per cent fewer hours, more leisure and more goods will be consumed.

Because the income and the substitution effects work in the same direction for the consumption of goods, we can be sure that a rise in the wage rate will lead to a rise in goods consumed. Because, however, the two effects work in opposite directions for leisure:

> **a rise in the wage rate leads to less leisure being consumed (more work) when the substitution effect is the dominant force,**

FIGURE 17.7 The Derivation of the Supply Curve of Effort

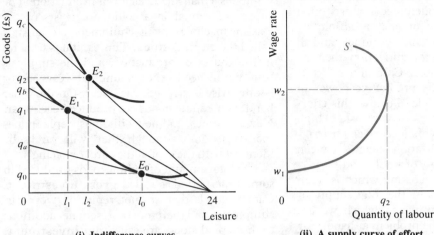

(i) Indifference curves (ii) A supply curve of effort

Because a change in the wage rate has an income and a substitution effect that pull in opposite directions, the supply curve of effort may slope upwards or downwards. Part (i) of the Figure plots leisure on the horizontal axis and the consumption of goods (measured in £s) on the vertical axis. The budget line always starts at 24, indicating that everyone is endowed with 24 hours a day that they may either consume as leisure or trade for goods by working.

At the original wage rate, the individual could obtain q_a of goods by working 24 hours (i.e. the hourly wage rate is $q_a/24$). Equilibrium is at E_0, where the individual consumes l_0 of leisure and works $24 - l_0$ hours in return for q_0 of goods.

The wage rate now rises so that q_b becomes available if 24 hours are worked (i.e. the hourly wage rate is $q_b/24$). Equilibrium shifts to E_1. Consumption of leisure falls to l_1, and the individual works $24 - l_1$ hours in return for a consumption of q_1 goods. The rise in wages increases hours worked.

The hourly wage rate now rises further to $q_c/24$ and equilibrium shifts to E_2. Consumption of leisure rises to l_2, while $24 - l_2$ hours are worked in return for an increased consumption of q_2 goods. This time, therefore, the rise in the wage rate lowers hours worked.

Part (ii) of the Figure shows the same behaviour as in part (i), using what is called a supply curve of effort. It plots the number of hours worked against the wage rate. At wage rates of up to w_1, the individual is not in the labour force since no work is offered. As the wage rate rises from w_1 to w_2, more and more hours are worked so the supply curve of effort has the normal, positive slope. The wage rates that result in E_0 and E_1 in part (i) of the Figure lie in this range. Above w_2 and q_2, the quantity of effort falls as wages rise, so that the supply curve has a negative slope. This latter case is often referred to as a *backward-bending supply curve of effort*. The wage that gives rise to equilibrium E_2 in part (i) lies in this range.

and to more leisure consumed (less work) when the income effect is the dominant force.

These alternative cases are analysed in Figure 17.7.

Much of the long-run evidence tends to show that as real hourly wage rates rise, people wish to reduce the number of hours they work. (This evidence is, of course, concerned with the supply of effort to the whole economy; there is also evidence to suggest that a rise in earnings in one industry will increase the supply of effort to that industry by attracting workers from other industries.)

Land

If by 'land' we mean the total area of dry land, then its supply is pretty well fixed. A rise in the earnings of land cannot increase the supply by much, except where land can be reclaimed from swamp or sea. For simplicity, economists often assume that the supply of land is absolutely inelastic. However, if by 'land' we understand all the fertile land available for cultivation, then the supply of land is variable. Care and effort is required to maintain the productive power of land, and if the return to land is low, this effort may not be forthcoming. In contrast, a high return to land may provide incentives for irrigation, drainage and fertilization schemes that can greatly increase the supply of arable land.[1]

There is no value in debating which is 'real' land, the total land area or the total supply of arable land. The magnitude in which we are interested depends on the problem at hand. For most problems in agricultural economics – for example, what are the effects of land taxes on the prices of agricultural goods – we need to know the elasticity of the total supply of arable land.

The total supply of arable land can be expanded by irrigation and reclamation, and it can be contracted as a result of poor farming practices.

Land is usually defined to include the natural resources found in it or on it. The quantity of each natural resource existing in the world is, of course, limited. But the problem of actual exhaustion does not arise as frequently as one might think. Often a large undiscovered, or unexploited, quantity exists, and a shortage of the resource that raises its price encourages the discovery of new sources, as well as the development of already known, but previously unprofitable, sources. The world's proven, and exploitable, supply of any natural resource thus tends to vary considerably with the price of the resource. This is certainly true today of both petroleum and natural gas – worries about the 'energy crisis' notwithstanding. Of course, there is an upper limit, and resources can be totally exhausted. Worse, they can be polluted or otherwise despoiled, so that they are rendered useless before they have been consumed.

---

[1] It used to be common practice, following David Ricardo, a British economist of the early nineteenth century, to define land as the *original and inexhaustible powers of the soil*. Ricardo wrote before it was widely known that many present-day deserts had once been fertile areas.

Capital

Capital is a man-made factor of production. The supply of capital in a country consists of the existing machines, plant, equipment, etc. and it is called the **capital stock**. This capital is used up in the course of production, and the supply is thus diminished by the amount that wears out, or is otherwise destroyed, each year. On the other hand, new capital goods are produced each year. New machines, and new buildings, replace ones that wear out (although they will rarely be identical with the capital they are 'replacing').

The total amount of capital goods produced in some time-period is called **gross investment**. Capital goods that are not replacing worn-out equipment, and therefore represent net additions to the capital stock, are called **net investment**. Expenditure on capital goods is called **investment expenditure**. To distinguish the two types of investment we talk of *gross* and *net investment expenditure*.

The volume of net investment determines the rate of increase of the capital stock. Net additions to this stock vary over the trade cycle, being low in periods of slump and high in periods of boom.

Taking the long view and ignoring cyclical fluctuations, there has been a fairly steady tendency for the capital stock to increase over a very long period of time.

The theory of investment, which we shall develop in subsequent sections of this book, is thus a theory of changes in the stock of capital.

The Supply of Factors to Particular Uses

Each type of factor of production has many uses. A given piece of land can, for example, be used to grow a variety of crops, and it can also be subdivided for a housing development. A machinist from Coventry can work in a variety of automobile plants, or in a dozen other industries, or even in the physics laboratories at Cambridge. Factors must be allocated among industries and among firms in the same industry.

Equal Net Advantage

Owners of a factor who wish to maximize their money incomes will move the factor to its most profitable use. Factors will thus move to more profitable uses until the earnings of any one type of factor in all of its various possible uses are equalized. For example, if land can earn more growing sugarbeet than any other crop, land will be transferred into sugarbeet production. As a result, the output of sugarbeets will rise and their price will fall. This will go on until land in sugarbeets can earn no more than land devoted to other crops. There will then be no further shift of land into sugarbeet production.

Owners of factors sometimes take other things besides money into account, including, for example, risk, convenience and a good climate. Factors will, therefore, be moved among uses until there is no *net* advantage in further movement, allowing for both the monetary and non-monetary advantages.

This discussion can be restated as the **hypothesis of equal net advantage**:

> **owners will choose that use of their factors that provides them with the greatest net advantage. Net advantage includes both monetary and non-monetary elements. Movements of units of a factor will occur among its various uses until the net advantage in all uses are equalized.**

This hypothesis plays the same role in the theory of distribution that the profit-maximization hypothesis plays in the theory of production. It leads to the prediction that factors of production will be allocated among various uses in such a way that they receive the same net return in each use.

The importance of non-monetary advantages: Suppose we observe that a mechanic is working in London for £2,000 a year less than he could make in Newcastle. Does this merely mean that the non-monetary benefits of living in London (or of *not* living in Newcastle) are £2,000 a year? To make the hypothesis of equal net advantage useful, we must do one of two things: either we must define in a measurable way the non-monetary benefits that are important to choices, or we must make an assumption about the relative stability of monetary and non-monetary advantages. The first alternative is difficult, if not impossible. The second alterna-

tive is more promising. If, for example, the difference in non-monetary advantages between two uses remains constant, variations in monetary advantages will cause variations in net advantages and resources will move in response. This leads to the following important prediction:

> **any change in the relative price paid to a factor in two uses will lead owners of the factor to increase the quantity they supply to the use in which the relative price has increased, and decrease the quantity they supply to the use in which the relative price has decreased.**

This prediction implies a rising supply curve for a factor in any particular use. Such a supply curve (like all supply curves) can shift in response to changes in other variables. One of these is the size of the non-monetary benefits.

Factor Mobility

How fast will factors move among uses when net advantages vary? **Factor mobility** refers to the readiness of factors to respond to signals that indicate where factors are wanted. If a factor is mobile in the sense that owners will quickly shift from use A to use B in response to a change in the relative factor price, then supply will be elastic. If, on the other hand, factor owners are 'locked in' to some use and will not, or cannot, respond quickly, the supply will tend to be inelastic. In earlier chapters, we discussed the mobility of capital as a result of entry into and exit from an industry as well as the barriers that impede that mobility. We will now generalize that discussion to include all factors.

Mobility of land: Consider agricultural land. Many crops can be harvested within a year and a totally different crop planted. A farm on the outskirts of a growing city can be sold for subdivision and development at very short notice. Once land is built upon, as urban land usually is, its mobility is much reduced. One can convert a hotel site into an office-building site, but it takes a very large differential in the value of land use to make tearing down the hotel worthwhile.

> **Land, which is physically the least mobile of all factors, is one of the most mobile in an economic sense.**

Although the land is highly mobile among alternative uses, it is completely immobile as far as location is concerned. There is only so much land within the borders of any given city, and no increase in the price offered can induce more land to relocate within the city. This locational immobility has, as we shall see, important consequences.

Mobility of capital: Most capital equipment, once constructed, is immobile. A great deal of machinery is specific: it must either be used for the purpose for which it was designed, or not be used at all. It is the immobility of most specialized capital equipment that makes exit of firms from declining industries a slow process.

During the life of a piece of capital, the firm may make allowances for depreciation so that capital goods can be replaced when they wear out. If conditions of demand and cost have not changed, the firm may spend money to replace the worn-out piece of equipment with an identical one. It may also do other things with its funds: buy a newly designed machine to produce the same goods, buy machines to produce different goods, or lend money to another firm. In this way, the long-run allocation of a country's stock of capital among various uses changes.

Physical capital is often immobile in the short run, but depreciation and replacement allow the capital stock to change greatly in its composition and allocation among uses in the long run.

Mobility of labour: Landlords may live in a place of their choice while obtaining income from renting out land located anywhere in the world. Capital can be used throughout the world while its owners never leave New York or Tokyo or London. If a capitalist decides to invest in steel mills, he need never visit one; if a labourer decides to work in a steel mill, he must be on the premises. If a worker employed by a firm in Wolverhampton decides to offer her labour services to a firm in south London, she must physically travel to south London to do so.

Labour is unique as a factor of production in that the supply of the service implies the physical presence of the owner.

This quite obvious point has one important consequence: non-monetary factors are much more important in the allocation of labour than in the allocation of other factors of production. If the rate of return is even slightly higher in steel mills than in other comparable investments, capital will move into steel. The wage paid in steel mills can be substantially above that paid in other industries without inducing an analogous flow of labour – if people find working in steel mills unpleasant.

An important variable affecting labour mobility is *time*. In the short term, it is difficult for people to change occupations. It is not difficult for a file clerk to move from one company to another, or to take a job in London instead of Colchester, but it will be difficult for him to become an editor or an advertising executive in a short period of time. There are two considerations here: ability and training. Lack of either make some people immobile.

Over long periods, labour mobility among occupations is great. Young people enter the labour force from school, older persons exit through retirement or death. The turnover due to these causes, makes it possible to reallocate 3 or 4 per cent of the labour force annually merely by directing new entrants to jobs different from those left vacant by persons leaving the labour force. Over a period of twenty years, a totally different occupational distribution can appear without a single individual ever changing his or her job.

Studies of labour mobility over the generations, or *social stratification* as the sociologists call it, indicate impressive mobility.

The data show very substantial movement, both up and down the scales of education, skill, training and social status, over the course of two or three generations.

Man-made barriers to labour mobility: Many organizations, private and public, adopt policies that influence labour mobility. Seniority rights not only protect older employees from being laid off because of cutbacks in production, but also make them reluctant to change jobs. Likewise, if a firm provides employees with a non-transferable pension plan, they may not want to forfeit this benefit by changing jobs.

Licensing is required in dozens of trades and professions. Barbers, electricians, solicitors and, in some places, even peddlers must have licences. There is, of course, a generally acceptable reason for requiring licences when the public must be protected against incompetents, quacks or nuisances. But licensing can also restrict supply. Racial prejudice, discrimination against women and other similar attitudes also limit the mobility of labour.

THE PRICING OF FACTORS IN COMPETITIVE MARKETS

If all units of any one factor of production were identical, and if non-monetary advantages were the same in all uses, then the prices of all units of any one factor would tend towards equality. Units of the factor would move from occupations in which prices were low, and the resulting shortage would tend to force the price up. Units would move into occupations in which prices were high, and the resulting surplus would tend to force the price down. The movements would continue until there was no further incentive to transfer, i.e. until the price paid to the factor was the same in all its uses.

This simple application of the hypothesis of equal net advantage helps us to highlight conditions for different units of the same factor (to be paid different prices).

Factor Price Differentials

When different units of one factor are paid different prices in different uses we speak of **factor price differentials**. These are of two sorts: disequilibrium differentials and equilibrium differentials.

Disequilibrium differentials are associated with changing circumstances, such as the rise of one industry and the decline of another; such differences set up movements in factors that will act to remove the differences.

The differences in prices may persist for a long time, but there is a tendency for them to be reduced, and in equilibrium they will be eliminated.

A rise in the demand for product A and a fall in the demand for product B increases the (derived) demand for factors in industry A and reduces it in B. As the prices paid to factors in the expanding industry A rise, relative to prices paid in B, a disequilibrium differential arises. Factors move from industry B to industry A in response to this differential, and their movement causes the differentials to lessen and eventually disappear. How long this process takes depends on factor mobility. Labour is sometimes relatively immobile in the short run so that disequilibrium differentials in wages persist. Other factors are often more mobile so that these differentials are eliminated almost as soon as they appear.

Equilibrium differentials persist in equilibrium without generating forces to eliminate them; they can be explained by intrinsic differences in the factors themselves, by differences in the cost of acquiring skills, or by different non-monetary advantages of different occupations.

Intrinsic differences: If various units of a factor have different characteristics, the price paid may differ among these units. Intelligent and manually dexterous workers earn more than less intelligent and less dexterous workers. Land that is highly fertile, or in especially good locations, earns more than land that is of poor quality or in unfavourable locations. These differences will persist even in long-run equilibrium.

Acquired differences: If the fertility of land can be increased by costly methods, landlords would not incur the costs of improving fertility unless that land earns enough to repay the costs. The same holds true for labour, because it is costly to acquire most skills. For example, a mechanic must train for some time, and unless the earnings of mechanics remain sufficiently above what can be earned in less skilled occupations, people will not incur the cost of training.

Non-monetary   advantages: Whenever working conditions differ among various uses for a single factor, that factor will earn different equilibrium amounts in its various uses. The difference between a test pilot's wage and a chauffeur's wage is only partly a matter of skill;

the rest is compensation for the higher risk of testing new planes compared to driving a car. If they were paid the same, there would be an excess supply of chauffeurs and a shortage of test pilots.

Academic researchers commonly earn less than they could earn in the world of commerce and industry because of the substantial non-monetary advantages of academic employment. If chemists were paid the same in both sectors, many chemists would prefer academic to industrial jobs. Excess demand for industrial chemists and excess supply of academic chemists would then force chemists' wages up in industry and down in academia until the two types of jobs offered equal net attractions.

The same forces account for equilibrium dif-ferences in regional earnings of otherwise identical factors. Construction workers in the North Sea oilfields earned more than they did in London. Without higher pay, not enough people would be willing to work in unattractive, remote or dangerous locations.

Transfer Earnings and Economic Rent

One of the most important distinctions in economics is that between transfer earnings and economic rent. The amount that a factor must earn in its present use to prevent it from moving (i.e. transferring) to another use is called its **transfer earnings**. Any excess it earns over this

---

BOX 17.3 THE HISTORY OF THE CONCEPT OF ECONOMIC RENT

Early in the nineteenth century, there was a controversy about the high price of 'corn' (the generic term for all grains). One group held that corn had a high price because the landlords were charging high rents to the farmers and, in order to meet these rents, farmers had to charge a high price for their product. Thus, it was argued, the price of corn was high because the rents of agricultural land were high. The second group, which included David Ricardo, one of the great figures of British classical economics, held that the reverse was true. The price of corn was high because there was a shortage caused by the Napoleonic Wars. Because corn had a high price, there was keen competition among farmers to obtain land. This competition bid up the rents of corn land. If the price of corn were to fall so that corn growing became less profitable, then the demand for land would fall, and the rent paid for the use of land would fall as well. Thus this group held that the rent of corn land was high because the price of corn was high, and not vice versa.

Modern students of economics will recognize in the Ricardian argument the idea of *derived demand*. Landlords, Ricardo was saying, cannot just charge any price they want for their land; the price they get will depend on demand and supply. The supply of land is pretty well fixed, and the demand depends on the price of the corn. The higher the price of corn, the more profitable corn growing will be, the higher the demand for corn land will be, and the higher the price that will be paid for its use.

The argument was elaborated by making the assumption that land had only one use, the growing of corn. The supply of land was given and virtually unchangeable, i.e. land was in perfectly inelastic supply and landowners would prefer to rent out their land for some return rather than leave it idle. Nothing had to be paid to prevent land from transferring to uses other than growing corn, because it had none. Therefore, all of the payment to land was surplus over and above what was necessary to keep it in its present use. *Given the fixed supply of land*, the price depended on the demand for land, which was itself a function of the price of corn.

Rent, which originally referred to the payment for the use of land, thus became the term for a surplus payment to a factor over and above what was necessary to keep it in its present use. Subsequently two facts emerged. First, it was realized that many factors of production, as well as land, earn a surplus over and above what is necessary to keep them in their present use. Film and TV stars, for example, are in short and relatively fixed supply, and their potential earnings in other occupations are often low. Because there is a huge demand for their services in the film industry, they may receive payments greatly in excess of what is needed to keep them from transferring to other occupations. Second, it was realized that land itself often has many alternative uses, so that *from the point of view of any one use*, part of the payment made to land is a *necessary* inducement to keep the land in its present employment. Thus all factors of production were pretty much the same in these respects: part of the payment made to them is necessary to keep them from transferring to other uses, and part is a surplus over and above that amount. This surplus came to be called economic rent, whatever the factor of production that earned it.

FIGURE 17.8 Economic Rent and Transfer Earnings

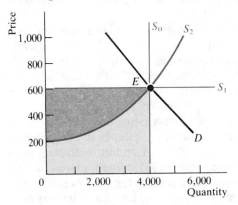

The division of total factor payments between economic rent and transfer earnings depends on the shape of the supply curve. A single demand curve is shown with three different supply curves. In each case the competitive equilibrium price is £600, and 4,000 units of the factor are hired. The total payment (£2.4 million) is represented by the entire shaded area.

When the supply curve is vertical (S_0), the whole payment is economic rent, because a decrease in price would not induce any unit of the factor to move elsewhere.

When the supply curve is horizontal (S_1), the whole payment is transfer earnings, because even a small decrease in price offered would lead all units of the factor to move elsewhere.

When the supply curve is positively sloped (S_2), part of the payment is rent and past is transfer earnings. As shown by the height of the supply curve, at a price of £600 the 4,000th unit of the factor is just receiving transfer earnings, but the 2,000th unit, for example, is earning well above its transfer earnings. The aggregate of economic rents is shown by the dark-shaded area above the supply curve and the aggregate of transfer earnings by the light-shaded area below the supply curve.

---

amount is called its **economic rent**. The distinction is crucial in predicting the effects of changes in earnings on the movement of factors.

The concept of economic rent, the surplus of total earnings over transfer earnings, is analogous to the economists' concept of profit as a surplus over opportunity cost.

The terminology can be confusing because economic rent is often called rent, but rent also

means the price paid to hire something, such as a machine or a piece of land. How the same term came to be used for these two different concepts is explained in Box 17.3.

Economists often drop the adjective 'economic' and speak of rent when they mean economic rent, causing a confusion between the concept described above and the payment made to landlords for the hiring of land and buildings. When tenants speak of 'rent' they are referring to what they pay their landlords, much of which is a transfer earning. When economists speak of rent, they may be referring to what is paid in excess of transfer earnings. It is important to guard against confusing these two uses of the term 'rent'.

The Division of Factor Earnings

In most cases the actual earnings of a factor of production are a composite of transfer earnings and economic rent. It is possible, however, to imagine cases in which earnings are all transfer earnings or are all economic rent. The various possibilities are illustrated in Figure 17.8.

When the supply curve is perfectly inelastic (vertical), the whole factor's income is an economic rent.

Even if price fell towards zero, the same quantity would be supplied. Transfer earnings are therefore zero. The price actually paid allocates the fixed supply to those most willing to pay for it.

When the supply curve is perfectly elastic (horizontal), the whole of the factor's income is a transfer payment.

If that amount is not paid, none of the factor can be obtained.

The more usual situation is that of a positively sloped supply curve. A rise in the factor's price serves the allocative function of attracting more units of the factor into employment, but the same rise provides additional economic rent to all units of the factor already employed. We know this increment is an economic rent because the owners of these units were willing to supply them at a lower price. This is a general result:

If a factor becomes scarce in any of its uses, its price will rise. This will serve the allocative function of attracting additional units, but it will also increase the

economic rent to all units of the factor already in that employment, whose transfer earnings were already being covered.

Determinants of the Division

How much of a given payment to a factor is economic rent and how much is transfer earnings varies from situation to situation. We cannot point to a factor of production and assert that some fixed fraction of its income is always transfer earnings and the remainder is always economic rent. The division depends on the mobility of the factor, that is, on the alternatives open to it. We consider two determinants of the mobility here, the type of transfer being considered and the length of time allowed for the transfer to occur.

Types of transfer: The mobility of a factor depends on the perspective of our analysis. If we focus on a narrowly defined use of a given factor, say the factor's use by a particular firm, then the factor will be highly mobile. Since the factor could readily move to another firm in the same industry, it has a number of alternatives open to it. Therefore, from the perspective of the firm a large proportion of the factor payment is transfer earnings.

If we focus on a more broadly defined use, for example the factor's use in an industry, then it is less mobile, because the factor will find it more difficult to gain employment quickly outside the industry. From the perspective of the particular *industry* (rather than the specific *firm* within the industry), a larger proportion of the factor payment is economic rent and a smaller proportion is transfer earnings.

From the even more general perspective of a particular *occupation*, mobility is likely to be even less, and the proportion of the factor payment that is economic rent is even larger.

As the perspective moves from a narrowly defined use of a factor to a broadly defined use, the mobility of the factor decreases; as mobility decreases, the share of the factor payment that is economic rent increases.

It would be tedious to spell out how these considerations apply to each factor in turn. We will, however, deal with one particular application that has proved troublesome: the division between rent and transfer payments in the payment to urban land.

Consider the movement of land between agricultural and urban uses. Land is very mobile between alternative agricultural uses because its location usually provides it with few advantages in one agricultural use over another. In the case of urban uses, however, location of the land is critical and, from this point of view, land is of course completely immobile. If there is a shortage of land in central London, such land as is available will command a high price, but no matter what price is paid, the land in rural areas will not move into central London. The very high payments made to urban land are economic rents. The land is scarce relative to demand for it, and it commands a price very much above that it could earn in agricultural uses. The payment that it receives is thus well in excess of what is necessary to prevent it from transferring from urban back to agricultural uses.

From the point of view of one particular type of urban use, however, high rents are transfer earnings. Cinemas, for example, account for but a small portion of the total demand for land in central London; if there were no cinemas at all, rentals of land would be about what they are now. Thus the cinema industry faces a perfectly elastic supply of land in central London, and the whole of the price that it pays for its land is a transfer earning which must be paid to keep the land from transferring to other urban uses.[1]

Time allowed for the move: In general, factors tend to be more mobile the larger the amount of time allowed for their movement. Thus a higher proportion of factor earnings may be rents in the short term than in the long term. An extreme but important illustration occurs with capital equipment that is so specialized that it has only one use. A car factory, for example, can be converted to making tanks during wartime but it has no significant alternative uses during

---

[1] Thus the old examination question 'Is it correct to say that the price of cinema seats is high in central London because the price of land is high?' should be answered in the affirmative, not in the negative, as examiners often seemed to expect. The view that the prices of all goods and services sold in central London are high because rents are high can, however, be denied.

peacetime. Either it produces cars or it lies idle (or is scrapped). Any income that is made from the operation of such specialized capital in the short run is rent. Assume, for example, that when some machine was installed it was expected to earn £5,000 per annum in excess of all its operating costs. If the demand for the product now falls off, so that the machine can earn only £2,000, it will still pay to keep it in operation rather than scrap it. Indeed, it will pay to do so as long as it yields any return at all over its operating costs.[1] Thus all of the return earned by the installed machine is economic rent because it will remain allocated to its present use – it has no other – as long as it yields even £1 above its operating costs. Thus, *once the machine has been installed*, any net income that it earns is rent.

The machine will, however, wear out eventually, and it will not be replaced unless it is expected to earn a return over its lifetime sufficient to make it a good investment for its owner. Thus, over the long run, much of the revenue earned by the machine is transfer earnings; if the revenue is not earned, a machine will not continue to be allocated to that use in the long run.

In the case just considered, whether a payment made to a factor is economic rent or a transfer earning depends on the time-span under consideration. In the short run all of the income of a machine with a specific use is a rent, while in the long run some (possibly all) of its income is a transfer earning. Factor payments which are economic rent in the short run and transfer earnings in the long run are called **quasi-rents**.

Some Implications of Rent and Transfer Earnings

Increasing the supply of a factor: Consider the effect of wage increases on the quantity of labour supplied. For example, if the central authorities want more physicists, should they subsidize physicists' salaries? As we have seen, such a policy may well have an effect on supply. It may influence schoolchildren uncertain about whether to become engineers or physicists to become physicists. But it will also mean that a great deal of money will have to be spent on extra

payments to people who are already physicists. These payments will be economic rents, since existing physicists have demonstrated that they are prepared to be physicists at their old salaries. Although some may have been considering transferring to another occupation, such movements are not common.[1] An alternative policy, which may produce more physicists per pound spent, is to subsidize scholarships and fellowships for students who will train to become physicists. The policy tends to operate at the margin on persons just deciding whether or not to enter the occupation. It avoids the payment of additional rents to persons already in the occupation. Graphically, it is shown by a rightward shift in the supply curve because there will now be *more* persons in the occupation at each price of the factor.

If a factor's supply curve is inelastic, an increase in the quantity supplied may be achieved more easily, and at less cost, by shifting the supply curve to the right rather than by moving along it by altering the factor's price.

Urban land values and land taxes: The high payments made to urban land are largely economic rents. The land is scarce relative to the demand for it, and it commands a price very much above what it could earn in agricultural uses. The payment it receives is thus well in excess of what is necessary to prevent it from transferring from urban back to agricultural uses. A society with rising population and rising per-capita real income tends also to have steadily rising urban land prices. This fact has created a special interest in taxes on land values.

Who ultimately pays taxes on the value of land? If the same tax rate is applied to land in all uses, the relative profitability of different uses will be unaffected, and thus landlords will not be tempted to change the allocation of their land. Land will not be forced out of use, because land that is very unprofitable will command little rent

---

[1] This is just another way of stating the proposition given in Chapter 12, that it pays a firm to continue in operation in the short run as long as it can cover its variable costs of production.

[1] International mobility is another matter. One of the reasons for the considerable migration of trained professionals of all ages from the United Kingdom to the United States is the higher monetary rewards to be earned in the US compared with the UK. When British professionals are being paid less than their international transfer earnings, the result is steady emigration.

and so pay little tax. Thus there will be no change in the supply of goods that are produced with the aid of land, and, since there is no change in supply, there can be no change in their prices. Thus farmers will be willing to pay exactly as much as they would have offered previously for the use of the land. Because the prices of agricultural goods and the prices paid by tenants for land

will be unchanged, the whole of the tax will be borne by the landlord. The incomes earned by landlords will fall by the full amount of the tax, and land values will fall correspondingly (because land is now less attractive to own than it was previously). One famous attempt to apply these ideas to government tax policy is discussed in Box 17.4.

BOX 17.4 HENRY GEORGE AND THE SINGLE-TAX MOVEMENT

Taxation of land values has had enormous appeal in the past. The peak of its appeal occurred about 100 years ago with the 'single-tax movement' led by the American economist Henry George. George's book *Progress and Poverty* is – as books on economic issues go – an all-time bestseller. It pointed out that the fixed supply of land, combined with a rapidly rising demand for it, allowed the owners of land to gain from the natural progress of society without contributing anything. Along with many others, George was incensed at this 'unearned increment' from which huge fortunes accrued to landlords. He calculated that most of government expenditure could be financed by a single tax that did nothing more than remove the landlords' unearned increment. A further appeal of taxes on land values arises from the fact that economic rent can be taxed away without affecting the allocation of resources. Thus, for someone who does not wish to interfere with the allocation resulting from the free play of market forces, the taxation of economic rent is attractive.

Two problems arise with any attempt to tax economic rent. First, the theoretical statement refers to *economic rent*, not to the payment actually made by tenants and landlords. What is called rent in the world is partly an economic rent and partly a return on capital invested by the landowner. The policy implications of taxing rent depend on being able in practice to identify *economic rent*. At best, this is difficult; at worst, it is impossible.

The second problem is a normative one. If, in the

interests of justice, we want to treat all recipients of economic rent similarly, we will encounter grave difficulties – because economic rent accrues to all factors of production. If there is, for example, a fixed supply of opera singers in the country, they earn rising economic rent as the society becomes richer and the demand for opera increases, without there being any corresponding increase in the supply of singers. No one has yet devised a scheme that will tax the economic rent, but not the transfer earnings, of such divergent factors as land, patents, football players and High Court judges.

When George died he left the huge royalties from his book to finance schools of 'economic science' which were to propagate his theories and policy recommendations. These schools are maintained throughout the world; one exists in London even today. The appeal of a single tax has, however, receded. This is partly because of the difficulties mentioned above, and partly because, with the great increase in the size of the government, even an effective tax on economic rent would finance only a tiny portion of government expenditures. The hostility towards unearned increments of landowners still survives in various forms of taxes in many modern countries. In Britain the most obvious example was in the land development tax, which sought to tax away most of the profit made by developing rural land for urban uses. This tax, introduced in the 1970s, severely curtailed the development of rural land for urban uses – at least until ways of avoiding it were developed. It was abolished by the Conservative government in the 1980s.

SUMMARY

1. According to neo-Classical theory, the problem of distribution can be reduced to the question of the determinants of the demand and supply of factors of production, plus the problem of determining the effect of the departures from a free market caused by such forces as monopolistic buyers, government action, and unions.

2. The marginal revenue product curve of a factor has the same shape as the firm's demand curve for that factor. The negative slopes of both curves show that a fall in the factor's price causes the firm to increase the quantity of the factor, and hence to increase output; hence the firm's demand curve for a factor is downward sloping.

3. The industry's demand curve for a factor is steeper than the sum of the firms' *ceteris paribus* demand curves because, as factor inputs are varied, the market price of the output must also vary.

4. An industry's demand for a factor will be more elastic (i) the less rapidly do diminishing returns set in, (ii) the larger is the proportion of total costs accounted for by the factor, (iii) the easier is it to substitute other factors for the one in question, and (iv) the more elastic is the demand for the industry's output.

5. The theory of household behaviour makes no prediction about the effect of an increase in wage rates on the overall supply of effort, which may rise, fall or remain unchanged, because the income and the substitution effect work against each other. Although the total land area of a country is fixed, the total supply of arable land is variable. The total supply of capital tends to rise over time as a result of positive net investment.

6. Labour is much more mobile in the long run than in the short run. Over a given time-period, it is more mobile among jobs in the same location and occupation than among locations (where movement of the family is a deterrent) or among occupations (where lack of training or skills is a deterrent).

7. The supply of factors to various uses is governed by the principle of equal net advantage: units of a factor move among uses until the net advantage – monetary and non-monetary gains – is the same in each use. How fast net advantages are equated depends on the mobility of a factor.

8. Disequilibrium factor differentials are a result of disequilibria in factor markets. They set up factor movements that eventually eliminate the differentials. Equilibrium differentials persist even in long-run equilibrium. They arise from: (i) intrinsic differences among units of a factor, (ii) differences that can be acquired at a cost, and (iii) different non-monetary advantages in different uses.

9. Transfer earnings are payments needed to keep a factor in its present use; any payments in excess of transfer earnings are economic rent. As the perspective moves from a narrowly defined use of a factor to a broadly defined use, the mobility of the factor decreases; as mobility decreases, the share of the factor payment that is economic rent increases.

TOPICS FOR REVIEW

- The size and the functional distributions of income
- The principles of derived demand
- The determinants of the elasticity of demand for a factor
- The determinants of the total supply of a factor
- The determinants of the supply of a factor to a specific use
- Monetary and non-monetary advantages
- Equilibrium and disequilibrium differentials
- Transfer earnings and economic rents

18

The Income
of Labour[1]

In this chapter we look specifically at labour markets. Do not forget that by *labour* we mean all human resources of both workers and management, and by *labour income*, or *wages*, we mean all income earned from work, whether in the form of wages or salaries.

WAGE DIFFERENTIALS

We noted in the previous chapter that if labour was a homogeneous factor of production, and was sold in perfectly competitive markets, every person would earn the same income in equilibrium. Disequilibrium differentials in wages would arise, but workers would move from the lower-income to the higher-income jobs until the differentials had disappeared.

In the real world, however, some workers scrape out a bare living, others earn modest but adequate incomes, while yet others earn enough to afford many of life's luxuries.

- *Incomes vary with the type of job*. Dustmen and charwomen earn less than coalminers and computer operators.
- *Incomes vary with education*. Average earnings of people with university degrees exceed the average earnings of those with only A-levels, which in turn exceed the average earnings of those with only O-levels.
- *Incomes vary with years on the job*. Generally, the longer one stays with one firm, the higher the income one earns.
- *Incomes vary with sex and race*. On average, men earn more than women, and West Indians earn less than Anglo-Saxons and Celts – even when differences in education and experience are allowed for.
- *Incomes vary with the type of market in which labour sells its services*. Workers who sell their labour in markets dominated by unions often earn more than similar persons who sell their labour in more competitive markets.

In what follows, we study some of the major causes of these equilibrium differentials in earnings of various types of labour.

---

[1] The descriptive and institutional background to this chapter is outlined in Chapter 4 of Harbury and Lipsey, *op. cit*.

Differentials Due to Genetics: Non-competing Groups

More highly skilled jobs pay better wages than less highly skilled jobs. Why does a movement from the latter to the former not erode these differentials?

One obvious answer lies in innate human differences. Some people are brighter than others, some people are more athletic, while some people are better endowed with manual skills.

Some of the earliest theories of the labour market dealt with income differentials among *non-competing groups*. These groups were assumed to sell their services in *segmented labour markets* which were separated by insurmountable barriers caused by innate human differences.

Figure 18.1 shows that wage differentials among non-competing groups arise from the positions of both the demand and the supply curves. One non-competing group will earn higher incomes than another only if its supply is

low *relative to the demand for it*. It is not good enough to have a rare skill; that skill must be rare in relation to the demand for it.

It follows that a high-income group can have its income differential eroded if either the demand for its services falls, or the supply of persons in that group increases. On the demand side, economic growth constantly alters the derived demand for many specific groups of labour, constantly creating new differentials and eroding old ones. On the supply side, human differences notwithstanding, substantial mobility between groups does occur – particularly in the long run when older people with specific skills leave the labour force and young people with different skills enter.

The shorter the period of time under consideration, the more useful is the hypothesis of zero labour mobility among markets. In a short time-period, differentials respond to shifts in demand and autonomous shifts in supply. The discussion in the previous paragraph suggests, however,

FIGURE 18.1 Wage Differentials in Segmented Labour Markets

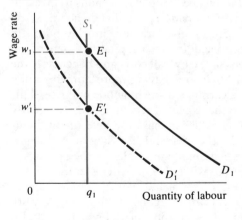 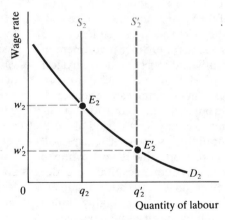

(i) **Occupation One**   (ii) **Occupation Two**

If labour cannot move from one market to another because of inability to acquire the necessary qualifications, wage differentials of any size can persist. Due to assumed genetic differences in abilities, the supply of labour is fixed at q_1 in occupation One, and at q_2 in occupation Two. Demand and supply curves intersect at E_1 and E_2 to produce the high wage of w_1 in occupation One, and the low wage of w_2 in occupation Two.

A fall in demand from D_1 to D'_1 in occupation One takes equilibrium to E'_1, lowering the equilibrium wage to w'_1.

An exogenous rise in supply in occupation Two, to q'_2, takes equilibrium to E'_2 and lowers the wage in occupation Two to w'_2.

that the hypothesis of completely segmented labour markets is not a satisfactory explanation of long-term wage differentials. Over time, supplies of different kinds of labour change endogenously as labour moves among markets in response to changing economic incentives.

Nonetheless, the lesson of the simple theory of non-competing groups is important:

some income differentials arise because innate human characteristics cause the supply of some types of labour to remain low relative to the demand for it, even in the long run.

Differentials Due to Human Capital

The key to mobility among occupations is education. Many skills are learned rather than inherited. These may be thought of as a stock of personal capital acquired by each worker.

A machine is physical capital. It requires an investment of time and money to create it and, once created, it yields valuable services over a long time. In the same way, labour skills require an investment of time and money to acquire and, once acquired, they yield an increased income to their owner over a long time. Since investment in labour skills is similar to investment in physical capital, acquired skills are called **human capital**. Because human capital can be acquired, different skill groups do not constitute non-competing groups over any long period of time. Instead, the supply of some particular skill increases when more people find it worthwhile to acquire the necessary human capital, and decreases when fewer do so. Because acquiring human capital is costly, the more highly skilled the job, the more it must pay if enough people are to be attracted to train for it.

The stock of skills acquired by individual workers is called human capital; investment in this capital is usually costly, and the return is usually in terms of higher labour productivity and hence higher earning power.

The two main ways in which human capital is acquired are through formal education and on-the-job training.

Formal Education

Compulsory education is an attempt to provide some minimum human capital for all citizens. Some people, either through luck in the school they attend, or through their own efforts, profit more from their early education than do others. They acquire more human capital than their less fortunate contemporaries. Subsequent income differentials reflect these differences in human capital acquired in the early stages of education.

Those who decide to stay in school beyond the years of compulsory education are deciding to invest voluntarily in acquiring further human capital. The costs and benefits of this decision are analysed in Figure 18.2. The cost is in terms of the income that could have been earned if the person had entered the labour force immediately, plus any out-of-pocket costs for such things as fees and equipment. The return is the higher income to be earned when a better job is obtained than is available to an early school-leaver. (There is also a consumption return whenever higher education is something that some students actually enjoy more than work.)

What influences people's decisions to invest in the type of human capital that is acquired by formal education? Variation in the numbers deciding to acquire such capital will depend on variations in the overall costs and benefits. If the demand for labour having more human capital rises, the earnings of such labour will rise. This will raise the expected return to those currently deciding whether to make the investment themselves. If the demand for labour with low amounts of human capital falls off, the earnings of such persons will fall. This will lower the costs of staying on in school and acquiring more capital, since the earnings forgone by not going to work are reduced. A rise in unemployment will also lower the costs, because the probability of earning a steady income will be reduced, and this will reduce the expected loss from not entering the labour force early.

As incentives change, so does the total amount of human capital change. But for any *given* state of these incentives, why do some people decide to acquire human capital while others do not?

First, there are differences among individuals. For reasons related to genetics or to early educational experience, some people at the age of

**FIGURE 18.2 The Costs and Benefits of Human Capital
Acquired Through Formal Education**

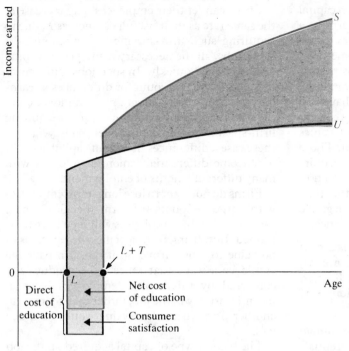

**Acquiring human capital through formal education beyond minimum
school-leaving age implies costs now and benefits later.** Age is plotted on the
horizontal axis and income earned on the vertical axis. Income is zero until age L,
which is the minimum school-leaving age. After that, the black line U shows the income
of a typical person who leaves school at age L and takes the relatively unskilled job
for which his his or her human capital is suitable.

The coloured line, S, shows the more complicated stream of payments and income
receipts of someone who stays on for T years of formal training after age L. At first,
receipts are negative, reflecting the out-of-pocket expenses related to attending school.
Deducting the consumption value placed on the experience of being in education
rather than in work (light-shaded area), yields the net cost associated with being in
school. Adding this to the income that could have been earned by going directly into
the labour force at age L, yields the total cost of the education, which is the medium-
shaded area.

The benefit is shown by the dark-shaded area, representing the difference between
the income earned in the skilled job that is acquired at year $L + T$ (line S) and the
income that would have been earned if the labour force had been entered at age L (line
U). The investment in human capital could not possibly be worth while unless the
dark-shaded benefit area exceeds the medium-shaded cost area. The net benefit to a
particular individual depends on how much he or she discounts the more distant gain
in order to compare it with the more immediate costs.

sixteen correctly decide that they have a low
chance of profiting from further formal education. For them, the return from such education
is lower than for others who have the necessary
aptitudes.

Second, some people have special talents for
types of work that do not require further human
capital. For them, the cost of acquiring more
human capital is higher than it is for others. The
earnings they would forgo by not entering the

labour force are higher than the earnings that would be forgone by the average school-leaver.

Third, different people have different time preferences. The cost of acquiring human capital is forgone income *now*, and the return is a *probability* of higher income *later*. Tastes differ. Some people put a high value on income now, and are not willing to pay the cost of postponing it. Others place a higher value on income to be earned later in life, and are willing to have less now in return for the chance of much more later.

Fourth, different people put different values on the consumption aspects of education. Those who enjoy the experience find the costs of acquiring human capital lower than those who do not. Those who would prefer to be at work rather than at school find the cost increased by the negative value they place on the educational experience.

Market forces adjust the overall costs and benefits of acquiring human capital, while individuals respond according to their varying personal assessments of costs and benefits.

In the long run, decisions to acquire human capital help to erode disequilibrium differentials in incomes. Market signals change the costs and benefits of acquiring human capital in such specific forms as skill in electronics, accountancy, law or medicine. By reacting to these signals, young people help to increase the supplies of high-income workers and reduce the supplies of low-income workers, thus eroding the disequilibrium differentials that exist at any moment in time.

On-the-job Education

Differentials according to age are readily observable in most firms and occupations. To a significant extent, these differentials are a response to human capital acquired on the job. This type of human capital falls into two types.

Firm-specific human capital refers to skills acquired on the job that are specific to that firm. Learning how one firm does such things as recording and retrieving its information, how it makes decisions, and how the personal relations among its employees are to be used to advantage are all firm-specific. As employees acquire this knowledge, they become more valuable to the firm. But the knowledge is not valuable to other firms. Workers who move to similar jobs with other firms will have to learn the new firm-specific characteristics of their jobs.

Firms can let their employees' pay increase at the same rate as their usefulness increases, due to acquiring such firm-specific human capital. In many jobs, all the necessary firm-specific capital can be learned quickly. In such jobs, differences in human capital account for differences in earnings between the relatively new employees and the rest. In other jobs, employees go on acquiring firm-specific human capital over many years. In these cases, differences in human capital account for income differentials among employees with many different lengths of employment.

Firms do not want to lose long-term employees with large amounts of firm-specific human capital since other employees will then have to be trained. But, being firm-specific, the capital is of no value to other firms. So if the firm pays the employee a wage that reflects the productivity conferred by this capital, employees have an incentive to stay in the job, rather than to move to another firm where their value would be much less.

The second type of capital acquired on the job is usually described as *general*. If firm A teaches an employee how to handle inventories on a computer, that skill will be useful to firm B. Similarly, if a firm trains a junior secretary through various ranks up to a senior secretary able to run the life of its general manager, the secretary's skills will be useful to other firms. Some of the secretary's human capital can only be acquired through on-the-job training. Hence, it must be acquired within the firm, but, unlike the firm-specific capital, a secretary who is paid the value of her marginal products at all times has no monetary incentive to stay with the firm that taught her these general skills. The same is true of any non-specific human capital acquired through on-the-job experience by any of the firm's employees.

Firms have no incentive to provide freely what can immediately be transferred to another firm. The solution is to pay each worker less than his or her marginal product in the early years, and more later. The low pay can be seen as the employee's recompense for acquiring marketable human capital. The high pay later in life is a return on that capital. This pay pattern also provides an incentive to employees to stay with the firm that trained them. Other firms would be willing to pay new employees the value of their marginal product, but would be less willing to pay the premium above marginal product that the original firm is paying.

Human capital acquired through on-the-job experience provides a reason why earnings rise with the length of time spent with a firm. Firms tend to pay employees the value of their current marginal products for firm-specific capital, but less than their marginal products early in life, and more later in life, for general human capital.

The above analysis shows the subtlety of market solutions to the issues posed by the human capital acquired through on-the-job experience. What looks arbitrary, or unfair, to the casual observer is often a rational response that has evolved to handle some aspect of the market – such as the fact that on-the-job training creates capital that is sometimes firm-specific and sometimes general.

To illustrate the significance of this lesson, consider two jobs that employ persons with equal initial requirements. One provides on-the-job training that is mainly firm-specific, and the wage follows the time-path of the employee's evolving marginal product fairly closely. The second job provides general training, and the wage paid is less than marginal product for younger employees and greater for older ones. Now assume government policy-makers get worried about the discrimination among workers in different jobs and that they introduce legislation requiring equal pay for 'work of equal value'. Both types of employees must now be paid the value of their marginal products. Firms then become reluctant to invest in helping their employees acquire general human capital because it is now illegal to use a time-pattern of wages that allows the firm to cover the cost of providing this human capital. However fair it may appear to some, this government policy, designed to enhance equity, may not be in the interests of all the workers affected by it.

Differentials Due to Sex and Race

Crude statistics show that incomes vary by race and sex. More detailed studies suggest that much of these differences can be explained by such factors as amount of human capital acquired through both formal education and on-the-job experience. A core of difference seems to remain, however, a difference that is consistent with discrimination based on race and sex.

Some forms of discrimination make it difficult, or impossible, for certain groups to take certain jobs, even if they are equipped by skill and education for these jobs. Until very recently, non-whites and women found many occupations closed to them. Even today when overt discrimination in hiring is illegal, many feel that more subtle forms of discrimination are applied.

To the extent that such discrimination occurs, it reduces the supply of labour in the exclusive jobs – by keeping out the groups who are discriminated against. It also increases the supply in non-exclusive jobs which are the only ones open to the groups subject to discrimination. This raises the wages in the exclusive jobs and lowers them in the non-exclusive jobs. Since discrimination prevents movement from the lower- to the higher-wage jobs, the resulting wage differences are equilibrium, not disequilibrium, differentials.

Differentials Due to Market Conditions

Evidence suggests that wages are higher in many markets dominated by unions than in more competitive markets. In this section, we see how differences among markets in the degree of competition can contribute to income differentials. We then go on to study unions in a little more detail.

The Determination of Wages Without Unions

We first look at the determination of wages in an individual labour market when labour is supplied competitively. Each individual worker must take the existing wage rate as given, and decide how much labour services to supply at that wage. We have seen that each worker has a supply curve showing how much effort he or she will supply at each wage (see pp.294–295). The sum of these curves yields a market supply curve showing the total supply of effort to this market as a function

FIGURE 18.3 Wages in a Competitive Market

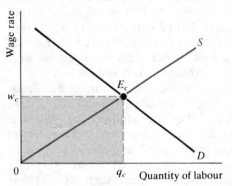

In a competitive labour market, no individual
worker or employer has the power to influence
the wage rate, which is determined by market
forces. The demand curve, D, and the supply curve,
S, intersect at E_c to produce a wage of w_c and
employment of q_c. The income earned by labour is
shown by the shaded area.

of the real wage rate. The determination of wages
under competitive supply now falls into two cases
depending on whether or not labour is demanded
under competitive conditions.

Case 1. Labour is supplied and demanded
competitively: We first assume that there are
so many purchasers of labour services that no one
of them can influence the market wage rate.
Instead, each merely decides how much labour to
hire at that rate. Since both demanders and
suppliers are price-takers and quantity-
adjusters, this labour market is perfectly
competitive. The wage rate and volume of employment is then determined by demand and
supply as shown in Figure 18.3.

Case 2. Labour is supplied competitively
but demanded monopsonistically: We now
consider a labour market containing so few firms
that each one realizes it can influence the wage
rate by varying the amount of labour that it
employs. The demanders are *not* price-takers in
this labour market. For simplicity, we deal with a
case in which the few purchasers form an employers' association and act as a single decision-
taking unit in the labour market.

When there is a single purchaser in any market,
that purchaser is called a **monopsonist**. A
monopsonist in some labour market can offer any

wage rate it chooses, and workers must either
work for that wage or move to other markets (i.e.
change occupation or location). For any given
quantity that is purchased, the labour supply
curve shows the price per unit that must be paid;
to the monopsonist, this is the average cost curve.

Consider an example. If 100 workers are
employed at £2 per hour, then total cost is £200
and average cost per worker is £2. If an extra
worker is employed and this drives the wage rate
up to £2.05, then total cost becomes £207.05
(101 × £2.05); the average cost per labourer is
£2.05, but the total cost has increased by £7.05 as
a result of hiring one more labourer.

> Whenever the labour supply curve is
> upward-sloping, the marginal cost to a
> monopsonist of obtaining an extra
> labourer will exceed the wage paid,
> because the increased wage rate necess-
> ary to attract the labourer must also be
> paid to all those already employed. Thus
> the monopsonist's marginal cost curve
> for labour lies above its average cost
> curve.

Figure 18.4 shows the result. The profit-

FIGURE 18.4 A Single Buyer of Labour Facing Many Sellers

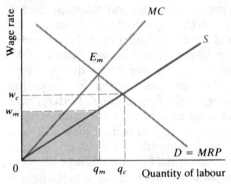

Under monopsony, employment and wages are
less than under competition. The competitive
wage and employment are w_c and q_c. The monopsonist
equates the marginal cost of hiring labour with
labour's marginal revenue product, which occurs at
point E_m. The firm hires q_m workers at a wage of w_m.
(According to the supply curve, w_m is the wage at
which q_m workers will be supplied.) Labour's income
is shown by the shaded area.

maximizing monopsonist will equate the marginal cost of labour with its marginal revenue product. In other words, it will go on hiring labour until the last unit hired increases total cost by as much as it increases total revenue. It follows that, in equilibrium, marginal cost, and not the wage rate, will be equated with the marginal revenue product of labour. Since marginal cost exceeds the wage rate, the wage rate will be less than the marginal revenue product. Also, since the supply curve of labour is upward-sloping, the volume of employment must be less than it would be if the market were perfectly competitive.

Monopsony results in a lower level of employment and a lower wage rate than when labour is purchased competitively.

The reason is that the monopsonistic purchaser is aware that, by trying to purchase more of the factor, it is driving up the price against itself. It will, therefore, stop short of the point that is reached when the factor is purchased by many different firms, none of which can exert an influence on its price.

The Determination of Wages With Unions

Unions affect wages and employment. To see how this can be done, we study a union that sets the wage in some labour market leaving the employers to decide how much to hire at that wage. There are two cases, depending on whether labour was hired competitively or monopsonistically before the union entered the market.

Case 3. Labour is supplied monopolistically but purchased competitively: Suppose a union enters a competitive labour market and raises the wage above its equilibrium level. By so doing it is establishing a minimum wage below which no one will work. This changes the supply curve of labour. The industry can hire as many units of labour as are prepared to work at the union wage, but no one at a lower wage. Thus the industry (and each firm) faces a supply curve that is horizontal at the level of the union wage up to the quantity of labour willing to work at that wage.

This is shown in Figure 18.5. The intersection of this horizontal supply curve and the demand

FIGURE 18.5 A Single Union facing Many Buyers of Labour

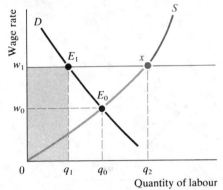

A union that faces many employers can raise wages above the competitive level. Competitive equilibrium is at E_0. When the union sets the wage at w_1, it creates a perfectly elastic supply curve of labour up to the quantity q_2, which is the amount of labour willing to work at the wage w_1. The supply curve follows the coloured line running from w_1 to x and then rises along the remainder of the supply curve, S. Equilibrium is at E_1, with q_1 workers employed, and $q_2 - q_1$ willing to work at the going wage rate but unable to find employment. Labour income is shown by the shaded area.

curve establishes a higher wage rate, and a lower level of employment, than would occur at the competitive equilibrium.

There will be a group of workers who would like to obtain work in the industry or occupation but cannot. This presents a problem for the union if it seeks to represent *all* the employees in the industry or occupation. A conflict has been created between serving the interests of the union's employed and unemployed members. Pressure to cut the wage rate may develop among the unemployed, but the union must resist this pressure if the higher wage is to be maintained.

A union can raise wages above the competitive-market level, but only at the costs of lowering employment and creating an excess supply of labour with its consequent pressure for wage-cutting.

Case 4. Labour is supplied monopolistically and demanded monopsonistically: We now consider the effects of introducing a union into the monopsonistic labour market first illustrated

FIGURE 18.6 A Single Union Facing a Single Buyer of Labour

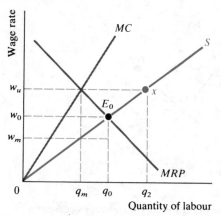

By presenting the monopsonist with a fixed wage, a union can raise both the wage and employment above their monopsonistic levels. The monopsonist facing competitively supplied labour is in the equilibrium analysed in Figure 18.4 with q_m workers employed at a wage of w_m.

If a newly entering union sets its wage at w_0, the supply curve follows the horizontal line from w_0 to E_0, and then rises along the line S. Equilibrium is E_0 with employment at q_0.

If the union seeks a wage higher than w_0 it must accept a lower level of employment than q_0. The union can, for example, set a wage of w_u creating a supply curve that runs from w_u to x, then up the S curve. This yields the same level of employment, q_m, as when the monopsonist dominated the market, but at the much higher wage of w_u. At that wage rate, there are $q_2 - q_m$ people who would like to work but who are unable to find employment.

in Figure 18.4. We shall see that this union can raise wages by a substantial margin and at the same time raise the volume of employment!

The union enters the monopsonistic market and sets a wage below which labour will not work. There will then be no point in the employer's reducing the quantity demanded in the hope of driving down the wage rate, nor will there be any point in holding off hiring for fear of driving the wage up. Here, just as in the case of a wage-setting union in a competitive market, the union presents the employer with a horizontal supply curve (up to the maximum number who will accept work at the union wage). The union raises wages and employment above the monopsony level. This result is demonstrated in Figure 18.6.

Because the union turns the firm into a price-taker in the labour market, it can prevent the exercise of the firm's monopsony power and thus raise both wages and employment to their competitive levels.

The union may be content merely to neutralize the monopsonist's power or may choose to raise wages further. If it does, the employer will no longer wish to hire all the labour offered at that wage. The amount of employment will fall, and unemployment will develop. This is also shown in Figure 18.6. Notice, however, that the union can raise wages substantially above the competitive level before employment falls to a level as low as it was in the pre-union monopsonistic situation. Indeed if the union is content with the monopsonistic level of employment, it can achieve this at a substantially higher wage than ruled when the monopsonist dominated the market.

A union entering a monopsonistic market will have a range over which it can raise wages and employment up to their competitive levels without creating a surplus of labourers eager to work at the going rate. It can raise wages further, but only at the cost of creating an excess supply of labour.

UNIONS

Having concluded our long discussion of the causes of equilibrium wage differentials with a study of the influence of unions, it is appropriate now to raise some further issues related to unions. We begin by discussing the rise of unions.

The Rise of Unions

One reason for the rise of unions was to turn Cases 1 and 2 that we studied above into Cases 3 and 4. Another was to provide the many workers with a collective, and hence effective, voice in dealing with the few employers on such other conditions of work as safety, hours, holidays and non-wage benefits.

Early in the history of unions their organizers perceived that ten or a hundred men acting together had more influence than one acting alone. The union was the organization that would provide a basis for confronting the monopsony power of employers with the collective (i.e. monopoly) power of the workers. But it was easier to see the solution than to achieve it. Employers did not accept organizations of workers passively. Agitators who tried to organize other workers were often dismissed and blacklisted; in many cases they were physically assaulted and occasionally they were murdered. In order to realize the ambition of creating some effective power over the labour market, unions needed to gain control of the supply of labour and to have the financial resources necessary to confront employers.

Since early unions did not have large re-

sources, employers had to be attacked where they were weakest. The unions that succeeded first were those which covered skilled artisans rather than semi-skilled or unskilled workers. Economic theory provides reasons that help to explain their success – reasons coming from both the demand and the supply side of the market.

Demand forces: Highly skilled specialists usually faced quite inelastic demands for their services, and thus could raise wages without facing major losses of employment. Inelastic demands are explained by two of the principles outlined in Chapter 17. First, these specialists were difficult to dispense with since their services had no real substitutes. (See rule 3 on page 292.) Second, labour in any one skilled occupation usually accounted for a very small proportion of total production costs, since large quantities of unskilled labour were employed in most production processes. (See rule 2 on page 291.)

Supply forces: We have seen that one of the problems of raising wages above their competitive levels is the emergence of a supply of workers who would like to work at the going wage rate, but cannot find employment. These would-be employees are tempted to work for less than the union wage, and thus can undercut the union's ability to maintain a high wage rate.

Fortunately for them, the skilled workers normally had guilds, and other associations, that controlled entry into their profession. Thus they did not have to rely on the strategy of fixing the wage and letting the employer decide quantity. Instead, they could restrict supply by restricting entry into their trade, and then accept the free-market wage rate. This method of raising wages, which is studied in Figure 18.7, had the advantage of avoiding a pool of unemployed workers ready to undercut the prevailing wage. Such a method was not, however, available to the semi-skilled and unskilled workers.

This is a method that has been used at many times and in many places. The key requirement is that the supply of persons offering themselves for employment can be controlled. This can be done by unions that can restrict membership and have closed-shop agreements preventing non-members from being employed. It can also be done by professional associations that license those allowed to practise the profession. Entry

FIGURE 18.7 Raising Wages by Restricting Supply

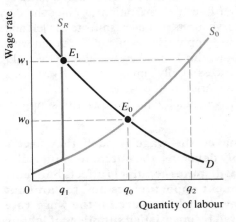

If wages are raised by restricting supply, any given target wage can be maintained without creating a pool of workers who are available to work at the going wage rate but are unable to find employment. With free entry into the occupation, the supply curve S_0 and the demand curve D intersect at E_0 to produce an equilibrium wage of w_0 with employment of q_0. If entry is restricted to the quantity q_1, the supply curve follows the curve S_0 up to that quantity and then becomes vertical (the dark supply curve in the Figure labelled S_R). The competitive market now reaches equilibrium at E_1, determining the wage rate at w_1. There is no excess supply.

If instead the wage had been fixed at w_1 without controlling entry, the supply of persons willing to work at that wage, but unable to find employment, would have been $q_2 - q_1$.

can then be reduced by raising standards for entry. This makes it difficult to decide whether the public is being protected by ensuring that practitioners are of a reasonable standard, or being exploited, by restricting entry through the imposition of unnecessarily high standards.

Unions Today

Compared with their early struggles, modern unions are successful over the whole industrialized world. They have won the right to bargain with employers over wages and working conditions, and to use their ultimate weapon, the *strike*, which is the concerted refusal of the members of a union to work. *Picket lines* are made up of striking workers who parade before the entrance to their plant or firm. Members of other unions will often not 'cross' a picket line. This means, for example, that if bricklayers strike against a construction firm, carpenters may not work on the project even though they themselves have no grievance against the firm, and lorry drivers may not deliver supplies to a picketed site. Pickets therefore represent an enormous increase in the negotiating power of a small union.

Modern unions are organized throughout the world along two main principles. In **trade** (or **craft**) **unions**, workers with a common set of skills are joined in a common association, no matter where, or for whom, they work. In **industrial unions**, all workers in a given plant, or a given industry, are collected into a single union, whatever their skills.

Industrial unions are common in the United States. Because of them, many firms including the great American automobile companies deal with one union. So also do the steel companies. A single agreement over wages, working conditions or union practices is sufficient to change the situation throughout the entire industry.

A single union covering an entire industry is less common in the UK (and in many other countries) because the main basis of organization is the trade union. As a result, a typical employer has to deal with many unions – twenty or more within a single firm is not uncommon in the UK. Under these circumstances agreement between labour and management can be hard to reach.

Furthermore, when many unions cover one operation, *demarcation disputes* often break out. The issue is which, of several competing unions, is to be responsible for a particular job. Of course, such demarcation disputes may merely reflect power struggles between the managements of various unions. They do, however, have at least one substantial economic cause. In situations in which unions are holding the wage above its competitive level, we have seen that there will be an excess supply of labour at the going wage rate. Since more people would like to work in the occupation than can do so, both the union leaders, and the rank and file, will be acutely aware of the trade-off between wages and unemployment. They will also be aware of the possibility that some workers who are currently employed may find themselves without work. (This does not mean, of course, that they must become permanently unemployed, but only that they must move to less remunerative occupations.) If the union loses a demarcation dispute, the demand curve for its members shifts to the left and the excess supply rises, while, if the union wins the dispute, the demand curve shifts to the right and the excess supply diminishes. Such problems could not arise if the wage were set so that quantity demanded equalled quantity supplied, but:

whenever the wage is such that excess supply develops, the outcome of jurisdictional disputes genuinely affects both employment opportunities and the amount of downward pressure on the wage rate exerted by unsatisfied suppliers of labour in a particular occupation.

Institutions

Unions do many things designed to influence the wages and conditions of work of their members. What they are able to accomplish depends partly on the institutional setting within which they operate.

Modern unions bargain under two basic types of arrangements: the open shop and the closed shop. In an **open shop** a union represents its members, but does not have exclusive negotiating rights for all the workers of one kind. Membership in the union is not a condition of getting or keeping a job. Unions usually oppose such an arrangement, and it is easy to see why.

Consider an open-shop negotiating situation. If, on the one hand, employers accede to union demands, the non-members achieve the benefits of the union without paying dues or sharing the risks. If, on the other hand, employers choose to fight the union, they can run their plants with the non-union members, thus weakening the power of the union.

Now consider what will happen if the union does succeed in obtaining a wage above the competitive level in an open-shop industry. We have already seen that when wages exceed the competitive level, there is an excess supply of labour *willing to work at less than the union wage*. With an open shop, there is nothing to prevent these workers from accepting work below the union wage, undermining the union's power to maintain high wages. If, however, all workers must join the union, then the union can prevent its members from accepting lower wages, and can thus maintain high wages in spite of the existence of excess supply.

The desire to avoid the open shop leads to other union arrangements. In a **closed shop**, only union members can be employed. (Closed shops may be either 'pre-entry', where the worker must be a member of the union before being employed, or 'post-entry', where the worker must join the union on becoming employed.)

FIGURE 18.8 Collective Bargaining Between One Union and One Employer

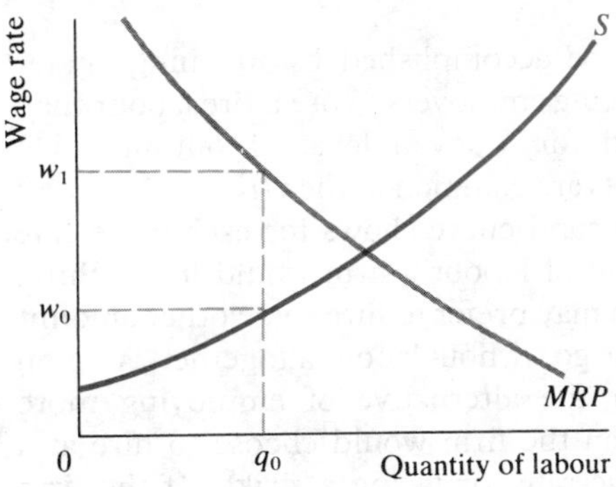

There is often more than one mutually acceptable outcome to the bargaining process. The supply curve of persons who would like to work in the job in question is given by S, but the union is assumed to have restricted entry to q_0. The single employer (one firm or an employers' association) has a marginal revenue product curve for this labour of MRP. The supply curve indicates that q_0 workers would be willing to work for w_0. The MRP curve indicates that the employer would be willing to employ q_0 workers at any wage up to w_1. Both sides would prefer any wage between w_0 and w_1 rather than have no agreement at all.

Objectives of Unions

Wages

One important difference between actual union wage bargaining and the theoretical analysis which we studied earlier in this chapter is that, in collective bargaining, both sides must agree to the wage, while, in our analysis, we assumed that the union set a wage and the employer decided how much labour to employ at that wage. In collective bargaining there is usually a substantial range for compromise. An example is shown in Figure 18.8.

Economic theory can usually set limits to the outcome, but where it settles within those limits may depend on a host of considerations. Just as in oligopolistic competition between firms, the outcome may be significantly influenced by such political and psychological factors as skill in bargaining, ability to bluff, and one side's assessment of the other side's reactions to its own moves. For example, the employers will ask, 'How much can we resist without provoking the unions into calling a costly strike?' and the union will ask, 'Will the employers force us to strike only for a token period so they can tell their shareholders they *tried* to resist, or do they think this is a really serious matter so that they intend to hold out to the bitter end against any strike that we might call?' It is because monopoly *versus* monopsony allows more than one acceptable economic solution, that these non-economic factors become so important.

Wages Versus Employment

We have already seen that in many situations the union faces a trade-off between wages and employment: an increase in wages can be obtained only at the cost of lowered employment.

In some cases it is possible to avoid the

conflict between wages and unemployment by bargaining with the employer about *both* wages and employment.

This can be accomplished by manning agreements forcing employers to use more labour than they need for a given level of output; such agreements are common in the UK.

The demand curve shows for each wage rate the amount of labour a firm would like to hire. But a firm may prefer to hire some other amount rather than go without labour altogether. A union may offer the alternative of employing more labour than the firm would choose to hire at a given wage rate, or facing a strike. If the firm accepts the former alternative, it will move to a point off its demand curve. The union's ability to raise the wage rate, and the employment of its members, will depend partly on the size of the profits in the industry (i.e. on the extent to which the industry departs from the perfectly competitive equilibrium), and partly on the current state of the firm's market. The current market conditions will determine the relation between the losses resulting from hiring more than the desired quantity of labour at the agreed wage rate, and the expected losses resulting from a strike. Under boom conditions, when profits are high, the union may succeed in holding firms off their demand curves for a long time. Under less buoyant conditions, when there may be no pure profits, firms may exit from the industry because their total costs now exceed their total revenues. Furthermore, employers are given a strong incentive to develop new technology that will eliminate the unneeded workers by replacing their jobs with machines. The workers will fight the introduction of the new technology but they cannot resist it indefinitely. When it is introduced, the demand curve shifts left and employment may be less than it would have been if employers had not been pushed off their demand curves in the first place. This is a reasonable description of the battle between newspaper unions and newspaper owners in which unions forced the owners off their demand curves for years while they successfully held off the introduction of new technology. Finally, when the new technology was introduced many of the union members lost their jobs. (The full story is of course more complex but the economic analysis needed to understand it is what has been outlined above.)

Wages Versus Job Security

Unions vary greatly in the extent to which they adopt a defensive or an offensive attitude to the labour market. Until recently the leaderships of unions, management and government were dominated by people who entered the labour force during the Great Depression of the 1930s. In those days of mass unemployment, the installation of a new machine in a factory condemned the worker it replaced to a long future on the dole. As a result, labour-saving machines were opposed bitterly, and job-saving restrictive practices were adhered to with tenacity. The defensive attitude which was so understandable in the 1930s survived in the UK into the post-war period, when circumstances were very different. This was a time of full employment. New jobs were available to replace old ones that had been destroyed by technological change. In such a world, the determination to preserve existing jobs at all costs made much less sense than in the 1930s. Let us see why.

Sustained economic growth means change, and change means that old jobs will be destroyed and new jobs created. The defensive attitude to old jobs was stronger in the UK than in both Europe – where the old order had been more disrupted by the Second World War – and the US – where unions were never as strong as in the UK. The net effect was that the process of changing the structure of employment, which must accompany growth, was slowed. Studies of comparable factories in Britain, France and Germany often showed up to twice as many workers used to produce the same output in Britain as on the Continent or in the US. Thus UK growth, and hence the rise in living standards of the average person, were slower than in Europe and North America. Although particular jobs were saved in the UK, there is no evidence that the overall level of unemployment was lower over the decades than in those countries where unions have been less defensive about preserving existing jobs.

Protecting existing jobs may be a successful way to protect the living standards of the average worker in the short

BOX 18.1   UNIONS AND THE FUNCTIONAL DISTRIBUTION OF INCOME

Are unions able to influence the share of total national income going to labour in general? This question does not concern the power of one small union to raise the wages of its members, possibly at the expense of workers in less powerful unions. It concerns, rather, the ability of unions to raise the earnings of labour in general at the expense of the earnings of land and capital. Early classical economists sought to develop theories that would explain the functional distribution of income. Early trade unionists were concerned to increase the share of total national income going to labour in general. Helping one group of labourers at the expense of other groups of labourers would not have had nearly the same general appeal of helping all the workers at the expense of the capitalists and the landowners. It may seem surprising that, in spite of all this early and continued interest, we cannot say very much about this question even now.

A well-developed micro-market theory does exist. It predicts the effect on relative wages of a particular intervention of a union, an employers' organization or the central authorities in any one market. We do not, however, have a workable theory of the functional distribution of national income that allows us to predict the consequences of a particular intervention, such as the growth of trade unions.

To illustrate this problem, let us consider trade-union intervention designed to raise wages above their competitive level in all industries. The predictions for one industry are that the wage rate rises but employment falls. If this intervention occurs simultaneously in *all* industries, however, we cannot apply the same analysis. The prediction for one industry uses demand curves, which are based on assumptions of other things being equal. If unions raise the wage rate for the whole labour force, they will cause incomes to change significantly; this will cause demand curves for consumers' goods to

shift, thus causing outputs to vary; which in turn causes shifts in the derived demand curves for labour. Unless we have a theory of how each of these changes is quantitatively related to the other, we cannot attempt to answer our question.

There is no doubt that unions are powerful organizations, particularly in the UK – although less so now than they were in the 1960s and 1970s – and that they have important effects on the economy. Just how much they succeed in changing the functional distribution in labour's favour, however, remains an unsettled question. For many years the share of total national income accounted for by wage income remained remarkably constant in the UK, and this caused a certain amount of scepticism concerning the claim that unions had significantly altered the functional distribution of income in favour of labour. From the mid-1960s to the early 1980s, however, labour's share rose significantly while the share going to profits fell. This occurred at a time when many observers felt that unions were becoming more powerful, both in terms of membership and in their ability to influence the labour market. This is at least consistent with the view that modern British unions did alter the functional distribution of income in favour of wages at the expense of profits over that period.

In recent years, union power has diminished. This has been due partly to changes in legislation affecting unions, partly to decline in the heavy industries where unions have traditionally been most powerful, partly to technological innovations which have increased the degree to which capital can be substituted for expensive labour, and partly to the rise of service industries which are often not heavily unionized. During this time, the share of national income going to wages stopped rising and fell somewhat, again consistent with the view that unions did have some effect on the functional distribution of income.

---

term, but over the long term it lowers living standards below what they would be if the structure of jobs were allowed to change according to the requirements of a growing, changing economy.

During the 1980s the last of those who had undergone the traumas of the 1930s retired from the labour force. With a fuller appreciation of the importance of flexibility in the economy, some unions became less defensive about old jobs and

more concerned about the creation of new jobs to replace lost old ones.

Unions and the Structure of Relative Wages

So far we have considered the influence of one particular union, operating in a small section of the total labour market, on the wages of its members. Our theory predicts that a powerful union can in such circumstances raise the wages earned by its members, possibly at the expense of lowering the volume of employment. This prediction seems to be supported by substantial empirical evidence that unions do influence the structure of relative wages by raising wages in some industries and occupations where they are particularly strong, without a corresponding rise in wages elsewhere.

Research suggests that British unions have been able to raise wages on average around 10 per cent above what they would have been if the occupation had not been unionized. If one group gets a larger share of total national income some other groups must get less, but the identity of the other group is not always obvious. A substantial amount of the extra earnings of unionized labour appears to be at the expense of lower wages for some groups of unorganized workers, as well as lower incomes for others who are unemployed but would have had a job if wages had not been raised above their competitive levels. The possible influence of unions on the functional distribution of income is discussed in Box 18.1.

SUMMARY

1. Equilibrium wage differentials can arise among jobs because: (i) each requires different degrees of innate physical or mental abilities, (ii) each requires different amounts of human capital acquired through costly formal education or on-the-job training, (ii) some jobs are closed to some who could fill them as a result of sex or race discrimination, and (iv) the factor markets related to different jobs have different competitive structures.
2. In perfectly competitive factor markets, wages are set by demand and supply and there is no unemployment in equilibrium. In monopsonistic markets, wages and employment are less than their competitive levels, but there is no unemployment in equilibrium.
3. If a union enters a perfectly competitive market, it can raise wages above the competitive level at the cost of lowering employment and creating a pool of persons who would like to work at the union wage but cannot. If a union enters a monopsonistic labour market, it can raise wages *and* employment to the competitive level. If it raises wages beyond that point, employment will fall.
4. Unions and professional associations can sometimes restrict the supply of labour and thereby achieve wages above the competitive equilibrium without creating a pool of unemployed.
5. Modern unions are organized either on trade or on industrial lines and they bargain either in open or closed shops. When a union bargains about wages and employment it can drive wages above the competitive level without reducing employment by forcing employers off their demand curves – at least until employers leave the industry or develop new techniques to replace the unneeded workers.

TOPICS FOR REVIEW

- Causes of equilibrium wage differentials
- Human capital
- Formal education and on-the-job training
- Wage differentials due to departure from perfect competition on the demand and the supply sides of labour markets
- The significance of unions

19

The Income of Capital

To many Marxists, capitalists are villains. To many socialists, capitalists are dispensable drones at best. To many liberals, capitalists are an important part of the productive process, as necessary as the providers of land and labour. To many conservatives, capitalists are heroic figures captaining the economy along risky channels that raise living standards.

This chapter examines the determinants of capital's share in the functional distribution of income. Capital theory, however, is one of the most difficult branches of economics and we can barely touch on it in an introductory treatment. Box 19.1 deals with some basic misconceptions.

Roundabout Production

The use of capital renders production processes *roundabout*. Instead of making what is wanted directly, with the aid of only those simple tools that nature provides freely, producers engage in the indirect process of first making capital goods and then using them to make commodities for sale to consumers.

In many cases, production is highly roundabout. For example, a worker may be employed in a factory making machines that are used in mining coal; the coal may be burned by a power plant to make electricity; the electricity may provide power for a factory that makes machine tools; the tools may be used to make a tractor; the tractor may be used by a potato farmer to help in the production of potatoes; and the potatoes may be eaten by consumers. This kind of indirect production is worthwhile, *if* the farmer, using his tractor, can produce more potatoes than could be produced by applying all the factors of production involved in the indirect chain directly to the production of potatoes (using only such tools as were provided by nature). In fact, the capital-using, roundabout method of production usually leads to more output than the direct method. The difference between the flows of output that would result from the two methods is a measure of the underlying *productivity of capital*.

Capital-using production is achieved at a cost, which is the reduction of current consumption while the capital goods are being made.

A decision to increase the amount of capital usually entails a present sacrifice and a future gain.

The present sacrifice occurs because resources are diverted from producing consumption goods to producing capital goods. The future gain occurs because production will be higher with the new capital than without it.

The Rate of Return on Capital

Capital yields a return over all costs of production. To calculate this return, take the receipts from the sale of the output and subtract all variable costs of production to obtain the **gross return on capital**[1]. It is convenient to divide this gross return into four components using concepts defined in Chapter 10 (see p. 172).

(1) *Depreciation* is an allowance for the decrease in the value of a capital good as a result of using it in production.

(2) The *pure return on capital* is the amount that capital could earn in a riskless investment in equilibrium. This is also called the **pure rate of interest**.

(3) The *risk premium* compensates the owners for the actual risks of the enterprise.

---

[1] This simplified example assumes that capital is the only fixed factor of production.

(4) *Pure* or *economic profit* is the residual after all other deductions have been made from the gross return. It may be positive, negative or zero. The gross return on capital is the sum of these four items. The *net return* is the sum of the last three – i.e. the gross return minus depreciation.

In a competitive economy, positive and negative pure profits are a signal that resources should be reallocated, because earnings exceed opportunity costs in some lines of production and fall short of costs elsewhere. Profits are thus a product of disequilibrium. The *equilibrium* net return on capital is composed of items (1), (2) and (3).

To study the return to capital in its simplest form, we consider an economy that is in equilibrium with respect to the allocation of existing factors of production among their possible uses. Thus profits are zero in every productive activity. This does not mean that the owners of capital get nothing; it means only that the gross return to capital does not include an element signalling the need to reallocate resources.

To simplify things further at the outset, we

BOX 19.1 QUESTIONS ABOUT CAPITAL AND INVESTMENT

Is capital itself either a villain or a dispensable drone in the productive process? None but the most extreme members of the back-to-nature school would answer yes. A primitive society in which there are no capital goods – not a spear, a lever, a washing tub nor a stone axe – is almost impossible to imagine.

Is a charge for the use of capital necessary? Early Communist societies thought not. Such charges were officially barred during the early years after the Russian Revolution of 1917. The trouble with doing this, however, is that capital is scarce; all producers would like to have more of it than they now have. If it does not have a price, how is the available supply to be allocated among the virtually limitless demands for it? Of course the state could allocate it. But how? Any state that is interested in maximizing production will want to allocate its scarce capital to its most productive uses. For this reason, virtually all Communist states today assign a price to capital. They allow firms to use more of it only if the capital will earn enough to cover its costs. Furthermore, the planners in these societies worry about setting the right

price of capital. The answer to this question is therefore yes.

Does capital need to be in private hands so that the price of capital becomes an income for its private owners? This time the answer is clearly no. In many socialist countries, capital is owned by the state, and the payments made for its use go to the state rather than to private 'capitalists'. People have differing views on the advantages of private versus public ownership of the 'means of production' (the term often used in socialist and Communist literature to describe capital), but either arrangement is possible.

Capital is indispensable, and its efficient use requires that it be priced. When capital is privately owned, its price becomes the income of its owners; when it is publicly owned, its price goes to the state.

Notice that if nationalized industries raise their capital by selling bonds to the public, much of the return on capital goes to private bond-holders, even though the capital is owned by the state.

deal with a world of perfect certainty: everyone knows what the return to an existing new unit of capital will be in any of its possible uses. Since there is no risk, the gross return to capital does not include a risk premium.

We have now simplified to the point where the net return to capital is all pure return (item (2) on the list), while the gross return is pure return plus depreciation (items (1) and (2)).

Do we now have a case that is too unrealistic to be interesting? The answer is No. All we have done is to focus on the pure return to capital. This is the return that varies from time to time and from place to place under the influences of economic forces. Risk and dynamic differentials are merely additions to that pure return.

WHAT DETERMINES THE PURE RETURN ON CAPITAL?

As a preliminary to answering the question posed in the heading we need to distinguish two different prices of capital.

Two Prices of Capital

If you wish to use the services of a house, you may either buy it for one lump sum, or you may rent it on a periodic basis. Similarly, if a firm wishes to use a machine, it may buy it or rent its use. The house, machine or any other factor of production thus has two prices, a purchase price and a rental price.

The only factor of production that does not have a purchase price is labour. In a slave economy, you could buy a slave outright, or you could rent its services. Current laws, however, only allow rental of labour services, not the purchase of the person who supplies those services. (The purchase of long-term contracts, such as are sometimes used for film and sports stars, comes close, however, to purchasing the factor for a lump sum rather than renting its services.)

Consider a machine that can be purchased for £10,000, or rented for £1,000 per year. These are its purchase and its rental prices. It is useful when talking about capital to express the rental price as a ratio of the purchase price. In this case the rental price is 0.10 times the sale price

(1,000/10,000). This tells us that, if you rent the piece of equipment, you will have to pay 10 per cent of its purchase price as a rental each year.

Now we ask, what determines the price of a piece of capital?

The Present Value of Future Returns

Capital equipment produces a stream of output extending into the future that, as it is sold, yields a stream of returns to the firm. To know what price a firm would be willing to pay for a piece of capital, we must be able to put a value on the stream of gross returns that the capital will yield into the future. (For the present, we assume that the price level is constant; later we consider the effects of inflation.)

The value of a single future payment: For purposes of illustration, we assume that the rate of interest on a perfectly safe loan is 5 per cent. We now ask three separate questions.

(1) *How much money would you have to invest today if you wished to have £100 in one year's time?* Letting X stand for the answer, we have: $X(1.05) = £100$.   Or $X = 100/1.05 = £95.24$. What this tells us is that, if you lend out £95.24 today at 5 per cent interest, you will receive £100 a year from now (£95.24 as repayment of the principal of the loan and £4.76 as interest).

(2) *What is the maximum amount you would be prepared to pay now to acquire the right to £100 in cash in one year's time?* Surely, this is £95.24. If you paid more you would be losing money since you can loan out £95.24 at 5 per cent and receive £100 in a year's time. If you could buy the right to £100 cash for anything less than £95.24 it would be profitable to do so, since you could borrow £95.24 now in return for your promise to repay £100 one year from now.[1]

(3) *What is the most you could borrow today in return for your promise to repay £100 a year from now?* If lenders were perfectly certain you would meet your promise, they would lend you £95.24.

---

[1] Suppose, for example, you were offered the right to £100 a year from now for £90 now. If the market rate of interest is 5 per cent, you could borrow £95.24 now, buy the right to £100 next year for £90 and pocket £5.24 as your profit. Next year you claim the £100, which is just enough to repay the loan of £95.24 plus 5 per cent interest which is £4.76.

No one would lend you any more since the lender has the option of lending his or her money elsewhere at 5 per cent. If you offered to take less (say £90) then everyone would rush to lend you money since lending to you would yield more than the going rate of return on safe loans of 5 per cent.

The three questions just considered can be reduced to one question: 'How much money now is equivalent to £100 payable for certain a year from now when the interest rate on perfectly safe loans is 5 per cent?' The answer is £95.24, and that amount is called the present value of £100 a year from now at a 5 per cent interest rate. In general, **present value (PV)** refers to the value now of payments to be received in the future. When a future sum is turned into its equivalent present value, that sum has been *discounted*.

Because discounting must take place at some particular rate of interest, present value depends on the rate of interest that is used in the calculation. Thus the numerical example given above depended on the 5 per cent interest rate that was chosen to illustrate the calculations. If the interest rate is 7 per cent, the present value of the £100 receivable next year is £100/1.07 = £93.45. In general, the present value of £X one year hence, at an interest rate of i per cent per year,[1] is:

$$PV = \frac{X}{(1 + i)} \ .$$

Now consider what would happen if the payment date is further away than one year. If we lend £X at 5 per cent for one year, we will be paid £(1.05)X. But if we immediately re-lend that whole amount, we would get back at the end of the second year an amount equal to 1.05 *times* the amount lent out, i.e. (£1.05)(1.05)X. Thus £100 payable two years hence has a present value (at 5 per cent) of

$$\frac{£100.00}{(1.05)(1.05)} = £90.70 \ .$$

The amount £90.70 lent out now, with the

interest that is paid at the end of the first year lent out for the second year, yields £100 in two years.[1] In general, the present value of £X after t years at i per cent is

$$PV = \frac{X}{(1 + i)^t} \ .$$

Inspection of the above expression shows that, as either i or t is increased, the denominator increases and hence *PV* decreases. This leads to the following conclusion:

> **The farther away the payment date and the higher the rate of interest, the smaller the present value of a given sum payable in the future.**

The present value of an infinite stream of payments: So much for a single sum payable in the future; now consider the present value of a stream of income that continues indefinitely. At first glance that might seem very high, since the total received grows without reaching any limit as time passes. The previous section suggests, however, that people will not value the far-distant money payments very highly. To find the *PV* of £100 a year, payable for ever, we ask: how much would you have to invest now, at an interest rate of i per cent per year, to obtain £100 each year? This is simply $iX = £100$, where i is the interest rate and X the sum required. This tells us that the present value of the stream of £100 a year for ever is

$$PV = £100/i \ .$$

If the interest rate were 10 per cent, the present value would be £1,000, which merely says that £1,000 invested at 10 per cent would yield £100 per year, forever. Notice that here, as above, *PV* is negatively related to the rate of interest: the higher the interest rate, the less the (present) value of distant payments.

The present value of a finite stream of income: The present value of some finite stream of income can be found and then converted into an equivalent infinite stream. This is of considerable theoretical value, since it allows us *always* to deal with the equivalent infinite stream,

---

[1] In all these calculations the interest rate is expressed as a ratio of interest divided by principal, so that a rate of 100 per cent is written 1, while 10 per cent is written as 0.1, and so on.

[1] Readers familiar with this type of calculation will realize that the argument in the text assumes annual compounding of interest.

even if the problem we are considering concerns a finite and irregular stream. Consider, for example, a machine that yields the following stream of gross returns: £100 now, £275 in one year, £242 in two years, £133.10 in three years, £87.84 in four years and nothing thereafter. The present value of this flow of income, when the market rate of interest is 10 per cent (and hence, $1 + i = 1.1$), is

$$PV = £100 + \frac{£275}{1.1} + \frac{£242}{(1.1)^2} + \frac{£133.10}{(1.1)^3}$$
$$+ \frac{£87.84}{(1.1)^4}$$
$$= £100 + £250 + £200 + £100 + £60$$
$$= £710 .$$

But £710 invested at 10 per cent interest will yield a flow of £71 per annum in perpetuity. Thus the irregular finite flow listed above is equivalent to (i.e. has the same present value as) the smooth flow of £71 for ever. Thus, in any practical problem concerning an irregular flow we can substitute the equivalent regular flow, which can be handled with much greater ease.

A Single Firm's Demand for Capital

We now know how to put a present value onto the flow of receipts conferred by a piece of capital (or any other asset). The next question is when will it pay a firm to buy a piece of capital. To answer the question we calculate what is called the *efficiency of capital.*

> **The efficiency of capital is measured by the rate of discount, *e*, that will just make the present value of the flow of receipts it generates equal to the purchase price of the piece of capital.**

Taking a constant flow for ever, we can show this easily. Find *e* such that

$$P = X/e ,$$

where P is the purchase price of the piece of capital, X is its constant flow of gross returns and e is the unknown value of the efficiency of capital. In this simple case we can solve for *e* as:

$$e = X/P .$$

If we think of a firm having an array of capital equipment and making a marginal decision to install one more piece of capital, we may call the *e* associated with this marginal increment that firm's *marginal efficiency of capital* (*mec*). Thus *e* is the efficiency of *any* unit of capital and *mec* is the efficiency of the *marginal* unit. (We use lower-case *mec* to refer to one firm and upper-case *MEC* to refer to the whole economy.) The value to the firm now of a flow of gross receipts is its present value, while the purchase price is the cost to the firm now of the capital that produces that flow of receipts. The former is the addition to revenue of a unit of capital; the latter value is its addition to cost. Profit-maximizing firms will go on adding units of any factor of production as long as its marginal revenue product exceeds its marginal cost. Thus they will go on adding capital as long as the present value of the flow of receipts from the marginal unit exceeds the purchase price.

The value of *e* is the rate of discount at which these two are just equal. But present value is calculated from the market rate of interest, *i*. Thus when *mec* equals *i*, the present value of the returns to the marginal unit of capital equals its price. Thus the firm's capital would be of equilibrium size: it would not pay the firm to add another unit of capital.

This is an important and subtle point. It may thus be worth going over it again using a slightly different argument. How does the firm decide whether or not to buy a piece of capital? One way is to use the market rate of interest to calculate the present value of the gross return and then compare it with the purchase price. Suppose, for example, that for £8,000 a firm can purchase a machine that yields £1,000 a year net of all non-capital costs *into the indefinite future*. Also suppose that the firm can borrow (and lend) money at an interest rate of 10 per cent. The present value of the stream of income produced by the machine (the capitalized value of the machine) is £1,000/0.10 = £10,000; the present value of £8,000 now is (of course) £8,000. The firm can increase its value if it purchases for £8,000 something that is worth £10,000. Another way to see this is to suppose that the only uses a firm has for its money are to buy the machine or to lend out its £8,000 at 10 per cent interest. Buying the machine is the superior alternative since this yields £1,000 per annum while lending out the

£8,000 purchase price yields only £800 per annum.

In general, a profit-maximizing firm will purchase a capital good if

$$X/i > P$$

where X is the flow of gross returns expressed as an infinite stream of payments. The term X/i is the present value of the stream of gross returns produced by the capital good, i.e. the capitalized value of the asset.

It pays to purchase a capital good whenever the present value of its future stream of gross returns exceeds the purchase price of the good.

This same relationship can be looked at in another way, by rearranging the terms in the algebraic inequality above:

$$X/P > i \ .$$

But X/P is the marginal efficiency of capital. Thus we have the rule:

it pays to purchase a further unit of capital whenever its marginal efficiency exceeds the rate of interest.

Looked at in this way, *mec* is a measure of the return on a marginal unit of capital to the firm, while i is a measure of the opportunity cost of capital (always assuming that the firm can borrow and lend at the going rate of interest).

We now assume that capital is subject to the law of diminishing marginal returns within the firm. Every further investment in capital equipment that the firm makes yields a lower return than previous investments. The rule outlined above now implies the following equilibrium condition:

a profit-maximizing firm will be in equilibrium with respect to the size of its capital stock when its marginal efficiency of capital is equal to the interest rate (*mec* = *i*).

The Economy's Demand for Capital

It is convenient to think of society as having a quantity of capital that can be measured in physical units and is called the *capital stock*. As with any other factor of production, there is an average and a marginal product of capital.

The marginal product of capital is the flow of future output contributed by the last unit of capital that is added to a fixed quantity of other factors. Marginal product is a physical measure, the amount of output per unit of capital. To obtain a money measure, we value that output at its expected market value. To convert this stream of expected future values to a present value we use the concept of the **marginal efficiency of capital (MEC)**.[1] This is the rate at which the value of the stream of output of a marginal £1's worth of capital must be discounted to make it equal to £1. A schedule that relates the efficiency of each additional £1's worth of capital to the size of the capital stock is called the **marginal efficiency of capital schedule**.

The *MEC* schedule is constructed on the assumptions that the society's population is fixed, and that *technology is unchanging*. These assumptions are made in order to focus on changes in the quantity of capital, other things remaining equal. As more and more capital is accumulated, with unchanging technical knowledge and population, the ratio of capital to labour increases. This is called **capital deepening**. To see why it occurs, consider the difference between a single firm and the whole economy.

When a single firm wants to expand output, it can buy another piece of land, build a factory identical to the one it now has, and hire new labour to operate the new plant. In this way, the firm can replicate what it already has. Since each new factory is a mere replication of the existing factories, output per worker, and per unit of capital, can remain unchanged as total output rises. Increasing the quantity of capital without changing the proportions in which the factors are used is called **capital widening**.

For the economy as a whole, capital widening is possible only as long as there are unemployed quantities of labour and other factors of produc-

---

[1] Like the other *marginals* that we have encountered, the *MEC* is a calculus concept. It is the derivative of the total product curve relating capital to output, *ceteris paribus*, with respect to the quantity of capital. For a non-calculus treatment, we use the ratio of two numbers. In this case, it is the change in the output of capital divided by the (small) change in the capital stock that brought it about.

tion. Additional workers, for example, must be drawn from somewhere. In a fully employed economy, what one small firm can do, the whole economy cannot do. If the size of the capital stock is increased while the total employed labour force remains constant, the amount of capital per employed worker must increase. In other words, capital deepening, rather than capital widening, must occur.

What is the effect of capital deepening on the marginal efficiency of capital? Because capital is subject to diminishing returns, as are all other factors of production, the marginal and the average products of capital will fall as capital deepening occurs. Each unit of capital has, as it were, fewer units of labour to work with than previously. If each unit produces less, the rate of discount needed to make the present value of its output stream equal to a given purchase price must be falling. The *MEC* schedule when plotted graphically is thus downward-sloping, as shown in Figure 19.1.

The Determination of the Pure Rate of Interest

Since each firm in the economy is in equilibrium with respect to its capital stock when its *mec* is equated with i, this will also be true of the economy. It follows that:

> the *MEC* schedule is the economy's demand schedule for capital with respect to the rate of interest.

A Fixed Stock of Capital

The existing stock of capital can be changed only very slowly. Thus we may take the stock of capital as fixed over shortish time-periods.

The marginal efficiency of that fixed stock of capital is given by the *MEC* schedule. The pure rate of interest will also be equal to that value in equilibrium. If the rate were below the *MEC*, investment would look profitable to all firms and there would be a rush to borrow funds to invest in new capital equipment. The shortage of investment funds would bid up the rate of interest until it approached the *MEC*. Second, if the rate were above the *MEC*, no firm would wish to borrow money for investment purposes, and the glut of funds will bring the interest rate down.

Over short periods of time the stock of capital and hence the marginal efficiency of capital is given, and the interest rate tends toward the current value of the MEC.

A Growing Stock of Capital

Over time, firms and households save and invest in new capital equipment, causing the capital stock to grow. This is shown by a slow rightward shifting of the vertical line indicating the given capital stock in Figure 19.1. This has the effect of moving the equilibrium point downwards along the *MEC* curve, thus reducing the marginal efficiency of capital and the equilibrium pure interest rate. Thus in an economy with static technology and fixed supplies of land and labour, capital accumulation will lower the marginal efficiency of capital and the rate of interest.

The growth of technical knowledge, however, provides new productive uses for capital. This

---

FIGURE 19.1 Determination of the Interest Rate and the Pure Return on Capital

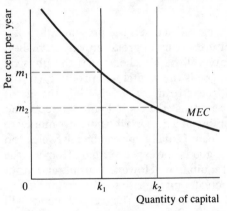

In equilibrium the rate of interest is equal to the marginal efficiency of the existing capital stock. The marginal efficiency of capital curve is labelled *MEC* and the current stock of capital is k_1. The marginal efficiency of this stock of capital is m_1. This value is also the equilibrium interest rate. If the rate is lower, people will want to hold more than the present capital stock, and the rush to borrow will drive the rate up. If the rate is higher, people will not wish to hold the existing stock, and no one will wish to borrow money, so the rate will fall.

When the capital stock grows to k_2, the *MEC*, and the equilibrium interest rate, falls to m_2.

tends to push the *MEC* schedule rightwards and *ceteris paribus* will raise the *MEC* and *i*.

THE PURE AND THE MARKET RATES OF INTEREST

The simple theory outlined above takes the stock of capital as exogenous (constant over a short period and growing slowly over a long period) and determines simultaneously the pure return on capital, called the marginal efficiency of capital, and the pure rate of interest which is the rate on a riskless loan made to purchase capital (see the assumptions on page 322). According to this theory the marginal efficiency of capital must in equilibrium be equal to the pure rate of interest.

To obtain a theory of the actual rate of interest that rules in the market, which is called the **market rate of interest** (usually just 'the' rate of interest), we must allow for a number of complications. These will cause the market rate of interest to diverge from the pure rate.

Risk

So far we have discussed the present value of a *certain* future stream of gross returns. In reality, uncertainty will be attached to (i) the physical stream of goods the capital will produce; (ii) the value of the stream of goods (i.e. the gross monetary returns) the capital will produce; and (iii) the ability of a person who borrows money to repay the loan. Usually one can be fairly clear on the flow of goods one expects to gain from a piece of capital equipment. However outputs and input prices fluctuate, giving rise to uncertainty about the flow of value that the capital good will produce.

These uncertainties vary among firms and among industries. People will only invest their money (e.g. by buying equities) in firms that are in high-risk industries if they expect a high yield from the capital that their money will be used to purchase. People will only lend their money to firms in high-risk industries (e.g. by purchasing their bonds) if they are offered a high rate of interest in return. For these reasons the return on capital, and the rate of interest paid on borrowed money, will differ among firms and industries.

The rate of interest will also differ systemati-

cally with the **term** (i.e. the duration) of a loan, for reasons that are ultimately related to uncertainty. Borrowers are usually willing to pay more for long-term loans than for short-term loans because they are certain of having use of the money for a longer period. Lenders usually require a higher rate of interest the longer the term of the loan, because the risk element is greater. (Will the borrower be able to repay? What will happen to the price level?) Thus, other things being equal, the shorter the term of a loan, the lower the interest rate.

All of these considerations affect the risk premium which is a part of the gross return to capital in addition to its pure return.

Inflationary Expectations

When the purchasing power of money is changing, it is necessary to distinguish between the real rate and the money rate of interest. The **money rate of interest** is measured simply in money paid. If you pay me £8 interest for a £100 loan for one year, the money rate is 8 per cent. The **real rate of interest** concerns the ratio of the *purchasing power* of the money returned to the *purchasing power* of the money borrowed, and it may be different from the money rate.

Consider further my £100 loan to you at 8 per cent. The real rate that I earn depends on what happens to the overall level of prices in the economy. If the price level remains constant over the year, then the real rate that I earn is also 8 per cent. This is because I can buy 8 per cent more real goods and services with the £108 that you repay me than with the £100 I lent you. If, however, the price level were to rise by 8 per cent, the real rate would be nil because the £108 you repay me will buy the same quantity of real goods as the £100 I gave up. If I were unlucky enough to have lent money at 8 per cent in a year in which prices rose by 10 per cent, the real rate would be minus 2 per cent. This example illustrates the general proposition that the real rate of interest is the difference between the money rate of interest and the rate of change of the general price level.

In discussing the relation between the real and the money rates of interest, it is important to distinguish between an inflation that is fully anticipated by everyone (as might be the case when say a steady 5 per cent inflation has been going on for a long time) and an inflation that is unanticipated (as might be the case when the rate of inflation suddenly accelerates). Consider first the case of a fully anticipated inflation. The relation between real and money rates of interest often leads to much misunderstanding during times of anticipated inflation. Say, for example, that the equilibrium value of the real rate of interest is a modest 3 per cent and that the rate of inflation is expected to be 5 per cent. The money rate will be 8 per cent. Now assume that the rate of inflation accelerates to 15 per cent per year and is expected to remain at that figure. The money rate will now rise to 18 per cent. The 18 per cent money rate combined with a 15 per cent inflation rate represents the same real burden on borrowers as did the 8 per cent money rate combined with a 5 per cent rate of inflation. Yet when such changes occur it is common for the public to become concerned at the 'crushing' burden of the rising interest rates on those with mortgages and other debts. But consider what would happen if in response to this worry the government legislated maximum interest rates of say 12 per cent in the face of the 15 per cent inflation. Now the real rate of interest would be negative: in real terms *lenders* would be paying for the privilege of being able to lend their money to the *borrowers*!

The real rate of interest is the money rate minus the rate of change of the general price level. A constant real rate of interest requires that the money rate increase by the same amount as any increase that occurs in the inflation rate.

If an inflation is fully expected, the money rate can be set to give any desired real rate of interest. Problems arise, however, when the inflation rate changes unexpectedly. Consider, for example, a loan that is supposed to carry a 3 per cent real rate of interest. If a 7 per cent inflation rate is expected, the money rate will be set at 10 per cent. But what if the inflationary expectations are wrong? If the inflation rate is only 4 per cent, the real rate of interest will be 6 per cent. If, on the other hand, the inflation rate is 12 per cent, the real rate of interest will be −2 per cent; the lender, after paying the interest on the loan, will give back less purchasing power at the end of the period than was borrowed at the beginning.

Unexpected changes in the rate of in-

flation cause the real rate of interest on contracts already drawn up to vary in unexpected ways. An unexpected fall in the inflation rate is beneficial to lenders; an unexpected rise is beneficial to borrowers.

Uncertainty about the rate of inflation is an added complication, because people are then uncertain about what the real rate of interest will be. If the rate of inflation accelerates unexpectedly, borrowers gain; if it decelerates unexpectedly, lenders gain. The effect on the current money rate of interest depends on how both borrowers and lenders react to uncertainty about the real rate of interest.

Other Influences

Other demands to borrow money: While capital equipment is a major source of the demand for funds, it is not the only source. Households borrow money to buy goods. The central authorities at all levels are major borrowers. Shifts in the demand to borrow money on the part of households or central authorities can cause the market rate of interest to change with no immediate change in the marginal efficiency of capital.

The influence of the central bank: Central banks often intervene in the market for bonds in an attempt to influence the yield of these bonds. The central bank is a large enough potential buyer and seller of bonds to be able to do so. The exact way in which it is accomplished is analysed in Chapter 38.

Bank administration of interest rates: The rate of interest does not fluctuate in response to every minor fluctuation in the demand to borrow money. Financial institutions, for example, consider many factors when they fix the rate of interest that they charge on loans. They are reluctant to change these rates every time changes occur in the demand to borrow money. If there is an excess demand for loanable funds (because the *MEC* is greater than i), rather than raising the rate of interest, lenders often ration the available supply of funds among their customers according to such criteria as the borrower's credit rating, how long he has been known and the amount of business he does.

When credit rationing holds the market rate of interest below the pure return on capital, money will appear 'tight' – difficult to borrow – to the typical businessman. The rapid growth of alternative sources of credit in recent decades has greatly reduced the power of specific lending institutions to administer interest rates by rationing credit. Firms that cannot get credit at home can look to many foreign sources in an increasingly 'globalized' financial system.

Differences in the cost of administering credit: There is a great variation in the costs of different kinds of credit transactions. It is almost as cheap (in actual numbers of pounds) for a bank to lend £1 million to an industrial firm that agrees to pay the money back with interest after one year as it is for the same bank to lend you £4,000 to buy a new car on a loan that you agree to pay back over two years in 24 equal instalments. The difference in the cost *per pound* of each loan is considerable. The bank may very well make less profit per pound on a £4,000 loan at 18 per cent per year than on a £1 million loan at 8 per cent per year. In general, the bigger the loan and the fewer payments, the less the cost per pound of servicing the loan. Why, then, do banks usually insist that you repay the loan in frequent instalments? They worry that, if you do not pay regularly, you will not have the money when the loan comes due.

Many rates of interest: In reality there are many rates of interest, not just a single one. Speaking in terms of *the* rate can, however, be a valid simplification for many purposes because the whole set of rates does *tend* to move upwards or downwards together. For some purposes, however, it is important to take into account the multiplicity of interest rates.

At the time that you receive an interest rate of 6 or 7 per cent on deposits at a building society, you may have to pay 10 or 11 per cent on a loan from the same building society to buy a house. Interest rates on hire-purchase credit of 16 per cent and 20 per cent are common. A small firm pays a higher interest rate than a giant corporation on funds it borrows from banks. Different government bonds pay different rates of interest, depending on the term of the bond. Company bonds tend to pay interest at a higher rate than government bonds, and there is variation among bonds of different companies. These differences

persist because they reflect such things as differences in risk, term and cost of administration among different loans.

THE PRICE OF AN INCOME-PRODUCING ASSET

The analysis of this chapter allows us to understand the determination of the market price of *any* asset that produces a stream of income over time. The asset might be a piece of land, a machine, a football player's contract or a block of flats. It will produce a stream of output and the market conditions of demand and supply will determine the price of this output. This allows us to convert the stream of output into a stream of money. The equilibrium market price of the asset will be equal to the present value of the stream of money associated with it.

What we have already seen for capital is true for any asset. If the market price of an asset is greater than the present value of the income stream it produces, no one will want to buy it, while if the market price is below its present value, everyone will want to buy it.

> **In a competitive market the equilibrium price of any asset will be the present value of the income stream it produces.**

To obtain the present value of any asset that yields a stream of future income, we *discount the future income stream* to get the **capitalized value** of the asset, which is merely the present value of the stream of income that the asset is expected to yield.[1]

An important application of these general considerations concerns the relationship between the rate of interest and the price of bonds.

Perpetuities: A *perpetuity* is a bond that pays

---

[1] A major problem in arriving at the present value of a future stream of money income is deciding on the appropriate interest rate to use in discounting the future stream. If the firm can borrow as much money as it wants at *i* per cent per year, it should discount at *i* per cent per year. If the firm cannot borrow all that it wishes, its internal rate of return on an extra pound invested may be substantially above the market rate of interest. In this case the firm should discount at its own opportunity cost of capital. The general principle is that the rate of discount should reflect the genuine opportunity cost of capital to the firm.

a fixed sum of money each year for ever. It has no redemption date. The price of a perpetuity promising to pay, for example, £100 per year, is £2,000 when the interest rate is 5 per cent and £1,000 when the rate is 10 per cent. *The price of a perpetuity varies inversely with the rate of interest.* (The most famous perpetuity in the UK is an issue called *consols* and this name is sometimes used to refer to all perpetuities.)

Now consider a world in which perpetuities are the only interest-earning asset, and assume that many people have excess money balances that they wish to invest. If everyone tries to buy perpetuities, their price will be bid up. If the price of a perpetuity paying £500 a year rises from say £5,000 to £10,000, this means that the interest rate that lenders are prepared to accept has fallen from 10 per cent to 5 per cent. (If existing bonds sell at £10,000 any new borrower can also sell a newly issued bond for £10,000.)

> **Any action of investors that causes the price of perpetuities to change also causes the rate of interest to change in the opposite direction: a rise in the price of bonds is the same thing as a fall in the rate of interest.**

Redeemable bonds: Most bonds are not perpetuities. Instead they pay a fixed sum of money in interest each year but also have a redemption date on which the principal of the loan will be repaid. A bond with a redemption value of £1,000 payable ten years hence and yielding £100 a year in the interim, is worth the present value of a ten-year stream of £100 per year *plus* the present value of £1,000 payable in ten years.

It is obvious that the same principles apply to redeemable bonds as to perpetuities:

> **(i) the price of bonds and the rate of interest vary inversely with each other;**
> **(ii) any action of investors that bids up the market price of existing bonds means that the rate of interest lenders are prepared to accept has fallen.**

A redeemable bond differs from a perpetuity, however, in that the present value of the former becomes increasingly dominated by the fixed redemption value as the redemption date approaches. Consider, for example, a bond that pays £100 interest one year from now and a further £100 plus the principal of £900 two years from now. At a rate of interest of 5 per cent the price of that bond (its PV) is £1,002.27, while at a rate of 10 per cent it is £917.36.[1] Thus a doubling of the rate of interest only reduces the value of that two-year bond to 91.5 per cent of its former value while it reduces the value of a perpetuity to half its former value. Taking an even more extreme case, if a bond is to be redeemed for £1,000 in a week's time, its present value will be very close to £1,000 and will hardly change if the rate of interest goes from 5 to 10 per cent.

> **The closer to the present the redemption date of a bond, the less its value changes with a change in the rate of interest.**

---

[1] The bond yields two payments: £100 and £1,000 in one and two years' respectively. The present value at 5 per cent is $100/1.05 + 1,000/(1.05)^2 = 1,002.27$, and at 10 per cent is $100/1.10 + 1,000/(1.10)^2 = 917.36$. The ratio of these two PVs is $917.36/1,002.27 = 0.915$.

SUMMARY

1. Production processes that use capital are roundabout. They are productive because more can be produced using the capital goods than could be produced by applying all the resources involved directly to the production of consumers goods.
2. The gross return on capital is composed of depreciation, the pure return on capital, a risk premium and profit.
3. A capital good has a rental value for its services and a purchase value for the good itself.
4. The value of a piece of capital to a user is the discounted present value of the flow of returns that it is expected to yield.

5. The marginal efficiency of capital is the rate of discount that will make the present value of its expected flow of receipts equal to its purchase price. It pays a firm to buy a piece of capital if its purchase price is less than its present value discounted at the current rate of interest, or, equivalently, if its *MEC* exceeds the rate of interest.

6. In equilibrium the pure rate of interest will be equal to the marginal efficiency of capital. The actual rate on various loans will be above the pure rate by the risk premium and the cost of making loans.

7. The value of any asset that produces an expected income stream into the future is the present value of that stream calculated at the going rate of interest. Its price on a competitive market will equal this present value.

TOPICS FOR REVIEW

- The productivity of capital
- The gross and net return on capital
- The rental and purchase price of capital
- The marginal efficiency of capital
- The pure and the market rate of interest
- Present value of an expected stream of future income

20

Criticisms and Tests

The previous chapters developed the neo-Classical theory of distribution in several contexts, repeating what is basically the same analysis in applications to land, labour and capital. This repetition helps to develop a 'feel' for the workings of the price system that is very important to the economist. It has the disadvantage, however, of making the theory appear to be more complex than it actually is. In fact, the whole of distribution theory depends on a very few basic hypotheses about the behaviour of factor owners and firms. Before going on to consider various criticisms and tests of the theory, it will be useful to repeat its underlying structure.

THE THEORY RESTATED

The traditional theory of distribution maintains that factor prices can be explained by supply and demand. The theory of factor supply is based on the assumption that factors will move among occupations, industries and places in search of the highest net advantage, taking both monetary and non-monetary rewards into account, until the net advantages in all possible uses are equalized. Because there are impediments to the mobility of factors, there may be lags in their response to changes in prices. The elasticity of supply will depend on what factor is being discussed and what time-horizon is being considered.

The demand for a factor is a derived demand. It depends for its existence on the demand for the commodity produced by the factor. The elasticity of an industry's demand curve for a factor is higher in the long run than in the short run, since more substitution is possible the longer the time considered. Also, as we saw in Chapter 6, the demand for any product made by the factor will itself be more elastic in the long run than in the short run – thus making the derived demand for the factors that it uses correspondingly more elastic.

In equilibrium, *all* profit-making firms will employ *all* variable factors up to the point at which the marginal unit of each type of factor adds as much to revenue as to costs. All profit-maximizing firms that are price-takers in the factor market will employ factors up to the point at which the price paid for the last unit of each factor equals the increase in revenue resulting from the sale of the additional output produced when that unit is employed. For firms selling goods in competitive markets, the increase in revenue is the marginal physical product *times* the price; for firms facing downward-sloping demand curves for their products, the increase in revenue is marginal physical product *times* marginal revenue.

The relations described in the above paragraphs all hold in equilibrium. They apply to all firms that succeed in maximizing their profits. On the one hand, the firm that is not equating the marginal revenue product of each of its factors with that factor's price is not maximizing its profits. On the other hand, a firm that is maximizing its profits is necessarily equating each factor's

BOX 20.1 SOME FALLACIOUS CRITICISMS OF MARGINAL PRODUCTIVITY THEORY

This Box deals with four common misconceptions, all of which have been drawn from real sources.

(1) *The theory assumes perfect competition in all markets (which is sometimes called pluperfect competition).* This is incorrect. The relationship between the marginal physical product and the marginal revenue product will be altered if the degree of competition alters, but the marginal revenue product will be equated with the price of a factor in perfect competition, imperfect competition, oligopoly and monopoly, provided only that firms are price-takers in factor markets.

(2) *The theory assumes that the amount and the value of the marginal product of a factor are known to the firm.* The theory assumes no such thing! Critics argue that firms will not pay factors the value of their marginal product because firms will usually have no idea what that marginal product is. It has already been pointed out, however, that payment according to marginal revenue product occurs *automatically* whenever firms are maximizing profits. It does not matter *how* firms succeed in doing this – by guess, luck, skill or by calculating marginal quantities. The theory does not purport to describe how firms calculate; it merely predicts how they will react to various situations, on the assumption that they are maximizers. The marginal productivity curve is a tool of analysis used by economists; it is not necessarily a tool for decision-taking by firms.

(3) *The theory is inhuman because it treats labour in the same way as it treats an acre of land or a wagonload of fertilizer.* One must be careful to distinguish one's emotional reaction to a procedure that treats human and non-human factors alike from one's evaluation of it in terms of positive economics. Those who accept this criticism must explain carefully why separate theories of the pricing of human and non-human factors are needed. Marginal productivity theory is only a theory of the *demand* for a factor. It predicts that firms' desired purchases of labour (and all other factors) depend on the price of the factor in question, the technical conditions of production and the demand for the product made by labour.

No evidence has yet been gathered to indicate that it is necessary to have separate theories of the *demand* for human and non-human factors of production. *Supply* conditions will differ between human and non-human factors, but these differences are accommodated within the theory. Indeed, one of the important insights of the theory of net advantage is that non-monetary considerations are more important in allocating labour than other factors. Non-monetary considerations do sometimes matter even with land and capital. For instance, concern over racial policies of the South African government has led some firms to reduce their investments in that country, even where they were highly profitable.

(4) *When all factors are paid according to their marginal products, the resulting distribution of income will be a just distribution.* Some supporters of the theory of marginal productivity believe that the theory describes an *equitable* distribution of income. It is just, they argue, that factors be rewarded according to the values of their contributions to the national product. Critics of the low levels of wages generally prevailing in the nineteenth century, and even in some sectors today, reacted with passion against a theory that claimed to provide moral justification for such wages.

The normative question of what constitutes a just distribution of income cannot be decided on the basis of economic analysis alone. It is, however, worth getting the facts straight. According to marginal productivity theory, each labourer (or each unit of any other factor) does *not* receive the value of what he or she personally contributes to production. Each labourer, instead, receives the value of what the last labourer employed would add to production *if all other factors of production were held constant*. Whatever the justice of the matter, it is not correct to say that each factor receives the value of *its own* contribution to production. Indeed, where many factors co-operate in production, it is generally impossible to divide up the *total production* into amounts contributed by each.

price to its marginal revenue product whether or not it knows it is doing so. The theory thus stands or falls with the theory of profit maximization. It is merely an implication of profit maximization, and the only reason for spelling it out in detail is that this helps us to develop interesting and useful hypotheses about the effects of various changes in the economy on the markets for factors of production.

When one thinks of all the heated arguments over the neo-Classical theory of distribution, and of all the passionate denunciations and defences that it has occasioned, it is surprising to observe how uncontroversial most of its predictions are. For example, the theory predicts that demand for a factor depends on, and varies with, the demand for the products made by the factor. This was undoubtedly a great discovery when it was first put forward; now, however, it is almost a platitude. The theory also predicts that (assuming the supply curve does not shift) changes in the factor price must reflect changes in the demand for the commodities made by the factor. On the supply side, the theory predicts that movement of resources will occur in response to changes in factor prices. It is hard to quarrel with these predictions, which are supported by much evidence. They are important since they frequently apply to practical issues of policy. Box 20.1 deals with some misconceptions about the theory that are commonly found in debate about its relevance and validity. In the text we deal with more serious criticisms.

DO FACTOR MARKETS ALLOCATE RESOURCES?

People sometimes advocate government intervention to determine factor prices such as wages in specific jobs, industries or parts of the country. When critics reply that the intervention will prevent the price mechanism from satisfactorily allocating resources, the advocates reply that the price system is ineffective in doing that job anyway. This debate involves a basic criticism that factor markets do not work as described by the theory. To make that case, one of two allegations must be established: *either* the theory does not explain relative factor earnings, *or* factors do not move in response to relative

earnings. Conversely, if the theory is to stand up to this criticism, *both* of these allegations must be shown to be substantially incorrect. We shall consider them in turn.

Do Market Conditions Determine Factor Earnings?

Factors Other Than Labour

Most non-human factors are sold on competitive markets. The overwhelming preponderance of evidence supports the hypothesis that changes in the earnings of these factors are associated with changes in market conditions. Consider just a few examples.

Raw materials: The prices of copper, tin, rubber and hundreds of other basic materials fluctuate daily in response to changes in the demand and supply of these products. Current shortages of certain key raw materials are almost always signalled by price increases. These prices also show a strong cyclical component. They rise on the upswing of the trade cycle when their (derived) demand rises, and fall on the downswing when their (derived) demand falls.

> **The theory of factor pricing in competitive markets successfully explains raw material prices and the incomes earned by their producers.**

Of course if monopoly elements arise, the theories of factor pricing under monopoly or monopsony needs to be applied. OPEC's escalation of prices in the 1970s, for example, led to a large rise in the prices of the petroleum-based inputs in many production processes and to increases in the profits of the owners of oilfields.

Land values: Values of land in the hearts of growing cities rise in response to increasing demand. Often it is even worthwhile to destroy buildings to convert land to more profitable uses. The New York and London skylines are monuments to the high value of urban land. The increase in the price of land on the periphery of every growing city is another visible example of the workings of the market.

Agricultural land appears at first glance to provide counter-evidence. The classical economists predicted 150 years ago that, as population and the demand for agricultural products grew, the price of the fixed supply of land would rise enormously. The price of agricultural land, however, has *not* skyrocketed throughout the world. Although the demand for agricultural produce did expand in the predicted fashion because of the rise in population, the productivity of agricultural land has increased in quite unexpected ways with the invention of the vast range of machines and techniques that characterize modern agriculture. The prediction was falsified, not because the price of agricultural land is not determined by market forces, but because some of the market forces were incorrectly foreseen.

The experience of the EC's common agricultural policy (CAP) provides another example. This policy has insulated the European market from cheap foreign imports, and has held up food prices. As a result, prices of agricultural land in Europe, and the incomes of landowners, have been much higher than prices and incomes for comparable land in such other food-producing countries as Australia and Canada. When Ireland entered the EC, prices of various types of agricultural land increased by between 100 and 500 per cent, a strong testimony both of the power of the CAP and to the applicability of the theory of derived demand.

Legal right to produce: In many instances the right to produce is restricted by regulations enforced either by governments or by private organizations. Many governments faced with agricultural surpluses due to over-generous price supports restrict output by issuing production quotas. The number of taxis operating in most North American cities is restricted by the local authorities who issue a fixed number of licences to operate. Sometimes the ability to produce a revenue requires admission to a professional society whose membership is controlled by quota. Also some products and production processes are controlled by patent.

In these, and similar cases, the quota, licence or patent are factors of production: without them, production is impossible. Often the right to produce is saleable. The market value of the right then becomes exactly the capitalized present value of the monopoly profits that accrue because of the restriction on output. Suppose, for example, each unit of a good that is produced

under quota restriction earns £1,000 of pure profit, i.e. £1,000 of revenue in excess of what it would have to yield to persuade firms to go on producing it. People who obtain a quota to produce a unit of the product can thus make £1,000 per year more than they could by producing in some other industry where freedom of entry and exit forces profits to zero. The quota will thus sell in the open market for the present value of a flow of £1,000 per year, $1,000/i$, which for example is £10,000 at a 10 per cent rate of interest.[1] As the demand for the product fluctuates and the supply restriction is held constant, the profits, and hence the present value of the quota, will fluctuate.

Various forms of output restrictions are found throughout the world, and the evidence supports the theory that the market determines their values.

> **Where output restrictions create monopoly profits, the market value of the instrument that confers the right to produce a unit of output equals the present value of the flow of monopoly profits earned by a unit of output.**

Labour

When we apply the theory to labour, we encounter two important sets of complications: first, labour markets are a mixture of competitive and non-competitive elements, the proportions of the mixture differing from market to market; second, labour being the human factor of production, non-monetary considerations loom large in its incentive patterns. These complications help to make labour economics one of the most difficult – and interesting – fields of economics.

Nevertheless, we do have a mass of evidence to go on. We do have cases in which a strong union – one able to bargain effectively and to restrict entry of labour into the field – has caused wages to rise well above the competitive level. Unions can and do succeed in raising wages and incomes when they operate in small sections of the whole economy; the high earnings do attract others to enter the occupation or industry; and the privileged position can be maintained only if entry can

---

[1] In practice there will be a further discounting of more distant profits because of the risk that government policy will change.

be effectively restricted. Closed-shop laws are one obvious way of doing this.

Not only can monopoly elements raise incomes above their competitive levels, they can also prevent incomes from falling and reflecting decreases in demand. Of course, if demand disappears more or less overnight (as it did for silent-movie stars and carriage-makers), there is nothing any union can do to maintain incomes. But the story may be different if, as is more usual, demand shrinks slowly over a few decades. In this case, unions *that are powerful enough virtually to prohibit new entry of labour into the industry* can often hold wages up in the face of declining demand. The industry's labour force thus declines, through death and retirement, in spite of the relatively high wage being paid to the employees who remain.

Wages also respond to fluctuations in competitive conditions of demand and supply. Consider some examples. With the advent of the motorcar, many skilled carriage-makers found the demand for their services declining rapidly. Earnings fell, and many craftsmen who were forced to leave the industry found that they had been earning substantial rents for their scarce, but highly specific, skills. Many silent-screen actors whose voices were unsuitable for the talkies suffered disastrous cuts in income and fell into oblivion when the demand for silent films disappeared. Much earlier, the same fate had met those music-hall stars whose talents did not project onto the flat, flickering screen of the early silent films. A similar fate hit many radio personalities who were unable to make the transition to television and had to compete in a greatly reduced market for radio talent. How soon will television entertainers who have enormous incomes due to the high demand for their services, go the same way when a yet newer mass entertainment medium sweeps away the present one? When in a competitive, changing society you hear the bell toll for some once-wealthy and powerful group, always remember that someday it could be tolling for you!

These variations in factor earnings are caused by changes in market conditions, not by changes in our notions of the intrinsic merit of various activities. To illustrate, ask yourself why, if you have the talent, you can make a lot of money writing copy for a London advertising agency, whereas even if you have great talent you are unlikely to make a lot of money writing books of poetry. This is not because any economic dictator or group of philosophers has decided that advertising is more valuable than poetry, but because there is a large demand for advertising and only a tiny demand for poetry. A full citing of all such evidence would cover many pages, and it would point to the following conclusion.

Earnings of labour do respond to changes in market forces. Some factor markets are competitive and some are monopolistic, and the evidence is that the theory of competitive and monopolistic market behaviour helps to explain factor incomes.

Do Factors Move in Response to Changes in Earnings?

In the previous section we saw that earnings do tend to change in response to changes in the conditions of demand and supply. Changes in earnings are signals that attract resources into those lines of production in which more are needed and out of lines in which less are needed. But do changes in factor prices produce the supply responses predicted by the theory?

Land: In the case of land, there is strong evidence that the theory is able to predict the actual course of events quite accurately. Land is transferred from one crop to another in response to changes in the relative profitabilities of the crops. Land on the edge of town is transferred from rural to urban uses as soon as it can earn substantially more as a building site than as a corn field. Although physically immobile, land is constantly transferred among its possible uses as the relative profitabilities of these uses change. Little more needs to be said here; the most casual observation will show the allocative system working with respect to land much as described by the theory.

Capital: The location of, and products produced by, the nation's factories have changed greatly over the last two centuries. Over a period of, say, fifty years the change is dramatic; from one year to the next, it is small. Most plant and machinery is relatively specific. Once installed, it will be used for the purpose for which it was designed as long as the variable costs of production can be covered. But if full, long-run opportunity costs are not covered, the capital will not be replaced as it wears out. Investment will take place in other industries instead.

Long-run movements in the allocation of capital clearly occur in response to market signals.

The mechanism works as long as there is freedom of entry and exit. Exit is difficult to prevent (other than by government legislation and subsidy), but monopolies and oligopolies, government regulations, and nationalized industries do erect barriers to entry. Profits of monopolists or oligopolists where entry is blocked, do not induce flows of new investment, and they therefore serve no apparent long-run allocative function.

Although the profits that arise from market power do not cause capital to move when entry is blocked in the long run, we cannot be so sure in the very long run. These profits may cause other firms to develop competing products and innovate in other ways so as to attack the firms with market power in a process of what Schumpeter called creative destruction (see pages 392–394). If so, then monopoly profits do influence the allocation of capital in the very long run.

Labour: Countless studies of labour mobility show that labour moves in response to monetary incentives. High relative wages do attract and hold labour in such unattractive parts of the world as the North Sea oilfields, the Canadian North, Siberia and the Amazon jungles, while occupations with much leisure and pleasant working conditions pay lower wages *ceteris paribus*. There is a supply as well as a demand element at work here. Unpleasant but unskilled jobs are often poorly paid because anyone can do them, but, even so, dustmen in the frozen Canadian North are paid more than dustmen in Montreal because otherwise they would not stay in the unattractive climate.

At the risk of grossly oversimplifying a complex situation, the following generalizations seem consistent with the evidence.

(1) There exists a fairly mobile compo- **nent of labour in any group. It tends to consist of the younger and more adaptable members of the group.**
(2) This mobile group can be attracted from one area, occupation or industry to another by relatively small changes in economic incentives.
(3) Provided that the pattern of demand for resources does not shift too fast, most of the necessary reallocation can be accomplished by movements of this mobile group. Of course, the same individual need not move over and over again. The group is constantly replaced by new entrants into the labour force.
(4) As we go beyond these very mobile persons, we get into ranges of lower and lower mobility until, at the very bottom, we find those who are completely immobile. The most immobile are the old, those with capital sunk in non-marketable assets, the timid, the weak and those who receive high rents in their present occupation or location. In extreme cases, even the threat of starvation may not be enough to induce movement since some people believe they will starve even if they do move.

Thus shifts in earnings may create substantial inflows of workers into an expanding occupation, industry or area and an outflow of workers from a depressed occupation, industry or area. Over long periods of time, outflows have been observed from depressed areas such as Appalachia and parts of New England in the US, the Maritime Provinces of Canada, Sicily and southern Italy, the Highlands of Scotland, declining areas of north-eastern England and rural parts of central France. Although *some* out-migration occurs readily, it is difficult for large transfers to take place in short periods of time. When demand falls rapidly, pockets of poverty tend to develop. Labour has been leaving each of the geographical areas mentioned above, but poverty has increased too. The reason is that the rate of exit has been slower than the rate of decline of the economic opportunities in the area. Indeed, the exit itself causes further decline, for when a family migrates, all the locally provided goods and services that it once consumed suffer a reduction in demand, leading to a further decline in the demand for labour.

The modern non-market theories of wage determination suggest an additional force. According to these theories, wages reflect the long-term value of labour to the firm but do not fluctuate with every change in labour's short-term value. This leaves employment and unemployment to do much of the short-term equilibrating. Assume, for example, a fairly rapid fall in the demand for labour in area A and a rise in demand in area B. If wages, being responsive to long-term considerations, do not respond quickly, employment will. There will be unemployment in region A and a labour shortage in region B. Labour may then move from A to B not in response to a wage differential but to a differential in the probability of obtaining employment. Indeed, there is some substantial evidence that at some times and places, differences in probability of finding a job motivates the movement of labour at least as much as differences in wage rates.

Factor movements can to a great extent be explained by demand-and-supply theory – using mixtures of competitive and market forces and the assumption that factors do move in response to changes in relative factor prices.

MARGINAL PRODUCTIVITY THEORY AND THE MACRO-DISTRIBUTION OF INCOME

The theory of distribution discussed above concentrates on the pricing of factors in each of the many markets of the economy. But what does the theory say about the determinants of the functional distribution of income among land, labour and capital? What, for example, determines the share of total income going to labour as a class? What influences do unions and government policy have on this share? Questions of distribution at this level of aggregation are often referred to as questions about *macro-distribution* (as opposed to *micro-distribution*, which refers to such questions as what determines the share of total income going to some small group of labour operating in a single labour market).

Marginal Analysis and Macro-distribution

Questions of the macro-distribution of income among the great social classes of the society, labourers, landlords and capitalists, were central issues to classical economics. With the development of marginal analysis in the last half of the nineteenth century, emphasis shifted to the determination of factor prices and quantities in millions of individual markets. The theory that grew out of this development (often called marginal productivity theory after its demand half) offers few general predictions about the macro-distribution of income. It holds that to discover the effect of some change, say a tax or a new trade union, on the macro-distribution between wages, profits and rent, we would need to be able to discover what would happen in each individual market of the economy and then aggregate to find the macro-result. To do this we would need to know the degree of monopoly and monopsony in each market, we would need to be able to predict the effect on oligopolists' prices and outputs of changes in their costs, and we would need to have a theory of the outcome of collective bargaining in situations of monopoly and monopsony. We would also need to know how much factor substitution would occur in response to any resulting change in relative factor prices. Finally, we would need a general equilibrium theory linking all these markets together. In recent years the development of *computable general equilibrium models* has gone a long way towards doing just this! Nonetheless, with our present state of knowledge, marginal productivity theory provides few if any predictions about the effects on macro-distribution of such changes as shifts in total factor supplies, taxes on one factor, and the rise of trade unions.

This conclusion is not necessarily a criticism of the theory. It may well be that relative shares are determined by all the detailed interactions of all the markets in the economy, and that general predictions about the effects of various events on macro-distribution can be obtained only after we have enough knowledge to solve the general equilibrium problem outlined in the previous paragraph. Nor does this conclusion mean that we can never identify forces that will affect the macro-distribution in a predictable way. If some common cause were to act on the demands for labour in most individual markets, the average return to all labour, and hence labour's share in total national income, would be significantly affected in predictable ways.

Many economists argue that we should not expect to get further than this. They hold that the great macro-questions on the scale of *labour versus capital* are largely unanswerable. The ability of the traditional theory to deal with micro-questions is nonetheless a remarkable triumph – although, they admit, it is much less dramatic than would be 'solutions' to the great macro 'puzzles'.

One reason advanced for the view that the great macro-distribution questions are unanswerable is that it makes sense to talk about laws governing macro-distribution only if labour, capital and land are each relatively homogeneous and each subject to a common set of influences not operating on the other two factors, whereas in fact (so goes the view) there is likely to be as much difference between two kinds of labour as between one kind of labour and one kind of machine. On the one hand, the micro-distribution of income can be thought of as subject to understandable influences because it deals with innumerable relatively homogeneous factors. On the other hand, macro-distribution is nothing more than the aggregate of the micro-distributions, and there is no more reason to expect that there should be simple laws governing the macro-distribution among land, labour and capital than to expect that there should be simple laws governing the macro-distribution between blondes and brunettes.[1]

Alternative Theories of Distribution

Many economists have been dissatisfied with the answer that there is no answer to the great questions of macro-distribution. This dissatisfaction has led to alternative theories which deal explicitly with macro-distribution problems.

[1] In case it is not obvious to the reader trying to guard against the author's biases, I am in general agreement with the view expressed in this paragraph (although, like most other economists who believe that their subject can explain some of what we see in society, I should be overjoyed if someone did succeed in getting a workable theory of macro-distribution that stood up to some serious empirical tests).

Macro-marginal Productivity Theories

An attempt that is in the tradition of marginal productivity theory is based on the postulated existence of a *macro-production function* for the whole economy. Assume that total national output can be treated as a simple composite commodity that varies in amount according to the inputs of three homogeneous factors: labour, land and capital. This allows us to write a single production function for the economy as a whole:

$$Y = Y(L, N, K) \; ,$$

where Y stands for output and L, N and K for inputs of land, labour and capital respectively. If the total supply of each factor is fixed at any one time, and if the economy is usually at, or near, full employment of all factors, then the inputs of L, N and K are determined and so, through the production function, is Y.

Each factor of production will have a marginal product – the change in output that would occur if the quantity of the factor were varied slightly, the quantity of the other factors being held constant – and this will determine the price of the factor.[1] The total payment going to the factor

[1] The Cobb-Douglas production function was an early attempt to explain labour's share. In the two-factor version, real national output (Y) is determined by inputs of labour (N) and capital (K), according to the single macro-production function applying to the whole economy:

$$Y = AN^{\alpha}K^{1-\alpha} \; ,$$

where A and α are positive constants and α is also less than unity. The real wage of labour (w) is its real marginal product which those who know calculus will recognise as the partial derivative of Y with respect to N:

$$w = \frac{\partial Y}{\partial N} = \alpha AN^{\alpha-1}K^{1-\alpha} \; .$$

The total wage bill is

$$wN = \frac{\partial Y}{\partial N} \cdot N = \alpha AN^{\alpha}K^{1-\alpha} \; ,$$

and the share of wages in the national product is

$$\frac{wN}{Y} = \frac{\alpha AN^{\alpha}K^{1-\alpha}}{AN^{\alpha}K^{1-\alpha}} = \alpha \; .$$

Thus the Cobb-Douglas national production function leads to the prediction that labour's share of the national product will be a constant, α. This share depends only on the nature of the production function and is independent of the size of the labour force.

measured in real terms will be the quantity of the factor multiplied by its marginal product. The macro-distribution of income is thus determined by the nature of the production function (which determines marginal products) and the total available supplies of the three factors. Although aggregate production functions of this sort are commonly used in theoretical models, there is little evidence to suggest that they are good descriptions of the behaviour of total output or its distribution over long periods of time.

Nonetheless, at a broad level, they do better than any of the other macro-theories of distribution. What we see in the world is in broad conformity with their predictions. In particular, when capital-rich societies are compared to those where capital is scarce, labour's wage tends to be higher in the former and lower in the latter. The reverse is true of capital. The share going to each group depends on price *and* quantity, and different production functions will produce different results for changes in the share of income going to any factor as it becomes more or less plentiful.

The Degree-of-Monopoly and Keynesian Theories

A more radical departure from traditional theory was expounded by Michael Kalecki, who sought to explain labour's share by the economy's overall degree of monopoly. Mention should also be made of the many 'macro-theories' that followed from Keynes's general theory. Theories of this sort make use of the Keynesian aggregates that we shall not study until much later in this book, so we will say no more about them here. We can observe, however, that, in spite of the obvious appeal of being able to relate distribution to only a few measurable variables, such theories have received little significant empirical support.

The Cambridge School

Finally, and perhaps most important in the list of critics of orthodox distribution theory, we should mention a group of radical dissenters centred at Cambridge University. The most famous of these were the late Professors Joan Robinson and Nicholas Kaldor. Professor Robinson wrote numerous influential attacks on orthodox distribution theory. She propounded the view that the theory went off on the wrong track with the late-nineteenth-century development of marginal productivity theory. In her view, we need to go back to the classical theories of Ricardo and Marx and develop them into satisfactory theories of macro-distribution. It is impossible to do justice to Professor Robinson's view, to say nothing of criticizing it in depth, within the confines of this book. Rather than present a capsule summary that would inevitably be a caricature, it is probably fairer to refer interested readers to Professor Robinson's own writings in which she attacks the traditional theory of distribution and propounds her own 'classical' alternative.[1] Two specific criticisms of capital theory that were made by the Cambridge School should, however, be mentioned. These concern the concept of the quantity of capital and the so-called reswitching problem.

The quantity of capital: In the simple development of the theory of capital and interest in Chapter 19, we talked of changes in 'the' quantity of capital and invoked the 'law' of diminishing returns to predict that the marginal efficiency of capital would decline as the stock of capital grew. But society's stock of capital is in fact a very heterogeneous collection of tools, factories, equipment, etc. How can we speak of 'the' stock of capital? How can we reduce this heterogeneous collection of capital goods to a single number so that we can say that the capital stock is increasing or decreasing?

The obvious way is to use a price. If we take the price of capital we can value all these diverse physical things and obtain the total value of the economy's capital stock. But if we then use this quantity of capital in combination with the *MEC* schedule to determine the price of capital, we

---

[1] See, in particular, Joan Robinson and John Eatwell, *An Introduction to Modern Economics* (London: McGraw Hill, 1973). Cambridge critics are often unwilling to give any points at all to the 'marginal productivity theory'. It seems to me, however, that when new theories replace old ones they should save what is valid in the old theories as well as discard what is invalid. Traditional theory is very successful in explaining micro-distribution problems. If it were to be supplanted by new theories, it would be a serious blunder to throw away the baby of successful micro-applications along with the admittedly dirty bathwater of unsuccessful macro-applications. Furthermore, it is not clear to me how Cambridge-style classical distribution theories can even be brought to bear on the sort of micro-distribution problems outlined earlier in this chapter. It seems only fair to add that I think Professor Robinson's 'classical alternative' says very little of a positive nature about the economy. Thus I do not so much think it is wrong as nearly empty of positive content.

may be involved in circular reasoning. We cannot use 'the' quantity of capital in conjunction with 'the' production function *to determine the price of capital* (and hence the share of total income going to the owners of capital) and use the price of capital to determine the quantity of capital.

For over a decade a debate raged over the possibility of calculating a single measure of the quantity of capital that could, without circularity, be placed into a macro-production function to determine the price of capital. The outcome of the debate appears to be that this cannot be done.[1] For the economist who wishes to combine marginal productivity theory with a macro-production function in order to deal with the macro-distribution of income, this is a serious matter. To the economist who accepts only the traditional micro-theory of distribution, it is not so upsetting. Such an economist believes that there are thousands of distinct factors, which it may sometimes be convenient to group into such broad classes as land, labour and capital, but which get separately priced, and which are more or less substitutable for each other. In this view, there is no particular reason to believe that labour as a whole will be subject to one set of influences, land as a whole to another distinct set and capital as a whole to yet a third distinct set. Thus the inability to measure *the* quantity of capital (and

[1] Note that the same problems exist with land and labour. The society's stock of land is a heterogeneous collection of good, bad and indifferent land, some suited for some crops and some for others. The society's stock of labour is a heterogeneous collection of human beings, no two of whom are the same: if identical quantities of other factors are combined first with individual A and then with individual B, very different quantities of output may result. To talk about 'the' quantity of labour and 'the' quantity of land is just as heroic an oversimplification as to talk about 'the' quantity of capital. Furthermore, just as with capital, to obtain 'the' quantities of labour and land by aggregating their values (i.e. multiplying each kind of labour by its price and then aggregating, and similarly for land), and then to use these aggregate quantities to determine the price of land and labour is to engage in circular reasoning.

the quantities of labour and land) is not a serious matter.

Reswitching: A second controversy concerning capital theory revolves around the 'reswitching debate' that arose out of Professor Sraffa's famous book, *Production of Commodities by Means of Commodities*.[1] This debate is too technical to be discussed here, but its burden is the view by the Cambridge School that a smoothly declining MEC schedule cannot necessarily be derived. Once again this appears to be correct. The possibility of other situations has been established by numerical illustrations. However, the empirical relevance of the possibilities raised by the Cambridge School remains to be demonstrated.[2]

Conclusion

For the traditional theorist there are at least two distinct issues: 'Does a demand-and-supply model of factor pricing shed any light on micro-distribution problems?' and 'Does marginal productivity theory adequately explain the demand for factors of production, particularly the demand for capital?' Some traditional theorists would answer Yes to both questions. Others would say that the answer to the second question may be No, particularly in respect to capital, but that the answer to the first question is surely Yes. They would hold that the questions of macro-distribution theory are not really interesting, whereas questions of micro-distribution concerning both functional shares among many factors and the size distribution among households are important and relevant to most government policies that attempt to change the distribution of income.

[1] Cambridge: Cambridge University Press, 1975.
[2] An excellent summary and critique of the Cambridge School from the standpoint of orthodox theory is given by M.Blaug, *The Cambridge Revolution: Success or Failure?*, Hobart Paperback No. 6 (London: Institute of Economic Affairs, 1975).

SUMMARY

1. The neo-Classical theory of distribution is an implication of profit maximization. Each factor is paid the value of its marginal revenue product and units of the factor move among uses to equalize net advantages, taking monetary and non-monetary rewards into account.
2. The satisfactory working of factor markets to allocate resources depends on two conditions: that factor prices reflect market conditions, and that factors move in response to changes in relative factor prices.
3. Both of the above conditions are clearly fulfilled in those competitive markets in which most non-human factors are bought and sold. It is not so obvious that they are fulfilled for labour since many labour services are traded in markets that have monopolistic elements on the demand and/or the supply side, and because non-monetary aspects are an important part of labour's remuneration. The evidence suggests, however, that long-term changes in wage rates do occur in response to changing market conditions, and that the allocation of labour does respond to market signals at least over the long run.
4. Neo-Classical theory sees the functional, macro-distribution of income as the aggregate result of what happens in millions of separate but interlinked factor markets. According to that theory, there is no reason to suspect that the heterogeneous labour, land and capital that we encounter in the real world will each be subject to its own distinct, small set of common forces which is necessary if macro-distribution among three functional classes is to be governed by a small list of identifiable macro causes.
5. Macro-distribution theories, such as those that relate macro-distribution to a macro-production function or to the degree of monopoly, have not had significant success in being used to explain observed phenomena. Such theories require that single magnitudes for the quantity of land, of labour and of capital can be meaningfully measured. The greater the difficulty in doing so, the more fruitful does the neo-Classical micro approach to distribution seem to be.

TOPICS FOR REVIEW

- The effect of market conditions on factor prices
- The effect of factor prices on the allocation of factors among uses
- Neo-Classical, micro- and macro-distribution theories

PART 6

International Trade

21

The Gains from Trade

The British buy Volkswagens, Germans take holidays in Italy, Italians buy spices from Tanzania, Africans import oil from Kuwait, Arabs buy Japanese cameras, and the Japanese depend heavily on American soy-beans as a source of food. *International trade* refers to exchanges of goods and services that take place across international boundaries.

The founders of modern economics were concerned with foreign trade problems. The great eighteenth-century British philosopher and economist David Hume, one of the first to work out the theory of the price system as a control mechanism, developed his concepts mainly in terms of prices in foreign trade. Adam Smith in his *Wealth of Nations* attacked government restriction of trade. David Ricardo in 1817 developed the basic theory of the gains from trade that is studied in this chapter. The repeal of the Corn Laws – tariffs on the importation of grains into the UK – and the transformation of that country during the nineteenth century from a country of high tariffs to one of complete free trade were to a significant extent the result of agitation by economists whose theories of the gains from trade led them to condemn all tariffs.

In this chapter we explore the fundamental question of what is gained by international trade. In Chapter 22 we will deal with the pros and cons of interfering with the free flow of such trade.

SOURCES OF THE GAINS FROM TRADE

An economy that engages in international trade is called an **open economy**. One that does not is called a **closed economy**. A situation in which a country does no foreign trade is called one of **autarky**. The advantages realized as a result of trade are called the **gains from trade**. The source of such gains is most easily visualized by considering the differences between a world with trade and a world without it. Although politicians often regard foreign trade differently from domestic trade, economists from Adam Smith on have argued that the causes and consequences of international trade are simply an extension of the principles governing domestic trade. What is the advantage of trade among individuals, among groups, among regions, or among countries?

Interpersonal, Interregional and International Trade

Consider trade among individuals. Without trade each person would have to be self-sufficient; each would have to produce all the food, clothing, shelter, medical services, entertainment and luxuries that he or she consumed. A world of individual self-sufficiency would be a world with extremely low living standards.

Trade among individuals allows people to specialize in those activities they can do well and to buy from others the goods and services they cannot easily produce. A good doctor who is a bad carpenter can provide medical services not only for his or her own family, but also for an excellent carpenter without the training or the ability to practice medicine. Thus trade and specialization are intimately connected. Without trade everyone must be self-sufficient. With trade everyone can specialize in what he or she does well and satisfy other needs by trading.

The same principles apply to regions. Without interregional trade, each region would be forced to be self-sufficient. With trade, each region can specialize in producing commodities for which it has some natural or acquired advantage. Plains regions can specialize in growing grain, mountain regions in mining and forest products, and regions with abundant power in manufacturing. Cool regions can produce wheat and other crops that thrive in temperate climates, and hot regions can grow such tropical crops as bananas, sugar and coffee. The living standards of the inhabitants of all regions will be higher when each region specializes in products in which it has some natural or acquired advantage and obtains other products by trade than when all regions seek to be self-sufficient.

The same principle also applies to nations. A national boundary seldom delimits an area that is naturally self-sufficient. Nations, like regions or persons, can gain from specialization. More of the goods in which production is specialized are produced than residents wish to consume, while less domestic production of other goods that residents desire is available.

International trade is necessary to achieve the gains that international specialization makes possible.

This discussion suggests one important possible gain from trade.

With trade, each individual, region or nation is able to concentrate on producing goods and services that it produces efficiently while trading to obtain goods and services that it does not produce efficiently.

Specialization and trade go hand in hand because there is no motivation to achieve the gains from specialization without being able to trade the goods produced for goods desired. Economists use the term *gains from trade* to embrace the results of both.

We shall examine two sources of the gains from trade. The first is differences among regions of the world in climate and resource endowment that lead to advantages in producing certain goods and disadvantages in producing others. These gains occur even though each country's costs of production are unchanged by the existence of trade. The second source is the reduction in each country's costs of production that results from the greater production that specialization brings.

The Gains from Specialization with Given Costs

In order to focus on differences in countries' conditions of production, suppose that there are no advantages arising from either economies of large-scale production or cost reductions that are the consequence of learning new skills. In these circumstances, what leads to gains from trade? To examine this question we shall use an example involving only two countries and two products, but the general principles apply as well to the real-world case of many countries and many commodities.

A Special Case: Absolute Advantage

The gains from trade are clear when there is a simple situation involving absolute advantage. **Absolute advantage** concerns the quantities of a single product that can be produced using the same quantity of resources in two different regions. One region is said to have an absolute advantage over another in the production of commodity X when an equal quantity of resources can produce more X in the first region than in the second.

Suppose region A has an absolute advantage over B in one commodity, while region B has an absolute advantage over A in another. This is a case of *reciprocal absolute advantage*: each country has an absolute advantage in some commodity. In such a situation the total production of both regions can be increased (relative to a situation of self-sufficiency) if each specializes in the commodity in which it has the absolute advantage.

Table 21.1 provides a simple example, using

TABLE 21.1 Gains from Specialization with Absolute Advantage

Part A: Amounts of wheat and cloth that can be produced with one unit of resources in the US and the UK

	Wheat (bushels)	Cloth (yards)
US	10	6
UK	5	10

Part B: Changes resulting from the transfer of one unit of US resources into wheat and one unit of UK resources into cloth

	Wheat (bushels)	Cloth (yards)
US	+10	− 6
UK	− 5	+10
Total	+ 5	+ 4

When there is a reciprocal absolute advantage, specialization makes it possible to produce more of both commodities. Part A shows the production of wheat and cloth that can be achieved in each country by using one unit of resources. The US can produce 10 bushels of wheat or 6 yards of cloth; the UK can produce 5 bushels of wheat or 10 yards of cloth. The US has an absolute advantage in producing wheat, the UK in producing cloth. Part B shows the changes in production caused by moving one unit of resources out of cloth and into wheat production in the US and moving one unit of resources in the opposite direction in the UK. There is an increase in world production of 5 bushels of wheat and 4 yards of cloth; worldwide, there are gains from specialization. In this example the more resources are transferred into wheat production in the US and cloth production in the UK, the larger the gains will be.

---

hypothetical data for wheat and cloth production in the US and the UK. In the example, total world production of both wheat and cloth increases when each country produces more of the good in which it has an absolute advantage. As a result there is more wheat *and* more cloth for the same use of resources.

These gains from *specialization* make the gains from *trade* possible. The UK will now be producing more cloth and the US more wheat than when they were self-sufficient. Thus, the US will be producing more wheat and less cloth than US consumers wish to buy, and the UK will be producing more cloth and less wheat than UK consumers wish to buy. If consumers in both countries are to get cloth and wheat in the desired proportions, the UK must export cloth to the US and import wheat from the US.

A First General Statement: Comparative Advantage

When each country has an absolute advantage over the other in a commodity, the gains from trade are obvious. But what if the US can produce both wheat and cloth more efficiently than the UK? In essence this was David Ricardo's question, posed over 170 years ago. His answer underlies the theory of comparative advantage and is still accepted by economists as a valid statement of the potential gains from trade.

To start with, assume that US efficiency increases tenfold above the levels recorded in the previous example, so that a unit of US resources can produce either 100 bushels of wheat or 60 yards of cloth. UK efficiency remains unchanged (see Table 21.2). It might appear that the US, which is now better at producing both wheat and cloth than is the UK, has nothing to gain by trading with such an inefficient foreign country. That it *does* have something to gain, is shown in Table 21.2. Even though the US is 10 times as efficient as in the situation of Table 21.1, it is still possible to increase world production of both wheat and cloth by having the US produce more wheat and less cloth, and the UK produce more cloth and less wheat.

What is the source of this gain? Although the US has an absolute advantage over the UK in the production of both wheat and cloth, the margin of advantage differs in the two commodities. The US can produce twenty times as much wheat as the UK by using the same quantity of resources, but only six times as much cloth. The US is said to have a **comparative advantage** in the production of wheat and a comparative disadvantage in the production of the cloth. (This statement implies another: the UK has a comparative disadvantage in the production of wheat in which it is twenty times less efficient than the US, and a comparative advantage in the production of cloth, in which it is only six times less efficient.)

One of the theory's key propositions is:

The gains from specialization and trade depend on the pattern of comparative, not absolute, advantage.

A comparison of Tables 21.1 and 21.2 refutes the notion that the absolute *levels* of efficiency of two areas determine the gains from specializ-

TABLE 21.2 Gains from Specialization with Comparative Advantage

Part A: Amounts of wheat and cloth that can be produced with one unit of resources in the US and the UK

	Wheat (bushels)	Cloth (yards)
US	100	60
UK	5	10

Part B: Changes resulting from the transfer of one-tenth of one unit of US resources into wheat and one unit of UK resources into cloth

	Wheat (bushels)	Cloth (yards)
US	+10	− 6
UK	− 5	+10
Total	+ 5	+ 4

When there is comparative advantage, specialization makes it possible to produce more of both commodities. The productivity of UK resources is left unchanged from Table 21.1; that of US resources is increased tenfold. The UK no longer has an absolute advantage in producing either commodity. Total production of both commodities can nonetheless be increased by specialization. Moving one-tenth of one unit of US resources out of cloth and into wheat and moving one unit of resources in the opposite direction in the UK causes world production of wheat to rise by 5 bushels and cloth by 4 yards. Reciprocal absolute advantage is not necessary for gains from trade.

TABLE 21.3 Absence of Gains from Specialization When There is No Comparative Advantage

Part A: Amounts of wheat and cloth that can be produced with one unit of resources in the US and the UK

	Wheat (bushels)	Cloth (yards)
US	100	60
UK	10	6

Part B: Changes resulting from the transfer of one unit of US resources into wheat and ten units of UK resources into cloth

	Wheat (bushels)	Cloth (yards)
US	+100	−60
UK	−100	+60
Total	0	0

Where there is no comparative advantage, no reallocation of resources within each country can increase the production of both commodities. In this example the US has the same absolute advantage over the UK in each commodity (tenfold). There is no comparative advantage, and world production cannot be increased by reallocating resources in both countries. Therefore, specialization does not increase total ouput.

ation. The key is that the margin of advantage one area has over the other must differ between commodities. Total world production can then be increased if each area specializes in producing the commodity in which it has a comparative advantage.

Comparative advantage is necessary as well as sufficient for gains from trade. This is illustrated in Table 21.3, showing the US with an absolute advantage in both commodities and neither country with a comparative advantage over the other in the production of either commodity. The US is ten times as efficient as the UK in the production of wheat and in the production of cloth. Now there is no way to increase the production of both wheat and cloth by reallocating resources within the US and within the UK. The lower half of the Table provides one example of a resource shift that illustrates this. Absolute advantage without comparative advantage does not lead to gains from trade.

A Second General Statement: Opportunity Costs

Much of the previous argument has used the concept of a unit of resources. It assumes that units of resources can be equated across countries, so that statements such as 'The US can produce ten times as much wheat with the same quantity of resources as the UK' are meaningful. Measurement of the real resource cost of producing commodities poses many difficulties. If, for example, the UK uses land, labour and capital in proportions different from those used in the US, it may not be clear which country gets more output per unit of resource input. Fortunately, the proposition about the gains from trade can be restated without reference to so fuzzy a concept as units of resources.

To do this, go back to the examples of Tables 21.1 and 21.2. Calculate the *opportunity cost* of wheat and cloth in the two countries. When resources are assumed to be fully employed, the only way to produce more of one commodity is to reallocate resources and produce less of the other commodity. Table 21.1 shows that a unit of resources in the US can produce 10 bushels of wheat *or* 6 yards of cloth. From this it follows that the opportunity cost of producing a unit of wheat is 0.60 units of cloth, while the opportunity cost of producing a unit of cloth is 1.67 units of wheat. These data are summarized in Table 21.4. The Table also shows that in the UK the opportunity cost of a unit of wheat is 2.0 units of cloth

TABLE 21.4 Opportunity Cost of Wheat and Cloth in the US and the UK

	Wheat (bushels)	Cloth (yards)
US	0.60 yards cloth	1.67 bushels wheat
UK	2.00 yards cloth	0.50 bushels wheat

Comparative advantages can be expressed in terms of opportunity costs that differ between countries. These opportunity costs can be obtained from Tables 21.1 or 21.2. The UK opportunity cost of one unit of wheat is obtained by dividing the cloth output of one unit of UK resources by the wheat output. The result shows that 2 yards of cloth must be sacrificed for every extra unit of wheat produced by transferring UK resources out of cloth production and into wheat. The other three cost figures are obtained in a similar manner.

forgone, while the opportunity cost of a unit of cloth is 0.50 units of wheat. Table 21.2 also gives rise to the opportunity costs in Table 21.4.

The sacrifice of cloth involved in producing wheat is much lower in the US than it is in the UK. World wheat production can be increased if the US rather than the UK produces it. Looking at cloth production, we can see that the loss of wheat involved in producing one unit of cloth is lower in the UK than in the US. The UK is the lower (opportunity) cost producer of cloth. World cloth production can be increased if the UK rather than the US produces it. This situation is shown in Table 21.5.

The gains from trade arise from differing opportunity costs in the two countries.

Although Table 21.4 was calculated from Table 21.1 (or Table 21.2), we do not need to be able to compare real resource costs to calculate comparative advantages. The existence of a production-possibility boundary implies opportunity costs, and the existence of different opportunity costs implies comparative advantages and disadvantages.

The conclusions about the gains from trade arising from international differences in opportunity costs may be summarized.

(1) Country A has a comparative advantage over country B in producing a commodity when the opportunity cost (in terms of some other commodity) of production in country A is lower. This implies, however, that it has a comparative disadvantage in the other commodity.

(2) Opportunity costs depend on the relative costs of producing two commodities, not on absolute costs. (Notice that the examples in Tables 21.1 and 21.2 each give rise to the opportunity costs in Table 21.4.)

(3) When opportunity costs are the same in all countries, there is no comparative advantage and there is no possibility of gains from specialization and trade. (You can illustrate this for yourself by calculating the opportunity costs implied by the data in Table 21.3.)

(4) When opportunity costs differ in any two countries, and both countries are produc-

TABLE 21.5 Gains from Specialization with Differing Opportunity Costs

Changes resulting from each country's producing one more unit of a commodity in which it has the lower opportunity cost

	Wheat (bushels)	Cloth (yards)
US	+1.0	−0.6
UK	−0.5	+1.0
Total	+0.5	+0.4

Whenever opportunity costs differ between countries, specialization can increase the production of both commodities. These calculations show that there are gains from specialization given the opportunity costs of Table 21.4. To produce one more bushel of wheat, the US must sacrifice 0.6 yards of cloth. To produce one more yard of cloth, the UK must sacrifice 0.5 bushels of wheat. Making both changes raises world production of both wheat and cloth.

ing both commodities, it is always possible to increase production of both commodities by a suitable reallocation of resources within each country. (This proposition is illustrated in Table 21.5.)

Factor Proportions and Climate as Sources of Comparative Advantage

We have seen that comparative advantages are the source of the gains from trade. But why do comparative advantages exist? Why do different countries have different opportunity costs?

What has become the traditional answer to this question was provided early in this century by two great Swedish economists, Eli Heckscher and Bertil Ohlin and is now incorporated in the so-called Heckscher-Ohlin model. According to their theory, the international cost differences that lie behind comparative advantages, arise because national factor endowments differ. To see how this works, consider an example.

A country that is well endowed with fertile land but has a small population will find that land is cheap while labour is expensive. It will, therefore, produce land-intensive agricultural goods cheaply, and labour-intensive goods, such as machine tools, only at a high cost. The reverse

will be true for a second country that is small in size but possesses abundant, and efficient, labour. As a result, the first country will have a comparative advantage in agricultural production, and the second in goods that use much labour and little land. Another country that is unusually well endowed with energy will have low energy prices. It will thus have a comparative advantage in such energy-intensive goods as chemicals and aluminium.

According to the Heckscher-Ohlin theory, countries have comparative advantages in the production of commodities that are intensive in the use of the factors of production with which they are abundantly endowed.

This is often called the *factor-endowment theory of comparative advantage*.

Modern research suggests that this theory has considerable power to explain comparative advantages, but that it does not provide the whole explanation. One obvious additional influence comes from all those natural factors that can be called *climate* in the broadest sense. If you combine land, labour and capital in the same way in Nicaragua, and in Iceland, you will not get the same output of most agricultural goods. Sunshine, rainfall and average temperature also matter. If you seek to work with wool, or cotton, in dry and damp climates, you will get different results. (You can, of course, artificially create any climate you wish in a factory, but it costs money to create what is freely provided elsewhere.)

Climate, interpreted in the broadest sense, undoubtedly affects comparative advantage.

Gains from Specialization with Variable Costs

So far we have assumed that unit costs are the same whatever the scale of output, and we have seen that there are gains from specialization and trade as long as there are interregional differences in opportunity costs. If costs vary with the level of output, or as experience is acquired via specialization, *additional* sources of gain are possible.

Economies of Scale

Real production costs, measured in terms of

resources used, generally fall as the scale of output increases. The larger the scale of operations, the more efficiently large-scale machinery can be used and the more a detailed division of tasks among workers is possible. Smaller countries such as Canada, Belgium and Israel whose domestic markets are not large enough to exploit economies of scale would find it prohibitively expensive to become self-sufficient by producing a little bit of everything at very high cost.

Trade allows smaller countries to specialize and produce a few commodities at high enough levels of output to reap the available economies of scale.

Bigger countries, such as the United States and the USSR, have markets large enough to allow the production of most items at home at a scale of output great enough to obtain the available economies of scale. For them, the gains from trade arise mainly from specializing in commodities in which they have a comparative advantage. Yet even for such countries, a broadening of their markets permits achieving scale economies in subproduct lines as specialty steels or blue jeans.

The importance of product diversity and specialization in specific subproduct lines has been one of the important lessons learned from patterns of world trade since the Second World War. When the European Common Market (now called the European Community) was set up in the 1950s, economists expected that specialization would occur according to the classical theory of comparative advantage, with one country specializing in cars, another in refrigerators, another in fashion clothes, another in shoes, and so on. This is not the way it worked out. Today one can buy French, English, Italian and German fashion goods, cars, shoes, appliances and a host of other goods in London, Paris, Bonn and Rome. Ships loaded with Swedish furniture bound for London pass ships loaded with English furniture bound for Stockholm, and so on.

What free European trade did was to allow a proliferation of differentiated products with different countries each specializing in different subproduct lines. Consumers have shown by their expenditures that they value this enormous increase in the range of choice among differentiated products. As Asian countries have expanded into European and American markets with textiles, cars and electronic goods, European and American manufacturers have increasingly specialized their production and now export textiles, cars and electronics equipment to Japan even while importing similar but differentiated products from Japan.

Learning by Doing

The discussion so far has assumed that costs vary only with the *level* of output. They may also vary with the time a good has been produced.

Early economists placed great importance on a factor that we now call learning by doing. They believed that as countries gained experience in particular tasks, workers and managers would become more efficient in performing them. As people acquire expertise, costs tend to fall. There is substantial evidence that such learning by doing does occur.

The distinction between this phenomenon and the gains from economies of scale is illustrated in Figure 21.1. It is one more example of the difference between a movement along a curve and a shift of the curve.

Recognition of the opportunities for learning by doing leads to an important implication: policy-makers need not accept *current* comparative advantages as given. Through such means as education and tax incentives, they can seek to develop new comparative advantages.[1] Moreover, countries cannot complacently assume that an existing comparative advantage will persist. Misguided education policies, the wrong tax incentives, or policies that discourage risk-taking, can lead to the rapid erosion of a country's comparative advantage in a particular product. So, too, can developments in other countries.

A changing view of comparative advantage: The classical theory of the gains from trade assumes given cost structures based largely on a country's natural endowments. This leads to a given pattern of international comparative advantage. It leads to the policy advice that a government interested in maximizing its citizens' material standard of living should encourage production to be specialized in those goods where

---

[1] Of course, they can, foolishly, use the same policies to develop industries in which they do not have, and will never achieve, comparative advantages.

FIGURE 21.1 Gains from Specialization with Variable Costs

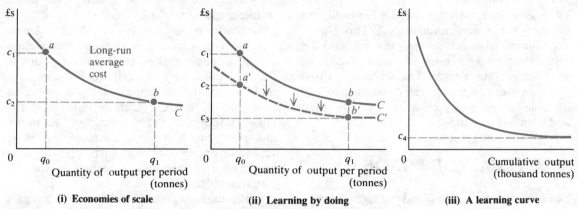

(i) Economies of scale   **(ii) Learning by doing**   **(iii) A learning curve**

Specialization may lead to gains from trade by permitting economies of larger scale output, by leading to downward shifts of cost curves, or both. Consider a country that wishes to consume the quantity q_0. Suppose that it can produce that quantity at an average cost per unit of c_1. Suppose further that the country has a comparative advantage in producing this commodity and can export the quantity $q_1 - q_0$ if it produces q_1. This may lead to cost savings in two ways. (i) The increased level of production of q_1 compared to q_0 permits it to *move along* its cost curve, C, from a to b, thus reducing costs per unit to c_2. This is an economy of scale. (ii) As workers and managements become more experienced, they may discover means of increasing productivity that lead to a downward shift of the cost curve from C to C'. This is learning by doing. The downward *shift*, shown by the arrows, lowers the cost of producing every unit of output. At output q_1 costs per unit fall to c_3. The movement from a to b' incorporates both economies of scale and learning by doing.

Part (iii) shows a learning curve, which is another way of showing the effects of learning by doing. This curve shows the relation between the costs of producing a given output per period and the total output over the whole time during which production has taken place. Growing experience with making the product causes costs to fall as more and more is produced. When all learning possibilities have been exploited, costs reach a minimum level, shown by c_4 in the Figure.

it currently has a comparative advantage. When all countries follow this advice, the theory predicts that each will be specialized in a relatively narrow range of distinct products. The British will produce engineering products, Canadians will be producers of resource-based primary products. Americans will be farmers and factory workers, Central Americans will be banana growers, and so on.

There is today a competing view. In extreme form it says that comparative advantages are certainly there, but they are typically acquired, not nature-given – and they change. This view of comparative advantage is *dynamic* rather than static. New industries are seen to depend more on human capital than on fixed physical capital or natural resources. The skills of a computer

designer, a videogame programmer, a sound mix technician or a rock star are acquired by education and on-the-job training. Natural endowments of energy and raw materials cannot account for the UK's prominence in modern pop music nor for the leadership in computer technology of Silicon Valley in California. When countries such as the UK, and latterly the US, find their former dominance (based on comparative advantage) declining in such smokestack industries as cars and steel, their firms need not sit idly by. Instead they can begin to adapt by developing new areas of comparative advantage.

There are surely elements of truth in both extreme views. It would be unwise to neglect resource endowments, climate, culture, social patterns and institutional arrangements. But it would also be unwise to assume all of them were innate and immutable.

To some extent, these views are reconciled by the theory of human capital discussed in Chapter 18. Comparative advantages that depend on human capital are consistent with traditional Heckscher–Ohlin theory. The difference is that this type of capital is acquired through conscious decisions relating to such matters as education and technical training.

THE TERMS OF TRADE

So far, we have seen that world production can be increased when countries specialize in the production of the commodities in which they have a comparative advantage, and then trade with one another. We now ask: how will these gains from specialization and trade be shared among countries? The division of the gain depends on what is called the **terms of trade**, which relates to the quantity of imported goods that can be obtained per unit of goods exported. They are measured by the ratio of the price of exports to the price of imports.

A rise in the price of imported goods, with the price of exports unchanged, indicates a *fall in the terms of trade*; it will now take more exports to buy the same quantity of imports. Similarly, a rise in the price of exported goods, with the price of imports unchanged, indicates a *rise in terms of trade*; it will now take fewer exports to buy the same quantity of imports. Thus the ratio of these prices measures the amount of imports that can be obtained per unit of goods exported.

In the example of Table 21.4, the UK domestic opportunity cost of 1 unit of wheat is 2 yards of cloth. If UK resources are transferred from cloth to wheat, 2 yards of cloth are given up for every bushel of wheat gained. But, if the UK can obtain its wheat by trade on more favourable terms, there are gains in producing and exporting cloth to pay for wheat imports. Suppose, for example, that international prices are such that 1 bushel of wheat exchanges for (i.e. is equal in value to) 1 yard of cloth. At those terms of trade, the UK can obtain 1 bushel of wheat for every 1 yard of cloth exported. It gets more wheat per unit of cloth exported than it can obtain by moving resources out of cloth into wheat production at home.

These terms of trade thus favour specializing in the production of cloth and trading it for wheat on international markets.

Similarly, in the example of Table 21.4, American consumers gain when they can obtain cloth abroad at any terms of trade more favourable than 1.67 units of wheat sacrificed. If the terms of trade permit the exchange of 1 bushel of wheat for 1 yard of cloth, the terms of trade favour the US obtaining its cloth by exporting wheat rather than producing it at home: a unit of cloth costs 1.67 units of wheat sacrificed when produced at home and only one unit of wheat when obtained through trade.

In this example, both the UK and the US gain from trade. Each can obtain units of the commodity in which it has a comparative disadvantage at a lower opportunity cost through international trade than through domestic production. The way in which the terms of trade affect the gains from trade is illustrated graphically in Box 21.1.

Because actual international trade involves many countries and many commodities, a country's terms of trade are computed as an index number:

$$\text{Terms of trade} = \frac{\text{index of export prices}}{\text{index of import prices}} \times 100 \ .$$

A rise in the index is referred to as a *favourable* change in a country's terms of trade. A favourable change means that more can be imported per unit of goods exported than previously. For example, if the export price index rises from 100 to 120 while the import price index rises from 100 to 110, the terms of trade index rises from 100 to 109. At the new terms of trade, a unit of exports will buy 9 per cent more imports than at the old terms.

A decrease in the index of the terms of trade, called an *unfavourable* change, means that the country can import less in return for any given amount of exports or, equivalently, it must export more to pay for any given amount of imports. For example, the sharp rise in oil prices in the 1970s led to large unfavourable shifts in the terms of trade of oil-importing countries. When oil prices fell sharply in the mid-1980s, the terms of trade of oil-importing countries changed favourably. The converse was true for oil-exporting countries.

BOX 21.1 THE GAINS FROM TRADE ILLUSTRATED GRAPHICALLY

International trade leads to an expansion of the set of goods that can be consumed in the economy in two ways: by allowing the bundle of goods consumed to differ from the bundle produced, and by permitting a profitable change in the pattern of production. Without international trade, the bundle of goods produced is the bundle consumed. With international trade, the consumption and production bundles can be altered independently to reflect the relative values placed on goods by international markets.

The graphical demonstration of the gains from trade proceeds in two stages.

Stage 1: Fixed Production
In each part of the Figure, the black curve is the economy's production possibility boundary. If there is no international trade, the economy must consume the same bundle of goods that it produces. Thus the production possibility boundary is also the consumption possibility boundary. Suppose the economy produces, and consumes, at point *a*, with x_1 of good *X* and y_1 of good *Y*, as in part (i) of the Figure.

Next, suppose that with production point *a*, good *Y* can be exchanged for good *X* internationally. The consumption possibilities are now shown by the line *tt* drawn through point *a*. The slope of *tt* indicates the quantity of *Y* that exchanges for a unit of *X* on the international market.

Although production is fixed at *a*, consumption can now be anywhere on the line *tt*. For example, the consumption point could be at *b*. This could be achieved by exporting $y_1 - y_2$ units of *Y* and importing $x_2 - x_1$ units of *X*. Since point *b* (and all others on line *tt* to the right of *a*) lies outside the

production possibility boundary, there are potential gains from trade. Consumers are no longer limited by *their* country's production possibilities. Let us suppose they prefer point *b* to point *a*. They have achieved a gain from trade by being allowed to exchange some of their production of good *Y* for some quantity of good *X* and thus to consume more of good *X* than is produced at home.

Stage 2: Variable Production
There is a further opportunity for the expansion of the country's consumption possibilities: with trade, the production bundle may be profitably altered in response to international prices. The country may produce the bundle of goods that is most valuable in world markets. That is represented by the bundle *d* in part (ii). The consumption possibility set is shifted to the line *t't'* by changing production from *a* to *d* and thereby increasing the country's degree of specialization in good *Y*. For every point on the original consumption possibility set, *tt*, there are points on the new set, *t't'*, which allow more consumption of both goods, e.g. compare points *b* and *f*. Notice also that, except at the zero-trade point, *d*, the new consumption possibility set lies *everywhere* above the production possibility curve.

The benefits of moving from a no-trade position, such as *a*, to a trading position such as *b* or *f* are the *gains from trade* to the country. When the production of good *Y* is increased and the production of good *X* decreased, the country is able to move to a point such as *f* by producing more of good *Y*, in which the country has a comparative advantage, and trading the additional production for good *X*.

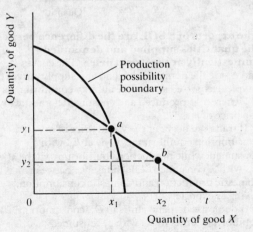

(i) Stage 1: fixed production

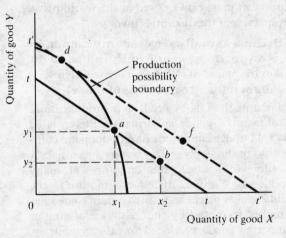

(ii) Stage 2: variable production

TRADE IN A SMALL OPEN ECONOMY

So far, we have discussed the gains from trade between two, more or less equal-sized nations. For many policy issues, however, we need a more realistic model.

The Price-taking Condition

Many countries, including the UK, are too small an actor on the international scene to influence the prices of most of the goods they import or export. The world prices of Swedish Volvos, Japanese tape-recorders or IBM computers will be unaffected if consumers in the UK buy more or less of these products. Similarly the prices of UK cars, aircraft and engineering products are constrained by the existence of similar products produced elsewhere in the world. UK producers could not drive up the prices of these exports significantly by withholding some supplies from foreign markets. The UK thus comes close to being a price-taker in both its import and its export markets. UK goods and services are bought and sold under conditions that come closer to those of perfect competition than to monopoly.

These conditions, which face all small and most middle-sized economies in international markets, are formalized in the model of the **small open economy (SOE).** This is an economy that is a price-taker for both its imports and its exports. It must buy and sell at the world price, irrespective of the quantities involved.

> **Because a small open economy cannot, by its own actions, significantly influence the world price of traded commodities, it cannot influence its terms of trade.**

Treating the UK as a SOE is a simplification. Manufactured goods are usually differentiated and sold under conditions of monopolistic competition or oligopoly. However, as a small actor on the world stage, and only one of many producers of differentiated commodities, the ability to alter prices and still maintain some sales is highly restricted by the existence of similar competing goods produced in other countries. Treating the UK as a SOE, therefore, comes closer to reality than treating it as a large trader

faced with negatively sloped demand curves for its exports and positively sloped supply curves for its imports.

Imports and Exports in a SOE

We can now use demand and supply analysis to show how the quantities of imports and exports are determined in a SOE. We first divide all goods into two types. **Tradeables** are goods and services that enter into international trade. For a small economy, the prices of tradeables are given since they are set on international markets. **Non-tradeables** are goods and services that are produced and sold domestically but do not enter into international trade. Their prices are set on domestic markets by domestic supply and de-

FIGURE 21.2 Exports in a Small Open Economy

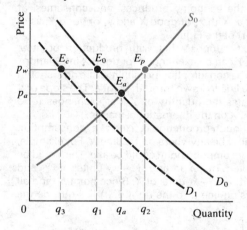

The exports of a SOE are the difference between the quantities supplied and demanded domestically at the world price. The curves D_0 and S_0 are the domestic demand and supply curves for a typical exported good. The autarky equilibrium is at E_a, where q_a is produced and consumed domestically at a price of p_a.

If trade can occur at the world price of p_w, consumption equilibrium will be at E_0, with q_1 consumed; while production equilibrium will be at E_p, with q_2 consumed. The difference between domestic production and domestic consumption, $q_2 - q_1$, is exported.

If domestic demand shifts to D_1, consumption equilibrium shifts to E_c, with q_3 consumed domestically. With unchanged domestic production, exports rise to $q_2 - q_3$.

mand, and they are unaffected by market conditions for the same products in other countries.

Exports: Figure 21.2 shows the domestic demand and supply curves for a typical commodity. For a small open economy, the world price is given and the country can buy or sell all that it wishes at that price. Notice that trade raises the price of the exported good above its autarky level. Notice also that the equilibrium is no longer where quantity demanded domestically equals domestic quantity supplied. Instead, the equilibrium price is the given world price, and the excess of domestic quantity supplied over domestic quantity demanded at that price is exported.

Imports: Figure 21.3 gives the domestic demand and supply curves for a typical imported commodity. If imports are to occur, the world price must be below the autarky price. Notice that trade lowers the price of the imported good below its autarky level. Notice also that the equilibrium is once again not where quantity demanded domestically equals quantity supplied domestically; price is given by the world price and the excess of domestic quantity demanded over domestic quantity supplied at that price is met by imports.

> **For an open economy, equilibrium in particular markets is consistent with domestic demand for that product being different from domestic supply. If at the world price, quantity demanded domestically exceeds quantity supplied domestically, the good will be imported; if quantity supplied domestically exceeds quantity demanded domestically, the good will be exported.**

Effects of changes in domestic supply and demand: Suppose that domestic residents experience a change in tastes. At the given prices, and values of the other variables that influence quantity demanded, they decide to consume less of their exported good and more of their imported good. This decision is shown in Figure 21.2, where the demand for the exported good shifts to the left, and in Figure 21.3, where the demand for imported goods shifts to the right. At the prevailing world prices, these shifts lead to an increase in the quantity of the good that is exported (Figure 21.2), and to an increase in the quantity of the good that is imported (Figure 21.3).

FIGURE 21.3 Imports in a Small Open Economy

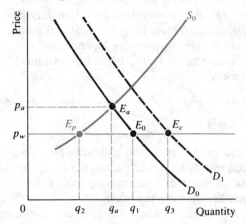

The imports of a small open economy are the difference between the quantities demanded and supplied domestically at the world price.
The curves D_0 and S_0 are the domestic demand and supply curves for a typical imported good. The autarky equilibrium is at E_a, where q_a is produced and consumed domestically at a price of p_a.

If trade can occur at a world price of p_w, consumption equilibrium will be at E_0, with q_1 consumed; while production equilibrium will be at E_p, with q_2 produced. The shortfall of domestic production below domestic consumption, $q_1 - q_2$, is imported.

If domestic demand shifts to D_1, consumption equilibrium shifts to E_c, with q_3 consumed. With unchanged domestic production, imports rise to $q_3 - q_2$.

good that is imported (Figure 21.3).

Since the economy we are studying is assumed to be small relative to the whole world, these demand shifts have no noticeable effects on world prices. The only results are changes in the *quantities* of imports and exports. The assumption that world prices are constant means that, in effect, the country can buy, or sell, any quantities it wants in world markets.

The effects of a change in domestic supply can also be studied. For example, an increase in domestic wages would increase the cost of producing both the imported and the exported good. This would reduce the quantity that would be supplied domestically at each price, i.e. the supply curves shift upwards. The reader can verify that *ceteris paribus* this would lead to an increase in the quantity of imports and a decrease in the quantity of exports. Later on we shall see that these changes are not the end of the story. The rise in imports combined with a fall in exports would lead to exchange-rate adjustments that would restore the previous balance between imports and exports. In the meantime, we have reached a key result:

in a small open economy, other things being equal, shifts in domestic supply and demand lead to changes in quantities imported and exported rather than to changes in domestic prices.

We shall have occasion to use this model of the SOE many times throughout this book.

SUMMARY

1. One country (or region or individual) has an absolute advantage over another country (or region or individual) in the production of a commodity when, with the same input of resources in each country, it can produce more of the commodity than can the other.
2. In a situation of reciprocal absolute advantage, total production of both commodities will be raised if each country specializes in the production of the commodity in which it has the absolute advantage. However, the gains from trade do not require absolute advantage on the part of each country, only comparative advantage.
3. Comparative advantage is the relative advantage one country enjoys over another in production of various commodities. It occurs whenever countries have different opportunity costs of producing particular goods. World production of all commodities can be increased if each country transfers resources into the production of the commodities in which it has a comparative advantage.
4. The most important proposition in the theory of the gains from trade is: Trade allows all countries to obtain the goods in which they do not have a comparative advantage at a lower opportunity cost than they would face if they were to produce all commodities for themselves; this allows all countries to have more of all commodities than they could have if they tried to be self-sufficient.
5. As well as gaining the advantages of specialization arising from the comparative advantage, a nation that engages in trade and specialization may realize the benefits of economies of large-scale production and of learning by doing.
6. Classical theory regarded comparative advantage as largely determined by natural resource endowments and thus difficult to change. Economists now believe that comparative advantage can be acquired and thus can be changed. A country may, in this view, influence its role in world production and trade. Successful intervention leads to a country acquiring a comparative advantage; unsuccessful intervention fails to develop such an advantage.
7. The terms of trade refer to the ratio of the prices of goods exported to those imported, which determines the quantity of imports that can be obtained per unit of exports. The terms of trade determine how the gains from trade are shared. A favourable change in terms of trade – that is, a rise in export prices relative to import prices – means a country can acquire more imports per unit of exports.
8. A small open economy is a price-taker in markets for internationally traded goods and services. It will export goods for which its domestic supply exceeds its domestic demand at the world price and import goods for which domestic demand exceeds domestic supply at the world price.

TOPICS FOR REVIEW

- Interpersonal, interregional, and international specialization
- Absolute advantage and comparative advantage
- Gains from trade: specialization, scale economies, and learning by doing
- Opportunity cost and comparative advantage
- Dynamic comparative advantage
- Terms of trade
- Determination of imports and exports in a small open economy

22

Barriers to Trade

Conducting business in a foreign country is always difficult. Differences in language, in local laws and customs, and in currency all complicate transactions. Our concern in this chapter is not, however, with these difficulties, but with the government's policy towards international trade, which is called its **commercial policy**. At one extreme is a policy of **free trade**, which means an absence of any form of government interference with the free flow of international trade. Any departure from free trade designed to give some protection to domestic industries from foreign competition is called **protectionism**.

THE THEORY OF COMMERCIAL POLICY

Today, debates over commercial policy are as heated as they were 200 years ago when the theory of the gains from trade was still being worked out. Should a country permit the free flow of international trade, or should it seek to protect its local producers from foreign competition? Such protection may be achieved either by **tariffs**, which are taxes designed to raise the price of foreign goods, or by **non-tariff barriers**, which are devices other than tariffs that are designed to reduce the flow of imports. Examples include quotas and customs procedures that are deliberately made more cumbersome than is necessary.

The Case for Free Trade

The case for free trade is based on the analysis presented in Chapter 21. We saw that whenever opportunity costs differ among countries, specialization and trade will raise world living standards. Free trade allows all countries to specialize in producing commodities in which they have a comparative advantage.

> Free trade allows the maximization of world production, thus making it *possible* for every household in the world to consume more goods than it could without free trade.

This does not necessarily mean that everyone *will* be better off with free trade than without it. Protectionism could allow some people to obtain a larger share of a smaller world output so that they would benefit even though the average person would lose. If we ask whether it is *possible* for free trade to be advantageous to everyone, the answer is 'yes'. But if we ask whether free trade is in fact *always* advantageous to everyone, the answer is 'not necessarily'.

There is abundant evidence that significant differences in opportunity costs exist and that large gains are realized from international trade because of these differences. What needs explanation is the fact that trade is not wholly free. Why do tariffs and non-tariff barriers to trade continue to exist two centuries after Adam Smith and David Ricardo stated the case for free trade? Is there a valid case for protectionism? Before addressing these questions, let us examine the methods used in protectionist policy.

Methods of Protection

The three main types of protectionist policy are illustrated in Figure 22.1. All three may end up affecting both the price and quantity of exports. They differ, however, in what the policy changes *in the first instance*.

The first policy initially raises the *price* of the imported commodity. A tariff, also often called an *import duty*, is the most common price-raising device. Others are rules and regulations that fulfil three conditions. They are costly to comply with; they do not apply to competing domestically produced commodities; and they are more than is required to meet legitimate purposes other than restricting trade.

Tariffs come in two main forms: **specific tariffs**, which are so much on each unit of the product, and **ad valorem tariffs**, which are a percentage of the price of the product. Tariffs raise revenue as well as acting as a protective device. For some less-developed countries which have limited sources of revenue, import duties can be an important revenue source. For more developed countries such as the UK, the revenue-raising function is unimportant and can be ignored.

As shown in part (i) of Figure 22.1, tariffs have effects on both efficiency and distribution. First, they transfer surplus from domestic consumers, who now pay a higher price, to domestic producers, who now receive a higher price. Second,

they reduce efficiency. A measure of this efficiency loss, which is called the *deadweight loss* of the tariff, is the lost consumers' surplus. Part of the loss stems from the reduction in consumption. The other part stems from the replacement of low-cost, foreign-produced units by higher-cost, domestically produced units. This amount goes to domestic factors of production to persuade them to produce in that industry rather than in some other. Since they could produce more value in the other industries, their transfer to the inefficient tariff-protected industry represents a loss.

The second type of protectionist policy initially restricts the *quantity* of the imported commodity. A common example is the **import quota**, by which the importing country sets a maximum of the quantity of some commodity that may be imported each year. Increasingly popular, however, is the **voluntary export restriction (VER)** by which an exporting country agrees to limit the amount it sells to a second country.

The EC and the US have used VERs extensively, while the EC also uses import quotas quite frequently. Japan has been pressured into negotiating several VERs with the EC and the US. These arrangements limit sales of some of the Japanese goods that have had most success in international competition.

As shown in part (ii) of Figure 22.1, the quota has the effect of driving up the domestic price and restricting domestic consumption. So its effect on domestic consumers and producers is the same as a tariff that has the equivalent effect in limiting imports. The major difference is that when a government levies a tariff, it gets the revenue, while when it levies a quota or negotiates a VER, the same sum of money is transferred as additional revenue to foreign producers.

The third type of policy to restrict imports consists of domestic policies that initially reduce the demand for imported commodities. For example, the US government recently required that all imported steel pipe be marked with its country of origin, which is both costly and alleged to reduce the quality of certain types of pipe. Whatever the apparent purpose of the legislation, its effect was to reduce the demand for imported steel pipe. Other countries restrict the ability of their citizens to purchase the foreign

FIGURE 22.1   Three Ways of Reducing Imports

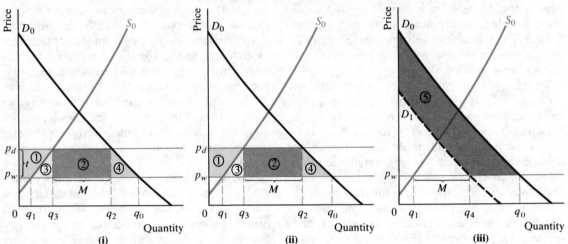

The government can restrict imports by policies that raise the price of the commodity, that directly reduce the quantity imported, or that reduce the demand for the commodity. In all the diagrams, D_0 and S_0 are domestic demand and supply. At the world price of p_w consumption is q_0, domestic production is q_1 and imports are $q_0 - q_1$. The government now wishes to reduce imports to the quantity indicated by M in all three figures.

In part (i), a tariff of t per unit is levied, raising the domestic price to p_d. Domestic production rises from q_1 to q_3, domestic consumption falls to q_2 while imports fall to $q_2 - q_3$. The surplus area (1) is transferred from consumers to producers. The surplus area (2) is transferred from consumers to the government as tariff revenue. The area (3), which is transferred from consumers' surplus to factor costs, is the extra cost of producing $q_3 - q_1$ at home rather than importing it. Area (4) is consumers' surplus lost when consumption falls from q_0 to q_2. The deadweight loss is areas (3) and (4).

In part (ii), an import quota of M is imposed. All changes are the same as in part (i) except that the consumers' surplus shown in area (2) now goes to the foreign producers (because the imports of $q_2 - q_3$ now yield their foreign sellers a price of p_d instead of p_w). In the tariff case shown in (i), this amount went to the domestic government as tax revenue.

In part (iii), the government uses domestic controls to shift the demand curve to D_1. Total consumption falls from q_0 to q_4 and imports fall by the same amount from $q_0 - q_1$ to $q_4 - q_1$. The lost consumers' surplus is the shaded area labelled (5). This policy succeeds in reducing imports, but unlike the other two it does nothing to increase domestic production (because it leaves the price in the domestic market unchanged).

exchange needed to pay for the imports. This shifts the demand curve for imports to the left.

Since the domestic price, and the level of domestic production, remains unchanged in this case, the full cost of the tariff is borne by consumers, as shown in part (iii) of Figure 22.1. They suffer a loss of consumers' surplus as a result of buying a lower quantity of the commodity at the same price. The policy is successful in reducing imports, but it does nothing to encourage domestic production of the commodity.

All import-restriction schemes cause efficiency losses. Restricting demand does not increase domestic output. Tariffs and quotas raise domestic prices and encourage domestic production; domestic firms gain at the expense of domestic consumers, and there is also a deadweight loss of consumers' surplus. A tariff also transfers surplus from domestic consumers to the government. An equivalent quota or VER transfers sur-

plus from domestic consumers to foreign producers.

In addition to devices designed to restrict imports for protectionist purposes, there is also a series of devices designed to prevent what are called 'unfair trade practices' by foreign firms or governments. The two most common of these are *anti-dumping duties* and *countervailing duties*. Although not intended as tools of protectionism, they can be used as such. For this reason they must be listed as potential protectionist devices. They are considered later in this chapter.

Nominal and Effective Rates of Tariff

The rate of tariff charged on each commodity, called the **nominal rate of tariff**, does not necessarily show the degree of protection given to that commodity. Nominal rates frequently understate the degree of protection offered to domestic manufacturing industries and a better measure is provided by what is called the **effective tariff rate**.

The distinction between nominal and effective rates of tariff arises whenever imported raw materials, or semi-finished goods, carry a lower rate of duty than do imports of the final manufactured goods that embody these intermediate products. When the final good is made abroad, the duty for manufactured goods is applied to the entire price of that good, even though the price includes the values of the raw materials and semi-finished goods that it embodies. When the final good is produced domestically, the raw materials and semi-finished goods enter at the lower rate of tariff. For this reason, a tariff of, say, 10 per cent on the final good will protect a domestic producer that is much more than 10 per cent less efficient than its foreign competitor.

To illustrate this important point, consider an example. A wood product is manufactured in both the UK and Norway using Norwegian wood. The wood is assumed to enter the UK duty-free, but the manufactured good is subject to a 10 per cent tariff. Further assume that when the product is manufactured in Norway the raw material accounts for half the cost of the final product and the other half is value added by the Norwegian manufacturer. Because of the 10 per cent tariff, a unit of output that costs £1 to produce in Norway will sell in the UK for £1.10.

Now consider the position of a UK manufacturer who is assumed to be less efficient than the Norwegian manufacturer. Let the UK firm's production costs be 20 per cent higher than those of the Norwegian firm. Thus to produce one unit of output, the raw material costs the UK firm £0.50, but its other costs – including the opportunity costs of its capital – are £0.60 (i.e. 20 per cent higher than the Norwegian manufacturer's costs of £0.50). This gives the UK firm a final price of £1.10, which is just low enough to compete against the tariff-burdened Norwegian import.

In this example, a tariff of 10 per cent on the value of the final product is sufficient to protect a UK firm that is 20 per cent less efficient than its Norwegian competitor. To measure this effect, the effective rate of tariff expresses the tariff as a percentage of the *value added* by the exporting industry in question. Thus the effective UK rate of tariff on the Norwegian manufacturing firm in the above example is 20 per cent, whereas the nominal tariff on manufactured goods is only 10 per cent.

The Case for Protectionism

Two kinds of arguments for protection are commonly offered. The first concerns national objectives other than output; the second concerns the desire to increase domestic national income, possibly at the expense of world national income.

Objectives Other Than Maximizing National Income

It is possible to accept the proposition that national income is higher with free trade, and yet rationally oppose free trade, because of a concern with policy objectives other than maximizing income. For example, comparative advantage might dictate that a country should specialize in producing a narrow range of commodities. The government might decide, however, that there are distinct social advantages in encouraging a more diverse economy. Citizens would be given a wider range of occupations, and the social and psychological advantages of diversification would more than compensate for a reduction in living standards by, say, 5 per cent below what they could be with complete specialization of production according to comparative advantage.

Specialization also involves the risk of cyclical fluctuations in the prices of basic commodities, which may alternate between very high and very low levels. The national income of a country specializing in the production of such commodities will be subject to wide fluctuations. The average income over a long period might be maximized by permitting specialization in a few basic commodities. The serious social problems associated with a widely fluctuating national income may, however, make the government decide to sacrifice some income in order to reduce fluctuations. The government might use protectionist policies to encourage the expansion of several less cyclically sensitive industries.

One non-economic reason for protectionism concerns national defence. It used to be argued, for example, that the UK needed an experienced merchant navy in case of war, and that this industry should be fostered by protectionist policies even though it was less efficient than the foreign competition. The same argument is sometimes made for the aircraft industry.

Other things being equal, most people prefer more income to less. Economists cannot, however, say that it is irrational for a society to sacrifice some income in order to achieve other goals. Economists can, however, do three things when faced with such reasons for adopting protectionist measures. First, they can ask if the proposed measures really do achieve the ends suggested. Second, they can calculate the cost of the measures in terms of lowered living standards. Third, they can see if there are alternative means of achieving the stated goals at lower cost in terms of lost output.

The Objective of Maximizing National Income

Next we consider four important arguments for the use of tariffs when the objective is to make national income as large as possible.

To alter the terms of trade: Trade restrictions can be used to turn the terms of trade in favour of countries that produce, and export, a large fraction of the world's supply of some commodity. They can also be used to turn the terms of trade in favour of countries that constitute a large fraction of the world demand for some commodity that they import.

When the OPEC countries restricted their output of oil in the 1970s, they were able to drive up the price of oil relative to the prices of other traded goods. This turned the terms of trade in their favour; for every barrel of oil exported, they were able to obtain a larger quantity of imports. When the output of oil grew greatly in the mid-1980s, the relative price of oil fell dramatically, and the terms of trade turned unfavourably to the oil-exploring companies. These are illustrations of how changes in the quantities of exports can affect the terms of trade.

Now consider a country that provides a large fraction of the total demand for some product that it imports. By restricting its demand for that product through tariffs, it can force the price of that product down. This turns the terms of trade in its favour because it can now get more units of imports per unit of exports.

Both of these techniques lower world output. They can, however, make it possible for a small group of countries to gain because they get a sufficiently larger share of the smaller world output. However, if foreign countries retaliate by raising their tariffs, the ensuing tariff war can easily leave every country with a lowered income.

To protect against 'unfair' actions by foreign firms and governments: Tariffs may be used to prevent foreign industries from gaining an advantage over domestic industries by use of predatory practices that will harm domestic industries and hence lower national income. Two common practices are subsidies paid by foreign governments to their exporters and dumping by foreign firms. Such practices are called 'unfair trade practices' and the laws that deal with them are called 'fair trade laws'. The circumstances under which dumping and foreign subsidization provide a valid argument for tariffs are considered in detail later in this chapter.

To protect infant industries: The oldest valid argument for protectionism as a means of raising living standards concerns economies of scale. It is usually called the **infant industry argument**. If an industry has large economies of scale, costs will be high when the industry is small, but will fall as the industry grows. In such industries, the country first in the field has a tremendous advantage. A newly developing country may find that, in the early stages of development, its industries are unable to compete with established foreign rivals. A trade restriction may protect these industries from foreign competition while they grow up. When they are large enough, they will be able to produce as cheaply as foreign rivals and thus be able to compete without protection.

To encourage learning by doing: Learning by doing, which we discussed in Chapter 21, suggests that the pattern of comparative advantage can be changed. If a country learns enough by producing commodities in which it currently is at a comparative disadvantage, it may gain in the long run by specializing in those commodities, developing a comparative advantage as the learning process lowers their costs.

Learning by doing is an example of what in Chapter 21 we called dynamic comparative advantages. The successes of such *newly industrializing countries* (the so-called NICs) as Brazil, Hong Kong, South Korea, Singapore and Taiwan seemed to many observers to be based on acquired skills and government policies that create favourable business conditions. This gave rise to the theory that comparative advantages can change, and that they can be developed by suitable government policies.

Protecting a domestic industry from foreign competition may give its management the time to learn to be efficient, and its labour force the time to acquire the needed skills. If so, it may pay in the very long run to protect the industry against foreign competition, while a dynamic comparative advantage is being developed.

Some countries have succeeded in developing strong comparative advantages in targeted industries, but others have failed. One reason such policies sometimes fail is that protecting local industries from foreign competition may make the industries unadaptive and complacent. Another reason is the difficulty of identifying the industries that will be able to succeed in the long run. All too often the protected infant grows up to be a weakling requiring permanent tariff protection for its continued existence. Or else the rate of learning is slower than for similar industries in countries that do not provide protection from the chill winds of international competition. In these instances the anticipated comparative advantage never materializes.

How Much Protectionism?

So far we have seen that there is a strong case for allowing much trade in order to realize the gains from trade, but that there are also some reasons for departing from completely free trade.

> **It is not necessary to choose between free trade on the one hand and complete protectionism on the other. A country can have some trade and some protectionism too.**

Free Trade Versus No Trade

It would be possible to grow a host of tropical products in English greenhouses, but the cost in terms of other commodities forgone would be huge, because these artificial means of production require lavish inputs of factors of production. It would likewise be possible for a tropical country, currently producing foodstuffs, to set up industries to produce all the manufactured products that it consumes. But for a small country without natural advantages in industrial production, the cost in terms of resources used could be enormous. These examples illustrate the large gains from free trade when no trade is the alternative. The consumption of all countries would be much lower if each chose to produce domestically all the goods it consumed.

> **In all-or-nothing choice, almost all countries would choose free trade over no trade.**

A Little More Trade Versus a Little Less Trade

Today we have trade among nations, but that trade is not perfectly free. Table 22.1 shows the levels of tariffs on selected commodities in force in 1990.

Would we be better off if today's barriers to trade were reduced or increased a little bit? This question shifts the focus of our discussion considerably, for it is quite a jump from the proposition that 'free trade is better than no trade' to the proposition that 'a little less trade restriction than we have at present is better than a little more'.

To see this latter issue, compare the effects of a 10 per cent uniform effective rate of tariff with those of free trade. Tariffs of 10 per cent will

TABLE 22.1 Tariffs on Selected Commodity Groups (*ad valorem* rates)

Commodity	USA	EC	Japan
Weighted average of all manufactured items	4.4	5.5	3.6
Fruits, vegetables	1.7	3.4	14.5
Tea, coffee, and spices	5.3	1.8	34.1
Paper, paperboard	0.3	4.0	1.4
Textiles	15.9	9.0	8.0
Transport vehicles	2.5	6.2	2.1
Tobacco	13.0	0.0	54.3
Petroleum and coal products	0.0	6.3	1.4
Oil and natural gas	4.0	0.0	0.0
All commodities (trade weighted)	3.2	3.7	5.4

Source: Post-Tokyo Round tariff rates, courtesy Special Trade Representatives Office, US government.

The European Community, the United States, and Japan all have a low average rate of tax on manufactured goods. These tariffs, the lowest in history, result from the General Agreement on Tariffs and Trade (GATT) Tokyo Round negotiations. They were phased in during the first half of the 1980s and will remain in force until the further reductions that may be agreed during the Uruguay Round are phased in during the 1990s.

protect industries that are up to 10 per cent less efficient than foreign competitors. If the costs of the various tariff-protected industries were spread out evenly, some would be 10 per cent less efficient than their foreign competitors and others only 1 per cent less efficient. Their average inefficiency would be about half the tariff rate, so they would be on average about 5 per cent less efficient than their foreign competitors.

Suppose that, as a result of tariffs, approximately 20 per cent of a country's resources are allocated to industries different from the ones to which they would be allocated if there were no tariffs. Approximately 20 per cent of a country's resources are thus producing on average about 5 per cent less efficiently than they would be if there were no tariffs. This reduces national income by about 1 per cent (i.e. 20 per cent of 5 per cent) as a result of tariff protection.[1]

[1] The above rough calculation is meant only to give some intuitive understanding of why the many careful measures of the cost of moderate tariffs commonly lead to figures closer to 1 per cent than to 10 per cent of the national incomes of the EC or the US.

Suppose that the efficiency loss caused by existing tariffs is equal to 1 per cent of our national income. Is the sacrifice of national income implied by existing tariffs large or small? Expressed as a percentage of GDP, the loss seems small, yet in 1988 prices it was nearly £3 billion *per year* in the UK. That amount every year for ever could buy a lot of hospitals, schools, medical research, solar energy research.

The previous calculations refer to gains from exploiting comparative advantage *when costs are given and constant.* More recent research allows for unexploited economies of scale in specific product lines, and for some forms of dynamic comparative advantages. They show gains from reducing the world's remaining tariffs that are much larger than the small gains suggested above. These gains tend to be in the range of 5–10 per cent of the national incomes of small and middle-sized economies. For large economies such as the EC and the United States, the gains tend to be somewhat smaller – because many of the scale and dynamic economies can be exploited within the existing large domestic markets.

Longer-run considerations: Some may be tempted to conclude that the seemingly small economic costs of the current amount of protectionism make it worthwhile to give in to the clamour to provide more protection for hard-pressed local industries. Before rushing to that conclusion, however, some long-run political and economic possibilities need to be considered. The world prosperity of recent decades has been built largely on a rising volume of relatively free international trade. There are real doubts that such prosperity could be maintained if the volume of trade were to shrink steadily because of growing trade barriers. Yet the pressure to use trade restrictions in troubled times is strong. If countries give in and begin to raise barriers moderately when the initial economic costs are not large, political pressures may make it hard to check the raising of trade barriers even when the costs become large.

In today's world, a country's products must stand up to international competition if they are to survive. Protection, by conferring a national monopoly, reduces the incentive for industries to fight to hold their own internationally. If any one country adopts high tariffs unilaterally, its domestic industries may become less competitive. Secure in their home market because of the tariff wall, they are likely to become less and less competitive in the international market. However, as the gap between domestic and foreign industries widens, any given tariff wall will provide less and less protection. Eventually, the domestic industries will have to meet the foreign competition, or else succumb to it. Meanwhile, domestic living standards will fall relative to foreign ones, as an increasing productivity gap opens between domestic, tariff-protected industries and foreign, internationally oriented ones.

Fallacious Trade-policy Arguments

We have seen that there are gains from a high volume of international trade and specialization. We have also seen that there can be valid arguments for a moderate degree of protectionism. There are also many claims that do not advance the debate. Fallacious arguments are heard on both sides, and they colour much of the popular discussion. These arguments have been around for a long time, but their survival does not make them true. We will examine them now to see where their fallacies lie.

Fallacious Arguments for Free Trade

Free trade always benefits all countries: This is not necessarily so. We saw above that a small group of countries may gain by restricting trade in order to get a sufficiently favourable shift in their terms of trade. Such countries would lose if they gave up these tariffs and adopted free trade unilaterally.

Infant industries never abandon their tariff protection: It is argued that granting protection to infant industries is a mistake because these industries seldom admit to growing up, and will cling to their protection even when fully grown. But infant-industry tariffs are a mistake *only* if these industries never grow up. In this case permanent tariff protection would be required to protect a weak industry never able to compete on an equal footing in the international market. But if the industries do grow up and achieve the expected scale economies, the real costs of production are reduced and resources are freed for other uses. Whether or not the tariff or other trade barriers remain, a cost saving has been effected by the scale economies.

Fallacious Arguments for Protectionism

Prevent exploitation: According to the exploitation theory, trade can never be mutually advantageous; one trading partner *must* always reap a gain at the other's expense. Thus the weaker trading partner must protect itself by restricting its trade with the stronger partner. By showing that both parties can gain from trade, the principle of comparative advantage refutes the exploitation doctrine of trade. When opportunity-cost ratios differ in two countries, specialization and the accompanying trade make it possible to produce more of all commodities. This makes it possible for both parties to consume more as a result of trade than they could get in its absence.

Keep the money at home: This argument says, if I buy a foreign good, I have the good and the foreigner has the money, whereas if I buy the same good locally, I have the good and our country has the money, too.

This argument is based on a misconception. It assumes that domestic money actually goes abroad physically when imports are purchased and that trade flows only in one direction. But when British importers purchase Japanese goods, they do not send sterling abroad. They (or their financial agents) buy Japanese yen and use them to pay the Japanese manufacturers. They purchase the yen on the foreign-exchange market by giving up sterling to someone who wishes to use it for expenditure *in the UK*. Even if the money did go abroad physically – that is, if a Japanese firm accepted a shipload of £5 notes – it would be because that firm (or someone to whom it could sell the notes) wanted them to spend in the only country where they are legal tender, the UK.

Sterling, or any other national currency, ultimately does no one any good except as purchasing power. It would be miraculous if UK money could be exported in return for real goods. After all, the Bank of England has the power to create as much new money as it wishes. It is only because

UK money can buy UK commodities, and assets, that others want it.

Protect against low-wage foreign labour:
Surely, this argument says, the products of low-wage countries will drive UK products from the market, and the high UK standard of living will be dragged down to that of its poorer trading partners. Arguments of this sort have swayed many voters through the years.

As a prelude to considering them, stop and think what the argument would imply if taken out of the international context and put into a local one, where the same principles govern the gains from trade. Is it really impossible for a rich person to gain from trading with a poor person? Would the local millionaire be better off if she did all her own typing, gardening and cooking? No one believes that a rich person cannot gain from trading with those who are less rich. Why then must a rich group of people lose from trading with a poor group? 'Well,' you say, 'the poor group will price their goods too cheaply.' Does anyone believe that consumers lose from buying in discount houses or supermarkets just because the prices are lower there than at the old-fashioned corner shop? Consumers gain when they can buy the same goods at a lower price. If the Koreans pay low wages and sell their goods cheaply, *Korean* labour may suffer, but the UK will gain by obtaining imports at a low cost in terms of the goods that must be exported in return. The cheaper our imports are, the better off we are in terms of the goods and services available for domestic consumption.

Stated in more formal terms, the gains from trade depend on comparative, not absolute, advantages. World production is higher when any two areas, say the UK and Japan, specialize in the production of the goods for which they have a comparative advantage than when they both try to be self-sufficient.

Might it not be possible, however, that Japan will undersell the UK in all lines of production and thus appropriate all, or more than all, the gains for itself, leaving the UK no better off, or even worse off, than if it had no trade with Japan? The answer is no. The reason for this depends on the behaviour of exchange rates, which are discussed in Chapter 39. As we shall see in that chapter, equality of demand and supply in foreign-exchange markets ensures that trade flows in both directions. In the meantime, the reason a country cannot import for long without exporting, may be stated intuitively as follows.

Imports can be obtained only by spending the currency of the country that makes the imports. Claims to this currency can be obtained only by exporting goods and services, or by borrowing. Thus, lending and borrowing aside, imports must equal exports. All trade must be in two directions; we can buy only if we can also sell.

In the long run, trade cannot hurt a country by causing it to import without exporting.

Trade, then, always provides scope for international specialization, with each country producing and exporting those goods for which it has a comparative advantage and importing those goods for which it does not.

Exports raise living standards; imports lower them:
Exports add to aggregate demand; imports subtract from it. Thus, other things being equal, exports tend to increase national income and imports to reduce it. Surely, then, it is desirable to encourage exports by subsidizing them and to discourage imports by taxing them. This is an appealing argument, but it is incorrect.

Exports raise national income by adding to the value of domestic output, but they do not add to the value of domestic consumption. In fact, exports are goods produced at home and consumed abroad, while imports are goods produced abroad and consumed at home. The standard of living in a country depends on the goods and services available for *consumption*, not on what is produced.

If exports were really good and imports really bad, then a fully employed economy that managed to increase exports without a corresponding increase in imports ought to be better off. Such a change, however, would result in a reduction in current standards of living, because when more goods are sent abroad while no more are brought in from abroad, the total goods available for domestic consumption must fall.

The living standards of a country depend on the goods and services consumed in that country. The importance of exports

is that they permit imports to be made. This two-way international exchange is valuable because more goods can be imported than could be obtained if the same goods were produced at home.

Create domestic jobs and reduce unemployment: It is sometimes said that an economy with substantial unemployment, such as that of the UK in the 1930s and the 1980s, provides an exception to the case for freer trade. Suppose that tariffs or import quotas cut the imports of Japanese cars, Korean textiles, US computers and Polish vodka. Surely, the argument maintains, this will create more employment in local industries producing similar products. The answer is that it will – initially. But the Japanese, Koreans, Americans and Poles can buy from the UK only if they earn sterling by selling things to (or by borrowing sterling from) the UK.[1] The decline in their sales of cars, textiles, computers and vodka will decrease their purchases of UK machinery, aircraft, insurance and holidays in the UK. Jobs will be lost in UK export industries, and gained in those industries that formerly faced competition from imports. The likely long-term effect is that overall unemployment will not be reduced but merely redistributed among industries. In the process, living standards will be reduced because employment expands in inefficient import-competing industries and contracts in efficient exporting industries.

Industries and unions that compete with imports often favour protectionism, while those with large exports usually favour more trade. Protection is an ineffective means to reduce unemployment.

INTERNATIONAL AGREEMENTS ON TRADE AND TARIFFS

In the past, any country could impose any desired set of tariffs on its imports. But when one country increased its tariffs, the action often triggered retaliatory changes by its trading partners. Just as an arms race can escalate, so can a tariff war. Extended negotiations were then required to undo the damage.

The General Agreement on Tariffs and Trade (GATT)

The 1930s saw a high-water mark of world protectionism as each country sought to raise its employment by raising its tariffs. The end result was lowered efficiency, less trade, but no more employment. One of the most notable achievements of the post-Second World War era was the creation of the General Agreement on Tariffs and Trade (GATT). Under this agreement, GATT countries meet periodically to negotiate bilateral cuts in tariffs that are mutually advantageous. They agree in advance that any tariff cuts negotiated in this way will be extended to all member countries on what is called the **most favoured nation (MFN)** principle. Significant tariff reductions have been effected by the member countries.

Two recent rounds of GATT agreements have each reduced world tariffs by about one-third. The Kennedy Round negotiations were completed in 1967, and new rates were phased in over a five-year period ending in 1972. The Tokyo Round negotiations began in 1975 and were completed in 1979. The reductions began to take effect in 1981 and were completed in 1986.

Ironically, as that new round of reductions began, pressure was mounting in many countries to protect jobs at home through trade restrictions. Protectionist policies grew alarmingly in the EC and many other areas. As time passed, even GATT itself came under attack. The worldwide recession that began in late 1981 was undoubtedly the main cause of this pressure. In addition, protectionist pressures in many countries were also created by the decline in the international competitiveness of traditional industries due to sharp changes in terms of trade. Also, under the impact of the high value of the US dollar, protectionist pressures grew throughout the 1980s in the United States.

In 1986 a preliminary meeting was held as a beginning towards a new round of GATT negotiations, which is called the Uruguay

---

[1] They can also get sterling by selling to other countries and then using their currencies to buy sterling. But this only complicates the transaction; it does not change its fundamental nature. Other countries must have earned the sterling by selling goods to the UK (or borrowing from the UK).

BOX 22.1 EUROPE 1992

'1992 will see the completion of the programme begun in 1958 when the Treaty of Rome set up the European Economic Community'

'1992 will see the creation of a single, integrated, European market of 320 million people'

So, at least, goes the rhetoric; but is there substance behind it all? Are the EC's plans for 1992 revolutionary, or are the European Commission's public relations officers merely working overtime? According to J. A. Kay, '1992 is perhaps the most successful marketing campaign of the decade. It has restored the political momentum of the European Community and broadened the horizons of many businessmen across the continent.'[1] In this sense, much of the real significance of 1992 does lie in the success of its publicity. Behind the publicity, however, lies a not insignificant amount of substance.

The substance of 1992 is to be found in programmes designed to come as close as possible to completing the liberalization of the internal European market. The three major plans for doing this are to abolish fiscal frontiers, to reduce non-tariff barriers to trade (NTBs), and to liberalize public procurement.

The first, and in many ways most contentious, plan is to dismantle fiscal frontiers between the member states. The Commission believes that what is needed for this is an approximate harmonization of VAT rates and excise duties. The Community already has a common set of tariffs against the outside world (by virtue of its being a common market rather than a free-trade area). If it also had a common set of NTBs this could, in principle at least, lead to the elimination of any form of border controls between the member states. In practice, differing national NTBs to imports from the rest of the world, particularly from Japan and the NICs, make some border control necessary. Even if this reason could be removed, member countries would no doubt still wish to maintain some border surveillance. Differences in laws (and the severity with which they are administered) on such matters as gun ownership, agricultural pests, animal diseases, and drugs would require border posts although the surveillance would be minimal by world standards.

A second way in which the Community's market is to be integrated is through reducing national restrictions on transportation. Airlines in Europe have never seen the dramatic effects that deregulation brought to airlines in the US and Canada. North American fares fell significantly, and passenger miles rose dramatically. Trucking, and some

---

[1] J. A. Kay, 'Myths and Realities' in *1992, Myths and Realities* (London: Centre of Business Strategies, 1989), p. 28. This whole Box relies heavily on Kay's excellent essay.

Round. This round is attempting to deal with four pressing issues: the growing worldwide use of non-tariff barriers to trade, and the need to develop rules for liberalizing trade in services, which is the most rapidly growing component of foreign trade; the distorting effect on trade in agricultural goods caused by heavy domestic subsidization of agricultural production; and the need to develop more effective methods of settling disputes that arise from violations of GATT rules. An interim report at the end of 1988 suggested that substantial progress was yet to be made. The final result will not be known, however, until at least 1991.

Common Markets

A **common market** is an agreement among a group of countries to eliminate barriers to free trade among themselves, and to present a common barrier to trade with the rest of the world. The most important example came into being in 1957 when the Treaty of Rome brought together France, Germany, Italy, Holland, Belgium and Luxemburg in what was first called the European Common Market (ECM), then the European Economic Community (EEC), and now just the European Community (EC). The original six were joined in 1973 by the United Kingdom, the Republic of Ireland and Denmark; Greece entered in 1983 and Spain and Portugal in 1986.

This organization is dedicated to bringing about free trade, complete mobility of factors of production, and the eventual harmonization of fiscal and monetary policies among the member countries. Many tariffs for manufactured goods have been eliminated and much freedom of movement of labour and capital achieved. Substantial monetary integrations have also been achieved, but there is still a long way to go to fully integrating the monetary system of the EC countries. At the time of writing, a major push is underway to remove most of the remaining restrictions by 1992. How far it will succeed

wholesale activities, are also highly regulated in some EC countries. Increasing competition in transportation should help significantly to integrate the EC market.

A third way in which large potential gains might be realized is to liberalize public procurement (the purchases made by governments). Such purchases, which are at present often restricted to nationals, are to be opened to international competition. However, the scope for persuading governments seriously to entertain bids from companies in other Community countries is probably limited.

The countries of the EC have been no exception to the world trend towards increased use of NTBs. A significant reduction in NTBs on intra-Community trade would represent real progress in the fight to contain the use of these threats to liberalized trade.

One important NTB that is signalled out for attack is the misuse of technical standards and regulations. Their purpose is consumer protection, but they are easily used to inhibit international trade – particularly in food products, pharmaceuticals, and engineering goods, as well as in financial services. The Community's original approach to this problem was to try to impose European standards on all products. This led to complaints about bureaucratic excesses which took the distinctiveness out of such national products as beer and salami. The new approach is to set minimum common standards for consumer safety and agree that any product meeting these must be admitted to the markets of all Community countries – leaving member countries free to impose further standards on commodities produced within their own borders if they wish to do so.

A series of barriers that restrict the entry of firms from one country into the markets of other member countries are also to be removed. The object is to increase intra-Community competition.

For these, and many other reasons, the EC countries are looking forward to 1992. But they are not alone. The rest of the world is also waiting for 1992, and doing so with a mixture of interest, well wishes, and apprehension. To them, the key question is, will 1992 make the Community more inward-looking or more outward-looking with respect to world trade? The liberalized trading system overseen by the GATT has served the world well for 45 years. Now, however, it is under heavy attack. Many observers fear the advent of a new era of managed trade, with more trade taking place within various blocs, and less between the blocs. By the way in which it removes its own internal barriers, Europe can make a significant difference one way or the other, lending its push either to restricting, or encouraging, world trade. Which way will Europe go in 1992? At the time of writing in 1989, no one – either within the Community or without – knows the answer to that momentous question.

remained uncertain in 1989. It is discussed further in Box 22.1.

Other common markets have been formed, such as the Central American Common Market and the East African Community, but none has yet achieved the success of the EC, and some have collapsed.

Free Trade Associations

A **free trade association** allows for tariff-free trade between the member countries but, unlike a common market, it leaves each member free to levy its own tariffs on imports from other countries. As a result, members must maintain customs points at their common border (if they have one) to make sure that imports into the free-trade area do not all enter through the country levying the lowest tariff on each item.

The first important free-trade association in the modern era was the European Free Trade Association (EFTA). It was formed in 1960 by a group of European countries unwilling to join the European Community because of its all-embracing character. Not wanting to be left out of the gains from trade, they formed an association whose sole purpose was tariff removal. They removed all tariffs on trade among themselves. Each of the EFTA countries also signed a free-trade-area agreement with the EC. This makes the EC–EFTA market the world's largest market (over 300 million people) in which goods can move largely unhindered by tariff barriers.

In 1985 the US signed a limited free-trade agreement with Israel. In 1988 a sweeping agreement was signed with Canada, instituting free trade on all goods and many services, and covering what is the largest flow of international trade between any two countries in the world. The US was also negotiating with Mexico over a limited free-trade agreement. Australia and New Zealand have also entered into an association removing restrictions on trade in goods and services between the two countries.

Trade Remedy Laws and Non-tariff Barriers

Early rounds of negotiations under the GATT concentrated on the reduction of tariffs. As these were lowered, countries wishing to protect domestic industries began using a series of trade restrictions that came to be known as non-tariff barriers (NTBs). Most NTBs are ostensibly levied for purposes other than protectionism. These other purposes are often called trade-relief purposes.

An effort to control the growing use of NTBs was made in the Tokyo Round of GATT negotiations. These measures were classified and the circumstances under which their use was legitimate were laid down. The ironic result was that, by making all countries aware of these measures, and by making their use respectable under some circumstances, these GATT agreements led to an increased use of NTBs for purposes of trade restrictions.

Escape clause: One procedure is the so-called 'escape clause action'. A rapid surge of imports may temporarily threaten the existence of domestic producers. These producers may then be given temporary relief by raising tariff rates over and above those agreed to during the GATT negotiations. The trouble is that, once imposed, these 'temporary' measures are hard to eliminate.

One 'temporary' measure that is still in force provides a cautionary tale. In the late 1950s, the textile and clothing industries in many advanced industrial nations saw their market shares reduced by a rising volume of trade from Hong Kong, Korea, the Philippines and other newly industrializing nations. In response to a United States initiative, international meetings were held in 1961. Out of these meetings came the *multi-fibre agreements* (MFAs), providing maximum annual quotas for each exporting textile-producing country for a twenty-year period. Starting in 1981, many of these agreements were renegotiated, generally leading to more, rather than less, restrictive policies. At the end of the decade they were still in existence.

Similar 'orderly marketing agreements' have been accepted by many countries with respect to footwear in 1977, colour television sets in 1977, and citizens' band radio sets in 1978.

Dumping: When a commodity is sold in two countries at a price that differs for reasons not related to costs, it is called **dumping**. This is a form of price discrimination of the kind studied in the theory of monopoly (see Chapter 13). Most governments have anti-dumping duties which protect their own industries against unfair foreign pricing practices.

Dumping, if it lasts indefinitely, can be a gift to the receiving country. Its consumers get goods from abroad at less than their real cost. Dumping is more often a temporary measure designed to get rid of unwanted surpluses or a predatory attempt to drive competitors out of business. In either case, domestic producers complain about unfair foreign competition. In these cases, it is accepted international practice to levy *anti-dumping duties* on foreign imports. These duties are designed to eliminate the discriminatory elements in their prices.

Unfortunately, anti-dumping laws have been evolving over the last two decades in ways that allow anti-dumping duties to become barriers to trade rather than redresses for unfair trading practices. The United States has led the way in making these changes, but many other countries, including those of the EC, have been quick to imitate the US.

Two features of the anti-dumping system now in effect in many countries make it highly protectionist. First, *any* price discrimination is classified as dumping and thus subject to penalties. Thus prices in the producer's domestic market become, in effect, minimum prices below which no sales can be made in foreign markets whatever the circumstances in the domestic and foreign markets.

Second, many countries' laws now calculate the 'margin of dumping' as the difference between the price charged in that country's market and the foreign producer's 'full allocated cost' (average total cost). This means that when there is global excess demand so that the profit-maximizing price for all producers is below average total cost (but above average variable cost), foreign producers can be convicted of dumping. This gives domestic producers enormous protection whenever the market price falls temporarily below ATC. Furthermore, it is very difficult to allocate overheads among individual products in many multi-product industries.

This is particularly so in industries such as chemicals, where fixed costs are a high proportion of total costs and there are many individual products which have widely differing development costs.

Countervailing duties: Countervailing duties provide another case where the evolution from a trade-relief measure to a covert NTB has been pioneered by the US. Since the early 1980s, one of the most potent American measures affecting trade has been the countervailing duty. This measure was designed to act not as a tariff barrier, but rather as a means of creating a 'level playing field' on which fair international competition could take place. American firms rightly complain that they cannot compete against the bottomless purses of foreign governments. Subsidized foreign exports can be sold indefinitely in the United States at prices that would guarantee losses in the absence of the subsidy. The original object of countervailing duties was to counteract the effect on price of the presence of such foreign subsidies.

If a US firm suspects the existence of such a subsidy and registers a complaint, the American government is then required to make an investigation. For a countervailing duty to be levied consistent with GATT rules, the investigation must find, first, that the foreign subsidy to the specific industry in question does exist and, second, that it is large enough to be a potential injury to competing American firms.

There is no doubt that countervailing duties have sometimes been used to remove the effects of 'unfair' competition caused by foreign subsidies. Other governments complain, however, that countervail is also sometimes used as a thinly disguised barrier to trade. At the early stages of the development of countervailing duties, only subsidies whose prime effect was to distort trade were subject to countervail. Even then, however, the existence of equivalent domestic subsidies was not taken into account when deciding to put a countervailing duty on subsidized imports. Over time, the type of subsidy that is subject to countervail has evolved until almost any government programme that affects industry now risks becoming the object of countervailing duty. Since all governments have many programmes that provide some direct or indirect assistance to industry, the potential for the use of countervailing duties as thinly disguised trade barriers is enormous.

Conclusion

While there are cases in which a policy to restrict trade has been pursued following a rational assessment of the approximate cost, it is hard to avoid the conclusion that, more often than not, such policies have been pursued for flimsy objectives, or on fallacious grounds, with little idea of the actual costs involved. The very high tariffs that marked the 1920s and 1930s are a conspicuous example. Clamour for Western governments to do something about the competition from Japan, South Korea and other newly industrializing countries may well be another. So may be the heavy pressures currently put on the governments of the world's major trading countries to 'solve' their serious unemployment problems by discouraging imports and encouraging exports. When all countries try to do this, there is no net increase in employment. All that happens is that each country produces inefficiently more goods for domestic production while decreasing its efficient production of goods for export. The net effect is a fall in world living standards with no alleviation of the problem of unemployment.

SUMMARY

1. Total world output will be higher under free trade than when protectionism restricts regional specialization.
2. Free trade among nations may be restricted intentionally by protectionist policies which seek to raise prices, lower quantities, or reduce the demand for imports.
3. Protection is sometimes urged as a means to ends other than maximizing world living standards. Examples are to produce a diversified economy, to reduce

fluctuations in national income, and to improve national defence.

4. Protection can also be urged on the grounds that it may lead to higher living standards for the protectionist country than would a policy of free trade. Such a result might come about through exploiting a monopoly position, or by developing a dynamic comparative advantage allowing inexperienced or uneconomically small industries to become efficient.

5. Almost everyone would choose free trade if the only alternative were *no* trade. Cutting existing tariff barriers offers gains that may seem small expressed as a percentage of GNP, but which are large in terms of the total of goods and services involved.

6. Some fallacious free-trade arguments are: (i) because free trade maximizes world income, it will maximize the income of every individual country; and (ii) because infant industries seldom admit to growing up, and thus try to retain their protection indefinitely, the whole country necessarily loses by protecting its infant industries.

7. Some fallacious protectionist arguments are that (i) mutually advantageous trade is impossible because one trader's gain must always be the other's loss; (ii) buying abroad sends our money abroad, while buying at home keeps our money at home; (iii) our high-paid workers must be protected against the competition from low-paid foreign workers; (iv) imports are to be discouraged because they lower national income and cause unemployment.

8. International agreements have lowered trade barriers from the high levels of 50 years ago. After the Second World War, the GATT began a series of multinational rounds of tariff reduction that have greatly lowered tariffs and are now trying to address non-tariff barriers as well. Nevertheless, the recent clamour for protection in many trading nations threatens the free-trade trend that GATT has fostered. Non-tariff barriers have been prominent in the attempt to raise trade restrictions in spite of GATT-negotiated reductions in tariffs.

TOPICS FOR REVIEW

- Free trade and protectionism
- Tariff and non-tariff barriers to trade
- Countervail and voluntary export agreements
- Fallacious arguments for protectionism
- Dumping and anti-dumping duties
- General Agreement on Tariffs and Trade (GATT)
- Common markets and free-trade associations

PART 7

Microeconomic policy

23

The Case for
the Free Market

Those who have read this far, understand that markets are impressive institutions. Consumers' tastes and producers' costs help to generate price signals. These signals co-ordinate decisions taken by millions of independent agents, all pursuing their own self-interest and oblivious of national priorities. The power of this automatic co-ordinating function is painfully obvious to any central planner who has sought to co-ordinate a modern command economy by consciously calculating all its needs, directing its allocation of resources, and determining its distribution of income.

In this chapter, we first summarize some of the key aspects of market economies, drawing together what we have learned in earlier chapters. Then we lay out the explicit arguments that have been made for 'letting the market do it'. These arguments are all variations on the theme that markets provide an *efficient* means of allocating the nation's resources. Finally, we go beyond efficiency considerations to deal with some broader issues of the behaviour of markets in the long and very long runs.

CHARACTERISTICS OF THE MARKET

We discuss four points that are important to understanding how markets behave. First, markets provide a social control mechanism; second, markets function without conscious central direction; third, in allocating resources, markets also determine the distribution of income; and fourth, the long-term behaviour of markets often exhibits a cycle in which products are born, grow to maturity, pass into old age, and eventually die.

A Social Control System

A co-ordinator of decisions: Every day millions of people make millions of independent decisions concerning production and consumption. These decisions are usually motivated by fairly immediate considerations of personal or group self-interest, rather than by a desire to contribute to the social good. The price system co-ordinates these decisions.

Economists have long emphasized price as the signalling agent. When a commodity such as oil becomes scarce, its free-market price rises. Firms and households that use it are led to economize on it and look for alternatives. Firms that produce it are led to produce more of it. This system works best when price is determined on free markets where there are many buyers and many sellers. Scarcities, and surpluses, are then signalled through prices that are set by the impersonal, aggregate forces of demand and supply.

Administered prices: The prices of oligopolistic industries do not, however, fluctuate in response to ever-changing market conditions. Oligopolies have administered prices set by firms, rather than impersonal market forces. The price system still works under oligopoly; but it works slightly differently (and possibly less efficiently) than when prices are determined on competitive markets. Oligopolistic firms respond to price signals on the input side, since the prices of their inputs are usually determined on competitive markets. On the output side, however, these firms respond to quantity signals. Firms adjust their outputs in response to changes in their sales and inventories, rather than in response to changes in market prices. What matters, however, is that markets co-ordinate decisions even when prices are administered.

Windfall profits: The basic engine that drives the adaptations of the economy is profit, in the case of capital, and disequilibrium differentials in the case of other factors of production. The general public has come to know these as *windfall profits*. All of these terms refer to earnings that rise above, or fall below, transfer earnings as a result of shifts in demands for, or supplies of, factors in particular uses. In the long run, windfall profits are eliminated because factors move among alternative uses until net advantages are equalized.

A rise in demand, or a fall in costs, produces windfall profits for producers, while a fall in demand, or a rise in costs, produces windfall losses. Profits signal that there are too few resources devoted to that industry. In search of these profits, more resources will enter, increasing output and driving down price, until the windfall profits fall to zero. Windfall losses signal the reverse. Resources leave the industry until those left behind are no longer making losses. If the government taxed away *all* windfall profits and replaced by subsidy *all* windfall losses, it would effectively destroy the market economy by removing its driving force.

An illustration of market co-ordination: Say, for example, that every family in the Greater London area decides that it wants to own a detached house with a garden. This would be physically impossible, because there is not nearly enough land to house London's population in such a manner. If the entire populace tried to move to such dwellings, they would vastly bid up the price of land and the price of existing housing, while causing the prices of multiple-unit dwellings to plummet. Reacting to these signals, many people would decide that, although they preferred to live in single-family dwellings at the original prices, they preferred to live in multi-family units at the new prices. With a price system, no central administrator has to calculate scarcities and decide what proportion of the population must live in multi-family dwellings, or have the unenviable task of saying which individuals must live in each type of dwelling. If there is excess demand for one type and excess supply of the other, the relative price will change. As this happens, some people will switch from demanding the type that is becoming more expensive to demanding the type that is becoming relatively cheaper. Once the excess demand and supply are eliminated, the relative prices of the two will be in equilibrium.

Lack of Conscious Direction

The market economy fulfils its function of co-ordinating decisions without anyone having to understand how it works. As Professor Tom Schelling puts it:[1]

> 'The dairy farmer doesn't need to know how many people eat butter and how far away they are, how many other people raise cows, how many babies drink milk, or whether more money is spent on beer or milk. What he needs to know is the prices of different feeds, the characteristics of different cows, the different prices ... for milk ... the relative cost of hired labour and electrical machinery, and what his net earnings might be if he sold his cows and raised pigs instead.'

---

[1] T. C. Schelling, *Micromotives and Macrobehaviour* (New York: Norton and Co., 1978).

By responding to such public signals as the costs and prices of what he buys and sells, the dairy farmer helps to make the whole economy fit together, to produce more or less what people want, and to provide it more or less where, and when, they want it.

It is, of course, an enormous advantage that all the citizens of a country can collectively make the system operate without any one of them having to understand how it works. This becomes a disadvantage, however, when they are asked, as voters or as legislators, to pass judgement on schemes for consciously intervening to improve the economy's operation. *Ignorance of how the system works then becomes a serious drawback.*

The Distribution of Income

The third important characteristic of a market economy is that it determines a *distribution* of the total income that it generates. People whose services are in heavy demand relative to supply, such as TV comedians and football players, earn large incomes, while people whose services are not in heavy demand relative to supply, possibly because they have low IQs or poor muscular co-ordination, earn low incomes.

The distribution of income produced by the market can be looked at in equilibrium or in disequilibrium. In equilibrium, similar efforts by similar people will be similarly rewarded everywhere in the economy. In disequilibrium, however, windfall profits and losses abound, so that similar people making similar efforts of work, or investment, are not similarly rewarded. People in declining industries, areas and occupations suffer the punishment of windfall losses through no fault of their own. Those in expanding sectors earn the reward of windfall gains for no extra effort of their own. These rewards and punishments serve an important function of causing decentralized decision-takers to respond appropriately to changes in demands and costs. The advantage is that individuals can take their own decisions about how to alter their behaviour when market conditions change. The disadvantage is that temporary rewards and punishments are dealt out for reasons that are beyond the control of the individuals affected.

The Product Cycle

The motto of a market economy might be 'No-thing is permanent'. New products appear continually, while others disappear. At the early stage of a product, total demand is low, and costs of production are high. Many small firms are each trying to get ahead of their competitors by finding the variations in the commodity's specifications that most appeal to consumers, or the technique that slashes costs. Sometimes new products never get beyond that phase. They prove to be passing fads, or else they remain as high-priced items catering to a small demand; others, however, do become items of mass consumption. Successful firms in growing industries buy up, merge with or otherwise eliminate their less successful rivals. Simultaneously their costs fall, due to scale economies. Competition drives prices down along with costs. Eventually at the mature stage the industry is often dominated by a few giant firms. They become large, and conspicuous, parts of the nation's economy. Sooner or later, new products are introduced to erode the position of the established giants. Demand falls off, and unemployment occurs as the few remaining firms run into financial difficulties. A large but declining industry appears to many as a national disgrace. People ask themselves if the market system has failed because yesterday's healthy giants have become today's ailing firms. Large declining industries are, however, as much a natural part of a healthy changing economy as are small growing ones.

THE INTUITIVE CASE FOR THE MARKET SYSTEM

Economists have used two types of argument to demonstrate the advantages of a market system. The first, which can be called the intuitive case, is as old as economics itself. The case is intuitive in the sense that it is not laid out in equations leading to some mathematical, maximizing result. But it does follow from some hard reasoning, and it has been subjected to some searching intellectual probing. (What follows seeks to *present* the intuitive case, *not* to evaluate it.)

The best co-ordinator: It is argued that the market system co-ordinates economic decisions better than any known alternative. Compared with the alternatives, the decentralized market system is more flexible and leaves more scope for personal adaptation at any moment in time, and for quick adjustment to change over time. If, for example, a scarcity of oil raises its price, one individual can elect to leave her heating up high and economize on her driving, while another may wish to do the opposite. In order to obtain the same overall effect by non-price rationing, the authorities must force the same reduction in heating and driving on both individuals, independent of their tastes, doctor's advice and other perceived needs.

Furthermore, as conditions change over time, prices change, and decentralized decision-takers can react continuously, while government quotas, allocations and rationing schemes are slower to adjust. The market provides automatic signals *as a situation develops*, so that all the adjustments to some major economic shock do not have to be anticipated, and allowed for, by a body of central planners. Millions of adaptations to millions of changes in tens of thousands of markets are required every year; and it would be a Herculean task to anticipate these and plan the necessary adjustments.

A producer of growth: The flexibility of the market system induces growth. It does so by having every avenue for innovation explored by decentralized decision-takers employing privately owned capital. It is also powerful in allowing adaptations to change. The outlook is for major changes in resource availabilities in all economies over the next few decades. New products, new inputs and new techniques will have to be devised to cope with the changes that can already be foreseen, such as the exhaustion of fossil fuels. A decentralized economy will be more responsive in producing the necessary adaptations than will a bureaucratic, centrally planned economy, provided that its taxation system does not eliminate the profits that are the incentive for these adaptations.

Impersonal decisions: Another important part of the case for a market economy is that it tends to decentralize power and thus involves less coercion than does any other type of economy. Nonetheless, large firms and large unions are still left with substantial power – a point that many existing defences of market economies tend to ignore.

Probably the best attempt to make a case for the market, while recognizing the existence of market power, was made by Joseph Schumpeter. He argued that the economic power of particular firms and labour groups would not persist indefinitely. High profits and wages, earned by monopolistic firms and unions, are the spur for others to invent cheaper or better substitute products and techniques that allow their suppliers to gain some of these profits. He called this process **creative destruction**, which is the erosion of seemingly well-entrenched positions of economic power by new products and new production processes introduced to appropriate some of an existing monopoly's profits.

Command economies tend to put larger and more permanent concentrations of power into the hands of the central authorities than market economies put into the hands of large firms and unions. If markets are not to deal with allocation of people to jobs and of outputs to consumers, then some centralized coercive power is *necessary* to do the same thing. Such power creates incentives for bribery, corruption and allocation according to the tastes of the central administrators. If, at the going prices and wages, there are not enough flats or plum jobs to go around, the local bureaucrat will often allocate some to those who pay the largest bribe, some to those with religious beliefs, hairstyles or political views that he likes, and only the rest to those whose names come up on the waiting list.

Prices are related to costs: Competition tends to force the price of each commodity to bear a close relation to its costs of production. Assuming that private costs to firms reflect social costs to society, consumers are encouraged to choose, from among alternatives that they value equally, the one that uses fewer of the nation's resources. Minimizing the cost of satisfying any specific set of wants helps to maximize living standards because it frees resources to satisfy other wants.

THE FORMAL CASE FOR THE FREE MARKET

Professional economists wanted to be more precise about just what the market economy did so well. To do so they developed the proof that an idealization of the market economy (perfect competition) would lead, in equilibrium, to an *optimum* allocation of resources. This is an equilibrium situation which is *efficient* in the sense that it is impossible to make anyone better off without simultaneously making someone else worse off. We must now study that case. The first step is to clarify our understanding of the concept of efficiency.

Economic Efficiency

Efficiency requires avoiding the waste of resources. When labour is unemployed and factories lie idle (as occurs in serious recessions), their potential current output is lost. If these resources could be employed, total output would be increased and hence everyone could be made better off.

But full employment of resources by itself is not sufficient to prevent the waste of resources. Even when resources are being fully used, they may be used inefficiently. (i) If firms do not use the least costly method of producing their chosen outputs, resources are being wasted. (ii) If some firms produce at high cost while other firms produce at low cost, the industry's overall cost of producing its output is higher than necessary. (iii) If products on which people place a low value are being produced while products which people would value highly go unproduced, resources are also being used inefficiently.

To refine our ideas of the waste of resources we must define precisely the concepts of efficiency and inefficiency in resource use.

> **Resources are said to be used *inefficiently* when it would be *possible*, by using them differently, to make at least one household better off without making any household worse off. Conversely, resources are said to be used *efficiently* when it is *impossible*, by using them differently, to make any one household better off without making at least one other household worse off.**

Efficiency in the use of resources is often called **Pareto-optimality** or **Pareto-efficiency** in honour of the great Italian economist Vilfredo Pareto (1848–1923), who pioneered the study of efficiency. The three sources of inefficiency noted above suggest important conditions that must be fulfilled if economic efficiency is to be attained. These conditions are conveniently collected into two categories, productive efficiency and allocative efficiency.

Productive efficiency ensures that any bundle of goods and services is produced at the lowest possible resource cost. If productive efficiency is not achieved, the resource cost of producing the present bundle of goods can be lowered. The resources saved can then be used to produce more goods, and so allow someone to be made better off without making anyone worse off. (In the simplest case, all of the extra production can be given to one person, while everyone else gets the same as before.)

Allocative efficiency ensures that the bundle of goods produced is an efficient bundle. If allocative efficiency is not achieved, resources can be reallocated to produce a different bundle of goods which will allow someone to be made better off while no one is made worse off.

These two types of efficiency can be illustrated by the production possibility curve shown in Figure 1.1 on page 6. Productive efficiency ensures that the economy is on, rather than inside, its production possibility curve. Allocative efficiency ensures that the economy is at a point on that curve that is optimal. Being at an *optimal point* means that it is impossible to move to another point on the boundary and make someone better off without anyone else being made worse off. What is required to obtain these two types of efficiency?

Productive Efficiency

Productive efficiency requires that the output of any one commodity entails the lowest possible opportunity cost in terms of forgone outputs of other commodities. When this is not true, an unnecessary sacrifice of other commodities is being incurred; costs could be reduced and more resources spared for the production of other commodities.

The Conditions for Productive Efficiency

Two specific conditions must be fulfilled if productive efficiency is to be achieved.

Firms must be on their relevant cost curves: The first condition is that:

each firm should be on, rather than above, its relevant cost curve.

If the firm is making a short-run decision, it must be on the lowest achievable short-run cost curve. If the firm is making a long-run decision, it must be on, rather than above, its long-run cost curve. If not, there is (by definition) a less costly way for the firm to produce its present output. This kind of efficiency is often called *X-efficiency*, and its absence *X-inefficiency*.

All firms in an industry must have the same level of marginal cost: The second condition for productive efficiency ensures that production of any given total industry output is distributed among the producing firms so as to minimize total industry costs. This condition is that:

the marginal cost of producing the last unit of output should be the same for every firm in the industry.

To see the importance of this condition, assume that it is not fulfilled. Suppose that the Jones Brothers shoe manufacturing firm has a marginal cost of £40 for the last pair of shoes of some standard type that it produces, while Abercrombie Limited has a marginal cost of only £35 for the same type of shoe. If the Jones plant produces one less pair of shoes and the Abercrombie plant produces one more, total shoe output is unchanged, but total industry costs are reduced by £5. Thus £5 worth of resources will be freed to increase the production of other commodities.

Achieving Productive Efficiency

Any profit-maximizing firm will wish to produce *whatever output it produces* at the lowest possible cost. Not to do so would be to sacrifice profits by having higher costs than necessary. Thus profit maximization ensures that all firms will be motivated to satisfy the condition for X-efficiency by producing on, rather than above, their relevant cost curves.

Though easy to state, this condition is, however, often difficult to fulfil in practice. We know that firms sometimes, perhaps often, do not take advantage of all the cost-reducing opportunities available to them. This may be so, for example, if the opportunities arise out of some new technology that existing managers have not learned about, or are not trained to use. Or it may be due to lack of access to sufficient investment funds. One major reason for takeovers occurs when the existing management is not achieving the lowest costs, and the acquiring firm sees a chance to raise profits by cutting costs.

The second condition for productive efficiency concerns the allocation of production among producers. In perfect competition, this occurs automatically. Since all firms in an industry are faced with the same market price and all maximize their profits by equating marginal costs to price, all firms end up having the same marginal cost. For example, if the price of the type of shoe we considered above is £37 a pair, all perfectly competitive, profit-maximizing firms will produce that type of shoe until the marginal cost of the last pair that they produce is £37.

A multi-plant monopoly will wish to divide its production efficiently among its plants. It will thus allocate production so that all plants produce outputs that give rise to the same marginal cost. The efficient allocation among plants becomes a matter of internal organization with a monopoly that owns all of the plants. There is, however, no inherent barrier to doing so.

When firms face downward-sloping demand curves they do not equate marginal cost to price. There is then no reason why all of the firms in one industry should have the same marginal costs.

Allocative Efficiency

Allocative efficiency is achieved when the allocation of resources cannot be changed so as to make someone better off without making someone else worse off. Reallocating resources implies producing more of some goods and less of others – that is, changing the mix of production.

Although the basic concept is simple, allocative efficiency has some surprisingly subtle aspects. For this reason, we will analyse it in three ways: first intuitively; second, using the partial equilibrium tools of consumers' and producers' surplus; third, using the general equilibrium tools of production possibility curves and indifference curves. All three of these approaches yield the same result, but each has its own insights to offer.

The Intuitive Approach to Allocative Efficiency

The Condition for Allocative Efficiency

How many shoes should be produced for allocative efficiency? How many dresses? How many hats? The answer is that the economy's allocation of resources is efficient when, for every good produced, the marginal cost of production is equated to its price.

To understand the significance of this condition, assume that shoes sell for £30 a pair but have a marginal cost of £40. If one less pair of shoes were produced, the value that households place on the pair of shoes not produced would be £30. But by the meaning of opportunity cost, the resources that would have been used to produce that pair of shoes could instead produce other goods (say, a coat) valued at £40. If society can give up something its members value at £30 and obtain in return something its members value at £40, the original allocation of resources is inefficient. Someone can be made better off, and none need be worse off.

This is easy to see when the same household gives up the shoes and gets the coat. But it follows even when different households are involved, for the gaining household *could* compensate the losing household and still come out ahead.

Assume next that the shoe production is cut back until the price of a pair of shoes rises from £30 to £35, while its marginal cost falls from £40 to £35. The efficiency condition is now fulfilled in shoe production because *price = MC* = £35. Now if one less pair of shoes were produced, £35 worth of shoes would be sacrificed, while at most £35 worth of other commodities could be produced with the freed resources.

In this situation, the allocation of resources to shoe production is efficient because it is not possible to change it so as to make someone better off without making someone else worse off. If one household were to sacrifice the pair of shoes, it would give up goods worth £35, and would then have to obtain for itself all of the new production of the alternative commodity produced just to break even. It cannot gain without making an-

other household worse off. The same argument can be repeated for every commodity, and it leads to this conclusion:

> **the allocation of resources is efficient when each commodity's price equals its marginal cost.**

Achieving Allocative Efficiency

Perfect competition: We have already seen that perfectly competitive firms maximize their profits by equating marginal cost to price. Thus, when perfect competition is the prevailing market structure across the whole economy, price is equal to marginal cost for all production, and allocative efficiency is assured.

> **An economy in which output is produced under conditions of perfect competition is allocatively efficient.**

Monopoly: The monopoly price is greater than marginal cost. This violates the conditions for allocative efficiency because consumers pay for the last unit an amount that exceeds the opportunity cost of producing it. Consumers would be prepared to buy additional units for an amount greater than the cost of producing these units. Some consumers could be made better off, and none need be made worse off, by shifting extra resources into the production of the product. As a consequence, the monopoly produces an output that is *not* allocatively efficient. From this follows the classic, efficiency-based preference for competition over monopoly:

> **An economy which contains monopolies will not be allocatively efficient.**

Note also that this result extends beyond the case of a simple monopoly. Whenever a firm has any power over the market, in the sense that it faces a downward-sloping, rather than a horizontal demand curve, its profit-maximizing behaviour will lead it to produce where *MC* equals *MR*, *not* where *MC* equals price.

A command economy: We have seen that in a free-market economy, perfect competition achieves allocative efficiency by the decentralized decisions of millions of independent households and firms, each responding to market price. We have also seen that all profit-maximizing firms are motivated to achieve productive efficiency.

There are thus powerful decentralized forces pushing the economy toward efficient results.

Where a centrally planned (command) economy replaces the market mechanism and the profit motive, it must find ways to allocate resources across different products and industries and to allocate production across plants in the same industry. It must also find ways to motivate producers to minimize costs of whatever output they do produce.

These are not impossible tasks, but they have proven among the most difficult to do well in the Soviet Union, Yugoslavia, China and other countries that have, to some degree, rejected the profit motive and the price system.

The Consumers' Surplus Approach to Allocative Efficiency

The previous discussion of allocative efficiency can be formalized by using the concepts of consumers' and producers' surplus.

We first met consumers' surplus in Chapter 6. Faced with a single price for all units of some commodity, a consumer goes on buying more until the last unit is valued the same as its price. Consumers' surplus arises because the consumer would be willing to pay more than the given price for all but the last unit bought. Consumers' surplus, which is shown in Figure 23.1, is the difference between the total value consumers place on all the units consumed of some commodity and the payment consumers must make to purchase the commodity.

We now define the parallel concept of **producers' surplus**. This is the earnings of firms over and above their variable costs of production, i.e. total revenue minus total variable cost; it is the market value that the firm creates by producing goods, net of the value of the resources currently used to create these goods. (Fixed costs are not deducted from total revenue to determine producers' surplus because the fixed resources have no short-run opportunity cost by virtue of their being fixed. Of course, for long-run decisions all costs are variable.)

Producers' surplus is easily defined in terms of total revenues and total costs. For graphical analysis, however, we wish to show it on demand

FIGURE 23.1   Consumers' Surplus and Producers' Surplus

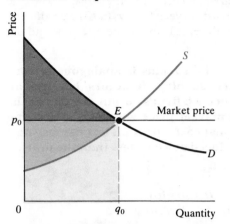

Consumers' surplus is the area under the demand curve and above the price line. Producers' surplus is the area above the supply curve and below the price line. The equilibrium price and quantity in this competitive market are p_0 and q_0. The total value consumers place on q_0 of the commodity is given by the sum of the three shaded areas. The amount they pay is p_0q_0, the rectangle consisting of the two lighter-shaded areas. The difference, shown as the dark-shaded area, is *consumers' surplus*.

The receipts to producers from the sale of q_0 units are also p_0q_0. The area under the supply curve, the colour-shaded area, is total variable cost, the minimum amount producers require to supply the output. The difference, shown as the light-grey shaded area, is *producers' surplus*.

and supply diagrams, all of which use average and marginal concepts. This is done in Figure 23.1, which should be studied now. It is described verbally below.

Note first that the market value of output is shown by the area defined by the equilibrium price and quantity. Graphically, that is the rectangle below the price line up to the quantity sold. Second, note that the total variable cost of producing *n* units is the sum of the marginal cost of each of those *n* units. For example, if the first unit adds £5 to costs, the second unit £6 and the third unit £7, the total variable cost of producing all three is £18. Graphically, the sum of all the marginal costs of the first *n* units of output, and hence the total variable cost of producing *n* units of output, is the area under the marginal cost curve up to *n* units of output.[1] Since the market value of output is the area below the price line, while variable costs are the area below the marginal cost curve, it follows that the producers' surplus is the area between the price line and the *MC* curve.

> **Producers' surplus is analogous to consumers' surplus. It occurs because all units of each firm's output are sold at the same market price while, given a rising marginal cost curve, all but the last unit is produced at a cost less than the market price.**

The Conditions for Allocative Efficiency

If the sum of the consumers' and producers' surplus is not maximized, output could be changed to increase the sum, and the extra surplus produced could be used to make someone better off without making anyone else worse off.

> **Allocative efficiency occurs at the point where the sum of consumers' plus producers' surplus is maximized.**

Achieving Allocative Efficiency

Perfect competition: The point where the sum of consumers' plus producers' surplus is maximized is where the demand curve intersects the supply curve, that is, the point of equilibrium in a competitive market. This is shown graphically in Figure 23.2.

The argument is along the following lines. For any output less than the competitive output, the demand curve is above the supply curve, which means that consumers value the last unit at an amount greater than its marginal cost of produc-

---

Those who know elementary calculus will find this idea easy. Letting C be total cost, V total variable cost, F total fixed cost and q output, we can write $C = V(q) + F$. This reads: total cost equals total variable cost, which varies with output, plus total fixed cost, which is a constant. To get to marginal cost, we merely differentiate total cost: $MC = dC/dq$. To get from marginal cost to total variable cost, we merely integrate the marginal cost function and subtract the constant of integration: $V = \int(MC)dq - F = V(q) + F - F$.

FIGURE 23.2 The Allocative Efficiency of Perfect Competition

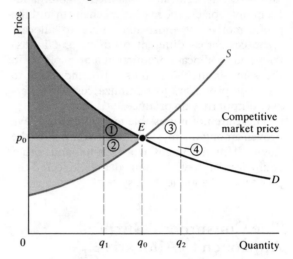

Competitive equilibrium is allocatively efficient because it maximizes the sum of consumers' plus producers' surplus. The competitive equilibrium occurs at the price-output combination, $p_0 q_0$. At that equilibrium, consumers' surplus is the dark-shaded area above the price line, while producers' surplus is the light-shaded area below the price line.

For any output less than q_0 the sum of the two surpluses is less than at q_0. For example, reducing output to q_1, but keeping price p_0, lowers consumers' surplus by area 1 and lowers producers' surplus by area 2.

For any output greater than q_0 the sum of the surpluses is also less than at q_0. For example, if producers are forced to produce output q_2 and sell it to consumers, who are forced to buy it at price p_0, producers' surplus is reduced by area 3 (the amount by which variable costs exceed revenue on those units), while the amount of consumers' surplus is reduced by area 4 (the amount by which expenditure exceeds consumers' satisfactions on those units).

Only the competitive output, q_0, maximizes the sum of the two surpluses.

---

tion. Suppose, for example, that the current output of shoes is such that consumers value at £45 an additional pair of shoes that adds £35 to costs. If it is sold at any price between £35 and £45, both producers and consumers gain; there is £10 of potential surplus to be divided between the two groups. In contrast, the last unit produced and sold at competitive equilibrium adds nothing to either consumers' or producers' surplus, since consumers value it at exactly its market price, and it adds the full amount of the market price to producers' costs.

If production were pushed beyond the competitive equilibrium, the sum of the two surpluses would be diminished. Assume, for example, that firms were forced to produce and sell further units of output at the competitive market price, and that consumers were forced to buy these extra units at that price. (Note that neither group would do so voluntarily.) Firms would lose producers' surplus on those extra units because their marginal costs of producing the extra output would be above the price they received for it. Purchasers would lose consumers' surplus because the valuation that they placed on these extra units, as shown by the demand curve, would be less than the price they would have to pay.

The sum of producers' and consumers' surplus is maximized *only* at the com- **petitive output, which is thus the only output that is allocatively efficient.**

If some authority wanted to 'maximize the sum of producers' and consumers' surplus', it could instruct firms to produce every unit up to the point at which the cost of making the last unit was just equal to the valuation the purchasers placed on that unit. The perfectly competitive market price provides exactly that signal.

Monopoly: Figure 23.2 shows that the perfectly competitive equilibrium output maximizes the sum of consumers' and producers' surplus. It follows immediately that the lower monopoly output must result in a smaller total of consumers' plus producers' surplus.

Why would producers and consumers agree to reduce their surpluses? The answer is that the monopoly equilibrium is not the outcome of voluntary agreement between the one producer and the many consumers. Instead it is imposed

FIGURE 23.3 The Allocative Inefficiency of Monopoly

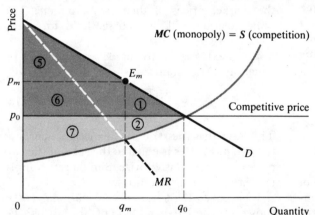

Monopoly is allocatively inefficient because it produces less than the competitive output and thus does not maximize the sum of consumers' and producers' surplus. If this market were perfectly competitive, price would be p_0, output q_0 and consumers' surplus would be the sum of areas 1, 5 and 6 (the dark-shaded area). When the industry is monopolized, price rises to p_m, and consumers' surplus falls to area 5. Consumers lose area 1 because that output is not produced; they lose area 6, because the price rise has transferred it to the monopolist.

Producers' surplus in a competitive equilibrium would be the sum of areas 7 and 2 (the light-shaded area). When the market is monopolized and price rises to p_m, the surplus area 2 is lost because the output is not produced. But the monopolist gains the area 6 from consumers (6 is known to be greater than 2 because p_m maximizes profits).

While area 6 is transferred from consumers' to producers' suplus by the price rise, *areas 1 and 2 are lost*. They represent the deadweight loss resulting from monopoly and account for its allocative inefficiency.

by the monopolist by virtue of the power it has over the market. When the firm reduces output below the competitive level, market price rises. As a result, consumers' surplus is diminished and producers' surplus is increased. In this way the monopoly gains at the expense of its customers. But that is not the whole story.

When output is lowered from the competitive level, there is a *net* loss of surplus. More is given up by consumers than is gained by the monopolist. Some surplus is lost because output between the monopolistic and competitive levels is not produced. This loss of surplus is called the *deadweight loss of monopoly*, and it arises because output between monopolistic and competitive levels is not produced. This is illustrated in Figure 23.3.

To recapitulate, there are two effects when a monopoly replaces competition:

Because monopoly output is below the competitive output, a smaller total of surplus is available to be shared between the consumers and the producer; but by raising price, the monopolist gets a larger share of this smaller pie for itself. As a result, the monopolist is better off, consumers are worse off, and the two groups taken together are worse off.

The General Equilibrium Approach to Allocative Efficiency[1]

So far, we have demonstrated the efficiency of perfect competition, using the tools of consumers' and producers' surpluses. These are the tools of partial equilibrium analysis which use demand and supply curves to study markets one at a time. They are based on *ceteris paribus* assumptions, looking at each market in isolation without explicitly studying the interrelations among markets.

We now study another approach, based on indifference curves and transformation curves, that looks beyond single markets. These are general equilibrium tools because they explicitly allow for the interrelations among markets.

[1] This section can be omitted without loss of continuity.

When the production and consumption of one commodity changes, for example, all consequent changes in the production and consumption of other commodities are allowed for.

Market Equilibrium

To analyse allocative efficiency using these tools, we look first at producers and then at consumers.

Producers' equilibrium: To begin, consider an economy where n different commodities are produced under conditions of perfect competition. Look first at any two, which we call commodities a and b. Because these are produced under perfectly competitive conditions, we know that in equilibrium:

$$MC_a = p_a \qquad (1)$$

and

$$MC_b = p_b \qquad (2)$$

where MC_a and MC_b are marginal costs of industries a and b respectively, and p_a and p_b are the market prices of their two products. The same relation will, of course, hold for every commodity.

The next step is to divide equation (1) by equation (2) to obtain:

$$\frac{MC_a}{MC_b} = \frac{p_a}{p_b} \,. \qquad (3)$$

This says that the ratio of the marginal costs in the two industries is equal to the ratio of the two prices – i.e. the relative price. Similar ratios apply to every pair of commodities.

What does the ratio of the marginal costs, shown on the left-hand side of (3), tell us? To illustrate, assume that the marginal cost of good a is £16, while that of good b is £4. Now assume that the production of good a is reduced by one unit, and the resources that are freed are used to produce more of good b. Sixteen pounds' worth of resources are freed from production of a, and, at b's marginal cost of £4 per unit, these can produce four units of good b. Using these illustrative figures, the ratio in (3) above takes on a value of four (£16/£4). This is the extra amount of good b that can be obtained by giving up one unit of good a.

This ratio is called the **marginal rate of**

transformation. The word transformation is not to be taken literally. We do not take units of good a and magically transform them into units of good b (as the ancient alchemists wished to transform base metals into gold). Instead, the 'magic' is performed by reallocating resources, so that the production of good a falls by one unit, and the production of good b rises by whatever amount the freed resources can produce.

Now we can rewrite (3), replacing the ratio of the marginal costs with the term marginal rate of transformation, which we abbreviate MRT:

$$MRT = \frac{p_a}{p_b} \cdot \qquad (4)$$

Figure 23.4 shows the graphical interpretation of this result for an economy with only two commodities.

In perfect competition the marginal rate of transformation between any pair of commodities is equal to the ratio of their market prices.

The result just stated in colour is important. Be sure that you understand the reasoning behind it.

Consumers' equilibrium: We saw in Chapter 8 that each consumer is in equilibrium when the marginal rate of substitution between each pair of commodities is equal to those commodities' relative price. (See Figure 8.7 on page 132.) The marginal rate of substitution shows the amount of good b that a consumer must be given to compensate for sacrificing one unit of good a. Using the abbreviation MRS for this concept, we can write the consumers' equilibrium as:

$$MRS = \frac{p_a}{p_b} \cdot \qquad (5)$$

The Condition for Allocative Efficiency

The condition for allocative efficiency is that the marginal rate of substitution should equal the marginal rate of transformation:

$$MRS = MRT \ . \qquad (6)$$

To understand why this is the efficiency condition, we will study a numerical example which involves changing the economy's allocation of resources and hence the bundle of goods produced. While this is being done, we will hold constant the bundle of goods consumed by all households except one. Then all the changes in total output will be reflected in changes in the consumption of this one household. Since, in equilibrium, all households have the same MRS, it does not matter which household we choose. The argument applies to each of them. This simple device allows us to see whether or not a reallocation of resources allows one consumer to be made better off while no other household is made worse off.[1]

We assumed in the previous section that the MRT between goods a and b was four. Now let us assume that the MRS for consumers is only two. The MRT tells us that we can get four units of b by giving up one unit of a. The MRS, however, tells us that households will be satisfied if they receive only two units of b for every unit of a given up. Now let the production of a fall by one unit and the production of b rise by four units. The household that we have chosen can be given two units of b to compensate it for the loss of a unit of a, according to its MRS. There are now two further units of b left over. This can be used to make someone better off while no one else is made worse off.

Now take the opposite case by letting the MRS be six, while the MRT remains at four. In these circumstances, more of b cannot be produced while compensating consumers for the loss of a. But resources could be reallocated in the other direction. The MRT tells us that, in order to produce one more unit of a, four units of b must be sacrificed. But the MRS tells us that consumers would be willing to sacrifice six units of b to get one unit of a. If one more unit of a is produced, the sacrifice is only four units of b. Since our household is willing to give up six units of b, it can be given the unit of a and only four units of b taken away, leaving it better off while all other households are in an unchanged position.

Finally, let the MRS and the MRT be equal at four. In this case, it is necessary to produce four less units of b to get one more unit of a, and that is the amount households are prepared to give up.

---

[1] An alternative device is to assume that the changes in output are shared out *equally* among all m households in the economy. Thus each change of one unit in the *production* of a commodity changes each household's *consumption* of that commodity by $1/m^{\text{th}}$ of a unit.

**FIGURE 23.4 The Marginal Rate of
Transformation**

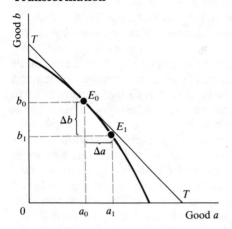

**The slope of the production possibility curve is
the *MRT*, and it equals the relative price of the
good under perfect competition.** The graph
illustrates the case of an economy that produces only
two goods, a and b. The curve is the economy's
production possibility curve showing all the
combinations of a and b that can be produced. It is
also called a transformation curve. When production
is at E_0, output is a_0 of commodity a and b_0 of
commodity b. Production then moves to point E_1 with
a_1 and b_1 of the two commodities. The changes are
shown by Δa and Δb in the Figure. The marginal rate
of transformation is the ratio of $\Delta b/\Delta a$, which is the
amount of b that can be obtained per unit of a given
up.
   The line TT is drawn tangent to the curve at the
point E_0. (Technical limitations in the artwork make
tangents hard to draw, but the line TT is supposed to
touch the production-possibility curve at E_0 *and lie
above it everywhere else*.) When the changes in a and b
are very small, the ratio $\Delta b/\Delta a$ along the production
possibility curve is approximately equal to the slope
of the tangent to the curve at the point from which
changes are being measured. *Graphically the slope of
the tangent to the curve at any point measures the* MRT
at that point. In the Figure, therefore, the slope of TT
measures the MRT at E_0.

So if the change is made, there is just enough
extra a to compensate for the forgone b. So the
household is neither better nor worse off. Now
consider a change in the other direction. Producing one less unit of a allows four more units of b to
be produced. Four units of b, however, is what

any household requires as compensation for
giving up one unit of a. So, if the change is made,
no one can be made better off while keeping
everyone else in an unchanged position.

**Whenever the *MRS* does not equal the
MRT, it is possible to reallocate resources and make someone better off
without making anyone else worse off.**

   Above we have illustrated this proposition
with an example. Figures 23.4 and 23.5 show the
same result graphically for a two-commodity

**FIGURE 23.5 The Conditions for Allocative
Efficiency**

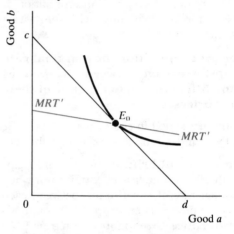

**For allocative efficiency the *MRS* must equal
the *MRT*.** The diagram shows a typical household in
equilibrium at point E_0 on the budget line cd. Because
the household faces the same price as do producers,
the slope of the budget line is equal to the MRT
(which is the slope of the line TT in Figure 23.4).
Because the consumer reaches a tangency with the
budget line, the MRS at E_0 must be equal to the
MRT.
   If producers face a relative price *different* from that
faced by households, the MRT will have a slope
different from the budget line. An example is shown
in the Figure by the line MRT', whose slope does not
equal that of the budget line cd. Consumers remain in
equilibrium at E_0. However, by altering the allocation
of resources, holding the consumption of all other
households constant, production – and hence this
consumer's consumption – could, by assumption, be
moved along the line MRT'. In this case, higher
indifference curves could be attained by moving to the
right along MRT'. Hence the equilibrium at E_0 is not
efficient.

example.[1] The common sense of the result is that, if people are willing to trade one good for another at a rate different from that at which these goods can be substituted for each other in production, there must be room for gain. More should be produced of the good that people value higher than its opportunity cost in production. For example, if people are willing to give up more *a* to get a unit of *b* than it is necessary to sacrifice when resources are reallocated, there is room to make someone better off without making anyone else worse off.

Achieving Allocative Efficiency

The condition for allocative efficiency is that $MRS = MRT$. We already know that consumers equate their MRSs between pairs of commodities to the ratio of those commodities' relative prices (equation (6) above). We also know that in perfect competition the marginal rate of transformation between any pair of commodities will equal the ratio of their prices (equation (4)). Since both consumers and producers face the same set of relative prices, it follows (by equating (4) and (6)) that in perfect competition the MRS will equal the MRT and allocative efficiency will be established.

This is the key result. It is also an example of a chain of reasoning referred to in the Foreword. Each step is obvious enough, but the cumulative effect of several steps, built one on the other, can seem forbidding on first encounter. The ideas involved are not difficult, but to reinforce them we now review the entire argument in summary form.

Recapitulation

(1) The efficiency condition is that the marginal rate of substitution in consumption (MRS) should equal the marginal rate of transformation in production (MRT). This is the type of condition we have encountered on several previous occasions. If goods can be transformed into each other at a rate that differs from the rate consumers are willing to trade one for the other, there is room for profitable substitution. More of the goods that consumers value (in terms of the quantities of other goods they are willing to forgo) more highly than their opportunity cost can be produced to everyone's gain. Only when consumers value goods at their opportunity cost is there no room for further gain.

(2) Under perfect competition, each product is produced where its marginal cost equals its price.

(3) For any pair of commodities produced under perfect competition, therefore, the ratio of their marginal costs will equal the ratio of their prices.

(4) The ratio of two commodities' marginal costs is equal to the marginal rate of transformation of one into the other.

(5) In consumption, each household equates its marginal rate of substitution between any pair of goods to the slope of its budget line. The slope equals the ratio of the prices of the two goods.

(6) Since under perfect competition, both MRT and MRS between any pair of commodities are made equal to the ratio of these commodities' prices, it follows that MRS must equal MRT. The condition for allocative efficiency is fulfilled under perfect competition.

Can an Optimum Allocation of Resources be Achieved?

Can an optimum, or Pareto-efficient, allocation of resources be achieved in the real world? Achieving it requires, among other things, that the following conditions be met.

(1) *For an optimal allocation of resources, there should be perfect competition in all sectors of the economy, therefore ensuring that marginal cost will equal price everywhere.* This condition is sometimes called *pluperfect* competition. If it does not exist, we cannot be sure what the effect will be of making marginal cost equal marginal revenue somewhere in the economy. Specifically, if in a world of mixed-market structures we break up one monopoly and make it into a competitive

---

[1] You may be tempted to put the two Figures together, plotting the indifference curve from 23.5 against the production possibility curve in 23.4. Indeed some elementary books do just that. But remember that 23.4 refers to a whole economy while 23.5 refers to a single consumer. We could only combine the two diagrams if the economy contained but one consumer – in which case we could not have price-taking behaviour. To be able to combine indifference curves with production possibility curves on a single diagram, we need to construct what are called *community indifference curves*. This requires procedures well beyond the scope of any introductory textbook.

industry, we have no general presumption, even in a theoretical model, that this will move us closer to an optimum position.

(2) *For an optimal allocation of resources under perfect competition, there should be no external economies or diseconomies of scale.* An external economy or diseconomy is beyond the influence of a single firm, and thus does not enter into the firm's calculations, even though it may be important for society.

(3) *For perfect competition to produce an optimal allocation of resources, there should be no divergence between private and social cost anywhere in the economy.* From society's point of view it pays to maximize consumers' plus producers' surplus only if the demand curve indicates the value the society places on output of each commodity and if the marginal cost curve represents the opportunity cost to society of the resources used in production. We will see in the next chapter that social and private costs often diverge.

It is clear that these conditions for an optimal allocation of resources are not fulfilled in any modern economy. In particular, perfect competition does not prevail everywhere, since many firms face downward-sloping curves. These firms will not take production to the point where marginal cost equals price.

The theory of the optimal allocation of resources under perfect competition provides uncertain guidance to practical policies of market intervention by the central authorities. Economic theory does *not* predict that in our societies of mixed-market structures *every* increase in the degree of competitiveness will always increase the efficiency of resource allocation. To evaluate current policy, we need to know the effects on the efficiency of resource allocation of interventions designed to produce a little more or a little less competition in some sectors of the economy. Unfortunately, this is just what we cannot do in general, and every case must be studied and evaluated in terms of its own specific circumstances.[1]

The theory of the optimal allocation of resources under perfect competition also has a substantial political appeal which is briefly discussed in Box 23.1.

UNSETTLED QUESTIONS

The Classical condemnation of non-competitive forms of behaviour was based on the belief that

---

[1] This important proposition upsets much of the basis of piecemeal welfare economics. We know how to identify the best of all possible worlds (from the limited point of view of the optimum we are discussing), but we have little clear idea of how to order two states of the very imperfect world in which we live. If this were not so, economists could not disagree as much as they do about specific policy measures. More advanced students may wish to consult one of the early demonstrations of this proposition given in R. G. Lipsey and K. J. Lancaster, 'The General Theory of Second Best', *The Review of Economic Studies*, Vol. XXIV, No. 63, 1956–7.

BOX 23.1   THE POLITICAL APPEAL OF PERFECT COMPETITION

A long time ago, the historian Lord Acton said something that is no less true today than it was in his own time: 'Power tends to corrupt and absolute power corrupts absolutely.' To anyone who fears concentrations of power, the perfectly competitive model is almost too good to be true. In it, no single firm, and no single consumer, has any power over the market. Individually they are passive quantity-adjusters. If we add to this the assumption that firms are profit maximizers, all firms become passive responders to market signals, doing what is most desirable from the society's point of view. The great impersonal force of the market produces an appropriate response to every important change. For example, if tastes change, prices will change, and the allocation of resources will move in the appropriate direction.

In perfectly competitive markets, countless firms react to the same price changes. If one refuses to react, others will be eager to make the appropriate changes. If one firm refuses to take coloured employees, or takes any other decision based on prejudice, thousands of other firms will recognize that profit maximization is not consistent with discrimination on the basis of race, colour, creed or anything other than how hard a person works.

It is a noble model: no one has power over anyone, and yet the system behaves in a co-ordinated way. Many will feel that it is a pity that it corresponds so imperfectly to reality as we know it today. Not surprisingly, some people still cling tenaciously to the belief that the perfectly competitive model describes the world in which we live; so many problems would disappear if only it did.

the alternative to monopoly was perfect competition. Today we realize that the effective choice is often not between monopoly and perfect competition, but between more or less oligopoly, so that we are not sure what effects a specific intervention will have on price and output. Thus, even if we accept the perfectly competitive result as being more desirable than a completely monopolistic one, this does not in itself tell us much about the real decisions that face us. In this section we shall discuss competitive and monopolistic situations in general terms. We do this because we wish to study and evaluate the effects of encouraging a little more or less competition than we now have.

The Importance of the Given-cost Assumption

The Classical predictions about monopoly depend critically on the assumption that costs are unaffected when an industry is monopolized. If any savings are effected by combining numerous competing groups into a single integrated operation, then the costs of producing any given level of output will be lower than they were previously. If this reduction does occur, then it is possible for output to be raised and price to be lowered as a result of the monopolization of a perfectly competitive industry. Such a case is shown in Figure 23.6.

> **The monopolization of an industry, combined with a sufficiently large consequent increase in efficiency, can result in a fall in price and a rise in quantity produced, as compared to the competitive industry.[1]**

Of course, the monopolization of an industry might reduce the efficiency of production and so shift the marginal cost curve upwards. In this case, monopolization will, *a fortiori*, raise price and lower output as compared to the competitive industry. You should draw your own diagram, showing the effects of a monopolization that caused costs to rise above those ruling under competition.

---

[1] You should be able to show for yourself that if the elasticity of demand were less than one at the competitive price, the monopolist would reduce output and raise price, no matter how large the reduction in its costs.

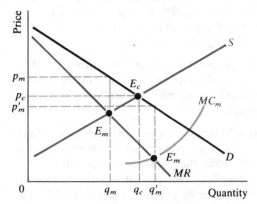

FIGURE 23.6 A Monopoly That Reduces Costs

If a monopoly reduces costs sufficiently, it may result in a lower price and higher output than would perfect competition. The competitive equilibrium is at E_c, with price p_c and quantity q_c. Monopolization with unchanged costs raises price to p_m and lowers output to q_m. If the integration of the industry reduces costs to MC_m, equilibrium shifts to E'_m with an output q'_m and price p'_m.

The Effect of Market Structure in the Very Long Run

The Classical case against monopoly concerns the allocation of resources within the context of a fixed technology. In the very long run, however, the production function is changing due to both the discovery of lower-cost methods of producing old products and the introduction of new and improved products. Does market structure affect the rate of innovation in the very long run?

The Incentive to Innovate

Both the monopolist and the perfect competitor have a profit incentive to introduce cost-reducing innovations. A monopoly can always increase its profits if it can reduce costs. Furthermore, since it is able to prevent the entry of new firms into the industry, these additional profits will persist into the long run. Thus, a monopoly has both a short- and a long-run incentive to reduce its costs.

Firms in perfect competition or in monopolistic competition have the same incentive in the short run, but not in the long run. In the short run, a reduction in costs will allow a firm that was just covering costs to earn profits. In the long run, other firms will be attracted into the industry by these profits. Existing firms will copy the cost-saving innovation, and new firms will enter the industry using the new techniques. This will go on until the profits of the innovator have been eliminated.

Monopolies have both a short- and a long-run incentive to innovate; perfectly competitive firms have only a short-run incentive.

The effectiveness of profits as an incentive to reduce costs for a firm in perfect competition will thus depend on the magnitude of the extra profits and on how long they persist. For example, if an innovation can be copied in a few months the profits earned over that period may not be sufficient to compensate the innovating firm for the costs of risks involved in making the innovation.

Funds for research and development: So far we have considered the profit incentive to innovate. Another consideration is the availability of the resources needed to finance research to develop new methods and new products. The large profits available to monopolistic firms provide a ready fund out of which research and development will be financed. The typical, perfectly competitive firm, however, is only earning enough to cover all its costs, and it will have few funds to spare for research and development. For example, few of the innovations that have vastly raised agricultural productivity over the last century were developed by the typical competitive farming unit; they were developed, rather, by a few oligopolistic manufacturers of farm equipment and by researchers in universities and in government-financed research institutions.

Penalties for not innovating: A further argument is that competitive firms *must* innovate or they will lose out to their competitors, while, although monopolists have an incentive to innovate, they do not need to do so because they are insulated from potential competition by their barriers to entry. Those who do not accept this argument say that it is wrong to think of a monopolist or oligopolist as shielded from all competition. It is always possible that some new firm will be able to break into the market by developing some new, similar, but superior product that evades existing patents and other

barriers to entry. Furthermore, the larger the monopoly profits of the existing firm(s), the larger the incentive for new firms to break into the market. Thus, it is argued, all monopoly and oligopolistic firms are in potential competition with possible new entrants, and the firm that sits back and does not innovate will not long remain profitable. A second argument that opponents advance is that the penalty for not innovating is not always high in perfect competition. If innovations are hard to copy, then there *is* a strong incentive for a competitive firm to innovate and a big penalty for firms who do not innovate because a long time will be needed before other firms can copy and catch up with the innovator. On the other hand, if innovations are easy to copy, there is smaller incentive for the competitive firm to innovate and a smaller penalty for the firm that fails to innovate, since it is easy for it to copy and catch up with the innovator. The above discussion may be summarized as follows.

All firms have an incentive to innovate since they can increase their profits with a successful innovation. The greater the barriers to entry and the harder it is for other firms already in the industry to copy the innovation, the longer will the profits of innovating persist and, thus, the larger will be the incentive to innovate. In competitive industries without barriers to entry, there will be little incentive to make innovations that are very easily copied, since both the profits of innovating and the losses from not innovating ahead of other firms will be very short-lived.

Schumpeter's defence of oligopoly and monopoly: The greatest opponent of the Classical preference for perfect competition was the distinguished Austrian (and later American) economist, Joseph A. Schumpeter. Schumpeter's theory relies on many of the forces just discussed. His basic argument has two main parts.

The first part is that innovations that lower costs of production – by increasing output per head and creating economic growth – have a much larger effect on living standards than any 'misallocation' of resources which causes too much production of one kind of commodity and too little of another at any one time. Modern measures made since Schumpeter wrote have tended to support his contention. It appears unlikely that the losses due to monopolistic and oligopolistic misallocations are more than 2 or 3 per cent of a country's national income. But the national income of most countries was for many years growing near that rate *each year*, and a growth rate of 3 per cent per year doubles material living standards in under 25 years.

The second part of Schumpeter's argument is that monopolistic and oligopolistic market forms are more conducive to growth than perfect competition. He claimed that only the incentive of

profits leads people to take the great risks of innovation, and that market power is much more important than competition in providing the climate under which innovation occurs. The large short-run profits of the firms with market power provide the incentive for others to try to usurp some of these for themselves. If a frontal attack on the major barriers to entry is not possible, then the barriers will be circumvented by such dodges as the development of similar products against which the established firms will not have entry protection. Schumpeter called the replacing of one entrenched position of market

---

BOX 23.2 INNOVATION AND CREATIVE DESTRUCTION: BALLPOINT PENS

In 1945, the American businessman Milton Reynolds developed a new type of pen that wrote with a ball-bearing rather than the then-conventional nib. He formed the Reynolds International Pen Company, capitalized at $26,000, and began production on 6 October 1945.

The Reynolds pen was introduced with a good deal of fanfare by Gimbels, the New York department store, which guaranteed that the pen would write for two years without refilling. The price was set at $12.50. Gimbels sold 10,000 pens on 29 October 1945, the first day they were on sale. In the early stages of production the cost of production was estimated to be around $0.80 per pen.

The Reynolds International Pen Company quickly expanded production. By early 1946, it employed more than 800 people in its factory and was producing 30,000 pens per day. By March 1946 it had $3 million in the bank.

Macy's, Gimbels' traditional rival, introduced an imported ballpoint pen from South America. Its price was $19.98 (production costs unknown).

The heavy sales quickly elicited a response from other pen manufacturers. Eversharp introduced its first model in April, priced at $15.00. In July 1946 *Fortune* magazine reported that Shaeffer was planning to put out a pen at $15.00, and Eversharp announced its plan to produce a 'retractable' model priced at $25.00. Reynolds introduced a new model, but kept the price at $12.50. Costs were estimated at $0.60 per pen.

The first signs of trouble emerged. The Ball Point Pen Company of Hollywood put a $9.95 model on the market, and a manufacturer named David Kahn announced plans to introduce a pen selling for less than $3.00. *Fortune* reported fears of an impending price war in view of the growing number of manufacturers and the low cost of production. In October Reynolds introduced a

new model, priced at $3.85, that cost about $0.30 to produce.

By Christmas 1946 approximately 100 manufacturers were in production, some of them selling pens for as little as $2.98. By February 1947 Gimbels was selling a ballpoint pen made by the Continental Pen Company for $0.98. Reynolds introduced a new model priced to sell at $1.68, but Gimbels sold it for $0.88 in a price war with Macy's. Reynolds felt betrayed by Gimbels and introduced a new model listed at $0.98. By this time ballpoint pens had become economy rather than luxury items, but they were still highly profitable.

In mid-1948 ballpoint pens were selling for as little as $0.39 and costing about $0.10 to produce. In 1951 prices of $0.25 were common. Within six years the power of the monopoly was gone for ever. Since that time ballpoint pens have become *the* writing instrument over most of the world. Although elaborate models can be bought in the UK at prices of over £1, perfectly good, basic pens sell for less than 20p. They are a universally accepted commodity – at least until some new writing innovation sweeps them away – and the firms manufacturing them long since ceased to do more than cover their full opportunity costs.

Monopoly power is worth having even if the attempt to perpetuate it is sure to fail eventually. The lag between an original monopoly and its subsequent erosion by competition may be long enough to ensure large profits to the monopolist. It is estimated, for example, that Milton Reynolds earned profits as high as $500,000 *in a single month* – about twenty times his original investment. The lessons are clear: monopoly profits are a spur to innovation and also to the entry of competitors that eventually eliminate these profits.

power by another through the invention of new products or new production techniques the *process of creative destruction*.

Since, in Schumpeter's theory, monopoly and oligopoly are more conducive to growth-creating innovations than perfect competition, it follows that the 'worse' the allocation of resources at any moment of time, i.e. the greater the amount of monopolization, the more rapid the rate of innovation and the resulting long-run rise in living standards. This important hypothesis cannot be handled with normal long-run theory, because long-run theory *assumes* constant technology.

Schumpeter's theory is not easy to test. Empirical work does suggest, however, that there may be more to his argument when it is applied to oligopolies than to textbook monopolies. Box 23.2 discusses an example of the kind of creative destruction that does occur in oligopolistic industries. Although spectacular, the ballpoint-pen case is not an isolated illustration. Pocket calculators provide one of the many recent examples. When they were first introduced in the early 1970s, their capacities were limited, prices were high, and so were the profits on each calculator sold. Customer acceptance was, however, immediate. As a result, many firms producing other products, and many new firms, rushed into production. Technological advance was rapid. While the capacities of the machines expanded, competition forced prices down. Today, consumers can choose from a vast array of calculators. Their prices are closely related to costs, so that producing firms find these lines only moderately profitable. A similar process occurred with personal computers, which started as expensive luxuries and evolved into low-cost items for everyday use.

The Effect of Market Structure on Consumers' Range of Choice

It is sometimes argued that one of the virtues of competition among several producers is that it presents consumers with a wide range of differentiated commodities, while complete monopoly tends towards uniformity of product. This is a very-long-run problem because we are concerned with changing the number of products to be produced.

An example from radio and television: An interesting case, in which competition tends to produce a nearly uniform product while monopoly tends to produce widely differentiated ones, is the case of radio and television. Consider an example in which there are two potential radio audiences: one group, comprising 80 per cent of the total audience, wishes to hear pop music; the other group, comprising 20 per cent, wishes to hear classical music. Each individual radio station seeks to maximize its own listening audience.

If there is only the one station, it will produce pop music. If a second competing station is now opened up, its most profitable policy will be to produce a similar pop-music programme because half of the large audience is better than all of the small one. A third station would also prefer a third of the large audience to all of the small one. Indeed five stations would be needed before it would be profitable for any one station to produce classical music. Thus competition between a few stations tends to produce two or three almost identical pop-music programmes, each competing for a share of the large audience.

A monopoly controlling two stations would not, however, pursue this policy. To maximize its total listening audience it would produce pop music on one station and classical music on the other. The monopoly might spend more money on preparing the programme for the larger audience, but it would not spend money to produce a similar programme on its second station – the optimal policy for its second station is to go after the other 20 per cent of potential listeners so that, between the two channels, the monopoly would have the maximum audience.

In both cases, of monopoly and competition, each individual firm tries to maximize its own listening audience, but two competing stations will both go after the same large audience, ignoring the minority group, while two stations owned by one monopoly will go after both audiences, one for each station. Under these circumstances, competition produces a uniformity of product which ignores the desires of the minority, while monopoly produces a varied product catering to the desires of both the majority and the minority group.

Product selection: The above example illustrates the problem of product choice that has recently concerned modern theorists of industrial organization. The Classical model takes commodities as given. With differentiated products, however, the number of conceivable products is infinite and the firm must *choose* which products to develop and then market. Think, for example, of the endless alternative types of cars which could be produced by varying the characteristics of existing cars. How do firms decide which of the many possible products to produce? Why do competing firms sometimes choose very similar products and at other times seek to establish substantial differences from competitors' products? These are interesting issues on which modern industrial organization theory has shed substantial light.[1]

Conclusion

The theory of the optimality of perfect competition is an intellectual triumph in providing an abstract demonstration of the power of decentralized decision-taking. It shows what seems counter-intuitive to many non-economists:

> conscious co-operation is not always the best route to desirable social outcome; the atomistic pursuit of self-interest can sometimes produce a better outcome than the co-operative route.

The analysis of efficiency is also an important aid to understanding the real world. Most economists who have spent time in countries where price signals have been seriously distorted – by such policy interventions as price controls, subsidies, import restrictions, state trading boards, and profit restraints – do not doubt the power of major inefficiencies to reduce living standards.

The intuitive defence for placing significant reliance on the price system to influence the nation's allocation of resources is a very strong one. The world over, governments of the left and the right have been accepting that message more and more during the last few decades. Soviet Premier Mikhail Gorbachev is but the latest in a long line of leaders to come to understand the

power of the market through the experience of running non-market systems. As a result, governments of all political persuasions have been placing more reliance on decentralized decision-taking, operating through markets. An understanding of how such decision-taking works, and why it tends to produce an effective use of the society's resources, is one of economists' most important insights.

Another great insight concerns the power of competitive behaviour to protect consumers from exploitation in the short and the long-run, and to produce increases in living standards via profit-seeking, innovative behaviour in the very long run. The other side of this pro-competitive coin is the Classical mistrust of monopoly. Schumpeter's support of profits as an engine of creative destruction can be applied to oligopoly, without having to embrace textbook monopoly as a desirable market structure. Ever since Adam Smith, economists have repeated the warning that the behaviour of established monopolists is usually not in the social interest. Many Marxists have seen good and bad social behaviour as being the prerogative of particular classes. The Classical economists' message, however, was that *any monopoly power* is against the social interest. Adam Smith observed that businessmen rarely got together, even for a picnic, without plotting some new action to exploit consumers. The same might be said for monopolies of labour unions and government bodies.

> The Classical prescription is that monopoly power is something to be avoided whenever possible; it should be discouraged in any form in which it might arise in both the private and the public sectors.
> The Schumpeterian prescription is that market forces will break up monopoly power *provided* that governments do not support that power by taking action to restrict entry – which they often do.

All of these insights are powerful and valuable. Problems arise, however, when attempts are made to prove the *perfection* of any real market economy. Does the economy, as we know it, produce an optimal allocation of resources? Economic theory answers this question with a

---

[1] For further discussion, advanced students may wish to consult B. C. Eaton and R. G. Lipsey, 'Product Differentiation', in R. Schmalensee and R. Willig (eds), *Handbook of Industrial Organization* (Elsevier Science Publishers, 1989).

BOX 23.3 POLITICAL FLAWS IN THE FORMAL DEFENCE OF THE PRICE SYSTEM

Although the proof of the optimality of perfect competition was an intellectual triumph, basing the practical case for the market system on this proof had some serious consequences. While professional economists went on studying and refining the model, and their academically bound graduate students went on learning it, the great bulk of their students were sent out into the world with an intellectual defence of the market economy that would not stand up to five minutes' rough handling by anyone who knew anything about the actual behaviour of real markets.

It was obvious to most non-economists who were exposed to the economists' model that the assumptions of perfect competition are not fulfilled in the world in which we live. Many people would have accepted the proposition that market economies were superior to other attainable forms of economic organization. They were not willing, however, to join Voltaire's Dr Pangloss in holding that, whatever misery and injustice it produced, a real-world market economy was the best of all possible economic worlds (i.e. the only *optimal* economy).

The concentration of the economists' case for the market economy on the formal defence had some disastrous consequences. First, many graduate students who found the case unconvincing went into the civil service and elsewhere in the 1950s, 1960s and 1970s convinced that there was no strong case for the price system.

Second, a vulnerable flank was exposed to any critics who were prepared to admit that perfect competition bore little relation to real-world market economies. It was not long before orthodox economists suffered a crushing defeat in the battlefield for public opinion. The defeat was administered by the man who, as a result, was the most commonly read and best-known academic economist in the 1960s and 1970s, John Kenneth Galbraith.

In the first hundred pages of his classic *American Capitalism*, Galbraith has a wonderful time ridiculing the picture of the workings of the American economy painted by the perfectly competitive model. He has no trouble in showing that the case for the price system based on the optimality of perfect competition fails when applied to any modern economy. Galbraith's main point is that prices of goods and factors do not fluctuate with every movement of demand or supply as they

do in the model of perfect competition. Instead they are administered by large firms and unions having market power. In this he is undoubtedly correct, and his point is sufficient to destroy the possibility that actual market economies could be optimal. Academic economists who rested their case for market economies on perfect competition had no effective reply, and Galbraith was left in possession of the field. The academics returned to the classroom to continue to show that the optimality of perfect competition survived a host of purely formal obstacles that were suggested by the new, set-theoretic approach to mathematics.

Had academic economists rested more of their case on the intuitive justification, they would not have had so much difficulty dealing with Galbraith's critique. After all, the general case for the price system – as being *relatively* effective in co-ordinating decentralized decisions – is still valid with administered prices, even if full optimality is not achieved. This is because economies with administered prices still allocate resources in response to consumer demand and relative scarcities of basic materials. Furthermore, arbitrary power of firms and unions is severely limited in the long term by Schumpeter's process of creative destruction.

As it was, however, Galbraith's attack was widely read and no really popular statement of the modern intuitive case for the free market received one-tenth as wide a distribution. Main-line economists have only themselves to blame for this.

Too little effort has been devoted to developing the theoretical case for *more or less* government intervention in the kinds of market economy actually found in the real world. Even today, graduate students are, as a matter of course, put through a rigorous training in proving all the theorems about the optimality of perfect competition, and often left with the view that this is the intellectual basis of the case for the market economy. They are seldom given help in core courses in thinking about the issue of more or less intervention into existing market economies.

Few really good intellectual defences of actual market economies have been publicized by those capable of doing so at the popular level; the intellectual case for our mixed market societies has yet to be made with a popular force equal to that of Galbraith's attack which is contained in his book *The New Industrial State*.

clear 'no', since many of the conditions needed for Pareto optimality are absent from any modern economy. Consider, for example, the many giant manufacturing firms who sell in oligopolistic markets. Whatever else they may be, they are certainly not price-takers. The attempt to defend the *perfection* of the price system is doomed to failure by the economists' own analysis of the necessary conditions for optimality. Some of the consequences for political economy of relying primarily on the formal defence of the price system are briefly discussed in Box 23.3.

Pluperfect competition is unattainable. A mixture of competitive, oligopolistic and monopolistic markets is attainable. Furthermore, most economists agree that oligopolies are preferable to monopolies. As we observed in Chapter 14:

the defence of oligopoly is that, given the efficiency of large-scale production, oligopoly may be the most competitive system that is available in the real world. The challenge to policy-makers is to keep oligopolists competing with each other, rather than co-operating to obtain monopoly results.

The realistic defence of the price system, then, has to be that it is better than any known alternative for making the majority of decisions concerning the allocation of resources. Those who accept this position are still free to disagree on the extent that government intervention is needed to alter the results that would be achieved by unhindered markets. After all, virtually everyone agrees that some intervention is desirable. Most debates among most social observers, therefore, concern the degree of government intervention that is called for – intervention into a system where decentralized market decisions exert the predominant influence on the allocation of resources. This range of debate, within the framework of agreement about the general value of the market, is sufficient to encompass the major parties in the UK, as well as most non-communist parties in the world's developed nations.

SUMMARY

1. Key characteristics of market economies are (i) their ability to co-ordinate decentralized decisions, (ii) their ability to do so without conscious control, (iii) their determination of the distribution of income, and (iv) the product cycle.
2. The intuitive defence of the price system argues that feasible market economies provide a better means for allocating a nation's resources than any known alternative in its ability to co-ordinate decisions, create growth, minimize personal power over economic decisions and provide efficiency by having relative prices reflect relative costs.
3. The formal defence of the price system lies in the demonstration that perfect competition leads to an optimal allocation of resources. Such an economy is Pareto-efficient in that there is *no* reallocation of resources that will make someone better off without making at least one other person worse off.
4. Productive efficiency requires that all firms be producing on, rather than above, their relevant cost curves (X-efficiency) and that any two firms producing the same product equate their marginal costs. Profit maximization is sufficient to produce X-efficiency but not the equating of marginal costs, which requires perfect competition.
5. Allocative efficiency requires that the mix of products produced be Pareto-efficient. The conditions are that marginal cost should equal price in all markets (which maximizes the sum of producers' and consumers' surplus) or that the marginal rate of transformation in production should equal the marginal rate of substitution in consumption. These conditions are fulfilled under universal perfect competition, but not when firms face negatively sloped demand curves.
6. Optimality is a long-run proposition concerned with making the most of given factor supplies when production occurs with given production functions. A different set of issues concerns the influence of alternative market structures on very-long-run behaviour. Some economists argue that oligopolies will be more

conducive to growth than perfect competition even where they succeed in erecting entry barriers – which will inevitably prove to be temporary.

7. Another very-long-run issue concerns the effect of market structure on the variety of differentiated products available to satisfy a diversity of consumers' tastes. Several competing firms will sometimes result in less variety than would a monopoly.

TOPICS FOR REVIEW

- Characteristics of the price system as a social control mechanism
- The intuitive defence of the price system
- Producers' surplus
- Pareto optimality
- Productive and allocative efficiency
- The optimality of perfect competition and the non-optimality of monopoly
- The equality of marginal rate of substitution and the marginal rate of transformation
- The effect of market structure on long-term growth
- The effect of market structure on consumers' range of choice

---

24

The Case for Government Intervention

An unkind critic of economics once said that economists have two great insights: *markets work* and *markets fail*. An unkind critic of politics once added that economics was thus a step ahead of both the political left and the political right, each of which accepts only one of these insights. Whatever may be true of others, economists do try to take the critical step of showing when each of these insights applies, and why.

We have seen that the general case for reliance on free markets lies in the belief that decentralized decision-taking is more efficient than fully centralized decision-taking. We have also seen that the general case for some government intervention is that most people wish to mitigate the disastrous results that the market produces for some people, and to improve the functioning of those markets which they believe do not work well. Thus, the practical issue is not to choose between unhampered free-market economies and fully centralized, command economies. It is, instead, to choose the mix of market and government determination that best suits people's hopes and needs.

In this chapter, we study the reasons for government intervention. In the next chapter we study the choice of the methods and the amounts of such interventions.

THE CASE AGAINST COMPLETELY FREE MARKETS

The term **market failure** describes any market performance that is judged to be less good than the best possible performance. The word *failure* in this context is potentially misleading:

> **market failure means that the best *attainable outcome* has not occurred; it does *not* mean that nothing good has happened.**

There are two somewhat different senses in which the phrase is sometimes used. One is the failure of the market system to achieve efficiency in the allocation of society's scarce resources; the other is the failure to serve social goals other than efficiency, such as a desired distribution of income or the preservation of value systems.

We divide our discussion between failure to achieve efficiency and failure to achieve other goals.

Failure to Achieve Efficiency

The sources of market failure that are related to efficiency mainly concern allocative efficiency. They cause a non-optimal bundle of goods to be produced. Some, however, concern productive efficiency. They cause goods to be produced at a higher cost than is necessary.

Public Goods

The most dramatic form of market failure, within the category of efficiency, concerns goods that would not be produced at all under a market system.

There are certain goods and services which, once produced, can be consumed by everyone in the society. Such goods are called **public goods** or **collective consumption goods**. National defence is a prime example. An adequate defence establishment protects all people in the country whether they want it or not, and there is no market where one individual can buy more of it and another individual less. The quantity of national defence must be decided collectively. Other examples of collective consumption goods are the beautification of a city, an embankment to protect a city from a flood, lighthouses and traffic lights, and a marine weather-forecasting system.

Market systems cannot compel payment for a collective consumption good since there is no way to prevent a person who refuses to pay for the good from receiving its services. Private, profit-seeking firms will thus fail to produce a public good. Governments, by virtue of their power to tax, can provide the services and collect from everyone.

Externalities

A major source of market failure under the general category of efficiency stems from what are called external effects. When these occur, some quantities of the goods in question will be produced. Compared with the optimal quantities, however, there will be too much of some goods and too few of others. To understand externalities, we must first look at the concept of costs.

Costs, as economists define them, concern the value of resources used in the process of production. According to the opportunity-cost principle, this value is measured by what the resources would produce in their best alternative use. But what is this best alternative?

When a timber company buys a forest, it perhaps regards the alternative to cutting the trees this year as cutting them five years hence. But citizens in the area may value the forest as a nature sanctuary or recreation area. The firm values the forest for the trees; the local residents may value the trees for the forest. The two values need not be the same.

Private and social costs: This difference in the way the firm and the residents value the forest, illustrates the important distinction between private cost and social cost. **Private cost** measures the best alternative use of the resources available to *the producer*. Private cost is usually measured by the market price of the resources that the firm uses. **Social cost** measures the best alternative use of the resources that is available to the whole society.

For some resources, social cost may be the same as private cost. For them, the price set by the market reflects the value of the resources in their best alternative use. For other resources, as will soon be clear, social cost differs from private cost.

Discrepancies between private and social cost lead to market failure.

Efficiency requires that prices reflect social cost. Private producers, adjusting to private costs, will neglect those elements of social cost that are not included in private costs. When an element of social cost is not part of a private firm's profit-and-loss calculation, it is *external* to its decision-making process.

Discrepancies between social and private cost lead to **externalities**. These are costs of a transaction that are incurred by members of the society, or benefits that are received by them, but not considered by the parties to the transaction. They are also called **third-party effects**, because parties other than the primary participants in the transaction (the buyers and the sellers) are affected. Externalities arise in many different ways, and they may be beneficial or harmful.

Some externalities are beneficial. When I paint my house, I enhance my neighbours' view and the value of their property. When an Einstein or a Rembrandt gives the world a discovery or a work of art whose worth is far in excess of what he is paid to produce it, he confers an external benefit. Private producers will tend to produce too little of commodities that generate beneficial externalities because they bear all of the costs, while others reap part of the benefits.

Other externalities are harmful. Private producers produce too much of commodities that generate harmful externalities because they bear none of the costs suffered by others.

> **Externalities, whether adverse or beneficial, cause market failure because they lead to allocations of resources that are non-optimal from society's point of view.**

We will now consider several examples of harmful externalities, which are often referred to as *negative externalities*.

Pollution: A major source of differences between private cost and social cost occurs when firms use resources they do not regard as scarce. This is a characteristic of most examples of pollution. When a paper mill produces pulp for the world's newspapers, more people are affected than its suppliers, employers and customers. The effluent that it discharges into the water hurts the fishing boats that ply nearby, and its smog makes many resort areas less attractive, thereby reducing the tourist revenues of local hotel operators and boat renters. The firm neglects these external effects of its actions, because its profits are not affected by them.

Dumping of hazardous wastes, air pollution and water pollution may occur as a result of calculated decisions as to what and how to produce or consume, or as a result of private producers taking risks that inflict injury on others. Even an apparent accident, such as an oil blowout, or the break-up of a tanker, which is desired by no one, may be caused by a private firm's insufficient avoidance of the risk, since it bears only part of the costs. When the tanker sinks the owner loses the cost of its cargo; society loses the cost of clean-up, plus the value of any ecological damage that cannot be removed.

Common-property resources: The world's oceans once teemed with fish, but today overfishing has caused a worldwide fish shortage. How could this happen?

Fish are an example of what is called a **common-property resource**, a resource that is owned by no one and may be used by anyone. No one owns the ocean's fish until they are caught. The world's international fishing grounds are common property for all fishermen. If, by taking more fish, one fisherman reduces the catch of other fishermen, he does not count this as a cost, but it is a cost to society.

It is socially optimal to add to a fishing fleet until the last boat increases the *value of the fleet's total catch* by as much as it costs to operate the boat. This is the size of fishing fleet that a social planner would choose.

The free market will not, however, produce that result. Potential new entrants will judge entry to be profitable if the *value of their own catch* is equal to the costs of operating their boats. But a new entrant's catch is *partly* an addition to total catch, and *partly* a reduction of the catch of other fishermen – because of congestion, each new boat reduces the catch of all other boats. Thus under free entry there will be too many boats in the fleet. Indeed, boats will continue to enter until there are no longer any profits for the marginal boat. In other words, boats will enter until the *average* value of the catch of a typical boat is equal to the cost of running that boat. At this point, however, the *net* addition to the *total* catch brought about by the last boat will be substantially less than the cost of operating the boat.

> **With common-property resources, the level of activity will be too high because each new entrant will not take account of the cost that it imposes on existing producers by reducing their catches.**

Fishing grounds and other common-property resources usually show a typical pattern of over-exploitation. Most of the world's fishing grounds do so today, except where the catch is effectively regulated by government intervention.

Congestion: Collisions between private planes and commercial airliners are headline news when they occur. They cannot occur unless *both* planes are in the air; this is what creates the externality. Suppose that the probability of a mid-air plane crash is roughly proportional to the number of planes in the air. Suppose, too, that I have the choice of flying from Edinburgh to London in my own plane or on a commercial airliner that has only 120 of its 150 seats filled. In choosing to fly by myself, I decide that the slight extra risk to me of a mid-air collision is more than balanced by the fun or convenience of my own plane.

What I have neglected is the social cost of my action: the increased risk for every other person in the air on my flight route that results from one more plane in the air. Since I do not consider other travellers' increased risk, my private decision may have been the wrong social decision – and I might not have taken that decision had I to bear its full costs.

Principal-agent Problems Once Again

The efficiency of the price system depends on firms and households receiving, and responding to, the signals provided by prices, costs and windfall profits. Forces that seriously distort these signals, or distort the required response to them, may cause a market to fail to perform efficiently. These forces are often referred to as *market imperfections* and *market impediments*.

If profits are the spur to efficient performance, it is clear that when a firm's managers (the agents) choose to pursue their own goals, rather than the profits desired by the firm's owners (the principals), they impede the functioning of the market system. A manager or a salesperson may incur unnecessary costs because some costly activities provide them with enjoyment. On a small scale, this occurs whenever a purchasing agent is swayed by the Christmas present from a salesperson, or when a person hiring a car is motivated to hire a more expensive car by some bonus she will receive, while her employer pays the bill. More serious are cases where managers regularly pursue their own goals that conflict with the minimization of production costs.

The above are examples where principal-agent problems cause productive inefficiency. They can also lead to allocative inefficiency. For example, managers may seek to increase the size of their firm in order to add to their own prestige. If they produce more than the profit-maximizing output, they may cause allocative inefficiency. As

we observed in Chapter 16:

> one of the most challenging problems facing a firm is to provide incentives that will give agents a self-interest in achieving the goals of the principals. When this does not happen, markets will fail.

Coping With Risk

All economic decisions have their effects felt over time. Since the future is never certain, all such decisions involve uncertainties. For example, will the anticipated demand be there when the new factory is built?

Much economic activity is designed to cope with risk. Although it is often effective in doing so, risk can also be a source of market failure.

Moral hazard: Suppose a person who has ample fire insurance does not take quite the precautions he should against fire; or suppose because of the availability of unemployment insurance a person refuses to accept a job she would otherwise have taken. Suppose you are on your way out for the evening and realize you have left your house unlocked. You decide to accept the risk knowing that you are fully covered by theft insurance. If everyone behaves in this way, there will be more fires, more unemployment and more theft in total than there would be if there were no insurance.

The socially beneficial purpose of insurance is to permit people to share given risks, not to increase the size of the aggregate risk. But in these three examples the behaviour described does increase the aggregate risk and thus the social cost. **Moral hazard** arises when people take actions that increase social costs because they are insured against private loss.

Adverse selection: Closely related to moral hazard is the problem of **adverse selection**. A person fearing a heart attack may seek to increase his life insurance coverage by purchasing as much additional coverage as is available, especially if it can be obtained without medical examination. People taking out insurance almost always know more about themselves as individual insurance risks than do their insurance companies. The company can try to limit the variation in risk by setting up broad categories based on variables, such as age and occupation. The rate charged is

BOX 24.1 USED-CAR PRICES: THE PROBLEM OF 'LEMONS'

It is common for people to regard the large loss of value of a new car in the first year of its life as a sign that consumers are very style-conscious and will always pay a big premium for the latest in anything. Professor George Akerloff of the University of California suggests a different explanation based upon the proposition that the satisfaction expected from a one-year-old car purchased on the used-car market will be lower than the utility of the average one-year-old car. Consider his theory.

Any particular model year of cars will include a certain proportion of 'lemons' – cars that have serious defects. Purchasers of new cars of a certain year and model take a chance that their car will turn out to be a lemon. Say, for purposes of illustration, that the chances are one in 100. Those who are unlucky and get a lemon are more likely to resell their cars than those who are lucky and get a quality car. Hence, in the used-car market, there will be a disproportionately large number of lemons for sale. There might, for example, be five in every 100. Similarly, not all cars are driven in the same manner. Those that are driven long distances or under bad conditions are much more likely to be

traded in, or sold used, than those that are driven on good roads and in moderate amounts.

Thus buyers of used cars are right to be on the lookout for low quality, while salespeople are quick to invent reasons for high quality ('It was owned by a little old lady who drove it only on Sundays'). Because it is difficult to identify a lemon or a badly maintained car before buying it, purchasers are prepared to buy a used car only at a price low enough to offset the higher probability that it is of poor quality.

This is a rational consumer response to uncertainty and may explain why one-year-old cars typically sell for a discount much larger than can be explained by the average amount of physical depreciation that occurs over one year. The probability that a used car of a given type and vintage will be a lemon is higher than was the probability of selecting a lemon from among those cars when they were new. This reduces the satisfaction to be expected from buying the used car, and means that rational consumers will only do so if they get them at a discount high enough to compensate for the extra risk.

---

then varied across categories based on the average risk in each category. But there must always be variability of risk *within* any one category. Those who know they are well above average risk within their category are offered a bargain. They will be led to take out more car, health, life or fire insurance than they otherwise would. Those who know they are low risks must pay more than their own risk really warrants and are motivated to take out less insurance than they otherwise would.

More generally, any time either party lacks information that the other party has, market results will tend to be inefficient. Unequal information is also involved in many other situations that do not necessarily lead to inefficiencies. One example is discussed in Box 24.1.

Transactions Costs

The costs incurred in negotiating and completing a transaction, such as the costs of billing or the bad-debt cost of those who never pay, are examples of **transactions costs**. They are always present to some degree, and they are a necessary cost of doing business. For a private firm to stay in business, it must be able to recover both its production and its transactions costs. If

transactions costs for a product are higher than they need to be because of imperfections in the private market, less than the optimal amount of that product will be produced. The market will have failed. Consider an example.

Could a private firm provide a road system for Birmingham, covering its costs by collecting tolls? The answer is probably no (at least with today's technology).[1] It would be prohibitively expensive, both in money and in delays, to erect and staff a toll booth at every road exit. Requiring collection of revenues via tolls would impose a prohibitive transactions cost. The users of a road system may be more than willing to pay the full costs of its construction and maintenance, but, without an inexpensive way to make them pay, no private firm will produce the road. The government, collecting revenue by means of a tax, can do what the private market fails to do. (Whether it can do so without making a different mistake –

---

[1] The warning about technology merits an additional comment. Technology changes rapidly. For example, the electronic metering of road use may make the toll booth unnecessary, just as the postage meter has made licking stamps unnecessary. Thus what a private market cannot do today, it may be able to do at low transactions cost tomorrow.

BOX 24.2 MISSING MARKETS AS A SOURCE OF MARKET FAILURE

For complete optimality there has to be a market in which each good and service can be traded to the point where the marginal benefit equals the marginal cost. Missing markets for such things as public goods are a source of inefficiency.

One important set of missing markets are those covering most risks. You can insure your house against burning down. This is because your knowledge of the probability of this occurrence is not much better than your insurance company's, and because the probability of your house burning down is independent of the probability of other houses burning down.

If you are a farmer, however, you cannot usually insure your crop against bad weather. This is because the probability of you and your neighbour's crop suffering from bad weather are interrelated. If the insurance company has to pay you, the probabilities are it will also have to pay your neighbour, and everyone else in the county – perhaps even the country. An insurance company survives by pooling independent risks. It cannot survive if the same event affects all its clients in the same way. (This is why, although you can insure your house against a fire from ordinary causes, you cannot insure it against fires caused by war.)

If you are in business, you cannot insure against bankruptcy. Here the problem is adverse selection. You know much better than your would-be insurance company the chances that your business will fail. If insurance was offered against such failure, it would mainly be taken out by people whose businesses had recently developed a high chance of failure.

For these and other reasons, many risks cannot be insured against. Optimality cannot occur because these markets are not there.

Another set of missing markets are many futures markets. You can buy certain well-established and unchanging products, such as corn or pigs, on futures markets. But you cannot do so for most manufactured products such as cars and TV sets, because no one knows the precise specifications of future models. Because these markets are missing, there is no way that the costs and benefits of planned future expenditure on these products can be equated by economic transactions made today.

---

producing more of the product than users are willing to pay for – is discussed below.)

> **Market imperfections may lead to market failure by preventing firms and households from completing transactions that are required for efficient resource allocation, or by causing too much or too little production of particular goods.**

Another reason for inefficiency is that some needed markets do not exist. This point, which follows from some rather advanced general equilibrium theory, is discussed briefly in Box 24.2.

Failure to Achieve Other Social Goals

Equity

An important characteristic of a market economy is the *distribution* of the income that it determines. People whose services are in heavy demand relative to supply, such as popular disc-jockeys and superior football players, earn large incomes, while people whose services are not in heavy demand relative to supply, such as Ph.D.s in English and early school-leavers without work experience, earn much less.

In Chapter 18, we distinguished between equilibrium and disequilibrium income differentials. Disequilibrium differentials serve the important function of motivating people to adapt. The 'advantage' of such a system is that individuals can make their own decisions about how to alter their behaviour when market conditions change. The 'disadvantage' is that temporary rewards and punishments are dealt out as a result of changes in the market conditions that are beyond the control of the individuals affected. Very high disequilibrium differentials often offend our sense of equity.

Equilibrium differences may also conflict with our views on equity. Should those who are unlucky enough to be born with skills on which the market places a low value receive only a subsistence wage? Should those lucky enough to have rare, highly prized talents feast while their less fortunate fellow citizens starve?

Income differentials also emerge from luck and personal accident that have no place in the theories of market adjustment or market equilibrium. Should heads of households be forced to bear the full burden of their misfortune if, through no fault of their own, they lose their jobs? Even if they lose their jobs through their own fault, should they and their families have to bear the whole burden, which may include starvation? Should the ill and aged be thrown on the mercy of their families? What if they have no families? What about the widowed mother of five whose husband had been meaning to take out a life-insurance policy for several months before his unexpected heart attack?

Both private charities, and many government policies, are concerned with modifying the distribution of income that results from such things as where one starts, how able one is, how lucky one is, and how one fares in the free-market world.

When the market produces a distribution of income that offends our sense of equity we can say that, in a sense, there has been a market failure. Government intervention designed to alter the distribution of income will then be considered.

Protecting Individuals from Others

People can use, and even abuse, other people for economic gain in ways that the members of society find offensive. Very young children may be employed, working standards may be degrading, and employers may take unnecessary risks with unsafe machinery.

Direct abuse is not the only example of this kind of market failure. In an unhindered free market, the adults in a household would usually decide how much education to buy for their children. Selfish parents might buy no education, while egalitarian parents might buy the same quantity for all their children regardless of their abilities. The members of society may want to interfere in these choices, both to protect the child of the selfish parent, and to ensure that some of the scarce educational resources are distributed according to intelligence rather than wealth. All households are then forced to provide a minimum of education for their children, and strong inducements are offered – through public

universities, scholarships and other means – for gifted children to consume more education than they or their parents might choose if they had to pay the entire cost themselves.

Part of the justification of these expenditures concerns efficiency effects – since education confers beneficial externalities on the whole society. Part, however, is to protect the interests of the young from decisions taken by their own parents.

Protecting Individuals from Themselves: Paternalism

Earlier we considered reasons for intervention based on improving the efficiency with which the market responds to household demand. Accepting market demand as a major determinant of the allocation of resources depends on believing that householders are the best judges of their own interests. This view is called *individualism*.

An alternative view, called *paternalism*, holds that the central authorities are sometimes better judges of households' self-interest than are the households themselves. Paternalistic intervention may take the form of downright prohibition on the consumption of such goods and services as hard drugs and gambling. In many countries, for example, off-track betting is illegal – as it was until the 1960s in the UK – on the grounds that would-be punters must be protected against themselves. In Canada, for another example, pubs were once forced to close for an hour from 6.30 to 7.30 on the grounds that this would force the man of the house to go home, where his wife could get her hands on some of his pay before he had spent it all on beer.

Paternalism often takes more subtle forms. For example, commodities such as milk and housing may be subsidized on the grounds that it is in households' own interests to consume more of these commodities than their members would consume voluntarily. The individualist's view is that, if households are thought to be too poor, they should be given a simple income supplement and left to spend it as they wish.

The issue of individualism versus paternalism raises many fascinating questions concerning human freedom and social justice. We can do no more here than note that much existing economic policy is paternalistic; it can only be justified on the grounds that the central authorities understand the best interests of many households better than do the households themselves.[1]

Merit goods: If the government decides that more of some commodity should be produced than people would choose to consume left to themselves, that commodity is sometimes called a **merit good**. If the government decides that less than people would choose of some other good should be produced, that commodity is sometimes called a **merit bad**. These terms cover several different motives. A commodity may be treated as a merit good because it confers positive externalities, or because the government feels people are not the best judges of their own best interests, or because it feels that production of the good contributes to the maintenance of certain social values that cannot be expressed in market terms.

Social Obligations

If you persuade someone else to clean your house in return for £15, presumably both parties to the transaction are better off. You prefer to part with £15 than clean the house yourself, and the person you hire prefers £15 to not cleaning your house. Normally, society does not interfere with people's ability to negotiate such mutually advantageous contracts.

   Some activities, however, are regarded as social obligations. For example, when military service is compulsory, some people could pay enough to persuade others to do their tour of service for them. By the same argument as we used in the previous paragraph, we can presume that both parties would be better off if they were allowed to negotiate such a trade. But such contracts are usually prohibited. Why? Because people, acting through their governments, wish to give weight to values other than those expressible in a market. In wartime, military service by all healthy males may be held to be a duty independent of an individual's tastes, wealth or

social position. Because it is felt that everyone *ought* to do this service, exchanges between willing persons are prohibited.

   Military service is not the only example. Citizens cannot buy their way out of jury duty, nor legally sell their votes to another, even though in many cases they could find willing trading partners.

> Even if the price system allocated goods and services efficiently, members of a society may not wish to rely solely on the market if they wish to pursue goals in addition to material living standards.

THE CASE FOR GOVERNMENT INTERVENTION

Because markets fail, improvements over market outcomes are conceivable. The next issue concerns the ability of governments to alleviate market failure.

   When we considered the case for the free-market system, we saw that asking if the idealized market form of perfect competition would produce optimal results was not enough. We also had to ask if the imperfect market systems of our actual experience – oligopolies, monopolies and all – would produce acceptable results. Similarly, when considering the case for government intervention, it is not sufficient to show that an idealized, perfectly functioning government could reduce market failures. We must also ask if governments as we know them are likely to achieve the potential gains. In the rest of this chapter, we consider the following three questions: first, could a perfectly functioning, costless government intervene to improve the workings of the market system, i.e. does it have the tools to do the job? Second, would there be net gains from the interventions of a perfectly functioning government, when the costs of such interventions are taken into account? Third, would the imperfect governments of the real world actually achieve any of the potential net gains that are available?

Tools

The main sets of tools available to governments

---

[1] The distinction between individualism and paternalism would be much clearer than it actually is if all households contained only one member. Because households typically have many members, including minors, some apparently paternalistic interventions can be understood as protecting some members from the paternalism of others. This really replaces one form of paternalism with another. Difficult cases aside, however, influencing actions that primarily affect the person taking the action is clearly paternalistic.

to deal with market failure are rules, public ownership, taxation and expenditure.

Rules

Rules and regulations are potent tools for redressing market failures. Governments use rules both to set the framework within which market forces operate and to alter the workings of unhindered markets. Rules pervade economic activities. Shop hours and working conditions are regulated. Rules govern the circumstances under which various types of unions can be formed and operated. Discrimination between labour services provided by males and females is illegal in the UK and in a large number of other countries. There is growing pressure in many countries to make termination of employment solely on account of age illegal. Children cannot be served alcoholic drinks. They must attend school in most countries, and be inoculated against communicable diseases in many. Laws prohibit people from selling or using certain drugs. Prostitution is prohibited in many societies even though it usually involves a willing buyer and a willing seller. In many countries, you are forced to purchase insurance for the damage you might do to others with your private motorcar. In some countries, people who offer goods for sale cannot refuse to sell them to someone just because they do not like the customer's colour or religion. There are rules against fraudulent advertising and the sale of substandard, adulterated or poisonous food. In some countries, such as the United States, anyone can purchase a variety of firearms ranging from pistols to machine-guns. In other countries, it is difficult for a private citizen to obtain a handgun.

Most business practices are controlled by rules and regulations. In many countries, agreements among oligopolistic firms to fix prices, or divide up markets, are illegal. The mere existence of monopoly is outlawed in some countries. When the cost advantages of monopoly resulting from scale economies are considerable, the prices a monopolistic firm can charge, and the return it can earn on its capital investment, are often regulated.

Public Ownership

Assume the government feels that, under free-market conditions, the firms in some industry would charge an 'excessive' price and earn 'unnecessary' profits. The government could use rules and regulations to force the firms in that industry to charge a 'reasonable' price and so eliminate the 'unnecessary' profits. Alternatively, the government could nationalize the industry and then instruct the managers to follow the desired pricing policy. Government ownership is thus a tool for exerting control over production and distribution. It brings the production in question under public ownership as an alternative to using rules and regulations to control the behaviour of private owners.

Expenditure

Some government expenditures are in return for goods and services that count as part of current output. They create a claim by the central authorities on the economy's resources. When the government purchases factors of production to produce goods and services in the public sector of the economy, the factors are unavailable to produce private-sector output. This type of expenditure is sometimes called **exhaustive expenditure**. Among their many uses, exhaustive expenditures are the tool for filling in gaps in what the free market provides. Public goods, such as national defence, the legal system and coastal navigation aids, must be produced by the government or not at all. In those cases, the failure of the free market, and the potential for a remedy by government action, are obvious.

The remainder of government expenditure consists of **transfer payments**, which are payments *not* made in return for any contribution to current output. Old-age pensions, unemployment insurance and supplementary benefits, welfare payments, disability payments and a host of other expenditures made by the modern welfare state are all transfer payments. They do not add to current marketable output; they merely transfer the power to purchase output from those who provide the money (usually taxpayers) to those who receive it. Transfer payments do not represent a claim by the government on real productive resources. Revenue must nonetheless be raised to pay them.

Taxation

Taxes are of major importance in the pursuit of many government policies. They provide the funds to finance expenditure, but they are also used as tools in their own right for a wide range of purposes. They are used to alter the incentives to which private maximizing agents react, and to alter the distribution of income.

Direct and indirect taxes: Taxes are divided into two broad groups, depending on whether persons or things are taxed. An **indirect tax** is levied on a thing, and is paid by an individual by virtue of his or her association with that thing. Local rates on property are indirect taxes. They vary with the value of the real estate and are paid by either the owner or the occupier of the real estate, independent of his or her circumstances. Taxes and stamp duties on the transfer of assets from one owner to another are also indirect taxes, since they depend on the assets being transferred. Estate duties which depend on the size of the estate being inherited, and not on the circumstances of the beneficiaries, are also an indirect tax.

The most important indirect taxes in today's world are those on the sale of currently produced commodities. These taxes are called excise taxes when they are levied on manufacturers, and sales taxes when they are levied on the sale of goods from retailer to consumer. The EC countries levy a comprehensive tax of this sort on all transactions whether at the retail, wholesale or manufacturer's level, called the *value added tax* (VAT). Value added is the difference between the value of factor services and materials that the firm purchases as inputs and the value of its output. It therefore represents the value that a firm adds by virtue of its own activities. The VAT is an indirect tax because it depends on the value of what is made and sold, not on the wealth or income of the maker or seller. Thus two self-employed fabric designers, each with a 'value-added' of £30,000 in terms of designs produced and sold, would pay the same VAT even if one had no other source of income while the other was independently wealthy.

Indirect taxes may be levied in two basic ways. An **ad valorem tax** is a percentage of the value of the transaction on which it is levied. An 8 per cent retail sales tax would mean, for example, that the retail firm had to charge a tax of 8 per cent of the value of everything it sold. A **specific** or **per unit tax** is a tax expressed as so much per

unit, independent of its price. Taxes on cinema and theatre tickets, and on each gallon of petrol or alcohol, and on each packet of cigarettes independent of the price at which they are produced or sold, are specific, indirect taxes.

Direct taxes are levied on persons, and vary with the status of the taxpayer. The most important direct tax is the income tax. The personal income tax falls sometimes on the income of households and sometimes separately on each member of the household. It varies with the size and source of the taxpayer's income and various other characteristics laid down by law, such as marital status and number of dependants.

Joint-stock companies also pay taxes on their income. This is a direct tax both in the legal sense that the company is an individual in the eyes of the law, and in the economic sense that the company is owned by its shareholders so that a tax on the company is a tax on them. An expenditure tax (as advocated for the UK by the Royal Commission headed by Nobel-prize-winning economist James Meade) is also a direct tax. It is based on what a person spends, rather than on what he or she earns, and has exemptions that are specific to the individual taxpayer. A poll tax, which is simply a lump-sum tax levied on each person, is also a direct tax. Inheritance taxes, based on the amount of money an individual inherits from someone else's estate, are also direct taxes.

The rate of tax is the tax expressed as a percentage of the base on which it is levied. The rate of income tax, for example, is the tax paid expressed as a percentage of the income on which it is levied. It is important in the discussion to distinguish average from marginal rates. The *average rate* of income tax paid by a person is that person's total tax divided by his or her income. The *marginal rate* of tax is the rate he or she would pay on another unit of income.

Progressivity: The general term for the relation between income and the percentage of income paid as a tax is **progressivity**. A **regressive tax** takes a *smaller percentage* of people's incomes the larger is their income. A **progressive tax** takes a *larger percentage* of people's incomes the larger is their income. A **proportional tax** is the boundary case between the two: it takes the *same percentage* of income

FIGURE 24.1 Income Taxes with Different Progressivities

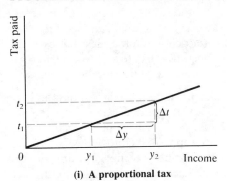

(i) A proportional tax

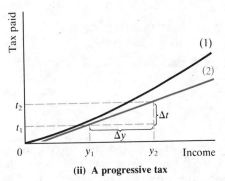

(ii) A progressive tax

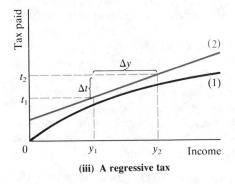

(iii) A regressive tax

Income taxes may be proportional, progressive or regressive. Part (i) shows a proportional tax. The average rate of tax does not change as income changes, $t_1/y_1 = t_2/y_2$, and the average rate is equal to the marginal rate $t_1/y_1 = \Delta t/\Delta y$. A change in the tax rate would change the slope of the line.

Part (ii) shows two progressive taxes. Tax (1) has rising average and marginal rates. Tax (2) has a constant marginal rate, shown by $\Delta t/\Delta y$, but a rising average rate, $t_2/y_2 > t_1/y_1$.

Part (iii) shows two regressive taxes. Tax (1) has falling average and marginal rates. Tax (2) has a constant marginal rate, $\Delta t/\Delta y$, but a falling average rate, $t_1/y_1 > t_2/y_2$.

from everyone. Taxes on food, for example, tend to be regressive because the proportion of income spent on food tends to fall as income rises. Taxes on alcoholic spirits tend to be progressive since the proportion of income spent on spirits tends to rise with income. Taxes on beer, on the other hand, are regressive. Different progressivities are shown in Figure 24.1.

Progressivity can be defined for any one tax, or for the tax system as a whole. Different taxes have different characteristics. Inevitably some will be progressive and some regressive. The impact of a tax system as a whole on high-, middle- and low-income groups is best judged by looking at the progressivity of the whole set of taxes taken together. For example, income taxes are progressive in the UK, rising to a maximum marginal rate of 40 per cent. The overall tax system is also progressive, but much less so than one would guess from studying only the income-tax rates. This is because much revenue is raised by indirect taxes, all of which are less progressive than income taxes, and some of which are regressive.

Conclusion

It is clear that the government controls a wide variety of instruments that might be used to reduce market failures. For example, it can alter the distribution of income by raising money through a progressive income tax and spending the money on services mainly used by people with low incomes. For another example, it can try to move a natural monopoly's output towards the optimal level by rules and regulations governing privately owned firms, by nationalizing the industry or by levying taxes and subsidies that provide an incentive for profit-maximizing firms to produce the socially optimal output. We shall consider such policies in greater detail in the next chapter. In the meantime, we go on to our next question: given that government action could alleviate some market failures, what are the costs of doing so?

The Benefits of Government Intervention Versus the Costs

To evaluate government intervention, we need to consider costs as well as benefits.

> Large potential benefits do not necessarily justify government intervention, nor do potential costs necessarily make it unwise. What matters is net benefits – the balance between benefits and costs.

Three types of costs of government intervention are considered below: costs that are internal to the government, costs that are external to the government but directly paid by others, and costs that are external to the government and felt more generally throughout the entire economy.

Internal Costs

When government inspectors visit plants to check on compliance with government-imposed health standards, industrial safety or environmental protection, costs are incurred in such forms as the salaries and expenses of the inspectors. When the government solicitors spend time on an anti-monopoly case, they are incurring costs. The costs of the judges, the clerks and the court reporters, who are needed when the case is heard, are likewise costs imposed by regulation. All these activities use valuable resources, resources that could have been used to produce other goods and services.

Everything the government does uses resources. Armies of clerks, backed up by computers and other modern equipment, keep track of income tax and VAT receipts. Inspectors take the field to enforce compliance, and the courts deal with serious offenders. Unemployment and supplementary benefits must be administered, and so on. The size of the body of public employees at the national and local level attests to the significant resource costs of government activity, costs that need to be set against the benefits produced.

Direct External Costs

Increases in production costs: Regulation and control often add directly to the costs of producing goods. Firms must inspect machinery to ensure that it meets government safety standards. For 50 years (until the mid-1970s), the

price of cars was falling relative to the prices of other commodities because of continuing advances in automotive engineering. Recent safety and emission standards have added so much to the cost of producing automobiles that over the last decade consumers had to adjust to an increasing relative price of cars for a number of years.

Costs of compliance: Much business activity is devoted to understanding, reporting and contesting regulatory provisions. Occupational safety and environmental control have increased the number of employees not working on the shopfloor. The legal costs of a major joint-stock company can run into large sums each year.

The same can be said of the costs of complying with tax laws. Firms, and wealthy individuals, spend substantial sums on lawyers and accountants. These advisers help them to comply with tax laws. They also assist in choosing tax-minimizing courses of action. These resources have alternative uses. So do firms' time and planning energies whose social product might be higher if devoted to maximizing growth potential rather than minimizing their tax payments.

Losses in productivity: Quite apart from the actual expenditures, government intervention may reduce the incentive for experimentation, innovation and the introduction of new products. Requiring advance government clearance before introducing a new method, or product (on grounds of potential safety hazards or environmental impact) can reduce the incentive to develop it. New lines of investment may be chosen more for their tax implications than for their potential for reducing production costs and so contributing to productivity growth.

Indirect External Costs

Ironically, government intervention to offset adverse externalities can create new adverse externalities. For example, government regulations designed to ensure the safety of new drugs delay the introduction of all drugs, including those that are safe. The benefits of these regulations are related to the unsafe drugs kept off the market. The cost includes the delayed availability of new safe drugs.

Indirect taxes and efficiency: Almost all taxation instruments have adverse efficiency

FIGURE 24.2 The Efficiency Loss of an Indirect Tax

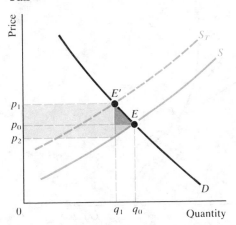

An indirect tax lowers output and causes a deadweight loss of consumers' surplus. The original demand and supply curves are D and S. Equilibrium is at E, with q_0 bought at a price of p_0. A tax is added to producers' costs, whose supply curve now shifts upwards to S_T. Equilibrium then shifts to E'. The quantity sold falls to q_1 while the market price rises to p_1. This is the price that purchasers pay. Producers, however, only receive p_2 per unit, net of tax.

As a result of the fall in consumption from q_0 to q_1, purchasers suffer a loss of consumers' surplus. This is the amount shown by the dark-shaded area between the demand curve and the original price over the range of the reduction in consumption.

As a result of the same fall in production, producers suffer a loss of producers' surplus. This is shown by the medium-shaded area between the supply curve and the original equilibrium price. Because these areas look like triangles (they are not unless the demand and supply curves are straight lines), they are often referred to as the 'triangles of surplus'.

The government gains the tax revenue given by the light-shaded area, whose height is $p_1 - p_2$, and whose length is q_1. This revenue is raised partly at the expense of consumers, and partly at the expense of producers. But no one gains the lost consumers' and producers' surpluses between q_1 and q_0. These lost-surplus triangles constitute the *deadweight loss* from the tax.

---

effects. These have played an important part in the so-called supply-side criticisms of government policy, and we need to look at them in some detail.

First, consider a sales tax on one specific good. The tax raises the relative price of that good faced by consumers so they will buy less of it, and more of other commodities. Production falls below the competitive equilibrium level, which is the one that maximizes the sum of consumers' and producers' surplus. The result, as shown in Figure 24.2, is a loss of consumers' surplus exactly analogous to the deadweight loss of monopoly. An alternative demonstration of the efficiency loss of taxes on commodities is given in Box 24.3.

This result applies to any taxes that affect the prices of commodities in different proportions and hence change relative prices. It thus applies to VAT whenever different commodities are taxed at different rates. The key is that:

> consumers adjust their *MRS*s to prices including tax, while producers adjust their marginal costs, and hence the *MRT*, to the prices excluding tax. Any set of taxes that alters relative prices will cause inefficiency by facing producers and consumers with different relative prices.

The income tax and efficiency: The income tax creates an inefficiency by distorting the work-leisure choice. Each individual, reacting to after-tax wage rates, sees a rate of substitution between work and leisure that differs from the rate implied by the pre-tax wage the employer is prepared to pay.

To understand the source of the inefficiency, compare the income tax with a **poll tax**, which takes the same lump sum from everyone. Because it is not related to income, a poll tax leaves the marginal rate of substitution between goods and leisure unaffected. Employees see a wage rate that correctly reflects the wage the employers are ready to pay. The tax exerts no disincentive to work at the margin, and is thus more efficient than the income tax.

Figure 24.3 demonstrates the inefficiency of the income tax. It shows that the household achieves a higher indifference curve when it is forced to pay a given amount of tax revenue through a poll tax, rather than through an income tax. The poll tax is more efficient because it leaves each person facing a choice at the margin that reflects the wage rate actually paid in the market.

Although local rates in the UK are being replaced by a poll tax – called the *Community Charge* – no one suggests doing the same with the income tax. In Figure 24.3, we selected the poll

BOX 24.3 THE EFFICIENCY LOSS FROM A TAX ON ONE COMMODITY

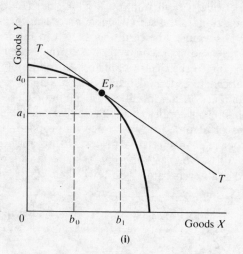

(i)

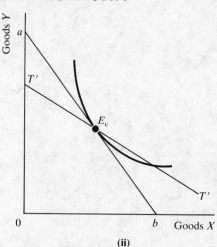

(ii)

The analysis of Figure 24.2 uses demand and supply curves which are based on the assumption that other things remain equal. It can only be used, therefore, to measure the loss resulting from a tax placed on a commodity that is a relatively small part of the total expenditure, so that the *ceteris paribus* assumptions remain approximately correct. If an indirect tax is placed on many commodities, many prices will change and the demand curve in the market being studied will shift. Until we know the amount of the shift, we cannot use demand and supply curves to calculate the effects of the tax.

An alternative, more satisfactory analysis uses the general-equilibrium tools of indifferences and production possibility curves. It applies to any indirect set of taxes that alter relative prices and so causes consumers to react to one set of relative prices (those including the taxes they must pay), while producers react to another set (those excluding the taxes, which they do not receive). The analysis relates to the Figure shown below.

Part (i) shows the production possibility curve for an economy that produces only two goods, X and Y. Production is at the point E_p and the marginal rate of transformation is given by the slope of the line TT which is tangent to the production possibility curve at E_p.

Part (ii) shows the position of a typical con-

sumer whose budget line is given by ab, and who is in equilibrium at E_c, where the slope of the indifference curve (the *MRS*) is equal to the slope of the budget line.

A tax on commodity X causes consumers to see a higher relative price of X than do producers, who do not receive the tax paid by consumers. The slope of the budget line ab in part (ii) is thus steeper than the slope of the TT line in part (i). Thus the *MRS* is not equal to the *MRT*. The line $T'T'$, drawn through the consumer's equilibrium point E_c, has the same slope as the line TT shown in part (i). Society can 'transform' good Y into X at the rate given by TT. For a small change, production moves along the line TT in part (i), which means that consumption can move along the line $T'T'$ in part (ii). But such a movement can make the consumer better off, since $T'T'$ intersects higher indifference curves to the right of E_c in part (ii). Thus, if all other consumers are left unchanged, the consumer shown in part (ii) can be made better off when less Y and more X is produced.

A sales tax on one commodity means that consumers and producers adjust to different relative prices and, as a result, the *MRS* in consumption will not equal the *MRT* in production. Allocative inefficiency is the result.

tax that caused the household to pay the same amount of money as it would pay under an income tax. But this equality cannot be maintained for all taxpayers. The poll tax takes the same amount from everyone, and thus is a highly regressive tax. If it was used to replace the

income tax, it would take much more from lower-income persons, and much less from higher-income persons, compared with an income tax that yielded the same total revenue for the government.

The importance of Figure 24.3 lies in its

FIGURE 24.3 The Distortion of the Work-Leisure Choice by an Income Tax

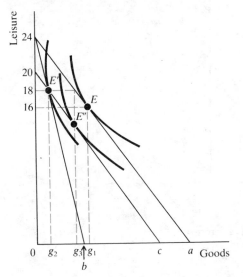

An income tax upsets the optimum condition between work and leisure. A household faces a pre-tax wage rate shown by the slope of the budget line running from 24 to a. Equilibrium is at E where g_1 of goods and 16 hours of leisure are consumed. This individual can be thought of as starting with 24 hours of leisure and no goods, then trading down the budget line to reach E by giving up 8 hours of leisure to gain g_1 of goods.

An income tax is now levied at the rate $(a-b)/a$. The pre-tax budget line is unchanged but the after-tax budget line shifts to the line running from 24 to b. The horizontal distance between the two lines shows the amount of the tax at each amount of work. For example, if 24 hours a day were worked, pre-tax income would be a, but the tax would be $a-b$, making after-tax income b. Equilibrium now shifts to E' where g_2 of goods and 18 hours of leisure are consumed. When the individual works six hours, the pre-tax return is g_3 along the original budget line. But $g_3 - g_2$ is paid in taxes, leaving after-tax consumption at g_2.

The budget line running from 20 to c corresponds to a poll tax that takes the same amount from the individual as did the income tax. (It goes through the point E'.) This line has the same slope as the pre-tax budget line, but it is shifted inwards horizontally by the amount of the poll tax which is $a-c=g_3-g_2$. After paying the poll tax, the consumer's budget line runs from 20 to c. Equilibrium is now at E'' where, compared to the income tax, the same tax is paid, but a higher indifference curve is reached.

demonstration that any practical tax does have negative efficiency effects, because it distorts relative price signals. The only tax that does not do so, under normal conditions, is the poll tax. It has no negative efficiency effects because the amount paid does not vary with any of the taxpayer's economic decisions.[1] But, precisely for this reason, many people find it unacceptable (on equity grounds) as anything other than a minor source of revenue.

Exceptional circumstances: Two extreme circumstances provide exceptions to the rule that all taxes upset efficiency conditions. These occur, as shown in Figure 24.4, where either the demand or the supply curve is perfectly inelastic. In either case, the same amount will be bought and sold both before and after the tax. Because the quantity is insensitive to price changes caused by the tax, it does not have adverse effects. If decisions do not respond to changes in the price signals then these changes have no effects, unfavourable or favourable.

There are few, if any, markets where these extreme conditions are met. It is sometimes alleged that taxes on cigarettes and alcohol come close because demand is highly inelastic. But there is plenty of room for substitution among types of alcohol with people shifting to cheaper sources as prices rise. Although elasticities of demand for alcohol and tobacco may be less than unity, they are not zero. Thus taxes on these products have efficiency effects. The very high rates charged on them may be justified on grounds of negative externalities, since a significant proportion of medical and hospital care goes to treat alcohol- and tobacco-related ailments. They may also be explained, however, by a government seeking to maximize its tax revenue from commodities which, although inelastic in demand, are not socially regarded as necessities.

---

[1] The argument in the text assumes a closed economy in which everyone actually pays the tax. In practice, however, even the poll tax will have some efficiency effects. A large enough poll tax might cause people to emigrate. It might also cause people to choose jobs, and lifestyles, that facilitated evasion. People with no fixed addresses, and no regular jobs, would find evasion easier than people who stuck with one job and owned their own houses or flats. Thus, at the margin, the poll tax might influence people's job and residence decisions, in which case it would have adverse efficiency effects.

FIGURE 24.4 Taxes that do not Cause Inefficiencies

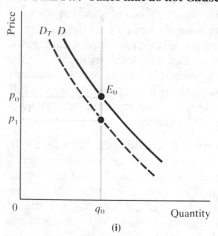 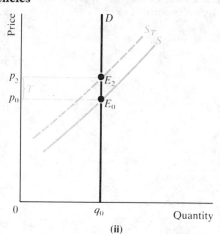

      (i)   (ii)

Any tax that does not alter economic behaviour will not cause economic inefficiency. In both parts of the Figure a demand curve, D, and supply curve, S, intersect at E_0 to produce equilibrium price and quantity of p_0 and q_0. A tax of T per unit is then placed on the sale of the commodity.

In part (i), the supply curve is completely inelastic and the market equilibrium remains at E_0. The after-tax receipts of suppliers are shown by the curve D_T, and their after-tax price by p_1. The quantity produced, and hence the allocation of resources, is unaffected by the tax, all of which is paid by suppliers.

In part (ii), the demand curve is perfectly inelastic. The after-tax supply curve shifts to S_T and market equilibrium goes to E_2, taking market price to p_2. Once again, the allocation of resources is unaffected. This time, however, the whole tax is paid by consumers.

FIGURE 24.5 Work Disincentives of Welfare Schemes

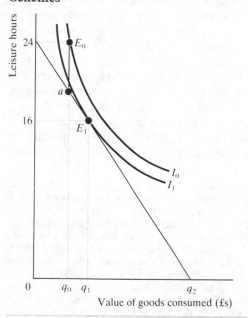

Income-tested benefits provide disincentives for work. The individual is not employed but is receiving benefits from some welfare scheme of q_0. Consumption is at point E_0, with 24 hours of leisure and q_0 of goods.

The opportunity for work now rises. The wage rate is $q_2/24$ per hour. (Twenty-four hours' work earns q_2 of goods.) If the welfare scheme did not exist, the budget line would be the line from 24 to q_2. Equilibrium would be at E_1 on indifference curve I_1 with 8 hours being worked in return for q_1 income.

For the individual at E_0, however, the benefits are reduced £1 for every £1 of income earned. The effective budget line thus starts at E_0 and is vertical down to a, where q_0 is earned by work rather than being received as benefits. (As the individual moves down the segment from E_0 to a, more of q_0 is being earned by work and less received as benefits, but total consumption remains fixed at q_0.) The budget line then runs from a to q_2 indicating that all income comes from work with no benefits being received.

Faced with these choices, a rational household will reject the work offer and remain at E_0 on indifference curve I_0, even though it would have worked if the benefits were unavailable.

Welfare and Work Incentives

Expenditures can have efficiency effects as well as taxes. We illustrate these with a single example. Payments designed to help certain low-income groups are often means-tested. Sometimes the welfare payments are reduced by £1 for every £1 of income the household earns. The household in effect faces a marginal tax rate of 100 per cent on every unit of income earned up to the level of the benefit payments. This introduces a severe disincentive to work, and we should not be surprised when households respond rationally to these market signals.

Say, for example, benefit payments are £50 a week and are cut by £1 for every £1 of income earned. If the household makes £10 a week, benefits fall to £40; if £20 is earned, benefits fall to £30, and so on. Only when more than £50 per week is earned will the household's disposable income begin to rise. Even if the benefits are reduced at a less sharp rate, say 50p per £1 earned, the disincentive of the high implicit tax rate is strong. Figure 24.5 illustrates this disincentive effect by showing how such schemes induce many people to reject employment that they would have accepted if the schemes were not there.

Benefit payments are required to help those in real need. If they are income-related, however, they tend to discourage rational recipients from working.

This does not argue against welfare payments, but it does suggest the desirability of comparing the efficiency effects of alternative schemes.

Benefits Versus Costs: Optimal Intervention

We have seen that government intervention can have benefits in removing market failure, but that it also has costs of many sorts. Government intervention is justified only when the benefits exceed the costs. Consideration of this issue leads us into the question: how much government intervention is optimal? We illustrate how to handle this question by studying the example of preventing pollution and we start by assuming that government intervention is free from error.

Costless intervention: Start with the simplest case where the only costs of government intervention are those associated with the changes in production techniques that are imposed by the government.

Suppose a factory is emitting noxious sulphur dioxide (SO_2) and the government wishes to correct this externality. Choice of method is a difficult problem, but for the moment we assume that the government has correctly determined that the best control method is to install filters on the chimneys.

The government must now decide how much of the pollution should be eliminated. Suppose that simple recirculation of the gases through the chimney filters would reduce the discharge of SO_2 by 50 per cent; after that, the cost would double for each further 10 per cent reduction in the remaining SO_2. At most it would be possible to eliminate 99.44 per cent of all SO_2, but the cost would be vast. The marginal costs of removal rise sharply as the amount of SO_2 eliminated rises from 50 per cent to 99.44 per cent.

What percentage of the gases should be eliminated? The answer depends on the marginal benefits relative to marginal costs. The marginal benefits of pollution control are the external effects avoided. The optimal amount of prevention occurs where the marginal costs of further prevention equal the marginal benefits. This is illustrated in Figure 24.6.

The optimal amount of pollution prevention will be less than the maximum possible when pollution is costly to prevent. Thus the optimal amount of pollution is not zero.

Costs of intervention: We know that government intervention brings with it enforcement costs – costs to the government, to the firm and to third parties – as well as possible inefficiencies introduced elsewhere in the economy. These costs have to be added to the direct costs we have just considered. Suppose, for simplicity, that these costs are variable and rise with the level of pollution to be eliminated.

The marginal costs of enforcement must be added to the marginal direct costs of prevention, thereby shifting upwards the marginal cost curves shown in the Figure. The addition of such costs will decrease the amount of prevention that is optimal. If the costs are large enough, they may

FIGURE 24.6 The Optimal Amount of Pollution Prevention

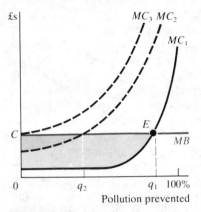

The optimal amount of pollution control occurs when the marginal cost of prevention equals the marginal benefit. MB represents the marginal benefit achieved by pollution prevention, assumed in this example to be constant at £C per percentage point. MC_1 represents the marginal cost of preventing pollution. For all units up to q_1, marginal benefits from pollution prevention exceed marginal costs. For all units beyond q_1, marginal costs exceed marginal benefits. The optimal level of pollution control is thus q_1, where $MB = MC_1$. Total net benefits are shown by the area that is light- and dark-shaded.

If the marginal cost curve shifts to MC_2, due, say, to the addition of enforcement and other external costs, the optimal quantity of prevention will decrease to q_2. The net benefits are then reduced to the darker shaded area.

If costs increase to MC_3, the optimal amount of prevention becomes zero.

even make any prevention uneconomical.

> **The optimal amount of government intervention to avoid market failure will be lower, the greater are the costs of prevention and intervention.**

Will Real-world Governments Achieve Potential Gains?

Governments are far from perfect. This is not because bureaucrats and politicians are worse than other people, more stupid, more rigid or more venal. Instead, it is because they are like others, with flaws as well as virtues. So, having found potential net benefits from perfect but costly government intervention, the final issue is,

would the imperfect governments that we encounter in the real world achieve some of these benefits? Where they do not succeed in achieving potential benefits, we speak of **government failure**.

Governments may sometimes make isolated mistakes just as private decision-makers do. What is interesting, however, are reasons why governments may tend, under certain circumstances, to be more systematically in error than would unhindered markets. Here are a few of the many possible causes of systematic government failure.

Rigidities

Rules and regulations, tax rates and expenditure policies are hard to change. Market conditions, however, change continually and often rapidly. A rule requiring the use of a certain method to reduce pollution may have made sense when the cost of that method was low. It may, however, become a wasteful rule when some alternative becomes the least costly method.

Today's natural monopolies are often made into tomorrow's competitive industries by technological innovations. For example, the near monopoly of the early railways was eliminated by the development of cheap road transport, and the falling cost of air transport is currently providing potent competition for surface transport in the movement of many commodities. One danger of government intervention is that it will be too slow in adapting to a constantly changing environment.

> **A centralized decision-taking body has difficulty in reacting to changing conditions as fast as decentralized decision-takers react to market signals.**

The results of using the wrong method of control – either because of an initial mistake in the choice of method, or because circumstances have changed – are analysed in Figure 24.7.

As well as rigidities in reacting to changing market conditions, governments are often slow to admit mistakes even when they are aware of them. It is often politically easier to go on spending money on a project that has turned sour, than to admit fault. A classic example was the development of Concorde. Successive governments realized it was an enormous money-

FIGURE 24.7   The Effects of Government Failure

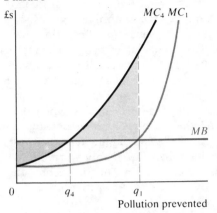

Choice of the wrong method of control will reduce the optimal amount of intervention and may convert the gains from intervention into losses. The MB and MC_1 curves are similar to those in Figure 24.6. Suppose the government specifies a method of pollution control that leads to the costs shown by MC_4 when costs shown by MC_1 could have been achieved by another method. The optimal level of prevention falls to q_4, with net benefits shown by the dark-shaded area. Government failure reduces the amount of prevention that is optimal.

The government will compound its failure if it insists on the level of prevention q_1 while requiring use of the inefficient method. The cost of every unit of pollution prevented beyond q_4 exceeds its benefits by the amount of the light-shaded area. In the case shown, the result is worse than no intervention (the light-shaded area is larger than the dark-shaded area). While the best possible government intervention would have produced a net gain, government failure in this case produces a net loss.

loser, but went on supporting it long after any chance of commercial success was gone.

Markets are much harsher in judging success. When people are investing their own money, the principle that bygones are bygones is usually followed. No firm could raise fresh financial capital for what was currently a poor prospect just because the prospects had seemed good in the past, or because much money had already been spent on it.

Decision-makers' Objectives

By far the most important cause of government failure arises from the nature of the government's own objectives. Until recently, economists did not concern themselves greatly with the motivation of government. The theory of economic policy implicitly assumed that governments had no objectives of their own. As a result, all that economists needed to do was to identify places where the market was best left on its own, and places where government intervention could improve the market's functioning. Governments would then stay out of the former markets, and intervene as necessary in the latter.

This model of government behaviour never fitted reality, and economists were gradually forced to think more deeply about the motivation of governments. Why was economists' advice followed closely in some cases, while it was systematically ignored in others? Today, economists no longer assume that the central authorities are faceless robots doing whatever economic analysis shows to be in the social interest. Instead, they are modelled just as are firms and households – as units with their own objectives which they seek to maximize.

Central authorities undoubtedly do care about the social good to some extent, but public officials have their careers, their families and their prejudices as well. Public officials' own needs are seldom wholly absent from their consideration of the actions they will take. Similarly, their definition of the public interest is likely to be influenced heavily by their personal views of what policies are best. The resulting problems are similar to the principal-agent issues mentioned earlier as a source of market failure. In the present case, the *principals* are the public. They want policies that are for the public good. The problem is that their *agents* – elected and appointed – are motivated by considerations that sometimes pull against the public good.

Modelling governments as maximizers of their own welfare, and then incorporating them into theoretical models of the working of the economy, was a major breakthrough. One of the pioneers of this development was the American economist, James Buchanan, who was awarded the 1986 Nobel Prize in economics for his work in this field. The theory that he helped to develop is called *public-choice theory*.

The key breakthrough was to view the government as just another economic agent engaging in its own maximizing behaviour. When this is done, there is still room for many competing theories, depending on what variables are in the government's preference function (i.e. what things the government cares about). Consider the other two main decision-taking bodies in orthodox economics. Firms have only profits in their utility functions, and they seek to maximize these. Households have only goods in their utility functions, and they seek to maximize their satisfactions from consuming goods. An analogous theory of the government allows only one variable in its utility function, the variable being votes! Such a government takes all its decisions with a view to maximizing its votes at the next election.

Of course, real government behaviour is more complex. For one thing, some government decisions are genuinely intended to improve people's welfare, even when those decisions reduce the government's popularity. But crude though it is, a surprising amount of behaviour can be understood by using the assumption that governments care only about votes, and operate to increase social welfare only when such action also happens to be vote-maximizing. Two examples will illustrate the power of this hypothesis.

Why do governments of so many countries continue to maintain rent controls in spite of the evidence that in the long run these controls harm the very people they are supposed to protect? The public-choice explanation looks at the effect of controls on the voting behaviour of the gainers and the losers.

Those who gain from controls are the large group of tenants. They gain significant amounts, and they command votes – votes that would be turned against any party that abolished controls. Those who lose are in two groups. First are the landlords, who are far less numerous than tenants and, therefore, wield far fewer votes. The second group are the would-be tenants of the future. They will be forced to find other types of accommodation because of the control-induced shortage of rental housing. But their problem is always in the future. At any moment in time, existing tenants will be the short-term losers from decontrol, while the long-term gainers are future tenants. But many future tenants are too young to vote now, and others are not yet born. Many of those who are of voting age today do not understand the link between present rent controls and difficulties they will experience in the

future. As a result of this balance of gainers and losers, the vote-maximizing government has a strong incentive to retain rent controls. Economists can produce evidence until they are blue in the face, but will have no effect on vote-maximizing governments, whose behaviour is uninfluenced by the fact that abolishing controls would increase social welfare and improve social justice in the long run. According to this theory, rent controls will be abolished only when they have reduced the supply of rental housing so much that there are few remaining tenants whose votes the government needs to worry about losing. This appears to have finally become the case in the UK in the late 1980s after 60 years of rent controls.

A second example concerns the policy of agricultural supports that is plaguing most modern governments. Why, in spite of strong advice from economists, have governments persisted in subsidizing agriculture for decades, until many now have major farm crises on their hands? Public-choice theory looks again at the gainers and the losers among the voters.

The gainers from agricultural supports are farmers. They are a large, politically powerful group, who are aware of what they would lose if farm supports were reduced. They would show their disapproval of such action by voting against any government that even suggests it. The entire group of consumers lose. Although more numerous than farmers, and although their total loss is large, each individual consumer suffers only a small loss. For example, a policy that gives £50 million a year to British farmers need only cost each citizen £1 per year.[1] Consumers have more important things to worry about and so do not vote against the government because it supports farmers. As long as the average voter is unconcerned and often unaware of the losses suffered, the vote-maximizing government will ignore the interests of the many, and back the interests of the few. Only when the cost of agricultural support becomes so large that ordinary taxpayers

---

[1] 'Why worry?' you may ask. 'Isn't the small loss to each consumer a reasonable price to pay?' It may be in this one case. The problem, however, lies not in one such policy, but in the cumulative effects of many. If each of many special-interest groups secures a policy that costs each member of the public a small amount, the total bill over all such policies can be, and in many countries is, very large indeed.

begin to count the cost, does the vote-maximizing government consider changing the agricultural policy. What is required for a policy change, according to this theory, is not that the amount of the loss be increased, but that those who lose become sufficiently aware of their losses for it to affect their voting behaviour.

The Effect of Government Failure

Suppose that, for any of the reasons discussed above, the central authorities make a mistake in regulation. Say they mistakenly specify a method of pollution control that is less effective than the best method. As we saw in Figure 24.7, this will increase the cost of achieving any given level of prevention. If they insist on the level of control appropriate to the correct method, but choose the incorrect method, they can convert a social gain from control into a social loss.

If governments pursue their own objectives such as vote maximizing, they may sometimes fail to act in the public interest by design rather than by mistake. If government economists foresee that a politically popular policy will increase the degree of market failure in the long term, while seeming beneficial in the short term, the government may adopt the harmful policy, in spite of the unfavourable long-run consequences. The government could plead in such cases that it was only being democratic in following the public will. But if governments are to follow exactly where public opinion leads, they do not require experts who are able to foresee consequences not obvious to casual observers.

Government Intervention Today

Do governments intervene too little, or too much, in response to market failure? This question reflects one aspect of the continuing debate over the role of government in the economy.

The Role of Analysis

Economics can help to eliminate certain misconceptions that cloud and confuse the debate. We have earlier noted one such misconception: the optimal level of a negative externality, such as pollution, is not, as some urge, zero.

Another mistake is to equate market failure with the greed of profit-motivated corporations. Externalities do not require callous, thoughtless

or deliberately deceptive practices of private, profit-seeking firms; they occur whenever the signals, to which rational decision-takers respond, exclude significant benefits and costs. Local authorities and nationalized industries pollute just as much as privately owned industries when they neglect externalities in their operations, as they often do.

A third mistake is to think that the profits are related to externalities. Both a profitable industry (such as chemicals) and an unprofitable one (such as coal) are capable of spending too little on pollution control or on safety. They may also spend too much. The existence of profits provides no clue one way or the other.

The Role of Ideology

While positive analysis has a part to play, there are reasons why ideology plays a large role in evaluating government intervention. First, measuring the costs of government intervention is difficult, particularly with respect to indirect costs, because some of the trade-offs are inherently uncertain. How important and how unsafe is nuclear power? Does the ban on some pesticides cause so much malnutrition as to offset the gains in the ecology that it brings? What cannot be readily measured can be alleged to be extremely high (or low) by opponents (or supporters) of intervention.

Second, classifying the actual pattern of government intervention as successful or not is in part subjective. Has government safety regulation been (choose one) useful if imperfect, virtually ineffective or positively adverse? All three views have been defended.

Third, specifying what constitutes market failure is sometimes difficult. Does product differentiation represent market success (by giving consumers the variety they want) or failure (by foisting unwanted variations on them)?

In many of the advanced industrial countries in the mid-1980s, confidence in the existing mix of free-market and government regulation seems to be relatively low. No one believes that government intervention can, or should be, reduced to zero. But many governments seem to have become more cautious in evaluating the potential net gains from specific interventions and willing to leave an increasing variety of decisions to be taken through the market mechanism.

SUMMARY

1. Free markets can fail to achieve efficiency because of such influences as: the existence of public goods, a divergence of social from private costs caused by pollution, common-property resources and congestion, principal-agent problems, the moral hazard and the adverse selection associated with insurance, and high transaction costs that inhibit private provision of particular goods and services.

2. Markets are sometimes also said to fail when they do not achieve other objectives held by members of the society, such as achieving a distribution of income regarded as equitable, protecting individuals from abuse by others (or sometimes by themselves), providing too few merit goods and too many merit bads, and allowing transactions that violate those social obligations that transcend the market. Although no one would disagree that these reasons sometimes provide valid grounds for government intervention, they are a different kind of 'market failure' than inefficiencies, because they refer to failure to achieve results whose evaluation depends on personal value judgements.

3. Governments may intervene in order to correct market failures using the tools of rules and regulations, nationalization of industry, expenditures and taxes.

4. A rational assessment of government intervention requires an assessment of the costs as well as the potential benefits. Internal costs refer to the government's costs of administering its policies. Direct external costs refer to the costs imposed on the non-government sector by these policies in such terms as extra production costs, costs of compliance and losses in productivity. Indirect external costs refer to the efficiency losses resulting from the alteration in price signals caused by government tax and expenditure policies.

5. As well as showing the potential for benefits to exceed costs in a world where the government functioned perfectly, it is necessary to consider the likely outcome in the imperfect world of reality. Government failure – not achieving some possible gains – can arise because of rigidities causing a lack of adequate response of rules and regulations to changing conditions, poorer foresight on the part of government regulators compared with private participants in the market, and government objectives – such as winning the next election – that conflict with such objectives as improving economic efficiency.

TOPICS FOR REVIEW

- Sources of market failure
- Public goods
- Externalities
- Common property resources
- Merit goods
- The tools of government intervention
- The benefits and costs of government intervention
- Sources of government failure
- Public-choice theory
- Direct and indirect taxes
- Progressive, regressive and proportional taxes

25

Aims and Objectives of Government Policy[1]

The central authorities play a major role in all of the world's economies. The nature and amount of their intervention differs from country to country, with the UK being somewhere between the extremes to be found in such command economies as the USSR, and in such relatively free-market economies as the USA. Even in so-called free-market economies, however, the government's economic activities are widespread, and many individual markets are regulated and controlled. In the 1980s, privatization and deregulation have been moving many countries, including the UK, towards a greater reliance on markets.

POLICY GOALS IN OUTLINE

The major goals of microeconomic policy, as traditionally seen by economists, are *efficiency* and *equity*. A third goal, growth, must now be added to this list.

Efficiency: Recall from Chapter 23 that efficiency is concerned with getting the most out of limited economic resources. When an economy is productively efficient, it is producing its current bundle of goods at the lowest possible resource cost. When an economy is allocatively efficient, the bundle of goods currently being produced is optimal. Achieving complete efficiency is an unattainable goal. Much government policy is devoted, however, to increasing efficiency.

Equity: The second traditional goal of economic policy is equity. An equitable distribution of income is one that satisfies our ideas of justice or fairness. Notice that this is not necessarily an equal distribution. Many people feel that income differentials related to differentials in effort, or in contributions to output, are just. Others feel that justice calls for an equal distribution of income and are willing to accept income differentials only where needed to avoid extreme inefficiencies.

Whatever their stand on the above issue, most people feel that social justice can be improved by some alteration in the distribution of income that would result from the unhindered market. Thus a major goal of government policy in all market economies is to influence the distribution of income.

[1] Factual and institutional background for this chapter can be found in Harbury and Lipsey, *op. cit.*, Chapter 6.

Growth: A third major goal of policy is economic growth. In the recent past, growth has often been treated as a purely macroeconomic issue – the assumption being that growth depended mainly on such macroeconomic aggregates as total saving and total investment. In the last decade or so, under the influence of the so-called supply-side critics, economists have rediscovered the teaching of the Classical economists:

> **as well as being related to such macro magnitudes as total saving and total investment, growth is closely related to the micro-behaviour of the economy, to how well individual markets work, and to the extent to which government policy avoids distorting market signals.**

Since the early 1980s, governments have no longer set their microeconomic policies without considering the effects of these policies on the microeconomic adjustments necessary for growth.

Two preliminaries: Before proceeding, two preliminary points deserve mention. First, because most policies have more than one goal, the classification of policies according to goals cannot be precise. We deal as far as possible, however, with policies according to their major goal. Second, since the importance of microeconomic policy to growth has only recently been re-emphasized, few micro policies have growth as their sole objective. Growth effects thus tend to be considered from time to time in the context of policies whose main objective is either efficiency or equity.

EFFICIENCY

Many government policies are designed to increase efficiency.

Improving Knowledge and Imposing Standards

People cannot make maximizing decisions if they are poorly informed or deceived about the things they are buying or selling. Rules requiring that products and prices be described correctly are meant to improve the efficiency of choices by providing people with correct and relevant information.

In many cases where the consequences of errors are not dramatic, consumers can be left to discover, through trial and error, what is in their own best interests. In other cases, however, the results of error can be too drastic to allow consumers to learn from their own experiences which products are reliable and which unreliable. For example, botulism, caused by poorly preserved foods, can cause death. In such cases, the state intervenes to impose standards in consumers' own best interests.

Standards are also set in the workplace. The individualist might argue that firms should be left to set their own safety standards, in which case high-risk firms would have to pay wage premiums to induce workers to accept these risks voluntarily. Those who favour government regulation argue it on two grounds. First, firms are often better informed than workers on changing safety conditions in work, particularly in small factories. Government regulation compensates for the inefficiencies caused by this unequal access to information. Second, people who are desperate for work will take risks that are socially unacceptable, or that their own desperation causes them to assess imperfectly. In this case, the purpose of government intervention is either to impose social values not held by specific individuals or to act paternalistically in the knowledge that the state can assess the self-interests of the workers better than do the workers themselves.

Provision of Public Goods

Because everyone can consume a public good once it is produced, private producers cannot market it. Lighthouses, weather notices broadcast to shipping, defence and a host of other similar public goods would not be provided if the market were the sole determinant of production.

When should a public good be provided? To illustrate the basic principle, consider a community composed of just two consumers. The government must decide whether or not to provide some public good which comes in a single indivisible unit; it is either produced, or it is not. Say that the first individual is prepared to pay £100 to have the use of the good, while the second individual is prepared to pay £75. On efficiency grounds, the good should be produced as long as its cost of production is no more than £175. Say it is £150. Producing the good provides services that the community values at £175 at an opportunity cost of only £150. There is a £25 gain on the operation.

The optimal quantity of a public good: The above example reveals a key point about public goods.

> The community's demand curve for a public good is the *vertical* sum of the demand curves of the individual consumers.

If one person consumes a unit of an ordinary commodity, another person cannot also consume that unit. Thus, to satisfy all the demand at any given price, the *sum of all the quantities demanded* must be produced. With a public good, however, a given unit can be consumed by everyone. Thus the demand for any quantity of the good is represented by the sum of the prices that each individual consumer would be willing to pay for it.

> If the amount of a public good can be varied continuously, the optimal quantity to produce is where the marginal cost of the last unit is just equal to the sum of the prices all consumers would be willing to pay for that unit.

This equilibrium, which is analysed in Figure 25.1, guarantees that the last unit of the public good costs as much to produce as the value that it gives to all its consumers.

Who pays?: One way to pay for a public good would be to charge each person the same fraction of the maximum amount he or she would be prepared to pay rather than go without the good, while fixing the fraction so as to cover the total costs of production. Consider, for example, a community of two persons, one of whom was prepared to pay £400 and the other £200 for some public good rather than go without. If the good costs £400 to produce, then each person would be charged two-thirds of their own maximum, making £267 for the first person and £133 for the second. Their payments would just cover

FIGURE 25.1 The Optimal Output of a Public Good

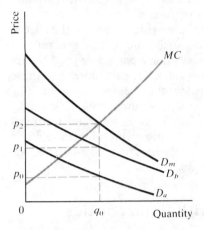

The society's demand curve for a public good is the vertical sum of the demand curves of all the individuals who consume that good. The demand curves D_a and D_b refer to two individual consumers of a public good. Their collective demand is shown by D_m, which is the vertical summation of D_a and D_b. For example, individual a would pay p_0 for quantity q_0, while individual b would pay p_1 for the same quantity. Together they are willing to pay the sum of p_0 and p_1, which is p_2.

The optimal quantity of the good to produce is q_0, where the marginal cost curve, MC, cuts the demand curve. At this point, the marginal cost of another unit is just equal to the sum of the values that each person places on that unit.

total costs of production, leaving a consumers' surplus of £200.

The problem with any formula of this type lies in getting people to reveal what they would be willing to pay. Suppose, for example, that the government is considering building a public good to serve a community of 1,000 persons. It asks each of them how much he or she is prepared to pay. If I am one of those 1,000, it is in my interests to understate my true valuation, as long as everyone else does not do the same. Indeed, I might say I valued the good at zero, while others reported enough value to cover the costs. The public good would then be produced, and I would get the use of it for no payment at all.

This **free rider problem** makes it difficult to cover the costs of public goods by any formula based on people's individual valuations of that good. If enough people try to be free-riders, the reported valuations will fall short of the cost. The public good will then not be built and everyone will be worse off than if they told the truth and paid their share of the cost.

Because of the free-rider problem, the cost of public goods is usually met out of general taxation. Those who value a particular good higher than the average valuation gain more than those who value it below the average valuation. The hope is that, over a large number of public goods, these individual differences will tend to cancel out. Everyone will then gain on balance as a result of the government's provision of public goods out of tax revenue.

Dealing with Externalities

Divergences between private and social costs and benefits are an important source of market failure. Firms that impose costs on society, that they do not bear themselves, will be motivated to produce too much. Firms that confer benefits on society, for which they cannot receive payment, will be motivated to produce too little.

In Figure 24.6, we studied the optimal correction of pollution. Here we go a little deeper into methods.

Rules and regulations: One method of correcting an externality is to make rules and regulations. Consider, for example, an industry containing a number of firms, each with a number of factories all emitting some pollutants.

The crudest rule would set a maximum daily amount of pollutant that each plant could emit. This is a wasteful rule if the costs of conforming with it differs among plants. For example, if preventing the last unit of pollution costs £100 for plant A and only £10 for plant B, society could get the same prevention at lower cost by switching prevention efforts from plant A to Plant B. If one more unit of pollution were allowed to be emitted by plant A, this would save £100 in anti-pollution costs. This expenditure could be used to reduce pollution emitted by plant B by 10 units at £10 per unit.

To get around this inefficiency, the regulating body could give each firm a pollution quota. The firm would then be free to meet that quota by allocating pollution-reduction expenditures where the return was highest.

But what if one firm has plants where the costs of pollution reduction are low, while another has different sorts of plants where costs are higher. For any given total expenditure on pollution reduction, society will get more return if expenditures are concentrated on those firms, and plants, where reduction costs are least.

An all-seeing administrator could achieve this result by ordering just the right amount of pollution reduction in each plant. But it is hard for administrators to obtain the requisite knowledge. Furthermore, if the administrators did get sufficient information to establish just the right quotas, plant by plant and firm by firm, that information would need continual updating as technology changed over time.

Internalization: A more efficient method is to **internalize the externality** which means doing something that makes it enter into the firm's own calculations of its private costs and benefits. A tax per unit of pollution can be imposed. Firms then see the social cost of pollution as a private cost. They will reduce pollution until the marginal cost of reducing a unit of pollution from every plant is equal to the per-unit pollution tax. This policy uses the flexibility of the price system to decentralize decisions. In an attempt to minimize their tax, firms will spend money where it has most effect in reducing pollution.

The government's only decision is then to set the rate of tax so that the total amount of pollution is at its optimal level.

The most efficient regulation of externalities tends to occur when the government sets an overall target, and then uses price incentives, in the form of taxes or subsidies, to induce decentralized decision-takers to achieve that target in the most efficient manner.

Two other policies would also do the same job. First, the firms creating the pollution could be required to compensate those affected. The firms would then only carry out polluting activities when the private benefit from a unit of activity exceeded the external cost. Second, mechanisms could be set up so that those affected could bribe the polluting firms not to produce. Payments would be made to induce the firm to cut back on

FIGURE 25.2 Correcting Externalities

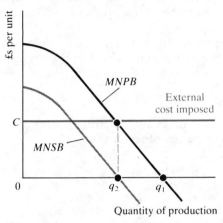

Internalizing an externality can correct market failure. The black curve labelled *MNPB*, marginal net private benefit, shows the contribution to the firm's profits of each unit of production. Its height at any output is the marginal revenue of that unit minus its marginal cost. The firm is motivated to produce all units that make a positive contribution to its profits. Its equilibrium output is thus q_1 where *MNPB* is zero (i.e. $MR = MC$). Production of each unit of this commodity is assumed to impose an external cost of £C on outsiders, as shown by the coloured line. Subtracting this additional social cost from the *MNPB* yields the marginal net social benefit curve, *MNSB*, shown by the grey line. The socially optimal output is q_2, where the *MNSB* equals zero. At this output, *MNPB* is just equal to the external cost imposed on outsiders for each unit of production.

Suppose the firm is required to pay an 'effluent tax' of £C per unit. Its *MNPB* now becomes the grey line. The externality has been *internalized*, and the profit-maximizing firm is motivated to reduce its output from q_1 to q_2. It does this because any units produced beyond q_2 would now subtract from total profits.

The same result occurs if the firm has to pay £C per unit compensation directly to those affected rather than as a tax to the government.

If those affected can bribe the firm to reduce its output, they will be willing to pay a maximum of £C per unit and the firm will accept that amount until production is reduced to q_2. Below that, the minimum bribe the firm would accept exceeds £C.

In all three cases – tax, compensation or bribe – production is in equilibrium at q_2 (although the distribution of gains and losses differs among the cases).

all those units of production where the private benefits exceeded the cost. In both cases production would be at the point where the net private benefit to the firm of the last unit of polluting activity equalled the external cost imposed on society by that unit of activity. This result is demonstrated in Figure 25.2.

The problem of externalities arises because of the absence of property rights. The polluting firm uses the free air to dump its waste. If it owned the air, it would worry about the loss of the value of its property caused by the pollution. If those affected by the pollution owned the air, they would not allow it to be used unless they were paid sufficient compensation.

> **Many externalities arise from an absence of property rights. One way to internalize the externality is to create appropriate property rights.**

Policy Towards Competition and Monopoly

Most governments have policies concerning the behaviour of firms. These policies usually have three main objectives, which are considered below: to prevent firms from colluding where competition is technically possible; to regulate the behaviour of firms that are made into monopolies by virtue of the technology of production; and to encourage activities that contribute to the long-run growth of the economy.

Preserving Competition Where Possible

The UK government has several policies designed to discourage the joint profit-maximizing behaviour which occurs when, by actual or tacit agreement, all firms in an industry act as if they were a single monopoly. Mergers that seem aimed at monopolization can be investigated by the Monopolies and Mergers Commission (MMC). Restrictive practices, which are explicit co-operative agreements among independent firms on matters such as prices and market shares, must be registered with the Director General for Fair Trading, and may then be referred to the Restrictive Practices Court.

Notice that, for alleged restrictive practices, the burden of proof lies with the firms, which must prove that they are not acting against the public interest. In contrast, the authorities must prove that mergers are not in the public interest.

The MMC has investigated a wide range of restrictive practices. It has sometimes found in the industry's favour, and at other times recommended that specific practices be abandoned.

Only once has it recommended that a firm be split up. Even in this one case, the recommendation was not accepted by the government.

Concentration in the UK: Concentration has been increasing in the UK over many years, with the percentage of industrial production

---

BOX 25.1   MORE ON MERGERS

Mergers, which unite two or more formerly independent firms, are a way in which monopoly power can grow. There are, however, several different types of merger and they do not all have the same consequences for market power. The type we usually think of is called a **horizontal merger**, where firms at the same stage of production unite. Since these firms are selling the same commodities, horizontal mergers usually represent an increase in market power.

Vertical mergers occur when firms at different stages of production unite. Usually the output of one of the merging firms is the other merging firm's input. The motive for such mergers is not to gain more power over one market, but rather to obtain a secure supply of some raw material or a secure set of outlets for one's products (as when brewery firms buy up public houses).

The third form of merger, the so-called **conglomerate** or **lateral merger**, occurs when firms selling quite unrelated products merge. The resulting firm is often called a *conglomerate*. Again, the motive is not to gain more power over any single market; more usually, it is one of risk-reduction. Firms in declining industries may seek to gain a share of expanding industries, and so avoid being permanently depressed. Firms selling products that are very sensitive to trade-cycle fluctuations may seek to expand into industries that are less cyclically sensitive. Firms selling many products may feel better insulated from unforeseen and unforeseeable events that can depress the market for one particular product.

Conglomerates can, however, engage in certain anti-competitive actions. For example, they can *cross-subsidize* various activities. This means using profits earned in a market insulated against entry to subsidize losses suffered in another market. If the losses are due to predatory price behaviour designed to drive competitors out of that market, the behaviour is anti-competitive.

Policy-makers who are concerned to control the power of firms to earn large profits by raising price well above opportunity cost will regard different types of mergers differently. Some types of mergers increase the market power of the participants, others do not.

Building societies recently engaged in a series of horizontal mergers. Bradford & Bingley Building Society has merged with the Yorkshire Building Society, Anglia Building Society with Nationwide Building Society, Leeds Permanent Building Society with the Town & Country Building Society. The London *Times* suggested in August 1987 that it was unlikely that more than 40 of the 123 building societies then in existence would survive the next five years.

Other recent examples of *horizontal mergers* (including takeovers) are the acquisition of Safeway supermarkets in the UK by the Argyll Group, which already ran Presto supermarkets, and Ratner's merger with H. Samuel (both retail jewellers).

It is sometimes difficult to decide whether or not a merger is horizontal. When Next, a chain of clothes shops, bought Dillons, a chain of 270 newsagents shops, and when Woolworth made a takeover bid for Underwoods, the chain of chemist shops, the firms involved were both retailers yet of a different type. Another example which *might* be regarded as horizontal was Perrier's purchase of Buxton Mineral Water. (Economists have a technical answer: if there is a high cross-elasticity of demand between the products of the firms concerned, then they are close substitutes, and the merger should be regarded as horizontal.)

A merger which can be regarded as *vertical* is Grand Metropolitan's takeover of Ruddles, Britain's best-known brewer of 'real ale', on the assumption that Ruddles beer would be sold in Grand Met's hotels and public houses. Of course, if one took account of the fact that Grand Met already owned the major brewer Watney's, one might consider the merger as horizontal.

Examples of *lateral* and *conglomerate* mergers are the combinations of Associated Dairies (which operate ASDA supermarkets) with MFI Furniture Groups; British Electric Traction (a very diversified group) with Initial (the laundry firm), and Sear (owner of show shops, department stores and jewellers) with Foster Brothers Clothing.

accounted for by the 100 largest firms growing steadily. Much of this has been the result of the growth of large firms at the expense of smaller ones, but much has also been the result of mergers of existing firms.

Box 25.1 gives some further discussion of the kinds, and the practice, of mergers in the UK. Only a small fraction of mergers have been referred to the MMC, and only some of them have been found to be against the public interest. The very threat of referral, however, may prevent the more anti-social mergers from occurring in the first place.

Should one be alarmed over the growing concentration of UK industries? The main reason why many economists answer this question in the negative is the growing internationalization of competition. The absence of trade barriers within the EC, and the decline in world transportation costs, has extended the size of most markets well beyond the boundaries of single nations. An apparent monopoly in the UK may well be operating in a highly competitive market that includes German, French and even Japanese firms.

Control of Natural Monopolies

We saw in Chapter 12 that perfect competition can exist only in industries in which the *MES* is small in relation to the total market demand. In this case, total output can be produced by many competing firms, all producing at minimum average total costs. If the *MES* is large in relation to the market demand, perfect competition is impossible. Firms will expand under the incentive of falling long-run costs, until the market is dominated by a few large producers, or possibly by only one. Such industries are **natural monopolies** or **natural oligopolies** since competition among many firms would quickly give way to monopoly or oligopoly.

Where *MES* is large, there are cost advantages in having only a few large firms in the industry rather than many small, high-cost firms. In the extreme case of natural monopoly, costs can only be minimized when the number of firms has been reduced to one. Although prices may be kept near to costs due to competition among oligopolists, no such force exists under monopoly. We shall concern ourselves, therefore, with natural monopoly. In such industries, costs are minimized by

the monopolization, while governments usually intervene to hold price to its competitive level.

Pricing policies: Whether the state nationalizes, or merely regulates, privately owned, natural monopolies, the industry's pricing policy is a matter for the state to determine. Usually, the industry is asked to follow some policy other than profit maximization.

Marginal Cost Pricing. Sometimes the state dictates that the natural monopoly should try to set price equal to short run marginal cost in an effort to maximize consumers' plus producers' surpluses in that industry. This policy is called **marginal cost pricing**. But there are problems here. The natural monopoly may still have unexploited economies of scale, and hence be operating on the falling portion of its *ATC* curve. In this case, *MC* will be less than *ATC* and pricing at marginal cost will lead to losses. This is shown in part (i) of Figure 25.3.

A falling-cost, natural monopoly directed to price at marginal cost will suffer losses.

Now assume, however, that demand is sufficient to allow the firm to produce on the rising portion of its *ATC* curve, where *MC* exceeds *ATC*. If the firm is directed to equate *MC* to price, it will earn profits. This is shown in part (ii) of the Figure.[1]

When a rising-cost, natural monopoly is directed to price at marginal cost, it will earn profits.

Average Cost Pricing. Sometimes natural monopolies are directed to produce the output that will just cover total costs, thus earning neither profits nor losses. This means the firm produces to the point where average revenue equals average total cost, which is where the demand curve cuts the average total cost curve. Part (i) of Figure 25.3 shows that, for a falling-cost firm, this pricing policy requires producing at less than the optimal output. This avoids the

---

[1] Some books define a natural monopoly as one where long-run costs are falling when price equals marginal cost. This, however, is only sufficient; it is not necessary. Demand may be such that one firm is producing, when price equals marginal cost, on the rising portion of its long-run cost curve, while there is no price at which two firms could both cover their costs.

FIGURE 25.3 Pricing Policies for Natural Monopolies

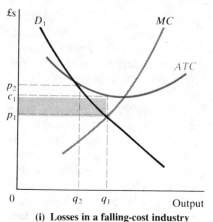 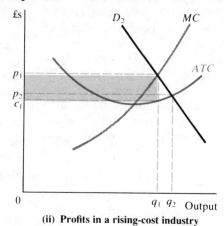

(i) **Losses in a falling-cost industry**   (ii) **Profits in a rising-cost industry**

Marginal cost pricing leads to profit or losses, while average cost pricing violates the efficiency condition. In each diagram the output at which marginal cost equals price is q_1 and price is p_1.

In part (i), average costs are falling at output q_1, so marginal costs are less than the average cost of c_1. There is a loss of $c_1 - p_1$ on each unit, making a total loss equal to the shaded area.

In part (ii), average cost of c_1 is less than price at output q_1. There is a profit of $p_1 - c_1$ on each unit sold, making a total profit equal to the shaded area.

In each part of the diagram, the output at which average cost equals price is q_2 and price is p_2. In part (i), marginal cost is less than price at q_2, so output is below its optimal level. In part (ii), marginal cost exceeds price at q_2, so output is greater than its optimal level.

---

losses that would occur under marginal cost pricing. Part (ii) shows that, for a rising-cost firm, the policy requires producing at more than the optimal output. This dissipates the profits that would occur under marginal cost pricing.

> **Generally, average cost pricing will not result in allocative efficiency.**

Investment policies: The optimal pricing policy makes price equal to short-run marginal cost. But we know that the position of the short-run MC curve (as well as the AC curve) depends on the amount of fixed capital that is currently available to be combined with the variable factor. What should determine the long-run decision on investment?

The answer, if marginal cost pricing is being followed, is to compare the current market price with the long-run marginal costs. The former expresses the value consumers place on a further unit of output. The latter expresses the full resource cost of providing an extra unit of output,

including capital costs. (To make the correct comparison, the cost of capital must be expressed at its current rental price so that it can be added to such other costs as wages and fuel.) If price exceeds $LRMC$, capacity should be expanded. If it is less, capacity should be allowed to decline as capital wears out. Thus:

> **The efficient pricing system rations the output of existing capacity by setting price equal to the short-run resource cost of producing another unit. It also adjusts capacity in the long run until the full marginal cost of producing another unit is equal to the price.**

The use of average cost pricing tends to distort investment decisions. Assume that there are two methods of generating electricity, cheap hydro-electric plants and expensive atomic energy plants. All of the hydro-electric sites have been utilized, so that new capacity must come from new atomic energy plants. The electricity authority uses average cost pricing, so that users pay more than the cost of hydro-electricity and less than the costs of atomic electricity. The authority finds that there is excess demand for electricity at its current market price and proposes to install new capacity. Should it be allowed to do so?

The relevant test is not, however, the existence of excess demand at the current price, because the long-run cost of providing more electricity exceeds that price. The cost is, in fact, the full long-run marginal cost of providing electricity from atomic plants. On efficiency grounds, another plant should be built only if there is excess demand at a price that equals that full long-run cost.

This case illustrates the error often made in nationalized and regulated industries that face rising long-run costs. If they priced at marginal cost, they would make profits. So in the interest of equity they price at average cost. But market price does not then provide the correct signal about the social value of further investment.

If a rising-cost industry installs enough capacity to meet all the demand when price is set equal to average cost, it will create more capacity than is socially optimal.

Industrial Policies for Growth

So far we have considered government policies towards industry that were primarily directed at efficiency. Other policies have long-term growth as their primary objective. Many of the disagreements over such policies depend on differing views on the micro-conditions needed to encourage growth-creating innovations. Some economists feel that maximizing the amount of competition at any point in time is the most important condition for growth. Others follow Schumpeter in holding that the existence of monopoly and oligopoly profits at any point in time is the most powerful incentive to growth-creating innovations.

Patents: Some economists who believe that competitive market structures best serve consumers by assuring them low prices, worry about a possible lack of incentives to innovate under competition. If an innovation can be easily copied, new firms may enter an industry so quickly that the innovating firm is not compensated for the costs and risks of innovation. The innovation is, in effect, a public good and private firms are not motivated to produce it.

Patent laws are designed to provide the needed incentives. They create a temporary property right over the invention, extending the short-run period during which the invention's owner can earn profits as a reward for inventing. Once the patent expires, and sometimes even before – as we saw in the case of ballpoint pens – other firms can copy the innovation. If there are no other barriers to entry, production will then expand until profits fall to normal.

Reduction of entry barriers: Those who accept Schumpeter's theory hold that anti-monopoly policy, and public utility regulations, are unnecessary as policies to influence behaviour in the very long run. They worry that state intervention will inadvertently create entry barriers that will protect existing firms from the growth-creating process of creative destruction. They see government policies directed at minimizing entry barriers as the only ones that are needed.

Nationalization: Those who reject Schumpeter's theory often support anti-monopoly and public utility regulation policies. They feel that such policies are required to prevent monopolies from earning large profits at the expense of consumers.

Supporters of Schumpeter's theory argue that nationalization and public regulation will defeat their own purposes in the long term by inhibiting the process of creative destruction. A government monopoly provides the most enforceable entry barrier. It may inhibit the introduction of new products, and new ways of producing old products, that would have occurred through new firms entering to attack the entrenched positions of existing firms. Supporters of this view, point to the USSR's evident desire to buy technology from Western countries, and argue that the rapid development of new products and processes in the oligopolistic and monopolistic industries operating in market-oriented economies gives some support to Schumpeter's view.

A short-term, long-term trade-off? Economists who accept both the force of the argument that monopolistic firms can earn large exploitative profits in the short term *and* Schumpeter's argument about the very long run, face a policy dilemma. In the short term, firms which gain monopoly power may earn very large profits at the expense of consumers. In the very long term, however, attempts to control these monopolies may inhibit the creative destruction that helps to raise living standards, through productivity growth. For these economists,

> **the policy world is not a simple place, and policies that help to achieve desired goals over one time-span must be constantly scrutinized for undesired effects over other time-spans.**

EQUITY

The central authorities attempt to change the distribution of income in countless ways. Some attempts are general in their effects, but some are quite specific and localized.

The Functional Distribution of Income

Governments have many policies with respect to the functional distribution of income. In the UK, for example, income arising from labour services – which was called *earned income* – was until 1985 taxed at lower income-tax rates than income arising from capital – which was called *unearned income*. This UK policy tended to redistribute income among the owners of factors away from those who provided capital and in favour of those who provided labour. Also, by reducing the return on invested capital, it may have provided a disincentive to save and invest.

Governments also have policies affecting the distribution of income within the broad functional class of labour income. Labour governments may try to redistribute income from professional-managerial and other middle-class groups to skilled and unskilled workers. Conservative governments may try to resist, or reverse, this redistribution.

Governments also change the distribution of income in favour of all sorts of relatively small special-interest groups. Special tax treatment, subsidies, legislation that restricts competition, and a host of other measures operate in many countries to turn the distribution of income in favour of various groups – small businessmen, farmers in general and poultry and milk producers in particular, households with large numbers of children, certain professional groups, some groups of skilled workers and unmarried mothers are examples. The treatment afforded to many – but of course not all – of these special-interest groups is often hard to explain on grounds of efficiency or equity. Many of these redistributive measures can, however, be explained by the theory of the vote-maximizing government. Such a government is tempted to adopt policies that greatly help each member of a small identifiable group, and slightly hurt each member of a large, diffuse, unorganized group. Those who are helped a lot will be grateful to the government, while those who are hurt a bit are less likely to notice, and, hence, unlikely to blame the government for their losses.

The Size Distribution of Income

In trying to alter the size distribution of income, the government is concerned with large and small incomes, irrespective of the source of that income. Most governments seek to narrow the range of the size distribution, reducing the incomes of those at the upper end and raising the incomes of those at the lower end. In doing so, however, governments face a trade-off between equality and efficiency. Some jobs are more skilled, more difficult, more unpleasant or more risky than others and, unless the former are more highly paid than the latter, people will not be persuaded to do them. Even Communist governments allows major inequalities in the size distribution of income in order to provide the incentives needed to make the economic system function.

Tax Policy

The first prong of any government's attempt to change the size distribution of income is its tax policy. A tax system that is progressive when viewed as a whole is helpful. Debate centres on the conflict between progressivity and adequate incentives.

Disincentive effects: The disincentive of high marginal rates of tax is still a subject of debate. If we consider a 'closed economy' where there is no possibility of emigration, then marginal rates of up to 50 per cent do not seem to have strong disincentive effects. Some people work less hard, but others work harder in order to restore their after-tax incomes to what they would have been if tax rates were lower. At some point over 50 per cent, however, high marginal tax rates begin to have more serious disincentive effects. As marginal rates approach 100 per cent, the disincentive effect becomes absolute.

Steeply progressive rates also have allocative effects among types of employment that reduce efficiency. People whose incomes are high for a few years and low thereafter pay high taxes, relative to others with the same lifetime incomes that are spread more evenly over the years. People with high incomes spend much time and expense on lawyers and accountants to shield their incomes from taxes. Such activities produce no other net output for the society.

In an open society where emigration is possible, very high marginal rates of tax have major effects. Authors, artists, pop groups and others who 'strike it rich' are strongly tempted to emigrate to countries that will allow them to keep a higher proportion of their incomes. The temptation is particularly strong when there are countries with common linguistic and cultural environments and substantially lower tax rates. Emigration of successful people of this type from the UK to the US, and various even lower-tax countries, has been significant over the past fifty years when UK marginal rates of income tax were often double those in the United States.

> **From the point of view of maximizing tax revenues, and reducing tax burdens on middle- and lower-income groups, it would be better to have high-income people still in the country paying tax rates of 40–50 per cent than out of the country, avoiding higher tax rates.**

Income taxes and the supply of effort: We have seen that income taxes cause an inefficiency by distorting the leisure- income trade off. But would a reduction of income taxes cause people to work more?

Economic theory makes no general prediction about the effect on the supply of effort of raising or lowering the rates of income tax. In Figure 17.7 on page 295, we showed that a rise in the wage rate might increase, or decrease, the supply of effort and, similarly, a fall in the wage rate might have either effect. Now observe that the after-tax wage rate is lowered by a rise in the rate of income tax, and raised by a fall in the rate. It follows immediately that any given change in the rate of income tax may either raise or lower the supply of effort.

The Laffer curve: The possibility that a cut in the rate of tax might increase the supply of effort so much that tax collections increased is illustrated in a famous curve called the **Laffer curve**, named after an American exponent of supply-side economics, Professor Arthur Laffer.

The general shape of the curve, which is shown in Figure 25.4, is argued as a matter of simple logic. At a zero tax rate, no revenue will be collected. Similarly, at an average tax rate of 100 per cent, revenues will again be zero because no one would bother to earn taxable income just to support the government. At intermediate rates, people will both earn taxable income and pay taxes. Government tax revenues will reach a maximum value at some rate of taxation below 100 per cent. For rates higher than the rate that produces this maximum, every increase in tax rates will lead to a decrease in tax revenues. The curve cannot be a guide to practical policy, however, until we know where this maximum

FIGURE 25.4 The Laffer Curve

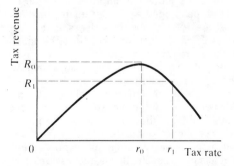

Increases in tax rates beyond some level will decrease rather than increase tax revenue. The curve relates the government's tax revenue to the tax rate. As drawn, revenue reaches a maximum level of R_0 at average tax rate r_0. If tax rates were at r_1, *reducing* them to r_0 would increase revenue to the government.

occurs. An interesting early precursor of Laffer's curve is discussed in Box 25.2.

Tax shifting: The **shifting** of a tax refers to the passing of its incidence from the person who initially pays it to someone else. The **incidence** refers to who finally bears it. One major problem with the use of taxes as a means of redistributing income is that market forces may shift the burden of the tax from the person who initially pays it to others. The major conclusion that follows from studying the effects of a tax levied in a single market (see Chapter 15, p. 266) is as follows:

if the supply curve is positively sloped, and the demand curve negatively sloped, the burden of a tax is shared between producers and consumers.

There will, however, be repercussions in other markets. As the price of one product rises, the demand curves for substitutes will shift to the right, while the demand curves for complements will shift to the left. The resulting changes in their market prices will induce changes in other related markets. The effects of a tax on one market will thus spread throughout the economy, making the final distribution of the burden difficult to ascertain.

Expenditure Policy

The second prong of redistributive policy is expenditure policy. The benefits received tend to vary with income. Many transfer payments benefit lower-income groups. Other expenditures, such as higher education, tend mainly to benefit middle-income groups.

BOX 25.2 THE LAFFER CURVE 600 YEARS BEFORE LAFFER

In the fourteenth century the Arabic philosopher Ibn Khaldun wrote:

It should be known that at the beginning of the dynasty, taxation yields a large revenue from small assessments. At the end of the dynasty, taxation yields a small revenue from large assessments. . . .

When the dynasty follows the ways of group feeling and (political) superiority, it necessarily has at first a desert attitude. The desert attitude requires kindness, reverence, humility, respect for the property of other people, and disinclination to appropriate it, except in rare instances. Therefore, the individual imposts and assessments, which together constitute the tax revenue, are low. When tax assessments and imposts upon the subjects are low, the latter have the energy and desire to do things. Cultural enterprises grow and increase, because the low taxes bring satisfaction. When cultural enterprises grow, the number of individual imposts and assessments mounts. In consequence, the tax revenue, which is the sum total of [the individual assessments], increases.

When the dynasty continues in power and their rulers follow each other in succession, they become sophisticated. The Bedouin attitude and simplicity lose their significance, and the Bedouin qualities of moderation and restraint disappear.

As a result, the individual imposts and assessments upon the subjects, agricultural labourers, farmers and all the other taxpayers, increase.

Every individual impost and assessment is greatly increased, in order to obtain a higher tax revenue. Customs duties are placed upon articles of commerce. Gradual increases in the amount of assessments succeed each other regularly, in correspondence with the gradual increase in the luxury customs and many needs of the dynasty, and the spending required in connection with them. Eventually, the taxes will weigh heavily upon the subjects and overburden them. Heavy taxes become an obligation and tradition, because the increases took place gradually, and no one knows specifically who increased them or levied them. They lie upon the subjects like an obligation and tradition.

The assessments increase beyond the limits of equity. The result is that the interest of the subjects in cultural enterprises disappears, since when they compare expenditures and taxes with their income and gain and see the little profit they make, they lose all hope. Therefore, many of them refrain from all the activity. The result is that the total tax revenue goes down.

Finally, civilization is destroyed, because the incentive for cultural activity is gone. It is the dynasty that suffers from the situation, because it [is the dynasty that] profits from cultural activity.[*]

---

[*] *From the Muqaddimah: An Introduction to History*, translated from the Arabic by Franz Rosenthal (Bollingen Series XLIII. Copyright © 1958 and 1967 by Princeton University Press. Reprinted by permission of Princeton University Press.)

The redistributive effects of expenditures depend on how the overall benefits are related to income. The redistributive effects of the overall tax system depend on how the balance between taxes paid and benefits received from expenditures varies with income. To take an extreme case, assume that government expenditure benefited people in proportion to the taxes they paid. The overall redistributive effect of the government's tax and expenditure system would then be zero: what it took away with one hand it would give back with the other. An effective redistribution scheme requires that the tax system be more progressive than the expenditure system. (A proportional tax system and a regressive expenditure system would do.)

Transfer payments help to fulfill this criterion since many of them are welfare payments to various classes of needy such as the aged, the incapacitated, the unemployed, the unemployable and the very young. Most of these expenditures are negatively related to incomes. For goods and services that are provided by the government at a subsidized, or zero price, the case is not so clear. Education, for example, tends to be consumed more by higher- than by lower-income groups, since the higher a household's income, the more likely it is that its children will stay on beyond the minimum school-leaving age. This kind of relation, which exists for other commodities as well, means that much of the non-transfer part of the expenditure system is progressive, with benefits received tending to rise with income.

The Distribution of Wealth

It is sometimes argued that egalitarian economic policy should concern itself more with the distribution of wealth and less with income than it now does. Wealth confers economic power, and wealth is more unequally distributed than is income. Heavy estate duties in the UK have, however, caused a substantial reduction in the inequality of wealth distribution over this century.

There are two main ways in which the distribution of wealth can be made less unequal. The first is to levy taxes on wealth at the time that wealth is transferred from one owner to another, either by gifts during the lifetime of the owner or by bequest after death. In the UK, such transfers are subject to a *capital transfer tax*. The rate of tax is progressive and rises to 60 per cent on taxable transfers in excess of £2 million. Recently, however, gifts among individuals during their lifetime have been exempted. As far as individuals are concerned, the transfer tax is now an estate duty levied at death.

The second method is an annual tax on the value of each person's wealth. A wealth tax of this sort has been under consideration since 1975 in the UK. It has aroused much controversy because it poses some formidable difficulties and could cause some serious disincentive effects.

Free Goods and Services as a Redistributive Device

Public goods must, by their very nature, be paid for out of general tax revenue. Many other goods and services that could be sold to cover costs are provided by the government at a subsidized price (zero in the limit). The shortfall between price and costs is then made up out of tax revenue. Such goods and services may be produced by a nationalized industry or by a private industry that receives a subsidy to cover the difference between its costs and the amount it receives from selling its products below the free-market prices.

The grounds for adopting such policies are partly efficiency, partly equity and possibly sometimes the mistaken belief that costs can be avoided. To the extent that the goal is to increase efficiency by encouraging the consumption of goods with positive externalities, there is no problem. The optimal policy is to provide a subsidy equal to the externality.

In what follows, we consider the provision of goods at a price below costs, which includes a price of zero in the extreme cases, as a device for redistributing income, and for avoiding costs.

The Opportunity Cost of 'Free' Goods

Voters sometimes opt to have the government subsidize a product, or even provide it free, because avoiding cost wherever possible seems a good idea. The opportunity cost of using resources to produce one commodity is the other commodities that could have been produced instead. The money measure of this cost is the market value of the resources being used. Whenever a commodity is provided free by the government, the costs are met by taxes.[1] The taxpayers thus forgo what they would have consumed by spending their tax money, and the free commodity is consumed by its users instead. Insofar as they are the same people, the consumers merely pay in a different form: taxes rather than purchase prices. Insofar as they are different people, there is a transfer of income: from taxpayers to the consumers of the free commodity.

> **Providing a commodity free of charge does not remove the opportunity cost, it merely transfers it from consumers of the product to taxpayers.**

The Inefficiency of Free Goods

Consider a commodity that has neither positive nor negative externalities so that private and social costs and benefits coincide. If such a commodity is provided free and all demand is met, then households will go on consuming it until the last unit has a zero value to them. Thus resources will have to be used up in producing units of the commodity which have zero value to each and every household. Since resources are scarce, they must be taken from the production of other goods that have positive values for all households (i.e. households would like to have more of them). To use scarce resources to produce commodities with low values, when the same resources could produce commodities with higher values, ensures that households will have a lower total value of consumption than they could have. If a price were charged for the commodity, its consumption would decline and resources would be freed to move to uses where their product would have higher values in the eyes of all households.

> **Providing a commodity free of charge, or at any price below marginal cost, is allocatively inefficient.**

The magnitude of the resource waste depends

on the elasticity of the demand curve for the subsidized commodity. With an inelastic demand curve, the policy induces only a small increase in output, so only a small amount of resources are inefficiently allocated. With an elastic demand, the quantity of misallocated resources is large.

The above discussion gives an intuitive statement of the argument for the inefficiency of a free-good policy. The formal case is given in Figure 25.5. It shows that:

> **any given expenditure of state funds will increase people's satisfactions more if it is used to give them an income transfer than if it is used to subsidize the prices of some of the commodities that they consume.**

FIGURE 25.5 The Case Against Free Goods

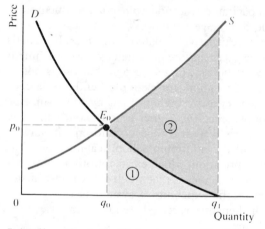

It is allocatively inefficient to provide goods free. Competitive equilibrium is at E_0 with q_0 produced and sold at price p_0. If the government supplies the commodity free of charge, q_1 will be produced and consumed. The addition to consumers' surplus resulting from the extra consumption is equal to the shaded area 1. But since every unit adds its marginal cost to the total costs of production, these costs rise by the sum of areas 1 and 2 – the area under the supply curve which is the industry's marginal cost curve. By the definition of opportunity cost, these two areas give the values of other goods forgone when resources are drawn into the production of the subsidized good. Thus the net loss of surplus to consumers is the shaded area 2.

The steeper is the demand curve through E_0, the smaller will be the increase in quantity from q_0 to q_1 and hence the smaller will be the area of loss labelled 2.

---

[1] This assumes that government expenditure is financed by taxes. We shall see in later chapters that there are other methods of finance. These do not, of course, avoid the cost; they merely shift it to yet other groups.

The free-commodity policy has a second major shortcoming. Much of the money spent goes to subsidize the consumption of higher-income groups. Since there are few goods that are not bought by all income groups, the policy is much like shooting at a target with a shotgun – the bull's eye will be hit but so will everything else.

Transfer payments can be targeted at specific income groups, free goods cannot.

This lack of targeting makes the free-good policy an unnecessarily expensive way of helping low-income groups.

The Case for Free Commodities

The case for providing some commodities, such as medical services and education, at a price below cost (zero in the limit) rests partly on a divergence between social and private costs which is an efficiency consideration, partly on compassion, and partly on more subtle welfare arguments which involve equity considerations.

To see what is involved, compare water with hospitals and schools. In some countries, water is provided free, or at a flat rate that does not vary with consumption. Water has a highly elastic demand at low prices – even though its demand becomes highly inelastic as consumption falls toward the minimum needed to sustain life. Thus a no-price policy causes significant amounts of the economy's scarce resources to be committed to producing units of water which have a very low value to consumers. There are no obvious positive or negative externalities from water and, since everyone consumes it, free water is an ineffective redistributive device. Here is a case where there is little rationale for the zero-price policy.

Now consider free hospital care and education. First, recall that the magnitude of the resource cost of a free-good policy depends on the elasticity of demand between the free-market price and the subsidized price (which in the limit will be zero). It is not clear, however, that many people waste free hospital care in the way they are observed to waste free water. Studies suggest low incidence of unnecessary hospitalization in a free-hospital system. In the case of education up to the statutory age, consumption is compulsory in any case.

Second, in both educational and medical care, social and private costs and benefits are thought to diverge substantially: if I do not cure my infectious disease, the effects are not felt by me alone. If all children are better educated, not only do they and their parents gain, but everyone gains from the rise in output that results from an increase in their labour productivity. Thus, there are arguments for reducing the private costs of these services below the market rate by means of a subsidy.

Third, whereas it is not a great burden for a household to pay a commercial rate for all the water that is necessary for a moderately civilized life, charging a price that covers costs of production would deny medical and educational services to many who have either neglected to, or who are unable to, obtain private insurance to cover the costs.

Finally, more subtle arguments concern social values. It has been argued that in richer societies decisions about basic medical care should be taken out of the economic arena. It is degrading for a person to have to balance medical care for a child against the other family needs. Therefore, it is argued, the inefficiency cost of providing basic medical care free is worth accepting in order to get the gain of creating a society where choices about basic medical services are eliminated.

Notice the use of the word 'basic' in the previous paragraph. The above position is arguable if it is confined to basic services for all. Modern medical technology is so expensive that the state could not afford to make all conceivable services freely available to all. The more expensive services must be rationed. This can be done either by prices or by decisions about need taken by medical and hospital authorities.

Specific Issues in Distribution Policy

In this section we consider some specific issues that arise in attempts to narrow inequalities in the size distribution of income.

Minimum Wages as a Redistributive Device

One other important market intervention designed to alter the size distribution of income is minimum-wage laws, which are a special case of the *price floors* that we discussed on page 107 of Chapter 7.

For a large fraction of all employment covered by the law, the minimum wage is below the actual market wage. Where this is true, the wage is said to be 'not binding'. But some workers are in occupations where the free-market wage rate is below the legal minimum, and for them the minimum wage is said to be 'binding'.

The value of minimum-wage laws is controversial. To the extent that they are effective, they raise the wages of employed workers. But, as our analysis in Chapter 7 indicated, an effective price floor may well lead to a market surplus – in this case, unemployment. Let us see to what extent this prediction applies to the minimum wage.

There are two main cases to consider. First, the minimum wage may be set in a market that is otherwise quite competitive, with many buyers and many sellers. Second, the wage may be set in a market where a few large employers buy from many unorganized sellers of labour services.

Effective minimum wages in a competitive market: In Figure 18.5 on page 313, we studied what happens when a union fixes a wage in an otherwise competitive market. The market outcome is unaffected by the identity of the organization fixing the wage – all that matters is that the wage is fixed. Thus the results of the earlier analysis apply directly to the case of a government-imposed minimum-wage law:

> **a minimum wage imposed on a competitive market will increase the wages of those employed, decrease employment, increase unemployment and create incentives to evade the law by working below the legal minimum wage.**

Effective minimum wages in a monopsonistic market: In Figure 18.6 on page 314, we studied what happens when a union fixes a wage in a market where monopsonistic employers were buying from unorganized labour. Since the source of the wage fixing does not affect the outcome, the results of the earlier analysis apply to the minimum-wage law introduced in this context:

> **a minimum wage, imposed on a monopsonistic market, can raise both wages and employment.**

In this case the minimum wage can protect the unorganized worker against monopsony power in the same way that a union can. It is possible, however, that minimum wages will be set above the competitive level. If so, while wages of those employed will be raised, no prediction can be made as to whether employment will increase or decrease compared to the monopsony level. (It depends both on how high the wage is and on the shapes of the curves.)

NATIONALIZATION

Finally we consider the policies of nationalization and privatization. We have left these to last because they concern all of the policy goals – efficiency, growth and equity.

One way of dealing with a natural monopoly is to nationalize it, and then direct it to follow the required pricing policy. Nationalization was a key part of the social democratic platform earlier in the twentieth century. In Britain the great wave of nationalization occurred under the Labour government that held power from 1945 to 1951. At that time, nationalization of the means of production was thought to be an important step towards achieving a more socially just society. Some people saw nationalization as an end in itself. It was good that the people should own the means of production. Others saw nationalization merely as a means to achieving goals of efficiency and equity. We assess five of the main reasons that were advanced on grounds of efficiency, growth and equity.

Efficiency Reasons

(1) To impose efficiency in the face of externalities: A typical argument was that nationalized industries would co-ordinate policies with other industries in order to take account of their external effects on these industries.

For example, the nationalized railways might take into account the costs and benefits that their decisions imposed on the road-haulage industry. A programme for a unified transport policy would have required, however, that all sectors of the transport industry be nationalized, and all directed to take account of externalities. In fact, important sectors, such as road transport, were left in private hands and few clear directives were issued to the rail industry – or any other nationalized industry for that matter – on how to internalize its externalities. As a result, British nationalized industries rarely attempted to look beyond their own parochial boundaries when taking decisions.

Rather than seek to co-ordinate policies among industries, most nationalized industries were given the task of avoiding losses. In industries that cannot make a profit given current demand and costs, minimizing losses is profit-maximizing behaviour. In industries that would make profits, the directive 'cover costs' ($AR = ATC$) leads to a higher output, and a lower price, than the directive 'maximize profits' ($MR = MC$). If more of something is produced, there must be less of something else. Thus the extra output of the nationalized industries which price at average costs represents a gain only if this production is valued more highly than the production of other commodities that are forgone.

In an effort to reduce the total amount of public-sector borrowing in the 1980s, British nationalized industries were often directed to finance their capital requirements out of retained earnings. This requirement tended to impose profit-maximizing behaviour on industries in need of funds for investment. It also meant that the customers of those industries were forced to provide the funds needed to purchase the industries' capital.

(2) To control a natural monopoly: At the time they were nationalized, industries such as the Post Office, water, telephone, gas and electricity came close to being natural monopolies. Those who believed that such industries cannot be regulated effectively favoured nationalization.

Natural monopoly is a long-run concept, meaning that, given *existing technology*, there is room for only one firm to operate profitably. In the very long run, however, technology changes. Not only does today's competitive industry sometimes become tomorrow's natural monopoly, but today's natural monopoly sometimes becomes tomorrow's competitive industry. A striking example is the telecommunications industry. Fifteen years ago, message transmission was a natural monopoly. Now, technological developments such as satellite transmission,

electronic mail and fax machines have made this activity highly competitive. In many countries an odd circumstance has now arisen: nationalized industries seek to maintain their profitability by prohibiting entry into what would otherwise become a fluid and competitive industry. With the full force of legal sanctions behind it, the public firm may be more successful than the privately owned firm in preserving its monopoly long after technological changes have destroyed its 'naturalness'.

Productive Efficiency

(3) To increase the efficiency of the production of goods and services: The relative productive efficiency of private versus public production has long been debated. Early Fabian socialists, such as George Bernard Shaw, argued that a single, co-ordinated, nationalized industry would avoid the wastes of duplication in having many competing firms do the same thing. Followers of Adam Smith, and many other Classical and neo-Classical economists, argued that even if facilities were duplicated, competition would yield lower-cost production than would monopoly.

A host of recent studies support a view that would not have surprised Adam Smith. The findings are that when industries are relatively competitive, privately owned firms tend to be more efficient than nationalized firms. When industries are close to being natural monopolies, the comparison is less clear. Publicly owned firms sometimes do better and sometimes worse than privately owned firms. This would not have surprised those who believed in the value of competition, and the inefficiency of monopoly, irrespective of ownership. An interesting case study of an alleged inefficiency that gave rise to the nationalization of an industry is discussed in Box 25.3.

Equity Reasons

(4) To confiscate the return on capital for the welfare of the general public instead of private capitalists: This is the standard egalitarian reason – stemming from both Marxist and Fabian socialist policies – for the production and sale of goods by government on the open market: the state should own the means of production

BOX 25.3 THE ECONOMICS OF DECLINING INDUSTRIES

Were coalmines productively inefficient? The view that public control was needed to save an industry from the dead hand of third-rate, unenterprising private owners was very commonly held about the British coal industry in the period between the First and Second World Wars. It was undoubtedly a factor leading to the nationalization of coal in 1946. The Commission which reported in 1926 on the state of the coal industry, had this to say:

> It would be possible to say without exagger-ation of the miners' leaders that they were the stupidest men in England, if we had not had frequent occasion to meet the owners.[1]

The late Sir Roy Harrod argued, however, that the run-down state of the industry in South Wales and Yorkshire, and the advanced state of the pits in Nottinghamshire and Derbyshire, represented the correct response of the owners to the signals of the market. He wrote:

> The mines of Derbyshire and Nottinghamshire were rich, and it was worth sinking capital in them. If similar amounts of capital were not sunk in other parts of the country, this may not have been because the managements were ineffi-cient, but simply because it was known that they were not worth these expenditures. Economic efficiency does not consist in always introduc-ing the most up-to-date equipment that an engineer can think of but rather in the correct adaptation of the amount of new capital sunk to the earning capacity of the old asset. In not introducing new equipment, the managements

may have been wise, not only from the point of view of their own interest, but from that of national interest, which requires the most profit-able application of available capital ... it is right that as much should be extracted from the inferior mines as can be done by old-fashioned methods (i.e. with equipment already installed), and that they should gradually go out of action.[2]

Declining industries always present a sorry sight to the observer. Because revenues have fallen below long-run costs, new equipment is not installed to replace old equipment as it wears out. The average age of equipment in use thus rises steadily. A declining industry will *always* display an old age-structure of capital, and thus 'anti-quated' methods. The superficial observer, seeing the industry's very real plight, is likely to blame the antiquated equipment, which is actually the effect, not the cause, of the industry's decline.

To modernize at high capital costs merely makes the plight worse, since output and costs will rise in the face of declining demand and prices. To nationalize a declining industry, as was done with coal, in order to install new plant and equipment which privately owned firms were unwilling to install (at least in some areas) was to use the nation's scarce resources inefficiently. Capital re-sources are scarce: if investment occurs in mines, there is less for engineering, schools, roads, com-puter research and a host of other things. To re-equip a declining industry which cannot cover its capital costs is to use scarce resources where, by the criterion of the market, their product is much less valuable than it would be in other industries. The efficient response to a steadily declining demand is not to replace old equipment, but to continue to operate existing equipment as long as it can cover its variable costs of production.

[1] Quoted in David Thomson, *England in the Twentieth Century* (Pelican Books, 1965), p. 110. But see also L.S. Amery's reply that the Commission had ignored the very strong claim of the government to be so considered. Some of the policies that gave the government that claim are discussed in Chapter 37.

[2] Roy Harrod, *The British Economy* (New York: McGraw-Hill, 1963), p. 54.

(capital), and the return on it should go to people, rather than to a capitalist class. After the expe-rience of running planned economies, commu-nists came to realize that capital had to be priced if it were to be allocated efficiently among its alternative uses. They continued to believe, how-ever, that this price should not produce an income for a group of households in the economy. In this view, the state – in the person of taxpayers – should provide the capital and receive its return. So taxpayers must be forced to save

and invest in the nation's industries and then receive the return – in the sense that profits will be available to be spent by the state. This compares with private ownership, where those who wish to save and invest do so and then receive the return on capital as a reward.

The experience of nationalized industries in the UK revealed two problems with the Fabian view. First, nationalized industries usually raised capital by reinvesting their own profits, by selling bonds to the public and by borrowing from the government money that was originally raised by selling bonds to the public. In these respects their behaviour was indistinguishable from that of private firms. When money is raised by selling bonds to the public, the return on capital is paid to the bondholders, not to the general public. Second, the nationalized industries rarely produced surpluses which they paid to the state as the return on capital belonging to the people rather than to private capitalists.

Growth Reasons

(5) To get a more rapid rate of growth: Early socialist literature on nationalization tended to concentrate more on static issues of efficiency and equity at a moment in time rather than on the dynamic issue of growth over time. Nonetheless, one of the major issues concerning public versus private ownership was the incentive to innovate.

The pro-public-ownership argument is as follows. First, private firms, particularly very large ones, are conservative and unwilling to take risks. Second, the state has the willingness, and the capital, to take risks and innovate where private firms either will not, or cannot. Third, the state is better than private firms at assessing the direction that research and innovation should take. Fourth, uncoordinated private activity will lead to much waste in 'going off in all directions at once', while a centrally co-ordinated effort will be much more effective. Fifth, the profits from innovation should go to the people, not to a private class of innovators.

The pro-private-ownership view answers these arguments as follows. First, although there is some evidence that large firms are risk-averse, even if they will not innovate, small firms will. Furthermore, the risk aversion is a function of size, not of ownership. Publicly owned giants will tend to be at least as risk-averse as privately owned ones. Second, the state's record in ability to innovate successfully seems worse than the private sector's. In the private sector, even if existing firms are slow to innovate, the Schumpeterian process of creative destruction will cause new firms to arise whenever conditions are ripe for successful innovations. Nationalization, its critics argue, places the full coercive power of the state behind the preservation of the existing state monopoly. It thus tends to frustrate the Schumpeterian process, which is the ultimate free-market protection against the inefficiencies of established monopolies. Fourth, there is protection in diversity. Co-ordinated state action can throw all of the economy's resources down what subsequently turns out to be a blind alley. Private enterprise will cause every promising direction to be explored. Those who go down blind alleys lose their money; those who find successful routes prosper. Fifth, in such an inherently risky business as innovation, it is better to risk the money voluntarily subscribed by private savers than the money forcibly extracted from taxpayers. Studies suggest that when losses are considered as well as gains, the overall private return to innovation may be negative. For every one who succeeds and makes a fortune, ten may lose all that they invest. From the public's point of view, private innovating activity is a great bargain. Private individuals risk their own money and lose most of it. The public gains the benefit of rising living standards created by the small fraction of innovating activity that is successful, and which produces large, highly visible fortunes for those who succeed.

Privatization

Experience with nationalized industries over the past few decades has shaken people's confidence in their superiority. Many thinkers who still support egalitarian social policies on equity grounds see no conflict with private ownership on efficiency grounds. Also the goals of economic policy have become more carefully specified over the last few decades. As a result, it has come to be understood that, except for the goal of nationalization as an end in itself, anything that can be done by nationalization can also be done by appropriate taxes, subsidies and directives aimed at privately owned firms. As a result, many countries, the UK included, have been moving to privatize their nationalized industries.

The first step towards privatization in the UK was the sale of council houses, which began in 1979. Over the succeeding decade this has accomplished a major reduction in the stock of publicly owned housing.

The next phase covered a number of relatively small operations in markets where competition was strong. These included the British Sugar Corporation, British Rail Hotels, Sealink

Ferries, British ports, Jaguar, British Aerospace and several others. These companies have operated successfully, under relatively competitive conditions, since their privatization.

The third phase covers the great industrial giants. It began with British Telecom in 1984 and continued with British Gas in 1986, British Airways in 1987 and British Steel in 1988. The electricity and water industries are scheduled for privatization in 1989 with coal, rail and the Post Office planned for later years.

With these industrial giants, the government faces a dilemma:

the government's sale price is maximized by selling an industry as a single unit, but this also maximizes the industry's subsequent allocative inefficiency.

The government can sell off a giant, such as British Airways or British Gas, as a single unit. This maximizes the monopoly power of its private owners, and hence maximizes the price that will be paid for it. The giant could also be broken up and sold in separate units as far as is feasible. This would seem possible, for example, in the forthcoming sale of British Coal. While this minimizes the monopoly power of the private purchasers (which will still be substantial), it also minimizes the price that will be paid for the industry.

On present evidence, the government appears to be succumbing to the temptation to maximize the sale price by selling off each giant as a single unit. This policy is likely to create more regulatory problems a decade from now than would have arisen if the government had sacrificed some short-term financial gain for the long-term advantages of enhanced competition. This behaviour cannot be explained by the theory of the disinterested government that always acts in the public interest, but it can be explained by the theory of the vote-maximizing government. Reducing the present budget deficit, at the cost of uncertain difficulties in the future, is probably a vote-maximizing strategy. This policy may also reflect a doctrinaire belief that privately owned firms always act more in the public interest than publicly owned ones. Such a view would not have commended itself to Adam Smith, who would have criticized any lost opportunity to enhance competitive forces.

CONCLUSION: EVALUATING THE ROLE OF GOVERNMENT

One of the most difficult problems for the student of the economic system is to maintain perspective about the scope of government activity in the market economy. One pitfall is to become so impressed with the many ways in which government activity impinges on the individual that one fails to see that these only change market signals in a system that basically leaves individuals free to make their own decisions.

A different pitfall is to fail to see that most of the taxes paid by the private sector buy goods and services that add to the welfare of individuals or make transfers designed to alleviate many types of hardship.

A related pitfall is to believe that the government's alleged inability to improve efficiency implies an inability to improve equity. Throughout the world, governments are placing more reliance on markets in order to improve economic efficiency and prospects for growth. Accepting the market for efficiency reasons does not, however, require grinding the faces of the poor. A search for social justice through government interventions directed at equity is quite compatible – providing appropriate means are carefully chosen – with a search for efficiency through increased scope for market determination.

Yet another pitfall is failing to recognize that the public and private sectors both make claims on the resources of the economy. Government activities are not without opportunity costs, except in those rare circumstances in which they employ resources that have no alternative use.

Public policies in operation at any time are not the result of a single master plan that specifies precisely where and how the public sector shall seek to complement, or interfere with, the workings of the market mechanism. Rather, as individual problems arise, governments attempt to meet them by passing ameliorative legislation. These laws stay on the books, and some become obsolete and unenforceable. Since this is true of systems of law in general, it is easy to find outrageous examples of inconsistencies and absurdities in any system.

The amount and type of government interference that is desirable has been one of the major political issues of the 1980s, and it will continue into the 1990s. A free-market system is valued for its lack of coercion and its ability to allocate resources efficiently. But we need not be mesmerized by it; governments can intervene in pursuit of various social goals. When doing so, however, we need to recognize that some interventions have been both inefficient and ineffective.

SUMMARY

1. The traditional goals of microeconomic policy of *efficiency* and *equity* are now augmented by *growth* as a result of the criticism of supply-side economists in the 1980s.
2. Efficiency-increasing policies include the provision of standards and knowledge, producing public goods, and dealing with externalities. The optimal quantity of a public good is provided when the marginal cost of production is equal to the sum of the prices that all its consumers would be willing to pay for the marginal unit produced. Externalities can be handled with rules and regulations, or by internalizing them through such measures as taxes and subsidies.
3. Most governments have policies to discourage monopolies and encourage competition. These can have all of the goals of efficiency, distribution and growth in view. Where natural monopolies exist, governments can regulate or nationalize them. Regulation of price calls for equating marginal cost to price on efficiency grounds, but that will lead to losses when long-run costs are declining and profits when long-run costs are rising. Average cost pricing always covers costs but leads to inefficiently small output when long-run costs are falling, and inefficiently large output when long-run costs are rising. Industrial policies for growth include patent laws, and reductions of entry barriers.
4. Governments use tax and expenditure policies in pursuit of equity objectives. All taxes have some disincentive effects, which must be balanced against their other benefits. Their incidence is often shifted from those who pay them, to a diffuse set of other persons that are often hard to identify. Free goods and services are often an unnecessarily costly redistributive device because their benefits go to all consumers, rich and poor. They also lead to inefficiently large amounts of production and consumption.

   Nonetheless, the provision of free commodities can be justified on economic grounds whenever there are externalities, or where social values call for removing some basic choices from the economic arena in spite of the efficiency costs of doing so. Minimum wages can serve as a redistributive device, but they benefit some who stay on at the higher wage and harm those who lose jobs as a result.
5. Today many believe that nationalization is not a reliable means to industrial efficiency, to a better distribution of income or to faster economic growth. As a result, privatization is a strong movement in many advanced industrial countries.
6. Accepting that the private sector, working through the market economy, is a means to economic efficiency and economic growth does not require accepting the distribution of income that the market provides. Redistributive policies in pursuit of equity are quite compatible with privatization in pursuit of efficiency – and with regulation of natural monopolies and oligopolies whenever they arise out of private market forces.

TOPICS FOR REVIEW

- The goals of microeconomic policy
- Rules for providing and pricing public goods
- Methods of dealing with externalities
- Internalization of externalities
- Marginal and average cost pricing
- The shifting and incidence of taxes
- Disincentive effects of taxes
- Reasons for nationalization and privatization

PART 8

The Elementary Theory of National Income: Interest Rates and the Price Level are Fixed

26

Macroeconomic Concepts and Variables

Inflation, unemployment, recession, economic growth, the balance of payments and the exchange rate are everyday words. Governments worry about how to reduce inflation and unemployment, how to prevent or cure recessions, how to increase the rate of growth, and how to achieve a satisfactory balance of payments. Firms are concerned with how inflation affects their earnings, how to increase their productivity, and how to insulate themselves from the consequences of recessions. Those firms that export also worry about the value of sterling on the foreign-exchange market. Workers are anxious to avoid the unemployment that comes in the wake of recessions and to protect themselves against the hazards of inflation. All of these issues relate to problems studied in macroeconomics.

WHAT IS MACROECONOMICS?

We saw on pages 54–57 of Chapter 4 that economics is divided into two main branches, microeconomics and macroeconomics. (That earlier discussion is a key part of the introduction to macroeconomics, and it is essential to reread it at this point. Once you have done this, we can move on to study the differences between the two branches of economics.)

Macroeconomics studies in broad outline the flow of income in the economy, as was illustrated in Figure 4.1. It does this without dwelling on much of its rich, but sometimes confusing, detail. In contrast, microeconomics deals with the behaviour of individual markets, such as the markets for wheat, coal and strawberries, without dwelling on their overall impact on the whole economy.

The following example illustrates the difference between the two branches of economics.

A microeconomic problem: Explaining the behaviour of energy prices is a typical microeconomic problem. For decades, energy prices fell in relation to the prices of most other commodities. Then, beginning in the early 1970s, this trend was reversed with energy becoming increasingly expensive relative to most other goods and services. In the mid-1980s, however, energy prices fell dramatically to almost their 1970 level (in relation to other prices). During the second half of the 1980s, energy prices fluctuated considerably but they never came near to the high levels reached at the beginning of the decade. In microeconomics, we seek to understand the causes and the effects of such changes in relative prices.

A macroeconomic problem: As well as changing relative to other prices, energy prices have tended to follow the rising trend of all prices over the past fifty years. Accounting for the average behaviour of all prices is a typical macroeconomic problem. This average is called the *general price level*. (Note, however, that the adjective 'general' is often dropped so that reference is made to 'the price level'.) Why, for example, does the general price level rise slowly in some decades and rapidly in others?

In this chapter, we introduce macroeconomics by considering the main variables whose behaviour we shall study in the remaining chapters. We also define a number of important terms. (Because some of these terms will not reappear again for several chapters, you are urged to make a list of their definitions.)

Six Macroeconomic Issues

Most macroeconomic issues fall under six main headings:

- employment and unemployment,
- inflation,
- the trade cycle,
- stagflation,
- economic growth, and
- the exchange rate and the balance of payments.

Employment and unemployment: Why was unemployment high in the 1930s and 1980s, and low in the 1950s and the 1960s? Why is there not always a job for everyone who would like to work? We know that all economies are characterized by *scarcity* – not nearly enough goods and services can be produced to satisfy everyone's wants. Why then should resources lie idle when what they could produce is wanted by consumers?

Inflation: Inflation refers to a rise in the general price level. Why did the pace of inflation accelerate during the 1970s, reaching levels never before seen in peacetime in most advanced Wes-

tern nations? Why was inflation quite low in the late 1980s? Why should we worry about inflation in any case?

The trade cycle: The trade cycle refers to the tendency of output and employment to fluctuate over time in a sequence of ups and downs. **Boom** periods of rising output and high employment alternate with **slump** periods of falling output and low employment. The latter are often referred to as *recessions* or, when they are extremely severe, as *depressions*. Why do market economies produce this cyclical behaviour? Why do they not settle into periods of stability, where all markets are in equilibrium at prices that produce full employment of all resources?

Stagflation: Alternating bouts of boom and recession have caused many policy headaches in the past. But the 1970s saw the emergence of a new economic ailment. Why were the recessions of that decade accompanied, not only by their familiar, and traditional, companion of earlier recessions – high unemployment – but also by an unexpected fellow traveller – rapid inflation? This new disease, called **stagflation**, is the simultaneous occurrence of a recession (with its accompanying high unemployment) *and* inflation. Will it be a recurrent problem of free-market economies in the future?

Economic growth: In spite of the short-term variations of output that are associated with the trade cycle, the long-term trend of total output has been upward for several centuries in all advanced industrial countries. The trend in the nation's total output over the long term is referred to as **economic growth**. Since rates of economic growth have typically exceeded rates of population growth in all advanced countries, there has also been an increase in *per capita* output – i.e. output per head of the population. Over recent centuries, the rise in per capita output has produced a trend towards rising living standards for the average person. Starting in the mid-1970s, there was a slowdown in worldwide growth rates which left *per capita* output stagnant. Did this represent a basic change in underlying trends, or is it just a temporary slowing in the long upward march of living standards? Recent evidence suggests that productivity growth has moved towards its long-term trend in most advanced industrial countries. Individual countries, however, are still experiencing big variations in productivity performance.

The exchange rate and the balance of payments: All international transactions are recorded in the country's *balance-of-payments* statistics. These transactions are influenced by the *exchange rate*, which is the rate at which a country's own currency exchanges for foreign currencies. The trend in the value of the pound sterling in terms of many other currencies, including the US dollar, has been downwards in the last 50 years. Economists wish to discover the causes and consequences of such changes.

FOUR KEY MACRO VARIABLES

The key variables of macroeconomics are:

- the overall level of employment and unemployment,
- the total national product,
- the general price level,
- the balance of payments and the exchange rate.[1]

We hear about these variables on television; politicians make speeches about them; economists theorize about them. To discuss their behaviour in a reasoned fashion, we must understand:

- How are these variables defined?
- Why are we concerned about them?
- How have they behaved in the past?

Employment and Unemployment

Definitions

The **employed** are those persons working for others and paid a wage or a salary, while the **self-**

employed are those who work for themselves. The **unemployed** are those who would be willing to accept work if jobs were available – an easier concept to understand than to measure. The **working population**, or **labour force**, is the total of the employed, the self-employed and the unemployed, i.e. those who have a job plus those who are looking for work.

In our earlier microeconomic analysis, we were concerned with employment and unemployment in individual markets – for example, the market for mechanics in Coventry. In macroeconomics, we are concerned with overall employment and unemployment in the whole economy.

Unemployment is usually expressed as a percentage of the labour force, and denoted by the symbol U:

$$U = \frac{\text{number unemployed}}{\text{labour force}} \times 100 \ .$$

Why Unemployment Matters

To understand the importance of unemployment, it is necessary to distinguish between voluntary and involuntary unemployment. **Voluntary unemployment** occurs when there is a job available, but the employed person is not willing to accept it at the existing wage rate. **Involuntary unemployment** occurs when a person is willing to accept a job at the going wage rate, but cannot find such a job. The undesirable social effects of unemployment, in terms of lost output and human suffering, are mainly related to involuntary unemployment.

Until the 1980s the social and political importance of the unemployment rate was enormous. It was widely reported in newspapers; the government was blamed when it was high and took credit when it was low; it was often a major issue in elections; and few economic policies were formed without some consideration of their effect on it. From 1945 to 1975 an unemployment rate of 4 per cent was regarded as politically intolerable – no government could survive it. In the 1980s, however, unemployment became a less politically sensitive issue. The official unemployment figure remained high in spite of being reduced by redefinitions. In mid-1986 the official rate peaked at 13 per cent and 11 per cent on the old and the new definitions respectively – after which it fell quite markedly.

---

[1]Earlier we discussed six groups of macroeconomic issues, but now we identify only four macroeconomic variables. All of the issues that were discussed earlier, however, concern the behaviour of these types of variables. Of the items that do not directly repeat the list of macroeconomic variables, the trade cycle and stagflation relate to the behaviour of the three variables: employment, national product and the price level, while economic growth concerns the rate at which the variable national product is growing.

FIGURE 26.1 Unemployment in the UK, 1930–1988

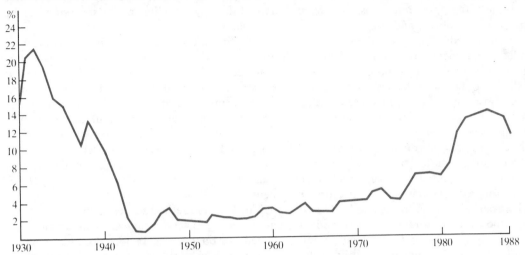

Unemployment, although fluctuating, remained low in the 1940s, 1950s and 1960s and high in the 1930s and 1980s. The figures show the average number of unemployed in each year as a percentage of the labour force in that year. The definitions have been changed substantially several times, making long-term comparisons risky. The changes introduced in 1982 greatly reduced the measured number of unemployed. If the figures were calculated on the basis used in earlier years, the line on the graph would be significantly higher for 1982–88.

There are two main reasons for worrying about unemployment: it wastes economic resources, and it causes human suffering.

The economic waste is obvious. If a fully employed economy has 25 million people who are willing to work, their labour services must either be used now or be wasted. If only 22 million are used because 12 per cent of the labour force is unemployed, the potential output of three million workers is lost. In an economy characterized by scarcity, where there is not nearly enough output to meet everyone's needs, any waste of the potential to produce that output is a serious matter.

In addition to economic waste, there is the human cost of unemployment. Severe hardship and misery can be caused by prolonged periods of unemployment, which have been observed to be associated with above-average incidences of ill health, alcoholism and divorce among those without work.

Experience of Unemployment

Figure 26.1 shows UK unemployment since

1930. During the period between the two world wars, UK unemployment was never less than 10 per cent in any single year. The first quarter-century following the Second World War provided a sharp contrast. Unemployment was always less than 3 per cent, and it was not until the mid-1970s that it exceeded that figure. Unemployment then rose steadily. By 1981, the rate had passed the 10 per cent level – or what is sometimes called the 'two-digit level' – and, on the definitions then in existence, it reached 13.8 per cent in October 1982. At the end of 1988 the official rate, based on the new definitions, was 7.2 per cent. (Although these data provide a reasonable general indication of the course of unemployment, great care must be taken when using them in detail since the statistical definition of unemployment has been changed several times.)

There are several reasons why the UK's unemployment experience over the last two decades has been regarded as particularly serious. First, there is a marked inequality of unemployment rates among regions. Northern Ireland and the north of England have had rates that were half as much again as those in the south-east. Much regional unemployment is connected with the decline of the old staple industries that were concentrated in the north, and the rise of new, technologically based industries in the south.

Second, current unemployment is particularly high among the young. Many school-leavers find it impossible to obtain jobs. When this happens, they not only lose incomes, they miss the valuable on-the-job training that usually accompanies early job experiences.

Third, experiences of unemployment have become much longer in duration than they were in previous decades. In the 1950s and 1960s, the typical unemployed person was without a job for a fairly short period of time. In the late 1970s and the 1980s, the average duration of a period of unemployment – the time between losing a job and finding a new one – increased significantly. Long-term bouts of unemployment are particularly upsetting to those who experience them.

Total National Product

Definitions

The nation's total output is loosely described as its *national product, national output* or *national income*. Precise measures and their definitions are discussed later in this chapter. In the meantime, note that this total product can be calculated by adding up the money values of all the goods and services that are produced in the economy over some period of time, usually taken as a year.

Index numbers to separate real and nominal output: A serious difficulty in calculating total product arises because of inflation. Say for example that, over one year, all prices remain unchanged while the quantities of all outputs increase by 10 per cent. The value of total output rises by 10 per cent. Next, say that over the following year, all quantities of output remain unchanged while the prices of everything that is produced rise by 10 per cent. The value of total output also rises by 10 per cent. But the two cases are different. In the first case, the value of output rises by 10 per cent because the *quantities* that are produced rise by that amount. In the second case, the value of output rises by 10 per cent because *prices* rise by that amount while quantities remain constant.

We shall shortly consider how to distinguish these two cases. First, however, we must notice two of the ways in which national product can be calculated.

The first method values each year's output at the market prices ruling in that year. The result is referred to as national product, *valued at current prices*, or as **nominal national product**, or as **money national product**. The measured value of nominal national product changes from year to year as a result of both price and quantity changes. For example, if all market prices, *and* all outputs, rise by 10 per cent, national product valued in current prices will rise by about 21 per cent.

The second method values each year's output at the set of prices ruling in some single year, called the **base year**. It does not matter which year is chosen as the base year. What matters is that some constant set of prices is used to value outputs. The result is then referred to as national product *valued at constant prices*, or as **real national product**. For example, if the base year is 1982, outputs in each year will be valued at 1982 prices and the result will be referred to as *national product valued at 1982 prices*. Because the prices used to value all the outputs are unchanged from year to year, changes in the measured value of output must be due *only* to changes in the quantities of output.

Actual and potential output: There is an important distinction between actual output and what is called **potential output**, or **full-employment output**. Actual output refers to what is actually produced over some time-period. Potential output refers to what the economy could produce over that time-period if all resources were fully employed. When the economy is producing its potential, or full-employment output, the actual output is on the production-possibility boundary shown in Figure 1.2 on page 6. When there are unemployed resources, so that actual output is less than potential output, the production point is somewhere inside the transformation curve.

Productivity: The secular rise in *per capita* living standards has been mainly due to increases in **productivity**, which is a measure of how much output is produced per unit of resources employed. If each unit of resources can produce more, it is possible for everyone in the nation to consume more.

Of the various possible productivity measures, most interest is focused on **labour productivity**. This is total output divided by the labour used in producing it, i.e. output *per unit of labour*. Dividing total output by the employed labour force gives output per employed person. This measure varies, however, not just as labour gets more or less productive, but also as hours worked vary. For example, a decline in the average weekly hours worked from 48 to 40 hours per week would, other things being equal, lower measured labour productivity by nearly 10 per cent – even though labour is no less productive per hour worked. For this reason, a more satisfactory measure of the productive ability of labour is to divide total output by the total number of hours worked. The result is *productivity per hour of labour* actually spent on the job.

FIGURE 26.2 UK Real National Product from 1948 to 1987, Measured at Constant Prices

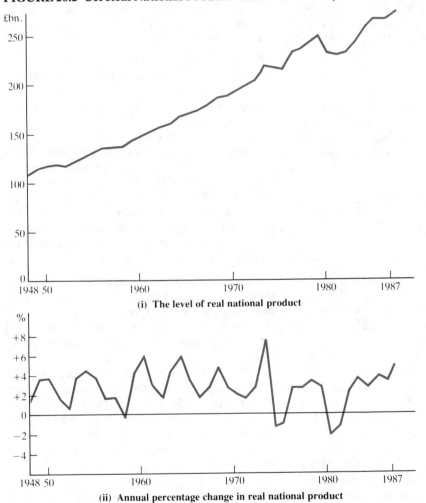

(i) **The level of real national product**

(ii) **Annual percentage change in real national product**

Although the rate of change of real national product has varied greatly, the overall trend has been upward. The data are for GDP measured at constant prices. The sharp recession in the late 1970s and early 1980s is clearly visible in both charts. The second chart shows the cyclical behaviour of the rate of growth of GDP that is associated with the trade cycle.

Why Output Matters

Short-run fluctuations of national product around its potential level reflect the ebb and flow of economic activity, called the trade cycle.

Policy-makers are concerned about short-term fluctuations in real national product because of the consequences for unemployment and lost output.

Long-run, trend changes in real national product have generally been upwards in recent centuries. This is the economic growth that has been the major cause of long-term increases in living standards. The worst horrors of the early industrial revolution are no longer with us, mainly because economic growth has removed the necessity of fourteen-hour days worked in extremely harsh conditions.

As long as growth continues, each generation can expect, on the average, to have substantially higher living standards than were enjoyed by each preceding generation.

Not surprisingly, therefore, policy-makers are greatly concerned with the nation's rate of economic growth.

Output Experience

Figure 26.2(i) shows the long-term trend of output, while Figure 26.2(ii) highlights the fluctuations from one year to the next. (In the Figure, output is measured by a statistic called the Gross Domestic Product (GDP) which we shall study later in this chapter.) The two parts are two ways of displaying the same output series. Part (i) shows the level of output each year from 1948 to 1987. Part (ii) shows the change in output from one year to the next over the same period.

Slow British growth rates from 1945 to the early 1980s have moved Britain down the list of present EC countries from the second highest per capita output in 1955 (only Luxemburg was higher then) to the second lowest in 1985. (The post-1985 entrants, Greece, Spain and Portugal, all have per capita output well below the UK's.) If the growth rates of output that have been typical over the last few decades persist to the end of this century, West Germany's per capita GDP will be six times Britain's. This is the same

relative discrepancy as now exists between Britain and the South American Republic of Colombia. Recently, however, the UK's growth rate has risen, and economists wonder if this is a change in the long-term trend or just some transitory fluctuation.

The General Price Level

Definitions

Prices are reported as levels, rates of change and changes in rates of change, and the distinction between these measures can be a rich source of popular confusion. Care must, therefore, be taken with definitions.

Changes in the price level: Macroeconomics uses the concept of the **general price level**, the average level of the prices of *all* goods and services produced in the economy. In practice, we are not interested in the average level of all prices itself, but in *changes* in this average. For example, you would not be much the wiser if you were told that the average level of all prices in the UK this year was £121.34. You would, however, be interested to know that the average level of all prices ruling this year was 7 per cent higher than the average ruling in the previous year. A rise in the general price level is called an **inflation**, while a fall is called a **deflation**.

Changes in the value of money: Changes in the price level cause changes in the **purchasing power of money**, or the **value of money**. Both of these terms refer to *the amount of goods and services that can be purchased with a given amount of money*.

Inflation, which is a rise in the general price level, reduces the purchasing power of money; deflation increases it. Say, for example, that all prices rise by 10 per cent. One pound sterling will now buy 10 per cent less goods and services than before the price level rose. Hence, the 10 per cent inflation reduces the purchasing power of money by 10 per cent. The same point may also be made by saying that the *value of money* (measured by what can be bought with it) has fallen by 10 per cent.

Now let all prices fall by 10 per cent. Any given amount of money will now buy 10 per cent *more* than it previously did. This deflation raises the purchasing power of money by 10 per cent.

These examples illustrate the following relation:

by definition, the purchasing power of money falls in inverse proportion to any rise in the price level, and rises in inverse proportion to any fall in the price level.

Measuring changes in the price level – index numbers: In practice, changes in the price level, and in the value of money, are measured by a **price index**. This is a statistical measure that expresses the average price of some group of commodities in some year as a percentage of the average price of the same commodities in some other year. The point in time from which the percentage is measured is called the **base period** (or base year), while the point in time to which the percentage is measured is called the **given period** (or given year). Thus, for example, an index of 200 in 1990 on a base year of 1980 tells us that prices have doubled between 1980 and 1990.

The definition of any price index raises several issues which need attention.

First, what group of prices should be used? This depends on the index. The *index of retail prices* (RPI) covers prices of commodities commonly bought by households. Changes in the RPI are meant to measure changes in the typical household's 'cost of living'. The *wholesale price index* measures a different group of commodities, one that is commonly bought and sold by wholesalers. The *implied deflator for the GNP* is a price index that covers virtually all of the goods and services produced in the economy: it includes not only the prices of consumer goods and services bought by households, but also the prices of capital goods such as plants and machinery bought by firms. (Be careful not to confuse a *deflator*, which is an index number designed to measure average price changes, and a *deflation*, which is a fall in the average level of all prices.)

Second, what kind of average should be used? If all prices were to change in the same proportion, this would not be an important question. A 10 per cent rise in each and every price means an average rise of 10 per cent, no matter how much importance we give to each price change when calculating the average. But what if – as is almost always the case – different prices change in different proportions? Now it does matter how much importance we give to each price change. A

rise of 50 per cent in the price of caviar is surely much less important to the average consumer than is a rise of 40 per cent in the price of bread, and this in turn is surely less important than a rise of 30 per cent in the cost of housing. The reason is that the typical household spends less on caviar than on bread, and less on bread than on housing.

In calculating any price index, statisticians seek to weigh each price according to its importance. For the RPI, government statisticians periodically survey a group of households to discover how they spend their incomes. The average bundle of goods bought is calculated, and the proportions of total expenditure devoted to each good within this bundle become the weights attached to the prices. Large weights are thus given to commodities on which consumers spend much, and small weights to commodities on which consumers spend only a little. The procedure is illustrated in Table 26.1.

The weighted average of prices in the given year is then expressed as a percentage of the weighted average of prices in the base year, and this figure is the index number for the new period. The price index is thus always 100 in the base year. It follows that the percentage change in the cost of purchasing the bundle is the index number minus 100. For example, an index number of 110 indicates a percentage increase in prices of 10 per cent over those ruling in the base year.

In summary:

an index number of prices with base-year weights is the ratio of the cost of purchasing a bundle of commodities in the given year to the cost of purchasing the same bundle in the base year, multiplied by 100.

Some difficulties with index numbers: An index number is meant to reflect the broad trend in prices rather than the details. This means that, although the information it gives is valuable, it must be interpreted with care. Here are three of the many reasons why care is required.

First, the weights in the index refer to an average bundle of goods. This average, although 'typical' of what is consumed in the nation, will not necessarily be typical of what each household consumes. The rich, the poor, the young, the old, the single, the married, the urban and the rural

TABLE 26.1 Calculation of an Index Number of Prices

(1) Calculation of Weights

Commodity	Price	Qty bought	Value of purchase	Proportion of total purchases
A	£1.00	496	£496	0.31
B	5.00	198.4	992	0.62
C	2.00	56	112	0.07
			1,600	1.00

(2) Base Year Average Price 1988

Commodity	Price	Weight	Price × Weight
A	£1.00	0.31	0.31
B	5.00	0.62	3.10
C	2.00	0.07	0.14
			$3.55 \div 3 = 1.18$

(3) Given Year Average Price 1989

Commodity	Price	Weight	Price × Weight
A	£2.00	0.31	0.62
B	7.00	0.62	4.34
C	9.60	0.07	0.67
			$5.63 \div 3 = 1.87$

Price Index

$$1988 = \frac{1.18}{1.18} \times 100 = 100 \qquad 1989 = \frac{1.87}{1.18} \times 100 = 158$$

The price index measures the average prices in the given year as a percentage of the average price in the base year. To calculate the average price in each year, weights are used. These are the proportions of total expenditure devoted to each commodity in the base year. Using these fixed weights, an average price for each year is calculated. The price index for the given year is the average price in that year expressed as a percentage of the average price in the base year.

households typically consume bundles that differ from one another. An increase in air fares, for example, will raise the cost of living of a middle-income globe-trotter, while leaving that of a poor stay-at-home unaffected. In the example of Table 26.1, the cost of living would have risen by 100 per cent, 40 per cent and 380 per cent respectively for three different families, one of whom consumed only commodity A, one only commodity B, and one only commodity C. The index in the Table shows, however, that the cost of living went up by 80 per cent for a family that consumed all three goods in the relative proportions indicated.

Second, households usually alter their consumption patterns in response to price changes. A price index that shows changes in the cost of purchasing a fixed bundle of goods, does not allow for this. For example, a typical cost-of-living index for middle-income families at the turn of the century would have given heavy weight to the cost of maids and children's nurses. A doubling of servants' wages in 1900 would have greatly increased the middle-income cost of living. Today, it would have little effect, for the rising cost of labour long ago ended the employment of full-time servants by most middle-income families. Furthermore, when the price of a commodity rises rapidly, a household that greatly reduces its consumption of that commodity, does not have its cost of living rise as fast as a household that continues to consume the same amount of that commodity.

Third, as time goes by, new commodities enter

the typical consumption bundle and old ones leave. A cost-of-living index in 1890 would have had a large item for horse-drawn carriages and horse-feed, but no allowance at all for motorcars and petrol.

The longer the period of time that passes, the less some fixed consumption bundle will be typical of current consumption patterns.

For this reason, the government makes periodic surveys of household expenditure patterns and revises the weights in the RPI. The base period is then often changed to conform to the year in which the new set of commodity weights was calculated. Nonetheless the choice of the base year and the choice of the year to use for weighting are two distinct choices.

Why Inflation Matters

The *level* of prices is irrelevant to living standards. For example, no economist argues that the British price level of 1788 was intrinsically better or worse than the price level of 1988.

The reason why one price level is just as good as any other price level is that, if all prices of goods, factors of production and everything else change in equal proportion, no relative prices have changed and there are no real consequences. For instance, if the amount of money you pay for everything you buy doubles, but the amount of money you receive also doubles, you are unaffected by the changes. You pay twice as much for everything you buy, but since your money income has also doubled, you can buy exactly as much as before prices rose. It follows that:

when all markets have reached full equilibrium, a change in the overall level of prices has no real effects.

Another way of seeing this important point is to observe that changing the number of zeros on the prices at which all transactions take place, has no real effect on anything.

Inflation causes harm during the *transition* from one price level to another. While the price level is changing, some prices adjust faster than others. As a result, relative prices change and real effects occur. The losers are those who find the prices of what they buy rising faster than the prices of what they sell; the gainers are those who find the prices of what they sell rising faster than the prices of what they buy. Thus:

while it is going on, inflation causes haphazard redistributions of income.

Those who are powerful enough, or smart enough, to keep ahead of the inflation, gain. Those who do not have the necessary economic power, or the needed foresight, lose.

Fixed money income: The extreme case of the redistributive effects of inflation occurs when some people's incomes do not rise at all as prices rise. For example, if a retirement pension specifies an income as so many pounds sterling, a rise in the price level lowers the purchasing power of that income. Anyone who retired on a fixed money income in 1974 found the purchasing power of that income cut in half by 1979 and then by a further 35 per cent by 1983. This meant that the person could buy in 1984 only 32 per cent of what could be bought in 1974. For such people, rapid inflation meant great suffering.

Note that the problems only arise with payments that really are fixed in money terms. State pensions in the UK have been adjusted from time to time as inflation has proceeded. Many private pensions, however, remained fixed in money terms, so that their recipients saw the purchasing power of their incomes shrink steadily as the price level rose.

Indexing: Some of the redistributive effects of inflation can be avoided by what is called 'indexing'. Such indexing arrangements allow the payments made under the terms of a contract to change as the general price level changes. For example, a retirement pension might specify that the beneficiary is to be paid £10,000 pounds per year starting in 1990, and that the amount paid will be increased each year in proportion to the increase in some specified index of the price level. If the price index rose by 10 per cent between 1990 and 1991, the pension payable in 1991 would be £11,000.

Foreseen inflations: Indexation provides an automatic correction that does not require anyone to foresee future changes in the price level. Even without formal indexation, however, it is possible to allow for the effects of an inflation, provided that the rise in the price level is *foreseen*. Wage contracts are major examples. If, say, a 10

FIGURE 26.3 Inflation in the UK, 1930–1988

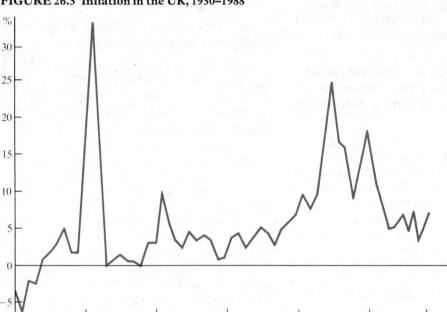

**The inflation rate was particularly high during the Second World War
(1939–45) and the 1970s.** The figures show the percentage change in the Retail Price
Index from one year to the next. The 1970s was a decade of inflation world wide.
During the 1980s the UK, along with most other industrial countries, brought the
inflation rate back to levels more typical of the 1950s and 1960s.

per cent inflation is expected over the next year, a
money wage that rises by 10 per cent over that
period will preserve the expected purchasing
power of wages. A money wage that increases by
13 per cent, will provide for an expected 3 per
cent increase in the purchasing power of wages.
This is made up of a 10 per cent increase in wages
to preserve purchasing power in the face of the
expected rise in prices, and a 3 per cent increase
to raise the real purchasing power of the wages.

**When an inflation is foreseen, many of its
effects can be allowed for in contracts
that take account of the expected rise in
prices.**

Unforeseen inflations: The most harmful
effects of inflation occur when the rise in the price
level is unforeseen.

**Contracts freely entered into when the
price level was expected to remain constant will mean hardships for some, and**

**unexpected gains for others, if the price
level rises unexpectedly.**

Consider, for example, a new wage contract
that specifies wage increases of 3 per cent, in the
expectation of a constant price level. Both employers and workers expect that the purchasing
power of wages paid will rise by 3 per cent as a
result of the new contract. Now assume that the
price level changes unexpectedly. If the price
level rises by 10 per cent over the course of the
wage contract, the workers' wages will buy less
than they would before the wage increase was
negotiated. (A 3 per cent increase in money wages
combined with a 10 per cent increase in prices
means a reduction in the purchasing power of
wages of about $6\frac{1}{2}$ per cent.)[1]

---

[1] The purchasing power of wages is W/P, where W stands for
the money wage rate and P the price level. Letting the original
real wage be W/P, the new purchasing power is
$1.03W/1.1P = 0.936W/P$. Thus the new purchasing power is
93.6 per cent of the original. This represents a fall of 6.4 per
cent in purchasing power.

The Experience of Inflation

Figure 26.3 shows the UK inflation rate for each year since 1930. Throughout the 1950s and the 1960s the rate, although low by current standards, was high enough to cut the purchasing power of the pound by more than half over those two decades, and to be a worry to policy-makers and voters.

Then, in the late 1960s, the United Kingdom, together with the rest of the developed world, moved into a period of *accelerating* inflation. After a slight deceleration in 1972, the rate rose dramatically in 1973–4 to levels never before seen during peacetime. By 1975 the annual rate of inflation reached a peak of approximately 25 per cent in the UK. The inflation rate did not, however, remain at that high level. Although prices continued to rise, the rate of inflation fell substantially until, at the end of 1982, it was below 10 per cent.

The inflation rate over that extraordinary decade was such that a household retiring in 1972 with comfortable income that was fixed in money terms saw 75 per cent of that income's purchasing power eroded over the ten years that followed.

In the 1980s, UK inflation fell dramatically, reaching a low of 3.4 per cent in 1986. This and the 4.2 per cent figure for 1987 were typical of the inflation rates achieved in the 1950s and early 1960s before the worldwide acceleration of inflation later in that decade. Although many observers were fearing a renewed acceleration of inflation at the end of the decade, the experience of the 1980s showed that the inflation rate could be substantially reduced given a determined enough anti-inflationary policy.

The Balance of Payments and Exchange Rates

Definitions

If you are going on a holiday in France, you will need French francs to pay for your purchases while you are there. Any bank will make this exchange of currencies for you. If you get 10 francs for every pound you give up, then these two currencies are trading at a rate of £1 = 10F or, what is the same thing, 1F = £0.10. The exchange rate refers to the rate at which two countries' currencies are traded.

The above example suggests that the exchange rate can be defined in either of two ways: (i) the amount of foreign currency that exchanges for one unit of domestic currency (10F for £1 in the above example), or (ii) the amount of domestic currency that exchanges for one unit of foreign currency (10p for 1F in the above example). It is customary in the UK to express the sterling exchange rate in the latter way. Thus the exchange rate between the pound sterling and the US dollar was £1 = $1.78 at the beginning of 1989. This means that £1 would buy you US$1.78 or, what is the same thing, US$1 would buy just over 56p.

Thus, in the UK the **exchange rate** between sterling and any one foreign currency is defined as the amount of that foreign currency that must be given up to purchase one pound sterling, i.e. the price of sterling in terms of a foreign currency.

Foreign exchange refers to foreign currencies themselves and claims to them in such forms as bank deposits, cheques and promissory notes payable in that currency. The **foreign-exchange market** is the market where foreign exchange is traded – at a price which is expressed by the exchange rate.

If the exchange rate is left free to be determined on the foreign-exchange market by the forces of demand and supply, the country is said to have a **floating exchange rate**. If the country's central bank intervenes in the foreign-exchange market to hold the exchange rate at some pre-announced fixed value, the country is said to have a **fixed exchange rate**.

The other important international concept that we need to mention at this point is the balance of payments. In order to know what is happening to the course of international trade and international capital movements, governments keep account of the transactions among countries. These accounts are called the **balance-of-payments accounts**, and they record all such international payments. They are considered in detail in Chapter 39.

Why Policy-makers Care

Unlike the other variables discussed above, such as unemployment and inflation, the exchange rate and the balance of payments do not provide obvious causes for concern. Most people agree

FIGURE 26.4 The Sterling–US Dollar Exchange Rate, 1945–1988

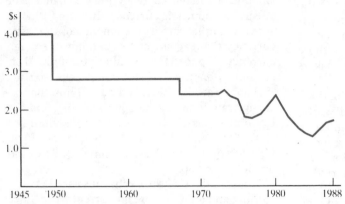

The long-term trend has been for sterling to fall in value relative to the US dollar. The Figure shows the average US$ price of £1 sterling during each year. It thus masks the substantial intra-year variability in the exchange rate, particularly in recent years. The Bretton Woods period of fixed but adjustable rates is clearly visible from 1945 to the mid-1970s, with its long periods of stable rates interrupted by two devaluations of sterling, one in 1949 and one in 1967. Since the breakdown of that system, rates have fluctuated on relatively free foreign-exchange markets.

that a *ceteris paribus* rise in either unemployment or inflation is undesirable. There is no reason, however, for feeling the same about a change in either the exchange rate or the balance of payments. A change in the exchange rate or the balance of payments may or may not be a matter of concern, depending on why the change occurred. For this reason, it is best to postpone asking why policy-makers are sometimes concerned about these variables until we have studied them in more detail.

Experience

Figure 26.4 shows the exchange rate between the pound sterling and the US dollar since 1945. The long periods of stability are periods when the exchange rate was fixed. The sudden changes were periods when the fixed rate was adjusted. More recently the rate has been left to find its level on the free market, and this shows up as a continuously varying rate on the chart – i.e. a floating exchange rate.

Balance-of-payments data can be understood only after you have learned more about the meaning of such data. For this reason we postpone looking at the balance of payments until a later chapter.

THE GOALS OF MACROECONOMIC POLICY

Macroeconomic policy is mainly concerned with the four key macro variables discussed above –

employment, output, the price level and the balance of payments. What follows is a short introductory survey designed to give the reader some general familiarity with the issues and terms. Everything discussed here will be gone over in detail later in this book. If you return at the end of your study of macroeconomics to re-read this part of the chapter, you will find that nothing here seems at all difficult.

Early Macro Goals

Until the twentieth century, governments were assumed not to have any responsibility towards, or even any ability to influence, most of the major macro variables. The main government responsibility towards the economy was thought to be to provide a stable background of law, order, and security of contracts. This background would allow citizens to get on with the private economic activity on which the material wealth of the nation depended.

The one major exception was the price level. Early in the history of economics, it was realized that the amount of money and credit that was available to 'grease the wheels of commerce' was at least partially under the control of the government. It was also realized that mismanagement of the monetary system could, as we shall see in detail later, cause inflation. The government's responsibility was therefore understood to include management of the monetary system in such a way that there was enough money to satisfy the needs of trade, but not so much as to cause inflation.

The other macro variables were not, however, considered the responsibility of policy. Good times and bad times seemed to follow each other – in the ebb and flow of the trade cycle – for reasons that were beyond government control.

Modern Macro Goals

In response to the so-called Great Depression of the 1930s, and the decade of heavy unemployment that accompanied it, modern macroeconomic theory was born. Since that time, economists have understood that government policy can have a significant influence on the nation's overall level of economic activity, while governments have, for better or for worse, accepted a responsibility for influencing the behaviour of each of the major macro variables that we have discussed above. The policies with respect to each of these variables are usually stated as full employment, a satisfactory growth rate, a stable price level, and a satisfactory balance of payments. We shall look briefly at each of these.

Full Employment

From 1945 onwards, the governments of most market-oriented, industrial countries accepted a responsibility for ensuring full employment. In the UK, this objective was stated in the *White Paper on Employment Policy* (Cmd 6527), published in 1944 by the Coalition government of that time.

Achieving the objective of full employment means holding national product at its potential, or full-employment, level. It does *not* mean achieving zero unemployment. Indeed, zero unemployment is an impossibility in any real economy because of the normal turnover of labour. Turnover occurs because people leave one job to take, or to look for, another, and because there are always some people leaving the labour force due to retirement, or death, and others entering it. As a result, there is always a pool of people who are unemployed because they are currently between jobs or looking for their first job. Such unemployment, which is due to the normal turnover of labour, is called **frictional unemployment**. It is the amount of unemployment that exists when output is at its potential level.

The 1944 White Paper defined full employ-

ment as existing when the recorded unemployment rate was 3 per cent. For a decade or so, starting in 1950, unemployment rates of 2 per cent, or less, became common. Then in the 1970s, the amount of unemployment associated with potential output rose steadily until, by the mid-1980s, it seemed to be somewhere between 6 and 8 per cent. In the 1980s the Conservative government officially ended the government's commitment to use its policy instruments to secure full employment. Governments do, however, still concern themselves about the level of employment.

A Satisfactory Rate of Growth of Output

Unfortunately, one of the least successful branches of economics has been growth theory. The theory does identify some influences, such as investment, and research and development, that are often associated with high growth rates. No one, however, has been able to sort out causes and effects in these relations to the extent that governments can easily influence the growth rates of their economies. Recent research has tended to emphasize the importance to growth of microeconomic policies, whereas growth was earlier thought to be influenced solely by macro policies.

Although many UK governments have had growth targets, few have been able to develop policy tools capable of raising the country's growth rate. Nonetheless governments do, as we shall see, continue to adopt growth policies.

Stable Prices

Governments still accept the responsibility, which was established centuries ago, for maintaining a stable price level, or at least a low rate of inflation. Figure 26.3 shows that the UK government has had a mixed success in meeting this objective. The Conservative government elected in 1979 gave high priority to this target, and by 1983 the rate of inflation had fallen well below what was typical of the 1970s.

A Satisfactory Exchange Rate and Balance of Payments

Most governments feel that large fluctuations in the exchange rate are undesirable, while also feeling that long-term trends in the exchange rate cannot be resisted.

Governments of various countries differ on how they regard the balance of payments. Some countries have active policies; others leave the balance of payments to be determined by market forces, without any serious government intervention. We have seen that the balance of payments does not present the same obvious policy objectives as do employment, output and the price level. For this reason, balance-of-payments objectives are sometimes said to be *secondary*, in contrast to the *primary* objectives of full employment, rapid economic growth and price stability.

Policy Instruments

There are two major sets of macroeconomic policy tools available to the government. One set, called demand-side policies, works on the demand side of the economy's markets. These are called the policies of **demand management**. The other set, called supply-side policies, works on the supply side of these markets.

Demand-side Policies

The major tools of demand management are fiscal and monetary policy.

Fiscal policy: Fiscal policy attempts to influence the *total demand for goods and services*. (This total demand is nothing other than the sum of all of the demands in the nation's individual markets that we studied in the micro half of this book.) A change in total demand can be achieved through the government's budget.

An increase in government expenditure means that the government is demanding more of the goods and services to which it allocates its extra expenditure. This means that the government is directly causing an increase in total demand. Reducing taxes has a similar, though less direct, effect on total demand. If, for example, the rates of personal income tax are reduced, taxpayers will be left with more after-tax income to spend. When they increase their spending, they will add to total demand for the goods and services that they buy. Thus, cutting taxes adds to total demand indirectly, because it leaves more money in people's pockets and relies on them to increase total demand by spending some of this money.

Although the British government is no longer commited to using fiscal policy in an attempt to maintain full employment, variations in the government's taxation and spending policies cannot help but have an impact on the economy.

Monetary policy: Monetary policy seeks to affect total demand by influencing the amount of money and credit available, and the cost of that credit to borrowers (interest rates). Since businesses and households borrow to finance much of their expenditure, changing the availability and the terms of credit can influence total demand. By making more funds available to be borrowed, and by exerting a downward pressure on interest rates which lowers the cost of borrowing, the government seeks to increase total demand. By making fewer funds available to be borrowed, and by exerting an upward pressure on interest rates, the government seeks to lower total demand. How the Bank of England can accomplish these changes in the conditions of credit will be studied in detail in a later chapter.

Supply-side Policies

As well as influencing total demand, the government can try to influence total national product by adopting what are called **supply-side policies**. These try to influence the total output that the private sector can, and will, produce. In general, supply-side policies are designed to cause rightward shifts in the supply curves in individual markets. Consider just two examples.

First let there be a reduction in the rates of personal income taxes. This *may* increase the amount of work that people wish to do. If it does, then the increased supply of labour will raise the economy's full-employment output. For a second example, let there be a large tax exemption for research and development. If this causes an increase in invention and innovation, the growth rate may be favourably affected. If such policies succeed in shifting enough individual supply curves, the aggregate supply of all goods will be significantly increased.

A CLOSER LOOK AT OUTPUT, INCOME, AND EXPENDITURE VARIABLES: THE NATIONAL ACCOUNTS

So far in this chapter, we have discussed the main variables of macroeconomics, and some of the reasons why policy-makers are concerned about them. The determinants of size of these variables, and the scope that governments have to influence them, is the subject-matter of macroeconomic theory to which we will soon turn our attention. First, however, we must look in more detail at the output and income variables of macroeconomics.

Three important macroeconomic concepts are output, income and expenditure. Firms produce the goods and services which in total are the nation's output (O). Production requires factors of production whose owners are paid for services provided. It thus generates income (Y). When the nation's output is sold, people spend money to purchase it, the value of expenditure (E) being the amount required to purchase the nation's output.

The most important empirical measure of these variables is called the **gross domestic product**, or the **GDP**. This is the value of total output actually produced in the whole economy over some period, usually a year (although quarterly data are also available). Statisticians measure the GDP by measuring the incomes generated in producing it, and by measuring the expenditure needed to purchase it. In doing this they define O, Y and E in such a way that they are the same thing, the value of total output. We shall review how this is done after we study the three approaches to measuring GDP.

The Income Approach

The first approach is to measure Y, the incomes generated by production. The main income items are shown for the UK in the first column of Table 26.2 on page 463.

Item (1) is straightforward: income from employment is wages and salaries. In microeconomics, self-employed persons are treated as firms, so item (2) would be partly wages and partly a return on the capital belonging to self-employed persons. The income from rent, item (3), includes not only the rent of land but also the rent of buildings, plus royalties earned from patents and copyrights. It is thus partly a return to land and partly a return to capital. The next two items, (4) and (5), are the major parts of the return on capital, item (4) for the private sector and item (5) for the public sector. Item (6)

represents depreciation, which is that part of the value of output that is not earned by any factor but is the value of capital used up in the process of production. This depreciation is part of the gross return on capital.

Item (8) involves stocks, and requires some explanation. Goods produced by a firm but not sold are part of a firm's stocks (sometimes also called inventories). These are valued at their market prices, i.e. the prices at which they could currently be sold. The difference between their cost of production and their market prices then shows up in the profit figures. Now consider what would happen if, with no change in real output, there is an increase in market prices of goods. Because of the method of valuation, the rise in market prices will cause a rise in the value of existing stocks. Unless some correction is made, all of this increase in value will be recorded as a profit, since the production costs of existing stocks have already been incurred. This would increase measured .GDP, even though stocks were unchanged. To avoid this distortion, a correction is made to eliminate changes in the value of stocks due to pure price changes. Thus, changes in stocks only contribute to changes in GDP when their physical quantities change. The correction for the change in the value of existing stocks yields gross domestic product, valued at factor cost and calculated from the income side of the economy. The residual error will be mentioned below.

The phrase 'valued at factor cost' deserves notice. When measured at factor cost, the GDP is the sum of the values of all factor services, including capital, that goes into making them. The GDP could also be measured at market prices, giving the market value of all output. The difference between the two measures arises from indirect taxes that affect market prices but do not create income for factors of production.

The income approach measures GDP in terms of the factor-income claims generated in the course of producing the total output.

The Output Approach

The second method of measuring the GDP is to add up the outputs of each firm to get the total value of the nation's output.[1] The outputs can be grouped into more or less aggregated categories corresponding to industries, to sectors or to any other desired category. One such grouping is shown in the second column of Table 26.2.

Adding up the value of output presents two conceptual problems. The first concerns the valuation of stocks of goods produced but unsold. We have already seen that these are valued at market prices. This has the effect of recording as part of current output (and income) the profits that will only be received by the firm when, and if, the goods are sold.[2]

The second problem concerns what is called *double counting* and it requires further attention. So far in this book we have proceeded as if all firms made goods and services which they sold for final use. In this case, the value of output is the sum of the values of all sales made by firms. In reality, however, production of commodities is divided into stages, with particular firms and industries often specializing in one stage of production. For example, one set of firms mine iron-ore; the ore may be sold to another set of firms for manufacturing into steel; the steel may be sold to another set of firms for use in making household tools; the manufacturer of the tools may sell them to a wholesaler; who sells them to a retailer; who in turn finally sells them to a household.

Stages of production, and the consequent inter-firm sales, raise a problem for measuring national income. If we merely added up the market values of the sales of all firms, we would obtain a total greatly in excess of the value of output actually available for use. Suppose we took the value of all farmers' sales of wheat and added to it the value of all flour mills' sales of flour, plus the value of the sales of bakeries, plus the value of the sales of bread by all retail shops. The resulting total would be much larger than the value of the final product – bread – produced by the economy. We would have counted the

value of the wheat four times, of the flour three times, of the bread produced by the bakery twice, and of the services of the retail shop once.

This is called the problem of **double counting**. *Multiple counting* would be a better term, since if we add up the values of all sales, the same output is counted *every time* it is sold from one firm to another. Double counting is avoided by using the important concept of value added. Each firm's **value added** is the value of its output *minus* the value of the inputs that it purchases from other firms. Thus a flour mill's value added is the value of its output *minus* the value of the grain it buys from the farmer and the values of any other inputs, such as electricity and fuel oil, that it buys from other firms. The relation between value added and total value of sales is further examined in Box 26.1.

> A firm's *output* is defined as its value added; the sum of all values added must be the value, at factor cost, of all goods and services produced by the economy.

The concept of value added suggests an important distinction between intermediate and final products. **Intermediate products** are all goods and services used as inputs into a further stage of production. **Final products** are the outputs of the economy after eliminating all double counting. In the previous example, grain, flour, electricity and fuel oil were all intermediate products used at various stages in the process leading to the final product, bread. We look in detail at what constitutes final products in the next section.

> The output approach measures GDP in terms of the values added by each of the sectors of the economy.

The Expenditure Approach

The third way of calculating the GDP is from the expenditure side, the flows of expenditure needed to purchase the nation's output. (The main income items for the UK are shown in the third column of Table 26.2.) National-income theory uses the categories defined by the expenditure approach, so we shall take some time on them here.

---

[1] These output data can be measured independently from the annual Census of Industry.

[2] This convention can cause a serious distortion of profit figures during times of slump. Goods that are produced but cannot be sold because of a lack of demand still produce reported profits even though the firm has not now seen, and (if prices fall in the future) may never see, these profits.

BOX 26.1 VALUE ADDED THROUGH STAGES OF PRODUCTION: AN EXAMPLE

Because the output of one firm often becomes the input of other firms, the total value of goods sold by all firms greatly exceeds the value of the output of final goods. This general principle is illustrated by a simple example in which firm R starts from scratch and produces goods (raw materials) valued at £100; the firm's value added is £100. Firm I purchases these raw materials valued at £100 and produces semi-manufactured goods that it sells for £130. Its value added is £30 because the value of the goods is increased by £30

as a result of the firm's activities. Firm F purchases the semi-manufactured goods for £130 and works them into a finished state, selling them for £180. Firm F's value added is £50. The value of final goods, £180, is found either by counting the sales of firm F or by taking the sum of the values added by each firm. This value is less than the £410 that we obtain by adding up the market value of the commodities sold by each firm. The following Table summarizes the example.

Transactions between firms at three different stages of production

	Firm R	Firm I	Firm F	All firms
A. Purchases from other firms	£ 0	£100	£130	£230 = Total inter-firm sales
B. Purchase of factors of production (wages, rent, interest, profits)	100	30	50	180 = Value added
Total A + B = value of product	£100	£130	£180 = Value of final goods and services	£410 = Total value of all sales

Consumption

Consumption expenditure is all purchases by households of currently produced goods and services, except new houses. There are several points to notice here. First, the purchases of new housing are counted as investment. (This will be considered below.) Second, we are only interested in currently produced goods and services. For example, the purchase of a used car (produced in an earlier year) represents a transfer of an existing asset, but does not represent current car production. Third, the measurement is of *purchases of the goods and services* made in the year, not of their *actual consumption* that occurs during the year (or other period under consideration). With services and non-durable goods, such as haircuts and eggs, there is no significant difference, since the consumption occurs at, or soon after, the time of purchase. With durable goods, such as cars and TV sets, however, there is a marked difference in timing. Expenditure occurs all at once, when the good is purchased, while consumption occurs as a flow over the lifetime of the good, which may be many years.

For example, if you bought a new car in 1988, your consumption expenditure occurred in 1988; however, you consume its services slowly over all of the years that you own it.

Investment

The terms *investment* and *investment goods* are used in the same way in macro- as in microeconomics. **Investment** is defined as the act of producing goods that are not for immediate consumption; the goods themselves are called **investment goods**.[1] They are produced by firms and they may be bought by firms, by households or by governments. The major components of investment goods are stocks, capital goods such as plant and equipment, and housing.

Investment in stocks: Virtually all firms hold stocks of their inputs and of their outputs. Stocks

---

[1] In common speech an individual speaks of 'investing' his money when he or she buys an equity or a bond. From the national-income point of view, this is a transfer of ownership of an existing asset; to count as investment expenditure in national income, it must be expenditure on currently produced investment goods.

of inputs allow production to continue at the desired pace in spite of short-term fluctuations in the deliveries of inputs bought from other firms. Stocks of outputs allow firms to meet orders in spite of temporary, unexpected fluctuations in the rate of output or sales.

Stocks are an inevitable part of the productive process, and they require an investment of the firm's money since the firm has paid for them but has not yet sold them. An accumulation of stocks counts as current investment because it represents goods produced but not used for current consumption. A drawing down of stocks – often called a decumulation – counts as negative investment or, as it is sometimes called, *dis*investment, because it is a reduction in the stock of goods produced in the past (see item (4) in Table 26.2).

Investment in capital goods: Capital was discussed in detail in Chapter 19. The production of new capital goods is a part of total investment and is often called **fixed investment** (because the goods are usually fixed to a location, unlike stocks which are moveable). Such investment may either replace capital that has been used up in production (or otherwise consumed) or make net additions to the stock of capital.

Investment in housing: A house yields its utility slowly over a long life. For this reason, housing construction is counted as investment, rather than as consumption. When the builder sells a house to someone intending to live in it, this is then a mere transfer of ownership that is not expenditure on current output. Behaviourally, however, investment in housing is different from investment in capital goods in that housing is sold to households, while other capital goods are sold to firms.

Total investment: The total of all investment expenditure is called **gross investment**. The amount necessary for replacement is called the **capital consumption allowance** and is often referred to as **depreciation**; the remainder is called **net investment**. Net investment increases the economy's total stock of capital, while replacement investment keeps the existing stock intact by replacing what has been worn out or otherwise used up. The national-income accounts record total spending on investment, as well as the breakdown into its various categories.

Government Expenditure

All government payments to factors of production in return for factor services rendered are counted as part of the GDP. These expenditures are called **government direct expenditures** or, sometimes, **exhaustive expenditures**. These represent the government's purchases of part of the economy's output of final goods (see item (2) in Table 26.2).

All government activity is counted as producing output of final goods or services, without any attempt to judge whether or not the activities are in some sense worthwhile. Very often government expenditure produces no marketable product. The Foreign Office and the Department of the Environment, for example, produce *public goods* (see page 400). They have no sale value, so the only feasible way to value them is at cost.

Valuation at cost does, however, have one curious consequence. If, due to a productivity increase, one civil servant now does what two used to do, and the displaced worker shifts to the private sector, the government's contribution to the GDP will register a decline. On the other hand, if two now do what one used to do, the government's contribution to GDP will rise. Both of these movements can occur in spite of the fact that what is actually done by the government is unchanged. This is an inevitable, but curious, consequence of measuring the value of the government's output by the value of the factors, mainly labour, used to produce it.

About half of total government expenditure is on what are called **transfer payments**. These are payments not made in return for any factor services rendered as part of current production. Examples are payments to those on welfare, or the unemployment rolls, or to the retired. These are transfers from taxpayers to the recipients. Although these payments may help to fulfil the nation's social goals, they do not of themselves create current production. Transfer payments are not, therefore, a part of expenditure on final output. For this reason, they are not a part of the GDP calculated from the expenditure approach.

Exports

Some domestic output is sold abroad. Although this represents expenditure by foreigners, it is expenditure on domestic output. Clearly, there-

TABLE 26.2 GDP and GNP of the UK, 1987 (current prices), £bn

THE INCOME APPROACH		THE OUTPUT APPROACH		THE EXPENDITURE APPROACH	
(1) Income from employment	226.4	Agriculture, forestry and fishing	5.9	(1) Consumer expenditure	258.3
(2) Income from self-employment	33.0	Energy and water	24.2	(2) General government final expenditure	85.8
(3) Income from rent	24.8	Manufacturing	85.6	(3) Gross domestic fixed investment	70.6
(4) Gross trading profits of companies	65.6	Construction	21.5	(4) Investment in stocks	0.6
(5) Gross trading surplus of public enterprises	6.4	Services and distribution	237.9	(5) Exports (goods and services)	107.5
(6) Imputed charge for consumption of non-trading capital	3.2	Total Domestic Output	375.1	(6) Total final expenditure (TFE), at market prices	522.8
(7) Total domestic income	359.4	Adjustment for financial services	−20.6	(7) *Less* imports (goods and services)	−112.0
(8) *Less* stock appreciation	−4.9	GDP at factor cost	354.5	(8) *Less* adjustment to factor costs	−62.0
(9) Gross Domestic Product at factor cost (from income)	354.5	Residual error	−2.3		
		GDP at factor cost (from expenditure)	352.2	(9) GDP at factor cost (from expenditure)	348.8
(10) Statistical discrepancy	−2.3			(10) Statistical discrepancy	3.4
(11) GDP at factor cost (average estimate)	352.2			(11) GDP at factor cost (average estimate)	352.2
				(12) Net property income from abroad	2.0
				(13) Gross National Product (GNP) at factor cost	354.2

Source: National Income and Expenditure (HMSO, 1988), Tables 1.2, 1.3 and 2.1

GDP can be measured by summing the incomes it generates, the values added by each sector of the economy, or the expenditures required to purchase it. The details of the three methods of calculation are given in the text.

fore, exports are a part of GDP (see item (5) of Table 26.2).

Total Final Expenditure

The sum of the four items just discussed – consumption, investment, government exhaustive expenditures, and exports – is called **total final expenditure (TFE)**. This is shown as item (6) in the expenditure column of the Table. It represents the total expenditure required to purchase all the goods and services produced domestically, when these are valued at market prices.

From TFE to GDP

We have seen that the output and income appro-

aches measure GDP at factor cost. To get to that value from the expenditure approach, some adjustments must be made to TFE.

Imports: Expenditure to purchase imports is part of total final expenditure, since some parts of consumption, investment and government expenditures go to purchase imports. These imports are not, however, a part of total domestic production. Imports are the converse of exports: they represent expenditure by *domestic* purchasers on *foreign* production. If we wish to measure domestic production, imports must therefore be deducted from TFE. This is shown in item (7) of the Table.

Indirect taxes and subsidies: Before we can

get from TFE to GDP, a second adjustment is required. Indirect taxes that are part of the sale price of commodities do not create incomes for factors of production since they are paid to the government. The principal tax in this category, in all EC countries, is the Value Added Tax (VAT). Such indirect taxes drive a wedge between the market value of output, and the factor incomes generated by its production. Indirect taxes must, therefore, be *deducted* from expenditure to get to GDP at factor cost.

By contrast, subsidies have the reverse effect. If a firm receives a subsidy, it will pay out the funds as wages, rent or profits. These incomes are not, however, generated by the sale of output. Subsidies must, therefore, be *added* to expenditure to get to GDP at factor cost. Consider, for example, a firm that pays its factors of production £10,000, of which £9,000 is raised from the sale of its output, and the other £1,000 comes from a government subsidy. If we start with the total final expenditure on its output of £9,000, we must add the £1,000 of subsidy to get to the £10,000 of incomes earned by the firm's factors of production.

The correction to TFE which is shown as item (8) combines the effect of taxes and subsidies. It is called *adjustment to factor cost*, and it is subsidies minus taxes. Since the latter usually exceeds the former, this correction is usually negative. In other words, the total factor income generated by output is usually less than the market value of that output because the government takes away more through indirect taxes than it gives through subsidies. When this net correction has been made, the result is GDP at factor cost (item 9).

From GDP to GNP

After correcting for the statistical error (item 10), a final adjustment (item 12) takes us from GDP at factor cost to what is called **gross national product (GNP)**. This latter concept measures incomes earned by UK residents in return for contributions to current production wherever that production is located. To get from GDP to GNP, we have to add receipts by British residents of dividends, interest and profits from assets that they own but which are located overseas. Clearly, this is part of the factor incomes earned by UK residents but it is not part of UK production. By the same token, dividends,

interest and profits earned on assets located in the UK, but owned abroad, must be deducted from GDP if we wish to arrive at income earned in the UK in the course of contributing to UK production. Item (10) is the sum of these two corrections, and it takes us from GDP to GNP. Since the correction is usually quite small, we shall ignore it in what follows and treat gross domestic product as being the equivalent of gross national product.

> **The expenditure approach measures the GDP in terms of the categories of expenditure required to purchase the total production.**

Residual Error

Finally we note that the two calculations of GNP, from income data and from expenditure data, are genuinely independent measures. Thus they will not give an identical result. The residual error reconciles the two to make the final estimate an average of the various estimates. The size of the discrepancy also gives some check on the accuracy of the overall measures.

The Identity of Output, Income and Expenditure

In all national-income accounting, the basic *overall* aggregate being measured is the total value of output at factor cost (either in constant or in current market prices). This can be looked at directly in terms of the output itself, O, or the income it generates, Y, or the expenditure required to purchase it, E. Although the details of each calculation give us independent information, the totals do not, since the three are defined so that they are identical:

$$Y \equiv O \equiv E \ .$$

(The three-bar identity sign reminds us that these magnitudes are equal by definition.) The reason for the identity of Y and O is that Y does not measure incomes actually paid out during the course of the year but, instead, measures the income claims generated by producing O. The identity of Y and O then follows from the accounting practice that all output must be matched by claims on that output: what is not wages, interest and rent becomes profits. Between them, they must account for all output, since someone must own the value that has been produced. Also, goods produced and not sold are valued at market prices, and the difference between their value and their cost of production is counted as part of profits.

The reason for the identity between O and E is that E does not measure actual expenditure but what *would have to be spent* to buy the output, O. This, of course, immediately makes E the same thing as O.

The interest in having all three measures, O, E and Y lies, not in their identical total, but in the separate components of each total.

In the case of O, the components are outputs of individual industries; in the case of E, they are types of expenditure, such as consumption and investment; in the case of Y, they are types of income, such as wages and salaries.

SUMMARY

1. Macroeconomics studies the economy in terms of broad aggregates and averages such as total employment and unemployment, total national product, the overall price level and the balance of payments.
2. Six major issues concern: (1) the amount of employment and unemployment, (2) the rate of inflation (changes in the price level), (3) the trade cycle (fluctuations in output and employment), (4) stagflation (the combination of high unemployment and high inflation), (5) economic growth (long-term trend of output), and (6) the behaviour of the exchange rate and the balance of payments.
3. High unemployment is undesirable because of the lost output and human misery involved. High output is desirable because the size of the national product determines (along with the size of the population) the average standard of living of a country's residents.
4. Changes in the price level are measured by an index number of prices. The index shows the cost of purchasing a given bundle of commodities in any year as a percentage of the cost of purchasing the same bundle in a base year.
5. Changes in the price level are undesirable in so far as they cause the price mechanism to allocate resources less efficiently and/or less equitably than would otherwise occur. This tends to be more likely when inflation is unanticipated than when it is anticipated.
6. The major primary goals of macroeconomic policy are (1) full employment (which does not mean zero unemployment), (2) a satisfactory rate of growth of national product, and (3) a stable price level. A satisfactory balance of payments is usually regarded as a secondary policy goal, since it is not so obviously desirable in itself, but may inhibit attainment of the primary goals if it is not achieved.
7. Two sets of macroeconomic policy instruments are usually distinguished: (1) demand-side policies, which include fiscal and monetary policies; (2) supply-side policies, which attempt to influence total output.
8. The income approach measures GDP as the total value of incomes generated by all production.
9. The output approach measures GDP as the total value of the nation's output by adding up the total value of final goods and services produced or the total of the *values added* by all producers in the economy.
10. The expenditure approach measures total final expenditure, TFE, as the total value of expenditure on final output in the categories of consumption,

investment, government expenditure and *net* exports (exports minus imports). The category of consumption includes goods and services currently produced for use by households, with the exception of residential housing (which counts as investment). Investment covers new construction of fixed capital, residential housing and *changes* in stocks. Government production covers all the government's exhaustive expenditures but excludes its transfer payments. Exports include everything that is produced at home and then exported.

11. To get from TFE to GDP it is necessary to subtract imports and indirect taxes and add subsidies. To get from GDP to GNP it is necessary to add net property income from abroad.

12. Because all three approaches measure the same total, the three measures – total output, total expenditure and total income – should give identical values. Each of the separate measures is valuable because of the specific details of output, expenditure and income that it provides. In all the theory of the following chapters, this total is referred to as *national income* and it is usually measured from the *expenditure approach*.

TOPICS FOR REVIEW

- Key macroeconomic variables
- Index numbers
- GDP, GNP and TFE
- The expenditure, income and output approaches to national income accounting
- The identity of output, income and expenditure

27

National Income in a Two-sector Model

GDP is the total output available to satisfy everyone's wants. The rising long-term trend in real GDP is the source of long-term growth that has made the living standards of each generation higher than those of all preceding generations. The short-term behaviour of GDP has, however, been characterized by oscillations. Rapidly rising real GDP often causes labour shortages, balance-of-payments problems and inflation. Declining or static real GDP often causes bouts of heavy unemployment, static or falling living standards and pockets of severe poverty, conditions which were found, for example, in the UK in the early 1980s.

Why does GDP behave as it does and can governments do anything to influence it? To deal with this and related questions, we need a theory of national income.

The theory that explains the size of and changes in national income is called the *theory of income determination*.

We begin with definitions and assumptions; then, because it is easier to study complex things one at a time rather than all at once, we proceed in a series of small steps. In the next three chapters, we study the forces that determine the GDP under the simplifying assumptions that both the rate of interest and the price level are constant. In the following three chapters, we consider the forces that determine the interest rate. Only then can we study inflation and all of its related problems. This may seem a circuitous route to get to one of the decade's key problems, the causes and control of inflation. However, everything that we do along the way is needed for a full understanding of inflation.

SOME PRELIMINARIES

First we introduce a few more definitions, some key concepts, and some assumptions.

A Further Definition

The measurement of national income in Chapter 26 distinguishes such concepts as TFE, GNP and GDP. In their theories, economists use the generic concept of **national income** (indicated by the symbol Y). National income, Y, may be thought of as interchangeable with constant-price GDP (i.e. the total real output produced in the nation). Note, however, that GDP is almost the same as GNP (i.e. total real income earned in the economy).

Key Concepts

We now introduce some key concepts that relate to flows of expenditure.

Expenditure Flows

The concept of a flow of expenditure is an important one in national-income theory and it has three important characteristics.

Expenditure flows are real (not nominal) flows: We saw in Chapter 26 that expenditure flows can be measured either in current, or in constant, prices. Economic *theory* is about real, not nominal, expenditures. Of course, if the price level is constant, current or constant prices give the same result. But when the price level does change, current and constant-price measures will give different results. The constant-price measure is used because we are concerned with changes in *real* values.

All expenditure flows are planned flows: The term **planned expenditure** refers to what people intend to spend; the term **realized expenditure** refers to what they actually succeed in spending. In economic theory, the term expenditure refers to planned expenditure. Realized expenditure will differ from what is planned whenever plans are frustrated, for example by a strike that interrupts production of the goods that consumers planned to buy. Planned expenditure is also described as **desired**, or **ex ante**, **expenditure**, while realized expenditure is often described as **actual** or **ex post expenditure**. (These terms, and the distinction they refer to, are important in what follows so they should be committed to memory now.)

All expenditure flows are aggregate flows: In macroeconomics, we are not concerned with the behaviour of individual households or firms, but with the aggregate behaviour of all households, and all firms.

Basic Assumptions

We start with some simplifying assumptions designed to isolate the main determinants of national income. Later we can drop these assumptions and move on to more realistic, but more complex, cases.

(1) Potential national income is constant: Because an economy's productive capacity changes slowly from year to year, its potential national income changes slowly. Assuming potential income to be constant is thus satisfactory for analyses covering only a few years. (In Chapter 36, we drop this assumption and study the growth of potential income over time.)

(2) There are unemployed supplies of all factors of production: This assumption implies that output can be increased by using land, labour and capital that is currently unemployed. In Chapter 33, we shall study the behaviour of national income under conditions of full employment. In this case it is difficult to increase output by employing factors of production that are currently unemployed.

(3) The interest rate and the general price level are constant: We seek first to understand the determination of income when the interest rate and the price level are constant. In Part 9, we allow them to vary.

The Microeconomic Underpinnings of the Basic Assumptions

The assumptions about unemployed factors and stable prices require some justification. The state of the economy described in assumption (2) is one of excess supply: firms are willing to sell more than they are now selling at existing prices, and unemployed workers are willing to work at the existing wage. The theory of competitive markets predicts, however, that prices and wages will fall when there is excess supply in product and labour markets. How then can assumptions (2) and (3) be valid simultaneously? Why do individual prices and wages, and hence the general price level, not fall when there is excess supply of all factors of production?

The basic microeconomic explanations are on pages 238–242 of Chapter 14, and pages 625–629 of Chapter 35. Let us recall how these work out. According to assumption (2), firms must be producing below normal capacity. We saw in Chapter 14 that oligopolistic firms often have flat

FIGURE 27.1 A Keynesian Aggregate Supply Curve

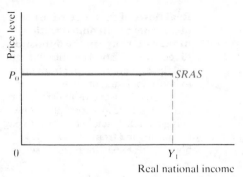

On a Keynesian *AS* curve, there is a range over which national income will vary with no change in the general price level. Real national income is measured horizontally and the price level vertically. The present price level is P_0, and output will vary over the range from zero to Y_1 at that price level. This means that firms will supply whatever is demanded over that range of national income without altering their prices. The level of output that is produced will be determined by total demand, which is not shown on the Figure.

cost curves, and find it costly to change their prices. In these circumstances, firms will vary their outputs (and hence their employment of factors of production) while holding their administered prices constant when responding to short-term fluctuations in demand. So part of the explanation is that goods markets are oligopolistic, not perfectly competitive, and oligopoly prices tend to be sticky in the short run.

Why does the price of labour not fall when there is heavy unemployment? If wages did fall, firms' cost curves would also fall, and firms would be induced to cut prices. One answer is given in Chapter 35, where we shall see that wages do not necessarily fluctuate so as to clear labour markets in response to short-term fluctuations in the demand for labour. When this is the case, wages stay fairly rigid in the short run; and when the demand for labour fluctuates, employment of labour fluctuates.

Under the circumstances just outlined, firms' cost curves, and hence their supply curves, are flat (perfectly elastic), at least up to capacity output. Nor do they shift down when there is unemployment because wages do not fall.

Given flat, stable cost curves, individual firms produce whatever they can sell, at the going price. Their outputs are demand-determined and their prices do not fluctuate as their output changes.

What is true for each firm is also true for the economy as a whole. We can illustrate this by drawing what is called an **aggregate supply curve**, which relates the economy's total output, Y, to the price level, P. If product and labour markets behave as just described, then the economy's aggregate supply curve will be perfectly elastic over some range of output. This is shown in Figure 27.1 by what is called *a Keynesian aggregate supply curve*. It tells us that, as far as the supply side of the economy is concerned, output can vary over the range shown in the Figure, without pressure for the price level to change. Thus, for the economy as a whole, the output that is produced in the aggregate – i.e. the level of Y – will be determined by total demand, which is usually called aggregate demand.

At this stage of our study, national income is demand-determined.

We do not yet enquire into the shape of the aggregate supply curve when output is near its potential level since we are concerned, by assumption (2), only with situations of substantial unemployment, when national income is below potential. Confining our attention to this case, allows us to concentrate on the forces that determine aggregate demand. Once this has been done, we can introduce the complications that arise when firms are not prepared to supply everything that is demanded at existing prices.

THE DETERMINATION OF INCOME

The Circular Flow of Income

We first encountered the circular flow of income on pages 55–57 of Chapter 4, which discussion should be reread now. The simplified circular-flow diagram in Figure 27.2 shows firms earning their incomes by selling their outputs to households, and households earning their incomes by selling their factor services to firms.

We now define the **circular flow of income**

FIGURE 27.2 The Circular Flow of Income

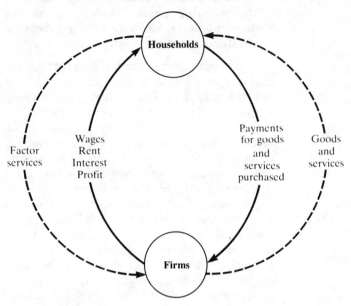

Real flows of factor services and of outputs are in one direction; money flows are in the opposite direction. The broken lines indicate real flows of output going from firms to households and of factor services going from households to firms. The solid lines indicate expenditure flows going from households to firms to pay for output and from firms to households to pay for factor services.

as *the flow of expenditures on output and factor services passing between domestic (as opposed to foreign) firms and domestic households.* Any other expenditure flow is not part of this basic circular flow, and must therefore be either an injection into, or a withdrawal from, the circular flow. An **injection** into the circular flow is income received, either by firms or households, that does not arise from the spending of the other group. A **withdrawal**, or **leakage**, from the circular flow is income received by either firms or households that is not passed on to the other group by buying goods or services from it.

The Basic Model

The economy that we consider in this chapter, and which we have shown in Figure 27.2, contains only domestic households and domestic firms. It produces only two kinds of commodities. The first is consumers' goods, which are sold by the firms that produce them to the households that consume them. The second is investment goods, which are sold by the firms that produce them to the firms that use them. To simplify, we assume that firms pay out all of their profits to their owners. Thus all of national income is paid out to households as their income. Households then decide how much of that income to spend for consumption purposes, C, and how much to save, S. Firms are willing to produce everything they can sell. Investment goods are paid for by raising money, either directly from households, or from the financial institutions where households deposit some of their savings.

According to these simple assumptions, all savings decisions are taken by households, and all investment decisions are taken by firms. The separation of these two decisions has one obvious, but important, implication:

> there is no reason why a change in the desire of households to save, or in the desire of firms to invest, should automatically be matched by a similar change on the part of the other group.

The Effects of Saving and Investment

Now consider the effects of saving on this simple economy's circular flow of income. Households receive income from firms and pass it back to firms through consumption expenditure. **Sav-**

ing is income received by households that they do *not* pass back to firms through consumption expenditure. Saving thus represents a withdrawal, or leakage, of expenditure from the circular flow of income between households and firms.

> **Since saving is a leakage out of the circular flow, it exerts a contractionary force on the flow.**

For example, if households suddenly decided to save all of their incomes, none would be passed back to firms. Sales would shrink to zero. Firms would soon stop producing goods that they could not sell, and hence would stop creating incomes for households. In this extreme case, the contractionary force of 100 per cent saving would shrink the circular flow of income to zero.

Now consider the effect of investment. Investment expenditure creates income for the firms that produce capital goods and for the factors they employ. This is income that does not arise from the expenditure of households. Investment expenditure thus creates an injection into, the circular flow of income.

> **Since investment is an injection into the circular flow of income, it exerts an expansionary force on that flow.**

For example, if investment expenditure increases greatly, firms will increase their outputs of investment goods, and take on new factors of production. This creates new incomes for the firms and for the households whose factor services they employ.

The full circular flow with savings and investment is shown in Figure 27.3 for the simple two-sector economy.

Total Demand: Aggregate Desired Expenditure

Definitions

Given our assumptions, total output will be determined by the total demand to buy that output. In this simple model, there are two elements of demand, desired consumption expenditure, C, and desired investment expenditure, I. The term **aggregate desired expenditure** is used to refer to the total amount of purchases that all spending units in the economy wish to make. (The term aggregate demand is reserved for another concept that we shall introduce in a later chapter.) Using E for aggregate desired expenditure, we have

$$E \equiv C + I . \tag{1}$$

FIGURE 27.3 The Circular Flow of Income in a Two-sector Economy

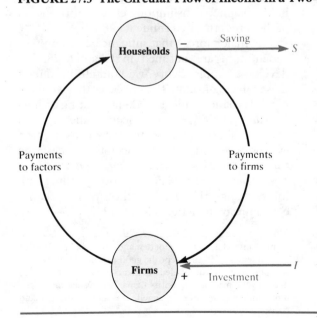

Saving is a withdrawal from, and investment is an injection into, the circular flow of income between firms and households. The black arrows show the circular flow of expenditure from domestic firms to domestic households and back again; the coloured arrows show the flow of saving as a withdrawal, or leakage, and the flow of investment as an injection.

The three-bar identity sign emphasizes that (1) is merely a definition of aggregate desired expenditure. It is defined as the sum of two components, consumption expenditure and investment expenditure.

Behavioural Assumptions

The next step is to make assumptions about the behaviour of the two elements of aggregate desired expenditure, investment and consumption.

Autonomous and induced expenditures: Our behavioural assumptions will divide expenditure flows into what are called autonomous and induced flows. The terms **autonomous** or **exogenous** are used interchangeably to refer to expenditure flows that are not influenced by any variable the theory is designed to explain. Because the current theory explains variations in national income, any expenditure flow that does not vary with national income is an autonomous, or exogenous, expenditure flow. Because autonomous expenditure flows are not explained by the theory, they are treated as constants. They can change, but not for reasons explained by theory.

Any expenditure flow that is related to national income (or any other variable explained by the theory) is referred to as an **induced** or an **endogenous** expenditure flow; the terms mean the same thing, and are used interchangeably. Variations in these expenditure flows are *induced* by changes in national income.

> **The distinction between autonomous (or exogenous) expenditure flows and induced (or endogenous) expenditure flows is basic to the whole of national-income theory; the former do not vary as national income varies, and can be treated as constants; the latter vary as national income varies, and are thus variables in the theory.**

Investment decisions: For the moment, it is convenient to study how national income adjusts to a fixed level of investment. Thus the three components of aggregate desired investment expenditure are assumed constant. Firms plan to spend a constant amount on plant and equipment each year; firms plan to hold their inventories

constant, and planned housing construction is constant from one year to the next. These assumptions make investment into an autonomous expenditure flow.

To indicate that investment is a constant we write:

$$I = I^* . \tag{2}$$

(Whenever an expenditure flow is assumed to be autonomous, this constant amount is indicated by an asterisk on the symbol for the variable.) Equation (2) says that desired investment expenditure, I, is a constant amount each year, which we call I^*. Depending on the size of the economy, I^* will be some specific number. It might, for example, be £5,000m or £50,000m per year.

The consumption-saving decision: Each household makes plans about how much to spend on consumption, C, and how much to save, S. These are not, however, independent decisions. Since saving is income not spent on consumption, it follows that households have to make a single division of their disposable income; they either save it or they spend it.

How do households in the aggregate actually divide their income between consumption and saving? The answer to this question is provided by what is called the **consumption function**, which states the relationship between households' planned consumption expenditure and all of the forces that determine it.

The major forces that influence consumption expenditure are outlined in Chapter 28. To develop a simple theory, we hold all but one of these forces constant. The one force that we allow to vary is national income. Concentrating on how consumption varies with income, allows us to derive a simple relation between consumption expenditure and national income. To describe this relation, we say that *consumption is a function of national income*. When the other influencing forces change, they will shift the function relating consumption to national income.[1]

---

[1] This is just what was done for demand curves in Part 2. All of the influencing forces except the good's own price were held constant, and a relation called a demand curve was established between the price and quantity demanded. When one of the other influencing forces changed, this *shifted* the demand curve.

FIGURE 27.4 Simple Saving and Consumption Functions

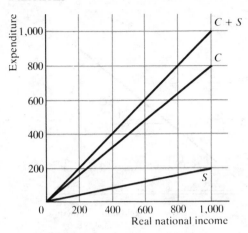

Saving and consumption are both related to household income, and together must account for all that income. The graph shows a consumption function in which desired consumption expenditure is always 80 per cent of income and desired savings is always 20 per cent. The line $C + S$ shows the sum of consumption plus saving which must yield all income.

The above assumptions have the effect of making consumption into what we have called an induced, or endogenous, expenditure flow: variations in consumption are explained by variations in national income. In this chapter we make the simple assumption that consumption is always a *constant fraction of income*. If, for example, every household spends 80 per cent of its income, and saves the remaining 20 per cent, then consumption will be 80 per cent of national income, and savings will be 20 per cent. We illustrate this assumption in the first three columns of Table 27.1 on page 476, and in Figure 27.4. Notice in the Figure that the line relating the sum of saving and consumption to income has a slope of unity. This is the graphical expression of the assumption that saving and consumption account for all of household income.

Our assumption about consumption expenditure is written:

$$C = cY . \tag{3}$$

In this equation C stands for the flow of consumption expenditure, and Y for the flow of household income. The third symbol, c, stands

for the fraction of income that is spent on consumption. Notice that in this, and all subsequent equations, capital letters stand for expenditure flows, while lower-case letters are used to express assumptions about behaviour. Since we are assuming that households always spend some part of their incomes, the value of c must be positive. Since we also assume that households do not spend all of their incomes – some of it is saved – c must be less than unity. In other words, c is a number greater than zero (positive consumption) but less than unity (positive saving).

To illustrate the interpretation of this equation, assume that households always devote 80 per cent of their incomes to consumption expenditure. The value of c is then 0.8. If, for example, total household income is £1,000m, equation (3) tells us that total consumption expenditure will be £800m.

Since what is not spent on consumption is by definition saved, we can also express our single assumption about household spending behaviour in the following savings function:

$$S = sY . \tag{3'}$$

Once again S and Y stand for flows – this time of income and saving – while the lower-case letter s describes behaviour. Since households save some, but not all, of their incomes, s will be greater than zero but less than unity. In our previous example, where households spent 80 per cent of income on consumption, the other 20 per cent must be saved. Thus s is equal to 0.2. If we consider an income of £1,000m, equation (3') with s set at 0.2 shows that saving is £200m.

Notice that, since saving and investment must account for all of household income, the fraction of income saved, plus the fraction of income spent, must add to unity. Another way of putting this point is that:

$$s = 1 - c . \tag{4}$$

This says that if c pence out of every pound of disposable income is spent on consumption, then $1 - c$ pence must be saved. In our previous numerical example c was 0.8, and s therefore had to be 0.2 (1 − 0.8).[1] Although simple, you must be

---

[1] Since income is either spent on consumption or saved, we write: $Y = C + S$. So if $C = cY$, we have $Y = cY + S$, or $S = (1 - c)Y$. So if $S = sY$, then $s = 1 - c$, which is the result stated in the text.

sure of equation (4) as we will have occasion to go back and forth between s and $1 - c$ many times in the discussion that follows.

Propensities to Consume and Save

Consumption propensities: To summarize the relation between consumption and income, Keynes developed two concepts. The **average propensity to consume (APC)** is the average amount of all income spent on consumption, i.e. total consumption expenditure divided by total income. This is C/Y. Since in our simple model $C = cY$, the APC is $cY/Y = c$. In our simple numerical example, the average propensity to consume is 0.8.

The **marginal propensity to consume (MPC)** is the proportion of each new increment of income that is spent on consumption. Recall that Δ stands for a change in the variable to which it is attached, so that ΔC and ΔY refer to changes in C and Y. Using this terminology, we can write the MPC as $\Delta C/\Delta Y$. First differencing[1] equation (3) shows that $\Delta C = c\Delta Y$. Dividing by ΔY shows the MPC, $\Delta C/\Delta Y$, is equal to c. This tells us that, if households spend £c out of every £1 of income, they will spend the fraction c out of any additional income that they get. In our numerical illustration where c is 0.8, the MPC is also 0.8.

Saving propensities: The savings propensities are similarly defined. The **average propensity to save (APS)** is total saving expressed as a fraction of total income ($S/Y = s$ in our model). The **marginal propensity to save (MPS)** is the fraction of any additional £1 of income that is saved ($\Delta S/\Delta Y = s$ in our model).

These definitions of consumption and saving are illustrated in Figure 27.5. As the Figure shows, our simple assumption about consumption makes the MPC equal to the APC. (It also makes MPS equal to the APS.) Of course, this is not necessary. Consider, for example, a household that was saving £2,000 each year out of its annual income of £20,000. Its APS and APC are thus 0.1 and 0.9. Now assume that, when its income rises to £21,000, its saving rises to £2,200. The household has saved £200 out of its

---

FIGURE 27.5 The Average and Marginal Propensities to Consume

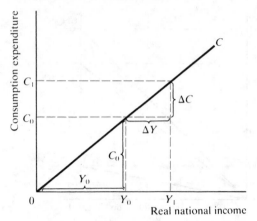

When the consumption function is a straight line through the origin, the average and marginal propensities to consume are equal.
The graph shows a consumption function whose equation is $C = cY$.

The APC is C_0/Y_0 at Y_0 and C_1/Y_1 at Y_1. Both of these are equal to the slope of the function which is c.

The MPC when Y goes from Y_0 to Y_1 and C from C_0 to C_1 is shown by the ratio $\Delta C/\Delta Y$, which is also equal to the slope of the consumption function, c.

---

additional income of £1,000, making its MPS 0.2 and its MPC 0.8. (To check your understanding, calculate the APS and the APC when the household's income is £21,000.)

The Aggregate Desired Expenditure Function

The aggregate desired expenditure function is merely the sum of the expenditure functions of each individual class of expenditure. It tells us how total desired expenditure varies with income. In the present model, there are only two classes of expenditure, consumption and investment, so desired aggregate expenditure is merely the sum of these two.

The construction of this function is illustrated numerically in column (5) of Table 27.1 on page 476, which uses a numerical example in which consumption is always 80 per cent of income and investment is constant at £100m. Figure 27.6 illustrates how this is done graphically. Notice that the aggregate expenditure line is labelled

AE. In the text we use the symbol E, but since E is used for equilibrium positions in all Figures we need another label for aggregate expenditure.

To derive the aggregate expenditure function algebraically, we substitute the behavioural equations (2) and (3) into the definition of aggregate expenditure in (1). This gives:

$$E = I^* + cY . \tag{5}$$

The aggregate expenditure function of equation (5) is just another way of saying that total expenditure is the sum of consumption and investment expenditure (equation (1)). Only now we have incorporated our assumptions about the behaviour of consumption (equation (3)) and

---

FIGURE 27.6 The Aggregate Expenditure Function

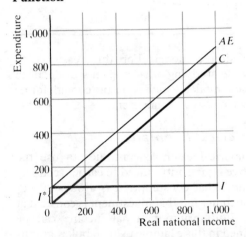

The aggregate expenditure function is the sum of the separate expenditure functions. The graph plots real national income on the horizontal axis and real desired expenditure flows on the vertical axis. In the present model, there are two elements of aggregate expenditure, investment and consumption. The investment function is shown as a horizontal straight line, labelled I, and drawn at a height of I^*. It shows investment remaining at that value whatever the level of income. The consumption function is the same positively sloped straight line as was shown in Figures 27.4 and 27.5. The aggregate expenditure function, AE, is the vertical summation of these two curves. It shows at each level of income the sum of the desired flows of investment and the desired consumption expenditures. Because investment is a constant, the AE line has the same slope as the C line, but is vertically above it by the amount I^*.

---

investment (equation (2)). Equation (5) expresses aggregate expenditure, E, as a function of the endogenous variable Y, and the autonomous expenditure I^*.

Equilibrium Conditions

The model is completed by adding an equilibrium condition. This can be expressed in either of two equivalent ways, which we now consider.

Desired Expenditure Equals Actual Income

Because firms will produce anything they can sell at existing prices, total output, Y, will be equal to total desired expenditure: whatever consumption and investment goods people and firms wish to buy, will be produced by firms eager to sell all they can. Thus, the equilibrium condition is:[1]

$$Y = E . \tag{6}$$

This condition says that actual output, Y, will be equal, in equilibrium, to desired expenditure, E. If actual output is less than what people want to buy, firms will increase output. If actual output exceeds what people want to buy, firms will have to reduce output to avoid an endless accumulation of unsold stocks.

Saving Equals Investment

An alternative way of expressing the same equilibrium condition is in terms of the equality of desired saving and desired investment. We know that, by definition, all income is either saved or consumed. This is written:

$$Y = C + S . \tag{7}$$

We also know that there are only two classes of expenditure in our model, so that all expenditure is either for consumption or investment (equation (1)). Substituting (1) and (7) into the equilibrium condition (6) yields:

$$C + S = C + I .$$

---

[1] This equilibrium condition has nothing to do with the identity between actual expenditure and actual income in the national-income accounts. In equation (6) above, Y does refer to actual GDP produced, but E refers to the amount households and firms *wish* to spend – which is not necessarily what they do spend.

TABLE 27.1 Equilibrium National Income for a Numerical Example (£m)

(1)	(2)	(3)	(4)	(5)	(6)
National income Y	Desired consumption[1] C	Desired saving[2] S	Desired investment I	Desired expenditure (2) + (4) E	Excess of desired expenditure over actual output (5) − (1)
100	80	20	100	180	80
300	240	60	100	340	40
400	320	80	100	420	20
500	**400**	**100**	**100**	**500**	**0**
600	480	120	100	580	−20
700	560	140	100	660	−40
900	720	180	100	820	−80

[1]$C = 0.8Y.$ [2]$S = 0.2Y.$

Equilibrium income occurs where desired expenditure equals actual output and desired saving equals desired investment. At income £500m, desired expenditure and actual output are equal. At that income, desired investment and desired saving are also equal with values of £100m.

Cancelling out the *C*s, which are common to both sides, yields

$$S = I . \qquad (8)$$

This is an alternative statement of the equilibrium condition given in equation (6). Saving, being a withdrawal or leakage, exerts a contractionary force on the circular flow of income, while investment, being an injection, exerts an expansionary force. As (8) shows, equilibrium occurs where the contractionary force of saving is just balanced by the expansionary force of investment.

> **Equilibrium income occurs when demanders are just willing to purchase everything produced, $E = Y$, or equivalently, when the contractionary force exerted by saving just equals the expansionary force exerted by investment.**

The Determination of Equilibrium Income

We must now see how equilibrium national income is established. We do this first in a numerical example, then graphically, and finally algebraically. Much of the more complex analysis that follows uses the results we are going to derive

for the simple model. For this reason it is worthwhile studying what happens in detail in the present model, which is simple enough for its workings to be readily apparent.

A Numerical Example

Our numerical example continues to use the illustrative figures introduced in earlier sections. We assume that consumption is always 80 per cent of income, and that investment is constant at £100m. Equilibrium national income can be determined in this example using tabular, graphical and algebraic methods.

(1) A tabular solution: Table 27.1 gives data for the numerical example. It is clear from the Table that if output were to be held at any level below £500m, people would wish to buy more than was being produced. Desired purchases would then exceed actual output. For example, if output were £400m, desired expenditure would be £420m. Since firms are assumed to produce enough to meet all demand, this is not a possible equilibrium position; firms will increase their outputs to meet the excess demand.

In contrast, if output is held above £500m, desired expenditure is less that actual output. For example, when output is £700m, desired expenditure is only £660m. Unsold stock worth

£40m would accumulate each period. To prevent such an accumulation from continuing indefinitely, firms will reduce output until they can sell all they produce.

Clearly, the only possible equilibrium in the Table is at an output of £500m. Demand is then just enough to buy what is produced, no more and no less. At that output, households spend £400m on consumption and save £100m. But firms spend £100m to buy investment goods, so total demand is £500m, which is just enough to buy the total output of £500m.[1]

The above discussion looks at the equilibrium in terms of the equality of desired expenditure and actual output (equation (6)). Now look at the same equilibrium in terms of the equality between saving and investment (equation (8)).

At the equilibrium level of income, desired saving of £100m is equal to desired investment of £100m. Below the equilibrium income, desired investment exceeds desired saving. The excess of injections over withdrawals exerts an expansionary force on national income. Above equilibrium, desired saving exceeds desired investment. The excess of desired withdrawals over desired injections exerts a contractionary force on national income. Finally, when saving and investment are equal, the addition to demand caused by investment expenditure just matches the subtraction from demand caused by households not spending all of their income. Desired expenditure is thus equal to output so that all the output that is produced will be bought, but no further output will be demanded.

(2) A graphical solution: The two parts of Figure 27.7 graph the data shown in Table 27.1. The first part also introduces a new relation, called the *45° line*. The 45° line graphs the equilibrium condition of equation (6) showing all the points where expenditure equals income. It shows all the points of possible equilibrium because anywhere on it buyers are just prepared to buy (E) as much as is being produced (Y).

Above the 45° line, desired expenditure exceeds national income; below the 45° line, desired expenditure falls short of national income. The 45° line has a slope of unity because it joins up all the points which have equal value on both axes.

Part (i) of the Figure shows that the equilibrium level of national income occurs where the aggregate expenditure function intersects the 45° line. This is the graphical solution of two simultaneous equations. One line indicates the amount of aggregate desired expenditure associated with each level of income, and the other line indicates the equilibrium condition, that aggregate desired expenditure should equal national income.

Part (ii) of the Figure shows that the equilibrium level of national income occurs where the saving curve intersects the investment curve.[1] Again, this is the graphical solution of two simultaneous equations, one line showing how much households wish to save at each level of income, and the other line showing how much firms wish to spend on investment. Only at the intersection point is income such that desired saving equals desired investment expenditure.

(3) An algebraic solution: To solve the example algebraically, we make two substitutions. First we substitute the behavioural assumption that investment is constant at £100m into equation (2). Then we substitute the assumption that consumption is always 80 per cent of income into equation (3). This yields:

$$I = 100 \; ,$$

and

$$C = 0.8Y \; .$$

Substituting these into the aggregate expenditure function of (1) gives:

$$E = 0.8Y + 100 \; .$$

This is the equation of the aggregate expenditure function graphed in part (i) of Figure 27.7.

The second equation of the model is (6), which expresses the equilibrium condition, and which is graphed as the 45° line in the Figure:

$$E = Y \; .$$

---

[1] Notice we have not said what would happen if the economy were temporarily at some disequilibrium level of income. To do this, we would need to specify the lags in the expenditure functions. All we have done is to argue that no output other than £500m could be an equilibrium because, if any other output were maintained indefinitely, demand would either exceed or fall short of that output.

[1] In our simple example the functions are all linear, and graphed as straight lines. In more general models they can be non-linear and graphed as curved lines. To allow for this possibility, it is customary to refer to them as curves, whether they are linear or non-linear functions.

FIGURE 27.7 The Determination of Equilibrium National Income

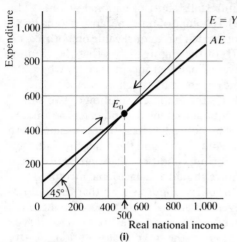

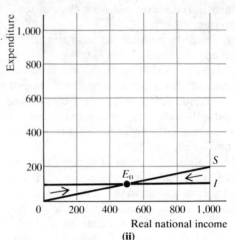

Real national income
(i)

Real national income
(ii)

Equilibrium occurs where the aggregate desired expenditure function intersects the 45° line, and where the desired saving function intersects the desired investment function. In part (i) of the Figure the line labelled AE graphs columns (1) and (5) of Table 27.1. It shows the amount of desired expenditure associated with each level of national income. The 45° line is a graph of the equilibrium condition that E should equal Y. Equilibrium is at E_0 where the two lines intersect. At any income below £500m, desired expenditure exceeds output and output will be increased, as indicated by the left-hand arrow. At any income above £500m, desired expenditure will be less than output and output will be reduced, as indicated by the right-hand arrow.

In part (ii) of the Figure, the line labelled S graphs columns (1) and (3). It is the saving function. The line labelled I graphs columns (1) and (4). It is the investment function. The latter is horizontal, indicating that investment remains constant at £100m whatever the level of income. Equilibrium occurs at E_0 where the two functions intersect. At any lower level of income, desired investment exceeds desired savings. The expansionary forces exceed the contractionary forces and income will rise. At any income above the equilibrium, desired saving exceeds desired investment. The contractionary forces exceed the expansionary forces and income will fall.

We now solve these two simultaneous equations by substituting the equation of the aggregate expenditure function into the equilibrium condition to eliminate E. This result is $Y = 500$.[1]

The Algebraic Solution More Generally

So far we have considered how to solve a numerical example using Tables, graphs and algebra.

---

[1] Substituting $E = 0.8Y + 100$ into $E = Y$ yields: $0.8Y + 100 = Y$. Subtracting $0.8Y$ from both sides: $Y - 0.8Y = 100$. Simplifying the left-hand side by completing the subtraction yields: $0.2Y = 100$. Dividing through by 0.2 gives: $Y = 100/0.2 = 500$.

Now let us deal in more general terms. The model is so simple that its formal solution is a trivial matter. Nonetheless, quite a bit can be learned from studying it. As a first step, we gather together its equations. Each of the equations listed below is repeated from the earlier discussion, and the original numbering is retained for ease of cross-reference.

Definitional equation:
$$E \equiv C + I \tag{1}$$
Behavioural equations:
$$I = I^* \tag{2}$$
$$C = cY \qquad 0 < c < 1 \tag{3}$$
Equilibrium condition:
$$Y = E \tag{6}$$

Equation (1) is what is called a definitional equation (or more properly a definitional identity), defining aggregate expenditure. Equations (2) and (3) are called behavioural equations. They tell us how investment behaves (it is autonomous), and how consumption behaves (it is an induced expenditure flow, varying with national income). Equation (6) is what is called an equilibrium condition. It tells us that in equilibrium desired expenditure must equal actual income.

Recall what we said earlier: as a matter of convention, the variables, whether autonomous or induced, are indicated by capital letters, while lower-case letters are reserved for the coefficients that describe decision-takers' behaviour in the model. These are called the *behavioural parameters*.[1] In the present case, there is only one behavioural parameter, *c*.

Usually, the values of behavioural parameters are restricted only in their signs, i.e. they are restricted to being positive or negative. The parameter *c*, however, is restricted to being positive but less than unity, indicating that consumption expenditure accounts for some but not all of household income.

Notice that the restrictions on behavioural parameters are given to the right of the equation where they occur. Specific examples, and empirical applications, arise by giving exact numerical values to these parameters (as well as to the autonomous variables). The numerical example used above arose from setting $c = 0.8$ and $I^* = 100$.

Now let us condense the model that we have just set out into the form in which we have graphed it. Substituting equations (2) and (3) into equation (1) yields the two equations whose solution is shown for a numerical example in part (i) of Figure 27.7. Equation (5) is the aggregate desired expenditure function. It is a linear relation in which I^* is the constant and c is the slope term. Equation (6) is the equilibrium condition that aggregate desired expenditure should equal actual national income. The algebraic solution is found by solving these two equations simultaneously:[1]

Aggregate desired expenditure function:
$$e = I^* + cY \tag{5}$$
Equilibrium condition:
$$E = Y \tag{6}$$
Solution:
$$Y = \frac{I^*}{1-c} \tag{9}$$

The solution is autonomous expenditure, I^*, divided by the reciprocal of one minus the *MPC*, i.e. $1 - c$. To compare this with later results, it is helpful to separate the two terms in the right-hand side by rewriting the above equation to read:

$$Y = I^* \frac{1}{1-c} \tag{9'}$$

Of course equations (9) and (9') say exactly the same thing. All we have done in (9') is to separate out the autonomous expenditure flow, I^*, from the term by which it is multiplied, $(1/(1-c))$.

We can also solve for equilibrium income using the saving equals investment condition. To do this, we use the following equations:

$$I = I^* \tag{2}$$
$$S = sY \tag{3'}$$
$$S = I . \tag{8}$$

The behavioural equations are (2) for investment and (3') for saving. Equation (8) is the equilibrium condition which says that desired saving should equal desired investment.

Substitution easily produces[2]

$$Y = \frac{I^*}{s} . \tag{10}$$

---

[1] When we consider how any two measures, X and Y, are related, X and Y are called variables. The nature of the relation between them is determined by what are called the parameters of the relation. For example, if the relation is $Y = a + bX$, the relation is linear; while if it is $Y = aX^b$, there is a power relation. In each case, a and b are the parameters that determine the nature of the relation. When these parameters are given specific values, they determine a specific example as with the numerical example used in the text. In that example the relation between C and Y is linear ($C = a + cY$) with the parameter values being $a = 0$ and $c = 0.8$. Parameter values are constant on one specific example, but they vary from example to example.

---

[1] Substituting (5) into (6): $Y = cY + I^*$. Subtracting cY from both sides: $Y - cY = I^*$. Factoring out the Y: $Y(1-c) = I^*$. Dividing through by $(1-c)$ then yields equation (9) in the text.

[2] Substituting (3') and (2) into (8): $sY = I^*$. Dividing through by s then produces equation (10) in the text.

This states that equilibrium national income is autonomous expenditure divided by the *MPS*. As with equation (9), it will help for future comparisons to write the right-hand side of (10) as two separate terms:

$$Y = I^* \frac{1}{s} \ . \tag{10'}$$

Of course, equations (10) and (10') say exactly the same thing. All we have done in (10') is to separate the autonomous expenditure from the term by which it is multiplied.

Finally, let us check that the two forms in which equilibrium income are stated, (9) and (10), are equivalent. We know from equation (4) that $s = 1 - c$ (what is saved out of every £1 of income is the part that is not spent on consumption). If we substitute $1 - c$ for s in equation (10), we obtain equation (9), or, if we substitute s for $1 - c$ in (9), we obtain (10). This shows that (9) and (10) are equivalent; they are just two ways of stating the one level of equilibrium national income implied by the model.

A Link Between Saving and Investment?

Earlier in this chapter, we stressed that saving and investment decisions were made by different groups, and that there was no necessary reason why households should decide to save the same amount that firms decided to invest. We have just concluded from our simple two-sector model, however, that equilibrium national income requires that saving be equal to investment. Does this not mean we have found a mechanism that ensures that households end up desiring to save an amount equal to what firms desire to invest? The answer is 'yes'. Is there not, then, a conflict between what we said at first and what have now concluded? The answer is 'no'.

The explanation of the apparent conflict provides the key to the theory of the determination of national income in the simple two-sector case. There is no reason why the amount that households wish to save, at a *randomly selected* level of national income, should be equal to the amount that firms wish to invest at the same level of income. This is the meaning of the statement made at the outset. But when desired saving is not equal to investment, there are forces at work that

cause national income to change until the two do become equal. This is the meaning of the latter statement.

The graphical expression of this is that the saving function does not coincide with the investment function in Figure 27.7(ii). At all levels of national income where the two curves have different heights, desired saving does not equal desired investment. But the two curves do intersect somewhere, and the equilibrium level of income, in the simple two-sector economy, occurs at the intersection point. To recapitulate:

> **there is no reason why desired saving should equal desired investment at any randomly chosen level of income, but when they are not equal in the two-sector economy, national income will change until they are brought into equality.**

CHANGES IN INCOME

Our next step is to study the forces that cause income to change in the simple two-sector economy. As a preliminary to this study, we shall review the important distinction, first made in Chapter 5, between movements along curves and shifts of curves.

If desired consumption expenditure rises, it makes a great deal of difference whether the rise is in response to a change in national income or to an increased desire to consume *at each level of national income*. The former change is represented by *a movement along* the aggregate consumption curve; it is the response of consumption to a change in income. The latter change is represented by *a shift* in the consumption curve, indicating a change in the proportion of income that households desire to consume at each level of income.

Figure 27.8 illustrates this important distinction. The slope of each of the expenditure lines is a measure of the responsiveness of the flow to a change in income; the steeper the line, the greater the responsiveness. The slope is called a **marginal propensity**. We have already met two such propensities, the marginal propensity to consume and to save. Similar propensities can be defined for any expenditure flow; each propensity

FIGURE 27.8 Shifts and Movements Along Curves

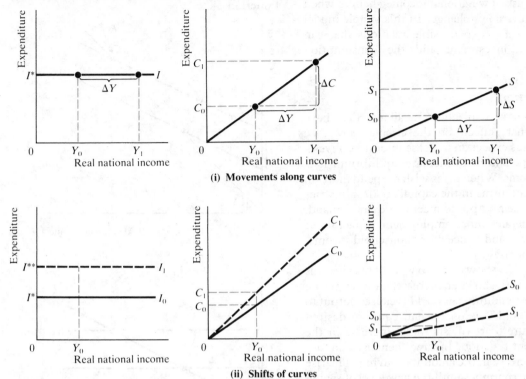

(i) Movements along curves

(ii) Shifts of curves

A movement along a curve indicates a change in expenditure in response to a change in income; a shift of a curve indicates a different level of expenditure associated with each level of income. Both parts of the diagram show an investment, a consumption and a saving function.

In part (i), income is initially at Y_0 and it then rises to Y_1, an amount indicated by ΔY in the Figure. Investment remains constant at I^*, so the ratio $\Delta I/\Delta Y$ is zero. Consumption increases from C_0 to C_1, which is shown by ΔC. The ratio $\Delta C/\Delta Y$ is the slope of the C line, which is the marginal propensity to consume (*MPC*). Saving increases from S_0 to S_1, an amount indicated by ΔS. The ratio $\Delta S/\Delta Y$ is the slope of the saving function, which is the marginal propensity to save (*MPS*).

In part (ii), the investment function shifts upward from I_0 to I_1, the consumption function shifts upward from C_0 to C_1 and the saving function shifts downwards from S_0 to S_1. At each level of income more is invested, and consumed, while less is saved. For example, at income Y_0, investment rises from I^* to I^{**}, consumption rises from C_0 to C_1, while saving falls from S_0 to S_1.

measures the ratio of the change in some expenditure flow to the change in income that initiated it.

Marginal propensities relate to movements along curves and tell us how much particular flows respond to changes in income.

Flows of expenditure, or of withdrawals, can change for a second reason: the curves *themselves* may shift, indicating a new level of the relevant flow for *each* level of national income. Such shifts are illustrated in part (ii) of Figure 27.8. The changes shown are not a consequence of changes in income, but of changes in the whole relationship with income.

Shifts in Expenditure Functions

We now ask how national income changes when expenditure flows change. In this simple model there are only two possible relations that can shift, the investment and the consumption functions.

Investment

Investment is an injection and all injections have expansionary effects on the circular flow. We would thus expect an increase in desired investment expenditure to increase equilibrium national income. When firms wish to spend more on investment, firms in the capital goods industries increase their output to meet this extra demand. This generates more employment of factors of production, and hence more household income. So income rises.

Figure 27.9 shows the two ways of proving this result. Part (i) shows an increase in the aggregate desired expenditure curve. This causes output to increase until it is once again equal to desired expenditure. Part (ii) shows an increase in the investment function. Income then rises, inducing an increase in the amount of saving. The rise in income continues until the new level of saving is equal to the new level of investment expenditure. When that occurs, the expansionary force of investment is again equal to the contractionary force of saving.

A rise in desired investment increases equilibrium national income, while a fall reduces it.

Consumption

Say that there is a rise in the proportion of income that households wish to spend on consumption and a corresponding fall in the proportion of income saved. In our numerical example, the propensity to consume might go from 0.8 to 0.9, taking the propensity to save from 0.2 to 0.1.

The effect is shown in part (i) of Figure 27.10. There is more desired consumption at each level of income so that at the original equilibrium income, desired expenditure now exceeds income. Firms will produce more to meet the new demand, and equilibrium income will rise. A fall in consumption reverses the process. There is less desired expenditure at each level of income

FIGURE 27.9 A Shift in the Investment Function

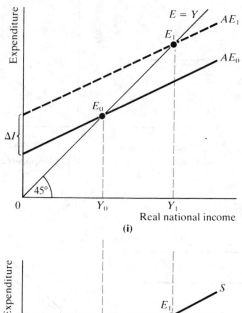

(i)

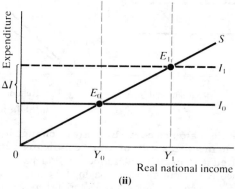

(ii)

Equilibrium national income changes in the same direction as does desired investment. In part (i), the original desired expenditure function is AE_0. Equilibrium is at E_0 with income at Y_0. Desired investment now increases by the amount ΔI, shifting the desired expenditure function upwards to AE_1. At income Y_0, desired expenditure now exceeds income. Equilibrium rises to E_1 with national income at Y_1.

In part (ii), the original saving and investment functions intersect at E_0 to give equilibrium income at Y_0. An upward shift in desired investment by ΔI shifts the function to I_1. At the original equilibrium level of income, Y_0, desired investment now exceeds desired saving and equilibrium shifts to E_1, with income Y_1.

The effect of a decrease in the desire to invest can be seen by starting with the expenditure function AE_1 with equilibrium at E_1, and letting the function change to AE_0, taking equilibrium to E_0. In part (ii), investment shifts from I_1 to I_0 taking equilibrium from E_1 to E_0.

FIGURE 27.10   A Shift in the Consumption and Saving Functions

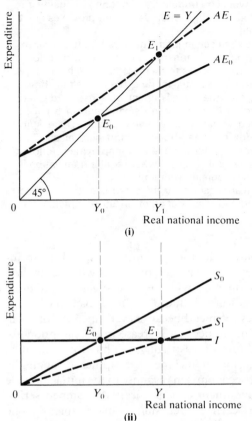

Real national income

(i)

Real national income

(ii)

An upward shift in the consumption function, which implies a downward shift in the saving function, increases equilibrium national income. The original expenditure function is AE_0 which produces equilibrium at E_0 with income Y_0. An increase in the fraction of income that households desire to spend at each level of income pivots the expenditure function to AE_1. At the original level of income of Y_0, desired expenditure now exceeds income. Equilibrium is now E_1 with income of Y_1.

In part (ii), the original saving and investment functions of S_0 and I intersect at E_0 to produce equilibrium income of Y_0. The increased desire to consume is reflected in a decreased desire to save, which pivots the saving function to S_1. At the income Y_0, desired saving is now less than desired investment. Equilibrium is now E_1 with income Y_1.

The opposite shifts are shown by letting the expenditure and saving functions start at AE_1 and S_1 and then shift to AE_0 and S_0. This shifts equilibrium from E_1 to E_0 and takes equilibrium income from Y_1 to Y_0.

so that, at the original equilibrium, desired expenditure is now less than income. In consequence, income falls.

The same result is shown in part (ii) of the Figure. Here the increase in the desire to consume is reflected in a fall in the desire to save. When desired saving falls, there is less contractionary pressure at the original equilibrium income, and income rises. When desired saving rises, there is more contractionary pressure, and income falls.

> **An upward shift in the consumption function (a downward shift in the savings function) increases equilibrium national income. The opposite shifts lower equilibrium income.**

The interpretation of these results is further considered in Box 27.1 on the paradox of thrift.

So far, our results have a strong commonsense appeal, since they follow from a model whose formal properties are really quite simple. Here are its characteristics in summary form.

(1) Firms are assumed to have perfectly elastic supply curves, so that output is demand-determined.
(2) Total desired expenditure exceeds output at zero income (by virtue of the constant investment assumption) and rises with income at a rate less than the rise in income (because the *MPC* is positive but less than unity).
(3) There exists, therefore, an equilibrium level of income at which total desired expenditure equals total output.
(4) Upward shifts in desired expenditure raise equilibrium income as firms increase production to meet the extra demand. Downward shifts in desired expenditure lower equilibrium income as firms decrease production in response to the fall in demand.

How Much Does Income Change?: the Multiplier

We now know the direction of the changes in income caused by a change in desired investment or desired consumption expenditure. Now consider the magnitude of the changes that result

BOX 27.1 THE PARADOX OF THRIFT

The simple prediction that equilibrium national income is increased when the desire to save falls and decreased when the desire to save rises, has been called the *paradox of thrift*. The paradox is no paradox at all. Instead it is the simple prediction of a model in which national income is demand-determined. More saving means less spending and thus reduces demand. Less saving means more spending and this increases demand.

The implication of the paradox of thrift is that a major recession is best combated by encouraging spending. The natural inclination to tighten one's belt when times are tough, to save more and spend less, will only make things worse. The idea that it is possible to spend one's way out of a depression sometimes offends the consciences of people who were reared in the belief that success is based on hard work and frugality, and not on prodigality. As a result, the suggestion very often provokes great hostility.

We shall see in later Chapters that the paradox refers only to a short-run phenomenon. In the long run, saving serves to increase national income by increasing potential income. It remains true, however, that the impact effect of a rise in desired spending is to increase demand and of a fall in desired spending is to lower demand. There is no paradox or even subtle relation here at all. The implications for income and employment follow, however, only in cases where equilibrium national income is demand-determined.

The applicability of the paradox of thrift will be considered at several points in later chapters.

---

from shifts in the expenditure function. Here we will concentrate on shifts in investment.

A key prediction of national-income theory is that a change in exogenous expenditure, whatever its source, will cause a change in national income that is greater than the initial expenditure change. The **multiplier** is defined as the ratio of the change in national income to the change in autonomous expenditure that brought it about. The change in expenditure might come, for example, from an increase in private investment. The importance of the multiplier in national-income theory justifies the use of more than one approach to develop it.

An Intuitive Statement

What would you expect to happen to national income if there were a rise in investment expenditure of £1m *per year*, say on the building of new factories? The answer is 'national income will rise by more than £1m'. The impact of the initial rise will be felt by the construction industry, and by all those industries that supply it. Income and the employment of factors used in these industries will rise by £1m as a result. But the newly employed factors will spend much of their new incomes buying food, clothing, shelter, holidays, cars, and a host of other products. This is the induced rise in the consumption expenditure. When output expands to meet this extra demand, employment will rise in all of the affected industries. When owners of factors that are newly

employed in these industries spend their incomes, output and employment will rise further; more income will then be created and more expenditure induced. The expansion finally comes to an end because every increase of £1 in income induces an increase in consumption expenditure of less than £1. Thus the multiplied expansion of income that ripples through the entire economy, in response to the initial increase in investment expenditure, is a damped series, where each repercussion is smaller than the one that preceded it.

This is as far as the intuitive argument can take us. Now we must look for a more formal demonstration of these propositions.

A Numerical Statement

Assume that there is an increase in investment expenditure of £1m *per year* in an economy where the marginal propensity to consume is 0.8. National income initially rises by £1m. That is not, however, the end of the story. The factors employed in producing the new investment goods spend £0.8m on consumption and save the remaining £0.2m. This second round of spending becomes new incomes for the people making the goods that are produced to meet the new demand. These people, in turn, spend 80 per cent of this £0.8m of new income, which is £0.64m of new expenditure. These people spend 80 per cent of their £0.64m; and so it continues, with each round of new income inducing a new round of expenditure of 80 per cent of the new income. Table 27.2 carries the process through 10 rounds. No matter how many rounds you calculate, you cannot make total spending exceed £5m. This is the limit that this multiplier process approaches. This approach is discussed more generally in Box 27.2 for those who wish to study it.

Notice in this example that the initial increase in expenditure was £1m and the final increase in income is £5m. This makes the multiplier, which is the ratio of the change in income to the change in autonomous expenditure, 5. This is also the reciprocal of the savings function, which in this case is $1/0.2 = 5$.

A Graphical Statement

Part (i) of Figure 27.11 repeats the saving and investment curves from Figure 27.10. It demonstrates that the multiplier is the reciprocal of the slope of the saving function, i.e. $1/s$. If we use equation (4), we can also see that the multiplier is the reciprocal of one minus the slope of the expenditure function $1/(1-c)$. Letting K stand

for the multiplier we can write this

$$K = \frac{1}{1-c} = \frac{1}{s} = \frac{1}{1-MPC} = \frac{1}{MPS}.$$

These are four ways of saying the same thing: the multiplier is the reciprocal of the marginal propensity to save, or one minus the marginal propensity to consume.

FIGURE 27.11   The Multiplier

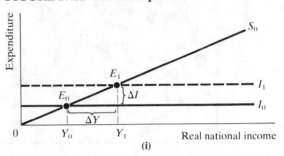

(i)

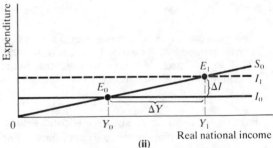

(ii)

The multiplier is equal to the reciprocal of the slope of the saving function, which is the marginal propensity to save. In both parts of the Figure, the initial saving and investment functions are S_0 and I_0. Equilibrium is at E_0 with income of Y_0. The investment function then shifts upwards to I_1 taking equilibrium to E_1 with income of Y_1.

The change in income from Y_0 to Y_1 is indicated by ΔY and the change in investment by ΔI. The slope of the saving function, which is given the symbol s in the text and is called the MPS, is shown in the diagram by $\Delta I/\Delta Y$. The multiplier K is defined as $\Delta Y/\Delta I$ which is the reciprocal of this slope.

The only difference between the two parts of the Figure is in the slope of the saving function. The line in the second part is flatter than in the first part. Thus the second part shows a lower MPS than the first part. Note that the increase in income for the given change in investment is larger in the second part than in the first. The general result is that the lower is the MPS, the larger is the multiplier.

TABLE 27.2   The Multiplier Process

Round of spending	Increase in expenditure (thousands of £s)	Cumulative total (thousands of £s)
Initial increase	1,000.0	1,000.0
2	800.0	1,800.0
3	640.0	2,440.0
4	512.0	2,952.0
5	409.6	3,361.6
6	327.7	3,689.3
7	262.1	3,951.4
8	209.7	4,161.1
9	167.8	4,328.9
10	134.2	4,463.1
11 to 20 combined	479.3	4,942.4
All others	57.6	5,000.0

An initial increase in autonomous expenditure induces a series of rounds of new expenditures. Initially the flow of investment expenditure rises by £1,000,000. With a marginal propensity to consume of 0.8, the £1,000,000 of new income induces £800,000 of new spending. This generates £800,000 of new income, which induces £640,000 of new spending, and so on. Equilibrium national income rises by £5,000,000 which is five times the original increase in autonomous expenditure.

BOX 27.2 THE MULTIPLIER AS THE SUM OF A CONVERGENT SERIES

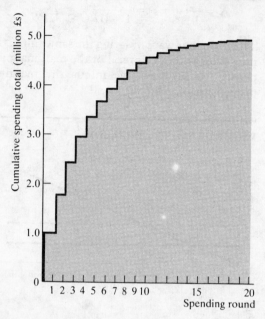

The multiplier is nothing more than the sum of a convergent series. An example is given in Table 27.2 in the text. In that example, the initial injection of new expenditure is £1m. This induces a new expenditure of 80 per cent of £1m which is £0.8m. This becomes new income and in turn induces a new round of expenditure of 80 per cent of £0.8m. And so it goes on, with each round of new induced expenditure being 80 per cent of the previous round. A graphical representation of this process is shown in the accompanying Figure. The height of the black line gives the total new expenditure after a certain number of rounds. Each increase is by 80 per cent of the previous round. The steps thus get smaller and smaller as the height of the line approaches its limiting value of five times the initial increase in autonomous expenditure.

The series involved in this example is £1m + £0.8m + £0.8²m + 0.8³m + …. As is well known from school mathematics, the sum of this series is £1m/(1 − 0.8) = £1m/0.2 = £5m.

Now let us drop the numerical example. We consider an initial new investment of £1m, and let c stand for the MPC. The initial increase in income is £1, so the first induced round of the new expenditure is £c. The next round is £$cc = c^2$, and so on. The multiplier thus becomes the sum of the series $1 + c + c^2 + c^3 + $ …. Once again we know from school mathematics that this sum is $1/(1 − c)$. By equation (4) in the text, this is also $1/s$.

Part (ii) of the Figure shows a second saving function. Comparison of the two parts shows that the lower the marginal propensity to save (the MPS), the larger the multiplier. Since the MPC is negatively related to the MPS, the multiplier is larger, the larger is the MPC.

The common sense of these results is that the lower the MPS, and the larger the MPC, the less of any new income is withdrawn through saving, and the more is passed on in new spending to generate new income. Thus, the larger is each round of induced expenditure that ripples through the economy as a result of an initial increase in autonomous expenditure.

An Algebraic Statement

The solution for the equilibrium value of income stated in equations (9′) is:

$$Y = I^* \frac{1}{1 - c} . \qquad (9')$$

Equation (9′) relates equilibrium national income to the size of autonomous expenditure on investment and to the slope of the consumption function – i.e. the MPC. If the equilibrium level of income is equal to investment expenditure multiplied by the reciprocal of $1 − MPC$, then the *change* in equilibrium income must be equal to the change in investment, multiplied by the reciprocal of $1 − MPC$. This result is obtained by first differencing[1] the above equation to obtain:

$$\Delta Y = \Delta I^* \frac{1}{1 - c} . \qquad (11)$$

If we now divide equation (11) through by ΔI^*, we get:

$$\frac{\Delta Y}{\Delta I^*} = \frac{1}{1 - c} . \qquad (12)$$

This is the multiplier expressed in terms of the MPC.

---

[1] The operation of first differencing is described in the Appendix to Chapter 3 (see page 44).

The expression in terms of the *MPS* can be derived from the solution given in equation (10) above:

$$Y = I^* \frac{1}{s} \ . \tag{10}$$

First differencing this equation yields:

$$\Delta Y = \Delta I^* \frac{1}{s} \ . \tag{13}$$

Dividing through by ΔI^* gives:

$$\frac{\Delta Y}{\Delta I^*} = \frac{1}{s} \ . \tag{14}$$

If we let *K* stand for the multiplier, defined as the change in income divided by the change in autonomous expenditure that brought it about, we can gather these results together as follows:

$$K = \frac{1}{s} = \frac{1}{1-c} \ . \tag{15}$$

This shows, once again, what we have already seen in a numerical example and using geometrical analysis:

the value of the multiplier is the reciprocal of the marginal propensity to save or, what is the same thing, the reciprocal of one minus the marginal propensity to consume.

Simple inspection of equation (15) also tells us what happens to the value of the multiplier if the *MPS* or the *MPC* changes. Since *K* is the reciprocal of the *MPS*, the multiplier is larger the smaller is *s*. Since *K* is the reciprocal of $1 - c$, an increase in *c* lowers $1 - c$ and hence raises the value of *K*. This is yet another proof of what we have already seen graphically:

the multiplier is larger, the larger is the *MPC* (i.e. the smaller is the *MPS*).

The Multiplier More Generally

There are two things to notice about the multiplier that we have just derived.

First, notice that the change in income is determined by the change in autonomous investment expenditure multiplied by *K*, the multiplier. This is the form that the multiplier always takes in this type of model, no matter how many sectors that we add to it. In the next chapters we

will find this result recurring.

Next, notice the form that the multiplier takes. It is the reciprocal of the *MPS* or, alternatively, the reciprocal of one minus the *MPC*. The marginal propensity to save is the proportion of any increase in income that leaks out of the circular flow of income at each round of expenditure. The *MPC* is the proportion that is passed on through further expenditure, i.e. the proportion that does *not* leak out. In the present model there is only one leakage, saving. In more complex models there may be several leakages. We will find, however, that the basic structure of the multiplier is unchanged when we move from model to model.

Conclusion

The multiplier predicts the magnitude of the change in national income that will accompany a shift in autonomous expenditure. In the real world, autonomous expenditures change quite often, and sometimes by quite large amounts. If the economy has a large multiplier, the result will be large swings in national income, in employment and in unemployment. If the economy has only a small multiplier, the resulting swings in national income will tend to be not much larger than the swings in autonomous expenditure.

The multiplier measures the magnitude of the swings in equilibrium national income that accompany shifts in autonomous expenditure.

In the 1940s and 1950s when modern macroeconomics was in its infancy, models of the determination of national income used the two-sector model outlined in this chapter. With most countries' marginal propensities to save measured at between 0.1 and 0.2, multipliers were often thought to be between 5 and 10. Such values suggested extreme instability for free-market economies. Relatively small shifts in desired investment expenditure would produce very large changes in national income and employment. Modern measures of most countries' multipliers are much smaller than these figures. To see why, we need to build more elaborate models, which we do in later chapters. First, however, we must turn to a more detailed consideration of the consumption function, which is our topic for Chapter 28.

SUMMARY

1. In the theory of the determination of national income all expenditure flows are real, desired and aggregated over the whole economy. The elementary theory assumes that potential national income is constant, that there are unemployed supplies of all resources, and that the interest rate and the price level are constant.

2. Saving is a leakage from the circular flow of income, because it is income that households receive but do not spend on purchasing goods and services from firms. Investment is an injection into the circular flow because it is income received by firms that does not arise from the spending of households.

3. In the simple theory of national-income determination, investment is an autonomous expenditure flow while consumption is an induced flow depending on income.

4. Equilibrium national income occurs in the simple theory where aggregate desired expenditure is equal to actual national income or, what is the same thing, where desired saving equals desired investment expenditure. Graphically, these are shown by the intersection of the aggregate desired expenditure curve and the 45° line or by the intersection of the saving and investment curves.

5. Equilibrium national income is increased by a rise in desired investment or consumption expenditure, and decreased by a fall in either of these two desired expenditure flows.

6. The multiplier is the ratio of the change in national income to the change in autonomous expenditure that brought it about. Because any increase in national income sets up rounds of induced expenditure, the multiplier always has a value greater than unity. In the simple two-sector model, it is the reciprocal of the marginal propensity to save or, what is the same thing, the reciprocal of one minus the marginal propensity to consume.

TOPICS FOR REVIEW

- Shifts of expenditure functions and movements along them
- Marginal and average propensities
- The consumption, saving, investment and aggregate desired expenditure functions
- The equilibrium condition that $E = Y$ and $S = I$
- The effect of changes in autonomous expenditure on equilibrium national income
- Why the value of the multiplier exceeds unity

28

The Consumption Function

There are two reasons for being concerned with the determinants of consumption at this stage in our study of macroeconomics. First, consumption is by far the largest component of aggregate expenditure of most countries. If we are to predict the effects of shifts in autonomous expenditure on equilibrium national income, we need to know the relation between consumption and national income. Second, in the simple two-sector model, consumption is the *only* expenditure flow that is induced (i.e. endogenous). All of the response of national income to shifts in autonomous expenditures depends on how consumption is related to national income.

Early in the history of macroeconomics all theories of the consumption function followed Keynes in relating current consumption expenditure to current disposable income as we have done in Chapter 27. More recent theories stress households' reactions to their longer-term expectations of income.

KEYNESIAN CONSUMPTION FUNCTIONS

The basic characteristic of Keynesian consumption functions is that current consumption expenditure is related to current disposable income.

Consumption as a Constant Fraction of Income

In Chapter 27 we used the simple case in which a constant proportion of current income is spent on consumption: $C = cY$. In this consumption function, both the marginal propensity to consume, $\Delta C / \Delta Y$, and the average propensity to consume, C/Y, are equal to c. For example, if c is 0.8, then total consumption expenditure will be 80 per cent of total income, *and* 80 pence will be spent on consumption out of each new £1 of income.

A Consumption Function with a Constant

Measured consumption functions that are based on annual data for aggregate consumption and aggregate household income, tend to fit the data better if they contain a constant: $C = a + cY$.

FIGURE 28.1 A Linear Consumption Function

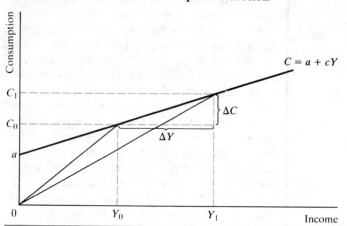

An example of such a consumption function is shown in Figure 28.1. The Figure shows that the average propensity to consume exceeds the marginal propensity. This is also easily seen algebraically.

First differencing the function $C = a + cY$ shows that $MPC = \Delta C/\Delta Y = c$. The c in equation (3) on page 473 is nothing more than the slope of the consumption function. The average propensity to consume is defined as C/Y. In the linear consumption function this is $APC = a/Y + c$.[1]

This tells us that for a linear consumption function, the *APC* always exceeds the *MPC*. Notice also that as Y gets very large the term a/Y gets very small. Thus, as Y gets larger and larger, the *APC* gets closer and closer to the *MPC*.

The linear consumption function has several other important characteristics.

(1) There is a 'breakeven' level of income at which all of income is consumed,[2] i.e. where the *APC* is unity.

(2) Above the breakeven level, there is positive saving, so that the *APC* is less than unity. Indeed, as we have already noticed, the *APC* falls towards the constant *MPC* as income gets larger and larger.

(3) Below the breakeven level, saving is nega-

tive (sometimes called dissaving), so that the *APC* exceeds unity. To sustain a level of consumption in excess of income, households must be reducing their net wealth either by consuming past savings or making new borrowings. Since this cannot continue indefinitely, the $C = a + bY$ consumption function above cannot describe long-term household behaviour. It does, however, describe behaviour that can persist over a trade cycle, since the dissaving that occurs in slumps can be matched by the positive saving that occurs in booms.

The Consumption Constant and Autonomous Expenditure

We now see that the model in Chapter 27 is not restricted to the case in which the consumption function has no intercept – although that is how we introduced it. Instead, the constant in the consumption function, and *any* other constant expenditure flow, is merely absorbed into the single constant which stands for *all* autonomous expenditures.

Although simple, this point is important, so let us be sure about it. Consider the two-sector model of Chapter 27, but using the linear consumption function given above:

Definitional equation:
$$E \equiv C + I$$
Behavioural equations:
$$C = a + cY$$
$$I = I^*$$

---

[1] Dividing the consumption function, $C = a + cY$, through by Y gives $C/Y = a/Y + cY/Y = a/Y + c$, which is the equation in the text.

[2] Substituting the definition of breakeven income, $C = Y$, into the consumption function, $C = a + cY$, yields $Y = a + cY$ or $Y = a/(1 - c)$.

To derive the equation of the aggregate expenditure function, we substitute the behaviour relations for consumption and investment into the definitions of aggregate expenditure:

$$E = I^* + a + cY.$$

Now we group the two constants together and call them A, for autonomous expenditures, $A = I^* + a$, and write:

$$E = A + cY.$$

This is the form of equation (5) on page 475, only now we write A for autonomous expenditure, whereas in the earlier treatment we wrote I^*.

All autonomous expenditure flows, and the constants on all expenditure functions, can be gathered together into a single autonomous expenditure term, A. An upward or downward shift in any of these autonomous expenditures is shown by an upward or a downward shift in constant A.

Other Determinants of Consumption

Several variables other than income exert a strong influence on consumption. These can be thought of as parameters that shift the simple relation between C and Y.

Changes in income distribution: If households have different *MPCs*, aggregate consumption depends not only on aggregate income, but also on the distribution of this income among households. In this case, a change in the *distribution* of income will cause a change in the aggregate consumption expenditure associated with any given *level* of national income.

Since the distribution of income tends to change fairly slowly, such changes do not typically upset a stable relation between aggregate consumption and aggregate income. Nevertheless, such changes can occur, and when something does significantly affect the distribution of income, the consumption function may shift.

Changes in the terms of credit: Many durable consumers' goods are bought on hire purchase, the terms on which may range from a few months to pay for a radio, to two or three years to

pay for a car. In other cases, money is first borrowed from the bank, and then used to purchase a durable consumers' good.

If credit becomes more difficult, or more costly to obtain, some households may postpone their planned, credit-financed purchases. Assume, for example, that the typical initial payment required for goods obtained on hire purchase increases from 10 to 20 per cent of the purchase price. Households that have just saved up 10 per cent of the purchase price of the goods they wish to buy will now find this sum inadequate. They will have to postpone their planned purchases until they have saved 20 per cent of the purchase price. There will be a *temporary* reduction in current consumption expenditures until these extra savings have been accumulated.

Anything that changes the cost and availability of credit will temporarily shift the consumption function and thus affect aggregate demand.

Changes in existing stocks of durable goods: Any period in which durables are difficult or impossible to purchase and monetary savings are accumulated is likely to be followed by an outburst of expenditure on durables. This is usually the case following a major war. Such a flurry of spending may also follow a period of unemployment, during which many families may have refrained from buying durables.

The emphasis here is on durable consumers' goods (e.g., cars and refrigerators) because purchases of non-durable consumers' goods (e.g., food and clothing) and of services (e.g., car repairs) cannot be long postponed.

While expenditures on non-durables tend to be relatively steady, purchases of durables are more volatile and can cause sharp shifts in the consumption function.

Changes in wealth: Most households appear to have target levels of wealth at each stage of their life-cycles. Unexpected changes in wealth cause deviations of actual from desired wealth and lead to corrective action.

If wealth falls unexpectedly, households will increase their savings, while if wealth rises unexpectedly they will cut savings.

Big changes in markets of equities can have

these effects. In 1987, for example, asset markets crashed leaving households with much less wealth at the end of the year than they had at the beginning. Savings rose as households sought to restore their desired wealth positions.

Changes in the price level: Periods of inflation tend to reduce household wealth. Bonds, and other assets that are denominated in money terms, fall in real value. To maintain their real wealth positions, households must save an extra amount measured in money terms to compensate for the erosion of the real value of their monetary assets. Periods of rapid inflation are usually observed, therefore, to be periods when nominal savings rise as a percentage of nominal income.

Commentators often express surprise at these high nominal savings during inflationary periods. The rise need not, however, represent a shift in real saving behaviour.

Consider, for example, a household with £10,000 deposited in a building society that pays 4 per cent on that deposit during a period of stable prices. The £400 received each year is properly regarded as income, and all of it can be spent without reducing the household's wealth. Now assume that the inflation rate rises to 10 per cent and the building society now pays 14 per cent on its deposits. The household cannot properly regard the £1,400 as income – although this amount will show up in the government's national-income figures as income. If the household spends the £1,400 each year, the real value of its £10,000 in the building society will be falling at 10 per cent a year. To preserve its real net wealth position the household must now 'save' £1,000 and add it to its deposit, regarding only £400 as income.

> **Each year to preserve the value of wealth denominated in money units households must 'save', and add to that wealth, an amount equal to the inflation rate. Only returns in excess of that amount are correctly regarded as income.**

MODERN THEORIES OF THE CONSUMPTION FUNCTION

The typical household in Keynesian theory is rather shortsighted. It spends a given portion of its income each year, and hence allows its expenditure to change every time its income changes even if the income change is perceived to be transitory. The typical household in modern theories is more farsighted. It has a longer-term view of its expected income. It smooths its consumption spending over time, allowing transitory increases and decreases in its income to be taken up mainly by transitory changes in its savings. The two best known of the modern theories are both associated with the name of American economists: the **life-cycle theory (LCT)**, associated with the name of Franco Modigliani, and the **permanent-income theory (PIT)**, associated with the name of Milton Friedman. We must now turn to a study of these theories.

Definitions

The first thing to establish in any theory is what variables are being considered, and how they are defined.

Consumption

Modern theories of the consumption function seek to explain the use of the services of consumption goods, rather than the purchases of these goods which is the subject of Keynesian consumption theory. This difference is important. Keynesian-type theories seek to explain the amounts that households spend on purchasing goods and services for consumption. This concept is called **consumption expenditure.** Modern theories seek to explain the actual flows of consumption of the services that are provided by the commodities that households buy. This concept is called **actual consumption.**[1]

With services and non-durable goods, expenditure and actual consumption occur more or less at the same time, and the distinction between these two concepts is unimportant. The consumption of a haircut, for example, occurs at the time it is purchased, and an orange, or a package of cornflakes, is consumed soon after it is pur-

---

[1] Because Keynes's followers did not always distinguish carefully between the concepts of consumption expenditure and actual consumption, the word 'consumption' is often used in both senses. We follow this normal practice, but where there is any possible ambiguity, we will refer to 'consumption expenditure' and to 'actual consumption'.

chased. Thus, if we knew purchases of such things over some time-period, say last year, we also know last year's consumption of them. This is not the case, however, with durable consumers' goods. A screwdriver is purchased at one point in time, but it yields up its services over a long time, possibly over the purchaser's entire life. The same is true of a house, a watch and, over a shorter period of time, of a car and a dress. For such products, if we know purchases last year, we do not necessarily know last year's consumption of the services that the products yielded.

One important characteristic of durable goods is that *expenditure* to purchase them is not synchronized with consumption of the stream of services that the goods provide.

Consider an example. In 1990, Mr Smith buys a car for £10,000, runs it for six years, and then discards it as worn out. His expenditure on automobiles is £10,000 in 1990, and zero for the next five years. His consumption of the services of automobiles, however, is spread out at an average annual rate of £1,666.67 for six years. Now assume that everyone follows Mr Smith's example by buying a new car in 1990 and replacing it in 1996. The automobile industry will undergo wild booms in 1990 and 1996, with five intervening years of slump even though the *actual consumption* of automobile services is spread more or less evenly over the years.

This example is extreme, but it illustrates an important possibility where consumers' durables are concerned. There can be quite different time-paths of *consumption expenditure*, which is the subject of Keynesian theories of the consumption function, and *actual consumption*, which is the subject of modern theories.

Saving

Now consider saving. The change in emphasis from consumption expenditure to actual consumption implies a change in the definition of saving. Saving is no longer income minus consumption expenditure; it is now income minus the value of actual consumption. When Mr Smith spent £10,000 on his car in 1990 but used only £1,666.67 worth of its services in that year, he was actually consuming £1,666.67 and saving £8,333.33. The purchase of a consumers' dur-

able is thus counted as saving, and only the value of its services actually consumed is counted as consumption.

Income

The third important variable is income. Instead of using current income, modern theories use some concept of long-term income. The precise definition varies from one theory to another, but basically it is related to the household's expected income stream over a fairly long planning period. In the *life-cycle theory*, it is related to the income that the household expects to earn over its lifetime.[1]

Every household is assumed to have a view of its expected lifetime earnings. This is not as unreasonable as it might seem. Students training to be doctors, for example, have a very different view of their expected lifetime incomes than those training to become primary-school teachers. Both of these expected income streams – for a doctor and for a primary-school teacher – will be different from that expected by an assembly-line worker, or a professional athlete.

One such possible lifetime income stream is illustrated in Figure 28.2. The graph shows a hypothetical expected income stream from work for a household whose planning horizon was 40 years starting from 1990. The current actual income rises to a peak, then falls slowly for a while, and then suddenly falls to a lower level on retirement. The household's expected lifetime income can be converted into a single figure for *annual* **permanent income** as shown in the Figure.

In the life-cycle theory, permanent income is the maximum amount the household can spend on consumption each year without reducing its real stock of wealth. If a household were to consume a constant amount equal to its permanent income each year, it would add to its debt in years when its current income was less than its permanent income and reduce its debt, or increase its assets, in years when its current income exceeded its permanent income. Over its whole lifetime, however, the household would just

---

[1] In the permanent-income theory, the household has an infinite time-horizon and the relevant permanent-income concept is the amount the household could consume for ever without increasing or decreasing its present stock of wealth.

FIGURE 28.2   Permanent and Actual Income

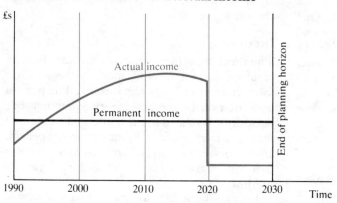

Actual income fluctuates over the life-cycle; permanent income is a constant flow. The Figure shows an expected stream of income for a household with a 40-year planning horizon starting in 1990 and a constant flow of expected permanent income. When actual income exceeds permanent income, the household will increase its net wealth through saving. When actual income is less than permanent income, the household will reduce its net wealth by dissaving. An unexpected change in actual income will have a large effect on permanent income if the change is expected to persist, and only a small effect if the change is expected to be transitory.

break even, leaving the same amount of net wealth to its heirs as it had received from its beneficiaries.

If the interest rate were zero, permanent income would be the sum of all expected incomes divided by the number of expected years of life. With a positive interest rate, however, permanent income diverges somewhat from this amount because of the costs of borrowing, and the extra income that can be earned by investing savings.

Assumptions

The basic assumption of the modern theories, whether *PIT* or *LCT*, is that the household's actual consumption is related to its permanent rather than to its current income. Two households that have the same permanent incomes (and are similar in other relevant characteristics) will have the same consumption patterns, even though their current incomes are very different.

Implications

The Effect on Consumption of Changes in Income

One major implication of these theories is that:

changes in a household's current income will affect its actual consumption only so far as they affect its permanent income.

Consider two income changes that could occur to a household with a permanent income of £20,000 per year, and an expected lifetime of 30 more years. In the first, suppose the household receives an unexpected extra income of £2,000 *for this year only*. The increase in the household's permanent income is thus very small. If the rate of interest were zero, the household could consume an extra £66.67 per year for the rest of its expected lifespan; with a positive rate of interest, the extra annual consumption would be more because money to spend this year could be invested and would earn interest.[1] In the second case, the household gets a totally unforeseen increase of £2,000 a year that is then expected to continue for the rest of its life. In this event the household's permanent income has risen by £2,000 because the household can actually consume £2,000 more every year without reducing its wealth. Although in both cases current income rises by £2,000, the effects on permanent income are different.

Keynesian theory assumes that *consumption expenditure* is related to current income and therefore predicts the same change in this year's consumption expenditure in each of the above cases. Permanent-income and life-cycle theories relate *actual consumption* to permanent income and, therefore, predict different changes in actual

---

[1] If the rate of interest were 7 per cent, the household could invest the £2,000, consume an extra £161 per year, and just have nothing left at the end of 30 years.

consumption in each of these cases. In the first case there would be only a small increase in actual consumption, while in the second case there would be a large increase.

> In permanent-income theories, any change in current income that is thought to be temporary will have only a small effect on permanent income, and hence on actual consumption.

From Actual Consumption to Actual Expenditure

Permanent-income theories tell us that the desired flow of households' consumption will not be significantly affected by transitory changes in current income. This is an important insight, but it cannot be immediately translated into an insensitivity of consumption *expenditure* to transitory changes in income. Here are two reasons why.

Saving, consumption and spending: Assume that households receive a transitory increase in income, say due to a tax cut expected to last for one year. Permanent-income theories tell us that most of this increment will be saved so that the consumption benefit can be spread over many years. This can be accomplished, however, in two very different ways. First, the household may buy a financial asset and slowly consume the interest and capital over many years. In this case, aggregate demand will not rise significantly as a result of the tax cut. Second, the household may buy durable consumers' goods, whose services it consumes over a long period of time. In this case, however, the tax cut does lead to a rise in current expenditure now.

> In so far as transitory fluctuations in household income lead to fluctuations in the purchases of durable consumers' goods, current expenditure is related to current income.

Capital-market constraints: Now consider a household that suffers a reduction in its income which it assumes to be transitory – possibly because of an announced temporary tax surcharge. The household will not revise its permanent-income estimate significantly downwards, and so will wish to absorb this transitory loss by reducing its wealth.

If the transitory loss of income is less than current money saving, there is no problem. The household merely cuts its flow of saving. But for many households this will not be the case. At their point in their life-cycles, they may be consuming all of their current incomes. For them, the only way to stick to their long-term consumption plans is to borrow or consume some of their wealth. But if – as it is for many ordinary people – their main wealth is their human capital and their stock of durable consumers' goods, they may not be able to borrow. Without marketable assets to pledge as collateral, banks are usually unwilling to lend money to people to allow them to sustain their consumption streams in the face of transitory reductions in income.

> Inability to borrow against human capital and consumers' durables may force households to respond to transitory reductions in income with cuts in expenditure even if this is not their preferred alternative.

Current consumption and current income: Thus transitory fluctuations in current income can leads to fluctuations in current expenditure of the type predicted by Keynesian theory even though the underlying determinants of expenditure are those analysed in the life-cycle theories. This is so for two basic reasons. First, desired fluctuations in saving designed to respond to short-term fluctuations in income will partly take the form of fluctuations in the expenditure on consumers' durables. Second, households may be forced to deviate from their desired spending plans because they are unable to sell, or borrow, against wealth held in the form of consumers' durables and human capital.

Changes in Permanent Income

Of course, if households encounter changes in their incomes that they assess to be permanent, their consumption expenditure will respond significantly. For example, when UK income-tax rates were cut twice during the 1980s, most people assumed the changes in disposable income to be permanent and reacted accordingly.

Consumption, Expenditure and Income

So the modern theory of consumption still leaves

room for a positive association between current expenditure and current income. However, the association is expected to be less reliable for transitory changes in income than for permanent changes. The effects of transitory changes in income depend on households saving through buying consumers' durables, rather than financial assets, or on being unable to sustain planned income streams because of inability to make short-term loans.

The net result is that there will be a **positive association between expenditure on consumption commodities and current disposable income. We call this the Keynesian consumption function although similar relations can arise, as we have just seen, from permanent-income theories.**

The relation is likely to be weaker for transitory changes in income than for permanent ones.

SUMMARY

1. The Keynesian consumption function relates current consumption expenditure to current income. In the linear version, $C = a + cY$, the constant a can be incorporated in the term for autonomous expenditure while the induced component of consumption is cY.
2. In a linear consumption function, the APC exceeds the MPC and falls towards the MPC as income increases. Above the breakeven level of income, savings are positive; below it savings are negative.
3. Major determinants of aggregate consumption expenditure, other than income, are the distribution of income, the terms and cost of credit, the existing stock of durable goods, wealth, and the price level (which affects wealth when it changes).
4. Modern theories of the consumption function relate the consumption of the flow of services provided by goods and services to lifetime, or permanent, income. Households tend to let their stock of wealth rise and fall in response to transitory fluctuations in income.
5. In spite of the behaviour described in 4, current consumption will be positively associated with current income because (i) some fluctuations in current income reflect permanent rather than transitory changes, (ii) some transitory reductions in income cannot be taken up by reductions in wealth even if households desire that result, and (iii) because some changes in wealth that accompany changes in transitory income will take the form of changes in the stock of consumers' durables, which means changes in current expenditure.

TOPICS FOR REVIEW

- The Keynesian consumption function
- The determinants of consumption
- Permanent-income and life-cycle theories of consumption
- Reactions to permanent and transitory changes in income
- Consumption expenditure and actual consumption

29

National Income in More Elaborate Models

In this chapter we expand the two-sector model of national income to deal with many sectors. As a first step, recall that the equilibrium condition for national income in the two-sector model can be stated in either of two ways.

(1) *Aggregate desired expenditure equals national income (equation (6) in Chapter 27).* When this equilibrium condition is fulfilled, desired expenditure is just sufficient to purchase the whole of the nation's output, and there is thus no tendency for output to change.

(2) *Saving equals investment (equation (8) in Chapter 27).* When this equilibrium condition is fulfilled, the contractionary force of income earned by households but not spent (saving) is just balanced by the expansionary force of income earned by firms that does not arise from household spending (investment). When these are in balance, national income will neither rise nor fall.

These equilibrium conditions generalize with surprising ease to cover all circular-flow models. The first applies, without amendment, to any circular-flow model.

When aggregate desired expenditure is less than national income, income will fall; when aggregate desired expenditure exceeds national income, income will rise. Equilibrium national income occurs when aggregate desired expenditure is equal to national income.

In moving from one circular-flow model to another, all we need to do is to identify any new components of aggregate expenditure, and make assumptions about how each is related to national income.

The second equilibrium condition, saving equals investment, requires reinterpretation before it can be extended to other circular-flow models. Saving and investment are examples of two more general categories of expenditure which we have called withdrawals and injections. Recall that a withdrawal, which is also called a leakage, is any income that is not passed on in the circular flow. Because withdrawals reduce expenditure, they are a contractionary force on national income. Recall also that an injection is an addition to the income of domestic firms that does not arise from the expenditure of domestic households, or an addition to the income of domestic households that does not arise from the spending of domestic firms. Because injections raise expenditure, they exert an expansionary force on national income.

In the two-sector model, saving is the only withdrawal and investment is the only injection. Thus, it makes no difference if we say that national income is in equilibrium when saving equals investment or when withdrawals equal injections. In more complex models, however, there are many withdrawals and many injections. In such models, national income will be in equilibrium when the aggregate contractionary force of all withdrawals is equal to the aggregate expansionary force of all injections.

> **When desired withdrawals exceed desired injections, national income will fall; when desired injections exceed desired withdrawals, national income will rise. Equilibrium national income occurs where desired withdrawals equal desired injections.**

Letting W and J stand for withdrawals and injections respectively, we write the equilibrium condition[1] $W = J$. All that is required in order to apply this theory to any particular model is to identify its withdrawals and injections and make assumptions about how each is related to national income.

GOVERNMENT TAXING AND SPENDING: A THREE-SECTOR MODEL

We now add a government sector to our model. This requires that we define some new terms, and make some further assumptions about behaviour.

Definitions

Following the discussion on page 462, government expenditure is divided into two parts. First comes the government's final (or exhaustive) expenditure. This is the government's expenditure on current production. We give this the symbol G. Second comes government transfer payments. These are not part of national income, but they do provide disposable income that is available to be spent. We give this the symbol Q.

> **The government's total expenditure is divided between expenditure on final goods and services, G, and expenditure on transfer payments, Q.**

Next we let T stand for the total tax revenues raised by the government.

Finally, we define the government's budget balance as its total tax revenue minus its total expenditures, i.e. $T - (G + Q)$. When this takes on a positive value, the government's budget is in **surplus** and there is an excess of tax revenue over expenditures. When this takes on a negative value, the government's budget is in **deficit** and there is an excess of expenditure over tax revenue. When the value is zero, the budget is said to be **balanced** and tax revenues just balance total expenditures.

Financial Implications of Deficits and Surpluses

The difference between expenditure and current revenue shows up as changes in the government's debt. A deficit requires an increase in borrowing, for which there are two main sources: the central bank and the private sector. The government borrows money from these sources by selling treasury bills and bonds. A **treasury bill**, or note, is a promise to repay a stated amount at some specified date between 90 days and 1 year from the date of issue. A government *bond* is also a promise to pay a stated sum of money in the future, but in the more distant future than a bill – sometimes as much as 25 years from the date of issue.[1]

When the government borrows from the pri-

---

[1] The general equivalence of $E = Y$ and $W = J$ is shown as follows. All income is either spent on consumption or withdrawn, $Y = C + W$, and all expenditure is either consumption expenditure or injections, $E = C + J$. So the equilibrium condition that $E = Y$ immediately reduces to $C + W = C + J$, or $W = J$.

[1] Bills carry a promise to return a fixed amount on maturity. Interest arises because they are initially sold at a discount; the difference between their current price and their redemption value represents interest. Bonds carry a fixed 'coupon rate of interest' on their redemption value. They guarantee not only the repayment of a fixed sum on the redemption date, but also the periodic payment of fixed sums between the sale and redemption.

vate sector, funds are merely shifted between the two sectors. When the government 'borrows' from the central bank, however, the central bank creates new money. Since the bank can create as much money as it likes, there is no limit to what the government can 'borrow' from this source.

A surplus allows the government to reduce its outstanding debt. Treasury bills and bonds may be redeemed using funds provided by the excess of tax revenue over expenditures.

Behavioural Assumptions

Next, we must make behavioural assumptions for our new spending unit, the government. We must also amend some of our previous assumptions to make them consistent with the new model.

The Government Sector

We assume that government expenditures on goods and services, and on transfer payments, are held constant in real terms. The justification for making this assumption is the same as with investment expenditure. We first want to see how income responds to a constant rate of government expenditure and transfer payments, before going on to see how it reacts to changes in these expenditures. We now write two equations that do no more than state that both G and Q are assumed to be autonomous expenditure flows.

$$G = G^* \qquad (1)$$

$$Q = Q^* . \qquad (2)$$

We also make three further assumptions whose sole purpose is to simplify matters so that we can study the basic impact of the government on the circular flow of income. Changing these assumptions would affect certain details, but would not affect the conclusions we reach in this chapter. First, we assume that all transfer payments are made to households. In the real world, firms also receive government transfer payments in such forms as subsidies. For the general results that we are going to derive, all that matters is that the government makes transfer payments; the precise identity of the recipients of these payments is not important. Second, we assume that all taxes are direct taxes on personal and company incomes. There are no indirect taxes on the

production and sale of output. Again, all that matters is that the government withdraws tax revenues from the circular flow of income. The precise points at which these withdrawals occur is not important for our results. Finally, we assume that the income tax is levied at a flat rate of t pence per £1 of income. This flat-rate assumption makes the algebra easier but, once again, does not affect the general results that we derive. It is stated in the following equation:

$$T = tY \qquad 0 < t < 1 . \qquad (3)$$

Notice that, following the procedure introduced in the last chapter, the flow of tax revenue is indicated here by a capital letter, T, and the behavioural parameter indicating how taxes are related to income is indicated by a lower-case letter, t. To illustrate the magnitudes involved, if national income is £1,000m and the tax rate is 20 per cent, then the tax revenue, T, is £200m (£1,000m × 0.2).

Equation (3) says that taxes are a constant proportion of national income. The restriction on the size of t tells us that the tax rate is positive but less than 100 per cent (the tax people are kind enough to leave some income behind them after taking their share from income earners).

We can now define two tax propensities. The **average propensity to tax** is the total tax revenue expressed as a proportion of total national income, T/Y. The **marginal propensity to tax** is the proportion of any increment in income that is taxed away, $\Delta T/\Delta Y$. Examination of equation (3) shows that the marginal and average propensities to tax are both equal to t in the simple case that we are considering here. This result is shown in Figure 29.1, which also shows the simple assumption about government expenditures.

The Firm Sector

There are no changes needed in our assumptions about the behaviour of firms: they supply all the goods that are demanded at the going price level, and their planned investment expenditure is constant:

$$I = I^* . \qquad (4)$$

The Household Sector

In the two-sector model used in the previous chapter, all of national income was paid out to

FIGURE 29.1 Tax and Expenditure Functions

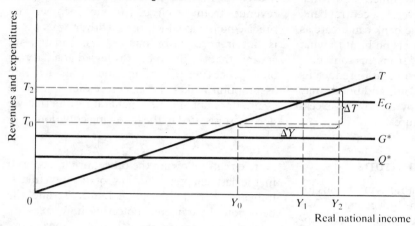

Government expenditure is assumed constant, while tax revenue is assumed to rise with income. The G and Q functions show government expenditure on goods and services and on transfer payments as constants, G^* and Q^*, which do not vary as national income varies. The sum of the two is the total government expenditure function E_G. The T function shows tax revenue positively associated with national income.

At income Y_1, the budget is balanced. At all lower levels of income, the budget is in deficit. For example at income Y_0, tax revenues of T_0 are less than expenditures of E_G. At incomes above Y_1, the budget is in surplus. For example at income Y_2, tax revenues of T_2 exceed total expenditures of E_G.

When income rises from Y_0 to Y_2, indicated by ΔY on the Figure, tax revenue rises from T_0 to T_2, indicated by ΔT. The ratio $\Delta T/\Delta Y$ is the marginal propensity to tax, MPT, and the diagram makes it clear that this is the slope of the tax function. Because the tax function goes through the origin, the average propensity to tax, T/Y, is the same as the marginal propensity to tax.

households, and all of it was thus available for households to spend on consumption or to save. Direct taxes and transfer payments, however, place a wedge between national income and what is called household **disposable income**. This is the income that households have at their disposal to spend or to save. On the one hand, actual disposable income is reduced below national income by the subtraction of direct taxes on income. On the other hand, disposable income is increased by the addition of transfer payments, which are receipts of households not in return for any contribution to current output. Disposable income is thus defined in our present model as national income, *minus* tax payments, *plus* transfer payments. Letting Y_d stand for the disposable income of households, we write:

$$Y_d = Y - T + Q \ . \tag{5}$$

Equation (5) tells us that:

if there were neither taxes nor transfer payments, as in Chapter 27, disposable income would equal national income. Taxes, however, reduce disposable income while transfer payments increase it.

We continue to assume that households spend a constant fraction, c, of their disposable income on consumption and save the rest. Since disposable income now differs from national income, we must specify that households respond to disposable income which is the income available to them to save or to spend:

$$C = cY_d \ . \tag{6}$$

Equation (6) is our basic behavioural assumption relating desired household consumption expenditure to *disposable* income. For a theory of the determination of national income, however, we need to know how desired household consumption expenditure varies as *national income* varies. Since this point is sometimes a source of difficulty to students, we illustrate it using a numerical calculation in Table 29.1 on page 503. The caption to the Table fully explains what is involved. The basic idea is, however, quite simple. We wish to relate consumption expenditure to national income. We start with the behavioural relation that relates consumption to disposable income and one that relates disposable income to national income. We then substitute the relation between disposable income and national income, and end with a relation between consumption and national income.

Algebraically, we start with equation (6) and then substitute equation (5) to eliminate disposable income. We then substitute equation (3) to replace total tax revenue, T, with the behavioural relation that tells us how T varies with Y. This gives the following relation between desired household consumption expenditure and national income:[1]

$$C = c(1-t)Y + cQ \ . \tag{7}$$

Let us see what this equation tells us.

Consider the first term on the right-hand side. Since t is the proportion of income that goes as taxes, $1 - t$ is the proportion that is *not* taxed and, hence, becomes disposable income. Of this amount, the fraction $c(1-t)$ is the proportion that gets spent. The rest $s(1-t)$ is saved. So $c(1-t)$ is the marginal propensity to consume out of national income. In the example given in the first row of Table 29.1, c is 0.8 and t is 0.2. Hence the *MPC* out of national income is $0.8(1-0.2)$ which is 0.64. This says nothing more than, if 80

per cent of disposable income is spent on consumption and if 80 per cent of national income becomes disposable income (because the other 20 per cent of disposable income is taxed away), expenditure will be 64 per cent of national income.

The other term on the right-hand side is cQ. This is the proportion of transfer payments that gets spent and hence adds to the demand for consumers' goods.

Taken together, the two terms on the right-hand side of (7) describe a linear relation between C and Y with $c(1-t)$ as the slope coefficient, and cQ as the constant.

The Income-expenditure Approach

We first study the behaviour of this model using the income-expenditure approach.

Equilibrium Income

In this model, aggregate desired expenditure has three components: consumption, investment and government expenditure:

$$E = C + I + G \ . \tag{8}$$

The equilibrium level of national income is, as always, where desired expenditure equals income:

$$E = Y \ . \tag{9}$$

The equilibrium of the model may now be determined using geometric or algebraic methods.

Geometric: The graphical solution is given in Figure 29.2. The Figure is similar to Figure 27.7, which showed the same solution for the two-sector model. However, the consumption line (which is the graph of equation (7) above) is flatter than it was in Figure 27.7 because the deduction of taxes reduces the fraction of national income that is spent on consumption. The consumption line also has a positive constant, because of the spending caused by transfer payments (cQ). Thus, even if income falls to zero, transfer payments will allow consumption to remain positive. Autonomous expenditure is now investment plus government expenditure.

The expenditure curve, AE, is now the sum of consumption, C, investment, I, and government expenditure, G. The equilibrium occurs where this curve intersects the 45° line, which expresses

---

[1] Substituting (5) into (6):

$$C = c(Y - T + Q) \ .$$

This merely replaces Y_d with its definition in terms of Y, T and Q. We then substitute (3) into the above equation to obtain:

$$C = c(Y - tY + Q) \ .$$

This merely replaces T with the behavioural relation, tY, that determines it. The rest is algebra. Writing only the right-hand side: first multiply out the bracket to obtain $cY - ctY + cQ$. Then factor out the Y to obtain $(c - ct)Y + cQ$. Now factor out the c to get $c(1-t)Y + cQ$.

the equilibrium condition that desired expenditure should equal national income.

Algebraic: The algebraic solution to the model is again simple. As a first step, let us gather together the equations that we have developed in this chapter.

Definitions:

$$E \equiv C + I + G \qquad (8)$$
$$Y_d \equiv Y - T + Q \qquad (5)$$

Behaviour:

$$G = G^* \qquad (1)$$
$$Q = Q^* \qquad (2)$$
$$T = tT \qquad 0 < t < 1 \qquad (3)$$
$$I = I^* \qquad (4)$$
$$C = cY_d \qquad 0 < c < 1 \qquad (6)$$

Equilibrium condition:

$$E = Y \qquad (9)$$

Solving the model is merely a matter of solving these simultaneous equations. First, however, let us derive the equation of the aggregate expenditure function. To begin, substitute the definition of disposable income (equation (5)) into the consumption function (equation (6)). Then substitute all of the behavioural assumptions (equations (1), (2), (3), (4) and (6)) into the definition of aggregate expenditure (equation (8)). This produces the equation of the aggregate expenditure function which is given as (10) below.[1] The second equation of the model is the equilibrium condition that E should equal Y which is graphed as the 45° line.

Aggregate expenditure function:

$$E = [c(1-t)Y + cQ^*] + I^* + G^* \qquad (10)$$

Equilibrium condition:

$$E = Y \qquad (9)$$

In the equation of the aggregate expenditure function, the term in square brackets is the consumption function which we derived as equation (7) and interpreted on page 501. The other two terms merely express the constant values of investment and government expenditure.

Next, the two equations are solved by substituting (10) into (9) to obtain:[1]

$$Y = [I^* + G^* + cQ^*]\frac{1}{1 - c(1-t)} . \qquad (11)$$

This equation shows equilibrium income depending on two main terms. The first, which is in square brackets, is the sum of the three autonomous expenditure flows, I^*, G^*, and expenditure out of transfer payments, cQ^*. The second is composed of the behavioural parameters. These determine how much national income becomes disposable income, t, and how much disposable income gets spent, c.

We have seen that $c(1-t)$ is the fraction of national income that is spent by households. We now call this the *marginal propensity to spend out of national income*, and denote it *MPE*. Whereas the marginal propensity to consume, *MPC*, is the fraction of an extra £1 of disposable income that is spent, the *MPE* is the fraction of an extra £1 of national income that is spent. If disposable income were equal to national income, as in Chapter 27, these two would be the same. With taxes, however, disposable income is less than national income and the *MPE* is less than the *MPC*.

The denominator of (11) is $1 - c(1-t)$ or $1 - MPE$. This value has three different names that are used by various writers. It is sometimes called the **marginal propensity not to spend**, sometimes the **marginal propensity to leak**, and sometimes the **marginal propensity to withdraw**. All those terms refer to the proportion of each additional £1 of national income that is not passed on in spending, and instead leaks out of (i.e. is withdrawn from) the circular flow of income.

The value of Y determined by (11) is the algebraic expression of equilibrium income, Y_0, shown in Figure 29.2.

Changes in Equilibrium Income

The next step is to examine the consequences of

---

[1] All of the key substitutions have already been made when we derived equation (7) relating consumption to national income. Since this has already been done, equation (10), the aggregate expenditure function, is derived just by substituting (7), (1) and (4) into (8).

[1] The steps are as follows. Putting (10) into (9): $Y = c[(1-t)Y + Q^*] + I^* + G^*$. Multiplying out the c and the Y: $Y = cY - ctY + cQ^* + I^* + G^*$, or $Y - cY + ctY = I^* + G^* + cQ^*$. Now look just at the LHS for a moment. First factor out the Y: $Y(1 - c + ct)$, then factor out the c: $Y[1 - c(1-t)]$. Now divide through by $1 - c(1-t)$ to obtain equation (11).

TABLE 29.1 The Relation Between Tax Rates and the Marginal Propensity to Spend Out of National Income

Marginal rate of tax	Change in national income (millions) ΔY	Change in tax revenue (millions) ΔT	Change in disposable income (millions) ΔY_d	Change in consumption (millions) ΔC	Marginal propensity to spend out of national income $\Delta C / \Delta Y$
0.2	£1,000	£200	£800	£640	0.64
0.4	£1,000	£400	£600	£480	0.48

The higher the marginal rate of tax, the lower the marginal propensity to spend out of national income. The marginal propensity to spend out of national income measures the change in spending associated with a change in national income. This Table illustrates how that marginal propensity changes when the tax rate changes. When national income changes by £1,000, disposable income changes by £800 when the tax rate is 20 per cent and by £600 when the tax rate is 40 per cent. Although the *MPC* out of disposable income is 0.8 in both examples, consumption changes by £640 in the first case and by only £480 in the second. Although the households' *MPC* out of their disposable income is unchanged, an increase in tax rates lowers the marginal propensity to spend out of national income on which the size of the multiplier depends.

changes in autonomous expenditure flows, and in the tax rate, t.

A change in investment or in final government expenditure: Because I and G are autonomous expenditure flows, changes in either have the same effect on equilibrium national income. A rise in either I or G is an increase in desired expenditure on goods and services. The aggregate expenditure function shifts upwards,

and output expands as a result.

A change in transfer payments: Next consider a change in transfer payments. For example, if the government increases its rates of supplementary benefits, the disposable incomes of recipients will rise. Aggregate desired expenditure will rise, and output will then rise to accommodate the extra demand. The end-result is an increase in equilibrium national income.

FIGURE 29.2 Equilibrium National Income in a Three-sector Model

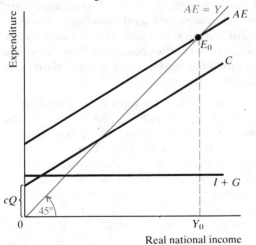

Equilibrium occurs where aggregate desired expenditure is equal to national income. The line labelled $I + G$ shows the sum of autonomous investment and government expenditures. The line labelled C is the relation between consumption and national income. Its slope is $c(1 - t)$, and it also has a constant which is equal to the spending out of transfer earnings, cQ. This is an autonomous expenditure since it does not vary with income. The sum of the $I + G$ and the C curves is the aggregate desired expenditure curve, AE.

Equilibrium occurs at the intersection of the AE line and the 45° line. At that point, labelled E_0, national income is Y_0. For incomes below Y_0, the AE line lies above the 45° line, indicating that desired expenditure exceeds national income, so income will rise. For incomes above Y_0, the AE curve lies below the 45° line, indicating that desired expenditure is less than national income, so income will fall.

The magnitude of changes: It follows that national income is increased if the government increases either its final expenditures, G, or its transfer payments, Q. However, an extra £1 spent on final expenditure will raise equilibrium by more than if the same amount were spent on transfer payments. Why is this so? When the government spends £1 more on goods and services, this increases national income by £1 in the first instance, and the multiplier then magnifies this amount. When the government spends £1 more on transfer payments, this raises disposable income by £1, but the initial effect on national income occurs only when the money is spent by its recipients. The impact of £1 of transfer payments depends, therefore, on the proportion of those receipts that are actually spent. This depends on the marginal propensity to consume, c. For example, if 10p out of every £1 of transfer payments is saved, and 90p is spent on consumption, the initial increase in demand is only 90p for every £1 that is distributed. The multiplier process then magnifies this effect, but it only has an initial increase in demand and output of 90p to work on.

> **Increases in government expenditure on goods and services, or on transfer payments, increase equilibrium national income (but not by the same amount); reductions in expenditure do the reverse.**

A warning: Readers should beware of a common error. It is sometimes argued that, because transfer payments only transfer money from taxpayers to the recipients, they have no net effect on aggregate desired expenditure. The taxpayers suffer a loss of income and will cut their expenditure, while the recipients gain an increase in disposable income and will increase their expenditure. The net effect is zero (except in so far as the recipients' marginal propensities to consume differ from the tax payers' propensities). This argument would be correct *if* the increased transfer payments were financed by increased taxes.

Note, however, that all the changes we have considered so far are *ceteris paribus* changes. When either G or Q are increased, t is not changed. Thus the extra government expenditure on goods and services, or on transfer payments, causes an increase in the government's budget deficit. If the government borrows the money to pay for its transfers, there is no corresponding decrease in anyone else's disposable income. Any new expenditure that the recipients make is thus totally new expenditure, and it will raise equilibrium national income.

A change in tax rates: A reduction in tax rates means that a larger proportion of each £1 of national income reaches households as disposable income. Hence, with a given marginal propensity to consume out of disposable income, the propensity to consume out of national income rises. This important proposition is illustrated numerically in Table 29.1.

A rise in the tax rate has the opposite effect. A smaller proportion of each £1 of national income will now reach households as disposable income. With a given MPC out of disposable income, a smaller proportion of each £1 of national income will then be passed on through household consumption expenditure.

The effect of changes in the tax rate can easily be seen by inspecting the aggregate expenditure function given in equation (10) on page 502. The slope of that function is $c(1-t)$. Since t enters with a negative sign, a reduction in t increases the slope of the function. This pivots the function upwards and raises equilibrium national income. An increase in t has the opposite effect. (The same conclusion can be reached by inspection of the solution for equilibrium national income given in equation (11).)

> **A cut in tax rates pivots the consumption function upward and increases equilibrium national income. An increase in tax rates pivots the consumption function downwards and lowers equilibrium national income.**

Note that a cut in tax rates has the same effect as a rise in c, the MPC. This is because the propensity to consume out of national income may rise either because (i) more of total income reaches households as their disposable income as a result of a fall in t, or (ii) more of a given total income is spent on consumption purchases as a result of a rise in c.

The discussion so far has all been in terms of the effects on the aggregate desired expenditure function and the results are shown graphically in Figure 29.3.

FIGURE 29.3 Changes in Equilibrium National Income: the Expenditure Approach

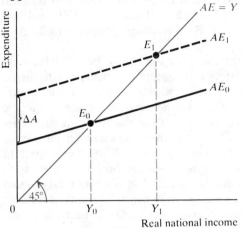

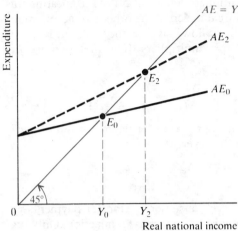

(i) **A rise in investment, government expenditure or government transfer payments**

(ii) **A reduction in tax rates or an increase in the *MPC***

Equilibrium income is increased by a rise in government expenditure on final goods, government transfer payments or a fall in tax rates. In both parts of the diagram, the AE function is the sum of the G, I and C functions as shown in Figure 29.2. That function intersects the 45° line at E_0 to produce an equilibrium income of Y_0.

In part (i), there is an increase in autonomous spending by ΔA because either I or G rose by ΔA, or Q rose by $\Delta A/c$ (so that cQ rose by ΔA). The aggregate expenditure function rises to AE_1. It now intersects the 45° line at E_1, making equilibrium national income Y_1. The reverse effect of a fall in investment, government final purchases or transfer payments is shown when the AE curve starts at AE_1 and then shifts downwards by ΔA to AE_0. Equilibrium income then falls from Y_1 to Y_0.

In part (ii), a fall in the tax rate (or a rise in the MPC) pivots the aggregate desired expenditure function from AE_0 to AE_2. The fall in the tax rate leaves a higher proportion of income in the hands of households and increases the percentage of national income that is devoted to consumption expenditure. Equilibrium shifts from E_0 to E_2, and income rises from Y_0 to Y_2. The effects of a rise in tax rates are shown by starting with AE_2 and shifting it to AE_0. Equilibrium national income then falls from Y_2 to Y_0.

The Multiplier

How large is the change in equilibrium national income associated with a given change in autonomous expenditure? To answer this question algebraically, we merely first difference equation (11) to obtain the following expression:

$$\Delta Y = [\Delta I + \Delta G + c\Delta Q] \frac{1}{1 - c(1 - t)} \quad . \quad (12)$$

Equation (11) gives the solution for equilibrium national income, while equation (12) tells us the change in income resulting from a change in autonomous expenditures. It shows that the effects of changes in G and I are the same. This is not surprising since a change in either type of expenditure shifts the aggregate desired expenditure curve in the same way. The households that earn the newly generated income then set up the same multiplier reaction in which further expenditure breeds further income, which breeds yet further expenditure.

To calculate the multipliers for each of the autonomous expenditure flows, we allow one of the changes in (12) to be positive while the other two are held at zero. We then divide through by the non-zero change. For example, if we let ΔG and ΔQ be zero, we have an expression for ΔY as a function of ΔI and the parameters c and t. We then divide through by ΔI to get the value of K (the multiplier) defined as $\Delta Y/\Delta I$. Repeating this procedure for each of the other two autonomous expenditure flows gives us the three autonomous expenditure multipliers. The first two are the same:

$$K = \frac{\Delta Y}{\Delta I} = \frac{\Delta Y}{\Delta G} = \frac{1}{1 - c(1 - t)} \quad . \quad (13)$$

The value of the transfer payments multiplier is smaller, however. It is

$$\frac{\Delta Y}{\Delta Q} = \frac{c}{1 - c(1 - t)} \quad . \quad (14)$$

This is so because not all transfer payments get into the income stream as an injection. Only that fraction that is consumed does so. Thus, the multiplier for transfer payments is lower than the other two multipliers to the extent that c is less than unity. (Inspection of (13) and (14) shows that if c is unity, all three multipliers are the same.)

Examination of (13) reveals its similarity to the multiplier from the two-sector model in Chapter 27. That earlier multiplier was $1/(1-c)$. It is the reciprocal of one minus the proportion of national income spent on consumption, which we have called the marginal propensity to spend out of national income, *MPE*. In (14) above, the multiplier is also the reciprocal of one minus the *MPE*, only now, because of taxes, that proportion is $c(1-t)$, rather than just c.

The generalization of this result is:

the multiplier for any change in autonomous expenditure is the reciprocal of one minus the proportion of any new income that gets passed on in terms of new expenditure, i.e. $1 - MPE$.

This result holds for any expenditure whose first impact is to raise Y by £1 for every £1 spent. For transfer payments the first impact is smaller, so the multiplier is correspondingly smaller.

The Withdrawals-Injections Approach

Identical results can be obtained by using the withdrawals-injections approach. In the three-sector economy, there are two withdrawals, sav-

ings and taxes. Taxes are national income that is not available to households to spend. Saving is disposable income that is not passed on through household spending. Thus total withdrawals are $W = S + T$. Both of these are positively related to national income.

There are three injections, two of which are straightforward: investment, which we discussed in the previous chapter, and government purchases of goods and services, which is income that does not arise from the spending of households. The third injection is transfer payments. These payments are not themselves a part of national income. They do, however, give rise to household spending that does not arise from income received from firms. The part of transfer payments that is spent (cQ) is, therefore, properly regarded as an injection.[1]

Thus total injections are $\mathcal{J} = I + G + cQ$. All three of these are assumed to be autonomous constants.

Equilibrium National Income

Geometric: The determination of equilibrium national income using the withdrawals-injections approach is shown in Figure 29.4. The withdrawals function is now the sum of two separate withdrawals, savings and taxes, both of which are positively related to national income. The injections function is the sum of three separate injections, I, G and cQ, all of which are assumed to be constant. Figure 29.4 is, of course, merely an alternative determination of the equilibrium value of national income already derived in Figure 29.3.

Algebraic: Some care is needed on how to treat savings out of transfer payments, sQ. Transfer payments only become an injection when they are spent. So the part that is saved never enters the income stream and cannot, therefore, be regarded as a leakage from it. It follows that the savings that are needed in the

---

[1] We could, if we wished, regard all transfer payments, Q, as an injection. The fraction that is saved, sQ, would then be an immediate withdrawal. For a geometric treatment, however, that would be awkward since a change in transfer payments would then shift both the injections and the withdrawals functions. It is simpler, therefore, to regard injections as *national* income that arises from outside the circular flow. Then injections are only the fraction of transfer payments that gets spent, cQ.

**FIGURE 29.4   Changes in Equilibrium National Income: the Withdrawals-
Injections Approach**

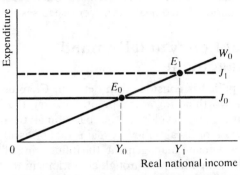

(i) **A rise in investment, government expenditure
or government transfer payments**

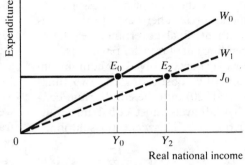

(ii) **A reduction in tax rates or an
increase in the MPC**

**Equilibrium national income is increased by an increase in the injections of
investment, final government expenditure or transfer payments, or a
decrease in the withdrawals of tax revenues.** The initial injection schedule of J_0
is the sum of the autonomous expenditures of I^*, G^*, and cQ^* (which are not
separately shown). The original withdrawal schedule of W_0 is the sum of the saving
and the tax schedules (which are not separately shown). These two schedules intersect
at E_0 to yield equilibrium income of Y_0.

A rise in any element of autonomous expenditure shifts the injections function in
part (i) upwards from J_0 to J_1. Equilibrium shifts from E_0 to E_1, taking national income
from Y_0 to Y_1. A fall in autonomous expenditure can be shown by shifting the
injections function downwards from J_1 to J_0.

In part (ii), a fall in the tax rate pivots the withdrawals schedule to W_1. At the initial
level of income, desired withdrawals are less than desired injections. Income will rise
until the new intersection at E_2 is reached with income at Y_2. A rise in the tax rate can
be analysed by allowing the withdrawals schedule to shift from W_1 to W_0.

withdrawals function are $S = s(Y - T)$, i.e. the
amount of *national* income that is saved, which is
national income, minus taxes, multiplied by the
propensity to save.

The model can now be summarized in the
following equations.

Definitions:
$$W \equiv S + T \tag{15}$$
$$J \equiv I + G + cQ \tag{16}$$
Behaviour:
$$S = s(Y - T) \tag{17}$$
$$T = tY \tag{3}$$
$$Q = Q^* \tag{2}$$
$$I = I^* \tag{4}$$
$$G = G^* \tag{1}$$
Equilibrium condition:
$$W = J \tag{18}$$

The first step in solving this model is to derive
a function relating saving to national income.

This is $S = s(1 - t)Y$.[1] The next step is to substitute this saving function, along with the rest of
the behavioural equations, into the equations
defining withdrawals (equation 15) and injections (equation 16). This yields the equations of
the withdrawals and the injections functions that
are graphed in Figure 29.4:

$$W = [s(1 - t) + t]Y \tag{19}$$
$$J = I^* + G^* + cQ^* . \tag{20}$$

Look first at the withdrawals function. Notice
that $s(1 - t)$ is the amount of each £1 of national
income that is withdrawn through saving, while
the second t is the amount that is withdrawn
through taxes. Thus $s(1 - t) + t$ is the fraction of
each new £1 of national income that is withdrawn
for one reason or another, i.e. all that is not passed

---

[1] Starting with (17), substitute (3) to eliminate T, yielding
$S = s(Y - tY)$. Now factor out the Y to get $S = s(1 - t)Y$.

on through consumption spending. We earlier called this the marginal propensity not to spend (or to leak or to withdraw). As usual, the injection schedule is merely the sum of a series of autonomous expenditures. There are three in this model, investment, final government expenditure, and spending out of transfer payments.

The model may now be solved for equilibrium national income by substituting the two functions in (19) and (20) into the equilibrium condition that withdrawals must equal injections given in equation (18). This yields the solution:

$$Y = [I^* + G^* + cQ^*]\frac{1}{s(1-t)+t} \quad . \quad (21)$$

The structure is the same as we obtained using the expenditure approach. Each of the autonomous expenditure flows is multiplied by a term that depends on the behavioural parameters which, in this case, are s and t.

The procedure for deriving the multipliers is also the same as for the expenditure approach. Equation (21) is first differenced. The changes in autonomous expenditure flows are allowed to take on non-zero values one at a time, and the equation is divided through by that change to obtain the ratio of the change in income to the change in autonomous expenditure. The multipliers for investment and final government expenditure that are derived in this way are:

$$K = \frac{\Delta Y}{\Delta I} = \frac{\Delta Y}{\Delta G} = \frac{1}{s(1-t)+t} \quad . \quad (22)$$

The multiplier for transfer payments is

$$\frac{\Delta Y}{\Delta Q} = \frac{c}{s(1-t)+t} \quad . \quad (23)$$

This suggests the simple generalization that

the expenditure multiplier is the reciprocal of the marginal propensity to withdraw income from the circular flow.

The effect of a change in the tax rates can be seen from equation (23) by rearranging the term $s(1-t)+t$ to read $s+t(1-s)$.[1] Since s, the *MPS*, is a positive fraction, $1-s$ is positive. Thus an increase in t increases the magnitude of the denominator and hence reduces the value of

equilibrium income in (21) and the value of the multipliers in (22) and (23). This checks with the result stated earlier that an increase in tax rates lowers national income while a decrease raises it.[1]

Fiscal Policy and Demand Management

Fiscal policy is considered in detail in Chapter 37. It is worth noting at this point, however, that we have now developed the basic analytical framework of fiscal policy. A major tool of fiscal policy is demand management, the influencing of aggregate expenditure through alterations in the government's budget. We have seen that a *ceteris paribus* rise in government expenditure on goods and services or transfer payments, or a fall in tax rates, increases total desired expenditure. As long as firms produce all they can sell, it also increases total output and employment. A *ceteris paribus* fall in government expenditure on goods and services or transfer payments, or a rise in tax rates, reduces aggregate desired expenditure. This also reduces total output and employment.

This is the basic theory behind the main tool of fiscal demand management:

> **Expansionary demand-management policies seek to raise total desired expenditure by increasing government expenditure on goods and services or on transfer payments or by lowering tax rates. Contractionary policies seek to do the reverse.**

FOREIGN TRADE: A FOUR-SECTOR MODEL

Our next step is to introduce foreign trade. This adds a fourth sector to our model, taking us from a closed to an open economy. We first define two new expenditure flows and then make assumptions about their behaviour.

---

[1] Multiply out $s(1-t)+t$ to get $s-st+t$ and factor the t out of the last two terms to get $s+t(1-s)$.

[1] The equivalence of the multiplier in (22) for the $W = J$ approach and the multiplier in (13) for the $E = Y$ approach is shown as follows. The denominator of (22) is $s(1-t)+t$. Replacing s by $1-c$, this yields $(1-c)(1-t)+t$ which expands to $1-t-c+ct+t = 1-c+ct = 1-c(1-t)$, which is the denominator of (13).

Definitions

Exports are defined as all those goods and services that are made domestically and sold abroad, while imports are defined as all those goods and services that are made abroad and sold domestically. The introduction of these two new expenditure flows requires that we look more carefully at the aggregate desired expenditure function, which refers to desired expenditure on *domestically produced output*. It is the demand for the country's national output. How do exports and imports fit into this expenditure function?

Exports, which we denote by X, constitute demand for domestic output and, when the demand is met, the production of goods for export creates domestic employment and income. Exports, therefore, represent an addition to aggregate desired expenditure.

In contrast, when domestic residents buy imports, this is a part of total final expenditure that does not go to purchase domestically produced commodities. Expenditure on imports, which we label M, is spending of domestic households, firms or governments, on foreign-produced output. If we want to obtain desired purchases of domestically produced output we must start with total spending on C, I, G and X, and subtract that part of it which goes to purchase imports, M.

The revised aggregate expenditure function now has X added and M subtracted. The two amounts of X and M are customarily grouped together to show desired expenditure on what is called **net exports**, so that the new aggregate expenditure function is as follows:

$$E = C + I + G + (X - M) . \qquad (24)$$

This value of net exports is usually small in relation to the total value of either X or M. Thus, the correction to aggregate expenditure when we move from a closed economy to an open economy will not usually be large. However, a change in either X or M, not matched by a change in the other, will cause aggregate expenditure to change in the same way as would an equivalent change in C, I or G.

Behavioural Assumptions

The next step is to make assumptions concerning the behaviour of X and M.

The amount of exports depends upon the domestic prices of these goods, on the exchange rate (which determines their foreign prices), on the prices of competing goods from other countries, and on foreign incomes. As with I and G, it is convenient to see how national income adjusts to a fixed level of exports before seeing how it reacts when exports change. Thus, exports are assumed to be an autonomous expenditure flow for the time being.

Imports, however, vary with national income. Domestic households spend a fraction of their consumption expenditure on imported consumers' goods. Furthermore, almost all domestic output contains some imported raw materials and semi-manufactured goods. Iron-ore, oil, paper and timber are but a few of the many examples. This means that all domestic expenditures on C, I and G have an import content. Thus, expenditure on imports is positively related to national income.

In what follows, we make the simplifying assumption that the only type of commodity that is imported is final consumers' goods. Note that consumption, C, refers to all expenditure on consumption goods wherever they are produced, and that M now refers to imported consumption goods. Thus, on our simple assumptions, $C - M$ is expenditure on domestically produced consumption goods. We also assume that imports are positively related to the level of national income.[1]

The above discussion can be captured in two behavioural equations:

$$X = X^* \qquad (25)$$

$$M = mY . \qquad (26)$$

The first equation says that exports are an exogenous constant. The second says that a constant fraction of national income goes to purchase imports. This fraction is labelled m. It is yet another *propensity*. It is both the **marginal propensity to import (M/Y)** and the **average**

---

[1] If the only imports are consumption goods, it might be better to relate imports to disposable income. No matter of substance would be changed if we did so, but the algebra would be a little more complex. Readers with a theoretical bent will find it instructive to write $M = mY_d$ in place of equation (26) and then to derive the corresponding multiplier. The trick is then to explain why the coefficients c, t and m are combined in the way they are in the new multiplier equation.

propensity to import $(\Delta M/\Delta Y)$. If, for example, m is 0.2, the equation $M = 0.2\,Y$ tells us the imports are always 20 per cent of income, and that any increase of £1 in income leads to an increase of 20p in imports.

These two behavioural equations, together with their combination into a net export function, are graphed in Figure 29.5.

Equilibrium Income

As usual, there are two ways of looking at the equilibrium conditions: either expenditure equals income, or withdrawals equal injections.

The Income-Expenditure Approach

Geometrical: For the graphical solution, we merely note that the aggregate desired expenditure function in Figures 29.2 and 29.3 now contains an added term for net exports, $X - M$. An increase in X, or a fall in m, shifts the E curve upwards while a reduction in X, or a rise in m, shifts it downwards. The common sense of this is that aggregate desired expenditure on domestic production rises if anyone, whether a domestic or a foreign resident, wishes to buy more domestic production; while aggregate desired expenditure on domestic production falls if domestic residents wish to shift expenditure from domestically produced to foreign-produced commodities. Equilibrium is where aggregate desired expenditure equals national income. Furthermore, anything that shifts the expenditure function upwards increases equilibrium national income, while anything that shifts the function downwards decreases equilibrium income. In this specific application:

> **equilibrium income is increased by a rise in exports and by a fall in the propensity to import: it is reduced by a fall in exports and a rise in the propensity to import.**[1]

Algebraic: The algebraic solution follows a now familiar path. It would, however, be a good check on your own understanding to follow through the steps for yourself. Starting with the model on page 502, substitute the new definition of E. Then add in the two new behavioural equations for X and M. Then substitute the behavioural equations into the new definition of aggregate expenditure. A bit of simplification, of the sort spelled out in the previous sections, produces the equation of the new aggregate desired expenditure function:

$$E = [I^* + G^* + X^* + cQ^*] + [c(1-t) - m]\,Y \quad (27)$$

Compare this new expenditure function with the expenditure function given in equation (10) on page 502. The two differ by the addition of X^* for exports, and the subtraction of mY for imports. Equilibrium national income is now found by substituting the new aggregate desired expenditure function into the equilibrium condition $E = Y$. The result is:

$$Y = [I^* + G^* + X^* + cQ^*]\frac{1}{1 - c(1-t) + m} \quad (28)$$

Once again the various expenditure multipliers are found by considering positive changes in the autonomous expenditure flows one at a time and then dividing by the change in the flow in question to obtain the following:

$$K = \frac{\Delta Y}{\Delta I} = \frac{\Delta Y}{\Delta G} = \frac{\Delta Y}{\Delta X} = \frac{1}{1 - c(1-t) + m} \quad (29)$$

Compare (29) with the multipliers for the closed-economy model given in equation (13) on page 506. The only difference is in the presence of m, the marginal propensity to import in the denominator of the multiplier. By raising the value of the denominator, m lowers the value of K. The common sense is that another leakage has been allowed for:

> **when autonomous expenditure increases, some of the spending induced by new income leaks out into demand for foreign goods.**

[1] This proposition requires that exports and imports can vary independently of each other. Under a fixed exchange rate this is possible, at least in the short term. Under a flexible-exchange-rate regime, however, a significant change in either X or M will affect the exchange rate, which will cause the other to change. Indeed, if the only source of demands and supplies on the foreign-exchange market were exports and imports (no capital flows), and the exchange rate were left perfectly free, it would fluctuate so as to keep exports equal to imports at all times. Under these circumstances, the net export term could be ignored since it would always be zero. Here we assume what is undoubtedly correct in today's world: that there is enough stabilization of the exchange rate, either through private capital flows or government intervention, that exports and imports can fluctuate independently of each other, at least in the short term.

FIGURE 29.5 Export and Import Functions

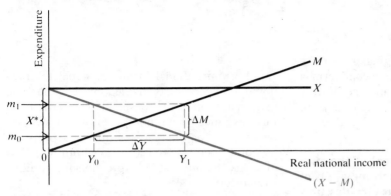

Exports are an autonomous expenditure flow, while imports and net exports are endogenous. The line labelled X shows exports as a constant amount X^* at all levels of national income. The line labelled M shows imports positively associated with national income. A rise in income from Y_0 to Y_1 raises imports from m_0 to m_1. These amounts are indicated by ΔY and ΔM in the Figure. The marginal propensity to import is indicated by the slope of the M function which is $\Delta M / \Delta Y$ in the Figure.

The line labelled $(X - M)$ is the net export function, which shows how net exports vary with national income. Since exports are constant, while imports are positively associated with national income, net exports must be negatively associated with national income.

The multiplier in (29) follows a now-familiar pattern. The proportion of new income that gets *passed on* in domestic spending in this model is $c(1 - t) - m$, i.e. the $c(1 - t)$ of the closed-economy model minus m, the fraction of the new spending that goes to imports. Thus the denominator of (29), which is $1 - [c(1 - t) - m]$, is one minus the proportion of new income that gets passed on – i.e. one minus the *MPE*. This illustrates once again the generalization stated at the end of Chapter 27.

The Withdrawals-Injections Approach

Exports are clearly an injection since they create income for domestic producers that does not arise from the spending of domestic households. Imports are clearly a withdrawal since they are income not passed on in the domestic circular flow, but which leaks out to foreign producers. Thus we now have

$$W = S + T + M \qquad (30)$$

and

$$\mathcal{J} = I + G + cQ + X . \qquad (31)$$

All that we have done here is to add one injection to our injection function and add one withdrawal to our withdrawal function.

Geometric: The graphical solution is obtained by adding these two terms to the W and $\mathcal{J}$ functions in Figure 29.4. An increase in X shifts up the injections line, just as does an increase in any other component of autonomous expenditure. It thus increases equilibrium income. An increase in m, the marginal propensity to import, pivots the withdrawal function upwards just as does an increase in the marginal propensity to save or to tax. It thus reduces equilibrium income.

Algebraic: The algebraic solution follows from substituting the behavioural assumptions into the new definitions of W and $\mathcal{J}$ just given, and then substituting them into the equilibrium condition, $W = \mathcal{J}$. Simple algebraic manipulation of a now familiar sort yields:

$$Y = [I^* + G^* + X^* + cQ^*] \frac{1}{s(1 - t) + t + m} \qquad (32)$$

Using the standard technique, the following expenditure multiplier is derived:

$$K = \frac{1}{s(1-t)+t+m} \; . \tag{33}$$

The first term, $s(1-t)$, is the marginal propensity to save out of national income, the second term is the marginal propensity to tax, and the third is the marginal propensity to import. All three are stated as propensities out of national income.

Again we see that:

the multiplier is a reciprocal of the sum of the proportions of each new £1 of income withdrawn from the circular flow for various reasons.

THE STRUCTURE OF NATIONAL-INCOME MODELS

All of the models considered so far have the same structure, they only differ in the number of sectors. There is a danger that the necessary algebraic manipulation will obscure the essential simplicity of the underlying model. So now that the four versions have been completed, let us outline that structure.

The basic assumption is that expenditure can be divided into two components, one that varies with national income, called induced expenditure, and one that does not, called autonomous expenditure. Letting A stand for all autonomous expenditure and letting z stand for the marginal propensity to spend out of national income, we can write these assumptions as follows:

$$E = A + zY \; . \tag{34}$$

Firms are assumed to supply all that is demanded at the going price, so equilibrium national income will be equal to aggregate desired expenditure. What everyone wants to buy will determine what is produced. This gives the now familiar equilibrium condition

$$E = Y \; . \tag{35}$$

To solve the model, we substitute the behavioural equation into the equilibrium condition to obtain

$$Y = A + zY \; .$$

Subtracting zY from both sides of the equation, factoring out the Y and dividing through by $(1-z)$ yields:

$$Y = A\frac{1}{(1-z)} \; . \tag{36}$$

Equilibrium national income is equal to autonomous expenditure divided by 1 minus the marginal propensity to spend out of national income. Since what is not spent is withdrawn, we have $1 - z = w$, where w is the marginal propensity not to spend (or to leak or to withdraw). This gives us the alternative expression for equilibrium income:

$$Y = A\frac{1}{w} \; . \tag{37}$$

This can also be derived by starting from the specification of withdrawals and injections and using the alternative equilibrium condition that $W = \mathcal{J}$.

The multipliers are found by studying what happens to Y when there is a change in autonomous expenditure. This is easily seen from equations (36) and (37) to be:

$$K = \frac{\Delta Y}{\Delta A} = \frac{1}{(1-z)} = \frac{1}{w} \; . \tag{38}$$

All of the various models merely differ in the elements of autonomous expenditure, and the components of z, the marginal propensity to spend, and w, the marginal propensity not to spend (both out of national income). Although some messy algebra may be involved in finding out how z and w change when some new assumption about spending flows is introduced, the basic structure of the model remains the simple one just laid out. No matter how many sectors are added, and no matter how complex are the behavioural assumptions about the expenditure flows, the result is always the same:

The multiplier is the reciprocal of the marginal propensity not to spend out of national income – i.e. the proportion of each new increment of national income that *is not passed on* through further spending. It can also be expressed as the reciprocal of one minus the marginal propensity to spend out of national income – i.e. the proportion of each new

increment of national income that *is* passed on through further spending.

The Value of the Multiplier

In Chapter 27 we saw that multipliers for the two-sector model were quite large. For example, with an *MPS* of 0.1, the multiplier in the two-sector economy is 10. In the four-sector model, however, the multiplier is much smaller. Assume, for example, the values $s = .10$, $t = .40$ and $m = .25$, which are in the approximate range of the British figures. Substituting these into equation (33) yields a multiplier value of 1.41.

This suggests vastly smaller fluctuations of Y in response to changes in autonomous expenditure flows than did the multiplier for the two-sector model. The difference between the two models is that taxes and imports create large withdrawals from the circular flow. Thus a much smaller part of every £1 of new income gets spent on domestic consumption, creating yet more new income.

Using realistic values for the behavioural parameters for open economies with large government sectors, multipliers are typically between 1 and 2 rather than between 5 and 10 as they are in two-sector models.

SUMMARY

1. If government expenditures on goods and services and transfer payments exceed tax revenues, the deficit must be covered by borrowing. This increases the national debt. If expenditures fall short of revenues, the surplus is used to reduce the debt.
2. Aggregate desired expenditure is increased by government expenditure on goods and services and by expenditure made out of transfer payments. These are injections into the circular flow of income (along with investment). Government revenue is a leakage (along with saving).
3. Equilibrium national income is increased by an increase in government expenditure on goods and services or transfer payments (providing these lead to increased consumption expenditure) or by a cut in tax rates.
4. Net exports $(X - M)$ are an element of aggregate desired expenditure; imports are a leakage and exports an injection into the circular flow.
5. Equilibrium national income is increased by an increase in exports or a decrease in the propensity to import.
6. The multiplier is the reciprocal of one minus the marginal propensity to spend out of national income $(1 - MPE)$. It is also the reciprocal of the marginal propensity to leak (or withdraw) income from the circular flow, MPL.
7. In a world of three main leakages – savings, taxes and imports – typical values of the *MPS*, *MPT* and *MPM* for countries such as the UK give multipliers of less than 2.

TOPICS FOR REVIEW

- Desired expenditure equals national income and withdrawals equal injections as equilibrium conditions
- The components of aggregate demand, withdrawals and injections in a four-sector model
- The causes of changes in equilibrium national income
- The relation between the multiplier and the *MPS*, the *MPT* and the *MPM*

PART 9

The Intermediate Theory of National Income: Interest Rates and the Price Level are Variable

30

Money and the Price Level

The previous chapters have developed the national-income model under the assumptions of a constant interest rate and price level. The interest rate is the price of borrowing money, and changes in the price level – called inflations and deflations – have long been understood to be related to the amount of money in the economy. In order to make interest rates and the price level endogenous, we must make a substantial digression to study the nature of money.

Anything that serves as money fulfils several related functions, which we study below. The most important function that distinguishes money from other assets, however, is its use as a medium of exchange. Indeed, **money** may be defined as any generally accepted medium of exchange, i.e. anything that will be accepted in exchange for goods and services.

THE FUNCTIONS AND CHARACTERISTICS OF MONEY

Four of the most important functions of money are to act as:

- a medium of exchange,
- a store of value,
- a unit of account, and
- a standard of deferred payments.

A medium of exchange: On pages 9–10 of Chapter 1 we saw that, where money does not exist, goods must be exchanged through barter, the direct exchange of one good for another. That discussion of the inefficiency of barter, and the efficiency of the use of money as a medium of exchange, should be re-read now. All modern economies are characterized by a high degree of specialization. As a result, most of what one produces is consumed by others, and most of what one consumes is produced by others. This requires a more efficient mechanism for the exchange of products than is provided by barter. Without money, therefore, our complicated economic system, based on specialization and the division of labour, would be impossible.

To serve as an efficient medium of exchange, money must have the following characteristics. (i) *It must be readily acceptable*, for if one is to take money in exchange for what one wants to sell, one needs to know that others will, in their turn, take the money in exchange for what one wants to buy. This is, of course, the fundamental characteristic that money must have. (ii) *It must be easily portable*, which requires that it must have a high value for its weight, for it would otherwise be a nuisance to carry around. (iii) *It must be divisible*, for money that comes only in large denominations is useless for transactions having only a small value. (iv) *It must not be easy to counterfeit*, for money that can be easily duplicated by anyone will quickly lose its value. All of these are characteristics that are found in virtually all types of modern money.

A store of value: Many goods, and all services, cannot be stored up for future needs. Money, however, allows us to store purchasing power: you can sell your goods today and store the money, giving you a claim to goods and services that you can exercise in the future.

To be a fully satisfactory store of future purchasing power, money must have a stable value in terms of the things that it can buy. If prices are stable, a given quantity of money stored up will command the same amount of goods and services when it is used in the future as it could have commanded when it was first set aside. If the general price level changes over time, the purchasing power of a given quantity of money stored over time will be varying.

A unit of account: Money may also be used purely for accounting purposes, without having any physical existence. For instance, a village commune might say that each person had so many 'roubles' at his or her disposal each month and might then establish these as credits on the books of the village's only shop. Goods would be given prices and purchases would be recorded. Consumers could buy all they wanted while their personal supply of 'roubles' lasted. The money would have no existence other than as entries in the shop's books, but it would be serving as a perfectly satisfactory unit of account.

A standard of deferred payments: There is a fourth function that is sometimes distinguished, although it is really implied by the other three. Acting as a standard of deferred payments means that a payment to be made in the future can be denominated in money terms in just the same way as can a payment to be made today. Here, money is acting as a unit of account, with the added dimension of time.

The History of Money

A surer understanding of what money is, and what it does, can be gained by studying some of the highlights in the history of money.

Metallic Money

All sorts of commodities have been used as money at one time or another, but gold and silver proved to have great advantages. They had a high and stable price both because their supply was relatively limited, and because they were in constant demand by the rich for ornament and decoration. They had the additional advantages of being durable and divisible into extremely small units. They were also easily recognized and readily accepted – their acceptability, of course, being the key characteristic they needed to develop as money.

Before the invention of coins, it was necessary to carry precious metals around in bulk, weighing the amount required for each transaction. The invention of coinage eliminated this need. The government made a coin using a fixed quantity of gold or silver for value, and an amount of cheap base metal to give the coin durability. It then affixed its own seal to guarantee the amount of precious metal contained in the coin.

This system worked well as long as the government played its part. From time to time, however, the temptation to cheat proved overwhelming. When the government had debts that it could not pay, it could *debase* the coinage. Gold and silver coins would be melted down and coined afresh, but, between the melting down and the recoining, further amounts of inexpensive base metals would be added. If the coinage were debased by adding, say, one ounce of new base metal to every four ounces of old coins, five coins could be minted for every four melted down. With these extra coins, the government could pay its debts. One consequence of currency debasement, called Gresham's Law, is discussed in Box 30.1.

The result was inflation. When the government paid its bills, the recipients of the extra coins would spend some or all of them, and this

BOX 30.1 GRESHAM'S LAW

The early experience of currency debasement led to a famous economic 'law' that has stood the test of time. The law states that 'bad money drives out good' and is called **Gresham's law** after the Elizabethan financial expert, Sir Thomas Gresham, who first explained its workings to Queen Elizabeth I. Monarchs before Elizabeth had severely debased the English coinage. Seeking to help trade, Elizabeth minted new coins containing their full face value in gold. But as fast as she fed these new coins into circulation, they disappeared. Why? Suppose that you possess one new and one old coin, each with the same face value but different gold contents. Now you have an account to settle. Which coin would you use? Clearly, you would pay with the debased coin and keep the undebased one. You part with less gold that way. If you wanted to obtain a certain amount of gold bullion by melting down the gold coins (as was frequently done), which coins would you use? Clearly, you would use new undebased coins

because to get a given amount of gold you would part with less 'face value' that way.

The debased coins would thus remain in circulation and the undebased coins would disappear. Whenever people got hold of an undebased coin, they kept it; whenever they got a debased coin, they would pass it on. Hence, the bad money stayed in circulation and drove the good money out of circulation.

Gresham's law has many modern applications. Here is one for illustration. Until about 25 or 30 years ago, most countries used some silver content in many of their coins, but the market value of the silver content was much less than the face value of the coin. Then in the 1960s, the price of silver soared. The value of the silver content exceeded the coins' face value and when this became known, they became 'good' money. True to Gresham's law, they disappeared from circulation. People melted them down and sold their silver content for more than the face value of the coin.

would cause a net increase in demand. The extra demand would bid up prices. Debasing the coinage thus led to a rise in the general price level. Such experiences led early economists to propound the *quantity theory of money and prices*. They argued that a change in the quantity of money would lead to a change in the price level in the same direction. (We shall have more to say about this theory later in the chapter.)

Paper Money

Paper money came into use in many ways. One was through the practice of storing gold for safekeeping with goldsmiths – craftsmen who worked with gold. The goldsmiths issued receipts, promising to hand over the gold to the bearer of the receipt on demand. These receipts soon became a medium of exchange. A buyer needed only to transfer a goldsmith's receipt for so much gold to a seller, who would accept it, secure in the knowledge that the goldsmith would pay over the gold whenever it was needed. As the receipts became *acceptable* for settling market transactions, they *became* money. The convenience of using easy-to-carry pieces of paper instead of gold is obvious.

Thus, when it first came into being, paper money was a promise to pay on demand so much gold, the promise being made first by goldsmiths

and later by banks. Early banks, too, undertook to store gold, and issued their promises to pay that gold on demand. These promissory notes were called **bank notes**. As long as the institutions were known to be reliable, their pieces of paper would be 'as good as gold'. Such notes remained an important part of the money supply until the early part of the twentieth century. When a country's money is *convertible* into gold, the country is said to be on a **gold standard**.

Fractionally backed paper money: Such was the convenience of paper money, that most people were content to use it for most of their transactions; and only occasionally did they ask to convert their notes into gold or silver. At any one time, therefore, some of the bank's customers would be withdrawing gold, others would be depositing it, and the great majority would be using the bank's paper notes without any need, or desire, to convert them into gold. For this reason, the bank was able to issue *more* money, redeemable in gold, than the amount of gold held in its vaults. This was good business, because the banks could use the money to make interest-earning loans. In such a situation, we say that the currency is *fractionally backed* by the reserves.

In the past, the major problem of a fractionally backed currency was to maintain its convertibility into the precious metal by which it was backed. The imprudent bank that issued too much paper money found itself unable to redeem its currency in gold when the demand for gold was even slightly higher than usual. This bank would then have to suspend payments, and the holders of its notes would suddenly find that no one would accept them because they could not be converted into gold.

The prudent bank, which kept a reasonable relation between its note issue and its gold reserve, found that it could meet the normal everyday demand for gold without difficulty. But if the public lost confidence and *en masse* demanded redemption of their bank notes, even prudent banks could find themselves unable to honour their pledges. Banks were sometimes ruined by 'panic-induced', sudden runs on their reserves.

Fiat currencies: Over time, bank notes came to be issued not only by ordinary commercial banks, but also by the government operating through its central bank (which we shall study in more detail later in this chapter). Originally central banks issued currency that was fully convertible into gold. The gold supply thus set some upper limit on the amount of paper money that the central bank could issue. But the central bank could issue (as bank notes) more currency than it had gold because only small amounts of the currency would be presented for redemption at any one time.

During the period between World Wars I and II, virtually all the countries of the world abandoned gold convertibility – the UK did so in 1931. From that time on, paper money has depended for its value on nothing more than its general acceptability – and the fact that the government has ordered it to be accepted. Inconvertible paper money that is declared by government order (or fiat) to be legal tender for settlement of all debts is called **fiat money**.

MODERN MONEY

Most of the terms referring to various kinds of money have been introduced already. In view of the large number of terms in use, some of which mean the same thing, it is worth pausing to recapitulate.

Coins refer to all metallic money. Examples are the 10p and 50p coins in your pocket. *Notes* refers to paper money. In England, virtually all paper money in circulation consists of notes issued by the Bank of England. In Scotland, notes issued both by the Bank of England and the Bank of Scotland are in common circulation. (The Bank of Scotland is the central bank of Scotland.) Examples are the £5, £10, and £20 notes that you carry around to make everyday purchases. Taken together, notes and coins are commonly referred to as *cash* or *currency*. *Deposit money* or *bank money* refers to deposits held at banks. Which types of bank deposits are properly regarded as money is discussed later in the chapter.

Legal tender is money that must be accepted if offered in payment for a purchase or settlement of a debt. In the UK, legal tender consists of coins (up to certain maximum amounts) and notes. Cheques drawn on bank deposits are not legal tender, although they are commonly used in purchases and in the settlement of debts.

Money is said to be *convertible* if it can be converted into some other form of money that is legal tender. In the UK, bank deposits are convertible money – and they are so converted every time a customer withdraws some of his or her bank account in the form of cash.

Convertible money is said to be *backed* by the legal tender into which it can be converted. It is *fully backed* if, for every unit of convertible money outstanding, a unit of whatever backs it is held in reserve. It is *partially* or *fractionally backed*, if the reserves held to back it are only a fraction of the amount of money that is outstanding. Money that is not convertible into anything is said to be *fiat* or *inconvertible* money.

Modern Fiat Currencies

Today, all notes and all coins in circulation are fiat money.

Modern coins, unlike their predecessors, contain a value of metal that is characteristically only a minute fraction of the face value of the coin. Modern coins, like modern paper money, are merely tokens. Nonetheless, they function satisfactorily as money. Since they are acceptable, they are a medium of exchange; since their purchasing power remains relatively stable in normal times, they are a satisfactory store of value; and since both of these things are normally true, they will also serve as a satisfactory unit of account and a standard of deferred payments.

Modern Deposit Money

Early in the twentieth century, most private banks lost the authority to issue *bank notes*. Yet they did not lose the power to create *money*. Let us see how banks create money in the modern world.

Banks' customers frequently deposit coins and paper money for safekeeping, just as in former times they deposited gold. Each deposit is recorded as an entry on the customer's account.

Customers who wish to pay debts might come to the bank to claim their money in notes and coins, and then pay the money to another person. This person might then redeposit the money in a bank. Like the gold transfers, this is a tedious procedure, particularly for large payments. It is more convenient to have the bank transfer claims to the money they hold on deposit. The common 'cheque' is an instruction to the bank to make the transfer. As soon as such transfers became easy and inexpensive, and cheques became widely accepted in payment for commodities, bank deposits on which cheques could be drawn became a form of money called **deposit money**. In the UK, this type of bank deposit is called a **sight deposit** or a **current account deposit**. The deposit can be transferred to others by means of cheque and it can be converted into cash on demand.

Cheques are in some ways the modern equivalent of old-time banknotes issued by commercial banks. The passing of a bank note from hand to hand transferred ownership of a claim against the bank. A cheque on a bank account is similarly an order to the bank to pay the designated recipient money credited to the cheque writer's account. Unlike bank notes, however, cheques do not circulate freely from hand to hand. Thus cheques themselves are *not* money. The balance in the bank deposit is money; the cheque transfers money from one person to another. Because cheques are easily used, and because they are relatively safe from theft, they are widely regarded as being virtually as good as the currency they stand for.

Thus, when banks lost the right to issue notes of their own, the form of bank money changed, but the substance did not. Today's banks hold reserves to back the convertibility of their deposit money, just as their predecessors did. Some is held as currency in their vaults, but in most countries the bulk is held as deposits held by the commercial banks with the central bank. These deposits are *claims* to currency that the commercial banks know the central bank will always honour, so they are as good as cash – indeed, they are often referred to as part of their 'cash reserves'.[1]

Since bank deposits are a generally accepted means of exchange that can be transferred among persons by the medium of cheques, they are money. The great majority of transactions (by value) take place by cheque; only a small proportion involve notes and coins.

> **Thus in the modern world, the greater proportion of the money supply is the deposit money that is created by commercial banks.**

The banks can, if they wish, contract the money supply by not creating deposits, or they can expand it by creating deposits up to the limit of prudence. It is, of course, in the bank's interest to expand deposits up to the limit because every £1 created can be used to acquire some income-earning asset.

THE MODERN BANKING SYSTEM IN THE UK[2]

The most visible units in the present-day banking system are the privately owned banks that deal with the ordinary public. These banks are variously called **commercial banks**, **listed banks** or **clearing banks**. (The latter term covers most, but not all, of the commercial

---

[1] Note the possible source of confusion here. 'Cash' strictly means notes and coins. Although the reserves that commercial banks hold on deposit with the Bank of England are called 'cash reserves', they are not cash. They are only entries on the Bank of England's books. But they are convertible into cash on demand. Furthermore, since the Bank of England is responsible for issuing notes and coins, there is no doubt about its ability to honour the commercial banks' deposits whenever the commercial banks wish to withdraw cash.

[2] This brief discussion is confined to essentials. More detail can be found in Harbury and Lipsey, Chapter 8.

banks.) These banks are profit-seeking firms. They accept deposits, they transfer certain kinds of deposits among their customers and other banks when ordered to do so by cheque, they make loans to customers, called **advances**, charging them interest in return, and they invest some of their funds by purchasing interest-earning financial assets on the open market.

In the United Kingdom, the most important commercial banks are the London clearing banks, located in England and Wales, and the clearing banks of Scotland and Northern Ireland. The four largest London clearing banks dominate the system in terms of value of deposits held. They have numerous branches throughout the country.

The banks require a mechanism to settle their interbank debts. If a depositor in Bank A writes a cheque to someone whose account is with Bank B, then a mere book transfer within Bank A will not do, because Bank A now owes money to Bank B. It is exactly the same as if one individual withdrew cash from Bank A and gave it to the second individual, who deposited it in Bank B. When the transaction is done by cheque, however, the banks rather than the individuals transfer the money.

Multibank systems make use of a **clearing house** where interbank debts are cancelled. At the end of the day, all of the cheques drawn on Bank A's customers and deposited in Bank B are totalled, and set against the total of all the cheques drawn by Bank B's customers and deposited in Bank A. It is only necessary to settle the difference between these two sums. This is done for every pair of banks. The actual cheques are passed through the clearing house back to the bank on which they are drawn. The bank is then able to adjust each individual's account by a set of book entries; a flow of cash between banks is necessary only if there is a *net* transfer of deposits from the customers of one bank to those of another.

The second main element of the UK banking system is the **discount houses**. These specialized institutions, which are peculiar to the UK, borrow money at call (i.e. repayable on demand) or at very short notice from banks and other lending institutions. They then use this money to purchase such short-dated financial assets as treasury bills and local authority bills. Since they

borrow money that is repayable on demand and lend it out for terms of up to a month or more (as they do when, for example, they buy a treasury bill that has 30 days to run to maturity), they are in the classic exposed position of borrowing short and lending (relatively) long.[1] The advantage to the clearing banks of this arrangement is that they can earn interest on the bulk of their cash reserves. (Loans to the discount houses are repayble at call, and hence are as good as cash.)

The third main element of the banking system is the **central bank**. The central bank was itself a natural outcome of the evolutionary process described earlier in this chapter. Where were the commercial banks to keep their cash reserves? Where were they to turn if they had made good loans and investments that would mature in the future, but were in temporary need of reserves to meet an exceptional demand to withdraw gold by their depositors? If banks provided loans to the public against reasonable security, why should not some other institution provide loans to *them* against the same sort of security? Central banks evolved in response to such needs. At first they were private profit-making institutions, providing services to ordinary banks, but their potential to influence the behaviour of commercial banks, and through them the behaviour of the whole economy, led to the development of close ties with governments. In most European countries these ties eventually became formalized as central banks were taken over by governments.

Almost all advanced countries have central banks, and their functions are similar: to be banker to the government and the commercial banking system, to manage the public debt, to control the money supply and to regulate the country's monetary and credit system. The central bank is always an instrument of the government, whether or not it is owned publicly. The main central bank in the UK is the Bank of England. It is one of the oldest and most famous of the central banks. It began to operate in the

---

[1] The discount houses provide a good example of the division of labour. They are specialists in the short-term money market. Institutions that specialize in other forms of loans do not find it worth their while to acquire detailed knowledge of the short-term market. They lend those funds that they can commit only for short terms to the discount houses who, guided by their specialist knowledge, can lend them profitably.

seventeenth century, but was not officially nationalized until 1947.

Most banking systems also have a variety of other specialized institutions. These are often called **financial intermediaries**, since they stand between those who save money and those who ultimately borrow it. Some of these accept time deposits from the public and lend money out on a longer-term basis. Two British examples are finance houses and building societies. Finance houses grant loans to finance hire-purchase acquisitions of durable goods; building societies grant mortgages for the purchase of real estate.

From our point of view, the most important thing about the banking system is its control of the money supply through the creation and destruction of deposit money. We must now look at this process in a little more detail.

The Creation of Deposit Money

Assume that, in a system with many banks, each bank obtains new deposits in cash. (This, as we shall see, is something that the central bank can engineer.) Say, for example, that the community contains ten banks of equal size and that each receives a new deposit of £100 in cash. Each bank now has on its books the new entries shown in Table 30.1. The banks are on a fractional reserve system and we assume *for purposes of this illustration that they wish to hold 10 per cent reserves against all deposits*. The new deposits put the banks into disequilibrium since they have 100 per cent reserves against all new deposits.

First, assume that only one of the banks begins to expand deposits by making new loans and buying bonds. Now when cheques are written on these deposits, the majority will be deposited in other banks. Thus the bank must expect much of its £100 in cash to be drained away to other banks

---

TABLE 30.1 A New Cash Deposit

Liabilities		Assets	
Deposit	£100	Cash	£100

A new cash deposit has 100 per cent backing.
The balance sheet shows the changes in assets and liabilities resulting from a new cash deposit. Both cash assets and deposit liabilities rise by the same amount.

---

as soon as it creates new deposits for its own customers.

If, for example, one bank has only 10 per cent of the total deposits held by the community, then, on average, 90 per cent of any new deposits it creates will end up in other banks. If other banks are not simultaneously creating new deposits, then this one bank will be severely restricted in its ability to expand deposits. The reason for the restriction is that the bank will suffer a major cash drain as cheques are written payable to individuals who deal with other banks.

One bank in a multibank system cannot produce a large multiple expansion of deposits based on an original accretion of cash, when others banks do not also expand deposits.

Now assume, however, that each bank begins to expand deposits based on the £100 of new reserves. On the one hand, since each bank does one-tenth of the total banking business, 90 per cent of the value of any newly created deposit will find its way into other banks as customers make payments by cheque to the community. This represents a cash drain to these other banks. On the other hand, 10 per cent of the new deposits created by each other bank should find its way into this bank. Thus, if all banks receive new cash, and all start creating deposits simultaneously, no bank should suffer a significant cash drain to any other bank. All banks can go on expanding deposits without losing cash to each other; they need only worry about keeping enough cash to satisfy those depositors who occasionally require cash. Thus the expansion can go on, with each bank watching its own ratio of cash reserves to deposits, expanding deposits as long as the ratio exceeds 1:10 and ceasing when it reaches that figure. Assuming no cash drain to the public, the process will not come to a halt until each bank has created £900 in additional deposits, so that, for each initial £100 cash deposit, there is now £1,000 in deposits backed by £100 in cash. Now *each* of the banks will have new entries in its books similar to those shown in Table 30.2 (where the division between bonds and loans is arbitrary and for purposes of illustration only.)

It might help to think of this process as taking place in a series of hypothetical steps. In the first

TABLE 30.2 Restoration of a 10 per cent Reserve Ratio

Liabilities		Assets	
Deposits	£1,000	Cash	£100
		Loans	£500
		Bonds	£400

With no cash drain, a new cash deposit will support a multiple expansion of deposit liabilities. The Table shows the changes in assets and liabilities when all banks engage in deposit expansion after each has received a new cash deposit of £100. New assets are £900 (divided between loans and bonds) and new deposits are £900. The accretion of £100 in cash now supports £1,000 in deposits, thus restoring the 10 per cent reserve ratio.

period, each bank gets £100 in new deposits and the books of each bank show new entries similar to those in Table 30.1. During the second period, each bank makes loans of £90 expecting that it will suffer a cash drain of £81 on account of these loans. Indeed, 90 per cent of the new loans made by Bank A do find their way into other banks, but 10 per cent of the new loans made by each other bank find their way into Bank A. Thus, there is no net movement of cash among banks. Instead of finding itself with its surplus cash drained away, each bank's books at the end of the day will contain the entries shown in Table 30.3.

TABLE 30.3 Deposit Expansion in Expectation of a Cash Drain

Liabilities		Assets	
Deposits	£190	Cash	£100
		Loans and bonds	£90
	£190		£190

If all banks expand deposits in the expectation of a cash drain, they will end up with excess reserves. The Table shows the position if all banks expand deposits on the basis of each receiving £100 in new cash deposits and in the expectation that 90 per cent of any new deposits will drain out of the bank in a cash flow. The banks obtain new assets of loans and bonds of £90 by creating new deposits of that amount. They expect £81 of these to be withdrawn in cash, leaving them with £19 to provide a 10 per cent reserve against £190 of deposits. Because there is no cash drain, they end up with cash reserves of close to 53 per cent.

Cash is now just over 50 per cent of deposits, instead of only 10 per cent as desired. Thus each bank can continue to expand deposits in order to grant loans and to purchase income-earning assets. As long as all banks do this simultaneously, no bank will suffer any significant cash drain to any other bank, and the process can continue until each bank has created £900 worth of new deposits and then finds itself in the position shown in Table 30.2.

A multibank system creates a multiple increase in deposit money when all banks with excess reserves expand their deposits in step with each other.

A Complication: Cash Drain to the Public

So far we have ignored the fact that the public actually divides its money holdings in a fairly stable proportion between cash and deposits. This means that, when the banking system as a whole creates significant amounts of new deposit money, the whole system will suffer a cash drain as the public withdraws enough cash from the banks to maintain its desired ratio of cash to deposits.

An example: Assume that the public wishes to hold 10 per cent of its money in cash and 90 per cent in the form of cheques. The 90 per cent will stay within the banking system; the other 10 per cent will be withdrawn as cash. This means that, if the banks receive new deposits of £100, the system cannot create as much as £900 of new deposits (assuming a 10 per cent reserve requirement). Banks will begin to expand deposits, but, as they do, they will all suffer a net cash drain. When their reserve ratios fall to 10 per cent of their deposits, their deposit expansion must cease. In the example, the results will be those shown in Table 30.4. The cash drain to the public is £52.63. This yields a ratio of cash held by the public to total money held (cash plus deposits) of $52.63/(473.68 + 52.63) = 0.10$. The banks are left with £47.37 of reserves which provide the necessary 10 per cent backing for deposits of £473.68.

A significant cash drain to the public greatly reduces the expansion of deposit

TABLE 30.4 Deposit Creation with a Cash Drain to the Public

Liabilities		Assets	
Deposits	£473.68	Cash	£47.37
		Loans and bonds	£426.31
	£473.68		£473.68

A cash drain to the public greatly reduces the amount of new deposits that can be created on the basis of a given accretion of cash. The bank has created new deposits of £373.68 and suffered a cash drain of £52.63. The initial £100 of new deposits plus the £373.68 created by the banking system gives £473.68 which is just enough to be sustained by the reserves of £47.37. Thus people are holding their new money in the ratio 1/10 of their new deposits.

money that can be supported by any new deposits accruing to the banking system.

The general case: This argument is easily generalized using simple algebra. Let there be new deposits of £N reaching the banking system. Banks find themselves with reserves and deposits of this amount. When they expand deposits, some of their reserves will be lost as a cash drain, C, to the public and the rest will remain as reserves, R. Thus

$$C + R = N . \qquad (1)$$

Now assume that there is a desired reserve ratio of x. This allows us to write

$$xD = R , \qquad (2)$$

where D is the total deposits that can be sustained as a result of the new deposit of £N. (It is the initial new deposit of £100 plus deposits that the banks themselves create.) Finally, assume that the public wishes to hold a fraction, b, of all its money in cash:

$$C = b(C + D) . \qquad (3)$$

Substituting the second and third equations into the first and solving for D yields:

$$D = \frac{1-b}{b+x-xb} N . \qquad (4)$$

If you substitute into equation (4) a bank's required reserved ratio of 0.10, and a public's desired cash to money ratio of 0.10, and then

substitute back through equations (1) to (3), you will be able to verify the numerical results given in Table 30.4.

Equation (4) shows if the public's desired cash ratio is zero, deposits rise by the reciprocal of the cash reserve ratio. A positive b, however, means that the resulting cash drain lowers the increase in deposits since it reduces the value of the numerator and raises that of the denominator in equation (4).

Kinds of Deposit Money

Customers who have deposits in banks can keep them in one of two forms: either as sight deposits (also called demand or current-account deposits), or as time deposits (savings or deposit accounts). The distinction between the two is commonly made throughout the world, although the terms applied to them vary.

The two main characteristics of **sight** or **demand deposits**, as they are variously called, are first that the owner can withdraw cash on demand, and, second, that the bank agrees to transfer such deposits from one person to another when ordered to do so by the writing of a cheque. The first characteristic makes sight deposits a satisfactory store of value, since they are as good as cash. The second characteristic helps to make sight deposits a medium of exchange. **Time deposits** or **deposit accounts** differ in both of these essential features. The owner of a time deposit must legally give notice of his intention to withdraw cash. Although banks often do not enforce this rule, they could do so. Furthermore, holders of time deposits cannot pay their bills by writing cheques ordering their banks to pay their creditors out of their deposits. Banks always pay a higher rate of interest on time deposits than on sight deposits. (Sight deposits frequently, although not invariably, carry a zero interest rate.)

Banks have recently created a number of new deposit instruments. The most important is the **certificate of deposit (CD)**. With a CD, money is deposited for a fixed period ranging from a month to several years. It earns a higher rate of interest than when deposited in a saving account where in effect the money can be withdrawn at any time. Some CDs are negotiable, others are not.

Evolution of Monetary Instruments

Over the centuries, what has been accepted as money has expanded from gold and silver coins to include, first, banknotes and then bank deposits subject to transfer by cheque. Until recently, most economists would have agreed that money stopped at this point. No such agreement exists today, and an important debate centres around the definition of money that is appropriate to the present world.

If we concentrate only on the medium-of-exchange function, money consists of notes, coins, and deposits subject to transfer by either cheque or by cheque-like instruments such as standing orders to transfer funds from one account to another. No other assets constitute generally accepted media of exchange. The problem of deciding what is money arises because anything that can fulfil the medium-of-exchange function can also fulfil the store-of-value function, but many things that can fulfil the store-of-value function do not fulfil the medium-of-exchange function.

Near money: Anything that fulfils the store-of-value function, and is readily *convertible* into a medium of exchange, but is *not* itself a medium of exchange is called **near money**. As long as all sales and purchases do not occur at the same moment, everyone needs a temporary store of value between the act of selling and the act of buying. Whatever serves the function of a medium of exchange can be held, and thus can also fulfil the function of a temporary store of value. But other assets can also be used for this store-of-value function.

Consider, for example, a deposit account on which cheques cannot be written. With such an account, you know exactly how much purchasing power you hold (at today's prices). Although this deposit is not a medium of exchange it can be turned into a medium of exchange – cash, or a sight deposit – whenever you desire. Additionally, your time deposit will earn interest during the period that you hold it.

Why then does everybody not keep their money in deposit accounts instead of in sight deposits or currency? The answer is that the inconvenience of continually shifting back and forth between sight and time deposits may outweigh the interest that can be earned. One week's interest on £100 at 12 per cent per year is less than 25p, not enough to cover the costs of transferring money needed in a week into an interest-earning account now, and back again next week.

Money substitutes: Near monies are assets that are not themselves media of exchange, but which can be easily converted into such at a secure rate (£1 in a time deposit can always be converted into £1 in a sight deposit). **Money substitutes**, on the other hand, are things that serve as temporary media of exchange but are not stores of value. Credit cards are a good example. With a credit card, many transactions can be made without either cash or a cheque. But the evidence of credit, in terms of the credit slip you sign, is not money because it cannot be used to effect further transactions. Furthermore, when your credit-card company sends you an account, you have to use money to pay that account which is, in effect, a delayed payment for the original transaction. The credit card serves the short-term function of a medium of exchange by allowing you to make purchases even though you have neither cash nor a positive bank balance currently in your possession. But this is only temporary; money remains the final medium of exchange for these transactions when the credit account is settled.

Operational Definitions of Money

What is an acceptable medium of exchange has evolved over time. Furthermore, new monetary assets are continually being developed to serve some of the functions of money, and these 'near monies' are readily convertible into money.

Economists who wish to measure the quantity of money in existence now find it necessary to distinguish several concepts of money. The most important of these in the UK are listed below.[1]

- **M0.** This is notes and coins, plus commercial bank deposits held with the Bank of England (excluding compulsory cash deposits). M0 is also called *high-powered money* or *the monetary base*.

[1] These definitions are taken from 'Measures of Broad Money', *Bank of England Quarterly Bulletin*, Vol. 7, No. 2, May 1987.

- **M1.** This is notes and coins, plus sight deposits of the private sector against which cheques can be drawn.
- **M2.** This is notes and coins, plus non-interest-bearing sight deposits, plus interest-bearing retail bank deposits, plus deposits with Building Societies.
- **M3.** This is M1, plus sterling time deposits of the private sector, plus holdings of bank certificates of deposit.
- **M3c.** This is M3, plus deposits of UK residents held in other currencies such as marks or francs.
- **M4.** This is M3, plus private-sector holdings of building society shares, deposits and sterling certificates of deposit, less building society holdings of bank deposits and bank certificates of deposit and notes and coin.
- **M5.** This is M4, plus holdings by the private sector of bank bills, Treasury bills and local authority deposits, certificates of tax deposit, and national saving instruments.

M0 includes the so-called clearing balances of the commercial banks – which they hold on deposit with the Bank of England to settle day-to-day net cash flows among themselves – plus all notes and coins in the hands of the public. The full importance of M0 can only be understood after we study monetary policy in Chapter 38. The M1 definition concentrates on the medium-of-exchange function of money. The M3 definition also includes time deposits with banks and building societies, which serve the temporary store-of-value function, and are in practice instantly convertible into a medium of exchange at a completely secure price. More and more of these deposits are becoming subject to transfer by cheque as financial institutions change their rules and regulations. As a result, more and more of these are becoming money rather than near money. M3c also includes – in addition to everything included in M3 – deposits held in foreign currencies that can quickly be converted into deposits held in sterling. The growing difference between the size of M3 and M3c is one indication of the degree to which the world's banking system has become internationalized over the past decade or two. (This is further discussed in Box 38.2 on pages 700–701.)

M1 and M2 are often called money, narrowly

defined. M3, M4, and M5 are measures of domestic money broadly defined to include assets that are not media of exchange but which can be easily converted into such media. As the financial system evolves under intense international competition, different measures of broad money are defined, and measured, by the Bank of England. Indeed, some new measures may be in use by the time this passage is being read. The details of such measures are not important at this stage, what matters is to understand that broadly defined money comprises a spectrum of closely related financial assets which their holders regard as highly substitutable for each other. Particular definitions, such as M4 or M5, pick out specific points along that continuous spectrum.

The supply of money: Economists use the terms **supply of money**, and **money supply** and **money stock**, to refer to the total amount of money available in the entire economy (defined in one of the ways just outlined). As we shall see in Chapter 38, the Bank of England has direct control over M0. By deciding how much deposit money to create, the commercial banks exert strong control over any of the broader concepts of money such as M1 or M3. One of the major tools of monetary policy, which we shall study in Chapter 38, seeks to influence the amount of deposit money that commercial banks create.

The nominal and the real money supply: It is also useful to distinguish the nominal from the real money supply. The **nominal money supply** is the money supply measured in monetary units. The **real money supply** is the money supply measured in purchasing-power units and expressed in constant prices – prices that were ruling in some base year. To obtain the real money supply, the nominal money supply is deflated by an index of the general price level.

For example, the nominal supply (as measured by M1) was £10,500 million in 1970 and £50,600 million in 1985. The real money supply, measured in 1970 prices, was £10,500 million in 1970 and £8,000 million in 1985. The latter figure is found by dividing the nominal money supply of £50,600 million by the index of retail prices for 1985 or 430 (1970 = 100) and then multiplying by 100. Thus, although the nominal money supply increased by nearly three and a half times between 1970 and 1985, the real money supply – the purchasing power of the existing money supply – actually fell over the period in question.

MONEY VALUES AND RELATIVE VALUES

Money is our measuring rod in most economic activities. We value our wealth, our incomes, what we buy and what we sell, all in money terms. When we think of a commodity's market value, we usually think of its money price. 'What', we might ask, 'is the value of this refrigerator?' 'It costs £X' might go the reply. 'Is this refrigerator worth more than this sound system?', is another type of value question we frequently ask. Assuming the hi-fi set costs £300, the answer is 'yes' if the refrigerator is priced at more than £300 and 'no' if it is priced at less.

Money prices are our measure of economic value. Money prices allow us to compare different values at any point in time, as with the refrigerator and the hi-fi set. They also allow us to compare values over time – for example, have I saved enough now to finance the holiday I intend to take next summer?

Money as a Veil

One of the great insights of the early economists was that any one money value is not important in itself. The value of money is always relative. A simple money price is meaningless unless it can be compared to the price of something else. What matters, therefore, is *the comparison of two or more money values*.

For example, you might tell a man, newly arrived from Patagonia, that the price of a refrigerator is £300. If he knows no other sterling values, this would convey no useful information to him. But let us say that he entered Britain with £3,000. Now he knows his funds are sufficient to buy 10 refrigerators. He has compared two money values: the market value of the refrigerator and the value of the funds he has brought with him.

But is the £3,000 he has with him a little or a lot? Now he needs to know the prices of all the things he might want to buy, either individually or expressed as an average. Here he is interested in the general purchasing power of his funds. This requires that he relate the amount of his funds to the *general level* of prices.

Consider a further example. How much meat, beer and travel can we buy for a day's wages? Such 'exchange rates' – between the labour that we sell and the goods that we buy – are what determine our living standards. If a worker sells his labour for £40 a day and buys a suit for £120, then what matters is that it costs him three days' work to buy the suit. If he only received £20 a day while a suit only cost him £60, the *real* exchange rate would be unchanged at three days' work to obtain the suit.

Adam Smith, writing in 1776, saw what the above examples illustrate; individual sums of money, and individual money prices, each looked at in isolation, convey no useful information. Instead, the comparison of two or more monetary values is what conveys significant information. Such comparisons allow us to look behind individual money prices to find real opportunity costs: how much of one thing must be given up to obtain a stated amount of something else.

A great insight is involved: value is *relative*; the monetary unit in which values are expressed is irrelevant. If, for example, wheat is worth twice as much as is barley per bushel, it does not matter, as far as their exchange rate is concerned, whether wheat is £2 and barley £1, or wheat £4 and barley £2 or wheat £100 and barley £50. Early economists thus talked of money as a veil behind which real economic relations occurred and were reacted to.

The monetary units in which commodity prices are measured (and the number of zeros on those units) are not relevant to the determination of real values. The only thing that is relevant for real values is the relation between values of different things measured comparably.

The Neutrality of Money

Out of this realization grew the doctrine of the *neutrality of money*. Correctly stated, this doctrine says that the units chosen to measure values have no effect on 'real values' – real values are 'relative values', and it is relative values that affect behaviour.

It follows from the doctrine of the neu-

trality of money that, when *all* monetary values are changed by the same proportion, nothing real happens.

The Real and the Monetary Parts of the Economy

The theory of the neutrality of money leads to a conceptual division of the economy into two parts. In the 'real part', *relative prices*, quantities of output and consumption, and the allocation of resources are all determined by such things as consumers' tastes, production technology, and the degrees of competition among buyers and among sellers. In the monetary part, the *absolute level of prices* is determined by monetary forces.

For example, the real forces of tastes and production possibilities operating through the markets for commodities and for factors of production might determine the relative price of wheat and barley at 1 bushel of wheat = 2 bushels of barley, their outputs at 3 and 5 million tonnes, and the resources of land and labour allocated to each at 1 and 2.5 million hectares, and 10 and 20 thousand person hours respectively. The monetary part of the economy might then set the price level such that either wheat was priced at £4 and barley at £2 a bushel and agricultural wages at £3 an hour, or wheat at £8 and barley at £4 and wages at £6. *Both* of these levels of absolute prices yield the same *price relatives*.

The neutrality of money is most easily seen with a currency reform, which usually follows a runaway inflation that takes the price of the cheapest things into thousands of units of the basic monetary unit. For example, an inflation in the UK that took the price of a box of matches to £100, and raised all other prices in proportion, would have inconvenient results. Useless zeros would be printed on all banknotes and carried in all transactions. By taking an appropriate number of zeros off the prices of all commodities, all factors of production and all contracts, nothing real is changed. The prices of cheap things can be lowered until they are once again only a fraction of the basic monetary unit. After the reform, the price of matches would be measured in pence rather than in hundreds of pounds, and all other prices would be lowered correspondingly. In the case in question, it would be appropriate to take three zeros off all prices. New five-pound notes would be issued which were each worth five thousand old pounds. Everyone's money incomes would be reduced by a factor of 1,000, but so would the money values of all debts, and all other contracts, as well as all money prices. As a result, everyone's real income, and wealth, would be unchanged. No new values would be created, and no existing values would be destroyed. The change would be solely in the 'monetary part' of the economy.

The process of price-level changes: Will changes in the general price level always leave real (relative) values unaffected? The answer is 'yes' when all adjustments have been fully made, but 'no' until then – and 'until then' may be a very long time. To see why, compare a currency reform with a change in the price level that comes about through the normal workings of the market.

A currency reform is carried out overnight by the stroke of a pen, and hence has virtually no real effects – the new long-run equilibrium set of money prices is established instantaneously. All prices, and all wealth holdings, are adjusted by legal decree at the same instant.

In most real-world situations, however, a major change in the price level is spread over a great deal of time – sometimes years, or even decades. Consider a case in which some unexpected disturbance doubles the equilibrium value of the general price level. It may take years for this new price level to be achieved through the operation of market forces. Some prices will adjust quickly, others will take time. At the outset, all existing contracts – wage contracts, mortgages, loans, orders to buy output not yet produced, etc. – will reflect the old price level. New contracts reflecting the new price level will be written as old ones expire. But many contracts last for years, so it will take years for the full adjustment to be completed. Thus, in the process of adjusting the price level, real changes in relative prices occur and, hence, the process of inflation has real effects.

The doctrine of the neutrality of money holds as a long-run equilibrium concept; it does not hold in transitory situations in which the price level is changing.

Relative and absolute prices: The micro-economics which we studied in earlier parts of this book is exclusively concerned with relative prices. Since we assumed that all money prices remain constant, except the one price being studied, all changes in money prices are changes in relative prices. A rise in the money price of a hamburger, for example, also raises its relative price, *if all other prices remain constant*.

Determination of changes in relative prices is a bit more difficult if the general level of prices is rising. Now a rise in the relative price of a hamburger requires that its price rise faster than other prices. Thus the same real forces of demand and supply that would cause the price of a hamburger to rise by 10 per cent in the context of a stable price level will cause its price to rise by 21 per cent if the price level rises by 10 per cent over the same time-period.[1]

THE CLASSICAL QUANTITY THEORY OF MONEY

What then determines the average level of all prices? Early in the history of economics the observations of the effects of currency debasement led economists to hypothesize that the price level is *positively related* to the quantity of money. This hypothesis was formalized in the **quantity theory of money**, which predicts that changes in the price level are proportionate to changes in the quantity of money. Thus, for example, a doubling of the quantity of money would lead to a doubling of the price level.

The demand for money: Before developing the quantity theory of money, we need to define a further concept. The **demand for money** is the amount of money the public wishes to hold as notes and coins and as bank deposits. Like any other demand, the demand for money is an *ex ante* concept – i.e. it tells us how much the public

wishes to hold, which is not necessarily the amount it succeeds in holding. In contrast, the *ex post*, or *realized*, holding of money is the amount the public actually ends up holding. As we have already observed, the *ex post* holdings of money will not necessarily equal the *ex ante* demand. Unlike the demand for goods and services, however, the demand for money is the demand for a stock. People wish to hold a stock of so much money (often called their *money balances*), not to consume so much money each period.

The 'Equation' of Exchange

One way to introduce the quantity theory is through the so-called *equation of exchange* that was made famous by the late American economist Irving Fisher. Although called an equation, it is in fact a definitional identity, which is something which is true simply by virtue of our definition of the terms involved. The 'equation' involves four terms.

Y is real national income, i.e. the physical volume of output.

P is the average level of all prices. (Thus PY is the money value of national income.)

M is the quantity of money, i.e. the supply of money.

V is what is called the **velocity of circulation**, which means the average number of times that the typical unit of money must change hands, in order to accomplish all the sales and purchases involved in producing and selling the national income.

We are already familiar with the concepts of real national income, Y, the price level, P, and money national income, PY. We have also discussed the concept of the supply of money, M, earlier in this chapter. For purposes of this theory, M can be thought of as M1. The only new thing we need to notice about M is that, since every unit of money in existence must be owned, and hence held, by someone – either in the form of cash or a bank balance – we can call M *the total money balances held by the public*.

Only the last term in the above list, V, has not already been discussed in this book. So we must consider it here. First, consider a simple example. Say in an imaginary economy with only

---

[1] Why 21 per cent and not 20 per cent? The intuitive answer is that the relation between the price of a hamburger and all other prices is multiplicative, not additive. Letting h stand for the price of a hamburger, and P for all other prices, the relative price of a hamburger is h/P. Letting period zero be the period before the change in relative prices and year one be the period after the change, we require that: $h_1/P_1 = 1.1\ h_0/P_0$. Rearranging yields $h_1/h_0 = 1.1\ P_1/P_0$. Only if P_1 is equal to P_0 is a 10 percentage point rise in the price of a hamburger called for. If, as in the text, $P_1 = 1.1\ P_0$, then $h_1/h_0 = (1.1)(1.1) = 1.21$.

two £1 notes, there are £4's worth of income-creating transactions. In this case, the velocity of circulation is *two* since the two £1 notes must have been used twice on average to effect £4's worth of transactions. If the value of income-creating transactions rises to £8 in the next period, then the velocity of circulation must have risen to four, if the £2's worth of money is to accomplish £8's worth of transactions. This use of the term velocity, implicitly defines it as PY/M, which is a measure of the average amount of work that a typical £1's worth of money must do to create a money national income of PY.

We can now set out the 'equation' of exchange:

$$MV \equiv PY \ . \tag{1}$$

What this tells us is that the quantity of money multiplied by its velocity of circulation must be identical to the money value of national income. So if, for example, money national income is £10 billion while the quantity of money is £2 billion, then velocity must be 10/2 which is 5. In other words, the average one pound unit of money must have been used five times in income-creating transactions to create £10 billion worth of national income.

Because this relation is a *definitional identity*, it tells us nothing about the real world. It does, however, provide a useful framework for classifying real-world data. When we see national income measured in current prices rise, we can ask how much of this is accounted for by an increase in the quantity of money, and how much by an increase in velocity. For example, if we observe PY to rise by 10 per cent, while M only rises by 5 per cent, then there must also have been a rise in velocity of about 5 per cent.

From the Equation of Exchange to the Quantity Theory of Money

The equation of exchange can be turned from an identity into a theory in two steps. First, we must define V independently of P, Y and M. Second, we must make empirical assumptions about the behaviour of all four variables.

To define V independently of P, Y and M, we first divide (1) through by V to obtain:

$$M \equiv \frac{PY}{V} \ . \tag{2}$$

Now define k as $1/V$ and substitute into (2) for k:

$$M \equiv kPY \ . \tag{3}$$

So far, (3) is still an identity but let us see what k means. We have defined k to be the reciprocal of V. This value tells us the proportion of money national income actually held as money balances in the whole economy, i.e. $k = M/PY$. For example, in the case considered above, PY was £10 while M was £2. This makes k equal to 2/10, which is 0.2. This tells us that the amount of money balances held by everyone in the economy was 1/5th (i.e. 20 per cent) of the money value of national income – which is the same thing as saying that the velocity of circulation of money is 5 in that economy.

What k does is to express the realized or *ex post* quantity of money actually held in the economy in terms of the proportion of PY that people actually hold as money balances. To turn what we have just said into a theory, we redefine k in *planned* or *ex ante* terms. To do this, we define k as the proportion of PY that people *wish* to hold in terms of money balances. We denote the amount of money balances that people wish to hold by M_D and call it the demand for money. According to our new *ex ante* definition of k we can now write:

$$M_D \equiv kPY \ . \tag{4}$$

Equation (4) says that the demand to hold money balances will be some proportion, k, of money national income, PY. To make sure you understand (4), consider an example. Say k is 0.2. This means that the public as a whole wishes to hold an amount of money balances equal to 20 per cent of their income-creating transactions. Now say the money national income is £15m. Then (4) tells us that the public will wish to hold money balances equal in value to £3m. But is there any reason for believing that the demand to hold money balances is related in this way to PY? To answer, we must look at what is called the transactions motive for holding money balances.

The Transactions Motive

We saw earlier in this chapter that money is a medium of exchange. People and firms must hold money balances in the form of cash and bank deposits to facilitate their exchanges. Let us see why such balances need to be held.

First, consider a firm. If that firm's payments and receipts were perfectly synchronized, so that every time it had to pay someone, someone else paid it, the firm would not need to hold transactions balances. But payments and receipts are not perfectly synchronized for any firm. As a result, the firm, like everyone else in the economy, must hold balances of money. When its customers pay, the firm's money balance is increased. When the firm settles its accounts, its money balance is diminished. At times of high receipts, the firm's money balance rises; at times of high payments, its money balance falls.

Similar considerations apply to households. They receive their incomes in periodic payments – usually every week or every month. They hold these receipts as money balances – currency, and, for many, a bank balance as well – in order to finance their payments until the next payday.

We may conclude from the above discussion that, given the way in which payments and receipts are timed, the public – households and firms – need to hold money balances in order to be able to receive money and pay it out according to their needs. The amount of money that the public wishes to hold for these reasons is called the *transactions demand for money*.

On what does the size of this demand depend? The answer is that it mainly depends on the demander's money income. If your income and your expenditures double, you will find yourself holding about twice as much money to finance your purchases between paydays. Similarly, if a firm's business doubles, it will need to hold larger amounts of cash in order to be able to meet its now-doubled volume of payments as they fall due. When we add up this behaviour over all firms and individuals, we find that

the public's transactions demand for money is positively related to the level of national income measured in current prices.

Thus, the demand for money balances, M_D, varies directly with PY. But this is exactly what equation (4) above says. The fraction of their transactions that the public wishes to hold as money balances is given by k.

We shall study the demand for money in greater detail in Chapter 31. All we need to note here is that the transactions motive is the only motive for holding money recognized in the Classical version of the quantity theory.

Other Assumptions

We have now seen the reasoning lying behind equation (4). Next, we outline the other assumptions of the quantity theory.

- The supply of money is an autonomous (i.e. an exogenous) variable. It is determined by the banking system, including the central bank, but it does not vary with P, Y or k.
- k depends on institutional factors, such as the frequency with which payments are made and received.[1] Since these do not vary greatly from one year to the next, k can be taken as a constant except for very long-term analysis.
- P rises when there is excess demand for output, and falls when there is an excess supply.
- Since we are dealing with long-term trends, departures from full-employment income can be ignored. Y will therefore be assumed to be constant at its full-employment, or potential, level.

Note that the last two assumptions represent major departures from the assumptions we have used so far in our study of macroeconomics. Up to now, we have assumed that the price level, P, was constant while real income was variable. In these circumstances, changes in aggregate desired expenditure caused real national income (and employment) to change. These were suitable assumptions for short-run analysis. To study long-run behaviour, however, we reverse these assumptions. We assume that, in the long run, actual national income will be equal to potential income (more precisely, that short-run deviations of actual from potential income can be ignored when studying long-run changes). We also assume, however, that the price level can change – which we know it does do over long periods of time. In these circumstances, variations in aggregate desired expenditure will affect the price level but not real income.

The assumptions set out above are the assump-

[1] For example, if households are paid each Friday and spend their money over the next week, they will hold money balances that average half a week's pay – i.e. about 1 per cent of annual income. If they are paid monthly, and spend their receipts over the month, they will hold money balances that average half a month's pay – i.e. about 4 per cent of annual income.

tions about the variables in the theory. We now need to make some assumptions concerning what happens when the demand to hold money balances is not equal to its supply.

- When the demand for money balances is less than the supply – i.e. the public has excess money balances – an attempt is made to spend the excess on the purchase of current output. In other words, the aggregate desired expenditure curve shifts upward.
- When the demand for money balances is greater than the available supply – i.e. there is a shortage of money balances – the public will attempt to add to its balances by reducing its purchases of current output. In other words, the aggregate desired expenditure curve shifts downward.

Implications

What happens when the demand for money does not equal its supply, i.e. when the public wishes to hold an amount of money balances different from the amount that is available to be held? We have already seen that when there is an excess supply of money balances, aggregate desired expenditure on current output increases. Because Y is fixed at its potential level, the upward shift in the aggregate expenditure curve creates excess demand for output and, according to the assumption just made, the price level rises. As P rises with national income constant at Y_0, PY rises and so, therefore, does the quantity of money that is demanded. (See (4) above.) The price level goes on rising until all the excess money balances are willingly held.

Now consider what happens when there is a shortage of money balances. People try to add to their balances by reducing their expenditure, which means that the aggregate desired expenditure curve shifts downward, creating an excess supply when output is at its potential or full-employment level. But unlike the theory we have considered in earlier chapters, the price level is now assumed to be flexible in a downward direction. Thus Y stays at its full-employment level and the price level, P, falls. As PY falls, less money is demanded to finance the falling value of money income. (See assumption (4) above.) The price level goes on falling until the demand for money balances equals the available supply.

Only when the demand for money balances equals the available supply, so that there is neither a surplus nor a shortage of money balances, will equilibrium be reached and the price level remain stable.

Let us now show what is happening in equation form. Equation (4) above gives the demand for money. Equation (5) below expresses the equilibrium condition just discussed, that the demand for money, M_D, should equal its supply, M^*:

$$M_D = M^* \qquad (5)$$

(M^* stands for the particular amount of money available at one time.) Note that (5) is an equation, not an identity. It does not hold as a matter of definition. Indeed, it only holds in equilibrium. Out of equilibrium, either M_D will exceed M^* – an excess demand for money – or M_D will be less than M^* – an excess supply of money.

Now we substitute the behavioural equation of (4) into the equilibrium condition of (5) to get:

$$kPY = M^* . \qquad (6)$$

Equation (6) expresses the equilibrium condition that the demand for money equals its supply just as does equation (5). The only difference is that (6) contains the relation that determines the demand for money, i.e. kPY.

Next, we divide (6) through by kY to get:

$$P = \frac{M^*}{kY} . \qquad (7)$$

This is the famous equation of the quantity theory of money. In it, both k and Y are assumed to be constant. Although the quantity of money is autonomous (which means it is unaffected by any of the variables in our theory, k, P and Y), it can be changed by the central bank. The equation tells us that the equilibrium price level will be positively related to M. Furthermore, the equation also implies that M^*, and equilibrium P, will vary in direct proportion to each other. For

---

[1] This can be shown as follows. Writing kY as x for simplicity: $P = M/x$. First differencing the equation gives $\Delta P = \Delta M/x$. Now divide through by P to get $\Delta P/P = \Delta M/Px$. Now eliminate the P from the denominator of the right-hand side by using $P = M/x$: $\Delta P/P = \Delta M/x(M/x)$. The x's cancel out to give the required proportionality result: $\Delta P/P = \Delta M/M$.

example, a 10 per cent increase in M^* will cause a 10 per cent increase in P.[1]

Conclusion

These, then, are the predictions of the Classical quantity theory of money – which is sometimes called the naive quantity theory. We shall see that modern theories of the relation between money and the price level are not quite as simple as this one. Most modern quantity theories rely on a more sophisticated version of the quantity theory than the one outlined above. Nonetheless, to understand the theory laid out in this chapter is to understand the fundamentals of the relation between the quantity of money and the price level.

Modern economists continue to accept the Classical insight that the quantity of money and the general level of prices are closely related to each other.

Many more complex and satisfactory theories also predict that changes in the quantity of money cause proportional changes in the price level. Current debate tends to be over the determinants of M and whether M is endogenous or exogenous. Few economists doubt, however, that major changes in M will be associated with major changes in P.

SUMMARY

1. Money functions as a medium of exchange – for which it needs to be acceptable, portable, divisible, and difficult to counterfeit – as a store of value – which works better the more stable is the general price level – as a unit of account and as a standard of deferred payments.
2. Modern notes and coins are fiat money whose value depends on their being legal tender and not on any backing. Deposit money is convertible into, and hence backed by, notes and coins.
3. Because bank deposits are only fractionally backed by the banks' cash reserves, the system as a whole can create many pounds worth of deposits on the base of a single pound of reserves.
4. The money supply is the stock of money in existence at a point in time, and it can be narrowly or broadly defined.
5. The doctrine of the neutrality of money holds that real values are relative values, and these are unaffected by the absolute level of prices. In full equilibrium the price level has no real consequences.
6. The Classical quantity theory of money recognizes only the transactions demand to hold money balances and, assuming this demand function as well as the level of national income to be given, it predicts that any given percentage change in the quantity of money will cause an equal percentage change in the price level.

TOPICS FOR REVIEW

- **The functions and characteristics of money**
- **Fractional backing of money**
- **Convertible and fiat money**
- **Deposit money and its creation by banks**
- **Near money and money substitutes**
- **The real and nominal money supply**

- **Money as a veil**
- **The neutrality of money**
- **The assumptions and predictions of the Classical quantity theory of money**

31

Monetary
Equilibrium

The Classical quantity theory provides a theory of how the price level is determined when real national income is held constant. Earlier chapters showed how real national income is determined if the price level is held constant. A full integration of money into the theory of income determination requires that we allow both income and the price level to be determined simultaneously.

We approach this integration in a series of steps. First, we return to a model in which the price level is held constant and national income varies. By elaborating the theory of the demand for money used in the Classical quantity theory, we are able to integrate monetary forces into the theory of the determination of national income when the price level is given. When this has been done, we can take the last step of making the price level into an endogenously determined variable.

Kinds of Assets

At any moment in time, households have a given stock of wealth. This wealth is held in many forms. Some of it is held as money in the bank or in the wallet; some is held as short-term securities such as certificates of deposit and treasury bills; some is held as long-term bonds; and some as real capital, which may be held directly (in such forms as farms, houses and family businesses) or indirectly (in the form of equities that indicate part ownership of a company's assets).

All these ways of holding wealth may be grouped into three main categories:

- assets that serve as a medium of exchange, that is, paper money, coins and bank chequing deposits;
- other financial assets, such as bonds earning a fixed rate of interest, that will yield a fixed money value at some future *maturity* date; some of these assets, such as deposits in building societies, have a fixed money value at all times, others, such as government bonds, can be converted into currency before their maturity date by selling them at a price that fluctuates on the open market; and
- claims on real capital, that is, physical objects such as factories and machines.

To simplify our discussion, it is helpful to assume that only two kinds of financial assets exist: *money*, which is perfectly liquid but earns no interest, and *bonds*, which are less liquid but earn an interest return. Thus the term *bonds* stands for all interest-earning financial assets plus claims on real capital such as equities.[1]

The Rate of Interest and the Price of Bonds

A bond is a promise to pay a stated sum of money as interest each year, and to repay the face value of the bond at some future 'redemption date', often many years distant. The time until the redemption date is called the **term to maturity**, or, more simply, the **term** of the bond. Some bonds, called perpetuities, pay interest for ever but never repay the principal.

The relationship between interest rates and bond prices was discussed in Chapter 19, pp. 330–331. The key conclusions that are important for present purposes are the following:

> **(1) the price of any bond is positively related to the value of the stream of future payments that its owner will receive;**
> **(2) the rate of interest and bond prices vary inversely with each other;**
> **(3) the closer is the redemption date of a bond, the less will the bond's value change when the interest rate changes.**

A full understanding of the reasoning behind these propositions is important for what follows, so if you are in any doubt about them you should review the earlier discussion now. To recall that reasoning, however, the next paragraphs illustrate these three propositions with numerical illustrations.

Proposition (1): Consider two bonds. Bond A pays £1,000 a year for ever, while bond B pays £2,000 for ever. At a rate of interest of 10 per cent, bond A will be worth £10,000 because that sum invested at 10 per cent will earn £1,000 per annum ($£10,000 \times .10 = £1,000$). At that rate of interest, bond B will be worth £20,000 ($£20,000 \times .10 = £2,000$).

Proposition (2): Let the rate of interest fall from 10 per cent to 5 per cent. Bond A's price will rise to £20,000 because it now takes that sum to

earn £1,000 a year at the interest rate of 5 per cent ($£20,000 \times .05 = £1,000$). Bond B's price rises to £40,000 ($£40,000 \times .05 = £2,000$).

Proposition (3): Bond A pays £1,000 per year for ever and is worth £10,000 now when the interest rate is 10 per cent. Now consider bond C, which pays £1,000 in interest a year from now, but is then redeemable for £10,000 an instant later. Like bond A, bond C will also be worth £10,000 now. (The present value of the £11,000 of interest and repayment of principal that can be gained from holding bond C for a year is $£11,000/1.1 = £10,000$.) If the interest rate does not change, holders of bonds A and C will do equally well over the next year. Now let the interest rate fall to 5 per cent. We have already noted that the value of bond A rises to £20,000. The value of bond C, however, will only rise to £10,416.19. (In a year's time the bond will pay its owner £1,000 in interest and the redemption value of £10,000. At a 5 per cent interest rate, the present value of this £11,000 to be paid a year from now is $£11,000/1.05 = £10,416.19$.) The difference is that bond C pays its face value in one year's time. So the present value of the £10,000 is only discounted for a year. Bond A, however, never repays a lump-sum face value. All it pays is a stream of income which goes on into the indefinite future. So when the interest rate changes, there is a big effect on the present value of those more distant income flows.

MONEY DEMAND AND SUPPLY

The Supply of Money

As used in this chapter, the supply of money is M1: the total quantity of currency plus demand deposits. We saw in the preceding chapter that deposit money is created by banks. We shall see in Chapter 38, how the Bank of England seeks to influence the amount of money created by the commercial banks. In the meantime, we assume that the commercial banks have created all the deposit money that they deem prudent, given their present situation and that the Bank of England does not alter that situation. These assumptions make the quantity of money an exogenous (or autonomous) variable, allowing us

---

[1] This simplification can take us quite a long way. For many problems, however, the simplest satisfactory model has three assets – money, debt (bonds) and real capital (equities).

to see how the economy adjusts to any given money supply. Later we can study changes in the money supply.

The Demand for Money

At any moment in time, everyone has a *given amount of wealth*. By summing this wealth over the whole economy, we can obtain the total stock of wealth in existence. We can think of that wealth being held in a *portfolio* of various assets. The decision on how to divide one's wealth between the various available assets is called a *portfolio balance decision* concerning the allocation of wealth. When people with wealth hold the portfolio of assets that they wish to hold, we say that they are in **portfolio equilibrium** or, as it is sometimes also called, **portfolio balance** or **asset equilibrium**. When wealth-holders have too much of some assets and too few of others in their current portfolios, they are in **portfolio disequilibrium** or **asset disequilibrium**.

The first step in studying portfolio equilibrium is to look at the demand for one particular asset that virtually all wealth-holders hold, money. In Chapter 30 we called the amount of wealth everyone in the economy wishes to hold in the form of money balances the *demand for money*.[1] We now study what determines this demand.

Note first that, because we have grouped all forms of wealth into only two classes called money and bonds, households must hold in the form of bonds that part of their wealth that they do not hold in the form of money. It follows that households have only one decision to make on how to divide their given stock of wealth.

For example, if a group of households having wealth of £5 billion, demand to hold £1 billion worth of money, their demand to hold bonds must be for £4 billion. If the demand for money rises to £2 billion, the demand for bonds must fall to £3 billion. In this case, people will be trying to reduce their holdings of bonds by £1 billion – by selling them on the open market – and increasing their holdings of money by £1 billion – by adding the proceeds of their bond sales to their money holdings. It also follows that, if households are in equilibrium with respect to their money holdings, they must be in equilibrium with respect to their bond holdings. They cannot, for example, feel that their current wealth is held in just the right amount of money and too many bonds. If too much of their wealth is held in bonds, then too little must be held in money, since there is, by definition, no other way in which their wealth can be held.

The Opportunity Cost of Holding Money Balances

There is a cost of holding any money balances: the money could have been used to purchase a bond which would have earned interest.

The opportunity cost of holding money is the return that could have been earned if the money had been used to purchase an income-earning asset.

Thus, money will be held only if it provides services to the holders that are at least as valuable as the opportunity cost of holding it.

If wealth can be held in the form of bonds which earn interest income, why hold it in the form of money which does not? Three reasons for doing so are important. They are called the transactions, the precautionary, and the speculative motives for holding money. We shall see that the first two relate to the function of money as a medium of exchange, while the third relates to the function of money as a store of value.

The Transactions Motive

The first motive for holding money is the one that we studied in the previous chapter in connection with the Classical quantity theory of money. This motive is briefly reviewed below. The amount of money that the public wishes to hold in order to finance their transactions is called their **transactions demand for money**. The need to hold such transactions balances arises because payments and receipts are not exactly synchronized. The transactions demand for money is positively

---

[1] Students sometimes have difficulty with the concept of the demand for money because they fail to appreciate that this demand is unlike the demand for goods and services that we considered earlier in this book. These demands were *flow* demands, describing the amount of some commodity that people wish to buy *in each period of time*. The demand for money describes the demand to hold a given *stock* of money. Once the stock is achieved, no further additions to it, or subtractions from it, will be made – at least until there is a change in one of the conditions that determines the demand for money.

related to the level of national income *measured in current prices*.

In the simple theory that we studied in Chapter 30, the transactions demand for money is proportional to nominal income: $M_D = kPY$ (where the variables are as defined in Chapter 30). It follows that:

the amount of money demanded for transactions purposes is positively associated with both real national income and the general price level.

The only reason for holding money in the Classical quantity theory is the transactions motive, and the resulting demand is related solely to PY. In the rest of this chapter, we go beyond the Classical theory by studying other influences on the transactions motive and also other motives for holding money.

The transactions demand and interest rates: The modern view of the transactions demand for money makes it depend not only on income but also on interest rates. This view was first put forward in two important articles by the American Professors William Baumol and James Tobin.

The Theory. The key to these theories lies in the opportunity cost of holding money balances – i.e. the rate of interest that could be earned if the money was invested in bonds rather than held as money. Because money balances have an opportunity cost, people and firms are motivated to reduce their transactions balances to a minimum. One way this can be done is to make frequent switches between money and other assets.

Consider a man who is paid a salary each month, and who spends all of it in a steady flow of payments over the month. Just after getting paid, his money holdings will equal his monthly salary. After that, his money holdings will steadily diminish as he spends his income, and will reach zero just before he receives his next salary payment.

Throughout the month, he will, therefore, be holding some unspent income. He might choose to hold this as a current-account deposit at his bank. In this case, he will hold, on average over each month (and hence over the year), transactions balances equal to half his monthly salary.

By dividing each month into fortnights, he could, however, keep only half of his salary in money at payday in order to finance the first fortnight's expenses. The other half of his salary he would invest in bonds. Then, at the start of the second fortnight, he would cash in the bonds that he bought on payday and obtain enough cash to finance the second fortnight's expenditure. In this way he reduces his average transactions holding to one-quarter of a month's income (compared to one-half before). At the start of each half of the month he has one-half of a month's income as a balance and at the end of the half he is down to nothing. Hence, he correspondingly increases his average holding of interest-earning assets.

A similar line of argument could be used to show that if the same man made *daily* transfers of funds, he could reduce his transactions balances yet further. But obviously the most profitable arrangement will depend on how much interest can be earned and how costly it is (in terms of such things as time spent making trips to the bank, inconvenience, and the cost of buying and selling assets) to switch assets. The higher the rate of return on interest-earning assets, the greater is the inducement to invest available funds rather than to hold transactions balances. But in order to hold a smaller quantity of transactions balances, an individual must make more frequent switches between money and other assets and thus incur higher total costs over the year. The modern theory of transactions balances predicts that these costs will be less of an inhibition the higher is the rate of interest, and thus that the amount of money held in transactions balances will be lower the higher is the rate of interest.

The Experience of the Late 1970s. Until the late 1970s, the theory of the influence of interest rates on the transactions demand for money remained a relatively unimportant adjunct to the theory that the transactions demand depended on income. Then interest rates soared from rates under 10 per cent to rates well over 20 per cent. At these new, higher rates, it paid firms, especially big ones with large transactions balances, to devote much attention to reducing their balances. After all, if a large firm could reduce its average balances by £1 million over the year, this is an extra £200,000 earned, at a 20 per cent interest rate. That sum would pay the salary of a full-time cash management official and still leave a handsome profit for the firm.

This is what happened on a grand scale in the 1970s with large firms lending out unwanted balances, sometimes for periods of no more than a few hours at a time. As a result, the average transactions balances fell dramatically.

The Precautionary Motive

Uncertainty plays no role in the need for transactions balances. If there is uncertainty about the exact timing of receipts and payments, households and firms may wish to hold additional balances called **precautionary balances**. The motivation is called the **precautionary motive** for holding money. Let us see how it works.

Many goods and services are sold on credit. The seller is uncertain when these goods will be paid for, and the buyer is uncertain of the day of delivery, and thus when payment will fall due. Nor can the buyer be certain of the degree to which his suppliers will be pressing for prompt payment. In order to be able to continue in business during times in which receipts are abnormally low and/or disbursements are abnormally high, firms carry money balances. The larger such balances, the greater the degree of insurance against being unable to pay bills because of some temporary fluctuation in either receipts or disbursements. If the firm is pressed for cash, or has other profitable uses for its funds, it may run down these balances and take the risk of being caught by some temporary fluctuations in receipts and disbursements. How serious this risk is depends on the penalties of being caught without sufficient reserves. A firm is unlikely to be pushed into insolvency. It will, however, incur costs if it is forced to borrow money at high interest rates for short periods to meet temporary shortages of cash. The cost depends on the lines of short-term credit open to the firm.

> **Whereas the transactions demand arises from the certainty of non-synchronization of payments and receipts, the precautionary demand arises from uncertainty about the degree of non-synchronization.**

The precautionary motive arises, therefore, out of stochastic disturbances in the flows of payments and receipts.

The protection provided by any given stock of precautionary balances depends on the degree to which payments and receipts fluctuate and on the value of the payments and receipts. If a firm does only £10,000 worth of business each week, it will need to hold an extra £500 to guard against receipts that are 5 per cent below normal or payments that are 5 per cent above normal. But if the firm does £100,000 worth of business each week, it will need to hold £5,000 to guard against the same percentage fluctuations in its receipts payments. Thus, the firm's demand for money can be expected to rise as its own sales rise. Aggregating over all firms and households, the total precautionary demand for money is found to be positively associated with nominal national income (PY). Firms can also be expected to hold more funds for precautionary purchases, the lower the opportunity cost of holding such funds, as measured by the market rate of interest.

> **The precautionary demand for money is negatively related to the rate of interest and positively related to the level of income.**

The importance of institutions: Both the transactions and the precautionary demands are influenced by institutional arrangements. Consider, for example, a shift from paying workers weekly to paying them fortnightly. Workers who spend all of their incomes evenly over the pay period, will hold money balances equal to a half a week's pay before the change, and one week's pay afterwards. Also the widespread use of credit cards significantly lowers the precautionary need for money. In the past, a traveller would have to carry a substantial precautionary balance in cash, but today her credit card covers her against almost any unforeseen expenses that may arise.

The Speculative Demand for Money

Firms and households will have to sell bonds if a temporary excess of payments over receipts exhausts their current money holdings. (Do not forget that 'bonds' stands for all financial assets other than money.) At one extreme, if a household or firm held all of its wealth in bonds, it would earn interest on all that wealth, but it would have to sell some bonds the first time its payments exceeded its receipts. At the other extreme, if a household or firm held all its wealth in money, the money would earn no interest, but bonds would never have to be sold to meet temporary excesses of payments over current receipts. Wealth-holders usually do not adopt either extreme position; instead, they hold part of their wealth as money and part as bonds.

Households and firms that hold bonds *and* money run the risk that an unexpected gap between their payments and receipts will force them to sell some bonds. Because the price of bonds fluctuates from day to day, the sale may have to be made when the price of bonds is unexpectedly low. Of course, if the household is lucky, the price may be unexpectedly high. Because no one knows in advance which way the price will go, firms and households must accept a risk whenever they hold their wealth in the form of bonds. Because many firms and households are *risk-averse*, they hold more money than they otherwise would, in order to reduce the risk of having to sell bonds in the future at a price that cannot be predicted in advance. (See Chapter 9, pages 149–150, for a discussion of attitudes toward risk.)

The motive that leads firms to hold more money *in reaction to the risks inherent in a fluctuating price of bonds* was first analysed by Keynes, who called it the **speculative motive**. Keynes' theory is discussed in Box 31.1. The modern analysis of this motive, which was sketched in the preceding paragraph, is due to Professor James Tobin of Yale University. Tobin's pioneering work on portfolio selection led to a whole branch of investigation into this and related problems. In 1981 he was awarded the Nobel Prize in economics for his work in this and other related aspects of macroeconomics.

Firms and households tend to insure against the risk of gains and losses by holding some fraction of their wealth in money and the rest in interest-earning assets. Thus the speculative demand for money is positively associated with wealth. For example, household A might elect to hold 5 per cent of its wealth in money and 95 per cent in bonds. If A's wealth is £50,000, its demand for money will be £2,500. If its wealth increases to £60,000, its demand for money will rise to £3,000. Although one household's wealth may rise or fall rapidly, the total wealth of a society changes only slowly. For the analysis of short-term fluctuations in national income, the

effects of changes in wealth are small enough to ignore. (Over the long term, however, variations in wealth have a major influence on money demand.)

The division of wealth between bonds and money is influenced by the cost of holding money. Wealth held in cash earns no interest; hence the reduction in risk involved in holding more money also carries a cost in terms of interest earnings forgone.

The speculative motive leads households and firms to add to their money holdings until the reduction in risk obtained by the last £1 added is just balanced (in the wealth-holder's view) by the cost in terms of the interest forgone on that £1.

Because the cost of holding money balances is the interest that could have been earned if wealth had been held in bonds instead, the demand to hold money is negatively related to the interest rate. When the rate of interest falls, the cost of holding money falls. This leads to more money being held for the speculative motive, to reduce risks associated with fluctuations in the market price of bonds. When the rate of interest rises, the cost of holding money rises. This leads to less money being held for the speculative motive.

The speculative demand for money has its source in uncertainty about future bond prices. It is negatively related to the rate of interest and positively related to wealth.

The Total Demand for Money: Recapitulation

The demand for money is defined as the total amount of money balances that everyone in the economy wishes to hold. The previous discussion about the motives for holding money can be summarized as follows:

(1) *The demand for money depends on institutional arrangements.* People who are paid monthly tend to hold larger transactions balances than people who are paid weekly. The invention of credit cards reduced the amount of precautionary balances that are held.

(2) *The demand for money is positively related to national income valued in current prices.* Both

BOX 31.1 KEYNESIAN THEORY OF THE SPECULATIVE MOTIVE

Keynes' theory of the speculative motive for holding money balances was published in 1936. It refers to the amount of money held over and above what is necessary to satisfy the transactions and precautionary motives. He assumed that each wealth-holder has an *expectation* of the *normal* rate of interest, i.e. the rate that he or she expects to rule, on average, over the near future. Since bond prices are directly related to interest rates, an *expected* rate of interest implies an *expected* price of bonds. Whether the individual will hold his or her wealth in money or bonds depends, according to this theory, on the relation between the *expected* rate of interest and the *actual* rate currently ruling.

To see what behaviour is implied by this theory, assume first that the actual market rate of interest lies below the expected normal rate. This means, using the relation between interest rates and bond prices, that the price of bonds lies above their expected normal price. Wealth-holders could sell bonds now at their high price and hold the proceeds as money, intending to repurchase bonds when their price fell to normal – i.e. when the rate of interest rose to normal. By so doing, they would make a capital gain.

Second, assume that the rate of interest lies above the rate people regard as normal. This means that the price of bonds is below normal. In this case, wealth-holders would use all the money available (above minimum transactions and precautionary needs) to buy bonds. Bonds would be sold to replenish money holdings when the price of bonds rose to normal (the rate of interest fell to normal). This transaction would yield a capital gain.

This theory predicts that individuals will want to hold money rather than bonds when the rate of interest is low relative to their expected normal rate (the price of bonds is high and expected to fall), and bonds rather than money when the rate of interest is high relative to the normal rate (the price of bonds is low and expected to rise).

Key Features of the Keynesian Theory

The Keynesian theory of the speculative demand for money predicts a negative relation between the interest rate and the demand for money. When it was first stated, it was revolutionary. By making the demand for money depend on the interest rate, as well as on income, it broke out of the straight-jacket of the Classical quantity theory of money. The theory does, however, have unsatisfactory features.

• If you are sure bonds are above their normal price, it will pay you to sell all your bonds now and hold only cash. You would then buy bonds again when their price falls back to normal. There would be no reason to hold *any* bonds. Similarly, if you are sure that bonds are below their normal price, it will pay you to put all the money you can spare into bonds now and sell some to replenish your cash balances when bond prices rise back to normal. Thus, on Keynes' explanation, an individual investor would either hold *all* of his or her available wealth in money – or *all* in bonds (over and above the minimum needed for transactions and precautionary purposes).

• In order to explain why *both* money *and* bonds are voluntarily held at any one time in the economy as a whole, Keynesian theory assumes that different people have different expectations about what is the normal rate of interest. Thus, if the current market rate of interest is 9 per cent, all those who believe that the normal rate is above 9 per cent will be holding bonds, while all those who believe that the normal rate is below 9 per cent will be holding money. Thus, over the whole economy, both money and bonds will be held.

Criticisms of the Keynesian Theory

There are two major criticisms that can be levied at the Keynesian theory of the speculative demand for money.

• Individuals are not observed to hold all of their wealth *either* in money *or* in bonds, nor to switch completely from one to the other as the actual rate of interest passes through some critical value (their own expected rate of interest).

• The Keynesian theory does not explain how people form their expectations about the normal rate of interest. Therefore the theory assumes what it sets out to explain; in order to explain the rate of interest it assumes the existence of a normal rate about which the actual rate gravitates. (This is the basis of the famous 'bootstraps' criticism of the theory – that in assuming what it sets out to explain, the theory is like a man who tries to pull himself into the air by pulling on his own bootstraps.)

Although no longer accepted as the theory of the speculative motive for holding money, Keynesian theory was an important advance when it was first put forward. Even today, it is useful for its emphasis on the role played by expectations about the future rate of interest in helping to determine the current demand for money.

transactions and precautionary motives lead to this hypothesis. The higher the level of income, the larger the amount of money needed for transactions purposes and the larger also is the amount required to provide a given level of security against unforseen fluctuations in receipts and payments.

(3) *The demand for money is negatively related to the rate of interest.* The higher the rate of interest, the higher the opportunity cost of holding money, and the less money will be held for transactions and precautionary purposes. The rate of interest also influences the amount of money held for speculative purposes, since the higher the rate of interest, the greater the cost of holding the money balances.

(4) *The demand for money is positively related to wealth.* If households and firms wish to hold some fraction of their wealth in money because of uncertainty over bond prices, the demand for money to hold will rise as wealth rises.

Note that although there are separately identifiable motives for holding money, money is not held in separate accounts labelled transactions, precautionary and speculative accounts. Each firm and household holds one money balance. We have separated the motives for holding these because we wish to understand the size of the balances and why that size changes.

When households and firms decide how much of their monetary assets they will hold as money rather than as bonds, they are said to be exercising their preference for liquidity. **Liquidity preference** thus refers to the demand to hold wealth as money rather than as interest-earning assets. The function that determines the demand to hold money balances is sometimes called the *liquidity preference function*, following Keynes' terminology. More usually today it is called the **money demand function**.

We can now write down the money demand function implied by the previous discussion. In doing so, however, we must be careful to distinguish real from nominal values, a distinction that is basic to much that follows. The reader is urged, therefore, to study the discussion carefully.

First, consider the demand for money *in real terms.* This refers to the number of units of purchasing power that the public wishes to hold

as money balances. In an imaginary one-product, wheat economy, this would be measured in the number of bushels of wheat that could be purchased with the money balances held. In a real economy it could be measured in terms of the number of weeks of national income. For example, the demand for money might be equal to one month's national income, represented by the money balances held by the public. Our previous discussion suggests that the demand for money measured in real, purchasing-power units, is related to the real value of national income, the real value of wealth and the rate of interest.[1] Let M_D stand for *the real demand for money measured in purchasing-power units*, and denote real national income by Y (as usual), the interest rate by r, and the real value of wealth by W. The letter L, which stands for liquidity preference, is used to indicate a functional relation that determines M_D from the values of Y, r and W. The demand for money is now written as follows:

$$M_D = L(Y, r, W) . \qquad (1)$$

This merely summarizes in functional notation what we have already said in words: the real amount of money demanded depends on real national income, the interest rate and the real value of wealth.

Next we determine *the nominal demand for money*. We do this by multiplying (1) through by the price level, P, which makes the nominal demand equal to $PL(Y, r, W)$. Thus the nominal demand for money varies in proportion to the price level, e.g. doubling the price level doubles nominal money demand.

The nominal demand for money is measured as so many million pounds sterling while the real demand is measured in so much purchasing power.

For short-term analysis, we can take the quantity of wealth as a constant, since it changes very

[1] When the price level is changing continuously, it is necessary to distinguish the real from the nominal rate of interest. This distinction will be introduced when it is needed. Right now, however, we are considering equilibrium situations where the price level is constant. There is no need to distinguish these two concepts of the interest rate since they are the same in these circumstances, and are measured by the market rate of interest.

FIGURE 31.1   The Demand for Money

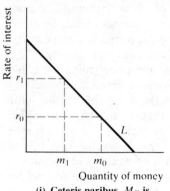
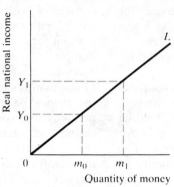
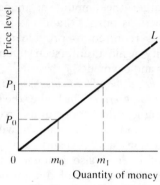

(i) **Ceteris paribus, M_D is negatively related to the rate of interest**

(ii) **Ceteris paribus, M_D is positively related to real national income**

(iii) **Ceteris paribus, M_D is positively related to the price level**

The quantity of money balances people wish to hold is related positively to real national income and the price level, and negatively to the rate of interest. The curve labelled L in part (i) shows the demand for money related to the interest rate, given a constant level of money national income. When the rate of interest is r_0, then m_0 of balances are demanded. When the rate rises to r_1, the money balances that are demanded fall to m_1.

The curve in part (ii) shows the demand for money varying positively with the level of real national income for a given rate of interest and a given price level. The demand for money balances is m_0 at income Y_0 and m_1 at income Y_1.

The curve in part (iii) shows the demand for money varying positively with the price level for given levels of real national income and the rate of interest. At price level P_0, m_0 of money balances are demanded, and at price level P_1, m_1 are demanded.

Compensating Changes: Let the initial values of the interest rate, real national income and the price level be r_0, Y_0 and P_0. Now let income rise to Y_1 with the price level constant at P_0, increasing the quantity of money demanded by $m_1 - m_0$ in part (ii). If the total quantity of money demanded is to remain constant (so that it can be equated to an unchanged supply), the interest rate must rise to r_1, reducing the quantity of money demanded by $m_0 - m_1$ in part (i).

---

slowly. For simplicity we assume the relation to be linear and write[1]

$$M_D = n + dY + er \qquad e < 0 < d, n \qquad (2)$$

We already know that M_D is the real demand for money, Y is real national income and r is the interest rate. We also have two behavioural parameters d and e and a constant n. The sign

restrictions are stated to the right of the equation. The parameter d is *positive*, indicating the fraction of annual income desired to be held in money balances. The parameter e is *negative*, showing how the demand for money responds to changes in the rate of interest.

The relation also contains a positive constant, n. This shows the amount of money demanded at a zero level of national income and a zero interest rate. Anything that increases the demand for money at *each* level of Y and r increases n. Anything that decreases it, lowers n. For example, changes in banking practices that allow firms to economize on transactions balances decrease the quantity of money demanded at each level of Y and r, and so decrease n.

---

[1] In the previous chapters, we have reserved lower-case letters for behavioural parameters. Here we make one exception by using r for the rate of interest, which is an endogenous variable. Consistency would call for the use of R rather than r but the lower-case r for the rate of interest (or sometimes i) is so hallowed by use that it seems better to stick with standard usage by allowing this one departure from our convention concerning lower-case and upper-case letters.

Figure 31.1 shows these three relations graphically:[1]

***Ceteris paribus* the quantity of money demanded is related negatively to the interest rate and positively to real national income and the price level.**

PORTFOLIO BALANCE

Since, in our simple model, there are only two assets in which wealth can be held, there is only one decision to take: how to divide wealth between bonds and money. We will concentrate on the demand to hold money (recognizing that, with given wealth, a demand to hold money implies a demand to hold bonds).[2] To see what is involved in equilibrium between the demand for, and supply of, money it is best to start with disequilibrium situations.

An Excess Demand for Money

If a single firm or household is short of money balances, it can sell some of its bonds and immediately replenish its stock of money. It is not possible, however, for everyone to do this simultaneously if the total stocks of money and bonds are constant. Under these circumstances, attempts to turn bonds into money balances will only succeed in altering the price of bonds. When all firms and households are short of money, they try to sell bonds to replenish their money holdings. This causes the price of bonds to fall which means, of course, a rise in the interest rate. As the interest rate rises, people will economize on cash holdings. Eventually, the rate will rise high enough so that people will no longer be trying to add to their cash balances by selling bonds. The quantity of money demanded will again equal its supply, and, since there will no longer be an excess supply of bonds, the interest rate will stop

rising. The net effect of the original excess demand for money will have been an increase in the rate of interest.

An excess demand for money causes firms and households to try to sell bonds. This raises the interest rate until the quantity of money demanded equals the supply.

An Excess Supply of Money

Now consider a case in which firms and households hold larger money balances than they wish to hold. A single household would purchase bonds with its excess balances. It would thus reach the desired holdings of money by adjusting quantities of money and bonds at given prices. What one household or firm can do, however, all cannot do. When all households and firms enter the bond market and try to purchase bonds with unwanted stocks of money, all they do is to bid up the price of existing bonds (i.e. bid down the rate of interest). As the rate of interest falls, households and firms are willing to hold larger quantities of money. This rise in the price of bonds continues until firms and households stop trying to convert money into bonds. Whereas a single wealth-holder reaches equilibrium by adjusting quantities of money and bonds at fixed prices, the whole society reaches equilibrium by having prices adjust so that people are willing to hold the existing, fixed quantities of money and bonds.

An excess supply of money causes firms and households to try to buy bonds. This lowers the interest rate until the quantity of money demanded equals its supply.

Demand Equals Supply

We have seen that when the supplies of money and bonds are fixed, the rate of interest must vary until people are satisfied to hold bonds and money in their existing proportions, indicating that they are in portfolio balance or asset equilibrium.

When the demand for money is equal to its supply, people are no longer trying to alter their portfolios of bonds and money. The rate of interest is then in equilibrium.

This is the so-called liquidity preference theory of interest. It stresses the role of the rate of

---

[1] Note that, as is usual with demand functions, economists reverse the normal labelling of the axes. The dependent variable, the quantity of money demanded, would be plotted on the vertical axis given normal mathematical conventions, but economic convention dictates that it be plotted on the horizontal axis. (See footnote 1, page 62.)

[2] Since wealth W, can only be held as either money or bonds we have (using B_D to indicate the demand to hold bonds): $M_D + B_D = W$, from which it follows that $B_D = W - M_D$. If we have determined M_D we have also determined B_D.

interest in equating the quantities of money and bonds that wealth-owners wish to hold to the fixed supplies of these assets.[1]

When portfolio balance is obtained, the demand and supply of both money and bonds are in equilibrium. Because emphasis is on monetary forces, this is often described as money-market equilibrium. The term bond market equilibrium would be more descriptive since the real action takes place in a market where people buy and sell bonds. Since they are in fact trading between bonds and money, we can equally think of them as buying or selling bonds in return for money or money in return for bonds. Either way, there is only one portfolio-balance condition, that people should be satisfied with the present division of their wealth between money and bonds.

It is now useful to restate what we have just done using simple algebra. First note that we have assumed the supply of money to be an exogenously determined constant. We use the symbol M_S to denote the money supply, while M^* is some specific value taken by the money supply at some point in time. M^* might for example be £20,000m. We can then write our behavioural assumption about the money supply as:

$$M_S = M^* . \qquad (3)$$

The equilibrium condition is simply that the demand for money should equal its supply. We have, however, defined M_D in real, purchasing-power units and M_S in nominal money units. To equate the two, we need to measure them in comparable units. To do this, we first multiply the real demand for money, which is measured in purchasing-power units, by the price level. This gives us the nominal demand for money which is measured in nominal money units: PM_D.

Let us illustrate this key operation with a numerical example. A simple economy produces only one commodity, wheat. Given its interest rate and price level, its citizens wish to hold money equal in value to 5 per cent of its national income of 200m bushels of wheat per year. This makes the real demand for money equal to 10 million bushels. People wish to hold as money balances the purchasing-power equivalent of that much wheat. If the price of wheat is £4 per bushel, the nominal demand for money is £40m; they wish to hold forty million pounds sterling in money.

To state the equilibrium condition in nominal money terms, we require that the nominal demand for money be equal to the nominal supply:

$$PM_D = M_S . \qquad (4)$$

We can also, however, restate the equilibrium condition in terms of the real demand and supply. To do this, we divide (4) through by P to obtain:

$$M_D = M_S/P . \qquad (5)$$

Equation (5) can be thought of as deflating the nominal money supply by the price level to express it in purchasing-power units, and equating that real money supply to the demand for money also expressed in purchasing-power units.

Equations (4) and (5) are two equivalent ways of stating the single equilibrium condition for portfolio balance, that the demand for money, measured in some appropriate units, should equal the supply of money, measured in the same units.

---

[1] Equilibrium between the demand for money, M_D, and the supply of money, M_S, implies equilibrium between the demand for bonds, B_D, and the supply of bonds, B_S. To see this, we reason as follows. The total quantity of wealth, W, in this two-asset model is the total quantities of bonds, B_S, and money, M_S. These are the supplies available to be held:

$$W = B_S + M_S . \qquad (i)$$

In a two-asset model, there are only two ways in which wealth can be held, so the total demand to hold money, M_D, and the total demand to hold bonds, B_D, must sum to total wealth:

$$W = B_D + M_D . \qquad (ii)$$

Substituting (ii) into (i) yields

$$B_S + M_S = B_D + M_D .$$

Rearranging:

$$B_S - B_D = M_D - M_S .$$

So an excess supply of bonds, $B_S > B_D$, implies an excess demand for money, $M_D > M_S$, and equilibrium between the demand for and supply of either bonds or money implies equilibrium between the demand for and supply of the other asset.

The *LM* Curve

We are now going to take the decisive step by deriving a famous relation called the *LM* curve. This curve is different from all of the curves we have encountered up to now, which have been graphs of behavioural relations or equilibrium conditions. The demand curve, for example, shows how the quantity demanded by households behaves as market price changes, while the aggregate desired expenditure curve shows the behaviour of desired expenditure as national income changes.

The new curve we are going to draw is *a locus of the equilibrium values of a pair of endogenous variables*. That mouthful is merely meant to warn the reader to be on the alert, because we are going to encounter something new. Fortunately, however, the manipulations involved are quite simple. It is the interpretation of the results that is a bit tricky.

We have used the symbol L (which is short for liquidity) to stand for the demand-for-money function in equation (1) above, and M to stand for the quantity of money. (We add an asterisk when we wish to indicate some specific quantity of money.) The LM relation is derived from the equilibrium condition that the demand for money, L, should equal the existing quantity of money, M – hence the name LM. We now need to see how it is derived.

The first step is to take the behavioural equations for the real demand for money from (2) above, and for the real supply of money from (3) above, and substitute them into the equilibrium condition given in equation (5). This gives us:

$$n + dY + er = M^*/P . \qquad (6)$$

Equation (6) merely expresses the condition that the real demand for money, measured in purchasing-power units, should equal the real supply, which is the nominal supply of money divided by the price level. The real demand is expressed in terms of the variables and parameters that determine it $(n + dY + er)$.

What we have just done should have become a familiar technique by now. Over and over again in the last few chapters, we have laid out the behavioural equations of the model and then substituted them into the equilibrium condition. The result is an equation that ensures that the behaviour expressed by the behavioural equations produces values that are consistent with equilibrium.

We are now in a position to derive the LM curve. To do this we merely subtract dY and n from both sides of equation (6) and then divide through by e. This gives us:

$$r = \left(\frac{M^*}{P} - n\right)\left(\frac{1}{e}\right) - \left(\frac{d}{e}\right)Y . \qquad (7)$$

The Mechanics of the LM Curve

Let us first look at equation (7) mechanically. After that, we can interpret the economic behaviour that lies behind it. The equation expresses the equilibrium value of r as a function of the fixed quantity of money, M^*, the price level, P, which we are currently treating as exogenous, the behavioural parameters d, e, and n, and the level of national income, Y. We cannot solve for r because we have one equation and two unknowns, r and Y. What we can do, however, is to find the equilibrium value of r for any *given value* of Y. So the whole LM curve shows the equilibrium value of r that corresponds to each given value of Y. That is why we said earlier that the LM curve is a locus of equilibrium values of the pair of variables Y and r. Pick any value of Y and the equation tells you the equilibrium value of r. The reverse is also true. Pick any value of r, and the equation tells you what the equilibrium value of Y must be.

> **The LM curve is the locus of all Y-r combinations that yield equilibrium between the demand for, and the supply of, money.**

Let us continue with the mechanical interpretation of equation (7), still postponing its economic interpretation. Notice that (7) describes a linear relation between Y and r. The slope of this relation is $-d/e$, and the constant is made up of two terms, the real money supply and the constant on the demand for money, both multiplied by the reciprocal of e, the term that determines the responsiveness of money demand to the rate of interest.

Finally consider the signs of these values. The constant may be either positive or negative since it is the difference between the exogenous money supply M^* and n and the amount of money demanded at zero Y and zero r. The slope coefficient is $-d/e$. The parameter d describes the relation between national income and demand for money, which we know is positive – the higher the level of real national income, the larger the amount of money balances people wish to hold. The parameter e describes the relation

FIGURE 31.2   The *LM* Curve

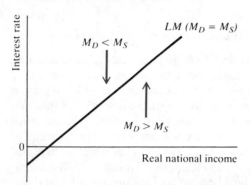

If portfolio equilibrium is to be maintained, a rise in national income must be accompanied by a rise in the interest rate. The *LM* curve plots national income against the rate of interest. It is the locus of *Y-r* combinations where the demand for money equals its supply.

Above the *LM* curve, there is an excess supply of money. The attempt to buy bonds with the excess money holdings raises their price, which means a lowering of interest rates. This pushes the economy back towards the *LM* curve, as shown by the arrow pointing downwards. Below the *LM* curve, there is excess demand for money. The attempt to sell bonds lowers their price, which means a rise in the interest rate. This pushes the economy back towards the *LM* curve, as shown by the arrow pointing upwards.

between the demand for money and the rate of interest, which we know is negative – the lower the rate of interest, the higher the amount of money people wish to hold. Since d is positive and e is negative, d/e is negative. This means that the actual slope coefficient, which is $-d/e$, is positive. So the slope of the *LM* relation is positive. The relation is graphed in Figure 31.2.

Our next step is to understand the economic behaviour that lies behind this curve. This involves nothing new since the *LM* curve embodies behaviour already studied in this chapter.

The Economics of the LM Curve

The *LM* curve graphs all the pairs of values of Y and r that will achieve portfolio equilibrium, i.e. the demand for money equals the supply of money. The critical aspect of the curve is its slope, which we have just shown, by algebraic analysis, to be positive. What is the economic behaviour that lies behind this slope?

The slope of the curve: Consider some combination of national income, Y, and the interest rate, r, that yields equilibrium. Now let national income increase to some higher level. We know that a rise in national income *increases* the quantity of money demanded (see part (ii) of Figure 31.1). But the supply of money is fixed at M^*. So, if the demand for money is to be equated to an unchanged supply, the quantity demanded must be reduced by a rise in the rate of interest.

How does this come about? The rise in national income means that more money is demanded for transactions and precautionary purposes. Firms and households seek to add to their money balances by selling bonds. But the supplies of money and bonds are fixed: so the attempt to sell bonds for money merely drives the price of bonds downwards. This means a rise in the rate of interest. As the rate rises, less money is demanded for speculative purposes. Equilibrium is re-established when the rise in the transactions demand for money, due to the increase in national income, just offsets the fall in demand due to the rise in the rate of interest.

So we now know two things. First, if equilibrium is to be maintained between the demand for money and a fixed supply, a rise in national income must be met by a rise in the interest rate. Second, the mechanism that brings this about is the attempt to sell bonds to add to money holdings which drives the interest rate up. The final part of the caption of Figure 31.1 provides an example of this process.[1]

Points off the curve: We have seen that, along the *LM* curve, the quantity of money demanded equals its (fixed) supply. What happens when the economy is off the *LM* curve to drive it back to that curve? Notice first that on all points below the *LM* curve, the quantity of money demanded exceeds its fixed supply, as indicated on Figure 31.2. To see this, start from any point on the *LM*

---

[1] The compensating nature of these changes can be seen by first differencing equation (6) to obtain $d\Delta Y + e\Delta r = \Delta(M^*/P)$. Since M^* and P are fixed, this yields $d\Delta Y + e\Delta r = 0$; i.e. since the real supply of money is constant, equilibrium requires that the quantity of money demanded does not change. Manipulation then produces $\Delta r/\Delta Y = -d/e$, which is the slope of the *LM* curve. This tells us that to hold M_D equal to the constant M_S, an increase in Y that increases M_D must be balanced by a rise in r that lowers M_D.

curve, and move to a point vertically below it, which lowers the rate of interest, keeping national income constant. If the rate of interest falls, *ceteris paribus*, the quantity of money demanded rises. If we started with portfolio balance, then there must now be an excess demand for money.

At any point below the *LM* curve, the demand for money exceeds the fixed supply.

We have gone over the next step several times. When decision-takers wish to hold more money than they now hold, they seek to sell bonds. This causes the rate of interest to rise. The rate goes on rising, thus reducing the quantity of money people wish to hold, until the excess demand for money has been eliminated. The pressure on interest rates is shown by the upward-pointing arrow in Figure 31.2.

When the economy is at any point below the *LM* curve, market forces cause the interest rate to rise; this pushes the point indicating national income and the interest rate upwards towards the *LM* curve.

Second, let the economy be moved from a point of equilibrium on the *LM* curve to a point above the curve. This means that the rate of interest is increased with national income held constant. Since a *ceteris paribus* rise in the interest rate lowers the quantity of money demanded, there must now be an excess supply of money. Households and firms do not wish to hold all of the money that they are now holding.

At any point above the *LM* curve, the demand for money is less than its fixed supply.

By now you should have no trouble in saying what will happen. When firms and households hold more money than they wish to hold, they seek to buy bonds with the excess. This pushes the price of bonds up (i.e. the rate of interest down) and people want to hold more money as a result. The rate goes on falling, increasing the quantity of money demanded, until the excess supply of money has been eliminated. The pressure on interest rates is shown by the downward-pointing arrow in Figure 31.2.

When the economy is at any point above

the *LM* curve, market forces cause the interest rate to fall; this pushes the point indicating national income and the interest rate downwards towards the *LM* curve.

Everything we have just gone over with the *LM* curve are applications of the general proposition that:

the demand for money, and for bonds, is equated to the fixed supplies of these assets through changes in the price of bonds (the rate of interest).

FIGURE 31.3 A Shift in the *LM* Curve

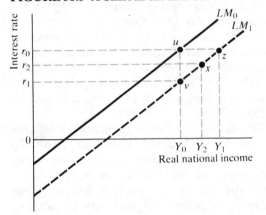

An increase in the real quantity of money shifts the *LM* curve to the right. The original *LM* curve is LM_0. Let the economy be at point *u* with national income of Y_0, and an interest rate of r_0. Now assume that the real quantity of money increases, taking the *LM* curve to LM_1. At *u* there is now excess supply of money. Equilibrium may be restored by an increase in national income to Y_1. This takes the economy to point *z*, and causes the demand for money to expand sufficiently to absorb the increased supply. Equilibrium can also be restored by a reduction in the interest rate to r_1. This takes the economy to point *v* and causes the demand for money to expand sufficiently to absorb the increased supply.

  These are the two changes that throw all of the adjustment onto one of the two variables. Appropriate *combinations* of the changes in the two variables will also do the job. For example, a fall in the interest rate to r_2, and a rise in national income to Y_2, takes the economy to point *x*. This restores portfolio equilibrium by increasing the quantity of money demanded, partly through the rise in income and partly through the fall in the interest rate.

Shifts of the LM Curve

A glance at the equation of the LM curve in (7) above, shows that the only three exogenous variables it contains are the money supply, M, and the price level, P, and the constant term in the demand-for-money function, n. Since M and P appear as a simple ratio, they can be thought of as being a single exogenous variable, the *real* money supply, M/P. What happens to the LM curve if the real money supply changes? Say, for example, that it increases, either because M rises or P falls.

The mechanical result is simple. The constant on the LM curve in equation (7) is $(M/P)(1/e)$, which is negative because e, the response of M_D to a change in r, is negative. Increasing M/P makes the absolute size of the constant larger, i.e. it shifts the LM curve downwards as shown in Figure 31.3. Increasing n has the opposite effect, since n enters the constant with the opposite sign to $M*/P$. So increasing n shifts the LM curve upwards, as shown by the shift from LM_1 to LM_0 in Figure 31.3.

We need to understand the market processes that are at work behind this algebraic result. To see what is involved start at some point on the LM curve, and let either of two events occur. First, the real money supply increases (either because the price level falls, or the nominal quantity of money increases). Second, the demand for money decreases (n falls). Either of these changes create an excess supply of money, and equilibrium can be restored in one of two ways. First, the rate of interest can fall so that people are prepared to hold the increased money supply at an unchanged level of national income. Second, the level of national income can rise. This will absorb the extra money into additional transactions and precautionary balances which will be needed as income rises.

A rightward shift in the LM curve is caused by an increase in the real money supply or a fall in money demand; it creates excess supply of money that can be eliminated by appropriate combinations of reduced interest rates and increased national income.

This important result will be used in later chapters. The reader should fully understand it and then commit it to memory.

A leftward shift in the LM curve is accomplished by a fall in the real money supply or a rise in the real demand, and its effects can be covered briefly. Either of these changes create excess demand for money that can be eliminated by appropriate combinations of increased interest rates and reduced national income, both of which lower the quantity of money demanded.

All we have done so far is to show what combinations of changes in Y and r are needed *if* monetary equilibrium is to be restored. In the next chapter we establish which of the possible Y-r combinations will actually be achieved.[1]

---

[1] For an alternative derivation of the LM curve and analysis of the causes of its shifts, see the Appendix to Chapter 32.

SUMMARY

1. The theory developed in this chapter concerns the allocation of private-sector wealth among the assets in which wealth can be held. It uses the simplest case in which 'money' means M1, and bonds means *all* income-earning assets (both of the debt and the equity type). Existing wealth must be held either in the form of bonds or as money.

2. Each wealth-holder's problem at any point in time is to reach portfolio balance or asset equilibrium by allocating the fixed amount of wealth among the two available assets. For the society, asset equilibrium occurs when all wealth-holders are in portfolio balance. Since the supplies of the wealth-holding assets (and the level of national income) are fixed at any moment in time, equilibrium must be achieved by fluctuations in the price of bonds – which means fluctuations in the interest rate.

3. The *LM* curve indicates those combinations of *Y* and *r* at which all wealth-holders are in portfolio equilibrium; the quantity demanded of each wealth-holding asset is equal to its given supply.
4. The *LM* curve slopes upwards because the demand for money is positively associated with national income and negatively associated with the rate of interest.
5. The *LM* curve is shifted to the right by an increase in the real money supply brought about either by an increase in the nominal money supply, *M*, or a decrease in the price level, *P*, or by a decrease in the demand for money (a fall in *n*). It is shifted to the left by a decrease in the real money supply, or a rise in the demand for money.

TOPICS FOR REVIEW

- **The effect of the yield and the term of a bond, and the rate of interest, on the price of the bond**
- **Motives for holding money**
- **Money demand as a function of the rate of interest, real income and the price level**
- **Portfolio equilibrium and the *LM* curve**
- **The positive slope of the *LM* curve**
- **Points off the *LM* curve**
- **Shifts of the *LM* curve**

32

The *IS–LM* Model

INVESTMENT IN NATIONAL-INCOME THEORY

We have seen how the rate of interest fluctuates to produce asset equilibrium, which means that all decision units are in equilibrium with respect to their holdings of money and bonds. We now come to the critical link between the financial-asset side of the economy and the real expenditure side: not only does the rate of interest influence people's portfolio-balance decisions – i.e. their demands and supplies of money and bonds – it also affects aggregate expenditure. To understand this link, we need to expand our earlier model of the determination of national income. Up to now we have treated investment as an autonomous expenditure flow. In this chapter we make this important component of aggregate expenditure endogenous. First, however, we must take a brief look at the effect of investment on both the demand and the supply side of the economy.

The Effects of Investment

Our theory of income determination is a short-run theory. It takes the economy's technology, supplies of factors of production, and hence potential national income, Y_F, all as given. Fluctuations in aggregate desired expenditure determine the degree to which resources are utilized and hence, also, the size of national income. A rise in investment expenditure increases national income because it increases aggregate expenditure.

In the long run, investment causes the capital stock to increase, and thus causes potential national income to rise.

In the long run, the decisive effect of investment on national income is through its effects on the capital stock, and hence on the size of potential national income. In the short run, the important effect of investment is on aggregate expenditure, hence on the degree to which existing resources are employed, and through that on national income.

The effect of investment on growth of potential national income will be discussed in Chapter 36.

In the meantime, we continue to study investment expenditure as a force influencing aggregate expenditure.

The Financing of Investment

To see the effects of making investment an endogenous variable, we must now look at the financing of investment. In circular-flow models it is common to speak of withdrawals and injections in pairs: imports and exports, government expenditure and government revenue, and saving and investment. This pairing is no accident and, in the case of saving and investment, it reflects the fact that the savings of firms and households are the major source of finance for investment.

If investment is typically financed by savings, what happens if the volume of investment does not equal the volume of saving. If the volume of investment expenditure exceeds the volume of funds currently saved, where does the money come from? Basically, there are three main sources: the money may come from funds accumulated in the past by domestic firms or households, or it may be money *newly created* by the banking system, or it may be borrowed from abroad. Since banks can, within very wide limits, create money, they can lend this money to firms for investment expenditure without there being any corresponding saving of funds on the part of households and firms. The other main possibility is that investment may fall short of saving. In this case the excess savings are added to idle balances held by households and firms, possibly in the form of bank balances.[1]

The Determinants of Investment

For the moment we concentrate on investment by firms, which is the largest single source of investment expenditure.

Profits provide the basic motive determining the investment decisions of private-sector firms.

Firms spend money on new investment, if they expect the investment to yield a profit over all of its costs. The forces that affect these expectations determine the amount of desired investment expenditure in the economy as a whole. We first list them, and then discuss how each influences investment decisions:

- the price and the productivity of capital goods,
- expectations about the future demand for the output of capital goods, and about the costs of producing that output,
- the development of new techniques of production and of new products,
- profits earned by firms and available for reinvestment, and
- the rate of interest.

The Price and Productivity of Capital Goods

The price and the productivity of capital equipment influences the profitability of investment in that equipment. Anything that reduces the price of capital goods will make investment more profitable. For example, if the price of a machine falls from £10,000 to £8,000, the machine is more likely to yield a profit, other things being equal.

Also, any new invention that makes capital equipment more productive will make investment more attractive. For example, if the machine that costs £10,000 can be made to produce a larger output, the income that can be earned by operating it will rise.

Expectations of the Future

Expectations of future demand conditions, and future cost conditions, exert a strong effect on investment decisions.

Expected demand conditions matter because the profitability of any investment depends on being able to sell the output of the capital goods, and to sell it at favourable prices. Current investment expenditure facilitates producing goods for sale in the future. If firms have favourable expectations about the future prices of their products, they will be inclined to invest more in new capital equipment than if they have unfavourable expectations about future prices.

Expected cost conditions also matter because the profits which motivate investment decisions

---

[1] This discussion about behaviour must not be confused with definitional identities. For example, in the two-sector model, realized saving is always equal to realized investment by definition. This definitional relation has no bearing on the issue of where the funds come from if firms succeed in spending on investment a different amount than households lay aside for voluntary saving.

depend on market prices for output, and on the costs of producing that output. When a machine is bought now, the cost of the machine is known now. But the cost of the labour that will operate the machine, and the cost of the materials that will be used over the lifetime of the machine, depend on prices that will rule in the future.

On occasion, these expectations about the future can change dramatically and suddenly – these are what Keynes called the animal spirits of businesspeople – and when they do change, desired investment will also change dramatically. A sudden swing from pessimism to optimism about the future can lead to a large increase in desired investment expenditure, while the opposite swing from optimism to pessimism can lead to a drastic curtailment of investment plans.

Innovations

The world changes constantly and dramatically as new inventions are put into commercial use in a process economists call innovation.

Process innovations: New ways of producing old products are usually embodied in new equipment. New investment is needed to set up these new processes. For example, robotization and the computerized ability to vary the specification of outputs, almost unit by unit, have radically changed assembly-line processes.

Product innovations: Creating the capacity to produce new products requires investment expenditure either to modify existing equipment or to create wholly new equipment.

Profits

Some investment is financed by borrowed funds, but much is financed by the firm's own money. Profits earned on past sales are retained by the firm – i.e. not paid out to its owners – and are re-invested in new capital equipment. Thus, one determinant of investment expenditure is current profits. Higher profits provide a larger flow of funds available for re-investment.

The Rate of Interest

The rate of interest measures the opportunity cost of capital to the firm. If the firm borrows money to spend on investment, it must pay interest to its creditors. If the firm uses its own funds, it must forgo the revenue that it could have obtained by lending those funds to others.

The lower is the rate of interest, the lower is the cost of capital, so the more new investment firms will tend to make. To see this, consider a simple example. Let there be four investment opportunities, each involving spending £100 now and obtaining a single sum one year hence. The most profitable pays £120, the next £115, the next £110, and the least profitable only £105. At interest rates in excess of 20 per cent, none of these four will be profitable. At rates between 15 and 20 per cent, only the first will be profitable. For example, if the rate were 17 per cent, then the £100 could be borrowed at a cost of £17. In a year's time the investment would yield £120, allowing a profit of £3 after repaying the £100 borrowed and paying interest of £17. At rates between 10 and 15 per cent, the two best opportunities will be profitable. A rate below 10 per cent makes the third one profitable, while any rate below 5 per cent makes even the fourth opportunity profitable. Thus, as the rate of interest falls, first one, then two, then three, then all four opportunities become profitable. As this happens, desired investment expenditure rises from £100 to £200 to £300 to £400 on account of these four investment possibilities.

In general:

the lower is the rate of interest, the greater the number of investment opportunities that will be profitable and, therefore, the greater the investment expenditure the firm will wish to make.[1]

We now consider in more detail the influence of interest rates on each of the major categories of investment expenditure.

The rate of interest and investment in capital equipment: If we assume that capital equipment is subject to diminishing returns, then the marginal efficiency of capital, the *MEC*, will be negatively related to the size of the stock of capital, as illustrated in Figure 32.1.[2] The capital

---

[1] Investment in new capital equipment requires committing funds for long periods into the future. The costs of these funds is the cost of borrowing over the term of the investment – i.e. the long-term interest rate.

[2] The marginal efficiency of capital was first introduced in Chapter 19. It relates the rate of return on a marginal unit of capital to the size of the capital stock.

FIGURE 32.1 Investment and the Interest Rate

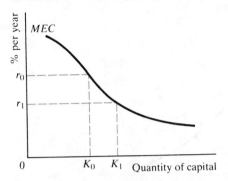

A change in the interest rate causes a change in the desired capital stock and leads to a temporary change in investment expenditure.
The Figure shows the marginal efficiency of capital schedule. The *MEC* curve relates the desired capital stock to the interest rate. A fall in the rate of interest from r_0 to r_1 causes an increase in the desired capital stock from K_0 to K_1. This requires $K_1 - K_0$ of new investment. A rise in the interest rate from r_1 to r_0 lowers the desired capital stock from K_1 to K_0. While the capital stock is depreciating to that level there will be no new investment expenditure.

stock will be of equilibrium size when *MEC* equals the rate of interest. From this it follows that *the equilibrium size of the capital stock* is related negatively to the rate of interest. In particular, a fall in the rate of interest will lead to a rise in the desired capital stock: firms will all wish to add to their capital, which is to say they will wish to engage in positive net investment.

But the timing of new investment depends on how fast the stock of capital is built up to its new desired level. The actual volume of investment in plant and equipment that takes place each year is limited by the capacities of the capital-goods and construction industries.

To illustrate what is involved, assume that, as a result of a fall in the interest rate, firms decide that they want a total of 3,000 new factories in operation next year, but that factories can only be built at the rate of 1,000 a year. It will now take three years before the desired addition to the capital stock is achieved. Next, assume that after one year has passed a rise in the rate of interest decreases the desired overall addition to the capital stock to 2,000 factories instead of 3,000. This new change will have no effect on invest-

ment in 'year two' because the capital-goods industries would still have to work to capacity to create the desired addition. Alternatively, if a fall in interest rates at the end of the first year raised the desired overall addition from 3,000 to 5,000 this, too, would not affect the rate of *current* investment, which is already at its maximum.

The upper limit to annual investment in plant and equipment is set by the capacity of the capital-goods producing industries. Whenever the desired increase in the capital stock is more than can be produced in a year, there will be a backlog of orders. Whenever substantial variations in the interest rate mainly affect order-books, they affect the *duration* of an investment boom generated by changes in desired capital stock, but without necessarily affecting the *amount of investment* in any one year during that boom.[1]

For the reasons outlined above, changes in interest rates are associated with changes in the relation between the existing and the desired capital stock. They often lead to changes in the rate at which the capital stock is growing, i.e. the rate of new investment. But there is no reason in theory to expect a permanent, stable relation between the rate of interest and the amount of investment. The permanent relation, *ceteris paribus*, is between the rate of interest and the stock of capital.

A fall in the rate of interest will lead to spurts of investment in plant and equipment that are temporary.

The rate of interest and investment in stocks: The opportunity cost of holding stocks is what the firm could earn by selling the inventories and investing their value in something else. A measure of this is the interest rate, since the firm could certainly lend out its funds and earn the market rate of interest. A rise in the rate of interest thus raises the cost of holding stocks. This causes firms to reduce their stocks until the

---

[1] This picture is somewhat over-simplified, since it is always possible to increase the rate at which capital goods are being produced by working overtime. This extra capital will usually be produced at higher cost, and so will not be profitable unless there is a particularly urgent demand for new capital. The urgency will depend on the expected profitability of new investment, which will tend to be higher the lower the rate of interest.

advantage of the marginal unit of stocks is just equal to the rate of interest. Thus the desired holding of stocks tends to be negatively related to the rate of interest. But as with physical capital, investment in stocks occurs only when stocks are being changed. Thus,

a fall in the rate of interest usually leads to a temporary spurt of investment in stocks, while a rise usually leads to temporary disinvestment in stocks.

The rate of interest and investment in housing: Interest payments are a large part of total mortgage payments. At an interest rate of 8 per cent, about half of the money paid on a twenty-year mortgage is interest, and only half is for repayment of principal. Because interest is such a large part of the total payments on a mortgage, small changes in the rate of interest cause relatively large changes in annual mortgage payments. For instance, a rise in the rate of interest by two percentage points from 8 to 10 per cent increases the monthly payments on a 20-year mortgage by over 15 per cent (from £8.37 to £9.66 per thousand pounds borrowed). Changes in interest rates can therefore have large effects on the demand for new housing.

A fall in the rate of interest will lead to a temporary spurt of investment in new housing. A rise will reduce the demand for new housing.

The rate of interest and total investment expenditure: Although, for the reasons outlined above, investment does not necessarily bear a precise, permanent relation to the rate of interest, most econometric studies show a significant negative relation between the rate of interest and investment expenditure.

The Investment Demand Function

In what follows, we isolate the relation between investment and the rate of interest by assuming all of the other influences are held constant. This relation is called either the **marginal efficiency of investment (MEI)** or, more simply, the *investment-demand function*. It relates the quantity of desired investment expenditure to the opportunity cost of obtaining investment funds. It is negatively sloped, as shown in Figure 32.2. As with any other demand curve, a change in the

FIGURE 32.2 The Marginal Efficiency of Investment

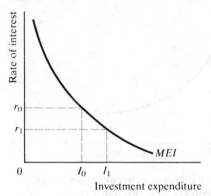

In the short term a fall in the interest rate leads to an increase in the volume of desired investment expenditure. The curve graphs desired investment expenditure against the interest rate and is called either the *marginal efficiency of investment curve* or the *demand curve for investment*. A fall in the rate of interest from r_0 to r_1 leads to a rise in desired investment expenditure from I_0 to I_1.

factors impounded in the *ceteris paribus* clause will shift the investment demand curve.

THE *IS* CURVE

We are now ready to make investment expenditure into an endogenous variable. To do this, we use a general version of the prototype model of income determination laid out in linear form on pages 512–513.

The Prototype Model of Income Determination

The aggregate desired expenditure function is

$$E = A + \mathrm{E}(Y) \tag{1}$$
$$E = Y \tag{2}$$

Equation (1) states that all expenditure is divided into two categories, one that is autonomous, and one that is endogenous, depending on the level of national income. (Recall that $\mathrm{E}(Y)$ is a general functional notation indicating all expenditure flows that vary with national income.)

Equation (2) is the equilibrium condition that

desired expenditure should equal actual income. Given a specific behavioural assumption about how desired expenditure depends on national income, the two equations can be solved simultaneously to determine the equilibrium value of Y, as was done on page 512.

Endogenous Investment

To reflect our new assumption about investment, we must remove that expenditure flow from the category of autonomous expenditure and make it depend instead on the rate of interest. This gives us a new expenditure function:

$$E = A + \mathrm{E}(Y) + \mathrm{I}(r) \ . \qquad (3)$$

The A term stands for all those expenditure flows that are autonomous – they vary with neither Y nor r. The $\mathrm{E}(Y)$ term stands for those expenditure flows that vary with income – this is consumption expenditure in the simple model. The $\mathrm{I}(r)$ term stands for all those expenditure flows that vary with the rate of interest – this is investment in the present model, but it may include other flows in more complex models.

The next step is to make behavioural assumptions about the endogenous expenditure flows. We already have our assumption about consumption, and any other elements that vary with national income:

$$\mathrm{E}(Y) = zY \qquad 0 < z < 1 \qquad (4)$$

Equation (4) states that this component of desired expenditure is positively associated with national income according to the marginal propensity to spend out of national income, z.

The discussion earlier in this chapter tells us that investment is negatively associated with the interest rate. In linear form this is written:

$$\mathrm{I}(r) = a + br \qquad b < 0 < a \qquad (5)$$

The coefficient b will be a large negative number since it tells us the absolute amount that desired investment expenditure changes for each unit change in the interest rate. The positive constant, a, will be a very large positive number showing the amount of investment expenditure if the interest rate were zero.

The next step is to substitute our two behavioural equations into the definition of the expenditure function to obtain the new aggregate

desired expenditure function:

$$E = A + zY + br \ . \qquad (6)$$

Equation (6) summarizes our new assumptions by showing this function as having three components. The first is autonomous expenditure, A, which is desired government expenditure, exports, and the constants in any of the other expenditure functions including the constant a in the investment function.[1] The second is an endogenous component that is positively associated with national income. The third is an endogenous component that is negatively associated with the interest rate.

Our new model consists of two equations. The aggregate desired expenditure function of (6) above, which is repeated below, and the familiar equilibrium condition that aggregate desired expenditure should equal national income:

$$E = A + zY + br \qquad (6)$$

$$E = Y \qquad (2)$$

These two equations refer to expenditure on the economy's flow of output of goods and services – what is called the *expenditure sector* or the *goods sector* of the economy, meaning all final output. This sector is distinguished from the *asset sector* whose equilibrium we studied in the previous chapter.

Derivation of the *IS* Curve

In the previous chapter we derived one famous relation called the *LM* curve. We are now ready to derive a second famous relation, called the *IS* curve.[2] It is derived by substituting the aggregate expenditure function of equation (6) into the

---

[1] Recall the discussion on page 491, showing that we do not have to write out the separate constants in each of the expenditure functions; they are all gathered together in the one constant, A.

[2] Its name derives from the two-sector model where investment is the only injection and saving the only withdrawal. The equilibrium condition is then that saving equals investment. We know that in more general models, the equilibrium condition is that withdrawals equal injections. For this reason the curve would be better named the $W\mathcal{J}$ curve. But the name *IS* is hallowed by decades of usage and we cannot change it now. All that matters is to realize that the name alludes to the condition for national income to be in equilibrium – that withdrawals equal injections, or alternately, that desired expenditure equals actual output.

equilibrium condition given by equation (2), giving a new equation:

$$Y = A^* + zY + br \ . \tag{7}$$

The equation is then rearranged to give the solution for the equilibrium value of r in terms of autonomous expenditure, A^*, the behavioural parameters, z and b, and the other endogenous variable, Y:[1]

$$r = -\left(\frac{A^*}{b}\right) + \left(\frac{1-z}{b}\right)Y \ . \tag{8}$$

This is the equation of the IS curve. It is a type of equation similar to the LM curve. It is a locus of pairs of equilibrium values showing all the combinations of Y and r that yield an equilibrium. This time, however, the equilibrium is in the goods market. (Recall that the LM curve gives combinations of Y-r values that yield equilibrium in the asset market.)

> **The IS relation gives all those combinations of national income, Y, and the rate of interest, r, that make desired expenditure equal to national income.**

Equation (8) can be plotted on a graph showing r on one axis and Y on the other. It gives graphically the same information that (8) gives algebraically: the combinations of Y and r that yield equilibrium in the goods market.

We cannot solve the IS relation for the equilibrium value of Y because it is one equation with two unknowns. If we take the interest rate as exogenous, as we did in Chapters 27 and 29, we can then solve equation (8) for Y. Now that r is endogenous, however, we need to determine Y and r simultaneously. Before we do this, we need to inspect the slope of the IS curve.

The Slope of the IS Curve

Algebraic derivation: Algebraically, it is clear from equation (8) that the IS curve is negatively sloped. The coefficient z is the marginal propensity to spend out of national income. Since it is positive but less than unity, $1 - z$ is also positive. But b, which indicates the effect on

aggregate expenditure of a rise in the interest rate, is negative, so $(1 - z)/b$ is also negative.

Geometric derivation: Figure 32.3 shows a geometric derivation of the IS curve from the familiar 45° diagram. This derivation emphasizes the relation between the aggregate desired expenditure curve and the IS curve. You should follow the Figure through carefully at this point.[1]

Intuitive explanation: The intuitive explanation of the downward slope of the IS curve follows from the fact that the curve shows equilibrium positions where desired expenditure equals national income. Let us start from some combination of Y and r that yields equilibrium. Given the amount of investment expenditure associated with that particular rate of interest, desired aggregate expenditure is equal to national income. Now let there be an increase in national income of some arbitrary amount, which we call ΔY. This moves the economy along the desired expenditure function. Desired expenditure increases, but by less than ΔY (the marginal propensity to spend is less than unity). In order, therefore, to make the higher level of income an equilibrium income, it is necessary to do something to shift the expenditure function upwards. This is done by lowering the rate of interest, shifting the aggregate desired expenditure function upwards until the increased desire to spend due to the fall in the interest rate makes desired expenditure equal to income at the new level of income.

Put more simply, the reason is that *equilibrium* national income can be increased only if the aggregate desired expenditure function shifts upwards, which is done by reducing the interest rate and so raising investment expenditure.

Note that we have not been describing any economic behaviour that will put the economy on one point on the IS curve rather than another. All

---

[1] The steps are: (i) subtract zY, and A, from both sides, (ii) factor out the Y to obtain $Y(1 - z)$, (iii) and then divide through by b.

[1] Notice that we have drawn IS as a curve rather than a straight line. Our algebraic derivation has used linear versions of all the behavioural relations and so the resulting equations are all linear in form. This was only to make the manipulations easy. Usually we expect the relations to be non-linear and we show them as such on the diagrams.

To handle the non-linear version mathematically we would use general functions instead of our specific linear approximations – e.g. $E = \mathrm{E}(Y, r)$ instead of $E = zY + br$. The final result is qualitatively the same, with partial derivatives replacing the constant-slope coefficient in each equation.

FIGURE 32.3 The Derivation of the *IS* Curve From the *AE* Curve

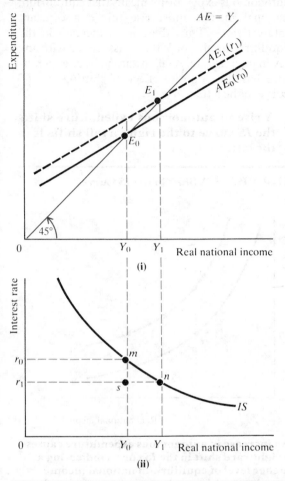

(i)

(ii)

Each point on the *IS* curve plots the rate of interest against the equilibrium level of income that results from the investment expenditure associated with that rate. The two parts of the diagram both plot national income so, by placing them one over the other, the levels of income determined in part (i) can be transferred directly to part (ii).

Let the interest rate be r_0. This gives rise to a given volume of investment, and hence a given aggregate expenditure function in part (i). This is the curve labelled $AE_0(r_0)$, where the term in parentheses reminds us that AE_0 occurs when the interest rate is r_0. Equilibrium income of Y_0 occurs at E_0 where AE_0 intersects the 45° line. Plotting Y_0 against the interest rate of r_0 in part (ii) of the Figure, gives rise to one point on the *IS* curve (labelled *m*).

Now let the interest rate fall to r_1. Investment now increases by the amount shown in Figure 32.2. As a result, the *AE* curve shown in (i) above shifts upwards to $AE_1(r_1)$. Equilibrium is now at E_1, with national income of Y_1. Plotting that level of income against the interest rate r_1 in part (ii), gives rise to a second point on the *IS* curve, this time labelled *n*. Since the *fall* in the interest rate from r_0 to r_1 leads to an *increase* in national income from Y_0 to Y_1, the *IS* curve that plots these two variables against each other has a negative slope.

Repeating the process for each rate of interest traces out the whole *IS* curve.

Point *s* is a point of disequilibrium. At interest rate r_1, and national income Y_0, the aggregate expenditure line $AE_1(r_1)$ in part (i), lies above the 45° line. This indicates that desired expenditure exceeds national income. National income will thus rise.

we know so far is that, given the behaviour of aggregate desired expenditure, the economy can only be in equilibrium if its r-Y combination puts it on the *IS* curve. Given any value of r, there is only one level of Y that will do this. Until we can determine r, we cannot, however, determine Y.

Income-expenditure Disequilibrium

Now let us look at situations off the *IS* curve, i.e. at situations where aggregate desired expenditure does not equal income. If we start from any point on the *IS* curve and then lower income by moving to a point to the left of the curve, actual

income will be less than its equilibrium value. We know from the 45° diagram that desired expenditure exceeds national income whenever actual income is less than equilibrium. Thus forces are at work to raise national income, which implies moving back towards the *IS* curve.

Now, starting once again from a point on the *IS* curve, increase national income, thus moving to some point to the right of the curve. National income is now above its equilibrium value. We know that in this circumstance, desired expenditure is less than actual income, and income will tend to fall. This pushes the economy back towards the *IS* curve.

This argument is illustrated for one point off the *IS* curve in the last paragraph of the caption

FIGURE 32.4 The *IS* Curve and Equilibrium National Income

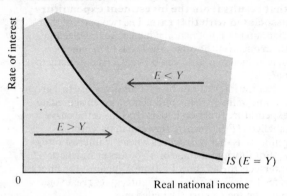

IS (E = Y)

0   Real national income

When the economy is off the *IS* curve, forces operate to push national income in the direction of the curve. As argued in the last paragraph of the caption of Figure 32.3, at any point to the left of the *IS* curve (the light-shaded area), desired expenditure must exceed national income. National income will rise, as shown by the right-pointing arrow. At any point to the right of the *IS* curve (the darker-shaded area), desired expenditure must be less than national income, so national income will tend to fall, as shown by the left-pointing arrow.

to Figure 32.3. It is summarized in Figure 32.4.

Shifts in the *IS* Curve

A glance at equation (8) shows that the only exogenous variable in the *IS* curve is *A*, which stands for the sum of all autonomous components of aggregate expenditure. This includes government expenditure and exports, as well as the constants on the consumption and investment functions (i.e. those parts of consumption and investment expenditure that do not vary with *Y* or *r*). Changing *A* allows us to study the effects of changes in government expenditure, and exports, as well as shifts in the consumption and investment functions. Equation (8) shows that an increase in *A* increases the positive constant in the *IS* curve, thus shifting it to the right, as shown in Figure 32.5. (Although *b* is negative, the negative sign on the whole term converts it into a positive number.)

The economic behaviour that lies behind this shift can be seen by starting at an equilibrium point on the *IS* curve. Now let autonomous

expenditure increase. The initial point is no longer an equilibrium position. The increase in autonomous expenditure means that equilibrium national income must rise (given a constant interest rate). Thus there is an increase in the equilibrium value of *Y* that is associated with any given interest rate. A fall in autonomous expenditure has the opposite effect of shifting the *IS* curve to the left.

> **A rise in autonomous expenditure shifts the *IS* curve to the right; a fall shifts it to the left.**

FIGURE 32.5 A Shift in the *IS* Curve

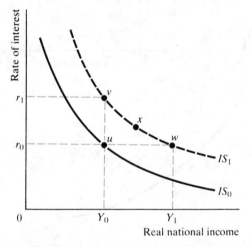

0   Y_0 Y_1

Real national income

An increase in autonomous expenditure causes a rightward shift in the *IS* curve, indicating a higher level of equilibrium national income associated with each interest rate. The initial curve is IS_0. Select some point, say *u*, on that curve. Here the interest rate is r_0 and national income is Y_0. Now let autonomous expenditure increase. This shifts the *IS* curve to IS_1. Starting from *u*, equilibrium can be restored either with the interest rate held constant at r_0 and national income rising to Y_1 (point *w*), or with national income held constant at Y_0, and the interest rate increased to r_1 (point *v*). In this latter case, the rise in *r* reduces aggregate desired expenditure just enough to offset the initial increase in autonomous expenditure. This leaves desired expenditure unchanged at the original level of national income.

These are the cases in which all of the adjustment is taken by either *Y* or *r*. Any suitable combination of changes in *Y* and *r* can also restore equilibrium. For example, a rise in *Y*, and a rise in *r*, that takes the economy to point *x* on IS_1, will restore equilibrium.

THE *IS-LM* MODEL

We have seen that the *IS* curve gives pairs of r-Y values that are consistent with equilibrium in the goods market. We could not, however, determine the equilibrium value of Y and of r because we had only one equation and two endogenous variables. In Chapter 31 we developed the *LM* curve, which gave equilibrium pairs of r-Y values that are consistent with portfolio equilibrium. Again we could not determine the equilibrium values of Y and r because we had only one equation and two endogenous variables. Readers who are at home with school algebra will be way ahead of where we now are. They will have seen that we have two simultaneous equations, the *LM* and the *IS* relations, with two unknowns, Y and r, and that if the two are brought together, they can be solved simultaneously to determine both Y and r.

The Solution of the Model

The *IS* curve shows the combinations of Y and r that give equilibrium in goods markets, while the *LM* curve shows combinations of Y and r that give equilibrium in asset markets. Economy-wide equilibrium occurs when both the goods markets and the asset markets are in equilibrium. To discover this simultaneous equilibrium of the two markets, we bring together the *IS* curve from equation (8) above and the *LM* curve from equation (7) on page 545 of Chapter 31.

A Graphical Solution

We first do this graphically. Figure 32.6 brings

TABLE 32.6 Equilibrium and Disequilibrium in the *IS–LM* Model

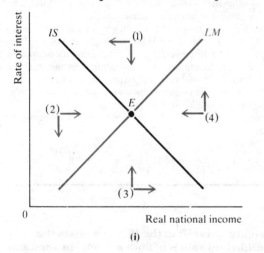

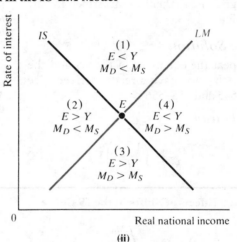

Equilibrium occurs at the intersection of the *IS* and *LM* curves. When the economy is off the two curves, changes in the interest rate and national income push the economy towards the curves. The *IS* and *LM* curves intersect at E which indicates the national income and interest rate at which the goods and asset markets are simultaneously in equilibrium. The two curves divide the Figure into four segments.

The arrows in part (i) of the Figure bring together those shown in Figures 31.2 and 32.4. They show the direction of the pressures on the interest rate and income.

The relations in part (ii) show the disequilibria that give rise to the arrows in part (i). In segment (1), desired expenditure is less than income, so income falls. Also the demand for money is less than its supply, so interest rates fall as well. In segment (2), desired expenditure exceeds income, so income rises. But the demand for money is less than its supply, so interest rates fall. In segment (3), desired expenditure exceeds income, so income rises. Also the demand for money exceeds its supply, so interest rates rise as well. Finally, in segment (4), desired expenditure falls short of income, so income falls. Here, however, the demand for money exceeds its supply so interest rates rise.

together the *IS* curve of Figure 32.4 and the *LM* curve of Figure 31.2.

Equilibrium: Simultaneous equilibrium in the two aggregate markets for goods and assets occurs where the two curves intersect. At that point, and only at that point, are both equilibrium conditions satisfied.

> **The intersection of the *IS* and *LM* curves indicates the unique *Y-r* combination that simultaneously produces goods-market and asset-market equilibrium.**

Disequilibrium: As summarized in Figure 32.6, when the economy is not on its *IS* curve, national income will change, moving the economy towards the *IS* curve. When the economy is not on its *LM* curve, the interest rate will change, moving the economy towards the *LM* curve. These two sets of pressures are shown by the arrows in part (i) of Figure 32.6. The forces that give rise to them are described in part (ii) of the Figure.

Algebraic Solution

We first repeat the equations of the *IS* and the *LM* curves that we have already derived (see pages 544–545 and 555–556):

The IS-LM Model
IS curve:

$$r = -\left(\frac{A^*}{b}\right) + \left(\frac{1-z}{b}\right)Y \qquad (8)$$

LM curve:

$$r = \left(\frac{M^*}{P} - n\right)\left(\frac{1}{e}\right) - \left(\frac{d}{e}\right)Y \qquad (9)$$

To solve these two equations simultaneously, we merely equate them to eliminate r. We then rearrange the equation to get Y on the left-hand side, and all of the exogenous variables and behavioural parameters on the right-hand side. This yields:[1]

$$Y = \left(\frac{1}{(1-z) + bd/e}\right)A^* \qquad (10)$$

$$+ \left(\frac{1}{d + e(1-z)/b}\right)\left(\frac{M^*}{P^*} - n\right)$$

---

[1] Straightforward manipulation of (8) and (9) produces the solution shown in (10). Anyone who can do O-level algebra can do it. Before reading on, try it for yourself. When you succeed, you will have gone a long way towards gaining self-confidence in formal proofs. Here are the steps: (i) eliminate r by equating the RHSs of (8) and (9); (ii) multiply through by be; (iii) gather the two terms containing Y on the LHS and the other terms on the RHS; (iv) factor out the Y to obtain $Y[(1-z)e + bd]$ on the LHS; (v) divide through by the coefficient of Y just given; (vi) clear the e from the numerator of the term containing A by dividing denominator and numerator by e; (vii) clear the b from the numerator of the M^*/P^* term by dividing numerator and denominator by b; this gives you equation (10).

Similar manipulation of (8) and (9) shows the solution for r to be:

$$r = -\left(\frac{1}{b + e(1-z)/d}\right)A^* + \left(\frac{1}{e + db/(1-z)}\right)\left(\frac{M^*}{P} + n\right).$$

FIGURE 32.7 Effects of Shifts in the *IS* Curve

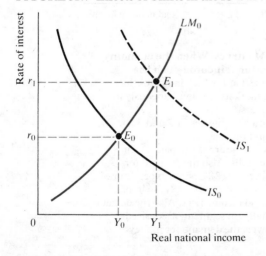

A rightward shift in the *IS* curve raises the equilibrium values of both national income and the interest rate. The initial curves are IS_0 and LM_0, yielding equilibrium at E_0, with values of Y_0 and r_0 for income and the interest rate. An increase in autonomous expenditure now shifts the *IS* curve to IS_1. At the original equilibrium values, there is now an excess of desired expenditure over actual income. This causes income to rise. The rise in income increases the quantity of money demanded, and the excess demand for money forces up the interest rate. At the new equilibrium, E_1, the values for income and interest rate are Y_1 and r_1.

A reduction in autonomous expenditure reverses the process, shifting the *IS* curve from IS_1 to IS_0, which lowers income and interest rate from Y_1 and r_1 to Y_0 and r_0.

Equation (10) expresses the value of Y_0 shown in Figure 32.7 – given all the values of the exogenous variables and behavioural parameters that determine the location of the IS_0 and the LM_0 curves in that Figure. It is an important equation. It is not the ultimate end of a complex analysis, it is instead the point from which some basic analysis begins. It is, therefore, worth spending time to ensure that you understand it.

First, you should follow the algebraic steps that are used to derive it, and which are listed in the footnote. Then you also need to understand the economic behaviour that lies behind it by studying the caption to Figure 32.6 carefully. To those whose algebra is rusty, what we have done will seem like pretty complex stuff. To a mathematician, however, what we have done by way of formal analysis is trivial. The economic behaviour that it describes is, however, quite subtle. Those who are at home with simple algebraic manipulation must be warned against thinking that the economic behaviour that lies behind this equation is as simple as the algebra used to derive it. We repeat – although the algebra is elementary, the economics is subtle.

Comparative Statics

We saw in Figures 32.5 (page 558) and Figure 31.3 (page 547), and their surrounding discussions, that changes in autonomous expenditure shift the IS curve, while changes in the real money supply (M/P) and money demand (n) shift the LM curve. The effects on Y and r of each of these shifts is shown in Figures 32.7 and 32.8. Several conclusions follow from the analysis in these Figures:

> **An increase in autonomous expenditure shifts the IS curve to the right and raises the equilibrium values of both national income and the interest rate. A decrease does the reverse.**

We know from our earlier chapters that an increase in any autonomous expenditure flow increases equilibrium national income. We now also know that it increases the interest rate. The reason is that an increase in national income increases the amount of money that people wish to hold for transactions and precautionary reasons. In an attempt to add to their money

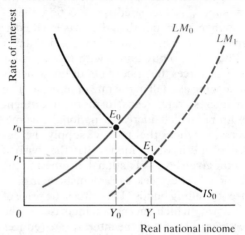

FIGURE 32.8 Effects of Shifts in the LM Curve

A rightward shift in the LM curve increases national income but decreases the interest rate. An increase in the real money supply, or a fall in money demand, shifts the LM curve from LM_0 to LM_1. At the original equilibrium values of Y_0 and r_0, there is now an excess supply of money. Thus market pressures are for r to fall and Y to rise. The new equilibrium is at E_1, with national income and interest rate of Y_1 and r_1.

A reduction in the real money supply, or a rise in money demand, is analysed by letting the LM curve shift from LM_1 to LM_0, thus reducing income from Y_1 to Y_0 and raising the interest rate from r_1 to r_0.

holdings, people seek to sell bonds. But if the stocks of money and bonds are fixed, all they succeed in doing is forcing up the interest rate until they are satisfied with their existing stocks. The rise in income, which increases the amount of money demanded, is just balanced by the rise in interest rates, which decreases the amount of money demanded.

The second main result is:

> **An increase in the real money supply or a reduction in real money demand shifts the LM curve rightward, lowering the equilibrium interest rate, while raising equilibrium national income. A decrease in real money supply or an increase in real money demand does the reverse.**

Do not forget that the real money supply can be changed by either a change in the nominal money supply M or the price level P. For the moment we concentrate on changes in the nominal money supply with the price level constant. When the money supply is increased, people find themselves with more money than they wish to hold at the given level of national income and interest rate. They seek to buy bonds with their surplus funds. This forces the price of bonds up, which is the same thing as a fall in the rate of interest. The fall in interest rates leads to more investment expenditure, which increases national income. Conversely, when the money supply is decreased, people have less money than they wish to hold at the given levels of national income and the interest rate. They seek to replenish their cash balances by selling bonds. This forces the price of bonds down, which means an increase in the interest rate. The rise in the interest rate reduces desired investment, which in turn reduces equilibrium national income.

These two conclusions lead to an interesting result.

Fluctuations in autonomous expenditure flows cause changes in national income and in interest rates to be positively associated with each other, rising and falling together. Fluctuations in the money supply cause changes in national income and changes in the interest rates to be negatively associated with each other, one rising while the other falls.

The Monetary Transmission Mechanism

The shifts in the *LM* curve just studied provide the integration between the monetary and the real side of the economy. The linkage is often referred to as the **monetary transmission mechanism**, which means the transmission of a monetary shock into an effect on real expenditure. The importance of the mechanism makes a further summary statement worthwhile.

The basic linkage is through the interest rate:

Portfolio disequilibrium leads to attempts to buy or sell bonds. These attempts cause the interest rate to change. The change in the interest rate causes desired investment to change, and this in turn alters desired aggregate expenditure. In the new equilibrium, both the interest rate and national income are changed.

The sequence of changes is laid out in Figure 32.9 and only a few additional comments are required. Monetary disequilibrium refers to a state in which the demand for money does not equal its supply. Starting from monetary equilibrium, a disequilibrium can be brought about by a shift in either the supply of, or the demand for, money. The real money supply is increased either by a rise in the nominal money supply or a fall in the price level. This causes an excess supply of money. An excess supply can also be brought about by a fall in the demand for money. Say, for example, that changes in banking practices allow firms to reduce the amount of transactions balances they need to hold. All three of these changes will cause an excess supply of money which sets up an expansionary process that increases equilibrium national income.

The opposite monetary disequilibrium is brought about by a fall in the real money supply (through a fall in *M* or a rise in *P*) or a rise in the demand for money. These changes create excess demand for money, and set in train a contractionary process that reduces equilibrium national income.

One further point to notice is that the link to real expenditure refers to 'interest-sensitive expenditure' rather than just 'investment'. In our model, investment is the only expenditure flow that responds to interest rates. In practice, other flows may also respond. For example, hire-purchase expenditures may fall off when interest rates rise. To allow for such possibilities, the reference is to interest-sensitive expenditures, which, of course, includes investment.[1]

---

[1] This transmission mechanism can now be contrasted with that of the Classical quantity theory of money. In the Classical theory, the transmission mechanism runs directly from a monetary disequilibrium to the goods market. If the people have excess money balances, they seek to spend these directly on goods. If they have a shortage of money balances, they cut down on their purchases of goods in an attempt to add the unspent amounts to their holdings of money. In contrast, the modern theory recognizes that money balances are a part of people's wealth. If people wish to alter these balances, they will substitute among the portfolio of assets that constitute their wealth. In particular, an attempt will be made to buy bonds with excess money balances and to sell bonds to replenish deficient money balances. The transmission of a monetary shock into an expenditure shock operates through the interest rate: widespread attempts to buy or sell bonds affect the interest rate, which in turn affects interest-sensitive expenditures.

FIGURE 32.9 The Monetary Transmission Mechanism

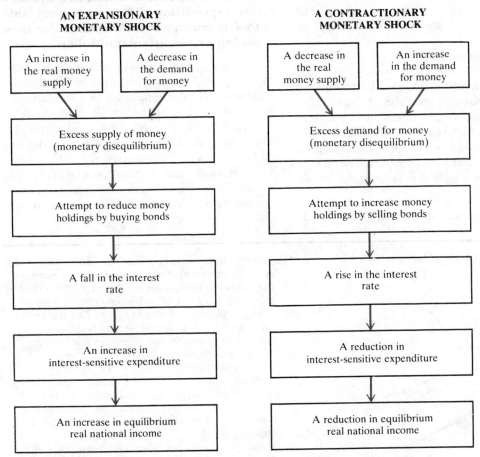

The transmission mechanism causes monetary shocks to be transmitted into real expenditure effects. An expansionary shock arises from either an increase in the real supply of money or a decrease in the real demand for money. Opposite changes cause a contractionary shock. The flow-chart shows how the shock works through asset adjustments, to the interest rate, and to real expenditure flows.

The IS-LM *Multiplier*

In Chapter 29 on page 512 we developed a simple multiplier that took the form[1]

$$\frac{\Delta Y}{\Delta A} = \frac{1}{1-z} = \frac{1}{w} \ . \qquad (11)$$

In these equations, z is the marginal propensity to spend out of national income, and w is the marginal propensity not to spend. This multiplier is often called the *naive multiplier* or, more descriptively, the *interest-constant multiplier*. It tells us how national income changes in response to the sum of marginal propensities to withdraw income from the circular flow. So the simple multiplier given in equation (11) above, can be taken quite generally, as long as z is understood to be the overall propensity to spend out of national income and $1 - z$ is understood to be the overall propensity not to spend, i.e. to leak or withdraw.

---

[1] In Chapter 29, the interest-constant multiplier for the four-sector model was shown to be

$$\frac{1}{1 - z(1 - t) + m} = \frac{1}{s(1 - t) + t + m} \ .$$

The interest-constant multiplier is always the reciprocal of

to a change in autonomous expenditure, on the assumption that the only endogenous variable is national income. (In particular, the interest rate and the price level are treated as exogenous variables.)

In the present model, however, the interest rate is endogenous. This leads to a now-familiar story. When income increases, the amount of money demanded also increases. Given a constant money supply, this forces up the rate of interest. This in turn reduces desired investment expenditure and chokes off some of the expansion that would otherwise have occurred. The reasoning behind this conclusion is laid out in the caption to Figure 32.10.

The interest-constant multiplier is

shown by the horizontal shift in the *IS* curve in response to a shift in autonomous expenditure. The interest-variable *IS-LM* multiplier is always smaller than the interest-constant multiplier.

The term **crowding-out effect** refers to the lowering of desired investment expenditure because a rise in national income is accompanied by a rise in the interest rate; expenditure is 'crowded out' due to the rise in the interest rate that occurs when the quantity of money demanded rises because income rises.

Algebraically the effect is shown by calculating the multiplier for a shift in autonomous expenditure in the *IS-LM* model. This is done by first differencing equation (10), treating M, P and n as

FIGURE 32.10 Various Multipliers

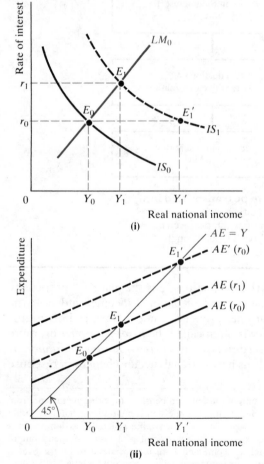

The rise in the interest rate that normally accompanies a rise in national income reduces the value of the multiplier. In part (i), the initial curves are IS_0 and LM_0, which intersect at E_0 to give equilibrium values of Y_0 and r_0. The *IS* curve then shifts to IS_1. If the interest rate had remained constant at r_0, equilibrium income would be at E'_1 with income rising to Y'_1. This is the interest-constant multiplier. The actual new equilibrium, however, is at E_1, with income Y_1 and interest rate r_1. National income rises to Y_1 rather than Y'_1 because the rise in the interest rate from r_0 to r_1 chokes off some investment expenditure. The crowding-out effect is $Y'_1 - Y_1$.

Part (ii) shows what is happening in terms of the 45° diagram. Initially the aggregate expenditure curve is $AE(r_0)$. Equilibrium is at E_0, with income Y_0 and interest rate r_0. Now autonomous expenditure rises, shifting the aggregate expenditure curve to $AE'(r_0)$. If the interest rate remained constant at r_0, equilibrium would shift to E'_1 with income at Y'_1 and the interest rate still at r_0. This is the interest-constant multiplier that was developed in previous chapters. However, the increase in income increases the transactions demand for money, and raises the equilibrium interest rate. The rise in the interest rate lowers desired investment expenditure, which shows up as a downward shift in the AE function to $AE(r_1)$. Thus equilibrium is at E_1 rather than at E'_1. The rise in income is smaller than would occur with a fixed interest rate because the rise in the interest rate from r_0 to r_1 shifts the AE curve downwards.

BOX 32.1 AN EVALUATION OF THE *IS-LM* MODEL

The *IS-LM* model is the simplest model that integrates the monetary-asset side of the economy with the real-expenditure side. There is a strong reaction in some circles against its alleged naivety and crudity. It is worth noting, however, that this model is a prototype version of the demand side of most econometric models. More subtle models allow for much more detail, splitting aggregate expenditure into dozens of components, each with its own determinants, and splitting 'bonds' into many assets, each with its own demand and supply function. Nonetheless, most such models are elaborations on the basic *IS-LM* model, which remains an intellectual prototype, or 'mark I' version of the more detailed expenditure-asset models of the demand side of the economy.

The *IS-LM* model is a pure flow model. Although wealth is in the consumption function, wealth is treated as a constant. Also the portfolio equilibrium, on which the *LM* curve is based, equates the demand for money and bonds with the *fixed* quantities of each of these assets that exist at a given moment in time. Changes in the quantities of money or bonds are *exogenous* changes causing once-and-for-all shifts in the *LM* curve.

We know, however, that stocks of both real capital and monetary assets are changing endogenously. Saving means that people are adding to their stocks of assets to be held in either money or bonds. Investment means that the physical stock of capital is rising. The financing of this investment provides the new bonds that people must add to their asset stocks. The new capital itself increases the size of potential income.

The *IS-LM* model is short-run in the sense that it treats as constant, variables that are in fact changing endogenously. The usefulness of the model depends on the possibility that changes in the stocks of assets are small enough to be ignored over the period of time being studied. For many short-term studies of variations in the economy from one year to the next, this may be an accept-

able assumption. For other longer-term problems, it clearly is not. In the long term, changes in the stocks of assets will have important effects on the behaviour of the model. Allowance must then be made for changes in stocks.

At the opposite extreme from a pure flow model, is a stock equilibrium model. This is one in which all stock variables are allowed to reach their equilibrium values – i.e. they are not changing in equilibrium. Comparative-static analysis then consists of introducing some disturbance and studying the changes between two positions of stock equilibrium. Although some interesting insights can be gained from such models, they are even further from reality than are pure flow models. Allowing the stock of capital to reach to an equilibrium level implies studying what the Classical economists called the 'stationary state', with *no* capital accumulation, and *no* net saving and hence *no* growth of national income.

The moral is that one must be careful about using any form of *IS-LM* model to study the economy over time-spans in which changes in the stock of 'bonds' and real capital exert significant effects on the equilibrium. One must also be careful, however, about drawing conclusions from models where all stocks are at equilibrium levels.

An alternative type of model studies economies that are on equilibrium growth paths. This means that all relevant variables are *changing* at constant or 'equilibrium' rates. For example, the supplies of all factors of production, and the size of potential national income, might be all growing at 3 per cent per year. The equilibrium can then be disturbed by some shift, and the model studied as it moves to some new equilibrium of steady growth path. Equilibrium growth models shed some light on economic problems but they are also far from reality since they typically assume technology to be given, whereas the effects of technological changes dominate longer-run behaviour, moving the economy from one growth path to another.

constants and dividing through by ΔA to obtain:[1]

$$\frac{\Delta Y}{\Delta A} = \frac{1}{(1-z)+bd/e} \ . \qquad (12)$$

---

[1] Equation (10) is in two parts. The first term relates to A and the second term to $M/P - n$. Since we wish to hold $M/P - n$ constant, the second term is a constant and disappears when we take first differences. The result is then $\Delta Y = z\Delta A$, where z stands for the term attached to A in equation (10). Dividing through by ΔA produces $\Delta Y/\Delta A = z$, which is equation (12) in the text.

Equation (12) is the *IS-LM, interest-variable multiplier*. To understand it, assume first that investment is totally insensitive to interest rates, which means $b = 0$. The multiplier then becomes $1/(1-z)$, which is the interest-constant multiplier. This confirms that, if expenditure is completely insensitive to interest rates (or if interest rates do not change), the interest-constant multiplier gives correct results. If, however, expenditure does respond to interest rates then b takes on a negative value. The term bd/e is then operative;

it is called the *crowding-out term*. Since *d* and *e*, the responses of the demand for money to income, and to interest rates, are respectively positive and negative, the whole term *bd/e* is positive. The term thus has the effect of increasing the value of the denominator in (12). This reduces the value of the whole expression. *The crowding-out term lowers the value of the multiplier.* The larger is this effect, the less is the increase in national income brought about by any given increase in autonomous expenditure.

The Crowding-out of Private-sector Expenditure

Assume that the government increases its public-sector investment programme in an attempt to expand the economy back toward full employment. If interest rates remain constant, the rise in income will be made up of the initial increase in autonomous expenditure, ΔA, and an induced increase in expenditure as given by the reciprocal marginal propensity to leak.

Under normal circumstances, however, interest rates will rise as national income rises. This will crowd out some private investment expenditure, offsetting some of the expansionary effect of the initial increase in income. Thus:

although the expansionary fiscal policy does succeed in increasing total expenditure and total national income, it also leads to the crowding-out of some private expenditure – i.e. some private expenditure is replaced by some public expenditure.

This change in the balance between private- and public-sector investment expenditure is an inevitable side-effect of increased government expenditure designed to remove a recessionary gap.

This completes our integration of money and interest rates into the circular-flow model of national income. We are now equipped to investigate the effects of shifts in exogenous variables on the equilibrium level of national income and the interest rate. Some of this has already been done in this chapter; more will be done later. Our next step, however, is to make the price level into an endogenous variable. In the meantime Box 32.1 discusses some points concerning an evaluation of the *IS-LM* model.

SUMMARY

1. The long-run effects of investment work on the supply side, increasing potential national income; the short-run effects work on the demand side, increasing aggregate desired expenditure.
2. Many factors influence investment. One of these is the interest rate, which is negatively related to investment.
3. The *IS* curve shows all the combinations of real national income and the interest rate that yield equilibrium in the goods market – i.e. for which desired aggregate expenditure equals actual national income (output). It is negatively sloped because a fall in the interest rate increases interest-sensitive expenditure and so increases equilibrium national income.
4. The *IS-LM* model shows the combinations of real national income and interest rate that produce simultaneous equilibrium in both goods and asset markets. Geometrically it is the intersection of the *IS* and *LM* curves. Algebraically it is the simultaneous-equation solution of the equilibrium conditions for the goods and the asset markets.
5. The *IS-LM* model makes the interest rate an endogenous variable and predicts that when expenditure shocks are the cause, national income and interest rates will vary in opposite directions, while when monetary shocks are the cause, income and interest rates will vary in the same direction.

6. The *IS-LM* model explains the crowding-out effect: any expansionary shock will cause interest rates to rise, reducing interest-sensitive expenditure and hence damping the expansionary effects of the initial shock.

7. An implication of the crowding-out effect is that an increase in government expenditure designed to move the economy towards its potential income will cause a shift in total expenditure away from the private sector and towards the public sector.

8. The workings of the model under the impact of monetary shocks are explained by the transmission mechanism. A monetary shock that creates excess supply of money forces the interest rate down, increasing interest-sensitive expenditure and hence increasing equilibrium national income. A monetary shock that creates excess demand for money has the opposite effects.

TOPICS FOR REVIEW

- The effects of investment in the short and the long run
- The determinants of investment
- The effects of changes in interest rates on the desired stock of capital and the quantity of investment
- The *IS* curve as a locus of equilibrium values
- Why the *IS* curve has a negative slope
- The *IS-LM* equilibrium
- Causes and consequences of shifts in the *IS* and the *LM* curves
- The crowding-out effect

APPENDIX to Chapter 32

An Alternative Derivation of the *LM* and *IS* Curves

In Chapters 31 and 32 we derived the *LM* and *IS* curves using algebra, words and simple geometry. In many ways the simple algebraic derivation is most satisfactory. Many students, however, feel much more at home with geometry than with algebra. This Appendix is designed for those who would like to see a more detailed geometric derivation where every individual relation that lies behind the *LM* and *IS* curves is displayed on its own graph. Those who are fully satisfied with the textual material in Chapters 31 and 32 can either skip this Appendix or read it as a check on their understanding. Deep economic understanding takes a long time to develop, and the more times one goes through a given argument from different approaches, the greater one's understanding becomes.

The *LM* Curve

Derivation

To derive the *LM* (and the *IS*) curves geometrically we start by introducing the so-called four-quadrant diagram. This diagram measures positive quantities in four different directions from a common origin. The advantage is that four different but linked relations can be shown on the one diagram. The disadvantage is that you have to get used to seeing some relations upside down and/or back to front from the way they are displayed on the usual graph. For reference, we label the four quadrants geographically: SE (bottom right), SW (bottom left), NW (top left) and NE (top right).

Figure 32A.1(i) shows the derivation of the *LM* curve. Our text discussion shows the demand for money depends on income and the rate of interest. These relations are depicted by the line $M_D(Y)$ in the SE quadrant, which shows the demand rising as Y rises, and by the line $M_D(r)$ in the NW quadrant, which shows the demand falling as r rises.

The line labelled 45° in the SW quadrant shows the equilibrium condition that the total demand for money (measured in real terms) should equal the real money supply M^*/P. The given real supply is measured along the two axes labelled M/P. Because these two distances are the same, the line joining the two M^*/P points has a slope of 45°. It is a characteristic of this line that any point on it represents two M/P values that sum to M^*/P.

Now, to derive the *LM* curve, start with any arbitrarily chosen level of real national income, say Y_1. The quantity of money demanded as a result of Y_1 is m_a. The 45° line in the SW quadrant then tells us that if the total demand for money is to equal its supply of M^*/P, then m_b must be demanded in addition to m_a. This occurs, according to the relation in the NW quadrant, if the interest rate is r_1. Now Y_1 and r_1 are projected into the NE quadrant to obtain the point x on the *LM* curve.

Next, pick another level of income, say Y_2. The transactions demand for money, given Y_2, is now m_e. This means that to maintain equality of M_D and M_S a further m_d must be demanded. This in turn requires an interest rate of r_2. Extending Y_2 and r_2 into the NE quadrant yields a second point, z, on the *LM* curve.

FIGURE 32A.1 A Four-quadrant Interpretation of the *LM* Curve

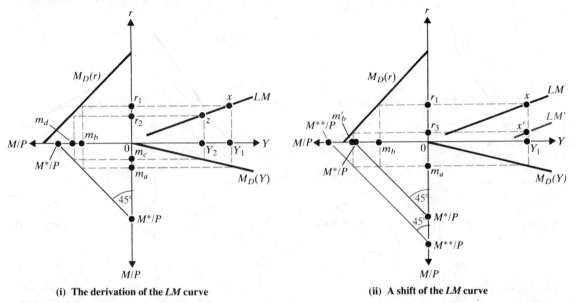

(i) The derivation of the *LM* curve

(ii) A shift of the *LM* curve

If the procedure is repeated for every level of Y, the results plot out an upward-sloping LM curve in part (i) of the Figure. All we have done is to lay out geometrically the two relations that the demand for money varies positively with Y and negatively with r, and to show that if the quantity of money demanded is to equal a fixed supply, Y and r must vary directly with each other (an increase in Y raising quantity demanded and an increase in r lowering it).

Shifts in the LM curve

Figure 32A.1(ii) repeats the curves from 32A.1(i) and repeats the derivation of the point x on the LM curve. Now let the real money supply increase, either because M increases or P falls. To be specific, assume that the nominal money supply increases from M^* to M^{**}. This shifts the 45° line in the SW quadrant outwards to its new intercepts on each axis of M^{**}/P. Now consider how to equate the demand for money with the newly increased supply at a level of income of Y_1. Following around the quadrants, we see that the original level of income is still associated with a transactions demand for money of m_a. With the larger supply of money, however, equality of M_D and M_S required that a further amount m'_b now

be demanded. This in turn requires a fall in the interest rate to r_3.

Now plotting Y_1 against r_3 yields the point x' on the new LM curve, LM'. What we have shown is that since the quantity of money demanded varies positively with Y and negatively with r, a rise in the supply of money requires, to restore the equality of demand and supply, a fall in the equilibrium rate of interest associated with each given level of national income.

The downward shift in the LM curve in Figure 32A.1(ii) can be caused by a decrease in the amount of money demanded at each level of income or by a decrease in the amount demanded at each rate of interest. Readers can now work out for themselves the various possible shifts in the LM curve caused by various possible shifts in the behavioural relations which relate the quantity of money demanded to Y and r.

The *IS* Curve

Derivation

Figure 32A.2(i) shows the derivation of the IS curve. The diagram is now familiar and the techniques used are similar.

The graphical derivation is simpler, however,

FIGURE 32A.2 A Four-quadrant Interpretation of the *IS* Curve

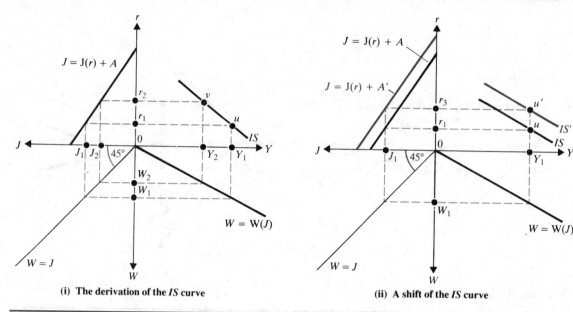

(i) **The derivation of the *IS* curve**   (ii) **A shift of the *IS* curve**

if we use the $W = J$ version rather than the $E = Y$ version, which we have learned are identical in any case. The *IS* curve in Chapter 32 is derived for the simple case of one injection, I, and one withdrawal, S. In more complex models, withdrawals are savings, taxes and imports, while injections are investment, government expenditure and exports. All that matters, however, is that withdrawals depend on income, so we write $W = W(Y)$, and that injections depend partly on the rate of interest and are partly autonomous, so we write $J = J(r) + A$.

The withdrawals-injections version of the model is shown in Figure 32A.2(i). In the SE quadrant we have the withdrawals function, relating withdrawals positively to income. In the NW quadrant we have the injections function, relating injections negatively to the rate of interest and also showing the exogenous component, A. The SW quadrant shows the equilibrium condition that withdrawals should equal injections. This is the familiar 45° line, only it now goes off to the SW because of the quadrant in which it is plotted.

To construct the *IS* curve, pick an arbitrary level of income, Y_1. The withdrawals function tells us that, for this level of income, withdrawals are W_1. Following around through the equilib-

rium condition in the SW quadrant tells us that this requires an interest rate of r_1. Plotting Y_1 against r_1 in the NE quadrant yields the point u on the *IS* curve.

Now pick a different level of income, say Y_2. This yields W_2 of withdrawals and, if injections are to equal withdrawals at J_2, then the interest rate must be r_2. Plotting Y_2 against r_2 in the NE quadrant yields a second point, v, on the *IS* curve. Repeating this procedure for every level of income yields a downward-sloping *IS* curve.

What this tells us is that, since withdrawals vary positively with income while injections vary negatively with the rate of interest, the two flows of withdrawals and injections can only be kept equal if Y and r vary inversely with each other.

Shifts in the *IS* Curve

Part (ii) of Figure 32A.2 repeats part (i) and shows the single equilibrium combination of income Y_1 and interest rate r_1. Now let autonomous expenditure rise. At every level of r there is now a higher level of injections (due to an increase in I, G or X). Now, following around the diagram with the new J function, it is clear that any given level of Y, say Y_1, is associated with a higher interest rate. The new Y, r combination is plotted by the point u', which is one point on the new *IS* curve, *IS'*, that arises from the new injections function. Thus the rise in autonomous injections' expenditure shifts the *IS* curve upwards.

Again this tells us something that is quite obvious. If withdrawals vary positively with *Y* while injections vary negatively with *r*, an autonomous rise in injections requires a rise in *r* if injections are to remain equal to withdrawals at a given level of income.

Finally, the reader can be left the exercise of showing the shifts in the *IS* curve caused by a shift in the withdrawals function: if there are more withdrawals associated with each level of income, the *IS* curve shifts downwards.

33

The Aggregate Demand, Aggregate Supply Model

In our study so far, we have assumed that all firms were operating at less than normal capacity, and were willing to sell whatever was demanded at the current price level. Such behaviour makes the economy's aggregate supply curve perfectly elastic. We are now ready to allow the price level to vary. Adding an equation to determine the price level is sometimes referred to as the problem of *closure*.

What would happen if a shift in the *IS* curve increased national income sufficiently to push firms beyond their normal-capacity outputs, or possibly even to the upper limits of their capacities to produce? Surely, prices would then rise. If so, the price level is an endogenous variable: *it changes in response to changes in real national income*.

Making the price level endogenous has serious consequences for the *IS-LM* model. Recall that, when the rate of interest was an exogenous variable, we were able to use the aggregate desired expenditure (*AE*) curve to determine national income (as we did in Chapters 27 and 29). When the rate of interest was made endogenous, however, we could not use that function as our primary tool of analysis. As we moved along the *AE* curve, due to a change in income, the curve shifted, due to changes in the interest rate. An analogous limitation now arises with the *LM* curve, which has M/P, the real money supply, as an exogenous variable in its equation.

To see the problem, consider an outward shift in the *IS* curve which increases Y and r along a given *LM* curve. This is fine, as long as the economy has a perfectly elastic aggregate supply curve so that the price level stays constant. If, however, the price level rises as income rises, the real money supply, M/P, must fall. Under these circumstances the *LM* curve shifts as soon as we move along it. Determining the final outcome requires knowing by how much the *LM* curve shifts.

To surmount this problem, we need curves that do not themselves shift when Y, r, or P change. The curves that we require are called aggregate demand and aggregate supply curves.

TWO OUTPUT GAPS

Before we begin, we need to define a key concept. What is variously called potential output, potential income, full-employment output and full-employment income is what the economy could produce if all available productive resources were fully employed at their normal levels of capacity utilization. This is given the symbol Y_F. Actual output is the output that the economy is currently producing. It is given the symbol Y. The **output gap**, or **GNP gap**, is the difference between potential output and actual output, $Y_F - Y$. When this difference is positive, actual national income falls short of potential national income and the difference is referred to as the **recessionary gap**. When this difference is negative, actual national income exceeds potential national income and the difference is referred to as the **inflationary gap**.

The existence of a recessionary gap signals that the economy is in the depressed part of the trade cycle. Resources are either unemployed or, if employed, are being used at less than their normal rates of capacity utilization. Many factories, and their employees, will be working short time, and many others will be fully unemployed.

The existence of an inflationary gap signals that the economy is in the boom part of the trade cycle. Resources are being used above their normal rates of capacity utilization. Factories are being operated in the range where average costs are rising; labour is being used beyond normal hours, at overtime rates of pay.

These terms are important and their definitions need to be committed to memory now:

> **A positive output gap, $Y < Y_F$, is called a recessionary gap; a negative output gap, $Y > Y_F$, is called an inflationary gap.**

THE AGGREGATE DEMAND CURVE

As a first step towards making the price level an endogenous variable, we develop a new tool called the **aggregate demand**, or **AD, curve**. This curve is derived by allowing the price level, P, to take on various values, one at a time. We are still treating the price level as exogenous, but we are allowing it to take on alternative exogenously determined values. Each value gives rise to a specific LM curve, and hence to a specific IS-LM equilibrium. The AD curve is drawn by plotting each equilibrium level of national income, Y,

BOX 33.1 AGGREGATE DEMAND TERMINOLOGY

From 1936 when Keynes first introduced it, until the early 1970s, the aggregate desired expenditure function was the major tool of macroeconomic analysis. It was referred to interchangeably as the 'aggregate expenditure' or the 'aggregate demand' function (or curve, when graphed). In the 1970s, the relation between the price level and equilibrium national income, that was always implicit in the basic macro model, was introduced as an explicit tool of analysis. When the American economist, William Branson, popularized its use, he called it *the economy's demand curve*. This distinguished it from the aggregate desired expenditure (E) function, which was then still commonly called the aggregate demand function.

With the solution to the mystery of stagflation, the key tools of macro analysis became the two functions relating aggregate supply and aggregate demand to the price level. By the early 1980s the term aggregate demand curve was firmly established as the name for the latter function, and the term aggregate expenditure function was reserved for the E function. This terminology, which is the one used in this book, has become standard in the advanced literature, common in intermediate texts and is just entering usage in elementary texts. It will be a long time, however, before the usage becomes universal. People educated in the earlier tradition, and not doing research at the frontiers of macroeconomics, may be expected to use the term aggregate demand to refer to the aggregate desired expenditure function for a long time to come. Readers should be warned of possible confusions that may arise from this evolution of terminology.

Definitions and terminology should be our tools, not our masters. There is no right or wrong about definitions or terms, but there are customary usages. Problems arise when, as is often the case, different terms for the same concept or different definitions of the same term are in common use, because the subject is evolving. There is no harm in this as long as people are aware of what is going on. Confusion can occur, however, when various people unknowingly use different definitions of the same term and, therefore, talk past each other.

against the value of the price level, P, that gave rise to it. Hence:

> the *AD* curve plots all combinations of the price level and national income that yield equilibrium in the goods and the asset markets – i.e. that yield *IS-LM* equilibrium.

Box 33.1 discusses a possible source of confusion in the terminology used to describe the aggregate demand and the aggregate desired expenditure functions.

Although it is easy to derive the *AD* curve formally, it is a little harder to see what market behaviour lies behind it. We first study the curve, using graphical techniques. We then go over the same ground again, using simple algebra.

A Graphical Treatment of the *AD* Curve

The first part of Figure 33.1 plots the *IS* and *LM* curves. Nothing that we are going to do affects the *IS* curve, which remains fixed at IS_0 throughout.

Derivation of the AD *Curve*

We know that the position of any given *LM* curve depends on the magnitudes of the behavioural parameters and the exogenous variables. With the *LM* curve, the exogenous variables are the real money supply, M/P, and the constant in the money demand curve, n. Since we are going to study how the equilibrium value of Y changes as the price level changes, we can no longer hold P constant. Instead, P will be allowed to vary while the nominal money supply is held constant at some value M^*. This changes the real money supply and shifts the *LM* curve. Since the position of any particular *LM* curve depends on the values given to M and P, we put the values on which a particular *LM* curve depends in parentheses after the curve's name in Figure 33.1. Thus the curve $LM_0(M^*/P_0)$ is the *LM* curve when the price level is P_0 and the nominal money supply is M^*. Changing the price level, shifts the *LM* curve and produces a new equilibrium level of national income. Plotting that national income against the given price level, yields one point on the *AD* curve. This process is shown in detail in

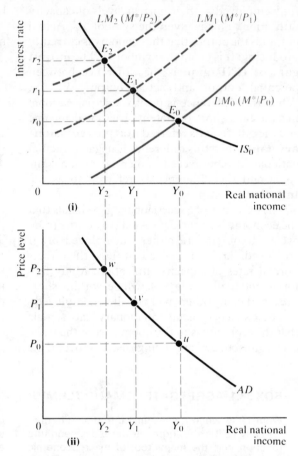

FIGURE 33.1 The Derivation of the Aggregate Demand Curve

The *AD* **curve shows how the equilibrium value of national income produced by the *IS-LM* model changes as the price level changes.** The *IS* curve remains constant at IS_0 and the money supply at M^*. When the price level is P_0, the corresponding *LM* curve is LM_0. Equilibrium is at E_0 with national income Y_0 and the interest rate r_0. Plotting Y_0 against P_0 in part (ii) of the Figure, gives the point u on the *AD* curve. A rise in the price level to P_1 shifts the *LM* curve to LM_1. Equilibrium shifts to E_1 with income of Y_1 and interest rate r_1. Plotting Y_1 against P_1 in part (ii), gives the point v on the *AD* curve. A further rise in the price level to P_2 shifts the *LM* curve to LM_2 and takes equilibrium national income to Y_2. Plotting Y_2 against P_2 in part (ii) yields the point w on the *AD* curve.

Figure 33.1, which needs careful study at this point.

The Slope of the AD Curve

The *AD* curve is negatively sloped because a rise in the price level shifts the *LM* curve to the left, thus lowering equilibrium national income.

The monetary transmission mechanism and the slope of the AD curve: As is so often the case with economic models, the real challenge lies not in formal derivation, but in understanding the market behaviour that is going on behind the scenes to produce the relation in question.

The key in this case is the monetary transmission mechanism. A rise in the price level lowers the real quantity of money and creates a monetary disequilibrium. This sets in motion the mechanism that we laid out in Figure 32.9 on page 563. The attempt to replenish money balances by selling bonds, drives the price of bonds down, which means a rise in the rate of interest. This causes a reduction in interest-sensitive expenditure, which reduces equilibrium national income.

A fall in the price level has the opposite effect. It increases the real money supply and leads to an excess supply of real money balances. The attempt to use the excess supply of money to buy bonds forces the price of bonds up, which means a fall in the interest rate. This increases interest-sensitive expenditure, which in turn increases equilibrium national income.

> The negative slope of the *AD* curve reflects the working of the monetary adjustment mechanism. A change in the price level causes a monetary disequilibrium; this causes the interest rate to change; this causes desired expenditure to change; and this causes equilibrium national income to change.

Points on and off the AD Curve: Equilibrium and Disequilibrium

Part (ii) of Figure 33.2 shows the *AD* curve while part (i) shows the *IS-LM* equilibrium corresponding to one point on that curve. The Figure shows that points to the left of the *AD* curve are positions in which there is an excess of desired expenditure over national income and an excess supply of money. The asset-market disequilibrium tends to reduce the interest rate which increases desired expenditure. The goods-

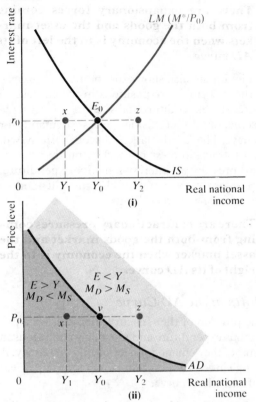

FIGURE 33.2 Points off the Aggregate Demand Curve

When the economy is off its *AD* curve, pressures come from the goods and the asset markets pushing national income back towards the *AD* curve. *IS-LM* equilibrium is at E_0, with income Y_0 and interest rate r_0. This puts the economy on point v on its *AD* curve in part (ii).

Now let the income be arbitrarily reduced, putting the economy at point x in both parts of the Figure. Figure 32.6 on page 559 tells us that at point x, desired aggregate expenditure exceeds national income and the demand for money is less than its supply. These disequilibria are noted to the left of the *AD* curve in part (ii) above. They apply to all points to the left of the *AD* curve – grey-shaded in the Figure.

Now let national income be arbitrarily increased, taking the economy to point z in both parts of the diagram. Figure 32.6 on page 559 now tells us that at point z, desired aggregate expenditure falls short of national income while the demand for money exceeds its supply. These disequilibria are noted to the right of the *AD* curve in part (ii) above. They apply to all points to the right of the *AD* curve – shaded in colour in the Figure.

market disequilibrium tends to increase national income. Thus:

> **There are expansionary forces coming from both the goods and the asset markets when the economy is to the left of its *AD* curve.**

The Figure also shows that points to the right of the *AD* curve are positions in which desired aggregate expenditure falls short of national income, and there is an excess demand for money. The asset-market disequilibrium will tend to raise interest rates, thus putting downward pressure on interest-sensitive expenditure. The goods-market disequilibrium will tend to lower national income. Thus:

> **There are contractionary pressures coming from both the goods market and the asset market when the economy is to the right of its *AD* curve.**

Shifts in the AD Curve

The position of the *AD* curve depends on autonomous expenditure and monetary conditions in terms of the demand for, and supply of, money. A change in any of these autonomous variables will shift the whole curve.

A change in autonomous expenditure: We saw in Chapter 29 that a rise in autonomous expenditure shifts the aggregate expenditure function upwards, and raises the equilibrium level of national income that is associated with any given interest rate and price level. This change is shown by a rightward shift in the *IS* curve (each rate of interest is associated with a higher equilibrium level of national income than previously). The outward shift in the *IS* curve raises the equilibrium values of national income and the interest rate that are associated with any given price level. This increase in the equilibrium value of Y from the *IS-LM* model for a given price level is shown by a rightward shift in the aggregate demand curve. Figure 33.3 gives a graphical derivation of this shift.

A change in nominal money supply or money demand: We know from Chapter 31 that an increase in the nominal money supply shifts the *LM* curve to the right, as does a reduction in money demand (as shown by a fall in

FIGURE 33.3 A Shift in the *IS* Curve Causes a Shift in the Aggregate Demand Curve

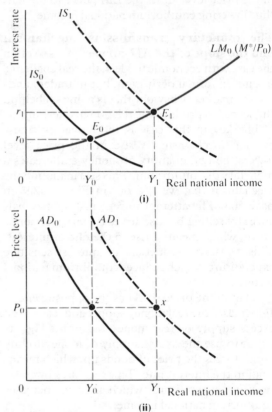

A rise in autonomous expenditure shifts the *AD* curve outwards, indicating a higher equilibrium level of national income associated with each given price level. In part (i) of the diagram, the original curves are IS_0 and $LM_0(M^*/P_0)$. They intersect at E_0 to yield national income of Y_0. Plotting Y_0 against P_0 gives the point z on the curve AD_0 in part (ii) of the Figure.

Autonomous expenditure now increases, shifting the *IS* curve to IS_1 in part (i). The intersection shifts to E_1 taking equilibrium income to Y_1. Plotting Y_1 against the price level P_0 yields the point x on the new curve AD_1.

The entire new curve, AD_1, can be derived by allowing the price level to vary with the new level of autonomous expenditure held constant. This shifts the *LM* curve in part (i), tracing out a series of equilibrium levels of Y along the new curve IS_1.

n). This lowers the interest rate, and increases equilibrium national income through the operation of the monetary transmission mechanism. Plotting the new equilibrium level of national

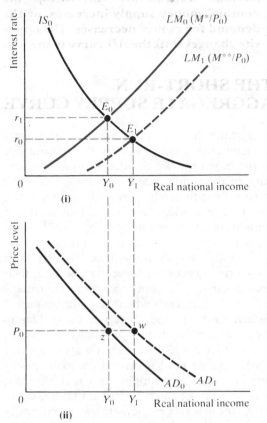

(i)

(ii)

A rightward shift in the *LM* curve causes a rightward shift in the *AD* curve. In part (i) of the diagram, the original curves IS_0 and $LM_0(M^*/P_0)$ intersect at E_0 to yield national income of Y_0. Plotting Y_0 against P_0 gives the point z on curve AD_0 in part (ii).

An autonomous increase in the nominal money supply, from M^* to M^{**}, now shifts the *LM* curve associated with the price level P_0 to $LM_1(M^{**}/P_0)$. The new intersection is at E_1 with national income of Y_1. Plotting Y_1 against P_0 yields point w on AD_1 in part (ii) of the Figure.

The whole curve AD_1 can now be derived by varying the price level, holding the nominal money supply constant at M^{**}.

income against the existing price level, shows that the aggregate demand curve has shifted rightwards. A new higher level of national income is associated with each price level because the increase in the nominal money supply (or a fall in money demand) exerts an expansionary

force on national income. This shift is shown graphically in Figure 33.4.

A rise in either autonomous expenditure or the nominal money supply, or a fall in money demand, shifts the *AD* curve to the right. The opposite changes in any of these three autonomous variables shift the *AD* curve to the left.

An Algebraic Treatment of the *AD* Curve[1]

For the algebraic derivation of the *AD* curve, we return to equation (10) on page 560. This equation gives the solution of the *IS-LM* model for equilibrium national income, when autonomous expenditure, A, the nominal money supply, M, and the price level, P, are all treated as exogenous variables. We repeat this equation:

$$Y = \left(\frac{1}{(1-z)+bd/e}\right)A^*$$

$$+\left(\frac{1}{d+e(1-z)/b}\right)\left(\frac{M^*}{P^*}-n\right). \tag{1}$$

We know from Chapter 32 that the level of national income determined by this equation ensures simultaneous goods-market, or *IS*, equilibrium $(E = Y)$, and asset-market, or *LM*, equilibrium, $(M_D = M_S)$.

To derive the *AD* curve, we merely treat the price level, P, as an endogenous variable. Equation (1), the *IS-LM* solution, now becomes one equation with two unknowns Y and P. It thus defines a locus of equilibrium P, Y combinations. This locus is the aggregate demand curve, and it shows all those combinations of the price level, P, and real national income, Y, that satisfy the twin equilibrium conditions $E = Y$ and $M_D = M_S$.

The aggregate demand curve is the locus of P, Y combinations that yield equilibrium in the *IS-LM* model. Its equation is obtained by treating P as an endogenous variable, rather than as an exogenous constant, in the equation for the solution of the *IS-LM* model.

---

[1] This section can be omitted without loss of continuity.

What we now know is that the aggregate demand curve relates P and Y. It is a negatively sloped curve[1] whose equation is given in (1) above, treating P as a variable. The curve shows that the price level is negatively associated with the equilibrium level of national income that satisfies the *IS-LM* model. Note also that, following the Marshallian convention when price and quantity variables are involved, the graph of the *AD* curve is drawn with price on the vertical axis and quantity on the horizontal axis.

If we write out the equation of the *AD* curve with all the behavioural parameters repeated, it will look much more complex than it really is. This is done in the Appendix. In the text, however, we rewrite equation (1) using g to stand for the combination of behaviour parameters attached to autonomous expenditure, and h to stand for the combination of parameters attached to the exogenous monetary variables, M^*, P^* and n. This gives us:

$$Y = gA + h\left(\frac{M^*}{P^*} - n\right), \qquad (2)$$

where g is the reciprocal of $[(1 - z) + bd/e]$ and h is the reciprocal of $[d + e(1 - z)/b]$. Treating P as a variable, produces an equation of the form:

$$Y = (gA - hn) + hM^*\left(\frac{1}{P}\right). \qquad (3)$$

This is an equation in two unknowns, Y and P. The equation's constant is $gA - hn$, and the coefficient attached to P is hM^*. If we want to write out the entire equation, we can replace g and h with the collection of coefficients that each stands for.

The equation of the aggregate demand curve contains the three exogenous variables, the money supply, M, the constant in the money-demand function, n, and autonomous expenditure, A. Inspection of equation (1) shows that a rise in A or a fall in n – larger autonomous expenditure or a smaller demand for money – increase the value of the constant term, while a rise in M increases the value of the term attached to $1/P$. All of these changes increase the value of Y associated with any given P.

---

[1] Proving the curves' negative slope algebraically is not as easy as it might seem. This matter is taken up in the Appendix to this Chapter.

The aggregate demand curve is shifted upwards, and to the right, when autonomous expenditure increases, the nominal money supply increases, or the demand for money decreases. The opposite changes shift the *AD* curve to the left.

THE SHORT-RUN AGGREGATE SUPPLY CURVE

Everything that we have done so far in macroeconomics has concentrated on the demand side of the economy. We avoided serious consideration of the supply side by assuming that firms were willing to produce everything they could sell at current prices. This could only be true if firms were producing at rates of output below capacity.

To study changes in the price level, we must allow firms to get close to, or even beyond, their normal-capacity outputs. Since firms usually encounter rising costs when their outputs exceed normal capacity, they will not be willing to supply everything that is demanded unless the prices of their products rise. To allow for this possibility, we need to amend the assumptions about the aggregate supply curve that were first introduced in Chapter 27. Recall that this curve relates the general price level to the total quantity of output that all of the economy's firms are willing to produce.

Our final objective is to see how aggregate demand and aggregate supply jointly determine national income and the price level. First, however, we must study the slope of the aggregate supply curve, and to do so, we study how arbitrary changes in the price level influence national income. This leads us to distinguish between a short-run and a long-run aggregate supply curve.

The **short-run aggregate supply curve (SRAS)** shows the total amount that will be produced and offered for sale at each price level *on the assumption that all firms' factor prices – wages, rent, etc. – are fixed.*

The Slope of the *SRAS* Curve

Figure 33.5 shows two *SRAS* curves, the short-run Keynesian curve that we have been using so far, and a positively sloped curve that we will use from now on. This positive slope indicates that, *other things being equal*, the price level and the total quantity produced are positively associated with each other.

The other things that are held constant along a *SRAS* curve are the prices of all factors.

The microeconomic behaviour that lies behind this curve has been studied in Chapter 14, where we saw that many manufacturing firms had saucer-shaped average variable cost curves and allowed output rather than price to vary in response to cyclical shifts in demand *that did not take output beyond plant capacity*. (Average variable costs are often called *unit costs*.) If all firms were oligopolies such as were shown in Figure 14.4, they would sell everything that was

demanded without changing their prices, at least up to normal-capacity output. This would give rise to the perfectly elastic Keynesian *SRAS* curve. If all firms were in perfect competition, and all had U-shaped cost curves, they would equate marginal costs to market price, and would raise output only if that price rose. This would give rise to an upward-sloping *SRAS* curve.

In fact, the economy contains a mixture of oligopolistic firms who are price-setters and perfectly competitive firms who are price-takers. Many manufacturing firms do vary their outputs as demand varies with little or no change in their prices, as long as output is below normal capacity. Other firms are price-takers, and face rising marginal cost curves. They have rising short-run supply curves, and only produce more when the market price rises. The aggregate behaviour of all these firms – as shown by $SRAS_1$ in Figure 33.5 –

FIGURE 33.5 Two Short-run Aggregate Supply Curves

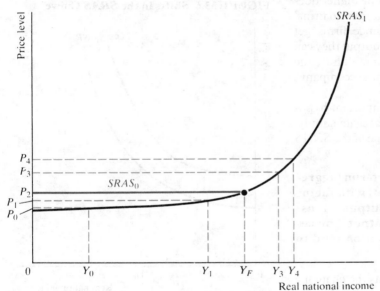

The Keynesian *SRAS* curve is horizontal; the more usual curve is upward-sloping. The curve labelled $SRAS_0$, which runs from 0 to Y_F, is the perfectly elastic Keynesian aggregate supply curve. It shows any output up to potential output Y_F being produced at the going price level of P_2.

The curve labelled $SRAS_1$ is positively sloped over its whole range. This indicates that the higher the price level, the larger will be the total output firms will be willing to produce. Below potential income, Y_F, a small increase in the price level from P_0 to P_1 is accompanied by a large rise in desired output from Y_0 to Y_1. Above potential income, Y_F, a similar increase in the price level from P_3 to P_4 is accompanied by a much smaller increase in output from Y_3 to Y_4.

is that any increase in overall output is associated with some rise in the price level. The amount of the rise will depend, however, on the proportion of total output that is produced by firms whose prices remain constant, and by those whose prices rise as output approaches full capacity. Since much output is accounted for by oligopolistic firms, the change in the price level when output varies below full capacity is usually quite small. Hence the curve labelled $SRAS_1$ is quite flat below potential output. (This is why using the Keynesian, perfectly elastic, aggregate supply curve – labelled $SRAS_0$ in the Figure – is a reasonable approximation to reality, as long as output is fluctuating below potential output.)

When output rises above potential, virtually all firms face rising marginal costs. They will not produce more unless they can be compensated by higher prices that at least cover their marginal costs. Thus, increases in output will be accompanied by larger increases in the price level than when output is below potential. The higher does output rise above potential, the steeper do firms' marginal cost curves become, since firms get closer and closer to the maximum output they can squeeze out of their existing plants. Thus, the smaller will be the increase in output accompanying any given increase in prices.

We have now developed two important hypotheses about the behaviour of aggregate supply. The first relates to the positive slope of the $SRAS$ curve:

the positively sloped, short-run aggregate supply curve shows that, with factor prices constant, higher output is associated with higher output prices because unit costs of production tend to vary directly with output.

Our second hypothesis concerns the changing slope of the $SRAS$ curve as one moves along it. This refers to what may be called the first of two important asymmetries of the economy's macroeconomic behaviour:

below potential income, small price level changes are accompanied by large changes in output. As output rises above potential income, given changes in the price level are associated with smaller and smaller changes in output.

This asymmetry is a consequence of the microeconomic behaviour discussed above. Its graphic expression is in the flatness of the $SRAS$ curve to the left of Y_F, and its increasing steepness to the right of Y_F.

Shifts in the $SRAS$ Curve

Shifts in the $SRAS$ curve are often called **supply-side shocks**. The short-run aggregate supply curve will shift if there is *any* change which affects the output that firms offer for sale at each given price level. Here we consider two of the most important of such changes.

Changes in input prices: Because factor prices are held constant along the $SRAS$ curve, shifts in factor prices are one important reason why the curve shifts. When factor prices rise,

---

FIGURE 33.6 Shifts in the $SRAS$ Curve

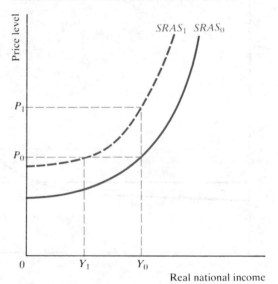

A shift to the left of the $SRAS$ curve reflects a decrease in supply, a shift to the right, an increase in supply. Starting from P_0 and Y_0 on $SRAS_0$, suppose there is an increase in input prices. This shifts the aggregate supply curve to $SRAS_1$, which is above, and to the left, of $SRAS_0$. At price level P_0, only Y_1 will be produced: to get output Y_0 would require a rise to price level P_1. A fall in input prices or a rise in labour productivity shifts the curve to the right, say from $SRAS_1$ to $SRAS_0$.

oligopolistic firms find that the profitability of their current production has been reduced. Their response is to raise output prices to cover their increased costs. Firms in perfect competition produce less because their marginal cost curves have shifted to the left. The consequence of the reactions of firms in both types of market situation is that the *SRAS* curve shifts up and to the left.

Using the terminology we used in the theory of price in Chapter 5, an upward shift in the *SRAS* curve is referred to as a *decrease in supply* because, at any given price level, less output will be produced. Putting the same point another way: for any given level of output to be produced, an increase in price will be required. This is illustrated in Figure 33.6.

A fall in factor prices shifts all firms' cost curves downwards. This increases the amount each will be willing to supply at any given price. For the whole economy this is shown by a rightward shift in the *SRAS* curve. Once again, we can look at this shift in two equivalent ways. The curve shifts right, indicating more is supplied at each price. The curve also shifts down, indicating that a lower price level is required to induce firms to produce any given output.[1]

Increases in productivity: A rise in labour productivity, meaning that each worker can produce more, reduces the unit costs of production as long as wage rates remain constant. Perfectly competitive firms find their marginal cost curves shifting downwards and produce more at any given set of output prices. Competing oligopolistic firms cut prices in attempts to raise their market shares, and the net result of such competition is lower prices. As we saw in Chapter 13, even a monopoly will cut its prices and raise its output when its marginal costs fall.

These responses cause the *SRAS* curve to shift to the right. This shift is an *increase in aggregate supply*, as is also illustrated in Figure 33.6.

Combined effects: Now consider what happens when both wages and productivity are changing, as is usually the case. It follows from the above that, if wages and productivity are both increasing at the same rate, unit costs – and hence the position of the *SRAS* curve – will be unchanged. If, for example, each worker produces 3 per cent more and is paid 3 per cent more, the labour cost of producing a unit of output will be unchanged.

An important conclusion follows immediately from this discussion:

> **the *SRAS* curve shifts upwards, remains unchanged, or shifts downwards, according as the rate of increase of wages is faster than, the same as, or slower than, the rate of increase of productivity.**

Profit margins: Changes in profit margins can cause the *SRAS* curve to shift. Say, for example, that with no change in costs, oligopolistic firms feel that economic conditions justify raising prices in order to increase their profit margins. This will raise the prices associated with any given level of output and so shift the *SRAS* curve upwards.

Although variations in profit margins can cause small, occasional shifts in the *SRAS* curve, they do not cause sustained shifts that go on year after year. This is an important point, so we must be sure it is understood. Say, for example, that profits count for 20p out of £1 of the market price of a good. A 10 per cent upward shift in the *SRAS* curve, in the face of constant unit costs of production, would require that profits rise to 30p in the first year and to 41p in the second year. Such enormous changes in the mark-up of prices over costs (from $20/80 = 25$ per cent, to $30/80 = 37$ per cent, to $41/80 = 51$ per cent) never occur. So *sustained* upward shifts in the *SRAS* curve cannot be caused by continual increases in profit margins, any more than they can be long held in check by continual decreases in profit margins.

> **Even over a few years, shifts in the *SRAS* curve must follow shifts in unit costs quite closely, since variations in profit margins cannot cause a *sustained* divergence of the former from the latter.**

---

[1] If you are worried that we have violated the assumption of the neutrality of money by making real output respond to the level of money prices, think again! The money prices of factors of production are held constant along the *SRAS* curve. Thus a change in the general level of the prices of final output represents a change in output prices relative to input prices.

EQUILIBRIUM OF AGGREGATE DEMAND AND AGGREGATE SUPPLY

Our next step is to bring the AD and the $SRAS$ curves together in Figure 33.7 to determine the short-run equilibrium values for national income and the price level. Equilibrium occurs where the two curves intersect, and it is often called the *economy's macroeconomic equilibrium*. At the equilibrium price level, firms will produce the output indicated by the $SRAS$ curve. We know from the AD curve that desired expenditure will be just equal to output at that price level (since the AD curve is the locus of P–Y combinations that produce equilibrium in both goods and asset markets).

Now consider a price level below the equilibrium where aggregate demand exceeds aggregate supply. Firms will only produce the output that

FIGURE 33.7 Macroeconomic Equilibrium

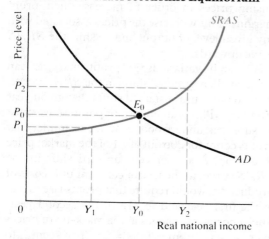

The intersection of the aggregate demand and supply curves simultaneously determines the equilibrium levels of national income and the price level. The $SRAS$ and the AD curve intersect at E_0 to determine equilibrium national income Y_0 and price level P_0. If the price level is P_1, aggregate supply will be Y_1. At that level of national income, desired expenditure exceeds national income. The resulting excess demand raises output and prices. If the price level is P_2, aggregate supply is Y_2. If firms produced their desired output, they could not sell it all because, to the right of the AD curve, desired expenditure falls short of national income.

FIGURE 33.8 Aggregate Demand Shocks

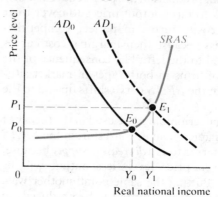

Shifts in aggregate demand cause the price level and real national income to move in the same direction. An increase in aggregate demand shifts the AD curve to the right, say from AD_0 to AD_1. Equilibrium moves from E_0 to E_1. The price level rises from P_0 to P_1 and real national income rises from Y_0 to Y_1, reflecting a movement along the $SRAS$ curve.

A decrease in aggregate demand shifts the AD curve to the left, say from AD_1 to AD_0. Equilibrium moves from E_1 to E_0. Prices fall from P_1 to P_0 and real national income falls from Y_1 to Y_0, again reflecting a movement along the $SRAS$ curve.

is indicated by the $SRAS$ curve. But this puts the economy to the left of the AD curve. We know that, at this level of national income, desired expenditure exceeds actual output. There will be excess demand for output and, since firms will not be willing to meet the demand at existing prices, the excess demand will bid up prices. So the price level will rise, and output will expand. This will continue until the intersection point is reached where firms will produce an output that just equals desired expenditure.

Next let the price level be above its equilibrium value where aggregate supply exceeds aggregate demand. Firms will want to produce a larger output than will be purchased. If they insist on producing that output, stocks of unsold output will accumulate. In this model, the excess supply will lead to a cutting back on output, and to some fall in prices. Once again, the economy is pushed towards its unique macroeconomic equilibrium, at which aggregate supply and aggregate demand are equal.

Shifts in the *AD* Curve

We can isolate the effects of a shift in aggregate demand by assuming that the *SRAS* curve stays constant. This is done in Figure 33.8, and it leads to the following conclusions.

> **An increase in aggregate demand increases equilibrium national income and the price level. A decrease has the opposite effects.**

We know from our earlier analysis that the *AD* curve is shifted to the right by any increase in autonomous expenditure, such as a rise in exports or government expenditure, as well as by an expansionary monetary shock – a rise in the nominal quantity of money or a fall in the demand of money. So now we know the effects of such shifts on equilibrium national income and the price level.

The Multiplier Yet Again

We saw in Chapter 27 that when the rate of interest and the price level remain constant, the multiplier is equal to the reciprocal of the mar-

---

FIGURE 33.9 The Multiplier When the *SRAS* Curve is Not Perfectly Elastic

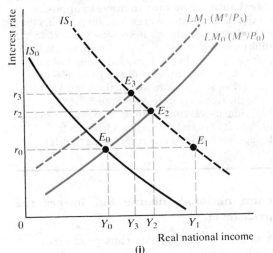

(i)

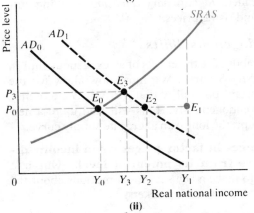

(ii)

When the *SRAS* curve has a positive slope, part of the effect of an increase in exogenous expenditure is dissipated in a rise in the price level. In part (i), the original curves of IS_0 and LM_0 intersect at E_0 to produce national income of Y_0 and interest rate of r_0. In part (ii), the initial curves of AD_0 and *SRAS* intersect at E_0 to produce income Y_0 and price level P_0. An increase in autonomous expenditure shifts the *IS* curve to IS_1 and the aggregate demand curve to AD_1. We can now distinguish three multipliers.

The multiplier with the interest rate and the price level constant. If both the price level and the interest rate are held constant, national income would increase to Y_1. There is no asset equilibrium, and the only equilibrium condition to be satisfied is that desired expenditure should equal national income. This holds at Y_1 on IS_1, given the initial price level P_0 and interest rate r_0.

The multiplier with the interest rate variable. If the interest rate is variable, but the price level is constant, equilibrium is given by the intersection of IS_1 and the initial *LM* curve, $LM_0(M^*/P_0)$. Equilibrium income only rises from Y_0 to Y_2. This amount is also shown by the horizontal shift of the *AD* curve in part (ii). (Recall that the *AD* curve plots the equilibrium Y given by the intersection of the *IS* and *LM* curves for a given price level.)

The multiplier with a variable interest rate and price level. Y_2 is not an equilibrium in part (ii), because firms are not prepared to increase output from Y_0 to Y_2 at the original price level P_0. The excess demand for output raises the price level and takes the economy to its macroeconomic equilibrium at E_3. The rise in the price level to P_3 lowers the real quantity of money and shifts the *LM* curve to the left, yielding the final equilibrium level of national income of Y_3.

Given the whole model, the *only* equilibrium for IS_1, AD_1 and *SRAS* is at E_3. E_1 and E_2 only fulfil some of the equilibrium conditions, but leave others unfulfilled.

ginal propensity not to spend (i.e. to withdraw expenditure from the circular flow). Then in Chapter 32 we saw that, if the interest rate is made endogenous, the multiplier is reduced by the crowding-out effect. The rise in national income drives up the interest rate and reduces private investment expenditure. This reduces the expansionary effect of any increase in autonomous expenditure below what it would be if the interest rate had remained constant.

Now that we have made the price level endogenous, we have a further force tending to reduce the value of the multiplier. If the *SRAS* curve is upward-sloping, the expansion of national income drives up the price level. This means that more money is needed for transactions purposes and this leads to a further upward pressure on interest rates. Yet more private expenditure is crowded out.

These modifications to the multiplier are laid out in Figure 33.9. The Figure provides an important summary statement of the various restraints on the multiplier and therefore deserves careful study.[1]

Any increase in the price level that is caused by an increase in autonomous expenditure reduces the multiplier effect.

Shifts in the *SRAS* Curve

Exogenous Shifts

So far, we have assumed that the position of the *SRAS* curve is fixed. Figure 33.10 shows the effects of shifts in the curve. The conclusions demonstrated in the Figure are the following:

A reduction in aggregate supply, shown by a leftward shift in the *SRAS* curve, lowers equilibrium national income but raises the price level. An increase in aggregate supply, shown by a rightward shift in the *SRAS* curve, raises equilib-

---

[1] When studying the Figure, note that the curves in parts (i) and (ii) are not independent of each other. The *AD* curve shows the equilibrium level of national income as the price level is varied so as to shift the *LM* curve over a fixed *IS* curve. Thus, if you go vertically up from any point on the *AD* curve corresponding to some given price level, say P_0, you must hit an intersection of the *IS* curve and the *LM* curve drawn for that price level – in this case (M^*/P_0).

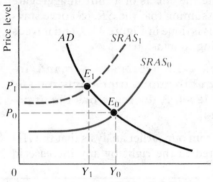

FIGURE 33.10 Aggregate Supply Shocks

Shifts in aggregate supply cause the price level and real national income to move in opposite directions. A decrease in aggregate supply shifts the *SRAS* curve to the left, say from $SRAS_0$ to $SRAS_1$. Equilibrium moves from E_0 to E_1. The price level rises from P_0 to P_1, but real national income falls from Y_0 to Y_1, reflecting a movement along the *AD* curve.

An increase in aggregate supply shifts the *SRAS* curve to the right, say from $SRAS_1$ to $SRAS_0$. Equilibrium moves from E_1 to E_0. The price level falls from P_1 to P_0, but real national income rises from Y_1 to Y_0, again reflecting a movement along the *AD* curve.

rium national income but lowers the price level.

A negative supply shock thus produces what are called *stagflationary conditions* – falling output and rising prices.

Endogenous Shifts

The above are the effects of an exogenous shift in the *SRAS* curve. We must now allow for the important possibility that the *SRAS* curve may shift endogenously. This will lead us to a new concept, the long-run aggregate supply curve.

Changes in factor prices when income diverges from its potential level: Our first step to make a key set of assumptions about the behaviour of factor markets.

Assumption 1: At potential income, total demand is equal to total supply when summed over all factor markets.

A sufficient set of conditions to justify this

assumption would be that each and every individual factor market was in equilibrium. This would be appropriate to a static economy, but it is never true of a changing economy. So we allow for continual adjustment and hence disequilibrium in individual markets. But at potential income, there is no *aggregate* disequilibrium in the economy's micro factor markets. Any excess demand in one market is balanced by excess supplies in some other markets for the same factor. Summed over all individual factor markets, there is neither excess demand nor excess supply for each factor. There is thus no overall demand pressure for factor prices to change.

Assumption 2: Above potential income, there is excess demand, while below potential income, there is excess supply, summed over all factor markets.

Assumption 2 can be deduced from assumption 1 if one also assumes that the demands for factors are positively associated with national income, while the supplies are not.

The next assumption refers to factor prices. We must, however, treat labour slightly differently than other inputs.

Assumption 3: (a) The prices of non-labour factors rise when they are in excess demand and fall when they are in excess supply. (b) When labour markets are in equilibrium, labour will get an increase in money wages equal to the increase in its productivity; excess demand for labour causes money wages to rise faster than productivity, excess supply causes them to rise more slowly than productivity (they may even fall).

In other words, money wages will be rising at a rate faster than, the same as, or slower than, the rate at which productivity is rising, according as national income exceeds, is equal to, or falls short of, its potential level. In what follows we concentrate on the most important factor price, which is labour costs. But what we say covers, with necessary corrections, all factor prices that are aff cted by the economy's demand (some may be imported at prices unaffected by home demand).

Shifts in *SRAS*:   We have already observed that what happens to the *SRAS* curve depends on the relation between money wages and pro-

ductivity. So the above assumptions lead to a key proposition:

> **when national income exceeds potential income (an inflationary gap), the *SRAS* curve will be shifting upward; when national income falls short of potential income (a recessionary gap), the *SRAS* curve will be shifting downwards; only when national income equals potential income will the *SRAS* curve be stable.**

The Long-run Effects of an Increase in Aggregate Demand

We are now ready to study the long-run effects of shifts in the *AD* curve. We start by assuming that the economy is producing its potential income and enjoying a stable price level as shown in Figure 33.11.

A rise in autonomous expenditure, perhaps caused by an investment boom, shifts the aggregate demand curve to the right. The immediate effects are that the price level, and national income, both rise. But since national income started at its potential level, firms will now be producing beyond their normal-capacity output. According to the assumption made in the previous section, this will cause the price of labour to rise faster than productivity is rising.

This means increased unit costs. These, as we have already seen, lead to upward shifts in the *SRAS* curve. Oligopolistic firms pass on their increases in unit costs by increasing their output prices, and the supply curves of price-taking firms shift upward. For this reason, the rise in the price level that occurred as income expanded along a given *SRAS* curve is not the end of the story. The *SRAS* curve shifts upward, and this causes a further rise in the price level. This time, however, the price rise is associated with a fall in output. Only when income returns to its potential level does the excess demand for labour disappear. At this point, the shift in the short-run aggregate supply curve has taken equilibrium income back to its original level, but has raised the price level even further.

Figure 33.11 shows this sequence.

> **Starting from potential income and a stable price level, the sequence of events following a demand shock is as follows:**

FIGURE 33.11   The Long-run Effects of an Expansionary Demand Shock

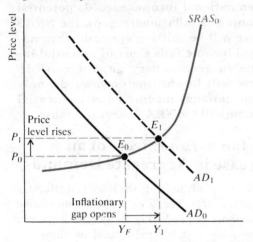

(i)

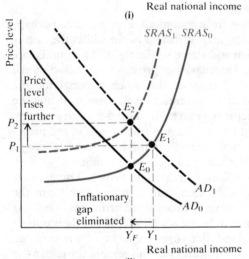

(ii)

A rightward shift of the *AD* curve first raises the price level and output along the *SRAS* curve. It then induces shifts of the *SRAS* curve that further raise prices, but lower output along the *AD* curve. In part (i) the economy is initially in equilibrium with potential output Y_F and price level P_0. The *AD* curve then shifts to AD_1. Equilibrium is at E_1, with income Y_1 and price level P_1, and an inflationary gap of $Y_1 - Y_F$.

In (ii), the inflationary gap results in an increase in wages and other input costs, shifting the *SRAS* curve leftward. As this happens, income falls and the price level rises along AD_1. Eventually, when the *SRAS* curve has shifted to $SRAS_1$, income is back to Y_F, the inflationary gap has been eliminated, but the price level has risen further to P_2.

(1) A rise in aggregate demand raises the price level, and raises income above its potential level as the economy expands along a given *SRAS* curve.

(2) The expansion of income beyond its potential level puts pressure on factor markets; factor prices then begin to rise faster than productivity, shifting the *SRAS* curve upward.

(3) The shift of the *SRAS* curve causes output to fall along the given *AD* curve; this process continues *as long as* actual output exceeds potential output.

(4) Actual output eventually falls back to its potential level. The price level will, however, now be higher than it was after the initial impact of the increased aggregate demand.

The ability of an aggregate demand shock to increase output beyond the economy's potential output is only a short-term success. Inflationary pressures shift the *SRAS* curve upwards, pushing national income back to its potential level.

Long-run Effects of a Decrease in Aggregate Demand

The economy with full employment and stable prices appears again in Figure 33.12, which duplicates the initial conditions of Figure 33.11. Now assume a *decline* in aggregate demand, perhaps due to a major reduction in investment expenditure.

The impact effect of this decline is a fall in national income and some downward adjustment of the price level, as the economy moves to the right along its given *SRAS* curve. Excess supply now develops in factor markets. This causes wage rates to rise more slowly than productivity, lowering unit costs and shifting the *SRAS* curve downwards.

The Importance of the Labour Market

We must now re-examine our earlier assumptions about the behaviour of wage costs when national income diverges from its potential level. If the labour market were perfectly competitive, money wages would rise or fall as was necessary to clear the market and maintain potential income. Wages, however, respond very slowly to

FIGURE 33.12 The Long-run Effects of a Contractionary Demand Shock

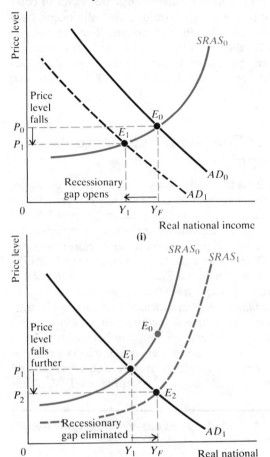

A leftward shift of the *AD* curve first lowers price and output along the *SRAS* curve and then induces a (slow) shift of the *SRAS* curve that further lowers prices, but raises output along the *AD* curve. In (i), the economy is in equilibrium at E_0, at its level of potential output Y_F and price level P_0. The *AD* curve then shifts to AD_1, moving equilibrium to E_1, with income Y_1 and price level P_1, and opens up a recessionary gap of $Y_F - Y_1$.

Part (ii) shows the adjustment back to full employment that occurs from the supply side when wages are sufficiently flexible. The fall in unit labour costs shifts the *SRAS* curve to the right. Real national income rises, and the price level falls further along the *AD* curve. Eventually, the *SRAS* curve reaches $SRAS_1$, with equilibrium at E_2. The price level stabilizes at P_2 when income has returned to Y_F, eliminating the recessionary gap.

excess labour supply. Trade unions exert substantial monopoly power in many labour markets, and they are often able to resist downward pressure on wages. Furthermore, as we shall see in Chapter 35, modern wage rates are often strongly influenced by longer-term forces than the current state of demand and supply in labour markets. To show the importance of the reaction of wage costs, we will study two cases – one where wages are fully flexible, and one where they are not.

Downward wage flexibility: Consider what would happen *if* the unemployment did cause wage rates to fall as fast as they rose when there was excess demand for labour. When there was a large recessionary gap, rapidly falling wage rates would lower unit costs. Competition among firms to sell in a depressed market would lead them to cut prices, once their falling costs gave them scope to do so. This in turn would cause a rapid downward shift in the *SRAS* curve. As a result, the economy would move along its fixed *AD* curve with falling prices and rising output, until potential national income was restored and a lower price level reached.

We conclude that *if* wages were to fall rapidly whenever there was unemployment – a condition called downward flexibility of wages – the resulting fall in the *SRAS* curve would restore full employment quickly. In other words, downwardly flexible wages would provide an automatic adjustment mechanism that would push the economy back toward full employment whenever output fell below potential.

Wages that are equally flexible in both an upward and a downward direction make the economy's adjustment to increases and decreases in demand symmetrical, eliminating inflationary and recessionary gaps with equal speed.

Downward wage inflexibility: The symmetrical world does not exist in reality. Instead, wages often respond rapidly to excess demand but only sluggishly to excess supply. Therefore, although the adjustment mechanism described in Figure 33.11 can act quickly to remove excess demand, the adjustment mechanism described in Figure 33.12 is weak and slow-acting in its removal of excess supply.

Raw materials prices, many of which are competitively determined, fall in recessions. This will push the *SRAS* curve downwards. But since wages account for the majority of costs in most lines of production, full employment cannot be restored from the cost side alone unless unit wage costs fall.

Notice that for the *SRAS* curve to shift downwards, it is not necessary for money wage rates actually to fall – something which workers tend to resist as strongly as possible. All that is needed is for wage rates to rise more slowly than productivity. For example, if output per worker is rising at 3 per cent per year, while money wages are rising at one per cent per year, unit labour costs will be *falling* at 2 per cent per year and the *SRAS* curve will be shifting slowly downwards. For this reason, the downward adjustment can occur even if no worker ever agrees to a cut in money wages. But since productivity increases have rarely exceeded 4 per cent per year in advanced industrial countries, and are more usually closer to 2 per cent, the downward shift in the *SRAS* curve will be very slow unless money wage rates actually fall.

Notice that the weakness of the automatic adjustment mechanism does not mean that slumps must last indefinitely. All that it means is that, if the economy is to avoid a lengthy recession in conditions of downward wage inflexibility, recovery must come from the demand side. A speedy recovery requires an upward shift in the *AD* curve.

The Second Asymmetry of Aggregate Supply

We have now arrived at what may be called the second asymmetry of the supply side of the economy. (The first is the slope of the *SRAS* curve, flat below Y_F and steep above Y_F.) The second asymmetry runs as follows:

Boom conditions, with severe labour shortages, do cause wages to rise rapidly, thereby causing rapid upward shifts of the *SRAS* curve; but slump conditions, with heavy unemployment, do not cause wages to fall with corresponding speed and, hence, do not cause the *SRAS* curve to shift down rapidly.

The second asymmetry of aggregate supply

explains two key characteristics of our economy. First, unemployment *can* persist for quite long periods without causing large decreases in costs and prices (which would, if they did occur, help to remove the unemployment). Second, booms, with labour shortages and production beyond normal capacity, *cannot* persist for long periods without causing large increases in wages and prices.

The Long-run Aggregate Supply Curve

Although the downward adjustment of wages may not remove recessionary gaps fast enough to be acceptable to policy-makers, the *possibility* of automatic adjustments gives rise to an important concept. The **long-run aggregate supply (*LRAS*) curve** relates the price level to equilibrium real national income, *after all input costs, including wages rates, have been fully adjusted to eliminate any excess demand or supply*. It thus shows the national income that would occur *if* wages were flexible enough in both directions to eliminate any excess demand or excess supply of labour. Full employment would then prevail and output would be at its potential level, Y_F. This

FIGURE 33.13 The Long-run Aggregate Supply Curve

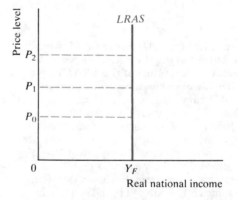

The vertical *LRAS* indicates that potential income is independent of the price level in the long run. The long-run neutrality of money implies that the potential income of Y_F can be equally well produced at a price level of P_0 or P_1 or P_2 or any other price level.

means that the long-run aggregate supply curve is a vertical line at potential output, as shown in Figure 33.13. It is called the long-run aggregate supply curve because it refers to adjustments that require a substantial amount of time.

Along the *LRAS* curve, the prices of *all outputs* and *all inputs* have been fully adjusted to eliminate excess demands or supplies in all markets. Various points on the *LRAS* curve thus refer to situations where the prices of *all* outputs and *all* inputs have changed equi-proportionately. Equal proportionate changes in money wages and in the price level (which, by definition, will leave real wages unaltered) will also leave equilibrium employment and output unchanged. The

key concept is this: if the price of absolutely everything (including labour) changes in the same proportion, then nothing real changes. (We discussed this in detail on pages 527–529 of Chapter 30.)

The perfectly inelastic long-run aggregate supply curve is nothing more than an expression of the long-run neutrality of money. The absolute level of prices need not have any effect on any real variable, including national income and employment, provided that the prices of absolutely everything have been adjusted to that price level.

SUMMARY

1. The aggregate demand curve plots the equilibrium level of national income that is associated with each price level. All points on the *AD* curve give equilibrium in the goods market – desired expenditure equals national income – and in the asset market – money demand equals money supply.

2. The *AD* curve is negatively sloped because a rise in the price level lowers real money balances and, through the operation of the monetary transmission mechanism, lowers equilibrium national income.

3. The *AD* curve is shifted to the right by a rise in any element of autonomous expenditure, a rise in nominal money supply, or a fall in money demand. The opposite changes shift it to the left.

4. The short-run aggregate supply curve plots the total desired output that is associated with each price level. It is drawn on the assumption that all factor prices are held constant. The first asymmetry of aggregate supply is that the *SRAS* curve tends to be flat below potential income and steep above it.

5. The *SRAS* curve is positively sloped because, even when factor prices are constant, unit costs tend to rise with output, so higher prices are required to induce firms to expand output.

6. The *SRAS* curve shifts to the left when unit labour costs of production rise either because wages rise faster than productivity or because other input prices rise. The opposite changes shift it to the right.

7. Macroeconomic equilibrium occurs where the *AD* and the *SRAS* curves intersect. This determines national income and the price level.

8. Changes in national income and in the price level are positively associated when the *AD* curve shifts, and negatively associated when the *SRAS* curve shifts. A leftward shift in the *SRAS* curve causes a stagflation with a rising price level and a falling national income.

9. When macroeconomic equilibrium causes an inflationary gap ($Y > Y_F$), wages rise faster than productivity and the *SRAS* curve shifts upwards until the gap is removed ($Y = Y_F$). When there is a recessionary gap ($Y < Y_F$), wages tend to rise slower than productivity, shifting the *SRAS* curve downwards until the gap is removed ($Y = Y_F$). The second asymmetry of

aggregate supply is that the $SRAS$ curve shifts upwards rapidly in the face of an inflationary gap but tends to shift downwards only slowly in the face of a recessionary gap.

10. The long-run aggregate supply curve relates real national income to the price level on the assumption that all markets have cleared to eliminate any excess demands or excess supplies. It is a vertical line at potential income. Its shape follows from the long-run neutrality of money: in equilibrium the level of prices at which all transactions take place has no real effects on the real values of those transactions.

TOPICS FOR REVIEW

- The shapes of the AD and $SRAS$ curves
- Causes of shifts in the AD and $SRAS$ curves
- The effects on macroeconomic equilibrium of shifts in the AD and $SRAS$ curves
- Induced shifts in the $SRAS$ curve
- The long-run tendency for Y to gravitate to Y_F
- The two asymmetries of aggregate supply
- The meaning of the vertical $LRAS$ curve

APPENDIX to Chapter 33

The Slope of the *AD* Curve

The *AD* curve has a simple form:

$$Y = F + G(1/P) . \tag{A1}$$

Both the constant term F and the coefficient G are each made up of combinations of the behavioural parameters and the exogenous variables. Written out in full, the equation looks more complex than it really is. To put signs on F and G, however, we need to consider each of these terms in detail.

To do this, let us write out the equation of the *AD* curve in full detail. We take equation (1) on page 577 and treat P as a variable. The term containing n becomes part of the constant and the whole equation is:

$$Y = \left(\frac{A^*}{(1-z) + bd/e} - \frac{n}{d + e(1-z)/b} \right)$$
$$+ \left(\frac{M^*}{d + e(1-z)/b} \right)\left(\frac{1}{P} \right) \tag{A2}$$

The terms containing A^* and n make up the constant term, indicated by F in (A1) above, while the term with M^* in the numerator is the coefficient attached to the variable P, indicated by G in (A1) above. The variable P itself appears as a reciprocal, $1/P$.

To find the signs of F and G we use the sign restrictions on the behavioural parameters. These are repeated below for easy reference.

Parameter Definitions and Sign Restrictions

b = the response of desired aggregate expenditure to a change in the interest rate <0.

d = the response of the real demand for money to a change in real national income >0.

e = the response of the real demand for money to a change in the interest rate <0.

n = the constant in the real demand for money function >0.

z = the response of aggregate desired expenditure to a change in national income: $0 < z < 1$.

Now let us sign the terms in the above equation. Consider first the term involving M^* which is:

$$\frac{M^*}{d + e(1-z)/b} .$$

To find its sign we use the sign restrictions to write out the sign pattern of parameters and exogenous variables. This is done by replacing each variable by its sign written in parentheses, and writing without parentheses any $+$ or $-$ signs that occur in the original expression. Using this convention,

$$\frac{M^*}{d + e(1-z)/b} \text{ is written } \frac{(+)}{(+)+(-)(+)/(-)}$$

Since this is the first time we have done such an operation, let us be clear on how we move from the left- to the right-hand expression. The $(+)$ in the numerator tells us that M^* is a positive number. The first $(+)$ in the denominator tells us that d is positive. The $+$ without a parenthesis repeats the $+$ from the left-hand expression. The $(-)$ tells us that e is negative, the next $(+)$ that $1-z$ is positive. The $/$ repeats the division sign from the left-hand expression and the final $(-)$ tells us that b is negative.

Now let us find the sign of the whole expression. The second term in the denominator is $(-)(+)/(-)$. This is positive, since a negative divided by a negative is a positive. Putting a single plus for this term yields:

$$\frac{(+)}{(+)+(+)} = (+) \ .$$

So the coefficient attached to P, indicated by G in (A1) above, is positive. But since P appears as a reciprocal, Y and P are negatively related to each other – the AD curve has a negative slope.

Also, notice that, because P enters as a reciprocal, the relation is non-linear. As P approaches zero, the term involving P gets indefinitely large and so does the solution for Y. As P gets larger and larger, the term involving P approaches zero so that Y approaches the value of the constant. Given the linear IS relation, extreme values of P will involve negative values of either Y or r, which makes no economic sense. Thus, we are only interested in values of M^*, n and P that yield positive values of Y and r. Given a linear IS curve, this requires limitations on the values of the exogenous variables, and parameters of the LM curve, that will make the two curves intersect in the positive quadrant. Those who are theoretically inclined will find it instructive to investigate this problem further. For all our purposes in this book, however, we merely rule out those extreme cases of very large, or very small, real money supplies that would yield nonsense results. These possibilities arise solely because we have linearized our behavioural relations, not from any inherent fault in the model.

Now look at the constant in equation (A2). It was called G in (A1). We already know that $[(1-z)+bd/e]$ is positive because it appears in the solution to the IS-LM model (see page 560), and we have just determined that $[d+e(1-z)/b]$ is positive. Since autonomous expenditure, A, and the constant in the demand-for-money function, n, are also positive, the whole constant term is the difference between two positive numbers. It follows that we cannot put a sign on this constant from a knowledge of the sign restrictions only. Because the variable P enters equation (A2) as a reciprocal, it follows that the constant is the value that Y approaches as P gets indefinitely large. Being unable to sign this constant is just another way of seeing what we observed already. For extreme values of P, the model may give nonsense results because all behaviour relations have been linearized.

PART 10

Macroeconomic Issues, Policies and Controversies

34
Inflation

Our discussion of macroeconomic equilibrium in the previous chapter has already touched on increases in the price level, which are loosely called inflations. We shall soon see that continued inflation is intimately associated with the money supply. This association presents us with a choice. We can first study how the central bank exerts a control over the money supply, and then return to study inflation, or we can carry on to study inflation now, taking some control over the money supply by the central bank as given. We take the latter course, because a study of inflation – one of this century's great problems – flows so naturally out of the previous chapter. To do this, we assume that the Bank of England can set the money supply at any level that it wishes. The money supply, M, continues to be an exogenous variable, but it is now a variable whose magnitude, M^*, is set by the Bank.

INFLATIONARY SHOCKS

We start by noting a key distinction.

It is important to distinguish between the forces that cause a once-and-for-all increase in the price level, and the forces that can cause a continuing (or sustained) increase.

In the text we refer to any increase in the price level as an inflation and distinguish between inflations of various durations.

Any event that tends to drive the price level upward is called an *inflationary shock*. To examine these, we begin with an economy in long-run macroeconomic equilibrium: the price level is stable, and national income is at its potential level. We then study the economy as it is buffeted by different types of inflationary shocks.

Supply Shocks

Suppose there is a decrease in short-run aggregate supply, that is, that the *SRAS* curve shifts up and to the left. This might be caused, for example, by a rise in the costs of imported raw materials, or by a rise in domestic wage costs per unit of output. The price level rises and output falls. The rise in the price level shows up as a temporary burst of inflation.

What happens next depends, first, on whether the shock to the *SRAS* curve is an isolated event or one of a series of recurring shocks, and second, on how the central bank reacts. If it responds by increasing the money supply, we say that the supply shock has been *accommodated*. If it holds the money supply constant, the shock is not accommodated.

Isolated Supply Shocks

Suppose that the leftward shift in the *SRAS* curve is an isolated event; it might, for example, be caused by a once-and-for-all increase in the cost of imported raw materials.

No monetary accommodation: The leftward shift in the *SRAS* curve causes the price level to rise and pushes income below its full-employment level, opening up a recessionary gap. Market pressures tend to cause wages and other factor costs to fall relative to productivity.

FIGURE 34.1 A Single Supply Shock

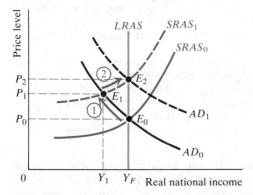

The final effect of a single supply shock depends on whether or not it is accommodated by monetary expansion. A supply shock causes the *SRAS* curve to shift leftward from $SRAS_0$ to $SRAS_1$, as shown by arrow 1. Short-run equilibrium is established at E_1.

If there is no monetary accommodation, the unemployment would put downward pressure on wage costs, causing the *SRAS* curve to shift slowly back to the right to $SRAS_0$. Prices would fall, and output would rise, until the original equilibrium was restored at E_0.

If there is monetary accommodation, the *AD* curve shifts from AD_0 to AD_1, as shown by arrow 2. This re-establishes full-employment equilibrium at E_2, but with a higher price level, P_2.

When this happens, the *SRAS* curve shifts downward, causing a return of income to full employment, and a fall in the price level. The period of inflation accompanying the original supply shock is followed by a period of deflation, which continues until long-run equilibrium is re-established. This sequence is discussed in the second paragraph of the caption to Figure 34.1. Since money wages tend to react only sluggishly to excess supply in the labour market, unit costs of production only fall slowly so the recovery to full employment may take a long time.

Monetary accommodation: Now suppose the Bank reacts by increasing the money supply. This shifts the AD curve to the right, causing both the price level and output to *rise*. When the recessionary gap is eliminated, the price level, rather than falling back to its original value, will have risen further. The effects are also illustrated in Figure 34.1.

The monetary authorities might decide to accommodate the supply shock because relying on cost deflation to restore full employment forces the economy to suffer through an extended slump.

> **Monetary accommodation can return the economy to full employment quickly, but at the cost of a once-and-for-all increase in the price level.**

Repeated Supply Shocks

As an example of a repeated supply shock, assume that powerful unions are able to raise money wages faster than productivity is increasing even in the face of significant excess supply of labour. Firms then pass these higher wages on in the form of higher prices. This type of supply shock causes what is called a **wage-cost push inflation**: an increase in the price level due to increases in money wages that are not associated with excess demand for labour.

No monetary accommodation: Suppose the Bank does not accommodate these supply shocks. The initial effect of the leftward shift in the *SRAS* curve is to open up a recessionary gap, as shown in Figure 34.1. If unions continue to negotiate increases in wages, subjecting the economy to further supply shocks, prices continue to rise while output and unemployment continue to fall. Eventually the trade-off between higher wages and unemployment will become obvious to everyone. Long before everyone is unemployed, unions will cease forcing up wages in order to maintain jobs for those who are still employed.

Once the wage-cost push ceases, there are two possibilities. First, the unions may succeed in holding on to their high real wages, but not push for further increases of money wages in excess of productivity increases. The economy then comes to rest with a stable price level and a large recessionary gap. Second, the persistent unemployment may eventually erode the power of the unions, so that real wages and hence unit costs begin to fall, because money wages rise more slowly than productivity is rising. In this case, the supply shock is reversed, and the *SRAS* curve shifts downward until full employment is eventually restored.

> **Non-accommodated wage-cost push tends to be self-limiting because the rising unemployment that it causes tends to restrain further wage increases.**

Monetary accommodation: Now suppose that the Bank accommmodates the shock with an increase in the money supply, thus shifting the *AD* curve to the right, as shown in Figure 34.2. In the new full-employment equilibrium, both money wages and prices have risen. The rise in wages has been offset by a rise in prices. Workers are no better off than they were originally, although those who remained in jobs were temporarily better off in the transition when wages had risen (taking equilibrium to E_1 in Figure 34.1) but before the price level had risen enough to restore full employment (taking equilibrium to E_2).

The stage is now set for the unions to try again. If they succeed in negotiating further increases in money wages, they hit the economy with another supply shock. If the Bank again accommodates the shock, full employment is maintained, but at the cost of a further round of inflation. If this process goes on repeatedly, it can give rise to a continual wage-cost push inflation as shown in Figure 34.2. The wage-cost push tends to cause a stagflation, with rising prices and falling output. Monetary accommodation tends to reinforce the rise in prices and to offset the fall in output.

FIGURE 34.2 Monetary Accommodation of a Repeated Supply Shock

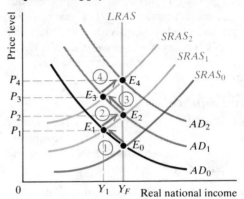

Monetary accommodation of a repeated supply shock causes a continuous inflation in the absence of excess demand. The initial equilibrium is at E_0. A supply shock then takes equilibrium to E_1, just as in Figure 34.1. This is the stagflation phase of rising prices and falling output; it is indicated by arrow 1.

If the central bank then accommodates the supply shock by increasing the money supply, the *AD* curve shifts to AD_1 taking equilibrium to E_2. This is the expansionary phase of rising prices and rising output (arrow 2).

A second supply shock takes equilibrium to E_3 (arrow 3) and a second round of monetary accommodation takes it to E_4 (arrow 4). As long as the supply shocks and the monetary accommodation continue, the inflation continues.

There are two requirements for continuing wage-cost push inflation. First, powerful groups, such as industrial unions or government employees, must press for, and employers must grant, increases in money wages in excess of productivity growth, even in the absence of excess demand for labour and goods. Second, the central bank must accommodate the resulting inflation by increasing the money supply, and so prevent the rising unemployment that would otherwise occur. The process set up by this sequence of wage-cost push, and monetary accommodation, is often called a *wage-price spiral*.

Is monetary accommodation desirable?
Once started, a wage-price spiral can be halted only if the Bank stops accommodating the supply shocks that are causing the inflation. The longer

the Bank waits to do so, the more entrenched will become the expectations of continuing inflation. These entrenched expectations may cause wages to continue to rise after accommodation has ceased. Because employers expect prices to rise, they go on granting wage increases. If expectations are firmly enough entrenched, the wage push can continue for quite some time, in spite of the downward pressure caused by the rising unemployment associated with the growing recessionary gap.

Because of this possibility, some economists argue that the process should not be allowed to begin. One way to ensure this is to refuse to accommodate any supply shock whatsoever.

Some people fear that accommodating any supply shocks risks setting off a wage-price spiral. Others are willing to risk accommodating isolated shocks, in order to avoid the recessions that otherwise accompany them.

Demand Shocks

Now suppose that an initial equilibrium is disturbed by a rightward shift in the aggregate demand curve; a shift that could have been caused by either an increase in autonomous expenditure or an increase in the money supply. This causes the price level and output to rise. If the Bank reacts to an increase in autonomous expenditure by increasing the money supply, it is said to be *validating* the shock. (Notice that this terminology distinguishes between the Bank's response to a supply shock, which is described as *accommodating* the shock, and its response to a demand shock, which is described as *validating* the shock.)

No monetary validation: This case is shown in Figure 33.11, on page 586. Because the initial *AD* shock takes output above the full-employment level, an inflationary gap opens up. The pressure of excess demand soon causes wages to rise faster than productivity, shifting the *SRAS* curve up. As long as the Bank holds the money supply constant, the rise in the price level moves the economy upwards along its fixed *AD* curve. The rise in the price level thus eventually eliminates the inflationary gap. In this case, the initial period of inflation is followed by further

inflation that continues until the new long-run equilibrium is reached. Full-employment income and a stable price level are then restored.

The monetary adjustment mechanism: We have just described a process whereby a demand inflation is halted because the *SRAS* curve shifted upwards along a fixed, negatively sloped *AD* curve, removing the inflationary gap. This is an important process. It is one whose operation is often misunderstood, and whose existence is sometimes even denied.[1] We must, therefore, pause to make sure that we understand it.

The basis of the proposition that the rise in the price level removes the inflationary gap is the negative slope of the *AD* curve. This we saw on pages 562–563 is due to the monetary transmission mechanism, which links the real and the monetary parts of the economy. Let us recall how it works. As the price level rises, more money is needed for transactions and precautionary purposes. The attempt to obtain money balances by selling bonds bids up the interest rate. This reduces interest-sensitive expenditures, and so reduces equilibrium national income. The process continues until national income is restored to its potential level, which means the inflationary gap is removed.

This is an aspect of the sense in which inflation is a monetary phenomenon. The rise in the price level creates an increased demand for money. If it is not satisfied by the creation of new money, the shortage of money will eventually end the inflation. What happens, to repeat, is that the rise in the price level pushes up the interest rate and crowds out enough expenditure to remove excess demand.

This mechanism is sometimes called the *monetary adjustment mechanism*. It is really just an aspect of the monetary transmission mechanism. But since this aspect is so important there is no harm in giving it a name of its own as long as it is not thought to be some new force, different from the transmission mechanism.

A sufficiently large rise in the price level will eliminate any inflationary gap, *pro-*

---

[1] In recent years, A-level examiners have more than once asked students to explain why a rise in the price level will not remove an inflationary gap.

vided the nominal money supply remains constant.

Monetary validation: Next, suppose that once the initial demand shock has created an inflationary gap, the Bank frustrates the monetary adjustment mechanism by increasing the nominal money supply when output starts to fall.

FIGURE 34.3 A Validated Demand-shock Inflation

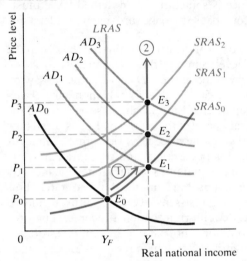

Monetary validation will cause the *AD* curve to shift, offsetting the leftward shift in the *SRAS* curve, and maintaining an inflationary gap in spite of the ever-rising price level. An initial demand shock shifts equilibrium from E_0 to E_1 (along the path indicated by arrow 1), taking income to Y_1 and the price level to P_1. The resulting inflationary gap then causes the *SRAS* curve to shift to the left. This time, however, the money supply is increased, shifting the *AD* curve to the right. By the time the aggregate supply curve has reached $SRAS_1$, the aggregate demand curve has reached AD_2, taking equilibrium to E_2. Income remains constant at Y_1, while the price level rises to P_2.

The persistent inflationary gap continues to push the *SRAS* curve to the left, while the continued monetary validation continues to push the *AD* curve to the right. By the time the aggregate supply reaches $SRAS_2$, the aggregate demand has reached AD_3. The price level has risen still further to P_3, but because of the frustration of the monetary adjustment mechanism, the inflationary gap remains unchanged at $Y_1 - Y_F$. As long as this monetary validation continues, the economy moves along the vertical path of arrow 2.

This is the case illustrated in Figure 34.3. Two forces are now brought into play. Spurred by the inflationary gap, the wage increases cause the *SRAS* curve to shift to the left. Fuelled by the expansionary monetary policy, the *AD* curve shifts to the right. As a result of both of these shifts, the price level rises, but if the shift in the *AD* curve offsets the shift in the *SRAS* curve, the inflationary gap does not diminish. The validation of an isolated demand shock thus creates a series of repeated demand shocks that permit the inflation to continue.

> **Validation of a demand shock turns what would have been a transitory inflation into a sustained inflation fuelled by monetary expansion.**

We can now see two reasons why a rise in the price level may not remove an inflationary gap. First, the central bank may choose, as a matter of policy, to validate the inflation by increasing the nominal money supply at the same rate as prices are rising, thus holding the real money supply constant. Second, the central bank might have insufficient control over the money supply. If the money supply expands endogenously to meet any demand for it, there is no monetary adjustment mechanism to eliminate the inflationary gap. As the price level rises, the nominal money supply rises sufficiently to keep the real money supply constant, and the inflationary gap is not reduced.

Although there is controversy over how much control the central bank can have over the money supply, few economists doubt that a determined enough anti-inflationary policy can stop the nominal money supply from expanding as fast as prices are rising. (Most central banks have done so at one time or another over the past few decades, thereby ending a galloping inflation in their own country.) Thus, in the world in which we live, inflations cannot go on indefinitely unless they are validated by policy decisions taken by the central bank.

Inflation as a Monetary Phenomenon

Economists have debated the extent to which inflation is a monetary phenomenon. Does it have purely monetary causes – changes in the demand for, or the supply of, money? Does it have purely monetary consequences – only the price level is affected? One slogan stating an extreme position on this issue was made popular by the American economist Milton Friedman: 'Inflation is *everywhere* and *always* a monetary phenomenon.'

Causes: To consider these issues, let us summarize what we have already learned about the causes of inflation.

(1) Many forces can cause the price level to rise. On the demand side, anything that shifts the *AD* curve to the right will have this result – *ceteris paribus* increases in desired expenditure on exports, government, investment and consumption, as well as increases in the money supply or decreases in money demand. On the supply side, anything that increases unit costs of production will shift the *SRAS* curve to the left and cause the price level to rise.

(2) Such inflations can continue for some time without any increases in the money supply.

(3) The rise in prices must eventually come to a halt, unless monetary expansion occurs.

Points (1) and (2) provide the sense in which, looking at causes, a temporary burst of inflation may or may not be a monetary phenomenon. It need not have monetary causes, and it need not be accompanied by monetary expansion. Point (3) is the sense in which, looking at causes, a sustained inflation must be a monetary phenomenon. If a rise in prices is to continue, it must be accompanied by continuing increases in the money supply (or decreases in money demand). This is true regardless of the cause that set the rise in prices in motion.[1]

Consequences: Next we summarize what we have learned about the consequences of an inflation, assuming that the economy begins from a situation of full employment and a stable price level.

(1) In the short run, a demand-shock inflation tends to be accompanied by an increase in national income.

(2) In the short run, a supply-shock inflation tends to be accompanied by a decrease in national income.

(3) When all adjustments have been fully made (so that the relevant supply-side curve is the *LRAS* curve), shifts in either the *AD* or *SRAS* curves leave national income unchanged and affect only the price level.

Points (1) and (2) provide the sense in which, looking at consequences, inflation is not, in the short run, a purely monetary phenomenon, it has real consequences in output and employment. Point (3) provides the sense in which, looking at consequences, inflation is a purely monetary phenomenon from the point of view of long-run equilibrium.

We have now established three important conclusions.

(1) Without monetary accommodation, supply shocks cause temporary bursts of inflation accompanied by recessionary gaps. The gaps are removed if, and when, unit costs of production fall, restoring equilibrium at potential income and at the initial price level.

(2) Without monetary validation, demand shocks cause temporary bursts of inflation accompanied by inflationary gaps. The gaps are removed as wages rise, returning income to its potential level, but at a higher price level.

(3) With an appropriate response from the central bank an inflation, initiated by either supply or demand shocks, can continue indefinitely; an ever-increasing money supply is necessary for an ever-continuing inflation.

THE PHILLIPS CURVE, OR HOW FAST DOES THE *SRAS* CURVE SHIFT?

Up to now it has been enough to say that an inflationary gap implies excess demand for labour, low unemployment, pressure on wages to

---

[1] The statement that inflation is everywhere and always a monetary phenomenon depends on a restricted and specific definition of the term *inflation*. To justify the statement, a temporary burst of inflation with non-monetary causes must be called a rise in the price level, and the term *inflation* must be reserved for increases in the price level that are sustained for long enough that they must be accompanied by monetary expansion.

rise faster than productivity, and, hence, an upward-shifting *SRAS* curve. But now we need to look in more detail at the influence of wages on inflation. To do this, we make use of a famous relation called the Phillips curve, which we first present in its original form and then transform into a form more applicable to the *AD-AS* model. Since the original curve uses *unemployment* rather than *national income* as its indicator of excess demand in labour markets, we must first show the relation between the two.

The NAIRU: We saw in Chapter 26 that when current national income is at its potential level, unemployment is not zero. Instead, there may be a substantial amount of frictional unemployment caused by the movement of people among jobs and structural unemployment caused by a mismatch between the characteristics of the demand for labour and the characteristics of its supply. The amount of unemployment (all of it frictional and structural) that exists when national income is at its potential level is called the **NAIRU** or the **natural rate of unemployment (U_N)**. We use the term NAIRU rather than natural rate because the latter term may create the erroneous impression that nothing can be done to reduce unemployment below a rate that is 'natural'.[1]

It follows from the definition of the NAIRU that when national income exceeds potential income $(Y > Y_F)$, unemployment will be less than the NAIRU $(U < U_N)$. When national income is less than full-employment income $(Y < Y_F)$, unemployment will exceed the NAIRU $(U > U_N)$.

We can now use the NAIRU terminology to restate our earlier assumptions about the pressure that is put on wage rates, and through them on the *SRAS* curve, by inflationary and recessionary gaps.

When the unemployment rate is below the NAIRU, demand forces put pressure on wages to rise faster than productivity. When the unemployment rate is above the NAIRU, demand forces put pressure

on wages to rise more slowly than productivity, or even to fall. When unemployment is at the NAIRU, demand forces exert neither upward nor downward pressure on wages relative to productivity.

The Nature of the Phillips Curve

In the 1950s, the late Professor A.W. Phillips was doing research on stabilization policy. He was interested in the question of the speed with which input prices responded to excess demand and excess supply. To study this question, he looked at the rate of change of money-wage rates in the UK over a period of 100 years. By relating these wage changes to the level of unemployment, he discovered a remarkable relation that came to be known as the Phillips curve.

The **Phillips curve** relates the percentage rate of change of money-wage rates (measured at an annual rate) to the level of unemployment (measured as the percentage of the labour force unemployed). Unemployment is plotted on the horizontal axis, and wage changes on the vertical axis. Thus, any point on the curve relates a particular level of unemployment to a particular rate of increase of money wages.

The Phillips curve is a new type of curve. So far in this book we have dealt with the magnitudes of our variables. The Phillips curve relates the amount of unemployment to the *rate of change* of money wages. Letting ΔW stand for the change in money-wage rates from one year to the next, and W for the level of wage rates in the first year, the equation of the Philips curve is:

$$(\Delta W / W)\, 100 = P(U)\,, \qquad (1)$$

where P stands for a functional relation. Hereafter we denote $(\Delta W / W)100$ by the symbol $\dot{W}$, which is a lot easier to write and a commonly used symbol for the percentage rate of change of a variable. We have used the letter P to indicate the functional relation to remind ourselves that this is the relation that bears Phillips' name.

A numerical example of a Phillips curve is shown in Figure 34.4. The numbers on the Figure are hypothetical – although they are not unrealistic. Because this is an unfamiliar type of curve, a numerical example may help in understanding it.

We shall see that, appropriately interpreted,

---

[1] The term NAIRU is the initials of *non-accelerating inflationary rate of unemployment*. The disadvantage of using this term is that not only is this a mouthful, but the reason for this name cannot be explained until much of the analysis in this chapter is completed.

FIGURE 34.4 A Phillips Curve

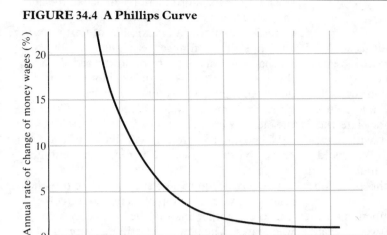

The Phillips curve relates the level of unemployment to the rate of change of money wage rates. The Figure shows a numerical example of a Phillips curve. According to the example, an increase in unemployment by four percentage points, from 8 to 12 per cent, will lower wage inflation from 3 to 2 per cent, while a reduction in unemployment by four percentage points, from 8 to 4 per cent, raises wage inflation from 3 to 14 per cent.

the Phillips curve can handle all of the causes of inflation. For the moment we shall concentrate on the influence of demand forces.

The Shape of the Phillips Curve

A negative slope: Note first that the Phillips curve has a negative slope, showing that the lower is the level of unemployment, the higher is the rate of change of money wages. This should not surprise us. Low rates of unemployment are associated with boom conditions when excess demand for labour will be causing money wages to rise rapidly. High rates of unemployment, on the other hand, are associated with slump conditions when the slack demand for labour will lead to low increases in money wages, or possibly even to decreases.

A flattening slope: Moving along the Phillips curve from left to right, the curve gets flatter. This shape is another way of showing what we have called the second asymmetry of aggregate supply – namely that input prices change more rapidly upwards than downwards. Let us recall why.

First, assume that a growing boom is increasing the excess demand for labour. As the boom develops, the unemployment rate will decrease towards, but never reach, zero (there will always be *some* frictional and structural unemployment).

At the same time, the growing excess demand for labour will be bidding up wage rates more and more rapidly. This behaviour causes the Phillips curve to get very steep and to lie far above the axis at its left-hand end. The further is the curve above the axis, the faster are wages rising.

The steepness of the curve in the range of low unemployment shows that wage inflation is very responsive to changes in unemployment in that range.

Second, consider a growing recession that raises unemployment. This recession restrains wage increases. As a result, the Phillips curve comes closer and closer to the horizontal axis, indicating less and less upward pressure on wages the higher is the level of unemployment. If the curve fell below the axis, then money wages would actually be falling over some range of high unemployment. We do not show this case in the Figure but instead assume that, as unemployment gets very large, the rate of increase in money wages approaches zero but never becomes negative.

The flatness of the Phillips curve in the range of high unemployment shows that the rate of wage inflation is relatively unresponsive to changes in unemployment over that range.

The Phillips Curve and Unit Labour Costs

To see what is happening to unit costs of production, we need to relate the increase in wage rates to the increase in labour productivity. For simplicity in the rest of the discussion, we will assume that labour is the only variable factor used by firms. This allows us to associate the labour costs of each unit of output with total variable costs per unit of output. (We could equally well have assumed that all input prices change at the same rate as does the price of labour.)

What happens to unit costs of production now depends only on the *differences* between what labour costs the firm and what labour produces for the firm.

To illustrate what is involved, we repeat in part (i) of Figure 34.5 the Phillips curve from Figure 34.4. We then add to it a horizontal line labelled 'g', for growth in output per unit of labour input, which shows the rate at which labour productivity is growing year by year. In the hypothetical example of the Figure, we have assumed that productivity is rising at 3 per cent per year. The intersection of the Phillips curve and the productivity line at the point x now divides the graph into an inflationary and a deflationary range described in the numbered points below. Given the assumptions about wage behaviour made earlier, and reiterated in the coloured passage on page 600, point x must occur at the NAIRU – which corresponds to a level of output equal to potential national income.

(1) At unemployment rates less than the intersection point, wages are rising faster than productivity and, thus, unit costs of production (input costs per unit of output) are rising. If unit costs are rising, the SRAS curve must be shifting upwards.

(2) At unemployment rates greater than the intersection point, money-wage rates are rising more slowly than productivity is rising. Thus, unit costs are *falling*. If unit costs are falling, the SRAS curve must be shifting downwards.

Notice that, although we have drawn the Phillips curve to show complete downward inflexibility of money wages, this does *not* imply complete downward inflexibility of unit costs. As long as money wages rise less than productivity

rises, unit costs of production will be falling, and the SRAS curve will be shifting downwards. Complete downward inflexibility of unit costs – and thus the total absence of the equilibrating mechanism that comes from downward shifts in the SRAS curve – requires more than the downward inflexibility of money wages; it requires that money wages *never* rise by *less than* the increase in productivity.

We now derive from the Phillips curve a new curve that expresses the verbal argument just given.

Part (ii) of Figure 34.5 shows a new curve that relates the rate of unemployment to the change in unit costs, rather than to the change in money-wage rates. The new curve still measures unemployment on the horizontal axis, but it now measures the rate of increase in unit costs on the horizontal axis. Since this is merely the rate of increase in money-wage rates *minus* the rate of increase of productivity, the new diagram is the same as part (i) of Figure 34.5 except that the origin on the vertical axis has been shifted by the rate of productivity growth.

The new curve tells us the rate at which unit costs of production are changing – and thus the rate at which the SRAS curve is shifting upwards or downwards – at each level of unemployment.

So far, we have followed Phillips in plotting unemployment on the horizontal axis. The SRAS curve, however, plots national income on its horizontal axis. To get a curve that relates the change in unit costs of production to the level of national income, we recall that unemployment is negatively related to the level of national income. As national income rises, unemployment tends to fall.

To make the relation precise, we assume that the labour force remains constant. Now any short-run increase in national income, which means more labour is employed, must mean that less labour is unemployed. In this case, any *increase* in national income must mean a *decrease* in unemployment.

We can now transform the curve in part (ii) of Figure 34.5, which plots changes in unit costs of production against the *unemployment rate*, into a new relation, shown in part (iii) of the Figure. This curve shows the same rate of change in unit costs of production, but plots it against the level of national income. Since national income and

FIGURE 34.5 The Phillips Curve Transformed

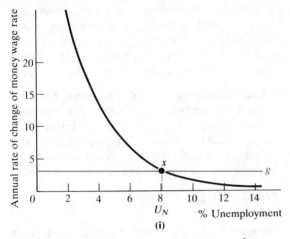

(i)

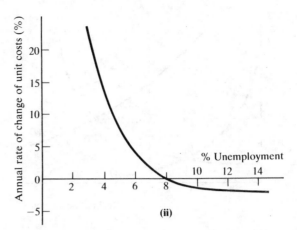

(ii)

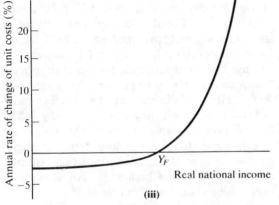

(iii)

The Phillips curve is transformed in two steps into a curve relating national income to the rate of change of unit costs. Part (i) repeats the numerical example from Figure 34.4. It also adds a straight line labelled *g*, indicating a 3 per cent rate of increase in labour productivity.

Part (ii) shows unemployment related to the rate of change of unit costs, which is the rate of change of money wages minus the rate of change of productivity.

Part (iii) substitutes *Y* for *U*, making use of the negative relation between the two variables. It shows the rate of change of unit costs positively related to national income.

unemployment vary negatively with each other, the curve in part (iii) of Figure 34.5 has the opposite slope to the curve in part (ii) of the same Figure.[1] We call this new curve the *transformed Phillips curve*. (Notice that to emphasize that we are dealing with rates of change we place a dot over the variable to indicate its annual percentage rate of change – in this case the symbol is *ċ*).

The Upward Shift in the SRAS Curve Explained

Figure 34.6 draws the familiar aggregate-

demand/aggregate-supply diagram in part (i). Part (ii) shows the transformed Phillips curve (TPC), relating the rate of change of unit costs to national income. Both parts have national income on their horizontal axes, and, by lining these up, we can compare one with the other. The *AD* and *SRAS* curves in part (i) determine the short-run levels of prices and national income. Given the national income so determined,

> the transformed Phillips curve tells us the rate at which the *SRAS* curve is shifting.

Since we will always be working with this transformed curve hereafter, we will just call it a Phillips curve.

The long-run equilibrium of the economy is at potential income. All that the curve in part (ii) tells us is how fast the *SRAS* curve in part (i)

---

[1] We have started with the relation $\Delta W/W = P(U)$, which is the original Phillips curve. We then subtracted productivity growth, *g*, to get a unit-cost-increase curve: $\Delta c/c = P(U) - g$. Then we substituted a relation between unemployment and national income, $U = U(Y)$ to get a curve relating the rate of increase in unit costs to the level of unemployment: $\Delta c/c = P[U(Y)]$.

FIGURE 34.6 The Phillips Curve and the AS-AD Relation

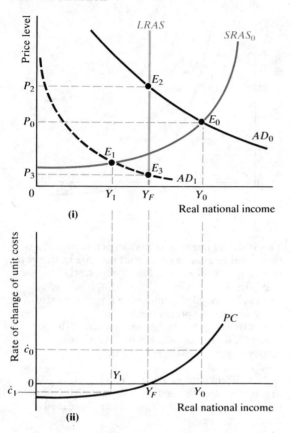

(i)

(ii)

shifts to move the economy towards its long-run equilibrium. The steepness of the curve for Y greater than Y_F shows the rapid adjustment towards equilibrium after a single expansionary shock. The flatness of the curve below equilibrium shows the slowness of adjustment towards equilibrium after a single contractionary shock.

> **The non-linearity of the transformed Phillips curve expresses the second asymmetry of aggregate supply, that costs, and hence prices, rise rapidly in the face of an inflationary gap, but only fall slowly in the face of a recessionary gap.**

The Micro Underpinnings of the Asymmetry

The micro behaviour that lies behind the flat part of the Phillips curve to the left of Y_F is explained in two parts.[1] The first concerns the theory of short-run oligopoly pricing described in Chapter 14: firms absorb cyclical demand fluctuations by varying their outputs rather than their prices. The second concerns the theory that wage costs do not fall rapidly in the face of an excess supply of labour, although they can rise rapidly in the face of excess demand for labour. One reason for this is suggested by the long-term, implicit-contract theory of wage determination outlined on pp. 627–629 of Chapter 35. An alternative explanation is discussed in Box 34.1.

Whatever the details of the explanation of wage behaviour, the overall microeconomic behaviour is envisioned to be as follows. When demand falls, firms reduce their outputs and their demands for labour, holding their mark-ups approximately constant. The unemployment does not force money wage rates down significantly, so firms' unit costs, and hence their prices, fall no faster than productivity is rising. There will also be some downward pressure on money wages (particularly in non-unionized markets) and on prices in more competitive markets, and the result will be a slow downward drift of the price level. When demand rises above potential income, firms try to expand output by hiring more

The transformed Phillips curve shows the speed with which the *SRAS* curve is shifting upwards. When the curves are AD_0 and $SRAS_0$ in part (i), they intersect at E_0 to produce equilibrium national income of Y_0.

Part (ii) shows that when income is Y_0, unit costs, and hence the rate of increase in the *SRAS* curve, is $\dot{c}_0$ per cent per year. Thus equilibrium national income is moving rapidly toward Y_F as the point of macroeconomic equilibrium moves up the fixed *AD* curve toward the long-run equilibrium at E_2.

When the curves are AD_1 and $SRAS_0$, equilibrium is at E_1, with income Y_1. Part (ii) shows that when income is Y_1, unit costs and hence the *SRAS* curve, will be shifting downwards at the rate of $\dot{c}_1$ per cent per year. Thus equilibrium national income is moving slowly along AD_1 towards a long-run equilibrium at E_3.

Each long-run equilibrium has the same level of national income, but a different price level.

---

[1] I have discussed the micro underpinnings of the Keynesian macro model in some detail elsewhere. See R. G. Lipsey, 'The Understanding and Control of Inflation: Is There a Crisis in Macroeconomics?', *Canadian Journal of Economics*, XIV, No. 4, November 1981.

BOX 34.1 WAGE RESPONSES TO EXCESS SUPPLY

In the neo-Classical model discussed on page 625, there is a single homogeneous supply of labour which sells its services for a real wage W/P, which is the money wage, W, divided by the price level, P. Rejecting this model, Keynes observed that there are many different kinds of labourers selling their services in many imperfectly linked labour markets. To this he added the hypothesis that workers care, not only about their own real wage, but also about their wage relative to other similar labour groups – a possibility ignored in the neo-Classical model where people care about their own levels of income and consumption, but not about their neighbours'.

Keynes argued that, in a world of multiple labour markets, a 5 per cent fall in real wages accomplished by a cut in money wages would be very different in its transitional effects from the same fall accomplished by an increase in the price level. *The latter preserves wage relativities in the transition, the former does not.* Consider a disequilibrium requiring a fall in W/P. No one can be quite sure in advance how much the fall must be. Thus, if one group's money wage falls too much, the affected workers will lose until their wage can be raised to its equilibrium position. Also, those who adjust sooner will lose more than those who adjust later. Furthermore, before the full adjustment is accomplished, conditions may change once again, requiring, say, that real wages return to their initial levels. Those who have not yet made the first adjustment will then have lost nothing. For these, and many other reasons, it is rational for people who can influence their wages to resist downward adjustment, making others adjust first. If, however, the adjustment is made through an increase in the price level, all wage relativities are preserved, and all workers gain or lose equally from any temporary overshooting or undershooting of W/P.

In the neo-Classical model, where a single homogeneous factor called labour is sold

on a perfectly competitive market, it is irrational to resist a fall in W/P accomplished by a fall in W while accepting it when it is accomplished by a rise in P. But in a set of disaggregated labour markets where transactions occur out of equilibrium for a long time, the real transitional effects of a fall in W/P accomplished by a fall in W are not the same as the effects of the same fall in W/P accomplished by a rise in P. Thus it is not necessarily irrational to accept the operation of the latter while resisting the former.

So Keynesian theory makes wages relatively rigid downwards, owing to concern over relativities in a dynamic, uncertain, non-homogeneous world.

The clearest modern statement of this line of reasoning is to be found in the writings of James Tobin. Tobin's theory is really Keynes' transferred to a modern setting. Tobin claims that wage-setters are concerned about their wages relative to other closely related rates. He adds that wage bargains are made only infrequently. Union wages are rarely negotiated more often than once a year and, in some countries, two- and three-year contracts are not uncommon. Thus when a particular wage is set, all other closely related wages are predetermined and, on average, for a period of one-half the length over which the wage in question is now to be set. Thus, independent of their expectations about the future rate of inflation, each group of workers will resist cutting their wages relative to other existing wages. There is also an asymmetry between raising and lowering relative wages: workers accept getting ahead of other closely related groups, but resist falling behind. Therefore, the wage stickiness is more serious on the down side of reducing wage inflation. This provides one explanation of the Phillips curve's slope, flat below Y_F and steep above it.

labour, and the labour shortages that develop cause wages to rise. As costs rise, firms pass these on in higher prices. This is a *continuing process* that goes on as long as excess demand holds income above its full-employment level.

Expectational Forces

We must now consider influences on costs and prices other than demand. A second force that can influence wage costs is *expectations*. Suppose,

for example, that both employers and employees expect a 4 per cent inflation next year. Unions will start negotiations from a base of a 4 per cent increase in money wages, which would hold their real wages constant. Firms may also be inclined to begin bargaining by conceding at least a 4 per cent increase in money wages, since they expect that the prices at which they sell their products will rise by 4 per cent. *Starting from that base,* unions will attempt to obtain some desired increase in their real wages. At this point such factors as profits, productivity and bargaining power become important.

> **The general expectation of an *x* per cent inflation creates pressures for wages to rise by *x* per cent more than productivity and hence for the *SRAS* curve to shift upwards by *x* per cent.**

The key point is that the *SRAS* curve can be shifting upwards even if there is no inflationary gap. As long as people expect prices to rise, their behaviour will push money wages and unit costs up. This brings about the rise in prices that was expected. This is another example of the phenomenon of self-realizing expectations: if everyone thinks event *x* is going to occur, their actions in anticipation of *x* may make *x* occur.

Expectations Formation

Backward-looking theories: Keynesian theories of expectations make this expectational component difficult to change. These are the theories of extrapolative and adaptive expectations. The theory of *extrapolative expectations* says that expectations depend on extrapolations of past behaviour and respond only slowly to what is currently happening to costs. In the theory's simplest form, the expected future inflation rate is merely a moving average of past actual rates. The rationale is that, unless a deviation from past trends persists, firms and workers dismiss the deviation as transitory. They do not let it influence their wage and price-setting behaviour.

The theory of *adaptive expectations* makes the expectation of future inflation rates adjust to the error in predicting the current rate. Thus if you thought the current rate was going to be 6 per cent and it turned out to be 10 per cent, you might revise your estimate of the next period's rate upwards by, say, half of your error, making the new expectation 8 per cent.

These two theories make expectations about future inflation depend on past actual rates. In an obvious sense, such expectations are *backward-looking*.

Forward-looking theories: An alternative theory assumes that people look to the government's current macroeconomic policy to form their expectations of future cost and price inflation. They understand how the economy works, and they form their expectations rationally by predicting the outcome of the policies now being followed. In an obvious sense, such expectations are *forward-looking*. They are usually called **rational expectations.** Rational expectations are not necessarily always correct; instead, *the rational expectations hypothesis merely assumes that people do not continue to make persistent, systematic errors in forming their expectations.* Thus, *if the economic system about which they are forming expectations remains stable*, their expectations will be correct *on average*. Any individual's expectations at any moment of time about next year's price level can thus be thought of as the actual price level that will occur next year, plus a random error term which has a mean of zero.

> **Rational expectations have the effect of speeding up the downward adjustment of expectations. Instead of being based on past inflation rates, expected inflation is based on a correct anticipation of the outcome of existing policies.**

Evaluation: Backward-looking expectations are overly naïve. People do look ahead to the future and assess future possibilities rather than just blindly reacting to what has gone before. Yet the assumption of unbiased forward-looking expectations requires that workers and firms have a degree of understanding about the effects of government policy on inflation that few economists would claim to have. Although pure theorists are currently investigating all the ramifications of rationally formed expectations, many observers suspect that wage-setting is a mixture of rational, forward-looking behaviour, and expectations based on the experience of the recent past. Depending on the circumstances, expectations will sometimes tend to rely more on past experience, and at other times more on present events whose effects are expected to influence the future.

Of course, people will not make the same error of consistently underpredicting (or overpredicting) the inflation rate for decades, but it can happen for several years whenever people do not fully understand the causes of current inflation. Every past period of inflation has led to intense debate among economists about its causes, cures and probable future course. If professionals are uncertain, it would be surprising if wage and price setters got these matters right on average.

Random Shocks

Wage changes are also affected by forces other than excess demand and expected inflation. These forces can be positive, pushing wages higher than they otherwise would go, or negative, pushing wages lower than they otherwise would go. One such shock occurs when an exceptionally strong union, or an exceptionally weak management, comes to the bargaining table and produces a wage increase that is a percentage point or two higher than would have occurred under more typical bargaining conditions. Another example is when a government policy that is favourable to management causes this year's negotiated wage rates to be a percentage point or two *below* what they would otherwise have been.

A simple theory assumes that there are many sources of shock, and that they are independent of one another. This means that, overall, they exert a random influence on wages – sometimes speeding wage changes up a bit, sometimes slowing them down a bit, but having a net effect that more or less cancels out when taken over several years. Over the long term, they may be regarded as random events and are referred to as *random shocks*.

Random shocks may have a large positive or negative effect in any one year. Over the period of a sustained inflation, however, positive shocks in some years will tend to be offset by negative shocks in other years so that, in total, they contribute little to the long-term trend of the price level.

Overall Effect

The overall change in wage costs is a result of the three basic forces just studied. We may express this as:

$$\text{percentage increase in unit wage costs} = \text{demand effect} + \text{expectational effect} + \text{shock effect} \quad (2)$$

The Expectations-augmented Phillips Curve

We can now add the forces of expectations and random shocks to the Phillips curve determining the behaviour of unit labour costs. The Phillips curves in Figure 34.5 show the effects only of demand pressures. It will predict actual inflation only if the expected inflation rate is zero and there are no random shocks.

The relation shown in (2) above defines a whole set of Phillips curves. Each curve is drawn

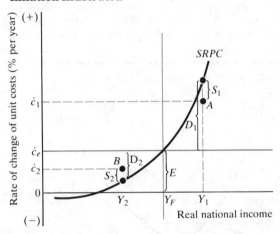

FIGURE 34.7 The Components of Cost Inflation Illustrated

The rate of cost inflation can be separated into three components: expectational inflation, demand inflation, and shock inflation. The short-run Phillips curve is drawn for a given expected rate of inflation and hence is labelled as a short-run Phillips curve. The given expected inflation rate, $\dot{c}_e$, is shown by the height of the horizontal coloured line.

Point A indicates a national income of Y_1 combined with a rate of cost inflation of $\dot{c}_1$. This rate is composed of the following: a rate to match expected inflation, shown by the brace E; a positive demand component, shown by the brace D_1 (determined by the shape of $SRPC$); and a negative shock component, shown by the brace S_1.

Point B indicates a national income of Y_2 combined with an rate of cost inflation of $\dot{c}_2$. This rate is composed of the following: a rate to match expected inflation, once again shown by the brace E; the demand component, shown by the brace D_2, which is now negative (since income Y_2 is less than Y_F); and a positive shock component, shown by the brace S_2.

for zero shocks, and a given expected rate of inflation, which enters as an additive constant. At Y_F there are no demand pressures on wages, so the height of the Phillips curve above the axis at that point is determined by the expected rate of inflation. The Phillips curve then shows how much the rate of change of unit costs varies from the expected inflation rate as a result of excess demand or excess supply in the labour market. Any particular Phillips curve drawn for a given expected rate of inflation is called a **short-run Phillips curve (SRPC)** or an **expectations-augmented Phillips curve**.

Figure 34.7 gives an example of one short-run curve, and uses it to illustrate the relations shown in equation (2). It shows unit costs rising due to increases in wage costs brought about by demand pressures (shown by the Phillips curve), expectations of inflation (which determine the height of

the Phillips curve above the axis at Y_F), and random shocks (which are shown as deviations from the Phillips curve).

ACCELERATING INFLATION

Now consider attempts to sustain a steady inflation. Assume that the economy starts out in macro equilibrium at potential income and steady prices as shown in Figure 34.8. The government then increases its expenditure. This shifts the AD curve, raising national income above its potential level so that unemployment falls below the NAIRU. Inflation then sets in at a rate determined by the Phillips curve, and by validating that inflation the low unemployment and high output can be sustained.

If that were the end of the story, the outcome might seem like a reasonable bargain. At the cost

---

FIGURE 34.8 An Accelerating Inflation

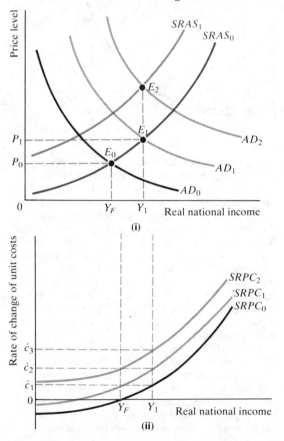

(i)

(ii)

The attempt to hold national income above its potential level and unemployment below the NAIRU will sooner or later lead to an ever-accelerating inflation. Macroeconomic equilibrium is orginally at E_0 with income Y_F and a stable price level of P_0.

The government then adopts measures to shift the AD curve to AD_1, taking national income to Y_1 and the price level to P_1. Now, however, unit costs begin to rise at a rate of $\dot{c}_1$. This shifts the $SRAS$ curve to the left and, to offset its effects, the government validates the inflation with monetary expansion. As long as the Phillips curve in part (ii) stays constant, the inflation proceeds at a constant rate.

Say that, when the curves in part (i) have reached $SRAS_1$ and AD_2, people come to expect the inflation to continue at the rate $\dot{c}_1$. The short-run Phillips curve now shifts upwards to $SRPC_1$, which passes through the point $(Y_F, \dot{c}_1)$. With income at Y_1, the inflation rate now accelerates to $\dot{c}_2$. The $SRAS$ curve now shifts upwards more rapidly and, to maintain income at Y_1, the rate of monetary validation must be increased to allow the AD curve to shift more rapidly. (Further shifts in $SRAS$ and AD are not shown in the Figure.)

Sooner or later, the inflation rate of $\dot{c}_1$ comes to be expected and the Phillips curve shifts to $SRPC_2$, which passes through the point $(Y_F, \dot{c}_2)$. The inflation rate now accelerates to $\dot{c}_3$ and the rate of monetary expansion must be further accelerated to hold income at Y_1.

of some inflation, extra output and extra employment have been obtained. Indeed, this is what many governments thought they had done in the 1960s, which decade saw the hey-day of Phillips curve trade-offs between inflation and unemployment.

We now know, however, that there is more to the story. Whatever theory of the formation of inflationary expectations we adopt, any persistent inflation will come to be expected sooner or later. The expected inflation rate will then rise, and the *SRPC* will shift upward. If the same level of national income is to be maintained, the Bank will have to raise its rate of monetary expansion to prevent the more rapid inflation from shifting the *AD* curve to the left.

Nor is this all. Ignoring shock inflation, we know that the actual inflation rate is the sum of the expected rate and the demand component. We also know that, when national income is above Y_F, the demand component is positive. It follows that whenever actual income exceeds potential income, actual inflation must exceed expected inflation. It also follows that the expected rate will itself continue to rise as it adjusts towards the actual rate. This means that the short-run Phillips curve will continue to shift upward.

An upward shift of the Phillips curve means that any given level of national income is associated with higher and higher rates of inflation. To maintain that income level, the Bank must then engage in a faster and faster rate of monetary expansion.

This gives us what is called the accelerationist hypothesis:

if the central bank validates any rate of inflation that results when national income is held above its potential level, then the inflation rate itself will accelerate continuously, *and* the rate of monetary expansion required to frustrate the monetary adjustment mechanism will also accelerate.

The Long-run Phillips Curve

Is there any level of income in this model that is compatible with a constant rate of inflation? The answer is yes, potential income. When income is at Y_F, the demand component of inflation is zero,

FIGURE 34.9 The Vertical Long-run Phillips Curve

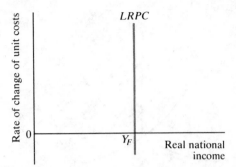

When actual inflation equals expected inflation, there is no trade-off between inflation and unemployment. In long-term equilibrium, the actual rate of inflation must remain equal to the expected rate (otherwise expectations would be revised). This can only occur at potential income Y_F, that is, along the *LRPC*.

At Y_F there is no demand pressure on the price level; hence the only influence on actual inflation is expected inflation. Any stable rate of inflation (provided it is validated by the appropriate rate of monetary expansion) is compatible with Y_F and its associated NAIRU.

as shown in Figure 34.6. This means that actual inflation equals expected inflation. There are no surprises. No one's plans are upset, so no one has any incentive to alter plans as a result of what actually happens to inflation.

> **Providing the inflation rate is fully validated, any rate of inflation can persist indefinitely as long as income is held at its potential level.[1]**

We now define the **long-run Phillips curve** (**LRPC**) as the relation between *national income and stable rates of inflation* that neither accelerate nor decelerate. This occurs when the expected and actual inflation rates are equal. On the theory just described, the long-run Phillips curve is vertical, because only at Y_F can the expected and actual rates of inflation be equal. The long-run Phillips curve is shown in Figure 34.9.

---

[1] We now see why the level of unemployment associated with potential income is called the *non-accelerating inflationary rate of unemployment*, NAIRU. At any lower level of unemployment, income exceeds potential income and the inflation rate will tend to accelerate.

FIGURE 34.10 Monetary Accommodation and Steady Inflation

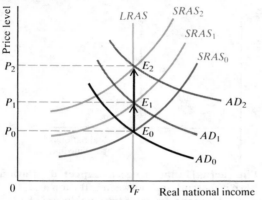

(i) **Upward-shifting** *AD* **and** *SRAS* **curves**

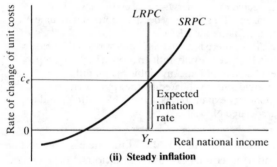

(ii) **Steady inflation**

Positive expected inflation means unit costs will be rising even when income is only at its potential level; monetary accommodation can then keep national income constant and sustain the inflation rate. The expected inflation rate is shown in (ii) by $\dot{c}_e$, which determines the height of the short-run Phillips curve above the axis at Y_F. This translates into an *SRAS* curve that is shifting upward at a constant rate from $SRAS_0$ to $SRAS_1$ to $SRAS_2$ in part (i). Monetary accommodation means that the *AD* curve in (i) also shifts upward, from AD_0 to AD_1 to AD_2. As drawn, the monetary accommodation just keeps national income constant at Y_F so inflation persists at the expected rate $\dot{c}_e$.

The inflation of unit costs in part (ii) is reflected in a constant rate of price increase, with the price level going from P_0 to P_1 to P_2 in part (i). Since the economy is on its *LRPC*, expected inflation is constant and the *SRPC* is stable.

Maintaining a point on the *LRPC* leads to steady inflation at the expected rate. This is illustrated in Figure 34.10, which shows a positive expected inflation rate being fully accommodated by the Bank's monetary expansion.

Because national income is at its potential level, there is no demand effect on inflation. Thus the actual and the expected inflation rates are equal. As a result, the situation is sustainable (as long as the Bank continues to validate the inflation). The *SRAS* curve shifts upwards at a constant rate while the short-run Phillips curve stays stable. Since everyone's expectations are being fulfilled, there is no reason for anyone to change their behaviour.

> **The long-run Phillips curve is vertical at Y_F; only Y_F is compatible with a stable rate of inflation; and any stable rate is, if fully accommodated, compatible with Y_F.**

BREAKING AN ENTRENCHED INFLATION

When an inflation has been going on for a long time, can it be reduced without inflicting major hardships in terms of unemployment and lost output?

This question greatly worried policy-makers in the early 1980s when they set out to break the existing two-digit inflation. It also worried those who, later in the 1980s, were unsatisfied with the 4 per cent inflation rate that had persisted for several years. The issue was then, and still is, how to reduce inflation when people have come to accept the existing rate as normal and have adapted their behaviour to the belief that the rate will continue.

Our analysis begins with a situation of a continuing, fully validated inflation, with actual income at its potential level. The inflation has been going on for some time, and people expect it to continue. Firmly held expectations of a continuation of the current inflation rate are what leads to the concept of *an entrenched inflation*. What is entrenched is the expectation of further inflation.

Now suppose that the central bank decides to reduce the inflation rate by reducing its rate of monetary validation. The events that follow such a decision fall into three phases.

Phase 1 – removing the inflationary gap: The first phase of the anti-inflationary policy, shown in Figure 34.11, consists of slowing the

FIGURE 34.11 Eliminating an Entrenched Inflation

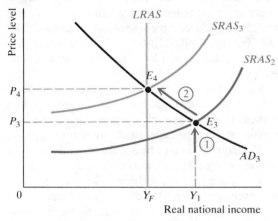

(i) **Phase 1: removing the inflationary gap**

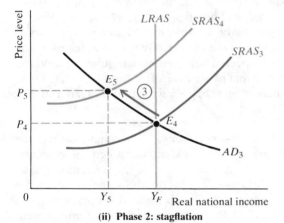

(ii) **Phase 2: stagflation**

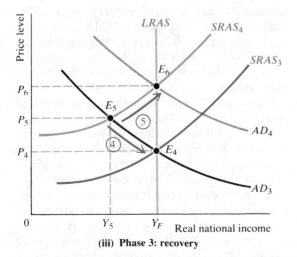

(iii) **Phase 3: recovery**

When monetary restraint is used to stop an entrenched inflation, a period of stagflation will usually be suffered. A fully validated inflation of the type shown in Figure 34.3 is taking the economy along the path shown by arrow 1 here. When the curves reach $SRAS_2$ and AD_3, the central bank stops expanding the money supply, thus stabilizing aggregate demand at AD_3.

(i) Phase 1. Wages continue to rise faster than productivity, taking the *SRAS* curve leftward. The economy moves along arrow 2, with income falling and the price level rising. When aggregate supply reaches $SRAS_3$, the inflationary gap has been removed, national income is Y_F and price level is P_4.

(ii) Phase 2. Expectations of inflation cause wages to continue to rise faster than productivity. Unit costs continue to rise, leading to a stagflation, with a growing recessionary gap and continuing inflation. The economy moves along the path shown by arrow 3. The driving force is now the $SRAS$ curve, which continues to shift because of inflationary expectations. The recessionary gap grows as income falls. The inflation continues, but at a diminishing rate. If wages stop rising faster than productivity when national income has reached Y_5 and the price level P_5, the stagflation phase is over, with equilibrium at E_5.

(iii) Phase 3. After expectations are revised, recovery takes income to Y_F and the price level is stabilized. There are two possible scenarios for recovery. In the first, the recessionary gap causes wage costs to fall (slowly), taking the $SRAS$ curve back to $SRAS_3$ (slowly) as shown by arrow 4. The economy retraces the path originally followed in part (ii) back to E_4. In the second scenario, the central bank increases the money supply sufficiently to shift the AD curve to AD_4. The economy then moves along the path shown by arrow 5. This restores potential income at the cost of a further temporary inflation that takes the price level to P_6. Full employment and a stable price level are now achieved.

rate of monetary expansion below the current rate of inflation. This slows the rate at which the aggregate demand curve is shifting upward. To illustrate what happens, we take an extreme case: the 'cold turkey approach', where the rate of monetary expansion is cut to zero so that the upward shift in the *AD* curve is halted suddenly.

Under the combined influence of an inflationary gap and expectations of continued inflation, wages continue to rise and the *SRAS* curve thus continues to shift upwards. Eventually, the gap is removed and income returns to Y_F. If the only influence on wage costs were current demand, that would be the end of the story. At Y_F there is no inflationary gap and hence no upward demand pressure on wages. Wages would stop rising, the *SRAS* curve would be stabilized, and the economy would remain at full employment with a stable price level.

Phase 2 – stagflation: Governments around the world have many times wished that things were really that simple. However, instead of settling into full employment and stable prices, economies tend to overshoot and develop a recessionary gap. The reason is, as we have already seen, that wages depend not only on current excess demand, but also on inflationary expectations. Once inflationary expectations have been established, it is not always easy to get people to revise them downward, even in the face of changed monetary policies. Thus the *SRAS* curve continues to shift to the left, causing the price level to rise and income to fall further.

> **Expectations may cause an inflation to persist after its original causes have been removed. What was initially a demand inflation due to an inflationary gap becomes a purely expectational inflation, fuelled by the expectation that it will continue.**

We have now entered phase 2, shown in part (ii) of Figure 34.11. Even though the inflationary gap has been eliminated, the expectation of further inflation leads to further wage increases. This shifts the *SRAS* curve to the left. The price level continues to rise in spite of a growing recessionary gap. This is the stagflationary phase.

The growing recessionary gap has two effects. First, there is rising unemployment. Thus the demand influence on wages becomes negative.

Second, as the recession deepens, people revise their expectations of inflation downward. When they have no further expectations of inflation, there are no further increases in wage costs and the *SRAS* curve stops shifting upwards. The stagflationary phase is over. The inflation has come to a halt, but a large recessionary gap now exists.

Keynesian and monetarist economists have often differed strongly on what they expect in a typical phase 2 period. Keynesians tend to be pessimistic and to expect a severe slump in phase 2. Monetarists tend to be optimistic and to expect a relatively mild recession in phase 2.

The main reason for these differences lies in a disagreement over what determines the expected inflation rate. Keynesians tend to believe that people adjust their expected inflation rates quite slowly, even in the face of substantial recessionary gaps. They believe, therefore, that phase 2 tends to be quite long. Monetarists are more likely to believe that downward adjustments in the expected rate can occur quite rapidly and hence that phase 2 can often be quite short. These sharply opposing views are investigated in Box 34.2.

Phase 3 – recovery: The final phase is the return to full employment. When the economy comes to rest at the end of the stagflation phase, the situation is exactly the same as when the economy is hit by an isolated supply shock (see Figure 34.1). The move back to full employment can be accomplished in either of two ways. First, the recessionary gap can be relied on to reduce wage costs, thus shifting the *SRAS* curve to the right to eliminate the effects of the overshooting caused by inflationary expectations. Second, the money supply can be increased sufficiently to shift the *AD* curve to a level consistent with full employment. These two possibilities are illustrated in part (iii) of Figure 34.11.

Those economists who worry about waiting for wages and prices to fall fear that the process will take a very long time. Those who worry about a temporary burst of monetary expansion fear that expectations of inflation may be rekindled when the central bank increases the money supply. If inflationary expectations are revived, the central bank will then have an unenviable choice. Either it must let another severe recession develop to break these new inflationary expect-

BOX 34.2 HOW SOON CAN AN ENTRENCHED INFLATION BE BROKEN?

Keynesian View

Keynesians cite two reasons for believing that the stagflation phase in the process of breaking a sustained inflation will often tend to be long and painful. The first has to do with wage momentum and the second with expectations.

Keynesians allege the existence of a self-perpetuating momentum to wage increases. This is the process discussed in Box 34.1.

The second main reason concerns expectations. In its simplest version, this reason is based on extrapolative expectations. People are assumed to believe that recent past trends will continue, and to require much new evidence before they conclude that an established inflationary trend has changed. The argument is that, unless a deviation from the past trend persists, people tend to dismiss a deviation – say, a fall in the inflation rate – as a transitory change and do not let it influence their long-term wage- and price-setting behaviour.

The combination of the momentum of wage increases, even in the face of large recessionary gaps, and slowly adjusting expectations means that phase 2 will be long. The stagflation will persist as rising wages shift the *SRAS* curve to the left until both the wage-price spiral, and expectations of further inflation, are finally broken.

Monetarist View

Monetarists expect phase 2 to be over rapidly. Some say that under ideal circumstances it may never occur at all. They offer two reasons.

First, monetarists deny that significant wage momentum exists. They believe that new wage bargains respond to current market conditions. Thus a large recessionary gap with unemployment above the NAIRU will lead quickly to new wage settlements well below the expected rate of inflation. The only lag in the adjustment of wage costs to current demand conditions is caused by the length of wage contracts. Thus, it will take only the duration of existing wage contracts before *all* wages adjust to depressed market conditions.

Second, many monetarists argue that expected inflation falls rapidly during phase 2. They accept

one version of the theory of rational expectations, according to which people look to the government's *current* macroeconomic policy when forming their expectations of future inflation.

Rational expectations have the effect of shortening the deflationary period. Instead of being strongly influenced by past inflation rates, people act on an anticipation of the outcome of current government policies. Once they realize that the Bank has stopped validating the inflation, they will quickly revise their inflationary expectations downward, and their consequent wage- and price-setting behaviour will produce a rapid slowdown in the actual inflation rate. Expected inflation falls quickly to zero, and there is no further upward push to wages arising from expectations.

This happy result occurs only if people believe the Bank is going to stick to its restrictive policies. If they are sceptical about the Bank's resolve, they may expect the inflation to continue. They will then increase wages and prices in anticipation of the inflation, and their actions will generate the very inflation that they expected. Thus, monetarists lay heavy stress on the credibility of the Bank's monetary policy.

Keynesians argue in response that sophisticated financial-market analysts may understand the underlying monetary causes of inflation, but the general public, and most labour leaders and business managers, hold different, sometimes crude, theories of inflation. They will tend, so the Keynesians argue, to extrapolate from past experience and will not even know what the Bank is doing to the money supply, let alone base their expectations on it.

The experience of the early 1980s suggested that the truth lay somewhere between these two extremes. When governments throughout the world adopted restrictive monetary policies, inflation rates fell faster than most Keynesians had predicted. But they did not fall fast enough to prevent a prolonged stagflation phase, lasting one to three years in most countries.

---

ations, or it must validate the inflation in order to reduce unemployment. In the latter case it is back where it started with a validated inflation on its hands.

Additional Anti-Inflationary Policies

The most commonly used anti-inflationary

policy, other than restricting demand, has been so-called **incomes policies**. This is a generic term. It refers to a wide range of policies running from the government's setting of voluntary guidelines for wage and price increases, through consultation on wage and price norms between unions, management and government to compulsory controls on wage, price and profit increases. They are basically interventionist policies that call for government action to alter the results that would otherwise have emerged from private-sector bargaining.

Incomes policies have a long history in Britain and Europe. They have been used in all sorts of circumstances.

The first major use of such policies is to contain demand inflations. Assume, for example, that there is an inflationary gap such as is shown by the curves $SRAS_0$ and AD_0 in Figure 34.6 (page 604). Effective wage-price controls may succeed in maintaining a zero inflation rate in spite of an inflationary gap. If, however, nothing is done to remove the excess demand, so that the $SRAS$ and the AD curves remain in their present positions, then the inflation will return as soon as the controls are removed.

Furthermore, if the government is indulging in excessive monetary expansion, the AD curve will be shifting to the right. This will cause the excess demand to grow. Experience shows that, in the face of growing excess demand, ways to circumvent the controls are found, the controls break down, and inflation proceeds to take the price level to where it would have gone if the controls had never existed.

Incomes policies can at best postpone, but cannot prevent, an inflation caused by excess demand.

A second use of incomes policies is as a temporary supplement to demand restraint to help reduce an entrenched inflation. The great attractiveness of incomes policies in such situations is that they may shorten the stagflationary phase by forcing the expected rate of inflation to fall much faster than it would on its own. The policies must be used in conjunction with a monetary policy that reduces the rate of growth of the money supply to what is compatible with the target rate of inflation. But instead of waiting for a growing recessionary gap, and rising unemployment, to curb the inflation, incomes policies would be used. Say that, starting from Y_F and an 8 per cent inflation, the rate of monetary expansion were cut from 8 to 5 to 3 to 0 per cent over four years and, at the same time, incomes policies were used to force unit-cost inflation down from 8 to 5 to 3 to 0 per cent over the same four years. In that case, the real money supply stays constant, so the AD curve does not shift left to create

a recessionary gap. The inflation is reduced by a combination of restrictive demand policy and an incomes policy. When the target inflation rate is achieved and stabilized, the controls can be removed. If everyone then expects the new lower rate to persist, inflation will have been broken without the phase 2 recession shown in Figure 34.11. *If* such a policy package had been tried, and *if* it had worked in the early 1980s, the largest world recession since the 1930s, with all its consequent suffering and lost output, would have been avoided.

A third use of incomes policies is advocated by those who believe in the existence of a permanent inflationary bias caused by an exogenous wage-push, which will not go away merely because the inflation rate is forced to a low level for a year or two. Instead, inflationary pressure will always be present when the economy is anywhere near full employment. Economists who believe in exogenous wage-push, advocate *permanent* incomes policies as the only way to achieve anything approaching full employment and relatively stable prices.

Wage-price controls are poor tools for such long-term policies since there is substantial evidence that they severely distort incentives when applied for long periods of time. General 'social contract' type agreements between unions, management and governments seem more attractive as long-term measures. But such agreements, when they have been struck in the past, have proved notably fragile, usually lasting for only a few years (although occasionally for much longer).

The checking of inflation by restrictive demand-management policies proved very costly for the world's economies in the 1980s. Several years of low inflation have restored some confidence in the belief that inflation may not be endemic in twentieth-century market economies. Although the UK economy continued to have a large recessionary gap up to the mid 1980s, the US economy moved back to full employment quite quickly without notable accelerations in inflation. The American experience tentatively suggests that the tendency for inflation to break out at levels of unemployment above the NAIRU may have been overstated, at least in that country. Experience with a full trade cycle following the end of the Great Inflation in the early 1980s is still not available. So as yet there is too little evidence to take a strong stand on the existence of permanent wage-cost push inflation.

Throughout the history of economics, inflation has been recognized as a harmful phenomenon. This view was given renewed strength as a result of the worldwide experiences of high inflation rates from the late 1960s to the mid-1980s. The governments of most advanced industrial coun-tries have resolved to prevent another outbreak of rapid inflation. Should one occur for reasons of unavoidable supply-side shocks, they resolve to prevent the inflation from continuing long enough to become firmly entrenched in people's expectations. The resolve for a strong anti-inflationary policy grew over the decade from 1975 to 1985; the success in fulfilling this resolve is a matter to be tested in the 1990s.

SUMMARY

1. A shift in the *SRAS* curve is called a supply shock, while a shift in the *AD* curve is called a demand shock.

2. A single leftward shift in the *SRAS* curve causes a rise in the price level and a fall in national income. Full employment can be restored either by a fall in unit wage costs that shifts the *SRAS* curve to the right, or by a monetary expansion that shifts the *AD* curve to the right.

3. Repeated supply shocks in terms of leftward shifts of the *SRAS* curve carry their own restraining force in terms of ever-rising unemployment if they are not accommodated by monetary expansion. If accommodated, they can give rise to a sustained supply-side inflation.

4. An isolated expansionary demand shock leads to a temporary rise in income and a rise in the price level. If it is not validated, income will fall while the price level rises when national income returns to its potential level.

5. Sustained demand shocks that are validated by monetary expansion lead to sustained inflation with income remaining above potential.

6. The original Phillips curve relates wage inflation to the level of unemploy-ment and, suitably transformed, it relates unit-cost inflation to national income. It thus determines the rate at which the *SRAS* curve is shifting.

7. Unit-cost inflation depends on the state of demand – being positive when $Y > Y_F$ and negative when $Y < Y_F$ – on expectations of inflation and random shocks. The expectations-augmented Phillips curve relates national income to unit-cost inflation and is displaced from the zero-demand-inflation point at $Y = Y_F$ by the amount of expectational inflation.

8. When $Y > Y_F$, actual inflation must exceed expected inflation. If expected inflation adjusts towards actual inflation, then the expectations-augmented Phillips curve must be shifting upwards. Hence if national income is held above potential by a constant amount, inflation must be accelerating.

9. A sustained inflation at a constant rate is only possible when $Y = Y_F$ and the monetary authorities validate the inflation. Expected inflation is then equal to actual inflation.

10. The economy reacts to breaking a sustained inflation in three phases. First, the rate of monetary accommodation is slowed until the inflationary gap is removed. Second, expectations of continued inflation cause the *SRAS* curve to continue shifting upwards, causing a stagflation with income falling below Y_F while prices continue to rise. Third, when expectations are fully adjusted, price stops rising and full employment is restored, either by a single *AD* shock, or a downward drift of unit costs causing a rightward shift in *SRAS*.

TOPICS FOR REVIEW

- Causes and consequences of demand and supply shocks
- Once-and-for-all and sustained inflations
- The original, the transformed and the expectations-augmented Phillips curves
- Starting and stopping sustained inflations
- Incomes policies

35

Employment and Unemployment[1]

In the 1980s, worldwide unemployment rose to levels that were unprecedented since the end of the Second World War. The rates were higher than during some of the years of the 1930s, although not as high as the peak unemployment rates of the 'Great Depression'. Not only was the overall level of unemployment wastefully large, the structure of unemployment was highly varied – in Britain in 1986, the unemployment rate was about 25 per cent among males under 25 and 5 per cent among women over 55. Regional disparities were significant, although not so large as they were a decade or two before. Currently, the most serious problem of localized unemployment is the very high rates among the many unskilled residents of the decaying inner cores of large industrial cities.

Economic conditions, as well as social and economic policies instituted since the 1930s, have made the economic consequences of short-term unemployment less serious than they were in earlier times. But the effects of high, long-term unemployment are still serious. Disillusioned workers give up trying to succeed within the system and sow the seeds of social unrest. The existence of two worlds – the affluent employed and the unemployed – strains the social fabric, and offends many people's sense of social justice.

KINDS OF UNEMPLOYMENT

The unemployed can be classified in various ways: by age, sex, occupation, degree of skill, and even by ethnic groups. We may classify by location – e.g., unemployment in the South East, the North West, and Scotland. We may also classify by the duration of unemployment between, say, those who are out of jobs for long periods of time and those who suffer relatively short-term bouts of unemployment. Finally, we may classify the unemployed by the reasons for their unemployment.

In the present chapter, we concentrate on the reasons for unemployment. Although it is not always possible to attach a specific cause to each unemployed person, we can estimate the total numbers of people unemployed for each major

---

[1] Details of employment and unemployment in the UK may be found in Harbury & Lipsey, Chapter 9.

cause. Different economists find it convenient to identify different causes, and there is no right or wrong about any system of classification. In what follows we take one common scheme for classifying unemployment by types:

- frictional unemployment
- structural unemployment
- real-wage (or Classical) unemployment
- demand-deficient unemployment.

Frictional Unemployment

Unemployment that is associated with the normal turnover of labour is called **frictional unemployment**. People leave jobs for many reasons, and they take time to find new jobs; young persons enter the labour force, but new workers do not often fill the jobs vacated by those who leave. This movement takes time and gives rise to a pool of persons who are 'frictionally' unemployed. They are moving between jobs. Frictional unemployment would occur even if the occupational, industrial, and regional structure of employment were unchanging.

Frictional unemployment is the irreducible minimum amount of unemployment caused by the labour turnover when new people enter the labour force and look for jobs and existing workers change jobs.

Structural Unemployment

Structural changes in the economy can cause unemployment. As economic growth proceeds, the patterns of demands and supplies change constantly. Some industries, occupations and regions suffer a decline in the demand for what they produce while other industries, occupations and regions enjoy an increase in demand. These changes require considerable economic readjustment. Structural unemployment occurs when the adjustments are not fast enough. Severe pockets of unemployment then arise in areas, industries and occupations in which the demand for labour is falling faster than its supply. **Structural unemployment** is defined as the unemployment that exists because of a mismatching between the unemployed and the available jobs in terms of any relevant dimension such as regional

location or required skills. In Britain today, structural unemployment exists, for example, in Wales, in the motorcar industry, and among machine-tool operators.

Structural unemployment occurs because changes in the regional, occupational and the industrial structure of the demand for labour do not match the changes in the structure of the supply of labour.

Structural unemployment can increase because either the pace of economic change accelerates or the pace of adjustment to change slows down. Natural forces and social policies that discourage movement among regions, industries and/or occupations can raise structural unemployment. Policies that prevent firms from replacing labour with new machines may protect employment in the short term. If, however, such policies lead to the decline of an industry because it cannot compete with more innovative foreign competitors, they can end up causing severe pockets of structural unemployment.

Real-wage Unemployment

Unemployment due to a disequilibrium real wage is called **real-wage unemployment**. It is also called *Classical unemployment*. The reference here is to the many economists who held that unemployment in the 1930s was due to excesssive real-wage rates, and whom Keynes called 'Classical economists'. Their remedy for unemployment was to reduce wages. Keynes argued that the unemployment of the 1930s was caused by deficient aggregate demand rather than by excessively high real wages.

The Keynesian view of the causes of the Great Depression eventually prevailed. But, the debate of the thirties aroused such strong emotions that many modern economists have refused to believe that *any* unemployment could be caused by excessive real wages. There was concern, however, that some of the unemployment occurring in Britain and Europe at the beginning of the 1980s was traceable to high real wages. Evidence seemed to suggest, however, that high real wages were not the most important cause of unemployment in the UK throughout the decade. They may have been a significant cause of unemployment, however, in certain areas and occupations.

We can distinguish two types of real-wage unemployment, one associated with relative wages among different groups of labour and one associated with wages in general. The former involves microeconomic issues of resource allocation that we discussed in Chapters 17 and 18. In those chapters we were concerned with unemployment caused by setting the wage rate above equilibrium in individual markets. We outlined the circumstances under which high wages would be likely to create unemployment in a particular occupation or industry. What we did not do in those microeconomic chapters was to discuss the causes of *general* unemployment. This we now do.

Disequilibrium Relative Wages

Typical microeconomic causes of unemployment are minimum floors to wages, union agreements that narrow wage differentials, nationally agreed wage structures that take no account of local market conditions, and equal-pay laws where employers perceive unequal marginal value products among the groups concerned.

Figure 35.1 shows the effect of such a minimum-wage law on the market for unskilled labour. This is the only group that will be affected, since semi-skilled and skilled workers will earn wages above the minimum in any case. The Figure shows the conflict of interest set up by minimum-wage laws:

> **those who keep their jobs receive higher wages as a result of a minimum-wage law. Others lose their jobs.**

There is evidence that minimum-wage laws cause unemployment of new entrants to the labour force. Young, inexperienced workers tend to have lower marginal productivities than do experienced workers and their low starting wages reflect this. But the young tend to learn quickly, so as they gain experience, their marginal productivities, and hence their free-market wages, rise. If a high minimum wage makes it hard for them to obtain their first job, they are delayed in gaining the work experience that would lift their market-determined wage above the minimum.

To see what is involved, consider an inexperienced school-leaver who would accept $£X$ for her first job. A potential employer is willing to pay this, but the minimum is $£1.5X$. So the employer hires someone overqualified for the job on the grounds that, if he has to pay more than he needs to, he might as well get something extra in return.

Similar results follow from wage structures that raise any group's wages above what their free-market wage would be. These structures set up a conflict of interest between those who obtain jobs at the higher wage, and are thus better off, and those who would like to work at that wage but cannot, and hence are worse off. This is true whether the higher wage is imposed by government intervention or agreed to in a union-negotiated contract.

> **Setting wages above their equilibrium levels in some markets, can cause unemployment in those markets.**

This unemployment adds to the overall level of unemployment in the whole country. Next, we turn to the possibility that wages may be above their equilibrium levels in *all* labour markets.

FIGURE 35.1 A Disequilibrium Relative Real Wage

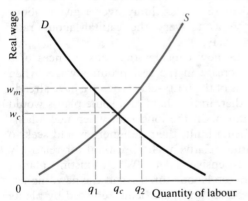

A real wage that is held above its free-market level causes unemployment in that market. The equilibrium wage is w_c, with employment of q_c. A minimum wage of w_m is now imposed. Wages rise to w_m, but employment falls to q_1. The q_1 workers who keep their jobs earn higher wages. But the $q_c - q_1$ workers who lose their jobs join the ranks of the unemployed. Also, a further $q_2 - q_c$ workers would now like employment at the higher wage, but cannot find work.

A Disequilibrium Average Real Wage

The real wage usually refers to the purchasing power of money wages. This can be measured by deflating the money wage by the retail price index.

Now we introduce a second type of real wage: the **real product wage**, which is the money wage earned in a particular industry, deflated by the value of that industry's product. For example, if labour costs £300 a week, and produces a weekly output whose market value is £400, then the real product wage is £300/£400, which is 0.75. What this means is that 75p out of every £1 of sales goes to pay for labour inputs.

Note that what matters to the employer is the full cost of hiring labour. This includes the pre-tax wage rate, any extra benefits such as pension plan contributions, and such government payroll taxes as employers' contribution to national insurance.

The real product wage can affect employment through forces operating both in the short run and in the long run. We shall consider each of these time-periods.

Before we do, a few terms must be recalled from earlier chapters. The **capital-labour ratio** is the ratio of the amount of capital to the amount of labour used to produce any given output. If that ratio is high, indicating the use of much capital relative to labour, production is called *capital intensive*. If the ratio is low, indicating relatively little capital per unit of labour, production is called *labour intensive*.

First, consider the short run, where the amount of capital is fixed. The currently existing technology was embodied in factories and machines when they were made. Since investment is a continuous process, any industry will have an array of capital, some of which can do little more than cover its variable costs and some which will make a handsome return over variable costs. Now assume that the real product wage rises by, say, 15 per cent. As a result, some plants will no longer be able to cover their variable costs, and they will close down. For example, a plant that had wages of 64p and other direct costs of 30p, in every £1 of sales, would find production worthwhile since 6p of every £1 of sales would be available as a return on already invested capital. If, however, the real product wage rose by 15 per

cent to 73.6p in every £1 of sales, then the plant would immediately be shut down, since it would not even be covering its variable costs – which would now be £103.6 in every £1 of sales. The plant's employees would then lose their jobs.

Now consider the long run, when the amount of capital can be changed. It is usually the case that, at the design stage, more or less capital can be spread over a given labour force, thus varying the capital-labour ratio by any desired amount. Once built, however, the ratio in which capital and labour is used is often determined by existing equipment, and cannot be significantly varied. For example, an engineer can design a highly automated, capital-intensive textile plant, and can also design one that uses simple, labour-intensive techniques. This allows him to vary the capital-labour ratio on the drawing board. Once a capital-intensive, automated plant is built, however, the plant manager cannot shift to a labour-intensive method of production by applying masses of labour to the automated machinery.

Capital of this type is referred to as *putty clay*. Before it is built, any amount of capital can be used in conjunction with each labourer. The capital is like putty. Once built, however, the capital has a rigid requirement for labour inputs. The capital is then like baked clay. It cannot be spread more or less thinly over a given labour force so as to vary the capital-labour ratio continuously.

Let us now consider the consequences of a large increase in the real product wage, when capital is of the putty-clay type. We have already noted that, in the short run, some plants would close down. In the long run, when new plants were being built, their designers would seek to substitute relatively cheap capital for relatively more expensive labour. When existing plants, that are too labour-intensive at the new, higher, real product wage, are being replaced by plants that are more capital-intensive, unemployment will develop. Although this may last for several years, it is a transitional phase. The final result depends on whether or not the real product wage is too high to encourage sufficient investment. Two general cases need to be distinguished.

First, the real product wage may be raised so high that no new plants that can be built with existing technology are profitable. Then, old plants that cannot cover variable costs will be closed down, no new plants will be built, and an alleviation of the unemployment (assuming the real product wage is not lowered) must await the very long run, when technologies that are profitable at existing relative prices are developed.

Second, capital-intensive plants may be profitable at existing prices, in which case some will be built. While older, more labour-intensive plants are being scrapped and new, capital-intensive ones are being built, severe unemployment may develop. Although the new plants will create some new employment, this may not be enough to match the employment lost as the old, labour-intensive plants close down. But how many new plants will be built? If the profitability of investment diminishes at the margin as the capital stock grows, then construction of new plants will stop when further units of capital are not sufficiently profitable. Will this happen before the whole labour force is re-employed? The answer depends on the height of the real wage, and on the rate at which returns to investment decline at the margin as the capital stock grows.

Demand-deficient Unemployment

The term **demand-deficient unemployment** (or cyclical unemployment) refers to unemployment that occurs because aggregate desired expenditure is insufficient to purchase all of the output of a fully-employed labour force. It is the main subject of the national-income theory studied through the macro part of this book. This theory seeks, among other things, to explain the unemployment that is caused by variations in the total demand for the nation's output – as shown by variations in both the aggregate desired expenditure curve and the aggregate demand curve.

National-income theory seeks to explain the causes of, and cures for, unemployment in excess of frictional and structural unemployment. Indeed, when we speak of 'full employment' we do not mean zero unemployment, but rather that all unemployment is frictional or structural.

Figure 35.2 shows demand-deficient unemployment as the amount of unemployment associated with a recessionary gap. This unemployment can be eliminated by raising aggregate demand sufficiently to raise equilibrium national income to coincide with potential income.

FIGURE 35.2 Demand-Deficient Unemployment

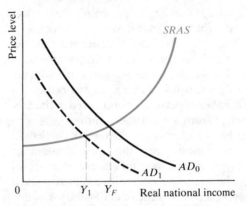

Demand-deficient unemployment occurs when the aggregate demand curve cuts the *SRAS* curve at a level of national income below potential income. When aggregate demand is given by AD_0, short- and long-run equilibrium is at Y_F. If the AD curve shifts to AD_1, equilibrium income falls to Y_1 and a recessionary gap of $Y_F - Y_1$ opens up. The accompanying unemployment is called demand-deficient unemployment.

'Full employment' means only that there is no demand-deficient unemployment. When the economy is fully employed, all remaining unemployment is frictional or structural. This unemployment, which we have called NAIRU and is sometimes called the natural rate of unemployment, cannot be reduced permanently by the tools of demand management. Because the volume of structural and frictional unemployment changes from time to time, so does the amount of unemployment regarded as full employment.

The brevity of our discussion of demand-deficient unemployment does not imply that it is unimportant. Having studied this type of unemployment throughout macroeconomics, little more needs to be said about it at this time.

THE MEASUREMENT OF UNEMPLOYMENT

There are two main problems of measurement that need to be addressed: the measurement of the overall rate of unemployment and the measurement of different types of unemployment.

Measurement of the Overall Rate

The measured overall rate of unemployment tries to identify the rate of *involuntary* unemployment. Problems arise both because we may not count some of those who are involuntarily unemployed, and because we may count some who are voluntarily unemployed or actually working.

The number of persons unemployed in the UK is estimated from a monthly count of those who are eligible to claim unemployment benefits.[1] There are reasons why this measurement of unemployment may not reflect the number of people who are truly unemployed, in the sense that they would accept the offer of a job for which they were qualified. On the one hand, the measured figure may understate involuntary unemployment by missing people who are genuinely willing to work at going wage rates. For example, some people who have worked in the past are not eligible for unemployment benefits and, therefore, are not counted. Also, those who have not worked before are not eligible for benefits. School-leavers and housewives, who would work if a booming economy offered them jobs, will not show up on the statistics as unemployed. On the other hand, the measured figure may overstate unemployment by including people who are not truly unemployed in the sense that we defined above. Some people cheat on the system by collecting unemployment benefits when they are employed. Some people do not really wish to work because the difference between their unemployment benefits and what they can earn in work is not sufficient to induce them to work. These people have voluntarily withdrawn from the workforce, but register as unemployed to collect their benefits. Others, for reasons of age or disability, are unemployable but register to receive benefits.

Measuring Types of Unemployment

Can we discover how much of total unemployment is due to each of the major causes that we have mentioned?

---

[1] Prior to 1982, the count was of those persons registered for work at job centres. The change caused an apparent fall of nearly $\frac{1}{4}$ million in the numbers of jobless.

Frictional and Structural Unemployment

Most studies provide estimates of the total of frictional and structural unemployment but not of their separate amounts. This is because, as we have already observed, frictional and structural unemployment shade into each other at the margin.

The total of frictional plus structural unemployment is measured by the percentage of the labour force unemployed when the number of unfilled job vacancies is equal to the number of persons seeking jobs.

When these two magnitudes are equal, there is some kind of job opening to match every person seeking a job. The unemployment that then occurs is either frictional or structural.

The unemployment-vacancies relation: This measure makes use of two statistics – the number of unfilled job vacancies, denoted by v, and the number of people looking for jobs, denoted by u. Figure 35.3 shows the relation between these two variables that is typically found in those countries where these data are available. The curve is called the *u-v curve*, and its negative slope indicates that, as the number of vacancies rises, the number of unemployed tends to fall, while when the number of vacancies falls, the number of unemployed tends to rise. This should not surprise us. On the one hand, when the demand for labour is high, there will be many job vacancies and, since it will be easy to find work, the number of unemployed will be low. On the other hand, when the demand for labour is low, there will be few job vacancies and, since it will be hard to find work, the number of unemployed will be high.

The shape of the u-v relation: Not only is the $u-v$ relation negatively sloped, it is also roughly the shape of a rectangular hyperbola. (This means its equation is $uv = c$, where c is a constant.) Why does the $u-v$ curve approach, but never reach, each axis. The answer lies in the behaviour of unemployment and vacancies at the extremes of the trade cycle. During a boom, the number of unemployed falls while the number of unfilled job vacancies rises, so that the economy

FIGURE 35.3 The Unemployment-Vacancies Relation

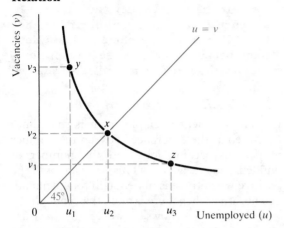

Alternations between boom and slump cause unemployment and vacancies to be negatively associated. The *u-v* curve shows a negative relation between unemployment and vacancies. At any point on the 45° line, $u = v$.

At point x, frictional plus structural unemployment is given by u_2 (and since $u = v$ along the 45° line, this unemployment is also measured by v_2). Now let a boom develop. The economy moves to some point such as y, where there are more vacancies (v_3) than unemployed (u_1). Next let a slump develop. The economy moves to some point such as z, where there are fewer vacancies (v_1) than unemployed (u_3).

moves upward to the left along its *u-v* curve. As aggregate demand gets greater and greater, the number of unfilled vacancies can increase without limit but the number of unemployed can never fall to zero – since some people always move between jobs and hence are frictionally unemployed. This is shown by the *u-v* curve getting very steep as the economy moves upwards to the left.

During a slump, the number of unemployed rises while the number of unfilled vacancies falls, so that the economy moves downwards to the right along its *u-v* curve. Unemployment can rise until it covers the whole labour force. Unfilled vacancies, however, can never reach zero, since there will always be some jobs just vacated by those who are changing jobs or leaving the labour force. This causes the curve to get flatter and flatter moving along it to the right.

The 45° line: Figure 35.3 also includes a 45° line. It shows all the points where $u = v$, i.e. where there is some job available (v) to match every unemployed person (u). Thus there is sufficient demand to put everyone to work. Unemployment occurs either because the unemployed have not yet located the jobs that are available (frictional unemployment) or because the unemployed are not suitable for the available jobs (structural unemployment).

The Figure shows how the alternation of booms and slumps moves the economy back and forth along a given *u-v* curve. A boom takes the economy above the 45° line, where the number of job vacancies exceeds the number of unemployed. A slump takes the economy below the 45° line, where the number of unemployed exceeds the number of job vacancies. When income is at its potential level, the economy is on the 45° line (at point x in the present case): every unemployed person is matched by some available job. The amount of unemployment that then exists is due to frictional and structural causes.

Changes shift the *u-v* curve: Now consider what happens if there is an increase in the total of structural plus frictional unemployment. An increased mismatching between the type of labour looking for jobs and the type of jobs available, means that, for any given state of aggregate demand, there will be more unemployed *and* more unfilled job vacancies. This shifts the *u-v* curve outwards away from the origin, as shown in Figure 35.4, indicating a rise in structural plus frictional unemployment. There will thus be more people unemployed when national income is at its potential level.

Experience of *u-v* shifts: On the measurement just described, frictional plus structural unemployment remained fairly stable in the UK until 1966 and then began to rise for adult males. Today there is substantially more unemployment than there used to be at times when, in the aggregate, the number of unfilled jobs equals the number looking for jobs. Similar shifts in the *u-v* curve have been observed in many other developed economies. Although the reasons are still subject to debate, the change is certainly consistent with a rise in structural unemployment occurring in the late 1970s and early 1980s.

FIGURE 35.4 A Shift in the Unemployment-Vacancies Relation

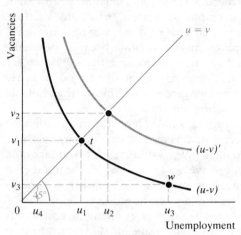

An increase in structural plus frictional unemployment shifts the *u-v* relation outwards. The curve labelled (*u-v*) is copied from Figure 35.3. A rise in frictional plus structural unemployment, shifts the (*u-v*) curve to (*u-v*)'. Originally frictional plus structural unemployment was $u_1 = v_1$ *and after the shift* it becomes $u_2 = v_2$.

Assume the curve (*u-v*) applies and a severe recession has taken the economy to point *w*. Measuring demand-deficient unemployment as unemployment minus vacancies makes it $u_3 - v_3$. By the construction of the 45° line, this is the same as $u_3 - u_4$. Now let a recovery of aggregate demand take the economy to point *t*, where there is no longer any demand-deficient unemployment (*u = v*). The rise in aggregate demand has reduced unemployment by $u_3 - u_1$, not by $u_3 - u_4$. When the economy is at point *w*, the correct measure of demand-deficient unemployment is thus $u_3 - u_4$, i.e. unemployment minus what unemployment would be if unemployment and vacancies were equal.

Real-wage Unemployment

How will real-wage unemployment affect the *u-v* relation? Let there be an economy-wide rise in real product wages. Plants and firms that can no longer cover their variable costs will shut down, and unemployment will rise throughout the country. In Figure 35.3 or 35.4 this will show up, approximately, as a movement *along* the existing *u-v* curve rather than as a *shift* of that curve. This is because there will be a large rise in unemployment and a small fall in vacancies (which would

otherwise have resulted from the normal turn-over of labour in the now-closed plants).

> A rise in the real product wage can lead to a general rise in unemployment that looks like demand-deficient unemployment because there is a rise in unemployment with some fall in unfilled vacancies.

Demand-deficient Unemployment

Demand-deficient unemployment is sometimes measured as the difference between the number of persons seeking jobs and the number of unfilled job vacancies. This statistic will be positive when there is not enough total demand, and negative when there is more than enough.

As Figure 35.4 shows, however, this measure overstates demand-deficient unemployment. As the economy moves back towards full employment, not only does *u* fall but *v* rises. Thus the difference between *u* and *v*, measured during a time of recessionary gap, overstates the amount by which unemployment can be reduced by returning to equilibrium where *u = v*.

This analysis suggests a second, more satisfactory measure of demand-deficient unemployment as total unemployment *minus estimated* frictional plus structural unemployment. This is current unemployment minus the unemployment where the *u-v* relation cuts the 45° line.

Both measures agree that demand-deficient unemployment exists whenever the economy is below and to the right of the 45° line on its *u-v* relation. The first measure (*u* minus *v*), however, gives a larger total of demand-deficient unemployment than does the second in times of recession. This measurement thus overstates the amount by which unemployment can be reduced by raising aggregate demand to move the economy back to potential income where unemployment equals vacancies.

EXPLAINING THE PERSISTENCE OF DEMAND-DEFICIENT AND REAL-WAGE UNEMPLOYMENT

The emergence of unemployment is no mystery. The puzzle is to explain why the labour market does not respond so as to restore full employment. Why, in other words, are wages relatively unresponsive to the downward pressures caused by excess demand in the labour market. We noted this phenomenon of downward 'stickiness' in Chapter 34, where we discussed the second asymmetry of the labour market: wages rise much more rapidly in response to excess demand than they fall in response to excess supply. We did not at that time attempt a full explanation of this observed behaviour.

We begin its further study by reviewing the relevant parts of the neo-Classical theory of labour markets that we introduced in Chapter 18.

The Neo-Classical Theory

In the neo-Classical theory, the wage rate adjusts to equate the demand for and supply of labour, unless monopoly or monopsony elements intervene. The macroeconomic version of the neo-Classical theory is shown in Figure 35.5. It assumes a single market for all labour and shows the demand and supply curves for labour as a function of the real wage rate. (The price level is assumed constant, so we need only plot the money wage rate.) The supply curve is drawn to illustrate the empirical evidence, first, that it is rather steeply sloped over the relevant range, and, second, that there is some maximum quantity of labour that will be supplied under free-market conditions.

If the wage rate fluctuates freely so as to clear the labour market, there will be no involuntary unemployment. Everyone who wishes to work at the equilibrium wage has a job. It is true that employment is below its maximum possible level. But the people who account for the short-fall are *voluntarily* unemployed; they would work only if the wage rate exceeded its equilibrium level.

It follows that persistent involuntary unemployment can occur in this world only if the real wage is held above its competitive equilibrium level. The remedy for involuntary unemployment is thus to reduce the wage rate.

In the neo-Classical model, the wage fluctuates (unless interfered with by monopoly or monopsony elements) so as to equate current demand for and supply

FIGURE 35.5   Unemployment in a Neo-Classical Labour Market

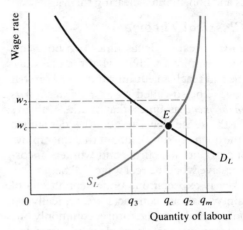

When wages fluctuate freely in competitive labour markets, all unemployment must be voluntary. The total quantity of labour that could be persuaded to work under the most favourable circumstances is q_m. The total demand and supply curves for labour plotted against the real wage rate are D_L and S_L. The competitive equilibrium is at E, with q_c labour employed at the wage rate w_c. The quantity of labour $q_m - q_c$ is voluntarily unemployed. Involuntary unemployment occurs at the disequilibrium wage rate of w_2 where q_2 labour would like to work but only q_3 can find employment. The solution to this involuntary unemployment is to lower the wage rate to w_c.

of labour; involuntary unemployment can occur only if the wage is held above its equilibrium value.

Alternative Theories

Economists have long sought to explain the persistence of involuntary cyclical unemployment that was neither frictional nor structural. For several decades, economists were satisfied with the explanation offered by early Keynesian economists. They argued that workers would stubbornly resist any downward movement in their money wage rate. Thus when the real wage rate was too high, competitive forces would not reduce it by forcing money wages down because workers would resist such a fall.

Recently, economists have sought better explanations of persistent unemployment by re-examining the behaviour of the labour market.

Many new theories have developed, but they fall into two general classes called New Classical theories and non-market-clearing theories.

New Classical Theories

The neo-Classical model assumes that both employers and employees know what the real wage would be and reach an equilibrium based on that knowledge. The so-called *New Classical theories of unemployment* assumes that markets always clear, in the sense that the quantity demanded equals the quantity supplied, but that unemployment appears because firms and workers incorrectly perceive what the real wage will be.

The key is expectations under conditions of uncertainty. Labour contracts are typically set over some period into the future, commonly one year. The money wage is agreed at the outset, but the real wage that rules over the period of the contract depends on what the price level turns out to be (i.e. on the rate of inflation over the contract period). In this theory, mistaken expectations about the price level generate market clearing with unemployment. To see how this comes about, assume that labour expects the price level over the contract period to be P_2, while firms expect the price level to be some lower level, P_1. Also assume that the money wage rate fluctuates until the quantity demanded equals the quantity supplied.

When employees and employers are bargaining, each possible money wage rate will be interpreted as indicating a particular real wage rate by each group. This will lead to a particular quantity of labour being demanded and being supplied. For any suggested money wage, w_0, the workers expect the real wage w_0/P_2, while employers expect the real wage w_0/P_1. Because of the different expectations about the price level that we have assumed, any agreed money wage rate will be interpreted as a higher real wage rate by firms than by labour. If the quantity demanded by firms exceeds the quantity supplied by labour at that money wage rate, the rate would be bargained upwards. If the quantity supplied exceeded the quantity demanded, the money wage rate would be bargained down. The bargaining process would end, and contracts would be drawn up, when there was neither excess demand nor excess supply of labour. Because each group thinks the relevant real wage is

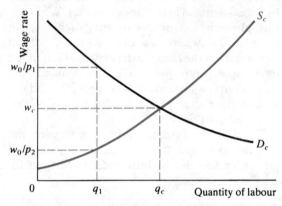

FIGURE 35.6 Unemployment Due to Mistaken Expectations

When labour expects the price level to be higher than firms expect it to be over the period of the wage contract, unemployment can occur even though the labour market clears. Over the period of the wage contract being negotiated, firms expect the price level to be P_1 while labour expects it to be P_2, which is higher than P_1 ($P_1 < P_2$). Thus, at the agreed wage rate of w_0, firms expect the real wage to be higher than does labour ($w_0/P_1 > w_0/P_2$). The quantity of labour demanded by firms and supplied by workers is in equilibrium at q_1. Employment is less than the level, q_c, it would reach if both sides had the same expectation of the price level. But the $q_c - q_1$ labourers who are without jobs have voluntarily withheld their labour because their expected real wage of w_0/P_2 is lower than the competitive equilibrium wage.

different, equilibrium will occur – as shown in Figure 35.6 – at a level of employment different from the one where the demand and supply curves intersect.

In this situation, the labour market clears in the sense that the quantity demanded is equal to the quantity supplied, and there is no involuntary unemployment. But employment is less than the equilibrium that would rule if both sides had the same expectations of the price level. The shortfall of employment is, however, voluntary. Because labour expects the price level to be higher than do firms over the contract period, workers expect a low real wage and voluntarily withhold their labour from the market.

In the New Classical model, all unemployment is voluntary. Employment falls below the competitive equilibrium level

because workers and firms have different expectations about the price level over the contract period; they thus interpret the same money wage as representing a different real wage.

This theory has had enormous influence, and many economists adhere to some of its more subtle versions. It is certainly an ingenious way to account for deviations of employment from the neo-Classical equilibrium while still assuming that markets always equate the quantities demanded and supplied. There is no evidence, however, that labour and management systematically have different expectations about the price level. Nor is there evidence that the unemployed are voluntarily withholding their labour from the market because, year after year after year, they expect the price level to be higher, and thus the real wage to be lower, than it turns out to be.

Non-market-clearing Theories

The second set of theories that we shall consider are called *non-market-clearing theories*. They deny the existence of forces that cause wages to fluctuate so as to equate the demand and supply of labour continuously. These theories start with the obvious observation that labour markets are not perfectly competitive markets in which wages respond quickly to eliminate any excess demand or excess supply. When unemployed workers are looking for jobs, employers do not go around to their existing workers and reduce their wages; instead they hang out a sign saying 'No vacancies'. This suggests something is wrong with the neo-Classical and New Classical theories, both of which view the labour market as a market where, in the absence of monopolies or monopsonies, excess supply quickly forces wages down.

Non-market-clearing theories build on the observation that many workers hold their jobs for quite long periods of time. Many employers and employees thus have long-term relations with each other. Under these circumstances, wages become, in effect, *regular payments* reflecting the employer's obligation to transfer a certain amount of wealth to the employee during the period of employment. (The discussion on pages 308–311 of Chapter 18 is relevant here.) As a result, wages become insensitive to current economic conditions.

When employers 'smooth' the income of employees by paying a steady wage, profits must fluctuate to absorb the effects of temporary increases and decreases in demand for the firm's product.

To see what is involved, consider a simple example in which a man is obligated by an unbreakable contract to work for an employer for seven years. Scheme 1 for paying the worker would be to give him a lump sum at the outset, leaving him to invest the money and spread its use for consumption over the seven years. Scheme 2 would give him a larger lump sum at the end of the seven years, leaving him to borrow against that payment so as to spread its use for consumption over the seven years. Scheme 3 would be to give him equal payments at regular intervals over the seven years.[1]

In the real world, however, the worker's obligation to stay in his job for seven years would be unenforceable. He may quit. Also, the employer may dismiss him before the seven years are up. Under scheme 1 the employee has an incentive to quit at an early date since he is in debt to his employer for the remaining years of work for which he has already been paid. Under scheme 2 the employer has an incentive to dismiss the worker before the seven years are up, since he is increasingly in debt to the employee until the end of the contract. Long-term arrangements that depend only on unenforceable understandings, will be frequently broken if either side becomes heavily in debt to the other at some points in the contract. This is one reason why actual compensation is paid as a steady stream of income, leaving neither side heavily in debt to the other at any point in time. A second reason is that this arrangement makes it unnecessary for workers to engage in large capital transactions (of investing as in scheme 1, or borrowing as in scheme 2).

Inevitably, however, some indebtedness will arise from time to time. Because of the trade cycle, and other unexpected shocks, the demand for the firm's product fluctuates. Hence the marginal revenue product of a stable workforce will also fluctuate. Under these circumstances, paying a steady compensation to employees

---

[1] The amounts could be set so as to make the present value of entering into the seven-year contract the same to the employee under each of these payment schemes.

means that indebtedness will arise on one side or the other from time to time. When the marginal revenue product has been low for some time, workers will be getting ahead because they are being paid more than their MRPs. When the marginal revenue product has been high for some time, workers will be falling behind, because they are being paid less than the MRPs. If the arrangement of paying a steady wage in spite of fluctuations in the MRP is to work, there must be some adhesive that prevents workers from quitting when they are in debt to employers, or from being dismissed when employers are in debt to them.

One institution by which the employee tends to be held to the firm is the pay-by-age tradition. Generally, the marginal product of workers rises as they gain experience, reaches a peak and then falls off as their age advances. The pay pattern, however, is often one that rises steadily with age and seniority. Thus experienced workers will get less than the value of their marginal products at earlier ages and more at later ages. This tends to hold workers to their firms.[1] But what stops the employers from dismissing workers once the value of their current marginal product begins to fall below their current wages? Union contracts requiring that least-senior employees be laid off first prevent this from happening.

The two institutions – wages that rise with age, and dismissal in ascending order of seniority – help to bind employers and employees to each other, allowing payment of a steady wage in the face of fluctuating economic circumstances.

This theory applies more to stable labour forces in established industries, and less to markets where turnover is high and long-term attachment of employees to firms rare. In such stable labour markets, the wage rate does not fluctuate so as to clear the market. Wages are written over what has been called the 'economic climate' rather than the 'economic weather'. Because wages are thus insulated from short-term fluctuations in demand, any market clearing

that does occur is through fluctuations in the volume of employment rather than in the wage.[1] In the words of the American economist Robert E. Hall: 'There is no point any longer in pretending that the labour market is an auction market cleared by the observed average hourly wage. In an extreme case, wages are just instalment payments on a long-term debt and reveal essentially nothing about the current state of the market.'[2]

Efficiency wage models: Much theoretical and empirical work is currently attempting to improve our understanding of the reasons for the persistence of involuntary unemployment. One interesting line of enquiry concerns the so-called efficiency wage models. These make use of the principal-agent analysis discussed on page 275. The principals are the firms' owners and the agents are the employees. The object is to make the employees work efficiently rather than slacking on the job. The punishment for slacking is to sack an employee. But sacking is costly in terms of lost firm-specific human capital and the costs of creating new capital in the employee's replacement. Also there is no guarantee that the replacement will work any harder.

One response to this problem is for the firm to pay its workers more than could be earned in other competitive labour markets. The penalty for workers who are caught slacking is now to lose the wage premium paid by the firm.

This theory can account for the existence of two markets. In the first market, it is difficult to monitor employees' efforts, and the cost to the firm of sacking and retraining new labour is high. Here wages are set above the competitive wage as a method of retaining labour and providing them with the incentive to work diligently. In the second market, which includes many smaller firms, wages are set at the competitive level.

This theory explains the existence of non-market-clearing wages in the first market, and may give rise to unemployment if people are willing to work for the higher wage ruling in the

---

[1] Mandatory retirement is an essential feature of this arrangement, since without it workers could decide to stay on the job for an unpredictable amount of time when their current wage was more than the value of their marginal product.

[1] Of course wages must respond to permanent shocks to a market, such as, for example, the permanent and unexpected decline in the demand for the output of a particular industry.
[2] Robert E. Hall, 'Employment Fluctuations and Wage Rigidity', *Brookings Economic Papers*, Tenth Anniversary Issue, 1980, p.120. This whole section draws heavily on Hall's excellent survey paper.

first market but not the lower wage in the second market. The circumstances under which the theory would explain general cyclical unemployment are not so obvious.

One thing that is suggested by this, and other similiar theories, is that the full explanation of persistent involuntary unemployment may be the sum of many different causes, each contributing to the persistence of non-market-clearing wages, and collectively interacting to create cyclical involuntary unemployment.

> **The basic message of non-market-clearing theories is that freely functioning labour markets, even those completely free from monopoly and monopsony elements, cannot be relied on to prevent outbreaks of involuntary unemployment by constantly equating current demand for labour with current supply.**

CURES FOR UNEMPLOYMENT

Frictional Unemployment

Labour turnover, which causes frictional unemployment, is an inevitable part of the functioning of the economy. There will always be some turnover, as people of all ages change jobs for any reason. Furthermore, some frictional unemployment is an inevitable part of the learning process. One reason why there is a high turnover rate, and hence high frictional unemployment, among the young is that one has to try jobs to see if they are suitable. New entrants – whether the young, or older women who have just decided to take a job rather than stay at home – often try several jobs before settling into the one that most satisfies, or least dissatisfies, them.

> **Frictional unemployment can be reduced by reducing the amount of time taken between jobs.**

Insofar as frictional unemployment is caused by ignorance, increasing the knowledge of labour-market opportunities can help.

Demographic and behavioural changes should lead to a national decline of frictional unemployment over the 1990s. First, the proportion of the labour force made up of youth will probably decline. Since young people have high rates of frictional unemployment, this will cause a fall in frictional unemployment. Similarly, the long-term upward trend in the female participation rate must soon slow down as participation rates approach equilibrium levels. This means that the proportion of female workers who are recent entrants to the labour force will also decline, and with that, frictional unemployment among female workers will decline.

Finally, policy changes that make it easier for youths to find jobs from which they can learn, and hence raise their productivity, could help. Youth training, and schemes aimed at subsidizing the wage rate for young workers, have also helped.

Structural Unemployment

Changes in the structure of the economy that cause bouts of structural unemployment are an inevitable result of the economic growth which is the main cause of long-term increases in average living standards. Although this does not make structural unemployment any the less unpleasant, it does put such unemployment into some perspective.

Two basically different approaches can be taken to reducing structural unemployment, and to alleviating the hardship that it causes. The first, which has sometimes found expression in British economic policy, is to try to prevent, or at least to slow, the changes in the economy that cause structural unemployment. The second, which has been pioneered in Sweden, is to accept the economic change that accompanies economic growth and to design policies to make the economy more adaptive to change.

> **Structural unemployment can be reduced by measures that increase the degree of labour mobility between regions, occupations and industries.**

Reducing the amount of change: Throughout the centuries many governments and workers have sought to combat the threat of structural unemployment by preventing, or slowing, structural changes.

One way in which this has been done in the past is through *manning agreements*. These seek to prevent people from being declared redundant, and thus becoming structurally unemployed, because of new innovations. For example, the replacement of coal by diesel in railway engines thirty years ago made firemen who shovelled coal into the boiler unnecessary, but existing firemen were kept to sit in the cabs of diesel engines by agreement between British Rail and the firemen's union. A second way is through the support of declining industries by public funds. For example, if some industry could sell an output of X on the free market but government subsidizes it to produce $2X$, jobs are provided for the 50 per cent of the industry's labour force who would otherwise have become unemployed.

Both of these policies will be attractive to the industry's workers. They may have trouble finding other jobs and, when they do, their skills may not turn out to be highly valued in their new industries. Policies that manipulate the rate at which jobs disappear in particular categories, or in whole industries, can be successful. If, however, the policies resist change indefinitely, they will not in the end be sustainable. Manning agreements raise costs and hasten the decline of an industry threatened by competitive products. An industry that is declining due to market forces, but supported by government subsidy, becomes an increasingly large charge on the public purse as the market becomes less and less favourable to its success. Sooner or later, public support is withdrawn, and precipitous decline in output and employment can ensue.

Measures that attempt to reduce structural unemployment by reducing the amount of structural change in the economy are self-defeating in the long run.

In assessing the above remedies for structural unemployment, it is important to realize that, although not viable in the long run for the economy, they may be the best alternative for the affected workers. Thus, there is often a real conflict between those threatened by structural unemployment, whose interests lie in preserving their old jobs, and the general public, whose interests lie in encouraging economic growth.

Increasing adaptability to change: The conflict just stated can be at least partly reduced by accepting the changes that accompany economic growth. Some industries decline and

some jobs are lost; other industries rise and other jobs are created. Policies can then be designed to reduce the costs, and increase the speed, of the adjustments that must be made by those who are affected by growth.

For example, retraining and relocation grants can make it easier for labour to move among jobs and geographic areas. They can also reduce the hardship involved in making these movements. Such policies have the advantage of helping the economy adjust to inevitable change and, by speeding up the change, of reducing the number of persons who are structurally unemployed.

To reduce structural unemployment, policies that inhibit adjustment can be avoided, and policies that encourage it can be adopted.

British housing policy is a good example of a policy that inhibits the geographical reallocation of labour and hence increases structural unemployment. Rent controls discourage the private construction of rental accommodation in expanding areas. By contributing to housing shortages, they make it harder for people to move. Geographic movement is also discouraged by the provision of council housing at low rents, accompanied by an inadequate supply of such housing in expanding centres. To leave a declining area often means giving up cheap, and available, council housing in return for nothing more than a place on a long waiting list in the expanding area. English laws and procedures governing sales of real estate make selling one's house to move to another area more long-drawn-out, more costly and more uncertain than in many other countries where an offer to purchase is legally binding on the purchaser and acceptance of that offer is legally binding on the seller.

Unemployment and supplementary benefits sometimes make the margin between the income from unemployment in contracting areas and the income from employment in expanding areas less than the costs, and risks, of moving. Such benefits discourage geographic mobility and so contribute to structural unemployment. This does not make policies to reduce the suffering from involuntary unemployment undesirable. Designing such policies without concern for their potential to increase structural unemployment, however, is self-defeating in the long run.

Designing policies that encourage mobility and adaptability while not denying assistance to those in need is not an easy task. The payoff, however, can be great compared with policies that give equal assistance, but discourage adaptability.

Demand-deficient and Real-wage Unemployment

Real-wage and demand-deficient unemployment arise from different causes. A rise in the real product wage that makes it unprofitable to operate many existing plants will cause widespread unemployment. This real-wage unemployment arises from a leftward shift in the *SRAS* curve. A major reduction in any of the components of planned aggregate expenditure will also cause unemployment, this time by shifting the *AD* curve to the left.

It may not be so obvious, however, that both of these types of unemployment can be removed from either the demand or the supply side. Consider demand-side cures first.

A rightward shift in the *AD* curve will remove demand-deficient unemployment by restoring sufficient demand to return the economy to its potential income in the manner shown in Figure 35.2 on page 621. A rightward shift in the *AD* curve will also remove real-wage unemployment. It will drive up the price level with wages constant and so restore full employment at a lower real product wage. This is shown in Figure 34.1 on page 595 where a leftward shift in the *SRAS* curve (which could have been caused by a rise in the real product wage) is offset by a rightward shift in the *AD* curve. (The adjustment will, of course, be frustrated if unions insist on raising money wages at the same rate as the general price level is rising. This will shift the *SRAS* curve to the left as fast as the *AD* curve is shifting to the right, setting up the type of wage-cost push inflation that is shown in Figure 34.2 on page 596.)

Now consider supply-side cures. A rightward shift in the *SRAS* curve is bought about by a lowering of the real product wage. This can happen either because money wage rates fall or because labour productivity rises, thus lowering the labour cost of each unit of output. Real-wage unemployment is caused by a rightward shift in the *SRAS* curve, and a leftward shift in that curve can clearly remove it. Demand-deficient unemployment is caused by a leftward shift in the *AD* curve, and a rightward shift is the *SRAS* curve can clearly remove it (by reducing the price level).

Conclusion

Most economists agree that, throughout most of the 1980s, there was significant demand-deficient unemployment. This unemployment was accepted by government policy-makers as a necessary, although unfortunate, consequence of their anti-inflationary policies and their drive to reduce the public-sector borrowing requirement. Some economists felt that these policies were not worth the price that was entailed in terms of unemployment. They called for expansionary demand-management policies to eliminate the demand-deficient unemployment.

Most economists agreed that there was more structural unemployment in the UK in the 1980s than there had been at any time since the end of the Second World War. Many called for policies to increase the adaptability of the economy and reduce inhibitions to the movement of labour. Others were more attracted by government intervention, mainly in the form of moving work to the places where unemployment was highest. Grants to encourage unemployed persons to start regional, service-oriented industries contained a bit of both approaches.

Whether or not real-wage unemployment was a serious problem in Britain and Europe throughout the 1980s, it was probably the most contentious issue concerning unemployment. Advocates of the real-wage explanation argued that British real wages were some 10–15 per cent too high in the early 1980s and, as a result, significant amounts of capital were being scrapped. They also pointed out that the first sign of such an unhappy situation is a rise in recorded labour productivity such as occurred in the early 1980s. Since the least efficient plants are scrapped first, the average output per head of those remaining in employment will rise steadily. Economists who held this view argued that the unemployment could not be eliminated until the real product wage fell significantly – as it did in many American industries in the early 1980s.

Whatever was true earlier in the decade, the evidence in the last half of the 1980s suggested the existence of substantial demand-deficient unemployment. As the British economy was expanding during the latter part of the decade, unemployment fell, showing that a recovery of demand was sufficient to remove much of the existing unemployment.

SUMMARY

1. Frictional unemployment is related to the natural dynamics of the labour force. It can be reduced by cutting the time labour takes in moving between jobs, but it can never be eliminated.

2. Structural unemployment is related to the changing structure of the demand for labour by regions, occupations and industries. It arises because of a mismatching of the structures of supply and demand; there is no deficiency of total jobs but there is a mismatching between the kind and place of the available jobs and the available labour supply. It can vary as the speed and efficiency with which the structure of labour supply adjusts to the structure of labour demand, but it can never be eliminated as long as change occurs and does not happen instantaneously.

3. Real-wage unemployment occurs because the real product wage is too high. At the existing real product wage and state of technology, it does not pay to employ all the labour force. It can be eliminated by reducing the real product wage or by changing the capital-labour ratio among the employed labour force in the long and very long runs until it is profitable to employ all the labour.

4. Demand-deficient or cyclical unemployment occurs because aggregate desired expenditure is not sufficient to employ all the available labour. It is the amount of unemployent caused by a recessionary gap when national income falls short of potential income. It can be eliminated by any demand or supply side measure that removes the recessionary gap.

5. Involuntary unemployment occurs when there are no jobs available for some who would like to work at the going wage rate. If the labour market is competitive and everyone knows the real wage rate, unemployment can occur in equilibrium if workers expect a real wage rate that differs from what employers expect (New Classical theories). This occurs when workers and employers have different expectations about the inflation rate. Such unemployment is voluntary. Involuntary unemployment can occur when wages are set by longer-run considerations and do not fluctuate to clear the labour market in the short run (non-market-clearing theories.)

6. The overall number of people willing to work but not working may be overestimated because people who appear unemployed do not really want a job, or it may be underestimated because people who want a job do not appear to be unemployed (because, e.g., they have withdrawn from the labour force).

7. The NAIRU or natural rate of unemployment occurs when the aggregate number of job vacancies equals the aggregate number of unemployed. All remaining unemployment is structural and frictional.

TOPICS FOR REVIEW

- Frictional, structural, demand-deficient and real-wage unemployment
- Causes of each type of unemployment
- The u-v curve
- Unemployment due to misperceptions of the inflation rate
- Efficiency wage hypothesis
- Neo-Classical, New Classical and non-market-clearing theories of unemployment

36

Fluctuations and Growth

The economic magnitudes that we observe in the real world are constantly changing. These changes can be seen as two basic movements: an up-and-down oscillatory movement called *cyclical fluctuations* and a trend rate of change which in the case of the GDP is positive and is called *economic growth*.

FLUCTUATIONS IN NATIONAL INCOME

Output, employment and living standards have all shown an upward trend in advanced countries over the last two centuries. If you compare any year in the 1980s with any year in the first decade of this century, your overwhelming impression will be one of growth, even if you choose a recent year of low activity and compare it with a boom year from the 1900s.

If, however, you take each year of the 1970s and 1980s and compare it with the year following, you will find that economic activity proceeds in an irregular path, with forward spurts being followed by pauses and even relapses. These short-term fluctuations are commonly known as **trade cycles** in Britain and *business cycles* in North America. At some times and places the patterns have been remarkably regular, at other times less so.

Some investigators have thought that they could discern several types of cycles in economic activity. One type, which is clearly observable in the nineteenth-century British data, had a duration of about nine years from peak to peak. This nine-year cycle was the one usually identified in the past as *the* trade cycle. A second type of cycle lasted anywhere from 18 to 40 months, and was sometimes associated with variations in stocks. Finally, some economists have thought that they could perceive a third, very long cycle, of about 50 years' duration, that was associated with, among other things, major fluctuations of investment activity following some fundamental innovation. Of all the 'cycles', this long-wave one is the most conjectural, and we shall say nothing further about it in this book except to notice that the depressed 1980s are five decades after the depressed 1930s, which were fifty years after the 'hungry eighties' (the 1880s).

The Terminology of Business Fluctuations

Although recurrent fluctuations in economic activity are neither smooth nor regular, a vocabulary has developed to denote their different stages. Figure 36.1 shows stylized cycles that illustrate some terms.

Trough: A trough is simply the bottom. It is characterized by high unemployment of labour and a level of consumer demand that is low in relation to the capacity of industry to produce, causing a substantial amount of unused industrial capacity. Business profits are low; for some companies they are negative. Confidence in future sales is low, and firms are consequently unwilling to risk making new investments. If a trough is deep enough, it may be called a **depression**.

Recovery: When something sets off a **recovery**, the lower turning point of the cycle has been reached. The symptoms of a 'recovery' (or expansion) are many: worn-out machinery is replaced; employment, income and consumer spending all begin to rise; expectations become more favourable as a result of increases in production, sales and profits. Investments that once seemed risky may now be undertaken as the climate of business opinion starts to change from pessimism to optimism. As demand expands, production can be expanded with relative ease merely by re-employing the existing unused capacity and unemployed labour.

Peak: A peak is the top of the cycle. At the peak there is a high degree of utilization of existing capacity; labour shortages may be severe, particularly in key skill categories; and shortages of essential raw materials may develop. Output can be raised further only by investment that increases capacity. Because such investment takes time, further rises in demand are now met more by increases in prices than by increases in production. As shortages develop in more and more markets, a situation of general excess demand for factors develops. Costs rise, but prices rise also, and business remains generally profitable.

Recession: A **recession**, which often follows a peak, is a sustained fall in the level of economic activity. Demand falls off, and as a result production and employment fall. As employment falls, so do households' incomes; falling income causes demand to fall further. Profits drop and more and more firms get into difficulties. Investments that looked profitable on the expectation of continually rising demand suddenly appear unprofitable, and investment is reduced to a low level. It may not even be worth replacing capital goods as they wear out because much existing capacity is unused.

Booms and slumps: Two non-technical but very graphic terms are often used to describe the cycle. The whole falling half is often called a *slump* and the whole rising half a *boom*. These are useful terms which we use when we do not wish to be more specific about the economy's position in the cycle.

FIGURE 36.1 A Stylized Trade Cycle

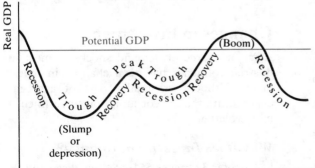

Although the phases of business fluctuations are described by a series of commonly used terms, no two cycles are the same. Starting from a lower turning point, a cycle goes through a phase of recovery, or expansion, reaches an upper turning point, and then enters a period of recession. Cycles differ from one another in the severity of their troughs and peaks and in the speed with which one phase follows another. Severe troughs are called *depressions*; extreme peaks are called *booms*.

Explaining Trade Cycles

An explanation of the trade cycle must answer two questions: (1) What are the factors that cause GDP and other key macro variables to fluctuate? (2) What are the factors that cause those fluctuations to form a cyclical pattern? These two questions are taken up in the two main sections that follow.

WHY DO INCOME AND EMPLOYMENT FLUCTUATE?

Figure 36.2 presents an explanation of the fluctuations of national income in terms of a fluctuating *AD* curve and a stable *SRAS* curve.

There is general agreement that over the course of economic history, the trade cycle has been driven mainly by fluctuations in aggregate demand. Nevertheless, particular cycles can sometimes be explained in part by aggregate supply shocks. Indeed, events of the mid-1970s

made the citizens of advanced industrial countries acutely aware of supply-side causes.

> **Aggregate demand shocks are a major historical source of fluctuations in GDP; aggregate supply shocks are a secondary source.**

Sources of Aggregate Demand Shocks

Aggregate demand shocks that cause income and employment to rise or fall have numerous sources. Occasionally, there are sufficient shifts in the consumption function to raise or lower aggregate expenditure significantly and hence alter income and employment. Major shifts in government expenditure and tax policies can raise or lower aggregate expenditure. Monetary policy can also have a major influence. A tight monetary policy that shifts the *LM* curve to the left and forces up interest rates can reduce expenditure, income and employment. A lax monetary policy that lowers interest rates can do the reverse. Increases in exports or decreases in imports that increase domestic production, can give a major upward push to aggregate expenditure, income and employment. All of these forces can result in significant demand shocks to the economy. Possibly the most important factor from the demand side, however, is investment expenditure and we shall look at this in more detail in the next section. First, to complete our preliminary list, we must add supply shocks. An upward shift in the aggregate supply function can, as we saw in the discussion surrounding Figure 34.1, cause a recession in which income falls in the face of a rising price level.

Changes in Investment

A major source of demand shocks in most industrial countries has been changes in investment. Although a smaller part of aggregate expenditure than is consumption, investment is more volatile.

Why Does Investment Change?

In Chapter 32 (pages 551–554) we discussed the major determinants of investment and that discussion should be re-read now. The theory of

FIGURE 36.2   A Demand-driven Trade Cycle

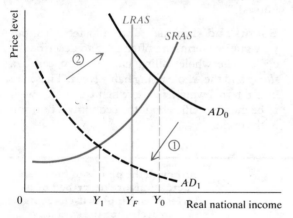

Fluctuations in aggregate demand can cause fluctuations in income and employment.
Assume that over the course of the trade cycle, aggregate demand oscillates regularly. The economy starts with a high level of aggregate demand, AD_0, and income at its peak, Y_0. The *AD* curve then falls continuously, as shown by arrow 1, until it reaches AD_1. Income falls through Y_F and reaches its trough at Y_1.
The *AD* curve then rises continuously, as shown by arrow 2. Income is taken back through Y_F and reaches Y_0 at the next peak.

aggregate demand already takes account of the response of investment (and other types of expenditure) to variations in interest rates. That responsiveness is a major determinant of the slope of the *IS* curve. Shifts in the *AD* function caused by investment must arise from changes in determinants of investment other than the interest rate – these are variables that are incorporated in the *AD* curve's *ceteris paribus* clause. A brief review of each, as a source of shifts in investment, follows.

Investment in capital equipment provides capacity for future production. Its expected profitability depends on expected future market conditions. Expectations are uncertain at the best of times and may occasionally be influenced by waves of optimism or pessimism that sweep over the trading community.

Product and process innovations are not developed at an even pace. Key new products such as the mass-produced car in the 1920s, cheap radios and record-players in the 1930s, computers in the 1960s, high-tech products based on semiconductors in the 1980s, and a host of others can lead to bouts of investment spending. Similarly, innovations in production such as robotization and computerization of assembly-line processes and the replacement of one energy source by another can require large rounds of new expenditure, particularly where the new technology must be embodied in new capital equipment.

Major changes in the rate of family formation can cause major changes in the demand for housing.

All of these changes, and more, can cause shifts in desired investment expenditure that are large enough to initiate major demand shocks.

THEORIES OF THE CYCLE

The many theories of the cycle fall into two main types. The first relies on random or haphazard shocks to aggregate demand being turned into systematic fluctuations in national income. The second relies on systematic fluctuations in the initiating shocks.

Random Shocks

Theories of this type rely on lags. Most empirical macro-models that are designed to fit the data have quite long lags in their behavioural relations. For example, if a fall in the rate of interest makes a new investment programme profitable, it may take six months to plan it, three months to let contracts, six more months before spending builds up to its top rate and another twenty-four to complete the project. This means that investment expenditure will be subject to a *distributed time-lag*; changes in the rate of interest will cause a reaction in investment expenditure that is distributed over quite a long period of time.

A pioneering study by two American economists, Irma and M. A. Adelman, established that, if occasional random shifts in exogenous expenditure disturb a system of expenditure-determining equations all of which contain long lags, a cycle is generated. Here the disturbing influences are random or erratic, but the consequences are a cyclical path for the major endogenous macro-variables such as national income and unemployment.

Each of the major components of aggregate expenditure have sometimes undergone shifts large enough to disturb the economic system significantly. The long lags in the expenditure function can then convert these shifts into cyclical oscillations in national income.

A recent line of theorizing has developed what are called equilibrium theories of the trade cycle. These rely on microeconomic models of markets which are always in equilibrium – a micro underpinning of cycle theory that has yet to gain major acceptance. Nonetheless, they rely on the basic process used in the Keynesian empirical models where random shocks have systematic effects due to long lags that smooth these effects out over time.

Systematic Shocks

The second main type of cycle theories rely on systematic disturbances to create systematic fluctuations. The most famous of these is called the multiplier-accelerator theory. No one believes any longer that it provides *the* explanation of cycles. Many economists still accept, however, that it captures one major element of cyclical fluctuations. To understand it, we need first to study a further major cause of variations in investment.

The Accelerator Theory of Investment

The **accelerator theory of investment** relies on a second way in which investment can become an endogenous variable. (The first is through its dependence on the interest rate.) This theory relates investment to national income. The possibility of systematic fluctuations arises because the *level* of investment is related to *changes* in national income.

The need for plant and equipment is obviously derived from the demand for the goods the plants and equipment are designed to produce. If there is a demand that is expected to persist, and that cannot be met by increasing production with existing industrial capacity, then new plants and equipment will be needed.

Investment expenditure occurs while the new capital equipment is being built and installed. If the desired stock of capital goods increases, there will be an investment boom while the new capital

is being produced. But if nothing else changes, and even though business conditions continue to look rosy enough to justify the increased stock of capital, investment in new plant and equipment will cease once the larger capital stock is achieved.

This makes investment depend on changes in sales, and hence on changes in national income, as illustrated in Table 36.1. The more formal derivation of the theory is outlined below.

Let there be a simple relationship between the GDP and the amount of capital needed to produce it:

$$K = \alpha Y \,, \qquad (1)$$

where K is the required capital stock. The coefficient α (the Greek letter alpha) is the capital-output ratio; $\alpha = K/Y$ and is also called the accelerator coefficient. First differencing (1) and noticing that investment is, by definition, the change in the capital stock, yields

$$I = \Delta K = \alpha \Delta Y \,, \qquad (2)$$

TABLE 36.1 An Illustration of the Accelerator Theory of Investment

(1)	(2)	(3)	(4)	(5)
Year	Annual sales	Change in sales	Required stock of capital[1]	Net investment: increase in required capital stock
1	£10	£0	£50	£0
2	10	0	50	0
3	11	1	55	5
4	13	2	65	10
5	16	3	80	15
6	19	3	95	15
7	22	3	110	15
8	24	2	120	10
9	25	1	125	5
10	25	0	125	0

[1] Assuming a capital-output ratio of 5:1.

With a fixed capital-output ratio, net investment occurs only when it is necessary to increase the stock of capital in order to change output. Assume that it takes £5 of capital to produce £1 of output per year. In years 1 and 2 there is no need for investment. In year 3 a rise in sales of £1 requires investment of £5 to provide the needed capital stock. In year 4 a further rise of £2 in sales requires an additional investment of £10 to provide the needed capital stock. As columns 3 and 5 show, the amount of net investment is proportional to the *change* in sales. When the increase in sales tapers off in years 7–9, investment declines. When sales no longer increase in year 10, net investment falls to zero because the capital stock of year 9 is adequate to provide output for year 10's sales.

i.e. investment is a constant proportion of the change in national income. This is called the 'simple', or sometimes the 'naive', accelerator.

The main insight which the accelerator theory provides is its emphasis on the role of net investment as a *disequilibrium* phenomenon – something that occurs when the stock of capital goods differs from what firms and households would like it to be. This gives the accelerator its particular importance in connection with *fluctuations* in national income. As we shall see, it can itself contribute to those fluctuations.

Limitations of the accelerator: Taken literally, the accelerator posits a mechanical and rigid response of investment to changes in sales (and thus, aggregatively, to changes in national income). It does this by assuming a proportional relationship between changes in income and the size of the desired capital stock, and by assuming a fixed capital-output ratio. Each assumption is to some degree questionable.

Changes in sales that are thought to be temporary in their effect on demand will not necessarily lead to new investment. It is usually possible to increase the level of output from a given capital stock by working overtime or extra shifts. While this would be more expensive per unit of output in the long run, it will usually be preferable to making investments in the new capital equipment that would lie idle after a temporary spurt of demand had subsided. Thus expectations about what is the required stock may lead to a much less mechanistic response of investment to income than the accelerator suggests.

A further limitation of the accelerator theory is its view of what constitutes investment. The fixed capital-output ratio emphasizes investment in 'capital widening', which we first encountered in Chapter 19 and which is investment in additional capacity that uses the same ratio of capital to labour as does existing capacity. It does not explain 'capital deepening', also encountered in Chapter 19, and which is the kind of increase in the amount of capital per unit of labour that occurs in response to a fall in the rate of interest. Nor does the theory say anything about investments stimulated by new processes or products. Furthermore, it does not allow for the fact that investment in any period is likely to be limited by the capacity of the capital-goods industry.

For these and other reasons, the accelerator does not by itself give anything like a complete explanation of variations in investment in capital goods, and it should not be surprising that a simple accelerator theory provides a relatively poor overall explanation of changes in investment. Yet accelerator-like influences do exist, and they play a role in the cyclical variability of investment.[1]

Multiplier-accelerator Theory

The theory linking systematic fluctuations in national income to systematic fluctuations in investment expenditure unites the accelerator theory just discussed with the version of Keynesian multiplier theory that sees the multiplier as a process working over time as successive rounds of induced expenditure build up in response to some initiating shock. (See pages 483–487, especially Box 27.2.)

This **multiplier-accelerator theory** of the cycle is divided into three steps: first, a theory of cumulative upswings and downswings explains why, once started, movements tend to carry on in the same direction; second, a theory of floors and ceilings explains why upward and downward movements are eventually brought to a halt; and third, a theory of instability explains how, once a process of upward or downward movement is brought to a halt, it tends to reverse itself.

Cumulative movements: Why does a period of expansion or contraction, once begun, tend to develop its own momentum? First, the multiplier process tends to cause cumulative movements. As soon as a revival begins, some unemployed labourers find work again. These people, with their newly acquired income, can afford to make much-needed consumption expenditures. This new demand causes an increase in production and creates new jobs for other unemployed workers. As incomes rise, demand rises; as demand rises, incomes rise. Just the reverse happens in a downswing. Unemployment in one

---

[1] In spite of decades of attempts to refute the accelerator empirically, *flexible accelerators* continue to provide significant explanations of much investment expenditure in many econometric models. (The flexible accelerator avoids some of the simple accelerator's mechanical rigidities referred to in the text.)

sector causes a fall in demand for the products of other sectors, which leads to a further fall in employment and a further fall in demand.

A second major factor is the accelerator theory. New investment is needed to expand existing productive capacity and to introduce new methods of production. When consumer demand is low and there is excess capacity, investment is likely to fall to a very low level; once income starts to rise and entrepreneurs come to expect further rises, investment expenditure may rise very rapidly. Furthermore, when full employment of existing capacity is reached, new investment becomes one of the few ways available for firms to increase their output.

A third major explanation for cumulative movements is expectations. All production plans take time to fulfil. Current decisions to produce consumer goods and investment goods are very strongly influenced by business expectations. Such expectations can sometimes be volatile, and sometimes self-fulfilling. If enough people think, for example, that bond prices are going to rise, they will all buy bonds in anticipation of the price rise, and these purchases will themselves cause prices to rise. If, on the other hand, enough people think bond prices are going to fall, they will sell quickly at what they regard as a high price and thereby actually cause prices to fall. This is the phenomenon of *self-realizing expectations*. It applies to many parts of the economy. If enough managers think the future looks rosy and begin to invest in increasing capacity, this will create new employment and income in the capital-goods industries, and the resulting increase in demand will help to create the rosy conditions whose vision started the whole process. One cannot lay down simple rules about so complicated a psychological phenomenon as the formation of expectations, but there is a bandwagon effect. Once things begin to improve, people expect further improvements, and their actions, based on this expectation, help to cause further improvements. On the other hand, once things begin to worsen, people often expect further worsening, and their actions, based on this expectation, help to make things worse.

The multiplier-accelerator process, combined with changes in expectations that cause expenditure functions to shift, **can explain the cumulative tendencies of recessions and recoveries.**

Floors and ceilings: The next question that arises is: why do these upward and downward processes ever come to an end?

A very rapid expansion can continue for some time, but it cannot go on for ever because eventually the economy will run into bottlenecks (or ceilings) in terms of some resources. For example, if investment funds become scarce, interest rates will rise. Firms will now find new investments more expensive than anticipated, and some will now appear unprofitable. In another case, the expansion may be halted by exhaustion of the reservoir of unemployed labour. The full-employment ceiling guarantees that any sustained rapid growth rate of real income and employment will eventually be slowed. At this point the accelerator again comes into play. A slowing down in the rate of increase of production leads to a decrease in the investment required in new plant and equipment. This causes a fall in employment in the capital-goods industries and, through the multiplier, a fall in consumer demand. Once consumer demand begins to fall, investment in plant and equipment will plummet because firms will have excess productive capacity. Unemployment begins to mount, and the upper turning point has been passed.

A rapid contraction, too, is eventually brought to an end. Consider the worst sort of depression imaginable, one in which every postponable expenditure of households, firms or governments has been postponed. Even then, aggregate demand will not fall to zero. Households can and will use up savings, or go into debt, to buy the necessities of life. This creates employment, and income for people to spend. Moreover, transfer payments to households in the form of unemployment compensation and welfare payments provide the funds to support minimum consumption expenditures. Much government expenditure is committed by statute and so must be sustained. Civil service salaries and defence expenditures will continue. Even business investment, in many ways the most easily postponed component of aggregate demand, will not fall to zero. In the industries providing food, basic clothing, and shelter, demand may remain fairly high in spite of quite large reductions in national income. These industries will certainly be carrying out some investment to replace equipment as it wears out, and they may even undertake some new investment. Furthermore, new innovations may provide opportunities for new investment even in the midst of a serious general depression. For example, even in the depths of the Great Depression, the electronics industries, based on such newly popular products as radios and record-players, underwent a boom that held unemployment low and investment high in south-east England.

Taken together, the minimum levels of consumption, investment and government expenditure will assure a minimum equilibrium level of national income that, although possibly well below the full-employment level, will not be zero. This is the floor. (This may be small comfort to those affected. It is possible for the economy to settle into a period of heavy unemployment for a long time, and if it does, many people will suffer long-term unemployment.)

Turning points: The final aspect of this theory explains why, once floors and ceilings stop income from changing at a rapid rate, income does not stabilize at the high of the ceiling or the low of the floor, but instead tends to change direction.

We saw earlier that the accelerator theory of investment may help to explain the cumulative nature of upswings and downswings. It also can explain reversals of direction of expansions and contractions. We have seen that the accelerator makes the desired level of *new* (not replacement) investment depend upon the rate of change of income. If income is rising at a constant rate, then investment will be at a constant *level*. If there is a slackening in the speed at which income is rising, the level of investment will decline. This means that a *levelling off* in income at the top of a cycle may lead to a *decline* in the level of investment. The decline in investment at the upper turning point will cause a decline in the level of income that will be intensified through the multiplier process.

> **The accelerator thus provides one theory of the upper turning point.**

What about the possible stabilization of income at a floor? Investment theory predicts that,

sooner or later, an upturn will begin. If nothing else causes an expansion of business activity, there will eventually be a revival of replacement investment. As existing capital wears out, the capital stock will eventually fall to the level required to produce current output. At this stage new machines will be bought to replace those that subsequently wear out. The rise in the level of activity in the capital-goods industries will then cause, by way of the multiplier, a further rise in income. The economy has turned the corner. An expansion, once started, may trigger the sort of cumulative upward movement already discussed.

Policy-induced Cycles

Some theories suggest governments may be one of the major causes of systematic shocks to aggregate demand. Here are three such theories.

A political trade cycle: As early as 1944, the Polish-born Keynesian economist Michael Kalecki warned that once governments had learned to manipulate the economy, they might engineer an election-geared trade cycle. In pre-election periods they would raise spending and cut taxes. The resulting expansionary demand shock would create high employment and good business conditions that would bring voters' support for the government. But the resulting inflationary gap would lead to a rising price level. So, after the election was won, the government would depress demand to remove the inflationary gap, also providing some slack for expansion before the next election.

This theory invokes the image of a vote-maximizing government, manipulating employment and national income solely for electoral purposes. Few people believe that governments deliberately do this all the time, but the temptation to do it some of the time, particularly before close elections, may prove irresistible.

Alternating policy goals: A variant of the policy-induced cycle does not require vote-maximizing government and an easily duped electorate. Instead both sides need only be rather short-sighted. In this theory, when there is a recession and relatively stable prices, the public and the government identify unemployment as the number-one economic problem. The government then engineers an expansionary demand shock. This, plus such natural cumulative forces as the multiplier and accelerator, expands the economy and cures unemployment. But as Y rises above Y_F, the price level begins to rise. At this point the unemployment problem is declared cured. Now inflation is seen as the nation's number-one economic problem and a contractionary policy shock is engineered. The natural cumulative forces again take over, reducing income to a recessionary level. The inflation subsides but unemployment rises, setting the stage once again for an expansionary shock to cure the unemployment problem.

Many economists have criticized government policy over the last few decades for causing fluctuations by shortsightedly pursuing expansion to cure unemployment, then contraction to cure inflation. This phenomenon has occurred often enough in the UK that it has been given a name: **stop-go policy** or more simply just *stop-go*.

We have cast the stop-go cycle in its modern form of alternating concern over inflation and unemployment. Historically, when the UK operated under a fixed exchange rate, the two competing policy goals were the balance of payments and full employment. The balance of payments could always be improved by depressing national income and so reducing imports which are positively related to income, but this would raise unemployment. The conflict encouraged policy alternations whereby income was depressed to remove a balance-of-payments deficit and then expanded to remove the heavy unemployment. This open-economy aspect of policy conflicts is considered further in Chapter 40.

Misguided stabilization policy: In a variant of the previous theory, the government tries to hold the economy at its potential level of national income by countering fluctuations in private-sector expenditure functions with offsetting changes in its own spending and taxes. This is the theory of *stabilization policy* which we shall cover in the next chapter. For now, we can observe that cycles in income and employment can be induced, or at least unwittingly exaggerated, by poorly conceived government stabilization policies. Unless the authorities are very sophisticated, bad timing may accentuate rather than dampen cyclical fluctuations.

An Exogenous Theory of the Cycle

All of the theories considered so far look to forces within the economy as the cause of cycles. Of course the world as a whole is a closed economy, and cyclical movements in world income and employment must have endogenous causes (although once upon a time a plausible theory was advanced linking trade cycles to cyclical activity in sun spots!). Small parts of the world, such as the UK, or any one of the other EC countries, are open economies. For these economies, cyclical fluctuations often have exogenous causes. A foreign recession may be transmitted to the UK through an induced fall in foreign demand for UK exports. This appears from the UK's point of view as an exogenous shock which then sets up a downward multiplier effect, just as would follow from a decline in domestic investment or government expenditure.

The more open an economy, the more vulnerable it is to 'imported' cyclical fluctuations in its national income. Since exports are a larger part of the UK's total final expenditure than is investment expenditure, it is clear that the UK is open to such international effects, and some sharp year-to-year changes in exports have occurred in both directions.

There is a second mechanism by which cycles have been transmitted internationally. Today there are large international flows of capital. A recession in a capital-exporting country that makes its firms and households less willing to invest abroad as well as at home, will show up in the capital-importing countries as exogenous reductions in their investment expenditure.

A third mechanism concerns interest rates. The sharp rise in American interest rates caused by restrictive monetary policy in the US in 1981 and 1982 forced up interest rates in the rest of the world and helped to worsen the already serious worldwide recession.

There is some evidence that UK fluctuations since 1945 were partly domestic in origin. There can be no doubt, however, that they were also in some measure exogenous to the UK economy, being 'imported' through the links of international trade and capital flows.

Causes of Trade Cycles: a Consensus View?

Economists once argued long and bitterly about which was the best explanation of cyclical behaviour.

Today most economists agree that there is not a single cause or class of causes governing trade cycles.

In an economy that has tendencies for both cumulative and self-reversing behaviour, any large shock, whether from without or within, can initiate a cyclical swing. Wars are important; so are major technical inventions. A rapid increase in interest rates and a general tightening of credit can cause a sharp decrease in investment. Expectations can be changed by a political campaign or a development in another part of the world. The list of possible initial impulses, autonomous or induced, is long. It is probably true that the characteristic cyclical pattern involves many outside shocks that sometimes initiate, sometimes reinforce, and sometimes dampen the cumulative tendencies that exist within the economy.

Cycles differ also in terms of their internal structure. There are variations in timing, duration and amplitude. In some cycles, full employment of labour may be the bottleneck that determines the peak. In others, high interest rates and shortages of investment funds may nip an expansion and turn it into a recession at the same time that the unemployment of labour is still an acute problem. In some cycles the recession phase is short; in others a full-scale period of stagnation sets in. In some cycles the peak develops into a severe inflation; in others the pressure of excess demand is hardly felt and a new recession sets in before the economy has fully recovered from the last trough. Some cycles last a long time, others are short.

In this chapter we have suggested some reasons why an economy that is subjected to periodic external shocks will tend to generate a continually changing pattern of fluctuations, as cumulative and then self-reversing forces alternatively come into play. In the next two chapters we study how governments sometimes seek to influence the cycle and to remove some of its extremes of boom and slump through the use of fiscal and monetary policy.

ECONOMIC GROWTH

Economic growth is the increase in the economy's potential, or full-employment, real national income, Y_F. It may be shown graphically by either of two outward shifts: (1) in the long-run aggregate supply curve, and (2) in the production-possibility curve that we first saw in Figure 1.2.

Growth and Living Standards

In the circumstances facing most countries, the single most important force leading to long-run increases in living standards is economic growth.

To see this, compare the effects of growth with policies that increase economic efficiency or redistribute income.

Increasing efficiency by pushing the economy on to its production-possibility curve (e.g., from point c to point b in Figure 1.1 on page 6) can increase national income somewhat. But a once-and-for-all increase of 5–10 per cent would be an optimistic estimate of what could be obtained by removing all economic inefficiencies.

Redistributing income can make some people better off at the expense of others; but increasing the incomes of the bottom 20 per cent of the people by, say, 10 per cent would be an optimistic prediction of what could be done with further redistribution policies.

Economic growth, however, can go on raising national income for centuries on end. Provided the population is constant, even the modest rate of growth of 2 per cent per year takes a little less than 5 years to raise everyone's income by 10 per cent, and just over 9 years to raise the living standards of the poor (and everyone else) by 20 per cent. Indeed, it doubles average living standards about every 35 years, so that if there is no change in the distribution of income, everyone's living standards will double and then double again over one biblically alloted lifetime of three score years and ten.

Total and per capita growth: Economic growth, as we have defined it, refers to the growth of total (potential) national income. What happens to living standards depends also on the growth of population. To measure the growth in a country's average living standards, we use **per capita economic growth** which is the rate of growth of per capita national income (national income divided by the population).

The Cumulative Nature of Growth

The dramatic effects of growth rates are further illustrated in Table 36.2. It compares the real incomes of five different countries that all start in 'year zero' with national incomes of 100, and then experience five different growth rates. Even modest growth rates work wonders over one human lifetime. The more rapid growth rates in the 6–8 per cent range, which countries such as Japan have achieved, produce truly dramatic results.

The continued importance of efficiency and redistribution: We observe that economic growth is the most important force for raising living standards over the long term, but this in no way implies that policies designed to increase economic efficiency or to redistribute income are unimportant.

If at any moment in time we could get a larger national income by removing certain ineffici-

encies, such gains would be valuable. After all, any increase in national income is welcome in a world where many wants go unsatisfied. Furthermore, inefficiencies may themselves serve to reduce the growth rate. For example, the policy of rent control, which can be criticized for violating efficiency conditions in the housing market, can also be criticized for reducing the geographic mobility of labour that is a necessary part of the growth process.

Next consider redistribution. It may be some consolation for the poor to know that economic growth has made them vastly better off than they would have been if they had lived 100 years ago. Yet it is not any the less upsetting if they cannot afford the basic medical treatment for themselves, or schooling for their children, *that is currently available to higher-income citizens.* After all, the comparison with others in their own society is what is thrust on people, not how they compare with their counterparts at other times or in other places. Because we care about relative differences among individuals, we continue to have policies to redistribute income, and to make such basic services as health and education available to everyone, at least at some minimum acceptable standards.

TABLE 36.2   Real National Incomes Over Time at Alternative Growth Rates

YEAR	GROWTH RATES				
	1%	2%	3%	5%	7%
0	100	100	100	100	100
10	111	122	135	165	201
30	135	182	246	448	817
50	165	272	448	1,218	3,312
70	201	406	817	3,312	13,429
100	272	739	2,009	14,841	109,660

Small differences in national growth rates can cause enormous differences in different countries' national incomes. The figures in the body of the Table show real national income at alternative growth rates after the elapse of time shown in the first column. The effects of growth rates on living standards can be seen by looking down any column. For example, assuming a constant population, a 3 per cent growth rate doubles real national income in about 24 years, and at the end of 70 it has raised national income by over 700 per cent!

The effects of differences in growth rates can be seen by comparing across any row, showing national incomes in one particular year at various growth rates. For example, in year 10 the country with a growth rate of 1 per cent has a real income of 111, while the country with a growth rate of 7 per cent has a real income of 201! A 7 per cent growth rate doubles real income in 10 years, while a 1 per cent rate only increases it by 11 per cent!

Nonetheless, over the long term:

the income-raising potential of economic growth vastly exceeds that of removing inefficiencies, or redistributing the existing national income.

Inter-relations among the policies: One important implication of the above discussion is that policies attempting to reduce inefficiencies or redistribute income must be scrutinized for any effect they may have on economic growth. Consider, for example, a hypothetical redistributive policy that raises the incomes of lower-income people by 5 per cent but lowers the rate of economic growth from 2 to 1 per cent. In 10 years, those who gain from the redistribution will be no better off than if they had not received the redistribution of income and the growth rate had remained at 2 per cent (and, of course, everyone who did not gain from the redistribution would be worse off from the beginning). After 20 years' time, those who had gained from the redistribution would have 5 per cent more of a national income that is 12 per cent smaller than it would have been if the growth rate had remained at 2 per cent. Thus, as a result of the lower growth rate, *everyone* will be substantially worse off than if the redistributive policy had not been adopted.

Of course, not all redistribution policies have unfavourable effects on the growth rate. Some may have no effect, and others – by raising health and educational standards of ordinary workers – may raise the growth rate.

Two Sources of 'Growth'

National income may rise for two distinct reasons: (1) a recessionary gap is being eliminated so that national income is increasing towards its potential level; and (2) potential income is itself increasing. This important distinction is illustrated in the two parts of Figure 36.3.

The removal of a typical, large, recessionary gap might cause a once-and-for-all increase in national income of 10 per cent. This is not to be disdained because it will remove unemployment, which is desirable, as well as raising output and, hence, average living standards. Yet a growth rate of 3 per cent per year raises potential national income by 10 per cent in just over 3 years – and then goes on to *double* real income in 24 years.

FIGURE 36.3 Ways of Increasing National Income

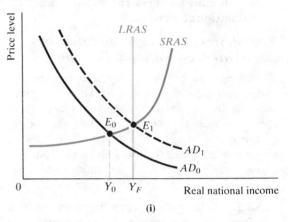

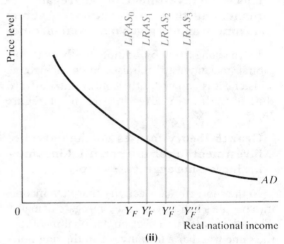

A once-and-for-all increase in national income can be obtained by raising aggregate demand to remove a recessionary gap. Continued increases in national income are possible by shifting the *LRAS* curve through continued economic growth. In part (i) with the aggregate demand curve at AD_0, there is a recessionary gap of $Y_F - Y_0$. An increase in aggregate demand from AD_0 to AD_1 takes equilibrium from E_0 to E_1, achieving a once-and-for-all change in national income which rises from Y_0 to Y_F.

In part (ii), increases in factor supplies and productivity lead to increases in potential income. This *continually* shifts the long-run aggregate supply curve outward. In successive periods it moves from $LRAS_0$ to $LRAS_3$, and so increases potential income as long as growth continues.

Over any long period of time, economic growth, rather than variations in aggregate demand, exerts the major effect on real national income.

The Short- and Long-run Effect of Investment on National Income

The theory of income determination studied earlier in this book, is a short-run theory. It takes potential income as constant and concentrates on the effects of all types of expenditure – including investment – on aggregate demand and thus on variations of actual national income around a given potential income. This short-term viewpoint is the focus of part (i) of Figure 36.3.

National-income theory focuses on the effects of investment on aggregate demand, and thus on variations of actual income around a given potential income.

In the long run, by adding to the nation's capital stock, investment raises potential income. This effect is shown by the continuing outward shift of the *LRAS* curve in part (ii) of Figure 36.3.

Growth theory focuses on the effects of investment in raising potential income – i.e. increasing aggregate supply.

In the short run, any activity that puts income into people's hands will raise aggregate demand. Thus the short-run effect on national income is the same whether a firm invests in digging holes and refilling them or in building a new factory. In terms of growth, however, we are concerned only with that part of investment that adds to a nation's productive capacity.

The Short- and Long-run Effect of Saving on National Income

The short-run effect of an increase in saving is a reduction of aggregate demand. When households elect to save more, they must spend less. The resulting downward shift in the consumption function lowers aggregate demand and thereby lowers equilibrium national income.

In the longer term, however, higher savings provide the funds out of which investment is financed. If full employment is more or less maintained in the long run, then the volume of investment will be strongly influenced by the volume of savings. The higher the savings, the higher the investment – and the higher the investment, the greater the rate of growth due to capital accumulation.

In the long run there is no paradox of thrift; societies with high savings rates have high investment rates and, other things being equal, high growth rates.

MACRO THEORIES OF GROWTH

To discuss the causes of economic growth, we first concentrate on theories that stress the macroeconomic relations of total investment and the overall productivity of capital.

Growth Without Learning

Nineteenth-century economists viewed growth as a long-run process which was primarily determined by the growth of the labour force and the growth of the capital stock, taking place in the framework of fixed (or at least very slowly changing) technical knowledge.

To understand such theories, assume that the supply of land and labour is fixed, while the capital stock grows.[1] Also assume that there is a known and fixed stock of investment projects that can be undertaken. Suppose also that nothing ever happens to increase the supply of such projects. Whenever the opportunity is ripe, some of the investment opportunities are utilized, thereby increasing the stock of capital goods, and depleting the reservoir of unutilized investment opportunities. Of course, the most productive opportunities will be used first.

Such a view of investment opportunities can be represented by the fixed *marginal efficiency of capital* curve first introduced on page 327 and now shown in Figure 36.4. The downward slope of the *MEC* curve indicates that, with knowledge constant, increases in the stock of capital bring smaller and smaller increases in output per unit

---

[1] Nineteenth-century economists were also interested in the consequences of the growth of population, but what we need for our purposes can be shown by the simple case in which capital is the only factor whose supply is increasing.

FIGURE 36.4 The Marginal Efficiency of Capital Schedule

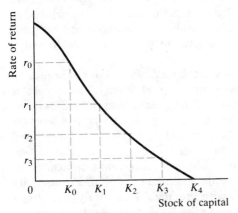

A declining *MEC* schedule shows that successive increases to the capital stock bring smaller and smaller increases in output and thus a declining rate of return. A fixed *MEC* schedule can represent the theory of growth in an economy with some unutilized investment opportunities but no learning. Increases in investment that increase the capital stock from K_0 to K_1 to ... K_4 lower the rate of return from r_0 to r_1 to ... zero. Because the productivity of successive units of capital decreases, the capital-output ratio rises.

of capital. This shape is a consequence of the law of diminishing returns. If, with land, labour and knowledge constant, more and more capital is used, the net amount added to output by successive increments will diminish and will eventually reach zero.

As capital is accumulated in a state of constant knowledge, the society moves down its *MEC* schedule. In such a 'non-learning' world, where new investment opportunities do not appear, output grows as the capital stock grows. For a given rate of capital accumulation, however, the growth rate of output will fall until eventually, when the marginal efficiency of capital reaches zero, no further growth is possible.

The *average* efficiency of capital refers to the average output produced in the whole economy per unit of capital employed – i.e. to total output divided by the total capital stock (Y/K). If each unit of new capital adds less to total output than did each previous unit, the average amount of output per unit of capital – i.e. the average efficiency of capital – must be declining.

In the theory of growth it is common to use the reciprocal of the average efficiency of capital (K/Y) and to call this new ratio the *capital-output ratio*. In a world without learning, the average efficiency of capital is declining and hence the capital-output ratio is increasing.

To illustrate these ratios, assume that in 'year one' an economy has an output of 1,000 and a capital stock of 5,000. In this case, the average efficiency of capital is 1,000/5,000 which is 0.20, while the capital-output ratio is 5,000/1,000 which is 5. All that these ratios tell us is that, on average, every pound's worth of capital produces 20p worth of output per year (the average efficiency of capital) and that the value of the capital stock is 5 times the value of annual output (the capital-output ratio). Next assume that some years later the economy's capital stock has grown to 6,000, while its annual output has grown to 1,100. Now the average efficiency of capital has fallen to 1,100/6,000, which is 0.183, and the capital-output ratio has risen to 6,000/1,100, which is 5.454. Thus, each unit of capital now produces on average less than it did before, and, what is the same thing, there are more units of capital per unit of output than there were before. This numerical example is consistent, therefore, with the case of growth in a world without learning.

In a world of static technology, the accumulation of capital is the main source of growth. As capital accumulates, however, the capital-output ratio rises while the marginal return on capital falls towards zero, at which point growth will stop completely.

Growth With Learning

Modern economists look at the process of growth more optimistically than did economists of the nineteenth century. The main reason lies in the recognition of the importance of technological change. Experience has taught economists that models of long-run growth based on a fixed technology are not very helpful in understanding the dynamic world in which we live. Instead, modern growth is seen to take place in a context of the very long run, where the influence of technological changes is pervasive.

The Very Long Run

In the long run, all factor inputs can be varied, but the firm must do the best it can within the confines of known technology – i.e. the production function is fixed. The *very long run* is defined as a period of time over which the techniques of production, factors of production and products, all change. Changes in production techniques cause downward *shifts* in long-run cost curves. When the *quality* of factors increases, more output can be obtained from given quantities of inputs. These two forces, along with the development of new products, are major sources of economic growth.

New techniques: First, consider changes in the techniques available for producing existing products. Over the average lifetime in the twentieth century, such changes have been dramatic. Eighty years ago, roads and railways were built by gangs of workers using buckets, spades, and draft horses. Today bulldozers, steam shovels, giant trucks, and other specialized equipment have banished the workhorse from construction sites and to a great extent have displaced the pick-and-shovel worker.

Increases in productive capacity can be either 'embodied' or 'disembodied' technical change. Those that are the result of changes in the form of particular capital goods in use are called **embodied technical change**. Examples are: the assembly line, automation, computerization and robotization which transformed much of manufacturing, the aeroplane which revolutionized transportation, and electronic devices which now dominate the communications industries. These innovations along with less well known but no less profound ones – for example, improvements in the strength of metals, the productivity of seeds, and the techniques for recovering basic raw materials from the ground – all create new investment opportunities.

Less visible, although important changes occur through **disembodied technical change**, which concerns changes in the organization of production that are not embodied in specific capital goods. One example is improved techniques of managerial control.

Changes in the quality of factors: The quality of labour and capital has changed greatly over the years. A given value of capital, say a pound's worth, is much more productive today than it was in 1900 (even when the values are measured at constant prices). This is mainly due to the kind of embodied technological progress referred to above, so we say no more about it here.

Increases in the quality of labour are reflected in increases in its productivity. One cause is better health. This is desired as an end in itself, but it also increases productivity per worker-hour by cutting down on illness, accidents and absenteeism. A second cause is the accumulation of human capital. Education and technical training have added to human capital. Productivity improves with literacy. More subtly, the longer people are educated, the more adaptable they are to new and changing circumstances – and thus, in the very long run, the more productive.

New goods: Finally, consider changes in outputs. Television, polio vaccine, nylon, pocket calculators, quartz watches, personal computers, detergents and even ballpoint pens have all come onto the market within living memory. Other products are so changed that the only connection they have with their predecessors is their name. A 1988 Jaguar car is very different from a 1938 Jaguar. The European Airbus is revolutionary compared with the DC-3, which itself barely resembled the Wright Brothers' original flying machine which flew on its historic flight in this century. All such new products are a major source of economic growth in the very long run.

Growth With a Shifting MEC Curve

The steady depletion of growth opportunities in the 'Classical case' occurred because investment opportunities were fixed. We have just seen, however, that as new knowledge is acquired, new investment opportunities are created. This causes the *MEC* schedule to shift outward over time as illustrated in Figure 36.5. Three possibilities are shown in the Figure. In each case, the economy's capital stock grows by the same amount. In each case, learning shifts the *MEC* curve outwards.

Gradual reduction in investment opportunities: Part (i) of Figure 36.5 illustrates a slightly more subtle version of the Classical 'no-learning case'. No longer are investment opportunities unchanging because of an absence of

FIGURE 36.5 Shifting Investment Opportunities: Three Cases

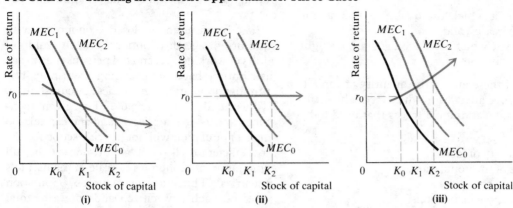

When both knowledge and the capital stock grow, the actual marginal
efficiency of capital depends on their relative rates of growth. In each case the
economy at period 0 has the MEC_0 curve, a capital stock of K_0, and a rate of return of
r_0. In period 1 the curve shifts to MEC_1 and there is investment to increase the stock of
capital to K_1. In period 2 the curve shifts to MEC_2 and there is new investment that
increases the capital stock to K_2. It is the relative size of the shift of the MEC curve
and the additions of the capital stock that are important.

In part (i) investment occurs more rapidly than increases in investment
opportunities, and the rate of return falls along the black arrow. In part (ii) investment
occurs at exactly the same rate as investment opportunities, and the rate of return is
constant. In part (iii) investment occurs less rapidly than increases in investment
opportunities, and the rate of return rises.

learning. Instead, learning occurs but not fast
enough to counteract the decline in the marginal
productivity of capital due to the growth in the
capital stock.

**Constant or rising investment opportun-
ities:** Parts (ii) and (iii) of Figure 36.5 show
cases in which invention and innovation create
new investment opportunities as fast, or faster,
than these opportunities have been used up
through capital accumulation. The former is seen
as an outward shift of the MEC curve; the latter
as a movement downwards along any given MEC
curve. The Figures show that in a world with
rapid innovation, the capital-output ratio may be
constant or decreasing. Despite large amounts of
capital accumulation, the marginal efficiency of
new capital may remain constant, or even increase, as new investment opportunities are
created.

The historical record suggests that modern
economies have been successful in generating
new investment opportunities at least as rapidly
as old ones were used up. As a result, modern
economists devote more attention to understand-

ing the *shifts* in the MEC schedule over time and
less to discovering its shape in a situation of static
knowledge.

In a world of improving technology, the
marginal efficiency of capital curve will
be shifting outwards. If it shifts outwards
as fast as the capital stock is growing, the
return on capital will not fall, and the
capital-output ratio will not rise.

Such growth can go on indefinitely
without any fall in the marginal return to
new capital, creating a world dominated
by 'very long-run' changes in production
techniques, the quality of factors of production, and the development of new
products.

Additional Factors Affecting Growth Rates

We have seen so far that an economy's growth
rate is influenced by:

- the rate at which capital is accumulated,

- the rate at which new technologies are put in place,
- the rate at which the quality of the labour force increases, and
- the rate at which new products are brought into production.

The first of these affects the quantity of capital, the other three affect its productivity. There are, however, some additional forces that need to be considered:

- the quantity of labour.
- the size of the population.
- structural changes.
- the country's institutions.

The Quantity of Labour: Population Theory

For any given state of knowledge and supplies of other factors of production, the size of the population affects the level of output per capita. Thus, from an economic point of view, it is meaningful to speak of overpopulated or under-populated economies, depending on whether the contribution to production of additional people would raise or lower the level of per capita income. Because population size is related to income per capita, we can conceive of an **opt-imum population**, which is defined as the population that maximizes national income per capita.

Start by assuming a closed economy with an equilibrium age distribution between children, adults of working age, and old persons (i.e. an age distribution that is not changing over time). The optimum population, under these circumstances, is illustrated in Figure 36.6. For given technology and given supplies of land and capital, too small a population will not provide scope for the most efficient division of labour, nor for the full exploitation of economies of scale in the nation's industries. Thus, as the nation's population increases, each new citizen adds more to total output than did each previous citizen. As the population goes on increasing, however, all of the opportunities for improving the division of labour and for exploiting scale economies will eventually be exhausted. From that point on, further new inhabitants will add less to total production than did each previous addition to the population. Now the marginal product of further additions to the population will fall.

Eventually, the falling marginal product of new inhabitants will cause the average product of all the population to reach a maximum and then begin to fall. This maximum is the population that maxim-izes output per person.

Notice that, from the point of view of maximizing living standards, it pays to increase the population beyond the point of diminishing *marginal* returns. It does not matter if each new inhabitant raises income by less than did the previous new inhabitant. What matters is that each new inhabitant raises income by more than the *average* income produced by the existing population – i.e. that the marginal product of a new inhabitant exceeds the average product of all existing inhabitants.

Notice that the optimum population is defined for a particular stock of land and capital and given technology. The very-long-run changes that we have already studied will cause *upward shifts* in the average and marginal product curves shown in Figure 36.6. This will certainly increase the size of per capita income when the population is optimal; it may or may not also increase the size of the optimum population by shifting the max-

FIGURE 36.6 Optimum Population

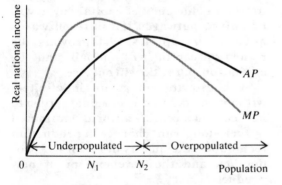

The optimum population occurs where average output per head of population is at a maximum. The diagram plots average and marginal national income against the size of the population. Falling marginal product sets in after the population reaches N_1. Average national income continues to rise, however, until the optimum population of N_2 is reached.

imum point of the *AP* curve to the right.

We now drop the assumption of a closed economy with an equilibrium age distribution. This raises two issues.

First, the balance of the population between the non-working (the young, housewives, and the old) and the working population influences the optimum size of the population. Total output depends on the size of the working population while real income depends on total output and the size of the whole population. On the one hand, if the birth rate is rising, a large proportion of the population will be young and not yet in the labour force. They will consume while not producing, and so tend to lower per capita living standards, even if the working population is unchanged. On the other hand, if the birth rate is declining, the proportion of the population over retirement age will eventually be rising. Again, this increases the proportion of people who are consuming without currently producing and tends to lower current, per capita, living standards.

Second, what do policy-makers do if they perceive their current population is far different from the optimum? If the population is too low, various inducements can be given for the size of families to be increased. After a long time, the working population will rise, but for nearly two decades after the birth rate rises, the net effect of such a policy will be a rise in the proportion of the population who are below working age. During this period, the pressure is for per capita living standards to fall. A more immediately effective policy is to encourage immigration. Through immigration, the population can be increased rapidly, and it is also possible to increase it in a 'balanced' way with children, working adults and older persons all entering the country. Immigration policies sometimes go further by favouring people who are at working age and who have significant skills. This increases the proportion of the population at working age and gives a twofold upward pressure on living stanadards: first, as the working population gets closer to the optimum level, the average product of the working population rises and second, as the proportion of non-working people in the population falls, each working person has, on average, fewer non-working persons to support.

Many countries have had conscious population policies. North America in the nineteenth century sought immigrants, as did Australia until very recently. Germany under Hitler paid bonuses for the birth of additional Aryan children and otherwise offered incentives to create Germans. Greece in the 1950s and 1960s tried to stem emigration to Western Europe. All are examples of countries that believed they had insufficient population, though the motives were not in every case purely economic. In contrast, many underdeveloped countries of South America, Africa and Asia desire to limit population growth in the belief that they are at or above their optimum populations. The Chinese People's Republic, in particular, has used strong economic incentives to limit the number of children to one per family.

We can summarize the effects of population changes on per capita growth rates as follows.

A country's growth rate will be higher:
- **the more rapidly its working population is growing if it is currently below the optimum;**
- **the more rapidly its working population is shrinking (or the less rapidly it is growing) if it is currently above the optimum; and**
- **the more rapidly is the working population growing relative to the non-working population.**

Structural Change

Changes in the structure of the economy's output can cause changes in its measured growth rate. On the one hand, a decline in such low-productivity sectors as distribution and an expansion in such high-productivity sectors as manufacturing, will temporarily boost the measured aggregate growth rate as labour moves from the declining to the expanding sectors. On the other hand, a decline in the high-productivity manufacturing sector, and a rise in the size of the lower-productivity service sector, will lower the measured rate of growth while the movement is occurring. The first, growth-increasing shift was typical of the 1950s and the 1960s, while the second, growth-reducing shift was typical of the 1980s.

Another example occurs when one type of energy (say, solar) supplants another type (say, oil). Much existing capital stock specifically geared to the original energy source will become too costly to operate and will be scrapped. New capital geared to the new energy source will be built. *During the transition*, gross investment expenditure is high, thus stimulating aggregate demand. But there is little if any increase in the economy's potential national income because the old capital goods have been scrapped.

A rise in the international price of *imported* energy will also lower productivity. The higher-priced imported energy means that domestic *value added* falls, and with it GNP per worker. Although the same volume of goods can be produced with a given input of labour, a smaller portion of the output's value is now earned as income by domestic workers and firms, while a larger proportion is used to pay for the energy imports. These changes show up in the statistics as a decline in productivity and a temporary fall in growth rates.

These are some of the many factors that were operative throughout the world in the late 1970s and early 1980s. They worked to depress growth rates for some considerable period of time. But they are not permanent factors. When the structural adjustments are complete, their depressing effects pass.

Institutional Considerations

Almost all aspects of a country's institutions can encourage or discourage the efficient use of natural and human resources. Social and religious habits, legal institutions and traditional trading patterns are all important. So, too, is the political climate.

Supply-side View of Growth

Much of the criticisms by the so-called supply-side economics has been directed at growth policy. The general supply-side view is that growth has many microeconomic causes and that obstacles to growth cannot be understood without studying obstacles to the efficient workings of individual markets. The extreme supply-side view is that, given a stable environment free from government interference, growth will take care of itself. The government's task is to create such a stable environment by establishing law and order, security of contract and the absence of

major inflations. Beyond that, government intervention is likely to be harmful rather than helpful.

As a result of these views, supply-side economists advocate reducing the current level of government intervention. Given the web of government rules, regulations, and perverse tax incentives that has grown up over many years, the supply-side agenda for reducing government intervention is usually a long one. Such an agenda was adopted by so-called supply-siders during the late 1970s and 1980s, and parts of it have been taken up by many governments including those of the UK and the US. The agenda includes *eliminating* the following policies:

Supporting declining industries: This policy causes resources that could be more productively employed elsewhere to leave the declining industry more slowly. Most economists agree that such policies are costly, harmful to growth, and in the end self-defeating.

Encouraging monopolies and discouraging competition: Most economists tend to oppose such policies, although there is disagreement over how much competition is desirable in certain industries. For example, some support complete deregulation of fare and route setting by airlines, while others tend to worry that cut-throat competition may reduce airline quality and safety.

Taxing income rather than consumption: Consider a woman in the 30 per cent tax bracket who earns an extra £1,000 and pays £300 income tax. If she spends her after-tax income she will be able to buy £700 worth of goods. If she saves the money, she will be able to buy a £700 bond. If the bond pays a 4 per cent real return, she will earn £28 real interest per year. But a 30 per cent tax must then be paid on the interest earnings, leaving only a £19.60 annual income. This is a 2.8 per cent after-tax return on the bond and a *1.96 per cent after-tax return on the original £1000 of income.* Supply-side economists argue for taxes on consumption, not on income, so that any income that is saved would be untaxed. A tax would be levied only when the interest earned on the savings was actually spent on consumption.

High rates of income tax: Supply-siders

BOX 36.1 PRODUCTIVITY GROWTH IN THE UK

Between 1950 and 1980, the rate of growth of UK labour productivity was slow relative to other major industrial countries. There was a burst of higher productivity growth in the mid-1960s but over the whole period the UK economy remained, on average, near the bottom of the league table of productivity growth in advanced industrial countries. During the 1970s, British industrial productivity became nearly stagnant. From 1973 to 1979 it grew at an average annual rate of well under 1 per cent, as compared with figures in the ranges 2–2.9 per cent for Italy and Canada, 3–3.9 per cent for West Germany, France and the US, and 4+ per cent for Japan. As a result of the long-term lag in UK productivity growth, UK living standards fell from the second highest in Western Europe in the 1950s to one of the lowest in the 1980s.

Low rates of productivity growth for the UK implied a relative fall in industrial efficiency, leading to declining price competitiveness in markets for exports and import-competing goods. If exchange rates had responded only to current-account transactions, this decline in competitiveness would have been to a large extent offset by an accompanying decline in the external value of sterling. However, capital movements had an increasing influence on exchange rates over the period, sometimes causing the sterling exchange rate to change in the *opposite direction* from that needed to offset changes in competitiveness for several years at a time.

These developments tended to set up a 'positive feedback loop': low export and high import growth implies low growth of output, which in turn implies low exploitation of scale economies and low investment for both the replacement of old, and the creation of new, capacity; in its turn, low investment implies a low rate of innovation of embodied technical progress – the form of technological progress that requires plants embodying the old technology to be replaced by plants embodying the new technology; this in turn tends to slow the rate of producitivity growth, and the feedback loop has gone the full circle back to poor international competitiveness.

In the 1980s, however, the UK had one of the highest rates of productivity growth of all the advanced industrial countries, surpassing even Japan. What were the causes?

One cause was the closing of older plants. The deep and prolonged recession of the early 1980s caused many manufacturing plants to close permanently. When falling demand and prices lead to major rounds of plant closings, it is usually the least efficient, higher-cost plants that are first to close. As a result, there is a rise in the average productivity of all the establishments that continue to operate. This is not, however, because anyone is becoming more efficient but because the less efficient are just not operating at all. This in itself causes a reduction in total output. National output and national living standards will be increased *only when*, *and if*, the displaced workers are put to work in other occupations where their productivity is higher than it had been in the plants that closed down.

A second reason was the shake-out of the overmanning that had become widespread during the 1970s. The recession of the 1980s forced industry to become much leaner. The same output was achieved with a lower labour force, and productivity came closer to levels already achieved in similar establishments in other industrial countries. This was a once-and-for-all gain in output per person in the surviving plants with no necessary fall in total output. In this case, national output and living standards began to rise when the displaced workers moved to *any* other productive employment.

Although important, both of these are one-time effects, having only a transitory influence on growth rates.

Although unemployment remained high through most of the decade (partly due to larger numbers of new entrants into the labour force), employment began to rise in 1983 and continued to do so through the rest of the decade. This gave rise to a third transitory force that raised productivity, this time in all sectors. In most lines of production, some of each firm's labour force is overhead labour that does not rise or fall over the trade cycle. For this reason, employment often changes less than output over the trade cycle with the result that, *ceteris paribus*, productivity falls in the cyclical downswing and rises in the upswing.

The continued rise in both employment and productivity in the late 1980s gave rise to the hope that longer-term forces had also come into play. British manufacturing had lowered costs and raised competitiveness, while investment and innovation seemed to be at a higher level. In 1989, it was too early to say whether or not these forces would be sustained or whether the UK's productivity performance would fall once again to the lower end of the international league table. Only time will tell. The experience of the early 1990s will bring important evidence of any longer-term productivity effects following from the profound changes that occurred in the UK economy in the 1980s.

allege that high taxes discourage work. But the effect of high taxes may actually be to make people work either more or less hard. Theory is silent on which is more likely, and no hard evidence has yet shown that lowering current tax rates makes people work harder. It does, however, reduce the incentive to emigrate to lower-tax jurisdictions and to spend effort avoiding taxes while one remains a resident.

'Double taxation' of business profits: Business profits are taxed first as income of firms and second as income of households when paid out as dividends. This and other policies that reduce business profits, and hence discourage the return to investing in equities, are alleged to discourage households from saving and investing in business that are the mainspring of economic growth.

Supply-siders argue that all these policies reduce the rate of growth below what it would otherwise be. Most economists would agree to some extent, but problems arise in assessing the existence and importance of the alleged harmful effects of each policy and also, since the government needs revenue, in finding alternative revenue sources that will have less harmful effects than the ones being criticized. In the 1980s, supply-side measures were directed at increasing the UK's rate of economic growth by making many microeconomic improvements designed, either directly or indirectly, to raise labour productivity. It is too early to assess the full effects of these measures, but Box 36.1 discusses the UK's actual productivity performance over this, and previous decades.

Benefits and Costs of Growth

In the remainder of this chapter, we shall outline some of the costs and benefits of growth.

Benefits of Growth

Growth and living standards: We observed at the beginning of this chapter that economic growth is the most important single force leading to long-run increases in living standards. This point is so fundamental that we chose to make it at the outset. So now we have only to recall it, and pass on to discuss some of the other advantages of growth.

Growth and income redistribution: Economic growth makes many kinds of redistributions easier to achieve than when national income is static. For example, if a constant national income is to be redistributed, someone's standard of living will actually have to be lowered. However, when there is economic growth, it is possible, by redistributing some of *the increment* in income, to reduce income inequalities without actually having to lower anyone's income. It is thus much easier for a rapidly growing economy to be generous towards its less fortunate citizens – or neighbours – than it is for a static economy.

Growth and lifestyle: As well as producing more of what we already consume, growth changes consumption patterns and lifestyles in more profound ways. Not only are more cars produced, but the government is led to produce more roads and to provide more recreational areas for its newly affluent (and mobile) citizens. At yet a later stage, a concern about litter, pollution, and ugliness may become important, and their correction may then begin to account for a significant fraction of national income. Such 'amenities' usually become matters of social concern only when growth has assured the provision of the basic requirements for food, clothing, and housing of a substantial majority of the population.

Growth and national power: When one country is competing with another for power or prestige, rates of growth are important. If our national income is growing at 2 per cent while the other country's is growing at 5 per cent, the other country will only have to wait for our relative strength to dwindle. Moreover, the faster its productivity is growing, the easier a country will find it to bear the expenses of an arms race, or a programme of foreign aid.

Costs of Growth

The benefits discussed above suggest that growth is a great blessing. Some of the consequences can, however, be a curse.

Social and personal costs of growth: Industrialization can cause deterioration of the environment. Unspoiled landscapes give way to motorways, factories, and billboards; air and

BOX 36.2 AN OPEN LETTER FROM THE GROWTH-IS-GOOD SCHOOL

Dear Ordinary Citizen:

You live in the world's first civilization that is devoted principally to satisfying *your* needs rather than those of a privileged minority. Past civilizations have always been based on leisure and high consumption for a tiny upper class, a reasonable living standard for a small middle class, and hard work with little more than subsistence consumption for the great mass of people. In the past the average person saw little of the civilized and civilizing products of the economy, except when he or she was toiling to produce them.

The continuing Industrial Revolution is based on mass-produced goods for you, the ordinary citizen. It ushered in a period of sustained economic growth that has raised consumption standards of ordinary citizens to levels previously reserved thoughout history for a tiny privileged minority. Reflect on a few examples: travel, live and recorded music, art, good food, inexpensive books, universal literacy, and a genuine chance to be educated. Most important, there is leisure to provide time and energy to enjoy these and thousands of other products of the modern industrial economy.

Would any ordinary family seriously doubt the benefits of growth and prefer to go back to the world of 150 or 500 years ago in its same relative social and economic position? Surely, the answer is no. But we cannot say the same for those with incomes in the top 1 per cent or 2 per cent of the income distribution. Economic growth has destroyed much of their privileged consumption position. They must now vie with the masses when visiting the world's beauty spots and are annoyed, while lounging on the terrace of a palatial mansion, by the sound of charter flights carrying ordinary people to inexpensive holidays in faraway places. Many of the rich resent the loss of exclusive rights to luxury consumption. Some complain bitterly, and it is not surprising that they find their intellectual apologists.

Whether they know it or not, the anti-growth economists are not the social revolutionaries they think they are. They are counter-revolutionaries who would set back the clock of material progress for the ordinary person. They say that growth has produced pollution and wasteful consumption of all kinds of frivolous products that add nothing to human happiness. But the democratic solution to pollution is not to go back to where so few people consume luxuries that pollution is trivial; it is to accept pollution as part of a transitional phase connected with the ushering in of mass consumption, to keep the mass consumption, and to learn to control the pollution it tends to create.

It is only through further growth that the average citizen can enjoy consumption standards (of travel, culture, medical and health care, etc.) now available to people in the top 25 per cent of the income distribution – which includes the intellectuals who earn large royalties from the books they write denouncing growth. If you think that extra income confers little real benefit, just ask those in that top 25 per cent to exchange incomes with the average citizen. Or see how hard *they* struggle to reduce their income taxes.

Ordinary citizens, do not be deceived by disguised elitist doctrines. Remember that the very rich and the elite have much to gain by stopping growth and even more by rolling it back, but you have everything to gain by letting it go forward.

Onward!

A. Growthman

water become polluted; and in some cases unique and priceless relics of earlier ages – from flora and fauna to ancient ruins – disappear. Urbanization tends to move people away from the simpler life of farms and small towns and into the crowded, sometimes crime-ridden life of urban areas. Those remaining behind in the rural areas find that rural life, too, changes. Larger-scale farming, the decline of population, and the migration of children from the farm to the city all have their costs. The stepped-up tempo of life brings joys to some but tragedy to others. Accidents, ulcers, crime rates, suicides, divorces, and murder all tend to be higher in periods of rapid growth and in more developed societies. To what extent the latter is the cause of the former remains uncertain, but the association is unmistakable.

When an economy is growing, it is also changing. Innovation leaves obsolete machines in its wake, and it also leaves partially obsolete people. No matter how well trained you are at age 25, in another 25 years your skills may be partially or wholly obsolete. A rapid rate of growth requires rapid adjustments, which can cause upset and sometimes misery to the individuals affected.

The opportunity cost of growth: In a world of scarcity, almost nothing is free. Growth re-

BOX 36.3 AN OPEN LETTER FROM THE GROWTH-IS-BAD SCHOOL

Dear Ordinary Citizen:

You live in a world that is being despoiled by a mindless search for ever higher levels of material consumption at the cost of all other values. Once upon a time, men and women knew how to enjoy creative work and to derive satisfaction from simple activities undertaken in scarce, and hence highly valued, leisure time. Today the ordinary worker is a mindless cog in an assembly line that turns out ever more goods that the advertisers must work overtime to persuade the worker to consume.

Statisticians and politicians count the increasing flow of material output as a triumph of modern civilization. Consider not the flow of output in general, but the individual products that it contains. You arise from your electric-blanketed bed, clean your teeth with an electric toothbrush, open with an electric tin opener a tin of the sad remnants of a once-proud orange, and eat your bread baked from super-refined and chemically refortified flour; you climb into your car to sit in vast traffic jams on exhaust-polluted roads. And so it goes, with endless consumption of high-technology products that give you no more real satisfaction than the simple, cheaply produced equivalent products used by your great-grandfathers: soft woolly blankets, natural bristle toothbrushes, real oranges, coarse but healthy bread, and public transport that moved on uncongested roads and gave its passengers time to chat with their neighbours, to read, or just to daydream.

Television commercials tell you that by consuming more you are happier. But happiness lies not in increasing consumption but in increasing the ratio of *satisfaction of wants* to *total wants*. Since the more you consume the more the advertisers persuade you that you want to consume, you are almost certainly less happy than the average citizen in a small town in 1900 whom we can visualize sitting on the family porch, sipping a cool beer or a lemonade, and enjoying the antics of the children as they play with scooters made out of old crates and skipping ropes made from pieces of old clothesline.

Today the landscape is dotted with endless factories producing the plastic trivia of the modern industrial society. They drown you in a cloud of noise, air, and water pollution. The countryside is despoiled by slag heaps, acid rain, and dangerous nuclear power stations producing energy that is devoured insatiably by modern factories and motor vehicles.

Worse, our precious heritage of natural resources is being fast used up. Spaceship Earth flies, captain-less, in its senseless orgy of self-consuming consumption.

Now is the time to stop this madness. We must stabilize production, reduce pollution, conserve our natural resources, and seek justice through a more equitable distribution of existing total income.

A long time ago Malthus taught us that if we do not limit population voluntarily, nature will do it for us in a cruel and savage manner. Today the same is true of output. If we do not halt its growth voluntarily, the halt will be imposed on us by a disastrous increase in pollution and a rapid exhaustion of natural resources.

Citizens, awake! Shake off the worship of growth, learn to enjoy the bounty that is yours already, and reject the endless, self-defeating search for increased happiness through ever-increasing consumption.

Upward!

A. Non-growthman

---

quires investments of resources in capital goods and education. These investments absorb factors of production that could otherwise be used to produce goods and services for current consumption – hence there is a current sacrifice. When, after a time, the new capital goods come into use, or the better-educated people enter the labour force, the economy's potential income will rise – hence future gain.

Table 36.3 illustrates the cost in terms of time paths of consumption. How expensive is the 'invest now, consume later' strategy? On the assumed figures, it takes 10 years for the actual amount of consumption to catch up to what it would have been had no reallocation been made. In the intervening 10 years, a good deal of consumption is lost, and the cumulative losses in consumption must be made up before society can really be said to have broken even. It takes an additional 9 years before total consumption over the whole period is as large as it would have been if the economy had remained on the 2 per cent path.

In market economies, individuals decide how much current sacrifice will be made. They do this by deciding how much of their current incomes not to spend on current consumption. This part of their income is saved and can be made available

TABLE 36.3 The Opportunity Cost of Growth

Year	(1) Level of consumption at 2% growth rate	(2) Level of consumption at 3% growth rate	(3) Cumulative gain (loss) in consumption
0	85.0	77.0	(8.0)
1	86.7	79.3	(15.4)
2	88.5	81.8	(22.1)
3	90.3	84.2	(28.2)
4	92.1	86.8	(33.5)
5	93.9	89.5	(37.9)
6	95.8	92.9	(40.8)
7	97.8	95.0	(43.6)
8	99.7	97.9	(45.4)
9	101.8	100.9	(46.3)
10	103.8	103.9	(46.2)
15	114.7	120.8	(28.6)
20	126.8	140.3	19.6
30	154.9	189.4	251.0
40	189.2	255.6	745.9

Transferring resources from consumption to investment goods lowers current income but raises future income. The example assumes that income in year zero is 100 and that consumption of 85 per cent of national income is possible with a 2 per cent growth rate. It is further assumed that to achieve a 3 per cent growth rate, consumption must fall to 77 per cent of income. A shift from (1) to (2) decreases consumption for 10 years but increases it thereafter. The cumulative effect on consumption is shown in (3); the gains eventually become large.

for current investment. In planned economies, governments make the decisions by deciding how many of the nation's factors of production will be allocated to producing investment goods, and how many to producing output for current consumption.

Growth as a Goal of Policy: Do the Benefits Justify the Costs?

In the 1960s and early 1970s, when the industrialized world had sustained economic growth, a great debate raged on whether or not such growth was desirable. When growth rates fell in the late 1970s and 1980s, most policy debate centred on how to get a return to growth – few appeared to welcome the actual onset of the low-growth society. Nonetheless, the issues raised in that debate were important ones, and two views on it are laid out in Boxes 36.2 and 36.3.

Today, most people think that already developed countries need yet more growth. Poverty is now a solvable problem in many of the richer western European countries as a direct result of its enhanced average living standards. Clearly, people in the top quarter of the income distribution in any industrialized country have more opportunities for leisure, travel, culture, fine wines and gracious living than have persons with much lower incomes. Most of those now in the bottom half of the income distribution would like these opportunities too. Only growth can give it to them.

Today, many countries that have not yet experienced sustained periods of economic growth are urgently seeking to copy those that have done so in order to obtain the benefits of growth, despite its costs.

How seriously the costs are taken depends in part on how many of the benefits of growth have already been achieved. With mounting population problems, the poorer countries are increasingly preoccupied with creating growth. With mounting awareness of pollution, the richer countries are devoting more resources to overcoming the problems caused by growth – at the same time that they are understandably reluctant to give up further growth.

Indeed, a similar conflict can often be seen within the same country at one time. A relatively poor community fights to acquire a new paper mill for the employment and income it will create; another, relatively affluent, community seeks to keep a mill away because of the pollution it will create.

SUMMARY

1. National income grows as a long-term trend over time, and fluctuates around that trend in the short term.
2. Short-term cyclical fluctuations take the economy through recoveries, peaks, recessions, troughs and then back to recoveries.

3. Fluctuations in aggregate desired expenditure can exert demand-side shocks, causing national income to change. Fluctuations in aggregate supply can also cause income to fluctuate.

4. One set of theories looks to random or haphazard demand-side shocks to cause systematic fluctuations in income because of long lags in the channels through which the effects of these shocks are transmitted into income changes.

5. Another set of theories looks to systematic fluctuations in demand shocks as an explanation of systematic fluctuations in income. The best known of this set is the multiplier-accelerator theory. The accelerator relates investment to changes in income and thus explains why the level of spending may fall off simply because income stops growing. The multiplier helps to reinforce any initial shock in either the upward or the downward direction.

6. Other systematic-shock theories look to changes in government policy (a) following the political cycle; or (b) following an alternation between two policy goals, one calling for expansion and the other for contraction; or (c) misguided stabilization policy leading to alternative bouts of expansionary and contractionary policies.

7. Growth theory concerns the long-term growth of potential income, which is the most potent single force leading to long-term increases in income.

8. In the long run, there is no paradox of thrift. Saving helps to finance investment, and investment raises potential income.

9. In a world of growth without learning, the growth of capital leads to rising output and a rising capital-output ratio, hence a falling real return to capital.

10. Learning, and other very-long-run developments, shift the *MEC* curve outwards. The growth of the capital stock will raise, leave constant or lower the return on capital depending on the relative speeds with which the *MEC* curve and the stock of capital are increasing.

11. The optimum population maximizes output per capita.

12. Supply-side theories emphasize microeconomic policies to encourage growth by making the economy more adaptable, its people more inclined to save and to work, and its firms more competitive.

13. The benefits of growth include long-term increases in living standards, greater room for redistributive policies, favourable changes in lifestyle and (for some) greater national power. The costs include forgone current production of consumption commodities, unfavourable changes in lifestyle and pollution.

TOPICS FOR REVIEW

- Causes of demand shocks
- Theories of cyclical behaviour
- The accelerator theory of investment
- The multiplier-accelerator theory of the cycle
- Government as a possible cause of the cycle
- Short- and long-term effects of saving and investment
- Outward shifts in the *MEC* curve and the accumulation of capital
- Optimum population
- Costs and benefits of growth

37

Demand Management 1: Fiscal Policy[1]

There is no doubt that government can exert a significant influence on national income. For example, during major wars, when governments throw fiscal caution to the winds and engage in massive military spending, both national income and employment rise. It is this ability of government to influence the macroeconomic behaviour of the economy that gives rise to macroeconomic policies.

A hierarchy of policies can be distinguished. At the top is **macroeconomic policy** itself, which includes any measure directed at influencing such macroeconomic variables as the overall levels of employment, unemployment, national income and the price level. One part of macroeconomic policy is **demand management**, which seeks to influence macroeconomic variables by working through aggregate demand. One aspect of demand management is *fiscal policy*, which seeks to influence aggregate demand by working through the *IS* curve. A second aspect is *monetary policy*, which seeks to influence aggregate demand by working through the *LM* curve.[1] The other branch of macroeconomic policy works through aggregate supply. Such policies have recently been dubbed 'supply-side economics'. **Stabilization policy** is the attempt to reduce fluctuations in income, employment and the price level, stabilizing national income at its full-employment level, if possible. Stabilization policy is normally pursued using the tools of demand management.

Background to Fiscal Policy

Any one of a large number of shocks can shift either the *AD* or the *SRAS* curve, taking equilibrium national income away from potential national income. In the long run, when all markets are fully adjusted, there will be neither inflationary nor recessionary gaps. In the short run, however, if the adjustment process is slow, and if

[1] The term demand management is sometimes used in Britain to mean only fiscal policy. This is an historical accident because fiscal policy was for decades the main tool of demand manipulation. Demand management seeks to influence the aggregate demand curve. Both monetary and fiscal policy affect that curve. They are both instruments for operating on the demand side of the economy and are distinct from the instruments of supply management that seek to operate on the aggregate supply curve.

[1] For background material for this chapter, see Harbury and Lipsey, Chapter 9.

shocks follow on each other before the effects of earlier shocks are fully worked out, the average performance of the economy may show significant inflationary or deflationary gaps over quite long periods of time.

> **Stabilization policy is operated by using the tools of demand management to reduce inflationary and recessionary gaps when they appear.**

The major fiscal tools of stabilization policy are government expenditures and tax rates. Changes in these will affect the government **budget balance**, the difference between its expenditures and its receipts. **Fiscal policy** can thus be defined as attempts to influence the aggregate demand curve by altering government expenditures and government revenues.

Fiscal impact: As we shall see, active attempts to use fiscal policy to stabilize the economy have fallen into disfavour in the UK. Nonetheless the impact that government taxing and spending have on the economy cannot be denied. This chapter helps us to understand that impact, whatever the motives may be for altering taxing and spending policies.

The public-sector borrowing requirement: The importance of public-sector production by nationalized industries in Britain has caused attention to be focused on a larger concept of the deficit. This is called the **public-sector borrowing requirement (PSBR)**, which is the combined excess of expenditure over revenue of the central government, the local authorities and public corporations. The PSBR is, therefore, the deficit of all branches of government plus the deficit of all publicly owned corporations.

A deficit means more is spent than is taken in. Is this a cause for public concern? Any private firm knows that it often must borrow now to pay for capital that will yield revenue in the future. For this reason, budget deficits are common in private industries that are borrowing for expansion. Thus a positive PSBR does not necessarily mean government prodigality. If the borrowing is to meet current expenditures such as transfer payments or civil service salaries, there may be real cause for concern, but if the borrowing is to cover capital expenses on, say, new power stations that will produce revenues sufficient to cover their capital cost, there may be no need for concern.

> **The PSBR records the excess of expenditure for current and capital purposes of governments and public corporations over all of their current revenues.**

THE THEORY OF FISCAL POLICY

A general discussion of how fiscal policy shifts the aggregate demand curve is given below. Box 37.1 provides an optional algebraic treatment for those who would like to see the analysis done formally.

Fiscal Policy When Private Expenditure Functions Do Not Shift

A relatively easy problem faces policy-makers when private-sector expenditure functions for consumption, investment and net exports are given and unchanging. What is needed is a once-and-for-all fiscal change to reduce any existing recessionary or inflationary gap.

A Change in Government Expenditures

Government expenditure on final goods is autonomous in our model. An increase in G thus represents a rise in the aggregate desired expenditure associated with each interest rate. This raises the level of national income at which desired expenditure equals national income at each given interest rate, which means an outward shift in the IS curve. The result is an increase in the equilibrium national income and the interest rate associated with any given price level. This in turn causes a rightward shift in the AD curve. By an analogous argument, a decrease in government spending shifts the AD curve to the left.

The above is just a summary of the analysis detailed in Chapter 29. It was shown graphically in Figures 29.3 and 29.4 on pages 505 and 507.

A Change in Tax Rates

Reductions in personal tax rates leave more income in the hands of households. If households

BOX 37.1 AN ALGEBRAIC TREATMENT OF HOW FISCAL POLICIES SHIFT THE AGGREGATE DEMAND CURVE

Fiscal policy that alters government expenditure or tax rates can exert an expansionary or a contractionary pressure on the economy. This can be seen as shifts in the aggregate desired expenditure curve, *E*, the *IS* curve and the aggregate demand curve, *AD*.

The Aggregate Desired Expenditure Curve
From Chapter 29 (see page 510), we know that the equation of the expenditure function for the four-sector model is the following:

$$E = [c(1-t)-m]Y + I^* + G^* + X^* + cQ^* \quad (1)$$

Inspection of equation (1) tells us that the aggregate desired expenditure is increased by an increase in G^* or in Q^*. It also tells us that it is increased by a fall in t, since t enters with a negative sign.

> **Aggregate desired expenditure is positively related to government expenditure on final goods, *G*, transfer payments, *Q*, and negatively related to the tax rate, *t*.**

The IS Curve
From Chapter 32 (see page 560), we know that the equation of the IS curve is

$$r = \left(\frac{1-z}{b}\right)Y - \left(\frac{A}{b}\right) \quad (2)$$

This is the condensed form where *A* stands for all autonomous expenditure and *z* for the marginal propensity to spend out of national income. In the four-sector model, *z* is equal to $[c(1-t)-m]$. It follows immediately that the *IS* curve is shifted to the right by a rise in *G* or *Q* which are elements of *A*. A little more care is required about *t*. The tax rate enters *z* with a negative sign, as just shown above. Thus, lowering *t* raises *z*. But *z* enters equation (2) with a negative sign, so raising *z* lowers the

absolute value of the coefficient attached to *Y*. The coefficient *b*, which shows the response of desired investment expenditure to the interest rate, is negative, which gives the *IS* curve its negative slope. It follows from all this that lowering *t* lowers the absolute value of the negative slope of the *IS* curve and hence pivots it outwards. This indicates a higher equilibrium level of national income associated with each interest rate.

> **The equilibrium level of national income associated with any given interest rate (as shown by the *IS* curve) is positively related to government expenditure on final goods and transfer payments, and negatively related to the tax rate.**

The Aggregate Demand Curve
Chapter 33 gives the equation of the aggregate demand curve as:

$$Y = \left(\frac{1}{(1-z)+bd/e}\right)A^* - \left(\frac{n}{d+e(1-z)/b}\right)$$
$$+ \left(\frac{M^*}{d+e(1-z)/b}\right)\frac{1}{P} \quad (3)$$

Inspection of equation (3) shows that the *AD* curve is shifted to the right by an increase in A^* which in turn can follow from an increase in G^* or Q^*. The reasoning used above for the *IS* curve tells us that lowering *t* lowers the value of $(1-z)$. This raises the value of the multiplier attached to A^*, which shifts the *AD* curve to the right indicating a higher value of *Y* associated with any given *P*.

> **The equilibrium value of national income associated with any given price level (as shown by the AD curve) is positively associated with government expenditure on final goods and transfer payments and negatively associated with the tax rate.**

spend some of this extra disposable income, the aggregate expenditure function shifts upwards. From that point on, the analysis is the same as for an increase in government expenditure. The upward shift in the desired expenditure function raises the equilibrium national income associated with each interest rate, which means a rightward shift in the *IS* curve. This raises the national income and interest rate that provides an *IS-LM* equilibrium at each price level, which in turn means a rightward shift in the aggregate demand

curve. An increase in tax rates has the opposite effects, ending in a leftward shift in the *AD* curve.

Notice one difference between a change in government expenditure and in tax rates. A rise in expenditure causes the same increase in autonomous expenditure at all levels of national income. This has the effect of shifting the aggregate desired expenditure curve upward, and the *IS* and *AD* curves outward parallel to themselves. A fall in tax rates has a proportionate effect, because this increases disposable income by the percentage reduction in the tax rate. If national income is low, then the increase in disposable income is also low. If national income is high, the increase in disposable income is also high. As a result, every point on the *AE* curve shifts up, while every point on the *IS* and *AD* curves shifts right in proportion to the level of income indicated by that point.

A rise in government expenditure or a fall in tax rates shifts the aggregate demand curve to the right; a fall in government expenditure or a rise in tax rates shifts it to the left.

Balanced-budget Changes

Another policy available to the government is to make a balanced-budget change by changing spending and tax revenues equally. Say the government increases tax rates enough to raise an extra £1 billion that it then uses to purchase goods and services. Aggregate expenditure would remain unchanged if, and only if, the £1 billion that the government takes from the private sector would otherwise have been spent by the private sector. In that case the government's policy would reduce private expenditure by £1 billion and raise its own spending by £1 billion. Aggregate demand, and hence national income and employment, would remain unchanged – although its composition would be shifted away from private-sector and towards public-sector spending.

This, however, is not the result predicted by our model. When an extra £1 billion in taxes is taken away from households, they reduce their spending on domestically produced goods by less than £1 billion. If the marginal propensity to consume out of disposable income is, say, 0.75, consumption expenditure will fall by only £750 million. If the government spends the entire £1 billion on domestically produced goods, aggregate expenditure will increase by £250 million. In this case, the balanced-budget increase in government expenditure has an expansionary effect. It shifts the aggregate desired expenditure curve upward, and hence shifts the *AD* curve to the right.

A balanced-budget increase in government expenditure will have an expansionary effect on national income, and a balanced-budget decrease will have a contractionary effect.

The **balanced-budget multiplier** measures the change in income divided by the balanced-budget change in government expenditure that brought it about. Thus, if the extra £1 billion of government spending, financed by the extra £1 billion of taxes, causes national income to rise by £500 million, the balanced-budget multiplier is 0.5; if income rises by £1 billion, it is 1.0.

Now compare the sizes of the multipliers for a balanced-budget and a deficit-financed increase in government spending. With a deficit-financed increase in expenditure, there is no increase in tax rates, and hence no consequent decrease in consumption expenditure to offset the increase in government expenditure. With a balanced-budget increase in expenditure, however, an offsetting increase in tax rates and decrease in consumption does occur. Thus, the balanced-budget multiplier is much lower than the multiplier that relates the change in income to a deficit-financed increase in government expenditure with tax rates constant.[1]

Fiscal Policy When Private Expenditure Functions Are Shifting

Thus far we have considered fiscal policy when the expenditure function is given (and unchanged by anything other than the fiscal policy

---

[1] The balanced-budget effect is most simply seen using the *IS* curve. To do this, return to equations (1)–(6) on pages 554–555, and add a new equation, $G + Q = T$, and treat t as a variable. In other words, the rate of tax, t is to be varied to ensure a balanced budget. Substitution then produces the following equation for the *IS* curve:

$$r = \left(\frac{1-z}{b}\right)Y - \left(\frac{(1-z)G + A}{b}\right).$$

The tax rate no longer appears as a parameter affecting behaviour since it is no longer a policy parameter; it must be set so as to balance the budget. Notice that *G* still appears in the autonomous expenditure term, but now multiplied by $(1-z)$. This tells us that the impact of a balanced-budget increase in *G* is only that part, $1 - z$, that would *not* have been spent if it had been left in private hands. The condition $G + Q = T$ used above assumes a globally balanced budget. For a balanced-budget *change* in expenditure, one must use the appropriate multiplier expression and add the condition $\Delta G + \Delta Q = \Delta T$.

itself). But as we saw in Chapter 36, private-sector expenditure functions change continually. This makes stabilization policy much more difficult than it would be if it were necessary only to identify a stable inflationary or recessionary gap and then to take steps to eliminate it once and for all.

What can stabilization policy be expected to achieve when private expenditure functions are shifting continually? We can distinguish two objectives that differ in the scope of required policy intervention. The first objective is the more ambitious of the two. In this case, the authorities try to keep national income at exactly its full-employment level by trying to offset every fluctuation in the private investment, consumption and export expenditure functions. The second objective is much less ambitious. In this case, the authorities accept fluctuations as inevitable. They recognize, however, that sometimes large and persistent inflationary or recessionary gaps will develop. The task of stabilization policy is then seen as offsetting these major gaps to prevent both deep and persistent recessions and long and rapid inflations.

Discretionary Fine-tuning

In the 1950s and 1960s many economists advocated the use of fiscal policy to remove even minor fluctuations in national income around the full-employment level. This attempt was called **fine-tuning** the economy. During that period, British Chancellors of the Exchequer introduced budgets each year, sometimes more often, that varied taxes and expenditures with the intention of influencing aggregate demand so as to stabilize national income. Careful assessment of the results, where such policies were followed, shows that their successes fell short of expectations.

Fiscal stabilization policies seek to stabilize the economy by creating *negative feedback*, which means that, when income deviates from its potential level, changes are made to push it back *towards* its potential level. Thus, when demand is too high, so that inflationary conditions prevail, demand is reduced; when demand is too low, so that unemployment prevails, demand is increased. Negative feedback is a necessary but not a sufficient condition for stabilizing income. If the economy operates with lags that are large relative to the fluctuations that stabilization

policy is seeking to control, the intervention can actually accentuate rather than dampen fluctuations.

The importance of time-lags: Controls operate with lags for many reasons. We mention two. The first is called the **decision lag**: it takes time to assess a situation and decide what corrective action should be taken. At a minimum it takes a month, and often much longer, to gather data about current happenings. Our current information thus tells us not what is happening today, but what was happening anytime from a month to six months ago. The data must then be interpreted. Questions such as 'Is the downturn the beginning of a large potential slide or just a temporary aberration?' need to be answered. After the situation is assessed, alternative corrective actions need to be considered and finally a decision taken on what action is appropriate.

A second source of lag is called the **execution lag**: it takes time to initiate corrective policies and for their full influence to be felt. For example, if the corrective action is an increase in new road-building, months may be needed to make surveys, to hear objections from persons affected by chosen routes and to sign contracts. Once the government has done its work, it will take time before the effects on the private sector are felt. A strike in the cement industry could delay still further the flow of wage payments to construction workers.

Destabilizing policy: Now consider an economy in which a downturn begins. The government must first decide whether it is faced with a major downturn or just a minor adjustment that will quickly be reversed. Then it must decide what measures to take, and with what strength to take them. Say it decides to cut tax rates. It must get the necessary legislation drafted, discussed in Parliament and passed. Then it must wait for the measures to take effect. People will find themselves with more disposable income and will then decide by how much to alter their expenditure plans. By that time, however, the recession may be over and a recovery underway. If so, the expenditure cut will reinforce the recovery phase, rather than dampen the recession phase.

Now suppose that the recovery proves a strong one, and an inflationary gap opens up. Once again, the government must diagnose the situation, decide on what action to take – say a rise in tax rates – take it, and wait for the effects to be felt. If it is unlucky, the expenditure-curtailing effects of the tax increase may be felt just as the economy is turning into a recession. The government's action will then be accentuating cyclical swings rather than working against them.

This simple example is sufficient to show that the problem of controlling the economy is not so simple as comparative-static analysis can make it seem. Stabilization policies will have differing effects depending on the time-lags both in the actual working of the economy and in the functioning of the stabilization scheme.

The decline of fine-tuning as a goal of policy: Towards the end of the 1960s a series of applied studies suggested that stabilization policy had sometimes succeeded in destabilizing the economy, making fluctuations in income and employment larger than they would have been in the absence of any intervention. As a result of this work, most economists and government policy-makers set much less ambitious objectives for fiscal policy in the 1970s and 1980s than they had done in the 1950s and 1960s.

Automatic Fine-tuning: Built-in Stabilizers

If a successful fine-tuning policy appears to be impossible, because of time-lags, is there no room for fiscal policy to correct short-term economic fluctuations?

Fortunately, much of the job of adjusting fiscal policy to an ever-changing economic environment is done automatically by built-in stabilizers. A **built-in stabilizer** is anything that reduces the economy's cyclical fluctuations and that is activated without a conscious governmental decision. Two major ways to achieve this result are to reduce the magnitude of destabilizing shifts in expenditure functions, and to reduce the size of the multiplier which determines the economy's response to such shifts.

Government expenditure: Government expenditure on goods and services tends to be relatively stable in the face of cyclical variations in national income. Much expenditure is already committed by earlier legislation, so only a small proportion can be varied at the government's discretion from one year to the next; and even this

small part is slow to change. In contrast, private consumption and investment functions are subject to both autonomous and induced shifts, tending to expand and contract the economy.

The twentieth-century rise in the size of government expenditure may have been a mixed blessing. One benefit, however, has been to transfer expenditure from the private sector, where it is subject to major disturbances, to the public sector, where it is not. Consumption and investment expenditures are of smaller absolute size than they would have been if the government sector had been substantially smaller than it now is. As a result, the absolute magnitude of *given percentage shifts* in the private investment and consumption functions has been reduced.

Taxes: Direct taxes act as a built-in stabilizer because they reduce the marginal propensity to consume out of national income and thus reduce the value of the multiplier. Consider an example. If there were no taxes in our model, every change in national income of £1 would cause a change in disposable income of £1. With a marginal propensity to consume out of disposable income of, say, 0.8, consumption would change by 80p. But with a marginal direct-tax rate of, say, 35p in £1, disposable income only changes by 65p for every change in national income of £1. Thus with an *MPC* out of disposable income of 0.8, consumption only changes by 52p for every change in national income of £1. By reducing the *MPC* out of national income, direct taxes act as a built-in stabilizer, reducing the size of the multiplier.

Transfer payments: So far we have treated government transfer payments as an exogenous constant, Q^*. In fact both unemployment payments and supplementary benefits tend to vary counter-cyclically. In a slump, when employment is low, these payments are high; in a boom, when employment is high, these payments are low. Such transfer payments have the effect of partially stabilizing disposable income and, hence, of partially stabilizing consumption expenditure. Consider an example. Assume that when disposable income from income sources drops by 65p, transfer payments rise by 30p, so that disposable income only drops by 35p. With an *MPC* out of disposable income of 0.8, consumption expenditure would only drop by 28p.

By partially stabilizing disposable income, national insurance and supplementary benefits reduce the value of the multiplier and thus reduce the magnitude of fluctuations in response to shifts in exogenous expenditure.

Agricultural-support policies: A slump causes a general decline in the demand for all goods, including agricultural produce. The free-market price of agricultural goods tends to fall, and government agricultural supports come into play. This ensures that support expenditure will rise as national income falls. This is as true of EC agricultural-support policies as it is true of policies in most developed countries.

If the supports take the form of purchasing surplus produce, then this element of government *expenditure* is rendered counter-cyclical. If the supports take the form of grants or subsidies, then it is *transfer payments* that are made counter-cyclical. Either way, the government policies reduce fluctuations by damping the multiplier process that acts through variations in agricultural incomes.

The shocks impinging on the economy are weaker, the larger is the (stable) government-expenditure sector and the smaller are the (less stable) consumption and private-investment sectors. The multiplied swings in income in response to expenditure shocks are smaller, the more are tax receipts pro-cyclical and transfer payments counter-cyclical.

Box 37.2 provides an optional algebraic analysis of built-in stabilizers for those who would like to study it.

The origin of built-in stabilizers: Most of these built-in stabilizers are fairly new phenomena. Sixty years ago agricultural-stabilization policies, steeply progressive income taxes and large unemployment and other national-insurance payments were unknown in the UK. Each of these built-in stabilizers is the unforeseen by-product of policies originally adopted for other reasons. But, unforeseen or not, they work as stabilizers.

BOX 37.2 A FORMAL ANALYSIS OF BUILT-IN STABILIZERS

Consider the equation of the *IS* curve on page 556 with G^* and cQ^* separated from the rest of the constants, A^*.

$$r = -\frac{G^* + A^* + zQ^*}{b} + \left(\frac{1-z}{b}\right)Y \ . \qquad (1)$$

Now take first differences to yield

$$\Delta r = -\Delta G^*/b - \Delta A^*/b - z\Delta Q^*/b \\ + \Delta Y(1-z)/b \ . \qquad (2)$$

We are interested in the horizontal shift in the *IS* curve. The larger is this shift, *ceteris paribus*, the larger is the increase in equilibrium income. The property of the *horizontal* shift of any point on the *IS* curve, when the whole curve shifts, is that the interest rate is held constant. Thus $\Delta r = 0$ in the above expression. Now we can, by setting the LHS at zero, write the constant-interest-rate multipliers (i.e. the horizontal shifts in the *IS* curve) as

$$\frac{\Delta Y}{\Delta G^*} = \frac{\Delta Y}{\Delta A^*} = \frac{\Delta Y}{c\Delta Q^*} = \frac{1}{1-z} \ . \qquad (3)$$

Increasing the size of G lowers the size of A and hence the magnitude of the ΔA disturbances that impinge on the economy. (ΔA stands for shifts in all exogenous components of expenditure including the constants on the consumption and invest-ment functions.)

We know from Chapter 29 that $z = c(1-t) - m$. Thus, increasing t lowers z, raises $1-z$ and lowers the value of the multiplier, $1/(1-z)$.

Finally to show the effects of counter-cyclical transfer payments we replace $Q = Q^*$ with the following:

$$Q = q_0 + qY \qquad q < 0 < q_0 \qquad (4)$$

This makes some transfer payments, q_0, independent of national income while the rest varies negatively with income according to the coefficient q.

If you re-solve the *IS* curve, and the relations just given, using (4) instead of $Q = Q^*$, you obtain an autonomous expenditure multiplier of

$$\frac{\Delta Y}{\Delta G^*} = \frac{\Delta Y}{\Delta A^*} = \frac{\Delta Y}{c\Delta Q^*} = \frac{1}{1-z-cq} \ . \qquad (5)$$

Consider the new term $-cq$. Since c is positive while q is negative, $-cq$ is positive. The coefficient $-q$ gives the amount that transfer payments rise for every £1 fall in Y, and $-cq$ gives the amount that consumption rises as a result. Inspection of the above equation shows that the addition of a positive term to the denominator of the multiplier lowers the value of the multiplier. Hence counter-cyclical transfer payments are a built-in stabilizer.

Discretionary Policy to Eliminate Persistent Gaps

The economy occasionally develops inflationary or recessionary gaps that are both severe and persistent. Such gaps last long enough for their major causes to be studied and for possible fiscal remedies to be carefully planned and executed without worrying too much about short-term lags.

Many economists who do not believe in the viability of fine-tuning believe that fiscal policy can be used to help remove persistent recessionary and inflationary gaps.

The techniques are the same as with fine-tuning but the more persistent is the gap the less likely is it that corrective fiscal measures will be destabilizing.

When the government decides to change its fiscal policy consciously, it must decide whether to use taxes or expenditures, or both, to achieve the desired shifts in aggregate demand. What issues are involved in this decision?

Location of effects: The multiplier effects of an increase in aggregate demand tend to spread over the whole economy, increasing the demand for virtually every commodity. If a slump is general, with widespread unemployment, this is an advantage. If, however, a slump has severely localized characteristics, for example, a major depression in a particular industry, such as the car industry, or area, such as South Wales, it may be desirable to achieve a disproportionate effect in the depressed sector. In this case, raising expenditure has some advantage over cutting taxes. The tax cut will have its initial impact on the entire economy, but by careful choice of projects much of the initial effect of extra expenditure can be channelled into particular sectors.

If specific impact effects are important, expenditure has an advantage over tax changes.

The duration of the time-lag: Long time-lags in fiscal policy are undesirable both because they delay the desired effects, and because they increase the possibility of destabilizing the economy.

Tax cuts have a substantial advantage over expenditure increases with respect to the execution lag.

Although the execution lag can be extremely long for a new road-building programme, it can be very short for changes in taxes and transfer payments. Only a matter of weeks after a tax cut has been legislated, wage-earners may find themselves with more take-home pay because their employers are withholding tax payments at a lower rate than before. Similarly, transfer payments can be changed only weeks after the enactment of the necessary legislation.

The reversibility of the policy: Private-sector spending undergoes continual oscillations. Even when a persistent gap develops, one thing that is clear from past experience is that the gap will sooner or later change as a result of shifts in private expenditure functions.

Fiscal changes made in the interests of stabilizing the economy must be easily and quickly reversible.

On this count, tax policy seems superior both to government expenditure on goods and services and to transfer payments. Transfer payments are usually part of social policy, and it would seem callous to change the rates on such payments every time inflationary or recessionary gaps developed. Government expenditures can be increased, but experience shows that they are not easy to cut since most of them become committed through statutory programmes. Although they can be reduced over a decade by a really determined effort – as happened in the 1980s – the degree of discretion that any government has to reduce them rapidly is very small. Furthermore, a new line of expenditure following from a decision to increase G usually requires a new set of civil servants to administer it. These people become a vested interest who will resist any cuts in the expenditure flows that support them. This behaviour helps to explain why expenditure changes are not wholly satisfactory tools for stabilization policies. Tax rates, on the other hand, do not suffer from this inertia. They can be changed quickly and the civil servant apparatus required to administer taxes is usually independent of the rates being levied.

The public's reaction to short-term changes: Stabilizing a fluctuating economy through tax policy calls for temporary tax increases to remove an inflationary gap and temporary tax reductions to remove a deflationary gap. These tax changes change household disposable income, and, according to the Keynesian theory of the consumption function, the resulting changes in expenditure would be stabilizing. Consumption expenditure would increase as taxes were cut in times of deflationary gaps, and decrease as taxes were raised in times of inflationary gaps.

This theory of the stabilizing effects of short-term tax changes relies on the assumption that household consumption expenditure depends on current disposable income. The more recent theories of the consumption function discussed in Chapter 28 emphasize households' expected *lifetime* or *permanent income* as the major determinant of consumption. According to such theories, households have expectations about their lifetime incomes, and their consumption responds to these expectations. Thus, a temporary rise in income may be saved, while a temporary fall may leave households maintaining their long-term consumption plans by using up some of their past savings.

Let us consider the consequences of this type of behaviour for the stabilizing effects of tax cuts and tax increases.

A tax increase that households regard as temporary has only a small effect on permanent income. Households may find the funds to pay the taxes by temporarily cutting savings, selling some of their wealth, or borrowing against it. If everyone does this, the effect on current consumption expenditure of a temporary increase in tax rates will be small.

In practice, however, the effect may be somewhat larger. First, some people operate from day to day, without a long-term consumption plan. For them, consumption really does depend on little more than current disposable income. Second, many people's capital is held in two forms: human capital – skills, experience and education – and ownership of a house or flat. Neither of these forms of wealth are easy to borrow against for short-term consumption purposes.

A tax cut that is perceived to be temporary will also have a small effect on expected lifetime income. As a result, much of the 'tax bonus' may be saved. To the extent that it is, the stimulating effects of tax cuts on current expenditure will be reduced.

The effect of temporary tax increases is smaller the more household consumption responds to permanent, rather than to current, income. It is larger the less do households have the resources that allow them to maintain consumption in the face of temporary reductions in disposable income.

Doubts about the possible efficacy of short-term variations in tax rates provide a reason for favouring government expenditure. Since government expenditure is itself a direct injection into the circular flow, its effect on income and expenditure is more reliable. Its initial impact does not rely on giving money to others and then having the effect depend on what they elect to do with it.

FISCAL POLICY IN PRACTICE

Keynesian economics in general, and fiscal policy in particular, has recently come under very severe criticism. It is not uncommon to hear it said that the Keynesian model is totally 'wrong' and its policy recommendations totally misguided. We will not go into these extreme views here. Suffice to say that the view that the *basic* theory of income determination is misguided is difficult to sustain. The concept of the circular flow of income long predates Keynes.[1] Almost every econometric model in existence today uses it. Of course certain behavioural relations used in particular models, and certain policy recommendations based on these models, may be open to criticism; but the view that the model itself – and all of the aggregates based on it – are useless is hard to sustain.

What can fiscal policy accomplish? In the

---

[1] A very clear statement is to be found in Chapter 1 of Schumpeter's great book, *The Theory of Economic Development: An Inquiry into Profits, Capital, Interest and the Business Cycle* (English translation, Harvard University Press, Cambridge, Mass., 1934, first published in German in 1912).

United States, where fiscal policy was not seriously used until the 1960s, there is a school of extreme monetarists who argue that fiscal policy does not influence the economy because the crowding-out effect is 100 per cent: every increase of £1 in government expenditure causes a reduction of £1 in private expenditure. The experience of Britain and other countries where fiscal policy has been used over the past 30 years makes it very hard to take this view seriously.[1]

In the latter part of the 1980s, while most of the Western world was experiencing a very sluggish recovery from a deep recession, the United States enjoyed a major boom. The boom coincided with the largest government budget deficits in American peacetime history, brought on by a combination of increased military expenditures and major cuts in tax rates – both of which our theory predicts to be expansionary. Many economists were critical of some of these policies, but few doubted that they had stimulated the economy massively. Indeed, it was something of an irony that the greatest Keynesian boom since the publication of the *General Theory* was instituted by a conservative president who in his election campaign disavowed Keynesian theory and promised balanced budgets.

Judging the Stance of Fiscal Policy

An expansionary fiscal policy is one that increases national income; a contractionary fiscal policy reduces national income. How can we judge changes in the stance of fiscal policy from one year to the next?

In popular discussion, a change in the government's current budget deficit (or the PSBR) is often taken as an indicator, a rise in the

---

[1] See page 566 for a discussion of the crowding-out effect. Fiscal policy has gone through some extraordinary variations in the UK over the last two decades. There is substantial debate about the wisdom of some of these budgetary changes. Indeed, one well-known authority writing about the period referred to '... this extraordinary combination of self-inflicted errors and externally imposed misfortunes ...' (M. V. Posner writing in M. V. Posner (ed.), *Demand Management*, Heinemann, London, 1978). Saying that fiscal policy should not be used because its potent effects are often harmful is quite different from saying it should not be used because it is impotent.

PSBR indicating an expansionary change and a fall indicating a contractionary change. Changes in the PSBR depend on changes in the balance between public-sector expenditures and revenues. Tax revenues, however, are the result of the interaction of tax rates, which the government does set, and the level of national income, which is mainly beyond the government's control. Thus, to judge changes in the stance of fiscal policy from changes in the government's budget deficit, or the PSBR, can be very misleading. It confuses endogenous changes in the deficit due to changes in national income with exogenous changes due to changes in the stance of fiscal policy.

> **The major tools of fiscal policy are government expenditure and tax *rates*. The government's deficit or surplus is the relation between its expenditure and its tax *revenues*.**

The distinction between the two causes of changes in the budget balance is easily seen in what is called the public-sector's **budget deficit function**. This function, which relates the budget deficit, B, to national income, is graphed in Figure 37.1. Its equation is

$$B = (G^* + Q^*) - tY .$$

Endogenous changes in the government's budget balance due to changes in national income are shown by movements along a given function. Changes in the budget balance due to policy-induced changes in government expenditure, G^*, transfer payments, Q^*, or in tax rates, t, are shown by shifts in the function. Such shifts indicate a different budget balance at *each* level of national income.

When measuring changes in the stance of fiscal policy, it is common to calculate changes in the estimated budget balance at some base level of national income. Doing so ensures that measured shifts in the budget balance are due to policy-induced shifts of the deficit function rather than income-induced movements along the function. The base most commonly used is potential national income, and the measure calculated is called the **cyclically adjusted deficit (CAD)**. This is an estimate of expenditures minus tax revenues, not as they actually are, but as they would be if potential national income had been

FIGURE 37.1 The Budget Deficit Function

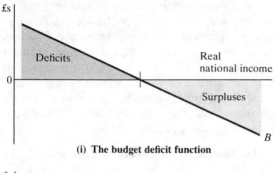

(i) The budget deficit function

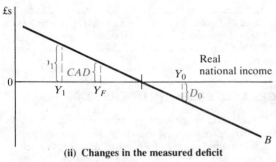

(ii) Changes in the measured deficit

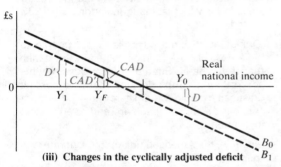

(iii) Changes in the cyclically adjusted deficit

Endogenous changes in national income move the economy along a given deficit function; exogenous changes in the stance of fiscal policy shift the entire function. The curve labelled B in part (i) shows the budget balance as negatively related to national income, with deficits at low levels of national income and surpluses at high levels.

In part (ii), a fall in national income from Y_0 to Y_1 causes the actual budget balance to go from a small surplus of D_0 to a much larger deficit of D_1. Government expenditure and tax rates are unchanged. The unchanged fiscal stance is correctly captured by the constancy of the cyclically adjusted deficit, CAD, measured at the (constant) potential level of national income, Y_F.

Part (iii) illustrates a contractionary change in the stance of fiscal policy. A government expenditure cut or a tax-rate increase shifts the budget deficit function from B_0 to B_1. Now there is a smaller budget deficit *at each level of national income*. This contractionary change is correctly measured by the fall in the cyclically adjusted deficit from CAD to CAD'.

Suppose national income had fallen from Y_0 to Y_1 at the same time that the budget deficit function shifted from B_0 to B_1. In that case, the measured deficit would have gone from surplus (D) to deficit (D'), despite the fall in the cyclically adjusted deficit from CAD to CAD'. Thus, judging the fiscal stance from the measured budget balance would have indicated an expansionary change in fiscal policy, while the fiscal stance actually changed in a contractionary direction.

---

achieved (i.e. if there were neither an inflationary nor a recessionary gap).

Changes in the cyclically adjusted deficit are an indicator of changes in the stance of fiscal policy.[1]

Figure 37.1 analyses the use of the full-employment deficit, as well as the errors that can

arise from use of the current deficit as an indicator of the stance of fiscal policy.

Balanced-budget Proposals

Concern over what some people feel is wastefully high government spending, and alleged inflationary pressures resulting from deficit-financed government spending, has led to proposals to balance budgets. For example, in the UK the Conservative government put great emphasis on its medium-term plan to reduce the PSBR during the 1980s. In order to accomplish this, the government abandoned any attempt at discretionary stabilization policy.

---

[1] The cyclically adjusted deficit is the simplest adequate measure, and it is vastly superior to the current surplus for estimating year-to-year changes in the stance of fiscal policy. More sophisticated measures exist and are often used in detailed empirical work. These use what is called the *weighted, standardized surplus.*

An Annually Balanced Budget

Some people advocate an annually balanced budget, or a PSBR of zero every year. With fixed tax rates, however, tax revenues fluctuate endogenously as national income fluctuates. We have seen that much government expenditure is fixed by past commitments and that most of the rest is hard to change quickly. Thus, an annually balanced budget is probably unfeasible. But suppose it were feasible. Would it be desirable?

We saw earlier that a large government sector, whose expenditures on goods and services are not very sensitive to the cyclical variations in national income, is itself a major built-in stabilizer. To insist that annual government expenditure be tied to annual tax receipts would be to abandon much of the built-in stability provided by the government. Government expenditure would then become a major destabilizing force. Tax revenues necessarily rise in booms and fall in slumps; an annually balanced budget would force government expenditure to do the same. Changes in national income would then cause induced changes not only in household consumption expenditure but also in government expenditure. This would greatly increase the economy's marginal propensity to spend and hence increase the value of the multiplier.[1]

An annually balanced budget would ac-

---

[1] To see this, solve the three-sector IS–LM model for Y, with the added equation $T = G$ (with G treated as a variable). You will then see that the value of the IS–LM multiplier is increased.

BOX 37.3 THE PARADOX OF THRIFT AND THE GREAT DEPRESSION OF THE 1930s

In the text, we have shown that balancing the budget year by year, destabilizes the economy by accentuating both slumps and booms. This result was stated by early Keynesians in what they called the *paradox of thrift*, which we first encountered in Box 27.1. It is nothing more than a simple implication of the theory of income determination: *ceteris paribus*, aggregate demand is decreased if the private sector saves more and spends less, or if the public sector increases taxes or reduces spending.

The paradox of thrift leads to the prediction that substantial unemployment is corrected by encouraging governments, firms and households to spend rather than to save. In times of unemployment and depression, frugality will only make things worse. The paradox was not generally understood during the Great Depression of the 1930s. At that time, many mistaken policies were followed. One such is suggested in a message by King George V to the House of Commons on 8 September 1931, on the occasion of the formation of a new national government after the collapse of the Labour administration:

'The present condition of the National finances, in the opinion of His Majesty's Ministers, calls for the imposition of additional taxation, and for the effecting of economies in public expenditure.'

At the time, the unemployment rate stood at 21 per cent of the labour force!

In the US, President Roosevelt, though he achieved the reputation of grappling vigorously with the problems of the decade while others shilly-shallied, showed no more appreciation of the real nature of the situation than did the British leaders. In his very first inaugural address in 1933 he stated:

'Our greatest primary task is to put people to work ... [This task] can be helped by insistence that the Federal, State and local governments act forthwith on the demand that their cost be drastically reduced. ... There must be a strict supervision of all banking and credits and investments.'

At the time, the American unemployment rate was 23 per cent.

National-income theory predicts that the correct response to the Great Depression of the 1930s was to encourage firms, households and governments to spend and not to save. Attempts to save or to cut government expenditure would only serve to lower national income and raise unemployment even further. The suffering and misery of that unhappy decade would have been greatly reduced had those in authority known even as much economics as is contained in this chapter.

Recall the very important warning given on page 646. The paradox of thrift is a short-run proposition based on the effect of saving and spending on the aggregate demand function. In the long run, saving raises national income by facilitating investment, and hence it increases potential income. The result is a shift of the long-run aggregate supply curve to the right.

centuate the swings in national income that accompany autonomous shifts in private-sector expenditure functions.

Box 37.3 discusses the harm done by the failure to appreciate this important proposition during the Great Depression of the 1930s.

A Cyclically Balanced Budget

Balanced-budget proposals are aimed at two major problems: first, they seek to avoid the alleged harmful consequences of chronic budget deficits; second, they seek to prevent stabilization policy from leading to a long-term increase in the size of the public sector. The process creating the second problem might be as follows. During a slump, the government increases expenditures to stimulate the economy, but during a boom it allows inflation to occur rather than cut expenditure; then, in the next slump, government expenditure is raised once again. The greater willingness to follow an expansionary fiscal policy in slumps than to follow a contractionary

policy in booms can lead to a long-term increase in the size of the government sector. The annually balanced budget would prevent this – but at the cost, as we have seen, of destabilizing the economy.

An alternative policy would prevent perpetual deficits as well as inhibiting the growth of the government sector. This is to balance the budget over the period of one business cycle – called a **cyclically balanced budget**. This would be more feasible than the annually balanced budget and would not make government expenditure a destabilizing force. This policy is illustrated in Figure 37.2.

> **An annually balanced budget is a destabilizer; a cyclically balanced budget is a stabilizer.**

Although more attractive in principle than the annually balanced budget, a cyclically balanced budget would carry problems of its own. The government might, for example, spend in excess of revenue just before an election, leaving the

---

FIGURE 37.2 Balanced and Unbalanced Budgets

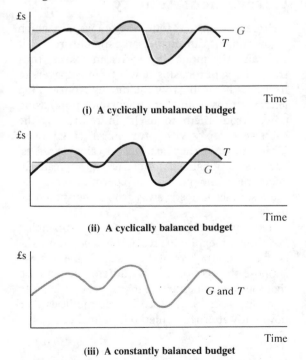

(i) A cyclically unbalanced budget

(ii) A cyclically balanced budget

(iii) A constantly balanced budget

An annually balanced budget is a destabilizer; a cyclically balanced budget is a stabilizer. The flow of tax receipts, T, is shown varying over the business cycle, while in parts (i) and (ii) government expenditure, G, is shown at a constant rate.

In part (i) deficits (grey areas) are common and surpluses (coloured areas) are rare because the average level of expenditure exceeds the average level of taxes. Such a policy will tend to stabilize the economy against cyclical fluctuations, but the average fiscal stance of the government is expansionary.

In part (ii) government expenditure has been reduced until it is approximately equal to the average level of tax receipts. The budget is now balanced cyclically. The policy still tends to stabilize the economy against cyclical fluctuations because of deficits in slumps and surpluses in booms. But the average fiscal stance is neither strongly expansionary nor strongly contractionary.

In part (iii) a constantly balanced budget has been imposed. Deficits have been prevented, but government expenditure now varies over the business cycle, tending to destabilize the economy by accentuating the cyclical swings in aggregate expenditure.

next government to spend less than revenue in subsequent years.

Although the cyclically balanced budget is both more feasible and less undesirable than the annually balanced budget, there is nonetheless serious doubt that enforcing a balanced budget over any time-period is sensible. Many economists believe that a superior alternative to insisting on a precise balance is to pay attention to the balance, without making a fetish of never adding to the public debt. After all, private firms borrow to finance capital expenditures; there seems no reason in principle why governments and public corporations should not do the same. To insist on a balanced public-sector budget is to insist that current taxpayers, and users of the output of public corporations, should pay for capital expenditures that will benefit future taxpayers and consumers. We shall see in the next section that a country can live satisfactorily for ever with a growing public-sector debt – provided the rate of growth is not excessive.

The Costs of Government Activity

We have seen that the operation of fiscal policy may well entail government expenditure in excess of tax receipts. This implies increases in the public debt. In recent decades, increases have far outweighed decreases in most Western countries, so that the trend of the debt has been upward. Does an increasing debt matter? Would an ever-increasing debt lead to an ultimate collapse of market economies? Does the debt represent a burden we are passing on to our heirs?

In discussing the significance of the debt, it is important to keep the cost of the *actual expenditure* distinct from the costs of the *method of financing* the expenditure. Both are important, but only the second is a 'cost of the *debt*'. Before discussing the particular consequences of debt financing, let us note certain costs of government expenditures that exist no matter how the expenditures are financed. This turns out to have a bearing on the questions of financing.

What are the Costs?

The opportunity cost of a particular government expenditure depends on what resources the government project will use, and from where they are

drawn. In times of heavy unemployment, most of the resources used in government activity might otherwise have remained unemployed. In this case, there is no opportunity cost in employing them in the government activity because there is no alternative current production sacrificed by so doing. In contrast, if, in a fully employed economy, the government builds dams, roads, schools and nuclear submarines, their opportunity cost is the consumer goods and capital goods that could have been produced instead.

To the extent that the resources for the government activity are drawn away from the production of consumer goods and services, the opportunity cost is necessarily borne by the present generation in terms of a reduced consumption of goods produced by the private sector of the economy. To the extent that the resources are drawn away from the production of capital goods, the opportunity cost will be spread out over the future, because the current generation is giving up capital goods. This reduces the stock of capital, and the capacity to produce goods and services for consumption in the future.

Alternative Means of Financing Government Activity

There are essentially four different ways in which a government can finance an expenditure: (1) it can raise the money by increasing taxes, thus transferring purchasing power from taxpayers to itself; (2) it can borrow the money from willing lenders, thus transferring current purchasing power from them to itself, in return for the promise to repay with future purchasing power; (3) it can, while they last, sell off valuable assets, such as nationalized industries; (4) it can (in effect) print enough money to permit itself to bid the resources it needs away from other potential users.

The major effect of the method of financing government expenditures is on *who* bears the costs, not on the size of the costs. To see this, we suppose the economy is at full employment, so that the government must incur real opportunity costs in order to produce its commodities. We now study alternative methods of finance.

Taxes

First, if the cost of a new government programme

is met by increases in taxes, then the current taxpayers bear the cost by having their purchasing power reduced.

Borrowing

Second, if the government expenditure is financed by borrowing from domestic households and firms, the reduction in purchasing power for current consumption is incurred by those who lend their money to the government instead of spending it on currently produced goods and services. (People who do not lend to the government do not postpone current consumption, and thus do not bear any of the current cost of the government activity.)

Foreign complications: So far, we have assumed that all transactions were with domestic residents. What if the government borrows from abroad to cover its budget deficits? Now, liabilities to foreigners will be building up – liabilities which will have to be met in the future by exporting goods and services to earn the necessary foreign exchange. In this case, the standards of living of future generations are being sacrificed in order to sustain the consumption of the present generation.

Selling Assets

The third possibility is that the government may cover some of its deficit by selling off assets such as nationalized industries. This was the policy followed by the Thatcher government through all of the 1980s. There are many microeconomic reasons related to efficiency and innovation why one might wish to privatize formerly nationalized industries. (Some of these reasons were discussed in Chapter 25.) Here, we are concerned only with the macroeconomic effects.

If the industries are sold to domestic savers, the issue is what they would otherwise have done with their savings. If they would have invested in other industries, then the policy results in a decline in capital formation that will reduce growth and hence future income. If they would have spent the money on consumption, then all that has happened is a transfer of ownership of assets from the public to the private sector and a transfer of consumption decisions from the private to the public sector. By saving money, private savers gives up their right to decide how

this money will be spent; by spending the money for current uses, the government decides how it will be spent.

When foreign citizens provide funds to buy the newly privatized industries, they are forgoing current consumption in order to buy British industries. The recipients of the benefits of UK government spending are consuming now. Future British citizens will have to forgo consumption in order to make exports available to earn the foreign exchange needed to pay interest and dividends to the foreign owners of these firms. Of course, if privatization greatly raises the profitability of these firms, the foreign payments may come out of new profits.

In either case, this is only a temporary solution. The government will have to decide what to do with the deficit once the assets have been sold off.

Printing New Money

The fourth possibility is that the activity is financed by creating new money. (As we shall see later, the way this is done in the modern world is for the government to sell bonds to the central bank. In return, the central bank credits the government with a deposit on which the government can draw cheques to pay for its purchases.) If resources are already fully employed, this method of finance must create an inflationary gap and thus cause a rise in the price level. Aggregate demand, already high enough to purchase all the output the economy is producing, becomes excessive as the government enters the market with its own new demand. The rise in prices will mean that households and firms will be able to buy less than they would otherwise have bought, and the government will be able to obtain resources for its own activities. Thus, fewer resources will be available for private consumption and private capital formation. The result in the aggregate is the same as if the government has reduced private expenditure by taxation.

As far as distributing the opportunity cost is concerned, inflationary finance is similar to financing by taxes, although the identity of the groups forced to cut back on their own purchases is likely to be different in the two cases. By choosing which taxes to increase, a government using tax finance can exert a considerable influence on the distribution of the burden (although taxes may be shifted from the groups

Box 37.4 THE MEDIUM TERM FINANCIAL STRATEGY: THE END OF STABILIZATION POLICY?

The 1944 White Paper committed the UK government to maintaining full employment. It was understood at the time that demand management would be the main tool of full-employment policy and that its use would cause deficits in slumps and surpluses in booms.

Stabilization policies were followed with varying degrees of success over the intervening 35 years. In the 1970s, however, budget deficits began to rise through recessions and recoveries. Disturbingly, however, employment showed less and less response to variations in fiscal stimulus. Investment became increasingly sluggish through boom and slump, and various empirical studies suggested that the fiscal multiplier had fallen to less than one. (The multiplier cannot be less than one for a £1 increase in spending on *domestic* output, but since all types of spending have an import content, the multiplier for £1 spent by the government may be less than one. In the text we avoided this complication by assuming that the only imports were of consumers' goods so that government expenditure did not have an import content.)

Critics argued that the problems of the UK economy were no longer ones that could be solved by demand management. The real product wage had risen so much during the 1970s that only increasing tax concessions made investment profitable. Even these were losing their power. As a result, successive bouts of fiscal stimulus during

the 1970s left the deficit large, and rising, through recession and recovery.

In 1979, the newly elected Conservative government announced a set of supply-side measures to deal with the problems of the economy. Tax incentives were altered to encourage work and risk-taking; union power was curtailed as part of a programme to reduce the real product wage sufficently to give profit incentives for new investment. The objectives for monetary and fiscal policy were to be set by the Medium Term Financial Strategy (MTFS). The object of this strategy was to achieve a steady reduction in the rate of inflation; the methods were to reduce both the rate of monetary expansion and the budget deficit.

The first Thatcher budget of 1979 signalled the end of demand management by taking steps to reduce the budget deficit in the face of unemployment that exceeded one million persons. Monetary policy took the form of adopting strict targets for the rate of growth of £M3, and a reduced deficit was planned. The reduction of income-tax rates and the increase of rates of VAT caused a once-and-for-all increase in the price level. This upset the inflation targets as the VAT increase passed through the price system. The needed increase in transactions balances made it impossible to keep to the monetary targets.

The MTFS was officially introduced in the 1980 budget, which planned a further cut in the deficit in the face of a predicted world downturn in

---

on which they are levied to other groups in surprising ways). Under inflationary finance, the government bids up prices and leaves it to the market to determine those groups that are to reduce their consumption and thus to pay the current cost. Retired persons and others on fixed incomes will bear much of the cost. Those whose incomes respond only slowly to changes in price levels will bear more of the cost than those whose incomes rise nearly as fast as prices. Some will not pay any of the cost. Inflationary finance is usually regarded as a less just method of taxation than income taxes, because it places much of the burden on the economically weak, the unfortunate, and the least burden on those who can adjust to rising prices, often the richer and more powerful groups.

The opportunity cost of government ac-

tivity in terms of forgone alternatives is incurred whether the money to pay for the projects is raised by taxes, by borrowing from the public, or by creating new money. Methods of finance determine who bears the costs but do not necessarily affect the total cost.

Post-expenditure Problems

Now consider what happens once the government project is finished. To the extent that it was financed by current taxes (or by inflationary creation of new money) the matter is finished once the government expenditure has been made. Resources can then be transferred back to the production of goods and services for private-sector purchases, and households' real disposable income can be allowed to rise by reducing taxes. But to the extent that the government activity

economic activity. The 1981 budget continued the fiscal squeeze although the country was in the midst of a severe recession. It also introduced measures to control government spending in the face of severe inflation by removing the automatic indexing of expenditure plans.

The budget aroused widespread protest for being contractionary in the face of major recession, but the government stuck to its medium-term targets, resisting calls for a revival of short-term stabilization measures. Just as the MFTS seemed to be revealed as an expensive failure, a mild recovery began with output and employment rising slowly. More dramatically, inflation tumbled to levels not seen in over a decade.

Subsequent budgets continued to reduce the PSBR, until by 1987, a balanced budget was achieved. Then in 1988, the top rate of personal income tax was slashed from 60 to 40 per cent and the standard rate was cut once again. The government's employment policy relied on microeconomic measures. In 1985 employers' (and employees') National Insurance contributions for low-paid workers were cut, thus reducing the cost to firms of employing such persons. Youth training schemes, and community projects, were expanded and minimum wages were reduced in some instances. Job counselling services were developed and a subsidy was paid on low-wage jobs for youths. Whatever the success of these schemes, they showed the major shift from reliance on demand management to microeconomic tools for dealing with macroeconomic problems from the supply rather than the demand side.

Although the MTFS had been successful in reducing – even in some years eliminating – the PSBR, it has done so to a great extent through once-and-for-all sales of assets of formerly nationalized industries. Between 1979 and 1986, the PSBR fell from 4.8 to 0.8 per cent of GDP while the PSBR, adjusted for public-sector asset sales, fell only to 3.1 per cent from its 1979 value of 4.2 per cent.

One further aspect of this use of asset sales is that the government has not been able to resist the temptation to sell off the industries in larger, more concentrated, chunks than is necessary. By maximizing the market power of privatized firms, the government maximizes their sale value while minimizing the subsequent amount of competition. Efficiency would call for maximizing competition by selling the industries in the smallest economically viable units.

Some observers have pronounced the death of demand management for all time. Past history suggests, however, that predictions of finality for any current government policy stance are usually misguided; conditions change, and appropriate government policies change as a result. A future government, faced with a budget that was balanced or even in surplus in a time of prolonged recession, might well feel itself justified in injecting some demand stimulus into an economy whose ills were clearly on the demand side, rather than the supply side.

was financed by borrowing from the private sector, the debt remains after the activity has been completed. It is necessary to pay interest each year to the bondholders and eventual redemption of the bonds is made from tax revenue, so taxpayers suffer a reduction in their consumption. The transfer is thus reversed. In return for bearing the original reduction in consumption, bondholders (or their heirs) now enjoy a rise in consumption and taxpayers who are not bondholders suffer a reduction. For the society, the cost in terms of forgone output was borne during the original activity. Once the activity is finished, total production returns to normal. The opportunity cost could not be postponed, but individuals who did not buy bonds must now pay for their share of the cost of the activity by transferring some claims on current production to the bondholders.

Worries About Debt Financing

Worries about public-sector deficits come under three headings. First, they may cause inflations. Second, public-sector borrowing may crowd out private-sector investment. Third, the growing public-sector debt may cause a crisis of confidence as investors begin to doubt the government's ability to repay.

Do Budget Deficits Cause Inflation?

The Conservative government elected in the UK in 1979 clearly took the view that reductions in the PSBR were a necessary condition for controlling inflation. They instituted the *medium term financial strategy* (MTFS). This used deficit reduction as part of an attack on the UK inflation that seemed to have become endemic. Some of the broader aspects of the MTFS are discussed in

Box 37.4.

In spite of the fall in inflation that accompanied the MTFS, the effects of budget deficits on inflation are still debated. The predictions of the theory of income determination are quite clear on this matter: sometimes deficits will cause inflation, and sometimes not.

If the government engages in a deficit-financed increase in expenditure, this shifts the *IS* curve to the right and raises equilibrium income. Further effects depend on *how* the deficit is financed. If it is financed by selling bonds to the central bank, then the money supply goes on increasing as long as the deficit persists. This means that the *LM* curve shifts continuously to the right. Sooner or later this opens up an inflationary gap and initiates an inflation. The inflation will then continue as long as the deficit causes the nominal money supply to increase.

If, however, the deficit is financed by the sale of bonds to the public, there is no monetary expansion and no rightward shift in the *LM* curve. There are still two possibilities. First, the deficit has only a small effect on the price level, if equilibrium national income does not rise above potential income. Second, the deficit causes a once-and-for-all rise in the price level and some crowding out of private expenditure, if the shift of the *IS* curve temporarily takes income above potential.

Deficits cause sustained inflation when they are financed by monetary expansion. When they are financed by borrowing from the private sector, they cause either a small change in the price level when they leave income below potential, or a significant but once-and-for-all rise in the price level if they take income temporarily above potential.

Does Debt Financing Cause Crowding-out?

To study the crowding-out issue, we need to consider separately the cases of full employment and substantial unemployment. Figure 37.3 shows the case where the economy is initially in equilibrium with a recessionary gap. An increase in government expenditure shifts the *IS* curve to the right. If interest rates remained constant, national income would have gone up by the full

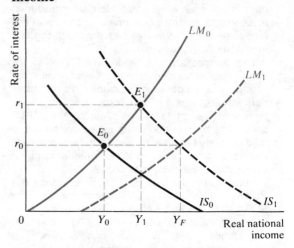

FIGURE 37.3 Crowding-out Below Potential Income

When income is below potential there is some crowding-out of new expenditure unless the money supply is also increased. The original curve of IS_0 and LM_0 yield equilibrium at E_0. Then an increase in government expenditure takes the *IS* curve to IS_1. If the interest rates were held constant, income would rise to Y_F. Instead, however, equilibrium is reached at E_1, the interest rate rises from r_0 to r_1 and income only rises to Y_1.

If the money supply is also increased, shifting the *LM* curve to LM_1, income does rise to Y_F and the crowding-out effect is avoided.

The above analysis assumes that the price level remains constant. If the *SRAS* curve is upward-sloping, some of the expansionary pressure is dissipated in terms of a rising price level. To get the same real effect, a larger increase in both expenditure and the money supply is needed, compared with the case where the price level does not change.

interest-constant multiplier. Instead, interest rates rise and private interest-sensitive expenditure falls. This fall in private expenditure is the crowding-out effect. It partially offsets the expansionary effects of the increase in government expenditure.

Of course, in the situation shown here, the avoidance of crowding-out is a simple matter. All the government has to do is to increase the money supply in line with the increase in the quantity of money demanded, so as to keep the rate of interest constant. If an increase in the money supply shifts the *LM* curve outwards sufficiently to hold the interest rate constant, there is no crowding-out of private expenditure.

Figure 37.4 shows the case when full employment initially prevails. The government expenditure does increase national income to some extent, but by less than before, because the rise in the price level causes a further rise in the interest rate and hence further crowding-out of private expenditure. But that is not the end of the story.

When new government spending raises national income above potential, the resulting inflationary gap raises factor prices and shifts the *SRAS* curve upwards. The process continues until national income has returned to its potential level. Now the crowding-out effect is complete. All that has happened between the initial and final positions is that government expenditure has replaced an equivalent amount of private

expenditure, with the interest rate and the price level higher than they were initially.

Three important conclusions have now been reached.

(1) When there are unemployed resources, a debt-financed increase in government expenditure combined with an increase in the money supply sufficiently to hold interest rates constant causes no crowding-out of private-sector expenditures.

(2) When resources are unemployed, a debt-financed increase in government expenditure combined with a constant money supply will cause some crowding-out of private-sector expenditure.

FIGURE 37.4 The Crowding-out Effect Above Potential Income

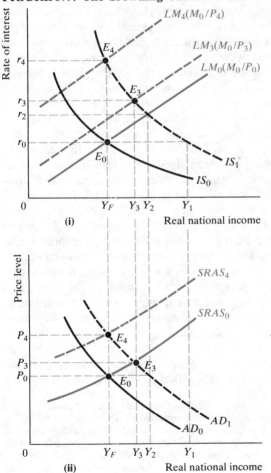

(i)

(ii)

When income starts at its potential level, the crowding-out effect is 100 per cent in the long run. The original curves are IS_0, LM_0, AD_0 and $SRAS_0$. Equilibrium is at E_0 in both parts of the Figure with equilibrium values of Y_F, r_0 and P_0. An increase in government expenditure then takes the IS curve to IS_1 and the AD curve to AD_1.

If the rate of interest and the price level were constant, income would rise to Y_1. Because the LM curve slopes upward, the rate of interest rises to r_2, crowding out some of the increased expenditure. If the price level remained constant, income would rise to Y_2. Because the $SRAS$ curve is upward-sloping, however, the price level rises, producing a short-run equilibrium at E_3 with interest rate r_3 and income Y_3. The rise in the price level from P_0 to P_3 weakens the real impact effect of the expansionary impulse. This weakening of the expansionary impulse is shown in part (i) by a leftward shift in the LM curve to $LM_3(M_0/P_3)$.

An inflationary gap of $Y_3 - Y_F$ has now been opened up. Over time, this will cause factor prices to rise, shifting the $SRAS$ curve upwards. This pushes the equilibrium back along AD_1, lowering income and raising the price level. In part (i), the LM curve is shifted left, taking equilibrium upwards along IS_1. The process stops when the $SRAS$ and LM curves reach $SRAS_4$ and LM_4. National income has returned to Y_F while the price level and the interest rate have risen to P_4 and r_4. In this final long-run equilibrium, the crowding-out effect is 100 per cent.

(3) When there is full employment of resources, any increase in government expenditure will crowd out exactly the same amount of real private expenditure through an increase in the price level and the rate of interest.

There is also a much more subtle crowding-out argument. It is an extreme form which makes crowding-out 100 per cent in all cases. It is outlined in Box 37.5 for those who wish to study it.

Does Debt Financing Risk Government Solvency?

Local authorities in the UK, and all those branches of governments in other countries that do not have their own central banks, must worry about their solvency. Their ability to service their debt depends on their taxing capacity. Such governments have, in the past, occasionally had to default on their debts.

Central governments, however, are in a different position. If they cannot raise enough tax revenue, or borrow enough by selling bonds to the private sector, they can sell an unlimited quantity of bonds to their central banks. This is the so-called 'printing-press method of finance' because the central bank buys the government's bonds with newly created money. At full employment such finance is, as we have seen, inflationary.

For central governments there can be no fear of ultimate insolvency with respect to domestic debt; the fear is, rather, that if the government is forced to printing-press finance, the ensueing inflation will destroy much of the real purchasing power of government debt that is denominated in nominal money terms. Such worries would cause lenders to demand a substantial interest premium to protect themselves against the purchasing-power erosion coming from the anticipated inflation. Such concern only arises, however, when investors feel that the growth of debt is outstripping the future capacity to service it.[1]

A Non-Keynesian View of the National Debt

The view of the national debt that we have just discussed may be called a Keynesian view. Its basic points are: (1) within quite broad limits, the size of the debt is of no great practical importance, and (2) the debt should be increased or decreased according to the needs of stabilization policy.

An alternative view, which may be called *fiscal conservatism*, uses the theory of government behaviour first discussed on pages 417–419. Its first premise is that governments are not passive agents doing what is necessary to create full employment and otherwise to maximize social welfare; instead they seek to maximize their own utility functions. This they do by spending as much as they can and by levying as few taxes as they can get away with. Spending is attractive to the central authorities because some of it, such as civil service salaries, expense accounts and pensions, is for the authorities' own consumption, and because much of the rest benefits the public, helping to gain votes to keep the present party in power. Taxation is undesirable because heavy taxes tend to lose votes for the party in power and may also cause pressure for reductions in spending which may reduce the consumption of the central authorities themselves. In this view, many governments are irresponsible: they seek to increase their own welfare by making their budget deficits as large as possible. (The criticism clearly did not apply to the Thatcher government of the 1980s, although it seemed much closer to the mark with respect to the Reagan administration in the US over the same time-period.)

The non-Keynesian view takes a broad historical perspective. It says that in the eighteenth century spendthrift rulers habitually spent more than their tax revenues and created inflationary gaps. The resulting inflations were harmful because they reduced the purchasing power of everyone's savings and disrupted trade. All through that century a battle was fought between

---

[1] Lack of confidence in the government's ability to pay interest on the debt and to repay the principal on time should not be confused with an unwillingness to take up new debt at too low a money rate of interest in the face of inflationary expectations. Few investors would be willing, for example, to buy new government bonds yielding an 8 per cent nominal interest rate if they expected a 16 per cent annual rate of inflation. The inability to sell bonds on these terms has nothing to do with investors' confidence in the government's ability to meet its contractual obligations. The problem is rather that investors would not wish to make a perfectly safe loan to anyone on such unfavourable terms.

BOX 37.5 DOES DEFICIT-FINANCED SPENDING REALLY RAISE AGGREGATE DEMAND?

It is possible to imagine circumstances under which deficit-financed spending does not raise aggregate demand. The basic idea is simple. When the government finances its spending by selling bonds to the public, it creates a future liability to service those bonds. Taxpayers' future disposable incomes will be reduced by the taxes needed to raise the funds required to service that debt. The present value of that future liability is the current value of the bonds.

In other words, government spending on final goods, or transfer payments, makes the recipients better off, but makes future taxpayers worse off by exactly the same amount. If future taxpayers understand what is happening and react by reducing their present expenditures, they will offset the increase in government expenditure. In a perfectly calculating world, the offset would be exact, and the aggregate demand curve would be unaffected by an increase in government expenditure financed by selling bonds to the public.

This possibility was originally analysed by David Ricardo in the nineteenth century, and, as a result, it is often referred to as the *Ricardo Invariance Principle*. Ricardo was showing what had to be true for fiscal policy to be impotent; he did not argue that the necessary conditions were fulfilled in the real world.

The modern analysis of this issue is due to Robert Barro's model of overlapping generations.[1] It is beautifully formulated in abstract terms but its essence is as follows.

(1) The population consists of people of different ages – the young, the working, and the retired.

(2) Each household has a plan for its lifetime consumption, and for a positive amount of net wealth that it wishes to pass on to its heirs.

(3) The government now introduces some new deficit-financed expenditure. Assume for illustration that it sells perpetuities on the open market and hands out the proceeds as extra unemployment benefits. The recipients will spend much of the money, while taxpayers, and their heirs, will be left with the future liability to pay the taxes needed to service the debt. The fiscal policy stimulates the economy by inducing extra expenditure on the part of the recipients of the government's 'transfer' payments and the overall effect will be stimulating if taxpayers do not react to the change in their future tax liability. But this violates the assumption that everyone has a rational plan for their own

future consumption and for the net wealth they wish to hand on to their heirs. In order to fulfil this plan, the present generation must save an amount equal to the new budget deficit and carry these new savings into the future. This will exactly offset the future tax liabilities required to pay interest on the debt. As a result, the new transfer payments induce no net increase in spending. The unemployed increase their spending but taxpayers reduce theirs by exactly the same amount.

So the government spends £x on unemployment benefits, which is financed by selling £x of bonds on the open market. These bonds carry interest payments of £rx per year for ever (where r is the interest rate). Taxpayers understand this new liability and save £x so as to earn £rx which will allow themselves, and their heirs, to pay the taxes that the government must levy to service this debt.

This is a valuable exposition of the conditions needed for full offsetting of deficit-financed spending. Some of this offset may well occur. It is unlikely, however, that all the people will behave in this way. Some people have no children; others, having educated their now-grown children, do not have a positive target for further net wealth that they wish to leave to them on death. Others who do, will not be paying close attention to the stock of national debt, and trying to offset any increased tax liabilities their heirs incur as a result of the rise in the stock of debt. The unemployed, themselves, are likely to be glad of the money to spend, and are unlikely to save enough to offset their increased future tax liabilities.[1]

Few economists believe that this offset is complete, for the reasons outlined in the previous paragraph. But as government debt piles up, many current taxpayers do become aware of their own liability to pay taxes to meet future interest payments. This raises the important empirical question: under what circumstances, and by how much, will the impact effects of deficit-financed increases in government expenditure be reduced by offsetting increases in saving.

There is a further subtle point. Because they cannot use their human capital as security for borrowing, some unemployed may be consuming less than their own expected lifetime incomes would justify. By borrowing for them, the government allows them to consume more now and less in the future. In this case, by removing an imperfection from the loan market, the government will have caused aggregate expenditure to rise.

[1] R. Barro, 'Are Government Bonds Net Wealth?', *Journal of Political Economy*, Nov./Dec. 1974.

[1] For further criticisms see J. Tobin, *Asset Accumulation and Economic Activity* (Univ. of Chicago Press, 1980).

Parliament – advocating fiscal responsibility – and the rulers – practising fiscal irresponsibility. Parliament won the battle by imposing on the rulers the obligation to balance their budgets.

Thus the balanced-budget doctrine was not the silly irrational doctrine that Keynesians made it out to be. It was, instead, the symbol of the people's victory in a century of struggle to control the spendthrift proclivities of the nation's rulers. The doctrine that had been well established by the end of the nineteenth century was that a balanced budget is the citizen's only protection against profligate spending and run-away inflation. The Keynesian revolution swept that view away. Budget deficits became, according to Keynesians, the tool by which a benign, enlightened government sought to ensure full employment. But, say the anti-Keynesians, this let the tiger out of the cage. Released from the nearly century-old constraint of balancing the budget, governments went on a series of wild spending sprees. Inflationary gaps, deflationary gaps or full employment notwithstanding, governments spent and spent. Deficits accumulated, national debts rose, and inflation became the rule of the day. Inflation robbed the people of the real value of their savings by lowering the purchasing power of the money they saved. In the end, the inflations even defeated the full-employment goal: when governments were finally forced to accept the need to reduce inflation, they imposed massive deflationary gaps in order to reduce the inflations that had developed an inertia of their own. The late 1970s and early 1980s saw the legacy of these disastrous policies: the simultaneous occurrence of high inflation, high unemployment rates and large budget deficits.

Here is an issue in political economy that is important for one's view on the functioning of the modern state. The interested student will want to pursue this matter further.[1]

---

[1] The pro-Keynesian view can be found in the majority of modern textbooks on macroeconomics. The view of the fiscal conservatives is well expounded in J.M. Buchanan, J. Burton, and R.E. Wayne, *The Consequences of Mr Keynes* (Institute of Economic Affairs, London, 1978).

SUMMARY

1. Macroeconomic policies seek to influence such macroeconomic variables as national income, the interest rate and the price level. Demand-management policies work through the aggregate demand curve. Fiscal policy influences the *AD* curve by shifting the *IS* curve. Monetary policy influences the *AD* curve by shifting the *LM* curve. Supply-management policies work through the aggregate supply curve. Stabilization policy uses the tools of demand management in an attempt to hold national income at its potential level.

2. A balanced government budget means that revenues equal expenditures. A budget deficit increases the national debt, while a surplus reduces it.

3. When fiscal policies have only to remove a given inflationary or recessionary gap, the job is simple. Increases in government expenditure or reductions in tax rates increase aggregate demand, and so can eliminate a recessionary gap. Cuts in expenditure, or increases in taxes, reduce aggregate demand, and so can eliminate an inflationary gap.

4. Fine-tuning an economy to hold it at its potential income when expenditure functions are changing continually, is a difficult, possibly impossible task, due primarily to time-lags, of which the decision and execution lags are examples.

5. Much of the job of stabilization policy is done by built-in stabilizers, which do not require conscious government decisions to bring them into play.

6. Fiscal policy can still be used to eliminate persistent gaps. When this is done, decisions must be made on tax versus expenditure changes, taking account of the location of the impact effects of the fiscal change, the need for policy

reversibility, and the effect of temporary fiscal changes on private expenditure plans.

7. Changes in the stance of fiscal policy are appropriately judged by changes in the cyclically adjusted deficit, which calculates what the deficit would be at a given, and unchanging, level of national income.

8. An annually balanced budget is probably impossible to achieve, given the endogenous nature of tax receipts. It would also be destabilizing. A budget balanced over a longer period of time would be stabilizing because there would be budget deficits in slumps and budget surpluses in booms.

9. The opportunity cost of government resource-using activity is in terms of the commodities that would have been produced instead. This cost can approach zero in times of unemployment but it is always significant in times of full employment of any factor of production. To the extent that the commodities forgone are consumers' goods, the cost is all borne currently; to the extent that the commodities forgone are capital goods, the cost is spread out over the future. Financing government expenditure by taxes, domestic borrowing, selling assets such as the nationalized industries, and printing money cause different distributions of the costs among groups in the society, and over time.

10. Government expenditure does not cause a sustained inflation unless it is financed by printing new money. New government expenditure, initiated at full employment, will eventually crowd out private expenditure pound for pound because the long-run equilibrium must be at full employment. Thus the price level, and the interest rate, will rise to restore equilibrium in response to new expenditure.

11. According to fiscal conservatism, the long hard struggle to enforce a balanced-budget policy on the state was a victory for the common people against the forces of government prodigality. When Keynes swept the balanced-budget doctrine away, he released the selfish forces that would lead governments back into a position of chronic deficits. This caused chronic inflationary gaps which inflicted suffering and misery on all those who could not protect themselves against the ensuing inflations.

TOPICS FOR REVIEW

- Budget deficits and surpluses
- Balanced-budget and deficit-financed increases in government expenditure
- Fiscal policies to remove recessionary and inflationary gaps
- Fine-tuning
- Policy lags
- Expenditure increases versus tax cuts as an expansionary device
- Built-in stabilizers
- The stance of fiscal policy
- Crowding out
- Annually and cyclically balanced budgets
- The costs of government resource-using activity

38

Demand
Management 2:
Monetary
Policy

In Chapter 37 we studied how fiscal policy shifts the aggregate demand curve by shifting the *IS* curve. A second way in which the central authorities can induce a major shift in the aggregate demand is through **monetary policy**. Monetary policy is traditionally seen as working through the *LM* curve, shifting aggregate demand by altering the supplies of monetary aggregates, and regulating the terms and availability of credit.

In the first part of this chapter we look at this traditional view on the assumption that the central bank can exercise exact control over the money supply. In the second part we consider arguments that this way of looking at monetary policy is based on too naive a view of the monetary adjustment mechanism.

THE TRADITIONAL THEORY OF MONETARY POLICY

Monetary policy has traditionally been based on the *IS–LM* model. To study the traditional theory that this policy acts by shifting the *LM* curve, consider the equation of that curve. We first derived it in Chapter 31 and we repeat it below:

$$r = \left(\frac{M^*}{P} - n\right)\left(\frac{1}{e}\right) - \left(\frac{d}{e}\right)Y . \qquad (1)$$

Inspection of this equation shows that an increase in the nominal money supply, M, or a decrease in the demand for money, n, shifts the *LM* curve upwards and to the right, while a decrease in M, or an increase in n, shifts it downwards and to the left. (Any given Y is associated with a higher r in the first case and a lower r in the second case.)

We know from Figure 33.4 on page 577 that a rightward shift in the *LM* curve causes a rightward shift in the aggregate demand curve. This is because the equilibrium national income associated with any given price level rises when the *LM* curve shifts to the right. That Figure also tells us that a leftward shift in the *LM* curve shifts the *AD* curve to the left.

At its simplest level, the traditional view of monetary policy consists in manipulating the nominal money supply so as to shift the *LM* curve and thus to shift the aggregate demand curve – the nominal

quantity of money and aggregate demand being positively associated with each other, *ceteris paribus.*

We shall see later in this chapter that the central bank may manipulate the nominal money supply either by trying to do so directly, or by achieving a target interest rate. The theory of the *LM* curve says, however, that effective monetary policy must end up changing *M* whether consciously or unconsciously.

The State of the Economy

The consequences of monetary-induced shifts in the aggregate demand curve will vary depending on the state of the economy when the monetary shock is introduced. We need, therefore, to study three key situations in which actual national income is below, equal to or in excess of its potential level.

A recessionary gap: Figure 38.1 shows a short-run equilibrium in which actual income is below potential income. An increase in the quantity of money of the appropriate size reduces the interest rate and removes the recessionary gap, restoring income to its potential level. This result uses the monetary transmission mechanism that we first encountered on page 562. An increase in the money supply creates an excess supply of money balances. The attempt to eliminate the excess money by buying bonds increases their prices, which means a fall in interest rates. As a result, interest-sensitive expenditure increases.

A reduction in the quantity of money puts the monetary transmission mechanism into reverse, raising interest rates and lowering equilibrium national income.

When income is below potential, the nominal quantity of money is related negatively to the interest rate and positively to equilibrium national income.

Income at potential: Figure 38.2 shows equilibrium income initially at its potential level. An increase in the quantity of money then shifts the *LM* and the *AD* curves to the right. A new short-run equilibrium is reached with a lower interest rate, and a higher national income and price level. But there is now an inflationary gap

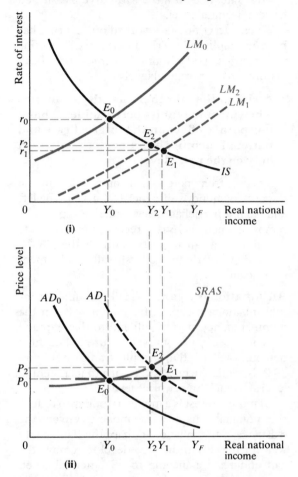

FIGURE 38.1 A Change in the Money Supply in the Presence of a Recessionary Gap

·**An increase in the money supply reduces the interest rate and increases national income.**
The original curves intersect at E_0 in both parts of the diagram to yield equilibrium values of Y_0, r_0 and P_0. An increase in the money supply shifts the *LM* curve to LM_1 and the *AD* curve to AD_1. With a horizontal *SRAS* curve, shown by the unlabelled dashed line through E_0, the equilibrium is at E_1 with national income of Y_1 and interest rate r_1.
If the *SRAS* curve has a positive slope, the final equilibrium position will be at E_2 because the rise in the price level will shift the *LM* curve to the left and dissipates some of the effect of the monetary expansion. In the Figure the final result is income Y_2, interest rate r_2 and price level P_2.

which causes the *SRAS* curve to shift because unit wage costs rise. The price level, and the interest rate, rise until the *LM* curve has shifted back to its initial level.

When everything has worked out, all that has been accomplished is a rise in the price level. The interest rate, and national income, have been restored to their original levels.

A rise in the nominal quantity of money when income is at its potential level has a temporary effect on the interest rate and national income, but a permanent effect only on the price level.

Starting from potential income, a fall in the quantity of money shifts the *AD* curve to the left and opens up a deflationary gap. The gap will be removed when there is a recovery of aggregate demand, or a fall in costs, shifting the *SRAS* curve downwards to establish full employment once again.

An inflationary gap: Finally assume an initial inflationary gap. A further increase in the nominal money supply will add to that gap and thus increase inflationary pressures. The final outcome will be the one illustrated in Figure 38.2. National income will return to its potential level at a much higher price level.

Of more interest is a monetary policy to reduce the nominal quantity of money. Given the existence of the inflationary gap, the Bank could wait for the rise in the price level to remove the gap and restore income to its potential level. Instead, if the Bank wishes to avoid the inflation, it can lower the nominal quantity of money. This shifts the *LM* curve to the left and restores potential income at the present price level.

An inflationary gap is removed from the monetary side of the economy by a fall in the real money supply (M/P), which can be accomplished by any combination of a market-induced rise in the price level or a policy-induced fall in the nominal quantity of money.

Monetary Policy for Sustained Inflation

The central bank can frustrate the monetary adjustment mechanism just described by in-

FIGURE 38.2 A Change in the Quantity of Money in the Absence of a Recessionary Gap

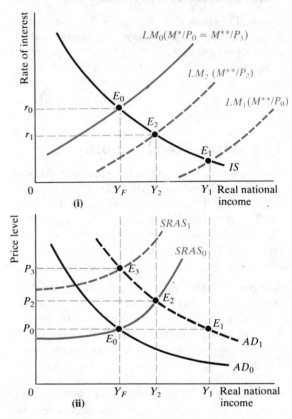

A monetary impulse designed to reduce interest rates when income is at potential, affects only the price level in equilibrium. The original curves intersect at E_0 to produce equilibrium values of r_0, Y_F and P_0. The money supply is then increased from M^* to M^{**}, shifting the *LM* curve to the right. The *AD* curve shifts to AD_1 taking equilibrium in part (ii) to Y_2 and P_2. (The rise in the price level from P_0 to P_2 shifts the *LM* curve part of the way back from LM_1 to LM_2, as explained in the caption to Figure 38.1.)

The inflationary gap now causes the *SRAS* curve to shift upward until it reaches $SRAS_1$. The rise in the price level to P_3 shifts the *LM* curve back to LM_0. The price level has now risen in proportion to the increase in the money supply so that $M^{**}/P_3 = M^*/P_0$. National income and the interest rate are returned to Y_F and r_0.

creasing the nominal quantity of money as fast as the price level is increasing. This holds the real money supply constant and leaves the *IS–LM* equilibrium unchanged. On the *AD–AS* diagram, the rise in unit production costs shifts the *SRAS* curve upwards, but the rise in the nominal money supply shifts the *AD* curve upwards. The price level rises, with national income staying constant. This is the path of inflation first shown in Figure 34.3 on page 598.

As was shown in Chapter 34, however, once the inflation comes to be expected, the actual rate accelerates as the excess-demand component of inflation is augmented by an accelerating expectational component. Thus, to hold national income above its potential level, the Bank will have to accelerate the growth in the nominal money supply to match the accelerating inflation rate. This is a recipe for runaway inflation that will sooner or later become unacceptable to policy-makers. So in the long term, any attempt to hold national income above its potential level by monetary policy is self-defeating.

Monetary Policy and Interest Rates

Governments are often called upon to use monetary policy to lower interest rates. We start by studying once-and-for all increases in the money supply, which allows us to compare situations in which the price level is constant. A constant price level means that the real and the nominal interest rate is the same. The previous sections yield two relevant conclusions.

(1) If national income is below potential, an increase in the nominal money supply can lower the interest rate permanently.

(2) If national income starts at its potential level, an increase in the nominal money supply leads to a temporary equilibrium in which the interest rate is lowered and national income is increased, but in the long run the interest rate and national income return to their original level.

Now consider what happens in case (2) if the Bank frustrates the monetary adjustment mechanism. It stops the *LM* curve from shifting left by making appropriate increases in the nominal money supply. A sustained inflation will set in, and we must now digress to distinguish between the real and the nominal rate of interest.

Real and Nominal Interest Rates

Before we can work with a model of continuous inflation, we must reintroduce the distinction between nominal and real interest rates first encountered in Chapter 19 (see page 328). The nominal, or market, rate of interest is the rate actually paid. The real rate of interest is the nominal rate minus the expected rate of inflation. In this calculation the expected rate of inflation is called the *inflationary premium*. Only after deducting this premium does the lender know if any real return has actually been received on a loan. Negative real rates are not uncommon in some inflationary situations. They mean that the interest on the loan is lower than the rate at which the inflation is eroding the purchasing power of the principal of the loan.

For example, a loan at 10 per cent interest in the face of a 10 per cent inflation earns a zero real rate of interest. The purchasing power of the capital sum loaned is depreciating at 10 per cent per year because of the inflation; the interest is adding 10 per cent per year to the money value of the sum which the lender has loaned. So the two effects exactly cancel out. If the interest is saved, and added to the principal, the real purchasing power of the total remains constant. So in this example, the nominal rate of interest is 10 per cent while the real rate is zero.

When nominal and real rates diverge, we must look more carefully at the role of interest rates in the *IS–LM* model. The theory of investment predicts that investment expenditure varies positively with the *real interest rate*. This means that the *IS* curve depends on the real interest rate, which we designate by r.

Portfolio balance theory, however, predicts that wealth-holders deciding how to divide their holdings between money and bonds, respond to the opportunity cost of holding money, which is the difference between the rate of return on money and the rate of return on bonds. This difference depends on the *nominal interest rate*, which we designate by i. We can see why i is the relevant variable by comparing either the nominal or the real interest rates.

Consider nominal rates first. The nominal rate of return on money is zero while on bonds it is i. Therefore, the opportunity cost of each £1 held in money balances is a forgone nominal return of *i*. Now consider real returns. The expected *real* rate of return on money balances held is not zero. Instead it is the negative of the expected inflation rate, $-\dot{P}^e$, since if you hold money during an inflation its purchasing power *depreciates* at the rate of inflation. The real rate of return on bonds is the nominal rate minus the expected inflation rate, $r = i - \dot{P}^e$. So the difference in the real return on bonds and on money is the $i - \dot{P}^e$ for bonds *minus* the $-\dot{P}^e$ return on money, i.e. $i - \dot{P}^e - (-\dot{P}^e) = i$, the nominal rate of interest. Thus, the opportunity cost to wealth-holders of holding money rather than bonds is given by i, and the higher is i the less money and the more bonds will they wish to hold. This means that the rate of interest in the equation for the *LM* curve is i, the nominal interest rate.

To illustrate, consider two situations. In the first, the inflation rate is zero and the real and the nominal interest rates are both 4 per cent; in the second, the inflation rate is 10 per cent and the nominal interest rate is 14 per cent, leaving the real interest rate at 4 per cent. *Ceteris paribus*, investment expenditure will be the same in both situations because the real cost of borrowing money is unchanged at 4 per cent. The proportion of wealth held in money balances will be smaller in the second situation because the opportunity cost of money is 14 per cent compared to 4 per cent in the first situation.

Interest Rates Under Sustained Inflation

We can now return to the original question that required the digression on real and nominal interest rates. Starting from a situation of full employment, can the Bank use monetary policy to reduce the interest rate? If it tries to do this, it must hold income above potential, which means validating an accelerating inflation. The Bank must increase the nominal money supply sufficiently to stop the *LM* curve from shifting left.[1]

---

[1] Due to the inflation, people will wish to hold a lower proportion of their assets in money. This decline in the demand for money shifts the *LM* curve to the right, partially offsetting the leftward shift caused by the rise in the price level. Thus the Bank will need to increase the nominal money supply by less than the rate of inflation. Basically its object is to let the real money supply decline only as fast as the real demand is declining at a constant real interest rate and an accelerating inflation rate.

The real rate of interest will remain constant, but the nominal rate will rise as the rate of inflation rises.

> **Only as long as the Bank is willing to tolerate an accelerating rate of inflation, can the real rate be held at a level below its full-employment equilibrium value: the nominal rate will be rising continually.**

MONETARY VERSUS FISCAL POLICY

Monetary and fiscal policies are both tools of demand management, which will sometimes rely more heavily on one and sometimes on the other. This is emphasized in Figure 38.3, which shows the transmission mechanisms for monetary, fiscal and supply-side policies.

In the past, however, there have been heated disputes over the relative effectiveness of the two policies. Early Keynesians argued that monetary policy would be relatively ineffective in shifting aggregate demand – and they may have been right in the extreme circumstances of the early 1930s, although even that is disputed. Some early monetarists argued that fiscal policy is totally ineffective. (Although how they explain the experience during the rearmament leading up to World War II, remains a mystery.)

It is worth noting that there are circumstances in which either policy can lose much of its effectiveness. Figure 38.4 shows that any given fiscal stimulus is less effective, the steeper is the *LM* curve. Inspection of the equation of the *LM* curve on page 682 shows that the slope of the curve is $-d/e$, where d and e are the effects on the demand for money of national income and the interest rate respectively. For any given dependence of the demand for money on income (any given value of d), the unfavourable case occurs if e is small, and the favourable case if e is large.

What is happening here is that the expansion of national income increases the quantity of money demanded and this puts upward pressure on the interest rate. If the demand for money is highly sensitive to interest rates, then only a small rise in interest rates is sufficient to restore the quantity of money demanded to its original level. If there is only a small rise in interest rates, then there is

FIGURE 38.3 Policy Transmission Mechanisms to Influence Real Income, *Y*, and the Price Level, *P*

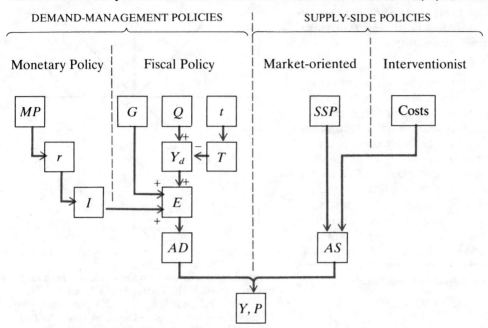

Monetary and fiscal policies act through the *AD* curve; supply-side policies act through the *AS* curve. Monetary policy works through monetary aggregates to the interest rate, r, to interest-sensitive expenditure, I, to aggregate desired expenditure, E, and thence to aggregate demand. Fiscal policy affects aggregate desired expenditure, E, and hence aggregate demand, through three channels: government expenditure on final goods, G, transfer payments, Q (which affect disposable income Y_d) and tax rates, t (which affect tax revenues, T, and hence disposable income).

Market-oriented supply-side policies (see page 652) work through incentive systems in an attempt to shift the *LRAS* curve to the right. Interventionist supply-side policies such as wage controls (see page 613) seek to control costs and prices directly and so to stop the *SRAS* curve from shifting upwards.

---

only a small crowding-out effect to reduce the efficacy of the fiscal expansion. If, on the other hand, the demand for money is not very interest-sensitive, then a large rise in the interest rate is needed to restore the quantity of money demanded to its original level (and thus make it equal to the unchanged money supply). In this case, there is a large crowding-out effect to reduce the efficacy of the fiscal expansion.

The less interest-sensitive is the demand for money, the steeper the *LM* curve, and the smaller is the increase in equilibrium income caused by any given expansionary fiscal stimulus.

Next look at monetary policy. Figure 38.5 shows that any given monetary stimulus is less effective the steeper is the *IS* curve. Inspection of the equation for the *IS* curve on page 556 shows its slope to be $(1 - z)/b$. Taking the propensity to spend out of national income, z, as given, the slope varies with b, which measures the sensitivity of investment expenditure to the interest rate. A large absolute value of b gives a flat *IS* curve, while a small absolute value gives a steep curve. The expansive monetary policy pushes down the interest rate and expenditure rises in response. The more responsive is expenditure to interest rates, the larger is the increase in equilibrium income resulting from the monetary stimulus.

The less sensitive is aggregate expenditure to the interest rate, the steeper is the *IS* curve, and the less is the increase in equilibrium income resulting from any given monetary stimulus.

Those who were involved in this particular controversy and who wished to favour monetary policy over fiscal policy have sought to show that variations in the interest rate have a large effect on aggregate expenditure and a small effect on the demand for money. Those who wished to favour fiscal policy over monetary policy sought to show that the interest rate has a large effect on the demand for money and a small effect on expenditure. This is why early Keynesians went to such lengths to argue that investment was not sensitive to the interest rate. Evidence suggests, however, that both desired expenditure (on such items as

FIGURE 38.4 The Effect of Fiscal Policy

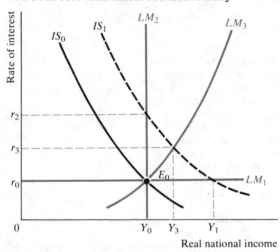

A fiscal stimulus which shifts the *IS* curve has more effect on national income the flatter is the *LM* curve. The initial equilibrium is at E_0 where IS_0 intersects an *LM* curve with interest rate r_0 and income Y_0. A fiscal stimulus now shifts the *IS* curve to IS_1. With the perfectly elastic *LM* curve, LM_1, income rises to Y_1 while the interest rate remains constant at r_0. With a perfectly inelastic *LM* curve, LM_2, incomes remains constant at Y_0 while the interest rate rises to r_2. One intermediate curve is shown by LM_3, where income and the interest rate rise to Y_3 and r_3 respectively. (This analysis assumes a constant price level and so the various changes in income measure the horizontal shifts in the *AD* curve.)

FIGURE 38.5 The Effect of Monetary Policy

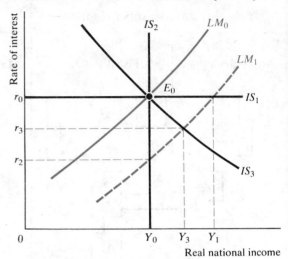

A monetary stimulus shifts the LM curve and has more effect the flatter is the IS curve. The initial equilibrium is at E_0 where LM_0 intersects some *IS* curve. A monetary expansion now shifts the *LM* curve to LM_1. With a perfectly elastic *IS* curve, IS_1, income rises to Y_1 with the interest rate unchanged at r_0. With a perfectly inelastic *IS* curve, IS_2, income stays constant while the interest rate falls to r_2. One intermediate case is shown by IS_3, with income rising to Y_3 and the interest rate falling to r_3. (This analysis assumes a constant price level and so the various changes in income measure the horizontal shifts in the *AD* curve.)

fixed investment, stocks and new housing) *and* money demand have sufficient interest-sensitivity to make both policies reasonably effective ways of influencing the economy.

As we saw in the analysis of Figure 37.3, when fiscal and monetary policy are co-ordinated, the crowding-out effect can be avoided for variations that do not take equilibrium income above its potential level.

HOW CENTRAL BANKS WORK

Up to now we have assumed the existence of a central bank with complete control over the money supply, M. We now need to study in more detail how this works in practice. We start with a digression on the functions of a central bank concentrating on the Bank of England, although most of what we say applies to any country's central bank.

The Bank of England

The Bank of England's activities are divided between two departments, the Issue Department and the Banking Department. The Issue Department is responsible for controlling the issue of notes and coins (although the actual manufacture of currency is in the hands of the Royal Mint). Notes and coins are put into circulation in return for securities obtained from the Banking Department. These appear as assets on the Issue Department's balance sheet, while the notes and coins appear as its liabilities.

The Banking Department acts as banker to the government and to the commercial banks. Deposits of the government (called public deposits), and of the commercial banks, appear as liabilities on this department's balance sheet. Other liabilities are deposits of nationalized industries, local authorities and the central banks of other countries. Assets of the Banking Department are government bonds (called securities) and bills (called Treasury Bills), loans to the banking system (called advances), and other assets such as bonds issued by local authorities and ordinary firms.

Functions of the Bank of England

Six of the Bank's most important functions are discussed below.

To be a Banker to the Government

Governments need to hold their funds in an account into which they can make deposits and against which they can draw cheques. Such government deposits are often held by the central bank.

The Bank of England 'manages' the National Debt. When the government issues new bonds, the Bank arranges their actual sale. The government's debt is also redeemed through the Bank. When a debt issue reaches maturity, the Bank will take in the bonds and pay out money to the bond-holders on behalf of the government.

The Bank also smooths over the effects that might otherwise ensue from uneven borrowing and lending requirements. The Bank purchases any part of new issues of the National Debt that is not taken up by other lenders on the day of issue, at what the Bank deems to be a reasonable interest rate. If it has judged the market correctly, the Bank will be able to sell the remaining part of the new debt over the next week or so. If it has guessed incorrectly, it may end up holding some of the new debt indefinitely. The Bank may enter the market if there is a large issue of government debt due for early redemption. The Bank buys up this issue over a period of time, thus preventing a sudden large accretion of cash to the public on redemption date.

The interest payments on the government debt are made by the Bank on behalf of the government. When interest must be paid on outstanding bonds, the Bank issues the cheques that go to the bond-holders. Finally, the Bank holds substantial amounts of the National Debt itself. These are bills and bonds that the Bank has purchased from the government, paying with a credit added to the government's account held at the Bank.

To be a Banker to Commercial Banks

The Bank of England acts as banker to the commercial banks. It holds some of their reserves against their outstanding deposit liabilities.[1] The Bank will, on order, transfer commercial banks' deposits from one bank to the other. In this way the Bank provides the commercial banks with the equivalent of chequing accounts, and with the means of settling debts among themselves. The Bank also ensures that the banking system is able to obtain funds when it is temporarily short of cash. The Bank does this either by lending funds to the system directly or by buying bills from the system in the open market in return for needed funds.

We shall see later in this chapter that these activities provide the Bank with the channels through which it operates its monetary policy.

To Control the Country's Currency

In most countries the central bank has the sole power to issue banknotes. In England this is done

---

[1] In many countries the central bank holds all such reserves. In the UK, however, the bulk of the reserves are, as we shall see, loaned out 'at call' to the discount houses.

by the Issue Department of the Bank of England.[1] The Bank allows the quantity of coins and banknotes in circulation to be determined by the tastes of the public for holding money as deposits or as cash.

The public does not decide the size of the whole money supply, as measured, say, by M1. What it can, and does, decide however is the *proportion* of M1 that will be held as notes and coins and the *proportion* that will be held as deposits. For example, if the public decides permanently to withdraw some of its deposits in the form of currency, the commercial banks will be faced with a cash drain to the public. To meet this, they will draw on their deposits with the Bank of England. The Bank will print new banknotes and give these to the commercial banks, reducing their deposits with the Bank by the corresponding amount.

The accounts are balanced by the Banking Department transferring financial assets to the Issue Department, which issues currency against them. Thus, when the commercial banks withdraw $£x$ cash from their deposits at the Bank, the Banking Department reduces its deposit liabilities to commercial banks by $£x$ and its holdings of interest-earning assets by the same amount. The Issue Department increases its holdings of interest-earning assets and increases its note liabilities by $£x$.

In contrast, if the public wants permanently to hold less currency than previously, people will bring the currency to the commercial banks and accept deposits in return. The commercial banks will deposit the notes and coins with the Bank. The Banking Department of the Bank will credit the deposits of the commercial banks with that amount and will hand the cash over to the Issue Department in return for securities that it holds. The Issue Department will then retire the currency from circulation.

To Operate in the Exchange Market

The Bank carries out the government's policy with respect to the exchange rate. It holds the country's official reserves of gold and foreign exchange, and it intervenes from time to time on the foreign-exchange market to influence the exchange rate between sterling and other currencies. These policies are discussed in detail in Chapters 39 and 40.

To Support the Financial System

The next function is often referred to as the Bank's *support function*, and it arose from the Bank's operation as a lender of last resort to the commercial banks. Today, the support function relates to the whole of the financial system and it consists of so managing the system as to avoid financial crises that could lead to failures of banks and other institutions that are in a basically sound position.

The two main aspects of the support are to provide financial institutions with sufficient liquidity and to prevent them from being put into difficulties by very rapid shifts in interest rates.

Many financial institutions are in the position of 'borrowing short' and 'lending long'. This means that they are obliged to pay their depositors and other creditors on demand, or on short notice, but they lend money out for longer terms. Thus, if too many depositors demand their money, the institutions cannot immediately raise the required funds by recalling loans. This puts the system in temporary need of liquidity. To provide the needed cash, the Bank can make loans to the system or provide the cash by buying up assets held by the system. Later in the chapter we shall study in detail how this is done.

If interest rates rise quickly, the banks, building societies, etc., will have to pay their depositors (other than those with sight deposits) more interest immediately to prevent them from taking their money elsewhere in search of higher rates. But they can raise the interest that they charge on many loans only as old loans mature and new loans are made.[1] Thus a rapid rise in interest rates may put some financial institutions in financial difficulties. Rather than let this happen, the central bank may try to slow down the rise in interest rates. To do this, the bank enters the open market and buys bonds, thus preventing

---

[1] Certain Scottish banks are allowed to issue banknotes, but the operation of monetary policies is solely in the hands of the Bank of England.

[1] This problem does not arise on loans, such as mortgages, where the interest rate is not fixed at the outset, because building-society interest varies as the market rate varies.

their prices from falling as much as they otherwise would.

The support function was one of the prime motives of the Bank's activities in the 1950s and 1960s. It tried to 'lean against the wind', slowing down changes in the interest rate in either direction. Today this motivation is somewhat less important, although the Bank still is the ultimate protector of the monetary system.

To Carry out Monetary Policy

The Bank is responsible for carrying out the government's monetary policy. One aspect of monetary policy concerns the manipulation of the commercial banks' cash reserves. By deciding how much of the government's debt to hold itself, and how much to sell to the public, the Bank can, as we shall see, influence the money supply. A second aspect of monetary policy is via the Bank's function as a 'lender of last resort' to the rest of the system. The Bank will lend on short term to the financial system whenever there is a short-term need for liquidity.

Open-market Operations and High-powered Money

In the UK, commercial banks hold most of their reserves as call loans with the discount houses. (See Chapter 30, page 521.) They also hold small quantities of reserves with the Bank of England and they hold 'clearing balances' to meet temporary imbalances between receipts from, and payments to, other commercial banks. Clearing balances are transactions and precautionary balances held because of fluctuations in receipts and payments.

The monetary magnitude that is under the direct control of the central bank is variously called **high-powered money** or **the cash base.** It is composed of cash in the hands of the public, bank reserves and clearing balances held by the commercial banks with the Bank of England. Why the term high-powered money is used will become clear from subsequent discussion.

To its holders, high-powered money is an asset. To the central bank, it is a liability. Indeed, the Bank has control over monetary affairs because high-powered money is nothing more than its liabilities looked at as assets from the public's point of view.

The Bank changes high-powered money by changing the composition of its own assets and liabilities through what are called *open-market operations*, which refer to the purchase and sale of assets – usually government bonds – by the Bank.

To see the effect of open-market operations we must follow through the balance-sheet changes that they cause.

Open-market Purchases

Assume that the central bank buys a bond from some holder in the private sector, say a household. The central bank pays for the bond by making out a cheque drawn on itself, payable to the household. The household deposits this cheque in its own bank. The commercial bank presents the cheque to the central bank for payment. The central bank makes a book entry increasing the deposit of the commercial bank at the central bank. At the end of these transactions, the central bank will have acquired a new asset in the form of a bond and new liability in the form of a deposit by the commercial bank. The household will have reduced its bond holdings and raised its cash holdings. The commercial bank

TABLE 38.1 An Open-market Purchase

CENTRAL BANK	
Liabilities	**Assets**
Deposits of commercial banks +£100	Bond +£100

COMMERCIAL BANKS	
Liabilities	**Assets**
Deposits of households +£100	Deposits with central bank +£100

PRIVATE HOUSEHOLDS	
Liabilities	**Assets**
No change	Bonds −£100
	Deposits with commercial banks +£100

When the Bank sells a bond, it reduces high-powered money. The Table shows the results of a sale of a £100 bond by the Bank. The purchaser (a household in this case) merely shifts assets, trading money for bonds. Commercial banks find themselves with less assets (reserves) and less liabilities (deposits).

will have a new deposit equal to the amount paid for the bond by the central bank. Thus the commercial bank will find its cash assets and its deposit liabilities increased by the same amount. The balance sheets of the three parties concerned will show the changes indicated in Table 38.1 after £100 worth of open-market purchases have been completed.

> **A central-bank purchase of any financial asset has the effect of increasing the high-powered money supply.**

Second, let the central bank enter the open market and sell bonds to the public. Now, follow through the set of transactions caused by this sale. The central bank sells a bond to a household in the private sector. It hands over the bond and receives the buyer's cheque drawn against its deposit at its own bank. The central bank presents this cheque to the commercial bank for payment. The payment is made merely by a book entry reducing the commercial bank's deposit at the central bank.

Now the central bank has reduced its assets by the value of the bond it sold, and reduced its liabilities in the form of cash owed to commercial banks. The household has increased its holding of bonds and reduced its deposits with its own

TABLE 38.2 An Open-market Sale

CENTRAL BANK	
Liabilities	Assets
Deposits of commercial banks − £100	Bond − £100

COMMERCIAL BANKS	
Liabilities	Assets
Deposits of households − £100	Deposits with central bank − £100

PRIVATE HOUSEHOLDS	
Liabilities	Assets
No change	Bonds + £100
	Deposits with commercial banks − £100

When the Bank purchases a bond, it increases high-powered money. The Table shows the results of a purchase of a £100 bond by the Bank. The seller (a household in this case) merely shifts assets, trading bonds for money. The commercial banks, however, find themselves with more assets (reserves with the central bank) and more liabilities (deposits of the public). This is a 100%-backed new deposit.

bank. The commercial bank has reduced its deposit liability to the household and reduced its deposits with the central bank by the same amount. Each of the asset changes is balanced by a liability change. The balance sheets of the three parties concerned will initially show the changes indicated in Table 38.2 after £100 worth of open-market sales have been accomplished.

> **A central-bank sale of any financial asset has the effect of decreasing the high-powered money supply.**

Any open-market purchase or sale by the central bank has the effects just analysed. If the Bank buys bills and bonds directly from the government, this also increases the cash base. In the first instance it is the government's account with the central bank that gains the new credit balance. But as soon as the government spends the money, writing cheques to households and firms, the money finds its way into the commercial banks, which are once again in the position of securing new deposits that simultaneously increase both their cash assets and their deposit liabilities by an equal amount. This permits a multiple expansion of deposit money.

Furthermore, it does not matter *why* the central bank engages in open-market operations; the effect is the same whatever the purpose of the purchase or sale. The open-market operations might have been engaged in for the express purpose of changing the cash base, or for the purpose of assisting the government to float new loans, or to prevent an anticipated rise in short-term interest rates. Whatever the reason for a particular open-market operation, the effect of this particular transaction on the cash base is unavoidable. (Of course, the Bank might do something else that offsets the effect of the initial transaction.)

Control of the Money Supply with Required Reserves

In many countries today, and in the UK until recently, the central bank required commercial banks to hold cash reserves equal to a fairly large proportion of their deposit liabilities. Central banks could then seek to control the quantity of deposit money by varying the cash reserves of commercial banks. How does such a system work?

We saw in Table 38.1 that an open-market purchase by the Bank creates a new deposit that is 100 per cent backed by reserves at the central bank. This puts the commercial bank in the position shown in Table 30.1 on page 522. The story is then taken up by that earlier discussion. (You should review pages 522–524 at this point.) As that discussion shows, the commercial banking system can create new deposits until the actual ratio of reserves to deposits is reduced to the required level.

We saw in Table 38.2 that an open-market sale by the Bank reduces deposits and reserves of the commercial banks by the same amount. This forces the ratio of reserves to deposits below their requirement ratio and, under this system, causes a multiple contraction of bank deposits until the required reserve ratio is restored.

Control Without a Required Reserve Ratio

The Bank of England, unlike most other central banks which really are lenders of last resort, is closer to *a lender of first resort*. When the clearing banks need cash, the *first* thing they do is to call in loans from the discount houses and the discount houses are forced to repay their loans. There are two ways in which the discount houses can obtain the money they need for repayment. First, they can borrow the money from the Bank. They put up approved financial assets (mainly short-term Treasury bills) as security, and they pay interest to the Bank on these loans. In these circumstances, the discount houses are said to be 'in the Bank'. Second, the Bank can provide funds through its open-market operations. If the discount houses tried to sell significant amounts of their holdings of Treasury bills, the prices would be forced down. The discount houses would then suffer large losses because the bills were being sold below their purchase prices. However, if the Bank enters the market and buys all the bills offered at, or near, their present price, the discount houses are able to obtain the cash that they need.

These arrangements tend to make the whole financial system more liquid than are systems where the central bank only makes loans as a last resort, and then often at a penal rate. The Bank of England now favours the open-market method

and no longer states a fixed rate at which it will lend money directly to the discount houses. The purpose of this change is to make the system more uncertain about the cost of having to obtain liquidity from the Bank. The intention is to make the system more cautious in expanding credit.

How can the Bank exercise monetary restraint when it cannot squeeze the reserves of commercial banks? It does this by raising the rates at which it will lend money to the discount houses, while making it clear that it will not accommodate them by buying their bills at a favourable price in the open market when they are under pressure to repay loans to the commercial banks. The Bank can put the commercial banks under pressure by selling bonds in the open market. This reduces their deposits and requires them to transfer funds to the Bank equal to the lost deposits (see Table 38.2). Instead of running down reserves held with the Bank, loans are called in from the discount houses. The discount houses are then forced to borrow at higher rates from the Bank. This makes the whole system less willing to expand loans and deposits. The constraint is not that lost reserves *force* a contraction of deposits, but that the high cost of maintaining reserves makes the system less willing to expand deposits to the point where it will be forced to obtain reserves by borrowing from the Bank.

To understand the forces that are at work, consider how the above discussion looks from the point of view of the discount houses. They borrow money on call from the commercial banks, and pay them an interest rate. They buy treasury bills that yield a higher interest rate and they earn the difference between the two rates. Say they fear that the Bank of England will force the commercial banks to recall some of their call loans to the discount houses. These houses will then be forced to borrow the funds they need to make their repayments from the Bank. If they fear that this borrowing will have to be at a penal rate of interest, they will not expect their practice of borrowing short to lend long to be so profitable – it could even bring losses. So they will be less inclined to borrow in order to bid for treasury bills. This pushes down the price of these bills and raises short-term interest rates. At the higher rates the public will wish to hold less money, and to borrow less for spending; so money, credit and spending will be curtailed.

FIGURE 38.6 Two Operating Regimes for Monetary Policy

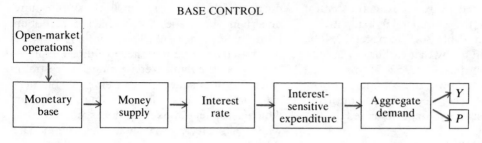

BASE CONTROL

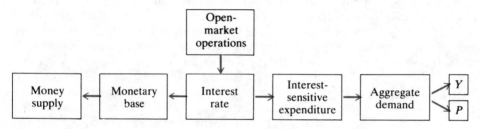

INTEREST-RATE CONTROL

The transmission mechanism is put into motion by altering the money supply under base control and the interest rate under interest-rate control. Base control uses the monetary adjustment mechanism as outlined in Figure 32.9 on page 563. Interest-rate control enters the mechanism at the interest-rate point, working one way to the money supply and the other way to aggregate demand.

Two Operating Regimes

The above two methods of control can be stylized into the two operating regimes set out in Figure 38.6. The traditional system works through the money supply to affect interest rates and interest-sensitive expenditure. The other system works through the interest rate to control the money supply in one direction, and interest-sensitive expenditure in the other direction.

Monetary Targets

If monetary policy is directed at a target money supply, M (or, in a changing world, at a target rate of growth of M), the two operating systems come to much the same thing, at least in a world of certainty. Figure 38.7 shows that controlling the money supply at some target value M_0, implies controlling the interest rate at some value r_0; while controlling the interest rate at r_0 implies controlling the money supply at M_0. Given a stable demand function for money, the two systems give the same result.

Figure 38.7 shows, however, that if there are unpredicted, and possibly unknown, shifts in the demand for money the two systems give different results. Stabilizing the money supply leads to wide fluctuations in the rate of interest, while stabilizing the rate of interest leads to wide fluctuations in the money supply.

MONETARISM

The Advice

The term **monetarism** means many things to many people – sometimes a whole system of political economy. Here we use it in the following restricted sense:

Monetarism is the doctrine that monetary magnitudes exert powerful influences on the economy, and control of these magnitudes is a potent means of affecting its macro behaviour.

FIGURE 38.7 Interest-rate Versus Money-supply Targets

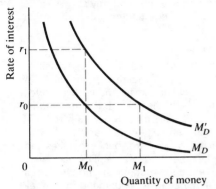

With a stable money-demand function, money-supply and interest-rate targeting are equivalent. On the money-demand function M_D, stabilizing the money supply at M_0 implies stabilizing the interest rate at r_0, while stabilizing the interest rate at r_0 implies stabilizing the money supply at M_0.

Let the money demand function be fluctuating unpredictably between M_D and M'_D. Stabilizing the interest rate at r_0 implies a money supply that fluctuates between M_0 and M_1. Stabilizing the money supply at M_0 implies an interest rate that fluctuates between r_0 and r_1.

Box 38.1 on pages 696–698 discusses in more detail the views of the main schools of economists who hold divergent views on the use of fiscal and monetary policy.

Monetarists urged central banks to follow the first operating system shown in Figure 38.6. Central banks were urged to work directly through the money supply, keeping the economy at a targeted level of the money supply (or its rate of growth). If, for institutional reasons, control had to be exercised through the interest rate (operating system two) monetarists advocated adjusting the interest rate so as to keep the money supply on its targeted value.

The American professor, Milton Friedman, who was for years the leading advocate of monetarism, called for the 'k per cent rule'. In his view, monetary policy was too potent, but too unpredictable in its short-run effects, to be used as a tool for short-run stabilization policy. Instead, the central banks were urged to expand their country's money supply, year in and year out, at k per cent per year. The value of k was to

be set equal to the long-run rate of growth of real national income. On the assumption of a unit income elasticity of demand for money, this would provide enough money to finance the increasing volume of transactions that would occur as a result of growth, but would not provide enough money to finance any significant rise in the general price level.

Multi-asset Difficulties

In the models we have used so far, the monetarists' advice is clear. There are only two financial assets, money and bonds. Controlling the money supply means controlling the transmission mechanism, which in turn means controlling aggregate demand. But, as we observed when we first introduced it on page 534, the two-asset model is a gross simplification, useful for only some purposes. It is not useful for evaluating the monetarists' advice.

To get a working picture of real links between money and aggregate demand we must allow for much more complexity in the spectrum of assets. Indeed, there is a whole series of assets that constitute alternative ways of holding wealth – from currency and sight deposits, through time deposits, to treasury bills and short-term bonds, to very long-term bonds and equities. With the exception of currency and demand deposits, each of these assets yields a return of interest or dividends, and (with the exception of currency and *all* deposit money) each carries uncertainty as to its market price before its maturity date. The longer the term of the bond, the larger the fluctuations in the bond's current price for a given fluctuation in the rate of interest.

Thus, financial assets can be thought of as forming a chain stretching from the assets with the least uncertainty attached to their money prices to the ones with the most uncertainty. Money itself has the least uncertainty as to its price (zero uncertainty); long-term bonds have the most. Wealth-holders will typically hold a portfolio that includes some money and quantities of some, or all, of these other assets. If households and firms find themselves with larger money balances than they require, they will transfer some money into short-term assets, and the extra demand will cause the prices of these assets to rise. This will make longer-term assets

BOX 38.1 SCHOOLS OF ECONOMIC THOUGHT: MONETARISTS AND KEYNESIANS

Because the real world is complex, there can be no absolute finality in any knowledge. As a result, when economists are called upon to analyse complex policy situations, and give policy advice based on that analysis, they often differ among themselves. These disagreements arise from their differences in assessing existing evidence, and from their judgements about which of several economic models best capture the essential behaviour of the world in which we live. This Box outlines some of the differences between today's main competing groups of economists – differences that are taken up again in Chapter 42.

For three decades, from 1945 to 1975, the major competing schools of thought in macroeconomics were what would now be called *eclectic, moderate* or *neo Keynesians*, on the one hand, and *moderate* or *traditional monetarists* on the other hand. Both of these positions evolved out of the debate that centred around the earlier more extreme versions of Keynesian theory.

Early Keynesianism

Early, and more extreme, Keynesian models had no place for monetary influences. They used perfectly elastic *LM* and *SRAS* curves. The perfectly elastic *LM* curve arose because the demand for money was assumed to be highly sensitive (in the limit, infinitely sensitive) to changes in the interest rate. As a consequence, the expansionary effects of rightward shifts in the *IS* curve were not in the least crowded out through interest-rate changes. The perfectly elastic *SRAS* curve arose because wages and prices were assumed to be inflexible downward. As a consequence, there was no crowding-out of the effects of expenditure changes through changes in the price level.

This early Keynesian model has several characteristics. First, changes in aggregate desired expenditure cause large changes in income and employment, changes that are not damped by variations in either the interest rate or the price level. Second, changes in monetary aggregates do not affect income because the perfectly elastic *LM* curve is unaffected by changes in the quantity of money. (Recall that a change in the quantity of money shifts the *LM* curve to the left or to the right; which means that the perfectly elastic curve 'shifts into itself' and thus undergoes no visible change.) Third, there is no automatic adjustment mechanism to restore full employment, since the downward rigidity of wages and prices prevents the *SRAS* curve from shifting downwards.

The main policy implication of the model is that government fiscal policy is needed to restore full employment whenever the economy shows signs of settling down into equilibrium with substantial unemployment.

Early Monetarism

Early monetarists disputed these conclusions while accepting the underlying model. For example, when challenged to outline his model, Milton Friedman, the leader of the monetarist school, used an *IS–LM* model in which the *LM* curve was steep, rather than flat, and the *SRAS* curve was flexible downwards because prices and wages were flexible downwards. The early versions of the extreme monetarist model had a vertical *LM* curve because the demand for money depended only on income and not on the interest rate. The consequence of this was 100 per cent crowding-out of any fiscal stimulus. Monetary policy, however, had powerful effects on the economy because any shift in the *LM* curve had a large effect on the *AD* curve. The early monetarist model also had an easily shifted *SRAS* curve because prices and wages were assumed to be quite flexible. This meant that any deviation from full employment would be corrected relatively quickly by adjustments in wages and prices that would shift the *SRAS* curve back to intersect the *AD* curve at full employment.

Modern Moderate Monetarism and Keynesianism

A great debate, accompanied by a vast amount of empirical work, raged between the two camps in the 1950s and 1960s. One by one, however, Keynesians and monetarists abandoned their extreme positions and moved towards a common ground until finally little but rhetoric divided the two groups. Eventually, both sides agreed on a downward-sloping *IS* and an upward-sloping *LM* curve, which allowed the economy to respond to both monetary and real expenditure shocks. Keynesians agreed that there was some downward flexibility in wages and prices. They argued, however, that it acted too slowly to be an effective mechanism for restoring full employment quickly after a downward shift in aggregate desired expenditure. Monetarists agreed that wages and prices were sufficiently inflexible downwards to cause serious deviations from full employment when the economy was hit by either a monetary or an expenditure shock.

Early monetarists also argued against fine-tuning, saying that the lags in the economy's response to monetary shocks were long and variable. Thus they believed that fine-tuning would be more likely to do harm than good.

Keynesians came to accept this view but continued to hold that the system often settled into slumps that were prolonged enough for there to be plenty of time to diagnose the situation. Corrective monetary and fiscal policies could then be applied at leisure, without having to worry about the pitfalls of fine-tuning against sharp, transitory fluctuations.

In 1980 the American Nobel Laureate, James Tobin, one of the leaders of the neo-Keynesians, debated with the British economist David Laidler, a moderate monetarist, in the pages of the *Economic Journal*. Neutral observers could find little real gulf between them. They disagreed, as one might expect, on matters of judgement about speeds of reactions and the precise slopes of some curves. They revealed, however, no discernable differences of underlying models or of fundamental assessment of what were the key relations that governed the economy's behaviour.

Indeed, the whole debate could have been regarded as a case study in positive economics. Although a great deal of heat had been generated over the decades, the end result was much light. Empirical evidence about such things as the income and the interest elasticities of the demand for money, and wage and price flexibility, was amassed. The extreme positions of the two schools were moderated in the light of the accumulating evidence, until their differences were slight compared with their agreements.

Just as that apparently satisfactory situation was being reached, two new schools became prominent. These schools offered radically divergent interpretations of economic reality. These were the *extreme Keynesians* centred at Cambridge and led by Wynne Godley and the late Nicholas Kaldor, and the *New Classicists* whose intellectual leader was the American economist Robert Lucas.

Modern Extreme Keynesiasnism

The extreme Keynesians harked back to many of the early views of the original Keynesians. This meant that they rejected much of the evidence that had convinced both the moderate Keynesians and the moderate monetarists. They maintained *the real wage hypothesis*, which states that *real* wages were quite inflexible downwards. This meant that there was no macroeconomic adjustment mechanism, even a slow-acting one, to take the economy out of a recessionary gap by shifting the *SRAS* curve downwards.

A second major part of their belief is that the *IS* and *LM* curves are not independent of each other. In particular, they believe that the money supply is mainly endogenous. Thus when the *IS* curve shifts

to the left, the nominal money supply, and hence the *LM* curve, will also shift left, further accentuating the recession. Furthermore, if the *SRAS* curve shifts downward taking the price level downward with it, this would normally increase equilibrium income by shifting the *LM* curve to the right. Extreme Keynesians believe instead that the nominal money supply will shrink as the value of nominal national income falls. This frustrates the working of the monetary adjustment mechanism: a fall in the price level is met by an equivalent fall in the nominal money supply, leaving the real money supply, and hence the *LM* curve, unchanged. So, basically, these economists believe that the original Keynesians had the story about right, and they wish to return economics to those Keynesian basics.

New Classicism

The New Classical theorists hold diametrically opposing views. They believe that markets clear continuously by acting *as if* they were perfectly competitive. This makes full employment the equilibrium position that would normally be achieved. The economy deviates from full employment either when mistakes are made or when rational agents (decision-takers are called agents) decide to work less than what is regarded as the full-employment amount of work. The New Classical theory also uses the theory of rational expectations in which agents make only random errors in forseeing the future course of market variables. Since markets always clear, and since agents do not make systematic errors, full-employment equilibrium is the normal state of the economy. Prices will always adjust to ensure that there are neither unsatisfied buyers nor unsatisfied sellers in any market, including the labour market.

Their critics in the three other camps argue that markets do not always clear. They believe that, even when a shock is foreseen so that no one misperceives what is happening, output will be affected because agents could not anticipate all of the economy's reactions in advance. Agents could not, therefore, establish the new equilibrium set of prices by anticipating what these will be. Instead, argue the critics, agents' reactions would have to be worked out slowly, and only as the price and quantity adjustments are observed to evolve over time.

Market Clearing

There are many subtle differences between the four groups. The two most fundamental differences concern market clearing, and expectations formation. New Classical theorists assume that markets always clear, moderate monetarists assume that markets do not clear; instantaneously, especially when downward adjustments are required. This sluggishness is sufficient to cause significant excess supplies to persist in goods and factor markets for some time. In the longer run, however, markets do tend to clear and full-employment equilibrium is the point to which the economy gravitates. Moderate Keynesians agree with the moderate monetarists, but think that the adjustment takes a little longer than the monetarists think. As a result, they are inclined to give a place to demand-management policies that will stabilize the economy against persistent recessionary and inflationary gaps – even if smaller, more transient gaps must be accepted as unavoidable. Extreme Keynesians believe that markets do not clear even in the long term and thus that government demand management must be used more or less continually to stabilize the economy at or near full employment.

Expectations Formation

On expectations, the New Classical theorists believe in fully rational expectations, in which prediction errors are 'pure white noise'. Loosely, this means that systematic errors of prediction are not made. Since prices always clear all markets, and systematic mistakes are not made, deviations from full employment cannot be reduced by government intervention. Other economists believe that expectations are formed by some mixture of rational calculation, extrapolation from the past, and customary behaviour. Different economists vary on how they believe the typical mix combines the rational, the extrapolative and the customary. Those economists who believe that the economy is too complicated for contemporary economists to understand fully are inclined to believe that private decision-makers can make major, often systematic, mistakes. They ask: if economists disagree as much as they clearly do over how the economy behaves, how can private agents be expected to get this behaviour right on average? (The material on non-linear dynamics, chaos theory, and bounded rationality, given in Box 42.2 on pages 772–773, is relevant at this point.)

This Book

The analysis in this book follows the moderate Keynesian position. That position is not far from moderate monetarists, and the model contained herein can be used to study their views. That also goes for the extreme Keynesian views which can be put in terms of *IS, LM, AD* and *SRAS* curves – although other analytical tools may sometimes be better for studying their results. The New Classical macro model is, however, quite different, and other books need to be studied to fully appreciate the New Classical view of the economy's macroeconomic behaviour.

seem more attractive and wealth-holders will move into them, making their prices rise in turn. Eventually a whole chain of substitutions will occur, with short- and long-term interest rates changing as households try to hold less money and more of all the other interest-earning assets. The change in interest rates will in turn affect interest-sensitive expenditures – investment in inventories, housing, fixed capital equipment, and credit-financed consumption expenditure.

Once the existence of a chain of assets is accepted, the simple transmission mechanism running from money directly to real expenditure that we have used so far becomes less exact. First, a change in the quantity of money must work through a whole chain of asset substitutions before it affects real expenditure. At each link there are possibilities of exogenous shifts in the demand and supply functions for the asset that may blur the simple transmission mechanism.

Second, we are no longer sure what asset, or group of assets, really is money? In the simple two-asset world, we had no problem – there was just money and bonds. The hectic pace of evolution of the financial system in the past 20 years has transformed monetary assets almost beyond recognition. One casualty has been the clear distinction between money and other financial assets. Today assets other than sight deposits can be transferred by cheque (or *automatically* transferred into deposits on which cheques can be drawn), and many sight deposits pay interest.

Today the policy directive to change the money supply by *x* per cent is not a completely clear directive, nor is the link between any one asset and real expenditure a perfectly predictable connection.

In a multi-asset world there is no simple dividing line between money and other financial assets. Twenty years ago the line was a little clearer – although even then it was more of a zone than a line. Then demand deposits and cash were the only media of exchange and they bore no interest. Other deposits were not subject to transfer by cheque and did bear interest. Money was then distinguishable as having two characteristics that it shared with no other financial asset. It was a medium of exchange and its nominal rate of return was zero.

Difficulties in Practice

Many Assets

When we move from the simplicity of the two-asset model to any real-world monetary system, we encounter, as we have just seen, a labyrinth of specialized assets and can quickly lose our bearings in our search for 'the' money supply. In the 1970s most of the world's central banks became more or less converted to two key views expounded by monetarists: that there is a stable relation between some monetary aggregate identified as 'the' money supply on the one hand, and the price level and real income on the other hand; and that these relations are robust enough so that the important macro variables can be manipulated by manipulating the money supply. But such relationships have been difficult to identify and often much less stable than many had hoped they would be.

There are so many highly substitutable monetary assets that control of any one group of assets can often lead to *disintermediation*, which means that the private sector holds more of a similar but uncontrolled asset and less of the controlled one, with little change in anyone's actual expenditures on currently produced goods and services.

Institutional Changes

Also a series of institutional changes in the 1970s have allowed firms and households to economize greatly on their holdings of typical transaction balances measured by M1. These financial innovations have occurred partly in response to exogenous innovations in the electronics industry, but may also have been partly in response to the monetary control exercised by the central banks. If, for example, you find yourself holding fewer transaction balances as a result of a tight monetary policy, one response is to engage in fewer transactions, as monetarists hoped would

happen; but another is to learn to handle the same volume of transactions with smaller money balances, which appears to have been what happened to a significant extent.

Another series of changes, which are discussed in Box 38.2, made the monetary system more international and hence less amenable to control by the central bank located in any one country.

Shifting Targets

Many central banks started out controlling M1. Those who were successful, however, often found the simple statistical relation between M1 and those macro aggregates they sought to control breaking down. The public learned to make do with assets not in M1, and the central banks then sought to control some wider monetary aggregate.

The search for the right monetary aggregate for central banks to control has led to the identification of a bewildering array of possible aggregates. In Britain these include the M1, M3 and M3c, which we have already identified; M2, a new measure not to be confused with an earlier M2 which went out of favour in the early 1970s; and PSL1 and PSL2 – private-sector liquidity, narrowly and broadly defined – now out of favour, being eclipsed by M4 and M5. The list on page 526 of Chapter 30 shows the aggregates being surveyed by the Bank of England in 1988. In all probability the list will be a different one by the time this passage is being read.

Control of the money supply proved more elusive than was first suspected when central banks became converted to monetarism. Even then, however, sceptics posed many difficult questions. Is there a right magnitude to control? Can it be controlled? Will there prove to be an enduring relation between that monetary magnitude and the macro variables in which the Bank is interested once the Bank starts to control the aggregate? As early as 1970 the late Nicholas Kaldor said 'No' to all of these questions. Charles Goodhart immortalized Kaldor's reasoning in his famous **Goodhart's law**: if you lean on a relation it will give way. He was referring to the statistical correlations that monetarists had established between various monetary aggregates on the one hand, and interest and prices on the other. Monetarists advocated controlling the former to influence the latter. Kaldor, Goodhart,

BOX 38.2 THE GLOBALIZATION OF FINANCIAL INSTITUTIONS

Technological innovations in communication, and the desire to avoid onerous government regulations, have been leading to an integration of financial-service firms and to a globalization of the financial-service industry.

Computers and satellite communication systems are the most important developments in information transfer. They put people in instantaneous contact through computer terminals located anywhere in the world. Reliable telephones with direct dialing, electronic mail, and fax machines are other key innovations. The next step is the telephone with a built-in TV screen for face-to-face conferences among persons who never leave their desks that are located in all parts of the world.

As a result, borrowers and lenders can learn about market conditions and then move their funds instantly anywhere around the world in search of the most favourable loan rates. Large firms need their transactions balances only while banks in their area are open, so they can move their transactions balances around the world on a daily basis. Once banks close for the day in each centre, the firms know that they will not need these balances until tomorrow's reopening. Funds are thus free to move between London, New York and Tokyo on a daily rota, being lent out in each market while they are needed during normal working hours. At the end of that market's day, the funds move on to the next market where they are used for its eight-hour day and then on to the next. This is a degree of global sophistication that was inconceivable before the advent of the computer, when international communication was both slower and costlier than it now is. To facilitate the movement in and out of various national currencies, increasing amounts of bank deposits in the UK and in other countries are denominated in foreign rather than domestic currencies.

The Growth of Euromarkets
One of the first developments in this movement towards internationalisation was the growth of the Euro Bond and Euro currency markets in the 1960s. At first, the main currency involved was the US dollar and hence Euro*dollar* markets were the first to develop.

Today, the *Eurobond* market is an international market where bonds that are of various types, and are denominated in various national currencies, are issued and sold to customers located throughout the world. The customers are mainly public corporations, international organizations and multinational enterprises (MNEs). The *Eurocurrency* market is a market for short-term bank deposits, and bank loans, denominated in various currencies. In both markets, the US dollar accounts for the largest single volume of transactions but many other currencies are also used.

The original attraction of this market was its freedom from the restrictions placed by the Federal Reserve System (the US central bank) on American commercial banks. By operating in offshore markets, the banks could avoid legal reserve requirements, and interest-rate ceilings imposed on various types of deposits. This allowed the banks to operate on lower reserve margins and to cut costs by dealing at a wholesale level (normally $1 million is the minimum unit dealt with). They could then offer rates that were higher for lenders, and lower for borrowers, than those ruling in the domestic US market. A further initial advantage of the Euromarkets was freedom from the exchange controls that were used by many countries to control capital movements in support of the fixed exchange rates that were imposed from the end of the Second World War until the early 1970s.

The development of the Eurodollar and Eurobond markets provides an excellent example of how difficult it is to control any economic system

and others like them replied that the relations were not cause and effect. Thus, they argued, as soon as the Bank started to manipulate the monetary magnitudes, the relations would break down. Today many central banks accept this view and reject the simple advice that monetary policy needs merely to hold the money supply on a prearranged target.

The simplistic view that 'the' quantity of money is a clearly defined magnitude, and that an effective monetary policy needs only to follow, mechanically, the *k* per cent rule, has been

rejected by most of the world's central banks on the basis experimental evidence – they tried it and it did not work.

This failure of naive monetarism should not be allowed, however, to obscure the real success of its less extreme versions. In the 1960s and 1970s, early monetariests fought a long, uphill battle to restore the view that was generally accepted by economists from the mid-eighteenth century until the 1930s: persistent inflation is mainly a monetary matter, and the responsibility for its control lies mainly with central banks. When, in

through government regulations. Regulations that are in the collective interest of those who are being regulated – e.g. regulations that impose desirable standards of safety, or prudence, on everyone – will tend to be successful. Regulations that go against the self-interests of those regulated tend to lead to the development of new institutions that avoid the regulations. These in turn lead to new regulations, and yet newer institutions to avoid the new regulations. These moves and counter-moves will continue as long as the government attempts to enforce such behaviour on the system.

The abandonment of fixed exchange rates in the early 1970s, and the progressive lifting of exchange controls, interest-rate ceilings and other capital-market restrictions, led to a further globalization of the financial markets. Although this removed some of the original reasons for their growth, the Euromarkets persisted. First, they allowed banks to avoid the remaining domestic restrictions, such as minimum reserve requirements. Second, the advantage of having an international market dealing in many different national currencies was sufficient to sustain the markets.

The Integration of Financial Firms
The increasing sophistication of information transfer also led to a breakdown of the high degree of specialization that had characterized financial markets in all earlier decades. When information was difficult to obtain, and analyse, an efficient division of labour called for a host of specialist institutions, each with expertise in a narrow range of transactions. As a result of the new developments in communication technology, economies of large scale came to dominate over the efficiencies of a detailed division of labour. The integration of various financial operations within one firm then became increasingly common. For example, banks have moved into the markets where securities are traded, while many security-trading firms have begun to offer a range of banking services. As the scale of such integrated firms increases, they find it easier to extend their operations geographically as well as functionally.

Government Regulations
It has often been difficult for government regulations to keep up with these rapid changes. Governments that were first to relax their regulations in the face of the evolving realities, often allowed their financial institutions to gain important advantages in international competition. The UK government has been quick to react to these developments and, as a result, London has retained its strong position in the international financial world. In contrast, the US government has been slow to adapt. For example, it still limits American banks to operating in only one of the 50 states and prevents them from extending their operations beyond the ones traditionally reserved for banks. As a result, the US banks have lost out heavily to European and Japanese banks.

The kinds of government intervention into domestic capital markets, and government control over international capital flows, that characterized the regime of fixed exchange rates of the 1950s and 1960s is no longer possible. International markets are just too sophisticated. The globalization is here to stay and, by removing domestic restrictions and exchange controls, governments in advanced countries are only bowing to the inevitable.

The banker bending over his computer terminal in London, moving funds from Hong Kong to New York in response to a change that just occurred in the New York rate is a long way from the British general, Sir Edward Pakenham, who on 8 January 1815 lost the battle of New Orleans (and his own life), 15 days after the war with the US had been ended by the Treaty of Ghent, but several days before the fast frigate arrived at his headquarters carrying the news that further fighting was unnecessary.

the late 1970s and early 1980s, governments finally decided to use monetary restraint to control the inflations that had been on an upward trend since the mid-1960s, central banks demonstrated that, given a tough enough monetary policy and a willingness to put up with large, unfavourable side-effects, inflations could be brought under control. Today, the majority opinion, even among many who would reject the label monetarist, is that the Classical economists had it right: inflation is intimately linked to the monetary system, and control of inflation is primarily the responsibility of the central banks. Opinion differs on the extent to which wage-cost push, and other non-monetary forces, are important at various times and places. However, no amount of wage-price controls, social-contract-type incomes policies, tight budgetary policies, or other non-monetary, anti-inflationary measures can prevent inflation from breaking out as long as the central bank follows a lax monetary policy that allows all monetary magnitudes to expand rapidly.

Recent UK Experience

Having discussed worldwide experience with monetarism, we need to consider the lessons of recent British experience.

Prior to 1971 the Bank of England operated a required reserve system much as was described in Chapter 30. Then in 1971 the Competition and Credit Control document introduced what is called a *reserve-asset system* for the UK banks. Instead of having a required ratio between deposit liabilities and reserves held at the Bank, a required ratio was defined between deposit liabilities and what are called *reserve assets*.

The reserve assets included 'normal' deposits of the banking system with the Bank of England (cash reserves), treasury bills, money loaned out at call to the discount houses and other similar institutions, UK local authority bills, British government stocks, and bonds of nationalized industries that were guaranteed by the government and had less than one year to run to maturity. This list makes it obvious that the total supply of assets held by the banks for their reserves could not be controlled by the Bank of England. To see this, assume that the commercial banks want more reserves than the Bank is willing to supply. Their alternative is to persuade the public to hold less of the given total supply so that the banks can hold more. With the UK reserve-asset base, it was possible to persuade the public to do this. The reserve assets were similar to, and hence substitutable for, other assets that were not in the reserve base. Hence, slight changes in prices of the assets, caused by the banks demanding more of them, made it possible for the banks to acquire more as people switched to other assets. Thus the reserve-asset system left the Bank of England unable to control the quantity of deposit money created by the banking system by controlling its reserves. The period following 1971 saw an unprecedented increase in the money supply as banks attracted reserve assets from the public and created deposit money.

Faced with a need to control the rapid monetary expansion, the Bank fell back on the Special Deposit scheme that had been introduced in the 1960s. From time to time the Bank of England could require that the commercial banks make special, non-interest-earning deposits with it.

This had the effect of increasing the required reserve ratio. At the end of 1973 a new variant of the scheme, which came to be called the 'corset', was introduced. The Bank of England announced a target for the expansion of deposit money, and if this target was exceeded, banks had to place amounts of money (determined on a sliding scale) into Special Deposits. This was intended to provide a disincentive against exceeding the target for growth in the money supply.

This system of control was abandoned in the early 1980s and a new set of measures was introduced.

(1) The required minimum reserve-asset ratio was abolished.

(2) The minimum lending rate (MLR), the stated rate at which the Bank would supply funds to the system, was abandoned. The intention was to make the banking system more uncertain about the terms on which the Bank would provide liquidity and thus make the system more cautious about expanding credit to the utmost limit dictated by financial prudence.

(3) All banks in the system must hold a small part (1 per cent was the original figure) of their eligible liabilities with the Bank (a required cash ratio). This is in addition to the clearing deposits held by the London clearing banks to settle their interbank transactions. Although this (small) cash reserve ratio is now required, the Bank of England did not, at the time, contemplate controlling the money supply through the cash base.

(4) The Bank seeks to keep interest rates within an *unannounced* band that will be changed whenever necessary.

Is There no Limit to the Money Supply?

Fierce international competition now rages among banks whose business has become increasingly globalized. One casualty of this competition is the required reserve system. Banks complain that being forced to hold non-interest-bearing reserves with the central bank puts them at a competitive disadvantage with banks in countries that do not operate that system – as well as with non-bank financial institutions not subject to such rules. So other countries are joining the Bank of England in dropping significant reserve requirements.

This does not, however, mean that banks can expand deposit money without limit. They need to keep minimum clearing reserves to meet fluctuations in payments and receipts (or in systems where these can be borrowed from the central bank, they need to worry about the cost of doing so). More importantly, the public continues to keep a significant part of its total money holdings in notes and coin. Thus, whenever banks engage in an expansion of deposit money, they can expect to suffer a significant cash drain to the public. Under these circumstances, the money multiplier still relates the total quantity of money to the high-powered money supply – only the size of the multipliers given on page 524 is now determined by a large cash-drain factor and a very small bank-reserve factor.

NON-MONETARY TARGETS

Disillusion with monetary targeting has led many central banks to a more eclectic view of monetary policy. In this view, the Bank's operating system works through the rate of interest. It watches targets on real national income, Y, and the price level, P. It also watches M for the information that changes in monetary magnitudes can give about shifts in the demand for money. Open-market operations are used to alter the rate of interest until satisfactory performance of Y and P is achieved, letting M be whatever it becomes. For example, when the Bank perceives a persist-ent inflationary gap, it forces interest rates up until the aggregate demand falls sufficiently to remove the gap and until the price level stops rising at a unacceptable rate.

This is a system that more and more central banks are following. It makes central banking once more into an art, rather than an exercise in blind rule-following. It recognizes that rigid links between any monetary aggregate and aggre-gate demand are unlikely to be maintained once the monetary aggregate is consciously manipu-lated. It accepts that monetary policy is a potent force for influencing aggregate demand as long as the central bank is willing to alter interest rates sufficiently to shift aggregate demand as required.

Knowledge of the long lags that characterize the monetary transmission mechanism leads to a scepticism about fine-tuning national income through monetary policy. As a result, setting targets for inflation has become the central con-cept of monetary policy – a return to the view-point of the early monetary theorists of the eighteenth century.

In the new system, central banks set targets for some combination of the rate of change of the price level and the gap between actual and potential national income. They eschew fine-tuning, and they adjust to longer-term trends. They no longer monitor a single monetary mag-nitude as *the* indicator of how their policy is doing. Instead they watch many variables, gain-ing information from each about exogenous dis-turbances and about the influence of their own policies. Among other things, they do pay close attention to changes in various measures of the money supply, which provide information about shifts in money demand functions when interest rates are being stabilized, at least in the short term. Banks accept that money matters; they accept the monetary transmission mechanism. They merely reject the view that they must fix the level, or rate of change, of some clearly defined M in order to use that mechanism effectively. In-stead, they enter the mechanism at the rate-of-interest link, and seek to influence aggregate demand letting M be what it may.

A Postscript on the *IS–LM* Model

The traditional view, introduced at the beginn-ing of this chapter, sees monetary policy working by changing M to shift the *LM* curve, bringing about a new *IS–LM* equilibrium. The view we have just been discussing breaks the simulta-neous *IS–LM* determination of Y and r. Instead, the central bank enters the transmission mechan-ism at the interest-rate point and monitors the effects of its changes in r on the inflationary or deflationary gap (and through that on the price level). This makes r exogenous and M endogen-ous in the *IS–LM* model. The central bank determines an r, in effect selecting the point on the *IS* curve that yields the desired Y. To maintain the desired rate of interest, the Bank is willing to engage in open-market operations to supply all of the money that is demanded at that rate. This means that the *LM* curve shifts to validate the Y, r position the Bank has chosen on the *IS* curve.

Of course, the world is full of uncertainties, exogenous shocks and difficulties of measurement, all of which make monetary policy more complex than the above discussion suggests. Nonetheless, this view of monetary policy is fundamentally different from the traditional one.

In the traditional view, the monetary authorities seek to change M – whether through the monetary-base or through interest-rate control – in an attempt to shift the *LM* curve to get the aggregate demand that it desires. In the other view, the monetary authorities target on the interest rate to get the level of aggregate demand they desire, and they produce whatever M is demanded so that the *LM* curve shifts passively to intersect the *IS* curve at the predetermined point.

Only time will tell how many central banks come to accept this view of monetary policy and how successful it will be. Either way, central bankers understand their obligation to prevent unacceptable inflation by controlling aggregate demand. Some will try by targeting the money supply and some by targeting interest rates. All have the power to prevent the persistence of large inflationary gaps provided they are willing to accept whatever short-run restrictive policies that are needed.

SUMMARY

1. The traditional theory of monetary policy sees it working by changing the quantity of money so as to shift the *LM* curve, and hence the *AD* curve.
2. Monetary expansion can lower interest rates and raise income, if it starts from a recessionary gap. If it starts from full employment it will have the same effects temporarily, but in full equilibrium, income and interest rates will return to their original levels and only the price level will be affected.
3. A restrictive monetary policy can remove an inflationary gap by shifting the *LM* and the *AD* curves to the left.
4. Starting from full employment, a monetary policy that attempts to lower the real interest rate for a sustained period will lead to an ever-accelerating nominal interest rate and inflation rate.
5. Properly understood, monetary and fiscal policy complement each other as tools of demand management, although it is possible to imagine extreme circumstances under which one or the other becomes impotent.
6. The Bank of England fulfils a number of functions, including being agent of the government's monetary policy. Its open-market operations affect the high-powered money supply which, on a reserve-base system, determines the quantity of bank reserves (and cash-holdings by the public) and through the money multiplier, the money supply.
7. UK commercial banks hold the bulk of their reserves in the form of call loans to the discount houses. The Bank of England stands ready to lend money to the discount houses should the commercial banks call in loans to replenish their reserves. The Bank exercises control by altering the terms on which it will accommodate the discount houses and by making the commercial banks more or less liquid through appropriate open-market operations.
8. Monetarism called for controlling aggregate demand by controlling the quantity of money. In a world of many assets, the right monetary magnitude was never found. The money supply can be influenced by either of two operating regimes where the Bank works (i) on interest rates or (ii) on high-powered money, altering either to maintain its monetary target.
9. Today many central banks have abandoned large compulsory reserve require-

ments as well as tight monetary targeting. They still use their open-market operations to influence aggregate demand through the monetary transmission mechanism, but they seek to work directly from interest rates to spending without trying to keep to rigid targets on monetary magnitudes. They still watch monetary magnitudes and real and nominal interest rates for the information each conveys about the development of inflationary pressures.

TOPICS FOR REVIEW

- Real and nominal interest rates
- Effects of an expansive monetary policy
- The degree of Bank power over interest rates
- Functions of a central bank
- Open-market operations
- Control of the money supply with a required reserve base
- Control of the money supply in the UK
- Monetary targets

39

Exchange Rates

So far we have discussed the problems of monetary and fiscal policy as they appear when there is no cause to be concerned about foreign implications. Unfortunately, things are not so simple. Foreign trade and foreign borrowing and lending have become increasingly important in the decades following the Second World War. Today no government can carry out its macroeconomic policies as if its own country was a closed economy. As a first step in allowing for open-economy effects, this chapter discusses the theory of the determination of exchange rates.

Concepts and Definitions

We must start by defining or recalling some key concepts. Some of these were introduced in Chapter 21, which should be reviewed at this stage. An economy that engages in international trade is called an *open economy*. One that does not is called a *closed economy* and a situation with no international trade is called *autarky* (see page 346). In this chapter we examine the simple case of a *small open economy*, which is an economy that can exert no influence on the world prices of traded goods. The quantities that it exports and imports are small in relation to the total volume of world trade, and, therefore, changes in these quantities do not influence the prices established in world markets. For many countries and commodities, this is an empirically applicable assumption.

Because a small open economy cannot by its own actions significantly influence the prices of world traded commodities, it cannot influence the terms on which it exchanges exports for imports on the international market. These terms are called *the terms of trade* and they are defined as the quantity of imported goods that can be obtained per unit of domestically produced goods that is exported (see page 354). The terms of trade may be measured by the relation: *prices of exports/prices of imports*. For example, if exports sell for £3 a unit while imports sell for £1.50, the terms of trade are *two*, indicating that two units of imports can be obtained for every unit of domestically produced goods that are exported.[1]

---

[1] When there is only one export and one import, as in the illustrations used in this chapter, the measurement is simple. When there are many exports and many imports, price indices need to be used.

We divide all goods into two types. *Tradeables* are goods and services that enter into international trade. For a small open economy the prices of tradeables, whether the economy imports or exports them, are given, since they are set on international markets. *Non-tradeables* are goods and services that are produced and sold domestically but do not enter into international trade. Their prices are set on domestic markets by domestic supply and demand and they are unaffected by the market conditions for the same products in other countries.

THE INFLUENCE OF EXCHANGE RATES

We are now ready to deal with exchange rates. One of the major differences between international trade and trade within one country is that while different regions of the same country use the same money, different nations do not. The currency of one country is generally acceptable within the bounds of that country, but usually it will not be accepted by households and firms in another country. When a British firm sells its products it requires payment in sterling. It must meet its wage bill, pay for its raw materials, and reinvest or distribute its profits. If it sells its goods to British purchasers there is no problem, since they will pay in sterling. If, however, it sells its goods to an Indian importer, either it must accept rupees or the Indian firm must exchange its rupees for sterling to pay for the goods. The British producer will accept rupees only if it knows that it can exchange them for the sterling that it requires. The same is true for producers in all countries; each must eventually receive payment in the currency of its own country.

> **In general, trade between nations can occur only if it is possible to exchange the currency of one nation for that of another.**

Foreign exchange refers to the actual foreign currency, or various claims on it such as cheques and promises to pay, that are traded for each other (see page 455). The *exchange rate* is the price at which purchases and sales of foreign currency, or claims on it, take place; it is the amount of one currency that must be paid in order to obtain one unit of another currency. For example, in the early 1980s the exchange rate between pounds sterling and American dollars was approximately £1 = $2.00, or, what is the same thing, £0.50 = $1.00. Thus one pound exchanged for two dollars, and one dollar exchanged for £0.50.

The Exchange of Currencies

What is the mechanism for exchanging currencies? International payments that require the exchange of one national currency for another can be made in a bewildering variety of ways, but in essence they involve the exchange of currencies between people who have one currency and require another.

Suppose an American dealer wishes to purchase a consignment of British fashion goods to sell in the United States. The British manufacturer requires payment in sterling. If the product is priced at, say, £2,000, the American importer can go to his bank, purchase a cheque for £2,000 and send it to the British seller. Given an exchange rate of $2.00 to £1, the US importer would write a cheque on its own account for $4,000 in payment of his £2,000 sterling cheque or 'draft'. The British producer would deposit the cheque in its own bank. When all this was done, the banking system would have exchanged obligations to Americans for obligations to the residents of the UK. The deposits of the American purchaser, which are liabilities of its bank, would be reduced by $4,000 and the deposits of the British seller, which are liabilities of the British bank, would be increased by £2,000. The banking system, as a whole, makes a profit by charging a commission on such transactions.

Now consider a second transaction. Assume that a British firm wishes to purchase ten American refrigerators for sale in Britain. If the refrigerators are priced at $400 each, the American seller will require a total payment of $4,000. To pay it, the British importer goes to its bank, writes a cheque on its account for £2,000 and receives in return a draft or money order payable for $4,000. This reduces the deposit liabilities of the British bank by £2,000. When the American seller deposits this payment, its deposits, which are liabilities of the US banking system, are

TABLE 39.1 The Monetary Effects of Foreign Trade

UK BANK			US BANK	
Liabilities		Assets	Liabilities		Assets
Deposits of fashion goods exporter	+£2,000	No change	Deposits of fashion goods importer	−$4,000	No change
Deposits of refrigerator importer	−£2,000		Deposits of refrigerator exporter	+$4,000	

The payments arising from imports and exports cause changes in the assets and liabilities of banks. The Table shows the offsetting changes in liabilities of two banks arising out of payment by an American to a British firm for the export of British fashion goods, and from a British to an American firm as a result of the import of American refrigerators.

increased by $4,000. Thus the banking system as a whole has merely switched liabilities, this time from the UK to the US.

These two transactions cancel each other out, and there is no net change in international liabilities. The balance sheets of the British and the American banks will show the changes set out in Table 39.1. No money need flow between the banks; each merely increases the deposits of one domestic customer and lowers those of another. Indeed, as long as the flows of payments between the two countries are equal, so that Americans are paying as much to UK residents as UK residents are paying to Americans, all payments can be managed as in this example and there is no need for a net payment between the two countries.

Reasons for exchange of currency: People buy and sell foreign exchange as a result of international transactions. These transactions are broadly divided into income-related and capital-related transactions. The former concern the purchase and sale of internationally traded goods and services, plus the international movement of income – such as interest and dividends – that is earned on investments. They are recorded in the *current account*. The latter arises from movement of capital itself. They are recorded in the *capital account*. We shall consider these divisions in more detail later in the chapter. For the moment we confine ourselves to items involving trade in goods and services.

The terminology of exchange rates: The exchange rates between two currencies can be expressed in either of two ways. First, the number of units of domestic currency required to

buy one unit of foreign currency and, second, the number of units of foreign currency required to buy one unit of domestic currency. Thus if £2 currently exchanges for $4, the exchange rate is £0.50 = $1.00 expressed the first way, and £1 = $2 expressed the second way.

When a change in the exchange rate raises the value of one currency, that currency is said to have **appreciated**; when a change in the exchange rate lowers the value of one currency, that currency is said to have **depreciated**. If sterling appreciates against the dollar, it becomes more valuable. It will thus take less sterling to buy a US dollar or, what is the same thing, more US dollars to buy a pound sterling. Say, for example, £1 used to exchange for $2 but now it exchanges for $3; sterling has appreciated and the dollar has depreciated. Whereas before it took 50p to buy a dollar and $2 to buy a pound sterling, it now takes only 33⅓p to buy a dollar and $3 to buy a pound sterling. Clearly sterling has become more valuable.

Exchange rates and the domestic prices of traded goods: The section on the determination of imports and exports in a small open economy given on pages 356–358 of Chapter 21 must be re-read at this point. As we saw in that earlier section, a small open economy faces prices of internationally traded goods that are fixed in foreign currency. The exchange rate translates these into domestic prices. If, for example, the price of wheat is $4 a bushel on international wheat markets, its sterling price in Britain depends on the exchange rate. When the rate is $2 to £1, the British domestic price of wheat is £2.

This is because £2 must be recovered from domestic sales in order to buy on the foreign-exchange market the $4 needed to buy a bushel of wheat on the international wheat market.

In Figures 21.2 and 21.3 on pages 356 and 358, we plotted the domestic demand and supply for British imports and exports and the world price of these goods in terms of the domestic currency, sterling. To do this we needed, although we did not say so at the time, an exchange rate so that we could convert world prices into local currency. *We express the exchange rate, e, as the number of units of domestic currency needed to buy one unit of foreign currency.* The *domestic* price of traded goods, p_d, is then the *world* price expressed in foreign currency, p_f, multiplied by the exchange rate:

$$p_d = (e)(p_f) .$$

For example: when the international price of wheat is $4 per bushel and the exchange rate is £0.50 = $1.00, the sterling price of wheat is $(0.50)(4) = £2.00$ per bushel.

It is now a simple matter to see the important effect of a change in the exchange rate on the domestic prices of traded goods. Say, for example, that sterling appreciates in value so that it only takes £0.33 to buy a US dollar. The sterling price of a bushel of wheat that costs US $4 is now only £1.33 since £$1\frac{1}{3}$ is sufficient to buy $4. Now say, for a second example, that sterling depreciates in value from 50p to 75p for one US dollar. Now the sterling price of wheat rises to £3 since it takes £3 to buy $4. (Our formula $(e)(p_f) = p_d$ gives the correct answer since $(0.75)(4) = 3$.)

> **An appreciation of the value of domestic currency lowers the domestic prices of tradeable goods, while a depreciation raises these prices.**

The influence of exchange rates on imports and exports:

Say that sterling depreciates so that it takes more sterling to buy a US dollar. This, as we have seen, raises the domestic price of tradeables. Figures 39.1 and 39.2 show that this raises the quantity of each good that is exported and lowers the quantity of each good that is imported.

> **For a small country, a depreciation of the domestic currency causes the domestic**

FIGURE 39.1 The Effect of a Change in the Exchange Rate on Exports

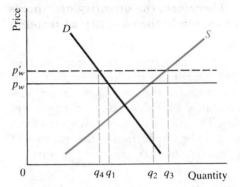

A depreciation of sterling raises the quantity of each good that is exported. *D* and *S* are the domestic demand and supply curves; p_w is the world price expressed in sterling at the original exchange rate; production, consumption and exports are q_2, q_1 and $q_2 - q_1$ respectively.

A depreciation of sterling raises the sterling price of imports from p_w to p'_w causing domestic production to increase to q_3, domestic consumption to fall to q_4, and exports to rise to $q_3 - q_4$.

An appreciation of sterling lowers the domestic price of exports, say from p'_w to p_w and lowers exports from $q_3 - q_4$ to $q_2 - q_1$.

FIGURE 39.2 The Effect of a Change in the Exchange Rate on Imports

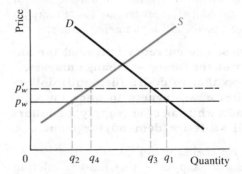

A depreciation of sterling lowers the quantity of each good that is imported. At the initial exchange rate the world price is p_w with q_2 produced at home, q_1 consumed and $q_1 - q_2$ imported. A depreciation of sterling raises the price of the imported good to p'_w. Domestic consumption falls to q_3 while domestic production rises to q_4. Imports thus fall to $q_3 - q_4$.

prices of traded goods to rise, thereby increasing the quantity supplied and reducing the quantity demanded domestically. Therefore, the quantity of exports increases, while the quantity of imports falls.

Now consider an appreciation of sterling. This means that it takes less sterling to buy a unit of foreign currency, so the sterling price of tradeable goods falls. This reduces the sterling price of tradeables. The effects are then easily seen from the diagram to be a reduction in the quantity of exports and an increase in the quantity of imports.

For a small country, an appreciation of the domestic currency causes the domestic prices of traded goods to fall, thereby reducing the quantity supplied and increasing the quantity demanded domestically. Therefore, the quantity of exports falls and the quantity of imports rises.

THE DETERMINATION OF EXCHANGE RATES

The theory that we develop here applies to all exchange rates, but for convenience we continue to deal with the example of trade between America and Britain and with the determination of the rate of exchange between their two currencies, dollars and pounds sterling. For a more general application, 'dollars' may be taken as 'all foreign exchange' and the US as all foreign countries.

Because one currency is traded for another on the foreign-exchange market, it follows that to desire (demand) dollars implies a willingness to offer (supply) pounds, while an offer (supply) of dollars implies a desire (demand) for pounds.

If at an exchange rate of £0.50 = $1.00 British importers demand $6.00, they must be offering £3; if American importers offer $6.00, they must be demanding £3. For this reason, the theory can deal either with the demand for, and the supply of, dollars, or with the demand for, and the supply of, pounds sterling; both need not be considered. Because we are interested in buying and selling *foreign* exchange, we shall conduct the

argument in terms of the supply, demand and price of dollars (quoted in pounds) which is foreign exchange from the point of view of Britain.

In our two-country model of the foreign-exchange market there are only two groups of private traders: people who have sterling and who want dollars, and people who have dollars and who want sterling. We shall assume for the moment that the Bank of England does not intervene in the market.

The demand for dollars: The demand for dollars arises because holders of sterling wish to make payments in dollars; it thus arises from imports of American goods and services into the UK. In addition to the purchase of imports studied before, there are purchases of assets previously owned or newly issued by Americans. Such purchases give rise to *capital flows*. These play an important role in exchange markets, and we shall study them later; for the present, we continue to focus on international trade in goods and services.

The supply of dollars: Dollars are offered in exchange for sterling because holders of dollars wish to make payments in sterling. The supply of dollars on the foreign-exchange market arises, therefore, because of British export of goods and services to the United States. In addition, dollars are supplied in order to purchase British assets such as government bonds and shares in joint stock companies. These capital flows are ignored until a later chapter.

The demand and supply curves for dollars: Now consider what changes in the exchange rate do to the demand for and the supply of dollars. As the price of dollars falls, the dollar is depreciating and sterling is appreciating. The appreciation of sterling lowers the sterling price of internationally traded goods. This, as we have seen, lowers Britain's exports and raises its imports. The dollar prices of these goods are, however, unchanged. So the demand for dollars must rise since more imports are being bought at the same dollar price. British exports fall and, given their constant dollar price, the dollar value of these exports must fall, therefore the quantity of dollars offered to obtain sterling to pay for these goods falls.

A small open economy's demand curve for foreign exchange is negatively sloped, while its supply curve of foreign exchange is positively sloped plotted against the domestic price of a unit of foreign exchange.

The Exchange Rate Determined Graphically

Figure 39.3 plots the sterling price of a dollar on the vertical axis and the quantity of dollars on the horizontal axis. If the current price of dollars is too low, the demand for dollars exceeds the supply. Some people who require dollars to make payments to America will be unable to obtain them, and the price of dollars will be bid up. The value of the dollar *vis-à-vis* the pound will appreciate or, what is the same thing, the value of the pound *vis-à-vis* the dollar will depreciate. This rise in the price of the dollar reduces the quantity demanded and increases the quantity supplied. Where the two curves intersect, quantity demanded equals quantity supplied, and the

FIGURE 39.4 Changes in the Exchange Rate

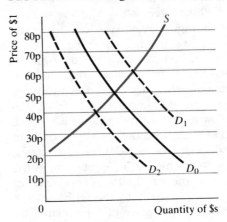

Shifts in the demand for foreign exchange cause the equilibrium exchange rate to change. The original demand and supply curves of D_0 and S intersect to produce an equilibrium exchange rate of 50p = \$1. A rise in the demand for dollars to D_1 raises the equilibrium rate to 60p (appreciates the dollar and depreciates sterling). A fall in the demand for dollars to D_2 lowers the equilibrium rate to 40p (depreciates the dollar and appreciates sterling).

exchange rate is in equilibrium.

If the price of dollars is too high, the demand for dollars will fall short of the supply; the dollar will be in excess supply, so that some people who wish to convert dollars into pounds will be unable to do so. The price of dollars will fall, fewer dollars will be supplied, more will be demanded and an equilibrium will be re-established.

Some Comparative Static Results

We may now use the theory of price determination in competitive markets to generate predictions about the effect of several important changes.

A rise in the world price of imports: First, consider the effect of a rise in the world price of some important imports from the US. This lowers the quantity imported but lowers the demand for dollars only if the fall in the quantity is more than proportionate to the rise in the price. If, for example, the world price of wheat rises 10 per cent from \$4 to \$4.40 and British demand falls 20 per cent from 10 to 8 million bushels per period, the demand for dollars to import wheat falls from \$40 million to \$35.2 million per period.

FIGURE 39.3 The Determination of the Exchange Rate

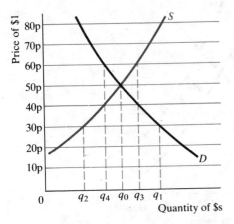

The exchange rate is in equilibrium when the quantity of foreign exchange demanded equals the quantity supplied. At a rate of 30p to the dollar, quantity demanded of q_1 exceeds quantity supplied of q_2. The price of the dollar will rise. At a rate of 60p to the dollar, quantity supplied of q_3 exceeds quantity demanded of q_4. The price of the dollar will fall. At the equilibrium price of 50p to the dollar (£1 = \$2), quantity demanded and quantity supplied are equal at q_0.

Assuming the quantity response to be large enough, the rise in the price of imports lowers the quantity of dollars demanded, shifting the demand curve in Figure 39.4 to the left, depreciating the dollar and appreciating sterling.

Now assume, however, that the demand response is less than in proportion to the price rise. Say, for example, the price of oil rises by 20 per cent while the quantity imported only falls by 10 per cent. Now more foreign exchange is needed. The demand curve for dollars shifts right in Figure 39.4. The price of dollars appreciates, which is the same thing as a depreciation of the pound. An example was the 1970s experience of oil-importing countries with the OPEC cartel. The large rise in the price of oil initiated by OPEC caused depreciations in the exchange rates of major oil-importing countries including the UK.

The development of an import-substituting domestic industry: Now assume that, sometime after the rise in price of an import,

Britain develops a low-cost domestic industry that captures some of the domestic market formerly served by the high-priced import. Imports will fall off drastically, so that at every exchange rate fewer dollars will be demanded (because fewer imports are demanded). The demand curve for dollars will now shift to the left. This lowers the sterling value of the dollars, which means an appreciation of sterling. This is what happened to sterling when North Sea oil came into production, largely replacing imported oil in the UK market.

A change in the price level of one country: Consider, for example, the case of an inflation in the UK. The effects are shown in Figure 39.5. When the British price level rises, domestically produced goods that are not traded, and hence do not have prices that are set on world markets, rise in price as do all domestic costs such as wages and rents. Prices of imports and exports which are set on world markets remain unchanged. The result is a shift in the supply curves of both imports and

FIGURE 39.5 A Local Inflation Affects Imports and Exports

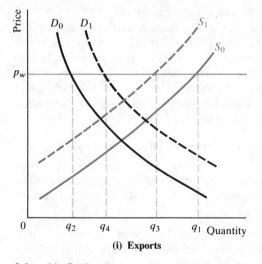
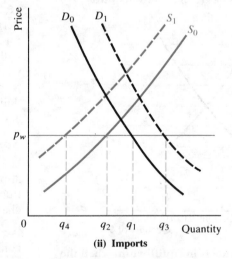

(i) **Exports**

(ii) **Imports**

A local inflation lowers exports and raises imports in a small open economy.
Part (i) refers to a typical exported good, while part (ii) refers to a typical imported good. In both parts of the Figure the original demand and supply curves are D_0 and S_0 and the original exchange rate gives a price of the good as p_w when expressed in domestic currency. The amount $q_1 - q_2$ indicates initial exports in part (i) and initial imports in part (ii).

A local inflation shifts the demand curves for both products to D_1 (because money incomes rise) and the supply curves to S_1 (because money costs rise). As a result, exports fall to $q_3 - q_4$ in part (i) and imports rise to $q_3 - q_4$ in part (ii).

exports, indicating that a higher money price is necessary to call forth any given quantity supplied because of the rise in costs. The demand curves for imports and exports also shift, indicating that the higher money incomes caused by the inflation allow consumers to pay a higher price for any given quantity, while the higher price of non-traded goods encourages the shift to goods whose prices are set on international markets. As a result of these shifts, the quantity of imports rises while exports fall.

> **A local British inflation raises the quantity of imports and lowers the quantity of exports.**

Since international prices are unaffected by the localized British inflation, the demand for dollars, to buy increased imports at a given dollar price, must rise. Similarly the supply of dollars, to buy fewer British exports at an unchanged price, must fall. The demand curve for dollars will shift to the right while the supply curve shifts to the left, so that the equilibrium price of dollars must rise as shown in Figure 39.6.

> **A local British inflation will lead to a depreciation of the exchange value of the pound (an appreciation of the value of the dollar).**

An equal percentage change in the price level in both countries: Now the demand and supply curves for imports and exports in Figure 39.6 shift upwards by 10 per cent as before but so does the world price of imports and exports. (The upward shift in p_w is not shown in the Figure.) These shifts are exactly offsetting so there is no change in imports or exports. The equal inflation in Britain and abroad leaves the relative prices of goods from Britain and from the rest of the world unchanged and hence has no effects on the patterns of trade. There is no reason to expect any change in either country's demand for imports at the original exchange rate and hence in the demands and supplies of foreign exchange. The inflations in the two countries leave the equilibrium exchange rate unchanged.

> **Offsetting inflations in two countries will leave the incentive to import and to export unchanged, and thus will cause no change in their exchange rates.**

FIGURE 39.6 A Local Inflation Affects the Exchange Rate

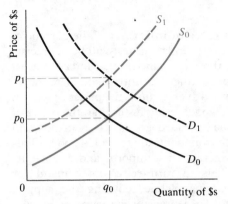

A local inflation in the UK appreciates foreign currencies and depreciates sterling. The original curves are D_0 and S_0 which yield an exchange rate of p_0 with q_0 dollars traded. A localized British inflation raises the demand for dollars to D_1 (because British residents buy more imports) and lowers the supply of dollars to S_1 (because American residents buy fewer British exports). The price of a dollar rises to p_1 (the dollar appreciates while sterling depreciates).

What happens to the quantity of dollars depends on the relative effects on British exports and British imports, since these may go either way. (No significance is to be attached, therefore, to the specific case shown in the Figure, where quantity is unchanged.)

Consideration of the last two cases of changes in price levels, shows that what matters is the relative rates of inflation between two trading countries. Differences in the inflation rates will cause changes in imports and exports and hence changes in quantities demanded and supplied on the foreign-exchange market. Thus the exchange rate between the two currencies will change. The general conclusion that follows from a simple extension of the two cases just studied is:

> **if the price level of one country is rising faster (falling slower) than that of another country, the equilibrium value of the first country's currency will be falling relative to that of the second country.**

What Causes the Exchange Rate to Change?

It follows from our theory that the simple answer to the question posed in this heading is: 'changes in demand or supply in the foreign-exchange market'. The question then needs to be rephrased as: 'What causes these changes in demand and supply?'

Differing rates of inflation: The currencies of countries that inflate fastest will be depreciating, while those of countries that inflate slowest will be appreciating. A country that inflates faster than the world average finds the prices of its own non-traded goods rising faster than the prices of internationally traded goods. Its demands will thus switch from domestic to traded goods. This tends to increase its imports and reduce its exports. This in turn raises its demand for foreign exchange while reducing the supply, which tends to depreciate the value of its currency on the foreign-exchange market.

On the other hand, a country that inflates slower than the world average finds the prices of its own non-traded goods rising slower than the prices of internationally traded goods. Its demands will thus switch from traded to non-traded goods. This tends to decrease its imports and increase its exports. This in turn lowers its demand for foreign exchange while increasing the supply of foreign exchange (offered to buy its exports). This tends to appreciate the value of its currency on the foreign-exchange market.

Structural changes: At the existing price levels, an economy can undergo structural changes that affect the exchange rate. 'Structural change' is an omnibus term for changes in cost structures, the invention of new products or anything else that affects the patterns of international competitiveness. For example, a country might be less dynamic than its competitors, so that at the initial set of prices consumers' demand shifts slowly away from the home-country products towards those of foreign countries. This would cause a slow trend depreciation in the home country's exchange rate.

Dramatic changes, such as major shifts in OPEC pricing policies, will have similar effects, except that they may occur suddenly over a space of months rather than gradually over a space of years. Big events such as the beginning or the end of the production of North Sea oil will also cause major changes in equilibrium exchange rates.

Long-term changes in exchange rates

that emanate from the current account can be accounted for mainly by the relative inflation rates and structural changes.

Capital Movements

So far we have confined ourselves to demands and supplies for foreign exchange that arise from trade in goods and services. Capital movements also exert a strong influence on exchange markets. If UK residents wish to buy American assets, they first need American dollars. This creates a demand for the dollars and a supply of sterling. The reverse is true when US residents want to buy British assets: a demand for sterling and a supply of dollars is created. When UK residents buy foreign assets, this is an export of British capital. Since this increases the demand for foreign exchange, it tends to appreciate the price of foreign exchange, hence to *depreciate* sterling. When foreign residents buy British assets, this is an import of capital into the UK. Since this raises the demand for sterling, it causes sterling to appreciate on the foreign-exchange market.

A movement of investment funds has the effect of appreciating the currency of the capital-importing country and depreciating the currency of the capital-exporting country.

This statement is true for all capital movements, short term or long term. Since the motives that lead to large capital movements are likely to be different in the short and long terms, however, it is worth considering each.

Short-term capital movements: A major motive for short-term capital flows is a change in interest rates. International traders hold transactions balances just as domestic traders do. These balances are often lent out on a short-term loan rather than being left idle. Naturally, the holders of these balances will tend to lend them, other things being equal, in the market where interest rates are highest. Thus if one major country's short-term rate of interest rises above the rates in most other countries, there will tend to be a large inflow of short-term capital into that country to take advantage of the high rate, and this will tend to appreciate the currency. If these short-term interest rates should fall, there will likely be a sudden shift away from that country as a short-term home for transactions balances, and its currency will tend to depreciate.

A second motive for short-term capital movements is speculation about a country's exchange rate. If foreigners expect sterling to appreciate, they will rush to buy assets that pay off in sterling; if they expect sterling to depreciate, they will be reluctant to buy or hold British securities.

Long-term capital movements: Such movements are largely influenced by long-term expectations about another country's profit opportunities and the long-run value of its currency. A British firm would be more willing to purchase an American factory if it expected that the dollar profits would buy more sterling in future years than the profits from investment in a British factory. This could happen if the American firm earned greater profits than the British firm, with exchange rates unchanged. It could also happen if the profits were the same but the British firm expected the dollar to appreciate relative to sterling.

The Trade-Weighted Exchange Rate

We have studied the determination of the exchange rate between two countries. When we consider foreign exchange in general, how do we calculate the appropriate exchange rate for sterling? One answer is to use what is called a **trade-weighted exchange rate**. This rate is an average of the exchange rate between sterling and each of the UK's major trading partners, with each rate being weighted by the amount of trade between the UK and the country in question. As a result, a movement in the sterling exchange rate with a major trading partner has a big effect on the trade-weighted exchange rate, while the equivalent movement with a minor trading partner has only a small effect.

The Effective Exchange Rate

Changes in the trade-weighted exchange rate are valuable indicators of changes in a country's international price competitiveness, but they do not tell the whole story. To illustrate, note that Sweden does little trade with Canada, so changes in the Swedish kroner–Canadian dollar exchange rate will have little effect on the Swedish trade-weighted exchange rate. But Sweden and Canada compete strongly in the sale of a number of commodities, such as pulp and paper, to the United States. If the kroner depreciates against the Canadian dollar, Swedish exports to the US will gain a price advantage over Canadian exports.

The International Monetary Fund calculates a series called the effective exchange rate. This attempts to weight changes on individual exchange rates by their importance in influencing competitiveness against each other's products and against those from other countries. Thus a change in the Swedish kroner–Canadian dollar rate would be weighted by the importance of Swedish sales to Canada *and* of Swedish sales to other countries that are made in competition with Canadian products.

What Determines the Value of the Exchange Rate in the Long Run?

So far in this chapter we have shown how demand and supply determine exchange rates. We have also shown how various forces can shift demands or supplies on the foreign-exchange market and so cause exchange rates to change.

We now ask why is the average value of the exchange rate taken over several years what it is, rather than something else? Why, for example, was the average sterling-dollar exchange rate, around $1.50 between 1983 and 1988, well down from what it had been a decade and a half previously?

The simple answer is that the relevant demand and supply curves intersected at a price for sterling of around $1.50 in that period, but at higher prices in earlier decades. But why did these curves intersect at those prices rather than at other very different ones? One theory that tries to answer this question seeks to explain the long-run trend around which the actual market rate fluctuates. It is called the **purchasing power parity (PPP) theory**, and the long-term rate predicted by this theory is called the **purchasing power parity (PPP) exchange rate**.

The PPP rate is the one that equates the costs of purchasing a representative bundle of traded goods and services between any two countries. Thus, if a representative bundle costs $100 in the US and £62.50 in the UK, the PPP exchange rate is $1 = £0.625 or, looked at the other way around £1 = $1.60. At this exchange rate, it would cost the same for a holder of sterling to buy the bundle for £62.50 in the UK or to convert sterling into dollars and buy the same bundle for $100 in the US.

We now need to explain a number of important points about the PPP rate.

(1) If the exchange rate between two countries is at the PPP rate, neither will have an overall competitive advantage over the other since, on average, each country's goods have the same prices as the other's. In these circumstances, each country will export to the other the goods that it can produce at home at a relatively lower price and will buy from the other the goods it can produce at home at a relatively high price.

(2) Changes in relative price levels change the PPP exchange rate. To illustrate, say that in the above example an American inflation increases the price of the bundle of goods from $100 to $125 in the US. Now the PPP rate changes to $1 = £2 or, what is the same thing, £1 = $0.50. In other words, the pound appreciates and the dollar depreciates. Notice that, if the actual rate follows the PPP rate, the American inflation does not put it at a competitive disadvantage. The rise in the US price level raises all of its costs and prices, but the depreciation of the exchange rate exactly offsets this so that the prices of the bundle of commodities remain the same in both countries. Indeed, the PPP rate has the effect of holding the relation between the price levels of the two countries constant when they are measured in a common currency.

(3) *If on the foreign-exchange market a country's currency is overvalued relative to its PPP rate, that country will tend to have a deficit on the balance of trade while, if it is undervalued, the country will tend to have a surplus.* Assume in the previous example that, although the cost of purchasing the representative bundle in the US rose from $100 to $125, the actual US exchange rate remained constant at $1 = £0.625. Now the US dollar is overvalued relative to its PPP rate. Converting the cost of the representative bundle from £62.50

to US dollars at the existing exchange rate yields $100 but, because of the inflation, the bundle costs $125 in the US. The same goods are, on average, cheaper in the UK than in the US. This will encourage Americans to buy more goods from the UK and discourage UK residents from buying American goods. American imports will rise and exports will fall, opening up a balance-of-trade deficit.

On the figures just considered, the UK exchange rate undervalues sterling relative to its PPP rate. (£1 is still only worth $1.60 when its PPP value is $2.) As we have seen, the UK will increase its exports to the US while reducing its imports from that country. This illustrates the second part of the italicized statement with which we opened this section.

(4) Finally, consider capital movements. We see in the next section that when a country is a net importer of capital (i.e. has a 'favourable' balance of payments on capital account) it also has a matching deficit on current account. Combining this with what we have just learned, leads to the conclusion that *capital-importing countries will tend to have exchange rates that are overvalued relative to their PPP rates – this will produce the deficit on current account needed to balance the surplus on capital account.*

Now consider countries that are net exporters of capital. Such countries have a deficit on capital account, which must be balanced by a surplus on current account. We have seen that surpluses are generated by having the country's actual exchange rate below its purchasing power parity rate. It follows that *countries that are net exporters of capital will tend to have exchange rates that are undervalued relative to their PPP rates.*

BALANCE-OF-PAYMENTS RECORDS[1]

In order to know what is happening to international payments, governments keep track of the actual transactions among countries. The record of such transactions is called the *balance-of-payments account* (see page 455). Each transaction, such as a shipment of exports or the arrival of imported goods, is recorded and classified

---

[1] For further details concerning these accounts see Harbury and Lipsey, Chapter 5.

according to the payments or receipts that would typically arise from it.

> **Any item that, from the home country's point of view, typically gives rise to a purchase of foreign currency is recorded as a debit item on the balance-of-payments accounts, and any item that typically gives rise to a sale of foreign currency is recorded as a credit item.**

If, for example, a British importer buys an American washing machine to sell in the United Kingdom, this appears as a debit in the UK balance of payments because when the machine is paid for, sterling will be sold and dollars purchased. On the other hand, if a US shipping firm insures with a member of Lloyd's of London a cargo destined for Egypt, this represents a credit

in the UK balance of payments, because when the insurance premium is paid, the shipping firm will have to buy sterling in order to pay the Lloyd's member.

The first thing that we need to notice about the record of international transactions is that the balance of payments always balances. Although it is possible for holders of sterling to want to purchase more dollars in exchange for pounds than holders of dollars want to sell in exchange for pounds, it is not possible for sterling holders actually to buy more dollars than dollar holders sell. Every dollar that is bought must be sold by someone, and every dollar that is sold must be bought by someone. Since the dollars actually bought must equal the dollars actually sold, the actual payments among countries must balance, even though desired payments may not.

TABLE 39.2 UK Balance of International Payments, 1988 (£m)

Current Account	
Visible Values	
Exports	80,157
Imports	100,714
Balance	−20,557
Invisible Balances	
Services	3,473
Interest, profits and dividends	6,001
Transfers	−3,582
Balance	+5,892
Current Account Balance	−14,665
Capital Account Balances	
Direct investment	−7,823
Portfolio investment	−6,738
Other capital items	16,760
Balance on Capital Flows	2,199
Balancing Item	15,227
Official Financing	−2,761
Sum of starred items	0

Source: Prest and Coppock's *The UK Economy* (12th edn, 1989), Table 3.1.

The overall balance of payments always balances, but the individual components do not have to. In 1988 the UK showed a negative merchandise trade balance with imports exceeding exports and a smaller negative (deficit) balance on current account. There is a positive (surplus) balance on capital accounts because capital imports exceeded capital exports. The capital *plus* current account balance is what is commonly referred to as the *balance of payments*. It is exactly matched by the balance in the official account, i.e. the use of official reserves.

Although the total number of pounds bought on the foreign-exchange market must equal the total number sold, the value of purchases and sales for a particular purpose may not be equal. It is quite possible, for example, that more pounds were sold for the purpose of obtaining foreign currency to import foreign cars than were bought for the purpose of buying British cars for export to other countries. In such a case, we would say that the UK had a balance-of-payments deficit on the 'car account', meaning that the value of UK imports of cars exceeded the value of its exports of cars. For most purposes, we are not interested in the balance of payments for single commodities but only for larger groups. The major divisions of the balance of payments are illustrated in Table 39.2.

The current account: The **current account** records all transactions in goods and services. **Visibles** are goods, i.e. things such as cars, pulpwood, aluminium, coffee and iron-ore, that we can see when they cross international borders. **Invisibles** are services, i.e. those things that we cannot see, such as insurance and freight haulage and tourist expenditures. Another main invisible item on the current account is the receipt of interest and dividends on loans and investments in foreign countries. If, for example, British residents hold shares in the International Telephone and Telegraph Company (IT & T), they will receive dividend payments in US dollars. If they wish to spend these at home, they will have to exchange the dollars for pounds. Interest and dividends on foreign loans and investment thus provide foreign exchange and are entered as a credit item.

The capital account: The **capital account** records transactions related to movements of long- and short-term capital. Consider, for example, holders of sterling who wish to invest abroad. We say that they are exporting capital. Suppose, for example, they wish to buy bonds being sold in New York by expanding American firms. In order to do this, they need to obtain dollars. They are demanders of foreign exchange and suppliers of sterling. Their transactions are, therefore, debit items in the UK balance-of-payments account.

Capital movements may be divided in several ways. One important division is between direct and portfolio investment. **Direct foreign investment** refers to changes in non-resident ownership of domestic firms and in resident ownership of foreign firms. Thus direct foreign investment in the UK is capital investment in a branch plant or subsidiary corporation in the UK in which the investor has voting control. It can also take the form of a takeover in which a controlling interest is acquired in a firm previously controlled by residents. **Portfolio investment**, on the other hand, is investment in bonds and other debt instruments that do not imply ownership or in minority holdings of shares that does not establish legal control.

Capital movements may also be classified according to their term. If a UK citizen buys a Brazilian tin-mining company's bond that will mature in 2010, this is a long-term capital outflow from the UK. If a British firm elects to transfer some of its working balances from London to its New York bank, this is an outflow of short-term capital, since the New York bank has the obligation to pay the deposit on demand. Short-term capital holdings arise in many ways. The mere fact of international trade forces traders to hold money balances. The funds can easily be moved from one currency to another in response to small changes in incentives. When this happens, purchases and sales of foreign exchange must occur.[1]

Official financing: The **official financing** items represent transactions involving the central bank of the country whose balance of payments is being recorded; in this case, the Bank of England. There are three ways in which credit items may occur on the official financing account. First, the Bank of England may borrow from the IMF. This represents a capital inflow and is thus a credit item on the balance of payments. (Repayment of old IMF loans is a debit item.) Second,

---

[1] Beginners sometimes find it confusing that the export of capital is a debit item and the export of a good is a credit item. The situation is, however, really very simple. The export of a good earns foreign exchange, and the export of capital uses foreign exchange. Therefore they have opposite effects on international payments. Another way of looking at it is that the capital transaction involves the purchase, and hence the *import* of a foreign bond or share; this has the same effect on the balance of payments as the purchase, and hence the import, of a foreign good. Both transactions use foreign exchange and are thus debit items in the UK balance of payments.

the Bank may borrow from other central banks through a network of arrangements built up in the 1960s to defend fixed exchange rates against speculative attacks. Such foreign borrowing by the Bank of England is a credit item on the balance of payments. Third, the Bank may run down its official reserves of gold and foreign exchange. This is a credit item because it gives rise to a sale of foreign exchange and a purchase of sterling. The running-down of reserves occurs when the Bank of England is supporting the value of sterling on the foreign-exchange market. The Bank then enters the free market selling foreign exchange and buying sterling.

Good and bad items?   The discussion above should have made it obvious that there is nothing necessarily good about credit items or bad about debit items on the balance of payments. For example, investment by UK firms in foreign countries that will yield future profits for UK owners is a debit item; the running-down of Bank of England reserves of foreign currencies is a credit item, as is the transfer of ownership of UK firms to foreigners.

Balances on Various Accounts

Specific balances: Earlier we have observed that when all transactions are taken into account, international payments must exactly balance, but that this is not true of particular sections of the accounts. Several sectional balances are important. The first is the balance on trade in visible goods. This is usually called the **balance of trade**. Next there is the balance on the invisible items in the current account. These are made up of two quite distinct balances: those on traded services, such as insurance and banking, and those on capital servicing items, such as interest and dividend payments. Together, the invisible and the trade balances make up the **current account balance**.

The rising importance of traded services in the modern world would make a different current-account grouping more useful. On the one hand would be the balance on traded goods *and* services. These are the items that respond quickly to changes in the exchange rate. On the other hand would be the balance on capital service items. These are items which change only slowly, since they are related to the total stocks of

foreign investment. In the short run, therefore, they do not respond to changes in the exchange rate. The net export term in national-income models is usually associated with the balance of trade, but it would be more useful to associate it with the balance on traded goods *and* services.

The next commonly used balance is the balance on capital account. This relates to the balance of all private-sector transactions that transfer capital into, and out of, the country for both short- and long-run purposes. Finally, there is the balance on official transactions, with relates to the movement of funds into, and out of, sterling by both the Bank of England and foreign central banks.

Good and bad balances?   A positive balance arises on any of these accounts when the sum of all credit items exceeds the sum of all debit items; a negative balance when the sum of debits exceeds the sum of credits. Such balances are often referred to as favourable and unfavourable balances respectively. This terminology is a carry-over from an old doctrine called **mercantilism**, which held that a country only gained from trade to the extent that its balance of trade was favourable. Since one country's export surplus must be another country's import surplus, the doctrine that a country only gains from trade to the extent that it has a favourable balance implies that, summed over all countries, the gains from trade are zero – one country's gains are another country's losses. This contradicts the Classical theory that trade benefits all countries by allowing each to specialize in its areas of comparative advantage. Box 39.1 further discusses the fallacy of judging the gains from trade by the balance of trade, rather than by its volume.

> Mercantilism holds that trade is a zero-sum game, in the sense that one country's gains from a favourable balance of trade must be another country's losses from an unfavourable balance. The Classical theory holds that trade is a positive-sum game, in the sense that the sum of all countries' gains, and any possible losses, from trade is positive.

The relation among the three main divisions: The relation among the three divisions of accounts follows simply from the fact that their

BOX 39.1 THE VOLUME OF TRADE, THE BALANCE OF TRADE, AND THE NEW MERCANTILISM

Media commentators, political figures, and much of the general public often judge the national balance of payments as they would the accounts of a single firm. Just as a firm is supposed to show a profit, the nation is supposed to secure a balance-of-payments surplus, with the benefits derived from international trade measured by the size of that surplus.

This view is related to the exploitation doctrine of international trade. Since one country's surplus is another country's deficit, one country's gain, judged by its surplus, must be another country's loss, judged by its deficit.

People who hold such views today are echoing an ancient economic doctrine called *mercantilism*. The mercantilists were a group of economists who preceded Adam Smith. They judged the success of trade by the size of the trade balance. In many cases this doctrine made sense in terms of their objective, which was to use international trade as a means of building up the political and military power of the state rather than raising the living standards of its citizens. A balance-of-payments surplus allowed the nation (then and now) to acquire foreign-exchange reserves. (In those days the reserves took the form of gold. Today they are a mixture of gold and claims on the currencies of other countries.) These reserves could then be used to pay armies, composed partly of foreign mercenaries; to purchase weapons from abroad; and generally to finance colonial adventures.

People who advocate this view in modern times are called *neo-mercantilists*. Insofar as their object is to increase the power of the state, they are choosing means that could achieve their ends.

Insofar as they are drawing an analogy between what is a sensible objective for a business interested in its own material welfare and what is a sensible objective for a society interested in the material welfare of its citizens, their views are erroneous, for the analogy is false.

If we take the view that the object of economic activity is to promote the welfare and living standards of ordinary citizens, rather than the power of governments, the mercantilist focus on the balance of trade makes no sense. The law of comparative advantage shows that average living standards are maximized by having individuals, regions, and countries specialize in the things they can produce comparatively best and trading to obtain the things they can produce comparatively worst. The more specialization, the more trade.

In this view the gains from trade are to be judged by the volume of trade. A situation in which there is a *large volume* of trade but where each country has a *zero balance* of trade can thus be regarded as quite satisfactory. Furthermore, a change in commercial policy that results in a balanced increase in trade between two countries will bring gain, because it allows for more specialization according to comparative advantage even though it causes no change in either country's trade balance.

To the business interested in private profit and to the government interested in the power of the state, it is the balance of trade that matters. To the person interested in the welfare of ordinary citizens, it is the volume of trade that matters.

sum must be zero:

$$C + K + F \equiv 0$$

where C, K and F are, respectively, the *balance* on current, capital and official settlement accounts.

A deficit on current account must be matched by a net surplus on capital plus official settlement accounts, which means borrowing abroad or running down exchange reserves. A surplus on current account implies a deficit on the sum of the other two accounts.

To illustrate this relation, assume that in a given year the value of UK imports exceeds the value of UK exports, considering all current-account transactions. The foreign exchange needed to finance the imports that were in excess of exports had to come from somewhere. It must have been lent by someone or else provided out of the government's reserves of gold and foreign exchange. If foreigners are investing funds in the UK, they will be selling foreign currency and buying sterling in order to be able to buy such assets as real estate or equities and bonds issued by UK firms. Such foreign investment can provide the foreign exchange necessary to allow the UK to have an excess of imports over exports. Another possibility is that the Bank of England financed the current-account deficit either by selling some of its reserves of foreign exchange or by borrowing from the IMF or other central banks.

Now consider a situation in which the value of exports is in excess of the value of imports. This means that foreigners will have been unable to obtain all the sterling they need in order to buy UK goods from the UK sources who wish to supply sterling in return for foreign currency in order to buy foreign goods. The excess of exports over imports could only have been paid for if foreigners obtained sterling from other sources. There are several possibilities. First, sterling may be provided by UK investors wishing to obtain foreign currency so that they can buy foreign equities and bonds. In this case, the excess of exports over imports is balanced by UK loans and investments abroad. Second, the UK Government, rather than its firms or citizens, may have lent money to foreign governments to finance their purchases of British-produced goods or services. Third, the UK Government may have given money away as aid, particularly to underdeveloped countries. Such gifts allow these countries to purchase more from the UK than they sell to it. The fourth main possibility is that the Bank of England has added to its reserves of foreign exchange by selling sterling on the foreign-exchange market.

We have already noted that when we add up all the uses of foreign currency, and all the sources from which it came, these two amounts are necessarily equal, and thus the overall accounts of all international payments necessarily balance. What, then, do we mean when we say that payments are not in balance, that there is a deficit or a surplus on the balance of payments?

When we speak of a balance-of-payments deficit or surplus, we refer to the balance on some part of the accounts. Usually, we are referring to the balance on current plus capital account.

A balance-of-payments deficit thus means that the reserves of the central bank are being run down or foreign ownership of its assets is rising, while a surplus means the opposite.

SUMMARY

1. International trade can occur only when it is possible to exchange the currency of one country for that of another. The exchange rate between two currencies is the amount of one currency that must be paid to obtain one unit of another currency.

2. The supply of foreign exchange arises from UK exports of goods and services and from long-term and short-term capital flows into the UK. The demand for foreign exchange arises from UK imports of goods and services and from capital flows out of the UK.

3. A depreciation of sterling raises the domestic price of traded goods. This increases the quantities of such goods supplied domestically and reduces the quantities demanded. As a result, the volume of exports rises and, with it, the supply of foreign exchange. But the volume of imports falls, and with it the demand for foreign exchange. Thus the supply curve for foreign exchange is upward-sloping and the demand curve for foreign exchange is downward-sloping when the quantities demanded and supplied are plotted against the price of foreign exchange measured in terms of sterling – that is, against the exchange rate.

4. A currency will tend to depreciate if there is a shift to the right of the demand curve for foreign exchange or a shift to the left of the supply curve. Shifts in the opposite directions will tend to appreciate the currency. Shifts are caused by such things as changes in the rates of inflation in different countries, capital movements, and structural changes.

5. In the long term, exchange rates tend to follow purchasing power parities, the rate that equates the purchasing power of two national currencies.

6. Actual transactions among the firms, households and governments of various countries are reported in the balance-of-payments accounts. In these accounts any transaction that, from the domestic country's point of view, uses foreign exchange is recorded as a debit item and any transaction that produces foreign exchange is recorded as a credit item. If all transactions are recorded, the sum of all credit items necessarily equals the sum of all debit items since the foreign exchange that is bought must also have been sold.

7. Major categories in the balance-of-payments account are the balance of trade (exports minus imports), current account, capital account, and official financing. The so-called balance of payments is the balance of the current plus capital accounts; that is, it excludes the transactions on official account. Ignoring official settlements, a balance on current account must be matched by a balance on capital account of equal magnitude but opposite sign.

TOPICS FOR REVIEW

- Foreign exchange and exchange rates
- Appreciation and depreciation
- Sources of the demand for and supply of foreign exchange
- Causes of changes in exchange rates
- Balance of trade and balance of payments
- Current and capital account
- Official financing items
- Mercantilist views on the balance and volume of trade

40

Macro Policy in an Open Economy[1]

[1] For background material, see Harbury and Lipsey, Chapters 7 and 9.

In the second half of this chapter we consider the serious complications brought to macroeconomic policy by the openness of an economy. As a prelude we consider, in the first half of the chapter, alternative exchange-rate regimes.

ALTERNATIVE EXCHANGE-RATE REGIMES

Two extreme regimes may be distinguished. The first is a system where exchange rates are fixed at pre-announced 'par' values that are changed only occasionally when the existing rate can no longer be defended. This is the system which operated from the end of the Second World War until the early 1970s. The second is a system of freely fluctuating rates determined by private-sector demand and supply in the complete absence of government intervention. This is a system that some countries have occasionally come close to since 1971. A third, intermediate system, called a *dirty float*, is one where the central bank seeks to have some stabilizing influence on the rate without trying to fix it at an official par value. This system is really a combination of the other two. We first study the two extreme cases of fully fixed and freely fluctuating rates, both because understanding them is a prerequisite to understanding the dirty float, and because many economists and policy-makers advocate returning to one or the other of the extreme systems. The fixed system is studied in the context of its most recent example, the Bretton Woods system, which lasted for nearly thirty years from the end of the Second World War in 1945.

Background

The onset of the Great Depression of the 1930s brought an end to the ancient stability of the gold standard and ushered in a period of experimentation in exchange regimes. Experiments were tried with both fixed and fluctuating rates. Often a rate would be allowed to fluctuate on the free market until it had reached what looked like equilibrium, and it would then be fixed at that level. Sometimes, as with the British pound, the rate was left to be determined by a free market throughout the whole period. Sometimes rates would be changed in an attempt to secure domestic full employment without any consideration of the state of the balance of payments.

The period of experimentation coincided with the Great Depression. This was a terrible period of mass unemployment, and governments began to cast around for any measure, no matter how extreme, that might alleviate their domestic unemployment problem. One superficially plausible way of doing this was to cut back on imports and produce those goods domestically. If one country managed to reduce its imports, then its unemployment might be reduced because people would be put to work producing replacement goods at home. Other countries would, however, find their exports falling and unemployment rising as a consequence. Because such policies attempt to solve one country's problems by inflicting them on others, they are called **beggar-my-neighbour policies**.

If the policies worked, there would at least be selfish arguments in their favour. But they work only as long as other countries do not try to protect themselves. Once they find their exports falling and unemployment rising, these other countries may retaliate by reducing their own imports and producing the goods at home, and the first country will find its exports falling and unemployment rising as a result. The simultaneous attempts of all countries to cut imports without suffering a comparable cut in exports is bound to be self-defeating. The net effect of such measures is to decrease the volume of trade, thereby sacrificing the gains from trade without raising worldwide employment.

> **When unemployment is due to insufficient world aggregate demand, it cannot be cured by measures designed to redistribute, among nations, the fixed and inadequate total of demand.**

Beggar-my-neighbour policies in the 1930s used such instruments of commercial policy as import duties, export subsidies, quotas, prohibitions, and, also, exchange-rate depreciation. If a country with a large portion of its labour force unemployed devalues its exchange rate, two effects can be expected: exports will rise, and domestic consumers will buy fewer imports and more domestically produced goods. Both of these changes will have the effect of lowering the amount of unemployment in the country.

If other countries do nothing, the policy succeeds. But again, the volume of unemployment in other countries will have increased because exports to the devaluing country will have been reduced. If other countries try to restore their positions, they may devalue their currencies as well. If all countries devalue their currencies in the same proportion, they will all be right back where they started, with no change in the relative prices of goods from any country and, hence, no change in relative prices from the original situation. When all countries devalue their currencies in an attempt to gain a competitive advantage over one another, we speak of **competitive devaluations**.

The Bretton Woods System

The one lesson that everyone thought had been learned from the 1930s was that either a system of freely fluctuating exchange rates, or a system of fixed rates with easily accomplished devaluations, was the road to disaster. In order to achieve a system of orderly exchange rates that would be conducive to the free flow of trade following the Second World War, representatives of most countries that had participated in the alliance against Germany, Italy, and Japan met at Bretton Woods, New Hampshire, in 1944. The international monetary system that developed out of the agreements reached at Bretton Woods consisted of a large body of rules and understandings for the regulation of international transactions and payments imbalances.

It was the first and so far the only international payments system that was consciously designed and then implemented through international governmental co-operation. In the words of Charles Kindleberger of MIT, the Bretton Woods meeting was 'the biggest constitution-writing exercise ever to occur in international monetary relations'. The system lasted until the early 1970s, when it broke down and was replaced by the piecemeal adoption of free-market exchange rates.

The object of the Bretton Woods system was to create a set of rules that would maintain fixed exchange rates in the face of short-term fluctuations; to guarantee that changes in exchange rates would occur only in the face of long-term, persistent deficits or surpluses in the balance of payments; and to ensure that when such changes did occur they would not spark a series of competitive devaluations.

The basic characteristic of the Bretton Woods system was that US dollars held by foreign monetary authorities were made directly convertible into gold at a fixed price by the US government, while foreign governments fixed the prices at which their currencies were convertible into US dollars. It was this characteristic that made the system a **gold exchange standard**: gold was the ultimate reserve, but other currencies were held as reserves because directly or indirectly they could be *exchanged* for gold.

The rate at which each country's currency was convertible into dollars was fixed within a narrow band on either side of a pre-announced par value or pegged rate. This rate could be changed from time to time in the face of a 'fundamental disequilibrium' in the balance of payments. A system with these two characteristics, a rate that is pegged against short-term fluctuations but that can be adjusted from time to time, is referred to as an **adjustable peg system**.

In order to maintain convertibility of their currencies at fixed exchange rates, the monetary authorities of each country had to be ready to buy and sell their currency in the foreign-exchange markets. In order to be able to support the exchange market by buying domestic currency, the monetary authorities had to have stocks of acceptable foreign exchange to offer in return. In the Bretton Woods system, the authorities held reserves of gold and claims on key currencies – mainly the American dollar and the British pound. When a country's currency was in excess supply, their authorities would sell dollars, sterling, or gold. When a country's currency was in excess demand, their authorities would buy dollars or sterling. If they then wished to increase their gold reserves they would use the dollars to purchase gold from the Federal Reserve System (the US central bank, hereinafter called the 'Fed'), thus depleting the US gold stock. The problem for the United States was to have enough gold to maintain fixed-price convertibility of the dollar into gold as demanded by foreign monetary authorities. The problem for all other countries was to maintain convertibility (on a restricted or unrestricted basis, depending on the country in question) between their cur-

rency and the US dollar at a fixed rate of exchange.

The Bretton Woods international payments system was an adjustable peg, gold exchange standard where the ultimate international money was gold. Countries held much of their exchange reserves in the form of US dollars, which they could convert into gold, and British pounds, which they could convert into US dollars.

The International Monetary Fund

The most important institution created by the Bretton Woods system was the International Monetary Fund (also called the IMF or the Fund). The Fund had several tasks. First, it tried to ensure that countries held their exchange rates pegged in the short run. Second, it made loans – out of funds subscribed by member nations – to governments that needed them to support their exchange rates in the face of temporary payments deficits. Third, the Fund was supposed to consult with countries wishing to alter their exchange rates to ensure that the rate was really being changed to remove a persistent payments disequilibrium, and that one devaluation did not set off a self-cancelling round of competitive devaluations. The importance of the Fund is attested by the fact that it has outlived the system that created it and is as active an instrument of international monetary co-operation today as it was under the Bretton Woods system.

Management of Fixed Rates

When rates were fixed at their average free-market rate, the demand and supply curves for foreign exchange intersected within the permissible band. In cases in which they did not, the government would take steps to shift the demand and supply curves so that they did intersect in that range. Exchange controls to limit the use of foreign exchange, and measures to encourage exports which earn foreign exchange, were commonly used for this purpose. Assuming the curves could be made to intersect in that range, where did the management problem lie?

The problem lay with seasonal, cyclical and random fluctuations that continually shifted the demand and supply curves for foreign exchange. To keep the exchange rate within the permissible band, the Bank must stand ready to enter the market, buying and selling as necessary.

When sterling threatened to depreciate, the Bank must sell foreign exchange and buy sterling to maintain the rate within the band. When sterling threatened to appreciate, the Bank must buy foreign exchange and sell sterling to maintain the rate within the band. These strategies are analysed further in Figure 40.1.

To operate such a system, the Bank requires reserves of foreign exchange to allow it to buy and sell as needed. If the average positions of the demand and supply curves for foreign exchange

FIGURE 40.1   Managing a Fixed Exchange Rate

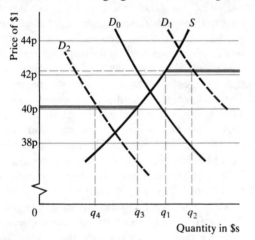

The Bank must be able to buy and sell any quantities of foreign exchange necessary to eliminate excess demand or supply at the controlled rate. The Bank has pegged sterling within the band $40\frac{1}{3}$p to $42\frac{1}{3}$p to the \$. This means the Bank must provide a perfectly elastic supply of foreign exchange at the upper limit of $42\frac{1}{3}$ and a perfectly elastic demand at the lower limit of $40\frac{1}{3}$. This is shown by the heavy horizontal lines at those prices.

If private-sector demand and supply curves are D_0 and S, the market rate is within the permissible band and no intervention is needed. If demand rises to D_1, the free-market rate would be outside the permissible band. To maintain the fixed rate, the Bank must sell $q_2 - q_1$ out of its reserves each period. This fills the gap between the quantity demanded of q_2 and the quantity supplied of q_1 at the rate of $42\frac{1}{3}$. If private-sector demand falls to D_2, the rate would once again go outside the band. This time the Bank must buy $q_3 - q_4$ to stop the excess supply of foreign exchange lowering its price (appreciating sterling).

intersect within the permitted band, the Bank's policy will be successful. In times of downward pressure on sterling, it will sell foreign exchange, depleting its reserves. In times of upward pressure on sterling it will sell sterling in return for foreign exchange, thus augmenting its reserves. Its reserves will fluctuate, but they will do so around a satisfactory average level.

If, however, the Bank tries to establish a band where the curves do not on average intersect, its average level of reserves will increase or decrease over time. If they decrease, the Bank's policy is threatened. If it runs out of reserves, it will have to allow sterling to depreciate.

If the Bank is fundamentally wrong in the rate it is trying to maintain, given the amount of exchange controls etc. it is willing and able to use, nothing can save the rate. Sooner or later the rate must be allowed to move towards its equilibrium level.

What if the Bank feels it is faced with a temporary fluctuation in demand but one that persists long enough to threaten to eliminate its reserves? The next line of defence is to induce capital movements. The Bank uses open-market operations to raise the short-term rate of interest, attracting short-term capital. People holding dollars now wish to obtain sterling in order to lend it out at the high UK rates. Thus the supply of dollars shifts to the right and less Bank sales of foreign exchange are needed. If the curve is shifted sufficiently, the inflow of short-term capital covers the deficit on current account, and the Bank's exchange reserves are not run down.

Provided the Bank guessed correctly that the demand was *abnormally* high, the policy will work. If the demand now falls to an abnormally low level, the Bank can lower interest rates, stopping the capital inflow. It can then buy dollars and add them to exchange reserves. When the reserves have been built up, the Bank can allow the short-term capital to flow abroad. It does this by lowering short-term rates of interest so that people who have lent money in Britain would now prefer to lend it in, say, New York. There will be a demand on the part of these investors to turn sterling into dollars. The government can now sell these dollars as required.

Short-term deficits in the balance of payments can be covered by attracting

short-term capital into a country. But this policy will be successful only if an equivalent short-term surplus subsequently develops, so that the capital can again be transferred out of the country.

Problems of an Adjustable Peg System

Three major problems of the Bretton Woods system were (1) providing sufficient reserves to iron out short-term fluctuations in international receipts and payments while keeping exchange rates fixed; (2) making adjustments to long-term trends in receipts and payments; and (3) handling speculative crisis. Since these problems would be present in any adjustable peg system that might be designed in the future, they are worth studying in detail in the forms in which they plagued the Bretton Woods system.

Reserves to accommodate short-term fluctuations: Reserves are needed to accommodate short-term balance-of-payments fluctuations arising from both the current and the capital accounts. On current account, normal trade is subject to many short-term variations, some systematic and some random. This means that even if the value of imports does equal the value of exports, taken on average over several years, there may be considerable imbalances over shorter periods.

On a free market, fluctuations in current and capital account payments would cause the exchange rate to fluctuate. To prevent such fluctuations when rates are fixed, the monetary authorities buy and sell foreign exchange as required, to keep the exchange rate pegged. These operations require that the authorities hold reserves of foreign exchange. If they run out of reserves, they cannot maintain the pegged rate, so they will want to hold some safety margin over the maximum they expect to use. It is generally felt that the absolute size of any gap they may have to fill with their own foreign-exchange sales increases as the volume of international payments increases. Since there was a strong upward trend in the volume of overall international payments, there was also a strong upward trend in the demand for foreign-exchange reserves.

The ultimate reserve in the Bretton Woods gold exchange standard was gold, which entailed

two serious problems. First, the world's supply of monetary gold did not grow fast enough to provide adequate total reserves for an expanding volume of trade. The gold backing needed to maintain convertibility of currencies became increasingly inadequate throughout the 1960s. Second, the country whose currency is convertible into gold must maintain sufficient reserves to ensure convertibility. During the 1960s the United States lost substantial gold reserves to other countries that had acquired dollar claims through their balance-of-payments surpluses with the United States. By the late 1960s the loss of US reserves had been sufficiently large to undermine confidence in America's continued ability to maintain dollar convertibility. *By 1970 there was an inadequate world supply of gold for monetary uses, and the United States had too small a proportion of the supply that did exist.*

Under the Bretton Woods system, the supply of gold was augmented by reserves of key currencies, the US dollar and the British pound. Because the need for reserves expanded much more rapidly than the gold stock in the period since the Second World War, the system required nations to hold an increasing fraction of their reserves in dollars and sterling. Of course they would do this only as long as they had confidence in the convertibility of these currencies, and maintaining confidence was made difficult by a continually declining percentage of gold backing for the dollar.

Adjusting to long-term disequilibria: With fixed exchange rates, long-term disequilibria (what the IMF used to call *fundamental disequilibria*) can be expected to develop because of secular shifts in the demands for and supplies of foreign exchange. There are three important reasons for these. First, different trading countries have different rates of inflation. Chapter 39 discussed how these cause changes in the equilibrium rate of exchange and, if the rate is fixed, cause excess supply or excess demand to develop in each country's foreign-exchange market. Second, changes in the demands for and supplies of imports and exports are associated with long-term economic growth. Because different countries grow at different rates, their demands for imports, and their supplies of exports, would be expected to be shifting at different rates. Third, structural changes, such as major new innovations or the rise in the price of oil, cause major changes in imports and exports.

The associated shifts in demand and supply on the foreign-exchange market imply that, even starting from a current-account equilibrium with imports equal to exports at a given rate of exchange, there is no reason to believe that equilibrium will exist at the same rate of exchange 5 or 10 years later.

The rates of exchange that will lead to a balance-of-payments equilibrium will tend to change over time; over a decade the changes can be substantial.

Governments may react to long-term disequilibria in at least three ways.

(1) The exchange rate can be changed whenever a balance-of-payments deficit or surplus clearly results from a long-term shift in the demands and supplies, rather than from some transient factor. During the period of the Bretton Woods system, there were three major rounds of exchange-rate adjustments.

(2) Domestic price levels can be allowed to change in an attempt to establish an equilibrium set of international prices. Changes in domestic price levels have all sorts of domestic repercussions (e.g., reductions in aggregate demand intended to lower the price level are more likely to raise unemployment than to lower prices), and one might have expected governments to be more willing to change exchange rates – which can be done by a stroke of a pen – than to try to change their price levels. A deflation is difficult to accomplish, while an inflation is accompanied by undesirable side-effects.

(3) Restrictions can be imposed on trade and foreign payments. Imports and foreign spending by tourists and governments can be restricted, and the export of capital can be slowed or even stopped. Surplus countries were often quick to criticize such restrictions on international trade and payments. As long as exchange rates were fixed and price levels proved difficult to manipulate, the deficit countries had little option but to restrict the quantity of foreign exchange their residents were permitted to obtain so as to equate it to the quantity available.

Handling speculative crises: When enough people begin to doubt the ability of the central authorities to maintain the current rate, speculative crises develop. The most important reason for such crises is that, over time, equilibrium exchange rates get further and further away from any given set of fixed rates. When the disequilibrium becomes obvious to everyone, traders and speculators come to believe that a realignment of rates cannot long be delayed. At such a time, there is a rush to buy currencies expected to be revalued and a rush to sell currencies expected to be devalued. Even if the authorities take drastic steps to remove the payments deficit, there may be doubt as to whether these measures will work before the exchange reserves are exhausted. Speculative flows of funds can reach very large proportions, and it may be impossible to avoid changing the exchange rate under such pressure.

Speculative crises were, and will always be, one of the most intractable problems of any adjustable peg system. The impact of such crises might be reduced if governments had more adequate reserves. If a speculative crisis precedes an exchange-rate adjustment, however, more adequate reserves may just mean that speculators will make larger profits since more of them will be able to sell the currency about to be devalued and to buy the currency about to be revalued before the monetary authorities are forced to act. During the Bretton Woods period, governments tended to resist changing their exchange rates until they had no alternative. This made the situation so obvious that speculators could hardly lose, and their actions set off the final crisis that forced exchange-rate readjustments.

Under an adjustable peg system, speculators get an easy opportunity for making large profits since everyone knows which way an exchange rate will be changed if it is to be changed at all.

As the equilibrium value of a country's currency changes, possibly under the impact of a high rate of inflation, it becomes obvious to everyone that the central bank is having more and more difficulty holding the pegged rate. So when a crisis arises, speculators sell the country's currency. If it is devalued, they can buy it back at its now lower price to earn a profit. If it is not devalued they can buy it back at the original price, losing only the transactions costs.

This asymmetry – speculators having a chance of a large profit by risking only a small loss – was what eventually undid the system. As trade became more unsettled, as differences in inflation rates became greater and as exchange reserves became smaller, more frequent adjustments in the pegged rates were necessary. Seeing these coming, speculators sold currencies under pressure to be devalued, and bought currencies under pressure to be revalued. There were massive movements of speculative funds, which destabilized the system and which were one of the major causes of its abandonment in the early 1970s.

Flexible Exchange Rates

Under a system of flexible exchange rates, demand and supply determine the rates without any government intervention. Since the market always clears with demand equal to supply, the central authorities can turn their attention to domestic problems of inflation and unemployment, leaving the balance of payments to take care of itself – at least so went the theory before flexible rates were introduced.

For reasons that we shall analyse later in this chapter, this optimistic picture did not materialize when the world went over to flexible exchange rates. Free-market fluctuations in rates were far greater – and hence more upsetting to trade – than many economists had anticipated. As a result, central banks have felt the need to intervene quite frequently, and heavily, to stabilize exchange rates at least against the more extreme short-term fluctuations. This has brought the world to the mixed regime of dirty floats.

Dirty Floats

Although many of today's exchange rates are determined on the free market, there is nevertheless substantial intervention in these markets by central banks. The difference between the present system and Bretton Woods is that central banks no longer have publicly announced par values for exchange rates that they are committed in advance to defending even at heavy cost. Central banks are thus free to change their exchange-rate targets as circumstances change. Sometimes they leave the rate completely free to fluctuate, and at other times they interfere ac-

tively to alter the exchange rate from its free-market value. Such a system is called a **managed float** or a **dirty float**.

To manage exchange rates, central banks must hold foreign-exchange reserves. One of the major forms in which reserves are held is US dollars; another, and one that is growing in importance, is the **special drawing rights (SDRs)** held with the IMF. SDRs, first introduced in 1969, were designed to provide a supplement to existing reserve assets by setting up a Special Drawing Account kept separate from all other operations of the Fund. Each member country of the Fund was assigned an SDR quota that was guaranteed in terms of a fixed gold value and that it could use to acquire an equivalent amount of convertible currencies from other participants. SDRs could be used without prior consultation with the Fund, but only to cope with balance-of-payments difficulties.

MACROECONOMIC POLICY IN AN OPEN ECONOMY: THE CURRENT ACCOUNT

The openness of an economy to trade and capital movements greatly complicates the operation of macro policy. To obtain some insight into these complex issues, we need to simplify. We do so by dealing with a single objective of domestic policy-makers: a target level of real national income. Limiting our attention to one domestic policy target is not as restrictive as it might at first seem. To illustrate, assume the objective is to reduce the domestic rate of inflation. We know from Chapter 34 that this can be accomplished by obtaining a target level of real national income below potential.

When real national income is at its target level, we say the economy has achieved **internal balance**.

In this section we focus on the trade account as the external policy target. When the trade account is equal to its target level, we say the economy has achieved **external balance**.

In this section we also treat the exchange rate as fixed. Later in the chapter we study the complications that arise when the capital account and a flexible exchange rate are considered. Studying these two extreme cases, helps us to

FIGURE 40.2 Internal and External Balance

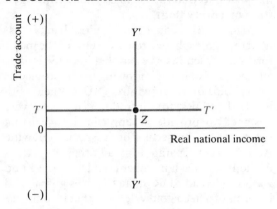

Internal and external balance are simultaneously attained at point Z. Internal balance is defined in terms of a target level of real national income and is depicted by the vertical line $Y'Y'$. External balance is defined in terms of a target level of the trade account and is depicted by the horizontal line $T'T'$. Only at the intersection, point Z, are both internal and external balance attained.

understand the policy problems associated with the current regime of dirty floats. To the extent that the Bank is stabilizing the exchange rate, it will encounter the problems associated with a fixed-rate regime; to the extent that the Bank allows the rate to fluctuate, it will encounter the problems associated with a flexible-rate regime.

The conditions for internal and external balance are illustrated in Figure 40.2.

The Potential for Conflict Between Objectives

When policies used to move the economy closer to one objective move the economy further from the other objective, the objectives are said to be in conflict.

Policies to eliminate a recessionary gap will also influence the trade account by causing a movement along the negatively sloped net export function (see page 511 where this function was last referred to). Whether there is a conflict between the objectives of internal and external balance depends on how the trade account and real national income compare to their target values.

For simplicity, we now make the assumption

that the target level of real national income is potential income and that the target for the trade account is a zero balance.[1] Hence we can identify the initial situation relative to the targets simply in terms of the signs of the output gap and the trade account balance. There are four possible cases:

(1) A trade account *deficit* combined with an *inflationary gap* poses no conflict, because the contraction of aggregate demand to eliminate the inflationary gap leads to a reduction in imports and hence reduces the trade deficit.

(2) A trade account *deficit* combined with a *recessionary gap* does pose a conflict, because the expansion of aggregate demand to eliminate the recessionary gap leads to an increase in imports and hence a worsening of the trade deficit.

(3) A trade account *surplus* combined with a *recessionary gap* poses no conflict, because the expansion of aggregate demand to eliminate the recessionary gap increases imports and hence reduces the trade surplus.

(4) A trade account *surplus* combined with an *inflationary gap* does pose a conflict, because the contraction of aggregate demand to eliminate the inflationary gap leads to a reduction in imports and hence an increase in the trade surplus.

The four cases are depicted in Figure 40.3. In case 2, the trade account deficit calls for a decrease in national income, but the recessionary gap calls for an increase. In case 4, the trade account surplus calls for an increase in national income, but the inflationary gap calls for a decrease.[2]

---

[1] We emphasize that this assumption is made only to simplify the discussion. The same principles apply regardless of the actual values of the targets. A nation with a large undeveloped natural resource base may have a low current national income yet anticipate a high future national income when the resource base is developed. High current investment to develop the resource base and high current consumption in anticipation of that high future income will together lead to high imports and a trade account deficit. Hence the *target* trade account in such a circumstance may well be a deficit.

[2] Case 2 has traditionally attracted the most attention, perhaps because a trade deficit is generally viewed as being a more serious problem than a trade surplus, and – at least in the past – unemployment has been considered a more serious problem than inflation. Case 2 is often referred to as a situation in which there is a 'balance-of-payments constraint' on domestic stabilization policy.

FIGURE 40.3 Conflicts Between Internal and External Balance

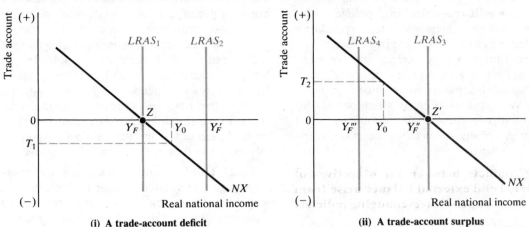

(i) A trade-account deficit   **(ii) A trade-account surplus**

Of the four different possible combinations of signs of the output gap and the trade account, only two pose conflicts. In both parts of the Figure, the net export function, which relates the trade-account balance to real national income, is shown by the black line labelled NX. The actual level of income is given by Y_0, so in part (i) there is a trade account deficit of T_1, while in part (ii) there is a trade account surplus of T_2.

In part (i), if potential output is given by Y_F so there is an inflationary gap (case 1), there is no conflict, since adjustment of actual real national income to achieve one target will also achieve the other target, at point Z. However, if potential output is given by Y_F' so there is a recessionary gap (case 2), there is a conflict, since movement of actual real national income to achieve either target will cause a movement away from the other target.

In part (ii), if potential income is given by Y_F'' so there is a recessionary gap (case 3), there is no conflict, since adjustment of actual real national income to achieve one target will also achieve the other target, at point Z'. However, if potential output is given by Y_F''' so there is an inflationary gap (case 4), there is a conflict, since a change in actual real national income to achieve either target will cause a movement away from the other target.

A conflict arises between the objectives of internal and external balance when the two call for opposite changes in the level of national income.

Basically, the conflicts arise from *movements along* the net export function through what are called *expenditure-changing policies*; they are resolved by *shifting* the net export function through what are called *expenditure-switching policies*.

Expenditure-changing and Expenditure-switching Policies

We start by repeating the basic equilibrium condition, that national income equals aggregate desired expenditure:

$$Y = C + I + G + (X - M) . \qquad (1)$$

The total $C + I + G$ is often referred to as *domestic absorption*, or simply *absorption*. This concept refers to total expenditure on goods for use in the economy. Denoting absorption by the letter A, we can rewrite the national-income equilibrium condition as

$$Y = A + (X - M) . \qquad (2)$$

This condition states that equilibrium national income is equal to aggregate desired expenditure, which in turn is equal to domestic absorption plus net exports.

Equation (2) is useful in distinguishing between two types of policies that might be used to maintain internal and external balance. Policies that maintain the level of aggregate desired

expenditure but influence its composition between domestic absorption and net exports are
called **expenditure-switching** policies. Policies that change aggregate desired expenditure
are called **expenditure-changing** policies.

Expenditure-changing policies involve moving along a given net export function, so changes
in the trade balance and national income must be
negatively related. If the initial situation calls for
them to move in the same direction, the use of
expenditure-changing policies necessarily involves a conflict.

**The conflicts between the objectives of
internal and external balance arise from
the use of expenditure-changing policies.**

An expenditure-switching policy shifts the net
export function. As we shall see, this can lead to
positively related changes in the trade balance and
national income. Devaluation or revaluation of
the domestic currency, restrictions on international trade such as tariffs or quotas, and
changes in the domestic price level relative to
foreign price levels, are all expenditure-
switching policies.[1]

With both expenditure-changing and expenditure-switching policies available, we can now see
how to deal with each of the four cases that we
described in the earlier section.

A Trade-account Deficit

As we have seen, a trade-account deficit means
that national income is less than domestic absorption. Now consider policies to eliminate the
trade-account deficit; to be successful, the
policies must raise national income *relative* to
absorption.

**Case 1. A deficit combined with an in-
flationary gap – no conflict:** If the economy
already has an inflationary gap, national income
should not be increased further. The trade-
account deficit indicates that domestic absorption is above the current level of national income
and hence, by virtue of the inflationary gap,

above the full-employment level. To eliminate
the deficit, absorption must be lowered. In other
words, if net exports are to rise, resources must
be released through a reduction in domestic
usage. This calls for *expenditure-reducing* policies
such as reductions in the money supply, cuts in
government expenditure, and increases in taxes.
No conflict for expenditure-changing policies
arises in this case, because the expenditure reduction cuts the inflationary gap and improves
the trade account by inducing a movement along
the net export function.

**Case 2. A deficit combined with a recess-
ionary gap – conflict:** When national income
is below its capacity level, income can be
expanded. But an expansion in national income
with a fixed net export function would worsen the
trade account, so expenditure-increasing policies
are not appropriate. A reduction in national
income to reduce the trade deficit would worsen unemployment, so expenditure-reducing
policies are not appropriate. What is needed is a
switch in expenditure away from foreign goods
(thus reducing the trade deficit) and toward
domestic goods (thus reducing the recessionary
gap).

**Policies to induce a *switch* of some ex-
penditure from foreign goods to domestic goods – thereby *shifting* the net export
function rightward and raising national
income – will alleviate the conflict posed
by a recessionary gap combined with a
trade deficit.**

Such policies include devaluation of the currency
and protective measures such as tariffs and
quotas. This is illustrated in Figure 40.4.

A Trade-account Surplus

Cases 3 and 4 in our list both involve a trade-
account surplus. An expansion of national income will therefore cause a move toward external
balance by raising imports. Hence in case 3,
where there is a recessionary gap, no conflict
arises, and expenditure-raising policies will lead
to movement toward both targets. In case 4,
where there is an inflationary gap, a conflict does
arise; external balance calls for expenditure increases, but internal balance calls for expenditure
reduction. What is needed is a *switch* in expenditure away from domestic goods (thus reducing

**FIGURE 40.4 A Trade Deficit and a
Recessionary Gap**

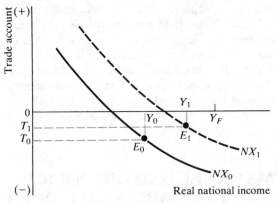

(i) Net export function

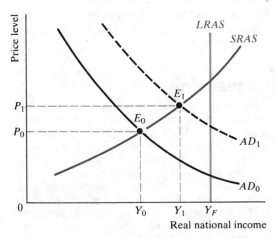

(ii) Determination of national income

**A policy to switch expenditure away from
foreign goods and toward domestic goods can
be used to resolve the conflict posed by a trade
deficit combined with a recessionary gap.**
Initially, the net export function is given by NX_0 in
part (i), and aggregate demand is given by AD_0 in part
(ii). Equilibrium is at E_0 with real national income
equal to Y_0. There is a recessionary gap of $Y_F - Y_0$ and
a trade deficit of T_0.

An expenditure-switching policy raises net exports
at each level of income, so the net export function
shifts right to NX_1 in part (i). The policy also raises
aggregate demand, so the AD curve shifts right to
AD_1 in part (ii). The new equilibrium is at E_1, with
real national income of Y_1 and a trade deficit of T_1.
Hence both the recessionary gap and the trade deficit
are reduced.

**FIGURE 40.5 A Trade Surplus and an
Inflationary Gap**

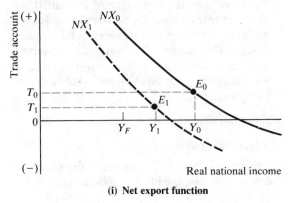

(i) Net export function

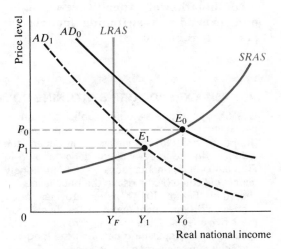

(ii) Determination of national income

**A policy to switch expenditure away from
domestic goods and toward foreign goods can
be used to solve the conflict posed by a trade
surplus combined with an inflationary gap.**
Initially, the net export function is given by NX_0 in
part (i), and aggregate demand is given by AD_0 in part
(ii). Equilibrium is at E_0 with real national income
equal to Y_0. This is an inflationary gap of $Y_0 - Y_F$ and
a trade surplus of T_0.

An expenditure-switching policy lowers net
exports at each level of income, so the net export
function shifts left to NX_1 in part (i). The policy also
lowers aggregate demand, so the aggregate demand
curve shifts left to AD_1 in part (ii). The equilibrium
moves from E_0 to E_1, real national income falls to Y_1,
and the trade surplus falls to T_1. Hence both the
inflationary gap and the trade surplus are reduced.

the inflationary gap) and toward foreign goods (thus reducing the trade account surplus).

> **Policies to induce a switch of expenditure from domestic goods to foreign goods – thereby *shifting* the net export function leftward and lowering national income – will alleviate the conflict posed by an inflationary gap combined with a trade surplus.**

This is illustrated in Figure 40.5.

A General Statement

We have now seen the difference in the effects of the two types of expenditure policies in an open economy.

> **To achieve internal and external balance, a combination of expenditure-changing and expenditure-switching policies is generally required.**

In the conflict situations, expenditure-switching policies will result in movement *toward* both targets. But they alone cannot be expected exactly to achieve both internal and external balance. Hence, both types of policies are generally required. Expenditure-switching policies are necessary to shift the net export function so that it cuts the horizontal axis at Y_F. Expenditure-changing policies can then be used to attain both internal and external balance simultaneously.

Some long-run aspects of such policies are taken up in Box 40.1.

MACROECONOMIC POLICY AND THE CAPITAL ACCOUNT

The capital account of the balance of payments records international movements of investment funds. When foreign investors buy securities

---

BOX 40.1 EXPENDITURE-SWITCHING POLICIES IN THE LONG RUN

Use of expenditure-switching policies, such as devaluation, has often been very controversial. Supporters point to the increase in output and the reduction in the trade-account deficit shown in Figure 40.4. Opponents focus on the inflationary impact indicated by the rise in the price level also shown in Figure 40.4. The controversy often hinges on disagreement about the relative size of these two effects. Some of the controversy can be defused by distinguishing between the long-run and short-run effects of such policies.

In the text we focused on the short-run effects of expenditure-switching policies, treating the *SRAS* curve as fixed and studying the shifts in the *NX* and *AD* curves. One alternative to using such policies is to do nothing, and let the monetary adjustment mechanism studied in Chapter 34 operate to eliminate the recessionary gap. (Similar automatic mechanisms also exist that establish external balance in the long run.) Justification for using devaluation, for example, in the face of a recessionary gap and a trade deficit is that these automatic adjustment mechanisms are very slow to operate. Hence support for devaluation and other expenditure-switching policies focuses on their ability to influence output and the trade account *in the short run.*

Note, however, that such policies do not alter potential output (they do not shift the *LRAS*

curve), and hence they have no effect on output in the long run. But by circumventing the monetary adjustment mechanism and stimulating aggregate demand, expenditure-switching policies ensure that when potential income is attained in the long run, the price level will be higher than it would have been in their absence. Opponents of such policies focus on this price-level effect, since that is the only long-run effect the policies have. Typically these opponents believe the automatic adjustment mechanisms are strong enough so that the long-run effect would be achieved fairly quickly without intervention or that devaluations set up expectations of price rises that quickly feed into wages and hence create very little real response of output and employment even in the short run.

The key policy implication of this debate is that when income is close to, or above, its potential level, devaluation and other expenditure-switching policies should be directed toward the external target, but they should be combined with expenditure-changing policies that focus on the internal target. In particular, a devaluation should be accompanied by expenditure-reducing policies to offset any inflationary gap caused by the devaluation in the short run and hence to avoid the price-level increase that would otherwise ensue in the long run.

issued by UK companies or governments or invest in British industry, this capital outflow is recorded as a receipt in the balance of payments, because it gives rise to an increase in the amount of foreign currency offered for sterling in the foreign-exchange market. Conversely, the acquisition of foreign assets by UK residents represents a capital outflow and is recorded as a payment because foreign currency is used up by such transactions.

The primary means by which capital flows can be influenced by the policy authorities is through domestic interest rates. International traders hold transactions balances just as domestic traders do. These balances are often lent out on a short-term basis rather than being left idle. Naturally enough, holders of these balances will tend to lend them, other things being equal, in markets where interest rates are highest. If short-term interest rates are raised in London, this will induce an inflow of short-run capital to take advantage of the higher UK rates. A lowering of UK interest rates will have the opposite effect, as capital moves elsewhere to take advantage of the now relatively higher foreign rates.

Long-term capital flows are typically less sensitive to interest-rate differentials, but they are, nevertheless, likely to show some response. In particular, British corporations and governments attempt to minimize the cost of long-term borrowing by selling bonds in foreign markets when the foreign interest rate is lower than the UK rate.

In discussing the trade account in the first part of this chapter, we did not need to distinguish between the effects of monetary and fiscal policy. However, capital flows respond to interest rates, and monetary and fiscal policies that have the same influence on income have opposite effects on interest rates. We saw in Chapter 37 that, in a closed economy, expansionary monetary policy exerts its influence on income by reducing interest rates, while an expansionary fiscal policy causes interest rates to rise. In discussing capital flows in an open economy it is therefore necessary to distinguish between the operation of monetary and fiscal policies.

Fiscal Policy and the Capital Account

The effects of fiscal policy on the capital account of an open economy are related to the interest-rate effects it would have in a closed economy. Expansionary fiscal policy, for example, leads to increased government borrowing in domestic capital markets. In a closed economy this pushes interest rates up; in an open economy it leads other domestic borrowers to import their capital requirements from foreign financial centres. Alternatively, the government may finance its deficit by itself borrowing abroad, thereby giving rise directly to a capital-account surplus. In summary:

> An expansionary fiscal policy will put upward pressure on interest rates and lead to an inflow of foreign capital, thereby moving the capital account towards a surplus. A contractionary fiscal policy will have the opposite effects.

Monetary Policy and the Capital Account

Since monetary policy influences interest rates in a closed economy, it will also influence the capital account in an open economy:

> An expansionary monetary policy will put downward pressure on interest rates and lead to an outflow of capital, thereby moving the capital account toward a deficit. A contractionary monetary policy will have the opposite effects.

An Alternative Target for External Balance

So far in this chapter we have used *external balance* to mean achieving the target level of the trade account. Consideration of international capital flows suggests an expansion of this target to incorporate the capital account and interest payments on the foreign debt as well.

> We now specify external balance in terms of a target level of the overall balance of payments.

For simplicity, we take external balance to mean a zero overall balance of payments on current and capital account with no need for transactions on the official settlements account. Thus any current-account imbalance is exactly offset by private-sector capital-account transactions.

Before turning to a discussion of how monetary

and fiscal policy might be combined to achieve internal and external balance in this circumstance, it will be useful to examine the relationship between the money supply and the overall balance of payments.

The Balance of Payments and the Money Supply

Suppose that the UK is experiencing a balance-of-payments deficit and that the Bank of England intervenes in the foreign-exchange market to maintain the value of sterling. The Bank will be selling foreign currency in exchange for sterling and thereby running down its stock of official reserves. Payment for the foreign currency acquired by private participants in the market will normally be made in the form of a sterling cheque drawn on one of the clearing banks. This cheque will be cleared by reducing the deposits of the bank at the Bank of England. These transactions are summarized in Table 40.1.

> **If there are no offsetting transactions, a balance-of-payments deficit will lead to a decrease both in bank reserves and in bank deposits equal to the amount of foreign exchange sold by the central bank. A surplus will lead to an increase in bank reserves and deposits.**

Thus a balance-of-payments deficit will lead to a contraction of the money supply. Of course, the central bank has the option of preventing this from happening by undertaking other offsetting transactions. For example, the decrease in bank reserves can be offset by an open-market purchase of bonds, which will have the effect of increasing bank reserves. This procedure of insulating the domestic money supply from the effects of balance-of-payments deficits or surpluses is known as **sterilization**.

Fixed Exchange Rates

Monetary Policy

To see the limitations of monetary policy under a fixed exchange rate, consider the following sequence of events. Suppose that interest rates in the UK are at levels similar to those in the rest of the world, and thus there is no inducement for large international movements of capital. Sup-

TABLE 40.1 Balance Sheet Changes Caused by a Sale of Foreign Currency by the Central Bank

NON-BANK PRIVATE SECTOR

Assets		Liabilities
Foreign exchange (equivalent value in Sterling)	+100	
Deposits	−100	

COMMERCIAL BANKS

Assets		Liabilities	
Reserve (deposits with central bank)	−100	Demand deposits	−100

CENTRAL BANK

Assets		Liabilities	
Foreign exchange	−100	Deposits of chartered banks	−100

The money supply is reduced when the central bank sells foreign exchange to maintain a fixed exchange rate when there is a balance-of-payments deficit. A deficit of 100 leads to an excess demand for foreign exchange of 100, which is met by a reduction of official reserves by this amount. When the Bank receives payment in the form of a cheque drawn on a commercial bank, bank reserves fall by 100.

pose now that the Bank, faced with a large recessionary gap, seeks to stimulate demand through an expansionary monetary policy. It buys bonds in the open market, thereby increasing the money supply and reducing interest rates.

Lower interest rates stimulate an outflow of capital from the UK and thus a deficit on the capital account. To the extent that national income rises, movement along the net export function creates a deficit on the trade account. Thus the overall balance of payments moves into deficit. To maintain the fixed exchange rate, the Bank will have to intervene in the foreign-exchange market and sell foreign currency. This will have the effect of *reducing* the money supply and thus *reversing* the increase brought about by the initial open-market operation.

If no other transactions are initiated by the Bank, national income and the money supply will fall and domestic interest rates will rise until they all return to their initial levels. Thus the deficit will be self-correcting, and the Bank's expansionary policy will be nullified.

Suppose now that the Bank attempts to sterilize the impact on the money supply of the balance-of-payments deficit. The difficulty with this strategy is that it can be continued only as long as the Bank has sufficient reserves of foreign exchange. If capital flows are highly sensitive to interest rates, as empirical evidence suggests is the case, these reserves will be run down at a rapid rate and the Bank will be forced to abandon its expansionary policy.

Under a fixed exchange rate, there is little scope for the use of monetary policy for domestic stabilization purposes because of the sensitivity of international capital flows to interest rates. The central bank will be forced to maintain domestic interest rates close to the levels existing in the rest of the world, and it will not be able to bring about substantial changes in the domestic money supply.

Fiscal Policy

Consider now the effectiveness of fiscal policy under fixed exchange rates. Suppose again that UK interest rates are in line with those of the rest of the world when an expansionary fiscal policy is introduced, aimed at reducing a large recessionary gap. The fiscal expansion raises the level of domestic interest rates and national income.

Higher interest rates stimulate a flow of capital into the UK, thereby leading to a surplus on the capital account. If the capital flows are large, as they are likely to be in the UK because of its close integration with world capital markets, the surplus on capital account will exceed the current-account deficit arising from the increased national income. Hence there will be an overall balance-of-payments surplus.

To maintain the fixed exchange rate, the Bank of England must intervene in the foreign-exchange market and buy foreign currency. This has the effect of increasing the money supply, thus reinforcing the initial fiscal stimulus.

Under a fixed exchange rate, interest-sensitive international capital flows stabilize the domestic interest rate and enhance the effectiveness of fiscal policy.

Combining Monetary and Fiscal Policy

Consider an attempt to increase employment with expansionary monetary policy that reduces interest rates and thereby stimulates investment and other interest-sensitive expenditures. The decline in domestic interest rates makes it more attractive to invest short-term capital abroad rather than at home. The outflow of short-term capital to be invested at more attractive rates in foreign financial centres worsens the balance of payments on the short-term capital account. Of course, if the expansionary policy succeeds in raising income, there will be additional strain on the balance of payments on current account as a consequence of the increased expenditure on imports caused by the rise in income.

In principle, the conflict can be removed by an appropriate combination of monetary and fiscal policy. Consider the country with full employment and a balance-of-payments deficit. It could eliminate the deficit by following a tighter monetary policy to increase domestic interest rates and attract short-term capital. At the same time, the contractionary effect of tight money on domestic expenditure and employment could be offset by raising government expenditure or cutting taxes. Thus the two goals can both be achieved through a combination of tight monetary policy and expansionary fiscal policy.

This strategy is unlikely to be a satisfactory solution to a persistent current-account deficit. The country will find it increasingly difficult to maintain its exchange rate by importing short-term capital. Short-term international capital flows are extremely volatile, and they are particularly sensitive to shifts in expectations concerning exchange rates. If investors lose confidence in a country's ability to maintain its existing exchange rate, capital outflows will build up, and ultimately a devaluation will be required to reduce the deficit and restore confidence.

Flexible Exchange Rates

A major advantage of a flexible exchange rate is that it removes conflicts between domestic stabilization objectives and the balance of payments, because deficits or surpluses are eliminated through movements in the exchange rate. In addition, a flexible rate often cushions the domestic economy against cyclical variations in economic activity in other countries. If, for example, the US economy goes into a recession, the decline in US income will lead to a reduction in demand for goods exported from the UK. The fall in exports will reduce income in the UK through the multiplier effect. But if the value of sterling is allowed to respond to market forces, there will also be a depreciation. This fall in sterling's external value will stimulate demand for UK exports and encourage the substitution of domestically produced goods for imports. Thus the depreciation will provide a stimulus to demand in the UK that will at least partially offset the depressing effect of the US recession.

Fiscal Policy

Suppose the government seeks to remove a recessionary gap by expansionary fiscal policy. An increase in government expenditure and/or a reduction in taxes will increase income through the multiplier effect and reduce the size of the gap. This will also tend to cause a movement along the net export function, leading to a deterioration of the trade account. However, this is not the whole story, for there will also be repercussions on the capital account and the exchange rate.

Capital flows and the crowding-out effect: In a closed economy, fiscal policy causes domestic interest rates to rise. This causes interest-sensitive private expenditures to fall, thus partially offsetting the initial expansionary effect of the fiscal stimulus. As we saw in Chapter 37, this *crowding-out effect* plays an important role in the analysis of fiscal policy in a closed economy. In an open economy the crowding-out effect will operate differently, due to international capital flows.

Higher domestic interest rates will induce a capital inflow and cause the domestic currency to appreciate. If capital flows are highly interest-elastic, the external value of the currency is likely to rise substantially. This will depress demand by discouraging exports and encouraging the substitution of imports for domestically produced goods. The initial fiscal stimulus will be *offset* by the expenditure-switching effects of currency appreciation.

Under flexible exchange rates there will be a strong crowding-out of net exports that will greatly reduce the effectiveness of fiscal policy.

However, it is possible to eliminate the crowding-out effect by supporting the fiscal policy with an accommodating monetary policy. Suppose that the Bank responds to the increase in the demand for money induced by the fiscal expansion by increasing the supply of money so as to maintain domestic interest rates at their initial level. There will then be no capital inflow and no tendency for the currency to appreciate. Income will expand by the usual multiplier process.

The effectiveness of fiscal policy under flexible exchange rates can be enhanced by an accommodating monetary policy.

Monetary Policy

We have seen that there is little scope under fixed exchange rates for the use of monetary policy for domestic stabilization purposes. Under flexible exchange rates the situation is reversed, and monetary policy becomes a very powerful tool.

Suppose the Bank seeks to stimulate demand through an expansionary monetary policy. It buys bonds in the open market, thereby increasing bank reserves and the money supply and reducing interest rates. Lower interest rates will cause an outflow of capital from the UK and thus a deficit on the capital account.

Under a fixed rate, we saw that the Bank may be forced to reverse its policy in order to stem the loss of foreign reserves. Under a flexible rate, however, sterling can be allowed to depreciate. This will stimulate exports and discourage imports so that the deficit on the capital account will be offset by a surplus on the current account.

Domestic employment will be stimulated not only by the fall in interest rates but also by the increased demand for domestically produced goods brought about by a depreciation of the currency. The initial monetary stimulus will be *reinforced* by the expenditure-switching effects of currency depreciation.

Under flexible exchange rates, monetary policy is a powerful tool for influencing domestic income and employment. If

capital flows are highly interest-elastic, the main channel by which an increase in the money supply stimulates demand for domestically produced goods is a depreciation of the currency.

Finally, consider a contractionary monetary policy. If the Bank wants to contract aggregate demand it reduces the money supply, shifting the *LM* curve to the left. This raises domestic interest rates and causes an inflow of short-term capital. The inflow in turn appreciates sterling, making it harder to export and so reinforcing the contractionary process.

The Theory of Exchange-rate Overshooting

Let us now consider this contractionary process in a little more detail. Assume that in pursuit of a restrictive monetary policy the Bank of England has forced British interest rates above those ruling in other major financial centres. A rush to lend money out at the profitable rates in London will lead to an appreciation of sterling. Where will this process stop? When will the short-term equilibrium be reached? The answer is that the rise in sterling's external value must be large enough so that investors expect it to fall in value subsequently, thus offsetting the interest premium from lending funds in the UK.

To illustrate this important point, assume that interest rates are 4 percentage points higher in London than in New York due to a very restrictive monetary policy in the UK. Investors believe the PPP rate is $2.00 = £1, but as they rush to

buy sterling they drive the rate to, say, $2.20. They do not believe this rate will be sustained and instead expect sterling to lose value at 4 per cent per year. Now foreign investors are indifferent between lending money in New York or London. The extra 4 per cent of interest they earn in London per year is exactly offset by the 4 per cent they expect to lose when they turn their money back into their own currency because they expect the external value of sterling to be falling (back towards its PPP) at that rate.

A restrictive monetary policy that raises domestic interest rates above world levels may lead to an inflow of capital that will appreciate the external value of the home currency so far that future expected depreciations just offset the interest differential.

If all the Bank wants to do is reduce aggregate demand, this added effect reduces it further, as the appreciation shifts the net export function downwards. But if the Bank is trying to achieve some long-run monetary target without causing too much short-term unemployment, these capital flows can be very disturbing. A central bank that is seeking to meet a monetary target must put up with some large fluctuations in the exchange rate. In particular, if a restrictive monetary policy is needed to hold the money supply on target, the resulting high interest rates may lead to a large overshooting of the external value of the currency above its PPP rate. This may put export and import-competing industries under temporary but very severe pressure from foreign competition.

SUMMARY

1. All systems of international monetary arrangements involve aspects of the two extremes of fixed exchange rates and flexible exchange rates.
2. Under fixed exchange rates the central bank intervenes in the foreign-exchange market to maintain the exchange rate within a narrow band around an announced par value. To do this, the Bank must hold sufficient foreign-exchange reserves. Reserves have historically been held in the form of gold or reserve currencies, particularly the US dollar. The SDR is a relatively new international paper money meant to provide additional international reserves linked neither to gold nor to the US dollar.
3. Any fixed-exchange-rate system will face three major problems: (1) providing

sufficient international reserves, (2) adjusting to long-term trends in receipts and payments, and (3) handling periodic speculative crisis.

4. Under a system of flexible, or floating, exchange rates, the rate is market-determined by supply and demand for foreign exchange.

5. Since their adoption in the mid-1970s, flexible exchange rates have fluctuated substantially. As a result, central banks have often intervened to stabilize the fluctuations. Thus the present system is called a managed, or dirty, float.

6. Policy-makers in an open economy are faced with policy targets or objectives relating to the foreign sector as well as to the domestic sector. Attainment of these targets is often called achieving external and internal balance, respectively. When policies to move the economy toward one target cause it to move away from the other, the targets are said to be in conflict.

7. Expenditure-changing policy used to control the level of national income will also influence the trade balance by altering imports. There will be a conflict of objectives if there is a trade-account deficit and a recessionary gap or if there is a trade-account surplus and an inflationary gap. Expenditure-switching policies that shift the net export function can be used to deal with conflict situations.

8. Usually, both expenditure-switching and expenditure-changing policies are needed to attain internal and external balance.

9. The capital account is influenced by both fiscal and monetary policy because both influence domestic interest rates.

10. Under a fixed exchange rate, there is little scope for the use of monetary policy to influence domestic national income. Because of the sensitivity of international capital flows to interest rates, the central bank will be forced to maintain domestic interest rates close to the levels in the rest of the world, and it will not be able to bring about substantial changes in the domestic money supply.

11. Under a fixed exchange rate, capital flows will act to reinforce the effectiveness of fiscal policy.

12. Under a flexible exchange rate, fiscal policy actions will be offset by a crowding-out effect unless they are accompanied by an accommodating monetary policy that prevents changes in interest rates and the exchange rate.

13. Under a flexible exchange rate, monetary policy is a powerful tool. When capital flows are highly interest-elastic, the main channel by which an increase in the money supply increases demand for domestically produced goods is a depreciation of the exchange rate.

TOPICS FOR REVIEW

- Fixed and flexible exchange rates
- Managed floats
- Adjustable peg
- Bretton Woods system
- International Monetary Fund
- Monetary and fiscal policy under fixed and flexible exchange rates
- Exchange-rate overshooting

41

Growth in Less Developed Countries

In the civilized and comfortable urban life of the highly developed countries, most people have lost sight of the fact that a very short time ago, *very* short in terms of the lifespan of the earth, people lived like any other animal, catching an existence as best they could from what nature threw their way. It has been less than 10,000 years since the agricultural revolution, when people changed from food gathering to food producing, and it has been only within the last century or two that a large proportion of the population of even the richest countries could look forward to anything but an endless struggle to wrest an existence from a reluctant nature. Most earlier civilizations were based on a civilized life for a privileged minority and unremitting toil for the vast majority.

THE UNEVEN PATTERN OF DEVELOPMENT

There are close to five billion people alive today, but the wealthy parts of the world – where people work no more than 40 or 50 hours per week, enjoy substantial leisure, and have a level of consumption at or above *half* of that attained by the citizens of the highest-income countries – contain less than 15 per cent of the world's population. Many of the rest struggle for subsistence. Many exist on a level at or below that enjoyed by peasants in ancient Egypt or Babylon.

Data on per capita income levels throughout the world (as in Table 41.1) cannot be accurate down to the last £100.[1] Nevertheless, such data do reflect enormous real differences in living standards that no statistical discrepancies can hide. The *development gap* – the discrepancy between the standards of living in countries at either end of the distribution – is real and large.

There are many ways to look at inequality of income distribution among the world's population. One way is a Lorenz curve, as in Figure 41.1. The more the curve bends away from the straight, 45° line, the greater is the inequality in income distribution. The Lorenz curve of in-

---

[1] There are many problems in comparing national incomes across countries. For example, home-grown food is vitally important to living standards in underdeveloped countries, but it is excluded, or at best imperfectly included, in the national-income statistics of most countries. So is the contribution of a warm climate.

**FIGURE 41.1 Lorenz Curves Showing
Inequalities Among the Nations of the World
and Within the United States**

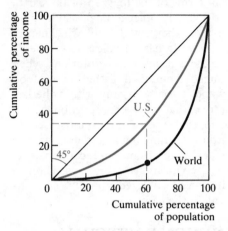

There is much less inequality in the
distribution of income within the United States
than among all the nations of the world. The
Lorenz curve for the world indicates a very unequal
distribution of income. For example, 60 per cent of
the world's population live in countries that earn only
10 per cent of the world's income, as shown by the
black dot. Contrast this with the distribution of
income within the United States. The poorest 60 per
cent of the American population earn 36 per cent of
the nation's income. This is not equality, but it is
much less unequal than the world distribution. The
UK Lorenz curve, shown on page 285, would lie
between the two existing curves if it were shown on
Figure 41.1, showing that the UK had more income
inequality than the US but less than the world
average.

---

come distribution among people in the United
States – who currently enjoy the highest real
incomes among developed nations – gives perspective on the disparity in income among countries. It is much closer to equality than the world
distribution.

The Consequences of Underdevelopment

The consequences of low income levels can be
severe. In a rich country such as the UK,
variations in rainfall are reflected in farm output
and farm income. In poor countries such as those
of the Sahel area of Africa variations in rainfall
are often reflected in the death rate. In these
countries, many live so close to subsistence that

slight fluctuations in the food supply bring death
by starvation. Other less dramatic characteristics
of poverty include inadequate diet, poor health,
short life-expectancy, and illiteracy.

For these reasons, reformers in underdeveloped countries, now often called **less-
developed countries (LDCs)**, feel a sense of
urgency not felt by their counterparts in rich
countries.[1] Yet, as the first two rows of Table 41.1
show:

**the development gap for the very poorest
countries has been widening.**

As we will see, this is a problem of both output
and population. It is also an international political problem.

Incentives for Development

Obviously the existence of relatively low national
living standards is nothing new. Concern with
them as a remediable condition, however, has
become a compelling policy issue only within the
present century. One early incentive behind this
new attention to development was the apparent
success of planned programmes of 'crash' development, of which the Soviet experience was the
most remarkable and the Chinese the most recent. Leaders in other countries asked: If they can
do it, why not us?

Demonstration effects should not be underestimated. It has been said that the real secret of the
atomic bomb was that it *could* be made, not how.
Much the same is true of economic development.
Observing other developing countries, people see
that it is possible to achieve better lives for
themselves and their children. It is bad enough to
be poor, but it is doubly galling to be poor when
others are escaping poverty.

A second incentive for development has come
from the willingness of developed countries to
aid less-developed countries. We shall discuss
such programmes and their motivation later.

---

[1] The terminology of development is often confusing. *Underdeveloped, less developed* and *developing* do not mean the same
thing in ordinary English, yet each has been used to describe
the same phenomenon. For the most part we shall refer to
these countries as the *less-developed countries*, or LDCs. Some
of them are developing; others are not. No value judgement is
implied by this choice of terms – some terms must be chosen
and no single one catches all of the characteristics of the
diverse set of countries being considered.

TABLE 41.1 Income and Population Differences Among Groups of Countries, 1985

Classification (based on gross domestic product per capita in 1980 US dollars) Group level	(1) Number of countries[a]	(2) GDP (billions)	(3) Population (millions)	(4) GDP per capita	(5) Percentage of world GDP	(6) Percentage of world population	(7) Growth rate[b]
I $400 or less	15	$548	2,099	$241	4.6	49.8	1.3
II $401–1,000	18	274	421	690	2.3	10.0	0.1
III $1,001–5,000	31	1,619	635	2,420	13.4	15.1	1.7
IV $5,001–10,000	13	4,175	613	6,794	34.7	14.5	2.0
V More than $10,000	16	5,417	448	13,251	45.0	10.6	1.4

Source: IMF International Financial Statistics Yearbook, 1987.

[a] Countries for which data are not available, and are therefore not represented in the table, account for about 9 per cent of the world's population and are mostly in the poorer categories.
[b] Average annual percentage rate of growth of real GDP per capita, 1975–1985.

Over half of the world's population lives in poverty. Many of the very poorest are in countries that have the lowest growth rates and thus fall ever farther behind. The unequal distribution of the world's income is shown in columns 5 and 6. Groups I and II, which have about 60 per cent of world population, earn less than 10 per cent of world income. Groups IV and V, with 25 per cent of world's population, earn 80 per cent of the world income. Column 7 shows that the poorest countries are not closing the gap in income between rich and poor countries.

A third incentive for development results from the emergence of a relatively cohesive bloc of LDCs within the United Nations. The bloc has attempted to use political power to achieve economic ends.

What are the causes of underdevelopment, and how may they be overcome?

BARRIERS TO ECONOMIC DEVELOPMENT

Income per capita grows when aggregate income grows faster than population. Many forces can impede such growth.

Population and Natural Resources

Rapid Population Growth

Population growth is a central problem of economic development. If population grows as quickly as national income, per capita income does not increase. Many less-developed countries have rates of population growth that are nearly as large as their rates of growth of gross

domestic product (GDP). As a result, their standards of living are barely higher than they were a hundred or even a thousand years ago. They have made appreciable gains in aggregate income, but most of the gains have been literally eaten up by the increasing population. This is shown in Table 41.2.

The population problem has led economists to talk about the *critical minimum effort* that is required not merely to increase GDP but to increase it fast enough so that the increase in output outpaces the increase in population. When population control is left to nature, nature often solves it in a cruel way. Population increases until many are forced to live at a subsistence level; further population growth is halted by famine, pestilence, and plague. This grim possibility was perceived early in the history of economics by Thomas Malthus.

In some ways, the population problem is more severe today than it was even sixty years ago because advances in medicine and in public health have brought sharp decreases in death rates. It is ironic that much of the compassion shown by wealthier nations for the people of the poor nations has traditionally taken the form of improving their health, thereby doing little to

TABLE 41.2 The Relation of Population Growth to Per Capita Income, 1975–1985 *(percentages)*

Classification of countries (based on GDP per capita in 1980 US dollars)		Average annual growth rate of			Population growth as percentage of real GDP growth
Group	Average income level	Percentage of world population	Real GDP	Population	Real GDP per capita	
I–II	$1,000 or less	59.8	3.2	2.6	0.6	81
III–IV	$1,001–10,000	29.6	3.6	1.8	1.8	50
V	More than $10,000	10.6	2.7	1.3	1.4	48

Source: Calculated from *IMF International Financial Statistics Yearbook,* 1987.

Growth in per capita real income depends on the difference between growth rates of real national income and population. The very poorest countries spend much of their increase in income on a rising population. Thus their increase in income per capita is less than half of the countries which are already richer.

avert their poverty. The medical personnel who brought modern medicine to the tropics are justifiably praised, but the elimination of malaria doubled population growth in Sri Lanka. Cholera, once a killer, is now largely under control. No one argues against controlling disease, but other steps must also be taken if the child who survives the infectious illnesses of infancy is not to die of starvation in early adulthood.

Figure 41.2 shows actual and projected world population growth. The population problem is not limited to less-developed countries, but about seven-eighths of the expected growth in the world's population is in Africa, Asia and Latin America, those areas where relatively low national living standards are the rule rather than the exception.

Insufficient Natural Resources

A country with ample fertile land and a large supply of easily developed resources will find growth in income easier to achieve than one poorly endowed with such resources. Kuwait has an income per capita above that of the United States because it is located on the world's greatest known oil field. A lack of oil proved a devastating setback to many LDCs when the OPEC cartel increased oil prices tenfold during the 1970s. Without oil, their development efforts would be halted, but to buy oil took so much scarce foreign exchange that it threatened to cripple their attempts to import needed capital goods.

The amount of resources available for production is at least in part subject to control. Badly fragmented land holdings may result from a dowry or inheritance system. When farm land is divided into many small parcels, it may be much more difficult to achieve the advantages of modern agriculture than it is when the land is available in tracts suitable for large-scale farming.

FIGURE 41.2 World Population Growth, 1400–2000

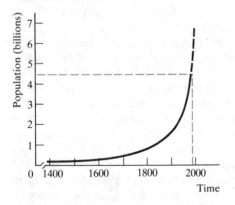

Time

The trend of growth in the world's population is explosive. The solid line shows past growth. The dashed line involves projections from observed trends. It took about 50,000 years from the emergence of modern human beings for the world's population to reach 1 billion. It took 100 years to add a second billion, 30 years to add the third billion, and 15 years to add the fourth billion. If these trends continue, the population will reach 7 billion by the year 2000.

Lands left idle because of lack of irrigation or spoiled by lack of crop rotation are well-known examples of barriers to development. Imperfect knowledge is another. The people of the Middle East lived through recorded history alongside the Dead Sea without realizing that it was a substantial source of potash. Not until after the First World War were these resources utilized; now they provide raw materials for Israel's fertilizer and chemical industries.

Inefficient Use of Resources

Low levels of income, and slower than necessary growth rates, may result from the inefficient use of resources as well as the lack of key resources.

In Chapter 23 we distinguished between two kinds of inefficiency. An hour of labour would be used inefficiently, for example, if a worker, even though working at top efficiency, were engaged in making a product that no one wanted. Using society's resources to make the wrong products is an example of *allocative inefficiency*.

In terms of the production-possibility boundary encountered in Chapter 1, allocative inefficiency represents operation at the wrong place on the boundary. It will occur if the signals to which people respond are distorted (both monopoly and tariffs are commonly cited sources of distortions) or if market imperfections prevent resources from moving to their best uses.

A second kind of inefficiency, called *X-inefficiency*, arises whenever resources are used in such a way that, even if they are making the right product, they are doing so less productively than is possible. Examples are workers too hungry, or too unmotivated, to concentrate on their tasks. X-inefficiency is not always undesirable. It may, for example, be the price societies pay when they give more weight to friendship, loyalty, and tradition than to productivity.

Inadequate Human Resources

A well-developed entrepreneurial class, motivated and trained to organize resources for efficient production, is often missing in less-developed countries. Its absence may be a heritage of a colonial system that gave the local population no opportunity to develop; it may result from the fact that managerial positions are awarded on the basis of family status or political patronage; it may reflect the presence of economic or cultural attitudes that do not favour acquisition of wealth by organizing productive activities; or it may simply be due to the absence of the quantity or quality of education or training that is required.

Poor health is likewise a source of inadequate human resources. When the labour force is healthy, less time is lost and more effective effort is expended. The economic analysis of medical advances is a young field, however, and there is a great deal to be learned about the drag of poor health on the growth of an economy.

Institutional and Cultural Patterns

Cultural Barriers

Traditions and habitual ways of doing business vary among societies, and not all are equally conducive to productivity. Max Weber argued that the 'Protestant ethic' encouraged the acquisition of wealth and hence encouraged more growth than systems of belief that directed activity away from the economic sphere.

Often in LDCs, personal considerations of family, past favours, or traditional friendship or enmity are more important than market incentives in motivating behaviour. One may find a too-small firm struggling to survive against a larger rival and learn that the owner prefers to remain small rather than expand because expansion would require use of non-family capital or leadership. To avoid paying too harsh a competitive price for built-in inefficiency, the firms' owners may then spend much of their energies influencing the government to prevent larger firms from being formed or securing restrictions on the sale of output. Such behaviour inhibits economic growth.

In an environment where people believe that it is more important who your father is than what you do, it may take a generation to persuade employers to change their attitudes and another generation to persuade workers that times have changed. In a society in which children are expected to stay in their fathers' occupations, it is more difficult for the labour force to change its characteristics and to adapt to the requirements of growth than in a society where upward mobility is itself a goal.

Structuring incentives is a widely used form of policy action in market-oriented economies. But if people habitually bribe the tax collector rather than pay taxes, they will not be likely to respond to policies that are supposed to work by raising or lowering taxes. All that will change is the size of the bribe.

There is lively debate on how much to make of the significance of differing cultural attitudes. Some believe that traditional considerations dominate peasant societies to the exclusion of economic responses; others suggest that any resulting inefficiency may be relatively small.

The fact that existing social, religious or legal patterns may make growth more difficult does not in itself imply that they are undesirable.

Instead it suggests that the benefits of these patterns must be weighed against the costs, of which the limitation on growth is one. When people derive satisfaction from a religion whose beliefs inhibit growth, when they value a society in which every household owns its own land and is more nearly self-sufficient than in another society, they may be quite willing to pay a price in terms of growth opportunities forgone.

Inadequate Infrastructure

Key services, called **infrastructure**, such as transportation and a communications network, are necessary to efficient commerce. Roads, bridges, railroads and harbours are needed to transport people, materials and finished goods. The most dramatic confirmation of their importance comes in wartime, when belligerents always place high priority on destroying each other's transportation facilities.

Reasonable phone and postal services, water supply, and sanitation are essential to economic development. The absence, whatever the reason, of a dependable infrastructure can impose severe barriers to economic development.

Money spent on a new steel mill seems to show more impressive results than money spent on automating the telephone exchanges. Yet private, growth-creating entrepreneurial activity will be far more discouraged by the absence of good telephone communications than by the lack of domestically produced steel.

Inadequate Financial Institutions

The lack of an adequate and trusted system of financial institutions is often a barrier to development. Investment plays a key role in growth, and an important source of funds for investment is the savings of households and firms. When banks and other financial institutions do not function properly, the link between private saving and investment may be broken and the problem of finding funds for investment greatly intensified.

People in many LDCs do not trust banks, sometimes with good reason, sometimes without. Either they do not maintain deposits or they panic periodically, drawing them out and seeking security for their money in mattresses, in gold, or in real estate. When banks cannot count on their deposits being left in the banking system, they cannot make the loans needed to finance investments. As a result, increases in savings do not become available for investment in productive capacity.

Developing countries must not only create banking institutions, they must create enough stability and reliability that people will trust their savings to such financial intermediaries.

Excessive Government Intervention

As noted above, the early successes of the growth policies of many socialist countries – particularly the USSR and China – inspired much of the belief that development of the LDCs was possible. Not surprisingly, the governments of many LDCs sought to copy the planning techniques that appeared to underlie these earlier socialist successes.

In recent decades, however, most of the more developed socialist countries have been forced to an understanding of the limitations of their planning techniques. Highly planned government intervention seems most successful in providing infrastructure and in developing basic industries such as electric power and steel where these are needed. It is now seen to be much less successful in providing the entrepreneurial activity, risk-taking and adaptivity to change that are key ingredients to sustained economic growth in the very long run. As a result,

the USSR, China and most of the other Eastern bloc countries are all moving towards putting more reliance on decen-

tralized, profit-oriented decision-taking, co-ordinated by markets rather than by central planning bodies.

The governments of many of the world's present LDCs have learned these lessons from their own bitter experience. Others have yet to learn them. As a result, growth is often hampered by excessive and rigid bureaucratic intervention. There is room for central government planning of the outlines of growth policies, but the experience of those countries that have gone furthest with central planning is that the limits of planning are quickly met. They find that decentralized markets are better adapted to unleashing the entrepreneurial activity that is critically important to growth in the very long run.

SOME BASIC CHOICES

There are many barriers to economic development that, singly and in combination, can keep a country poor.

Economic development policy involves identifying the barriers to the level and kind of development desired and then devising ways to overcome them. Although the problems and strategies vary greatly from country to country, there are common basic choices that all developing countries must face.

How Much Government Control?

How much government control over the economy is necessary and desirable? Practically every shade of opinion from 'The only way to grow is to get the government's dead hand out of everything' to 'The only way to grow is to get a fully planned, centrally controlled economy' has been seriously advocated.

These extreme views are easily refuted by historical evidence. Many economies have grown with very little government assistance: Great Britain in the industrial revolution, Holland during the heyday of its colonial period, Singapore, Hong Kong and Taiwan during modern times. Others, such as the Soviet Union and

Austria, have sustained growth with a high degree of centralized control. Other countries have successfully used almost every conceivable mix of state and private initiative.

As noted in the previous section, however, the evidence is that it is difficult to sustain growth over long periods under highly centralized planning systems. There is still room for debate, however, on the appropriate mix of government and market determination of economic decisions at various stages in the growth process.

The Case for Planning

The case for active government intervention in the management of a country's economy rests on the real or alleged failure of market forces to produce satisfactory results. The major appeal of such intervention is its power to accelerate the pace of economic development particularly in its early stages.

Many barriers to development may be lowered by appropriate government actions.

For example, when living standards are low, people have urgent uses for their current income, so savings tend to be low. Governments can intervene in a variety of ways and force people to save more than they otherwise would in order to ease a shortage of investment funds.

Compulsory saving has been one of the main aims of most development plans of centralized governments, such as those of the USSR and China. The goal of such plans is to raise savings and thus lower current consumption below what it would be in an unplanned economy. A less authoritarian method is to increase the savings rate through tax incentives and monetary policies. The object is the same: to increase investment in order to increase growth, and thus to make future generations better off.

Authoritarian central governments can be particularly effective in overcoming some of the sources of X-inefficiency. A dictatorship may suppress social and even religious institutions that are barriers to growth, and it may hold on to power until a new generation grows up that did not know and does not value the old institutions. It is much more difficult for a democratic government, which must command popular support at each election, to do currently unpopular things in the interests of long-term growth. Whether the gains in growth that an authoritarian government can achieve are worth the political and social costs is, of course, an important value judgment.

An important role of planning is to direct growth in a different direction, one that the planners guess will have the greatest chance of long-run success.

Unplanned growth will usually tend to exploit the country's present comparative advantages; planners may choose a pattern of growth that involves trying to change the country's future comparative advantages.

One reason planners seek to do so is their belief that they can evaluate the future more accurately than the countless individuals whose decisions determine market prices. As we saw in Chapter 21, a country need not passively accept its current comparative advantages. Many skills can be acquired, and fostering an apparently un-economic domestic industry may, by changing the characteristics of the labour force, develop a comparative advantage in that line of production.

The Case for the Market

Most people would accept that government must play an important part in any development programme, especially in programmes concerning education, transportation and communication. But what of the sectors usually left to private enterprise in advanced capitalist countries?

The advocates of relying on market forces in these sectors place great emphasis on human drive, initiative and inventiveness. Once the infrastructure has been established, they argue, an army of entrepreneurs will do vastly more to develop the economy than will an army of civil servants. The market will provide the opportunities and direct their efforts. People who seem lethargic and unenterprising when held down by lack of incentives will show bursts of energy when given sufficient self-interest in economic activity.

Furthermore, the argument goes, individual capitalists are far less wasteful of the country's capital than civil servants. Bureaucrats investing capital that is not their own (raised perhaps from the peasants by a state marketing board that buys

cheap and sells dear) may choose to enhance their own prestige at the public's expense by spending too much money on cars, offices, and secretaries and too little on truly productive activities. Even if the bureaucrats are genuinely interested in the country's well-being, the incentive structure of a bureaucracy does not encourage creative risk taking. If their ventures fail, their heads will likely roll; if they succeed, they will receive no profits – and their superior may get the medals. Thus they will be cautious about taking risks.

What Sorts of Education?

Most studies of LDCs suggest that under-education is a barrier to development and often urge increased expenditures on education. This poses a choice: whether to spend educational funds on erasing illiteracy and increasing the level of mass education or on training a small cadre of scientific and technical specialists.

To improve basic education requires a large investment in school building and in teacher training. This investment will result in a visible change in the level of education only after 10 or more years, and it will not do much for product-ivity even over that time span. The opportunity cost of basic education expenditures always seems high. Yet it is essential to make them because the gains will be critical to economic development a generation later.

Many developing countries have put a large fraction of their educational resources into train-ing a small number of highly educated men and women, often by sending them abroad for ad-vanced study, because the results of acquiring a few hundred doctors or engineers or Ph.D.s are relatively more visible than the results of raising the school-leaving age by a year or two, say, from age 10 to age 12. It is not yet clear whether the policy of 'educating the few' pays off, but it is clear that it has some drawbacks.

Many of this educated elite become highly dedicated specialists who work hard for their country's welfare. Others, however, regard their education as the passport to a new aristocracy rather than as a mandate to serve their fellow citizens; and an appreciable fraction emigrate to countries where their newly acquired skills bring higher pay than they do at home. Of those who return home, some seek the security of a government job, which they may utilize to advance their own status in what is sometimes a self-serving and unproductive bureaucracy.

What Population Policy?

The race between population and income has been a dominant feature of many less-developed countries.

Where population is growing rapidly, there are only two possible ways for a country to win this race. One is to make a massive effort to achieve an income growth rate well in excess of the population growth rate. The other is to control population growth.

The problem *can* be solved by restricting population growth. This is not a matter of serious debate, but the desirability of, and the means for, restricting it are disputed, for considerations of religion, custom and education are involved.

The consequences of different population policies are large. The birthrate in Sweden is 12 per thousand, in Venezuela it is 42 per thousand, and the two countries have similar death rates. The variations in birthrates have economic consequences. In Venezuela the net increase of population per year is 33 per thousand (3.3 per cent), but it is only 3 per thousand (0.3 per cent) in Sweden. If each country were to achieve an overall rate of growth of output of 3 per cent per year, Sweden's living standards would be increasing by 2.7 per cent per year, while Venezuela's would be falling by 0.3 per cent per year. In 1985 Sweden's income per capita ($9,000) was two and one-half times as high as Venezuela's ($3,600) – and Venezuela is the wealthiest country in South and Central America. The gap will widen rapidly if present population trends continue.

Population control can take forms as mild as public education programmes designed to alter attitudes toward family size and to encourage the avoidance of involuntary pregnancies. At the other extreme are massive programmes of compulsory sterilization, such as the then Prime Minister Indira Gandhi attempted in India in the mid-1970s. Between these extremes are many possibilities, most of which use various economic and legal incentives or penalties to encourage a lower birthrate.

Customs can be changed to raise the average marriage age and hence lower the birthrate. Prohibition of child labour and the establishment of compulsory education alters the costs and benefits of having children and may reduce desired family size. Changing the role of women and providing career alternatives outside the home can also lower the birthrate.

University of Maine Professor Johannes Overbeck reported recently that a comprehensive family-planning programme – involving the provision of a broad selection of birth-control techniques, a broad range of social services, and accelerated research to develop more effective and cheaper contraceptives – would have an annual cost of £0.50 per capita in a typical less-developed country. Excluding mainland China, this amounts to around £1 billion per year for all LDCs combined, a relatively modest sum compared with the over £250 billion currently spent annually on armaments. If this estimate is roughly accurate, population policy offers an extremely high return on spending to promote per capita growth in LDCs.

The political, religious and cultural dimensions of population policy lead some governments to resist population control. Positive economics cannot decide whether population control is desirable, but it can describe the consequences of any choice. Economic development is much easier to achieve with population control than without it.

How to Acquire Capital?

A country can raise funds for investment in three distinct ways: from the savings (voluntary or forced) of its domestic households and firms, by loans or investment from abroad, and by contributions from foreigners.

Capital from Domestic Saving: The Vicious Circle of Poverty

If capital is to be created by a country's own efforts, resources must be diverted from production for current consumption. This means a cut in present living standards. If living standards are already near the subsistence level, such a diversion will be difficult. At best, only a small proportion of resources can be reallocated to the production of capital goods.

BOX 41.1 DEBT AND THE LDCs

The 1970s and early 1980s witnessed explosive growth of the external debt of many LDCs. In the last half of the 1980s a number of these countries experienced difficulties in making the payments required to service their debt. 'Debt reschedulings' – that is, putting off until tomorrow payments that cannot be made today – have been common, and by the beginning of the 1990s many observers felt that major defaults were inevitable.

The trend to increased debt started when OPEC quadrupled the world price of oil in 1973. Because many LDCs relied on imported oil, their balance of trade moved sharply into deficit. At the same time, the OPEC countries developed massive trade surpluses. Commercial banks helped *recycle* the deposits of their OPEC customers into loans to the deficit LDCs. These loans financed some necessary adjustments and worthwhile new investment projects in the LDCs. However, not all of the funds were used wisely; wasteful government spending and lavish consumption splurges occurred in a number of borrowing countries.

A doubling of energy prices in 1979 led to a further increase in LDC debt. The severe world recession that began in 1981 reduced demand for the exports of many of the LDCs. As a result, the LDCs were unable to achieve many benefits from the adjustments and investment expenditures they had made. Furthermore, sharp increases in real interest rates led to increased debt service payments; as a result, many of the LDCs could not make their payments.

The lending banks had little choice but to reschedule the debt – essentially lending the LDCs the money to make interest payments while adding to the principal of the existing loans. The IMF played a central role in arranging these reschedulings, making further loans and concessions conditional on appropriate policies of adjustment and restraint. These conditions presumably were intended to limit wasteful government expenditure and consumption and thus increase the likelihood that the loans would eventually be repaid. Critics of the IMF's role, however, argued that much of the restraint resulted in reduced investment, and thus the IMF conditions were counterproductive.

In the mid-1980s, the world economy recovered and interest rates fell. As a result, the LDCs' export earnings grew, their debt service obligations stabilized, and the crisis appeared to subside. The sharp *fall* in the price of oil, which started in late 1985, further eased the problems of the oil-importing LDCs, but it also created a new debt problem.

Throughout the period of rising energy prices, a number of *oil-exporting* LDCs – including Mexico, Venezuela and Indonesia – saw in those high prices new opportunities for investment and growth. Based on their high oil revenues, their ability to borrow improved. Their external debt grew, and they were able to avoid many of the adjustments that the oil-importing LDCs had been forced to undertake. When oil prices fell, these oil-exporters found themselves in a very difficult position.

Mexico provides an illustrative case study. Its oil revenues doubled from around $8 billion in 1978 to $16 billion by 1982. This increased earning capacity led to increased borrowing, and its external debt also doubled in the same period, from $40 billion in 1978 to $80 billion in 1982. Even with its high oil revenues, however, not all was well; in the words of the *Economist* magazine,

---

Such a situation is often described as the **vicious circle of poverty**: because a country has little capital per head, it is poor; because it is poor, it can devote few resources to creating new capital rather than to producing goods for consumption; because little new capital can be produced, capital per head remains low, and the country remains poor.

The vicious circle can be made to seem an absolute constraint on growth rates. Of course it is not; if it were, we would all still be at the level of Neanderthal man. The grain of truth in the vicious circle argument is that some surplus must be available somewhere in the society to allow saving and investment. In a poor society with an even distribution of income, where nearly everyone is at the subsistence level, saving may be very difficult. But this is not the common experience. Usually there is at least a small middle class that can save and invest if opportunities for the profitable use of funds arise. Also in most poor societies today the average household is above the physical subsistence level. Even the poorest households will find that they can sacrifice some present living standards for a future gain. For example, presented with a profitable opportunity, villagers in Ghana planted cocoa plants at the turn of the century even though there was a seven-year growing period before any return could be expected!

'Mexico officially opened the international debt crisis in 1982.'

For a number of reasons, including bad investment decisions and the world recession, Mexico's export earnings did not increase as fast as its debt. Soaring real interest rates meant that by 1982 Mexico was unable to service its debt. Only a major debt rescheduling, conditional on severe fiscal restraint and a devaluation to stimulate exports, prevented a default.

Continued borrowing, much of it necessary just to service its existing debt, meant that Mexico's debt continued to rise; by 1986 the debt had risen to $100 billion. For much of this period, the spending restraint in Mexico combined with the recovery in the world economy and the fall in world interest rates led to a gradual improvement in Mexico's prospects for growing out from under its debt burden. But in 1986 world oil prices fell, and Mexico's oil revenues plummeted to around $8 billion. A new crisis emerged.

The situation in the late 1980s was different from the situation in 1982 in several important ways. The world economy and the international financial system were both healthier. Lower real interest rates and lower oil prices meant that other LDCs were able to service their loans; hence there was less fear of a collapse of the international financial system.

But for Mexico the later crisis was worse than the earlier one. Domestic restraint had been pushed virtually to the limit; the government deficit had been cut by over 6 per cent of GNP in just two years. Headlines in the international press proclaimed, 'With Mexico Focusing on Debt Repayment, Ports and Roads Suffer', and 'Mexican Children Scrounge for Food as Schools Drop Free Lunch'.

Projections showed that Mexico would require major foreign borrowing if it were to continue to meet its interest obligations on existing debt. Commercial banks were not anxious to lend any more on their own initiative. The IMF tried to negotiate a loan package based on further restraint, and the US proposed a plan with renewed lending conditional on major economic adjustment. But further restraint and rapid adjustment seemed politically impossible in a country already racked by massive restraint and plummeting export revenues; many economists argued that restraint would in any event retard growth and prove counter-productive.

A major impasse thus arose. Using the threat of default, Mexico demanded major concessions on the terms of its new borrowing. The 'crisis' situation stimulated innovative proposals. One proposal was for the banks to forgive some debt in return for equity participation in Mexico's oil and other industries; this would reduce the burden of Mexico's debt service payments while sharing some of the risks of the Mexican situation between Mexico and its creditors.

In mid 1986 an agreement was reached providing for major new borrowing; for the first time in IMF history, the terms not only included conditions that appropriate adjustment policies be undertaken but also a provision for repayment linked to the price of the borrowing country's exports, in this case oil. This provision was intended to forestall further crises by allowing the required payments to fluctuate with the country's ability to pay. By the end of the decade Mexico had still not solved the basic problem of how to eliminate the heavy burden that its foreign debt placed on its economy.

An important consideration is that in less-developed countries one resource that is often *not* scarce is labour. Profitable home or village investment that requires mainly labour inputs may be made with relatively little sacrifice in current living standards. However, this is not the kind of investment that will appeal to planners mesmerized by large and symbolic investments such as dams, nuclear power stations and steel mills.

Imported Capital

Another way of accumulating the capital needed for growth is to borrow it from abroad. When a poor country borrows from a rich country, it can use the borrowed funds to purchase capital goods produced in the rich country. The poor country thus accumulates capital and needs to cut its current output of consumption goods only to pay interest on its loans. As the new capital begins to add to current production, it is possible to pay the interest on the loan and also to repay the principal out of the increase in output. This method has the great advantage of giving a poor country an initial increase in capital goods far greater than it could possibly have created by diverting its own resources from consumption industries.

There are two ways to obtain foreign capital (other than by gift). First, governments or agencies and firms directly under government control may borrow it. This method was heavily used after the first OPEC oil shock in 1973. During the next 12 years reliance on foreign borrowing exploded to the point where it became a serious international problem, for both LDCs and their creditors. During the 1970s the rising cost of oil to many oil-importing less-developed countries combined with over-optimistic income expectations and led to massive borrowing by the LDCs. High interest rates in the 1980s greatly raised the cost of servicing this debt. World recession and rising protectionism in the developed world made it more difficult to earn the money necessary to pay interest on, let alone repay, the principal. For oil-importing countries the collapse of oil prices in 1985 provided some relief, but for oil exporters such as Mexico the oil price decline made things much worse. This problem had reached the dimensions of a crisis by the mid-1980s and is discussed with reference to Mexico in Box 41.1.

The second way in which foreign, non-gift capital can be obtained is through capital brought in by foreign companies – the so-called *multinational* or *transnational* corporations. Historically many countries, developed and undeveloped, have been suspicious of foreign capital. They fear foreign investors will gain control over their industries or their government.

The extent of foreign control depends on the form foreign capital takes. When foreigners buy bonds in domestic companies, they do not own or control anything. When they buy common stocks or shares, they own part or all of a company, but their control over management may be small. When foreign companies establish plants and import their own managers and technicians, they have much more control. Finally, when foreign firms subsidize an LDC government in return for permission to produce, they may feel justified in exacting political commitments.

Contributed Capital

Investment funds for development are being received today by LDCs from the governments of the developed countries. These governments sometimes act unilaterally (for example, the programme of the US Agency for International Development and a similar Soviet programme) and sometimes act through international agencies such as the World Bank, the Export-Import Bank, and the OPEC Fund established in January 1980. These funds are not really outright gifts, but are 'soft' loans, where repayment is not demanded in the near future. It is common to label them *contributed capital* to distinguish them from hard loans, where repayment is expected under normal commercial terms.

The heyday of contributed capital was the post Second World War cold-war period, when the United States, the Soviet Union and others sought to win the allegiance of Third World LDCs by making soft loans and outright gifts. Today Japan is the largest single source of contributed capital and other forms of aid to LDCs.

DEVELOPMENT STRATEGIES

In the search for development, individual LDCs have a number of policy options. The choice of options is in part a matter of what the planners believe will work and in part a question of the nature of the society that will be created once development has occurred.

In so far as they wish to influence the pattern of growth, governments must choose between agricultural and industrial emphases, between different kinds of industrial development, and between more or less reliance on foreign trade. Several possibilities have been widely advocated, and each has been tried. None is without difficulties.

Agricultural Development

Everyone needs food. An LDC may choose to devote a major portion of its resources to stimulating agricultural production, say, by mechanizing farms, irrigating land, and utilizing new seeds and fertilizers. If successful, the country will stave off starvation for its current population, and it may even develop an excess over current needs and so have a crop available for export. A food surplus can earn foreign exchange to buy needed imports.

India, Pakistan, Taiwan, and other Asian countries have achieved dramatic increases in food production by the application of new technology and the use of new seed in agricultural production. Increases of up to 50 per cent have been achieved in standards of living. But the gains from this strategy, while large at first, are subject to diminishing returns. Further gains in agricultural production have an ever higher opportunity cost, in the resources needed to irrigate land and to mechanize production. Critics of sole reliance on agricultural output argue that underdeveloped economies must start at once to develop other bases for economic growth.

One problem with heavy reliance on the agricultural strategy is that it frequently requires heavy initial subsidization of agricultural production and also some means of subsidizing consumption of increased quantities of food by a poor population. A common device is to provide artificially high prices to producers and artificially low prices to consumers. Once such a programme is put in place it creates a serious policy dilemma. Continuation of the artificially high prices for producers and low prices for consumers creates a substantial drain on the government's finances. Lowering the subsidy to producers risks a rural revolution; eliminating the subsidy to consumers risks an urban revolution. The government finds itself with an untenable policy, but with no room for manoeuvre.

Specialization in a Few Commodities

Many LDCs have unexploited resources such as copper, uranium or opportunities for tourism. The principle of comparative advantage provides the traditional case for the desirability of relying on such resources. By specializing in producing those products in which it has the greatest comparative advantage, the country can achieve the most rapid growth in the short run. To neglect these opportunities will result in a lower standard of living than would result from specialization accompanied by increased international trade.

These are cogent reasons in favour of *some* specialization. But specialization involves risks, and it may be worthwhile to reduce the risks by maintaining diversification even at the cost of loss of some income. Specialization in a few commodities makes the economy highly vulnerable to cyclical fluctuations in world demand and

supply. For example, a recession in developed countries or fear of terrorism decreases overseas travel and creates problems for an LDC that has relied on tourism for foreign exchange.

The problem is not only short run. When technological or taste changes render a product partially or wholly obsolete, a country can face a major calamity. Just as individual firms and regions may become overspecialized, so too may countries.

Import Substitution

During the Great Depression the collapse in world agricultural prices caused the value of the exports of agricultural countries to decline drastically relative to the prices of goods those countries imported. During the Second World War many countries found that the manufactured goods they wished to import were unavailable. In each of those situations dependence on foreign trade for necessities was unattractive. During the 1970s, the rising prices of fuel and other imports created enormous balance-of-payments problems for many LDCs. Such countries were forced to reduce imports, increase exports or resort to foreign borrowing.

Much of the industrialization by LDCs in the 1950s and 1960s was directed toward **import substitution**, that is, the production of home goods that were previously imported. It is often necessary both to subsidize the home industry and to restrict imports to allow the new industries time to develop.

LDCs sometimes pursue certain lines of production on a subsidized basis for prestige purposes or because of a confusion between cause and effect. Because most wealthy nations have a steel industry, the leaders of many underdeveloped nations regard their countries as primitive until they develop a domestic steel industry. Because several LDCs have succeeded in producing consumer durables, many others assume that they should try to do so. However, if a country has a serious comparative disadvantage in steel or in making consumer durables, fostering such industries will make that country even poorer.

The import-substitution strategy has many problems. It fosters industries that are currently inefficient, and in the long run countries do not get rich by being inefficient. It aggravates inequalities in income distribution by raising the prices of manufactured goods relative to agricultural goods and by favouring profits over wages.

Export Development

Most development economists believe that to maximize the changes of achieving sustained economic growth, industrialization ought to be encouraged only in areas where the country can develop a reliable and efficient industry that can compete in world markets.

Obviously, if Tanzania or Peru could develop steel, shipbuilding and manufacturing industries that operated as efficiently as those of Japan or West Germany, they might share in the rapid economic growth enjoyed by those industrial countries. Indeed, if a decade or two of protection and subsidization could give infant industries time to mature and become efficient, the price might be worth paying. After all, within living memory Japan and South Korea were underdeveloped countries.

Industrialization for export can sometimes be done by employing inexperienced workers in simple, labour-intensive enterprises, such as sewing clothing. But it often means devoting resources for a long period to education, training, infrastructure development, and overcoming any cultural and social barriers to efficient production. While this is hard, it is not impossible. Indeed, there have been some spectacular success stories. Brazil, South Korea, Hong Kong, Singapore and Taiwan are charter members in the category of **newly industrialized countries (NICs)** that are providing vigorous competition in manufactured goods in world markets.

Import substitution and export development do not need to be seen as alternative development strategies. Many now successful trading countries used import substitution in the first stages of their development strategy. The intention was to create the domestic industrial base and the human capital that were needed for industrial success. Once that base was in place, emphasis could be shifted to export encouragement.

Canada used import substitution to build its industries behind high tariff walls in the first half of the twentieth century. Then, throughout the second half of the century, it has lowered tariffs to integrate its developing export industries into the world economy. Singapore and Korea used import substitution policies in their early stages of development. Japan also did so in selected industries. The most recent example was in semiconductors (which include the chips that drive computers) where the domestic industry developed in a highly protected home market and then went on to lead the world in exports of semiconductors.

The challenge is not, therefore, to choose at an early stage of growth between import substitution and export development policies for all time. The challenge, if import substitution policies are adopted first, is to be able to shift into export-encouraging policies at a later stage. Such a shift will not occur if the wrong industries are chosen for import substitution so that they remain sickly infants indefinitely, or if strong vested interests in the sheltered industries are able to prevent the country's later transition to an export-oriented strategy.

Cartelization

When all or most producers of a commodity can agree on price and output levels, they can achieve monopoly profits not available in competitive markets. Many LDCs are heavily committed to the production and export of one or more basic commodities such as bananas, bauxite, cocoa, coffee, copper, cotton, iron ore, jute, manganese, meat, oil, phosphates, rubber, sugar, tea, tropical timber and tin. Why do not all producers of, say, bananas get together and create an effective cartel that gives producers the enormous profits that are potentially available?

Cartelization has been tried many times in history. Until OPEC it has always failed, yet everyone knows that OPEC transformed a handful of formerly poor LDCs into the wealthiest of nations.[1] OPEC's success was substantial, but proved impossible to sustain. The special reasons for its success for almost 10 years and its eventual failure were discussed in Chapter 15.

---

[1] This has added to the terminological confusion. It was once fashionable to speak of a non-aligned *third world* as another term for LDCs, the first two 'worlds' being the developed capitalist and developed socialist countries. Now some commentators divide the LDCs into a richer (oil-producing) *third world* and a still poor *fourth world*.

Wheat, coffee, cocoa, tin, rubber and copper have all been suggested as potential subjects for similar commodity price stabilization agreements, but they lack the small number of politically cohesive producers and inelastic short-run demand and supply conditions that gave the OPEC cartel its initial successes.

SOME UNSETTLED ISSUES

The Speed of Development

Reformers in underdeveloped countries often think in terms of transforming their economies within a generation or two. The sense of urgency is quite understandable but unless it is tempered by some sense of historical perspective, totally unreasonable aspirations may develop – only to be dashed all too predictably. Many underdeveloped countries are probably in a stage of development analogous to that of medieval England – they have not yet developed anything like the commercial sophistication of the Elizabethan era. It took 400 years for England to develop from that stage to its present one. To do the same elsewhere in half the time of 200 years would be a tremendous achievement; to aspire to do it in 25 or 50 years may be to court disaster. How fast an LDC can sensibly plan to develop remains an unsettled issue.

Population Policy

The view presented in this chapter is neo-Malthusian and constitutes the current conventional wisdom on underdevelopment. There are, however, opposing views.

The neo-Malthusian view gives no place for the value of children in parents' utility functions. Critics point out that the psychic value of children should be included as part of the living standards of their parents. They also point out that in rural societies even quite young children are a productive resource because of the work they can do; while fully grown children provide old-age security for their parents in societies where state help for the aged is negligible.

The neo-Malthusian theory is also criticized for asserting that people breed blindly like animals. Critics point out that traditional methods of limiting family size have been known and practised since the dawn of history. Thus they argue that large families in rural societies are a matter of choice. The population explosion came not through any change in 'breeding habits' but by medical advances that greatly extended life expectancy (which surely must be counted as a direct welfare gain for those affected). The critics argue that once an urban society develops, family size will be reduced voluntarily. This was certainly the experience of Western industrial countries and why, ask the critics, should it not be the experience of the now-developing countries?

The Cost of Creating Capital

Is it true that developing countries must sacrifice current living standards if they wish to invest in future growth? Production of consumption and capital goods are substitutes for each other only if factor supplies are constant. But, say the critics, the development of a market economy will lead people to substitute work for leisure. For example, the arrival of Europeans with new goods to trade led the North American Indians to collect furs and other commodities needed for exchange. Until they were decimated by later generations of land-hungry settlers, the standard of living of the Indians rose steadily with no immediate sacrifice. They created the capital needed for their production – weapons and means of transport – in their abundant leisure time so that their consumption began to rise immediately. This too, the argument runs, could happen in LDCs if market transactions were allowed to evolve naturally. The spread of a market economy would lead locals to give up leisure in order to produce saleable output that would provide the money needed to purchase new goods that private traders were introducing from the outside world.

Other controversies exist but this discussion should be sufficient to suggest that in development economics, as in all other branches of the subject, established views should always be regarded as open to challenge from conflicting theories and awkward facts.

SUMMARY

1. About one-fourth of the world's population still exists at a level of bare subsistence, and nearly three-fourths are poor by the standards of advanced countries. The gap between rich and poor is large, and is not decreasing.
2. Impediments to economic development include excessive population growth, resource limitations, inefficient use of resources, inadequate infrastructure, and institutional and cultural patterns that make economic growth difficult.
3. A series of basic choices face LDCs who are adopting development pro-grammes. How much should governments intervene in the economy, and how much should the economy be left to operate on the free market? History has demonstrated that growth is possible with almost any conceivable mixture of free-market and central control. Centralized planning can change both the pace and direction of economic development; it can also prove wasteful and hamper individual initiative.
4. Educational policy, while vitally important to the long-run rate of economic development, yields its benefits only in the future. Improvement of basic education for the general populace is sometimes bypassed for the more immediate results of educating a selected technical and political elite.
5. The race between output and population is a critical aspect of development efforts in many countries. Different countries have different attitudes towards limiting population growth and have chosen different population policies.
6. Capital for development is a major concern. It can be acquired from domestic savings, but the vicious circle of poverty creates a serious barrier. Importing capital rather than using domestic savings permits heavy investment during the early years of development, but imported capital is available only when the LDC has opportunities that are attractive to foreign investors. Much foreign capital for LDCs in the last three decades has been from soft loans or contributions by foreign governments and international institutions.
7. Development involves choices among different strategies: agricultural devel-opment, specialization based on natural resources, development of import-substitution industries, development of export industries, and cartelization.
8. A multipronged strategy that includes at least some agricultural development, some development of new export commodities, and some restraint on population growth has much to recommend it.
9. Controversial unresolved issues include the appropriate pace of development, the neo-Malthusian view of population growth as problem, and the size of the cost of creating capital in terms of the sacrifices of current consumption.

TOPICS FOR REVIEW

- The gap between LDCs and developed countries
- Barriers to development
- Infrastructure
- Role of planning in development
- Alternative development strategies

42

Macroeconomic Controversies

How well do markets work? Can government improve market performance? In various guises these two questions are the basis of most disagreements over economic policy. Different answers to these questions imply big differences in macroeconomic policy prescriptions.

ALTERNATIVE VIEWS: NON-INTERVENTIONIST AND INTERVENTIONIST

Macroeconomics is mainly concerned with the behaviour of three important variables: employment (and unemployment), the price level, and the rate of economic growth. Macroeconomic policy suggests goals for each: full employment, stable prices, and a satisfactory growth rate. The advantages of full employment and a positive growth rate are obvious and not subject to serious dispute. Although most people agree that inflation is harmful, there is much debate about what social ills can really be blamed on it.

Broadly speaking, we can identify a non-interventionist and an interventionist view with respect to each of the policy goals just specified. The non-interventionist view says that the unaided market economy can best achieve the goal. The interventionist view says that government policy can improve the economy's performance in terms of that goal. Since one can take a non-interventionist or an interventionist position with respect to each of these three goals, there are eight different possible policy combinations.[1]

Consider two extreme policy stances: *non-interventionists* oppose government intervention on all issues, while *interventionists* support government intervention at all times. A few people may actually be non-interventionist or interventionist in this sense. Most, however, would favour intervention on some issues and oppose it on others. They might still identify themselves as non-interventionist or interventionist because they were more often on one side than the other.

It is popular to identify monetarist with non-interventionist and Keynesian with interven-

---

[1] Since each of the three issues breaks up into hundreds of different sub-issues, there are thousands of different policy stances available by combining on one side or the other of each issue.

tionist. It is true that many monetarists are on the non-interventionist side, while many Keynesians are on the interventionist side. But it is not always so. For example, many economists are Keynesian in accepting the Keynesian macro model as a reasonable description of the economy's macro-economic behaviour, but non-interventionist in believing that the unaided market usually does a reasonably good job of allocating resources.

The Non-interventionist View

Non-interventionists believe that the free-market economy performs quite well on balance. Although shocks do hit the system, they lead rather quickly, and often painlessly, to the adjustments dictated by the market system. For example, relative prices in booming sectors rise, drawing in resources from declining sectors or regions. As a result, resources (and particularly labour) usually remain fully employed, so there is no need for full-employment policies.

> **Non-interventionists hold that macro-economic performance will be most satisfactory if it is determined solely by the workings of the free market.**

Of course, few believe that the market system functions perfectly, thereby ensuring *continuous* full employment. But the view is that the market system works well enough to preclude any constructive role for policy.

In addition, many non-interventionists believe that policy instruments are so crude that their use is often counter-productive. A policy's effects may be so uncertain, with regard to both strength and timing, that it may often impair rather than improve the economy's performance.

In a modern economy some government presence is inevitable. Thus a stance of no intervention is impossible; rather, what is advocated by noninterventionists is minimal direct intervention in the market system. The government is, however, responsible for providing a *stable environment* in which the private sector can function.

The Interventionist View

Interventionists believe that the functioning of the free-market economy is often far from satisfactory. Sometimes markets show weak self-regulatory forces and the economy settles into prolonged periods of heavy unemployment. At other times markets tend to 'overcorrect,' causing the economy to lurch between the extremes of large recessionary and large inflationary gaps.

This behaviour can be improved, argue the interventionists.

> **Interventionists hold that although interventionist policies are imperfect, they are good enough to improve the functioning of the economy with respect to all three main goals of macro policy.**

MACROECONOMIC ISSUES

Everyone agrees that the economy's performance is often less than perfectly satisfactory. Serious unemployment has been a recurring problem. Inflation was a serious problem throughout the 1970s and early 1980s. For most of that period, UK growth rates were unsatisfactorily low. Non-interventionists and interventionists differ in diagnosing the causes of these economic ills.

In this section, we consider four key macro-economic issues – the trade cycle, the behaviour of the price level, the existence of macroeconomic equilibrium, and economic growth. In the first two of these, we contrast the views of the monetarists with those of the Keynesians. Although these two groups do not exactly co-incide with non-interventionists and interventionists, the monetarist views do provide much of the intellectual underpinnings of the non-interventionist positions while the Keynesian views do provide much of the underpinnings of the interventionist case. In subsequent discussions, we deal directly with interventionist and non-interventionist views.

The Trade Cycle

We saw in Chapter 36 that cyclical ups and downs can be observed for as far back as records exist. Monetarists and Keynesians have long argued about the causes.

Monetarist views: Monetarists believe that the economy is inherently stable because private-sector expenditure functions are relatively stable. In addition, they believe that shifts in the aggregate demand curve are mainly due to policy-induced changes in the money supply.[1]

The view that trade cycles have mainly monetary causes relies partly on the evidence advanced by Milton Friedman and Anna Schwartz in their monumental *A Monetary History of the United States, 1867–1960*. They establish a strong correlation between changes in the money supply and changes in economic activity. Major recessions have been associated with absolute declines in the money supply and minor recessions with the slowing of the rate of increase in the money supply below its long-term trend.

The correlation between changes in the money supply and changes in the level of economic activity is accepted by many economists. But there is controversy over how this correlation is to be interpreted. Do changes in money supply cause changes in the level of aggregate demand and hence of business activity, or vice versa?

Friedman and Schwartz maintain that changes in the money supply cause changes in business activity. They argue, for example, that the severity of the Great Depression was due to a major contraction in the money supply that shifted the aggregate demand curve far to the left.

According to monetarists, fluctuations in the money supply cause fluctuations in national income.

This leads the monetarists to advocate a policy of stabilizing the growth of the money supply. In their view this would avoid policy-induced instability of the aggregate demand curve.

More recent work has shown that the Friedman-Schwartz relations are not as close, even in the US, as these authors tried to show. Attempts to establish a similar close relation for the UK have not been successful. Nonetheless, there is a broad association – even if a loose one –

between changes in the money supply and changes in money national income. When, for example, the latter rises rapidly during an inflation, the former rises as well.

Keynesian views: The Keynesian view on cyclical fluctuations in the economy has two parts. First, it emphasizes variations in investment as a cause of trade cycles and stresses the non-monetary causes of such variations.[1]

Keynesians reject what they regard as the extreme monetarist view that only money matters in explaining cyclical fluctuations. Many Keynesians believe that both monetary and non-monetary forces are important in explaining cycles. Although they accept serious monetary mismanagement as one potential source of economic fluctuations, they do not believe that it is the only, or even the major, source of such fluctuations. Thus they deny the monetary interpretation of trade-cycle history given by Friedman and Schwartz. They believe that most fluctuations in the aggregate demand curve are due to variations in the desire to spend on the part of the private sector and are not induced by government policy.

Keynesians also believe that the economy lacks strong natural corrective mechanisms that will always force it easily and quickly back to full employment. They believe that while the price level rises fairly quickly to eliminate *inflationary* gaps, the asymmetries noted in earlier chapters imply that prices and wages fall only slowly in response to recessionary gaps. As a result, Keynesians believe that recessionary gaps can persist for long periods of time unless they are eliminated by an active stabilization policy.

The second part of the Keynesian view on cyclical fluctuations concerns the alleged correlation between changes in the money supply and changes in the level of economic activity. In so far as this correlation exists, the Keynesian explanation reverses the causality suggested by the monetarists. Keynesians argue that changes in the level of economic activity often cause changes

[1] The view that fluctuations often have monetary causes is not new. The English economist R. G. Hawtrey, the Austrian Nobel Laureate F. A. von Hayek, and the Swedish economist Knut Wicksell were prominent among those who have given monetary factors an important role in explaining the turning points in cycles and/or the tendency for expansions and contractions, once begun, to become cumulative and self-reinforcing. Modern monetarists carry on this tradition.

[1] Like the monetarists, the Keynesians are modern advocates of views that have a long history. The great Austrian (and later American) economist Joseph Schumpeter stressed such explanations early in the present century. The Swedish economist Wicksell and the German Speithoff both stressed this aspect of economic fluctuations before the emergence of the Keynesian school of thought.

in the money supply. They offer several reasons for this, but only the most important need be mentioned.

Keynesians point out that from 1945 to the mid-1970s most central banks tended to stabilize interest rates as the target variable of monetary policy. To do this they had to increase the money supply during upswings in the business cycle and decrease it during downswings. When an expansion got under way, the demand for money tended to increase, and if there was no increase in the money supply, interest rates would rise. The central bank might prevent this rise in interest rates by buying bonds offered for sale at current prices, but in so doing it would increase banks' reserves and thereby inject new money into the economy. Similarly, in a cyclical contraction interest rates would tend to fall unless the central bank stepped in and sold bonds to keep interest rates up. Generally it did so, thereby decreasing the money supply. This behaviour caused the *LM* curve to shift in the same direction as the *IS* curve, and created the positive correlation between changes in money and changes in national income on which the monetarists rely.

According to Keynesians, fluctuations in national income are often caused by fluctuations in expenditure decisions. Further, they believe that fluctuations in national income often cause fluctuations in the money supply.

Nevertheless, most Keynesians also agree that policy-induced changes in monetary policy can cause national income to change.

The Price Level

As we saw in Chapter 34, sustained inflation requires a sustained expansion of the money supply.

Motives for such excessive monetary expansions have varied from time to time and place to place. Sometimes central banks have rapidly increased the money supply in an effort to end a recession. Then, when the economy expanded due to its own natural recuperative forces, the increased money supply allowed a significant inflation during the boom phase of the cycle. At other times central banks have tried to hold interest rates well below their free-market levels.

To do this they buy bonds to hold bond prices up. We have seen that these open-market operations increase the money supply and so fuel an inflation. At still other times central banks have helped governments finance large budget deficits by buying up the new public debt. These open-market operations provide what is popularly known as *printing press finance*. The steady increase in the money supply fuels a continuous inflation.

Monetarist views: Many monetarists hold that inflation is everywhere and always a monetary phenomenon. They thus focus on changes in the money supply as the key source of shifts in the *AD* curve.

According to monetarists, all inflations are caused by excessive monetary expansion and would not occur without it.

Keynesian views: Keynesians agree that a sustained rise in prices cannot occur unless it is *accompanied by* continued increases in the money supply. Keynesians also emphasize, however, that temporary bursts of inflation can be caused by shifts in the *AD* curve brought about by increases in private- or public-sector expenditure. If such inflations are not validated by monetary expansion, they are brought to a halt by the monetary adjustment mechanism.

Keynesians also accept the importance of supply-shock inflations. Again, they accept that such inflations cannot go on indefinitely unless accommodated by monetary expansion. But Keynesians argue that 'temporary' inflation due to either *AD* or *SRAS* shifts can go on long enough to be a matter of serious policy concern.

Many Keynesians also take seriously the possibility of wage-cost push inflation that we studied in Chapter 34. Whenever this type of inflation exists, it makes full employment incompatible with a stable price level.

Macroeconomic Equilibrium

In all previous chapters we have assumed a single completely inelastic long-run aggregate supply (*LRAS*) curve. This curve defines a unique level of national income towards which the economy gravitates in the long run. The associated level of unemployment is called the non-accelerating inflationary rate of unemployment (NAIRU), or the natural rate of unemployment. It is all frictional unemployment in a static economy, and frictional plus structural unemployment in a growing, changing economy.

The view that the economy has a unique macroeconomic equilibrium gained general acceptance in the 1970s. It has, however, come under serious criticism from some recent developments in Keynesian economics. To isolate the issues involved, we shall confine ourselves from here on to a static, non-growing economy.

The Evolution of the Concept

To understand the modern debate, we need to review briefly how the concept of macroeconomic equilibrium has evolved since the beginning of Keynesian economics. That evolution has been towards allowing less and less scope for interventionist fiscal policy – at least until the very recent developments that we discuss later.

Phase 1 – the diagonal cross: The earliest Keynesian models were of the type laid out in Part 8. Equilibrium national income occurred where the aggregate desired expenditure curve cut the 45° line. This equilibrium income would be equal to potential (i.e. full-employment) income only by accident. Whenever it was less than potential income, there was a place for interventionist fiscal policy designed to make the two coincide.

Phase 2 – the simple Phillips curve: In the 1960s, the Phillips curve was added to the Keynesian model. As long as wage costs were flexible upwards and downwards, the long-run equilibrium level of income was now uniquely determined at the non-inflationary level of unemployment and national income. This is where the Phillips curve cut the productivity growth line or, what is the same thing, where the unit-cost inflation curve cuts the zero axis. (See pages 603–604.)

In this model, however, the government could permanently select an inflationary level of national income as long as it was willing to validate the inflation with the necessary monetary expansion. In other words, the appropriate interventionist policy would allow the government to achieve any desired point on the Phillips curve.

To do this, fiscal policy would be used to shift the *IS* curve so that it intersected the *LM* curve at the desired level of real income. Monetary policy would then be used to prevent the resulting inflation from shifting the *LM* curve to the left. This is done by increasing the nominal money supply at the same rate as the price level is rising, thus holding the real money supply constant.

Phase 3 – the expectations-augmented Phillips curve: The accelerationist hypothesis removed the above-mentioned possibility by adding the expected inflation rate to the simple Phillips curve. If the government tried to hold the economy at any point on the expectations-augmented Phillips curve associated with some positive rate of inflation, the Phillips curve would begin to shift upwards. This is because the expected rate of inflation would be continually rising to catch up with the actual rate. Maintaining the target level of income and employment would thus require accepting an ever-accelerating rate of inflation. Since sooner or later such a policy would have to be abandoned, the unique NAIRU was the only viable objective for national income policy. Thus interventionist policy could not affect the level of income and employment at which the economy settled. All it could do, at best, was to speed up the adjustment when cyclical forces caused income to deviate from the NAIRU. Interventionists called for such a stabilization policy; non-interventionists rejected it because they felt it was likely to be perverse in its effects and because the economy's natural adjustment forces were thought to be strong.

Modern Controversies

The view given in phase 3 underlies the theories in the macro part of this book. We have already alluded, however, to a more modern controversy that calls this view into question.

Non-interventionist views: A key component of the non-interventionist view is that policy cannot affect the level of potential income – long-term economic growth aside. This view is based on the belief that at any point in time the economy has a unique equilibrium level of income and employment which cannot be altered by policy.

It is sometimes thought that uniqueness of

full-employment equilibrium is the same thing as a vertical *LRAS* curve. This is incorrect because the argument for the perfectly inelastic *LRAS* curve (see page 588) does not require a unique equilibrium. Instead it is based solely on the absence of money illusion. To see this, assume that there is an equilibrium level of national income consistent with some equilibrium in each of the economy's markets. If we now add a zero to all prices, nothing real changes and the same real equilibrium will be consistent with the new price level. This argument shows that any single equilibrium income that exists is consistent with any price level – provided only that there is no money illusion. In other words, any given equilibrium real national income is associated with a vertical *LRAS* curve, showing that income to be independent of the price level. This does not, however, prove uniqueness, because the argument applies to *any* equilibrium income, no matter how many equilibria there may be.

Now let us look further at the argument for uniqueness. It requires that there be a unique equilibrium in each of the economy's many markets. Aggregating output and employment over all of these markets, gives an equilibrium level of national income, and of total employment, that is unique at any moment in time. The theoretical underpinning of this view is a well-known result that is proven in the so-called Arrow-Debreu model – a model named after the two Nobel-prize winning, American economists who developed it. The result is that there is a unique equilibrium for an economy all of whose markets are perfectly competitive (and which also fulfil a number of other stringent conditions).

Working from this basic Arrow-Debreu result, non-interventionists argue that potential income is unaffected by the cyclical behaviour of the economy. Thus there is no need to worry about what happens to potential income and the NAIRU when the economy is left to follow whatever cyclical path is produced by private-sector, market forces. Government policy can thus be left to concentrate on controlling inflation and providing a stable climate in which private firms can flourish.

Interventionist views: The interventionist view starts by criticizing the assumption that the economy's macroeconomic equilibrium is unique. The Arrow-Debreu model, composed as it is, solely of perfectly competitive markets, presents a highly stylized view of the real economy. No one has yet proved that there is a unique equilibrium in a model that captures the mixture of perfectly competitive, oligopolistic and monopolistic markets that characterizes real modern economies. Without such a proof, there is not even a theoretical prediction of uniqueness of macroeconomic equilibrium for modern industrial economies. Furthermore, we cannot know if a given theoretical prediction is correct until it passes some reasonable empirical tests, and no such evidence for uniqueness has yet been gathered. Until uniqueness has been derived as a prediction from a model which captures modern market structures, and has been tested empirically, the assumption of the existence of a unique macroeconomic equilibrium remains a speculative leap in the dark.

The second part of the interventionist critique is based on the development of theories that cast doubt on the uniqueness assumption. These theories arose partly out of attempts to explain the prolonged resession that beset most of the countries of the EC during the 1980s.

One class of such theories is based on the idea of 'hysteresis', which describes situations in which the equilibrium state of a system depends on the path by which that equilibrium is approached. In such cases, the equilibrium is said to be *path-dependent*. Of course, it cannot then be unique.

One way in which an equilibrium can be path-dependent is related to capital. To see what is involved, let the economy start from a position of macroeconomic equilibrium and then consider two cases. In case 1, there is a short recession followed by a return to potential income and the NAIRU. In case 2, there is a prolonged recession, lasting most of a decade, followed by a return to potential income and the NAIRU.

Consider first the effect on physical capital. During the short recession, physical capital and labour will both be unemployed. When the recovery quickly follows, the unemployed capital and labour will be put back to work and the new full-employment equilibrium will be the same as the original one. In the long recession, however, capital may not be replaced as it wears out since demand is too low to employ all of the existing capital. When the economy eventually recovers, the remaining capital stock will become fully employed while there is still substantial unemployed labour. Thus the NAIRU will be met at a higher level of unemployment than after the short recession because the capital stock will be smaller due to the longer period of the recession. (This argument assumes a fixed capital/labour ratio embodied in existing capital – see the discussion on pages 326–327.)

Similiar results can occur with human capital. A short recession will have little effect on human capital. A prolonged recession will cause many young people entering the labour force for the first time to remain for years without a job, thus losing the on-the-job training that goes with early job experience. When the recovery comes, they are different people, with different attitudes and less human capital, than they would have been if they had worked during their early formative years. Others who did have jobs during the recession may have been less inclined to invest in further human capital because the prospects of moving to a better job were bleak. Since capital is productive, less human capital implies less output from any given amount of employment. When recovery finally comes, full-employment national income will thus be lower than it would have been if the recession had been short-lived. Furthermore, those who have lost out on the chance of developing human capital may remain in the ranks of the unemployed or semi-employed for a much longer period – some for the rest of their lives.

To see the other side of this coin, consider a period of boom characterized by an inflationary gap, income above potential and unemployment below the NAIRU. The boom may lead people to acquire more human capital than they would under full employment. When normal conditions return, potential income may be higher because more human capital means more output from a given amount of employment. Furthermore, the NAIRU may be lower because a better-trained, more adaptable workforce results in lower frictional and structural unemployment.

These possibilities provide reasons for the interventionist position that the government should use stabilization policy to prevent prolonged periods of slump. They also provide

reasons for saying that occasional recessionary gaps, with their accompanying unemployment, are more serious than occasional inflationary gaps with their mild inflations and high employment.

Another quite different source of non-uniqueness of macroeconomic equilibrium arises from possible union behaviour. Suppose unions understand the conflict between higher wages and higher employment that follows from a downward-sloping demand curve for labour. Suppose, however, that they care only about their members. A short recession leads to layoffs, but those without jobs stay in the union and are re-employed when the recovery occurs. Now let there be a prolonged recession. Once again employment falls, but this time the unemployed drift out of the union. The union who cares only about its members will then wish to protect the existing level of wages. The unemployed have no say in the matter because they are not union members. Having got to a period of low employment, the economy tends to stay there because the union protects the interests of the already employed who have no desire to cut wages to increase employment of non-members.

This possibility provides a rationale for altering institutions to give more representation in wage bargaining to the unemployed. But in the absence of such a major reform, it also provides a rationale for government intervention to prevent the emergence of prolonged periods of unemployment – periods which prevent the unemployed from having a say in making the trade-off between higher employment and higher wages.

These non-uniqueness theories are still in their infancy, although some evidence has already been gathered in their favour.

The key point in the present discussion is that the assumption of the uniqueness of macroeconomic equilibrium at any point of time is just that – an assumption which does not follow from any general equilibrium theory describing the economy as we know it, and which has, as yet, no strong empirical evidence in its favour.

Competing theories predicting the path-dependence of equilibrium provide genuine alternatives. Current empirical work is attempting to discriminate between the uniqueness and non-uniqueness hypotheses, and much more will no doubt be learned about them over the next decade.

Growth

Non-interventionist views: Non-interventionists feel that in a stable environment free from government interference, growth will take care of itself. Large firms will spend much on research and development. Where they fail, or where they suppress inventions to protect monopoly positions, the genius of backyard inventors will come up with new ideas and will develop new companies to challenge the positions of the established giants. Left to itself the economy will prosper, as it has in the past, provided only that inquiring scientific spirit and the profit motive are not suppressed.

Interventionist views: Interventionists, and indeed many Keynesians, are less certain than are non-interventionists about the ability of market forces to produce growth. While recognizing the importance of invention and innovation, they fear the dead hand of monopoly and cautious business practices that choose security over risk-taking. Therefore, they believe that the state needs, at the very least, to give a nudge here or there to help the growth process along.

THE ROLE OF POLICY

The non-interventionist and the interventionist diagnoses of the economy's ills lead, not surprisingly, to very different prescriptions about the appropriate role of economic policy.

Non-interventionist Prescriptions

It is not necessary to distinguish non-interventionist policies with respect to full employment and with respect to stable prices. This is because non-interventionists believe that both goals will be achieved by the same basic policy: provision of a stable environment in which the free-market system is to operate.

Full Employment and Stable Prices: Providing a Stable Environment

Creating a stable environment, as the non-interventionists advocate, may be easier said than done. We focus on the prescriptions for establishing stable fiscal and monetary policies.

One major problem to keep in mind is that macro variables are interrelated. The stability of one may imply the instability of another. In such cases, a choice must be made. How much instability of one aggregate can we tolerate to secure stability in another related aggregate?

Assume, for example, that the government decides to adopt the goal of stability in the budget balance as part of the stable environment. This 'stability' would require great *instability* in tax and expenditure policy. Tax revenues depend on the interaction between tax rates and the level of national income. With given tax rates, tax revenues change with the ebb and flow of the cycle. A stable budget balance would require that the government raise tax rates and cut expenditure in slumps and lower tax rates and raise expenditure in booms.

Not only does this squander the budget's potential to act as a stabilizer, but great instability of the fiscal environment is caused by continual changes in tax rates and expenditure levels. A stable fiscal environment requires substantial stability in government expenditures and tax rates. Stability is needed so the private sector can plan for the future within a climate of known patterns of tax liabilities and government demand.

> **Any target budget balance must be some average over a period long enough to cover a typical cycle. Stability from year to year should be found in tax rates and expenditure programmes, *not* in the size of the budget balance.**

This in turn requires that the budget deficit vary cyclically, showing its largest deficits in slumps and its largest surpluses in booms.

Advocates of a stable monetary environment are actually advocating stable inflation. Whether a *zero* rate is feasible or not is still debated. The central bank is urged to set a target rate of increase in the money supply and hold it. To establish the target, the central bank estimates the rate at which the demand for money would be growing if actual income equalled potential income and the price level were stable. As a first approximation this can be taken to be the rate at which potential income itself is growing.[1] This then becomes the target rate of growth of the money supply. The key proposition is that the money supply should be changing gradually along a stable path that is independent of short-term variations in the demand for money caused by cyclical changes in national income. This is referred to as a *k per cent rule*.

Will the *k* per cent rule really provide monetary stability? The answer is, not necessarily.

Assuring a stable rate of monetary growth does not assure a stable monetary environment. Monetary shortages and surpluses depend on the relation between the supply and the demand for money.

The *k* per cent rule looks after supply, but what about demand? Problems arise when the demand for money shifts. For example, payment of interest on checking deposits increases the demand for M1. In this event, if the Bank adheres to a *k* per cent rule for M1, there will be an excess demand for money and interest rates will rise. Thus contractionary pressure will be put on the economy.

Should the Bank commit itself to a specific *k* per cent rule or merely work toward unannounced and possibly variable targets? The announced rule makes it easier to evaluate how well the Bank is doing its job. It also helps to prevent the Bank from succumbing to the temptation to fine-tune the economy.

One disadvantage of the announced rule is that it sets up speculative behaviour. If, for example, when weekly money supply figures are announced there is too much money, speculators know that the Bank will sell more bonds in the future to reduce the surplus. This will depress the price of bonds. Speculators are thus induced to sell bonds, hoping to rebuy them at bargain prices once the Bank acts.

Stable pre-announced monetary targets can introduce instability into interest-rate behaviour.

---

[1] Such a rule assumes that members of the public wish to keep their money holdings in a fixed proportion to their real income. If other demand patterns are established, that is, if desired money holdings as a proportion of real income change as income rises, then the Bank can alter its monetary target appropriately.

A second disadvantage of such a rule is that the Bank, in order to preserve its credibility, may fail to take discretionary action that would otherwise be appropriate. For example, after an entrenched inflation is broken, the economy may come to rest with substantial unemployment and a stable price level. There is then a case for a once-and-for-all discretionary expansion in the money supply to get the economy back to full employment. The *k* per cent rule precludes this, condemning the economy to a slump.

Despite these problems non-interventionists believe the *k* per cent rule is superior to any known alternative. Some would agree that, in principle, the central bank could improve the economy's performance by occasional bouts of discretionary monetary policy to offset such things as major shifts in the demand for money. But they also believe that once given any discretion, the central bank would abuse it in an attempt to fine-tune the economy. The resulting instability would, they believe, be much more than any instability resulting from the application of a *k* per cent rule in an environment subject to some change.

Long-term Growth

Non-interventionists want to let growth take care of itself. They argue that governments cannot improve the workings of free markets and that their interventions can interfere with market efficiency. Thus they push for reducing the current level of government intervention as the best pro-growth policy.

Interventionist Prescriptions

Interventionists call for different policies for the three policy goals of full employment, price stability and growth. As we consider their prescriptions, we give their reasons for rejecting the non-interventionist case.

Full Employment

Interventionists call for discretionary fiscal and monetary policies to offset significant inflationary and recessionary gaps. Some of the major problems associated with discretionary stabilization policy have been discussed in earlier chapters.

A Stable Price Level

Some interventionists, particularly a group

called *post-Keynesians*, believe that the *k* per cent rule may not be enough to achieve full employment and stable prices simultaneously. This is because they accept the wage-cost-push theory of inflation discussed in Chapter 34.

These people call for incomes policies to restrain the wage-cost push and so make full employment compatible with stable prices. They believe that such policies should become permanent features of the economic landscape.

Wage-price controls might work as *temporary* measures to break inflationary inertias, but as permanent features they would introduce inefficiencies and rigidities.

More permanent incomes policies might be of the type commonly used in the past decades but now out of favour, a *social contract*. Labour, management and the government consult annually and agree on target wage changes. These are calculated to be non-inflationary, given the government's projections for the future and its planned economic policies.

Growth

Policies for intervention to increase growth rates are of two sorts. Some policies seek to alter the general economic climate in a way favourable to growth. They typically include subsidization or favourable tax treatment for research and development, for purchase of plant and equipment, and for other profit-earning activities. Measures to lower interest rates temporarily or permanently are urged by some as favourable to investment and growth. Most interventionists support these general measures.

Some also support more specific intervention, usually in the form of what is called *picking and backing winners* in one way or another. Advocates of this view want governments to pick the industries, usually new ones, that have potential for future success and then to back them with subsidies, government contracts, research funds, and all of the other encouragements at the government's command.

Opponents argue that picking winners requires foresight and that there is no reason to expect the government to have better foresight than private investors. Indeed, since political considerations inevitably get in the way, the government may be less successful than the market in picking winners. If so, channelling

funds through the government rather than through the private sector may hurt rather than help growth.

Many of the issues discussed in this chapter so far have been debated by economists for decades. Over the last decade, several theoretical issues, centring around the so-called New Classical model, have been hotly debated. Although the debates have subsided somewhat, and although there is much less confidence in it than there was a few years ago, the New Classical model deserves some attention in a chapter devoted to macroeconomic controversies.[1]

THE NEW CLASSICISM

Traditional monetarists tried very hard to establish a major difference in underlying theory between themselves and neo-Keynesians. In the main this was not successful and the Keynesian-monetarist debate was carried on mainly within the confines of the general model outlined in the present book.[2] However, during the late 1970s and the 1980s a radically different model was developed. This model refined many monetarist views and took them to their logical conclusion. This New Classical model really was a different theoretical model from Keynesian-style macro models. Traditional monetarists were then forced to decide whether or not they would accept the New Classical model. Some, such as Milton Friedman, did not. These economists then found the differences that divided them from the neo-Keynesians small relative to what divided them from the New Classicists.[3] At this point Milton Friedman ceased to be the intellec-

[1] My own views on this model coincide with those expressed by Alan Blinder in his paper, 'The Fall and Rise of Keynesian Economics', invited paper presented to the 1988 Australian Economics Conference and published in the *Australian Economic Record*.

[2] For a survey of these attempts, see D. Purvis, 'Monetarism: A Review', *Canadian Journal of Economics*, vol. XIII, No. 1, February 1980.

[3] For example, the reader is hard pressed to find really fundamental differences between the position taken by James Tobin, the leader of the American neo-Keynesians, and David Laidler, a monetarist who does not accept the New Classicism, in their exchange in the *Economic Journal*, vol. 99, No. 361, March 1981. Probably their biggest difference is some implicit disagreement over the shape of the short-run Phillips curve when Y is less than Y_F.

tual leader of the extreme monetarist school and the mantle passed to the leaders of the New Classical school such as Robert Lucas of Stanford University.

The major characteristics of the New Classical model are as follows.

(1) All markets behave as if they were perfectly competitive. In particular, price adjusts in all markets until there are neither unsatisfied buyers nor unsatisfied sellers. This means that involuntary unemployment does not occur, since this requires that there are unsatisfied sellers of labour who would like to work at the going wage rate but cannot find a job.

(2) Deviations from full-employment equilibrium occur only where people make mistakes. The really important mistake is the confusion of a change in the absolute price level with a change in relative prices.

(3) Since the theory of rational expectations implies that people do not make systematic mistakes, there is no systematic pressure for output and employment to diverge from its static equilibrium value.

(4) As we shall see, cyclical behaviour can nonetheless occur as a result of changes in people's willingness to trade off work and leisure between the present and the future. This in turn occurs as a result of anticipated changes in the relation between the current and the future real wage rate which determines the so-called inter-temporal terms of trade.

In the New Classical model, all unemployment is voluntary. Employment can fall below its static full-information, full-employment level because of a mistaken anticipation of a fall in real wage rates. Unemployment can show a cyclical path without anyone making errors because a change in the inter-temporal terms of trade causes people to decide to vary the amount that they work.

Let us see how these results are derived.

The Lucas Aggregate Supply Function

The New Classical model starts from the static full-information equilibrium. This is the equilibrium that is reached when everyone has complete information about all relevant economic magnitudes. Deviations from this complete equilibrium occur only because people make mistakes.

Employment deviations can be caused by mistakes either of the workers or the employers. For simplicity, we assume that it is the workers who make mistakes while employers correctly foresee all relevant market forces. The resulting variations in employment can be analysed by what is called the *Lucas aggregate supply function* after the American economist Robert Lucas, its originator.

In the Keynesian aggregate supply function, the direction of causality runs from aggregate demand to real national income to the price level. The Lucas aggregate supply function reverses the direction of causation, making it run from the price level to aggregate demand and national income.

Recall that in Chapter 34 inflation was broken up into three components – demand, expectational and shock inflation:

$$\dot{P} = \dot{P}_d + \dot{P}_e + \dot{P}_s . \tag{1}$$

First, assume zero shock inflation for simplicity. Second, recall that expectational inflation depends on expectations of future wage costs and hence future inflation. Third, note that demand inflation depends on $Y - Y_F$. Taking all of this into account, we write (1) as

$$\dot{P}_t = \mathrm{F}(Y - Y_F)_t + \dot{P}^e_{t-1} \tag{2}$$

where $\dot{P}_t$ is this period's inflation rate, $(Y - Y_F)_t$ is this period's recessionary or inflationary gap, F is the 'Phillips curve' function that translates the gap into demand inflation, and $\dot{P}^e_{t-1}$ is the expectation of inflation in period t formed in the previous period. This is the neo-Keynesian view where the inflation rate is the dependent variable which is determined by $Y - Y_F$ (which is in turn determined by the *IS-LM* part of the model) and by expectations of inflation (plus shocks, currently assumed to be zero for simplicity).

In the New Classical model, as we have already seen, output deviates from its full-employment level when mistakes are made in predicting price level. Thus in the New Classical model the output gap is the dependent variable determined by the prediction errors on the inflation rate. To see how this occurs, we need to go beyond the labour-market analysis of Chapter 35. Assume that everyone, employers and employees, expect a rise in the price level of 10 per cent over their current planning period. Assume that prices actually rise by 15 per cent. Each firm sees its price rise by 15 per cent and mistakes this for a rise of 5 per cent in its own relative price (since each only expects the general price level to rise by 10 per cent). Each firm, therefore, decides to produce more. Similar considerations apply to labour. Thus when everyone is underpredicting the rate of inflation, they are misinterpreting their own price increase in excess of their expected rate of inflation as an increase in their relative price (when it is really just a part of the actual rate of inflation). Similar considerations suggest that if everyone is overpredicting the actual rate of inflation, each will be incorrectly believing that their own relative price is falling. Assume for example that everyone expects a 10 per cent inflation but the actual rate is only 5 per cent. So they see their own price rise by 5 per cent and incorrectly think it has fallen relative to all other prices, which they expect to rise by 10 per cent.

For the above reasons, real output, Y, will exceed the equilibrium output Y_F if the actual rate of inflation exceeds the expected rate, while Y will fall below Y_F if actual inflation is less than the expected rate. This gives us

$$Y_t - Y_F = G(\dot{P}_t - \dot{P}^e_{t-1}) \ . \tag{3}$$

In other words the deviation of output from its 'full-employment' level depends on the deviation of actual from expected inflation. As a next step we introduce the rational expectations theory of inflationary expectations. As we saw in Chapter 34, this requires that people do not make systematic errors. Instead their prediction of what the inflation rate will be at time t, which they make at time $t-1$, will be equal to the actual inflation rate plus a random error term ε:

$$\dot{P}^e_{t-1} = \dot{P}_t + \varepsilon_t \ . \tag{4}$$

For some periods ε will be positive, indicating an overestimate of the inflation rate. In other periods it will be negative, indicating an underestimate. But on average over a large number of periods, ε will be zero, indicating no systematic, long-term tendency to over-or underestimate the inflation rate.

Substituting (4) into (3) yields

$$Y_t - Y_F = G(\varepsilon_t) \ . \tag{5}$$

But now we seem to have proved too much; there is no systematic business cycle; all departures of Y from Y_F are random. To avoid this obviously unrealistic prediction, the Lucas supply function introduces a lag so that

$$Y_t - Y_F = G(\varepsilon_t) + \alpha(Y_{t-1} - Y_F) \\ 0 < \alpha < 1 \tag{6}$$

This introduces an inertia that makes income behave cyclically. But the disturbances which cause income to change are essentially random, and if the disturbances were zero for a long time, the gap, $Y_t - Y_F$, would approach zero so that output would tend to settle down at Y_F.

In this model, variations in output around its full-employment level are caused by errors in predicting the inflation rate. When combined with the theory of rational expectations, this makes the impulse for variations essentially random.

This model has been named the rational expectations model. This is a misnomer, since rationally formed expectations can be used in any model. For example, rational expectations of the expected rate of inflation can be used in the Keynesian model of inflation without altering its basic conclusions. The Lucas supply function depends on a New Classical market-clearing model plus rationally formed expectations of the inflation rate. Hence 'the New Classical model' is a better description of the model rather than 'the rational expectations model'.

In this model, variations in output around its static equilibrium level are caused by errors in predicting the rate of inflation. In this case, all employed workers should say at the end of each decision period that they had been voluntarily unemployed, and that they wished they had taken one of the jobs that they could have had. If they had correctly predicted the real wage rate, they would have worked. As it was, however, they stayed unemployed because, by overpredicting the inflation rate, they predicted a real wage rate that was lower than it turned out to be.

No doubt this sort of error can occasionally occur. No evidence has, however, been gathered to show that bouts of sustained unemployment, such as experienced throughout the EC countries in the 1980s, stem from incorrect predictions of the inflation rate by workers causing them to work less than they would in static, full-informational equilibrium.

The Equilibrium Trade Cycle

The variations in employment that we have just studied are due to errors. According to the rational expectations part of the New Classical model, such errors cannot be systematic. They should therefore give rise to random variations of employment around its full-informational, static equilibrium level. One attempt to avoid this result is the ad hoc introduction of a lagged adjustment of the type shown in (6) above.

Another attempt attempt to reconcile the New Classical model with the observed, *systematic* cyclical variations in real national income, employment and unemployment which we call the trade cycle, lies in the *equilibrium theory of the trade cycle*. This theory assumes that markets always clear. There are no unsatisfied buyers or sellers, hence no involuntary unemployment. In contrast, Keynesians and traditional monetarists see the trade cycle as a largely disequilibrium phenomenon. Both prices and quantities are sluggish to adjust. Variations of output and employment from full equilibrium can thus be the result of disequilibria in which output and labour markets have not cleared. For example, *involuntary* unemployment may exist. Workers would like to sell their labour services at the going wage rate but cannot find willing buyers.

Although study of the equilibrium theory of the trade cycle lies beyond the scope of this introductory text, one or two comments are in order.

The theory explains variations in output by equilibrium variations of investment in physical capital and firms' stocks. One of its key problems, however, is to explain *systematic* variations in employment. The theory accounts for these as being workers' reactions to changes in the so-called *intertemporal terms of trade* – the current real wage rate relative to the real wage rate expected to exist in the future.

To illustrate what is involved, consider a household which works and consumes in two periods and wishes to save nothing for consumption beyond the second period. If the wage rate is high this period, it will be rational for the household to work longer hours this period, save some of the resulting income, and then work shorter hours next period when the wage is lower. The second period's consumption will be financed partly out of income earned in that period and partly out of funds saved in the previous period. Conversely, if the wage is expected to be high next period relative to this period, it will be rational for the household to consume more leisure this period, borrowing to finance some of its consumption expenditures, while working longer hours next period. Next period's income will finance that period's consumption and also pay off the debt accumulated in the first period. Thus, systematic, voluntary variations in employment can result from rational household responses to procyclical variations in the real wage rate. These employment variations are the result of variations in the economy's full-informational, static equilibrium.

One problem with this theory is that the real wage rate does not vary greatly over the cycle. Indeed, the variation is so small that there is even uncertainty about its direction. Is the real wage pro-cyclical, rising in booms and falling in slumps, or is it counter-cyclical, falling in booms and rising in slumps. For purposes of the rest of this discussion, we will assume that the variation is pro-cyclical.

Even this assumption, however, still leaves the problem that large swings in unemployment are to be explained by very small swings in the real wage rate. The theory explains this phenomenon by assuming that households' tastes show a very high degree of inter-temporal substitutability between work in the two periods. The theory thus gives a picture of people who do not care greatly about when they consume their leisure. If this period's wage falls even a bit below next period's expected wage, much more leisure is consumed this period and much more work done next period. Thus small changes in the intertemporal terms of trade lead to large substitutions between work done over the trade cycle. Opponents find it highly implausible that the observed variations in employment over the cycle – including the massive world-wide unemployment in the early 1980s – were caused by voluntary decisions to consume leisure in slumps when wage rates are slightly depressed while planning to work harder once the recovery raises wage rates slightly.

Policy Invariance

The New Classical model has an interesting characteristic called *policy invariance*: no systematic stabilization policy, neither fiscal nor monetary, has any influence on the economy! This startling result claims that generations of government policy-makers, and their critics, were completely fooling themselves. The fiscal and monetary stabilization policies they were using were without effect – except where they were unanticipated. Apparently, policy-makers throughout the world were unable to see that their policies were without systematic effect over the decades that these policies were actively practiced!

Similar remarks apply to their critics. Many of the criticisms of stabilization policy that we have studied in early chapters argued that the policies were less effective than they might have been, or even were perverse in their effects, because policy-makers did not understand the complexity of the economic system that they were trying to influence – as illustrated by the economy's long and variable lags between any disturbance and its full effects. According to the New Classical view, these critics also did not appreciate, over the decades of their research and detailed assessments, that they were fighting a sham battle – studying and criticizing the effects of something which had no effects. Only the general public understood the potential effects of the stabilization policy and took it into account sufficiently to cause it to have no effect!

The intuitive reasoning behind the policy-invariance result is as follows. The world of the New Classical model is fully inhabited by rational individuals whose mistakes are never systematic. Thus, all systematic behaviour of the economy is fully anticipated and cannot cause deviations from full-employment equilibrium. Only random and unpredictable forces can do this. Purposeful government stabilization policy must be systematic. It will follow some rule such as to adopt expansionary or contractionary policies depending on whether there is a recessionary or an inflationary gap. Since what we have now noted – systematic shocks cannot cause the economy to deviate from its equilibrium –

applies to all systematic shocks including those induced by the government, systematic stabilization policy has *no* effect on the economy.

This result is shown algebraically in Box 42.1 for the case of systematic monetary policy. The Box is there for those who would like to see the result demonstrated formally. Others can read on in the text.

It is important to understand that this result stems from two critical characteristics of the New Classical model. First, that deviations of Y from Y_F only occur because people make mistakes in predicting the inflation rate and, second, that according to the theory of rational expectations, people do not make systematic mistakes (which implies that they fully understand and act on anything systematic that the government does – as well as that there be no irrational speculative bubbles in stock or property markets, and that there be no cobweb cycles such as we studied in the Appendix to Chapter 7).

It is also interesting to note that there is here a sharp difference of prediction between the New Classical and traditional monetarists. Friedman and other traditional monetarists hold that monetary policy is such a powerful tool that it should not be used because it will do more harm than good. Lucas and other New Classicists hold that monetary (and any other systematic) policy is such an impotent tool that it should not be used.

In my view, the empirical evidence supports Friedman's view that monetary policy is potent (often destabilizing the economy) and conflicts with the New Classical view that it is impotent.

The neo-Keynesian model allows deviations of Y from Y_F where no one makes mistakes but which occur as a result of oligopolistic pricing policies and the working of the labour market. In these circumstances firms and workers can see a government policy coming and yet it will affect their behaviour because it will influence aggregate demand and total output. Assume, for example, that the Bank announces that one month from now it is going to contract the money supply by 20 per cent. According to the New Classical model, people will correctly perceive that this will reduce the price level by 20 per cent and will all cut their own wages or prices by 20 per cent. As a result, relative prices will be unchanged and neither output nor employment

BOX 42.1 POLICY INVARIANCE IN THE NEW CLASSICAL MODEL

Start by assuming a crude form of monetarism that makes this period's inflation rate $\dot{P}_t$ equal to last period's rate of growth of the money supply, $\dot{m}_{t-1}$:

$$\dot{P}_t = \dot{m}_{t-1} \ . \tag{1}$$

Next assume that the central bank varies the rate of growth of the money supply, partly following some systematic rule of stabilization policy and partly randomly. Thus for the rate of change of the money supply, we have

$$\dot{m}_{t-1} = \dot{m}^r_{t-1} + \dot{m}^u_{t-1} \ , \tag{2}$$

where $\dot{m}^r$ is that part of the monetary growth that follows a systematic rule, while $\dot{m}^u$ is that part that is unsystematic. Since $\dot{m}^u$ is unpredictable, it is always a surprise. It can be thought of as a random variable with mean zero. (If it were not random it would be systematic and hence would be a part of $\dot{m}^r$).

Now substitute the Bank's monetary rule from (2) into equation (1) that determines the inflation rate to obtain.

$$\dot{P}_t = \dot{m}^r_{t-1} + \dot{m}^u_{t-1} \ , \tag{3}$$

which merely says that inflation will have a systematic component as a result of the Bank's systematic monetary behaviour and a random component as a result of surprise variations in the money supply.

Next, make the added assumption that when expectations about period t's inflation rate are formed in period $t-1$, people know what the systematic component of $\dot{m}$ will be but they do not known what the random component will be. (The money-supply figures are available only with a lag, but the policy rule is known.) Thus we have

$$\dot{P}^e_{t-1} = \dot{m}^r_{t-1} + \varepsilon_t \ , \tag{4}$$

which says that rational agents predict at $t-1$ what the inflation rate will be at t by a knowledge of the systematic rule the Bank is following and that their predictions are subject to an error that is a random variable of mean zero. (In other words, on average over a very long time their errors cancel out and do not have any systematic bias to over- or under-predict.)

We have seen that the Lucas supply function explains deviations from potential income, $Y_t - Y_F$, in terms of errors in predicting the price level $G(\dot{P}_t - \dot{P}^e_{t-1})$ and a lagged adjustment back towards potential income, $\alpha(Y_{t-1} - Y_F)$. Writing this out in full gives

$$Y_t - Y_F = G(\dot{P}_t - \dot{P}^e_{t-1}) + \alpha(Y_{t-1} - Y_F) \ . \tag{5}$$

Now substitute the determinants of $\dot{P}_t$ from equation (3) and $\dot{P}^e_{t-1}$ from (4) to yield

$$Y_t - Y_F = G(\dot{m}^r_{t-1} + \dot{m}^u_{t-1} - \dot{m}^r_{t-1} - \varepsilon_t)$$
$$+ \alpha(Y_{t-1} - Y_F)$$
$$Y_t - Y_F = G(\dot{m}^u_{t-1} - \varepsilon_t) + \alpha(Y_{t-1} - Y_F) \ . \tag{6}$$

The systematic component of monetary policy $\dot{m}^r_{t-1}$ has disappeared, and deviations from potential income depend on the difference between two random variables $\dot{m}^u$ and ε_t and on the mechanical term that adjusts Y back towards Y_F whenever there are no other disturbances.

will be affected. According to the neo-Keynesian model, even though people see the monetary shock coming, there is little they can do about it. Labour markets will not miraculously become perfectly competitive. Instead, money wages will be more or less unchanged, and as a result, oligopolistic prices will also be more or less unchanged. Thus when the monetary shock hits, output and employment will fall. The shock will have real effects.

The evidence seems to me to favour the neo-Keynesian model in showing that output deviates from its full-employment level not just because people make mistakes in predicting inflation. The underlying theoretical reason is that the perfectly competitive model does not describe the real-world behaviour of markets for labour or for most manufactured goods.

Micro and Macro Economics

One of the most valuable results of the criticisms of traditional monetarists and New Classicists is that macro economists have been forced to examine in great detail the microeconomic underpinnings of assumed macroeconomic relations. We observed on page 50 that economics is about behaviour, the behaviour of households, firms and central authorities. Relations that cannot be traced back to the microeconomic behaviour of basic decision-taking units are a mystery. Scientists always have to live with some mysteries but they are never satisfied to leave them as mysteries. Progress comes by understanding what we observe in terms of our theoretical constructs so that it ceases to be a mystery (while always holding open the possibility that

BOX 42.2 NON-LINEAR DYNAMICS, CHAOS, AND BOUNDED RATIONALITY

Physics has seen at least two revolutionary changes in paradigm in this century. The 1900s began with the Newtonian view of the world still in ascendency. According to this view, the world behaves mechanically according to deterministic laws. God may have established the laws of physics in the first place, and set the initial conditions. From that point on, however, the world unfolded according to these laws, and any observer with enough knowledge could predict its entire future. If two situations were set up with identical initial conditions, they would unfold in an identical fashion as seen by someone who could stand outside the system and observe it.

In economics, equilibrium theory with perfectly rational agents is Newtonian in conception. In an individual market, for example, the underlying laws are those of demand and supply, while the initial conditions are the shapes of the curves and the initial market price. If the same market experiment – e.g. the same curve shift – is analysed over and over again, starting from the same initial conditions, the final result will be the same. For example, controls that fix price below the equilibrium will always lead to excess demand, the amount of which depends on the shapes of the demand and the supply curves.

The first revolution of the twentieth century was relativity theory, which swept away ideas of absolute time and position in space. The second came with quantum electrodynamics, which has already been discussed in Box 2.1 on page 18. The universe is now seen as statistical and the very act of observing the system changes its behaviour. For example, the better the accuracy in observing an electron's position, the poorer the accuracy in observing its velocity, and vice versa.

More recent developments in science have emphasized non-linear dynamic systems, which sometimes produce what is called chaotic behaviour (which isn't quite what the term means in ordinary speech). In classical linear dynamics, a system either settles down at a constant rate of change, or in a regular cycle. The system's behaviour can also be disturbed by random shocks, but their effects normally die out fairly quickly.

For example, in a model of economic growth that is built on linear dynamic equations real income may follow the growth path of potential income, or it may also exhibit regular trade-cycle fluctuations around that growth path. In such models, the observed time-path of real national income can be decomposed into a long-term growth trend and cyclical component (and possibly other systematic components such as seasonal patterns), plus random shocks whose effects do not influence the long-term behaviour of the system.

Non-linear Dynamics

Non-linear dynamic systems do not behave in this way. Instead, they may exhibit steady growth for quite a while, then, quite suddenly, move to regular cycles and then, quite suddenly again, produce irregular fluctuations that never repeat themselves. The laws that govern the system's behaviour may be fully understood, and may be fully deterministic – i.e. there may be no random disturbances at all. Nonetheless, the system as a whole may produce an irregular pattern of fluctuations that never repeats itself and that cannot be predicted from a knowledge of its past behaviour, no matter how many observations are available. In these systems, the apparently random behaviour is caused by the system's deterministic laws, and when the system is started out twice at what appears to be the same initial conditions, it will trace out quite different paths.

A system that behaves as just described is called a *chaotic* system. It is one that has the capacity to magnify small differences in its initial conditions into two paths that diverge from each other at a rate that is *at least* exponential. Such systems are characterized by *phase transitions* and 'positive feedback loops'.

Phase Transitions

A change of phase state occurs when a system that has been reacting smoothly to changes in the forces that influence it suddenly starts to react quite differently – usually without any warning whatsoever. For example, when water is cooled steadily, the speed of the random movement of its molecules falls continuously. Then, at freezing temperature, there is an abrupt change. The molecules stop moving about and become fixed in a definite pattern. The water has frozen. A similar phase transition occurs when the water is heated and goes abruptly from a liquid to a gaseous state.

Non-linear models of economic growth can go through two phase changes: first, when they begin to exhibit regular cycles around their growth trend and, second, when they begin to fluctuate in an irregular manner.

Positive Feedbacks

Positive feedback loops occur when a given divergence from any state of the system is magnified rather than damped. A normal competitive market is a negative feedback system. If price diverges from equilibrium, market forces push price back towards the equilibrium. Reverse the labels of the *D* and *S* curves, however, and you have a positive feedback system. Now a slight increase in price above the equilibrium value will create excess demand and this will cause price to rise even further.

Another example can occur when two different technologies that do the same job are competing with each other in the early stages of their development. The positive feedback mechanism is that most R & D expenditure tends to be allocated towards the technology that is currently the more successful. A slight advantage of one technology over the other will tend to cause more and more of the R & D effort to be directed to that technology, magnifying its lead over the other. The losing technology may be superior to the winning one in some fundamental way, but if a small – even random – advantage develops for the inferior technology, it may gain a decisive lead over the other because of the positive R & D feedback loop.

This is what may have happened when steam and petrol competed to be the technology to be used to power early automobiles. In many ways the steam engine, with its combustion outside of the cylinders, is superior to the petrol engine with its internal combustion. However, once the petrol-driven car got a small advantage over the steam car – partly due to some astute advertising by the manufacturers of petrol-driven cars exploiting some early accidents with the steam car – more R & D funds were then allocated to the internal-combustion engine. Ten years later, the steam car was hopelessly behind. The important point is that a positive feedback R & D loop has the potential to magnify small, possibly random, divergences into large, irreversible divergences within relatively short periods of time. With a positive feedback loop it is the first, rather than the best, technology to enter the field that has the best chance of winning.

Bounded Rationality

In standard economic models of rational behaviour, the individual decision-taker maximizes with respect to a full knowledge of the system in which he or she is operating. However, the behaviour of non-linear systems, especially if they produce chaotic behaviour, cannot always be predicted even by sophisticated mathematical models. Neither can they be predicted from a knowledge of their past behaviour. The behaviour is unlikely, therefore, to be predicted by the average businessperson operating on a mixture of experience, intuition and simple analysis. This realization has led many economists to move away from the rationality that is assumed in traditional economics, to say nothing of the super-rationality that is assumed in the theory of rational expectations. These economists use the theory of *bounded rationality*, which takes account of the limitations of decision-makers in terms of their ability to observe, and understand, the system in which they are operating.

Just as engineers still use Newtonian mechanics to build bridges, so economists will continue to use classical equilibrium theory to analyse the behaviour of markets that can be seen as being more or less isolated from outside influences and that are dominated by negative feedback systems. Many believe, however, that the behaviour of some individual markets, particularly those trading in bonds and equities, may be described by non-linear, even chaotic, systems. Many also believe that large systems, such as those describing economic growth – which involves invention, knowledge diffusion, and innovation in an economy containing a large number of interrelated markets – may be characterized by non-linear dynamic equations, positive feedback loops, occasional chaotic behaviour, and decision-taking that is at best bounded in its rationality.

---

the theoretical construct, and hence the 'understanding' that builds on it, may be wrong).

THE PROGRESS OF ECONOMICS

It is difficult to predict major shifts in the approach that is to be used by any science – major shifts in the way of looking at things are often called *paridigm shifts*. Economics has stayed with the Newtonian paridigm of deterministic, fully rational, equilibrium systems much longer that have most of the natural sciences. Signs of change are, however, on the horizon. By the next edition of this book these changes may have found their way into the mainstream of undergraduate teaching. In the meantime, Box 42.2 provides a brief discussion of some of the most exciting of these new approaches – approaches that may give insights into some of the subject's most difficult problems.

Whatever its current paridigm, useful economics must be related in some clear way to what we see in the real world. Applying the scientific method is not, however, a simple matter in economics. We lack laboratory conditions. We cannot get the holders of opposing views to agree on critical tests and then repeat them over and over until everyone must agree on the results. The call that economics try to be a science is a plea that economists try to relate their theories to observations. If we hold that the truth of economic theories is totally independent of successful empirical applications, it is difficult to see how economics can claim to be in any way useful in interpreting the world around us.

In economics, general acceptance that theories should be tested by confronting their predictions with the available evidence is fairly new. At this point you should re-read the quotation from Lord Beveridge given at the beginning of this book (see pages xiv and xv). The controversy that Beveridge was describing followed the publication in 1936 of Keynes' *General Theory of Employment, Interest and Money*. Keynes' work gave rise to the macroeconomics that we have developed in the macro part of this book. At many points, we have raised the question of how various parts of macroeconomic theory could be tested; we have also discussed some of the tests that have been conducted and some of the resulting changes in the theory. Reflect on the differences between this approach to the problem of accepting or rejecting theories and the one described by Beveridge.

There is no doubt that since economics first began, some progress, albeit irregular and halting, has been made in relating theory to evidence. This progress has been reflected in the superior ability of governments to achieve their policy objectives. The pathetic efforts of successive British governments to deal with the economic catastrophe that overwhelmed the country after the return to the gold standard in the 1920s and even more so during the Great Depression of the 1930s show measures adopted in all sincerity which in most cases actually served to make things worse. Across the Atlantic, President Roosevelt's attempts to reduce American unemployment in the same decade were greatly hampered by the failure of most economists to realize the critical importance of budget deficits in increasing aggregate demand and hence national income.

The debate between monetarists and neo-Keynesians is another illustration of the value of the rule of evidence. Monetarists have several times had to revise their positions in the face of evidence. For example, they no longer hold that the demand for money is completely interest-inelastic, nor that fiscal policy cannot affect aggregate expenditure. The anti-inflation experiments of the late 1970s and early 1980s have been closely watched and heavily documented. Already we have hard evidence on several issues on which economists could only conjecture 10 to 15 years ago. The debate between Nicholas Kaldor on the one hand, and Anna Schwartz and Milton Friedman on the other hand, that took place in *Lloyds Bank Review* in 1970 makes instructive re-reading. Several of the points that Kaldor could then only assert that he thought were right have now been shown by solid evidence to be right. Those monetarists and neo-Keynesians who are emotionally fully committed to their present views will never abandon their basic positions, but through the testing of their specific positions, those who have open minds really do learn about the economy.

In 1974, the new disease of stagflation burst on the world's economies. The coexistence of falling output and accelerating inflation seemed utterly paradoxical to observers familiar with the concept of a stable Phillips curve, along which inflation increased on cyclical upswings and decreased on cyclical downswings. Many observers spoke of the end of conventional economics, and the need to develop entirely new models for understanding the economy's radically new behaviour.

Such was the pace of theoretical and empirical research, however, that within a very few years, the phenomenon of stagflation was explained by, and incorporated into, conventional macro models. Today, a satisfactory explanation of what seemed so paradoxical to observers in the 1970s has found its way into standard first-year, university textbooks – as readers of this book well know.

The process of understanding, and explaining, stagflation greatly enriched economists' understanding in a number of ways. First, economists are now much more aware of the importance of supply-side phenomena, compared with earlier days when most attention was focused on the demand side of macro models. Second, economists are more aware of the influence of sectoral price shocks. In the 1970s, Milton Friedman, along with many other monetarists, argued that the oil price shock would not be inflationary because other prices would fall so as to hold the general price level constant. The experience was clearly otherwise. It is now clear that, in the face of equal amounts of excess supply and excess demand, prices do not fall as fast as they rise, so that a major sectoral price shock raises the whole price level. Thus it shifts the *SRAS* curve upwards, giving the economy a contractionary supply-side shock. Third, economists are more aware of the dangers of treating supply-side, stagflationary shocks as if they were demand-side shocks. The US government made this mistake in the period 1974–5 and exacerbated an already severe contractionary, supply-side shock by imposing restrictive demand measures.[1]

It is in such important policy areas as the curing of major depressions and the handling of major inflations that the general thrust of our theories is tested, even if all their specific predictions are not. In some general sense, then, economic theories have always been subjected to empirical tests. When they were wildly at variance with the facts, the ensuing disaster could not but be noticed, and the theories were discarded or amended in the light of what was learned.

What we do not know covers vast areas, which should give all economists a sense of humility.

---

[1] This whole period has been carefully studied, and explained, in a way that contemporary observers thought would be impossible by Alan Blinder in his valuable book *Economic Policy and the Great Stagflation* (London: Academic Press, 1979).

But those who feel that we know nothing need only involve themselves in a policy-making situation with non-economists to lose some of their feelings of inferiority. First, we really do know positive things about the behaviour of the economy that help us to evaluate policy choices. Second, many non-economists do not understand how price systems work, and thus fail to understand how decentralized decision-taking can be both co-ordinated and efficient. This leads them to misinterpret much of the economic behaviour that they observe, and to advocate policies that will work only if the price system does not. Third, economists have a method of looking at problems that is potentially enlightening to almost any problem whether or not it is conventionally described as economic.

The advance of economics in the last 60 years partly reflects a change in economists' attitudes towards empirical observation. Today, we are much less likely to dismiss theories just because we do not like them and to refuse to abandon theories just because we do like them. Today, we are more likely to try to base our theories as much as possible on empirical observation, and to accept empirical relevance as the ultimate arbiter of the value of those theories. As human beings, we suffer much anguish at the upsetting of a pet theory; as scientists, we should try to train ourselves to take pleasure in it because of the new knowledge we gain thereby. It has been said that one of the great tragedies of science is the continual slaying of beautiful theories by ugly facts. As economists, we are all too often swayed by aesthetic considerations. In the past, we have too often clung to our theories because they were beautiful or because we liked their political implications; as scientists, we must always remember that when theory and fact come into serious conflict, it is theory, not fact, that will eventually give way.

SUMMARY

1. Views about the role of policy in improving macroeconomic performance range between two extremes. The non-interventionist view is that there is only a minimum role for policy; macroeconomic performance will be most satisfactory when the market system is allowed to function as freely as possible. The interventionist view is that active use of policy will improve macroeconomic

performance. It is common on many issues to identify monetarists with non-interventionists and Keynesians with interventionists.

2. Non-interventionists believe that because the economy is inherently stable, the goal of damping the business cycle is best achieved by avoiding fluctuations in policy, especially monetary policy. Hence they advocate a stable rate of monetary expansion. Interventionists believe that the economy is inherently unstable in that expenditure functions shift frequently and the economy's self-corrective mechanisms are weak. Hence, they believe in an active role for demand management to reduce trade-cycle fluctuations.

3. Monetarists believe that inflation is everywhere and always a monetary phenomenon and so advocate the same policies to avoid price instability as they advocate to minimize policy-induced cycles in output. They also argue that in order to control inflation, the long-term growth rate of the money supply must be kept low and stable.

   Keynesians accept the view that monetary expansion is necessary for inflation to persist in the long term, but they take seriously the role of other factors in causing short-term but substantial inflation. Hence they believe in an active role for policy to offset these inflationary forces in the short term.

4. Non-interventionists believe in a unique macroeconomic equilibrium with its associated NAIRU – which is composed of frictional and structural unemployment. For them, the long-term Phillips curve is vertical so that demand management can have no long-term effect on national income and unemployment.

   Some interventionists question the uniqueness of macro equilibrium. They point out that the existence of equilibrium has only been proved in a highly abstract model that assumes perfect competition in all markets. They argue that hysterisis models, where the macroeconomic equilibrium is path-dependent, may capture an element of reality. If so, short-term stabilization policy can affect the position of long-term equilibrium.

5. Non-interventionists believe that long-term growth will be maximized when the profit motive is given relatively free reign, operating through relatively free markets. Interventionists see a need for special government programmes to channel resources into research and development and other investment expenditures designed to raise potential output.

6. Non-interventionists see a role for policy in terms of providing a stable environment for individual decision-makers. This involves maintaining a consistent set of 'fiscal rules of the game' in terms of expenditure and tax rates and providing a steady but gradual growth in the money supply.

7. Interventionists have specific prescriptions for each policy variable. They advocate active use of discretionary monetary and/or fiscal policy to stabilize output and employment. Despite imperfections caused by lags and incomplete knowledge, they believe such policies are helpful. Similar policies can sometimes be combined with incomes policies to stabilize the fluctuations in the price level that arise from various sources and are subject to an upward bias. They also sometimes support policies to promote growth through subsidization, tax concessions and more specific intervention.

8. The New Classical model allows departures from full-employment when people make mistakes in predicting the price level. When combined with the theory of rational expectations, this leads to the policy invariance proposition. New Classical monetarists support the *k* per cent rule because they believe an interventionist monetary policy will not influence output.

9. In the equilibrium theory of the trade cycle, systematic fluctuations in the equilibrium values of income and employment can result from systematic shifts in the inter-temporal trade-offs made between work and leisure today and work and leisure in the future. In contrast, Keynesians emphasize the non-perfectly competitive nature of the economy. As a result they believe that fluctuations in aggregate demand lead primarily to fluctuations in output rather than in the price level. In this view, an interventionist stabilization policy can be effective in stabilizing fluctuations in output.

TOPICS FOR REVIEW

- Interventionist and non-interventionist policies
- Macroeconomic equilibrium
- Hysterisis
- *k* per cent rule
- Traditional and New Classical monetarists
- Lucas aggregate supply curve
- Policy invariance proposition
- The equilibrium theory of the business cycle

Glossary

absolute advantage One region is said to have an absolute advantage over another in the production of some commodity when an equal quantity of resources can produce more of that commodity in the first region than in the second.

absolute price The price of a commodity expressed in monetary units; also called a *money price*.

accelerator theory of investment The theory that the level of investment depends on the rate of change of national income.

actual consumption The actual consumption of the services that are provided by the commodities that households buy.

actual expenditure See *realized expenditure*.

AD **curve** See *aggregate demand curve*.

ad valorem tariff A tariff levied as a percentage of the price of the product.

ad valorem tax A tax levied as a percentage of the value of some transaction.

adjustable peg system A system with these two characteristics: (i) the exchange rate is pegged at a publicly announced par value; (ii) the exchange rate is adjusted from time to time in the face of fundamental disequilibria.

administered prices Prices that are set by the decisions of individual firms rather than by impersonal market forces.

advances Banks loans.

adverse selection The tendency for people most at risk to insure, while people least at risk do not, so that the insurers get an unrepresentative sample of clients within any one fee category.

aggregate demand The total desired purchases of all the nation's buyers of final output.

aggregate demand curve A curve which plots all combinations of the price level and national income that yield equilibrium in the goods and the asset markets – i.e. that yield *IS–LM* equilibrium.

aggregate desired expenditure The total amount of purchases of currently produced goods and services that all spending units in the economy wish to make.

aggregate supply The total desired output of all the nation's producers.

aggregate supply curve A curve relating the economy's total desired output, Y to the price level, P.

allocative efficiency Resources cannot be reallocated to produce a different bundle of goods which will then allow someone to be made better off while no one is made worse off.

appreciated When a change in the free-market exchange rate raises the value of one currency.

arc elasticity Uses the incremental ratio along the demand curve $(\Delta q/\Delta p)/(p/q)$. See also *point elasticity*.

asset disequilibrium See *portfolio disequilibrium*.

asset equilibrium See *portfolio equilibrium*.

autarky Where a country does no foreign trade.

autonomous variable See *exogenous variable*.

average fixed cost Total fixed costs divided by the number of units produced.

average product Total output divided by the number of units of the variable factor used in its production.

average propensity to consume Total consumption expenditure divided by total income, C/Y.

average propensity to import Total imports divided by total income, M/Y.

average propensity to save Total saving divided by total income, S/Y.

average propensity to tax The total tax revenue divided by total national income, T/Y.

average revenue The total revenue divided by the number of units sold.

average total cost The total cost of producing any given output divided by the number of units produced, i.e. the cost per unit.

average variable cost Total variable cost divided by the number of units produced; also called *unit cost*.

balanced budget A situation in which current revenue is exactly equal to current expenditure.

balanced budget multiplier Measures the change in income divided by the balanced-budget change in government expenditure that brought it about.

balance-of-payments accounts A summary record of a country's transactions that involve payment or receipts of foreign exchange.

bank notes Paper currency issued by banks.

barriers to entry Anything that prevents new firms from entering an industry that is earning profits.

barter The trading of goods directly for other goods.

base period See *base year*.

base year A year, or other point in time, chosen for comparison purposes in order to express or compute index numbers. Also called *base period*.

beggar-my-neighbour policies Policies designed to increase a country's prosperity (especially by reducing its unemployment) at the expense of reducing prosperity in other countries (especially by increasing their unemployment).

black market A market in which goods are sold illegally at prices that violate the legal restrictions on prices.

bond In economic theory, any evidence of a debt carrying a legal obligation to pay interest and repay the principal at some stated future time.

boom Periods of high output and high employment.

budget deficit The shortfall of current revenue below current expenditure, usually with reference to the government.

budget deficit function This function relates the government budget deficit, or the PSBR, to national income.

budget line Shows all those combinations of commodities that are just obtainable, given the household's income and the prices of commodities.

budget surplus The excess of current revenue over current expenditure, usually with reference to the government.

built-in stabilizer Anything that reduces the economy's cyclical fluctuations and that is activated without a conscious government decision.

business cycle See *trade cycle*.

capacity The output that corresponds to the minimum short-run average total cost.

capital All those man-made aids to further production, such as tools, machinery and factories, which are used up in the process of making other goods and services rather than being consumed for their own sake.

capital account Records international transactions related to movement of long- and short-run capital.

capital consumption allowance An estimate of the amount by which the capital stock is depleted through its contribution to current production. Also called *depreciation*.

capital deepening Increasing the ratio of capital to labour.

capital-labour ratio The ratio of the amount of capital to the amount of labour used to produce any given output.

capital stock The total quantity of capital.

capital widening Increasing the quantity of capital without changing the proportions in which the factors are used.

cartel A group of firms that agree to act as if they were a single seller.

cash base See *high-powered money*.

central authorities All public agencies, government bodies and other organizations belonging to, or owing their existence to, the government; sometimes called the *government*.

central bank A bank that acts as banker to the commercial banking system and often to the government as well. In the modern world, usually a government-owned and -operated institution that controls the banking system and is the sole money-issuing authority.

centrally controlled economy See *command economy*.

ceteris paribus Other things being equal, as when all but one independent variables are held constant so as to study the influence of the remaining independent variable on the dependent variable.

change in demand A *shift* in the whole demand curve, that is, a change in the amount that will be bought at *every* price.

change in the quantity demanded An increase or decrease in the specific quantity bought at a specified price, represented by a movement along a demand curve; sometimes called an *extension* (increase) or a *contraction* (decrease) in demand.

circular flow of income The flow of expenditures on output and factor services passing between domestic (as opposed to foreign) firms and domestic households.

clearing house A place where interbank debts are settled.

clearing banks See *commercial banks*.

closed economy An economy that does not engage in international trade.

closed shop Only union members can be employed. Closed shops may be either 'pre-entry', where the worker must be a member of the union before being employed, or 'post-entry', where the worker must join the union on becoming employed.

collective consumption goods See *public goods*.

command economy An economy in which the decisions of the central authorities (as distinct from households and firms) exert the major influence over the allocation of resources.

commercial banks Privately owned banks that deal with the ordinary public.

commercial policy The government's policy towards international trade.

commodities Everything of value that is produced; commodities may be either goods or services.

common market An agreement among a group of countries to have free trade among themselves, a common set of barriers to trade with other countries, and free movement of labour and capital among themselves.

common property resource A resource that is owned by no one and may be used by anyone.

comparative advantage The ability of one nation (or region or individual) to produce a commodity at a lesser opportunity cost in terms of other products forgone than another nation.

comparative statics Short for *comparative static equilibrium analysis*; studying the effect of some change by comparing the positions of static equilibrium before and after the change is introduced.

competitive advertising Advertising by which firms seek to control market demand instead of being controlled by it.

competitive devaluations When several countries devalue their currencies in an attempt to gain a competitive advantage over one another.

complements Two goods are complements if the quantity demanded of one is negatively related to the price of the other.

conglomerate Units selling unrelated products who are united into one firm.

conglomerate merger When firms selling quite unrelated products merge; also called *lateral merger*.

constant returns to scale A firm's output increases exactly as fast as its inputs increase.

consumer Anyone who consumes goods or services

to satisfy his or her wants.

consumers' surplus The difference between the total value consumers place on all units consumed of a commodity and the payment they must make to purchase that amount of the commodity.

consumption The act of using goods and services to satisfy wants.

consumption expenditure The amount that households spend on purchasing goods and services for consumption.

consumption function The relationship between households' planned consumption expenditure and all of the forces that determine it.

creative destruction Schumpeter's theory that high profits and wages, earned by monpolistic or oligopolistic firms and unions, are the spur for others to invent cheaper or better substitute products and techniques that allow their suppliers to gain some of these profits.

cross-elasticity of demand The responsiveness of demand for one commodity to changes in the price of another commodity, defined as the percentage change in quantity demanded of one commodity divided by the percentage change in price of another commodity.

crowding-out effect The lowering of interest-sensitive expenditure because a rise in national income causes a rise in the interest rate; it explains the difference between the values of the interest-constant and the interest-sensitive multipliers.

current account Records all international transactions related to goods and services.

cyclically adjusted deficit (CAD) An estimate of expenditures minus revenues, not as they actually are, but as they would be if potential national income had been achieved (i.e. if there were neither an inflationary nor a recessionary gap). Also called *full-employment deficit* and *high-employment deficit*.

cyclical fluctuations Periodic (auto-correlated) oscillations of any economic time-series around its trend.

cyclical unemployment See *demand-deficient unemployment*.

cyclically balanced budget The budget is balanced over the period of one trade cycle.

debenture A certificate issued by a firm indicating a debt to the holder.

decision lag The time it takes to assess a situation and decide what corrective action should be taken.

decreasing returns to scale A situation in which output increases less than proportionately to inputs as the scale of production increases.

deficit The shortfall of current revenue below current expenditure.

deflation A decrease in the general price level.

demand The entire relationship between the quantity of a commodity that buyers wish to purchase per period of time and the price of that commodity, other things equal.

demand curve A graphical relation showing the quantity of some commodity that households would like to buy at each possible price.

demand-deficient unemployment Unemployment that occurs because aggregate desired expenditure is insufficient to purchase all of the output of a fully employed labour force. Also called *cyclical unemployment*.

demand deposit See *sight deposit*.

demand for money The amount of wealth everyone in the economy wishes to hold in the form of money balances. Also called *liquidity preferance*.

demand function A functional relation between quantity demanded and all of the variables that influence it.

demand management Policies that seek to shift the aggregate demand curve either by shifting the *IS* curve (fiscal policy) or the *LM* curve (monetary policy).

demand schedule A numerical tabulation showing the quantity that is demanded at selected prices.

deposit accounts See *time deposits*.

deposit money Bank deposits on which cheques can be drawn.

depreciated When a change in the free-market exchange rate lowers the value of one currency.

depreciation (1) The loss in value of an asset over a period of time due to physical wear and tear and obsolescence. (2) A fall in the free-market value of domestic currency in terms of foreign currencies. See also *capital consumption allowance*.

depression A prolonged period of very low economic activity with very high unemployment and high excess capacity.

derived demand The demand for a factor of production that results from the demand for the products it is used to make.

desired expenditure See *planned expenditure*.

differentiated product A product that is produced in several varieties, or brands, all of which are sufficiently similar to distinguish them, as a group, from other products (e.g. cars).

diminishing marginal rate of substitution The hypothesis that the less of one commodity that is presently being consumed by a household, the less willing will the household be to give up a unit of that commodity to obtain an additional unit of a second commodity; its geometrical expression is the decreasing absolute value of an indifference curve as one moves along it to the right.

direct foreign investment Changes in non-resident ownership of domestic firms and in resident ownership of foreign firms. Thus direct foreign investment in the UK is capital investment in a branch plant or subsidiary corporation in the UK in which the investor has voting control. It can also take the form of a takeover in which a controlling interest is acquired in a firm previously controlled by residents.

direct tax A tax levied on persons that can vary with the status of the taxpayer.

dirty float See *managed float*.

discount houses Specialized financial institutions, which borrow money at call (i.e. repayable on demand), or at very short notice, from banks and other lending institutions. They use this money to purchase short-dated financial assets such as treasury bills and local authority bills.

diseconomies of scale See *decreasing returns to scale*.

disembodied technical change Technical change that is the result of changes in the organization of production that are not embodied in specific capital goods, e.g. improved management techniques.

disequilibrium A state of imbalance between opposing forces so that there is a tendency to change.

disequilibrium differentials Differentials in the prices of similar factors due to economic disturbances; they disappear when equilibrium is reached. Also called *dynamic differentials*.

disposable income The after-tax income that households have at their disposal to spend or to save.

distribution of income The division of national income among various groups. (See also *size and functional distribution of income*.)

dividends Profits that are paid out to shareholders.

division of labour The breaking up of a production process into a series of repetitive tasks, each done by a different worker.

double counting In national-income accounting, adding up the total outputs of all the sectors in the economy so that the value of intermediate goods is counted in the sector that produces them *and* every time they are purchased as an input by another sector.

dumping When a commodity is sold in a foreign country at prices below its domestic sale price for reasons not related to costs.

duopoly An industry containing exactly two firms.

dynamic differentials See *disequilibrium differentials*.

economic growth The positive trend in the nation's total output over the long term.

economic rent Any excess that a factor is paid in excess of its transfer earnings.

economies of scale See *increasing returns to scale*.

economy Any specified collection of interrelated marketed and non-marketed productive activities.

effective tariff rate The tax charged on any imported commodity expressed as a percentage of the value added by the exporting industry.

elastic demand The percentage change in quantity

demanded is greater than the percentage change in price (elasticity greater than one).

elasticity of demand See *price elasticity of demand*.

elasticity of supply See *price elasticity of supply*.

embodied technical change A technical change that is the result of changes in the form of particular capital goods.

employed Those persons working for others and paid a wage or a salary.

endogenous variable A variable that is explained within a theory; also called an *induced variable*.

entrepreneur One who innovates, i.e. one who takes risks by introducing both new products and new ways of making old products.

envelope curve Any curve that encloses, by being tangent to, a series of other curves. In particular, the *envelope cost curve* is the *LRAC* curve, which encloses the *SRAC* curves by being tangent to each without cutting any of them.

equilibrium A state of balance between opposing forces so that there is no tendency to change.

equilibrium differentials Differentials in the prices of factors that persist in equilibrium without generating forces to eliminate them.

equilibrium price The price at which quantity demanded equals quantity supplied.

equilibrium quantity The amount that is bought and sold at the equilibrium price.

equities Certificates indicating part ownership of a joint stock company.

ex ante expenditure See *planned expenditure*.

ex post expenditure See *realized expenditure*.

excess-capacity theorem Each firm in a monopolistically competitive industry is producing its output at an average cost that is higher than it could achieve by producing its capacity output.

excess demand The amount by which quantity demanded exceeds quantity supplied at some price; negative excess supply.

exchange rate The rate at which two national currencies exchange for each other. Often expressed as the amount of domestic currency needed to buy one unit of a foreign currency.

excess supply The amount by which quantity supplied exceeds quantity demanded at some price; negative excess demand.

execution lag The time it takes to initiate corrective policies and for their full influence to be felt.

exhaustive expenditures Government purchases of currently produced goods and services, also called *government direct expenditures*.

exogenous variable A variable that influences other variables within a theory but is itself determined by factors outside the theory; also called an autonomous variable.

expenditure See *planned expenditure*.

expenditure changing Policies that change aggregate desired expenditure.

expenditure switching Policies that maintain the level of aggregate desired expenditure but change its composition between domestic absorption and net exports.

external balance When the value of the balance of payments is equal to some target level.

external economies Economies of scale that arise from sources outside of the firm.

externalities Costs of a transaction that are incurred by members of the society, or benefits that are received by them, but not considered by the parties to the transaction.

factor markets Markets where factor services are bought and sold.

factor mobility The readiness of factors to respond to signals that indicate where factors are needed.

factor price differentials These occur when different units of one factor are paid different prices in different uses.

factor services The services of factors of production.

factors of production Resources used to produce goods and services; frequently divided into the basic categories of land, labour, and capital. Sometimes entrepreneurship is distinguished as a fourth factor; sometimes it is included in the category of labour.

fiat money Inconvertible paper money that is declared by government order (or fiat) to be legal tender for settlement of all debts.

final products The outputs of the economy after eliminating all double counting.

financial capital The funds used to finance a firm, including both equity capital and debt (also called *money capital*).

financial intermediaries Financial institutions that stand between those who save money and those who invest it.

fine tuning The attempt to maintain national income at, or near, its full-employment level by means of frequent changes in fiscal and/or monetary policy.

firm The unit that employs factors of production to produce commodities that it sells to other firms, to households or to the central authorities.

fiscal policy Attempts to influence the aggregate demand curve by altering government expenditures and/or government revenues, thus shifting the *IS* curve.

fixed exchange rate The country's central bank intervenes in the foreign-exchange market to hold the exchange rate within a narrow band around some pre-announced par value.

fixed factor An input whose amount available in the short run is fixed.

fixed investment Investment in plant and equipment.

floating exchange rate The exchange rate is left free to be determined on the foreign-exchange market by the forces of demand and supply.

foreign exchange Foreign currencies and claims to them in such forms as bank deposits, cheques and promissory notes payable in the currency.

foreign-exchange market The market where foreign exchange is traded – at a price which is expressed by the exchange rate.

free-market economy An economy in which the decisions of individual households and firms (as distinct from the central authorities) exert the major influence over the allocation of resources.

free riders People who are unwilling to reveal the strength of their own preferences for a public good in the hope that others will pay for it.

free trade An absence of any form of government interference with the free flow of international trade.

free-trade association Allows for tariff-free trade between the member countries but, unlike a common market, it leaves each member free to levy its own tariffs on imports from other countries.

freedom of entry and exit Any new firm is free to set up production if it so wishes, and any existing firm is free to leave the industry if it so wishes.

frictional unemployment Unemployment that is associated with the normal turnover of labour.

full-capacity output The highest output at which minimum costs can be obtained.

full-cost pricing Instead of equating marginal revenue with marginal cost, firms set price equal to average cost at normal-capacity output, plus a conventional mark-up.

full-employment output See *potential output*

functional distribution of income The distribution of income among major factors of production.

gains from trade Advantages realized as a result of specialization made possible by trade.

general price level The average level of the prices of all goods and services produced in the economy, usually just called the *price level*.

Giffen good A good with a positively sloped demand curve.

given period Any particular period that is being compared with a base period.

GNP gap See *output gap*.

gold exchange standard A monetary system in which US currency is directly convertible into gold, and other countries' currencies are indirectly convertible into the gold-backed US dollar at a fixed rate.

gold standard A country's money is convertible into gold.

Goodhart's law The view that many statistical relations (particularly those established by monetarists)

cannot be used for policy purposes because they do not depend on causal relations.

goods Tangible production, such as cars or shoes.

goods markets Markets where goods and services are bought and sold.

government See *central authorities*.

government direct expenditures See *exhaustive expenditures*.

government failure Where the government achieves less than the benefits it could achieve through perfectly efficient action.

Gresham's law Bad money (i.e. money whose intrinsic value is less than its face value) drives good money (i.e. money whose intrinsic value exceeds its face value) out of circulation.

gross domestic product The value of total output actually produced in the whole economy over some period, usually a year (although quarterly data are also available).

gross investment The total value of all investment goods produced in the economy during a stated period of time.

gross national product Income earned by UK residents in return for contributions to current production, whether production is located at home or abroad.

gross return on capital The market value of output minus all non-capital costs; divided into depreciation, pure return, risk premium and pure profit.

high-employment deficit This is an estimate of expenditures minus tax revenues, not as they actually are, but as they would be if potential national income had been achieved (i.e. if there were neither an inflationary nor a recessionary gap). Also called *full-employment* or *cyclically adjusted deficit*.

high-powered money The monetary magnitude that is under the direct control of the central bank; it is composed of cash in the hands of the public, bank reserves and clearing balances held by the commercial banks with the Bank of England.

homogeneous product A product is homogeneous when, in the eyes of purchasers, every unit is identical to every other unit.

horizontal merger When firms at the same stage of production unite.

household All the people that live under one roof and who take, or are subject to others taking for them, joint financial decisions.

human capital The capitalized value of productive investments in persons; usually refers to value derived from expenditures on education, training, and health improvements.

hypothesis of equal net advantage Owners will choose that use of their factors that provides them with the greatest net advantage, which includes both monetary and non-monetary elements. Movements of units of a factor will occur among its various uses until the net advantages in all uses are equalized.

identification problem The problem of how to estimate both demand and supply curves from observed market data on prices and quantities actually traded.

import quota A maximum amount of some commodity that may be imported each year.

import substitutions A policy of producing goods domestically that were previously imported.

imputed costs The costs of using factors of production already owned by the firm, measured by the earnings they could have received in their best alternative employment.

income-consumption line On an indifference-curve diagram, a line showing how consumption bundles change as income changes, with prices held constant.

income effect The effect on quantity demanded of a change in real income.

income elastic The percentage change in quantity demanded exceeds the percentage change in income.

income elasticity of demand The responsiveness of quantity demanded to a change in income.

income inelastic The percentage change in quantity demanded is smaller than the percentage change in income.

incomes policies A wide range of policies running from the government's setting of voluntary guidelines for wage and price increases, through consultation on wage and price norms between unions, management and government, to compulsory controls on wages, prices and profits.

increasing returns to scale A situation in which output increases more than in proportion to inputs as the scale of a firm's production increases. A firm in this situation, with fixed factor prices, is a decreasing-cost firm.

incremental ratio When Y is a function of X, the incremental ratio is the change in Y divided by the change in X that brought it about, $\Delta Y/\Delta X$. The limit of this ratio as ΔX approaches zero is the derivative of Y with respect to X, $\mathrm{d}Y/\mathrm{d}X$.

index of retail prices An index that covers prices of commodities commonly bought by households. Changes in it measure changes in the typical household's 'cost of living'.

indifference curve A curve showing all combinations of commodities that yield equal satisfaction to the household.

indifference map A set of indifference curves.

indirect tax A tax levied on a thing, and paid by an individual by virtue of his or her association with that thing.

individualism The belief that individuals are the best judges of their own interests.

induced expenditure Any expenditure flow that is related to national income (or to any other variable explained by the theory).

induced variable See *endogenous variable*.

industrial unions All workers in a given industry belonging to a single union, whatever their trade.

industry A group of firms that sells a well-defined product or closely related set of products.

inelastic demand The percentage change in quantity is less than the percentage change in price (elasticity is less than one).

infant industry argument The argument that new domestic industries with potential economies of scale need to be protected from competition from established low-cost foreign producers so that they can grow large enough to achieve costs as low as those of foreign producers.

inferior good A commodity with a negative income elasticity; its demand diminishes when income increases.

inflation An increase in the general price level.

inflationary gap A negative output gap, i.e. actual national income exceeds potential national income.

informative advertising Advertising that seeks to inform consumers of the characteristics of the available products.

infrastructure The basic facilities (especially transportation and communications systems) on which the commerce of a community depends.

injection Income received, either by domestic firms or domestic households, that does not arise from the spending of the other group.

inputs The materials and factor services used in the process of production.

interest The amount paid each year on a loan, usually expressed as a percentage (e.g. 5 per cent) or as a ratio (e.g. 0.05) of the principal of the loan.

intermediate products All goods and services used as inputs into a further stage of production.

internal balance When real national income is at its target level.

internal economies Economies of scale that arise from sources within the firm.

internalizing an externality To do something that makes an externality enter into the firm's own calculations of its private costs and benefits.

invention The discovery of something new, such as a new production technique or a new product.

inventories See *stocks*.

investment The act of producing goods that are not for immediate consumption.

investment expenditure Expenditure on capital goods.

investment goods Goods produced not for present consumption, i.e. capital goods, inventories, and residential housing.

invisibles Services, i.e. those things that we cannot see, such as insurance and freight haulage and tourist expenditures.

involuntary unemployment Occurs when a person is willing to accept a job at the going wage rate, but cannot find such a job.

iso cost lines A line showing all combinations of inputs that have the same total cost to the firm.

isoquant A curve showing all technologically efficient factor combinations for producing a specified output.

isoquant map A series of isoquants from the same production function, each isoquant relating to a specific level of output.

joint stock company A firm regarded in law as having an identity of its own; its owners are not personally responsible for anything that is done in the name of the firm; called a *corporation* in North America.

Keynesian economics Economic theories based on *AE, IS, LM, AD* and *AS* curves and assuming enough short-run price inflexibility that *AD* and *AS* shocks cause substantial deviations of real national income from its potential level.

labour All productive human resources, mental and physical, both inherited and acquired.

labour force See *working population*.

labour productivity Total output divided by the labour used in producing it, i.e. output per unit of labour.

Laffer curve A curve relating total tax revenue to the tax rate.

land Those free gifts of nature, such as land, forests, minerals, etc., sometimes called natural resources.

lateral merger See *horizontal merger*.

law of diminishing returns This states that if increasing quantities of a variable factor are applied to given quantity of a fixed factor, the marginal product, and the average product, of the variable factor will eventually decrease.

leakages See *withdrawals*.

less developed countries The lower-income countries of the world, most of which are in Asia, Africa and South and Central America. Also called *underdeveloped countries* and *developing countries*.

life-cycle theory A theory that relates the household's actual consumption to its expected lifetime income.

liquidity preference The demand to hold wealth as money rather than as interest-earning assets. Also called the *demand for money*.

listed banks See *commercial banks*.

long run A period of time in which all inputs may be varied, but the basic technology of production cannot be changed.

long-run aggregate supply curve A curve that relates the price level to equilibrium real national income, after all input costs, including wages rates, have been fully adjusted to eliminate any excess demand or supply.

long-run average cost curve The curve showing the least-cost method of producing each level of output when all inputs can be varied. Also called long-run average total cost curve.

long-run industry supply curve Shows the relation between equilibrium price and the output all the firms in the industry will be willing to supply after all the desired entry or exit has occurred.

long-run Phillips curve The relation between national income and stable rates of inflation that neither accelerate nor decelerate.

macroeconomic policy Any measure directed at influencing such macroeconomic variables as the overall levels of employment, unemployment, national income and the price level.

macroeconomics The study of the determination of economic aggregates and averages, such as total output, total employment, the general price level, and rate of economic growth.

managed float Intervention in the foreign-exchange market by a country's central bank in pursuit of an unofficial exchange-rate target, but not to maintain a publicly announced par value. Also called a *dirty float*.

marginal cost pricing Price is set equal to marginal cost.

marginal cost The increase in total cost resulting from raising the rate of production by one unit.

marginal efficiency of capital The rate at which the value of the stream of output of a marginal unit of capital must be discounted to make it equal to £1.

marginal efficiency of capital schedule A schedule that relates the marginal efficiency of each additional £1's worth of capital to the size of the capital stock.

marginal efficiency of investment The relation between desired investment and the rate of interest, assuming all other things are equal.

marginal product The change in total product resulting from using one more (or less) unit of the variable factor. Also called *marginal physical product*. Mathematically the partial derivative of total product with respect to the variable factor.

marginal propensity not to spend The proportion of each additional £1 of income that is not passed on in spending, and instead leaks out of (i.e. is withdrawn from) the circular flow of income. Also called the *marginal propensity to withdraw* and the *marginal propensity to leak*.

marginal propensity to consume The proportion of each new increment of income that is spent on consumption, $\Delta C/\Delta Y$.

marginal propensity to import The proportion of any new increment of income that is spent on imports $\Delta M/\Delta Y$.

marginal propensity to leak See *marginal propensity not to spend*.

marginal propensity to save The proportion of any new increment of income that is saved, $\Delta S/\Delta Y$.

marginal propensity to spend The ratio of any increment of induced expenditure to the increment in income that brought it about.

marginal propensity to tax The proportion of an increment in income that is taxed away by the government, $\Delta T/\Delta Y$.

marginal propensity to withdraw See *marginal propensity not to spend*.

marginal rate of substitution Measures the rate at which one factor is substituted for another with output held constant; graphically, the slope of the isoquant.

marginal rate of transformation The slope of the production possibility curve, indicating the rate of substitution of one good for another.

marginal revenue The change in total revenue resulting from a unit change in the sales per period of time.

marginal revenue product The addition to a firm's revenue resulting from the sale of the output produced by an additional unit of the variable factor.

marginal utility The change in satisfaction resulting from consuming one unit more or one unit less of a commodity.

market An area over which buyers and sellers negotiate the exchange of a well-defined commodity.

market economy Refers to a society in which people specialize in productive activities and meet most of their material wants through exchanges voluntarily agreed upon by the contracting parties.

market failure Any market performance that is judged to be less good than the best possible performance.

market rate of interest The actual rate of interest that rules in the market.

market sector That portion of an economy in which producers must cover their costs by selling their output to consumers.

market structure Characteristics of a market that influence the behaviour and performance of firms that sell in the market; the four main market structures are perfect competition, monopolistic competition, oligopoly and monopoly.

mercantilism The doctrine that the gains from trade are a function of the balance of trade, in contrast with the Classical theory in which the gains from trade are a function of the volume of trade.

mergers When two or more formerly independent firms unite. See *horizontal, vertical* and *conglomerate mergers*.

merit goods Goods, more of which the government decides should be produced than people would choose to consume left to themselves.

microeconomics The study of the allocation of resources and the distribution of income as they are affected by the workings of the price system and by the policies of the central authorities.

minimum efficient scale The smallest level of output at which long-run average cost is at a minimum; the smallest output required to achieve the economies of scale in production and/or distribution.

mixed economies An economy in which some decisions about the allocation of resources are made by firms and households and some by the central authorities.

monetarism The doctrine that monetary magnitudes exert powerful influences in the economy, and control of these magnitudes is a potent means of affecting the economy's macroeconomic behaviour.

monetary policy Traditionally seen as working through the *LM* curve, shifting aggregate demand by altering the supplies of monetary aggregates, and regulating the terms and availability of credit.

monetary transmission mechanism The mechanism that turns a monetary shock into a real expenditure shock and thus links the monetary and the real side of the economy.

money Any generally accepted medium of exchange, i.e. anything that will be accepted in exchange for goods and services.

money demand function The function that determines the demand to hold money balances. (It is sometimes called the *liquidity preference function*.)

money income Measures a household's income in terms of some monetary unit.

money national product See *nominal national product*.

money price See *absolute price*.

money rate of interest The rate of interest as measured in monetary units.

money stock See *supply of money*.

money substitutes Things that serve as temporary media of exchange but are not stores of value, e.g. credit cards.

money supply See *supply of money*.

monopolist A single seller in any market.

monopolistic competition A market structure in which there are many sellers and freedom of entry but in which each firm sells a product somewhat differentiated from the others, giving it some control over its price.

monopoly A market structure that exists when an industry is in the hands of a single producer.

monopsonist A single purchaser in any market.

moral hazard When people take actions that increase social costs because they are insured against private loss.

most favoured nation An agreement between two

countries according to which each will give the other's goods treatment that is at least as favourable as the most favourable treatment given to any other countries' goods (where more favourable means lower tariffs).

multiplier The ratio of the change in national income to the change in autonomous expenditure that brought it about.

multiplier accelerator theory The theory that trade cycles are caused by the interaction of the multiplier and the accelerator.

NAIRU The amount of unemployment (all of it frictional and structural) that exists when national income is at its potential level and which, if maintained, will result in a stable rate of inflation.

national income In general, the value of the nation's total output, and the value of the income generated by the production of that output.

natural monopoly An industry whose market demand is sufficient to allow only one firm to produce at its minimum efficient scale.

natural oligopoly An industry whose market demand is sufficient to allow only a few firms to produce at their minimum efficient scales.

natural rate of unemployment See *NAIRU*.

near money Anything that fulfills the store-of-value function, and is readily convertible into a medium of exchange, but is *not* itself a medium of exchange.

negatively related Two variables are negatively related when an increase in one is associated with a decrease in the other.

net exports Total exports minus total imports ($X - M$).

net investment Gross investment minus replacement investment, which is new capital that represent net additions to the capital stock.

New Classical theory A theory that assumes the economy behaves as if it were perfectly competitive with all markets always clearing; deviations from full employment can only occur if people make mistakes and, given rational expectations, these mistakes will not be systematic.

newly industrialized countries (NICs) Formerly underdeveloped countries that have become major industrial exporters in recent times.

nominal money supply The money supply measured in monetary units.

nominal national product Total output valued at current prices.

non-market sector That portion of an economy in which producers must cover their costs from some source other than sales revenue.

non-tariff barriers Devices other than tariffs that are designed to reduce the flow of imports.

non-tradeables Goods and services that are produced and sold domestically but do not enter into international trade.

normal capacity output The level of output that the firm expects to maintain on average.

normal good A commodity whose demand increases when income increases.

normative Statements concerning what ought to be; they depend on our *value judgements*.

official financing These items represent international transactions involving the central bank of the country whose balance of payments is being recorded.

oligopoly An industry that contains only a few firms.

open economy An economy that engages in international trade.

open shop A place of employment in which a union represents its members but does not have bargaining jurisdiction for all workers in the shop and membership of the union is not a condition of getting or keeping a job.

opportunity cost The cost of using resources for a certain purpose measured by the benefit given up by not using them in their best alternative use.

optimum population The population that maximizes national income per capita.

organization theory A theory that predicts that the substance of the decisions of a firm is affected by its size and its form of organization.

output The goods and services that result from the process of production.

output gap The difference between actual output and potential output ($Y_F - Y$); positive output gaps are called *recessionary gaps*; negative output gaps are called *inflationary gaps*.

Pareto efficiency See *Pareto optimality*.

Pareto optimality A situation in which it is impossible, by reallocating production or consumption activities, to make at least one person better off without making anyone worse off. Also, called *Pareto efficiency*.

partnership An enterprise with two or more joint owners, each of whom is personally responsible for all of the partnership's debts.

paternalism The belief that the individual is not the best judge of his or her own self-interest; someone else knows better.

per capita economic growth The growth of per capita national income (national income divided by the population).

per unit tax See *specific tax*.

perfect competition A market structure in which all firms in an industry are price-takers and in which there is freedom of entry into, and exit from, the industry.

permanent income The maximum amount that a

household can consume per year into the indefinite future without reducing its wealth.

permanent-income theory A theory that relates actual consumption to permanent income.

perpetuity A bond that pays a fixed sum of money each year for ever and has no redemption date, sometimes called a consol.

Phillips curve Relates the percentage rate of change of money wages (measured at an annual rate) to the level of unemployment (measured as the percentage of the labour force unemployed).

planned expenditure What people intend to spend.

point elasticity Uses the derivative at a point on the demand curve $(\mathrm{d}q/\mathrm{d}p)/(p/q)$. (See also *arc elasticity*.)

poll tax A tax which takes the same lump sum from everyone.

portfolio balance See *portfolio equilibrium*.

portfolio disequilibrium When wealth-holders have too much of some assets and too few of others in their current portfolios.

portfolio equilibrium When wealth-holders have the desired proportion of assets in their current portfolios; also called *portfolio balance*.

portfolio investment Investment in bonds and other debt instruments that do not imply ownership, or in minority holdings of shares that do not establish legal control.

positive Statements concerning what is, was or will be; they assert alleged facts about the universe in which we live.

positively related Two variables are positively related when an increase in one is associated with an increase in the other.

potential output What the economy could produce if all resources were fully employed at their normal rates of utilization, Y_F. Also called *full employment output*.

precautionary balances The amount of money people wish to hold because of uncertainty about the exact timing of receipts and payments.

present value The value now of a sum to be received in the future. Also called *discounted present value*.

price-consumption line A line on an indifference curve diagram showing how consumption changes as the price of one commodity changes, *ceteris paribus*.

price controls Anything that influences prices by laws, rather than market forces.

price discrimination When firms sell different units of their output at different prices for reasons not associated with differences in costs.

price elasticity of demand The percentage change in quantity demanded divided by the percentage change in price that brought it about; often called *elasticity of demand*.

price elasticity of supply The percentage change in quantity supplied divided by the percentage change in price that brought it about; often called *elasticity of supply*.

price index A statistical measure of the average percentage change in some group of prices over some base period.

price level See *general price level*.

price system An economic system in which prices play a key role in determining the allocation of resources and the distribution of the national product.

price-taker A firm that can alter its rate of production and sales within any feasible range without having any effect on the price of the product it sells.

principal The amount of a loan.

private cost The value of the best alternative use of the resources used in production as valued by *the producer*.

private sector That portion of an economy in which the organizations that produce goods and services are owned and operated by private units such as households and firms.

producer Any unit that makes goods or services.

producers' surplus Total revenue minus total variable cost; it is the market value that the firm creates by producing goods, net of the value of the resources currently used to create these goods.

production The act of making goods and services.

production function A functional relation showing the maximum output that can be produced by each and every combination of inputs.

production possibility boundary A curve that shows the alternative combinations of commodities that can just be attained if all available productive resources are used; it is the boundary between attainable and unattainable output combinations.

productivity Output per unit of input employed.

progressive tax A tax which takes a *larger percentage* of people's income the larger is their income.

progressivity The general term for the relation between income and the percentage of income paid in taxes.

proportional tax A tax which takes the *same percentage* of people's income whatever the level of their income.

protectionism Any departure from free trade designed to give some protection to domestic industries from foreign competition.

PSBR See *public-sector borrowing requirement*.

public corporation A body set up to run a nationalized industry; it is owned by the state but is usually under the direction of a more or less independent, state-appointed board.

public goods Goods and services which, once produced, can be consumed by everyone in the society.

public sector That portion of an economy in which production is owned and operated by the central authorities, or bodies created by them such as nationalized industries.

public sector borrowing requirement (PSBR) The combined excess of expenditure over revenue of the central government, the local authorities and public corporations.

purchasing power of money The amount of goods and services that can be purchased with a given amount of money.

purchasing power parity exchange rate The exchange rate between two currencies that equates their purchasing powers and hence adjusts for relative inflation rates.

purchasing power parity theory The theory that the equilibrium exchange rate between two national currencies will be the one that equates their purchasing powers.

pure profit Any excess of a firm's revenue over all opportunity costs including those of capital.

pure rate of interest See *pure return on capital.*

pure return on capital The amount that capital can earn in a riskless investment; hence the transfer earnings of capital in a riskless investment; also called the *pure rate of interest.*

quantity actually bought and sold The amount of a commodity that households and firms actually succeed in purchasing and selling.

quantity actually purchased See *quantity actually bought and sold.*

quantity demanded The amount of a commodity that households wish to purchase in some time-period.

quantity supplied The amount of a commodity that firms are able, and willing, to offer for sale in some time-period.

quantity theory of money Predicts that the price level and the quantity of money vary in exact proportion to each other – i.e. changing M by X per cent changes P by X per cent.

quasi-rent Factor payments which are economic rent in the short run and transfer earnings in the long run.

rational expectations The theory that people understand how the economy works and learn quickly from their mistakes, so that while random errors may be made, systematic and persistent errors are not made.

reaction curve Shows one firm's profit-maximizing output for each given quantity sold by its competitor.

real capital Physical assets that constitute factories, machinery and stocks of material and finished goods (also called *physical capital*).

real income The purchasing power of money income.

real money supply The money supply measured in purchasing-power units.

real national product Total output valued at base-year prices.

real product wage The proportion of the sale value of each unit that is accounted for by labour costs (including the pre-tax nominal wage rate, benefits, and the firm's national insurance contributions).

real rate of interest The money rate of interest minus the inflation rate, which expresses the real return on a loan.

real wage The money wage deflated by a price index to measure the wage's purchasing power.

real wage unemployment Unemployment due to a disequilibrium real wage.

realized expenditure What people actually succeed in spending.

reallocation of resources Some change in the uses to which the economy's resources are put.

recession A sustained drop in the level of economic activity.

recessionary gap A positive output gap, when actual national income falls short of potential national income.

redemption date The time at which the principal of a loan is to be repaid.

regressive tax A tax which takes a *smaller percentage* of people's incomes the larger is their income.

relative price Any price expressed as a ratio of another price.

resource allocation The allocation of the economy's scarce resources among alternative uses.

risk-averse Risk-averse persons will only play games that are sufficiently biased in their favour to overcome their aversion to risk, but will be unwilling to play mathematically fair games, let alone ones that are biased against them.

risk-lover People who are willing to play some games that are biased against them, the extent of the love of risk being measured by the degree of bias that they are willing to accept.

risk-neutral Risk-neutral persons are indifferent about playing a mathematically fair game, will willingly play one that is biased in their favour, but will not play one that is biased against them.

risk premium The return on capital necessary to compensate owners of capital for the risk of loss of their capital.

SRAS curve See *short-run aggregate supply curve.*

satisficing An hypothesis that firms will strive to achieve certain target for their profits, but having achieved them, they will not strive to improve their profit position further.

saving Income received by households that they do *not* pass back to firms through consumption expenditure.

self-employed Those people who work for themselves.

sellers' preferences Allocation of commodity in excess demand by the decisions of sellers.

services Intangible production such as haircuts.

shares See *equities*.

shifting The passing of tax incidence from the person who initially pays it to someone else.

short run The period of time over which the inputs of some factors cannot be varied.

short-run aggregate supply (SRAS) curve The total amount that will be produced and offered for sale at each price level on the assumption that all input prices are fixed.

short-run equilibrium Generally, equilibrium subject to fixed factors or other things that cannot change over the time-period being considered.

short-run Phillips curve Any particular Phillips curve drawn for a given expected rate of inflation.

short-run supply curve A curve showing the relation of quantity supplied to price, when one or more factor is fixed; under perfect competition it is the horizontal sum of marginal cost curves (above the level of average variable costs) of all firms in an industry.

sight deposit A deposit that can be transferred to others by means of cheque and can be converted into cash on demand. Also called *demand deposit*.

single proprietorship An enterprise with one owner who is personally responsible for everything that is done.

size distribution of income A classification of income according to the amount of income received by each individual irrespective of the sources of that income.

slump Periods of low output and low employment.

small open economy An economy that is a price-taker for both its imports and its exports. It must buy and sell at the world price, irrespective of the quantities that it buys and sells.

social cost The value of the best alternative use of resources that are available to the whole society.

special drawing rights (SDRs) Financial liabilities of the IMF held in a special fund generated by contributions of member countries. Members can use SDRs to maintain supplies of convertible currencies when these are needed to support foreign exchanges.

specialization of labour An organization of production in which individual workers specialize in the production of particular goods or services (and satisfy their wants by trading) rather than producing everything they consume (and satisfy their wants by being self-sufficient).

specific tariffs Tariffs which are so much on each unit of the imported product, independent of its price.

specific tax A tax expressed as so much per unit, independent of its price.

speculative motive The motive that leads firms to hold money in reaction to the risks inherent in a fluctuating price of bonds.

stabilization policy The attempt to reduce fluctuation in national income, employment and the price level, stabilizing national income at its full-employment level, if possible.

stagflation The simultaneous occurrence of a recession (with its accompanying high unemployment) and inflation.

stock See *equities*.

stocks Accumulation of inputs and outputs held by firms to facilitate a smooth flow of production in spite of variations in delivery of inputs and sales of outputs. Sometimes called *inventories*.

stop-go policy Fluctuations caused by shortsightedly pursuing expansion to cure unemployment, then contraction to cure inflation.

structural unemployment Unemployment that exists because of a mismatching between the characteristics of the unemployed and the characteristics of the available jobs in terms of region, occupation or industry.

substitutes Two goods are substitutes if the quantity demanded of one is positively related to the price of the other.

substitution effect The change in quantity demanded of a good resulting from a change in the commodity's relative price, eliminating the effect of the price change on real income.

supply The whole relation between the quantity supplied of some commodity and its own price.

supply curve The graphical representation of the relation between the quantity of some commodity that producers wish to make and sell per period of time and the price of that commodity, *ceteris paribus*.

supply of effort The total number of hours people in the labour force are willing to work, also called *supply of labour*.

supply of labour See *supply of effort*.

supply of money The total amount of money available in the entire economy, also called the *money supply* or the *money stock*.

supply schedule A numerical tabulation showing the quantity supplied at a number of alternative prices.

supply-side policies Policies that seek to shift either the short-run or the long-run aggregate supply curve.

supply-side shocks A shift in any aggregate supply curve.

tariffs Taxes designed to raise the price of imported goods.

term The amount of time between a bond's issue date and its redemption date.

term of maturity The amount of time between the present date and the redemption date of a bond.

terms of trade The ratio of the average price of a country's exports to the average price of its imports.

theory of income determination The theory that

explains the size of, and changes in, national income.

third-party effects See *externalities*.

time deposits An interest-earning bank deposit, legally subject to notice before withdrawal (the notice requirement is not normally enforced) and, until recently, not transferable by cheque.

total cost The total of all costs of producing a firm's output, usually divided into fixed and variable costs.

total final expenditure The total expenditure required to purchase all the goods and services that are produced domestically, when these are valued at market prices.

total fixed costs The total of a firm's costs that do not vary in the short run.

total revenue The total amount of money that the firm receives from the sale of its output.

total variable costs The total of those of the firm's costs that do vary in the short run.

total utility The total satisfaction derived from consuming some amount of a commodity.

trade cycles More or less regular, long-term patterns of fluctuations in the level of economic activity. Also called *business cycles*.

trade union An organization of workers with a common set of skills, no matter where, or for whom, they work.

trade-weighted exchange rate The average of the exchange rates between a particular country's currency and those of each of its major trading partners, with each rate being weighted by the amount of trade with the country in question.

tradeables Goods and services that enter into international trade.

transactions demand for money The amount of money that people wish to hold in order to finance their transactions.

transfer earnings The amount that a factor must earn in its present use to prevent it from moving (i.e. transferring) to another use.

transfer payments Payments not made in return for any contribution to current output.

treasury bill A promise to repay a stated amount at some specified date between 90 days and 1 year from the date of issue, issued by the Treasury.

unit cost See *average variable cost*.

utility The satisfaction that a household receives from consumption.

value added The value of a firm's output *minus* the value of the inputs that it purchases from other firms.

value of money See *purchasing power of money*.

variable factors Inputs whose amount can be varied in the short run.

vertical merger When firms at different stages of production unite.

very long run A period of time over which the technological possibilities open to a firm are subject to change.

vicious circle of poverty When a country has little capital per head, it is poor; because it is poor, it can devote few resources to creating new capital rather than to producing goods for consumption; because little new capital can be produced, capital per head remains low, and the country remains poor.

visibles Goods, i.e. things such as cars, pulpwood, aluminium, coffee and iron ore, that we can see when they cross international borders.

voluntary export restriction An exporting country agrees to limit the amount it sells to a second country.

voluntary unemployment Occurs when there is a job available, but the unemployed person is not willing to accept it at the existing wage rate.

wage-cost-push inflation An increase in the price level due to increases in money wages that are not associated with excess demand for labour.

wage-price spiral The process set up by a sequence of wage-cost pushes that shifts the *SRAS* curve to the left and monetary accommodation that shifts the *AD* curve to the right.

withdrawals Income received by either firms or households that is not passed on to the other group by buying goods or services from it. Also called *leakages*.

working population The total of the employed, the self-employed and the unemployed, i.e. those who have a job plus those who are looking for work.

X-inefficiency Failure to use resources efficiently within the firm so that firms are producing above their relevant cost curves and the economy is inside its production possibility boundary.

Index

A page number in italics refers to a definition in the Glossary.